Introduction to Law
and the Legal System

Introduction to Law and the Legal System

TENTH EDITION

FRANK AUGUST SCHUBERT
Professor Emeritus
Northeastern University

WADSWORTH
CENGAGE Learning

Australia • Brazil • Canada • Mexico • Singapore • Spain • United Kingdom • United States

WADSWORTH
CENGAGE Learning

Introduction to Law and the Legal System
Tenth Edition
Frank August Schubert

Executive Editor: Carolyn Merrill

Development Editor: Kate Scheinman

Assistant Editor: Katherine Hayes

Editorial Assistant: Angela Hodge

Marketing Manager: Lydia LeStar

Marketing Coordinator: Josh Hendrick

Marketing Communications Manager: Heather Baxley

Content Project Manager: Jessica Rasile

Art Director: Linda Helcher

Print Buyer: Fola Orekoya

Senior Rights Acquisition Specialist, Image: Mandy Groszko

Rights Acquisition Specialist, Text: Shalice Shah-Caldwell

Production Service/Compositor: MPS Limited, a Macmillan Company

Cover Image: Junia/©istockphoto

For product information and technology assistance, contact us at
Cengage Learning Customer & Sales Support, 1-800-354-9706
For permission to use material from this text or product, submit all requests online at **www.cengage.com/permissions**.
Further permissions questions can be emailed to
permissionrequest@cengage.com

Library of Congress Control Number: 2010938458

ISBN-13: 978-0-495-89933-4
ISBN-10: 0-495-89933-X

Wadsworth
20 Channel Center Street
Boston, MA 02210
USA

Cengage Learning is a leading provider of customized learning solutions with office locations around the globe, including Singapore, the United Kingdom, Australia, Mexico, Brazil and Japan. Locate your local office at **international.cengage.com/region**

Cengage Learning products are represented in Canada by Nelson Education, Ltd.

For your course and learning solutions, visit **www.cengage.com**

Purchase any of our products at your local college store or at our preferred online store **www.cengagebrain.com**

Instructors: Please visit **login.cengage.com** and log in to access instructor-specific resources.

Printed in the United States of America
1 2 3 4 5 6 7 15 14 13 12 11

✳

To Barbara Macintosh
F. A. S.

Brief Contents

✳ Contents

Preface

Welcome to the tenth edition of *Introduction to Law and the Legal System*! The first edition was published thirty-five years ago. In recognition of this publication milestone, the publisher has produced a special cover; tribute is given to the original author, Harold J. Grilliot; and a Short Chronicle, which discusses the evolution of the book from 1975 to 2010, has been included in the Appendix.

Suited for undergraduate or graduate programs, this text is a survey of the American legal system and can be used in a variety of courses such as Survey of Law, Introduction to Law and the Legal System, Law and Society, Legal Environment and Business, and Legal Process. This text could be an integral part of business, criminal justice, political science, interdisciplinary, paralegal, or other similar courses in an institution of higher learning.

From its first edition to the present, the goal has been to provide readers with a general understanding of American substantive and procedural law. The premise is that this kind of knowledge is basic to a well-rounded education. Because this book is used in a wide variety of academic settings and disciplines it is expected that instructors will select topics and cases that are appropriate to the course and students. The length and complexity of cases varies from case to case because it is difficult to reduce a fifty-page opinion to three or four pages and still include all the fodder for class discussion. While it is true that many topics included in the text are fundamental to the typical law school's curriculum, this is not a textbook for law students. This book explains in a few pages fundamental principles that law students study for an entire semester. Law students study law so that they can become practitioners. Undergraduate students study law in order to obtain a basic understanding of law. This presentation's strength is that it provides readers with a brief peek at what are inherently complex concepts without getting students in over their heads.

Because this is an undergraduate/graduate level text, it also tries to show readers connections between law and topics typically covered in more detail in undergraduate/graduate courses taught in history, philosophy, political science, sociology/anthropology, and business departments. Thus, the text includes some legal and cultural history, jurisprudence, ethics, etc. in the hope that students will get a taste of the bigger picture and perhaps enroll in a corresponding course. Showing these connections helps to promote a better understanding of the role law plays in a complex, modern society. From this understanding, students can decide for themselves whether lawmaking institutions—the legislative, judicial, and administrative agencies—are adequately addressing our society's problems.

By reading cases and studying statutes in this text, students will learn to exercise their own powers of reasoning. Because the cases are continuously updated in every edition, students read about real-world problems and study appellate court discussions about how the problems should be resolved. This promotes class discussions about the relative strengths and weaknesses of the competing arguments made by the parties.

New to the Tenth Edition

The tenth edition has been updated with thirty-two new cases including many recent, controversial cases such as *Video Software Dealers Association v. Schwarzenegger, Caperton v. Massey, Herring v. U.S.,* and *Cable Connection Inc. v. DIRECTV.* Comments from reviewers and users have been carefully considered as decisions were made with respect to the replacement or retention of particular cases. As always, the goal has been to select cases that are interesting, teachable, and controversial, and that illustrate the theory being discussed in the corresponding chapter section. Some of the retained cases are classics and have proven to be useful for many years. *Katko v. Briney, Strunk v. Strunk,* and *Campbell Soup Company v. Wentz,* for example, have appeared in all ten editions. Other older cases have been included because they better illustrate the legal principle being addressed in the text than did the removed case.

Readers can find on the website other long-standing favorite cases that have been "retired" from the textbook such as *Du Pont v. Christopher* as well as additional cases, statutes, and materials that could not be included in the textbook because of space limitations. This website will be updated periodically with new and relevant cases, and often will include concurring and dissenting opinions that would be too lengthy to be included in the textbook. Additionally, students will find open access to learning objectives, tutorial quizzes, chapter glossaries, flashcards, and crossword puzzles, all correlated by chapter, as well as additional cases on the website. Instructors also have access to the Instructor's Manual.

For the first time, this edition offers an Instructor's Resource CD-ROM. This CD contains test banks in Microsoft® Word and ExamView® computerized testing and offers a large array of well-crafted true–false, multiple-choice, and essay questions, along with their answers and page references. An Instructor's Manual includes chapter objectives, court cases, and answers to chapter questions.

Teaching and Learning Aids

The text includes a glossary that was substantially expanded in the ninth edition. Please note that it focuses on terms as they are used in the text and is not intended to be as comprehensive as a legal dictionary. The Constitution of the United States is also reprinted for easy reference.

All cases have been edited to frame issues for classroom discussion and for length and readability. Most case footnotes have been deleted. Many citations have similarly been omitted, as well as less important portions of majority opinions. Ellipses have been inserted to indicate such omissions. Academic works that were relied upon as sources within each chapter have been acknowledged with endnotes. Case citations are occasionally provided so that interested students can consult the official reports for unedited cases.

Acknowledgments

This revision would not have been possible without the valuable contributions of many people. The following reviewers were instrumental in shaping the tenth edition:

Monique Chiacchia, Edmonds Community College

Collin K. C. Lau, Chaminade University of Honolulu

Lynnette Noblitt, Eastern Kentucky University

Susan Vik, Boston University

I am most pleased and proud that my daughter, Tracy, has prepared the index for this text. Her excellent assistance has made the tenth edition both better and more memorable.

This special edition of the textbook is dedicated to my wife, Barbara, who was there at the very beginning of this project way back in 1988 when all the legal research had to be completed the old-fashioned way—in an academic law library. She has helped me in countless ways to complete each of the seven editions I have worked on. An author's spouse makes many sacrifices so that deadlines can be met. Barbara's love, encouragement, patience, wisdom, and steadfastness have made it all possible. *Mahalo nui loa,* Barbara, *aloha au ia'oe.*

F.A.S.

A Tribute to Professor Harrold J. Grilliot

This textbook originated in the mind of its first author, the late Harold J. Grilliot. Professor Grilliot majored in accounting and received his undergraduate education at the University of Dayton (1960). He subsequently graduated from the University of Cincinnati Law School (1967). He taught briefly at the University of Detroit and then embarked on a fifteen-year academic career as a member of the University of Cincinnati College of Business, where he was an

Assistant Professor. What eventually became the first edition of the textbook began as a collection of "teachable" cases and materials Professor Grilliot assembled for use in an introduction to law class he taught in the UC College of Business. In 1975, Houghton Mifflin Company published the first edition of the textbook, and a second edition followed in 1979. The third edition appeared just prior to Professor Grilliot's untimely death in 1983.

Harold Grilliot explained his reasoning for the book's infrastructure and perspective in his preface to the first edition.

"This book is designed to provide an introduction to what every educated citizen should know about law and the American legal system. It provides an interesting and exciting means of developing an understanding of the strengths and weaknesses of law...

"A basic understanding of the law and the legal system in one's community promotes a better understanding of the role law plays in a complex modern society. This text is designed to stimulate students to exercise their powers of reasoning.... Case analysis stimulates thinking and consideration of the extent to which the law is addressing itself to the social and business problems of the time..."

Harold Grilliot was recognized postmortem by his colleagues at the University of Cincinnati College of Business for his teaching excellence and dedication to students. They established an annual award named in his honor that is presented to a deserving UC business faculty member.

The current author has included in the Appendix a chronicle of the textbook's thirty-five year history. This Chronicle contains a narrative and two figures that explain the evolution of the text. As longtime adopters know, Harold Grilliot's founding principles for this textbook have been continued by the current author. It is the current author's hope that Grilliot's approach continues to be reflected in future editions.

F.A.S.

✳

Introduction to Law
and the Legal System

1

✳

Introduction

CHAPTER OBJECTIVES

1. *Understand each of five jurisprudential approaches to answering the question, "What is law?"*
2. *Explain the legal objectives that are common to American public and private law.*
3. *Understand how our nation's legal history and culture have contributed to law and legal institutions as we know them today.*
4. *Develop the ability to read and brief an appellate court opinion.*
5. *Explain in general terms the concepts underlying the Due Process and Equal Protection Clauses.*
6. *Understand the basic differences between civil and criminal law.*
7. *Understand the basic differences between tort and contract law.*

WHAT IS LAW?

The study of legal philosophy is called **jurisprudence.** Many of the world's greatest philosophers have theorized about the nature and meaning of law. Jurisprudential philosophers ask questions like these: What is law? Is bad law still law? Is custom law? Is law what it says in the statute books, or what really happens in practice? Philosophers have debated the essential nature of law for centuries, yet there is no single commonly accepted definition. This chapter begins by summarizing some of the schools of legal philosophy in order to introduce students to different ways of answering this fundamental question: What is law?[1]

Law as Power

According to this view, the validity of a law does not depend on whether it is socially good or bad. It is apparent, for example, that tyrannies, monarchies, and democracies have produced socially beneficial laws. They have also produced laws that are unjust and "wrongful." What these different forms of government have in common is that each is based on power and that possessing the power to enforce its laws is central to each government's existence. This philosophy can be criticized for ignoring arbitrariness, abuses of power, and tyranny, and for producing bad law.

Natural Law

Natural law philosophers argued that law is that which reflects, or is based on, the built-in sense of right and wrong that exists within every person at birth. This moral barometer, which operates through the functioning of conscience, gives each person the capacity to discover moral truth independently. Some believed that this sense was God-given; others believed it was an intrinsic part of human nature.[2] Natural law philosophers argued that moral goodness is conceptually independent of institutional views of goodness or evil. Thus, no government can make a morally evil law good or a morally good law evil. Moral goodness exists prior to institutional lawmaking, and sets a moral standard against which positive law should be measured. Thus, even though during apartheid the all-white South African government may have had the power to enact racially discriminatory statutes, such statutes were not truly "law" because they were morally abhorrent. This natural law philosophy was very influential in seventeenth- and eighteenth-century Europe. Revolutionaries who sought to overthrow established monarchies were attracted to natural law because it established a philosophical foundation for political reform.

Natural law thinking has greatly influenced American law as well. American civil rights advocates currently use the same time-tested natural law arguments that were used thirty and forty years ago to oppose racial discrimination. They argue that discriminatory statutes should not be respected as law because they are so blatantly unfair. Constitutional provisions that require government to treat all persons fairly and impartially (the due process and Equal Protection Clauses) are other examples.

Our tort system is also a reflection of natural law thinking. It is "right" that people who intend no harm but who carelessly cause injury to other people should have to pay compensation for the damages. Similarly, if two people voluntarily enter into a contract, it is "right" that the parties comply with its terms or pay damages for the breach. (However, our law confers power in our judges to refuse to enforce contractual provisions that are too one-sided.) Finally, it is "right" to punish persons who commit crimes for those acts.

When there is no consensus in society about what is morally right and wrong, natural law loses its effectiveness as a basis for law. Current examples of this problem include issues such as abortion, physician-assisted suicide, and capital punishment.

Historical Jurisprudence

Historical jurisprudence evolved in response to the natural law philosophy. Aristocrats were attracted to this school because it provided a justification for preserving the status quo and the preferential treatment of powerful elites that was deeply rooted in cultural tradition. The historical philosophy of law integrated the notion that law is the will of the sovereign with the idea of the "spirit of the people."[3] That is, law is only valid to the extent that the will of the sovereign is compatible with long-standing social practices, customs, and values. Law, according to this view, could not be arbitrarily imposed by legislators whose legal source was "right" reasoning. Instead, the historical school insisted that only practices that have withstood the test of time could be thought of as law.[4] Further, these philosophers believed that law changes slowly and invisibly as human conduct changes.

A major advantage of historical jurisprudence is that it promotes stability in law. In fact, much law is largely grounded in judicially approved custom.

Our contemporary American real estate law,[5] property law,[6] and contract law[7] are some of the areas in which long-standing practices continue to be recognized as law. Custom has also played an important role in determining the meaning of the Constitution. Appellate courts such as the U.S. Supreme Court trace provisions of the Bill of Rights to their historical statutory and case law antecedents. They do this because they recognize that some beliefs, practices, procedures, and relationships between people and the state have become fundamental to our culture.

Occasionally a sovereign will enact legislation that significantly contravenes long-standing custom. A few years ago, the Massachusetts legislature enacted a mandatory seat belt law. Many citizens believed that the state was infringing on a matter of personal choice. They insisted that the matter be placed on the ballot, and the law was repealed in a statewide referendum.[8]

A major problem with historical jurisprudence is determining at what point a practice has become a custom. How long must a practice have been followed, and how widely must it be accepted, before it is recognized as customary?

Utilitarian Law

The utilitarian school of law concentrated on the social usefulness of legislation rather than on metaphysical notions of goodness and justice.[9] **Utilitarians** thought that government was responsible for enacting laws that promote the general public's happiness. They believed that the desire to maximize pleasure and minimize pain is what motivates people, and that legislatures were responsible for inducing people to act in socially desirable ways through a legislated system of incentives and disincentives.[10] For example, if the pain imposed by a criminal sentence exceeds the gain realized by an offender in committing the offense, future criminal actions will be deterred. Additionally, they thought that law should focus on providing people with security and equality of opportunity. They maintained that property rights should be protected because security of property is crucial to attaining

happiness. People, they thought, should perform their contracts because increased commercial activity and economic growth produce socially beneficial increases in employment.

Utilitarians also favored the simplification of legal procedures. They opposed checks and balances, legal technicalities, and complex procedures. They believed that these "formalities" increased the costs and length of the judicial process and made the justice system ineffective and unresponsive to the needs of large numbers of average people. Modern utilitarians would favor small claims courts, with their simplified pleading requirements, informality, low cost, and optional use of lawyers.

Utilitarian influence can be found in legislative enactments that require the nation's broadcasters to operate "in the public interest," in "lemon laws," and in other consumer protection legislation. A major problem with utilitarianism is that not everyone agrees about what is pleasurable and what is painful. And many, if not most, political scientists would dispute that legislators actually make decisions according to the pleasure–pain principle.

Analytical Positivism

Analytical positivists asserted that law was a self-sufficient system of legal rules that the sovereign issues in the form of commands to the governed. These commands did not depend for legitimacy on extraneous considerations such as reason, ethics, morals, or even social consequences.[11] However, the sovereign's will was law only if it was developed according to duly established procedures, such as the enactments of a national legislature.

Thus, the apartheid laws passed by the previously all-white South African legislature were "the law" of that country at that time to the same extent that civil rights legislation enacted by the U.S. Congress was the law of this country. Each of these lawmaking bodies was exercising sovereign power in accordance with provisions of a national constitution. Positivists would maintain that individuals and governmental officials have no right to disobey laws with which they personally disagree due to moral, ethical, or policy objections. Positivists would also maintain that trial jurors have a legal obligation to apply the law according to the judge's instructions, even if that means disregarding strongly held personal beliefs about the wisdom of the law or its application in a particular factual dispute.

Members of this philosophical school would view disputes about the goodness or badness of legal rules as extra-legal.[12] They would maintain that such issues do not relate to the law *as it is*. This approach promotes stability and security. It also legitimizes governmental line drawing (such as laws that specify the age at which people can lawfully drink or vote, or those that determine automobile speed limits).

In the United States, people often disagree with governmental decisions about foreign policy, as well as about such issues as housing, the financing of public education, health care, abortion, environmental protection, and the licensing of nuclear power plants. Many contend that governmental officials are pursuing wrongful, and sometimes immoral, objectives. Such concerns, however, are generally unpersuasive in our courts. If governmental officials are authorized to make decisions, act within constitutional limitations, and follow established procedures, even decisions that are unpopular with some segments of society are nevertheless law.

But is law really just a closed system of rules and the product of a sovereign? Doesn't international law exist despite the absence of a sovereign? Don't contracting parties routinely create their own rules without any sovereign's involvement unless a dispute arises that results in litigation? And is law really morally neutral? Shouldn't the positivist approach be criticized if it protects governmental officials who act unfairly?

SOCIOLOGICAL JURISPRUDENCE, LEGAL REALISM, AND LEGAL SOCIOLOGY

After the Civil War, the nation's economy rapidly expanded, and America moved toward a market economy. Along with this expansion came new technologies, new products, and changing legal attitudes about government's rights to interfere with private property. Laissez-faire was in vogue, and although it contributed to expanding the economy, it also produced monopolies, political corruption, environmental pollution, hazardous working conditions, and labor-management conflict. The U.S. Supreme Court often opposed social reforms initiated by state governments. In *Lochner v. New York*, for example, the Court struck down a reform statute that limited bakers to ten-hour workdays and sixty-hour work weeks.[13] The majority ruled that this statute unreasonably infringed on the rights of employees and employers to negotiate their own contracts. The Court also declared the Erdman Act unconstitutional in *Adair v. United States*.[14] Congress enacted the Erdman Act to stop the railroad monopolies from discharging employees who joined labor unions. Congress, said the Supreme Court, had no right under the interstate Commerce Clause to regulate labor relations in the railroad industry.

The excesses of laissez-faire produced social and economic unrest among farmers and laborers in particular, and produced political pressure for reforms. These factors culminated in the rise of the Progressive Movement. The Progressives sought an expanded governmental role in the economy. They wanted government to pay attention to reforming and to enact laws that would regulate special interests. The Progressives rejected the notion that law is based on immutable principles and deductive reasoning, and therefore is unrelated to political, social, and economic factors in society. Too often, they contended, the courts had ignored what Benjamin Cardozo would call the "pursuit of social justice."[15]

Sociological Jurisprudence

Roscoe Pound, of Harvard Law School, published an article in the 1911 *Harvard Law Review* that picked up on Progressive themes and announced a philosophy of law called **sociological jurisprudence**.[16] Pound argued against what he called "mechanical jurisprudence," with its backwardness and unjust outcomes in individual cases.

He advocated that governments become proactive in working to promote social and economic reforms and that judges become more socially aware of the impact of their decisions on society.[17]

Early sociologists were interested in examining jurisprudence from a social-scientific perspective. They focused on what they called the living law—not just the law declared by legislatures and courts, but the informal rules that actually influence social behavior. The sociological school maintains that law can only be understood when the formal system of rules is considered in conjunction with social realities (or facts). In this sense, it is similar to the historical school. However, the historical school approached time in terms of centuries, whereas the sociological school focused on ten- or twenty-year segments.

Sociological jurisprudence theorists, for example, would note that during the last sixty years the courts and legislatures have made many attempts to eliminate racial discrimination in voting, housing, employment, and education, and that the law on the books has significantly changed. It is equally clear from scholarly studies, however, that discrimination continues. The written law provides for equal opportunity, and on the surface racial discrimination is not as obvious as it once was. But the social facts continue to reveal subtle forms of racism that law has not been able to legislate or adjudicate away. Similarly, employment discrimination against women, older workers, and the disabled continues despite the enactment of federal and state legislation that legally puts an end to such practices. Informally enforced social norms that condone bigotry and inflict personal indignities and economic inequities on targeted segments of society are not easily legislated away.

Although this approach effectively points out the discrepancies between the promise and the reality of enacted law, it often fails to produce practical solutions to the problems. Should judges be encouraged to consider social consequences in addition to legal rules in reaching decisions? If so, might this not result in arbitrary, discretionary decisions that reflect only the personal preferences of one particular jurist or group of jurists?

Legal Realists

During the early decades of the twentieth century, the social sciences were emerging. Academics and judges were attempting to borrow the scientific methods that had been used to study the natural and physical sciences and use them to examine social institutions. From the late 1920s through the middle 1930s, juries, and judges in particular, were subjected to empirical scrutiny by reformists such as Jerome Frank and Karl Llewellyn, who called themselves *legal realists*. The realists focused on the extent to which actual practices varied from the formal legal rules.[18] They believed that judges were influenced more by their personal convictions than by established and immutable rules. Llewellyn made a very important distinction between the legal rules and precedent-setting cases that were often cited as the basis for deciding why cases were won and lost (which he called "paper" rules) and the "real" rules of decisions that were undisclosed unless revealed by behavioral research.[19] Llewellyn believed that judges made law instead of discovering it, and he went so far as to proclaim that law was merely "what officials do about disputes."[20] Rules, the realists pointed out, do not adequately account for witness perjury and bias, and neither do rules compensate for the differing levels of ability, knowledge, and prejudice of individual lawyers, judges, and jurors. Because the realists produced little theory and research, they primarily blazed a trail for the legal sociologists to follow.

Legal Sociologists

Legal sociologists such as Donald Black have gone beyond the legal realists. Using quantitative methodological tools, they examine such factors as the financial standing, race, social class, respectability, and cultural differences of those involved in disputes.[21] In addition, they evaluate the social facts of the lawyers and judges working on the case, as well as those of the parties. In theory, legal outcomes should not be affected by differences in the socioeconomic status of the litigants, because all are "equal" before the law. Individual plaintiffs, for example, should be able to win when suing multinational corporations. But legal sociologists claim that the facts do not support this theory.[22] The rule of law is a myth, they say, because legal rules fail to take into account the impact of social diversity on litigation. Discrimination is a fact of modern life, and different combinations of social factors will produce disparate legal outcomes.[23] Donald Black points out that disputes between friends, neighbors, and family members are rarely litigated because "law varies directly with relational distance."[24] It can be argued persuasively that well-trained lawyers should decide whether to settle a case or go to trial, whether to try a case to a judge or a jury, and whether to appeal only after carefully considering the relevant social factors and relationships.[25]

Legal sociologists raise issues that challenge fundamental postulates of our society. If people become convinced that legal outcomes are largely a function of sociological considerations, rather than the application of impartial rules, the integrity of the judicial process itself will be undermined, as will the legitimacy of government. If research, however, can reveal more precisely how various combinations of sociological factors influence legal outcomes, this information could be used either to eliminate the bias or to develop alternative mechanisms for resolving particular types of disputes.

OBJECTIVES OF LAW

One of the foundations of our society is the belief that ours is a nation committed to the rule of law. No person is above the law. Our shared legal heritage binds us together as Americans. We use law to regulate people in their relationships with each other, and in their relationships with government. Law reflects our societal aspirations, our culture, and our political and economic beliefs. It provides mechanisms for resolving disputes and for controlling government officials. Private law includes property, family, tort, probate, and corporate law. Public law includes constitutional, criminal, and administrative law. Common to both, however, are certain legal objectives.

Continuity and Stability

It is important that established laws change gradually. Litigants have greater confidence that justice has been done when preexisting rules are used to determine legal outcomes. Laws work best when people become aware of them and learn how they work and why they are necessary. Stable laws are also more likely to be applied uniformly and consistently throughout a jurisdiction, and will be better understood by those charged with enforcement.

Stable laws are also very important to creating and maintaining a healthy economy because they are predictable and serve as a guide for conduct. Businesspeople, for example, are not likely to incur risk in a volatile legal and political environment. They are likely to feel more comfortable in making investments and taking economic risks where it appears likely that the future will resemble the present and the recent past. This stability is threatened by society's appetite for producing rules. Various state and federal legislative and administrative rule-making bodies are currently promulgating so many regulations that it is difficult, if not impossible, for affected citizens to stay current.

Adaptability

In one sense, it would be desirable if society could create a great big "legal cookbook" that contained a prescribed law or rule for every conceivable situation. We would then only have to look in the cookbook for definitive answers to all legal problems. In reality, there is no such cookbook. Legislators produce statutes that have a broad scope and that are designed to promote the public health, safety, welfare, and morals. Judges make law in conjunction with resolving disputes that have been properly brought before the court. Experience has shown that legislative enactments and judicial opinions produce imperfect law. Lawmakers cannot anticipate every factual possibility. Courts, in particular, often feel compelled to recognize exceptions to general rules in order to provide justice in individual cases. Judges often find that there are gaps in the law that they have to fill in order to decide a case, or that a long-standing rule no longer makes any sense, given current circumstances and societal values. In this way, law adapts to social, environmental, and political changes within our evolving society.

Justice, Speed, and Economy

Although most people would agree with the preamble to the U.S. Constitution that it is the role of the government "to establish justice," there is no consensus about what that means. Some see justice as a natural law–type settlement, which means each party to a dispute receives what he or she is due. To other people justice means that a specified process was followed by governmental institutions. In some situations, justice requires the elimination of discretion so that law is applied more equally. In other situations, justice requires the inclusion of discretion (equity) so that the law is not applied too mechanically. In this respect, it is helpful to look at recent history. Our current notions of justice with respect to race, gender, and class differ from the views of many of our forebears. Posterity will probably have a concept of justice that differs from our own.

Rule 1 of the Federal Rules of Civil Procedure provides that procedural rules should be construed "to secure the just, speedy and inexpensive determination of every action." Although it would be desirable if our judicial systems could satisfy all three of these objectives, they are often in conflict. As a society we continually have to make choices about how much justice we desire and can afford.

Consider a society dedicated to achieving the highest possible levels of justice in its judicial system. Elaborate measures would be required to ensure that all relevant evidence has been located and all possible witnesses identified and permitted to testify. In such a society, all litigants would be entitled to the services of investigators, thorough pretrial discovery procedures, and qualified and experienced trial attorneys. Great care would have to be taken to ensure that jurors were truly unbiased and competent to render a fair verdict. Only highly probative evidence would be permitted as proof, and various levels of appellate review would be required to consider carefully whether significant substantive or procedural errors were made at trial. Obviously, such a process would be very slow and very expensive. Denying deserving plaintiffs a recovery until the process had run its course could itself be unfair, because a recovery would be denied for several years.

Instead, some judicial systems build in cost-cutting measures such as six-person instead of twelve-person juries. They also make it easier for juries to reach decisions by permitting less-than-unanimous verdicts. Although each cost-cutting step risks more error in the system, there are limits as to how much justice society is willing to provide. People have a multitude of needs, including medical care, housing, education, and defense, as well as a limited interest in paying taxes. These competing needs have to be prioritized. In recent years, governmental funding of poverty lawyers has been greatly reduced. This has occurred at a time when the costs of litigating average cases have risen substantially. As the costs of using the legal system increase, fewer persons will be able to afford to use litigation to resolve their disputes. Private attorneys often decline to represent a potential client if the likely recovery in the case will not produce an acceptable profit.

An example of how law balances the desire for justice with a concern for cost appears in the case of *Goss v. Lopez* (which can be read on the textbook website). In that case the U.S. Supreme Court determined that public school administrators only have to provide rudimentary procedural due process to students who face short suspensions. The Supreme Court explained that requiring schools to provide students with extensive trial-type procedures would make the disciplinary process too expensive. In Chapter XIV we examine alternative methods for resolving disputes.

Determining Desirable Public Policy

Historically, law has been used to determine desirable public policy. It has been used to establish and then abolish discrimination on the basis of race, gender, age, and sexual preference. Law has been used to promote environmental protection and to permit resource exploitation. Through law, society determines whether doctors can assist in suicides, whether people of the same sex can marry, and which kinds of video games minors can purchase.

ORIGIN OF LAW IN THE
UNITED STATES

The British victory over the French in the French and Indian War and the signing of the Treaty of Paris (1763) concluded the competition between the two nations for domination of North America. A French victory might well have resulted in the establishment of the French legal system in the colonies along the Atlantic seaboard. The British victory, however, preserved the English common law system for what would become the United States. The following discussion highlights some of the important milestones in the development of the common law.

The Origins of English Common Law

Anglo-Saxon kings ruled England prior to 1066. During the reign of Edward the Confessor (1042–1066), wealthy landowners and noblemen, called earls, gained power over local affairs. There was no central legislature or national judicial court. Instead, the country was organized into communal units, based on population. Each unit was called a hundred, and was headed by an official called the reeve. The primary function of the hundred was judicial; it held court once each month and dealt with routine civil and criminal matters. Local freemen resolved these cases in accordance with local custom.[26]

The hundreds were grouped into units called shires (counties), which in earlier times often had

been Anglo-Saxon kingdoms. The shire was of much greater importance than the hundred. The king used it for military, administrative, and judicial purposes. The king administered the shires through the person of the shire reeve (sheriff). Royal sheriffs existed in each of the shires throughout the country. The sheriff was the king's principal judicial and administrative officer at the local level. Sheriffs collected taxes, urged support of the king's administrative and military policies, and performed limited judicial functions.[27] The shire court, composed of all the freemen in the county, was held twice a year and was presided over by the bishop and the sheriff.[28] It handled criminal, civil, and religious matters that were too serious or difficult for the hundred court, as well as disputes about land ownership.[29] The freemen in attendance used local custom as the basis for making decisions, even in religious matters, resulting in a variety of regional practices throughout the country. Anglo-Saxon law did not permit a person to approach the king to appeal the decisions of these communal courts.[30]

The Anglo-Saxon king had a number of functions. He raised armies and a navy for the defense of the kingdom. He issued **writs,** which were administrative letters containing the royal seal.[31] The writs were used to order courts to convene, the sheriffs to do justice, and to award grants of land and privileges.[32] The king administered the country with the assistance of the royal household, an early form of king's council.[33] He also declared laws (called dooms),[34] sometimes after consulting with the Witan, a national assembly of important nobles.[35]

When Edward the Confessor died childless in 1066, the candidates to succeed him were his brother-in-law, Harold, Earl of Wessex, and his cousin, William, Duke of Normandy (a French duchy). Harold was English and the most powerful baron in the country. William was French. Each claimed that Edward had selected him as the next king. William also claimed that Harold had agreed to support William's claim to the throne.[36] Harold, however, was elected king by the Witan and was crowned. William's response was to assemble an army, cross the English Channel, and invade England.

The Norman Invasion

In 1066, Duke William of Normandy, with 5,000 soldiers and 2,500 horses, defeated the Anglo-Saxons, and killed King Harold at the Battle of Hastings.[37] William became king of England, and the Normans assumed control of the country. Although the Anglo-Saxons had implemented a type of feudalism before the invasion, the Normans developed and refined it. Feudalism was a military, political, and social structure that ordered relationships among people. Under feudalism, a series of duties and obligations existed between a lord and his vassals. In England, the Normans merged feudalism with the Anglo-Saxon institution of the national king. William insisted, for example, that all land in England belonged ultimately to the king, and in 1086 he required all landholders to swear allegiance to him.[38] In this way, all his barons and lords and their vassals were personally obligated to him by feudal law. At his coronation, King William decreed that Englishmen could keep the customary laws that had been in force during the reign of the Anglo-Saxon King Edward the Confessor. This meant that the communal, hundred, and shire courts could continue to resolve disputes between the English as they had in the past.[39] William did, however, make one significant change in the jurisdiction of the communal courts: He rejected the Anglo-Saxon practice of allowing church officials to use the communal courts to decide religious matters. Instead, he mandated that the church should establish its own courts and that religious matters should be decided according to canon (church) law, rather than customary law.[40] William also declared that the Normans would settle their disputes in the courts of the lords and barons in agreement with feudal law.

England at that time consisted of two societies, one French and the other English.[41] French was the language spoken by the victorious Normans, as well as by the king, the upper classes, the clergy, and scholars.[42] Following the invasion, English was only spoken by the lower classes, and it did not achieve prominence and become the language of the courts and the "common law" until 1362.[43]

The French legacy can be seen in many words used by lawyers today. **Acquit, en banc, voir dire, demurrer, embezzle,** and **detainer** are some examples of English words that were borrowed from the French. Although the Normans spoke French, formal documents were written in Latin. This may help to explain why students reading judicial opinions in the twenty-first century encounter Latin words such as **certiorari, subpoena, mens rea, actus reus, in camera, mandamus, capias,** and **pro se.**

The Development of the Common Law

Over time, marriages between Norman and English families blurred the old class system. William's son Henry (who became Henry I), for example, married a descendant of the Anglo-Saxon royal house.[44] It was not until after 1453, when the French drove the English out of France (except for Calais), however, that the Normans and English were unified as one nation.

William died in 1100. The most important of his successors—in terms of the development of the common law—were Henry I and Henry's grandson, Henry II. After the death of the very unpopular William II, the nobles elected Henry I as king. Henry I had promised the nobles that if elected he would issue a charter in which he pledged to respect the rights of the nobles.[45] He also promised to be a fair ruler in the manner of William I. This charter is significant because it was a model for the most famous of all charters, the **Magna Carta.**[46]

Henry I ruled during a prosperous period and strengthened the king's powers while making peace with the church and feudal barons. He also strengthened the judiciary by requiring members of his council, the **Curia Regis,** to ride circuit occasionally throughout the country to listen to pleas and supervise the local courts. During this period, the communal courts, the religious courts, and the feudal courts of the barons were still meeting, and there was much confusion over jurisdiction.[47] Henry I encouraged people who distrusted the local courts to turn to the king for justice.

Henry II was the king most involved in the development of the central judiciary and the common law.[48] He created a professional royal court to hear civil litigation between ordinary parties (common pleas) and staffed this court with barons who had learned how to judge from working as members of the Curia Regis.[49] The king had some of his judges sit with him at Westminster (in London), and others traveled throughout the country listening to pleas and supervising local courts.[50] These royal judges applied the same law in each of the jurisdictions in which they held court.[51] They did not treat each case as if it were a case of first impression, or apply the customary law of the particular region. Decisions were not based on abstract principles and theories. The royal judges decided disputes in a consistent manner throughout the country, based on slowly evolving legal rules adopted by the members of the court.[52]

There were important procedural incentives for bringing suit in the royal courts rather than in the local courts. One was that the losing party in a communal or feudal court could have the decision reviewed by common pleas. Another was that the king enforced royal court judgments. Last, royal courts used juries instead of trials by battle and ordeal.[53]

One type of problem that was often brought to the king involved land disputes between neighboring nobles. One noble would claim part of his neighbor's land and seize it without bringing the matter to the attention of any court. Henry II's response was to allow victims to petition him for issuance of a writ of right. This writ, which was purchased from the king, directed the communal courts to do full justice without delay or to appear in a royal court and give an explanation.[54] The development of the writ of right resulted in a law making it illegal to dispossess someone of land without a trial conducted according to a royal writ.

The Normans became very creative in the way they used writs. Under the Norman kings, prospective plaintiffs had to obtain writs in order to litigate any claim. As the demand for writs increased, the responsibility for issuing them was transferred from

the king to the chancellor,[55] and in later years to the courts themselves. Each writ conferred jurisdiction on a designated court to resolve a particular dispute. It also specified many of the procedures to be followed since there was no general code of civil procedure to regulate the conduct of litigation.[56] A writ, for example, would often be addressed to the sheriff and would require him to summons in the defendant and convene a jury. In Henry I's era, there were very few writs. By Henry III's reign, many writs existed, including entry, debt, detinue, account, replevin, covenant, and novel disseisin (wrongful ejection).[57] A few master registers of writs were developed to form a primitive "law library."

By roughly 1200, the principal components of the common law system were in place. National law had replaced local and regional customs of the shire and hundred. A body of royal judges applied a common law throughout the nation, a tradition of respecting precedent was established, and the writ system was functioning.[58]

The development of legal literature was important to the development and improvement of the common law.[59] Henry Bracton, a thirteenth-century English lawyer, wrote commentaries on the writs of the day during the reign of Henry III (Henry II's grandson) and collected cases from the preceding twenty years.[60] During the fourteenth and fifteenth centuries, lawyers and law students began a series of "Year Books," a collection of the cases that had been heard in the most important courts for each year. The Year Books were discontinued in 1535 and were replaced by case reports, which were informal collections by various authors. Some of these authors, such as Chief Justice Edward Coke (pronounced "cook"), were well known and highly respected.[61] Coke published thirteen volumes of cases between 1572 and 1616. The reports established a process that in 1865 resulted in the publication of official law reports. In 1765, Sir William Blackstone, an Oxford professor, published a collection of his lectures in a book titled *Commentaries on the Laws of England*, which was immensely popular in the American colonies. The first American judicial reports were published in

1789, and James Kent's influential *Commentaries on American Law* was published between 1826 and 1830.[62]

The common law came to what is now the United States as a result of Britain's colonization policies. In the early 1600s, British monarchs began awarding charters to merchants and proprietors to establish colonies along the Atlantic coast of North America. Over the next 150 years, a steady flow of immigrants, most of whom were British, crossed the Atlantic, bringing the English language, culture, law books, and the English legal tradition. The common law was one major component of that tradition; another was the court of equity.

The Origin of the English Equitable Court

Until the fourteenth century, the common law courts were willing to consider arguments based on conscience as well as law. The judges were concerned with equity (fairness and mercy) as well as legality. By the fifteenth century, however, the common law courts were sometimes less concerned with justice than with technicalities. Common law pleading was complex and jury tampering was common.[63] The courts often refused to allow parties to testify, and there were no procedures for discovering an opponent's evidence. Although the common law courts were able to act against land and would award money judgments, they refused to grant injunctive relief (court orders directing individuals to perform or refrain from engaging in certain acts).[64] Unusual situations arose for which there was no common law relief, or where the relief available was inadequate as a remedy. In addition, the law courts were often slow, and litigation was very costly. Increasingly, dissatisfied parties began to petition the king and his council to intervene in the name of justice. As the number of petitions rose, the king and council forwarded the petitions to the chancellor.[65]

The **chancellor,** originally a high-ranking member of the clergy, was part of the royal household. He was the king's leading advisor in political matters and was a professional administrator. The chancellor's staff included people with judicial experience who issued the writs that enabled suitors to litigate in the common law courts.[66] Because they were ecclesiastics, the early chancellors were not trained as common law lawyers. They were well educated,[67] however, and were familiar with the canon law of the Roman Catholic Church.[68] As a result, the chancellors were often more receptive to arguments based on morality than to arguments based exclusively on legality.

As chancellors began to hear petitions, the **court of chancery,** or **equity court,** came into being. It granted relief based on broad principles of right and justice in cases in which the restrictions of the common law prevented it. Chancellors began to use the **writ of subpoena** to speed up their hearings and the **writ of summons** to require people to appear in the chancery.[69] Chancery trials were conducted before a single judge who sat without a jury. The chancellor, who exercised discretion and did not rely on precedent in granting relief, would only act where extraordinary relief was required, because no writ applied to the wrong from which the petitioner sought relief. One such area was specific performance of contracts. Although a suit for what we would call breach of contract could be maintained in a common law court, that court could not require a contracting party to perform his bargain. The chancellor, however, could issue such an order directed to the nonperforming person and could enforce it with the contempt power.

The equity court became very popular and was very busy by the middle 1500s. For centuries, common law and equity were administered in England by these two separate courts. Each court applied its own system of jurisprudence and followed its own judicial rules and remedies. Much of traditional equity is based on concepts such as adequacy, practicality, clean hands, and hardship (matters we discuss in Chapter VII). The equity court's workload continued to grow, as did the chancellor's staff. By the seventeenth century, the most important of the chancellor's staff clerks were called masters in chancery. The chief master was called the Master of the Rolls. Masters in chancery helped the chancellor conduct the equity court, particularly while the chancellor was performing nonjudicial duties for the king.

Initially, despite their differing aims, the common law courts and the equity court cooperated with each other. Starting with Henry VIII's reign, common law lawyers rather than ecclesiastics were named chancellor, which improved relations between courts of law and equity[70] Sir Thomas More, as chancellor, invited the common law judges to incorporate the notion of conscience into the common law, but the judges declined, preferring to stand behind the decisions of the juries. Gradually, however, this dual-court system created a competition for business, and the common law courts became more flexible by borrowing from equity. The equitable courts were also changing, and chancellors began to identify jurisdictional boundaries between the equitable and common law courts. Equity, for example, agreed to furnish a remedy only when the common law procedure was deficient or the remedy at common law was inadequate.[71]

Beginning in 1649, the decisions of the chancellors were sporadically collected and published, a process that led to the establishment of equitable precedent.[72] Eventually, equitable precedent made the equity courts as formalistic and rigid as the common law courts had been in equity's early days.[73] This dual-court system continued in England until the passage by Parliament of the Judicature Acts of 1873 and 1875, which merged the equitable and common law courts into a unified court.

Some North American colonies along the Atlantic coast diverged from British precedent when it came to the establishment of equity courts. Massachusetts never established an equity court, and its trial courts were not permitted to exercise the equitable powers of the chancellor until 1870. Maryland, New York, New Jersey, Delaware, North Carolina, and South Carolina initially established separate courts for common law and equity. However, by 1900 common law and equity had merged into a single judicial system in most states.

As you read the cases included in this textbook, you will notice that plaintiffs often request legal and equitable relief in the same complaint. A plaintiff may demand money damages (common law relief), a declaratory judgment (equitable relief), and an injunction (equitable relief) in the complaint. This creates no problem for the courts. The legal issues will be tried by a jury (unless the parties prefer a bench trial), and the equitable issues will be decided by the judge sitting as a chancellor according to the rules of equity. In Chapter VII we look more closely at the differences between the common law and equitable remedies.

A PROCEDURAL PRIMER

The following highly simplified overview of litigation is intended to give you a sense of the big picture before we examine each stage of the process in more detail. Like a trial attorney's opening statement in a jury trial, it is intended to help you see how the various procedural stages fit together. This abbreviated treatment omits many of the details and is intentionally very limited in scope.

Every lawsuit is based on some event that causes a person to feel that he or she has been legally injured in some manner by another. The injured party will often contact an attorney to discuss the matter. The attorney will listen to the facts, make a determination about whether the client has a case, and present the client with a range of options for pursuing a claim. These options will often include informal attempts to settle the claim, alternative dispute resolution methods such as those discussed in Chapter XIV, and filing suit in court. After weighing the costs and benefits of each option and listening to the advice of the attorney, the client will make a decision as to how to proceed. If the decision is made to file suit, the lawyer will draft a document called a **complaint** and a **writ of summons,** and serve them on the defendant in accordance with the law. The complaint will explain the plaintiff's claims and requested relief. The summons will tell the defendant to serve a document called an **answer** in which the defendant responds to the claims made in the complaint, on the plaintiff's attorney by a statutorily determined date. If the defendant's attorney finds any legal defects in jurisdiction, venue, form, or substance in either the summons or the complaint, he or she can make motions seeking modification or dismissal of the action. Assuming that the motions are denied and any defects are corrected, the defendant will then draft and serve the answer. If the defendant fails to file a timely answer, the court can declare the plaintiff the winner by default due to the defendant's inaction.

Once the complaint has been properly served and filed with the court, the **discovery** phase begins. This is where each party learns as much as possible about the case. Virtually all relevant information can be obtained from friendly, neutral, or adverse sources, such as the opposing party. Obviously some information is not discoverable, such as an attorney's trial strategy, research notes (work product), and other material that is classified as privileged. Later in the chapter, we learn specific techniques lawyers use during the discovery phase.

After the facts have been sufficiently investigated, one or both parties will frequently request the court to dispose of the case and award a **judgment** (the court's final decision in a case), rather than proceeding to trial. This request, called a **motion for summary judgment,** is properly granted when the plaintiff and defendant substantially agree about the important facts in the case. If there is no dispute about the significant facts, there is no reason to conduct a trial. In that situation, the judge can resolve any dispute about what legal rule applies to this particular set of facts and award a judgment to the deserving party.

It is important to note that informal discussions between the attorneys often take place at all stages of the process, up to and even during the course of the trial, in an effort to settle the case. These discussions usually intensify once motions for summary judgment have been denied and it appears that the case will be tried. Assuming that summary judgment is denied and there is no negotiated settlement, what usually follows is the pretrial conference.

At a **pretrial conference,** the court and the attorneys will meet to define the issues, prepare for the trial, and discuss the possibility of settlement. At this meeting, the parties can indicate how many days they believe it will take to try the case, try to resolve evidentiary and discovery problems, and schedule any necessary pretrial hearings. After the meeting, the judge will sign a pretrial order that records the decisions that were made at the conference.

Before proceeding to trial, many jurisdictions will require or encourage the litigating parties to participate in **alternative dispute resolution (ADR).** Some form of ADR is practiced in every state, but it is more commonly used in some jurisdictions than in others. The situation in the federal district courts is somewhat similar. Although all districts are required by federal statute to offer at least one ADR procedure, its use varies greatly by district.[74] ADR is an umbrella concept for a variety of procedures designed to help parties resolve their disputes without trials. Jurisdictions participate in ADR to differing degrees. Some mandate cooperation, and others make participation optional. In Chapter XIV we explain such ADR techniques as mediation, arbitration, summary jury trials, and minitrials, but we emphasize that any party dissatisfied with the ADR process can insist on proceeding to trial. There is a continuing dispute as to whether ADR is living up to its proponents' claims and producing faster, less expensive, and higher-quality justice than litigation.[75]

Less than 2 percent of all federal lawsuits filed actually are decided at trial.[76] Nonjury trials (also known as **bench trials**), in which a judge decides the factual issues, are conducted differently from trials in which juries render a verdict. In bench trials, for example, there are no jurors to select, the attorneys generally do not make opening statements, the rules of evidence are often relaxed, and there are no jury instructions to prepare and deliver. The judge will consider the evidence presented by each party and determine whether the plaintiff has satisfied the burden of proof. At the end of a bench trial, the judge will announce findings of fact, state conclusions of law, and award a judgment.

Additional procedures are necessary for jury trials. The jurors have to be carefully selected, and in major trials, the lawyers may seek help from trial consultants. Because jurors generally know little about rules of evidence and the applicable law, the lawyers do not present their cases as they would in a bench trial. Judges must keep the lawyers in check and ensure that the jury is exposed only to evidence that is relevant, material, and competent (legally adequate). After each side has had the opportunity to present evidence and cross-examine opposing witnesses, the attorneys will conclude by arguing their cases to the jury. After the closing arguments, the judge instructs the jury on the law and sends it out to deliberate. The jury deliberates until it reaches a verdict, which it reports to the court. After deciding any postverdict motions, the court will enter a **judgment** in favor of one of the parties and award relief accordingly. Normally any party dissatisfied with the judgment will have a specified number of days after the entry of judgment in which to make an appeal, provided timely objections were made during the trial.

READING CASES

The application of law to factual situations is necessary when there is a controversy between two or more people or when parties seek guidance concerning the consequences of their conduct or proposed conduct. The court cases in this text involve disputes that the parties were unable to resolve by themselves and that were brought to the trial and appellate courts for a decision. Most disputes, however, are settled by the parties outside court based on professional predictions of what a court would do.

Students learn to understand the legal process and the relationship between judicial theories and practical legal problems by analyzing actual court cases. The cases in this text illustrate particular points of law. They also convey current legal theory. These cases should serve as points of departure for discussions about the legal response to current social problems. It is important to understand the strengths and weaknesses of law as an instrument of social change.

Case reports are official explanations of a court's decision-making process. They explain which legal principles are applicable and why they are controlling under the particular circumstances of each case. Thus, in analyzing each case decision, students should focus on the underlying factual situation, the law that the court applied, whether the decision was just, and the impact the decision will have when it is used as precedent.

Author's Comment about *E. I. Du Pont de Nemours & Co., Inc. v. Christopher*

Persons interested in reading *E. I. Du Pont de Nemours & Co., Inc. v. Christopher*, which was the first case in editions of this textbook published between 1975 and 2006, can find it online in the "retired cases" section of the textbook's website. Many students who initially struggled with the *Du Pont* case later came to appreciate that it previewed and contributed to their understanding of their entire course.

Introduction to *Video Software Dealers Association et al. v. Arnold Schwarzenegger*

Our first case concerns the State of California's attempt to make it a crime for minors to rent or purchase video games featuring what many would consider to be "morbid or deviant" content, such as *Grand Theft Auto* and *Postal 2*. The state contended the aforementioned products and other games with similar content were harming minors.

A bill was passed by the state legislature and signed into law by the governor, which was intended to prevent minors from engaging in "violent, aggressive, and antisocial behavior," and protect minors who do play video games from sustaining "psychological or neurological harm." The state justified the need for such legislation by pointing to the disturbing content contained on such videos—images of humans being killed, maimed, dismembered, or sexually assaulted. The state also emphasized its legitimate concern about the impact these images could have on minors playing these games.

The law provided that video games containing "serious literary, artistic, political, or scientific" content, which were clearly appropriate for minors and compatible with existing community standards, were exempted from the provisions of this law. The statute also exempted purchases or rentals of "violent video games" made by parents for their children.

The Video Software Dealers Association (VSDA) and another trade association filed suit against the state to prevent the law's implementation.

The issue before the court for decision related to whether the statute infringed on the right to freedom of speech protected by the First and Fourteenth Amendments to the U. S. Constitution.

Video Software Dealers Association et al. v. Arnold Schwarzenegger
U.S. Court of Appeals for the Ninth Circuit
556 F.3d 950
February 20, 2009

Callahan, Circuit Judge:
Defendants–Appellants California Governor Schwarzenegger and California Attorney General Brown (the "State") appeal the district court's grant of summary judgment in favor of…Video Software Dealers Association and Entertainment Software Association ("Plaintiffs")…. Plaintiffs filed suit for declaratory relief seeking to invalidate newly enacted California Civil Code sections 1746–1746.5 (the "Act"), which impose restrictions…on the sale or rental of "violent video games" to minors, on the grounds that the Act violates rights guaranteed by the First and Fourteenth Amendments….

I.

A.
On October 7, 2005, Governor Schwarzenegger signed into law Assembly Bill 1179 ("AB 1179"), codified at Civil Code §§ 1746–1746.5 …. The Act states that "[a] person may not sell or rent a video game that has been labeled as a violent video game to a minor." Cal. Civ. Code § 1746.1(a)…. Violators are subject to a civil penalty of up to $ 1,000. Id. at § 1746.

Central to this appeal, the Act defines a "violent video game" as follows:

(d)(1) "Violent video game" means a video game in which the range of options available to a player includes killing, maiming, dismembering, or sexually assaulting an image of a human being, if those acts are depicted in the game in a manner that does either of the following:

(A) Comes within all of the following descriptions:
(i) A reasonable person, considering the game as a whole, would find appeals to a deviant or morbid interest of minors.

(ii) It is patently offensive to prevailing standards in the community as to what is suitable for minors.
(iii) It causes the game, as a whole, to lack serious literary, artistic, political, or scientific value for minors.
(B) Enables the player to virtually inflict serious injury upon images of human beings or characters with substantially human characteristics in a manner which is especially heinous, cruel, or depraved in that it involves torture or serious physical abuse to the victim….

Borrowing language from federal death penalty jury instructions, the Act also defines the terms "cruel," "depraved," "heinous," and "serious physical abuse,"… and states that "[p]ertinent factors in determining whether a killing depicted in a video game is especially heinous, cruel, or depraved include infliction of gratuitous violence upon the victim beyond that necessary to commit the killing, needless mutilation of the victim's body, and helplessness of the victim…."

A.B. 1179 states that the State of California has two compelling interests that support the Act: (1) "preventing violent, aggressive, and antisocial behavior"; and (2) "preventing psychological or neurological harm to minors who play violent video games." A.B. 1179 also "finds and declares" that

(a) Exposing minors to depictions of violence in video games, including sexual and heinous violence, makes those minors more likely to experience feelings of aggression, to experience a reduction of activity in the frontal lobes of the brain, and to exhibit violent antisocial or aggressive behavior.

(b) Even minors who do not commit acts of violence suffer psychological harm from prolonged exposure to violent video games.

The State included in the excerpts of record several hundred pages of material on which the Legislature purportedly relied in passing the Act. While many of the materials are social science studies on the asserted impact of violent video games on children, other documents are varied and include legal analyses, general background papers, position papers, etc.

B.
The content of the video games potentially affected by the Act is diverse. Some of the games to which the Act might apply are unquestionably violent by everyday standards, digitally depicting what most people would agree amounts to murder, torture, or mutilation. For example, the State submitted a videotape that contains several vignettes from the games Grand Theft Auto: Vice City, Postal 2, and Duke Nukem 3D, which demonstrate the myriad ways in which characters can kill or injure victims or adversaries.... The record also contains descriptions of several games, some of which are based on popular novels or motion pictures, which are potentially covered by the Act. Many of these games have extensive plot lines that involve or parallel historical events, mirror common fictional plots, or place the player in a position to evaluate and make moral choices.

The video game industry has in place a voluntary rating system to provide consumers and retailers information about video game content. The Entertainment Software Rating Board ("ESRB"), an independent, self-regulated body established by the Entertainment Software Association, rates the content of video games that are voluntarily submitted. ESRB assigns each game one of six age-specific ratings, ranging from "Early Childhood" to "Adults Only." It also assigns to each game one of roughly thirty content descriptors, which include "Animated Blood," "Blood and Gore," "Cartoon Violence," "Crude Humor," "Fantasy Violence," "Intense Violence," "Language," "Suggestive Themes," and "Sexual Violence."

II.
We review a grant of summary judgment de novo and must "determine, viewing the evidence in the light most favorable to the nonmoving party, whether there are any genuine issues of material fact and whether the district court correctly applied substantive law...."

IV.
The Supreme Court has stated that "minors are entitled to a significant measure of First Amendment protection, and only in relatively narrow and well-defined circumstances may government bar public dissemination of protected materials to them.... The State does not contest that video games are a form of expression protected by the First Amendment.... It is also undisputed that the Act seeks to restrict expression in video games based on its content.... ("[A] law is content-based if either the main purpose in enacting it was to suppress or exalt speech of a certain content, or it differentiates based on the content of speech on its face." ...We ordinarily review content-based restrictions on protected expression under strict scrutiny, and thus, to survive, the Act "must be narrowly tailored to promote a compelling Government interest." *United States v. Playboy Entm't Group, Inc.*, [529 U.S. 803... (2000)]. "If a less restrictive alternative would serve the Government's purpose, the legislature must use that alternative...." see also *Sable Commc'ns of Cal., Inc. v. FCC*...(1989) ("The Government may...regulate the content of constitutionally protected speech in order to promote a compelling interest if it chooses the least restrictive means to further the articulated interest.")....

The State, however, urges us to depart from this framework because the Act concerns minors. It argues... that the Court's reasoning in [*Ginsberg v. New York*, 390 U.S. 629 (1968)]...that a state could prohibit the sale of sexually explicit material to minors that it could not ban from distribution to adults should be extended to materials containing violence. This presents an invitation to reconsider the boundaries of the legal concept of "obscenity" under the First Amendment.

In *Ginsberg,* the Court held that New York State could prohibit the sale of sexually explicit material to minors that was defined by statute as obscene because of its appeal to minors...Therefore, the state could prohibit the sale of "girlie magazines" to minors regardless of the fact that the material was not considered obscene for adults.... The Court stated that "[t]o sustain the power to exclude material defined as obscenity by [the statute] requires only that we be able to say that it was not irrational for the legislature to find that exposure to material condemned by the statute is harmful to minors."...The Court offered two justifications for applying this rational basis standard: (1) that "constitutional interpretation has consistently recognized that the parents' claim to authority in their own household to direct the rearing of their children is basic in the structure of our society"; and (2) the State's "independent interest in the well being of its youth." ...

The State suggests that the justifications underlying *Ginsberg* should apply to the regulation of violent content as well as sexually explicit material. The assertion, however, fails when we consider the category of material to which the *Ginsberg* decision applies and the First Amendment principles in which that decision was rooted. *Ginsberg* is specifically rooted in the Court's First Amendment obscenity jurisprudence, which relates to non-protected sex-based expression—not violent content, which is presumably protected by the First Amendment.... *Ginsberg* explicitly states that the New York statute under review "simply adjusts the definition of obscenity to social realities by permitting the appeal of this type of material to be assessed in term of the sexual interests of such minors".... The *Ginsberg* Court applied a rational basis test to the statute at issue because it placed the magazines at issue within a sub-category of obscenity—obscenity as to minors—that had been determined to be not protected by the First Amendment, and it did not create an entirely new category of expression excepted from First Amendment protection. The State, in essence, asks us to create a new category of non-protected material based on its depiction of violence. The Supreme Court has carefully limited obscenity to sexual content. Although the Court has wrestled with the precise formulation of the legal test by which it classifies obscene material, it has consistently addressed obscenity with reference to sex-based material....

In light of our reading of *Ginsberg* and the cases from our sister circuits, we decline the State's invitation to apply the *Ginsberg* rationale to materials depicting violence, and hold that strict scrutiny remains the applicable review standard.... We decline the State's entreaty to extend the reach of *Ginsberg* and thereby redefine the concept of obscenity under the First Amendment.

V.

Accordingly, we review the Act's content-based prohibitions under strict scrutiny. As noted above, "[c]ontent-based regulations are presumptively invalid."...and to survive the Act "must be narrowly tailored to promote a compelling Government interest."... Further, "[i]f a less restrictive alternative would serve the Government's purpose, the legislature must use that alternative."...

A.

The Legislature stated that it had two compelling interests in passing the Act: (1) "preventing violent, aggressive, and antisocial behavior"; and (2) "preventing psychological or neurological harm to minors who play violent video games." Although there was some early confusion over whether the State was relying on both of these interests, the State subsequently clarified that "[t]he physical and psychological well-being of children is the concern of the Act," as distinguished from the interest of protecting third parties from violent behavior. The State's focus is on the actual harm to the brain of the child playing the video game. Therefore, we will not assess the Legislature's purported interest in the prevention of "violent, aggressive, and antisocial behavior"....

The Supreme Court has recognized that "there is a compelling interest in protecting the physical and psychological well-being of minors".... Notwithstanding this abstract compelling interest, when the government seeks to restrict speech "[i]t must demonstrate that the recited harms are real, not merely conjectural, and that the regulation will in fact alleviate these harms in a direct and material way".... Although we must accord deference to the predictive judgments of the legislature, our "obligation is to assure that, in formulating its judgments, [the legislature] has drawn reasonable inferences based on substantial evidence"...

In evaluating the State's asserted interests, we must distinguish the State's interest in protecting minors from actual psychological or neurological harm from the State's interest in controlling minors' thoughts. The latter is not legitimate.... Violence has always been and remains a central interest of humankind and a recurrent, even obsessive theme of culture both high and low. It engages the interest of children from an early age, as anyone familiar with the classic fairy tales collected by Grimm, Andersen, and Perrault is aware. To shield children right up to the age of eighteen from exposure to violent descriptions and images would not only be quixotic, but deforming; it would leave them unequipped to cope with the world as we know it.... *Interactive Digital Software Ass'n*.... Because the government may not restrict speech in order to control a minor's thoughts, we focus on the State's psychological harm rationale in terms of some actual effect on minors' psychological health.

Whether the State's interest in preventing psychological or neurological harm to minors is legally compelling depends on the evidence the State proffers of the effect of video games on minors. Although the Legislature is entitled to some deference, the courts are required to review whether the Legislature has drawn reasonable inferences from the evidence presented.... Here, the State relies on a number of studies in support of its argument that there is substantial evidence of a causal effect between minors playing violent video games and actual psychological harm....

[T]he evidence presented by the State does not support the Legislature's purported interest in preventing psychological or neurological harm. Nearly all of the research is based on correlation, not evidence of causation, and most of the studies suffer from significant, admitted flaws in methodology as they relate to the State's claimed interest. None of the research establishes or suggests a causal link between minors playing violent video games and actual psychological or neurological harm, and inferences to that effect would not be reasonable. In fact, some of the studies caution against inferring causation. Although we do not require the State to demonstrate a "scientific certainty," the State must come forward with more than it has. As a result, the State has not met its burden to demonstrate a compelling interest.

B.

Even if we assume that the State demonstrated a compelling interest in preventing psychological or neurological harm, the State still has the burden of demonstrating that the Act is narrowly tailored to further that interest, and that there are no less restrictive alternatives that would further the Act.... We hold that the State has not demonstrated that less restrictive alternative means are not available....

Based on the foregoing, and in light of the presumptive invalidity of content-based restrictions, we conclude that the Act fails under strict scrutiny review....

VII.

We decline the State's invitation to apply the variable obscenity standard from Ginsberg to the Act because we do not read Ginsberg as reaching beyond the context of restrictions on sexually explicit materials or as creating an entirely new category of expression—speech as to minors—excepted from First Amendment protections. As the Act is a content-based regulation, it is subject to strict scrutiny and is presumptively invalid. Under strict scrutiny, the State has not produced substantial evidence that supports the Legislature's conclusion that violent video games cause psychological or neurological harm to minors. Even if it did, the Act is not narrowly tailored to prevent that harm, and there remain less restrictive means of forwarding the State's purported interests, such as the improved ESRB rating system, enhanced educational campaigns, and parental controls.... Accordingly, the district court's grant of summary judgment to Plaintiffs...is AFFIRMED.

Case Questions

1. What claim was made by the VSDA in its complaint about the California violent video games law?
2. From what decision did the California officials appeal to the U.S. Court of Appeals for the Ninth Circuit?
3. Assume that the Ninth Circuit ruled in favor of the state, and minors were prohibited from purchasing violent video games. Think through what the subsequent consequences of such a ruling might be.
4. What explanation did the U.S. Court of Appeals give for its decision?

CASE ANALYSIS

Because the case of *Video Software Dealers Association ... v. Arnold Schwarzenegger* is the first reported judicial decision in this book, a brief introduction to case analysis is appropriate. The case heading consists of four items. The first line contains the names of the parties to the suit. The Video Software Dealers Association and the Entertainment Software Association (hereafter called the VSDA), were the plaintiffs (the parties filing the complaint in this case). Governor Arnold Schwarzenegger and California Attorney General Edmund G. Brown, Jr.

(hereafter called the "California officials") were the defendants (the parties being sued). The next item in the heading describes the volume and page where the judicial opinion in the case can be found. In this instance, the case is reported in volume 556 of the third series of the Federal Reporter (F.3d), on page 950. The name of the appellate court that decided the appeal is next in the heading, followed by the date the decision was published. Although federal and state trials are presided over by a single judge, cases reviewed by U.S. Circuit Courts of Appeals are normally reviewed by a panel of three judges. The VDSA case was decided by

Alex Kozinski, Chief Judge, and Circuit Judges Sidney R. Thomas and Consuelo M. Callahan.

The first item in the body of the court opinion is the name of the judge who wrote the appellate court's majority opinion (also called the opinion for the court). Generally only one of the judges voting with the majority of the court is selected to write the majority opinion. The other members of the court who constitute the majority are said to have "joined in the opinion." The majority opinion explains the court's decision in the case and the majority's reasoning for reaching that outcome. A concurring opinion is written by a judge who, while voting with the majority, has additional comments to make that go beyond what is included in the majority opinion. Sometimes the majority will agree on the decision but disagree on the reasons for that result. In such a case, the court will announce the decision, but there will be no majority opinion. The judges constituting the majority will write concurring opinions explaining their differing reasons for what they agree is the correct result. A judge who disagrees with the majority opinion can explain why in a dissenting opinion.

In our first case, the VSDA filed suit against the governor and attorney general. It asked for declaratory relief. This means that the VSDA requested that the trial court (the United States District Court for the Northern District of California—hereafter called the district court) award it a **declaratory judgment.** This means that the VSDA wanted the court to declare that the California "violent video games law" (Civil Code §§ 1746–1746.5) violated constitutionally protected free speech rights. The plaintiffs also requested that the district court issue an **injunction** (a court order requiring someone to perform some act or refrain from performing an act). In this case the plaintiffs sought an injunction prohibiting California from enforcing the "violent video games law." Both parties filed pretrial summary judgment motions, with the district court ruling in favor of the VSDA. That decision was appealed to the U.S. Court of Appeals for the Ninth Circuit because the California officials believed the district court had incorrectly decided the case. On appeal, the California officials, the

parties seeking appellate review, acquired the status of appellants and the VSDA became the appellees.

Only courts with appellate jurisdiction are entitled to decide cases on appeal. Appeals courts review the decisions of lower courts to see if substantial error was committed in those lower courts. An appellate court can affirm, reverse, and/or remand a lower court's decision. It can also, when appropriate, dismiss an appeal. If an appellate court affirms the lower court, it rules that the lower court's decision is valid and reasserts the judgment. If it reverses, it vacates and sets aside the lower court's judgment. Note that a decision can be reversed in part. When a case is remanded, it is returned to the lower court, generally with instructions as to further proceedings to be undertaken by the trial court.

In order to maximize the benefits of the case study method, one must read each case carefully and pay close attention to detail. After reading a case, one should have not merely a general sense or the gist of what the case says, but a precise understanding of what the court did.

Careful attention should be given to the **holding** of the case—the rule of law that the court says applies to the facts of the case. Majority opinions are often discursive and their authors often stray into writing about issues not actually before the court for decision. Such unnecessary comments are classified as **dicta.** Although these statements may appear to be important, if they are dicta they lack the authority of the case's holding.

Most students new to reading judicial opinions often find it helpful to **brief** a case. With practice it becomes possible to write a brief without having to refer back constantly to the judicial opinion itself. Briefing the case from memory provides a check on understanding, as well as an incentive to careful reading. A brief should contain the parts of the case selected as important, organized for the purpose at hand rather than in the haphazard order in which they may be reported.

The following brief of the *Video Software Dealers Association v. Arnold Schwarzenegger* case illustrates one way of briefing. The elements in the example are usually found in most briefs, though writing style is often a matter of individual preference. It is usually desirable to keep copying from the text of the case to a minimum; briefs are not exercises in stenography. This brief was written to help students who have not previously read a judicial opinion. It is intended to help these students understand what is important in the case reports they are reading.

Sample Brief

Video Software Dealers Association v. Schwarzenegger, 556 F.3d 950 (2009)

Facts: California adopted a statute making it a crime for persons under eighteen to purchase or rent what the law termed "violent video games." Violent video games were defined as being products that focused on images that "reasonable people" would think too extreme for minors to see and which otherwise lacked any redeeming literary, artistic, political, or scientific value. Proponents contended that the video games targeted in this statute contained content that was physically and psychologically harmful to minors. The state also argued that the games emphasized "deviant and morbid images," a focus incompatible with "community standards."

Two video trade associations filed suit against the state in the local federal district court, claiming that the "violent video games" statute infringed on constitutionally protected rights to freedom of speech.

Both sides moved for summary judgment, each asserting that there were no material facts in dispute that needed to be resolved and each claiming that it was entitled to judgment as a matter of law with respect to the constitutional claims.

The district court ruled against the state and the state appealed that decision to the U.S. Court of Appeals for the Ninth Circuit.

Issues Presented or Questions of Law:

1. Is a California statute that restricts the right of minors to purchase video games containing violent content subject to strict scrutiny review?

    The district court ruled that strict scrutiny was required.

2. Did the state prove the existence of compelling interests sufficient to justify restricting the free speech rights of minors to purchase and view video games containing violent content?

    The district court ruled that the state had not proven its compelling interest claim and that even if it had, the statutory restrictions had not been narrowly tailored.

3. Did the state disprove the possibility that less restrictive alternative means exist, other than the statute, for remedying the alleged compelling interest, and was the statute narrowly tailored?

    The district court did not address this issue.

Holding: The U.S. Court of Appeals for the Ninth Circuit affirmed the district court's grant of summary judgment in favor of VSDA. It held that minors have the right to purchase violent video games because the California violent video games statute violated the right to freedom of expression protected by the First and Fourteenth Amendments.

Rationale: The appellate court explained the reasoning behind its holding as follows:

1. The statute is subject to strict scrutiny review. Freedom of expression has been recognized by the U.S. Supreme Court as one of the most fundamental of our constitutional rights. Normally state laws that restrict freedom of expression are presumed to be unconstitutional and can only survive constitutional challenge if they pass a rigorous level of judicial examination called *strict scrutiny*. The parties to this case disagreed about whether the court of appeals should examine the "violent video game" statute using the strict scrutiny test or should apply a less-demanding standard. The VSDA argued that strict scrutiny was required, and that to save the statute the state had to prove

the existence of a "compelling interest" that would justify overriding minors' right to freedom of expression. The state disagreed. It urged the court of appeals to use a "a more relaxed" level of scrutiny when examining the video game statute. It urged the court of appeals to use the same level of scrutiny that the U.S. Supreme Court had approved in the 1968 case of *Ginsburg v. New York*. *Ginsburg* was a case in which the Supreme Court found constitutional a New York state statute that prohibited minors from purchasing "sexually explicit" materials. The Supreme Court ruled in that case that the New York statute did not have to undergo strict scrutiny review. Statutes that restrict minors from purchasing "sexually explicit" materials can survive a constitutional challenge, said the Supreme Court, if there is a rational basis for such laws. To be constitutional under this more relaxed, rationally based standard, the state would only have to prove there was some rationality supporting the legislature's conclusion that "the exposure [of minors] to [sexually explicit] material condemned by the statute is harmful to others." The court of appeals rejected the state's compelling-interest claim, concluding that the *Ginsburg* precedent was "rooted in obscenity" law and had not been extended into "violence" jurisprudence. The Ninth Circuit, after researching the law, found no cases in which the definition of obscenity had been extended beyond sexually oriented materials. The Ninth Circuit declared itself to be unwilling to break new ground itself by defining obscenity as including violence. Thus it concluded that the California statute would only be constitutional if it could withstand strict scrutiny review.

2. The state failed to meet its burden of proving that a compelling interest exists, which is necessary to justify infringing on a minor's right to purchase video games containing violent content.

   The court of appeals, as part of its strict scrutiny review, examined the interests that the state claimed were so compelling as to warrant restricting minors' free speech rights. The state claimed the challenged statute would help to prevent minors from engaging in "violent, aggressive, and antisocial behavior" and would also protect them from sustaining "psychological or neurological harm." The court of appeals reviewed the research studies that the state claimed established a causal relationship linking the playing of violent video games to the occurrence of physical and neurological harm in minors. After identifying serious weaknesses in the proffered research and determining that its probative value was unimpressive, the court of appeals concluded that the state had not proven its compelling interest claim.

3. The state failed to meet either (a) its obligation to disprove the possibility that other nonstatutory, less restrictive options would be equally as effective as, or more effective than, the challenged statute in achieving the government's stated interests, or (b) its obligation to prove that the challenged statute was narrowly tailored.

   The Ninth Circuit was critical of the state's failure to disprove the efficacy of less restrictive alternatives to the challenged statute. This lack of proof led the appellate court to conclude that the statute was not narrowly tailored. The appellate court also objected to the related failure of the state to specifically respond to the video game industry's voluntary efforts to rate videos as to age appropriateness and to educate sellers and buyers of video games about the substantive content of each video.

Video Software Dealers Association Update

Governor Schwarzenegger successfully petitioned the U.S. Supreme Court for certiorari in this case. The high court is not expected to decide the case until spring 2011. The U.S. Supreme Court's decision will be posted on the textbook website once the justices announce their ruling.

DUE PROCESS

The Due Process Clauses of the Fifth and Fourteenth Amendments to the U.S. Constitution provide that no person shall be "deprived of life, liberty, or property, without due process of law." These clauses are deeply embedded in Anglo-American legal history, going back to 1215. In June of that year, English barons decided that King John had been acting arbitrarily and in violation of their rights. They sought protection from the king in the Magna Carta, a charter containing sixty-three chapters that limited the king's powers.[77] Chapter XXXIX of the Magna Carta is the predecessor of our Due Process Clauses.

It provided that "no man shall be captured or imprisoned or disseised or outlawed or exiled or in any way destroyed, nor will we go against him or send against him, except by the lawful judgment of his peers or by the law of the land."[78]

The barons amassed an army, confronted the king, and forced him to agree to the Magna Carta. Subsequent monarchs reissued the Magna Carta many times over the next two centuries.[79] In 1354 the words "by the law of the land" (which were initially written in Latin) were translated into English to mean "by due process of the law."[80] In the seventeenth century, these words were interpreted to include the customary rights and liberties of Englishmen.[81] English legal commentators further expanded the scope of due process by arguing that it included what philosopher John Locke called each individual's natural right to "life, liberty, and property."[82]

The Magna Carta's influence in this country is apparent in the 1776 constitutions of Maryland and North Carolina, which contain due process language taken verbatim from the Magna Carta. In 1791 the Due Process Clause was included in the Fifth Amendment to the U.S. Constitution. Every person in our society has an inherent right to due process of law, which protects him or her from arbitrary, oppressive, and unjust governmental actions. If a proceeding results in the denial of fundamental fairness and shocks the conscience of a court, a violation of due process has occurred. In addition, under both the Fifth and Fourteenth Amendments, a corporation, as well as a partnership or unincorporated association, is a person to whom that protection applies.

Due process of the law focuses on deprivations of "life, liberty, and property." "Life" refers to deprivation of biological life and to a person's right to have a particular lifestyle. "Liberty," as is further explained below, covers a vast scope of personal rights. It also implies the absence of arbitrary and unreasonable governmental restraints on an individual's person, as well as the freedom to practice a trade or business, the right to contract, and the right to establish a relationship with one's children. "Property" is everything that may be subject to ownership, including real and personal property, obligations, rights, legal entitlements such as a public education, and other intangibles.

Determining what due process means in a given factual situation has been a matter for the judiciary. In this, the courts are influenced by procedures that were established under English common law prior to the enactment of our constitution. They are also influenced by contemporary events, values, and political and economic conditions.

The due process guarantee protects people from unfairness in the operation of both substantive and procedural law. Substantive law refers to the law that creates, defines, and regulates rights. It defines the legal relationship between the individual and the state and among individuals themselves and is the primary responsibility of the legislative branch of the government. Procedural law prescribes the method used to enforce legal rights. It provides the machinery by which individuals can enforce their rights or obtain redress for the invasion of such rights.

The Fifth and Fourteenth Amendments

The Fifth Amendment guarantee of due process of law was included in the Bill of Rights in order to place limits on the federal government. It was intended to control the Congress, and prior to the Civil War, it was primarily used to protect property rights from governmental regulation. The Due Process Clause was also interpreted by the Supreme Court to overrule those parts of the Missouri Compromise that prohibited slavery. In the *Dred Scott* case (60 U.S. 393 [1861]), the Supreme Court ruled that slaves were property, and thus the Due Process Clause prohibited Congress from making slavery illegal. This is a historical irony, given the role due process has played in promoting civil rights in recent decades. Even during the Civil War era, many abolitionists interpreted due process differently and identified this Fifth Amendment clause as the basis for their convictions, maintaining that states had no right to deny slaves, or any other person, the right to life, liberty, or property without due process of law.

The addition of the Fourteenth Amendment to the Constitution in 1868 reflected the abolitionists' position. From that point forward, state governments were constitutionally required to provide due process of law and equal protection of the law to *all* people.

The Meaning of Substantive Due Process

The Bill of Rights contains many specifics regarding procedural fairness, particularly in criminal cases, but the meaning of substantive due process is less obvious. In our system of government, the U.S. Supreme Court has historically borne the responsibility for determining the degree to which the concept of due process includes a substantive dimension.

In substantive due process cases, the claimant challenges a statute on the grounds that the law excessively intrudes on individual decision making. The claimant argues that the infringement is against that person's due process liberty interest. When the court examines the facts, it often discovers that the government has no legitimate interest in the matter and is acting arbitrarily, and the claimant has an important, historically validated interest (a "fundamental right," in legalese) to make the decision. The court decides these claims on a case-by-case basis, and the claimant wins when a majority of justices conclude that the claimed right should be

classified as fundamental given these particular circumstances.

An example of such a case is found in Chapter IX of this textbook in a case decided by the U.S. Supreme Court in 1967, titled *Loving v. Virginia.* Richard Loving, who was white, and his wife, Mildred, who was black, brought suit challenging Virginia's antimiscegenation laws (statutes making it illegal for white people to marry black people). The U.S. Supreme Court ruled in favor of the Lovings. It concluded that the decision as to whether to enter into an interracial marriage was a matter for Richard and Mildred, not the Commonwealth of Virginia. The Court said that Virginia had no legitimate interest in the races of married people, and could not categorically prohibit black and white people from marrying one another.

But most persons seeking federal due process protection are unsuccessful. You will soon read the case of *Washington v. Glucksberg,* in which doctors unsuccessfully argued before the U.S. Supreme Court that they had a constitutionally protected due process right to assist their terminally ill patients to commit suicide. The Supreme Court ultimately decided that the doctors' claim was not within the scope of due process protection.

U.S. Supreme Court Justice David H. Souter commented in *Washington v. Glucksberg,* 521 U.S. 702 (1997), on substantive due process in his concurring opinion. Souter, although voting with the majority to sustain Washington's statute, recognized the conceptual legitimacy of substantive due process. He referred to substantive due process as the long-standing "American constitutional practice... [of] recognizing unenumerated substantive limits on governmental action" (e.g., rights not explicitly included in the text of the Constitution).

This "American constitutional practice" was also acknowledged by the late Chief Justice Rehnquist in *Cruzan v. Missouri Department of Health,* 497 U.S. 261 (1990), where he asserted in his opinion for the Court that "the principle that a competent person has a constitutionally protected liberty interest in refusing unwanted medical treatment may be inferred from our prior decisions." In *Cruzan,* as in *Glucksberg* and *Loving,* the fact that the

Due Process Clauses were textually silent about a substantive due process claim did not preclude the Court from recognizing that such an unenumerated right is protected within the scope of substantive due process.

Substantive Due Process and Economic and Social Regulation

In the years following the enactment of the Fourteenth Amendment, the U.S. Supreme Court began a slow process of expanding the substantive meaning of due process. As we learned in the earlier discussion of sociological jurisprudence, the Supreme Court in the 1890s was unsympathetic to the Progressives and state reform legislation. In the early cases, the states usually won if they were legislating to protect the public's health, welfare, safety, or morals. Gradually, however, the Court began using the Fourteenth Amendment to strike down state social and economic legislation. The justices often concluded that these laws exceeded the state's legislative power because they infringed upon the individual's due process right to contract. They maintained that the individual had the right to determine how many hours he or she wanted to work, at least in nonhazardous occupations. And legislative attempts to set minimum wages for women hospital workers were viewed by the Court as "price fixing." The Court was, in effect, sitting in judgment on the legislative policies themselves. The Court used the Due Process Clause as an instrument for striking down social and economic legislation with which it disagreed.

The depression of the 1930s resulted in New Deal legislative initiatives that were intended to stimulate the economy. Congress created numerous agencies and programs in order to benefit industry, labor, savers and investors, farmers, and the needy. However, the Supreme Court struck down many of these New Deal laws between 1934 and 1936. This made the Court very unpopular in the "court" of public opinion, and the president responded by proposing that Congress increase the size of the Court, presumably so that he could nominate people for the new seats who were sympathetic to

New Deal legislation. In 1936, the Supreme Court began to reverse itself and uphold New Deal legislation. In 1937, the Court's majority began using the Commerce Clause to sustain federal legislation, and they were no longer using the due Process Clause to overturn state reforms. The Court replaced the dual federalism doctrine, which attempted to enforce strict boundaries around the federal and state "zones of interest," with a general policy of deference to legislative preferences with respect to social and economic policies that are in its view neither arbitrary nor irrational.

However, the traditional deference shown to Congress was called into question in 1995 in the case of *United States v. Lopez* (a "Commerce Clause" case that can be read on this textbook's website), in which the Supreme Court explicitly held that Congress did not have the right under the Commerce Clause to criminalize the possession of a gun within a local school zone because there was no connection between the legislation and commerce. The Court also used this same rationale in 2000 to strike down a portion of the Violence Against Women Act in the case of *United States v. Morrison*. But as we will see in *Gonzales v. Raich* (the "medical marijuana" case you will read in Chapter III), the Supreme Court in 1995 upheld Congress's right to make it a crime for someone to grow their own marijuana for personal medicinal purposes. It is unlikely that the existing ambiguity about the Commerce Clause will be resolved in a clear-cut, doctrinaire manner. Rather, its meaning will probably evolve slowly on a case-by-case basis in the traditional common law manner.

The Scope of Substantive Due Process

In the 1920s, the Supreme Court began to recognize that an individual's liberty rights included more than just property rights. Individual "liberty" also required the constitutional protection of certain kinds of conduct. The justices of the U.S. Supreme Court differed, however, about whether such rights could be "found" within the meaning of due process. Although various justices on the Court proposed limits on the scope of substantive due process, the majority on the Court adopted what is called the selective incorporation approach. This approach recognizes that all rights that the Court deems to be fundamental are included in the concept of due process.

Fundamental rights include those that have historically been part of our legal tradition, such as the First Amendment freedoms. Other fundamental rights include intimate decisions relating to marriage, procreation, contraception, family relations, child rearing, and education. The determination of whether a right is fundamental is made by the U.S. Supreme Court on a case-by-case basis.

The following case of *Washington v. Glucksberg* illustrates conflicting approaches to the meaning of substantive due process. In this case, Dr. Harold Glucksberg and four other doctors brought suit for declaratory and injunctive relief against the state of Washington. They sought to enjoin the enforcement of a Washington statute that made it a crime for the doctors to help three of their mentally competent but terminally ill patients to commit suicide. The late Chief Justice Rehnquist first explains his views on the proper scope of substantive due process under the Fourteenth Amendment. Recently retired Associate Justice David Souter then explains that although he agrees with Rehnquist as to the correct decision in the case, he profoundly disagrees with the chief justice about the proper scope of substantive due process.

Washington et al., Petitioners v. Harold Glucksberg et al.
521 U.S. 702
U.S. Supreme Court
June 26, 1997

Chief Justice Rehnquist delivered the opinion of the Court.
The question presented in this case is whether Washington's prohibition against "causing" or "aiding" a suicide offends the Fourteenth Amendment to the United States Constitution. We hold that it does not.

It has always been a crime to assist a suicide in the State of Washington. In 1854, Washington's first Territorial Legislature outlawed "assisting another in the commission of self murder." Today, Washington law provides: "A person is guilty of promoting a suicide attempt when he knowingly causes or aids another person to attempt suicide."…"Promoting a suicide attempt" is a felony, punishable by up to five years' imprisonment and up to a $10,000 fine…. At the same time, Washington's Natural Death Act, enacted in 1979, states that the "withholding or withdrawal of life sustaining treatment" at a patient's direction "shall not, for any purpose, constitute a suicide"…

Petitioners in this case are the State of Washington and its Attorney General. Respondents Harold Glucksberg, M.D., Abigail Halperin, M.D., Thomas A. Preston, M.D., and Peter Shalit, M.D., are physicians who practice in Washington. These doctors occasionally treat terminally ill, suffering patients, and declare that they would assist these patients in ending their lives if not for Washington's assisted suicide ban. In January 1994, respondents, along with three gravely ill, pseudonymous plaintiffs who have since died and Compassion in Dying, a nonprofit organization that counsels people considering physician assisted suicide, sued in the United States District Court, seeking a declaration that Wash Rev. Code 9A.36.060(1) (1994) is, on its face, unconstitutional.

The plaintiffs asserted "the existence of a liberty interest protected by the Fourteenth Amendment which extends to a personal choice by a mentally competent, terminally ill adult to commit physician assisted suicide." …Relying primarily on *Planned Parenthood v. Casey*, 505 U.S. 833 (1992), and *Cruzan v. Director, Missouri Dept. of Health*, 497 U.S. 261 (1990), the District Court agreed… and concluded that Washington's assisted suicide ban is unconstitutional because it "places an undue burden on the exercise of [that] constitutionally protected liberty interest."…The District Court also decided that the Washington statute violated the Equal Protection Clause's requirement that "all persons similarly situated…be treated alike"…

A panel of the Court of Appeals for the Ninth Circuit reversed, emphasizing that "in the two hundred and five years of our existence no constitutional right to aid in killing oneself has ever been asserted and upheld by a court of final jurisdiction."...The Ninth Circuit reheard the case en banc, reversed the panel's decision, and affirmed the District Court.... Like the District Court, the en banc Court of Appeals emphasized our *Casey* and *Cruzan* decisions.... The court also discussed what it described as "historical" and "current societal attitudes" toward suicide and assisted suicide... and concluded that "the Constitution encompasses a due process liberty interest in controlling the time and manner of one's death—that there is, in short, a constitutionally recognized 'right to die.'"...After "weighing and then balancing" this interest against Washington's various interests, the court held that the State's assisted suicide ban was unconstitutional "as applied to terminally ill competent adults who wish to hasten their deaths with medication prescribed by their physicians."...The court did not reach the District Court's equal protection holding.... We granted certiorari...and now reverse.

I.

We begin, as we do in all due process cases, by examining our Nation's history, legal traditions, and practices.... In almost every State—indeed, in almost every western democracy—it is a crime to assist a suicide. The States' assisted suicide bans are not innovations. Rather, they are long-standing expressions of the States' commitment to the protection and preservation of all human life.... Indeed, opposition to and condemnation of suicide—and, therefore, of assisting suicide—are consistent and enduring themes of our philosophical, legal, and cultural heritages....

More specifically, for over 700 years, the Anglo American common law tradition has punished or otherwise disapproved of both suicide and assisting suicide.... In the thirteenth century, Henry de Bracton, one of the first legal treatise writers, observed that "just as a man may commit felony by slaying another so may he do so by slaying himself." ...The real and personal property of one who killed himself to avoid conviction and punishment for a crime were forfeit to the king; however, thought Bracton, "if a man slays himself in weariness of life or because he is unwilling to endure further bodily pain...[only] his movable goods [were] confiscated." ...Thus, "the principle that suicide of a sane person, for whatever reason, was a punishable felony was...introduced into English common law." Centuries later, Sir William Blackstone, whose *Commentaries on the Laws of England* not only provided a definitive summary of the common law but was also a primary legal authority for 18th and 19th century American lawyers, referred to suicide as "self murder" and "the pretended heroism, but real cowardice, of the Stoic philosophers, who destroyed themselves to avoid those ills which they had not the fortitude to endure...." Blackstone emphasized that "the law has... ranked [suicide] among the highest crimes," although, anticipating later developments, he conceded that the harsh and shameful punishments imposed for suicide "borde[r] a little upon severity." ...

For the most part, the early American colonies adopted the common law approach....

Over time, however, the American colonies abolished these harsh common law penalties. William Penn abandoned the criminal forfeiture sanction in Pennsylvania in 1701, and the other colonies (and later, the other States) eventually followed this example....

Nonetheless, although States moved away from Blackstone's treatment of suicide, courts continued to condemn it as a grave public wrong....

That suicide remained a grievous, though nonfelonious, wrong is confirmed by the fact that colonial and early state legislatures and courts did not retreat from prohibiting assisting suicide.... And the prohibitions against suicide never contained exceptions for those who were near death....

The earliest American statute explicitly to outlaw assisting suicide was enacted in New York in 1828 ... and many of the new States and Territories followed New York's example.... In this century, the Model Penal Code also prohibited "aiding" suicide, prompting many States to enact or revise their assisted suicide bans. The Code's drafters observed that "the interests in the sanctity of life that are represented by the criminal homicide laws are threatened by one who expresses a willingness to participate in taking the life of another, even though the act may be accomplished with the consent, or at the request, of the suicide victim." ...

Though deeply rooted, the States' assisted suicide bans have in recent years been re-examined and, generally, reaffirmed. Because of advances in medicine and technology, Americans today are increasingly likely to die in institutions, from chronic illnesses.... Public concern and democratic action are therefore sharply focused on how best to protect dignity and independence at the end of life, with the result that there have been many significant changes in state laws and in the attitudes these laws reflect. Many States, for example, now permit "living wills," surrogate health care decision making, and the withdrawal or refusal of life sustaining medical treatment.... At the same time, however, voters and legislators continue for the most part to reaffirm their States' prohibitions on assisting suicide.

The Washington statute at issue in this case...was enacted in 1975 as part of a revision of that State's criminal code. Four years later, Washington passed its Natural Death Act, which specifically stated that the "withholding or withdrawal of life sustaining treatment ...shall not, for any purpose, constitute a suicide" and that "nothing in this chapter shall be construed to condone, authorize, or approve mercy killing...." In 1991, Washington voters rejected a ballot initiative which, had it passed, would have permitted a form of physician assisted suicide. Washington then added a provision to the Natural Death Act expressly excluding physician assisted suicide....Wash. Rev. Code § 70.122.100 (1994).

Attitudes toward suicide itself have changed since *Bracton*, but our laws have consistently condemned, and continue to prohibit, assisting suicide. Despite changes in medical technology and notwithstanding an increased emphasis on the importance of end of life decision making, we have not retreated from this prohibition. Against this backdrop of history, tradition, and practice, we now turn to respondents' constitutional claim.

II

The Due Process Clause guarantees more than fair process, and the "liberty" it protects includes more than the absence of physical restraint.... The Clause also provides heightened protection against government interference with certain fundamental rights and liberty interests.... In a long line of cases, we have held that, in addition to the specific freedoms protected by the Bill of Rights, the "liberty" specifically protected by the Due Process Clause includes the rights to marry, *Loving v. Virginia*, 388 U.S. 1 (1967); to have children, *Skinner v. Oklahoma ex rel. Williamson*, 316 U.S. 535 (1942); to direct the education and upbringing of one's children, *Meyer v. Nebraska*, 262 U.S. 390 (1923); *Pierce v. Society of Sisters*, 268 U.S. 510 (1925); to marital privacy, *Griswold v. Connecticut*, 381 U.S. 479 (1965); to use contraception, ...*Eisenstadt v. Baird*, 405 U.S. 438 (1972); to bodily integrity, *Rochin v. California*, 342 U.S. 165 (1952), and to abortion.... We have also assumed, and strongly suggested, that the Due Process Clause protects the traditional right to refuse unwanted life-saving medical treatment. *Cruzan*, 497 U.S., at 278–279.

But we "ha[ve] always been reluctant to expand the concept of substantive due process because guideposts for responsible decision making in this unchartered area are scarce and open ended." ...By extending constitutional protection to an asserted right or liberty interest, we, to a great extent, place the matter outside the arena of public debate and legislative action.

We must therefore "exercise the utmost care whenever we are asked to break new ground in this field," ...lest the liberty protected by the Due Process Clause be subtly transformed into the policy preferences of the members of this Court....

Our established method of substantive due process analysis has two primary features: First, we have regularly observed that the Due Process Clause specially protects those fundamental rights and liberties which are, objectively, "deeply rooted in this Nation's history and tradition," ..."so rooted in the traditions and conscience of our people as to be ranked as fundamental," and "implicit in the concept of ordered liberty," such that "neither liberty nor justice would exist if they were sacrificed." ...Second, we have required in substantive due process cases a "careful description" of the asserted fundamental liberty interest.... Our Nation's history, legal traditions, and practices thus provide the crucial "guideposts for responsible decision making" ...that direct and restrain our exposition of the Due Process Clause. As we stated recently...the Fourteenth Amendment "forbids the government to infringe...'fundamental' liberty interests at all, no matter what process is provided, unless the infringement is narrowly tailored to serve a compelling state interest." ...Justice Souter, relying on Justice Harlan's dissenting opinion in *Poe v. Ullman*, would largely abandon this restrained methodology, and instead ask "whether [Washington's] statute sets up one of those 'arbitrary impositions' or 'purposeless restraints' at odds with the Due Process Clause of the Fourteenth Amendment," ...(quoting *Poe* ...[1961] [Harlan, J., dissenting]). In our view, however, the development of this Court's substantive due process jurisprudence, described briefly above...has been a process whereby the outlines of the "liberty" specially protected by the Fourteenth Amendment—never fully clarified, to be sure, and perhaps not capable of being fully clarified—have at least been carefully refined by concrete examples involving fundamental rights found to be deeply rooted in our legal tradition. This approach tends to rein in the subjective elements that are necessarily present in due process judicial review. In addition, by establishing a threshold requirement—that a challenged state action implicate a fundamental right—before requiring more than a reasonable relation to a legitimate state interest to justify the action, it avoids the need for complex balancing of competing interests in every case.

Turning to the claim at issue here, the Court of Appeals stated that "properly analyzed, the first issue to be resolved is whether there is a liberty interest in determining the time and manner of one's death"...or, in other words, "is there a right to die?"...Similarly, respondents assert a "liberty to choose how to die" and a right to "control of one's final days"...and describe the asserted liberty as "the right to choose a humane, dignified death" ...and "the liberty to shape death." ...As noted above, we have a tradition of carefully formulating the interest at stake in substantive due process cases. For example, although *Cruzan* is often described as a "right to die" case ...we were, in fact, more precise: we assumed that the Constitution granted competent persons a "constitutionally protected right to refuse life-saving hydration and nutrition." ...The Washington statute at issue in this case prohibits "aid[ing] another person to attempt suicide"...and, thus, the question before us is whether the "liberty" specially protected by the Due Process Clause includes a right to commit suicide which itself includes a right to assistance in doing so.

We now inquire whether this asserted right has any place in our Nation's traditions. Here, as discussed above...we are confronted with a consistent and almost universal tradition that has long rejected the asserted right, and continues explicitly to reject it today, even for terminally ill, mentally competent adults. To hold for respondents, we would have to reverse centuries of legal doctrine and practice, and strike down the considered policy choice of almost every State....

Respondents contend, however, that the liberty interest they assert is consistent with this Court's substantive due process line of cases, if not with this Nation's history and practice. Pointing to *Casey* and *Cruzan*, respondents read our jurisprudence in this area as reflecting a general tradition of "self sovereignty" ...and as teaching that the "liberty" protected by the Due Process Clause includes "basic and intimate exercises of personal autonomy." ...According to respondents, our liberty jurisprudence, and the broad, individualistic principles it reflects, protects the "liberty of competent, terminally ill adults to make end of life decisions free of undue government interference." ... The question presented in this case, however, is whether the protections of the Due Process Clause include a right to commit suicide with another's assistance. With this "careful description" of respondents' claim in mind, we turn to *Casey* and *Cruzan*.

Respondents contend that in *Cruzan* we "acknowledged that competent, dying persons have the right to direct the removal of life sustaining medical treatment and thus hasten death," ...and that "the constitutional principle behind recognizing the patient's liberty to direct the withdrawal of artificial life support applies at least as strongly to the choice to hasten impending death by consuming lethal medication." ...Similarly, the Court of Appeals

concluded that "*Cruzan*, by recognizing a liberty interest that includes the refusal of artificial provision of life sustaining food and water, necessarily recognize[d] a liberty interest in hastening one's one death." ...

The right assumed in *Cruzan*, however, was not simply deduced from abstract concepts of personal autonomy. Given the common law rule that forced medication was a battery, and the long legal tradition protecting the decision to refuse unwanted medical treatment, our assumption was entirely consistent with this Nation's history and constitutional traditions. The decision to commit suicide with the assistance of another may be just as personal and profound as the decision to refuse unwanted medical treatment, but it has never enjoyed similar legal protection. Indeed, the two acts are widely and reasonably regarded as quite distinct.... In *Cruzan* itself, we recognize that most States outlawed assisted suicide—and even more do today—and we certainly gave no intimation that the right to refuse unwanted medical treatment could be somehow transmuted into a right to assistance in committing suicide....

Respondents also rely on *Casey*. There, the Court's opinion concluded that "the essential holding of *Roe v. Wade* should be retained and once again reaffirmed." ...We held, first, that a woman has a right, before her fetus is viable, to an abortion "without undue interference from the State"; second, that States may restrict post-viability abortions, so long as exceptions are made to protect a woman's life and health; and third, that the State has legitimate interests throughout a pregnancy in protecting the health of the woman and the life of the unborn child.... In reaching this conclusion, the opinion discussed in some detail this Court's substantive due process tradition of interpreting the Due Process Clause to protect certain fundamental rights and "personal decisions relating to marriage, procreation, contraception, family relationships, child rearing, and education," and noted that many of those rights and liberties "involv[e] the most intimate and personal choices a person may make in a lifetime." ...

The Court of Appeals, like the District Court, found *Casey* '"highly instructive'" and '"almost prescriptive'" for determining '"what liberty interest may inhere in a terminally ill person's choice to commit suicide.'"

'"Like the decision of whether or not to have an abortion, the decision how and when to die is one of 'the most intimate and personal choices a person may make in a lifetime,' a choice 'central to personal dignity and autonomy.'"

By choosing this language, the Court's opinion in *Casey* described, in a general way and in light of our prior cases, those personal activities and decisions that this Court has identified as so deeply rooted in our history and traditions, or so fundamental to our concept of constitutionally ordered liberty, that they are protected by the Fourteenth Amendment…. That many of the rights and liberties protected by the Due Process Clause sound in personal autonomy does not warrant the sweeping conclusion that any and all important, intimate, and personal decisions are so protected …and *Casey* did not suggest otherwise.

The history of the law's treatment of assisted suicide in this country has been and continues to be one of the rejection of nearly all efforts to permit it. That being the case, our decisions lead us to conclude that the asserted "right" to assistance in committing suicide is not a fundamental liberty interest protected by the Due Process Clause. The Constitution also requires, however, that Washington's assisted suicide ban be rationally related to legitimate government interests…. This requirement is unquestionably met here. As the court below recognized…Washington's assisted suicide ban implicates a number of state interests….

First, Washington has an "unqualified interest in the preservation of human life." …The State's prohibition on assisted suicide, like all homicide laws, both reflects and advances its commitment to this interest….

Respondents admit that "the State has a real interest in preserving the lives of those who can still contribute to society and enjoy life." …The Court of Appeals also recognized Washington's interest in protecting life, but held that the "weight" of this interest depends on the "medical condition and the wishes of the person whose life is at stake." …Washington, however, has rejected this sliding scale approach and, through its assisted suicide ban, insists that all persons' lives, from beginning to end, regardless of physical or mental condition, are under the full protection of the law…. As we have previously affirmed, the States "may properly decline to make judgments about the 'quality' of life that a particular individual may enjoy." …This remains true, as *Cruzan* makes clear, even for those who are near death.

Relatedly, all admit that suicide is a serious public health problem, especially among persons in otherwise vulnerable groups…. The State has an interest in preventing suicide, and in studying, identifying, and treating its causes….

The State also has an interest in protecting the integrity and ethics of the medical profession. In contrast to the Court of Appeals' conclusion that "the integrity of the medical profession would [not] be threatened in any way by [physician assisted suicide]," …the American Medical Association, like many other medical and physicians' groups, has concluded that "physician assisted suicide is fundamentally incompatible with the physician's role as healer." American Medical Association, Code of Ethics §2.211 (1994)… And physician assisted suicide could, it is argued, undermine the trust that is essential to the doctor-patient relationship by blurring the time-honored line between healing and harming….

Next, the State has an interest in protecting vulnerable groups—including the poor, the elderly, and disabled persons—from abuse, neglect, and mistakes. The Court of Appeals dismissed the State's concern that disadvantaged persons might be pressured into physician assisted suicide as "ludicrous on its face." … We have recognized, however, the real risk of subtle coercion and undue influence in end of life situations…. Similarly, the New York Task Force warned that "legalizing physician assisted suicide would pose profound risks to many individuals who are ill and vulnerable…. The risk of harm is greatest for the many individuals in our society whose autonomy and well being are already compromised by poverty, lack of access to good medical care, advanced age, or membership in a stigmatized social group." …If physician assisted suicide were permitted, many might resort to it to spare their families the substantial financial burden of end of life health care costs.

The State's interest here goes beyond protecting the vulnerable from coercion; it extends to protecting disabled and terminally ill people from prejudice, negative and inaccurate stereotypes, and "societal indifference." …The State's assisted suicide ban reflects and reinforces its policy that the lives of terminally ill, disabled, and elderly people must be no less valued than the lives of the young and healthy, and that a seriously disabled person's suicidal impulses should be interpreted and treated the same way as anyone else's….

Finally, the State may fear that permitting assisted suicide will start it down the path to voluntary and perhaps even involuntary euthanasia. The Court of Appeals struck down Washington's assisted suicide ban only "as applied to competent, terminally ill adults who wish to hasten their deaths by obtaining medication prescribed by their doctors." …Washington insists, however, that the impact of the court's decision will not and cannot be so limited…. If suicide is protected as a matter of constitutional right, it is argued, "every man and woman in the United States must enjoy it." … See *Kevorkian*…527 N. W. 2d, at 727–728, n. 41. The Court of Appeals' decision, and its expansion reasoning, provide ample support for the State's concerns. The court noted, for example, that the "decision of a duly appointed surrogate decision maker is for all legal purposes the decision of the patient himself," ...that "in some instances, the patient may be unable to self administer the drugs and ...administration by the physician ...may be the only way the patient may be able to receive them," ...and that not only physicians, but also family members and loved ones, will inevitably participate in assisting suicide.... Thus, it turns out that what is couched as a limited right to "physician-assisted suicide" is likely, in effect, a much broader license, which could prove extremely difficult to police and contain.... Washington's ban on assisting suicide prevents such erosion.

We need not weigh exactingly the relative strengths of these various interests. They are unquestionably important and legitimate, and Washington's ban on assisted suicide is at least reasonably related to their promotion and protection. We therefore hold that Wash. Rev. Code § 9A.36.060(1) (1994) does not violate the Fourteenth Amendment, either on its face or "as applied to competent, terminally ill adults who wish to hasten their deaths by obtaining medication prescribed by their doctors."

Justice Souter, concurring in the judgment

When the physicians claim that the Washington law deprives them of a right falling within the scope of liberty that the Fourteenth Amendment guarantees against denial without due process of law, they are...[claiming] that the State has no substantively adequate justification for barring the assistance sought by the patient and sought to be offered by the physician. Thus, we are dealing with a claim to one of those rights sometimes described as rights of substantive due process and sometimes as unenumerated rights, in view of the breadth and indeterminacy of the "due process" serving as the claim's textual basis. The doctors accordingly arouse the skepticism of those who find the Due Process Clause an unduly vague or oxymoronic warrant for judicial review of substantive state law, just as they also invoke two centuries of American constitutional practice in recognizing unenumerated, substantive limits on governmental action.... The persistence of substantive due process in our cases points to the legitimacy of the modern justification for such judicial review...while the acknowledged failures of some of these cases point with caution to the difficulty raised by the present claim....

Respondents claim that a patient facing imminent death, who anticipates physical suffering and indignity, and is capable of responsible and voluntary choice, should have a right to a physician's assistance in providing counsel and drugs to be administered by the patient to end life promptly....

This liberty interest in bodily integrity was phrased in a general way by then Judge Cardozo when he said, "Every human being of adult years and sound mind has a right to determine what shall be done with his own body" in relation to his medical needs.... The familiar examples of this right derive from the common law of battery and include the right to be free from medical invasions into the body, ...as well as a right generally to resist enforced medication.... Thus "it is settled now ...that the Constitution places limits on a State's right to interfere with a person's most basic decisions about ...bodily integrity." ...Constitutional recognition of the right to bodily integrity underlies the assumed right, good against the State, to require physicians to terminate artificial life support, ... and the affirmative right to obtain medical intervention to cause abortion. See...*Roe v. Wade*....

It is, indeed, in the abortion cases that the most telling recognitions of the importance of bodily integrity and the concomitant tradition of medical assistance have occurred. In *Roe v. Wade*, the plaintiff contended that the Texas statute making it criminal for any person to "procure an abortion," ...for a pregnant woman was unconstitutional insofar as it prevented her from "terminat[ing] her pregnancy by an abortion 'performed by a competent, licensed physician, under safe, clinical conditions,'" ...and in striking down the statute we stressed the importance of the relationship between patient and physician....

The analogies between the abortion cases and this one are several. Even though the State has a legitimate interest in discouraging abortion, the Court recognized a woman's right to a physician's counsel and care... Like the decision to commit suicide, the decision to abort potential life can be made irresponsibly and under the influence of others, and yet the Court has held in the abortion cases that physicians are fit assistants. Without physician assistance in abortion, the woman's right would have too often amounted to nothing more than a right to self-mutilation, and without a physician to assist in the suicide of the dying, the patient's right will often be confined to crude methods of causing death, most shocking and painful to the decedent's survivors.

There is, finally, one more reason for claiming that a physician's assistance here would fall within the accepted tradition of medical care in our society, and the abortion cases are only the most obvious illustration of the further point. While the Court has held that the performance of abortion procedures can be restricted to physicians, the Court's opinion in *Roe* recognized the doctors' role in yet another way. For, in the course of holding that the decision to perform an abortion called for a physician's assistance, the Court recognized that the good physician is not just a mechanic of the human body whose services have no bearing on a person's moral choices, but one who does more than treat symptoms, one who ministers to the patient.... This idea of the physician as serving the whole person is a source of the high value traditionally placed on the medical relationship. Its value is surely as apparent here as in the abortion cases, for just as the decision about abortion is not directed to correcting some pathology, so the decision in which a dying patient seeks help is not so limited. The patients here sought not only an end to pain (which they might have had, although perhaps at the price of stupor) [but also] an end to their short remaining lives with a dignity that they believed would be denied them by powerful pain medication, as well as by their consciousness of dependency and helplessness as they approached death. In that period when the end is imminent, they said, the decision to end life is closest to decisions that are generally accepted as proper instances of exercising autonomy over one's own body, instances recognized under the Constitution and the State's own law, instances in which the help of physicians is accepted as falling within the traditional norm....

I take it that the basic concept of judicial review with its possible displacement of legislative judgment bars any finding that a legislature has acted arbitrarily when the following conditions are met: there is a serious factual controversy over the feasibility of recognizing the claimed right without at the same time making it impossible for the State to engage in an undoubtedly legitimate exercise of power; facts necessary to resolve the controversy are not readily ascertainable through the judicial process; but they are more readily subject to discovery through legislative fact finding and experimentation. It is assumed in this case, and must be, that a State's interest in protecting those unable to make responsible decisions and those who make no decisions at all entitles the State to bar aid to any but a knowing and responsible person intending suicide, and to prohibit euthanasia. How, and how far, a State should act in that interest are judgments for the State, but the legitimacy of its action to deny a physician the option to aid any but the knowing and responsible is beyond question....

The principal enquiry at the moment is into the Dutch experience, and I question whether an independent front line investigation into the facts of a foreign country's legal administration can be soundly undertaken through American courtroom litigation. While an extensive literature on any subject can raise the hopes for judicial understanding, the literature on this subject is only nascent. Since there is little experience directly bearing on the issue, the most that can be said

is that whichever way the Court might rule today, events could overtake its assumptions, as experimentation in some jurisdictions confirmed or discredited the concerns about progression from assisted suicide to euthanasia.

Legislatures, on the other hand, have superior opportunities to obtain the facts necessary for a judgment about the present controversy. Not only do they have more flexible mechanisms for fact finding than the Judiciary, but their mechanisms include the power to experiment, moving forward and pulling back as facts emerge within their own jurisdictions. There is, indeed, good reason to suppose that in the absence of a judgment for respondents here, just such experimentation will be attempted in some of the States....

I do not decide here what the significance might be of legislative foot dragging in ascertaining the facts going to the State's argument that the right in question could not be confined as claimed. Sometimes a court may be bound to act regardless of the institutional preferability of the political branches as forums for addressing constitutional claims.... Now, it is enough to say that our examination of legislative reasonableness should consider the fact that the Legislature of the State of Washington is no more obviously at fault than this Court is in being uncertain about what would happen if respondents prevailed today. We therefore have a clear question about which institution, a legislature or a court, is relatively more competent to deal with an emerging issue as to which facts currently unknown could be dispositive. The answer has to be, for the reasons already stated, that the legislative process is to be preferred. There is a closely related further reason as well.

One must bear in mind that the nature of the right claimed, if recognized as one constitutionally required, would differ in no essential way from other constitutional rights guaranteed by enumeration or derived from some more definite textual source than "due process." An unenumerated right should not therefore be recognized, with the effect of displacing the legislative ordering of things, without the assurance that its recognition would prove as durable as the recognition of those other rights differently derived. To recognize a right of lesser promise would simply create a constitutional regime too uncertain to bring with it the expectation of finality that is one of this Court's central obligations in making constitutional decisions....

Legislatures, however, are not so constrained. The experimentation that should be out of the question in constitutional adjudication displacing legislative judgments is entirely proper, as well as highly desirable, when the legislative power addresses an emerging issue like assisted suicide. The Court should accordingly stay its hand to allow reasonable legislative consideration. While I do not decide for all time that respondents' claim should not be recognized, I acknowledge the legislative institutional competence as the better one to deal with that claim at this time.

Case Questions

1. What was Dr. Glucksberg's argument in the U.S. Supreme Court?
2. On what grounds did Chief Justice Rehnquist justify his conclusion that Washington's statute did not violate the Due Process Clause?

Glucksberg Postscript

Eleven years after the U.S. Supreme Court ruled in favor of the State of Washington in the *Glucksberg* case, Washington voters redefined the state's public policy regarding assisted suicide. On November 4, 2008, 54 percent of voters supported Initiative 1000 and Washington joined with Oregon to become the only states to have enacted physician-assisted suicide laws. Oregon's 1994 "Death with Dignity" law was the first such law to be adopted in the United States.

More recently, the Montana Supreme Court decided in the 2009 case of *Baxter v. Montana* that physician-assisted suicide was permitted in that state. The court ruled in a 5–4 decision that there was no relevant statutory or case law prohibiting the practice. The Montana legislature, as of this writing, has not indicated whether it will maintain the status quo or enact legislation declaring physician-assisted suicide to be contrary to public policy. A legislative decision to prohibit physician-assisted suicides would likely result in this question returning to the Montana Supreme Court.

INTERNET TIP

An edited version of the Montana Supreme Court's opinion in *Baker v. Montana* and excerpts from the concurring and dissenting opinions can be found with the Chapter I materials in the textbook's website. Future developments in Montana law regarding physician-assisted suicides will be posted on the textbook's website with the Chapter I materials.

VAGUENESS AND OVERBREADTH

One of our fundamental legal principles is that laws must be written with sufficient precision or they will fail substantive due process requirements. Courts will declare unconstitutional statutes and ordinances that are overly broad and/or too vague. **Vagueness** exists where legislation fails to control the police exercise of discretion and fails to provide citizens with fair notice of what the law prohibits. **Overbreadth** exists where a statute is insufficiently focused. Thus, a disorderly conduct statute would be overly broad if it includes within its scope conduct that is clearly criminal as well as conduct that is protected by the First Amendment.

INTERNET TIP

An interesting Supreme Court vagueness case, *Chicago v. Morales* (1999), can be found on the textbook's website. This case involves a constitutional challenge to a Chicago ordinance intended to help combat loitering by members of Chicago street gangs.

Procedural Due Process

American law is very much concerned with procedure. The underlying premise is that justice is more likely to result when correct procedures have been followed. All states and the federal government have extensive rules that govern criminal and civil litigation; these are subject to modification by federal and state legislative and judicial bodies. Although some rules are essentially arbitrary—for instance, one that requires a defendant to file an answer within twenty days of being served with a summons and complaint—other procedures are thought to be essential to due process and have been given constitutional protection. This latter category of rules promotes accurate fact-finding and fairness and is used in all jurisdictions in every case.

Procedural due process rules play a major role in criminal cases, placing limits on police investigative techniques and prosecutorial behavior, and outlining how criminal trials should be conducted.

Even when the Supreme Court has interpreted the Due Process Clause of the Fourteenth Amendment to require a procedural right, however, it sometimes permits states to deviate from practices followed in federal courts. Procedural due process, for example, guarantees criminal defendants who are subject to more than six months' incarceration upon conviction the right to a jury trial. A defendant who stands trial in a state court, however, may not receive the same type of jury trial as in a federal court. Due process has been interpreted to permit states to accept nonunanimous jury verdicts in criminal cases where a unanimous verdict would be required in a federal court. Similarly, states are not constitutionally mandated to provide twelve-member juries even though twelve jurors are required in federal court.

In civil cases, due process rules are less extensive. They ensure that the court has jurisdiction over the parties, that proper notice has been given to defendants, and that the parties have an equal opportunity to present evidence and argument to the decision maker. In both types of litigation, procedural due process rules help ensure that decisions are made in a fair and reasonable manner.

As mentioned earlier, however, accuracy and fairness are not the only considerations. Elaborate procedural requirements are costly in terms of time, money, and utility. When the Supreme Court decides that a procedural right is fundamental to due process, there are often financial costs

imposed on government, society, and individual litigants. Due process requirements can also lengthen the time it takes to conclude litigation, adding to the existing backlogs in many jurisdictions. Courts therefore generally try to balance accuracy against its cost on a case-by-case basis. In criminal cases, the need for accurate decision making is paramount, and the requirements of due process are quite extensive.

It is important to emphasize that the Fifth and Fourteenth Amendment Due Process Clauses operate only as restraints on government. One of the consequences of this limitation is that private schools have considerably more procedural latitude than public schools. Private elementary and secondary schools can regulate what students wear, substantially restrict student expression and behavior, enforce a common moral code, and enforce rules that are so vague that they would not be constitutionally acceptable in a public school. If private schools contract with their students to provide due process, or if they violate public policy, commit torts, or act inequitably, courts have been increasingly willing to intervene. Over the years, there has been an expansion of the concept of "state action" and a closer relationship between private schools and government in the form of grants, scholarships, and research funds to institutions of higher education. Courts are beginning to require procedural due process in actions of those private colleges and universities that have such governmental involvement.

In recent years, state legislatures throughout the country have enacted controversial statutes intended to protect the public from future attacks by convicted sexual offenders. These statutes require convicted sexual offenders to register with one or more governmental agencies (often the police or state attorney general) and supply detailed personal information. Often these statutes are challenged on procedural due process grounds.

The following case from Idaho was brought by a convicted sex offender who successfully argued that he was denied procedural due process in a proceeding in which resulted in his designation as a violent sexual predator.

Jason C. Smith v. State of Idaho
203 P.3d 1221
February 10, 2009

Horton, Justice.

Jason Smith was incarcerated for the 1998 rape of a fifteen-year-old girl. Prior to his release, he was referred to the Sexual Offender Classification Board (the Board or SOCB) to determine whether he should be classified as a violent sexual predator (VSP). The Board classified Smith as a VSP. Smith sought judicial review of that decision. After conducting an evidentiary hearing, the district court upheld the Board's decision. We conclude Smith's designation was not constitutionally sound and, therefore, reverse and remand with instructions to vacate Smith's designation as a VSP....

Analysis

We begin by acknowledging the obvious: Smith's history of violent deviant sexual behavior is such that the Board's designation as a VSP may well be warranted. The important question presented by this appeal, however, is not whether he deserves that label. Rather, the question that is the focal point of this Court's inquiry is whether the State of Idaho has labeled Smith as a VSP in a fashion that comports with his constitutional right to due process....

A. The statutory framework for VSP designation in Idaho presents significant constitutional shortcomings.

1. The Statutory Framework

Designation as a VSP is based on the provisions of Idaho's Sexual Offender Registration Notification and Community Right to Know Act (the Act or SOR Act)..... Only offenders convicted of certain specified crimes are eligible for designation as VSPs.... The Board is charged with the duty of considering for VSP designation those inmates scheduled for release who have been referred by the department of correction or the parole commission.... Smith was such an inmate.... A VSP designation is based upon the Board's determination that the offender continues to "pose a high risk of committing an offense or engaging in predatory sexual conduct.".... The Board's rules provide that "[a] sexual offender shall be designated as a VSP if his risk of re-offending sexually or threat of violence is of sufficient concern to warrant the designation for the safety of the community."... In reaching this decision, the Board is required to "assess how biological, psychological, and situational factors may cause or contribute

to the offender's sexual behavior.... Once the Board determines whether to designate the offender as a VSP, it must make written findings that include a risk assessment of the offender, the reasons upon which the risk assessment is based, the Board's determination whether the offender should be designated, and the reasons upon which the determination is based....

Apart from submitting to a mandatory... psychosexual evaluation...the offender has no opportunity to provide input to the Board. "The Board and the evaluator conducting the psychosexual evaluation may have access to and may review all obtainable records on the sexual offender to conduct the VSP designation assessment." ...The offender is not given notice of the information being considered by the Board, much less an opportunity to be heard as to the reliability of that information. If the Board determines that the offender is to be designated as a VSP, the offender is notified of the Board's decision by way of a copy of the Board's written findings....

If the Board makes a VSP designation, the offender has 14 days from receipt of the notice to seek judicial review... An offender designated a VSP is only entitled to challenge the designation on two grounds:

(a) The offender may introduce evidence that the calculation that led to the designation as a violent sexual predator was incorrectly performed either because of a factual error, because the offender disputes a prior offense, because the variable factors were improperly determined, or for similar reasons; ... and (b) The offender may introduce evidence at the hearing that the designation as a violent sexual predator does not properly encapsulate the specific case, i.e., the offender may maintain that the case falls outside the typical case of this kind and, therefore, that the offender should not be designated as a violent sexual predator....

The scope of judicial review is limited to "a summary, in camera review proceeding, in which the court decides only whether to affirm or reverse the board's designation of the offender as a violent sexual predator."... Thus, the Act contemplates that judicial review will ordinarily occur without the offender having the opportunity to address the basis of the Board's decision. The Act does provide that "[w]here the proof, whether in the form of reliable hearsay, affidavits, or offers of live testimony, creates a genuine issue of material fact as to whether the offender is a violent sexual predator, the court should convene a fact-finding hearing and permit live testimony."... At the hearing, the State bears the burden of presenting a prima facie case justifying the Board's designation.... Despite this threshold burden of production, the offender ultimately bears the burden of proof... [The statute] provides that "[t]he court shall affirm the board's determination unless persuaded by a preponderance of the evidence that it does not conform to the law or the guidelines."

2. The Constitutional Shortcomings

The oddity lies herein: while both parties may introduce evidence, neither party is provided with the record utilized by the Board to make its determination, except for a written summary of information relied upon by the Board and documents that are available to the parties by other means.... All records that contain witness or victim names or statements, reports prepared in making parole determinations, or other "confidential" records are withheld from disclosure to the offender, his attorney, and even the prosecutor, and are available only to the district court for the purpose of reviewing the Board's determination.... The rules of evidence do not apply....

In our view, there are significant constitutional shortcomings in the statutory procedure as a result of the lack of procedural due process afforded an offender. "Where a person's good name, reputation, honor, or integrity is at stake because of what the government is doing to him, notice and an opportunity to be heard are essential." *Wisconsin v. Constantineau*, 400 U.S. 433, 437 (1971). "[C]ertainly where the State attaches 'a badge of infamy' to the citizen, due process comes into play. We take it as a given that the label of "violent sexual predator" is a "badge of infamy" that necessitates due process protections. The high court of New York has recognized that an individual's private interest, his liberty interest in not being stigmatized as a sexually violent predator, is substantial. The ramifications of being classified and having that information disseminated fall squarely within those cases that recognize a liberty interest where there is some stigma to one's good name, reputation or integrity, coupled with some more "tangible" interest that is affected or a legal right that is altered. More than "name calling by public officials," the sexually violent predator label "is a determination of status" that can have a considerable adverse impact on an individual's ability to live in a community and obtain or maintain employment....

Idaho provides a computerized sex offender registry that is accessible to the public via the internet complete with photos of all sex offenders, along with their personal information including name, address, date of birth, and offense history.... Furthermore, there is a special link for those sex offenders designated as VSPs. This Court has recognized "the fact that registration brings notoriety to a person convicted of a sexual offense ...prolong[s] the stigma attached to such convictions....

Designation as a VSP results in consequences beyond simply requiring the designee to register as a sex offender. Sex offenders need only update their information and photographs in the registry annually, while VSPs must do so every ninety days.... Non-VSP offenders may petition a court for relief from the duty to register after a period of ten years.... On the other hand, a VSP has no right to such relief. Thus, for an offender designated as a VSP, the scarlet letters are indelible.

While the duty to register as a sex offender is triggered simply by reason of conviction for a specified crime, classification as a VSP is based upon a factual determination of probable future conduct, i.e., that the offender poses a high risk of committing an offense or engaging in predatory sexual conduct. ... This distinguishes Idaho's VSP system from a sex offender registry based solely on the fact of conviction of a predicate offense. As to the latter, the United States Supreme Court has concluded that sex offender registration laws do not violate the offender's procedural due process rights, noting the offender "has already had a procedurally safeguarded opportunity to contest" the charge. *Conn. Dep't of Pub. Safety v. Doe*, 538 U.S. 1, 7 (2003). ... In reaching this conclusion, the Supreme Court emphasized that Connecticut's registry requirement is "based on the fact of previous conviction, not the fact of current dangerousness...[i]ndeed, the public registry explicitly states that officials have not determined that any registrant is currently dangerous."...

Under *Constantineau* and its progeny, procedural due process is a constitutional prerequisite to the state's ability to designate an individual a VSP. "Only when the whole proceedings leading to the pinning of an unsavory label on a person are aired can oppressive results be prevented."... This Court has stated:

> Procedural due process basically requires that a person, whose protected rights are being adjudicated, is afforded an opportunity to be heard in a timely manner. There must be notice and the opportunity to be heard must occur at a meaningful time and in a meaningful manner....

In spite of the existence of well-established standards of procedural due process, Idaho's statutory scheme for VSP designation minimizes, at every turn, the possibility that an offender has the constitutionally required notice and opportunity to be heard. The offender is not provided notice or opportunity to be heard before the Board. At the district court level, the offender is provided only a summary of the information considered by the Board, presenting little meaningful opportunity to respond to specific information considered by the Board. The offender is given his first opportunity to be heard only if he can persuade the district court that there is a genuine issue of material fact whether he is a VSP. In the event that the offender clears this threshold hurdle, he then bears the burden of disproving the propriety of the designation, all the while being denied access to many of the documents upon which the designation may have been based....

We do not question the legitimate state interest in identifying those offenders who pose a high risk of reoffending or engaging in predatory sexual conduct. However, the United States Constitution prohibits the state from doing so without affording the offender due process. In our view, Idaho's statutory scheme violates an offender's right to procedural due process by failing to provide notice and an opportunity to be heard at a meaningful time and in a meaningful manner and by placing the burden of proof on the offender... at the only hearing in which he is permitted to appear....

Conclusion
When information upon which the VSP designation is based is withheld from an offender it cannot be said that there is either notice or a meaningful opportunity to be heard. The procedures afforded by the statute must comport with constitutional standards of procedural due process.

[F]airness can rarely be obtained by secret, one-sided determination of facts decisive of rights.... [S]ecrecy is not congenial to truth-seeking and self-righteousness gives too slender an assurance of rightness. No better instrument has been devised for arriving at truth than to give a person in jeopardy of serious loss notice of the case against him and opportunity to meet it....

The statutory scheme for VSP designation is constitutionally infirm. The district court did not succeed in fashioning an *ad hoc* remedy to the invalid statute. Until Smith has the benefit of his constitutional right to notice and an opportunity to be heard, the State may not designate him as a VSP. Accordingly, we reverse the decision of the district court and remand this matter to the district court with direction to vacate Smith's designation as a VSP...

Case Questions

1. According to the Idaho Supreme Court, what fundamental constitutional rights were denied to Smith?
2. To what extent should judges consider the real-life consequences of their actions when deciding a case such as this one?
3. Were you surprised that legislation this flawed could be enacted into law?
4. How should citizens feel about the court's decision in favor of Smith?

CRIMINAL AND CIVIL LAW

The distinction between criminal and civil law is a very important concept in our legal system (see Figure 1.1). This text deals primarily with civil law. A civil suit involves a dispute between private individuals involving either a breach of an agreement or a breach of a duty imposed by law. A criminal action is brought by the government against an individual who has allegedly committed a crime. Crimes are classified as treason, felonies, and misdemeanors, depending on the punishment attached to the crime. **Treason** is a crime defined only by the Constitution, Article III, Section 3, clause 1. To commit treason—levying war against the United States, or adhering to or giving aid or comfort to its enemies—there must be an overt act and the intent to commit treason. A **felony** is a crime that is classified by statute in the place in which it is committed. That is, the severity of the punishment for a felony varies from place to place. A felony is generally regarded as being any criminal

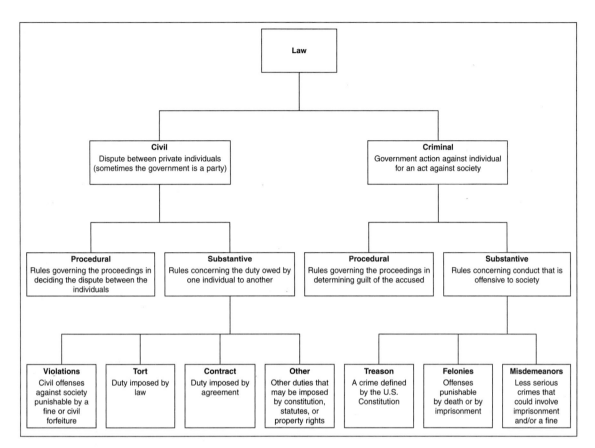

FIGURE 1.1 Criminal and Civil Law

offense for which a defendant may be imprisoned for more than one year, or executed. One determines whether a crime is a felony according to the sentence that might lawfully be imposed, not according to the sentence actually ordered. Felonies do not include **misdemeanors,** offenses that are generally punishable by a maximum term of imprisonment of less than one year.

In a civil suit, the court attempts to remedy the dispute between individuals by determining their legal rights, awarding money damages to the injured party, or directing one party to perform or refrain from performing a specific act. Since a crime is an act against society, the criminal court punishes

a guilty defendant by imposing a fine or imprisonment or both.

In a criminal prosecution, the rules of court procedure differ. In order to meet the burden of proof to find a person guilty of a crime, guilt must be proved beyond a reasonable doubt, a stricter standard than the preponderance of evidence usually required in a civil case.

As we will see in the next case, when the same act gives rise to both a criminal proceeding and a civil suit, the actions are completely independent of each other. *Katko v. Briney* involves a civil suit for damages brought against the victim of a criminal larceny, by the person convicted of committing the crime.

Katko v. Briney
183 N.W.2d 657
Supreme Court of Iowa
February 9, 1971

Moore, Chief Justice

The primary issue presented here is whether an owner may protect personal property in an unoccupied boarded-up farmhouse against trespassers and thieves by a spring gun capable of inflicting death or serious injury.

We are not here concerned with a man's right to protect his home and members of his family. Defendants' home was several miles from the scene of the incident to which we refer *infra*.

Plaintiff's action is for damages resulting from serious injury caused by a shot from a 20-gauge spring shotgun set by defendants in a bedroom of an old farmhouse, which had been uninhabited for several years. Plaintiff and his companion, Marvin McDonough, had broken and entered the house to find and steal old bottles and dated fruit jars, which they considered antiques. At defendants' request, plaintiff's action was tried to a jury consisting of residents of the community where defendants' property was located. The jury returned a verdict for plaintiff and against defendants for $20,000 actual and $10,000 punitive damages.

After careful consideration of defendants' motions for judgment notwithstanding the verdict and for a new trial, the experienced and capable trial judge overruled them and entered judgment on the verdict. Thus we have this appeal by defendants....

Most of the facts are not disputed. In 1957 defendant Bertha L. Briney inherited her parents' farmland in Mahaska and Monroe Counties. For about ten years, 1957 to 1967, there occurred a series of trespassing and housebreaking events with loss of some household items, the breaking of windows, and "messing up of the property in general." The latest occurred June 8, 1967, prior to the event on July 16, 1967, herein involved.

Defendants through the years boarded up the windows and doors in an attempt to stop the intrusions. They had posted "no trespass" signs on the land several years before 1967. The nearest one was 35 feet from the house. On June 11, 1967, defendants set a "shotgun trap" in the north bedroom. After Mr. Briney cleaned and oiled his 20-gauge shotgun, the power of which he was well aware, defendants took it to the old house where they secured it to an iron bed with the barrel pointed at the bedroom door. It was rigged with wire from the doorknob to the gun's trigger so that it would fire when the door was opened. Briney first pointed the gun so an intruder would be hit in the stomach but at Mrs. Briney's suggestion it was lowered to hit the legs. He admitted he did so "because I was mad and tired of being tormented" but "he did not intend to injure anyone." He gave no explanation of why he used a loaded shell and set it to hit a person already in the house. Tin was nailed over the bedroom window. The spring gun could not be seen from the outside. No warning of its presence was posted.

Plaintiff lived with his wife and worked regularly as a gasoline station attendant in Eddyville, seven miles from the old house. He had observed it for several years while hunting in the area and considered it as being abandoned. He knew it had long been uninhabited. In 1967 the area around the house was covered with high weeds. Prior to July 16, 1967 plaintiff and McDonough had been to the premises and found several old bottles and fruit jars, which they took and added to their collection of antiques. On the latter date about 9:30 P.M. they made a second trip to the Briney property. They entered the old house by removing a board from a porch window, which was without glass. While McDonough was looking around the kitchen area, plaintiff went to another part of the house. As he started to open the north bedroom door the shotgun went off, striking him in the right leg above the ankle bone. Much of his leg, including part of the tibia, was blown away. Only by McDonough's assistance was plaintiff able to get out of the house and after crawling some distance, he was put in his vehicle and rushed to a doctor and then to a hospital. He remained in the hospital 40 days.

Plaintiff's doctor testified he seriously considered amputation but eventually the healing process was successful. Some weeks after his release from the hospital plaintiff returned to work on crutches. He was required to keep the injured leg in a cast for approximately a year and wear a special brace for another year. He continued to suffer pain during this period.

There was undenied medical testimony that plaintiff had a permanent deformity, a loss of tissue, and a shortening of the leg.

The record discloses plaintiff to trial time had incurred $710 for medical expenses, $2056.85 for hospital service, $61.80 for orthopedic service and $750 as loss of earnings. In addition thereto the trial court submitted to the jury the question of damages for pain and suffering and for future disability.

Plaintiff testified he knew he had no right to break and enter the house with intent to steal bottles and fruit jars therefrom. He further testified he had entered a plea of guilty to larceny in the nighttime of property of less than $20 value from a private building. He stated he had been fined $50 and costs and paroled during good behavior from a 60-day jail sentence. Other than minor traffic charges, this was plaintiff's first brush with the law. On this civil case appeal, it is not our prerogative to review the disposition made of the criminal charge against him.

The main thrust of defendants' defense in the trial court and on this appeal is that "the law permits use of a spring gun in a dwelling or warehouse for the purpose of preventing the unlawful entry of a burglar or thief."...[T]he court referred to the early case history of the use of spring guns and stated under the law their use was prohibited except to prevent the commission of felonies of violence and where human life is in danger. The instruction included a statement that breaking and entering is not a felony of violence.

Instruction 5 stated: "You are hereby instructed that one may use reasonable force in the protection of his property, but such right is subject to the qualification that one may not use such means of force as will take human life or inflict great bodily injury. Such is the rule even though the injured party is a trespasser and is in violation of the law himself."

Instruction 6 stated: "An owner of premises is prohibited from willfully or intentionally injuring a trespasser by means of force that either takes life or inflicts great bodily injury; and therefore a person owning a premise is prohibited from setting out 'spring guns' and like dangerous devices which will likely take life or inflict great bodily injury, for the purpose of harming trespassers. The fact that the trespasser may be acting in violation of the law does not change the rule. The only time when such conduct of setting a 'spring gun' or a like dangerous device is justified would be when the trespasser was committing a felony of violence or a felony punishable by death, or where the trespasser was endangering human life by his act."

Instruction 7, to which defendants made no objection or exception, stated:

"To entitle the plaintiff to recover for compensatory damages, the burden of proof is upon him to establish by a preponderance of the evidence each and all of the following propositions:

"1. That defendants erected a shotgun trap in a vacant house on land owned by defendant, Bertha L. Briney, on or about June 11, 1967, which fact was known only by them, to protect household goods from trespassers and thieves.

"2. That the force used by defendants was in excess of that force reasonably necessary and which persons are entitled to use in the protection of their property.

"3. That plaintiff was injured and damaged and the amount thereof.

"4. That plaintiff's injuries and damages resulted directly from the discharge of the shotgun trap which was set and used by defendants."

The overwhelming weight of authority, both textbook and case law, supports the trial court's statement of the applicable principles of law."

Prosser on Torts, third edition, pages 116–118, states that:

"[T]he law has always placed a higher value upon human safety than upon mere rights in property. [I]t is the accepted rule that there is no privilege to use any force calculated to cause death or serious bodily injury to repel the threat to land or chattels, unless there is also such a threat to the defendant's personal safety as to justify a self-defense... spring guns and other man-killing devices are not justifiable against a mere trespasser, or even a petty thief. They are privileged only against those upon whom the landowner, if he were present in person, would be free to inflict injury of the same kind."

Restatement of Torts, §85, page 180, states that:

"the value of human life and limbs, not only to the individual concerned but also to society, so outweighs the interest of a possessor of land in excluding from it those whom he is not willing to admit thereto that a possessor of land has, as is stated in §79, no privilege to use force intended or likely to cause death or serious harm against another whom the possessor sees about to enter his premises or meddle with his chattel, unless the intrusion threatens death or serious bodily harm to the occupiers or users of the premises.... A possessor of land cannot do indirectly and by a mechanical device that which, were he present, he could not do immediately and in person. Therefore, he cannot gain a privilege to install, for the purpose of protecting his land from intrusions harmless to the lives and limbs of the occupiers or users of it, a mechanical device whose only purpose is to inflict death or serious harm upon such as may intrude, by giving notice of his intention to inflict, by mechanical means and indirectly, harm which he could not, even after request, inflict directly were he present."...

In *Hooker v. Miller*, 37 Iowa 613, we held defendant vineyard owner liable for damages resulting from a spring gun shot although plaintiff was a trespasser and there to steal grapes. At pages 614, 615, this statement is made: "This court has held that a mere trespass against property other than a dwelling is not a sufficient justification to authorize the use of a deadly weapon by the owner in its defense; and that if death results in such a case it will be murder, though the killing be actually necessary to prevent the trespass."... At page 617 this court said: "Trespassers and other inconsiderable violators of the law are not to be visited by barbarous punishments or prevented by inhuman inflictions of bodily injuries."

The facts in *Allison v. Fiscus*, 156 Ohio 120, decided in 1951, are very similar to the case at bar. There plaintiff's right to damages was recognized for injuries received when he feloniously broke a door latch and started to enter defendant's warehouse with intent to steal. As he entered, a trap of two sticks of dynamite buried under the doorway by defendant owner was set off and plaintiff seriously injured. The court held the question whether a particular trap was justified as a use of reasonable and necessary force against a trespasser engaged in the commission of a felony should have been submitted to the jury. The Ohio Supreme Court recognized the plaintiff's right to recover punitive or exemplary damages in addition to compensatory damages....

In *United Zinc & Chemical Co. v. Britt*, 258 U.S. 268, 275, the Court states: "The liability for spring guns and mantraps arises from the fact that the defendant has...expected the trespasser and prepared an injury that is no more justified than if he had held the gun and fired it."

In addition to civil liability many jurisdictions hold a landowner criminally liable for serious injuries or homicide caused by spring guns or other set devices....

In Wisconsin, Oregon and England the use of spring guns and similar devices is specifically made unlawful by statute....

The legal principles stated by the trial court in instructions 2, 5 and 6 are well established and supported by the authorities cited and quoted *supra*. There is no merit in defendants' objections and exceptions thereto. Defendants' various motions based on the same reasons stated in exceptions to instructions were properly overruled.

Plaintiff's claim and the jury's allowance of punitive damages, under the trial court's instructions relating thereto, were not at any time or in any manner challenged by defendants in the trial court as not allowable. We therefore are not presented with the problem of whether the $10,000 award should be allowed to stand.

We express no opinion as to whether punitive damages are allowable in this type of case. If defendants' attorneys wanted that issue decided, it was their duty to raise it in the trial court.

The rule is well established that we will not consider a contention not raised in the trial court. In other words, we are a court of review and will not consider a contention raised for the first time in this court....

Under our law punitive damages are not allowed as a matter of right. When malice is shown or when a defendant acted with wanton and reckless disregard of the rights of others, punitive damages may be allowed as punishment to the defendant and as a deterrent to others. Although not meant to compensate a plaintiff, the result is to increase his recovery. He is the fortuitous beneficiary of such an award simply because there is no one else to receive it.

The jury's findings of fact including a finding that defendants acted with malice and with wanton and reckless disregard, as required for an allowance of punitive or exemplary damages, are supported by substantial evidence. We are bound thereby.

This opinion is not to be taken or construed as authority that the allowance of punitive damages is or is not proper under circumstances such as exist here. We hold only that a question of law not having been properly raised cannot in this case be resolved.

Study and careful consideration of defendants' contentions on appeal reveal no reversible error.

Affirmed.

Larson, Justice, dissenting

I respectfully dissent, first because the majority wrongfully assumes that by installing a spring gun in the bedroom of their unoccupied house the defendants intended to shoot any intruder who attempted to enter the room. Under the record presented here, that was a fact question. Unless it is held that these property owners are liable for any injury to an intruder from such a device regardless of the intent with which it is installed, liability under these pleadings must rest on two definite issues of fact, i.e., did the defendants intend to shoot the invader, and if so, did they employ unnecessary and unreasonable force against him?

It is my feeling that the majority oversimplifies the impact of this case on the law, not only in this but other jurisdictions, and that it has not thought through all the ramifications of this holding.

There being no statutory provisions governing the right of an owner to defend his property by the use of a spring gun or other like device, or of a criminal invader to recover punitive damages when injured by such an instrumentality while breaking into the building of another, our interest and attention are directed to what should be the court determination of public policy in these matters. On both issues we are faced with a case of first impression. We should accept

the task and clearly establish the law in this jurisdiction hereafter. I would hold there is no absolute liability for injury to a criminal intruder by setting up such a device on his property, and unless done with an intent to kill or seriously injure the intruder, I would absolve the owner from liability other than for negligence. I would also hold the court had no jurisdiction to allow punitive damages when the intruder was engaged in a serious criminal offense such as breaking and entering with intent to steal....

Case Questions

1. Suppose that, instead of a spring gun, the Brineys had unleashed on the premises a vicious watchdog that severely injured Katko's leg? Would the result have been different? What if the watchdog had been properly chained?
2. When may one set a spring gun and not be subject to liability? What can one legally do to protect property or life?
3. What do you think the consequences would have been if the dissenting judge's suggestions had become law?
4. A case involving breaking and entering and shooting a gun might appear to be a criminal matter. What factors make this a civil lawsuit?

EQUAL PROTECTION OF THE LAW

The Equal Protection Clause of the Fourteenth Amendment has been used to strike down legislation that was enacted for the purpose of discriminating against certain groupings of people (called "classifications" in legalese). The Jim Crow laws, used to discriminate against African Americans, are one notorious example of an invidious (legally impermissible) classification scheme.

Earlier in this chapter, we learned about the U.S. Supreme Court's decision in the 1967 case of *Loving v. Virginia*. Virginia's miscegenation statute was found to violate substantive due process. We return to that case at this time because the Lovings had an additional ground for challenging the statute. They maintained that it also violated the Equal Protection Clause of the Fourteenth Amendment. The Supreme Court agreed. It ruled that the statute had deprived the Lovings of equal protection because "Virginia prohibit[ed] only interracial marriages involving white persons" and because there "is patently no legitimate overriding purpose independent of

invidious racial discrimination which justifies this classification."

The Equal Protection Clause has been invoked to invalidate discriminatory classification schemes that are based on national origin, alienage, religion, and gender (in some situations).

TORT AND CONTRACT LAW

A person has a right to bring a civil action against another for a wrongful act or omission that causes injury to him or her. The basis of the suit is a violation of some duty owed to the injured person. This duty arises either from an agreement of the persons or by operation of the law.

Torts

Tort law establishes standards of conduct that all citizens must meet. A plaintiff sues in tort to recover money damages for injuries to his or her person, reputation, property, or business caused by a breach of a legal duty.

A tort is any wrongful act, not involving a breach of an agreement, for which a civil action may be maintained. The wrongful act can be intentional or unintentional. Intentional torts are based on the defendant's willful misconduct or intentional wrongdoing. This does not necessarily mean the defendant had a hostile intent, but only that he or she had a belief that a particular harmful result was substantially likely to follow. *Katko v. Briney* was such a case. When Briney rigged the spring gun, he did so believing that serious bodily injury was very likely to occur to any intruder who opened the door. Briney was civilly found to have violated the standard of care owed by a property owner to a trespasser such as Katko under the circumstances of that case. A person who commits an intentional tort may also be committing a criminal act, for which the government may bring criminal charges. As we saw in *Katko v. Briney*, the tort and criminal actions would be independent of each other.

An unintentional tort occurs when a person acts negligently. That is, he or she unintentionally fails to live up to the community's ideal of reasonable care. Every person has a legal duty to act toward other people as a reasonable and prudent person would have acted under the circumstances. Torts are discussed more fully in Chapter XI.

Contracts

A contract is a promissory agreement between two or more people that creates, modifies, or destroys a legally enforceable obligation. People voluntarily enter into a contract in order to create private duties for mutual advantage. Thus, under ordinary conditions, contractual terms are not imposed by law. There are exceptions to this rule; however, the essence of contract law is the enforcement of a promise voluntarily made.

Although contract law is more thoroughly discussed in Chapter X, it will be helpful to introduce it here. In the legal sense, the term **contract does not mean the tangible document that contains evidence of an agreement.** Rather, a contract is the legally enforceable agreement itself. There are three parts to every contract: **offer, acceptance,** and **consideration.** An offer is a communication of a promise, with a statement of what is expected in return. An offer is made with the intention of creating an enforceable legal obligation. Acceptance is the evidence of assent to the terms of the offer. Consideration is the inducement each party has to enter into an agreement. Only legally enforceable obligations are called contracts.

A person who fails to perform a contractual obligation has breached the contract. The plaintiff brings a suit in contract to obtain legal relief from the breaching party. The normal remedy for a breach of contract is monetary damages, although in appropriate circumstances, the breaching party may be ordered to perform his or her agreement.

Contracts may be oral, written, express (explicit terms), implied in fact (inferred from the person's actions), or implied in law. In *Suggs v. Norris*, which follows, the trial court permitted the jury to find an implied-in-law agreement from the facts of the case, even though there was no proof of an oral agreement or written document evidencing a contract.

Suggs v. Norris
364 S.E.2d 159
Court of Appeals of North Carolina
February 2, 1988

Wells, Judge
The overriding question presented by this appeal is whether public policy forbids the recovery by a plaintiff partner to an unmarried but cohabiting or meretricious relationship, from the other partner's estate, for services rendered to or benefits conferred upon the other partner through the plaintiff's work in the operation of a joint business when the business proceeds were utilized to enrich the estate of the deceased partner.

Defendant argues under her first three assignments of error that any agreement between plaintiff and the decedent providing compensation to plaintiff for her efforts in the raising and harvesting of produce was void as against public policy because it arose out of the couple's illegal cohabitation. While it is well settled that no recovery can be had under either a contractual or restitutionary (*quantum meruit*) theory arising out of a contract or circumstances which violate public policy...defendant's application of the rule to the present case is misplaced.

This Court has made it clear that we do not approve of or endorse adulterous meretricious affairs, *Collins v. Davis*, 68 N.C. App. 588.... We made it clear in *Collins*, however, that cohabiting but unmarried individuals are capable of "entering into enforceable express or implied contracts for the purchase and improvement of houses, or for the loan and repayment of money."...Judge Phillips, writing for the majority, in *Collins* was careful to point out that if illicit sexual intercourse had provided the consideration for the contract or implied agreement, all claims arising therefrom, having been founded on illegal consideration, would then be unenforceable.

While our research has disclosed no other North Carolina cases which address this specific issue, we do find considerable guidance in the decisional law of other states. Most notable is Justice Tobriner's landmark decision in *Marvin v. Marvin*, 18 Cal.3d 660... (1976) which held that express contracts between unmarried cohabiting individuals are enforceable unless the same are based solely on sexual services....

The *Marvin* Court also held that an unmarried couple may, by words and conduct, create an implied-in-fact agreement regarding the disposition of their mutual properties and money as well as an implied agreement of partnership or joint venture.... Finally, the court endorsed the use of constructive trusts wherever appropriate and recovery in *quantum meruit* where the plaintiff can show that the services were rendered with an expectation of monetary compensation....

Other jurisdictions have fashioned and adhered to similar rules. In *Kinkenon v. Hue* [207 Neb. 698 (1981)], the Nebraska Supreme Court confirmed an earlier rule that while bargains made in whole or in part for consideration of sexual intercourse are illegal, any agreements not resting on such consideration, regardless of the marital status of the two individuals, are enforceable....

Likewise, the New Jersey Supreme Court held as enforceable an oral agreement between two adult unmarried partners where the agreement was not based "explicitly or inseparably" on sexual services. *Kozlowski v. Kozlowski* [80 N.J. 378 (1979)]. In *Fernandez v. Garza*, 88 Ariz. 214 (1960), the Arizona Supreme Court held that plaintiff's meretricious or unmarried cohabitation with decedent did not bar the enforcement of a partnership agreement wherein the parties agreed to share their property and profits equally and where such was not based upon sexual services as consideration....

We now make clear and adopt the rule that agreements regarding the finances and property of an unmarried but cohabiting couple, whether express or implied, are enforceable as long as sexual services or promises thereof do not provide the consideration for such agreements....

In the present case, the question is before this Court on an appeal of the trial court's denial of defendant's Motion for Judgment Notwithstanding the Verdict; therefore, our standard of review is whether the evidence, viewed in the light most favorable to plaintiff, is sufficient to support the jury verdict. *Wallace v. Evans*, [60 N.C. App. 145 (1982)]. Applying the foregoing standard, we find that plaintiff's evidence that she began work for the decedent in his produce business several years before she began cohabiting with him and that at the time she began work she believed the two of them were "partners" in the business, was sufficient evidence for the jury to have inferred that plaintiff's work comprised a business relationship with decedent which was separate and independent from and of their cohabiting relationship. Therefore, the jury may have inferred that sexual services did not provide the consideration for plaintiff's claim. We therefore hold that plaintiff's claim for a *quantum meruit* recovery was not barred as being against public policy. Defendant's first three assignments of error are overruled.

Defendant next argues under assignments of error 4 and 5 that the trial court erred in submitting a *quantum meruit* recovery issue to the jury because any services rendered by plaintiff were either gratuitous or incidental to an illegal relationship. As we have already addressed the issue of illegality, we are concerned here only with the question of whether there existed sufficient evidence to submit the issue of recovery in *quantum meruit* to the jury.

The trial court placed the following issue regarding a quasi-contract or *quantum meruit* recovery before the jury:

Issue Four:

Did DARLENE SUGGS render services to JUNIOR EARL NORRIS involving the raising, harvesting and

sale of produce under such circumstances that the Estate of JUNIOR EARL NORRIS should be required to pay for them?
ANSWER: Yes

Recovery on *quantum meruit* requires the establishment of an implied contract.... The contract may be one implied-in-fact where the conduct of the parties clearly indicates their intention to create a contract or it may be implied-in-law based on the restitutionary theory of quasi-contract, which operates to prevent unjust enrichment.... An implied-in-law theory required the plaintiff to establish that services were rendered and accepted between the two parties with the mutual understanding that plaintiff was to be compensated for her efforts.... Moreover, plaintiff's efforts must not have been gratuitous as is generally presumed where services are rendered between family or spousal members....

In the present case, the evidence clearly showed that the plaintiff had from 1973 until the death of the decedent in 1983 operated a produce route for and with the decedent. According to several witnesses' testimony, plaintiff had worked decedent's farm, disked and cultivated the soil, and harvested and marketed the produce. Plaintiff, working primarily without the decedent's aid, drove the produce to various markets over a 60-mile route. She handled all finances and deposited them in the couple's joint banking account. Finally, the evidence showed that the decedent, an alcoholic, depended almost entirely on plaintiff's work in the produce business and as well her care of him while he was ill. Because of plaintiff's efforts the couple had amassed seven vehicles valued at $20,000; some farm equipment valued at $4,000; $8,000 in cash in the account, and all debts which had attached to the farm when plaintiff began working with decedent in 1973 were paid—all due to plaintiff's efforts. Additionally, plaintiff testified that when she began work with the decedent in 1973 she believed they were partners and that she was entitled to share in one-half the profits.

The foregoing evidence clearly establishes a set of facts sufficient to have submitted a quasi-contractual issue to the jury and from which the jury could have inferred a mutual understanding between plaintiff and the decedent that she would be remunerated for her services. Plaintiff's efforts conferred many years of benefits on the decedent and the decedent, by all accounts, willingly accepted those benefits.

Because the evidence viewed in the light most favorable to plaintiff was clearly sufficient to permit the jury to find a mutual understanding between plaintiff and decedent that plaintiff's work in the produce business was not free of charge and because plaintiff's work in the produce business was not of the character usually found to be performed gratuitously...defendant's Motions for Directed Verdict and Judgment Notwithstanding the Verdict were properly denied.

No Error.

Case Questions

1. Darlene Suggs's suit against the estate of Junior E. Norris was based on what legal theories?
2. Under what circumstances does the court indicate that the contracts between unmarried but cohabiting persons would not be enforceable?
3. Why should a court be able to create a contract after a dispute arises for parties who never signed a binding contract?
4. Do you see any moral principles reflected in the court's opinion in this case?

CHAPTER SUMMARY

Chapter I began by raising a fundamental jurisprudential question, "What is law?" Many students who have not previously thought much about law are surprised to learn that there is no single universally accepted answer to the question and that the likely best answer is "it depends." After reading brief synopses of several differing philosophical schools, it becomes apparent why developing a consensus definition has proven to be so difficult. What followed next were a discussion of legal objectives that are common to both private and public law in this country and a review of Anglo-American historical and cultural heritage with a focus on how these have contributed to law as we know it today. Because students using this textbook need immediately to begin developing the ability to read excerpts from judicial opinions, the chapter included a highly simplified overview of civil procedure. This overview was necessary preparation for students about to read their first case. Civil procedure is a topic that is covered in considerably more detail in Chapter V. The chapter continued with some additional comments on reading cases immediately prior to the first judicial opinion, *Video Software Dealers Association v. Schwarzenegger*. An analysis of that case followed, along with a sample brief, both of which were intended to further help students learn how to read and understand judicial opinions in general, and the first case in particular. The chapter then turned to an overview of constitutional due process and equal protection, and a discussion of the differences between civil and criminal law. The chapter concluded with an explanation of the differences between tort and contract law.

CHAPTER QUESTIONS

1. Inmates in a state reformatory brought suit against the state department of corrections because corrections officials refused to permit certain persons to visit inmates. The inmates brought suit because receiving visitors is essential to inmates' morale and to maintaining contacts with their families. They argued that the state had established regulations to guide prison officials in making visitation decisions, thus the court should recognize that inmates have a constitutionally protected liberty right to a hearing whenever prison officials deny a visitation. Convening such a hearing would make it possible for inmates to determine whether prison officials had complied with the guidelines or had acted arbitrarily in denying a visitation. Should the inmates have a due process right to a hearing?

   Kentucky Department of Corrections v. Thompson, 490 U.S. 454 (1989)

2. Terry Foucha, a criminal defendant, was charged with aggravated burglary and a firearms offense. On October 12, 1984, Foucha was found not guilty by reason of insanity and was ordered committed to a mental institution until medically discharged or released pursuant to a court order. In March 1988, doctors evaluated Foucha and determined that he was "presently in remission from mental illness, [but] [w]e cannot certify that he would not constitute a menace to himself or to others if released." There was testimony from one doctor that Foucha had "an antisocial personality, a condition that is not a mental disease, and that is untreatable." Based on these opinions, the court ordered that Foucha remain in the mental institution because he posed a danger to himself as well as others. Under state law, a person who has been acquitted of criminal charges because of insanity but who is no longer insane can only be released from commitment if he can prove that he is not a danger to himself or to society. Does the statutory scheme violate Foucha's liberty rights under the Due Process Clause?

   Foucha v. Louisiana, 504 U.S. 71 (1992)

3. Rhode Island's legislature enacted laws that prevented liquor retailers from advertising the retail prices of their merchandise at sites other than their retail stores. It feared that allowing package stores to advertise their prices freely and honestly would lower the cost to consumers and increase the use of alcoholic beverages. 44 Liquormart, a liquor retailer, brought suit seeking a declaratory judgment on the grounds that Rhode Island's laws violated the store's First Amendment right to freedom of speech. The U.S. District Court made a

finding of fact that Rhode Island's law had "no significant impact on levels of alcohol consumption" and concluded that the law was unconstitutional. The district judge's rationale was that the statute in question did not further the goal of reducing alcohol consumption, and further, that its restrictions on commercial freedom of speech were unnecessary and excessive. The U.S. Court of Appeals for the First Circuit reversed, however, and the U.S. Supreme Court granted certiorari. Do you believe that Rhode Island's statute violates the package store's First Amendment and due process right to engage in commercial speech?

44 Liquormart, Inc. v. Rhode Island, 517 U.S. 484 (1996)

4. Margaret Gilleo is a homeowner in a St. Louis suburb. In December 1990, she placed a 24- by 36-inch sign on her lawn expressing opposition to Operation Desert Storm. She contacted police after her sign was stolen on one occasion and knocked down on another occasion. Police officials told Margaret that her signs were prohibited by city ordinance. Margaret unsuccessfully petitioned the city council for a variance, and then filed suit. In her civil rights action, she maintained that the city ordinance violated her First Amendment right of freedom of speech, which was applicable to the state through the Fourteenth Amendment Due Process Clause. The U.S. District Court agreed and enjoined the enforcement of the ordinance. Margaret then placed an 8½- by 11-inch sign in an upstairs window indicating her desire for "Peace in the Gulf." The city, in the meantime, repealed its original ordinance and replaced it with an ordinance that prohibited all signs that did not fit within ten authorized exemptions. The ordinance's preamble indicated that its purpose was to improve aesthetics and protect property values within the city. Margaret's peace sign did not fit within any of the authorized exemptions. She amended her complaint and challenged the new ordinance because it prohibited her from expressing her opposition to the war. The city

defended by arguing that its ordinance was content neutral and its purposes justified the limited number of exemptions. It noted that alternative methods of communication, such as hand-held signs, pamphlets, flyers, etc., were permissible under the ordinance. How would you decide this case?

City of Ladue v. Gilleo, 512 U.S. 43 (1994)

5. Keen Umbehr was in the trash collection business. He had an exclusive contract with Wabaunsee County and six of the county's seven cities to collect the trash from 1985 to 1991. Throughout his term as the primary trash collector, he publicly criticized the county board and many of its policies, successfully sued the board for violating the state open meetings law, and tried, unsuccessfully, to be elected to the board. The board's members retaliated against Umbehr by voting to terminate his contract with the county. Umbehr, however, successfully negotiated new agreements with five of the six cities whose trash he had previously collected. In 1992, Umbehr sued the two county board members who had voted to terminate his contract. He alleged that his discharge/nonrenewal was in retaliation for having exercised his right to freedom of speech. The U.S. District Court ruled that only public employees were protected by the First Amendment from retaliatory discharge. The U.S. Court of Appeals disagreed and reversed. Should independent contractors who have government contracts be protected by the Fourteenth Amendment's Due Process Clause from retaliatory contract discharges resulting from a contractor's exercise of speech? Should the well-known system of patronage, a practice followed by politicians of all stripes by which they reward their supporters with contracts and discharge those who are their political adversaries or who criticize their policies, take precedence over First Amendment considerations?

Board of County Commissioners, Wabaunsee County, Kansas v. Umbehr, 518 U.S. 668 (1996)

6. A Cincinnati, Ohio, ordinance makes it a criminal offense for "three or more persons to assemble, except at a public meeting of citizens, on any of the sidewalks, street corners, vacant lots, or mouths of alleys, and there conduct themselves in a manner annoying to persons passing by, or occupants of adjacent buildings." Coates, a student who became involved in a demonstration, was arrested and convicted for the violation of this ordinance. His argument on appeal was that the ordinance on its face violated the Fourteenth Amendment. Is this a valid contention?

   Coates v. City of Cincinnati, 402 U.S. 611 (1971)

7. Fuentes purchased a stove and stereo from Firestone Tire and Rubber Company. Payment was to be made in monthly installments over a period of time. After two-thirds of the payments were made, Fuentes defaulted. Firestone filed an action for repossession, and at the same time instructed the sheriff to seize the property pursuant to state law. The sheriff seized the property before Fuentes even knew of Firestone's suit for repossession. Fuentes claims that she was deprived of due process because her property was taken without notice or a hearing. What should the result be?

   Fuentes v. Shevin, 407 U.S. 67 (1972)

8. Plaintiff brought a class action on behalf of all female welfare recipients residing in Connecticut and wishing divorces. She alleged that members of the class were prevented from bringing divorce suits by Connecticut statutes that required payment of court fees and costs of service of process as a condition precedent to access to the courts. Plaintiff contended that such statutes violate basic due process considerations. Is her argument valid?

   Boddie v. Connecticut, 401 U.S. 371 (1970)

9. Like many other states, Connecticut requires nonresidents of the state who are enrolled in the state university system to pay tuition and other fees at higher rates than residents of the state who are so enrolled. A Connecticut statute defined as a nonresident any unmarried student if his or her "legal address for any part of the one-year period immediately prior to [his or her] application for admission...was outside of Connecticut," or any married student if his or her "legal address at the time of his application for admission...was outside of Connecticut." The statute also provided that the "status of a student, as established at the time of [his or her] application for admission... shall be [his or her] status for the entire period of his attendance." Two University of Connecticut students who claimed to be residents of Connecticut were by the statute classified as nonresidents for tuition purposes. They claimed that the Due Process Clause does not permit Connecticut to deny an individual the opportunity to present evidence that he or she is a bona fide resident entitled to state rates and that they were being deprived of property without due process. Is this a valid argument?

   Vlandis v. Kline, 412 U.S. 441 (1973)

NOTES

1. Special recognition goes to Bruce D. Fisher and Edgar Bodenheimer. Students seeking more extensive treatment of this material should see Fisher, *Introduction to the Legal System* (St. Paul, MN: West Publishing Co., 1977); and Bodenheimer, *Jurisprudence* (Cambridge, MA: Harvard University Press, 1967).

2. J. G. Murphy and J. Coleman, *An Introduction to Jurisprudence* (Totowa, NJ: Rowman and Allenheld Publishers, 1984), p. 13.

3. Bodenheimer, p. 71; and Fisher, p. 7.

4. Bodenheimer, p. 72.

5. Examples are adverse possession, delivery of a deed, the concept of escheat, estate, and the

covenant of seisin, and the rule against restraints on alienation.

6. Property law addresses the notion that property equals rights, the rights of a finder vis-à-vis everyone but the true owner, the importance of delivery in the making of a gift, or the right of survivorship in joint tenancies.

7. The concepts of consideration, silence as acceptance, and the Statute of Frauds are addressed by contract law.

8. The Massachusetts legislature has again enacted a mandatory seat belt law. An attempt to repeal this statute was unsuccessful.

9. G. Sabine, *A History of Political Theory*, 3d ed. (New York: Holt, Rinehart and Winston, 1961), pp. 681–684; and Bodenheimer, p. 85.

10. Bodenheimer, p. 84; and B. H. Levy, *Anglo-American Philosophy of Law* (New Brunswick, NJ: Transaction Publishers, 1991), pp. 19–23.

11. Bodenheimer, pp. 94, 99; and Levy, pp. 29–36.

12. Bodenheimer, p. 96; and Fisher, p. 11.

13. *Lochner v. New York*, 198 U.S. 45 (1905).

14. Adair v. United States, 208 U.S. 161 (1908).

15. B. Cardozo, *The Nature of Judicial Process* (New Haven, CT: Yale University Press, 1921), p. 65–66.

16. R. Pound, *The Scope and Purpose of Sociological Jurisprudence*, 24 *Harvard Law Review* 591 (1911).

17. Ibid., pp. 510–514.

18. Bodenheimer, p. 116.

19. K. Llewellyn, "A Realistic Jurisprudence—The Next Step," 30 *Columbia Law Review*, 431 (1930) 12.

20. K. Llewellyn, *The Bramble Bush* (1930), p. 12.

21. D. Black, *Sociological Justice* (New York: Oxford University Press, 1989), p. 5.

22. Ibid., p. 21.

23. Ibid., pp. 24–25 and Chapter II "Sociological Litigation."

24. Ibid., pp. 9–13, 21–22.

25. Ibid., p. 24–25, 95–96.

26. F. Marcham, *A History of England* (New York: Macmillan, 1937), p. 62.

27. G. Keeton, *The Norman Conquest and the Common Law* (London: Ernest Benn Limited, 1966), p. 14.

28. Ibid., p. 128; and Marcham, pp. 60–61.

29. T. F. F. Plucknett, *A Concise History of the Common Law* (Little, Brown and Co., 1956), p. 102.

30. F. Marcham, *A History of England* (New York: Macmillan, 1937), p. 62; and T. F. F. Plucknett, *A Concise History of the Common Law* (Boston: Little, Brown, 1956), p. 144.

31. Keeton, p. 23.

32. F. Barlow, *The Feudal Kingdom of England*, 4th ed. (Longman, 1988), p. 51; P. Loyn, *The Making of the English Nation* (Thames & Hudson, 1991), p. 78; C. Brooke, *From Alfred to Henry III* (Norton, 1961), p. 78.

33. Plucknett, p. 139.

34. A. K. R. Kiralfy, *Potter's Historical Introduction to English Law*, 4th ed. (London: Sweet and Maxwell Ltd., 1962), p. 11.

35. Plucknett, p. 141; and Keeton, p. 13.

36. Marcham, p. 80.

37. Plucknett, p. 11; and Barlow, p. 81.

38. Marcham, p. 83.

39. Ibid., p. 86.

40. Ibid., p. 90; and Plucknett, p. 12.

41. Marcham, pp. 110–111.

42. Keeton, p. 160.

43. A. C. Baugh and T. Cable, *A History of the English Language*, 3d ed. (Englewood Cliffs, NJ: Prentice Hall, 1978), pp. 145, 148–149.

44. Brooke, pp. 160, 192.

45. Ibid., p. 156; and Plucknett, p. 14.

46. Marcham, p. 118; and Plucknett, p. 22.

47. Plucknett, p. 15.

48. Brooke, pp. 182–185; and Loyn, p. 128.

49. Marcham, pp. 156–157.

50. Plucknett, p. 103.

51. Keeton, p. 125.

52. Ibid., p. 201.

53. Loyn, p. 139.

54. Marcham, p. 131; and Plucknett, p. 355.

55. Marcham, p. 295.

56. Plucknett, p. 408.

57. Plucknett, p. 357.

58. R. Walsh, *A History of Anglo-American Law* (Indianapolis: Bobbs-Merrill Co., 1932), p. 65.

59. P. H. Winfield, *Chief Sources of English Legal History* (Cambridge, MA: Harvard University Press, 1925).

60. Plucknett, p. 259.

61. Ibid., pp. 280–281.

62. M. Grossberg, *Governing the Hearth* (Chapel Hill: University of North Carolina Press, 1985), p. 15.

63. Marcham, p. 295.

64. Plucknett, p. 178.

65. Ibid., p. 180.

66. Ibid., p. 280; and Marcham, p. 295.

67. Cardinal Wolsey was educated at Oxford, and Becket was educated at the universities of Paris and Bologna (Brooke, p. 64).

68. Brooke, p. 64.

69. D. Roebuck, *The Background of the Common Law*, 2d ed. (Oxford University Press, 1990), p. 64; and Marcham, p. 295.

70. Plucknett, p. 688.

71. Ibid., p. 689; and Potter, pp. 581–584.

72. Potter, p. 280; and Plucknett, pp. 693–694.

73. Roebuck, p. 68.

74. E. Ward, "Mandatory Court-Annexed Alternative Dispute Resolution in the United States Federal Courts: Panacea or Pandemic?" 81 *St. John's Law Review* 77 (2007), 83.

75. Ibid, p. 87.

76. M. Galanter, "The Vanishing Trial: An Examination of Trials and Related Matters in Federal and State Courts," 1 *J. Empirical Legal Studies* 459 (2004), p. 463.

77. Loyn, p. 141; and Brooke, pp. 220–223.

78. Marcham, p. 143; and Brooke, p. 221.

79. Brooke, p. 223.

80. C. A. Miller, "The Forest of Due Process of Law: The American Constitutional Tradition," in J. R. Pennock and J. W. Chapman, *Due Process* (New York: New York University Press, 1977), p. 6.

81. Ibid.

82. Ibid., p. 9.

II

✳

Ethics

CHAPTER OBJECTIVES

1. *Increase awareness of the connection between ethics and law.*

2. *Encourage students to understand why there are different ways of thinking about moral questions.*

3. *Build on themes addressed in the philosophy of law discussion in Chapter I (especially natural law, utilitarianism, and analytical positivism).*

4. *Encourage students to think about current highly controversial moral issues (such as same-sex marriage, abortion, physician-assisted suicide, medical marijuana, and capital punishment), from differing ethical perspectives.*

This chapter builds on themes introduced in the philosophy section of Chapter I. It shows readers why people need to be sensitive to ethical issues and illustrates some of the problems that arise when members of our complex and diverse society disagree as to the proper boundaries of ethics and law. Because of the limitations of space, it is only possible to give the reader a taste of the ways law and ethics intertwine. However, this discussion can expand interest and understanding and stimulate thinking about this rich and intricate subject.

All human beings face ethical challenges in their personal, professional, and public lives. Ethical questions permeate our society. In charting public policy, for example, legislators choose from among alternative courses of action as part of the lawmaking process. Similarly, when appellate judges construe constitutions and statutes and review the decisions of lower courts in contract and tort cases, they also make choices about public policy. Is it morally right for the Supreme

Judicial Court of Maine to rule in a medical malpractice unintended pregnancy case that "a parent cannot be said to have been damaged by the birth and rearing of a healthy, normal child?"[1] Is the Massachusetts legislature morally justified in enacting an extremely short statute of limitations for the commencement of skiers' personal injury actions against ski area operators, to the detriment of injured skiers?[2]

South Dakota's legislature enacted the following statute, which permits pharmacists in certain circumstances to refuse to fill a customer's prescription if doing so would violate the pharmacist's moral beliefs.

South Dakota Codified Laws 36-11-70.
Refusal to dispense medication.

No pharmacist may be required to dispense medication if there is reason to believe that the medication would be used to:

1. Cause an abortion; or

2. Destroy an unborn child as defined in subdivision 22-1-2(50A); or

3. Cause the death of any person by means of an assisted suicide, euthanasia, or mercy killing.

No such refusal to dispense medication pursuant to this section may be the basis for any claim for damages against the pharmacist or the pharmacy of the pharmacist or the basis for any disciplinary, recriminatory, or discriminatory action against the pharmacist.

Should health care professionals be legally permitted to refuse to fulfill their patients'/customers' lawful requests because of the provider's deeply held moral beliefs? If so, do providers exercising this legal right have any moral obligation to inform their potential customers of this fact?

Reasonable people can differ about whether the ethical judgments embodied in these legislative and judicial decisions should be legally sanctioned as the public policy of the state. It is no wonder that there is great public concern about the morality of governmental policies regarding such topics as capital punishment, abortion, assisted suicide, same-sex marriages, homosexuality, interracial adoptions, the rights of landowners versus environmental protection, the meaning of cruel and unusual punishment, and the right of indigents to appellate counsel in capital cases.

The following case is an example of an ethical debate over public policy. The petitioner was a convicted robber and murderer who was sentenced to death pursuant to a Georgia statute. He failed to convince the courts in Georgia to overturn his sentence, but he did successfully petition the U.S. Supreme Court for certiorari.

In the case of *Gregg v. Georgia*, the Supreme Court justices debated the ethics and the legality of capital punishment. The case of *Gregg v. Georgia* was decided in 1976. In that case, seven justices ruled that Georgia's statute authorizing capital punishment was not inherently cruel and unusual under the Eighth and Fourteenth Amendments to the U.S. Constitution. The following excerpts from *Gregg* have been edited to focus on the argument about the morality of capital punishment. In the opinions below, you will find several references to an earlier case, *Furman v. Georgia*. *Furman* was a 1972 case in which the Supreme Court prohibited states from imposing the death penalty in an arbitrary manner. The justices wrote extensively on the ethical issue of capital punishment in Furman, and only summarized their views in *Gregg*. Because of limitations of space, *Gregg* has been excerpted below. However, you are encouraged to read the *Furman* case on the Internet.[3] You will better understand the following discussion of *Gregg* if you do so.

Gregg v. Georgia
428 U.S. 153
United States Supreme Court
July 2, 1976

Opinion of Justices Stewart, Powell, and Stevens

C

... We now consider specifically whether the sentence of death for the crime of murder is a per se violation of the Eighth and Fourteenth Amendments to the Constitution. We note first that history and precedent strongly support a negative answer to this question.

The imposition of the death penalty for the crime of murder has a long history of acceptance both in the United States and in England. The common-law rule imposed a mandatory death sentence on all convicted murderers..., And the penalty continued to be used into the 20th century by most American States, although the breadth of the common-law rule was diminished, initially by narrowing the class of murders to be punished by death and subsequently by widespread adoption of laws expressly granting juries the discretion to recommend mercy....

It is apparent from the text of the Constitution itself that the existence of capital punishment was accepted by the Framers. At the time the Eighth Amendment was ratified, capital punishment was a common sanction in every State. Indeed, the First Congress of the United States enacted legislation providing death as the penalty for specified crimes.... The Fifth Amendment, adopted at the same time as the Eighth, contemplated the continued existence of the capital sanction by imposing certain limits on the prosecution of capital cases:

> "No person shall be held to answer for a capital, or otherwise infamous crime, unless on a presentment or indictment of a Grand Jury ...; nor shall any person be subject for the same offense to be twice put in jeopardy of life or limb; ... nor be deprived of life, liberty, or property, without due process of law...."

And the Fourteenth Amendment, adopted over three quarters of a century later, similarly contemplates the existence of the capital sanction in providing that no State shall deprive any person of "life, liberty, or property" without due process of law.

For nearly two centuries, this Court, repeatedly and often expressly, has recognized that capital punishment is not invalid per se....

... In *Trop v. Dulles* ... Mr. Chief Justice Warren, for himself and three other Justices, wrote:

> "Whatever the arguments may be against capital punishment, both on moral grounds and in terms of accomplishing the purposes of punishment ... the death penalty has been employed throughout our history, and, in a day when it is still widely accepted, it cannot be said to violate the constitutional concept of cruelty."

Four years ago, the petitioners in *Furman* ... predicated their argument primarily upon the asserted proposition that standards of decency had evolved to the point where capital punishment no longer could be tolerated. The petitioners in those cases said, in effect, that the evolutionary process had come to an end, and that standards of decency required that the Eighth Amendment be construed finally as prohibiting capital punishment for any crime regardless of its depravity and impact on society. This view was accepted by two Justices. Three other Justices were unwilling to go so far; focusing on the procedures by which convicted defendants were selected for the death penalty rather than on the actual punishment inflicted, they joined in the conclusion that the statutes before the Court were constitutionally invalid.

The petitioners in the capital cases before the Court today renew the "standards of decency" argument, but developments during the four years since *Furman* have undercut substantially the assumptions upon which their argument rested. Despite the continuing debate, dating back to the 19th century, over the morality and utility of capital punishment, it is now evident that a large proportion of American society continues to regard it as an appropriate and necessary criminal sanction.

The most marked indication of society's endorsement of the death penalty for murder is the legislative response to *Furman*. The legislatures of at least 35 States have enacted new statutes that provide for the death penalty for at least some crimes that result in the death of another person. And the Congress of the United States, in 1974, enacted a statute providing the death penalty for aircraft piracy that results in death. These recently adopted statutes have attempted to address the concerns expressed by the Court in *Furman* primarily (i) by specifying the factors to be weighed and the procedures to be followed in deciding when to impose a capital sentence, or (ii) by making the death penalty mandatory for specified crimes. But all of the post *Furman* statutes make clear that capital punishment itself has not been rejected by the elected representatives of the people....

As we have seen, however, the Eighth Amendment demands more than that a challenged punishment be acceptable to contemporary society. The Court also must ask whether it comports with the basic concept of human dignity at the core of the Amendment.... Although we cannot "invalidate a category of penalties because we deem less severe penalties adequate to serve the ends of penology," ... the sanction imposed cannot be so totally without penological justification that it results in the gratuitous infliction of suffering....

The death penalty is said to serve two principal social purposes: retribution and deterrence of capital crimes by prospective offenders.

In part, capital punishment is an expression of society's moral outrage at particularly offensive conduct. This function may be unappealing to many, but it is essential in an ordered society that asks its citizens to rely on legal processes rather than self-help to vindicate their wrongs.

> "The instinct for retribution is part of the nature of man, and channeling that instinct in the administration of criminal justice serves an important purpose in promoting the stability of a society governed by law. When people begin to believe that organized society is unwilling or unable to impose upon criminal offenders the punishment they "deserve," then there are sown the seeds of anarchy—of self-help, vigilante justice, and lynch law." Furman v. Georgia ... (STEWART, J., concurring).

> "Retribution is no longer the dominant objective of the criminal law," *Williams v. New York* ... but neither is it a forbidden objective nor one inconsistent with our respect for the dignity of men.... Indeed, the decision that capital punishment may be the appropriate sanction in extreme cases is an expression of the community's belief that certain crimes are themselves so grievous an affront to humanity that the only adequate response may be the penalty of death.

Statistical attempts to evaluate the worth of the death penalty as a deterrent to crimes by potential offenders have occasioned a great deal of debate. The results simply have been inconclusive....

... In sum, we cannot say that the judgment of the Georgia Legislature that capital punishment may be necessary in some cases is clearly wrong. Considerations of federalism, as well as respect for the ability of a legislature to evaluate, in terms of its particular State, the moral consensus concerning the death penalty and its social utility as a sanction, require us to conclude, in the absence of more convincing evidence, that the infliction of death as a punishment for murder is not without justification and thus is not unconstitutionally severe....

We hold that the death penalty is not a form of punishment that may never be imposed, regardless of the circumstances of the offense, regardless of the character of the offender, and regardless of the procedure followed in reaching the decision to impose it.

Mr. Justice Brennan, dissenting

... In *Furman v. Georgia*,... I said:

> "From the beginning of our Nation, the punishment of death has stirred acute public controversy. Although pragmatic arguments for and against the punishment have been frequently advanced, this longstanding and heated controversy cannot be explained solely as the result of differences over the practical wisdom of a particular government policy. At bottom, the battle has been waged on moral grounds. The country has debated whether a society for which the dignity of the individual is the supreme value can, without a fundamental inconsistency, follow the practice of deliberately putting some of its members to death. In the United States, as in other nations of the western world, 'the struggle about this punishment has been one between ancient and deeply rooted beliefs in retribution, atonement or vengeance on the one hand, and, on the other, beliefs in the personal value and dignity of the common man that were born of the democratic movement of the eighteenth century, as well as beliefs in the scientific approach to an understanding of the motive forces of human conduct, which are the result of the growth of the sciences of behavior during the nineteenth and twentieth centuries.' It is this essentially moral conflict that forms the backdrop for the past changes in and the present operation of our system of imposing death as a punishment for crime."

That continues to be my view. For the Clause forbidding cruel and unusual punishments under our constitutional system of government embodies in unique degree moral principles restraining the punishments that our civilized society may impose on those persons who transgress its laws. Thus, I too say: "For myself, I do not hesitate to assert the proposition that the only way the law has progressed from the days of the rack, the screw, and the wheel is the development of moral concepts, or, as stated by the Supreme Court ... the application of 'evolving standards of decency.'"...

This Court inescapably has the duty, as the ultimate arbiter of the meaning of our Constitution, to say whether, when individuals condemned to death stand before our Bar, "moral concepts" require us to hold that the law has progressed to the point where we should declare that the punishment of death, like punishments on the rack, the screw, and the wheel, is no longer morally tolerable in our civilized society. My opinion in Furman v. Georgia concluded that our civilization and the law had progressed to this point and that therefore the punishment of death, for whatever crime and under all circumstances, is "cruel and unusual" in violation of the Eighth and Fourteenth Amendments of the Constitution. I shall not again canvass the reasons that led to that conclusion. I emphasize only the foremost among the "moral concepts" recognized in our cases and inherent in the Clause is the primary moral principle that the State even as it punishes, must treat its citizens in a manner consistent with their intrinsic worth as human beings—a punishment must not be so severe as to be degrading to human dignity. A judicial determination whether the punishment of death comports with human dignity is therefore not only permitted but compelled by the Clause....

I do not understand that the Court disagrees that "in comparison to all other punishments today ... the deliberate extinguishment of human life by the State is uniquely degrading to human dignity." ... For three of my Brethren hold today that mandatory infliction of the death penalty constitutes the penalty cruel and unusual punishment. I perceive no principled basis for this limitation. Death for whatever crime and under all circumstances "is truly an awesome punishment. The calculated killing of a human being by the State involves, by its very nature, a denial of the executed person's humanity.... An executed person has indeed 'lost the right to have rights.'" Death is not only an unusually severe punishment, unusual in its pain, in its finality, and in its enormity, but it serves no penal purpose more effectively than a less severe punishment; therefore the principle inherent in the Clause that prohibits pointless infliction of excessive punishment when less severe punishment can adequately achieve the same purposes invalidates the punishment....

The fatal constitutional infirmity in the punishment of death is that it treats "members of the human race as nonhumans, as objects to be toyed with and discarded. [It is] thus inconsistent with the fundamental premise of the Clause that even the vilest criminal remains a human being possessed of common human dignity." ... As such it is a penalty that "subjects the individual to a fate forbidden by the principle of civilized treatment guaranteed by the [Clause]." I therefore would hold, on that ground alone, that death is today a cruel and unusual punishment prohibited by the Clause. "Justice of this kind is obviously no less shocking than the crime itself, and the new 'official' murder, far from offering redress for the offense committed against society, adds instead a second defilement to the first."

I dissent from the judgments in ... Gregg v. Georgia ... Proffitt v. Florida, and ... Jurek v. Texas, insofar as each upholds the death sentences challenged in those cases. I would set aside the death sentences imposed in those cases as violative of the Eighth and Fourteenth Amendments.

Mr. Justice Marshall, dissenting

In Furman v. Georgia, 408 U.S. 238, 314 (1972) (concurring opinion), I set forth at some length my views on the basic issue presented to the Court in these cases. The death penalty, I concluded, is a cruel and unusual punishment prohibited by the Eighth and Fourteenth Amendments. That continues to be my view....

In Furman I concluded that the death penalty is constitutionally invalid for two reasons. First, the death penalty is excessive.... And second, the American people, fully informed as to the purposes of the death penalty and its liabilities, would in my view reject it as morally unacceptable....

... Assuming ... that the post-Furman enactment of statutes authorizing the death penalty renders the prediction of the views of an informed citizenry an uncertain basis for a constitutional decision, the enactment of those statutes has no bearing whatsoever on the conclusion that the death penalty is unconstitutional because it is excessive. An excessive penalty is invalid under the Cruel and Unusual Punishments Clause "even though popular sentiment may favor" it.... The inquiry here, then, is simply whether the death penalty is necessary to accomplish the legitimate legislative purposes in punishment, or whether a less severe penalty—life imprisonment—would do as well....

The two purposes that sustain the death penalty as nonexcessive in the Court's view are general deterrence and retribution. In Furman, I canvassed the relevant data on the deterrent effect of capital punishment....

The available evidence, I concluded ... was convincing that "capital punishment is not necessary as a deterrent to crime in our society." ... The evidence I reviewed in Furman remains convincing, in my view, that "capital punishment is not necessary as a deterrent to crime in our society." ... The justification for the death penalty must be found elsewhere....

The other principal purpose said to be served by the death penalty is retribution. The notion that retribution ... can serve as a moral justification for the sanction of death finds credence in the opinion of my Brothers Stewart, Powell, and Stevens, and that of my Brother White.... It is this notion that I find to be the most disturbing aspect of today's unfortunate decisions.

The concept of retribution is a multifaceted one, and any discussion of its role in the criminal law must be undertaken with caution. On one level, it can be said that the notion of retribution or reprobation is the basis of our insistence that only those who have broken the law be punished, and in this sense the notion is quite obviously central to a just system of criminal sanctions. But our recognition that retribution plays a crucial role in determining who may be punished by no means requires approval of retribution as a general justification for punishment. It is the question whether retribution can provide a moral justification for punishment—in particular, capital punishment—that we must consider.

My Brothers Stewart, Powell, and Stevens offer the following explanation of the retributive justification for capital punishment:

> "'The instinct for retribution is part of the nature of man, and channeling that instinct in the administration of criminal justice serves an important purpose in promoting the stability of a society governed ... by law. When people begin to believe that organized society is unwilling or unable to impose upon criminal offenders the punishment they "deserve," then there are sown the seeds of anarchy—of self-help, vigilante justice, and lynch law.'" ...

This statement is wholly inadequate to justify the death penalty. As my Brother Brennan stated in *Furman*, "There is no evidence whatever that utilization of imprisonment rather than death encourages private blood feuds and other disorders." ... It simply defies belief to suggest that the death penalty is necessary to prevent the American people from taking the law into their own hands.

In a related vein, it may be suggested that the expression of moral outrage through the imposition of the death penalty serves to reinforce basic moral values—that it marks some crimes as particularly offensive and therefore to be avoided. The argument is akin to a deterrence argument, but differs in that it contemplates the individual's shrinking from antisocial conduct, not because he fears punishment, but because he has been told in the strongest possible way that the conduct is wrong. This contention, like the previous one, provides no support for the death penalty. It is inconceivable that any individual concerned about conforming his conduct to what society says is "right" would fail to realize that murder is "wrong" if the penalty were simply life imprisonment.

The foregoing contentions—that society's expression of moral outrage through the imposition of the death penalty preempts the citizenry from taking the law into its own hands and reinforces moral values—are not retributive in the purest sense. They are essentially utilitarian in that they portray the death penalty as valuable because of its beneficial results. These justifications for the death penalty are inadequate because the penalty is, quite clearly I think, not necessary to the accomplishment of those results.

There remains for consideration, however, what might be termed the purely retributive justification for the death penalty—that the death penalty is appropriate, not because of its beneficial effect on society, but because the taking of the murderer's life is itself morally good. Some of the language of the opinion of my Brothers Stewart, Powell, and Stevens ... appears positively to embrace this notion of retribution for its own sake as a justification for capital punishment. They state:

> "The decision that capital punishment may be the appropriate sanction in extreme cases is an expression of the community's belief that certain crimes are themselves so grievous an affront to humanity that the only adequate response may be the penalty of death."...

They then quote with approval from Lord Justice Denning's remarks before the British Royal Commission on Capital Punishment:

> "'The truth is that some crimes are so outrageous that society insists on adequate punishment, because the wrongdoer deserves it, irrespective of whether it is a deterrent or not.'" ...

Of course, it may be that these statements are intended as no more than observations as to the popular demands that it is thought must be responded to in order to prevent anarchy. But the implication of the statements appears to me to be quite different, that society's judgment that the murderer "deserves" death must be respected not simply because the preservation of order requires it, but because it is appropriate that society make the judgment and carry it out. It is this latter notion, in particular, that I consider to be fundamentally at odds with the Eighth Amendment....

The mere fact that the community demands the murderer's life in return for the evil he has done cannot sustain the death penalty, for as Justices Stewart, Powell, and Stevens remind us, "the Eighth Amendment demands more than that a challenged punishment be acceptable to contemporary society." ... To be sustained under the Eighth Amendment, the death penalty must "compor[t] with the basic concept of human dignity at the core of the Amendment," ... the objective in imposing it must be "[consistent] with our respect for the dignity of [other] men." ... Under these standards, the taking of life "because the wrongdoer deserves it" surely must fall, for such a punishment has as its very basis the total denial of the wrongdoer's dignity and worth.

The death penalty, unnecessary to promote the goal of deterrence or to further any legitimate notion of retribution, is an excessive penalty forbidden by the Eighth and Fourteenth Amendments. I respectfully dissent from the Court's judgment upholding the sentences of death imposed upon the petitioners in these cases....

Case Questions

1. How does Justice Stewart justify his conclusion that capital punishment is a permissible form of punishment?
2. What is the moral principle that is the fundamental basis of Justice Brennan's dissent?
3. Does Justice Marshall believe that retribution provides a moral justification for capital punishment? Why or why not?
4. In your opinion, is the fact that capital punishment is popular with a majority of society a sufficient fact to conclude the debate about whether the death penalty is cruel and unusual under the Eighth Amendment?

People are also affected by ethical considerations in their professional interactions with others. Although we may not realize it at the time, our actions and inactions at work and school are often interpreted by others as evidence of our personal values and character—who we are and what we stand for. A person whose behavior is consistent with moral principles is said to have integrity. It is common for people to try to create at least the illusion that they have integrity. Integrity is prized by employers, who try to avoid hiring persons known to lie, cheat, and steal. Many companies also try to avoid doing business with firms that are reputed to engage in fraudulent practices, who try to take unfair advantage of those with whom they contract, who negotiate in bad faith, or are otherwise unscrupulous to their business partners. Students applying to professional schools quickly learn that integrity is important to members of admissions committees. Such committees generally require recommenders to include an evaluation of an applicant's character in their letters. People are also concerned about ethical behavior in their personal lives. They worry about whether a person with whom they have shared a confidence is trustworthy.

But it is often difficult to know the parameters of ethical behavior in particular situations. Is it ever permissible to break a promise not to tell? Are there any rules about lying? Who determines the rules? How are they enforced? Are there any circumstances when it is morally permissible to lie to a total stranger? A family member? A best friend? A business partner? When is it acceptable for other people to lie to you? What are the social and legal consequences of lying?[4]

In your role as a student you may have encountered situations in which you and/or some classmates have cheated on a test or paper. Have you ever seriously thought about the ethics of cheating? Is it always morally wrong for a student to cheat? Can circumstances make a difference? Does it make a difference if the teacher makes no effort to prevent dishonesty and virtually every other student in the class is cheating on a test or written assignment? Would it make a difference if you believed the teacher had been unfair to you on a previous assignment and cheating would enable you to get the final grade that you "really deserved"? If you observe classmates cheat, do you have any duty to tell the instructor? What would you think about some other student who did tell? What is the basis for your positions?

Who makes the rules for you? Is it up to you to decide, your peer group, your parents, or other significant people in your life? Perhaps you look to religious leaders for guidance. Religious groups have historically assumed a major role in setting moral standards, and religious leaders frequently take firm positions on contemporary ethical issues. How can anyone tell who is "right"? Thomas Jefferson in the Declaration of Independence said, "We hold these truths to be self evident…" Is that sufficient proof of the proposition that all people are created equal?

Philosophers have argued for centuries about the answers to questions such as those raised above. The following mini-introduction will help to provide some background and structure for the discussion of the cases that follow.

ETHICS

Ethics, which is the study of morality, is one of the five traditional branches of study within philosophy, as can be seen in Table 2.1. Ethicists are concerned with what makes conduct morally right or wrong and the essential nature of moral responsibility. They also investigate the application of ethical principles to the practice of professions such as law, medicine, and business.

We see in Table 2.2 that ethical theories are often classified as being either metaethical or normative in their approach.[5]

TABLE 2.1 Branches of Philosophy

Ethics	The study of morality
Metaphysics	The study of the nature of reality or being
Aesthetics	The study of beauty
Logic	The study of correct reasoning
Epistemology	The study of knowledge

TABLE 2.2 Ethics

Metaethics	Theoretical foundations of ethics
Normative ethics	Applied ethics

Metaethical scholars have centered on defining ethical terms and developing theories. They have tended to focus on abstract topics, such as identifying the fundamental characteristics of moral behavior. These discussions have tended to be extremely theoretical and have been often criticized for not having many practical applications.[6] The following example is intended to raise philosophical questions about the essential nature of integrity under circumstances when it is acknowledged that all of the actors have engaged in "correct" actions.

Karen, Keisha, and Kelly

Assume that Karen is a "goody-goody" and always tries to do the "right" thing in order to comply with what she perceives to be her moral duty. Assume that Keisha also does the "right" thing, but does so at least in part for selfish reasons (being seen doing the right thing will make the newspapers and will be good for business). What if Kelly selectively does the "right" thing only when she feels a personal connection with some other person in need, under circumstances when she feels she can help without putting herself at risk? Does Karen have more integrity than Keisha and Kelly?

Normative ethicians have been more concerned with answering practical questions such as "Is killing in self-defense wrong?" or "What should a physician do when a patient dying of a terminal disease asks for assistance in committing suicide?" Modern ethicians primarily focus on normative moral issues rather than metaethical ones, although this tendency is of recent origin and primarily began in the 1970s.[7]

Philosophers disagree about whether ethical judgments about right and wrong can be conclusively proven.[8] Some have argued that ethical judgments can be scientifically proven. Others have rejected science and insisted that such judgments be based on natural law, sounding intuitive notions of right and wrong,[9] or based on the logical soundness of the reasons underlying the ethical judgment.[10]

Another area of disagreement involves where those making ethical judgments should focus their attention. Some philosophers believe that whether an action is "good" or "bad" can only be determined after an act has occurred by examining the outcomes. Only by looking backward can the relative costs and benefits of an action be weighed and its worth assessed.[11] *Utilitarianism*, which was discussed in Chapter I, is such a theory. Thus, from a utilitarian perspective, publicly and brutally caning one prisoner for a given criminal offense would be moral if it could be proven later that it has deterred thousands of others from engaging in that same offense.

Deontologists would reject a focus on aftermaths in favor of studying the role of moral duty. Immanuel Kant, for example, argued that, to be ethical, an actor's *deeds* should be evaluated based on the reasoning that led to the act.[12] Kant believed that intent mattered and that an ethical actor should be motivated only by a desire to comply with a universally accepted *moral duty*. He did not view actions motivated by feelings of love, sympathy, or the potential for personal gain, as being ethically principled.[13] Caning a convicted person could not be a moral act if it amounted to torture. **Egoists** had yet a different approach. They believed that individuals were ethically "right" to act in their own self-interest, without regard for the consequences to other people.[14]

Many theorists have argued that conduct is moral only if it coincides with religious mandates such as the Ten Commandments or the Golden Rule. Society, however, has been unable to agree on any single, universally acceptable ethical theory. Serious disagreements exist about what constitutes ethical conduct in specific contexts. "Right" answers are not always obvious, and rules, interpretive opinions, and guidelines are needed to direct individuals toward "good" conduct.

Law and Morality

One of the unresolved debates revolves around what role law should play in making ethical rules. Should law supply the enforcement mechanism for enforcing moral norms? What should an ethical person do when confronted with "bad" laws? Should decisions about morality in some contexts be reserved to the individual?

Although law can contribute rules that embody moral norms, law in our democracy is not expected to play the primary role in promoting ethical behavior in society. Parents, churches, schools, youth organizations, athletic teams, and business, professional, and fraternal groups of all types are expected to fill the void. They often establish ethical codes, rules (such as those prohibiting "unsportsmanlike conduct" or "conduct unbecoming an officer"), and discipline and even expel members who violate their terms. A precise calculus of law's relationship to morality, however, remains illusive.

You may recall from reading Chapter I that there is a fundamental and unresolved disagreement between philosophers who are *natural law adherents* and those who are *analytical positivists* regarding the true nature of law. From the positivist point of view, laws are merely the rules that political superiors develop pursuant to duly established procedures that are imposed on the rest of the polity. Laws are viewed as being intrinsically neither good nor bad. They do establish norms of legal behavior, but such efforts sometimes amount to little more than arbitrary line drawing. Positivists would point out that law establishes a floor but not a ceiling. Individuals who satisfy their legal obligations always retain the right to self-impose additional restrictions on their conduct in order to satisfy a deeply felt moral duty. But law does not depend for its authority on an ad hoc assessment of whether the government ought to follow a different policy. It is clear, however, that defying the law can result in state-imposed sanctions. Assume, for example, that a taxpayer takes an unauthorized "deduction" off her income tax obligation and makes an equivalent dollar donation to a charity rather than to the Internal Revenue

Service. The fact that her conscience tells her that it is self-evident that the U.S. government is morally wrong to spend our dollars on some disfavored program is unlikely to save her from criminal and civil sanctions.

In the following passage, Martin Luther King Jr. distinguishes between just and unjust laws and argues that immoral laws should be civilly disobeyed.

*Letter from a Birmingham Jail**

You express a great deal of anxiety over our willingness to break laws. This is certainly a legitimate concern. Since we so diligently urge people to obey the Supreme Court's decision of 1954 outlawing segregation in the public schools, it is rather strange and paradoxical to find us consciously breaking laws. One may well ask, "How can you advocate breaking some laws and obeying others?" The answer is found in the fact that there are two types of laws: there are just and there are unjust laws....

... A just law is a man-made code that squares with the moral law or the law of God. An unjust law is a code that is out of harmony with the moral law. To put it in the terms of Saint Thomas Aquinas, an unjust law is a human law that is not rooted in eternal and natural law. Any law that uplifts human personality is just. Any law that degrades human personality is unjust. All segregation statutes are unjust because segregation distorts the soul and damages the personality. It gives the segregator a false sense of superiority, and the segregated a false sense of inferiority....

So segregation is not only politically, economically and sociologically unsound, but it is morally wrong and sinful....

... I submit that an individual who breaks a law that conscience tells him is unjust and willingly accepts the penalty by staying in jail to arouse the conscience of the community over its injustice, is in reality expressing the very highest respect for law....

We can never forget that everything Hitler did in Germany was "legal" and everything that Hungarian freedom fighters did in Hungary was "illegal." It was "illegal" to aid and comfort a Jew, in Hitler's Germany. But I am sure that if I had lived in Germany during that time I would have aided and comforted my Jewish brothers even though it was illegal....

Positive Law Rules

In our republic, the people are sovereign, but there is no law higher than the U.S. Constitution.[15] We have adopted the analytical positivist view that bills that have been enacted in conformity with constitutional requirements are the law. Individuals, for reasons of conscience, may defy these duly enacted laws, but they are lawfully subject to prosecution.

It is important to note, however, that political majorities in federal and state legislatures often enact statutes that reflect widely held moral beliefs in the electorate. Examples include the Civil Rights Act of 1964, the Americans with Disabilities Act, the Clean Air Act, the Clean Water Act, and the Sherman Act, to name just a few. Legislative bodies have also taken the ethical views of political minorities into consideration when drafting legislation. Congress, for example, exempted conscientious objectors from having to register with the Selective Service System. Similarly, Congress's 1998 omnibus spending bill contained a provision that permitted doctors opposed to birth control to refuse on moral grounds to write prescriptions for contraceptives requested by federal employees.[16] But one need only look at Article I, Section 9, of the U.S. Constitution to see an example of political expediency taking precedence over moral considerations. In that article, antislavery founders compromised their moral principles in order to win ratification of the Constitution in southern states.

Federal and state judicial bodies also impart moral views when they construe constitutions and statutes. Examples include the U.S. Supreme Court's interpretations of the Fourteenth Amendment in *Lawrence v. Texas* (the right of two same-sex, consenting adults, while at home, to determine the nature of their sexual intimacy), *Loving v. Virginia* (an individual's right to marry a person of a different race), and *Moore v. City of East Cleveland* (in which the court broadened the meaning of the term "family"), three famous cases involving interpretations of the Due Process Clause, which are included elsewhere in this textbook.

It is obvious that there are many instances in which moral rules and legal rules overlap. Our criminal laws severely punish persons convicted of murder, rape, and robbery, and they ought to do so. Such acts simultaneously violate legal and moral principles. Tort law provides another example. Damages in negligence cases should be borne by the parties based on the extent to which each was responsible for the damages. Because this decision is, with some exceptions, based on the relative fault of the parties, it can also be argued both on teleological and deontological grounds to be an ethical rule. We see another example of legal and ethical harmony in the *Iacomini* case (Chapter VII). In that case the court ruled that the law would permit a mechanic to claim an equitable lien against a motor vehicle that he had repaired, under circumstances when no other relief was possible. The court said that such a remedy was legally appropriate in proper circumstances to prevent unjust enrichment. The following materials raise interesting legal and moral questions about legal and moral duties as they relate to members of one's family.

Aiding and Abetting, Misprision, Informing, and the Family

Imagine how difficult it must be for a person who, after acquiring bits and pieces of information from various sources, ultimately concludes that a member of his or her family is probably involved in criminal activity. Suppose further that the crimes involved are a series of premeditated murders, and that the offender will probably be sentenced to the death penalty upon conviction of the charges. Assume further that you have to admit that, unless you inform authorities, other innocent persons may well become additional victims. Suppose there is a million-dollar cash award that will be paid to the person who provides the information that ultimately leads to the conviction of the offender. What would you do? Would you tell authorities and run the risk of being viewed as being disloyal to your family? Would you stay silent and hope that nobody else is harmed?[17]

If you were writing a statute to prevent people from harboring fugitive felons, would you carve out an exception for people protecting members of their own families? Examine the following New Mexico statute from ethical and legal perspectives.

New Mexico Statutes Annotated 30–22–4. Harboring or Aiding a Felon.

Harboring or aiding a felon consists of any person, not standing in the relation of husband or wife, parent or grandparent, child or grandchild, brother or sister, by consanguinity or affinity, who knowingly conceals any offender or gives such offender any other aid, knowing that he has committed a felony, with the intent that he escape or avoid arrest, trial conviction or punishment. Whoever commits harboring or aiding a felon is guilty of a fourth degree felony. In a prosecution under this section it shall not be necessary to aver, or on the trial to prove, that the principal felon has been either arrested, prosecuted or tried.

Do you agree with the way the legislature defined the scope of the legal duty? Should the scope of the moral duty be the same as the scope of the legal duty?

The above statute has its roots in the common law crime of accessory after the fact. With the exceptions indicated above, it creates a legal duty on everyone else to refrain from helping a known felon escape apprehension by authorities. You can see how this statute was applied in the following case. Read the case and think about whether you agree with the opinion of the court majority or the dissenting judges. What is the basis for your choice?

State v. Mobbley
650 P.2d 841
Court of Appeals of New Mexico
August 3, 1982

Wood, Judge

The criminal information charged that defendant did "knowingly aid Andrew Needham knowing that he had committed a felony with the intent that he escape arrest, trial, conviction and punishment.... The issue is whether the agreed upon facts are such that defendant may not be prosecuted for the offense of aiding a felon.

Defendant is married to Ricky Mobbley. Police officers went to a house and contacted defendant; they advised defendant that felony warrants had been issued for Ricky Mobbley and Andrew Needham. The officers asked defendant if "both were there." Defendant denied that the men were there, although she knew that both men were in the house. Hearing noises, the officers entered the house and discovered both men. Defendant could not have revealed Needham without also revealing her husband. The criminal charge was based on the failure to reveal Needham....

The power to define crimes is a legislative function....

Section 30–22–4, *supra*, applies to "any person, not standing in the relation of husband or wife, parent or grandparent, child or grandchild, brother or sister by consanguinity or affinity...." There is no claim that any of the exempted relationships applies as between defendant and Needham. As enacted by the Legislature, § 30–22–4, *supra*, applies to the agreed facts.

Defendant contends that such a result is contrary to legislative intent because statutes must be interpreted in accord with common sense and reason, and must be interpreted so as not to render the statute's application absurd or unreasonable.... We give two answers to this contention.

First, where the meaning of the statutory language is plain, and where the words used by the Legislature are free from ambiguity, there is no basis for interpreting the statute.... Section 30–22–4, *supra*, applies to "any person" not within the relationship exempted by the statute. Defendant is such a person.

Second, if we assume that the statute should be interpreted, our holding that § 30–22–4, *supra*, applies to the agreed facts accords with legislative intent. Statutes proscribing harboring or aiding a felon grew out of the common law of accessories after the fact. LaFave & Scott, Criminal Law § 66 (1972). However:

> At common law, only one class was excused from liability for being accessories after the fact. Wives did not become accessories by aiding their husbands. No other relationship, including that of husband to wife, would suffice. Today, close to half of the states have broadened the exemption to cover other close *relatives*.... This broadening of the excemption [*sic*] may be justified on the ground that it is unrealistic to expect persons to be deterred from giving aid to their close *relations*. (Our emphasis.)

LaFave & Scott, *supra*, at 523–24.

New Mexico legislative history accords with the discussion in LaFave & Scott, *supra*. In 1875 New Mexico adopted the common law.... The present statute ... was a part of the Criminal Code enacted in 1963....

Limiting the exemptions in § 30–22–4, *supra*, to *relatives* named in that statute accords with the legislative intent as shown by legislative history. In light of the limited exemption at common law, and legislation limited to relatives, it is not absurd and not unreasonable to hold that if defendant aided Needham, § 30–22–4, *supra*, applies to that aid.

Except for one fact, there would have been no dispute as to the applicability of § 30–22–4, *supra*. That one fact is that defendant could not have revealed Needham without also revealing her husband. The statute does not exempt a defendant from prosecution when this fact situation arises; to judicially declare such an additional exemption would be to improperly add words to the statute.... Also, such a judicial declaration would be contrary to the rationale for this type of statute; it is unrealistic to expect persons to be deterred from giving aid to their close relations. LaFave & Scott, *supra*.

We recognize that defendant was placed in a dilemma; if she answered truthfully she revealed the presence of her husband; if she lied she took the chance of being prosecuted....

Defendant contends we should follow two Arkansas decisions which support her position.... We decline to do so. Our duty is to apply the New Mexico statute, not the Arkansas law of accomplices.

The order of the trial court, which dismissed the information, is reversed. The cause is remanded with instructions to reinstate the case on the trial court's docket.

It is so ordered...

Lopez, Judge (dissenting)

I respectfully dissent. The majority holds that the defendant can be charged with the offense of harboring or aiding Andrew Needham ... because she does not qualify under any of the exemptions listed in the statute with respect to Needham. It arrives at this holding in spite of the fact that the defendant could not have revealed the presence of Needham in the house without also revealing the presence of her husband. This holding negates the legislative intent of the statute to exempt a wife from being forced to turn in her husband. Under the majority ruling,

the defendant would have had to turn in Needham to escape being charged under § 30–22–4, which would have been tantamount to turning in her husband.

Whether the rationale underlying the legislative exemption is a recognition "that it is unrealistic to expect persons to be deterred from giving aid to their close relations," LaFave and Scott, Criminal Law § 66 (1972), or an acknowledgment of human frailty, Torcia, Wharton's Criminal Law § 35 (14th ed. 1978), that rationale is ignored by requiring a wife to turn in her husband if he is with another suspect. Such a result requires a proverbial splitting of analytic hairs by attributing the defendant's action, in denying that Needham was at the house, to an intent to aid Needham rather than her husband....

The practical effect of the majority opinion, which requires a wife to turn in her husband if he is with a co-suspect, is to deny the wife's exemption in § 30–22–4. The reasons for refusing to force a wife to inform on her husband are the same whether or not he is alone. The statute should not be construed so narrowly as to frustrate the legislative intent to exempt a wife from turning in her husband.... Although the court should not add to the provisions of a statute, it may do so to prevent an unreasonable result.... Given the wife's exemption from turning in her husband contained in § 30–22–4, it would be unreasonable to require her to do just that by revealing Needham.

For the foregoing reasons, I cannot agree that the defendant in this case can be charged under § 30–22–4 for refusing to tell the police that Needham was in the house. I would affirm the action of the trial court in dismissing the information against the defendant.

Case Questions

1. Given the wording of the statute, did the majority have any flexibility in applying this law to the facts of this case? Do you think that Andrew Needham's presence in the house with Ricky Mobbley *ought* to warrant application of this legal rule?
2. Do you believe the statute should be amended to exempt individuals in Pam Mobbley's predicament from prosecution?
3. What would you have done if you had been in Pam's situation? Why?

Misprision of a felony is another common law crime. It makes it criminal for a person to fail to tell authorities of the commission of a felony of which he or she has knowledge. The history and rationale for this crime are explained in the following excerpt from the case of *Holland v. State*. In *Holland*, the court had to decide whether misprision is a crime in Florida.

Holland v. State of Florida
302 So.2d 806
Supreme Court of Florida
November 8, 1974

McNulty, Chief Judge

… As far as we know or are able to determine, this is the first case in Florida involving the crime of misprision of felony.

As hereinabove noted, we chose to decide this case on the fundamental issue of whether misprision of felony is a crime in Florida.

In any case, we now get on to the merits of the question we decide today. We begin by pointing out that almost every state in the United States has adopted the Common Law of England to some extent. Many of these states have done so by constitutional or statutory provisions similar to ours. But the nearly universal interpretation of such provisions is that they adopt the common law of England only to the extent that such laws are consistent with the existing physical and social conditions in the country or in the given state.

To some degree Florida courts have discussed this principle in other contexts. In *Duval v. Thomas*, for example, our Supreme Court said:

> "When grave doubt exists of a true common law doctrine … we may … exercise a 'broad discretion' taking 'into account the changes in our social and economic customs and present day conceptions of right and justice.' It is, to repeat, only when the common law is plain that we must observe it."

Moreover, our courts have not hesitated in other respects to reject anachronistic common law concepts.

Consonant with this, therefore, we think that the legislature in enacting § 775.01, *supra*, recognized this judicial precept and intended to grant our courts the discretion necessary to prevent blind adherence to those portions of the common law which are not suited to our present conditions, our public policy, our traditions or our sense of right and justice.

With the foregoing as a predicate, we now consider the history of the crime of misprision of felony and whether the reasons therefor have ceased to exist, if indeed they ever did exist, in this country. The origin of the crime is well described in 8 U. of Chi. L. Rev. 338, as follows:

> "Misprision of felony as defined by Blackstone is merely one phase of the system of communal responsibility for the apprehension of criminals which received its original impetus from William I, under pressure of the need to protect the invading Normans in hostile country, and which endured up

to the Seventeenth Century in England. In order to secure vigilant prosecution of criminal conduct, the vill or hundred in which such conduct occurred was subject to fine, as was the tithing to which the criminal belonged, and every person who knew of the felony and failed to make report thereof was subject to punishment for misprision of felony. Compulsory membership in the tithing group, the obligation to pursue criminals when the hue and cry was raised, broad powers of private arrest, and the periodic visitations of the General Eyre for the purpose of penalizing laxity in regard to crime, are all suggestive of the administrative background against which misprision of felony developed. With the appearance of specialized and paid law enforcement officers, such as constables and justices of the peace in the Seventeenth Century, there was a movement away from strict communal responsibility, and a growing tendency to rely on professional police…."

In short, the initial reason for the existence of misprision of felony as a crime at common law was to aid an alien, dictatorial sovereign in his forcible subjugation of England's inhabitants. Enforcement of the crime was summary, harsh and oppressive; and commentators note that most prosecutors in this country long ago recognized the inapplicability or obsolescence of the law and its harshness in their contemporary society by simply not charging people with that crime….

Many courts faced with this issue have also found, though with varying degrees of clarity, that the reasons for the proscription of this crime do not exist. Moreover, as early as 1822 in this country Chief Justice John Marshall states in *Marbury v. Brooks*:

> "It may be the duty of a citizen to accuse every offender, and to proclaim every offense which comes to his knowledge; but the law which would punish him in every case, for not performing this duty, is too harsh for man." …

We agree with Chief Justice Marshall … that the crime of misprision of felony is wholly unsuited to American criminal law…. While it may be desirable, even essential, that we encourage citizens to "get involved" to help reduce crime, they ought not be adjudicated criminals themselves if they don't. The fear of such a consequence is a fear from which our traditional concepts of peace and quietude guarantee freedom. We cherish the right to mind our own business when our own best interests dictate. Accordingly, we hold that misprision of felony has not been adopted into, and is not a part of, Florida substantive law.

Case Questions

1. The majority in *Holland* noted that American judges going back to the esteemed John Marshall have concluded that it is "un-American" for citizens to be criminally prosecuted for not reporting the commission of known felonies to the authorities. Is this position morally justifiable in your opinion?
2. Justice John Marshall is quoted in an 1822 case as follows: "It may be the duty of a citizen to accuse every offender, and to proclaim every offense which comes to his knowledge...." Do you think Marshall was referring to a moral duty, a legal duty, or both?

Traditionally individuals have not been legally obligated to intervene to aid other persons in the absence of a judicially recognized duty owed to that person. Courts have recognized the existence of a duty where a special relationship exists. The special relationships generally fall within one of the following categories: (a) where a statutory duty exists (such as the obligation parents have to support their children), (b) where a contractual duty exists (lifeguards are employed to try to make rescues on the beach), or (c) where a common law duty exists (such as when an unrelated adult has voluntarily assumed primary responsibility for bringing food to an isolated, incapacitated, elderly neighbor, and then stops without notifying authorities). In the absence of a legal duty to act, the law has generally left the decision as to whether or not to be a Good Samaritan up to each individual's conscience.

Good Samaritan Laws

Many people feel that Americans today are less willing than in times past to play the role of Good Samaritan. But do bystanders, who have no special relationship to a person in need, have a moral obligation to intervene? Should they have a legal duty to either intervene or inform authorities if they can do so without placing themselves in jeopardy? Consider the following 1997 Las Vegas case in which an eighteen-year-old young man enticed a seven-year-old girl into a ladies' room stall in a Las Vegas casino and sexually assaulted and murdered her. The attacker had a male friend who allegedly watched some of the events in that stall and presumably knew that the little girl was in danger. The friend made no attempt to dissuade the attacker, save the girl, or tell authorities. He was not subject to prosecution under the laws of Nevada.

Should a person who is a passive observer, as in the above situation, be subjected to criminal prosecution for failing to act? The following Massachusetts statute was enacted in 1983 in response to a brutal rape at a tavern. This crime was the basis for the movie *The Accused*.

Massachusetts General Law Chapter 268, Section 40. Reports of Crimes to Law Enforcement Officials.

Whoever knows that another person is a victim of aggravated rape, rape, murder, manslaughter or armed robbery and is at the scene of said crime shall, to the extent that said person can do so without danger or peril to himself or others, report said crime to an appropriate law enforcement official as soon as reasonably practicable. Any person who violates this section shall be punished by a fine of not less than five hundred nor more than two thousand and five hundred dollars.

Why do you believe the Massachusetts legislature limited the scope of this duty to only these five crimes? Do you see any potential problems that may result because of this statute? Do you think that such laws will influence more bystanders to intervene? Should society enact legislation primarily to make a moral statement and put society on record as expecting citizens to act as members of a larger community? Do you agree with Lord Patrick Devlin that our society would disintegrate if we didn't criminalize immoral conduct? Devlin argues that such statutes encourage citizens to think similarly about questions of right and wrong and that this helps to bind us together as a people.[18] The following discussion focuses on the society's right to promote a common morality by enacting statutes that prohibit certain types of private sexual conduct between consenting adults.

Individual Choice Versus Social Control: Where Is the Line?

Members of our society often disagree about the extent to which the states are entitled to promote a "common morality" by criminalizing conduct that the proponents of such legislation believe to be morally offensive. When such statutes are enacted into law, those prosecuted for alleged violations often ask the courts to rule that the state has crossed an imprecise constitutional line separating the lawful exercise of the state's police power from the constitutionally protected privacy rights of individuals to engage in the prohibited conduct. State legislatures and supreme courts during the last forty years have confronted this issue with respect to the constitutionality of their respective deviant sexual intercourse statutes. Kentucky and Pennsylvania are examples, because their state supreme courts accepted the argument that it was up to individual adults to determine for themselves the nature of their voluntary, noncommercial, consensual, intimate relationships. The state, through the exercise of the police power, should not use the criminal law to "protect" such adults from themselves where the conduct in question doesn't harm any other person. The supreme courts in these states declared unconstitutional criminal statutes that made it a crime for consenting adults to engage in prohibited sexual conduct that the legislature deemed to be morally reprehensible.

The constitutional right of the federal and state legislatures to enact laws is discussed more thoroughly on pages 89–98; however, before reading *Lawrence v. Texas* it is necessary that readers know more about a legal concept known as the **police power**.

In general, the police power is a term that refers to each state's inherent right as a sovereign ("autonomous") government to enact laws to protect the public's health, welfare, safety, and morals. You will recall that the states were in existence prior to the adoption of the U.S. Constitution, and that they had traditionally exercised broad lawmaking powers to protect the citizens of their states. Congress's right to legislate, however, has no such historical underpinning. Congress does not have the right to legislate based on the police power because it derives all its authority from powers granted in the federal constitution. Because the states retained their right to exercise the police power when the U.S. Constitution was adopted, they continue to enact laws pursuant to this right today.

The Texas legislature, in 1973, pursuant to the police power, repealed its laws that regulated noncommercial, sexual conduct taking place in private between consenting, heterosexual adults. At the same time, however, the legislature enacted a statute making it a misdemeanor for same-sex adults to engage in identical conduct, classifying such conduct in such circumstances as "deviate sexual intercourse."

In *Lawrence v. Texas*, the U.S. Supreme Court had to determine whether the Texas deviant sexual intercourse statute's restrictions on the behavior of same-sex adults constituted a lawful exercise of the police power or a constitutionally invalid infringement of individual liberty rights.

John Geddes Lawrence v. Texas
539 U.S. 55
U.S. Supreme Court
June 26, 2003

Justice Kennedy delivered the opinion of the Court.
Liberty protects the person from unwarranted government intrusions into a dwelling or other private places. In our tradition the State is not omnipresent in the home. And there are other spheres of our lives and existence, outside the home, where the State should not be a dominant presence. Freedom extends beyond spatial bounds. Liberty presumes an autonomy of self that includes freedom of thought, belief, expression, and certain intimate conduct. The instant case involves liberty of the person both in its spatial and more transcendent dimensions.

I

The question before the Court is the validity of a Texas statute making it a crime for two persons of the same sex to engage in certain intimate sexual conduct.

In Houston, Texas, officers of the Harris County Police Department were dispatched to a private residence in response to a reported weapons disturbance. They entered an apartment where one of the petitioners, John Geddes Lawrence, resided. The right of the police to enter does not seem to have been questioned. The officers observed Lawrence and another man, Tyron Garner, engaging in a sexual act. The two petitioners were arrested, held in custody over night, and charged and convicted before a Justice of the Peace.

The complaints described their crime as "deviate sexual intercourse, namely anal sex, with a member of the same sex (man)."... The applicable state law is Tex. Penal Code Ann. §21.06(a) (2003). It provides: "A person commits an offense if he engages in deviate sexual intercourse with another individual of the same sex." The statute defines "[d]eviate sexual intercourse" as follows:

(A) "any contact between any part of the genitals of one person and the mouth or anus of another person; or

(B) the penetration of the genitals or the anus of another person with an object." §21.01(1).

The petitioners exercised their right to a trial de novo in Harris County Criminal Court. They challenged the statute as a violation of the Equal Protection Clause of the Fourteenth Amendment and of a like provision of the Texas Constitution. Tex. Const., Art. 1, §3a.

Those contentions were rejected. The petitioners, having entered a plea of *nolo contendere*, were each fined $200 and assessed court costs of $141.25....

The Court of Appeals for the Texas Fourteenth District ... affirmed the convictions.... The majority opinion indicates that the Court of Appeals considered our decision in *Bowers v. Hardwick*, 478 U.S. 186 (1986), to be controlling on the federal due process aspect of the case. *Bowers* then being authoritative, this was proper.

We granted certiorari ... to consider three questions:

1. Whether Petitioners' criminal convictions under the Texas "Homosexual Conduct" law—which criminalizes sexual intimacy by same-sex couples, but not identical behavior by different-sex couples—violate the Fourteenth Amendment guarantee of equal protection of laws?

2. Whether Petitioners' criminal convictions for adult consensual sexual intimacy in the home violate their vital interests in liberty and privacy protected by the Due Process Clause of the Fourteenth Amendment?

3. Whether *Bowers v. Hardwick*, 478 U.S. 186 (1986) should be overruled?"...

The petitioners were adults at the time of the alleged offense. Their conduct was in private and consensual.

II.

We conclude the case should be resolved by determining whether the petitioners were free as adults to engage in the private conduct in the exercise of their liberty under the Due Process Clause of the Fourteenth Amendment to the Constitution. For this inquiry we deem it necessary to reconsider the Court's holding in *Bowers*. There are broad statements of the substantive reach of liberty under the Due Process Clause in earlier cases, ... but the most pertinent beginning point is our decision in *Griswold v. Connecticut*, 381 U.S. 479 (1965).

In *Griswold* the Court invalidated a state law prohibiting the use of drugs or devices of contraception and counseling or aiding and abetting the use of contraceptives. The Court described the protected interest as a right to privacy and placed emphasis on the marriage relation and the protected space of the marital bedroom....

After *Griswold* it was established that the right to make certain decisions regarding sexual conduct extends beyond the marital relationship. In *Eisenstadt v. Baird* ... (1972), the Court invalidated a law prohibiting the distribution of contraceptives to unmarried persons. The case was decided under the Equal Protection Clause ... but with respect to unmarried persons, the Court went on to state the fundamental proposition that the law impaired the exercise of their personal rights.... It quoted from the statement of the Court of Appeals finding the law to be in conflict with fundamental human rights, and it followed with this statement of its own:

> "It is true that in *Griswold* the right of privacy in question inhered in the marital relationship.... If the right of privacy means anything, it is the right of the individual, married or single, to be free from unwarranted governmental intrusion into matters so fundamentally affecting a person as the decision whether to bear or beget a child." ....

The opinions in *Griswold* and *Eisenstadt* were part of the background for the decision in *Roe v. Wade* ... (1973). As is well known, the case involved a challenge to the Texas law prohibiting abortions, but the laws of other States were affected as well. Although the Court held the woman's rights were not absolute, her right to elect an abortion did have real and substantial protection as an exercise of her liberty under the Due Process Clause. The Court cited cases that protect spatial freedom and cases that go well beyond it. *Roe* recognized the right of a woman to make certain fundamental decisions affecting her destiny and confirmed once more that the protection of liberty under the Due Process Clause has a substantive dimension of fundamental significance in defining the rights of the person.

In *Carey v. Population Services Int'l* ... (1977), the Court confronted a New York law forbidding sale or distribution of contraceptive devices to persons under 16 years of age. Although there was no single opinion for the Court, the law was invalidated. Both *Eisenstadt* and *Carey*, as well as the holding and rationale in *Roe*, confirmed that the reasoning of Griswold could not be confined to the protection of rights of married adults. This was the state of the law with respect to some of the most relevant cases when the Court considered *Bowers v. Hardwick*.

The facts in *Bowers* had some similarities to the instant case. A police officer, whose right to enter seems not to have been in question, observed Hardwick, in his own bedroom, engaging in intimate sexual conduct with another adult male. The conduct was in violation of a Georgia statute making it a criminal offense to engage in sodomy. One difference between the two cases is that the Georgia statute prohibited the conduct whether or not the participants were of the same sex, while the Texas statute, as we have seen, applies only to participants of the same sex. Hardwick was not prosecuted, but he brought an action in federal court to declare the state statute invalid. He alleged he was a practicing homosexual and that the criminal prohibition violated rights guaranteed to him by the Constitution. The Court, in an opinion by Justice White, sustained the Georgia law....

The Court began its substantive discussion in *Bowers* as follows: "The issue presented is whether the Federal Constitution confers a fundamental right upon homosexuals to engage in sodomy and hence invalidates the laws of the many States that still make such conduct illegal and have done so for a very long time." ... That statement, we now conclude, discloses the Court's own failure to appreciate the extent of the liberty at stake. To say that the issue in *Bowers* was simply the right to engage in certain sexual conduct demeans the claim the individual put forward, just as it would demean a married couple were it to be said marriage is simply about the right to have sexual intercourse. The laws involved in *Bowers* and here are, to be sure, statutes that purport to do no more than prohibit a particular sexual act. Their penalties and purposes, though, have more far-reaching consequences, touching upon the most private human conduct, sexual behavior, and in the most private of places, the home. The statutes do seek to control a personal relationship that, whether or not entitled to formal recognition in the law, is within the liberty of persons to choose without being punished as criminals.

This, as a general rule, should counsel against attempts by the State, or a court, to define the meaning of the relationship or to set its boundaries absent injury to a person or abuse of an institution the law protects. It suffices for us to acknowledge that adults may choose to enter upon this relationship in the confines of their homes and their own private lives and still retain their dignity as free persons. When sexuality finds overt expression in intimate conduct with another person, the conduct can be but one element in a personal bond that is more enduring. The liberty protected by the Constitution allows homosexual persons the right to make this choice.

Having misapprehended the claim of liberty there presented to it, and thus stating the claim to be whether there is a fundamental right to engage in consensual sodomy, the *Bowers* Court said: "Proscriptions against that conduct have ancient roots." ... In academic writings, and in many of the scholarly amicus briefs filed to assist the Court in this case, there are fundamental criticisms of the historical premises relied upon by the majority and concurring opinions in *Bowers*.... We need not enter this debate in the attempt to reach a definitive historical judgment, but the following considerations counsel against adopting the definitive conclusions upon which *Bowers* placed such reliance.

At the outset it should be noted that there is no longstanding history in this country of laws directed at homosexual conduct as a distinct matter. Beginning in colonial times there were prohibitions of sodomy derived from the English criminal laws passed in the first instance by the Reformation Parliament of 1533. The English prohibition was understood to include relations between men and women as well as relations between men and men.... Nineteenth-century commentators similarly read American sodomy, buggery, and crime-against-nature statutes as criminalizing certain relations between men and women and between men and men.... The absence of legal prohibitions focusing on homosexual conduct may be explained in part by noting that according to some scholars the concept of the homosexual as a distinct category of person did not emerge until the late 19th century.... Thus early American sodomy laws were not directed at homosexuals as such but instead sought to prohibit nonprocreative sexual activity more generally. This does not suggest approval of homosexual conduct. It does tend to show that this particular form of conduct was not thought of as a separate category from like conduct between heterosexual persons.

Laws prohibiting sodomy do not seem to have been enforced against consenting adults acting in private. A substantial number of sodomy prosecutions and convictions for which there are surviving records were for predatory acts against those who could not or did not consent, as in the case of a minor or the victim of an assault.... Instead of targeting relations between consenting adults in private, 19th-century sodomy prosecutions typically involved relations between men and minor girls or minor boys, relations between adults involving force, relations between adults implicating disparity in status, or relations between men and animals.

To the extent that there were any prosecutions for the acts in question, 19th-century evidence rules imposed a burden that would make a conviction more difficult to obtain even taking into account the problems always inherent in prosecuting consensual acts committed in private. Under then-prevailing standards, a man could not be convicted of sodomy based upon testimony of a consenting partner, because the partner was considered an accomplice. A partner's testimony, however, was admissible if he or she had not consented to the act or was a minor, and therefore incapable of consent....

American laws targeting same-sex couples did not develop until the last third of the 20th century. The reported decisions concerning the prosecution of consensual, homosexual sodomy between adults for the years 1880–1995 are not always clear in the details, but a significant number involved conduct in a public place....

It was not until the 1970s that any State singled out same-sex relations for criminal prosecution, and only nine States have done so.... Over the course of the last decades, States with same-sex prohibitions have moved toward abolishing them. See, e.g., *Jegley v. Picado*, 349 Ark. 600 ... (2002); *Gryczan v. State*, 283 Mont. 433 ... (1997); *Campbell v. Sundquist*, 926 S. W. 2d 250 (Tenn. App. 1996); *Commonwealth v. Wasson*, 842 S. W. 2d 487 (Ky. 1992); see also 1993 Nev. Stats. p. 518 (repealing Nev. Rev. Stat. §201.193).

In summary, the historical grounds relied upon in *Bowers* are more complex than the majority opinion and the concurring opinion by Chief Justice Burger indicate. Their historical premises are not without doubt and, at the very least, are overstated.

It must be acknowledged, of course, that the Court in *Bowers* was making the broader point that for centuries there have been powerful voices to condemn homosexual conduct as immoral. The condemnation has been shaped by religious beliefs, conceptions of right and acceptable behavior, and respect for the traditional family. For many persons these are not trivial concerns but profound and deep convictions accepted as ethical and moral principles to which they aspire and which thus determine the course of their lives. These considerations do not answer the question before us, however. The issue is whether the majority may use the power of the State to enforce these views on the whole society through operation of the criminal law. "Our obligation is to define the liberty of all, not to mandate our own moral code." ...

In all events we think that our laws and traditions in the past half century are of most relevance here. These references show an emerging awareness that liberty gives substantial protection to adult persons in deciding how to conduct their private lives in matters pertaining to sex. "History and tradition are the starting point but not in all cases the ending point of the substantive due process inquiry." ...

Two principal cases decided after *Bowers* cast its holding into even more doubt. In *Planned Parenthood of Southeastern Pa. v. Casey*... (1992), the Court reaffirmed the substantive force of the liberty protected by the Due Process Clause. The *Casey* decision again confirmed that our laws and tradition afford constitutional protection to personal decisions relating to marriage, procreation, contraception, family relationships, child rearing, and education.... In explaining the respect the Constitution demands for the autonomy of the person in making these choices, we stated as follows:

> "These matters, involving the most intimate and personal choices a person may make in a lifetime, choices central to personal dignity and autonomy, are central to the liberty protected by the Fourteenth Amendment. At the heart of liberty is the right to define one's own concept of existence, of meaning, of the universe, and of the mystery of human life. Beliefs about these matters could not define the attributes of personhood were they formed under compulsion of the State."...

Persons in a homosexual relationship may seek autonomy for these purposes, just as heterosexual persons do. The decision in *Bowers* would deny them this right.

The second post-*Bowers* case of principal relevance is *Romer v. Evans* ... (1996). There the Court struck down class-based legislation directed at homosexuals as a violation of the Equal Protection Clause. *Romer* invalidated an amendment to Colorado's constitution which named as a solitary class persons who were homosexuals, lesbians, or bisexual either by "orientation, conduct, practices or relationships," ... (internal quotation marks omitted), and deprived them of protection under state antidiscrimination laws. We concluded that the provision was "born of animosity toward the class of persons affected" and further that it had no rational relation to a legitimate governmental purpose....

As an alternative argument in this case, counsel for the petitioners and some amici contend that *Romer* provides the basis for declaring the Texas statute invalid under the Equal Protection Clause. That is a tenable argument, but we conclude the instant case requires us to address whether *Bowers* itself has continuing validity. Were we to hold the statute invalid under the Equal Protection Clause some might question whether a prohibition would be valid if drawn differently, say, to prohibit the conduct both between same-sex and different-sex participants.

Equality of treatment and the due process right to demand respect for conduct protected by the substantive guarantee of liberty are linked in important respects, and a decision on the latter point advances both interests. If protected conduct is made criminal and the law which does so remains unexamined for its substantive validity, its stigma might remain even if it were not enforceable as drawn for equal protection

reasons. When homosexual conduct is made criminal by the law of the State, that declaration in and of itself is an invitation to subject homosexual persons to discrimination both in the public and in the private spheres. The central holding of *Bowers* has been brought in question by this case, and it should be addressed. Its continuance as precedent demeans the lives of homosexual persons.

The stigma this criminal statute imposes, moreover, is not trivial. The offense, to be sure, is but a class C misdemeanor, a minor offense in the Texas legal system. Still, it remains a criminal offense with all that imports for the dignity of the persons charged. The petitioners will bear on their record the history of their criminal convictions. Just this Term we rejected various challenges to state laws requiring the registration of sex offenders.... We are advised that if Texas convicted an adult for private, consensual homosexual conduct under the statute here in question the convicted person would come within the registration laws of at least four States were he or she to be subject to their jurisdiction.... This underscores the consequential nature of the punishment and the state-sponsored condemnation attendant to the criminal prohibition. Furthermore, the Texas criminal conviction carries with it the other collateral consequences always following a conviction, such as notations on job application forms, to mention but one example.

The foundations of *Bowers* have sustained serious erosion from our recent decisions in *Casey* and *Romer*. When our precedent has been thus weakened, criticism from other sources is of greater significance. In the United States criticism of *Bowers* has been substantial and continuing, disapproving of its reasoning in all respects, not just as to its historical assumptions.... The courts of five different States [Arkansas, Georgia, Montana, Tennessee, and Kentucky] have declined to follow it....

The doctrine of stare decisis is essential to the respect accorded to the judgments of the Court and to the stability of the law. It is not, however, an inexorable command....

The rationale of *Bowers* does not withstand careful analysis. In his dissenting opinion in *Bowers* Justice Stevens came to these conclusions:

> "Our prior cases make two propositions abundantly clear. First, the fact that the governing majority in a State has traditionally viewed a particular practice as immoral is not a sufficient reason for upholding a law prohibiting the practice; neither history nor tradition could save a law prohibiting miscegenation from constitutional attack. Second, individual decisions by married

persons, concerning the intimacies of their physical relationship, even when not intended to produce offspring, are a form of 'liberty' protected by the Due Process Clause of the Fourteenth Amendment. Moreover, this protection extends to intimate choices by unmarried as well as married persons."...

Justice Stevens' analysis, in our view, should have been controlling in *Bowers* and should control here.

Bowers was not correct when it was decided, and it is not correct today. It ought not to remain binding precedent. *Bowers v. Hardwick* should be and now is overruled.

The present case does not involve minors. It does not involve persons who might be injured or coerced or who are situated in relationships where consent might not easily be refused. It does not involve public conduct or prostitution. It does not involve whether the government must give formal recognition to any relationship that homosexual persons seek to enter.

The case does involve two adults who, with full and mutual consent from each other, engaged in sexual practices common to a homosexual lifestyle. The petitioners are entitled to respect for their private lives. The State cannot demean their existence or control their destiny by making their private sexual conduct a crime. Their right to liberty under the Due Process Clause gives them the full right to engage in their conduct without intervention of the government. "It is a promise of the Constitution that there is a realm of personal liberty which the government may not enter."... The Texas statute furthers no legitimate state interest which can justify its intrusion into the personal and private life of the individual....

The judgment of the Court of Appeals for the Texas Fourteenth District is reversed, and the case is remanded for further proceedings not inconsistent with this opinion.

It is so ordered.

Case Questions

1. What did Justice Kennedy mean when he said in his opinion, "The Texas statute furthers no legitimate state interest which can justify its intrusion into the personal and private life of the individual"?
2. According to Justice Kennedy, what public policy objective that is impermissible under the Fourteenth Amendment was the State of Texas trying to accomplish through this criminal statute?
3. What conclusion does the U.S. Supreme Court reach?
4. Why does the Court say it reached this conclusion?

Business Ethics

Business managers often encounter ethical questions as they attempt to increase profits, lower costs, and secure and preserve markets in their never-ending quest to maximize earnings and the return that stockholders receive on their investments. One of the most interesting debates presently taking place in academic and professional circles involves ethical challenges to the traditional definition of the role of the corporation in society. The question, which encompasses both legal and ethical dimensions, is Do corporations have ethical obligations beyond increasing stockholder equity? Do corporations, for example, have any ethical obligations to such other stakeholders as employees, suppliers, customers, and the community?[19] To what extent should law attempt to influence business decision makers to expand their perspectives and include in their calculus the concerns of a broad range of constituencies? Some authors argue that ethical managers are more likely to flourish where businesses view themselves as a "corporate community." In such an environment, it is suggested, the need to weigh and balance the corporate community's competing needs and interests will naturally lead policymakers to make ethical choices.[20]

Business people often employ lawyers to help them monitor legal developments in such highly relevant subject areas as contract, tort, property, and employment law. You may be familiar with traditional common law doctrines such as privity of contract and caveat emptor, the preference traditionally shown to landlords over tenants, and the at-will employment doctrine. Implicit in these judicial doctrines are assumptions about what constitutes ethical business conduct. The trend in recent decades has been for legislatures and courts to use law as a catalyst for influencing companies to change or modify their business practices. Their apparent goal has been to encourage businesses to become more aware of the ethical implications and the societal consequences resulting from their business choices.

Between 1890 and 1914, Congress enacted a series of antitrust statutes to counter the perceived abuses of economic power by the dominant national monopolies of that era. The Sherman Act (1890), the Clayton Act (1914), and the Federal Trade Commission Act (1914) were intended to redress price discrimination and other monopolistic practices. Unethical business practices in the securities industry in the early 1930s led to the creation of the Securities and Exchange Commission. More recently, legal initiatives have produced implied warranty statutes, lemon laws, strict liability in tort, state and federal environmental protection standards, and protections against discrimination in employment.

The lawmaking process inherently requires legislative bodies to make prospective determinations as to what principles of fairness and equity require of people and interests in particular circumstances. For example, some states have laws that specify how the legislature believes financial responsibility for unintended injuries sustained by customers should be apportioned between businesses and their customers. This overlap between law and equity appears in the next case. The Connecticut statute involved in the case prescribed how that state's legislature believed financial responsibility for unintended injuries sustained by customers should be apportioned. In staking out its policy, the legislature expressed itself as to how the conflicting interests of business and consumers could best be reconciled with the public interest as a whole.

Author's Preview: *Reardon v. Windswept Farm, LLC*

The author has prepared a preview of the next case because some readers will need assistance in understanding it. The author hopes that this preview will give readers a clear understanding of the basic facts so that they can begin to think about the ethical and legal implications of the case.

The Parties and the Trial   Windswept Farm, the defendant in the next case, is a family-owned and operated horse-riding academy. Jessica Reardon, the plaintiff and the riding academy's customer, was seriously injured when she fell off of one of the defendant's horses while participating in a riding lesson. The plaintiff contended that the defendant had unintentionally violated a legal duty by not acting reasonably under the existing circumstances and was legally at fault for her having fallen from the horse. She argued that the defendant was obligated to compensate her financially for her injuries. The trial court disagreed, ruling that the defendant was entitled to summary judgment because the plaintiff had executed a release exempting the defendant from liability. The plaintiff appealed the trial court's ruling to the Connecticut Supreme Court.

The Appeal   The Connecticut Supreme Court turned to a state statute in which the legislature spelled out its views as to the equitable way to allocate financial responsibility for the risk of injury to riding academy customers.

The state legislature could have drafted its law to primarily benefit the riding academies by making the customers financially responsible for all injuries attributable to anyone's negligence. A "pro-business" approach would have made the customer responsible for injuries he/she sustained while engaged in academy-sponsored horse-riding activities irrespective of whether they were attributable to the customer's own negligence or were a result of negligent conduct on the part of riding academy employees. But would such a policy produce "the greatest good for the greatest number" of people? If riding academies were protected from all financial risk resulting from negligence, what incentive would they have affirmatively to develop policies and procedures that would reduce the known risks of injury and keep their customers safe?

Alternatively, the law could have been drafted to be primarily "pro-consumer" by making the riding academies exclusively responsible for injuries sustained by consumers irrespective of whether they were attributable to the customer or to the business. On the surface, the second option appears to be very advantageous to consumers because it would theoretically provide financial resources to all customers injured as a result of negligence. This would significantly benefit customers who lacked or had inadequate medical insurance. However, such a "pro-consumer" approach would likely devastate the riding academies. Because of the high cost of insurance, the cost of riding lessons and other sponsored programs would have to increase dramatically. These increases could easily translate into riding academies going out of business as their customers reluctantly decide to abandon horseback riding in favor of more affordable recreation.

The Connecticut legislature wisely chose a middle course. It provided that the customer was responsible for "any injury to … [his/her] person or property arising out of the hazards inherent in equestrian sports, unless the injury was proximately caused by the negligence of …. [the riding academy which was] providing the horse…." Thus, in this case, if the defendant exercised reasonable care in its dealings with the plaintiff and the plaintiff became injured, the plaintiff would be totally responsible for the costs resulting from her injury. The defendant would only be liable if it were determined that it was the legal cause (in legal jargon, the "proximate cause") of the plaintiff's injuries. To be the legal cause of plaintiff's injuries, the defendant's action or inaction would have to have directly or indirectly contributed to the plaintiff's injuries. Secondly, the conduct would have to have been very significant and important to justify holding the defendant legally responsible. And lastly, the defendant could only be held responsible for risks it could reasonably be said to have foreseen.

The Contract of Adhesion   The defendant, however, devised a strategy for evading the statute and achieving the "pro-business" outcome. It decided to require customers to "agree" contractually to release the riding academy of its statutory liability.

Some release "agreements" are substantively unfair because they are one-sided, overreaching, and exclusively for the benefit of the party drafting the document. They are often also procedurally unfair in that they typically consist of a printed form with "take it or leave it" (nonnegotiable) terms that are often presented to the other party for signature at the last minute. Agreements of this type are called *adhesion contracts*. Even though a party has voluntarily entered an agreement, courts will sometimes refuse to enforce adhesion contracts where the terms are both substantively and procedurally unfair to the non-drafting party to such an extent that the court finds the drafting party's conduct "unconscionable" and/or a violation of public policy.

The fact that Reardon presumably read the agreement and signed it was not contested. Her appeal was based on the hope that the Connecticut Supreme Court would refuse to enforce the liability release.

As you read this case, keep in mind that courts in other states might well have decided other cases with similar facts differently than did the Connecticut Supreme Court.

Jessica Reardon v. Windswept Farm, LLC
905 A.2d 1156
Supreme Court of Connecticut.
October 3, 2006.

Borden, J.

The … issue in this appeal is whether a release signed by the plaintiff, Jessica Reardon, indemnifying the defendants, Windswept Farm, LLC, and its owners, William Raymond and Mona Raymond, from an action brought in negligence, precludes the plaintiff from recovering damages. More specifically, the question before this court is whether the release signed by the plaintiff violates public policy pursuant to our holding *Hanks v. Powder Ridge Restaurant Corp*…. (2005). The plaintiff appeals from the judgment of the trial court granting the defendants' motion for summary judgment. The plaintiff claims that ... in light of this court's holding in *Hanks*, the release violates public policy....

The plaintiff brought this personal injury action against the defendants alleging negligence. The defendants moved for summary judgment, arguing that the release signed by the plaintiff was clear and unambiguous.... The trial court agreed that the plaintiff had signed a well-drafted waiver of liability in the defendants' favor, granted the defendants' motion for summary judgment, and rendered judgment thereon. This appeal followed.

The following facts are relevant to our analysis of the plaintiff's claims. The defendants are in the business of providing horseback riding lessons to the general public. In October, 2002, the plaintiff came to the defendants' property and requested a horseback riding lesson. As a condition to riding one of the defendants' horses, the plaintiff was required by the defendants to sign a release and indemnity agreement (release). The release was printed on a single page and consisted of three sections entitled, "Warning,"... "RELEASE,"... and "INDEMNITY AGREEMENT."... It is undisputed that the plaintiff signed and dated the release prior to commencing her horseback riding lesson with the defendants. Similarly, it is undisputed that the plaintiff identified herself on the release as an "[e]xperienced [r]ider" and as someone who had "[r]idden [horses] frequently" several years earlier.

Subsequent to the plaintiff signing the release provided by the defendants, the defendants paired the plaintiff with one of the horses from their stables and with one of the instructors in their employ. During the course of the plaintiff's horseback riding lesson, the horse provided by the defendants became excited, bucked back and forth suddenly and without warning, and threw the plaintiff to the ground, causing her serious injuries.

The plaintiff brought an action in August, 2003, alleging that she had been injured due to the defendants' negligence. In particular, the plaintiff alleged that her injuries were caused by the "carelessness, recklessness and negligence of the defendants" including, among other things, that (1) the "defendants failed to ensure that the horse on which [she] was placed was an appropriate horse commensurate with [the plaintiff's] skill and experience"; (2) the "defendants failed to prevent, warn or protect the plaintiff from the risk of a fall"; (3) the "defendants knew of the horse's propensity to buck yet failed to warn [the plaintiff] of the same"; and (4) the "defendants failed properly to hire and train their riding instructor...." In their answer, the defendants raised a special defense, namely, that "[t]he plaintiff [had] assumed the risk and legal responsibility for any injury to her person per ... General Statutes [§]52-557p,"... and that "[t]he plaintiff's claims [were] barred [due to the fact] that she signed a waiver/release of all claims in favor of the defendants."...

...[I]n *Hanks*, we concluded that the enforcement of a well drafted exculpatory agreement that releases a provider of a recreational activity from prospective liability for personal injuries sustained as a result of the provider's negligence may violate public policy if certain conditions are met.... In general, we noted that "[t]he law does not favor contract provisions which relieve a person from his own negligence .... This is because exculpatory provisions undermine the policy considerations governing our tort system ... [which include] compensation of innocent parties, shifting the loss to responsible parties or distributing it among appropriate entities, and deterrence of wrongful conduct...." Moreover, we recognized that "it is consistent with public policy to posit the risk of negligence upon the actor and, if this policy is to be abandoned, it has generally been to allow or require that the risk shift to another party better or equally able to bear it, not to shift the risk to the weak bargainer." ....

Additionally, when assessing the public policy implications of a particular release or waiver of liability, we concluded that "[n]o definition of the concept of public interest [may] be contained within the four corners of a formula," and that "[t]he ultimate determination of what constitutes the public interest must be made considering the totality of the circumstances of any given case against the backdrop of current societal expectations.".... Our analysis in *Hanks* [included]..., among other things, a consideration as to whether the release pertains to a business thought suitable for public regulation, whether the party performing the service holds himself out as making the activity available to any member of the public who seeks it, and whether the provider of the activity exercises superior bargaining power and confronts the public with a standard contract of adhesion.

In the context of snowtubing, which was the recreational activity at issue in *Hanks*, we placed particular emphasis on: (1) the societal expectation that family oriented activities will be reasonably safe; (2) the illogic of relieving the party with greater expertise and information concerning the dangers associated with the activity from the burden of proper maintenance of the snowtubing run; and (3) the fact that the release at issue was a standardized adhesion contract, lacking equal bargaining power between the parties, and offered to the plaintiff on a "'take it or leave it'" basis.... Moreover, we recognized the clear public policy in favor of participation in athletics and recreational activities.... ("[v]oluntary recreational activities, such as snowtubing, skiing, basketball, soccer, football, racquetball, karate, ice skating, swimming, volleyball or yoga, are pursued by the vast majority of the population and constitute an important and healthy part of everyday life").

We conclude that, based on our decision in *Hanks*, the totality of the circumstances surrounding the recreational activity of horseback riding and instruction that was offered by the defendants demonstrates that the enforcement of an exculpatory agreement in their favor from liability for ordinary negligence violates public policy and is not in the public interest. First, similar to the situation at issue in *Hanks*, the defendants in the present case provided the facilities, the instructors, and the equipment for their patrons to engage in a popular recreational activity, and the recreational facilities were open to the general public regardless of an individual's ability level. Indeed, the defendants acknowledged that, although the release required riders to indicate their experience level, it also anticipated a range in skills from between "[n]ever ridden" to "[e]xperienced [r]ider," and that the facility routinely had patrons of varying ability levels. Accordingly, there is a reasonable societal expectation that a recreational activity that is under the control of the provider and is open to all individuals, regardless of experience or ability level, will be reasonably safe.

Additionally, in the present case, as in *Hanks*, the plaintiff "lacked the knowledge, experience and authority to discern whether, much less ensure that, the defendants' [facilities or equipment] were maintained in a reasonably safe condition." ... Specifically, although the plaintiff characterized herself as an experienced rider, she was in no greater position then the average rider ... to assess all the safety issues connected with the defendants' enterprise. To the contrary, it was the defendants, not the plaintiff or the other customers, who had the "expertise and opportunity to foresee and control hazards, and to guard against the negligence of their agents and employees. They alone [could] properly maintain and inspect their premises, and train their employees in risk management.".... In particular, the defendants acknowledged that they were responsible for providing their patrons with safe horses, qualified instructors, as well as properly maintained working equipment and riding surfaces.

In the context of carrying out these duties, the defendants were aware, and were in a position continually to gather more information, regarding any hidden dangers associated with the recreational activity including the temperaments of the individual horses, the strengths of the various riding instructors, and the condition of the facility's equipment and grounds. As we concluded in *Hanks*, it is illogical to relieve the defendants, as the party with greater expertise and information concerning the dangers associated with engaging in horseback riding at their facility, from potential claims of negligence surrounding an alleged failure to administer properly the activity.

Furthermore, the release that the plaintiff signed broadly indemnifying the defendants from liability for damages resulting from the defendants' own negligence was a classic contract of adhesion of the type that this court found to be in violation of public policy in *Hanks*. Specifically, we have noted that "[t]he most salient feature [of adhesion contracts] is that they are not subject to the normal bargaining processes of ordinary contracts," and that they tend to involve a "standard form contract prepared by one party, to be signed by the party in a weaker position, [usually] a consumer, who has little choice about the terms ...." In the present case, signing the release provided by the defendants was required as a condition of the plaintiff's participation in the horseback riding lesson, there was no opportunity for negotiation by the plaintiff, and if she was unsatisfied with the terms of the release, her only option was to not participate in the activity. As in *Hanks*, therefore, the plaintiff had nearly zero bargaining power with respect to the negotiation of the release and in order to participate in the activity, she was required to assume the risk of the defendants' negligence. This condition of participation violates the stated public policy of our tort system because the plaintiff was required to bear an additional risk despite her status as a patron who was not in a position to foresee or control the alleged negligent conduct that she was confronted with, or manage and spread the risk more effectively than the defendants.

We are also mindful that ...recreational horseback riding is a business thought suitable for public regulation, but that the legislature has stopped short of requiring participants to bear the very risk that the defendants now seek to pass on to the plaintiff by way of a mandatory release. In particular, the legislature has prescribed that "[e]ach person engaged in recreational equestrian activities shall assume the risk and legal responsibility for any injury to his person or property arising out of the hazards inherent in equestrian sports, unless the injury was proximately caused by the negligence of the person providing the horse or horses to the individual ...." This language establishes that the plaintiff assumed the risk for certain injuries when riding at the defendants' facility due to the nature of horseback riding as an activity, but that an operator of such a facility can still be liable for injuries caused by its own negligence. For the reasons previously discussed, we conclude that the defendants' attempt contractually to extend the plaintiff's assumption of risk one step beyond that identified by the legislature in § 52-557p violates the public policy of the state and, therefore, is invalid....

Furthermore, the fact that there are certain risks that are inherent to horseback riding as a recreational activity, as the legislature recognized in § 52-557p, one of which may be that horses move unexpectedly, does not change the fact that an operator's negligence may contribute greatly to that risk. For example, the defendants may have negligently paired the plaintiff with an inappropriate horse given the length of time since she last had ridden or negligently paired the plaintiff with an instructor who had not properly been trained on how to handle the horse in question. Both of these scenarios present factual questions that, at trial, may reveal that the defendants' negligence, and not an inherent risk of the activity, was to blame for the plaintiff's injuries.

Moreover ... the plaintiff does not challenge the fact that there were risks inherent in the activity of horseback riding that she otherwise was prepared to assume. Rather, she challenges the defendants' claimed indemnity from the alleged neglect and carelessness of the stable operator and its employees to whom she entrusted her safety. Indeed, the inherent unpredictability of a horse is something that the legislature already has considered in providing to an operator of a horseback riding facility a defense to a claim of negligence pursuant to the assumption of risk doctrine codified in § 52-557p. This protection granted by the legislature, however, does not permit the operator to avoid liability entirely for its negligence or that of its employees. Accordingly, on the basis of our decision in *Hanks*, as well as the circumstances of the present case, we are unable to conclude that the recreational activity of horseback riding is so different from snowtubing that the release in this case should be enforced as a matter of law.

The judgment is reversed and the case is remanded to the trial court with direction to deny the defendants' motion for summary judgment, and for further proceedings according to law.

Case Questions

1. If you analyze the court's decision in this case from the natural law and utilitarian perspectives, what do you conclude?
2. Was the riding academy ethical in its dealings with the plaintiff?
3. Assume you are a judge on this case who disagrees with the decision of the court. Make an argument as to why this case was wrongly decided.

Author's Comment

The trial court, as a result of the Connecticut Supreme Court's decision, would have denied the motion for summary judgment, refused to enforce the release agreement, and scheduled the case for trial (if the parties were unable to negotiate a settlement of the case). At trial, the finder of fact (the judge in a bench trial or the jury in a jury trial) would hear the evidence and ultimately decide the factual questions necessary to a determination of each party's financial liability, and the judge would award a judgment in accordance with the provisions of the law.

Professional Ethics

We have learned that law is only one of society's resources for developing standards of ethical conduct. Professional associations also make significant contributions. It is common for persons in a trade or profession who share a common concern about competency, quality, and integrity to organize an association. Such an association typically will develop a code of ethics to which the members will subscribe. In this fashion, many of the do's and don'ts of a profession become codified, at least as far as the members are concerned. Theoretically, a member who fails to comply with the code will be expelled from membership. This process has the twin advantages of distinguishing the membership from predatory competitors and enabling the members to establish and maintain a positive image with consumers. Real estate brokers, undertakers, social workers, engineers, doctors, police chiefs, and lawyers, to name but a few, have formed associations, at least in part, to establish and maintain standards of ethical behavior for their memberships. In some of the regulated professions, membership in an association is required as a condition of licensure. This is true in the legal profession, where thirty states require attorneys to be dues-paying members of the state's bar association.[21]

The American Bar Association and many state bar associations have standing committees on ethics that issue advisory opinions at the request of members. These opinions are often highly respected and can be influential when used in conjunction with disciplinary proceedings. Bar associations are also heavily involved in developing proposed rules for consideration by the state supreme courts, and they often sponsor courses in continuing legal education for the benefit of the membership.

Ethics and Professional Responsibility Codes for Lawyers and Judges

The supreme court of each state is normally responsible for overseeing the practice of law within its jurisdiction. It fulfills this obligation in part by promulgating standards of professional conduct to protect the public from incompetent and/or unethical lawyers and from judges who prove to be unsuited or unfit to remain on the bench. Supreme courts also create administrative boards to investigate complaints and enforce rules, and increasingly require that all attorneys and judges participate in continuing legal education programs.

Typical codes of conduct for lawyers and judges will express concerns about competency, confidentiality, loyalty, honesty, candor, fairness, and avoiding conflicts of interest.

The West Virginia Supreme Court of Appeals, for example, has promulgated such codes of conduct for its lawyers and judges. It has established a special commission to investigate complaints against judges and to "determine whether probable cause exists to formally charge a judge with a violation of the Code of Judicial Conduct."

The West Virginia Code of Judicial Conduct, in Canon 3E(1), prohibits any judge from participating in any proceeding where "the judge's impartiality might reasonably be questioned ..."

West Virginia is one of thirty-nine states that elect rather than appoint some or all of their judges.

Judges everywhere appreciate that the only power they possess is the right to make decisions. They depend on the executive branch of government to enforce their orders and on the legislative branch of government for funding. Judges who are not fair and impartial threaten public support for the judiciary as an institution, and potentially undermine respect for all other judges. It is unusual, for a judge to refuse to voluntarily remove (in legal jargon, "recuse") himself/herself from a proceeding which fairly or unfairly involves circumstances that could be perceived as raising questions about whether that judge is biased or has a conflict of interest. It is even more rare for a sitting judge to deny three separate recusal motions brought by one of the parties to a highly publicized and contentious case.

In our country, whenever it appears that a federal or state court trial has been fundamentally unfair for procedural reasons, an aggrieved party, after exhausting all other available sources of relief, has the right to petition the U.S. Supreme Court for a writ of certiorari. This is what happened in the case of *Caperton v. Massey Coal Co.* The U.S. Supreme Court granted certiorari, and thereby agreed to decide this case, in part because the facts were so compelling. However, by accepting this case the Court was also reminding the lower courts, political operatives, and the country that the protections of the Due Process Clause can be invoked to remedy a procedural wrong, if it is necessary to the preservation of judicial integrity.

Hugh M. Caperton v. A. T. Massey Coal Company, Inc.
556 U.S.___
U.S. Supreme Court
June 8, 2009

Justice Kennedy delivered the opinion of the Court.
In this case, the Supreme Court of Appeals of West Virginia reversed a trial court judgment, which had entered a jury verdict of $50 million. Five justices heard the case, and the vote to reverse was 3 to 2. The question presented is whether the Due Process Clause of the Fourteenth Amendment was violated when one of the justices in the majority denied a recusal motion. The basis for the motion was that the justice had received campaign contributions in an extraordinary amount from, and through the efforts of, the board chairman and principal officer of the corporation found liable for the damages....

I
In August 2002 a West Virginia jury returned a verdict that found respondents A. T. Massey Coal Co. and its affiliates (hereinafter Massey) liable for fraudulent misrepresentation, concealment, and tortious interference with existing contractual relations. The jury awarded petitioners Hugh Caperton, Harman Development Corp., Harman Mining Corp., and Sovereign Coal Sales (hereinafter Caperton) the sum of $50 million in compensatory and punitive damages.

In June 2004 the state trial court denied Massey's post-trial motions challenging the verdict and the damages award, finding that Massey "intentionally acted in utter disregard of [Caperton's] rights and ultimately destroyed [Caperton's] businesses.... In March 2005 the trial court denied Massey's motion for judgment as a matter of law.

Don Blankenship is Massey's chairman, chief executive officer, and president. After the verdict but before the appeal, West Virginia held its 2004 judicial elections. Knowing the Supreme Court of Appeals of West Virginia would consider the appeal in the case, Blankenship decided to support an attorney who sought to replace Justice McGraw. Justice McGraw was a candidate for reelection to that court. The attorney who sought to replace him was Brent Benjamin.

In addition to contributing the $1,000 statutory maximum to Benjamin's campaign committee, Blankenship donated almost $2.5 million to "And For The Sake Of The Kids," a political organization formed under 26 U. S. C. §527. The §527 organization opposed McGraw and supported Benjamin.... Blankenship's donations accounted for more than two-thirds of the total funds it raised....This was not all. Blankenship

spent, in addition, just over $500,000 on independent expenditures—for direct mailings and letters soliciting donations as well as television and newspaper advertisements—" 'to support ... Brent Benjamin.'"...

To provide some perspective, Blankenship's $3 million in contributions were more than the total amount spent by all other Benjamin supporters and three times the amount spent by Benjamin's own committee....

Benjamin won. He received 382,036 votes (53.3 percent), and McGraw received 334,301 votes (46.7 percent)....

In October 2005, before Massey filed its petition for appeal in West Virginia's highest court, Caperton moved to disqualify now-Justice Benjamin under the Due Process Clause and the West Virginia Code of Judicial Conduct, based on the conflict caused by Blankenship's campaign involvement. Justice Benjamin denied the motion in April 2006.... In December 2006 Massey filed its petition for appeal to challenge the adverse jury verdict. The West Virginia Supreme Court of Appeals granted review.

In November 2007 that court [consisting of "then-Chief Justice Davis and joined by Justices Benjamin and Maynard"] reversed the $50 million verdict against Massey.... Justice Starcher dissented, stating that the "majority's opinion is morally and legally wrong...."

Caperton sought rehearing, and the parties moved for disqualification of three of the five justices who decided the appeal. Photos had surfaced of Justice Maynard vacationing with Blankenship in the French Riviera while the case was pending..... Justice Maynard granted Caperton's recusal motion. On the other side Justice Starcher granted Massey's recusal motion, apparently based on his public criticism of Blankenship's role in the 2004 elections. In his recusal memorandum Justice Starcher urged Justice Benjamin to recuse himself as well... He noted that "Blankenship's bestowal of his personal wealth, political tactics, and 'friendship' have created a cancer in the affairs of this Court."... Justice Benjamin declined Justice Starcher's suggestion and denied Caperton's recusal motion.

The court granted rehearing. Justice Benjamin, now in the capacity of acting chief justice, selected Judges Cookman and Fox to replace the recused justices. Caperton moved a third time for disqualification.... Justice Benjamin again refused to withdraw, noting that the "push poll" was "neither credible nor sufficiently reliable to serve as the basis for an elected judge's disqualification."… In April 2008 a divided court again reversed the jury verdict, and again it was a 3-to-2 decision. Justice Davis filed a modified version of his prior opinion, repeating the two earlier holdings. She was joined by Justice Benjamin and Judge Fox. Justice Albright, joined by Judge Cookman, dissented: "Not only is the majority opinion unsupported by the facts and existing case law, but it is also fundamentally unfair. Sadly, justice was neither honored nor served by the majority…." The dissent also noted "genuine due process implications arising under federal law" with respect to Justice Benjamin's failure to recuse himself….

Four months later—a month after the petition for writ of certiorari was filed in this Court—Justice Benjamin filed a concurring opinion. He defended the merits of the majority opinion as well as his decision not to recuse. He rejected Caperton's challenge to his participation in the case under both the Due Process Clause and West Virginia law. Justice Benjamin reiterated that he had no "'direct, personal, substantial, pecuniary interest' in this case.'"

We granted certiorari. 555 U. S. ___ (2008).

II

It is axiomatic that "[a] fair trial in a fair tribunal is a basic requirement of due process."… The early and leading case on the subject is *Tumey* v. *Ohio*, 273 U. S. 510 (1927)….

To place the present case in proper context, two instances where the Court has required recusal merit further discussion.

A

The first involved the emergence of local tribunals where a judge had a financial interest in the outcome of a case, although the interest was less than what would have been considered personal or direct at common law.

This was the problem addressed in *Tumey*. There, the mayor of a village had the authority to sit as a judge (with no jury) to try those accused of violating a state law prohibiting the possession of alcoholic beverages. Inherent in this structure were two potential conflicts. First, the mayor received a salary supplement for performing judicial duties, and the funds for that compensation derived from the fines assessed in a case. No fines were assessed upon acquittal. The mayor-judge thus received a salary supplement only if he convicted the defendant….. Second, sums from the criminal fines were deposited to the village's general treasury fund for village improvements and repairs….

The Court held that the Due Process Clause required disqualification "both because of [the mayor-judge's] direct pecuniary interest in the outcome, and

because of his official motive to convict and to graduate the fine to help the financial needs of the village…." It so held despite observing that "[t]here are doubtless mayors who would not allow such a consideration as $12 costs in each case to affect their judgment in it…" The Court articulated the controlling principle:

> "Every procedure which would offer a possible temptation to the average man as a judge to forget the burden of proof required to convict the defendant, or which might lead him not to hold the balance nice, clear and true between the State and the accused, denies the latter due process of law…."

The Court was thus concerned with more than the traditional common-law prohibition on direct pecuniary interest. It was also concerned with a more general concept of interests that tempt adjudicators to disregard neutrality….

B

The second instance requiring recusal that was not discussed at common law emerged in the criminal contempt context, where a judge had no pecuniary interest in the case but was challenged because of a conflict arising from his participation in an earlier proceeding. This Court characterized that first proceeding (perhaps pejoratively) as a "'one-man grand jury.'" *Murchison*, 349 U.S., at 133… In that first proceeding, and as provided by state law, a judge examined witnesses to determine whether criminal charges should be brought. The judge called the two petitioners before him. One petitioner answered questions, but the judge found him untruthful and charged him with perjury. The second declined to answer on the ground that he did not have counsel with him, as state law seemed to permit. The judge charged him with contempt. The judge proceeded to try and convict both petitioners….

This Court set aside the convictions on grounds that the judge had a conflict of interest at the trial stage because of his earlier participation followed by his decision to charge them. The Due Process Clause required disqualification. The Court recited the general rule that "no man can be a judge in his own case," adding that "no man is permitted to try cases where he has an interest in the outcome."… It noted that the disqualifying criteria "cannot be defined with precision. Circumstances and relationships must be considered."… That is because "[a]s a practical matter it is difficult if not impossible for a judge to free himself from the influence of what took place in his 'grand-jury' secret session…"

The *Murchison* Court was careful to distinguish the circumstances and the relationship from those where the Constitution would not require recusal. It noted that the single-judge grand jury is "more a part of the accusatory process than an ordinary lay grand juror," and that "adjudication by a trial judge of a contempt committed in [a judge's] presence in open court cannot be likened to the proceedings here." *Id.*, at 137. The judge's prior relationship with the defendant, as well as the information acquired from the prior proceeding, was of critical import....

Again, the Court considered the specific circumstances presented by the case.... The inquiry is an objective one. The Court asks not whether the judge is actually, subjectively biased, but whether the average judge in his position is "likely" to be neutral, or whether there is an unconstitutional "potential for bias."

III

Based on the principles described in these cases we turn to the issue before us. This problem arises in the context of judicial elections, a framework not presented in the precedents we have reviewed and discussed.

Caperton contends that Blankenship's pivotal role in getting Justice Benjamin elected created a constitutionally intolerable probability of actual bias. Though not a bribe or criminal influence, Justice Benjamin would nevertheless feel a debt of gratitude to Blankenship for his extraordinary efforts to get him elected. That temptation, Caperton claims, is as strong and inherent in human nature as was the conflict the Court confronted in *Tumey*... when a mayor-judge (or the city) benefitted financially from a defendant's conviction, as well as the conflict identified in *Murchison*... when a judge was the object of a defendant's contempt.

Justice Benjamin was careful to address the recusal motions and explain his reasons why, on his view of the controlling standard, disqualification was not in order.... We do not question his subjective findings of impartiality and propriety. Nor do we determine whether there was actual bias. ...

... [A] judge inquires into reasons that seem to be leading to a particular result. Precedent and *stare decisis* and the text and purpose of the law and the Constitution; logic and scholarship and experience and common sense; and fairness and disinterest and neutrality are among the factors at work. To bring coherence to the process, and to seek respect for the resulting judgment, judges often explain the reasons for their conclusions and rulings. There are instances when the introspection that often attends this process may reveal that what the judge had assumed to be a proper, controlling factor is not the real one at work. If the judge discovers that some personal bias or improper consideration seems to be the actuating cause of the decision or to be an influence so difficult

to dispel that there is a real possibility of undermining neutrality, the judge may think it necessary to consider withdrawing from the case.

The difficulties of inquiring into actual bias, and the fact that the inquiry is often a private one, simply underscore the need for objective rules. ... [T]he Due Process Clause has been implemented by objective standards that do not require proof of actual bias.... In defining these standards the Court has asked whether, "under a realistic appraisal of psychological tendencies and human weakness," the interest "poses such a risk of actual bias or prejudgment that the practice must be forbidden if the guarantee of due process is to be adequately implemented." ...

We turn to the influence at issue in this case. Not every campaign contribution by a litigant or attorney creates a probability of bias that requires a judge's recusal, but this is an exceptional case.... We conclude that there is a serious risk of actual bias—based on objective and reasonable perceptions—when a person with a personal stake in a particular case had a significant and disproportionate influence in placing the judge on the case by raising funds or directing the judge's election campaign when the case was pending or imminent. The inquiry centers on the contribution's relative size in comparison to the total amount of money contributed to the campaign, the total amount spent in the election, and the apparent effect such contribution had on the outcome of the election.

Applying this principle, we conclude that Blankenship's campaign efforts had a significant and disproportionate influence in placing Justice Benjamin on the case. Blankenship contributed some $3 million to unseat the incumbent and replace him with Benjamin....

Massey responds that Blankenship's support, while significant, did not cause Benjamin's victory. In the end the people of West Virginia elected him, and they did so based on many reasons other than Blankenship's efforts. Massey points out that every major state newspaper, but one, endorsed Benjamin.... It also contends that then-Justice McGraw cost himself the election by giving a speech during the campaign, a speech the opposition seized upon for its own advantage.... Justice Benjamin raised similar arguments....

Whether Blankenship's campaign contributions were a necessary and sufficient cause of Benjamin's victory is not the proper inquiry. Much like determining whether a judge is actually biased, proving what ultimately drives the electorate to choose a particular candidate is a difficult endeavor, not likely to lend itself to a certain conclusion. This is particularly true where, as here, there is no procedure for judicial factfinding and the sole trier of fact is the one accused of bias. .. Blankenship's campaign contributions—in comparison to the total amount contributed to the campaign, as well as the total amount spent in the election—had a significant and disproportionate influence on the electoral outcome. And the risk that Blankenship's influence engendered actual bias is sufficiently substantial that it "must be forbidden if the guarantee of due process is to be adequately implemented...."

The temporal relationship between the campaign contributions, the justice's election, and the pendency of the case is also critical. It was reasonably foreseeable, when the campaign contributions were made, that the pending case would be before the newly elected justice. The $50 million adverse jury verdict had been entered before the election, and the Supreme Court of Appeals was the next step once the state trial court dealt with post-trial motions. So it became at once apparent that, absent recusal, Justice Benjamin would review a judgment that cost his biggest donor's company $50 million. Although there is no allegation of a *quid pro quo* agreement, the fact remains that Blankenship's extraordinary contributions were made at a time when he had a vested stake in the outcome. Just as no man is allowed to be a judge in his own cause, similar fears of bias can arise when—without the consent of the other parties—a man chooses the judge in his own cause. And applying this principle to the judicial election process, there was here a serious, objective risk of actual bias that required Justice Benjamin's recusal. ...

We find that Blankenship's significant and disproportionate influence—coupled with the temporal relationship between the election and the pending case—'"offer a possible temptation to the average ... judge to ... lead him not to hold the balance nice, clear and true."'.... On these extreme facts the probability of actual bias rises to an unconstitutional level.

IV

Our decision today addresses an extraordinary situation where the Constitution requires recusal.... Massey and its ... [advocates] predict that various adverse consequences will follow from recognizing a constitutional violation here—ranging from a flood of recusal motions to unnecessary interference with judicial elections. We disagree. The facts now before us are

extreme by any measure. The parties point to no other instance involving judicial campaign contributions that presents a potential for bias comparable to the circumstances in this case.

It is true that extreme cases often test the bounds of established legal principles, and sometimes no administrable standard may be available to address the perceived wrong. But it is also true that extreme cases are more likely to cross constitutional limits, requiring this Court's intervention and formulation of objective standards. This is particularly true when due process is violated....

This Court's recusal cases are illustrative. In each case the Court dealt with extreme facts that created an unconstitutional probability of bias that "'cannot be defined with precision.'".... Yet the Court articulated an objective standard to protect the parties' basic right to a fair trial in a fair tribunal. The Court was careful to distinguish the extreme facts of the cases before it from those interests that would not rise to a constitutional level.... In this case we do nothing more than what the Court has done before....

"Courts, in our system, elaborate principles of law in the course of resolving disputes. The power and the prerogative of a court to perform this function rest, in the end, upon the respect accorded to its judgments. The citizen's respect for judgments depends in turn upon the issuing court's absolute probity. Judicial integrity is, in consequence, a state interest of the highest order..."

"The Due Process Clause demarks only the outer boundaries of judicial disqualifications. Congress and the states, of course, remain free to impose more rigorous standards for judicial disqualification than those we find mandated here today...." Because the codes of judicial conduct provide more protection than due process requires, most disputes over disqualification will be resolved without resort to the Constitution. Application of the constitutional standard implicated in this case will thus be confined to rare instances.

The judgment of the Supreme Court of Appeals of West Virginia is reversed, and the case is remanded for further proceedings not inconsistent with this opinion.

It is so ordered.

Case Questions

1. The Supreme Court split 5–4 in deciding this case. What do you suppose were some of the concerns of the dissenting four justices?
2. What single fact was most important to you as you went about making up your own mind as to whether this case was correctly decided?
3. Does this case have any possible ethical implications that might have relevance for appointed judges?

INTERNET TIP

Interested readers can find Chief Justice Roberts's dissent online at the textbook's website. Another interesting case is also available on the website. In 2005, the Florida Supreme Court disciplined two attorneys because their television advertisement featured a pit bull with a spiked collar and their firm's telephone number: 1-800-PIT-BULL. This form of advertising, said the Florida Supreme Court, violated the Florida Rules of Professional Conduct. You can read an edited version of *The Florida Bar v. John Robert Pape* on this textbook's website.

Ethics and Professional Responsibility Codes for Paralegals

Lawyers, law firms, businesses, and governments have increasingly been hiring people as legal assistants or paralegals (hereafter called simply paralegals) to do work previously performed by licensed attorneys. The primary reason for this trend is the financial savings realized by having legal work performed by nonlawyers.

Paralegals today perform a wide variety of tasks, depending on their training, education, and experience. Because they are not licensed attorneys, they cannot represent clients in court, give legal advice, or sign pleadings. Subject to these limitations, the scope of a paralegal's duties is largely a matter of what the supervising attorney is willing to permit. Often this includes interviewing clients, conducting research, preparing drafts of documents, undertaking investigations, preparing affidavits, and collecting and organizing materials for hearings.

Legally, a supervising attorney is responsible for providing oversight and regulating his or her paralegal's work and conduct. There have been proposals that paralegals be subject to rules of professional responsibility established by each state's supreme court. This was proposed in New Jersey, but rejected by that state's supreme court.[22] Several

states have established paralegal divisions within the state bar. One state that undertook this step in 1995 is New Mexico.

All three of the national paralegal associations—the National Federation of Paralegal Associations, the American Alliance of Paralegals, Inc., and the National Association of Legal Assistants—have recognized the need to provide paralegals with ethical guidelines, and each has promulgated a code of ethics to which its members subscribe. State and local paralegal organizations also promote ethical conduct within their memberships.

The New Mexico Supreme Court has been a leader in enhancing ethical conduct and professional responsibility on the part of paralegals. The court, through its "Rules Governing Paralegal Services," has helped to clarify the boundaries of the paralegal's role within that state. (Readers can see the complete text of the rules and commentary on the textbook's website.). The court has also recognized the importance of establishing general ethical guidelines for paralegals in its "Canons of Ethics" (see Table 2.3).

Many states have defined what it means to be a paralegal and require people holding themselves out to be paralegals to have satisfied minimum standards with respect to education, certification, and/or experience. These laws usually prohibit paralegals from advertising or offering their services to consumers and require that all paralegal work be performed at the direction and under the supervision of a licensed attorney of that state. Such laws are intended to prevent paralegals from engaging in the unauthorized practice of law. Some states, notably California, require paralegals to complete mandatory continuing legal education courses periodically.

The American Bar Association also has a Standing Committee on Paralegals, and has published "ABA Guidelines for the Approval of Paralegal Education Programs" and "ABA Model Guidelines for the Utilization of Paralegal Services."

T A B L E 2.3 State Bar of New Mexico, Canon of Ethics for Paralegal Division

It is the responsibility of every member of the Paralegal Division of the State Bar of New Mexico (hereinafter referred to as "Paralegal") to adhere strictly to the accepted standards of legal ethics. The Canons of Ethics set forth hereafter are adopted by the Paralegal Division of the State Bar of New Mexico as a general guide.

CANON 1. A Paralegal must not perform any of the duties that only attorneys may perform nor take any actions that attorneys may not take.

CANON 2. A Paralegal may perform any task which is properly delegated and supervised by an attorney, as long as the attorney is ultimately responsible to the client, maintains a direct relationship with the client, and assumes professional responsibility for the work product.

CANON 3. A Paralegal must not: (a) engage in, encourage, or contribute to any act which could constitute the unauthorized practice of law; and (b) establish attorney-client relationships, set fees, give legal opinions or advice or represent a client before a court or agency unless so authorized by that court or agency; and (c) engage in conduct or take any action which would assist or involve the attorney in a violation of professional ethics or give the appearance of professional impropriety.

CANON 4. A Paralegal must use discretion and professional judgment commensurate with knowledge and experience but must not render independent legal judgment in place of an attorney. The services of an attorney are essential in the public interest whenever such legal judgment is required.

CANON 5. A Paralegal must disclose his or her status as a Paralegal at the outset of any professional relationship with a client, attorney, a court or administrative agency or personnel thereof, or a member of the general public. A Paralegal must act prudently in determining the extent to which a client may be assisted without the presence of an attorney.

CANON 6. A Paralegal must strive to maintain integrity and a high degree of competency through education and training with respect to professional responsibility, local rules and practice, and through continuing education in substantive areas of law to better assist the legal profession in fulfilling its duty to provide legal service.

CANON 7. A Paralegal must protect the confidences of a client and must not violate any rule or statute now in effect or hereafter enacted controlling the doctrine of privileged communications between a client and an attorney.

CANON 8. A Paralegal must do all other things incidental, necessary, or expedient for the attainment of the ethics and responsibilities as defined by statute or rule of court.

CANON 9. A Paralegal's conduct is governed by the codes of professional responsibility and rules of professional conduct of the State Bar of New Mexico and the New Mexico Supreme Court. A member of the Paralegal Division of the State Bar of New Mexico shall be governed by the Rules Governing Paralegal Services (Rules 20-101 et seq. NMRA, as the same may be amended).

CHAPTER SUMMARY

Ethical questions permeate our society and are reflected in the laws enacted by our legislative bodies and the decisions of our judges and executive branch officials. Ethics is the study of morality and is a branch of the larger field of philosophy. Philosophers disagree about many things, including whether ethical judgments about right and wrong can be conclusively proven, whether "goodness or badness" is dependent on aftermaths, and whether there is such a thing as an "unjust" law. Because people differ in their moral beliefs, we have seen that there is ongoing ethical debate raging in this country as to where to draw the line between the right of individual choice and the right of society to promote a common morality. In this chapter, readers learned about codes of ethics and rules of professional responsibility. Readers also learned that establishing objective rules to govern complex ethical problems is often a difficult undertaking. We saw one contemporary example of this in conjunction with the financing of judicial elections in West Virginia. It is hard to draft objective rules that tell a sitting judge who has accepted campaign contributions precisely when recusal is required to insure judicial impartiality and avoid the possibility of bias. Justice Kennedy explained that in some circumstances the likelihood of bias is clear and a constitutional remedy is required. Kennedy and a majority of Supreme Court justices believed *Caperton v. Massey* was such a case.

But in providing a new Due Process Clause–based remedy in *Caperton*, the Court essentially opened Pandora's Box. They made it likely that future U.S. Supreme Court justices will find it difficult to draw clear-cut ethical lines. Because many states require that judges be elected, judicial candidates have difficult decisions to make as they attempt to fund their campaigns without creating the appearance of being biased in favor of large donors and without compromising their impartiality should they be elected to office.

CHAPTER QUESTIONS

1. Michael and Patricia Sewak bought a house from Charles and Hope Lockhart. Prior to the sale, the Lockharts had employed a contractor for $12,000 to renovate their basement. Somehow, the main structural support that held up the house was removed during the renovations. Shortly after moving in, the Sewaks noticed that the kitchen floor was not level, that doors were not in alignment, and that the first and second floors were sagging. They hired a consultant, who investigated and determined that the support column was missing and that an illegal jack, found in the back of a heater closet, was used to provide the needed structural support. The consultant predicted that the absence of the structural column would ultimately result in the collapse of the house. The Sewaks filed suit, alleging fraud and a violation of the Pennsylvania Unfair Trade Practices and Consumer Protection Law (UTPCPL). The Sewaks maintained that the Lockharts should have informed them that the support column had been removed. The trial evidence, according to the appellate court, permitted the jury to find that the Lockharts not only had knowledge of the column's removal, but also took steps to conceal its replacement with the illegal jack, and that they had not obtained the proper building permits before undertaking the renovations. Did the Lockharts act ethically in their dealings with the Sewaks? Should the law impose a legal duty on the Sewaks to investigate and discover the absence of the structural support column for themselves?

   Sewak v. Lockhart, 699 A.2d 755 (1997)

2. Jonas Yoder and Wallace Miller, members of the Amish religion, withdrew their daughters, Frieda Yoder and Barbara Miller, from school after they had completed the eighth grade. This refusal violated a Wisconsin compulsory school attendance law that required Frieda and Barbara to be in school until their sixteenth birthdays. The U.S. Supreme Court ruled that the Amish parents had a constitutionally protected right to control the religious education of their children under the First and Fourteenth Amendments. The Court's majority concluded that to require the children to attend public high school would undermine fundamental Amish values and religious freedoms. Frieda and Barbara were not parties to the lawsuit, and there is no record as to their positions on the issue in this case. Given the Supreme Court's holding in *Wisconsin v. Yoder,* what posture should the law take in a situation where Amish

children desire to attend high school over the objections of their parents?

Wisconsin v. Yoder, 406 U.S. 205 (1972)

3.   Raymond Dirks worked for a New York City broker-dealer firm. He specialized in analyzing insurance company investments. Dirks received a tip from Ronald Secrist, a former officer of Equity Funding of America (an insurance company), that Equity Funding had fraudulently overstated its assets. Dirks decided to investigate. Although neither Dirks nor his employer traded in Equity Funding shares, he told others in the securities industry about the tip, and soon thereafter Equity Funding's shares dropped precipitously in value. The Securities and Exchange Commission (SEC) investigated Dirk's role in disclosing the existence of the fraud and charged him with being a "tippee" who had aided and abetted violations of the Securities Act of 1933. This statute makes it illegal for persons with inside knowledge (nonpublic information) to take unfair advantage of a company's shareholders by trading in the affected securities before the news has become public. Can you make an argument supporting the conclusion that it would be unethical for Dirks to share the information he obtained from Secrist with other people in the industry? Can you make an argument that Dirk's conduct was not unethical?

Dirks v. Securities and Exchange Commission, 463 U.S. 646 (1983)

4.   Three separate federal suits were brought by gay men and lesbians who had been discharged from their jobs. One plaintiff, a schoolteacher, alleged that his firing was because he wore an earring to school. The second suit was brought by two lesbians who alleged that they were terminated from their jobs because of their sexual orientation. The third suit was filed by three homosexual plaintiffs who alleged that they were in one case denied employment, and in two cases fired from employment because

their employer had a corporate policy of not employing homosexuals. The U.S. District Court dismissed the complaints on the grounds that Title VII does not protect employees from discharges based on effeminacy or homosexuality. The U.S. Court of Appeals affirmed the decision of the District Court. Does the fact that two federal courts ruled that the plaintiffs were not entitled to legal relief affect the ethical merits of their claims?

De Santis v. Pacific Tel. & Tel. Co., Inc., 608 F.2d 327 (1979)

5.   In many regions of the country, it is customary for schools to take a break for school vacations during February. Many families arrange their schedules so that families can take very special trips to remote destinations. The airlines are beneficiaries of this tradition, and flights to popular vacation spots are often totally booked. In 1999, airline pilots involved in collective bargaining disputes with their employer engaged in a "sick-out" during the school vacation period. Analyze this scenario from the *egoist* perspective.

6.   The Massachusetts Supreme Judicial Court has interpreted a statute to require injured skiers who wish to sue ski area operators to give the operators notice of the skier's claims within ninety days of the injury and comply with a one-year statute of limitations. Failure to give timely notice of the claims will preclude bringing the suit at all. Both the court majority and the dissenting justices attributed these unusually short limitations to bringing actions to a legislative policy. Both concluded that the legislature evidently placed a higher value on the economic vitality of the Massachusetts ski industry than on the rights of injured skiers to seek recoveries in tort and contract from ski area operators. Analyze this case from a *utilitarian* perspective.

Atkins v. Jiminy Peak, Inc. 514 N.E.2d 850 (1987)

NOTES

1. See *Macomber v. Dillman* in Chapter VI.

2. See *Atkins v. Jiminy Peak, Inc.* in Chapter V.

3. You can find this case on the Internet at http://www.Findlaw.com. The case citation is *Furman v. Georgia*, 408 U.S. 238 (1972).

4. Telling a lie about a material fact while under oath is a crime called perjury. Theft by false pretense is another crime that is based on a fraudulent, actual, factual misrepresentation. In contracts, fraud in the formation of an agreement can result in rescission and an award of damages to the injured party.

5. Hancock, Roger N., *Twentieth Century Ethics*. (New York: Columbia University Press, 1974), p. 2.

6. An example is the debate about whether the concept we call "good" is composed of parts or is essentially indefinable. Moore, G. E., *Principia Ethica* (1903). (Cambridge, England: University Printing House, 1976.)

7. Rachels, James, *The Elements of Moral Philosophy*. (New York: McGraw-Hill, 2nd ed., 1986), pp. 8–14.

8. Hancock, p. 12.

9. Ibid., p. 12.

10. Rachels, pp. 12–24.

11. You will recall from Chapter I, for example, that utilitarians sought to produce the greatest good for the greatest number of people. This kind of calculation can only be undertaken by examining aftermaths.

12. Carol Gilligan and Jane Attanucci maintain that all people think about the morality of their relations with others from two perspectives. One perspective is based on a concern for treating people fairly (which they call the "justice perspective"), and the other focuses on responding to persons who are in need (which they call the "care perspective"). The authors suggested that males are more oriented toward concerns for "justice" and females toward "caring." See Gilligan, Ward, Taylor, and Bardige, *Mapping the Moral Domain* (Cambridge, MA: Harvard University Graduate School of Education, 1988), Chapter IV.

13. Kant, Immanuel, *Groundwork of the Metaphysics of Morals* (1785), Chapter I. http://www.earlymodern texts.com/pdfbits/kgw.html http://www.gutenberg.org/etext/5682

14. *Egoism* (Benedict Spinoza, 1632–1677): "The virtues that ethics seeks to inculcate are the qualities we require to have personally fulfilled lives." These, he said, included "courage, temperance, harmonious, cooperative and stable relations with others."

15. Under Article VI's Supremacy Clause, the federal Constitution is the ultimate authority as to matters arising under it, but the state constitutions are the ultimate authority as to matters that do not amount to federal questions.

16. *Boston Globe,* October 16, 1998, p. A17.

17. Note that these facts parallel the facts in the Unabomber case and that Ted Kaczynski's brother did tell authorities of his suspicions, he did receive a large cash reward, and he gave it all to charity.

18. P. Devlin, "Morals and the Criminal Law," in *The Enforcement of Morals* (Oxford University Press, 1965), pp. 9–10.

19. David Millon refers to this as a dispute between the "contractarians" and the "communitarians." See David Millon, "Communitarians, Contractarians, and the Crisis in Corporate Law," 50 *Washington & Lee Law Review* 1373 (1993).

20. See J. Nesteruk, "Law, Virtue, and the Corporation," 33 *American Business Journal* 473 (1996).

21. For a brief and critical history of the development of bar associations, see Howard Abadinsky, *Law and Justice* (Chicago: Nelson-Hall, 1991), p. 102.

22. The New Jersey Supreme Court in 1999 rejected its own Committee on Paralegal Education and Regulation's recommendation that the state supreme court adopt "a court directed licensing system." The New Jersey high court indicated that it supported in principle "the creation and adoption of a Code of Professional Conduct for Paralegals," but thought this should be produced by "paralegals and attorneys and their respective associations." New Jersey Supreme Court Press Release of May 24, 1999.

III

✳

Institutional Sources
of American Law

CHAPTER OBJECTIVES

1. *Identify the primary sources of American law.*
2. *Summarize each source's formal role in the making of American law.*
3. *Explain important aspects of our federal form of government such as federal supremacy, the police power of the states, full faith and credit, and conflict-of-laws rules.*
4. *Explain the judicial doctrine known as stare decisis.*
5. *Describe the fundamental differences between civil law and common law legal systems.*

It is important to understand that the rules constituting American law derive from several authoritative sources. The most important of these are the federal and state constitutions; legislation produced at the federal, state, and local levels of government; decisions of federal and state courts; and the regulations and adjudicatory rulings of federal, state, and local administrative agencies. In this chapter we preview each of these major sources of law and focus on the legislative and judicial branches of government.

COMMON LAW AND CIVIL LAW LEGAL SYSTEMS

From your reading of Chapter I, you have already seen how the English common law system developed over many centuries.[1] You know that as judges decided cases, rules slowly evolved and became recognized as judicial precedents, which began to be written down and followed. These practices made it possible for cases raising a particular issue to be decided in essentially the same way throughout England. With its emphasis on judge-made law, this approach differs markedly from the legal systems found in France, Germany, and Italy. Those countries follow a different approach, often referred to as the civil law system.[2]

Civil law systems are based upon detailed legislative codes rather than judicial precedents. Such a code is a comprehensive, authoritative collection of rules covering all the principal subjects of law. Civil law codes are often developed by academicians and then enacted by legislative bodies. They are based on philosophy, theory, and abstract principles. Civil law systems usually reject the use of precedent, dispense with juries in civil cases, and avoid complex rules of evidence. In civil law countries, judges are expected to base their decisions on the appropriate provisions of the relevant code, and they do not treat the decisions of other judges as authoritative sources.

The civil law tradition traces its roots to historically famous codes of law such as ancient Rome's **Corpus Juris Civilis** and the **Code Napoleon**. At present, Europe, Central and South America, the Province of Quebec, and the former French colonies of Africa have adopted the civil law system.

Although the common law system has had much more impact on American law, the civil law system has been of increasing influence. For example, early-nineteenth-century American legislatures wanted to replace the complex and ponderous system of common law pleading, and reformers campaigned in favor of replacing the traditional reliance on judge-made law with legislated codes. Today, codes of civil procedure regulate litigation in all federal and state courts. Many states have taken a similar approach with respect to probate law, criminal law, and commercial law. State legislatures in forty-nine states, for example, have adopted the Uniform Commercial Code to replace the common law with respect to the sale of goods. (Louisiana is the holdout.)

CONSTITUTIONS

The United States in its Constitution has adopted a federal form of government. Like the federal government, each of the fifty states is sovereign with a written constitution and legislative, executive, and judicial branches of government. The written constitution is the fundamental source of the rule of law within each jurisdiction. It creates a framework for the exercise of governmental power and allocates responsibility among the branches of government. It authorizes and restrains the exercise of governmental authority, protects fundamental rights, and provides an orderly vehicle for legal change. Laws and governmental actions that violate its terms are unconstitutional.

The U.S. Constitution grants certain powers to the federal government in Article I, such as the rights to regulate interstate commerce, operate post offices, declare war, and coin money. The states, however, retain many important powers and can implement significant change by enacting statutes and by amending their state constitutions. One strength of our federal form of government is that states can innovate and experiment without having to obtain permission from other states. Nebraska's constitution, for example, provides for a unicameral legislature (the only state to do so); Oregon's laws provide persons who are terminally ill with the option of physician-assisted suicide; Vermont was the first state to legalize civil unions; and Massachusetts was the first state to issue marriage licenses to same-sex couples. Because of federalism, it is not unusual for states to provide their residents with greater substantive and procedural protections as a matter of state law than are required by the U.S. Constitution.

LEGISLATION

To maintain social harmony, society needs uniformly operating rules of conduct. The responsibility for determining the rules lies primarily with legislative bodies. The legislative branch creates law by enacting statutes. An examination of legislation reveals the problems and moods of the nation. Legislatures write history through the legislative process. There have been legislative reactions to almost all political, social, and business problems that have faced society. Laws have been passed in response to wars, depressions, civil rights problems, crime, and concern for cities and the environment. Checks and balances have been built into the system in order to prevent overreaction by the legislature and to promote wise and timely legislation.

The process of enacting statutes is lengthy and complex. At the federal level, it is a procedure that involves 535 persons in the House and Senate who represent the interests of their constituents, themselves, and the country. A proposed bill may encounter numerous obstacles. Mere approval by the legislative bodies does not ensure passage, for at both federal and state levels the executive branch has the power to veto a bill. Another check on legislation can come once a bill becomes law. At that point, the constitutionality of the legislative act may be challenged in court.

With the exception of bills for raising revenue, which must originate in the House (Article I, Section 7 of the Constitution), it makes no difference in which body a bill is introduced, because a statute must be approved by both houses of the legislature. However, the legislative process varies slightly between the Senate and House. If differences exist between the House and Senate versions of a bill, a joint conference committee meets to reconcile the conflicts and draft a compromise bill.

After a bill has been approved by both houses and certain formalities have been completed, it must be approved and signed by the president of the United States to become effective. If the president vetoes a bill—which rarely occurs—it does not become law unless the veto is overridden by a two-thirds vote of both houses.

Defeat of a bill is far more common than passage. More than 95 percent of all legislation introduced is defeated at some point. Still, much legislation *is* signed into law each year. Legislative death can result at any stage of the process, and from many sources. For legislation to be successful in passing, assignment to the proper committee is crucial. However, committees can be cruel. They may refuse to hold hearings. They may alter a bill completely. Or they may kill it outright. If a proposed statute survives the committee stage, the House Rules Committee or the Senate majority leader determines the bill's destiny. Once a bill reaches the floor of the House or Senate, irrelevant proposals—known as riders—may be added to it. Or drastic amendments can so alter it that it is defeated. The possibilities are almost endless.

The need for certainty and uniformity in the laws among the states is reflected in federal legislation and uniform state laws. A great degree of uniformity has been accomplished among the states on a number of matters. An important example is the **Uniform Commercial Code** (UCC). With increased interstate business operations, business firms pressured for uniform laws dealing with commercial transactions among states. Judges, law professors, and leading members of the bar drafted the UCC for adoption by the individual states. The UCC was first adopted by the Pennsylvania legislature in 1953, and has now been adopted at least partially in all fifty states. The UCC covers sales, commercial paper, bank collection processes, letters of credit, bulk transfers, warehouse receipts, bills of lading, other documents of title, investment securities, and secured transactions.

The Power to Legislate

Legislative bodies are organized in accordance with the provisions of the U.S. and state constitutions, and are entrusted with wide-ranging responsibilities and powers. These powers include enacting laws, raising taxes, conductinginvestigations, holding

F I G U R E 3.1 The Commerce Clause

hearings, and determining how public money will be appropriated. Legislatures play a major role in determining public policy. It is widely understood, however, that today's legislatures actually share policymaking duties with the executive and judicial branches and with administrative agencies.

Federal Government

The federal government cannot exercise any authority that is not granted to it by the Constitution, either expressly or by implication. The U.S. Constitution, in Article I, Section 8 and in authorizing sections contained in various constitutional amendments, enumerates the powers granted to the Congress. The powers that the Constitution delegates to the federal government are comprehensive and complete. They are limited only by the Constitution. The power to regulate interstate commerce is one of the most important of the expressly delegated powers.

From 1900 until 1937, the U.S. Supreme Court often followed a formalistic approach in its interpretations of the Commerce Clause. The justices severely limited the scope of this clause in a series of controversial cases. The Court, for example, rejected Congress's claim that Article I, Section 8, permitted the federal government to address problems resulting from indirect as well as direct impacts on interstate commerce,[3] and it defined interstate commerce very narrowly in cases in which Congress sought to regulate mining,[4] protect workers wishing to join labor unions,[5] and discourage the use of child labor in factories.[6]

The Supreme Court reversed its direction in 1937 and began to defer to Congress in cases where a rational connection existed between the legislation and commerce. The Court often used the Necessary and Proper Clause in conjunction with the Commerce Clause to justify extensions of federal authority.[7] In one case it upheld a federal act that was jurisdictionally based on indirect effects on interstate commerce and that authorized the use of injunctions against companies engaging in unfair labor practices,[8] and in a second case it upheld minimum wage legislation.[9] The continued viability of the "deferential" standard was called into question because of the Court's decision in *United States v. Lopez*, a case in which the U.S. Supreme Court ruled that Congress did not have authority under the Commerce Clause to enact the Gun-Free School Zones Act of 1990.

INTERNET TIP

You can read edited versions of *United States v. Lopez* and the U.S. Supreme Court's recent 2010 decision in *United States v. Comstock* with the Chapter III materials on the textbook's website. In *Comstock*, the justices considered whether Congress's reliance on the U.S. Constitution's Necessary and Proper Clause was sufficient authority to enact the Adam Walsh Child Protection Act of 2006. The federal district court and court of appeals had ruled that Congress had exceeded its legislative powers. The Adam Walsh law, also known as 18 U.S.C. Section 4248, provided a process by which federal prisoners with mental illnesses who had been previously classified as "dangerous sexual offenders" could continue to be detained indefinitely after the expiration of their prison sentences.

The U.S. Supreme Court in 2005 had to decide whether Congress had the right under the Commerce Clause to prohibit California and eight other states from statutorily permitting the cultivation and use of marijuana for medicinal purposes.

Angel Raich and Diane Monson, the plaintiffs in the trial court, were both experiencing excruciating pain because of serious illnesses. They unsuccessfully tried to alleviate this pain with conventional medications. But when these medications proved ineffective, they obtained prescriptions written by their board-certified physicians that allowed them to use marijuana to treat the pain. Monson, in addition to using marijuana for pain relief, also grew marijuana for her own medicinal use. Both the women, as well as their physicians, concluded that the marijuana had been effective in alleviating their pain.

Federal and state officers jointly investigated Monson's cultivation and use of marijuana, with the state officers concluding that she was acting lawfully under California law. The federal officers, however, took a different view and seized the plants, believing Monson's possession and use of this controlled substance to be a violation of the federal Controlled Substances Act (CSA). Raich and Monson then filed suit in the **U.S. District Court** (a federal trial court) seeking a **prohibitory injunction** (a court order prohibiting the enforcement of the CSA against Raich and Monson because of their cultivation and/or use of medicinal marijuana). Although the district court ruled against the women, the **U.S. Court of Appeals** (the primary appellate court in the federal system) for the Ninth Circuit reversed the district court and ruled in favor of Raich and Monson. The justice department then successfully petitioned the U.S. Supreme Court to agree to decide the case.

Alberto R. Gonzales v. Angel Raich
545 U.S. 1
U.S. Supreme Court
June 6, 2005

Justice Stevens delivered the opinion of the Court. California is one of at least nine States that authorize the use of marijuana for medicinal purposes....The question presented in this case is whether the power vested in Congress by Article I, §8, of the Constitution "make all Laws which shall be necessary and proper for carrying into Execution" its authority to "regulate Commerce with foreign Nations, and among the several States" includes the power to prohibit the local cultivation and use of marijuana in compliance with California law.

I
California has been a pioneer in the regulation of marijuana. In 1913, California was one of the first States to prohibit the sale and possession of marijuana ...and at the end of the century, California became the first State to authorize limited use of the drug for medicinal purposes. In 1996, California voters passed Proposition 215, now codified as the Compassionate Use Act of 1996...The proposition was designed to ensure that "seriously ill" residents of the State have access to marijuana for medical purposes, and to encourage Federal and State Governments to take steps towards ensuring the safe and affordable distribution of the drug to patients in need....The Act creates an exemption from criminal prosecution for physicians,...as well as for patients and primary caregivers who possess or cultivate marijuana for medicinal purposes with the recommendation or approval of a physician...A "primary caregiver" is a person who has consistently assumed responsibility for the housing, health, or safety of the patient....

Respondents Angel Raich and Diane Monson are California residents who suffer from a variety of serious medical conditions and have sought to avail themselves of medical marijuana pursuant to the terms of the Compassionate Use Act. They are being treated by licensed, board-certified family practitioners, who have concluded, after prescribing a host of conventional medicines to treat respondents' conditions and to alleviate their associated symptoms, that marijuana is the only drug available that provides effective treatment. Both women have been using marijuana as a medication for several years pursuant to their doctors' recommendation, and both rely heavily on cannabis to function on a daily basis. Indeed, Raich's physician believes that forgoing cannabis treatments would certainly cause Raich excruciating pain and could very well prove fatal.

Respondent Monson cultivates her own marijuana, and ingests the drug in a variety of ways including smoking and using a vaporizer. Respondent Raich, by contrast, is unable to cultivate her own, and thus relies on two caregivers, litigating as "John Does," to provide her with locally grown marijuana at no charge. These caregivers also process the cannabis into hashish or keif, and Raich herself processes some of the marijuana into oils, balms, and foods for consumption.

On August 15, 2002, county deputy sheriffs and agents from the federal Drug Enforcement Administration (DEA) came to Monson's home. After a thorough investigation, the county officials concluded that her use of marijuana was entirely lawful as a matter of California law. Nevertheless, after a 3-hour standoff, the federal agents seized and destroyed all six of her cannabis plants.

Respondents thereafter brought this action against the Attorney General of the United States and the head of the DEA seeking injunctive…relief prohibiting the enforcement of the federal Controlled Substances Act (CSA)…to the extent it prevents them from possessing, obtaining, or manufacturing cannabis for their personal medical use. In their complaint and supporting affidavits, Raich and Monson described the severity of their afflictions, their repeatedly futile attempts to obtain relief with conventional medications, and the opinions of their doctors concerning their need to use marijuana. Respondents claimed that enforcing the CSA against them would violate the Commerce Clause, the Due Process Clause of the Fifth Amendment, the Ninth and Tenth Amendments of the Constitution, and the doctrine of medical necessity.

The District Court denied respondents' motion for a preliminary injunction….

A divided panel of the Court of Appeals for the Ninth Circuit reversed and ordered the District Court to enter a preliminaryinjunction….

The obvious importance of the case prompted our grant of certiorari….The case is made difficult by respondents' strong arguments that they will suffer irreparable harm because, despite a congressional finding to the contrary, marijuana does have valid therapeutic purposes. The question before us,

however, is not whether it is wise to enforce the statute in these circumstances; rather, it is whether Congress' power to regulate interstate markets for medicinal substances encompasses the portions of those markets that are supplied with drugs produced and consumed locally….

II

Shortly after taking office in 1969, President Nixon declared a national "war on drugs."…As the first campaign of that war, Congress set out to enact legislation that would consolidate various drug laws on the books into a comprehensive statute, provide meaningful regulation over legitimate sources of drugs to prevent diversion into illegal channels, and strengthen law enforcement tools against the traffic in illicit drugs…. That effort culminated in the passage of the Comprehensive Drug Abuse Prevention and Control Act of 1970….

This was not, however, Congress' first attempt to regulate the national market in drugs.

Rather, as early as 1906 Congress enacted federal legislation imposing labeling regulations on medications and prohibiting the manufacture or shipment of any adulterated or misbranded drug traveling in interstate commerce….Aside from these labeling restrictions, most domestic drug regulations prior to 1970 generally came in the guise of revenue laws, with the Department of the Treasury serving as the Federal Government's primary enforcer…For example, the primary drug control law, before being repealed by the passage of the CSA, was the Harrison Narcotics Act of 1914….The Harrison Act sought to exert control over the possession and sale of narcotics, specifically cocaine and opiates, by requiring producers, distributors, and purchasers to register with the Federal Government, by assessing taxes against parties so registered, and by regulating the issuance of prescriptions….

Marijuana itself was not significantly regulated by the Federal Government until 1937 when accounts of marijuana's addictive qualities and physiological effects, paired with dissatisfaction with enforcement efforts at state and local levels, prompted Congress to pass the Marihuana Tax Act….Like the Harrison Act, the Marihuana Tax Act did not outlaw the possession or sale of marijuana outright. Rather, it imposed registration and reporting requirements for all individuals importing, producing, selling, or dealing in marijuana, and required the payment of annual taxes in addition to transfer taxes whenever the drug changed hands…. Moreover, doctors wishing to prescribe marijuana for medical purposes were required to comply with rather burdensome administrative requirements….Noncompliance exposed traffickers to severe federal penalties, whereas compliance would often subject them to prosecution under state law....Thus, while the Marihuana Tax Act did not declare the drug illegal *per se*, the onerous administrative requirements, the prohibitively expensive taxes, and the risks attendant on compliance practically curtailed the marijuana trade.

Then in 1970, after declaration of the national "war on drugs," federal drug policy underwent a significant transformation...prompted by a perceived need to consolidate the growing number of piecemeal drug laws and to enhance federal drug enforcement powers, Congress enacted the Comprehensive Drug Abuse Prevention and Control Act....

Title II of that Act, the CSA, repealed most of the earlier antidrug laws in favor of a comprehensive regime to combat the international and interstate traffic in illicit drugs. The main objectives of the CSA were to conquer drug abuse and to control the legitimate and illegitimate traffic in controlled substances... Congress was particularly concerned with the need to prevent the diversion of drugs from legitimate to illicit channels....

To effectuate these goals, Congress devised a closed regulatory system making it unlawful to manufacture, distribute, dispense, or possess any controlled substance except in a manner authorized by the CSA....The CSA categorizes all controlled substances into five schedules. §812. The drugs are grouped together based on their accepted medical uses, the potential for abuse, and their psychological and physical effects on the body....Each schedule is associated with a distinct set of controls regarding the manufacture, distribution, and use of the substances listed therein....The CSA and its implementing regulations set forth strict requirements regarding registration, labeling and packaging, production quotas, drug security, and recordkeeping....

In enacting the CSA, Congress classified marijuana as a Schedule I drug....This preliminary classification was based, in part, on the recommendation of the Assistant Secretary of HEW "that marihuana be retained within schedule I at least until the completion of certain studies now underway."...Schedule I drugs are categorized as such because of their high potential for abuse, lack of any accepted medical use, and absence of any accepted safety for use in medically supervised treatment....These three factors, in varying gradations, are also used to categorize drugs in the other four schedules. For example, Schedule II substances also have a high potential for abuse which may lead to severe psychological or physical dependence, but unlike Schedule I drugs, they have a currently accepted medical use....By classifying marijuana as a Schedule I drug, as opposed to listing it on a lesser

schedule, the manufacture, distribution, or possession of marijuana became a criminal offense, with the sole exception being use of the drug as part of a Food and Drug Administration pre-approved research study....

The CSA provides for the periodic updating of schedules and delegates authority to the Attorney General, after consultation with the Secretary of Health and Human Services, to add, remove, or transfer substances to, from, or between schedules.... Despite considerable efforts to reschedule marijuana, it remains a Schedule I drug....

III

Respondents in this case do not dispute that passage of the CSA, as part of the Comprehensive Drug Abuse Prevention and Control Act, was well within Congress' commerce power....Nor do they contend that any provision or section of the CSA amounts to an unconstitutional exercise of congressional authority. Rather, respondents' challenge is actually quite limited; they argue that the CSA's categorical prohibition of the manufacture and possession of marijuana as applied to the intrastate manufacture and possession of marijuana for medical purposes pursuant to California law exceeds Congress' authority under the Commerce Clause.

In assessing the validity of congressional regulation, none of our Commerce Clause cases can be viewed in isolation. As charted in considerable detail in *United States v. Lopez*, our understanding of the reach of the Commerce Clause, as well as Congress' assertion of authority thereunder, has evolved over time....The Commerce Clause emerged as the Framers' response to the central problem giving rise to the Constitution itself: the absence of any federal commerce power under the Articles of Confederation....For the first century of our history, the primary use of the Clause was to preclude the kind of discriminatory state legislation that had once been permissible....Then, in response to rapid industrial development and an increasingly interdependent national economy, Congress "ushered in a new era of federal regulation under the commerce power," beginning with the enactment of the Interstate Commerce Act in 1887,... and the Sherman Antitrust Act in 1890....

Our case law firmly establishes Congress' power to regulate purely local activities that are part of an economic "class of activities" that have a substantial effect on interstate commerce....As we stated in *Wickard* [v.Filburn (1942)], "even if appellee's activity be local and though it may not be regarded as commerce, it may still, whatever its nature, be reached by Congress if it exerts a substantial economic effect on interstate commerce."...We have never required Congress to legislate with scientific exactitude. When Congress decides that the "'total incidence'" of a practice poses a threat to a national market, it may regulate....In this vein, we have reiterated that when "'a general regulatory statute bears a substantial relation to commerce, the *de minimis* character of individual instances arising under that statute is of no consequence.'"...

Wickard...establishes that Congress can regulate purely intrastate activity that is not itself "commercial," in that it is not produced for sale, if it concludes that failure to regulate that...activity would undercut the regulation of the interstate market in that commodity....

The similarities between this case and *Wickard* are striking. Like the [wheat] farmer in *Wickard*, respondents are cultivating, for home consumption, a fungible commodity for which there is an established, albeit illegal, interstate market....Just as the Agricultural Adjustment Act [of which Wickard was accused of violating] was designed "to control the volume [of wheat] moving in interstate and foreign commerce in order to avoid surpluses"...and consequently control the market price,...a primary purpose of the CSA is to control the supply and demand of controlled substances in both lawful and unlawful drug markets....

Regulation [of marijuana] is squarely within Congress' commerce power because production of the commodity meant for home consumption, be it wheat or marijuana, has a substantial effect on supply and demand in the national market for that commodity.... In assessing the scope of Congress' authority under the Commerce Clause, we stress that the task before us is a modest one. We need not determine whether respondents' activities, taken in the aggregate, substantially affect interstate commerce in fact, but only whether a "rational basis" exists for so concluding....Given the enforcement difficulties that attend distinguishing between marijuana cultivated locally and marijuana grown elsewhere,...and concerns about diversion into illicit channels,...we have no difficulty concluding that Congress had a rational basis for believing that failure to regulate the intrastate manufacture and possession of marijuana would leave a gaping hole in the CSA. Thus, as in *Wickard*, when it enacted comprehensive legislation to regulate the interstate market in a fungible commodity [wheat], Congress was acting well within its authority to "make all Laws which shall be necessary and proper" to "regulate Commerce... among the several States." U.S. Const., Art. I, §8. That the regulation ensnares some purely intrastate activity is of no moment. As we have done many times before, we refuse to excise individual components of that larger scheme.

IV

To support their contrary submission, respondents rely heavily on two of our more recent Commerce Clause cases. In their myopic focus, they overlook the larger context of modern-era Commerce Clause jurisprudence preserved by those cases. Moreover, even in the narrow prism of respondents' creation, they read those cases far too broadly. Those two cases, of course, are [*United States v.*] *Lopez*,...and [*United States v.*] *Morrison*....As an initial matter, the statutory challenges at issue in those cases were markedly different from the challenge respondents pursue in the case at hand. Here, respondents ask us to excise individual applications of a concededly valid statutory scheme. In contrast, in both *Lopez* and *Morrison*, the parties asserted that a particular statute or provision fell outside Congress' commerce power in its entirety. This distinction is pivotal for we have often reiterated that "where the class of activities is regulated and that class is within the reach of federal power, the courts have no power 'to excise, as trivial, individual instances' of the class."...

At issue in *Lopez*,...was the validity of the Gun-Free School Zones Act of 1990, which was a brief, single-subject statute making it a crime for an individual to possess a gun in a school zone....The Act did not regulate any economic activity and did not contain any requirement that the possession of a gun have any connection to past interstate activity or a predictable impact on future commercial activity. Distinguishing our earlier cases holding that comprehensive regulatory statutes may be validly applied to local conduct that does not, when viewed in isolation, have a significant impact on interstate commerce, we held the statute invalid. We explained:

> "Section 922(q) is a criminal statute that by its terms has nothing to do with 'commerce' or any sort of economic enterprise, however broadly one might define those terms. Section 922(q) is not an essential part of a larger regulation of economic activity, in which the regulatory scheme could be undercut unless the intrastate activity were regulated. It cannot, therefore, be sustained under our cases upholding regulations of activities that arise out of or are connected with a commercial transaction, which viewed in the aggregate, substantially affects interstate commerce..."

The statutory scheme that the Government is defending in this litigation is at the opposite end of the regulatory spectrum. As explained above, the CSA, enacted in 1970 as part of the Comprehensive Drug Abuse Prevention and Control Act,...was a lengthy and detailed statute creating a comprehensive framework for regulating the production, distribution, and possession of five classes of "controlled substances." Most of those substances—those listed in Schedules II through V—"have a useful and legitimate medical purpose and are necessary to maintain the health and general welfare of the American people." …The regulatory scheme is designed to foster the beneficial use of those medications, to prevent their misuse, and to prohibit entirely the possession or use of substances listed in Schedule I, except as a part of a strictly controlled research project.

While the statute provided for the periodic updating of the five schedules, Congress itself made the initial classifications. It identified 42 opiates, 22 opium derivatives, and 17 hallucinogenic substances as Schedule I drugs.…Marijuana was listed as the 10th item in the third subcategory. That classification, unlike the discrete prohibition established by the Gun-Free School Zones Act of 1990, was merely one of many "essential part[s] of a larger regulation of economicactivity, in which the regulatory scheme could be undercut unless the intrastate activity were regulated." …Our opinion in *Lopez* casts no doubt on the validity of such a program.…

The Violence Against Women Act of 1994,…created a federal civil remedy for the victims of gender-motivated crimes of violence.…The remedy was enforceable in both state and federal courts, and generally depended on proof of the violation of a state law. Despite congressional findings that such crimes had an adverse impact on interstate commerce, we held [in *U.S. v. Morrison*] the statute unconstitutional because, like the statute in *Lopez*, it did not regulate economic activity. We concluded that "the noneconomic, criminal nature of the conduct at issue was central to our decision" in *Lopez*, and that our prior cases had identified a clear pattern of analysis: "'Where economic activity substantially affects interstate commerce, legislation regulating that activity will be sustained.'"…

Unlike those at issue in *Lopez* and *Morrison*, the activities regulated by the CSA are quintessentially economic. "Economics" refers to "the production, distribution, and consumption of commodities." …The CSA is a statute that regulates the production, distribution, and consumption of commodities for which there is an established, and lucrative, interstate market. Prohibiting the intrastate possession or manufacture of an article of commerce is a rational (and commonly utilized) means of regulating commerce in that product.…Such prohibitions include specific decisions requiring that a drug be withdrawn from the market as a result of the failure to comply with

regulatory requirements as well as decisions excluding Schedule I drugs entirely from the market. Because the CSA is a statute that directly regulates economic, commercial activity, our opinion in *Morrison* casts no doubt on its constitutionality.

The Court of Appeals was able to conclude otherwise only by isolating a "separate and distinct" class of activities that it held to be beyond the reach of federal power, defined as "the intrastate, noncommercial cultivation, possession and use of marijuana for personal medical purposes on the advice of a physician and in accordance with state law." …The court characterized this class as "different in kind from drug trafficking." …The differences between the members of a class so defined and the principal traffickers in Schedule I substances might be sufficient to justify a policy decision exempting the narrower class from the coverage of the CSA. The question, however, is whether Congress' contrary policy judgment, *i.e.*, its decision to include this narrower "class of activities" within the larger regulatory scheme, was constitutionally deficient. We have no difficulty concluding that Congress acted rationally in determining that none of the characteristics making up the purported class, whether viewed individually or in the aggregate, compelled an exemption from the CSA; rather, the subdivided class of activities defined by the Court of Appeals was an essential part of the larger regulatory scheme.

First, the fact that marijuana is used "for personal medical purposes on the advice of a physician" cannot itself serve as a distinguishing factor.…The CSA designates marijuana as contraband for *any* purpose; in fact, by characterizing marijuana as a Schedule I drug, Congress expressly found that the drug has no acceptable medical uses. Moreover, the CSA is a comprehensive regulatory regime specifically designed to regulate which controlled substances can be utilized for medicinal purposes, and in what manner. Indeed, most of the substances classified in the CSA "have a useful and legitimate medical purpose." …Thus, even if respondents are correct that marijuana does have accepted medical uses and thus should be redesignated as a lesser schedule drug,…the CSA would still impose controls beyond what is required by California law. The CSA requires manufacturers, physicians, pharmacies, and other handlers of controlled substances to comply with statutory and regulatory provisions mandating registration with the DEA, compliance with specific production quotas, security controls to guard against diversion, recordkeeping and reporting obligations, and prescription requirements.…Furthermore, the dispensing of new drugs, even when doctors approve their use, must await federal approval.…Accordingly, the mere fact that marijuana—like virtually every other controlled substance regulated by the CSA—is used for medicinal purposes cannot possibly serve to distinguish it from the core activities regulated by the CSA.

Nor can it serve as an "objective marke[r]" or "objective facto[r]" to arbitrarily narrow the relevant class as the dissenters suggest...More fundamentally, if, as the principal dissent contends, the personal cultivation, possession, and use of marijuana for medicinal purposes is beyond the "'outer limits' of Congress' Commerce Clause authority,"'...it must also be true that such personal use of marijuana (or any other homegrown drug) for recreational purposes is also beyond those "'outer limits,'" whether or not a State elects to authorize or even regulate such use....That is, the dissenters' rationale logically extends to place *any* federal regulation (including quality, prescription, or quantity controls) of *any* locally cultivated and possessed controlled substance for *any* purpose beyond the "'outer limits'" of Congress' Commerce Clause authority. One need not have a degree in economics to understand why a nationwide exemption for the vast quantity of marijuana (or other drugs) locally cultivated for personal use (which presumably would include use by friends, neighbors, and family members) may have a substantial impact on the interstate market for this extraordinarily popular substance. The congressional judgment that an exemption for such a significant segment of the total market would undermine the orderly enforcement of the entire regulatory scheme is entitled to a strong presumption of validity. Indeed, that judgment is not only rational, but "visible to the naked eye,"...under any commonsense appraisal of the probable consequences of such an open-ended exemption.

Second, limiting the activity to marijuana possession and cultivation "in accordance with state law" cannot serve to place respondents' activities beyond congressional reach. The Supremacy Clause unambiguously provides that if there is any conflict between federal and state law, federal law shall prevail. It is beyond peradventure that federal power over commerce is "'superior to that of the States to provide for the welfare or necessities of their inhabitants,'" however legitimate or dire those necessities may be....

Respondents acknowledge this proposition, but nonetheless contend that their activities were not "an essential part of a larger regulatory scheme" because they had been "isolated by the State of California, and [are] policed by the State of California," and thus remain "entirely separated from the market."...The dissenters fall prey to similar reasoning....The notion that California law has surgically excised a discrete activity that is hermetically sealed off from the larger interstate marijuana market is a dubious proposition, and, more importantly, one that Congress could have rationally rejected.

Indeed, that the California exemptions will have a significant impact on both the supply and demand sides of the market for marijuana is not just "plausible" as the principal dissent concedes,...it is readily apparent. The exemption for physicians provides them with an economic incentive to grant their patients permission to use the drug. In contrast to most prescriptions for legal drugs, which limit the dosage and duration of the usage, under California law the doctor's permission to recommend marijuana use is open-ended. The authority to grant permission whenever the doctor determines that a patient is afflicted with "any other illness for which marijuana provides relief,"...is broad enough to allow even the most scrupulous doctor to conclude that some recreational uses would be therapeutic....And our cases have taught us that there are some unscrupulous physicians who overprescribe when it is sufficiently profitable to do so....

The exemption for cultivation by patients and caregivers can only increase the supply of marijuana in the California market....The likelihood that all such production will promptly terminate when patients recover or will precisely match the patients' medical needs during their convalescence seems remote; whereas the danger that excesses will satisfy some of the admittedly enormous demand for recreational use seems obvious....Moreover, that the national and international narcotics trade has thrived in the face of vigorous criminal enforcement efforts suggests that no small number of unscrupulouspeople will make use of the California exemptions to serve their commercial ends whenever it is feasible to do so....Taking into account the fact that California is only one of at least nine States to have authorized the medical use of marijuana, a fact Justice O'Connor's dissent conveniently disregards in arguing that the demonstrated effect on commerce while admittedly "plausible" is ultimately "unsubstantiated."...Congress could have rationally concluded that the aggregate impact on the national market of all the transactions exempted from federal supervision is unquestionably substantial.

So, from the "separate and distinct" class of activities identified by the Court of Appeals (and adopted by the dissenters), we are left with "the intrastate, noncommercial cultivation, possession and use of marijuana."...Thus the case for the exemption comes down to the claim that a locally cultivated product that is used domestically rather than sold on the open market is not subject to federal regulation. Given the findings in the CSA and the undisputed magnitude of the commercial market for marijuana, our decisions in *Wickard v. Filburn* and the later cases endorsing its reasoning foreclose that claim.

V

Respondents also raise a substantive due process claim and seek to avail themselves of the medical necessity defense. These theories of relief were set forth in their complaint but were not reached by the Court of Appeals. We therefore do not address the question whether judicial relief is available to respondents on these alternative bases. We do note, however, the presence of another avenue of relief. As the Solicitor General confirmed during oral argument, the statute authorizes procedures for the reclassification of Schedule I drugs. But perhaps even more important than these legal avenues is the democratic process, in which the voices of voters allied with these respondents may one day be heard in the halls of Congress. Under the present state of the law, however, the judgment of the Court of Appeals must be vacated. The case is remanded for further proceedings consistent with this opinion.

It is so ordered.

Justice O'Connor, with whom The Chief Justice and Justice Thomas join as to all but Part III, dissenting.
We enforce the "outer limits" of Congress' Commerce Clause authority not for their own sake, but to protect historic spheres of state sovereignty from excessive federal encroachment and thereby to maintain the distribution of power fundamental to our federalist system of government....One of federalism's chief virtues, of course, is that it promotes innovation by allowing for the possibility that "a single courageous State may, if its citizens choose, serve as a laboratory; and try novel social and economic experiments without risk to the rest of the country."...

This case exemplifies the role of States as laboratories. The States' core police powers have always included authority to define criminal law and to protect the health, safety, and welfare of their citizens.... Exercising those powers, California (by ballot initiative and then by legislative codification) has come to its own conclusion about the difficult and sensitive question of whether marijuana should be available to relieve severe pain and suffering. Today the Court sanctions an application of the federal Controlled Substances Act that extinguishes that experiment, without any proof that the personal cultivation, possession, and use of marijuana for medicinal purposes, if economic activity in the first place, has a substantial effect on interstate commerce and is therefore an appropriate subject of federal regulation. In so doing, the Court announces a rule that gives Congress a perverse incentive to legislate broadly pursuant to the Commerce Clause—nestling questionable assertions of its authority into comprehensive regulatory schemes— rather than with precision. That rule and the result it produces in this case are irreconcilable with our decisions in *Lopez, supra*, and *United States v. Morrison*.... Accordingly I dissent....

Case Questions

1. What exactly were Raich and Monson asking the Supreme Court to find?
2. What was the Supreme Court's decision?
3. What is your view of the decision in this case?

INTERNET TIP

You can read an edited version of the omitted portion of Justice O'Connor's dissent in the *Raich* case online at the textbook's website.

State Government

The authority that resides in every sovereignty to pass laws for its internal regulation and government is called **police power**. It is the power inherent in the state to pass reasonable laws necessary to preserve public health, welfare, safety, and morals. The states, as sovereigns, were exercising the police power prior to the adoption of the federal constitution, and they never delegated it to the federal government in the U.S. Constitution. In fact, the Constitution itself, in the Tenth Amendment, explicitly reserves to the states (or to the people) any power not delegated to the federal government. Although the police power exists without any express limitations in the U.S. Constitution, the federal and state constitutions set limits on its exercise.

The basis of the police power is the state's obligation to protect its citizens and provide for the safety and order of society. This yields a broad, comprehensive authority. The definition of crimes and the regulating of trades and professions are examples of this vast scope of power. A mandatory precondition to the exercise of police power is the existence of an ascertainable public need for a particular statute, and the statute must bear a real and substantial relation to the end that is sought. The possession and enjoyment of all rights may be limited under the police power, provided that it is reasonably exercised.

Limitations on the police power have never been drawn with exactness or determined by a general formula. The power may not be exercised for private purposes or for the exclusive benefit of a few. Its scope has been declared to be greater in emergency situations. Otherwise its exercise must be in the public interest, must be reasonable, and may not be repugnant to the rights implied or secured in the Constitution.

Powers delegated by the federal government and individual state constitutions also serve as a basis for state legislation. Any activity solely attributable to the sovereignty of the state may not be restrained by Congress.

Federal Supremacy

The U.S. Constitution divides powers between the federal government and the states. Certain powers are delegated to the federal government alone. Others are reserved to the states. Still others are exercised concurrently by both. The Tenth Amendment to the Constitution specifies that the "powers not delegated to the United States by the Constitution...are reserved to the states...or to the people." Unlike the federal power, which is granted, the state already has its power, unless expressly or implicitly denied by the state or federal constitutions. Each state has the power to govern its

own affairs, except where the Constitution has withdrawn that power.

The powers of both the federal and state governments are to be exercised so as not to interfere with each other's exercise of power. Whenever there is a conflict, state laws must yield to federal acts to the extent of the conflict. This requirement is expressed by the **Supremacy Clause** in Article VI of the Constitution.

Under the Supremacy Clause, Congress can enact legislation that may supersede state authority and preempt state regulations. The preemption doctrine is based on the Supremacy Clause. Hence state laws that frustrate or are contrary to congressional objectives in a specific area are invalid. In considering state law, one takes into account the nature of the subject matter, any vital national interests that may be involved, or perhaps the need for uniformity between state and federal laws, and the expressed or implied intent of Congress. It is necessary to determine whether Congress has sought to occupy a particular field to theexclusion of the states. All interests, both state and federal, must be examined.

Constitutionality of Statutes The power to declare legislative acts unconstitutional is the province and the duty of the judiciary, even though there is no express constitutional grant of the power. It is generally presumed that all statutes are constitutional and that a statute will not be invalidated unless the party challenging it clearly shows that it is offensive to either a state or federal constitution. When a court encounters legislation that it believes to be unconstitutional, it first tries to interpret the statute in a narrow way with what is called a limiting construction. An act of the legislature is declared invalid only as a last resort if it is clearly incompatible with a constitutional provision.

The right and power of the courts to declare whether the legislature has exceeded the constitutional limitations is one of the highest functions of the judiciary. The Supreme Court declared in *Marbury v. Madison*, 5 U.S. (1 Cranch) 137 (1803) that the judicial branch has the power to declare void an act of the legislature that conflicts with the Constitution. The issue of the supremacy of the U.S. Constitution, and the right of individuals to claim protection thereunder whenever they were aggrieved by application of a contrary statute, was decided in *Marbury*. Chief Justice John Marshall wrote the opinion for the Court, stating in part:

> The question, whether an act, repugnant to the Constitution, can become the law of the land, is a question deeply interesting to the United States; but, happily, not of an intricacy proportioned to its interest. It seems only necessary to recognize certain principles, supposed to have been long and well established, to decide it.
>
> That the people have an original right to establish, for their future government, such principles as, in their opinion, shall most conduce to their own happiness, is the basis on which the whole American fabric has been erected. The exercise of this original right is a very great exertion; nor can it, nor ought it, to be frequently repeated. The principles, therefore, so established, are deemed fundamental. And as the authority from which they proceed is supreme, and can seldom act, they are designated to be permanent.
>
> …It is a proposition too plain to be contested, that the Constitution controls any legislative act repugnant to it; or that the legislature may alter the Constitution by an ordinary act.
>
> Between these alternatives there is no middle ground. The Constitution iseither a superior paramount law, unchangeable by ordinary means, or it is on a level with ordinary legislative acts, and, like other acts, is alterable when the legislature shall please to alter it.
>
> If the former part of the alternative be true, then a legislative act, contrary to the Constitution, is not law; if the latter part be true, then written constitutions are absurd attempts, on the part of the people,

> to limit a power, in its own nature illimitable.…
>
> It is, emphatically, the province and duty of the judicial department to say what the law is. Those who apply the rule to particular cases must of necessity expound and interpret that rule. If two laws conflict with each other, the courts must decide on the operation of each.
>
> So, if a law be in opposition to the Constitution; if both the law and the Constitution apply to a particular case, so that the court must either decide that case, conformable to the law, disregarding the Constitution, or conformable to the Constitution, disregarding the law; the court must determine which of the conflicting rules governs the case. This is of the very essence of judicial duty.
>
> If, then, the courts are to regard the Constitution—and the Constitution issuperior to any ordinary act of the legislature—the Constitution, and not suchordinary act, must govern the case to which they both apply.

Ex Post Facto Laws and Bills of Attainder

Article I, Section 9, of the federal Constitution prohibits Congress from enacting **ex post facto** laws or **bills of attainder**. The state legislatures are likewise prohibited by Article I, Section 10.

An ex post facto law is a law that makes acts criminal that were not criminal at the time they were committed. Statutes that classify a crime more severely than when committed, impose greater punishment, or make proof of guilt easier have also been held to be unconstitutional ex post facto laws. Such laws deprive an accused of a substantial right provided by the law that was in force at the time when the offense was committed.

The Ex Post Facto Clause restricts legislative power and does not apply to the judicial function. The doctrine applies exclusively to criminal or penal statutes. A law's ex post facto impact may not be avoided by disguising criminal punishment in a civil form. When a law imposes punishment for certain activity in both the past and future, even though it is void for the punishment of past activity, it is valid insofar as the law acts prospectively. A law is not ex post facto if it "mitigates the rigor" of the law or simply reenacts the law in force when the crime was committed.

To determine if a legislative act unconstitutionally punishes past activity, courts examine the intent of the legislature. The court, after examining the text of the law and its legislative history, makes a determination as to whether an act that imposes a present disqualification is, in fact, merely the imposition of a punishment for a past event. The principle governing the inquiry is whether the aim of the legislature was to punish an individual for past activity, or whether a restriction on a person is merely incident to a valid regulation of a present situation, such as the appropriate qualifications for a profession.

A constitutionally prohibited bill of attainder involves the singling out of an individual or group for punishment. Bills of attainder are acts of a legislature that apply either to named individuals or to easily ascertainable members of a group in such a way as to impose punishments on them without a trial. For example, an act of Congress that made it a crime for a member of the Communist Party to serve as an officer of a labor union was held unconstitutional as a bill of attainder (*United States v. Brown*, 381 U.S. 437, 1965).

Statutory Construction

To declare what the law shall be is a legislative power; to declare what the law *is* is a judicial power. The courts are the appropriate body for construing acts of the legislature. Since courts decide only real controversies and not abstract or moot questions, a court does not construe statutory provisions unless doing so is required for the resolution of a case before it. A statute is open to construction only when the language used in the act is ambiguous and requires interpretation. Where the statutory language conveys a clear and definite meaning, there is no occasion to use rules of statutory interpretation.

Courts have developed rules of statutory construction to determine the meaning of legislative acts. For interpreting statutes, the legislative will is the all-important and controlling factor. In theory, the sole object of all rules for interpreting statutes is to discover the legislative intent; every other rule of construction is secondary.

It is the duty of the judiciary in construing criminal statutes to determine whether particular conduct falls within the intended prohibition of the statute. Criminal statutes are enforced by the court if worded so that they clearly convey the nature of the proscribed behavior. Legislation must be appropriately tailored to meet its objectives. Therefore it cannot be arbitrary, unreasonable, or capricious. A court will hold a statute void for vagueness if it does not give a person of ordinary intelligence fair notice that some contemplated conduct is forbidden by the act. The enforcement of a vague statute would encourage arbitrary and erratic arrests and convictions.

Penal statutes impose punishment for offenses committed against the state. They include all statutes that command or prohibit certain acts and establish penalties for their violation. Penal statutes are enacted for the benefit of the public. They should receive a fair and reasonable construction. The words used should be given the meaning commonly attributed to them. Criminal statutes are to be strictly construed, and doubts are to be resolved in favor of the accused. **Strict construction** means that the statute should not be enlarged by implication beyond the fair meaning of the language used. However, the statute should not be construed so as to defeat the obvious intention of the legislature.

A literal interpretation of statutory language can lead to unreasonable, unjust, or even absurd consequences. In such a case, a court is justified in adopting a construction that sustains the validity of the legislative act, rather than one that defeats it.

Courts do not have legislative authority and should avoid "judicial legislation." To depart from the meaning expressed by the words of the statute so as to alter it is not construction—it is legislative alteration. A statute should not be construed more broadly or given greater effect than its terms require. Nothing should be read into a statute that was not intended by the legislature. Courts, however, don't always adhere to the principle.

Statutes are to be read in the light of conditions at the time of their enactment. A new meaning is sometimes given to the words of an old statute because of changed conditions. The scope of a statute may appear to include conduct that did not exist when the statute was enacted—for example, certain activity related to technological progress. Such a case does not preclude the application of the statute thereto.

ADMINISTRATIVE AGENCIES

As we will see in more detail in Chapter XIII, legislative bodies often delegate some of their authority to governmental entities called agencies, boards, authorities, and commissions. Legislatures do this when they lack expertise in an area requiring constant oversight and specialized knowledge. Agencies such as the Environmental Protection Agency; the Securities and Exchange Commission; the boards that license doctors, attorneys, and barbers; and public housing authorities are other examples.

Legislative bodies often permit the agencies to exercise investigative and rulemaking powers. Administrative rules, if promulgated according to law, have the same force as statutes. Some agencies also are delegated authority to conduct adjudicatory hearings before administrative law judges who will determine whether agency rules have been violated.

JUDICIAL DECISION MAKING

Legislators are not able to enact laws that address every societal problem. Sometimes a court encounters a case that presents a problem that has not been previously litigated within the jurisdiction. In such a case, the court will try to base its decision on a statute, ordinance, or administrative regulation. If none can be found, it will base its decision on general principles of the common law (principles that have been judicially recognized as precedent in previous cases). This judge-made law has an effect similar to a statute in such situations. Legislatures can modify or replace judge-made law either by passing legislation or through constitutional amendment.

In this portion of the chapter, we will learn about the use of common law precedents and how judges determine which body of substantive law to apply when the facts of a case involve the laws of more than one state.

One of the most fundamental principles of the common law is the doctrine of **stare decisis**. A doctrine is a policy, in this case a judicial policy that guides courts in making decisions. The doctrine normally requires lower-level courts to follow the legal precedents that have been established by higher-level courts. Following precedent helps to promote uniformity and predictability in judicial decision making. All judges within a jurisdiction are expected to apply a rule of law the same way until that rule is overturned by a higher court.

Following Precedent

Literally, stare decisis means that a court will "stand by its decisions" or those of a higher court. This doctrine originated in England and was used in the colonies as the basis of their judicial decisions.

A decision on an issue of law by a court is followed in that jurisdiction by the same court or by a lower court in a future case presenting the same—or substantially the same—issue of law. A court is not bound by decisions of courts of other states, although such decisions may be considered in the decision-making process. A decision of the U.S. Supreme Court on a federal question is absolutely binding on state courts, as well as on lower federal courts. Similarly, a decision of a state court of final appeal on an issue of state law is followed by lower state courts and federal courts in the state dealing with that issue.

The doctrine of stare decisis promotes continuity, stability, justice, speed, economy, and adaptability within the law. It helps our legal system to provide guidelines so that people can anticipate legal consequences when they decide how to conduct their affairs. It promotes justice by establishing rules that enable many legal disputes to be concluded fairly. It eliminates the need for every proposition in every case to be subject to endless relitigation. Public faith in the judiciary is increased where legal rules are consistently applied and are the product of impersonal and reasoned judgment. In addition, the quality of the law decided on is improved, as more careful and thorough consideration is given to the legal questions than would be the case if the determinations affected only the case before the court.

Stare decisis is not a binding rule, and a court need not feel absolutely bound to follow previous cases. However, courts are not inclined to deviate from it, especially when the precedents have been treated as authoritative law for a long time. The number of decisions announced on a rule of law also has some bearing on the weight of the precedent. When a principle of law established by precedent is no longer appropriate because of changing economic, political, and social conditions, however, courts should recognize this decay and overrule the precedent to reflect what is best for society.

The Holding of the Case

Under the doctrine of stare decisis, only a point of law necessarily decided in a reported judicial opinion is binding on other courts as precedent. A question of fact determined by a court has no binding effect on a subsequent case involving similar questions of fact. The facts of each case are recognized as being unique.

Those points of law decided by a court to resolve a legal controversy constitute the **holding** of the case. In other words, the court holds (determines) that a certain rule of law applies to the particular factual situation present in the case being decided and renders its decision accordingly.

Sometimes, in their opinions, courts make comments that are not necessary to support the decision. These extraneous judicial expressions are referred to as **dictum**. They have no value as precedent because they do not fit the facts of the case. The reason for drawing a distinction between holding and dictum is that only the issues before the court have been argued and fully considered. Even though dictum is not binding under the doctrine of stare decisis, it is often considered persuasive. Other judges and lawyers can determine what the decision makers are thinking and gain an indication of how the problem may be handled in the future.

It is the task of the lawyer and judge to find the decision or decisions that set the precedent for a particular factual situation. In court, lawyers argue about whether a prior case should or should not be recognized as controlling in a subsequent case.

The Ohio Supreme Court had to make such a decision in the following 1969 case. Did the prosecution violate Butler's federal due process rights when it used his voluntary, in-custody statement (that was obtained without prior *Miranda* warnings) to **impeach** his trial testimony? The U.S. Supreme Court had ruled in a 1954 case (*Walder v. United States*) that prosecutors could impeach a testifying defendant with illegally obtained evidence once the defendant had "opened the door" with false testimony. The U.S. Supreme Court's *Miranda v. Arizona* (1966) opinion seemed to suggest that constitutional due process prevented the government from using such statements for any purpose. In *Miranda*, however, the prosecution had used the defendant's statement to prove guilt, not to impeach the defendant's testimony. Butler's lawyer argued to the Ohio Supreme Court that (1) the language contained in *Miranda* applied to impeachment uses, (2) *Miranda* should be recognized as controlling, and (3) Butler's statement was inadmissible. The lawyers for the State of Ohio disagreed. They argued (1) *Miranda* was not controlling, because

Butler's facts were distinguishable from the facts in *Miranda*;, (2) the *Walder* case was controlling;, and (3) Butler's statement was admissible for purposes of impeachment.

State v. Butler
19 Ohio St. 2d 55, 249 N.E.2d 818
Supreme Court of Ohio
July 9, 1969

Schneider, Justice

...The offense for which appellant was indicted, tried, and convicted occurred on August 30, 1964. He struck Annie Ruth Sullivan with a jack handle, causing an injury which resulted in loss of sight [in] her left eye. Appellant was apprehended and arrested by the Cincinnati police, and while in custody he was interrogated by police officers. Prior to the questioning, the police gave no explanation to appellant as to his rights to remain silent and have an attorney present. The interrogation was recorded and reduced to writing. Over objection by appellant's counsel, these questions and answers were repeated by the prosecutor at trial to impeach statements made by appellant during cross-examination.

Appellant appeared before the municipal court of Hamilton County on November 22, 1965. Probable cause was found and appellant was bound over to the Hamilton County grand jury. Bond was set at $500, which appellant posted. The grand jury returned an indictment for the offense of "maiming." Appellant was arraigned and pleaded not guilty, after which the court appointed counsel. Trial was set. A jury was waived and appellant was found guilty by the court of the lesser included offense of aggravated assault. The court of appeals affirmed the judgment of conviction.

Appellant raises [the question in this appeal as to] whether, in cross-examination of a defendant the prosecutor may use prior inconsistent statements of the defendant, made to police without *Miranda* warnings, in order to impeach his credibility....

Appellant's...contention is that the prosecution violated his Fifth Amendment right against self-incrimination by using statements of his which were made to police during in-custody interrogation with no warning of his right to silence or to counsel....The

United States Supreme Court...in *Miranda v. Arizona* [1966]...held there that the prosecution's use of statements of an accused, made to police without prior warnings of his rights to remain silent, to counsel and appointed counsel if indigent, was a violation of the accused's Fourteenth and Fifth Amendment right against self-incrimination....

The appellant took the stand and, on cross-examination by the prosecution, he made assertions as to the facts surrounding the crime. A recorded statement appellant made to a detective after arrest was then read to him to show a prior inconsistent statement. Counsel objected, but the court allowed the statement to be used as evidence to impeach the witness's credibility. Appellant contends that this use of the statements, made without cautionary warnings, violated his Fifth Amendment rights as defined by *Miranda v. Arizona, supra*....

We cannot agree. First, the statements used by the prosecution were not offered by the state as part of its direct case against appellant, but were offered on the issue of his credibility after he had been sworn and testified in his own defense. Second, the statements used by the prosecution were voluntary, no claim to the contrary having been made.

The distinction between admissibility of wrongfully obtained evidence to prove the state's case in chief and its use to impeach the credibility of a defendant who takes the stand was expressed in *Walder v. United States* [1954]...."It is one thing to say that the government cannot make an affirmative use of evidence unlawfully obtained. It is quite another to say that the defendant can turn the illegal method by which evidence in the Government's possession was obtained to his own advantage, and provide himself with a shield against contradiction of his untruths..."

Those words of Justice Frankfurter were uttered in regard to evidence inadmissible under the Fourth Amendment exclusionary rule. In the case of the Fifth Amendment, even greater reason exists to distinguish between statements of an accused used in the prosecution's direct case and used for impeachment in cross-examining the accused when he takes the stand. We must not lose sight of the words of the Fifth Amendment: "...nor shall be compelled to be a witness against himself..." This is a privilege accorded an accused not to be compelled to testify, nor to have any prior statements used by the prosecution to prove his guilt. We cannot translate those words into a privilege to lie with impunity once he elects to take the stand to testify...

We do not believe that...Miranda...dictates a conclusion contrary to ours. In Miranda, the court indicated that statements of a defendant used to impeach his testimony at trial may not be used unless they were taken with full warnings and effective waiver. However, we note that in all four of the convictions reversed by the decision, statements of the accused, taken without cautionary warnings, were used by the prosecution as direct evidence of guilt in the case in chief.

We believe that the words of Chief Justice Marshall regarding the difference between holding and *dictum* are applicable here. "It is a maxim not to be disregarded, that general expressions, in every opinion, are to be taken in connection with the case in which those expressions are used. If they go beyond the case, they may be respected, but ought not to control the judgment in a subsequent suit when the very point is presented for decision. The reason of this maxim is obvious. The question actually before the court is investigated with care, and considered in its full extent. Other principles which may serve to illustrate it are considered in their relation to the case decided, but their possible bearing on all other cases is seldom completely investigated."...

The court, in Miranda, was not faced with the facts of this case. Thus, we do not consider ourselves bound by the *dictum* of Miranda.

The "linchpin" (as Mr. Justice Harlan put it...) of Miranda is that police interrogation is destructive of human dignity and disrespectful of the inviolability of the human personality. In the instant case, the use of the interrogation to impeach the voluntary testimony of the accused is neither an assault on his dignity nor disrespectful of his personality. He elected to testify, and cannot complain that the state seeks to demonstrate the lack of truth in his testimony.

Finally, we emphasize that the statements used by the prosecution were voluntarily made. The decision in Miranda did not discard the distinction between voluntary and involuntary statements made by an accused and used by the prosecution...Lack of cautionary warnings is one of the factors to consider in determining whether statements are voluntary or not. However, appellant here has never claimed that the statements used to impeach were involuntary. Thus, we assume they were voluntary, and hold that voluntary statements of an accused made to police without cautionary warnings are admissible on the issue of credibility after defendant has been sworn and testifies in his own defense....

Judgment affirmed.

Duncan, Justice, dissenting

...The use of statements made by the defendant for impeachment without the warnings set forth in Miranda v. Arizona...having been given, is reversible error.

In Miranda, Chief Justice Warren stated...

"The warnings required and the waiver necessary in accordance with our opinion today are, in the absence of a fully effective equivalent, prerequisites to the admissibility of *any statement made by a defendant*. No distinction can be drawn between statements which are direct confessions and statements which amount to 'admissions' of part or all of an offense. The privilege against self-incrimination protects the individual from being compelled to incriminate himself in any manner; it does not distinguish degrees of incrimination. Similarly, for precisely the same reason, *no distinction may be drawn between inculpatory statements and statements alleged to be merely 'exculpatory.'* If a statement made were in fact truly exculpatory, it would, of course, never be used by the prosecution. *In fact, statements merely intended to be exculpatory by the defendant are often used to impeach his testimony at trial or to demonstrate untruths in the statement given under interrogation and thus to prove guilt by implication.* These statements are incriminating in any meaningful sense of the word and may not be used without the full warnings and effective waiver required for any other statement."...
[Emphasis supplied.]

This *specific* reference to impeachment, I believe, forecloses the use of defendant's in-custody statement in the instant case.

The United States Court of Appeals for the Second Circuit…arrived at a decision contrary to that arrived at by the majority in this case. Judge Bryan…stated:

"These pronouncements by the Supreme Court may be technically *dictum*. But it is abundantly plain that the court intended to lay down a firm general rule with respect to the use of statements unconstitutionally obtained from a defendant in violation of *Miranda* standards. The rule prohibits the use of such statements whether inculpatory or exculpatory, whether bearing directly on guilt or on collateral matters only, and whether used on direct examination or for impeachment."…

I would reverse.

Case Questions

1. Explain the difference between holding and dictum.
2. Can the holding of a case be broader than the precedent relied on?
3. Why should dictum not be considered binding under the doctrine of stare decisis?
4. Was *Miranda* properly relied on by the majority in the *Butler* case?
5. If this same case had been decided by the United States Court of Appeals for the Second Circuit, would the decision have been different or the same? Why?

Requirements for a Precedent

Only a judicial opinion of the majority of a court on a point of law can have stare decisis effect. A dissent has no precedential value, nor does the fact that an appellate court is split make the majority's decision less of a precedent. When judges are equally divided, as to the outcome of a particular case, no precedent is created by that court. This is true even though the decision affirms the decision of the next-lower court.

In addition, in order to create precedent, the opinion must be reported. A decision by a court without a reported opinion does not have stare decisis effect. In the great majority of cases, no opinion is written. Appellate courts are responsible for practically all the reported opinions, although occasionally a trial judge will issue a written opinion relating to a case tried to the court. Trial judges do not write opinions in jury cases.

Once a reported judicial precedent-setting opinion is found, the effective date of that decision has to be determined. For this purpose, the date of the court decision, not the date of the events that gave rise to the suit, is crucial.

The Retroactive-Versus-Prospective Application Question

A court has the power to declare in its opinion whether a precedent-setting decision should have retroactive or prospective application. **Retroactive effect** means that the decision controls the legal consequences of some causes of action arising prior to the announcement of the decision. **Prospective effect** means that the new rule will only apply to cases subsequently coming before that court and the lower courts of the jurisdiction. Prior to the U.S. Supreme Court's 1993 decision in *Harper v. Virginia Dep't of Taxation*, the general rule in civil cases was that unless a precedent-setting court had expressly indicated otherwise, or unless special circumstances warranted the denial of retroactive application, an appellate court decision was entitled to retroactive as well as prospective effect in all actions that were neither *res judicata* (not previously decided) nor barred by a **statute of limitations**, (meaning the plaintiff's lawsuit cannot go forward because of the plaintiff's failure to start the action within the period of time allowed for that purpose by state statute. This topic is more thoroughly discussed in Chapter IV). This pre-*Harper* approach was based on the U.S. Supreme Court's decision in a 1971 case, *Chevron Oil Co. v. Huson*. The U.S. Supreme Court's decision in *Harper* prohibited federal courts from applying a decision prospectively. Each state then had to decide whether or not to continue following the *Chevron* approach. This was the question before the Montana Supreme Court in the 2004 case of *Dempsey v. Allstate Insurance Company*.

The following excerpt from the majority opinion in *Dempsey* provides an excellent summary of the evolution of the law as it relates to retroactivity. Readers may recall from Chapter I references to Sir William Blackstone as an important figure in the development of the common law and to the philosophical school known as legal realism. Notice how Justice Leaphart in the *Dempsey* opinion contrasts Blackstone's belief that judges "discover law" with the view of the legendary legal realist, Justice Oliver Wendell Holmes, that judges make law.

Dempsey v. Allstate Insurance Company
104 P.3d. 483
Supreme Court of Montana
December 30, 2004

Justice W. William Leaphart delivered the Opinion of the Court
[The "Factual and Procedural Background" segment of this opinion has been omitted in order to focus on the court's discussion about whether decisions should apply prospectively.]

Discussion
In 1971 the United States Supreme Court announced *Chevron Oil Co. v. Huson* (1971), 404 U.S. 97....*Chevron* laid out a flexible three-factored test for whether a decision applies prospectively only. We adopted the *Chevron* test for questions of Montana law...and subsequently applied it several times...In the meantime, the United States Supreme Court revisited the question of prospective application several times and eventually overruled *Chevron* in *Harper v. Virginia Dep't of Taxation* (1993)....

...[I]t appeared that we would follow the rule of the United States Supreme Court's *Harper* decision. However, subsequent decisions did not bear that out ... [as] we applied the *Chevron* test to determine whether prospective application was appropriate....Given our long history of applying decisions prospectively we cannot ignore these recent decisions applying the *Chevron* test....As we explain later in this opinion, the two lines of cases may be comfortably merged into a rule of retroactivity in keeping with the last seventy years of this Court's jurisprudence....

A. A Brief History of Retroactivity
The retroactive/prospective distinction is relatively new to our common law tradition. In the days of Blackstone

the law was understood as something that the courts applied, not something that they made. Accordingly, it made no sense for a court to comment on whether its ruling applied retroactively or not. Its ruling was simply the law as it is and always was...("[T]he Blackstonian model takes law as a timeless constant, always (optimistically) assuming the correctness of the current decision. Prior inconsistent decisions are and always were incorrect.")

This view, of course, is no longer even remotely fashionable in today's climate of legal realism and aversion to castles in the clouds. Justice Holmes, the great realist of his time, was one of the first to see past Blackstone and spy the retroactive/prospective distinction. In endorsing what we now call "retroactivity" he characterized common law adjudication not as a search for an entity separate from the courts, but as an act of creation, stating "[t]he law of a State does not become something outside of the state court and independent of it by being called the common law. Whatever it is called it is the law as declared by the state judges and nothing else." *Kuhn v. Fairmont Coal Co.* (1910)... (Holmes, J., dissenting).

After flirting with the issue of prospective decisions in a handful of now defunct....common law cases, the Court ruled in 1932 that a state supreme court does not violate the United States Constitution by giving a decision mere prospective effect. *Great N. Ry. Co. v. Sunburst Oil & Ref. Co.* (1932),...("A state in defining the limits of adherence to precedent may make a choice for itself between the principle of forward operations and that of relation backward.")....

After receiving the United States Supreme Court's blessing in *Great Northern* this Court used its power to prospectively apply its decisions when it saw fit.... The United States Supreme Court fully endorsed and justified its own use of prospective application in 1965 with *Linkletter v. Walker*.... In *Linkletter* the Warren Court was faced with an extraordinarily explosive issue. Four years before, [in] *Mapp v. Ohio* (1961)... the Court had ruled that the exclusionary rule applies against the states. Linkletter argued that his conviction was obtained through evidence that should have been inadmissible under the exclusionary rule. Even though he was convicted and his case became final before the *Mapp* ruling, he reasoned that because the decisions of the United States Supreme Court apply retroactively he must be granted habeas corpus relief....

If the Court had granted Linkletter's request, thousands of otherwise properly obtained convictions would have immediately become suspect. The Court found such retroactive application too great a disruption of the criminal justice system.... Also, applying *Mapp* to cases closed before its issuance would do nothing to further the policy behind the exclusionary rule—deterrence of unconstitutional police actions..... Therefore, after weighing these factors and others, the Court concluded it was prudent to rule that cases final before the *Mapp* decision were unaffected by it.

In 1971 the Court extended this flexible approach to civil cases in *Chevron Oil Co. v. Huson* (1971).... In applying a prior decision that had greatly changed the operation of statutes of limitations under the Outer Continental Shelf Lands Act, the Court adopted a version of the nonretroactivity test used in its criminal cases. In the context of criminal appeals, the three factors of the test were as follows:

> First, the decision to be applied nonretroactively must establish a new principle of law, either by overruling clear past precedent on which litigants may have relied or by deciding an issue of first impression whose resolution was not clearly foreshadowed. Second, it has been stressed that "we must... weigh the merits and demerits in each case by looking to the prior history of the rule in question, its purpose and effect, and whether retrospective operation will further or retard its operation." Finally, we have weighed the inequity imposed by retroactive application, for "[w]here a decision of this Court could produce substantial inequitable results if applied retroactively, there is ample basis in our cases for avoiding the injustice or hardship by a holding of nonretroactivity."

...With this test in place the federal courts had flexibility to grant nonretroactive relief to litigants who had justifiably relied on old rules of law when there was no indication that the rule would change. Gone was any pretense that the law that the courts announce is the law as it has always been.

B. The Decline and Fall of Chevron.

The United States Supreme Court's tolerance of prospective decisions did not last long. After indicating several times that it was not satisfied with current doctrine, the Court finally overruled itself in 1987, jettisoning the *Linkletter* approach. *Griffith v. Kentucky* (1987),... The Court announced a new rule requiring that all criminal decisions apply retroactively to all cases "pending on direct review or not yet final."... It reasoned that it was unfair to announce a new rule that would affect some defendants and not others merely because of the timing of their prosecutions...

It was only a matter of time before this approach to retroactivity in criminal cases found its way into the Court's civil jurisprudence.... [T]he Court announced [in *Harper v. Virginia Dep't of Taxation,* 509 U.S. 86 (1993) that due to the inequities inherent in a flexible *Chevron* approach, federal rules of law may not be selectively applied prospectively....

After *Harper,* the *Chevron* test no longer had any applicability to interpretations of federal law, whether in federal or state court. The *Harper* decision is grounded in fairness and the arbitrariness of "temporal barriers," rather than a renewed embrace of Blackstone's theory of law "existing" independently of a court's decisions.

C. Revolt in the Provinces: Chevron *is Alive and Well in the State Courts*

Chevron concerned a federal question, and thus only governed issues of federal law. Therefore, although the United States Supreme Court has rejected *Chevron,* the states are free to continue employing the *Chevron* criteria in deciding questions of retroactivity of state law. Prior to *Harper,* the *Chevron* approach proved popular in state courts....

The state courts' reactions to *Harper* have been decidedly mixed, with many expressing disagreement, if not open hostility. For example, the Supreme Court of New Hampshire voiced support for the rejection of *Chevron....* However, inspired by Justice O'Connor's dissent in *Harper,* the court reserved for itself the authority to give new rules prospective effect, but that if a rule is applied retroactively to the parties before the court, it must be given uniform retroactive effect.... In contrast, the New Mexico Supreme Court took great issue with much of *Harper, ...* [constructing] a *presumption* in favor of retroactivity "in lieu of the hard-and-fast rule prescribed for federal cases in

Harper.".... Many states are uncomfortable with the harsh results that might follow if they abandon *Chevron* and completely disallow prospective decisions.

D. *Reserving* Chevron *as an Exception*

Our precedent allows for a compromise between the powerful arguments of the *Harper* court and the compelling need for prospective application in limited circumstances....

We agree with the *Harper* court that limiting a rule of law to its prospective application creates an arbitrary distinction between litigants based merely on the timing of their claims. Interests of fairness are not served by drawing such a line, nor are interests of finality. In the interests of finality, the line should be drawn between claims that are final and those that are not (the line drawn in *Harper*).... We have already recognized the arbitrary nature of prospective decisions in the criminal context...[and] ...in keeping with the United States Supreme Court's opinion in *Griffith,* we overruled all of our prior decisions which limited a new judicial rule of criminal procedure to prospective application....

We also understand, however, that what follows from civil litigation is different in kind from the consequences inherent in a criminal prosecution and conviction. On many occasions we have noted the disruption that a new rule of law can bring to existing contracts and to other legal relationships. Therefore today we reaffirm our general rule that "[w]e give retroactive effect to judicial decisions,"...We will, however, allow for an exception to that rule when faced with a truly compelling case for applying a new rule of law prospectively only.

The *Chevron* test is still viable as an exception to the rule of retroactivity. However, given that we wish prospective applications to be the exception, we will only invoke the *Chevron* exception when a party has satisfied *all three* of the *Chevron* factors....

Therefore, we conclude that, in keeping with our prior cases, all civil decisions of this court apply retroactively to cases pending on direct review or not yet final, unless all three of the *Chevron* factors are satisfied. For reasons of finality we also conclude that the retroactive effect of a decision does not apply ....to cases that became final or were settled prior to a decision's issuance....

Case Questions

1. Based what you have read about the history of the rule of retroactivity, do you see any fundamental problems with the *Harper v. Virginia Department of Taxation* decision that could in the future threaten its survival as a precedent?
2. Think about the positions advocated by Sir William Blackstone and Justice Oliver Wendell Holmes with respect to whether judges "discover law" or "make law." How would you characterize the decision-making process followed by the Montana Supreme Court in reaching its conclusions in *Dempsey*?

 Do you believe that ethical considerations played any role in the Montana Supreme Court's decision not to exclusively follow the rule promulgated by the U.S. Supreme Court in *Harper v. Virginia Department of Taxation*?

Absence of Precedent

When judges are confronted by a novel fact situation, they must rely on their own sense of justice and philosophy of law. The public interest, tradition, prevailing customs, business usage, and moral standards are important considerations in the decision-making process. Judges encountering a case of first impression first look for guidance within the forum state. When precedent is lacking in the forum state, decisions of other state and federal courts, as well as English decisions, may be considered persuasive on the legal point at issue.

The trial court in the following case encountered a problem that was unique. The trial and appellate courts were required to make decisions without being able to benefit from the experience of others as reflected in statutory law and common law opinions. They had to create new law when life and death were at stake. Note that three of the seven members of the appellate court dissented.

Strunk v. Strunk
445 S.W.2d 145
Court of Appeals of Kentucky
September 26, 1969

Osborne, Judge

The specific question involved upon this appeal is: Does a court of equity have power to permit a kidney to be removed from an incompetent ward of the state upon petition of his committee, who is also his mother, for the purpose of being transplanted into the body of his brother, who is dying of a fatal kidney disease? We are of the opinion it does.

The facts of the case are as follows: Arthur L. Strunk, 54 years of age, and Ava Strunk, 52 years of age, of Williamstown, Kentucky, are the parents of two sons. Tommy Strunk is 28 years of age, married, an employee of the Penn State Railroad and a part-time student at the University of Cincinnati. Tommy is now suffering from chronic glomerus nephritis, a fatal kidney disease. He is now being kept alive by frequent treatment on an artificial kidney, a procedure that cannot be continued much longer.

Jerry Strunk is 27 years of age, incompetent, and through proper legal proceedings has been committed to the Frankfort State Hospital and School, which is a state institution maintained for the feeble-minded. He has an IQ of approximately 35, which corresponds with the mental age of approximately six years. He is further handicapped by a speech defect, which makes it difficult for him to communicate with persons who are not well acquainted with him. When it was determined that Tommy, in order to survive, would have to have a kidney, the doctors considered the possibility of using a kidney from a cadaver if and when one became available, or one from a live donor if this could be made available. The entire family, his mother, father, and a number of collateral relatives, were tested. Because of incompatibility of blood type or tissue, none was medically acceptable as a live donor. As a last resort, Jerry was tested and found to be highly acceptable. This immediately presented the legal problem as to what, if anything, could be done by the family, especially the mother and the father, to procure a transplant from Jerry to Tommy. The mother as a committee petitioned the county court for authority to proceed with the operation. The court found that the operation was necessary, that under the peculiar circumstances of this case, it would not only be beneficial to Tommy but also beneficial to Jerry because Jerry was greatly dependent on Tommy, emotionally and psychologically, and that his well-being would be jeopardized more severely by the loss of his brother than by the removal of a kidney.

Appeal was taken to the Franklin Circuit Court where the chancellor reviewed the record, examined the testimony of the witnesses, and adopted the findings of the county court.

A psychiatrist, in attendance to Jerry, who testified in the case, stated in his opinion the death of Tommy under these circumstances would have "an extremely traumatic effect upon him [Jerry]."

The Department of Mental Health of this commonwealth has entered the case as *amicus curiae* and on the basis of its evaluation of the seriousness of the operation as opposed to the traumatic effect on Jerry as a result of the loss of Tommy, recommended to the court that Jerry be permitted to undergo the surgery. Its recommendations are as follows: "It is difficult for the mental defective to establish a firm sense of identity with another person. The acquisition of this necessary identity is dependent on a person whom one can conveniently accept as a model and who at the same time is sufficiently flexible to allow the defective to detach himself with reassurances of continuity. His need to be social is not so much the necessity of a formal and mechanical contact with other human beings as it is the necessity of a close intimacy with other men, the desirability of a real community of feeling, an urgent need for a unity of understanding. Purely mechanical and formal contact with other men does not offer any treatment for the behavior of a mental defective; only those who are able to communicate intimately are of value to hospital treatment in these cases. And this generally is a member of the family.

"In view of this knowledge, we now have particular interest in this case. Jerry Strunk, a mental defective, has emotions and reactions on a scale comparable to that of a normal person. He identifies with his brother Tom. Tom is his model, his tie with his family. Tom's life is vital to the continuity of Jerry's improvement at Frankfort State Hospital and School. The testimony of the hospital representative reflected the importance to Jerry of his visits with his family and the constant inquiries Jerry made about Tom's coming to see him. Jerry is aware he plays a role in the relief of this tension. We the Department of Mental Health must take all possible steps to prevent the occurrence of any guilt feelings Jerry would have if Tom were to die.

"The necessity of Tom's life to Jerry's treatment and eventual rehabilitation is clearer in view of the fact that Tom is his only living sibling and at the death of their parents, now in their fifties, Jerry will have no concerned, intimate communication so necessary to his stability and optimal functioning.

"The evidence shows that at the present level of medical knowledge, it is quite remote that Tom would be able to survive several cadaver transplants. Tom has a much better chance of survival if the kidney transplant from Jerry takes place."

Upon this appeal, we are faced with the fact that all members of the immediate family have recommended the transplant. The Department of Mental Health has likewise made its recommendation. The county court has given its approval. The circuit court has found that it would be to the best interest of the ward of the state that the procedure be carried out. Throughout the legal proceedings, Jerry has been represented by a guardian *ad litem*, who has continually questioned the power of the state to authorize the removal of an organ from the body of an incompetent who is a ward of the state. We are fully cognizant of the fact that the question before us is unique. Insofar as we have been able to learn, no similar set of facts has come before the highest court of any of the states of this nation or the federal courts. The English courts have apparently taken a broad view of the inherent power of the equity courts with regard to incompetents. *Ex parte Whitebread* (1816)…holds that courts

of equity have the inherent power to make provisions for a needy brother out of the estate of an incompetent.…The inherent rule in these cases is that the chancellor has the power to deal with the estate of the incompetent in the same manner as the incompetent would if he had his faculties. This rule has been extended to cover not only matters of property but also to cover the personal affairs of the incompetent.…

The right to act for the incompetent in all cases has become recognized in this country as the doctrine of substituted judgment and is broad enough not only to cover property but also to cover all matters touching on the well-being of the ward.…

The medical practice of transferring tissue from one part of the human body to another (autografting) and from one human being to another (homografting) is rapidly becoming a common clinical practice. In many cases, the transplants take as well when the tissue is dead as when it is alive. This has made practicable the establishment of tissue banks where such material can be stored for future use. Vascularized grafts of lungs, kidneys, and hearts are becoming increasingly common. These grafts must be of functioning, living cells with blood vessels remaining anatomically intact. The chance of success in the transfer of these organs is greatly increased when the donor and the donee are genetically related. It is recognized by all legal and medical authorities that several legal problems can arise as a result of the operative techniques of the transplant procedure.…

The renal transplant is becoming the most common of the organ transplants. This is because the normal body has two functioning kidneys, one of which it can reasonably do without, thereby making it possible for one person to donate a kidney to another. Testimony in this record shows that there have been over 2500 kidney transplants performed in the United States up to this date. The process can be effected under present techniques with minimal danger to both the donor and the donee.…

Review of our case law leads us to believe that the power given to a committee under KRS 387.230 would not extend so far as to allow a committee to subject his ward to the serious surgical techniques here under consideration unless the life of his ward be in jeopardy. Nor do we believe the powers delegated to the county court by virtue of the above statutes would reach so far as to permit the procedure which we [are] dealing with here.

We are of the opinion that a chancery court does have sufficient inherent power to authorize the operation. The circuit court having found that the operative procedures are to the best interest of Jerry Strunk and this finding having been based on substantial evidence, we are of the opinion the judgment should be affirmed. We do not deem it significant that this case reached the circuit court by way of an appeal as opposed to a direct proceeding in that court.

Judgment affirmed.

Hill, C.J., Milliken, and Reed, JJ., concur.

Neikirk, Palmore, and Steinfeld, JJ., dissent.

Steinfeld, Judge, dissenting

Apparently because of my indelible recollection of a government which, to the everlasting shame of its citizens, embarked on a program of genocide and experimentation with human bodies, I have been more troubled in reaching a decision in this case than in any other. My sympathies and emotions are torn between a compassion to aid an ailing young man and a duty to fully protect unfortunate members of society.

The opinion of the majority is predicated on the authority of an equity court to speak for one who cannot speak for himself. However, it is my opinion that in considering such right in this instance, we must first look to the power and authority vested in the committee, the appellee herein. KRS 387.060 and KRS 387.230 do nothing more than give the committee the power to take custody of the incompetent and the possession, care, and management of his property. Courts have restricted the activities of the committee to that which is for the best interest of the incompetent.... The authority and duty have been to protect and maintain the ward, to secure that to which he is entitled and preserve that which he has....

The wishes of the members of the family or the desires of the guardian to be helpful to the apparent objects of the ward's bounty have not been a criterion. "A curator or guardian cannot dispose of his ward's property by donation, even though authorized to do so by the court on advice of a family meeting, unless a gift by the guardian is authorized by statute."...Two Kentucky cases decided many years ago reveal judicial policy. In *W. T. Sistrunk & Co. v. Navarra's Committee*, ...105 S.W.2d 1039 (1937), this court held that a committee was without right to continue a business which the incompetent had operated prior to his having been declared a person of unsound mind. More analogous is *Baker v. Thomas*, ...114 S.W.2d 1113 (1938), in which a

man and woman had lived together out of wedlock. Two children were born to them. After the man was judged incompetent, his committee, acting for him, together with his paramour, instituted proceedings to adopt the two children. In rejecting the application and refusing to speak for the incompetent, the opinion stated: "The statute does not contemplate that the committee of a lunatic may exercise any other power than to have the possession, care, and management of the lunatic's or incompetent's estate."...The majority opinion is predicated on the finding of the circuit court that there will be psychological benefits to the ward but points out that the incompetent has the mentality of a six-year-old child. It is common knowledge beyond dispute that the loss of a close relative or a friend to a six-year-old child is not of major impact. Opinions concerning psychological trauma are at best most nebulous. Furthermore, there are no guarantees that the transplant will become a surgical success, it being well known that body rejection of transplanted organs is frequent. The life of the incompetent is not in danger, but the surgical procedure advocated creates some peril.

It is written in *Prince v. Massachusetts*, 321 U.S. 158 (1944), that "Parents may be free to become martyrs themselves. But it does not follow they are free, in identical circumstances, to make martyrs of their children before they have reached the age of full and legal distinction when they can make the choice for themselves." The ability to fully understand and consent is a prerequisite to the donation of a part of the human body....

Unquestionably, the attitudes and attempts of the committee and members of the family of the two young men whose critical problems now confront us are commendable, natural, and beyond reproach. However, they refer us to nothing indicating that they are privileged to authorize the removal of one of the kidneys of the incompetent for the purpose of donation, and they cite no statutory or other authority vesting such right in the courts. The proof shows that less compatible donors are available and that the kidney of a cadaver could be used, although the odds of operational success are not as great in such cases as they would be with the fully compatible donor brother.

I am unwilling to hold that the gates should be open to permit the removal of an organ from an incompetent for transplant, at least until such time as it is conclusively demonstrated that it will be of significant benefit to the incompetent. The evidence here does not rise to that pinnacle. To hold that committees, guardians, or courts have such awesome power, even in the persuasive case before us, could establish legal precedent, the dire result of which we cannot fathom. Regretfully I must say no.

Neikirk and Palmore, JJ., join with me in this dissent.

Case Questions

1. The Court of Appeals of Kentucky is the court of last resort in that state. The *Strunk* decision is now Kentucky law. Does the decision make mental institutions a storehouse of human bodies available for distribution to the more productive members of society whenever the state decides that someone's need outweighs the danger to the incompetent?
2. Which opinion, the majority or dissent, was more persuasive?
3. Where no legal cases have a direct bearing on the issue of a case, should the court turn to other disciplines for authority?

 What ethical considerations do you think convinced the dissenters in this case to oppose the operation on Jerry Strunk?

RECOGNIZING LAWS OF OTHER STATES

Conflict of Laws

Every person within the territorial limits of a government is bound by its laws. However, it is well recognized that law does not of its own force have any effect outside the territory of the sovereignty from which its authority is derived. Because each of the fifty states is an individual sovereignty that creates its own common and statutory law, there are often inconsistencies among the laws of the various states. When the facts of a case under consideration have occurred in more than one state or country, and a court must make a choice between the laws of different states or nations, a conflict case is presented.

Another type of conflict-of-laws case involves a situation in which an event occurred in one state and the suit is brought in another state. For example, a driver from Michigan might bring suit in Kentucky regarding an automobile collision in Ohio involving a driver from Kentucky. In this situation, the court must decide whether to apply its own substantive law, the law of the state in which the events occurred, or possibly the law of some other state.

Conflict-of-laws rules have been developed by each state to assist its courts in determining whether and when foreign substantive law (i.e., some other state's contract law, tort law, property law, etc.) should be given effect within the territory of the forum. Always remember that a state court always follows its own procedural law, even when it decides to apply the substantive law of some other state. The rules afford some assurance that the same substantive law will be used to decide the case irrespective of where the suit is tried.

Tort Cases

The traditional approach in tort cases is to apply the law of the place where the wrong was committed—**lex loci delicti commissi**. The place of the wrong is where the last event necessary to make the actor liable takes place or where the person or thing harmed is situated at the time of the wrong. The following case exemplifies a trend that had been occurring in recent years. The Indiana Supreme Court used the *Hubbard* case to replace the traditional lex loci delicti commissi rule with the **significant relationship rule**. The significant relationship approach is more flexible than a rigid lex loci approach. A court following the significant relationship rule can apply the law of the place that has the most significant contacts with the incident or event in dispute.

Hubbard Manufacturing Co., Inc., v. Greeson
515 N.E.2d 1071
Supreme Court of Indiana
December 1, 1987

Shepard, Chief Justice

The question is whether an Indiana court should apply Indiana tort law when both parties are residents of Indiana and the injury occurred in Illinois.

Plaintiff Elizabeth Greeson, an Indiana resident, filed a wrongful death action in Indiana against defendant Hubbard Manufacturing Co., Inc., an Indiana corporation. The defendant corporation built lift units for use in cleaning, repairing, and replacing streetlights.

On October 29, 1979, Donald Greeson, plaintiff's husband and also a resident of Indiana, happened to be working in Illinois maintaining street lights. He died that day while using a lift unit manufactured by Hubbard in Indiana.

Elizabeth Greeson's suit alleged that defective manufacture of Hubbard's lift unit caused her husband's death. When she raised the possibility that Illinois products-liability law should be applied to this case, Hubbard moved the trial court for a determination of the applicable law. The trial court found that Indiana had more significant contacts with the litigation but felt constrained to apply Illinois substantive law because the decedent's injury had been sustained there. The Court of Appeals expressed the opinion that Indiana law should apply but concluded that existing precedent required use of Illinois law....

We grant transfer to decide whether Indiana or Illinois law applies.

Greeson's complaint alleged two bases for her claim: "the defective and unreasonably dangerous condition of a lift type vehicle sold...by the defendant" and "the negligence of the defendant." Both theories state a cause for liability based on Hubbard's manufacture of the vehicle in Indiana.

The differences in Indiana law and Illinois law are considerable. First, in Indiana a finding that the product represented an open and obvious danger would preclude recovery on the product liability claim...to impress liability on manufacturers the defect must be hidden and not normally observable. Under Illinois law, the trier of fact may find product liability even if the danger is open and obvious.... Second, under Indiana law misuse would bar recovery...In Illinois misuse merely reduces a plaintiff's award....These differences are important enough to affect the outcome of the litigation.

Choosing the applicable substantive law for a given case is a decision made by the courts of the state in which the lawsuit is pending. An early basis for choosing law applicable to events transversing (*sic*) several states was to use the substantive law of the state "where the wrong is committed" regardless of where the plaintiff took his complaint seeking relief....

The historical choice-of-law rule for torts,...was *lex loci delicti commissi*, which applied the substantive law where the tort was committed. *Burns v. Grand Rapids and Indiana Railroad Co.* (1888).... The tort is said to have been committed in the state where the last event necessary to make an actor liable for the alleged wrong takes place.

Rigid application of the traditional rule to this case, however, would lead to an anomalous result. Had plaintiff Elizabeth Greeson filed suit in any bordering state the only forum which would not have applied the substantive law of Indiana is Indiana....To avoid this inappropriate result, we look elsewhere for guidance.

Choice-of-law rules are fundamentally judge-made and designed to ensure the appropriate substantive law applies. In a large number of cases, the place of the tort will be significant and the place with the most contacts....In such cases, the traditional rule serves well. A court should be allowed to evaluate other factors when the place of the tort is an insignificant contact. In those instances where the place of the tort bears little connection to the legal action, this

Court will permit the consideration of other factors such as:

1. the place where the conduct causing the injury occurred;
2. the residence or place of business of the parties; and
3. the place where the relationship is centered.

Restatement (Second) of Conflicts of Laws § 145(2) (1971). These factors should be evaluated according to their relative importance to the particular issues being litigated.

The first step in applying this rule in the present case is to consider whether the place of the tort "bears little connection" to this legal action. The last event necessary to make *Hubbard* liable for the alleged tort took place in Illinois. The decedent was working in Illinois at the time of his death and the vehicle involved in the fatal injuries was in Illinois. The coroner's inquest was held in Illinois, and the decedent's wife and son are receiving benefits under the Illinois Workmen's

Compensation Laws. None of these facts relates to the wrongful death action filed against Hubbard. The place of the tort is insignificant to this suit.

After having determined that the place of the tort bears little connection to the legal action, the second step is to apply the additional factors. Applying these factors to this wrongful death action leads us to the same conclusion that the trial court drew: Indiana has the more significant relationship and contacts. The plaintiff's two theories of recovery relate to the manufacture of the lift in Indiana. Both parties are from Indiana; plaintiff Elizabeth Greeson is a resident of Indiana and defendant Hubbard is an Indiana corporation with its principal place of business in Indiana. The relationship between the deceased and Hubbard centered in Indiana. The deceased frequently visited defendant's plant in Indiana to discuss the repair and maintenance of the lift. Indiana law applies.

The Court of Appeals decision is vacated and the cause remanded to the trial court with instructions to apply Indiana law.

Case Questions

1. Under lex loci delicti commissi, how should a court determine where a tort was committed?
2. Why did the Indiana Supreme Court decide to replace the traditional lex loci delicti commissi approach?
3. What contacts were evaluated by the court in determining which state had a more significant relationship with the occurrence and with the parties?

Contract Cases

All states have developed their own conflict-of-laws rules for contractual disputes, which differ from the rules that apply to tort cases. In contractual disputes, depending on the facts involved and jurisdictional preferences, courts have historically applied the law of place in any of the following ways: (1) where the action was instituted **(lex fori)**, (2) where the contract was to be performed **(lex loci solutionis)**, (3) which law the parties intended to govern their agreement, (4) the law of the state where the last act necessary to complete the contract was done and which created a legal obligation **(lex loci contractus)**, and (5) the law of the state that has the greatest concern with the event and the parties **(significant relationship rule)**. A court may choose to follow its own substantive law of

contracts and will do so if the application of the foreign law would offend its public policy.

Courts often honor the law intended by the parties to be controlling. The state chosen usually has a substantial connection with the contract, but courts have held that no such connection is necessary if the parties intended that that state's laws govern the agreement. For example, automobile and house insurance contracts generally included a choice-of-law clause, usually a forum selected by the lawyers for the insurance company, and "agreed to" by the insured. If a contract fails to include a choice-of-law clause, courts may still determine the parties' intent by examining the facts surrounding the contract.

One of the important developments in contract law has been the enactment by all states of at least some provisions of the Uniform Commercial Code (UCC). This code was created in order to enhance the uniformity of state laws regulating certain commercial transactions. The UCC does not apply to all types of contracts. It does not apply, for example, to employment contracts, services, or to the sale of real property. With respect to conflicts of law, the UCC basically follows the significant relationship rule when parties to contracts have not specified a choice of law.

Full Faith and Credit

Prior to learning about full faith and credit, readers may find it helpful to reread the "Procedural Primer" that begins on page 12 of Chapter I. There can be found a simplified overview of civil procedure, a topic that will be explored in much greater detail in Chapter V.

When beginning a discussion of full faith and credit, it is important to emphasize that each state in the United States is a distinct sovereignty. In the absence of a federal constitutional requirement to the contrary, each state would be entitled to totally disregard the constitutions, statutes, records, and judgments of other states. Clearly, the refusal of some states to recognize and enforce the judgments issued by other states would deny justice to those who had taken their disputes to court. A judgment debtor, the party ordered in the judgment to pay money to winner of the lawsuit (the "judgment creditor"), could flee to a state that refuses to recognize and enforce judgments from the issuing state, undermining public confidence in the law.

The authors of the U.S. Constitution anticipated this problem and addressed it in Article IV, Section 1, which provides that "full faith and credit shall be given in each state to the public acts, records, and judicial proceedings of every other state." Thus the Constitution requires the states to cooperate with each other and binds them together into one nation. Since final judgments of each state are enforceable in every other state, irrespective of differences in substantive law and public policy, the full faith and credit requirement also helps to preserve the legal differences that exist from state to state. There are some exceptions to the full faith and credit requirement. For example, the requirement does not apply if the judgment-issuing court lacked jurisdiction over the subject matter or person or if the judgment was fraudulently obtained.

Another important benefit of the full faith and credit requirement is that it puts teeth into the doctrine of *res judicata*. Once a valid judgment has been rendered on the merits in one jurisdiction, the claims adjudicated in that lawsuit cannot be relitigated by the same parties in some other jurisdiction.

A state can justifiably refuse to grant full faith and credit to another state's judgment under limited circumstances: for example, when the issuing court has failed to follow the mandates of the U.S. Constitution regarding due process of law. Full faith and credit can be denied when the issuing court did not have minimum contacts with the person of the judgment debtor, or when the judicial proceedings denied the judgment debtor the constitutionally required elements of notice and an opportunity for a hearing.

Article IV, Section 1, only requires that the states provide full faith and credit to other states. The federal Full Faith and Credit Act (28 USC Section 1738), however, also requires all federal courts to afford full faith and credit to state court judgments.

INTERNET TIP

You can read the excerpt from the federal Full Faith and Credit Act (28 USC Section 1738)), online at the textbook's website.

Although a properly authenticated judgment of an issuing state is presumptively valid and binding in all other states, it is not self-implementing. A judgment creditor who has to go to some other state to enforce a judgment will have to begin an action against the judgment debtor in the nonissuing state. Normally, the courts of the nonissuing state will then have to enforce the foreign judgment in the same manner as they would one of their own judgments, even if enforcing the judgment would contravene the enforcing state's public policy. This was the problem presented in the following case, in which three same-sex adoptive couples sought to overturn an Oklahoma statute which denied them recognition as the adoptive parents of their children. The parents of E.D sued to obtain a supplemental birth certificate, claiming that Oklahoma was obligated under the Full Faith and Credit Clause of the Constitution to recognize the judgment of adoption rendered by a California court.

Finstuen v. Crutcher
496 F.3d 1139
United States Court of Appeals, Tenth Circuit
August 3, 2007

Ebel, Circuit Judge

Defendant-Appellant Dr. Mike Crutcher, sued in his official capacity as the Commissioner of Health (hereinafter referred to as "Oklahoma State Department of Health ('OSDH')") appeals a district court judgment that a state law barring recognition of adoptions by same-sex couples already finalized in another state is unconstitutional. OSDH also appeals the district court's order requiring it to issue a revised birth certificate for E.D., a Plaintiff-Appellee who was born in Oklahoma but adopted in California by a same-sex couple....

I

Three same-sex couples and their adopted children have challenged the following amendment to Oklahoma's statute governing the recognition of parent-child relationships that are created by out-of-state adoptions.

§ 7502-1.4. Foreign adoptions

A. The courts of this state shall recognize a decree, judgment, or final order creating the relationship of parent and child by adoption, issued by a court or other governmental authority with appropriate jurisdiction in a foreign country or in another state or territory of the United States. The rights and obligations of the parties as to matters within the jurisdiction of this state shall be determined as though the decree, judgment, or final order were issued by a court of this state. Except that, this state, any of its agencies, or any court of this state shall not recognize an adoption by more than one individual of the same sex from any other state or foreign jurisdiction.

Okla. Stat. tit. 10, § 7502-1.4(A) (the "adoption amendment").

Each of the three families has a different set of circumstances. Mr. Greg Hampel and Mr. Ed Swaya are residents of Washington, where they jointly adopted child V in 2002. V was born in Oklahoma, and... the men agreed to bring V to Oklahoma to visit her mother "from time to time."...However, they do not... have any ongoing interactions with the state of Oklahoma. After V'sadoption, Mr. Hampel and Mr. Swaya requested that OSDH issue a new birth certificate for V. OSDH did so... but named only Mr. Hampel as V's parent. Mr. Hampel and Mr. Swaya contested that action, prompting OSDH to seek an opinion from the Oklahoma attorney general.... The attorney general opined that the U.S. Constitution's Full Faith and Credit Clause required Oklahoma to recognize any validly issued out-of-state adoption decree. OSDH subsequently issued V a new birth certificate naming both men as parents. The state legislature responded one month later by enacting the adoption amendment.

Lucy Doel and Jennifer Doel live with their adopted child E in Oklahoma. E was born in Oklahoma. Lucy Doel adopted E in California in January 2002. Jennifer Doel adopted E in California six months later ...OSDH issued E a supplemental birth certificate naming only Lucy Doel as her mother. The Doels have requested a revised birth certificate from OSDH that would acknowledge Jennifer Doel as E's parent, but OSDH denied the request.

Anne Magro and Heather Finstuen reside in Oklahoma with their two children. Ms. Magro gave birth to S and K in New Jersey in 1998. In 2000, Ms. Finstuen adopted S and K in New Jersey as a second parent, and New Jersey subsequently issued new birth certificates for S and K naming both women as their parents.

These three families brought suit against the state of Oklahoma seeking to enjoin enforcement of the adoption amendment, naming the governor, attorney general and commissioner of health in their official capacities. The Doels also requested a revised birth certificate naming both Lucy Doel and Jennifer Doel as E's parents.

On cross-motions for summary judgment, the district court found that Mr. Hampel, Mr. Swaya and their child V lacked standing to bring the action....However, the district court granted summary judgment for the remaining plaintiffs, determining that they had standing and that the Oklahoma adoption amendment violated the Constitution's Full Faith and Credit, Equal Protection and Due Process Clauses....The court enjoined enforcement of the amendment, and ordered that a new birth certificate be issued for E.D....

OSDH appeals from the district court's conclusion that the Doels and the Finstuen-Magro family have standing and its ruling that the adoption amendment is unconstitutional. The Oklahoma governor and attorney general did not appeal. In addition, Mr. Hampel, Mr. Swaya and their child V timely appeal from the denial of standing, and reassert their claim that the Oklahoma amendment violates their constitutional right to travel....

II

A. Jurisdiction

[The court's expansive discussion of standing, a topic examined in Chapter VI of this text is omitted . The Court concluded that it did could not decide the case brought by Hampel and Swaya (child V), primarily because this family had minimal connections with Oklahoma, and did "not establish the circumstances in which the non-recognition of the adoption would arise," and therefore lacked standing to sue. The court also found that Finstuen and Magro lacked standing. Magro was the children's birth mother and not an adoptive parent, and Finstuen, who was an adoptive mother, could point to "no encounter with any public or private official in which her authority as a parent was questioned." The court ruled that Lucy Doel and Jennifer Doel, the adoptive parents of child E.D., did have standing to maintain their suit].

B. Full Faith and Credit Clause

Having established jurisdiction, we proceed to consider the merits of OSDH's appeal. The district court concluded that the adoption amendment was unconstitutional because the Full Faith and Credit Clause requires Oklahoma to recognize adoptions—including same-sex couples' adoptions—that are validly decreed in other states....We affirm, because there is "no roving 'public policy exception' to the full faith and credit due *judgments*"...and OSDH presents no relevant legal argument as to why the Doels' out-of-state adoption judgments should not be recognized under the Full Faith and Credit Clause.

The Constitution states that "Full Faith and Credit shall be given in each State to the public Acts, Records, and judicial Proceedings of every other State." U.S. Const. art. 4, § 1. The Supreme Court has often explained the purpose and policies behind the Full Faith and Credit Clause.

The very purpose of the Full Faith and Credit Clause was to alter the status of the several states as independent foreign sovereignties, each free to ignore obligations created under the laws or by the judicial proceedings of the others, and to make them integral parts of a single nation throughout which a remedy upon a just obligation might be demanded as of right, irrespective of the state of its origin.

...The Clause is designed "to preserve rights acquired or confirmed under the public acts and judicial proceedings of one state by requiring recognition of their validity in other states."...The Clause "is one of the provisions incorporated into the Constitution by its framers for the purpose of transforming an aggregation of independent, sovereign States into a nation. If in its application local policy must at times be required to give way, such is part of the price of our federal system."..."To vest the power of determining the extraterritorial effect of a State's own laws and judgments in the State itself risks the very kind of parochial entrenchment on the interests of other States that it was the purpose of the Full Faith and Credit Clause and other provisions of Art. IV of the Constitution to prevent"....

In applying the Full Faith and Credit Clause, the Supreme Court has drawn a distinction between statutes and judgments....Specifically, the Court has been clear that although the Full Faith and Credit Clause applies unequivocally to the judgments...of sister states, it applies with less force to their statutory laws....*Nevada v. Hall*, 440 U.S. 410,... (1979) However, with respect to final judgments entered in a sister state, it is clear there is no "public policy" exception to the Full Faith and Credit Clause:

Regarding judgments...the full faith and credit obligation is exacting. A final judgment in one State, if rendered by a court with adjudicatory authority over the subject matter and persons governed by the judgment, qualifies for recognition throughout the land. For claim and issue preclusion (res judicata) purposes, in other words, the judgment of the rendering State gains nationwide force....

In numerous cases th[e] [Supreme] Court has held that credit must be given to the judgment of another state although the forum would not be required to entertain the suit on which the judgment was founded; that considerations of policy of the forum which would defeat a suit upon the original cause of action are not involved in a suit upon the judgment and are insufficient to defeat it.

OSDH stops short of arguing that the Full Faith and Credit Clause permits states to invoke a "policy exception," but contends that requiring Oklahoma to recognize an out-of-state adoption judgment would be tantamount to giving the sister state control over the effect of its judgment in Oklahoma....

Full faith and credit...does not mean that States must adopt the practices of other States regarding the time, manner, and mechanisms for enforcing judgments. Enforcement measures do not travel with the sister state judgment as preclusive effects do; such measures remain subject to the even-handed control of forum law. ...

A California court made the decision, in its own state and under its own laws, as to whether Jennifer Doel could adopt child E. That decision is final. If Oklahoma had no statute providing for the issuance of supplementary birth certificates for adopted children, the Doels could not invoke the Full Faith and Credit Clause in asking Oklahoma for a new birth certificate. However, Oklahoma has such a statute — i.e., it already has the necessary "mechanism[] for enforcing [adoption] judgments." ... The Doels merely ask Oklahoma to apply its own law to "enforce" their adoption order in an "even-handed" manner....

Oklahoma continues to exercise authority over the manner in which adoptive relationships should be enforced in Oklahoma and the rights and obligations in Oklahoma flowing from an adoptive relationship. And Oklahoma has spoken on that subject:

After the final decree of adoption is entered, the relation of parent and child and all the rights, duties, and other legal consequences of the natural relation of child and parent shall thereafter exist between the adopted child and the adoptive parents of the child and the kindred of the adoptive parents. From the date of the final decree of adoption, the child shall be entitled to inherit real and personal property from and through the adoptive parents in accordance with the statutes of descent and distribution. The adoptive parents shall be entitled to inherit real and personal property from and through the child in accordance with said statutes.

After a final decree of adoption is entered, the biological parents of the adopted child, unless they are the adoptive parents or the spouse of an adoptive parent, shall be relieved of all parental responsibilities for said child and shall have no rights over the adopted child or to the property of the child by descent and distribution....By way of illustration, the right of a parent in Oklahoma to authorize medical treatment for her minor child,...extends...to adoptive parents as well. Whatever rights may be afforded to the Doels based on their status as parent and child, those rights flow from an application of Oklahoma law, not California law....

The rights that the Doels seek to enforce in Oklahoma are Oklahoma rights....

We hold today that final adoption orders and decrees are judgments that are entitled to recognition by all other states under the Full Faith and Credit Clause. Therefore, Oklahoma's adoption amendment is unconstitutional in its refusal to recognize final adoption orders of other states that permit adoption by same-sex couples. Because we affirm the district court on this basis, we do not reach the issues of whether the adoption amendment infringes on the Due Process or Equal Protection Clauses.

We reverse the district court's order in this matter to the extent it held that the Magro-Finstuen plaintiffs had standing and directed OSDH to issue new birth certificates for the Magro-Finstuen plaintiffs. The order and judgment of the district court in all other respects is affirmed.

Case Questions

1. Why did the authors of the Constitution create the Full Faith and Credit Clause?
2. Why did Oklahoma refuse to recognize the California judgment?

CHAPTER SUMMARY

In this chapter readers have learned that federal and state constitutions, statutes, judicial opinions, and administrative rules constitute the primary sources of American law. Summary explanations were provided as to how each primary source contributes to the making of American law.

The importance of the federal and state constitutions as the fundamental sources of the rule of law was emphasized. Because of the federal constitution, Congress's right to legislate is confined, and because it is limited, the state legislatures, as sovereigns, retained the constitutional right to pass laws pursuant to the police power. But where state laws directly conflict with a constitutionally enacted federal statute, the federal law is supreme.

There was a major emphasis in this chapter on judicial decision making and the important role of the doctrine of stare decisis.

Readers have learned that laws can vary from state to state both procedurally and substantively. Federal and state laws can also differ. States, for example, can elect to provide a higher level of procedural protections than is required either under the U.S. Constitution or by federal statute. Last, we have seen that state choice-of-law rules provide methods for ensuring cooperation between states and that the Full Faith and Credit Clause of the U.S. Constitution helps to preserve differences between the states.

CHAPTER QUESTIONS

1. Elizabeth Fedorczyk slipped and fell in a bathtub in her cabin on board the M/V *Sovereign*, a cruise ship sailing in navigable waters. She brought a negligence suit against the ship's owners and operators in a state court in New Jersey. The defendants removed the case to the U.S. District Court for the District of New Jersey on the basis of diversity jurisdiction. Neither party addressed the admiralty issue in their pleadings. The trial court entered summary judgment in favor of the defendants. The plaintiffs appealed to the U.S. Court of Appeals. The appeals court, in order to rule on the appeal, had to determine whether it should apply admiralty law to this dispute or follow instead the substantive law of the state of New Jersey. Which option should the Court of Appeals choose, and why?

   Fedorczyk v. Caribbean Cruise Lines, LTD, No. 95-5462, (3rd Circuit 1996)

2. Sludge, Inc., entered into a contract with XYZ, Inc., whereby Sludge was to build a building for XYZ in Detroit, Michigan, at the price of $1 million. Sludge was incorporated in Ohio; its principal place of business was in Chicago, Illinois. XYZ is a Delaware corporation with its home office in New York. The contract was negotiated primarily in Chicago but became effective when it was signed at

   XYZ's home office. There was a dispute concerning the agreement, and XYZ sued Sludge in a federal district court in Ohio. Which state law would govern the dispute if the court follows (1) the lex fori approach, (2) the lex loci contractus approach, or (3) the lex loci solutionis approach?

3. Lorretta Klump, at the time a resident of Illinois, was injured in an automobile collision in which her vehicle was struck by a vehicle driven by Curt Eaves, also an Illinois resident. This incident occurred in Illinois. After the accident, Lorretta moved to North Carolina, where she retained a local attorney, J. David Duffus Jr., to represent her in a lawsuit she wanted to file in Illinois against Mr. Eaves. She subsequently moved back to Illinois, where she maintained regular contact with Attorney Duffus. Lorretta's doctor and her insurance carrier were both situated in Illinois. She filed a malpractice suit against Duffus when he failed to file her Illinois suit prior to the lapsing of the Illinois statute of limitations. The jury awarded a judgment in plaintiff's favor in the amount of $424,000, but the defendants appealed on the grounds that the trial court did not have *in personam* jurisdiction over them. Duffus argued on appeal that since his allegedly negligent acts occurred in North Carolina, he could not be

subject to personal jurisdiction in Illinois. Is Duffus correct? Why or why not?

Klump v. Duffus, Jr., No. 90-C-3772, U.S. Court of Appeals (7th Circuit 1995)

4. Evian Waters of France, Inc., a New York corporation, was an importer of natural spring water from France. Evian contracted in 1987 with Valley Juice Limited, of Boston, Massachusetts to become Evian's exclusive New England distributor. Valley came to believe that Evian was violating its exclusivity rights in New England and filed breach of contract and other claims in a suit it filed in Massachusetts state court. Evian, believing that Valley had not paid it for contract water it had delivered, also filed suit in Connecticut. Both suits were removed to federal court on the basis of diversity jurisdiction, and the two suits were consolidated in the U.S. District Court for the District of Connecticut. The case was tried to a jury, which found in favor of Evian. Valley appealed to the U.S. Court of Appeals for the Second Circuit. Before reviewing the appellant's claims, the appeals court had to determine what state's law applied when two suits, which were initially filed in different states, were consolidated for trial, as in this case. Evian argued that a provision in its agreement with Valley provided that New York law should apply. Valley contended that if the states' laws conflict, Massachusetts law should apply. How should the court of appeals resolve this dispute?

Valley Juice Ltd., Inc. v. Evian Waters of France, Inc., Nos. 94-7813, 94-7817, 95-7709, U.S. Court of Appeals (2nd Circuit 1996)

5. On May 20, Arnie Walters's car crashed into a train owned and operated by the Regional Transit Authority at its crossing in Smithville. As a matter of law, the court found that the "Smithville crossing is extremely hazardous." On December 1 of that same year, Ole and Anna Hanson ran into a RTA train at the same crossing while George was driving them home from a party. Does the doctrine of stare decisis require that the court in *Hanson* accept the conclusion announced in the *Walters* case?

6. While en route to jury duty, Evans sustained a personal injury as a result of carelessness on the part of the county commissioners in permitting the concrete steps at the El Paso (Colorado) county courthouse to deteriorate. The lower court dismissed the complaint under the doctrine of governmental immunity. On appeal, the Supreme Court of Colorado, in its opinion dated March 22, 1971, decided to abolish governmental immunity for that state. The courts stated, "Except as to the parties in this proceeding the ruling here shall be prospective only and shall be effective only as to causes of action arising after June 30, 1972." Why might a court make its decision effective as a precedent some fifteen months after the date of its decision?

Evans v. Board of County Commissioners, 174 Colo. 97, 482 P.2d 968 (1971)

7. P. Whitney, a West Virginia contractor, was under contract with the state of West Virginia to construct State Route 2 near East Steubenville, just across the border from Steubenville, Ohio. Since the area was very hilly, Whitney used high explosives, such as dynamite and nitroglycerin, to clear the way for the road. One particularly large blast damaged a storeroom of the Steubenville Plate and Window Glass Company, located across the border in Ohio. The damage was extensive, and most of the stored glass was broken and rendered unusable. Keeping in mind that the blasting was done in West Virginia and the damage occurred in Ohio, which state's law will govern the action brought in a West Virginia court by Steubenville Plate Glass against Whitney?

Dallas v. Whitney, 118 W. Va. 106 (1936)

NOTES

1. You might want to refresh your memory and review this material in conjunction with your current reading.

2. L. Fuller, *Anatomy of the Law* (New York: Praeger, 1968), p. 85.

3. *Schechter Poultry Corp. v. United States*, 295 U.S. 495 (1935).

4. *Carter v. Carter Coal Co.*, 298 U.S. 495 (1936).

5. *Adair v. United States*, 208 U.S. 161 (1908).

6. *Hammer v. Dagenhart*, 247 U.S. 251 (1981).

7. *Heart of Atlanta Motel, Inc. v. United States*, 379 U.S. 241 (1964).

8. *National Labor Relations Board v. Jones & Laughlin Steel Corp.*, 301 U.S. 1 (1937).

9. *West Coast Hotel v. Parrish,* 300 U.S. 379 (1937).

IV

✳

The Judicial System

CHAPTER OBJECTIVES

1. *Understand the basic underlying common law heritage from England.*
2. *Describe how the federal and state court systems are organized.*
3. *Identify the functions of the trial and appellate courts.*
4. *Summarize the procedural differences between cases tried to juries and cases tried to judges.*
5. *Summarize the fundamental requirements for jurisdiction and venue in the federal and state judicial systems.*
6. *Describe when cases can be removed from state court to federal court.*
7. *Understand the policy reason underlying the* Erie *doctrine.*

COURTS

A court is a governmental body that is empowered to resolve disputes according to law. Courts are reactive institutions. They do not undertake to adjudicate disputes by themselves, and can only act when someone files suit.

Courts are created in accordance with constitutional provisions and legislative acts. The legislative branch of the government usually has the right to establish and change courts, to regulate many of their procedures, and to limit their jurisdiction.

In the United States, we have a separate judicial system for each of the states and yet another for the federal government. These systems vary in size and complexity, although they usually have hierarchical structures. Since federal and state judicial systems function simultaneously throughout the nation, conflicts can arise with respect to jurisdictional issues, substantive law, supremacy, and the finality of decisions.

Trial Courts

Courts are classified by function: There are trial courts and appellate courts. A trial court hears and decides controversies by determining facts and applying appropriate rules. The opposing parties to a dispute establish their positions by introducing evidence of the facts and by presenting arguments on the law.

The right of a trial by jury provides litigants with a choice of trying the case to a single judge or to a jury of peers. When a case is litigated before a judge instead of a jury, it is called a bench trial. The judge controls the entire trial and determines the outcome. In a jury trial, the decision-making functions are divided between the judge and the jury, which provides a safeguard of checks and balances. The judge rules on the admissibility of evidence, decides questions of law, and instructs the jury. The jury listens to the testimony, evaluates the evidence, and decides what facts have been proven. In many instances, the testimony of witnesses is contradictory. In such cases, the jury can determine the facts only after deciding which witnesses should be believed. It then applies the law to those facts in accordance with the judge's instructions. The judge supervises the entire process. This includes ruling on pretrial motions, supervising discovery, and conducting the trial, matters that are addressed in Chapter V.

When the jury's verdict is submitted, the jury decides who wins and what the recovery will be. Over half of the states permit a less-than-unanimous verdict in civil cases. The usual requirement in such states is five jurors in agreement out of six. Unless the parties stipulate otherwise, the rule in federal civil trials is that the jury verdict must be unanimous.

The law may authorize the jury to use a special verdict. This means that the jury answers specific questions related to certain factual issues in the case. A special verdict is used to focus the jury's attention on the evidence and the factual disputes in the case. It discourages jurors from determining the case's outcome by deciding which party they would like to see win the lawsuit. When the jury returns a special verdict, the judge applies the law to the jury's answers and reaches a final judgment.

It is often said that questions of fact are for the jury and questions of law are for the judge. A factual issue is presented when reasonable people could arrive at different conclusions in deciding what happened in an actual event. When an inference is so certain that all reasonable people must draw the same conclusion, it becomes a question of law for the judge. It is often difficult to make a distinction between questions of fact and questions of law.

There is no need for a trial (either to a jury or to the court) unless there is a factual dispute between the parties. If the parties agree about the facts, but disagree about the law, the judge can determine the applicable law and dispose of the case by motion for summary judgment.

A jury was traditionally composed of twelve people. Today, many jurisdictions have authorized six-person juries. Jurors are chosen from the community, and their qualifications are reviewed before they are seated. At trial, they make their decision in private.

Although federal and state constitutions guarantee the right to a trial by jury, there is some dispute about the effectiveness of the jury system. Jury trials take more time to conduct than bench trials and contribute to the congestion of court dockets. Jury trials also are expensive. Because jurors do not know how to evaluate evidence, rules of evidence and trial procedures have been developed so that they are exposed only to competent evidence and permissible argument. In a bench trial, many of these procedures and rules can be eliminated or relaxed.

In addition, juries are known to be very unpredictable and sometimes arbitrary, and add uncertainty to the adjudication process. Lawyers deal with this uncertainty by attempting to discover jurors' hidden tendencies, biases, and attitudes. More and more trial attorneys employ jury research firms in big cases to help them select the jury and prepare and present their clients' cases. Attorneys who try such cases develop special skills and strategies that they would be unlikely to use in a bench trial before an experienced judge.

One of the most important benefits of the jury system is that it allows citizens to participate in the legal process. A jury is supposed to represent a cross section of the public, whereas a judge does not. Despite the weaknesses of the jury system, it is not likely that the right to a trial by jury will be eliminated in the near future.

Appellate Courts

Appellate courts review the decisions of trial courts. Usually, an appeal can only be taken from a lower court's judgment. In the case of *Du Pont v. Christopher* (a case you can read on the textbook's website), however, readers learn that some jurisdictions permit a limited interlocutory appeal to be made prior to a trial in some circumstances. That is, appellate review may be permitted to resolve a controlling question of law before the case itself is actually decided. In a civil action, any dissatisfied party generally may appeal to a higher court. In criminal cases, the defendant usually may appeal, but the prosecution generally may not.

The appellate court reviews the proceedings of the trial court to determine whether the trial court acted in accordance with the law, and whether the appellant properly preserved the error. This means that an attorney cannot observe error occurring in a trial court and do nothing. The attorney must inform the judge of the error and request specific relief. Failure to object results in a waiver of the right to raise the matter subsequently on appeal.

An appellate court bases its decision solely on the theories argued and evidence presented in the lower court. There are no witnesses or jury at the appellate level. The appellate court does not retry the facts of the case, and no new arguments or proof are permitted. The appellate court reaches its decision by using only the record of the proceedings in the lower court, the written briefs filed by both parties to the appeal, and the parties' oral arguments given before the appellate judges. The record of the proceedings in the lower court includes the pleadings, pre-trial papers, depositions, and a transcript of the trial proceedings and testimony.

STATE COURT SYSTEMS

The power to create courts is an attribute of every sovereignty. The various states of the United States have exercised this power either by constitutional provisions or by statutory enactments. The power to create courts includes the authority to organize them, including the establishment of judgeships, and to regulate their procedure and jurisdiction.

Although each of the states has developed its own unique structure, substantive law, rules, and procedures, there is an underlying common law heritage. In our nation's formative years Americans were greatly influenced by English structures, procedures, and substantive law. Yet from the earliest days, the states modified or replaced both substantive law and legal structures when necessary, and created new ones. Each of the various states was independently charged with dispensing justice in its courts. Each system had the capacity to adapt, reform, and experiment. From those early days down to the present, the states have borrowed from each other in order to improve the administration of justice.

Even though fifty-one judicial systems are available to resolve disputes, very few cases actually go to trial. Disputes are usually settled outside the courtroom on the basis of the lawyer's predictions of what would happen if the case were tried. Litigation is very expensive and time consuming, which encourages litigants to settle cases without a trial.

JURISDICTION

Jurisdiction is the power or authority of a court to determine the merits of a dispute and to grant relief. A court has jurisdiction when it has this power over the subject matter of the case **(subject matter jurisdiction)**, and over the persons of the plaintiff and defendant **(personal/*in personam* jurisdiction)** or the property that is in dispute **(*in rem* jurisdiction)**. The court itself must determine whether it has jurisdiction over a controversy presented before it. This is true even if neither party

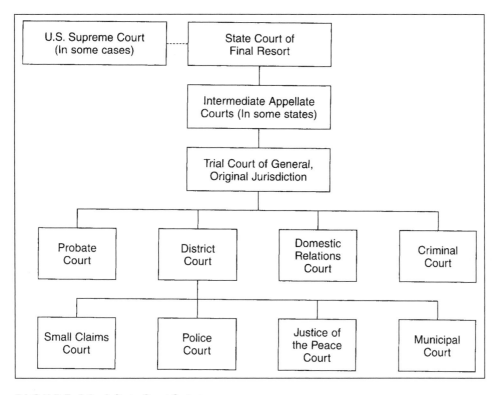

FIGURE 4.1 A State Court System

Source: Adapted from Arnold J. Goldman and William D. Sigismond, Business Law: Principles & Practices, 2d 3d. Copyright © 1988 by Houghton Mifflin Company.

questions the court's jurisdiction. Once a court has acquired jurisdiction, it keeps it throughout the case, even if a party changes domicile or removes property from the state. When more than one court has a basis for jurisdiction, the first to exercise it has exclusive jurisdiction until the case is concluded. Questions about jurisdiction should be resolved before the court concerns itself with other matters involved in the case.

The primary function of trial courts is to exercise original jurisdiction. This term refers to the court's power to take note of a suit at its beginning, try it, and pass judgment on the law and the facts of the controversy. In many states, trial courts also exercise appellate jurisdiction over decisions of courts of limited subject matter jurisdiction.

Some state judicial systems provide that appeals from the decisions of trial courts go directly to the state's highest court (usually, but not always, called the supreme court). Many states, however, usually require review by an intermediate appellate court (often called a court of appeals) before the matter can be heard by the state's highest court. The state's highest court reviews appeals of major questions emanating from the lower state courts, and at the state level, its decision is final. A typical example of a state court system can be seen in Figure 4.1.

Subject Matter Jurisdiction in State Court

Legislatures, in accordance with state constitutions, have the right to allocate the workload throughout the state's judicial system. This means that the legislature usually enacts statutes that define each court's subject matter jurisdiction (the types of controversies that can be litigated in that court). The parties to a lawsuit cannot by consent confer subject matter jurisdiction on a court.

Legislatures often create specialized trial courts, including the land court, probate court (which handles deceased persons' estates), juvenile court, environmental court, and housing court, to exercise original subject matter jurisdiction over particular types of controversies. Subject matter jurisdiction may also be limited by the dollar amount involved in the controversy, as in small claims court, or by territory such as in municipal courts. All these courts would be possessed of limited subject matter jurisdiction.

Legislatures also create trial courts to exercise original subject matter jurisdiction over all other controversies. These courts, which go by various names such as the court of common pleas, district court, superior court, circuit court, county court, or even—in New York State—the trial division of the supreme court, are classified as courts of general or residual jurisdiction.

In the following case, the plaintiff/appellant filed suit in the Franklin County Municipal Court against the defendant/appellee for breach of contract and was awarded a default judgment when the defendant failed to answer the plaintiff's complaint. Approximately 11 months later, the defendant filed a motion asking the municipal court to vacate its own judgment, claiming that the court lacked subject matter jurisdiction to rule in the case. The case was brought before the Ohio Supreme Court. Notice how Judge Moyer's opinion refers to an Ohio court known as the Court of Common Pleas. The first court bearing this name was established in 1178 by England's King Henry II. Besides Ohio, courts of common pleas also exist in Delaware, Pennsylvania, and South Carolina. The Court of Common Pleas in Ohio is a court with general jurisdiction over civil and criminal matters.

Cheap Escape Co., Inc. v. Haddox, LLC
900 N.E.2d 601
Supreme Court of Ohio
December 11, 2008

Moyer, C. J.

I

This appeal requires us to determine whether municipal courts have subject-matter jurisdiction over matters lacking connections to their geographical territories. . . .

II

Appellant, Cheap Escape Company, Inc., d.b.a. JB Dollar Stretcher ("Cheap Escape"), produces a magazine that features business advertisements. Haddox, L.L.C., a construction firm located in Summit County, entered into two contracts with Cheap Escape to run ads in this magazine; appellee, Jeffrey L. Tessman, signed both agreements as a guarantor. The contracts provided that "in the event either party is in noncompliance with any provision of this Agreement the proper venue for litigation purposes will be in the Franklin County Municipal Court or Franklin County Common Pleas." The parties agree that the events relevant to these transactions occurred outside Franklin County and that the only connection to that forum arises from the forum-selection clauses in the contracts between them.

After Haddox allegedly defaulted on the agreements, Cheap Escape filed a breach-of-contract action against Haddox and Tessman in the Franklin County Municipal Court, seeking $1,984 in damages. Neither defendant filed a responsive pleading, and the municipal court eventually entered default judgment for Cheap Escape. Nearly 11 months later, Tessman moved to vacate the default judgment, arguing that the municipal court lacked subject-matter jurisdiction because none of the relevant events occurred in Franklin County. . . . The municipal court denied this motion.

Tessman appealed. The court of appeals . . . held that the municipal court did not have subject-matter jurisdiction over the case, regardless of the forum-selection clause. . . . The court of appeals therefore reversed the municipal court's decision and remanded the case for dismissal. . . .

III

This case requires us to examine the limits of municipal court jurisdiction. Unfortunately, jurisdiction is a vague term. . . . Several distinct concepts, including territorial jurisdiction, monetary jurisdiction, personal jurisdiction, and subject-matter jurisdiction, must be demonstrated for a municipal court to be able to hear a specific case.

While the parties agree that the Franklin County Municipal Court had territorial jurisdiction [because the municipal court deciding the case was situated in Columbus Ohio, which is geographically within Franklin County], monetary jurisdiction [because the amount in dispute was less than $15,000 monetary statutory ceiling for breach of contract cases], and personal jurisdiction in this case, they disagree sharply on the issue of municipal court subject-matter jurisdiction. "Subject-matter jurisdiction of a court connotes the power to hear and decide a case upon its merits" and "defines the competency of a court to render a valid judgment in a particular action." Morrison v. Steiner (1972). . . .

Unlike courts of common pleas [which in Ohio is the name given to what other states call the county courts], which are created by the Ohio Constitution and have statewide subject-matter jurisdiction, . . . municipal courts are statutorily created, . . .and their subject-matter jurisdiction is set by statute . . . . R.C. 1901.18(A) provides the applicable law in this regard: "Except as otherwise provided in this division or section 1901.181 of the Revised Code, subject to the monetary jurisdiction of municipal courts as set forth in section 1901.17 of the Revised Code, a municipal court has original jurisdiction within its territory in all of the following actions or proceedings. . . ." The list of enumerated actions includes breach-of-contract cases, which is the cause of action here. . . .

To resolve this case, we must specifically determine what the phrase "original jurisdiction within its territory" means. Appellant interprets the phrase to mean that a municipal court has subject-matter jurisdiction over any statutorily prescribed action, regardless of where the underlying events occurred. Conversely, appellee argues that the phrase limits subject-matter jurisdiction to those actions with a territorial connection to the court (e.g., the relevant events occurred within the territorial limits of the court). . . .

Appellant argues that the words "within its territory" refer to "jurisdiction" and not the various types of actions listed in R.C. 1901.18(A)(1) through (12). Under this reading, R.C. 1901.18(A) grants a municipal court subject-matter jurisdiction to hear one of those actions if the court convenes within its geographical

territory, regardless of whether the case has a territorial connection to the forum. Thus, appellant claims that the Franklin County Municipal Court had jurisdiction over this case because it was operating in Columbus, as required by R.C. 1901.02(A), even though the relevant events occurred in Summit County. . . .

Appellee argues that this approach renders the phrase "within its territory" irrelevant and that R.C. 1901.18 should instead be read to give municipal courts subject-matter jurisdiction only over events having a territorial connection to the court. This interpretation requires us to read "within its territory" as referring to the types of actions that a municipal court may hear. . .

After reviewing these arguments and the plain text of R.C. 1901.18(A), we find the statute to be ambiguous. . . . It is simply unclear from the statutory language whether the General Assembly intended to limit municipal court subject-matter jurisdiction to territorial matters or to give municipal courts subject-matter jurisdiction over all matters suitable for municipal court review so long as the court sits within its territory when it disposes of a dispute. Both interpretations are reasonable. . . .

To resolve this ambiguity, we must rely on additional methods of statutory interpretation. Because R.C. 1901.18 is part of a complex series of statutes related to jurisdiction, it is appropriate to review the statutes in pari materia. . . . Under this canon of construction, we read all statutes relating to the same general subject matter together and interpret them in a reasonable manner that "give[s] proper force and effect to each and all of the statutes.". . . .

As noted above, appellant argues that "within its territory" means that a municipal court may hear any of the actions enumerated in R.C. 1901.18(A)(1) through (12) so long as it sits within its geographical territory. . . .

Thus, appellant's interpretation would make the phrase "within its territory" in R.C. 1901.18 mere surplusage. . . . If the General Assembly had intended to merely repeat the provisions of these statutes, it could have incorporated them by reference. . .

However, the General Assembly chose to use the unique phrase "original jurisdiction within its territory" in R.C. 1901.18, and we must afford those words some meaning. "It is axiomatic in statutory construction that words are not inserted into an act without some purpose." . . . .Because "within its territory" does not refer to the areas in which a municipal court may sit, the only other logical way to read the phrase is as a limit on the types of actions that a court may hear. Thus, the phrase "original jurisdiction within its territory in all of the following actions" means that a municipal court may hear only those matters listed in R.C. 1901.18(A)(1) through (12) that have a territorial connection to the court.

This reading makes sense in view of. . . R.C. 1901.20 [which] provides that municipal courts have subject-matter jurisdiction in criminal matters only when the crime was committed "within its territory" or "within the limits of its territory." R.C. 1901.20(A)(1) and (B). We find no reason that the General Assembly would have granted municipal courts statewide subject-matter jurisdiction over civil matters but only territorial subject-matter jurisdiction over criminal matters. Further, the fact that the General Assembly used the words "within its territory" in both sections suggests that the phrase should carry the same meaning in both.

We therefore hold that R.C. 1901.18(A) limits municipal court subject-matter jurisdiction to actions or proceedings that have a territorial connection to the court. Because the parties admittedly did not have territorial connections to the Franklin County Municipal Court, the court lacked subject-matter jurisdiction in this matter. Although the parties entered into contracts with what appear to be valid forum-selection clauses, such clauses may be used only to choose from among venues that have subject-matter jurisdiction; litigants cannot vest a court with subject-matter jurisdiction by agreement. . . .

Case Question

1. The parties to this case contractually agreed that in the event of a breach that suit could be brought in either the Franklin County Municipal Court or the Franklin County Court of Common Pleas. Why did the Ohio Supreme Court conclude that this contractual term could not be enforced?

Jurisdiction Over the Person

The establishment of personal jurisdiction is constitutionally required for a court to impose binding liability on a person.

Imagine what would happen in our country if there were no jurisdictional limits on a state judicial system's ability to exercise personal jurisdiction over nonresidents. Every state would try to maximize its power, and total chaos would result. It was for this reason that jurisdictional rules were created: to prevent courts from deciding the merits of a case unless they have jurisdiction over the particular parties to the suit.

In the 1860s there were two methods of establishing a basis for jurisdiction over a person (*in personam* jurisdiction). The first involved showing that the party had been served within the boundaries of the state in which the lawsuit was filed (called the forum state) with a summons originating from within the state (see Figure 4.2).

The constitutionality of this method was upheld by the U.S. Supreme Court in the 1990 case of *Burnham v. Superior Court*. The Court rejected Burnham's argument that basing personal jurisdiction on someone's mere presence within the forum state when served is unfair where minimum contacts between the person and the forum state do not exist. California, said the Court, was entitled to exercise personal jurisdiction over a nonresident from New Jersey, who voluntarily traveled to California and was served with a California summons while he was in San Francisco for the weekend to visit his children.[1] The summons had nothing to do with his actions within California.[2]

A second traditional method of establishing personal jurisdiction not involving the existence of "sufficient minimum contacts" was based on consent. For example, a plaintiff implicitly consents to personal jurisdiction in a state when he or she files a lawsuit with a clerk of court. Defendants can also consent to personal jurisdiction in the following circumstances:

1. The defendant makes a general appearance in a case. If the defendant argues the substantive facts of the case, he or she is implicitly consenting to personal jurisdiction. Thus, a defendant wishing to challenge *in personam* jurisdiction must notify the court that she or he is making a special appearance for the limited purpose of contesting jurisdiction.

STATE OF WISCONSIN _____ Court _____ County

_____, Plaintiff

v. Summons File No. _____

_____, Defendant

The State of Wisconsin

To each person named above as a defendant:

You are hereby notified that the plaintiff named above has filed a lawsuit or other legal action against you. The complaint, which is attached, states the nature and basis of the legal action.

Within 45 days of receiving this summons, you must respond with a written answer, as that term is used in chapter 802 of the Wisconsin Statues, to the complaint. The court may reject or disregard an answer that does not follow the requirements of the statutes. The answer must be sent or delivered to the court, whose address is . . . . , and to . . . . , plaintiff's attorney, whose address is . . . . . You may have an attorney help or represent you.

If you do not provide a proper answer within 45 days, the court may grant judgment against you for the award of money or other legal action requested in the complaint, and you may lose your right to object to anything that is or may be incorrect in the complaint. A judgment may be enforced as provided by law. A judgment awarding money may become a lien against any real estate you own now or in the future, and may also be enforced by garnishment or seizure of property.

Dated: . . . . . . , 20 . . .

[signed] _____
Attorney for Plaintiff

Address: _____

F I G U R E 4.2 State of Wisconsin Statutory Form of Summons Tort Actions [Sec. 801.095]

2. A nonresident defendant allegedly commits a tortious act within the forum state.

3. A nonresident drives a motor vehicle on the roads of the forum state and becomes involved in a collision. Under the laws of most states, the motorist impliedly appoints an official of the forum state to be his agent for receiving service of the plaintiff's summons arising from the accident.

Because nonresident defendants rarely consent to being sued, and can avoid being served within the forum state by never going there, a new theory for jurisdiction was necessary. To remedy this problem, the U.S. Supreme Court developed its "sufficient minimum contacts" rule.

The sufficiency of the defendant's contacts with the forum state is determined by looking at the particular facts of each case. Sufficient minimum contacts, for example, exist in the state in which the defendant is domiciled. A person's domicile is the state in which the defendant has established his or her permanent home and to which the defendant returns after temporary absences. Factors such as where a person is licensed to drive, votes, and is employed are considered in determining domicile.

Long-Arm Statutes

Every state has enacted what are called long-arm statutes (see Figure 4.3) that permit the exercise of personal jurisdiction over nonresident defendants who have had sufficient minimum contacts with the forum state. A long-arm statute allows the plaintiff to serve the forum state's summons on the defendant in some other state.

When a plaintiff successfully uses the long-arm statute, the defendant can be required to return to the forum state and defend the lawsuit. If the defendant fails to do so, he or she risks the entry of a default judgment.

The consequences of not establishing personal jurisdiction are significant. Assume, for example, that a plaintiff has won a lawsuit and been awarded a judgment (the court document declaring the plaintiff the victor and specifying the remedy) entitling the plaintiff (now called the judgment creditor) to collect money damages from the defendant (now called the judgment debtor) and the judgment debtor fails to pay. If the trial court had proper personal jurisdiction over the defendant, the judgment creditor would be entitled to take the judgment to any state in which the judgment debtor owns property and there have it enforced. If the court issuing the judgment lacked *in personam* jurisdiction over the defendant, however, that judgment would be unenforceable.

The advent of the Internet has impacted many aspects of contemporary life in this country. The following case is about a dispute resulting from the auction of a motor vehicle via eBay. The purchaser of the vehicle, a Kentucky resident, chose to file suit against the seller in Kentucky rather than in Missouri, the state in which the seller resided. Because the seller could not be served with a summons within Kentucky, the buyer sought to invoke the Kentucky long-arm statute, which permits the service of the Kentucky summons outside of Kentucky. In this case of first impression, the Kentucky Court of Appeals had to decide whether sufficient minimum contacts existed between Kentucky and the Missouri seller of the vehicle to permit the exercise of personal jurisdiction over the seller.

The procedural posture of the case is also interesting. The seller was served with a Kentucky summons within Missouri and filed both an answer and a motion to dismiss for lack of *in personam* jurisdiction. The Kentucky trial court denied the motion and shortly thereafter entered a default judgment against the seller. The seller subsequently appealed to the Kentucky Court of Appeals.

Robey v. Hinners
Court of Appeals of Kentucky.
May 29, 2009

Buckingham, Senior Judge:
Brad Robey, d/b/a as Robey's Pawn World, appeals from a default judgment of the Kenton Circuit Court in favor of Gerald S. Hinners resulting from Robey's sale of a vehicle to Hinners through eBay. Robey, a Missouri

resident, contends that the circuit court lacked personal jurisdiction to enter the judgment against him. . . .

Robey operates a pawn business in Sikeston, Missouri, and Hinners is a resident of Kentucky. eBay is a widely used auction site on the Internet. It provides an online forum for sellers to list items for auction and for prospective buyers to bid.

On or about September 15, 2005, Robey listed a 2002 Cadillac Escalade automobile for auction on eBay Motors, a division of the eBay auction site. The auction listing stated that the vehicle was "clean, better than average" and that "the engine runs like a dream." The listing also stated that there was a "1 month/1,000 mile Service Agreement."

Hinners successfully outbid others at $25,869 and won the auction. He traveled to Missouri to close the transaction, paid Robey the renegotiated amount of $23,000 rather than the bid amount, and took possession of the vehicle.

Hinners claims that after returning to Kentucky, he began to experience problems with the vehicle. After attempts to resolve his complaints were unsuccessful, on December 22, 2005, Hinners filed a civil complaint against Robey in the Kenton Circuit Court. The complaint alleged that the vehicle began to have mechanical troubles immediately after delivery and that a mechanic examined it and determined that it had been rolled and had suffered extensive physical damage. The complaint further alleged that the vehicle had severe electronic problems and was unsafe to drive.

Robey filed an answer and also a motion to dismiss on the ground of lack of personal jurisdiction. The trial court denied the motion. . . . Thereafter, Robey failed to respond to discovery requests, and the court entered an order compelling discovery. When Robey failed to comply with the order compelling discovery, the court granted Hinners's motion to strike Robey's answer and entered a default judgment. The judgment against Robey is in the amount of $36,320.05, an amount that exceeds the purchase price by more than $13,000. Robey's appeal herein followed. . . .

The U.S. Supreme Court stated . . . that personal jurisdiction is "an essential element of the jurisdiction" of a court and that without such jurisdiction a court is "powerless to proceed[.]". . . The Supreme Court stated . . . that "[i]t has long been the constitutional rule that a court cannot adjudicate a personal claim or obligation unless it has jurisdiction over the person of the defendant." . . . . The Sixth Circuit of the U.S. Court of Appeals explained that "[i]t is elemental that a judgment rendered by a court lacking personal jurisdiction over the defendant is void as to that defendant.". . .

Because judgments against defendants over whom the courts lack personal jurisdiction are void, the inquiry for our purposes becomes whether the issue of personal jurisdiction may be raised by Robey in this appeal even though a default judgment was entered . . . .

Foremost Ins. Co. v. Whitaker . . . is very similar to this case. In that case, the trial court entered a default judgment against a Michigan corporation. The nonresident corporation then moved the court to set aside the default judgment on the ground that the court lacked personal jurisdiction to enter the judgment . . . . The court denied the motion, and the corporation appealed. This court held as follows:

> A void judgment is not entitled to any respect or deference by the courts. *Mathews v. Mathews*. . . . A void judgment is a legal nullity, and a court has no discretion in determining whether it should be set aside. . . . Therefore, because the trial court had no jurisdiction over Foremost at the time default judgment was entered, the judgment was *void ab initio* [void from the beginning] and the trial court erred as a matter of law in refusing to set it aside. . . .

Even though this case involves a default judgment, Robey actually contested the issue of personal jurisdiction by moving the court to dismiss Hinners's complaint on that ground. By raising the issue of personal jurisdiction on appeal, Robey is alleging that the judgment against him is void. We conclude that under the foregoing authorities, he may raise this issue on appeal.

Hinners asserts that the court had personal jurisdiction over Robey under the Kentucky long-arm statute. . . .

The Kentucky long-arm statute "extends personal jurisdiction over nonresidents only to the limits of the Constitution's due process clause.". . . . The requirements of due process in this regard were set forth by the U.S. Supreme Court in the landmark case of *International Shoe Co. v. State of Washington*. . . . In that case, the Supreme Court stated as follows:

> [D]ue process requires only that in order to subject a defendant to a judgment in personam, if he be not present within the territory of the forum, he have certain minimum contacts with it such that the maintenance of the suit does not offend 'traditional notions of fair play and substantial justice.' . . .

In Kentucky, the courts have established a "three-pronged analysis to determine the outer limits of personal jurisdiction based upon a single act.". . . . The test is stated as follows:

> The first prong of the test asks whether the defendant purposefully availed himself of the privilege of acting within the forum state or causing a consequence in the forum state. The second prong considers whether the cause of action arises from the alleged in-state activities.

The final prong requires such connections to the state as to make jurisdiction reasonable. . . . The Wilson court [*Wilson v. Case*, 85 S.W.3d 589 (Ky. 2002)] also stated that "[e]ach of these three criteria represents a separate requirement, and jurisdiction will lie only where all three are satisfied." . . . .this court held that "[i]n terms of a due process analysis, the defendant's connection must be such `that he should reasonably anticipate being haled into court there.'". . . Further, the court in *Sunrise Turquoise* stated that "[t]he requirement of `purposeful availment' is significant since it assures that the defendant will not be haled into a jurisdiction as a result of `random,' `fortuitous,' or `attenuated' contacts.". . .

"Whether personal jurisdiction may be exercised over a defendant is a fact-specific determination, and `[e]ach case involving the issue of personal jurisdiction over a nonresident defendant must be decided on its own facts'". . . .

The issue of personal jurisdiction in the context of an eBay transaction between a resident buyer and a nonresident seller is an issue of first impression in the appellate courts of this state. . . .

. . . . The circuit court began its analysis by stating that Robey's listing of the automobile on eBay was "not alone sufficient for the exercise of personal jurisdiction over defendant to comport with due process requirements." The court further held that "at the time of the posting of the ad, the defendant did not demonstrate purposeful availment to Kentucky as a state of proper jurisdiction over him."

The court next stated that because Robey accepted Hinners's Application for Kentucky Certificate of Title/Registration when the car was picked up, the transaction became "more than a random, fortuitous or attenuated contact with this state. Acceptance of the application created a continuing obligation between the defendant and the plaintiff." The court further noted that "the consequences of the sale of the car are in Kentucky" and that "[t]he defendant clearly had knowledge that the car was being brought back into this state."

In addition, the court held that "jurisdiction in Kentucky is reasonable" because the plaintiff was an individual, "whereas defendant is in the business of selling cars through his pawn shop." The court

emphasized that Robey "placed the vehicle into the stream of commerce, sold it to a Kentucky consumer, and accepted the Kentucky resident's application for a Kentucky title." The court also stated that Robey had a "continuing obligation regarding the title and perhaps other matters (such as the alleged warranty) [.]" Finally, the court held that "Kentucky has a manifest interest in providing its resident, the consumer, a convenient forum to redress the damages, if any, caused by the defendant.". . .

However, in *Burger King Corp. v. Rudzewicz*. . . (1985) . . . the U.S. Supreme Court held that the formation of a contract with a nonresident defendant was not, standing alone, sufficient to create jurisdiction. . . .

Hinners argues in his brief that by advertising on eBay, Robey "solicited purchasers from all jurisdictions." Thus, he maintains that "[b]y engaging in such conduct, it is clear that [Robey] should foresee suits in foreign jurisdictions.". . .

We conclude, as did the trial court, that merely placing the vehicle for auction on eBay did not alone create personal jurisdiction over Robey in Kentucky. We further conclude that merely accepting the Application for Kentucky Certificate of Title/Registration did not create personal jurisdiction. In addition, the fact that Hinners took the vehicle to Kentucky and determined there that it was not as advertised did not create personal jurisdiction. Also, there was no evidence that Robey used eBay through which to sell automobiles on any occasion other than this one. Finally, we conclude that the language in the eBay listing referring to a "1 month/1,000 mile Service Agreement" also did not create jurisdiction.

Contrary to the conclusion of the circuit court, we conclude that the transaction was a random, fortuitous, and attenuated contact with this state. . . . In short, we conclude that Robey did not have sufficient minimum contacts with Kentucky to allow a Kentucky court to assert personal jurisdiction over him.

Based upon the foregoing authority from the U.S. Supreme Court and on the persuasive reasoning of the courts from other jurisdictions that have addressed this issue, we reverse the judgment of the Kenton Circuit Court and remand for the entry of an order dismissing Hinners's complaint.

Case Questions

1. What did the trial court conclude with respect to Hinners's assertion that Robey should have understood, when he auctioned the vehicle on eBay, that he would be subject to suits in jurisdictions other than Missouri?
2. As a result of the Kentucky Court of Appeals decision, does Hinners still have any other options?

454.210. Personal jurisdiction of courts over nonresident—Process, how served—Venue

(1) As used in this section, "person" includes an individual, his executor, administrator, or other personal representative, or a corporation, partnership, association, or any other legal or commercial entity, who is a nonresident of this Commonwealth.

(2) (a) A court may exercise personal jurisdiction over a person who acts directly or by an agent, as to a claim arising from the person's:

　　1. Transacting any business in this Commonwealth;

　　2. Contracting to supply services or goods in this Commonwealth;

　　3. Causing tortious injury by an act or omission in this Commonwealth;

　　4. Causing tortious injury in this Commonwealth by an act or omission outside this Commonwealth if he regularly does or solicits business, or engages in any other persistent course of conduct, or derives substantial revenue from goods used or consumed or services rendered in this Commonwealth, provided that the tortious injury occurring in this Commonwealth arises out of the doing or soliciting of business or a persistent course of conduct or derivation of substantial revenue within the Commonwealth;

　　5. Causing injury in this Commonwealth to any person by breach of warranty expressly or impliedly made in the sale of goods outside this Commonwealth when the seller knew such person would use, consume, or be affected by, the goods in this Commonwealth, if he also regularly does or solicits business, or engages in any other persistent course of conduct, or derives substantial revenue from goods used or consumed or services rendered in this Commonwealth;

　　6. Having an interest in, using, or possessing real property in this Commonwealth, providing the claim arises from the interest in, use of, or possession of the real property, provided, however, that such in personam jurisdiction shall not be imposed on a nonresident who did not himself voluntarily institute the relationship, and did not knowingly perform, or fail to perform, the act or acts upon which jurisdiction is predicated;

　　7. Contracting to insure any person, property, or risk located within this Commonwealth at the time of contracting;

　　…

(3) (a) When personal jurisdiction is authorized by this section, service of process may be made on such person, or any agent of such person, in any country in this Commonwealth, where he may be found, or on the Secretary of State who, for this purpose, shall be deemed to be the statutory agent of such person;
　　…

(4) When the exercise of personal jurisdiction is authorized by this section, any action or suit may be brought in the country wherein the plaintiff resides or where the cause of action or any part thereof arose.

(5) A court of this Commonwealth may exercise jurisdiction on any other basis authorized in the Kentucky Revised Statutes or by the Rules of Civil Procedure, notwithstanding this section.

F I G U R E 4.3 Excerpt from Kentucky Long-Arm Statute, KRS 454.210

INTERNET TIP

The Kentucky Supreme Court has agreed to review this case, and after it rules, the majority opinion will be posted on the textbook's website with the Chapter IV materials.

Interested readers can find a case discussing the sufficient minimum contacts rule, personal jurisdiction, and the Internet on the textbook's website. The case is captioned *David Mink v. AAAA Development LLC.*

In Personam Jurisdiction Over Corporations

Every corporation has been incorporated by one of the fifty states and is therefore subject to the *in personam* jurisdiction of that state's courts. A corporation may also consent to *in personam* jurisdiction in other states. Generally, a state will require that all corporations doing business within its borders register with it and appoint a state government official as its agent. This official will be authorized to receive service of process relating to litigation arising in the wake of its presence and its business activities conducted within that state. Soliciting orders, writing orders, and entering into contracts would establish a corporate presence that would be sufficient for *in personam* jurisdiction. The mere presence of corporate officers within the forum state or the occasional shipping of orders into the forum is not sufficient for personal jurisdiction.

Jurisdiction Over Property—*In Rem* Jurisdiction

A state has jurisdiction over property located within the state. The property may be real (land and buildings) or personal (clothes, cars, televisions, checking accounts, antique clocks, etc.). This is called *in rem* jurisdiction, or jurisdiction over things. An *in personam* decision imposes liability on a person and is personally binding. A decision *in rem*, however, is directed against the property itself and resolves disputes about property rights. A court can determine the rights to property that is physically located within the forum state regardless of whether the court has personal jurisdiction over all interested individuals. For example, if two parties—one of whom is from out of state—dispute the ownership of a piece of land in Montana, the courts of Montana can determine ownership because it relates to property located within that state.

Procedural Due Process Requirements

In addition to establishing a basis for jurisdiction over the person or the property that is in dispute, a court must give proper notice to a defendant. The statutes of each jurisdiction often make distinctions between the type of notice required for *in personam* actions and *in rem* actions. This subject is covered in more detail in Chapter V.

Venue

Venue requirements determine the place where judicial authority should be exercised. Once personal jurisdiction has been established, a plaintiff has to litigate in a court that has subject matter jurisdiction over the controversy and in a place that the legislature says is a permissible venue.

State legislatures enact venue statutes to distribute the judicial workload throughout the system. They often provide for venue in the county or district where the cause of action arose, the county or district in which the defendant resides, and the county or district in which the plaintiff resides. In cases where the venue requirements can be satisfied in more than one district, the plaintiff's choice will usually prevail.

Parties wishing to challenge venue must assert their objections promptly, or they may be waived. In both civil and criminal cases, venue may be considered improper for several reasons. A court may decline to hear a case for fear of local prejudice, for the convenience of litigants and witnesses, or in the interests of justice.

In a civil case, the most common reason given for a court to decline to exercise jurisdiction is that it believes the case can proceed more conveniently in another court. This is known as the doctrine of *forum non conveniens*. The doctrine is applied with discretion and caution. One frequent ground for applying the doctrine occurs when the event that gave rise to the suit took place somewhere other than in the forum state. The difficulties of securing the attendance of out-of-state witnesses and applying foreign law may make decision making inconvenient. The court balances the conveniences between the forum court and another court and weighs the obstacles to a fair proceeding against the advantages.

INTERNET TIP

You can see an example of a venue statute and read *Massey v. Mandell*, a Michigan venue case, on the textbook's website.

THE FEDERAL COURT SYSTEM

Article III, Section 1, of the U.S. Constitution is the basis of our federal court system. It provides that "the judicial power of the United States shall be vested in one supreme court, and in such inferior courts as the Congress may, from time to time, ordain and establish." Congress first exercised this power by passing the Judiciary Act of 1789, which has been amended and supplemented many times in order to establish the various federal courts, as well as their jurisdiction and procedures.

The federal court system consists of the district courts, exercising general, original jurisdiction; the courts of appeals, exercising intermediate appellate jurisdiction; and the U.S. Supreme Court, sitting as the highest court for both federal and state cases involving federal questions. Federal courts of limited jurisdiction include the U.S. Court of Federal Claims, which decides non-tort claims filed against the United States; the U.S. Tax Court, which reviews decisions of the secretary of the treasury with respect to certain provisions of the Internal Revenue Code; the U.S. Court of International Trade, which has jurisdiction over civil actions relating to embargoes on imports, customs duties, and revenues from imports or tonnage; the Federal Bankruptcy Court, which hears bankruptcy cases; and the Court of Appeals for the Armed Forces, which is a court of last resort in military criminal appeals. An organizational chart of the federal judiciary can be seen in Figure 4.4.

The U. S. Supreme Court is undoubtedly the best-known federal court, and at the opposite end of the continuum are probably the least known federal courts, the Foreign Intelligence Surveillance Court (FISC) and the Foreign Intelligence Surveillance Court of Review (FISCR). The FISC and FISCR were established in 1978 in the aftermath of a Senate Select Committee's groundbreaking and comprehensive study of the federal government's domestic intelligence operations over the preceding four decades. The Committee, which was appointed in 1975, was headed by the late U.S. Senator Frank Church. After an extensive investigation, the Church Committee concluded that "domestic intelligence activity has threatened and undermined the constitutional rights of Americans to free speech, association and privacy. It has done so primarily because the constitutional system for checking abuse of power has not been applied."[3] Among the many Church Committee recommendations was one urging the Congress to ". . . [T]urn its attention to legislating restraints upon intelligence activities which may endanger the constitutional rights of Americans."

Congress responded in 1978 by enacting the Foreign Intelligence Surveillance Act (FISA). The legislation centralized the federal government's surveillance activities and provided for judicial oversight of the surveillance process. Pursuant to this legislation, Congress established the FISC and FISCR to protect Americans from executive branch abuses such as had happened in the past and required that government obtain warrants from FISC.

Congress, however, did not require that federal officers investigating domestic espionage and terrorism comply with the same warrant requirements that apply in all other criminal prosecutions. Instead they established separate and less stringent requirements for national security operations.

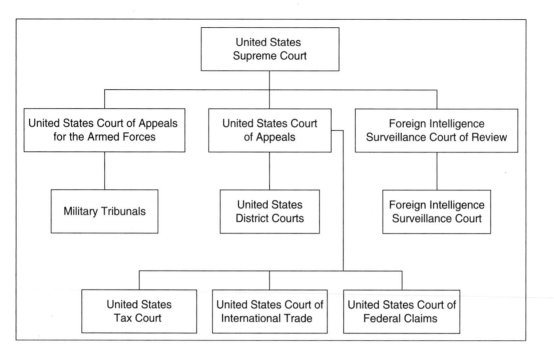

FIGURE 4.4 The Federal Court System

Source: Adapted from Arnold J. Goldman and William D. Sigismond, Business Law: Principles & Practices, 2d ed. Copyright © 1988 by Houghton Mifflin Company.

INTERNET TIP

Because of space limitations, it is not possible to continue this discussion to include the Protect America Act of 2007 and the FISA Amendments Act of 2008. The topic is fascinating and can readily be pursued online by interested readers.

The Chief Justice of the United States appoints the eleven members of the Foreign Intelligence Surveillance Court and chooses one of these appointees to be the Chief Judge. The judges serve nonrenewable seven-year terms.

FISC proceedings are closed and only Department of Justice (DOJ) lawyers are present at hearings. The DOJ attorneys try to persuade the FISC judges to approve the issuance of surveillance warrants. The FISC, which conducts its business in

secret, can approve an electronic surveillance upon Justice Department certification that "a significant purpose" of its intended surveillance is to gather foreign intelligence information. You will notice in Figure 4.5 that the FISC almost always approves the issuance of such warrants. Congress also permitted the government to appeal any adverse rulings handed down by the FISC to a specially created court called the Foreign Intelligence Surveillance Court of Review (FISCR). By creating a special appeals court for national security investigation appeals, Congress bypassed the traditional intermediate appellate courts in the federal system, the U.S. Courts of Appeal.

The FISCR has three federal judges, all of whom are appointed by the Chief Justice. These judges serve nonrenewable seven-year terms. It is interesting to note that the no cases were appealed

Action Taken	2006	2007	2008
New applications submitted for Court approval	2,181	2,371	2,081
Applications approved by Court	2,176	2,368	2,080
Applications denied by Court	1	3	1
Applications substantively modified by Court	73	86	2
Applications withdrawn prior to Court ruling and not resubmitted for approval	4	0	0

FIGURE 4.5 Foreign Intelligence Surveillance Court: Applications Submitted, Approved, Denied, Substantively Modified, and Withdrawn Prior to Court Ruling and Not Resubmitted

Sources: U.S. Department of Justice's Annual Reports to Congress for years 2006, 2007, and 2008, as required by Sections 1807 and 1862 of the Foreign Intelligence Surveillance Act of 1978.

to the FISCR between 1978 and 2002, when the DOJ appealed the FISC's decision in *In re: Sealed Case No. 02-001.*

Under FISCA, in the most unlikely event that the DOJ loses in both the FISC and the FISCR, the government can still seek review in the U.S. Supreme Court.

INTERNET TIP

It is unusual for FISC or FISCR opinions to be published in the Federal Reports. An exception to this rule was the opinion written in the first case ever appealed to the FISCR by the government in a case captioned *In re: Sealed Case No. 02-001,* 310 F.3d 717 (2002). It can be found by searching for that citation online.

INTERNET TIP

You can read selected excerpts from the Foreign Intelligence Surveillance Act (Title 50 United States Code Sections 1803–1805) on the textbook's website.

THE U.S. DISTRICT COURTS

There are ninety-four federal district courts, with at least one in each state and territory in the United States. They are the courts of original jurisdiction and serve as the trial court in the federal court system. The federal district courts are given limited subject matter jurisdiction by the Constitution and by Congress. Article III provides that federal courts have jurisdiction over "all cases . . . arising under . . . the laws of the United States."

Because there are no federal common law crimes, all federal criminal actions must be based on federal statutes. In civil actions, Congress has authorized federal courts to exercise subject matter jurisdiction in two categories of cases:

1. Federal question jurisdiction exists where the case involves claims based on the Constitution, laws, or treaties of the United States. Such claims would include suits by the United States and civil rights, patent, copyright, trademark, unfair competition, and admiralty suits.

2. Diversity of citizenship jurisdiction exists if a suit is between citizens of different states or between a citizen of a state and an alien, and if the amount in controversy exceeds $75,000 (the jurisdictional amount). Diversity jurisdiction provides qualifying plaintiffs with a choice of a federal or state forum for many types of civil actions. However, federal courts have traditionally declined to exercise diversity jurisdiction in divorce actions, child custody cases, and probate matters.

State citizenship is a key concept in diversity cases. For natural citizens, state citizenship is closely related to the establishment of a principal residence (domicile). Thus, a person who presently makes her home in Texas is a citizen of Texas. If she spends the summer working in Colorado and plans to return to Texas in September, she would still be a citizen of Texas.

Federal diversity jurisdiction requires that the diversity of citizenship be complete. This means that in a multiple-party suit, no one plaintiff and one defendant can be citizens of the same state. Thus, if a citizen of New York brings suit against two defendants, one a citizen of Wisconsin and one a citizen of Michigan, there would be total diversity of citizenship. A federal district court would have jurisdiction over the subject matter if the plaintiff were suing in good faith for over $75,000. If, however, one of the defendants were a citizen of New York, there would not be complete diversity of citizenship necessary for jurisdiction.

Congress has provided special citizenship rules for corporations. A corporation is considered a citizen in the state where it is incorporated, as well as in the state of its principal place of business. For example, a corporation incorporated in Delaware with its principal place of business in New York cannot sue or be sued by citizens of either of the two states in a diversity case in a federal district court.

Diversity jurisdiction avoids exposing the defendant to possible prejudice in the plaintiff's state court. There are many who argue against diversity jurisdiction, claiming that the fear of possible prejudice does not justify the expense of the huge diversity caseload in federal courts. See Figure 4.6 for data regarding civil cases brought in the U.S. District Courts from 2004 to 2008.

	Cases Commenced				
Type of Case	**2004**	**2005**	**2006**	**2007**	**2008**
Cases Total	**281,338**	**253,273**	**259,541**	**257,507**	**267,257**
Contract Actions, Total	29,404	28,020	30,044	33,939	34,172
Real Property Actions, Total	5,845	4,561	4,414	5,180	5,072
Tort Actions, Total	55,023	51,335	68,804	61,359	72,011
Personal Injury, Total	50,594	47,364	64,734	57,244	68,121
Personal Property Damage, Total	4,429	3,971	4,061	4,115	3,890
Actions under Statutes, Total	191,017	169,265	156,177	156,916	155,939
Civil Rights, Total	40,239	36,096	32,865	31,756	32,132
Voting	173	166	150	118	145
Employment	19,746	16,930	14,353	13,375	13,219
Housing & Accommodations	1,222	885	643	665	644
Welfare	61	54	56	27	48
Other Civil Rights	19,037	16,459	15,295	15,253	15,398
Environmental Matters	978	714	871	767	920
Deportation	316	201	130	115	130
Prisoner Petitions, Total	55,330	61,238	54,955	53,945	54,786
Habeas Corpus—General	23,344	24,633	22,745	22,192	21,298
Habeas Corpus—Death Penalty	225	240	239	246	192
Prison Condition	7,971	8,609	7,811	7,309	7,610
Intellectual Property Rights	9,590	12,184	11,514	10,783	9,592
Securities, Commodities & Exchanges	3,094	2,038	1,621	1,394	1,637
Social Security Laws	15,873	15,487	13,847	12,974	13,138
Constitutionality of State Statutes	317	310	304	277	254

FIGURE 4.6 U.S. District Courts-Civil Cases Commenced 2004–2008

Source: Administrative Office of the United States Courts, *2008 Annual Report of the Director: Judicial Business of the United States Courts*. Washington, D.C.: U.S. Government Printing Office, 2009.

The Plaintiff's Choice of Forum

There are various factors that influence plaintiffs in their choice of a federal or state forum. One forum may be more attractive than another because it is closer and more convenient for the plaintiff. The plaintiff's attorney may be influenced by the reputation of the county or court in terms of the size of verdicts awarded there, by whether the forum is rural or urban, by socioeconomic factors, or by the reputations of the plaintiff and defendant within the forum. Plaintiffs may also be influenced to file in a federal forum if the federal procedural rules are more liberal than the corresponding state rules.

In the following case, a plaintiff whose diversity suit was dismissed by a federal district court for failing to satisfy the jurisdictional amount requirement appealed that decision to the U.S. Court of Appeals for the Eighth Circuit.

Kopp v. Kopp
280 F.3d 883
U.S. Court of Appeals for the Eighth Circuit
February 19, 2002

Morris Sheppard Arnold, Circuit Judge
Donna Kopp appeals from the order of the district court dismissing her tort claim for lack of subject-matter jurisdiction. . . .

I
Ms. Kopp was attacked, restrained, and sexually assaulted in her own home by her ex-husband, Donald Kopp. When Mr. Kopp . . .pleaded guilty . . .and was sentenced to four years in prison, Ms. Kopp then sued Mr. Kopp in federal court, claiming violations of the Violence Against Women Act of 1994 . . .and of state tort law as well. After the district court dismissed the federal claim because of the decision in *United States v. Morrison*, 529 U.S. 598 (2000) [declaring the Violence Against Women Act unconstitutional], it also dismissed the state law claims because it concluded that they did not satisfy the requirements for diversity jurisdiction.

When the two parties to an action are citizens of different states, as they are here, a federal district court's jurisdiction extends to "all civil actions where the matter in controversy exceeds the sum or value of $75,000, exclusive of interest and costs," 28 U.S.C. § 1332(a). Although Ms. Kopp's medical bills fall well below the requisite amount, she argues that in the circumstances of this case she could well recover punitive damages and damages for emotional distress that would exceed $75,000.

We have held that "a complaint that alleges the jurisdictional amount in good faith will suffice to confer jurisdiction, but the complaint will be dismissed if it 'appear[s] to a legal certainty that the claim is really for less than the jurisdictional amount.'" *Larkin v. Brown* . . . (8th Cir. 1994). . . . If the defendant challenges the plaintiff's allegations of the amount in controversy, then the plaintiff must establish jurisdiction by a preponderance of the evidence. *McNutt v. General Motors Acceptance Corp.*, 298 U.S. 178 (1936) . . . .

. . .The district court has subject matter jurisdiction in a diversity case when a fact finder could legally conclude, from the pleadings and proof adduced to the court before trial, that the damages that the plaintiff suffered are greater than $75,000. We emphasize that McNutt does not suggest that . . . damages in some specific amount must be proved before trial by a preponderance of the evidence. . . .

Confusion may arise because the relevant jurisdictional fact, that is, the issue that must be proved by the preponderance of evidence, is easily misidentified. The jurisdictional fact in this case is not whether the damages are greater than the requisite amount, but whether a fact finder might legally conclude that they are: In other words, an amount that a plaintiff claims is not "in controversy" if no fact finder could legally award it. In one of our more extensive discussions of this issue, we upheld jurisdiction even though the jury ultimately awarded less than the statutory minimum, because jurisdiction is "measured by the amount properly pleaded or as of the time of the suit, not by the end result." . . .If access to federal district courts is to be further limited it should be done by statute and not by court decisions that permit a district court judge to prejudge the monetary value of [a] . . . claim." . . .

As we see it, the federal court has jurisdiction here unless, as a matter of law, Ms. Kopp could not recover punitive damages or damages for emotional distress, the amount of damages that she could recover is somehow fixed below the jurisdictional amount, or no reasonable jury could award damages totaling more than $75,000 in the circumstances that the case presents.

Under Missouri law, which is applicable here, punitive damages "may be awarded for conduct that is outrageous, because of the defendant's evil motive or reckless indifference to the rights of others. . . ." We have no trouble reconciling the facts of this case with those criteria, as the defendant admitted in his pre-trial deposition that he attacked, restrained, and raped his ex-wife who ultimately had to flee to a neighbor's house for safety. Furthermore, we have discovered no statutory or judicially created limits on punitive damages or damages for emotional distress in Missouri, nor has the defendant directed our attention to any. Finally, we conclude that an award of damages of more than $75,000 would not have to be set aside as excessive under Missouri law, nor would such an award be so "grossly excessive" as to violate the due process clause of the United States Constitution. . . .

Based on the present record, therefore, it seems clear to us that Ms. Kopp has demonstrated that her case falls within the diversity jurisdiction of the federal courts.

For the foregoing reasons, the order of the district court is reversed and the case is remanded to that court for further proceedings not inconsistent with this opinion.

Case Questions

1. Inasmuch as Ms. Kopp's medical bills were well below the jurisdictional amount, how could she make a good faith claim that she had enough damages to satisfy the jurisdictional amount requirement?
2. How closely do you believe federal district court judges should scrutinize a plaintiff's assertions in the complaint about having sufficient damages to satisfy the jurisdictional amount in cases in which federal subject matter jurisdiction is based on diversity of citizenship (i.e., plaintiff brings a diversity action)?
3. Assume that a plaintiff brings a diversity action in federal district court. Assume further that the plaintiff is ultimately awarded a money judgment for $60,000. Is the fact that plaintiff's damage award was for less than the jurisdictional amount of any jurisdictional significance if the case is appealed to a federal court of appeals?

In Rem and *In Personam* Jurisdiction

In order for a district court to hear a civil case, it must have, in addition to jurisdiction over the subject matter, jurisdiction over the property in an *in rem* proceeding or over the person of the defendant in an *in personam* proceeding. Jurisdiction over the person is normally acquired by serving a summons within the territory. In an ordinary civil action, the summons may be properly served anywhere within the territorial limits of the state in which the district court is located. A federal summons may also be served anywhere that a state summons could be served pursuant to the state's long-arm statute.

Venue in Federal Courts

Congress has provided that venue generally exists in the federal district where any defendant resides, if all defendants reside in the same state. It also exists where the claim arose or the property is located. If these choices are inappropriate, venue will exist in a diversity case in the federal district in which the defendant is subject to personal jurisdiction at the time the action is filed. In federal question cases, the alternative venue is the federal district in which any defendant can be found.[4]

A corporate defendant is subject to suit in any federal district in which it is subject to personal jurisdiction when the suit is filed.

Removal from State to Federal Courts (Removal Jurisdiction)

Except in those areas in which federal courts have exclusive jurisdiction, a suit does not have to be brought in a federal district court just because that court could exercise jurisdiction over the subject matter and over the person or property. A plaintiff may bring a dispute in any state or federal court that has jurisdiction.

A defendant sued in a state court may have a right to have the case removed to the federal district

Year	2004	2005	2006	2007	2008
Removals	34,443	30,178	29,437	30,282	30,065

F I G U R E 4.7 Removal from State Courts to U.S. District Courts 2004–2008

Source: Administrative Office of the United States Courts, *2008 Annual Report of the Director: Judicial Business of the United States Courts.* Washington, D.C.: U.S. Government Printing Office, 2009.

court. Any civil action brought in a state court that could originally have been filed in a district court is removable. Thus, removal jurisdiction is permissible where a federal question is raised or where the requirements for diversity of citizenship jurisdiction are met. Where the basis of removal jurisdiction is diversity of citizenship, that basis must exist at the time of filing the original suit and also at the time of petitioning for removal. To initiate the removal process, the defendant must file notice of removal with the federal court within thirty days after

service of the complaint. In recent years, U.S. District Court judges have approved the removal of approximately 31,000 cases per year from state to federal court (see Figure 4.7).

The plaintiff in the following case sought to prevent Wal-Mart from removing her tort action from the Louisiana court system to federal district court. The defendant asserted that the federal district court could exercise jurisdiction in this case because of diversity of citizenship.

Catherine Gebbia v. Wal-Mart Stores, Inc.
233 F.3d 880
U.S. Court of Appeals for the Fifth Circuit
December 4, 2000

Robert M. Parker, Circuit Judge

. . .Plaintiff brought this action on September 23, 1998, in the Twenty-First Judicial District Court of Louisiana, alleging claims arising from her injuries suffered in one of Defendant-Appellee Wal-Mart Stores, Inc.'s ("Defendant") stores in Hammond, Louisiana, on October 5, 1997. Plaintiff suffered her injuries when she went into the produce section of the store and slipped and fell in liquid, dirt, and produce on the floor. Plaintiff alleged in her original state court petition that she sustained injuries to her right wrist, left knee and patella, and upper and lower back. . . . Plaintiff alleged damages for medical expenses, physical pain and suffering, mental anguish and suffering, loss of enjoyment of life, loss of wages and earning capacity, and permanent disability and disfigurement. . . . . Consistent with Article 893 of the Louisiana Code of Civil Procedure, which prohibits the allegation of a specific amount of damages, Plaintiff did not pray for a specific amount of damages.

Defendant removed this action to the district court on October 13, 1998, pursuant to diversity jurisdiction as provided by 28 U.S.C. § 1332. It is undisputed

that the parties are completely diverse, as Plaintiff is a citizen of Louisiana and Defendant is a citizen of Delaware with its principle place of business in Arkansas. Defendant stated in its Notice of Removal that the $75,000 amount in controversy requirement was satisfied because Plaintiff's alleged injuries and damages, exclusive of interests and costs, exceeded that amount.

The district court scheduled this action for trial on March 20, 2000, and the parties proceeded with pretrial discovery until March 2, 2000, when Plaintiff questioned the court's diversity jurisdiction by filing a motion to remand arguing that the $75,000 amount in controversy requirement was not satisfied. In the motion, accompanied by Plaintiff's affidavit, Plaintiff argued that due to continuing medical treatment of her injuries, Plaintiff was unable to confirm the amount of damages claimed. Plaintiff added that only after conducting discovery and receiving information from her treating physicians was she able to ascertain that the amount of claimed damages would be less than $75,000. In light of such information, Plaintiff argued that the amount in controversy was less than

$75,000, and that the district court should remand this action for lack of subject-matter jurisdiction.

The district court denied the motion to remand on March 14, 2000, finding that the court had subject-matter jurisdiction because Plaintiff's petition at the time of removal alleged injuries that exceeded the $75,000 requirement. In the Revised Joint Pretrial Order filed on March 16, 2000, Plaintiff again disputed the court's jurisdiction because Plaintiff stipulated, based on medical evidence, that her claims did not amount to $75,000. Plaintiff then filed a motion to reconsider the district court's denial of her motion to remand in light of the stipulation, and re-urged the district court to remand for lack of subject-matter jurisdiction. On March 16, 2000, the district court denied Plaintiff's motion for reconsideration, restating its finding that because Plaintiff's claims at the time of removal alleged claims in excess of $75,000, the court was not inclined to reconsider its previous denial of the motion to remand.

Thereafter, this action was tried on March 20, and a jury found for Defendant on Plaintiff's claims. On March 22, the district court entered a judgment in favor of Defendant and dismissing Plaintiff's claims with prejudice. Plaintiff timely appealed the judgment, and now argues that the district court erred in denying her motion to remand.

Analysis

. . . Any civil action brought in a state court of which the district courts have original jurisdiction may be removed to the proper district court. 28 U.S.C. § 1441(a). District courts have original jurisdiction of all civil actions where the matter in controversy exceeds the sum or value of $75,000, exclusive of interests and costs, and is between citizens of different states. . . . §1332(a)(1). As noted above . . . the only issue on this appeal is whether the district court erred in deciding that the amount in controversy exceeded the sum or value of $75,000, exclusive of interest and costs.

We have established a clear analytical framework for resolving disputes concerning the amount in controversy for actions removed from Louisiana state courts pursuant to § 1332(a)(1) . . . Because plaintiffs in Louisiana state courts, by law, may not specify the numerical value of claimed damages . . .the removing

defendant must prove by a preponderance of the evidence that the amount in controversy exceeds $75,000. . . . The defendant may prove that amount either by demonstrating that the claims are likely above $75,000 in sum or value, or by setting forth the facts in controversy that support a finding of the requisite amount. . . .

Moreover, once the district court's jurisdiction is established, subsequent events that reduce the amount in controversy to less than $75,000 generally do not divest the court of diversity jurisdiction. . . . The jurisdictional facts that support removal must be judged at the time of the removal . . . . Additionally, if it is facially apparent from the petition that the amount in controversy exceeds $75,000 at the time of removal, post-removal affidavits, stipulations, and amendments reducing the amount do not deprive the district court of jurisdiction. . . .

In this action, the district court properly denied Plaintiff's motion to remand. It is "facially apparent" from Plaintiff's original petition that the claimed damages exceeded $75,000. In *Luckett* [*v. Delta Airlines, Inc.*, 171 F.3d 295, (5th Cir. 1999)], we held that the district court did not err in finding that the plaintiff's claims exceeded $75,000 because the plaintiff alleged damages for property, travel expenses, an emergency ambulance trip, a six-day stay in the hospital, pain and suffering, humiliation, and temporary inability to do housework after hospitalization. . . . In this action, Plaintiff alleged in her original state court petition that she sustained injuries to her right wrist, left knee and patella, and upper and lower back. Plaintiff alleged damages for medical expenses, physical pain and suffering, mental anguish and suffering, loss of enjoyment of life, loss of wages and earning capacity, and permanent disability and disfigurement. Such allegations support a substantially large monetary basis to confer removal jurisdiction . . . and therefore the district court did not err in denying Plaintiff's motion to remand. Because it was facially apparent that Plaintiff's claimed damages exceeded $75,000, the district court properly disregarded Plaintiff's post-removal affidavit and stipulation for damages less than $75,000, and such affidavit and stipulation did not divest the district court's jurisdiction. . . .

Affirmed.

Case Questions

1. In this case, which party had to prove that the jurisdictional amount requirement was met?
2. How did the court in this case assure itself as to the extent and nature of the plaintiff's damages?
3. What provision of the Louisiana Code of Civil Procedure makes it more difficult for litigants to determine the amount of a plaintiff's damages?

Federal statutes contain some limitations to removal jurisdiction. One statute limits a defendant who is a citizen of the state in which the lawsuit is filed to removing claims that raise a federal question. For example, if a citizen of New York sued a citizen of Ohio in a state court in Ohio for breach of contract or tort, the defendant could not have the case removed.

The plaintiffs in the next case filed suit in state court against the defendants after the plaintiffs defaulted on a loan and subsequently lost their home as a result of foreclosure. The defendants, not wishing to litigate in state court, sought to remove the case from the state court to the U.S. District Court for the Southern District of California. The defendants based their removal on the existence of a federal question. The plaintiffs responded by dismissing their federal claim and filing a motion seeking an order remanding the case to the state court.

The following opinion was written by the federal judge who ruled on the remand motion.

Gilmore v. Bank of New York
09-CV-0218-IEG
United States District Court, Southern District
July 9, 2009

Irma Gonzalez, District Judge
Plaintiffs Karen and Larry Gilmore ("Plaintiffs") have filed a motion to remand this case to state court. . . . Defendants Bank of New York ("BNY"), Countrywide Home Loans ("Countrywide"), America's Wholesale Lender ("AWL"), and Bank of America ("BOA") (collectively, "Defendants") have filed a motion to dismiss Plaintiffs' first amended complaint. . . .

Factual and Procedural Background
Plaintiffs Karen and Larry Gilmore's claim arises from a loan Ms. Gilmore received to purchase a home. The following facts are drawn from Plaintiffs' first amended complaint. On March 9, 2006 Karen Gilmore purchased an Oceanside, California home ("the property") for $780,000.

Using the services of a mortgage broker, Defendant American Mortgage Professional, Inc. ("AMP"), she obtained a loan from AWL for 80 percent ($624,000) of the purchase price. Ms. Gilmore agreed to make monthly payments on the loan in an amount of $4,591.74 at an interest rate of 7 percent for a period of 10 years . . . Ms. Gilmore financed the remaining 20 percent ($156,000) of the purchase price though a home equity line of credit ("HELOC"), allegedly funded by BOA. She agreed to monthly payments in an amount of $1,586.71 at an interest rate of 12.375 percent. The combined monthly payment on Plaintiffs' two loans equaled $6,178.45, at a time when Plaintiffs earned a combined monthly income of $7,500. At an undisclosed point in time, AWL allegedly transferred the servicing of the two loans to its parent company, Countrywide. Plaintiffs defaulted on their loans, resulting in a trustee's sale of the property on September 29, 2008 to BNY, as agent for Countrywide.

Plaintiffs brought the instant action in the Superior Court of California for the County of San Diego on January 12, 2009. Defendants removed the case to this Court on February 5, 2009. . . . The complaint alleged: "wrongful foreclosure;" "action to set aside trustee sale;" violation of California Civil Code §§ 1573 (constructive fraud) and 2923.5; violation of California Financial Code §§ 4973(f) and (n); violation of 12 U.S.C. §§ 2607(a) and (b) (the Real Estate Settlement Procedures Act, hereinafter "RESPA"); and "breach of fiduciary duties." Plaintiffs filed a first amended complaint on April 10, 2009 . . . alleging the following claims: "set aside of trustee sale;" conspiracy to defraud; violation of Cal. Civ. Code §§ 1573, 1667, 1708, 1770 and 2923.5; violation of Cal. Fin. Code § 4973; "breach of fiduciary duties;" and "contractual rescission."

On April 27, 2009, Defendants filed a motion to dismiss the first amended complaint. . . . On May 13, 2009 Plaintiffs filed a motion to remand the case to state court. . . . The Court finds the motions appropriate for disposition without oral argument. . . .

Discussion
I. Plaintiffs' Motion to Remand
A. Legal Standard
"Any civil action brought in a State court of which the district courts of the United States have original jurisdiction, may be removed by the defendant or the defendants, to the district court of the United States for the district and division embracing the place where such action is pending." 28 U.S.C. § 1441(a). . . . Removal jurisdiction may be based on diversity of citizenship or on the existence of a federal question. 28 U.S.C. § 1441 (b); . . . .The removal statute also provides that "[w] henever a separate and independent claim or cause of

action . . . is joined with one or more otherwise nonre-movable claims or causes of action, the entire case may be removed and the district court may determine all issues therein, or, in its discretion, may remand all matters in which State law predominates." 28 U.S.C. § 1441 (c). . . .

The Ninth Circuit "strictly construe[s] the removal statute against removal jurisdiction." . . . Accordingly, "[t]he `strong presumption' against removal jurisdiction means that the defendant always has the burden of establishing that removal is proper." . . . Whether removal jurisdiction exists must be determined by reference to the well-pleaded complaint. . . .

B. Analysis
Defendants originally premised their removal of this case upon Plaintiffs' allegations that Defendants violated RESPA, a federal statute. . . . Defendants further argued the Court had supplemental jurisdiction over Plaintiffs' state law claims . . . because those claims arose from the same set of operative facts as Plaintiffs' federal claim.

Plaintiffs' first amended complaint eliminates the RESPA claim. . . . However, Defendants argue the Court should retain supplemental jurisdiction over the amended complaint because Plaintiffs' "voluntary amendment to their complaint after removal to eliminate the federal claim does not automatically defeat federal jurisdiction." . . .

Plaintiffs' argument that the Court should remand the case . . . because they have abandoned their federal cause of action misstates the applicable legal rule. Section 1447 (c) provides, "[i]f at any time before final judgment it appears that the district court lacks subject matter jurisdiction, the case shall be remanded." . . . Notwithstanding this rule, removal jurisdiction based on a federal question is determined from the complaint as it existed *at the time of removal*. . . . Therefore, when removal, as in this case, is based on federal-question jurisdiction and all federal claims are eliminated from the lawsuit, "[i]t is generally within a district court's discretion either to retain jurisdiction to adjudicate the pendent state claims or to remand them to state court." . . . Accordingly, because Plaintiffs have abandoned their federal claim, the Court must exercise

its discretion to determine whether to retain supplemental jurisdiction over the remaining state claims.

The Supreme Court has held, and the Ninth Circuit has reiterated [sic] that "`in the usual case in which all federal-law claims are eliminated before trial, the balance of factors . . . will point toward declining to exercise jurisdiction over the remaining state-law claims.". . . . Moreover, this discretionary decision "depend[s] upon what `will best accommodate the values of economy, convenience, fairness, and comity. . . ." . . . The Court finds this case to be a "usual case" in which the balance of factors weighs in favor of remanding the remaining state claims to state court.

While Defendants argue the Court should exercise its discretion to retain the case because "Plaintiffs' filing of the [First Amended Complaint] is a blatant attempt to forum shop" . . . and the Supreme Court has held "[a] district court can consider whether the plaintiff has engaged in any manipulative tactics when it decides whether to remand a case," the Ninth Circuit has held it is not improper for a plaintiff to exercise the tactical decision to move for remand soon after removal . . . .("If the defendant rejects the plaintiff's offer to litigate in state court and removes the action, the plaintiff must then choose between federal claims and a state forum. Plaintiffs in this case chose the state forum. They dismissed their federal claims and moved for remand with all due speed after removal. There was nothing manipulative about that straight-forward tactical decision.") . . . Furthermore, Plaintiffs have abandoned their federal claim early in the case. There is also no indication that proceeding in state court would be wasteful or duplicative because no court or party has yet invested substantial resources into this case. The Court therefore finds that the concerns of economy, convenience, and comity would be served by returning this case to state court, and grants Plaintiffs' motion to remand. . . .

Conclusion
For the reasons stated herein, the Court orders that this action be remanded to the Superior Court of California for the County of San Diego. The Court denies as moot Defendants' motion to dismiss the complaint and request for judicial notice.

It is so ordered.

Case Questions

1. Why were the Gilmores allowed to file the amended complaint, manipulate the process to their advantage, and thereby deny the defendant the opportunity of removing the case to federal court?
2. Why, according to the court, does the defendant have the burden of proof in a removal proceeding?

The *Erie* Doctrine

In adjudicating state matters, a federal court is guided by a judicial policy known as the *Erie* doctrine. In the 1938 landmark case of *Erie Railroad Company v. Tompkins*, 304 U.S. 64, the U.S. Supreme Court decided that federal questions are governed by federal law. In other cases, however, the substantive law that should generally be applied in federal courts is the law of the state. The law of the state was defined as including judicial decisions as well as statutory law. In addition, there is no federal general common law governing state matters. A federal district court is bound by the statutes and precedents of the state in which it sits.

This restriction prevents a federal court and a state court from reaching different results on the same issue of state law.

The *Erie* doctrine, which goes to the heart of relations between the state and federal courts, is one of the most important judicial policies ever adopted by the U.S. Supreme Court. Many of the civil cases brought subsequent to this landmark case have been affected by the decision.

Where state and federal procedural rules differ, the *Erie* doctrine does not normally apply. Federal courts do not generally apply state procedural rules. Instead, the Federal Rules of Civil Procedure apply in federal courts unless they would significantly affect a litigant's substantive rights, encourage forum shopping, or promote a discriminatory application of the law. The Federal Rules of Civil Procedure were not designed to have any effect upon the rules of decision.

It is important to remember that the *Erie* doctrine does require that federal judges apply the same conflict-of-law rule that would be applied in the courts of the state in which the federal court is situated. In the following case, a district court sitting in Indiana had to determine whether it should apply Indiana law or that of California in reaching its decision.

INTERNET TIP

Interested readers will find an excellent case that illustrates the *Erie* doctrine, *Carson v. National Bank,* on the textbook's website. This case was "retired" in the ninth edition after initially appearing in the second edition of the textbook, twenty-eight years ago. It can be found with other "Retired Cases."

Readers may recall reading the Chapter III conflict of law case from Indiana of *Hubbard Manufacturing Co. v. Greeson*. In that 1987 case the Indiana Supreme Court decided to apply the significant relationship rule in tort cases where a conflict of law issue is raised but the place where the tort was committed was an unimportant fact in the case.

We see that precedent followed in the next 2001 federal appeals case, which illustrates the working of the *Erie* doctrine.

The federal district court, sitting in Indiana, at the request of Yamaha Motor Corporation granted Yamaha's motion for summary judgment, thereby declaring Yamaha the prevailing party in this lawsuit. Summary judgment is granted only if no genuine issues of material fact exist or the opposing party cannot possibly prevail at trial because the facts necessary to establish that party's case are not provable or are not true. This pretrial motion is not granted if there are important facts in dispute between the parties, because it would deprive them of their right to a trial.

The key issue at trial and on appeal was whether Indiana or California law should be applied to this product liability case. Yamaha argued that Indiana law should be applied, and Charles and April Land maintained that California law should control. As we learned in Chapter III, the outcome of disputes as to which state's law should be applied in a case depends on the conflict of laws rule (also known as choice of law rule) that has been adopted in the forum state. The district court, following the principles of the *Erie* doctrine, concluded after applying Indiana's choice of law rule that Indiana law should apply. It determined that an Indiana statute required that product liability suits like this one be brought within ten years of the date when *the product was first purchased from the manufacturer (here, Yamaha).* Therefore, said the district court, inasmuch as the Lands had not started their suit within that time period, there was no way that they could prevail at trial. Yamaha, the court concluded, was entitled to summary judgment. The Lands subsequently appealed to the Seventh Circuit, arguing that the district court had wrongfully applied Indiana law instead of California law.

Charles and April Land v. Yamaha Motor Corporation
272 F.3d 514
U.S. Court of Appeals for the Seventh Circuit
December 10, 2001

Flaum, Chief Judge.
The district court granted summary judgment in favor of defendants Yamaha Motor Corporation, U.S.A. ("YMUS") and Yamaha Motor Co., Ltd. ("YMC"), holding plaintiffs Charles and April Land's product liability suit [was] barred by the Indiana Statute of [Limitations]. . . .

When appellant Charles Land, an Indiana resident, attempted to start a Yamaha WaveRunner Model WR500G on Heritage Lake in Indiana on June 25, 1998, the vehicle exploded and caused Land permanent back injury. The plaintiffs contend that the WaveRunner was defective in design: it allowed fuel fumes to accumulate in the hull of the boat, posing serious risk of fire upon ignition. . . . For purposes of the summary judgment motion, the district court assumed that the plaintiffs could prove their product liability claim on the merits. That is, it assumed that when the WaveRunner left the possession and control of the defendants, it was in a defective condition unreasonably dangerous to anticipated users. Furthermore, it is undisputed that the Lands filed suit on December 23, 1999, and that both the injury and the filing of the suit occurred more than ten years after the WaveRunner was delivered to Wallace Richardson, the first user.

The Indiana Statute of Repose provides in relevant part that product liability actions must be commenced within ten years after the delivery of the product to the initial user or consumer. YMC, a Japanese corporation with its principal place of business in Japan, designed, manufactured, and tested the WaveRunner in Japan. It petitioned for an exemption from the United States Coast Guard's requirement that every vehicle like the WaveRunner have a fan to ventilate fuel fumes out of the hull of the boat. YMUS knew of the test results, and, according to the Lands, gave false information to the Coast Guard as to the known danger of the WaveRunner design in order to keep its exemption from the fan requirement. YMUS, which maintains its principal place of business in California, participated in developing the WaveRunner and imported it to the United States. YMUS, while it has no office in Indiana, is authorized and does business in the state. On July 7, 1987, YMUS sold and shipped the vehicle to a boating store in Kentucky. On July 28, 1987, Wallace Richardson, an Indiana resident, purchased the WaveRunner. Larry Bush, another Indiana resident, subsequently bought the WaveRunner in 1989 or 1990. Bush was the registered owner when the WaveRunner caused Land's injury. From the time of Bush's purchase, the boat was registered, garaged, and serviced in Indiana.

Between 1988 and 1998, 24 other WaveRunners were reported to have exploded. YMUS twice recalled certain models of WaveRunners for modifications to reduce the likelihood of fuel leakage. It never recalled the WR500 series. . . .

Appellants argue that although they did not commence their action until well over ten years after delivery to the initial user, their case is not barred because . . . California law, which includes no statute of repose, governs the action . . . .

We review a grant of summary judgment de novo [i.e., take a fresh look at the evidence], construing the evidence in the light most favorable to the nonmoving party. . . . Summary judgment is appropriate if there is no genuine issue as to any material fact and the moving party is entitled to judgment as a matter of law. . . .

Choice of Law
A federal court sitting in diversity jurisdiction must apply the substantive law of the state in which it sits, 304 U.S. 64 . . . (1938). . . . The *Erie* doctrine extends to choice-of-law principles and requires the court to apply the conflicts rules of the forum state. . . . Therefore, the district court properly applied the choice-of-law rule of Indiana.

Indiana applies a two-step conflicts analysis. *Hubbard Mfg. v. Greeson* (Ind. 1987). First, the court must determine if the place where the last event necessary to make the defendant liable—that is, the place of the injury—is insignificant. . . . If it is not, the law of that state applies. . . . Only if the court finds that the place of injury is insignificant does it move to step two which requires the court to consider "other factors such as: 1) the place where the conduct causing the injury occurred; 2) the residence or place of business of the parties; and 3) the place where the relationship is centered." . . . In the instant case, we, like the district court, arrive at the inevitable conclusion that the place of the injury—Indiana—is not insignificant. Therefore, we apply Indiana law and need not address the second prong in Indiana's choice-of-law analysis. . . .

Charles Land was injured while operating the WaveRunner in Indiana. He was a resident of Indiana, the owner of the boat was a resident of Indiana, and the boat had been garaged and serviced in Indiana for a decade before it caused Land's injury. There is no evidence in the record that the WaveRunner was ever used outside of Indiana. It was not mere fortuity that the injury occurred in Indiana, as the Lands suggest by comparing this choice-of-law determination with those involving pass-through automobile or airplane accidents in which the place of the injury is given little weight, and the argument that Indiana's contacts have little or no relevance to the legal action simply cannot withstand scrutiny. Therefore, our analysis of Indiana choice-of-law policy must end with step one.

The Lands argue that California, where YMUS was incorporated and where the defendant's tortious conduct occurred, has greater relevance. Maybe so. . . . This analysis belongs in step two of the Indiana

conflicts policy, however, which we cannot reach. Some states use the "most significant relationship" approach suggested by the Restatement (Second) of Conflict of Laws. If Indiana did so, we would skip step one of our analysis and instead "isolate the pertinent issue, examine each state's connection to the occurrence, identify the governmental policies espoused by each state relevant to the issue, and proclaim applicable the law of the state with the superior interest." . . . That case might have a different outcome from the one at hand. Indiana does not adhere to the most significant relationship analysis, however, and the Supreme Court of Indiana has not signaled that it intends to overrule *Hubbard*. Although *Hubbard* does note some discomfort with the rigid place of injury, or *lex loci delicti*, approach, it still adheres to an analysis that uses the place of injury as a baseline. . . . If the place of injury is not insignificant, we must apply its law regardless of the greater interest another state may have. The Lands propose an approach whereby the law of the place of the tortious conduct is controlling in product liability cases. The state of Indiana has given us no-indication that it intends to change its choice-of-law policy to reach such a result, and we decline to make that policy decision for it. Indiana's contacts to this case are not insignificant. Therefore, its law, including the Statute of Repose, applies.

Because Indiana law governs this case and because the Indiana Statute of Repose bars product liability actions that, like this one, are brought more than ten years after delivery of the product to the initial user or consumer, we find that the district court properly granted summary judgment in favor of the defendants. We AFFIRM.

Case Questions

1. What was the basis for federal jurisdiction in this case?
2. Since the case was heard in federal court, why didn't the judge apply the law as generally applied in the nation, rather than the law of Indiana?

THE THIRTEEN U.S. COURTS OF APPEALS

The United States has been divided by Congress into eleven circuits (clusters of states), and a court of appeals has been assigned to each circuit. A court

of appeals has also been established for the District of Columbia. In 1982, Congress created a new court of appeals with broad territorial jurisdiction and with very specialized subject matter jurisdiction. This court is called the Court of Appeals for the Federal Circuit. Its job is to review appeals from the U.S. district courts throughout the nation in such areas as patent, trademark, and copyright cases; cases in which the United States is the defendant; and cases appealed from the U.S. Court of International Trade and the U.S. Court of Federal Claims. Figure 4.8 shows the boundaries of the thirteen circuits.

These appellate courts hear appeals on questions of law from decisions of the federal district courts in their circuits and review findings of federal administrative agencies. For most litigants, they are the ultimate appellate tribunals of the federal system. Appeal to these courts is a matter of right, not discretion, so long as proper procedures are followed.

When attorneys wish to appeal decisions of lower tribunals, they must follow such procedures to get the cases before a court of appeals. Notice of appeal must be filed within thirty days from the entry of judgment (sixty days when the United States or an officer or agent thereof is a party). A cost bond (in civil cases) may be required to ensure payment of the costs of the appeal. Both the record on appeal and a brief must be filed.

Attorneys must then persuade the judges that the lower tribunals committed errors that resulted in injustices to their clients. On appeal, the court

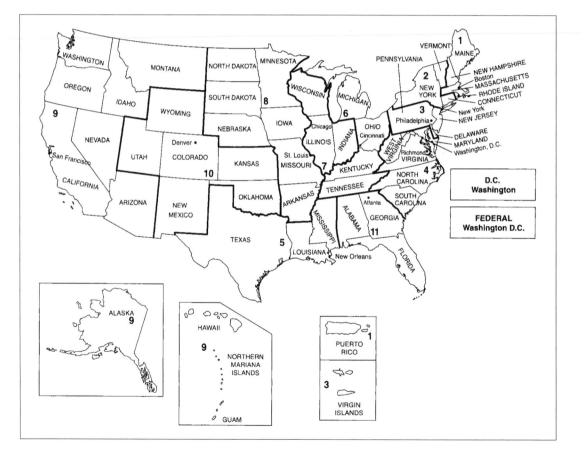

FIGURE 4.8 The Thirteen Federal Judicial Circuits

of appeals does not substitute its judgment for that of the lower tribunal's finding of fact. It does reverse the lower court's decision if that decision was clearly erroneous as a matter of law. See Figure 4.9 for statistical information regarding cases filed and terminated by U.S. Courts of Appeals between 2005 and 2008.

THE U.S. SUPREME COURT

The U.S. Supreme Court has existed since 1789. Today the court consists of a chief justice and eight associate justices. It exercises both appellate and original jurisdiction. Its chief function is to act as the last and final court of review over all cases in the federal system and some cases in the state system.

Supreme Court review is not a matter of right. A party wishing to have its case reviewed by the Supreme Court (called a petitioner) is required by statute to file a petition for a writ of certiorari with the court. The other party, called the respondent, will have the right to oppose the granting of the writ. The court grants certiorari only where there are special and important reasons for so doing. If four or more justices are in favor of granting the petition, the writ issues and the case are accepted. The court thus controls its docket, reserving its time and efforts for the cases that seem to the justices to deserve consideration. Figure 4.10 shows what happened to certiorari petitions filed by litigants in the U.S. Courts of Appeals seeking review by the U.S. Supreme Court over a twelve-month period in 2007–2008.

The U.S. Supreme Court is the only court specifically created in the Constitution. All other federal

	2005	2006	2007	2008
Cases Filed	68,473	66,618	58,410	61,104
Cases Terminated	61,975	67,582	62,846	59,096

F I G U R E   4.9 U.S. Court of Appeals—Appeals Commenced and Terminated During 48-Month Period Ending September 30, 2008

Source: Administrative Office of the United States Courts, *2007 & 2008 Annual Reports of the Director: Judicial Business of the United States Courts*. Washington, D.C.: U.S. Government Printing Office, 2008, 2009.

Nature of Proceeding	Pending on Oct. 1, 2007	Filed	Granted	Pending on Sept. 30, 2008
Total	3,861	6,154	259	3,300
Criminal	1,567	2,673	170	1,112
U.S. Civil	536	780	22	501
Private Civil	1,612	2,545	50	1,565
Administrative Appeals	146	156	17	122

F I G U R E   4.10 Petitions for Review on Writ of Certiorari to the Supreme Court during the 12-Month Period Ending September 30, 2008

Source: Administrative Office of the United States Courts, *2008 Annual Report of the Director: Judicial Business of the United States Courts*. Washington, D.C.: U.S. Government Printing Office, 2009.

courts are statutorily created by the Congress. The Constitution provides for the court's original jurisdiction. Original jurisdiction is the power to take note of a suit at its beginning, try it, and pass judgment on the law and the facts of the controversy. The Constitution has given the court the power to perform the function of trial court in cases affecting ambassadors, public ministers, and consuls, and in controversies in which a state is a party. Usually the power is not exclusive, nor is the court required to hear all cases over which it has original jurisdiction.

Article III authorizes Congress to determine the court's appellate jurisdiction. A history-making example occurred in 1983 when Congress enacted the Military Justice Act. This act conferred jurisdiction on the Supreme Court to directly review designated categories of appeals from the Court of Military Appeals. These appeals are brought to the court pursuant to the writ of certiorari procedure. This marked the first time in the history of the United States that any Article III court was authorized to review the decisions of military courts.

CHAPTER SUMMARY

In this chapter readers have learned how federal and state court systems are organized and about the different functions of trial and state courts. Explanations were also provided as to the procedural differences between jury trials and bench trials. The fundamental requirements for subject matter and personal jurisdiction in federal and state courts were summarized, and the importance of venue was explained. Students also learned the circumstances under which cases can be removed from state court to federal court and why federal trial courts need to be concerned about the *Erie* doctrine.

CHAPTER QUESTIONS

1. Bensusan Restaurant Corporation owns and operates a popular, large New York City jazz club called "The Blue Note." Richard King owns and has operated a small cabaret, also called "The Blue Note," in Columbia, Missouri, since 1980. King's establishment features live music and attracts its customers from central Missouri. In 1996, King decided to establish a website for the purpose of advertising his cabaret. King included a disclaimer on his website in which he gave a plug to Bensusan's club and made it clear that the two businesses were unrelated. He later modified this disclaimer by making it even more explicit and said that his "cyberspot was created to provide information for Columbia, Missouri area individuals only."

   Bensusan brought suit in the U.S. District court for the Southern District of New York against King seeking monetary damages and injunctive relief. The plaintiff maintained that King had infringed on his federally protected trademark by calling his cabaret "The Blue Note." King moved to dismiss the complaint for lack of personal jurisdiction. He contended that he had neither engaged in business within New York nor committed any act sufficient to confer *in personam* jurisdiction over him by New York. The U.S. District Court agreed with King, and the case was appealed to the United States Court of Appeals for the Second Circuit. Should the Second Circuit affirm or reverse the District Court? Why?

   Bensusan Restaurant Corporation v. Richard B. King, Docket No. 96-9344 (1997)

2. Dorothy Hooks brought a class action suit against Associated Financial Services, Inc. and others for breach of contract, fraud, and conspiracy. In her complaint, Hooks stipulated for the members of the class that the plaintiffs would waive both the right to recover more than $49,000 in damages and any right to recover punitive damages. The defendant nevertheless sought removal predicated on diversity of citizenship jurisdiction. Should the U.S. District Court grant the plaintiff's petition to remand this case back to the state courts?

   Hooks v. Associated Financial Services Company, Inc. et al. 966 F. Supp. 1098 (1997)

3. David Singer was injured when his automobile was struck by an uninsured motorist. David was insured against this type of accident up to a policy limit of $30,000 by State Farm Mutual Automobile Insurance Company. When State Farm stalled on paying on his insurance claim, David filed suit in state court, alleging breach of contract and breach of good faith and fair dealing. David did not demand any specified amount of money damages in his complaint because state law prohibited him from so doing. State Farm filed a removal petition in U.S. District Court, alleging that the federal court had subject matter jurisdiction based on diversity of citizenship. The defendant alleged that damages existed in excess of $50,000 (the jurisdictional amount at the time the suit was filed). Has the defendant followed the correct procedure, under these circumstances, for establishing the existence of the jurisdictional amount? How should the U.S. Court of Appeals for the Ninth Circuit rule?

   Singer v. State Farm, No. 95-55441 (1997)

4. Sludge Inc., a Wisconsin corporation, has a website in Wisconsin in which it advertises its wares. This website is accessible in every state in the nation. Can a Colorado corporation that believes Sludge has infringed on its trademarks successfully establish a basis for *in personam* jurisdiction if suit is brought in a Colorado court? Shout it make a difference if the website had generated several thousand messages, as well as 500 contacts, and 10 percent of its sales from Colorado? What argument would you make in favor of jurisdiction over Sludge? What argument would you make in opposition to jurisdiction over Sludge?

5. Mr. and Mrs. Woodson instituted a product liability action in an Oklahoma state court to recover for personal injuries sustained in Oklahoma in an accident involving a car that they had bought in New York while they were New York residents. The Woodsons were driving the car through Oklahoma at the time of the accident. The defendants were the car retailer and its wholesaler, both New York corporations, who did no business in Oklahoma. The defendants entered a special appearance, claiming that the Oklahoma state court did not have personal jurisdiction. Would there be enough "minimum contacts" between the defendants and the forum state for the forum state to have personal jurisdiction over the defendants?

   World-Wide Volkswagen Corp. v. Woodson, 444 U.S. 286 (1980)

6. In this hypothetical diversity of citizenship case, federal law requires complete diversity of citizenship between plaintiffs and defendants and an amount in controversy greater than $75,000 in order for federal courts to entertain jurisdiction of an action. Tom Jones and Leonard Woodrock were deep-shaft coal miners in West Virginia, although Leonard lived across the border in Kentucky. Tom purchased a new Eureka, a National Motors car, from Pappy's Auto Sales, a local firm. National Motors Corporation is a large auto manufacturer with its main factory in Indiana, and is incorporated in Kentucky. When Tom was driving Leonard home from the mine, the Eureka's steering wheel inexplicably locked. The car hurtled down a 100-foot embankment and came to rest against a tree. The Eureka, which cost

$17,100, was a total loss. Tom and Leonard suffered damages of $58,000 apiece for personal injuries. Can Tom sue National Motors for damages in a federal court? Why? Can Leonard? Can Leonard and Tom join their claims and sue National Motors in federal court?

7. National Mutual Insurance Company is a District of Columbia corporation. It brought a diversity action in the U.S. District Court of Maryland against Tidewater Transfer Company, a Virginia corporation doing business in Maryland. National Mutual contends that, for diversity purposes, a D.C. resident may file suit against the resident of a state. Tidewater Transfer disagrees. What should be taken into consideration in deciding whether the District of Columbia can, for diversity purposes, be regarded as a state?

National Mutual Insurance v. Tidewater Transfer Co., 337 U.S. 582 (1949)

8. Several Arizona citizens brought a diversity suit in a federal district court against Harsh Building Company, an Oregon corporation. All parties involved in the suit stipulated that the defendant had its principal place of business in Oregon. During the trial, evidence showed that the only real business activity of Harsh Building Co. was owning and operating the Phoenix apartment complex, which was the subject of the suit. The plaintiffs lost the suit. On appeal, they claimed that the district court did not have jurisdiction because of lack of diversity of citizenship. Did the plaintiffs waive their right to challenge jurisdiction?

Bialac v. Harsh Building Co., 463 F.2d 1185 (9th Cir. 1972)

ENDNOTES

1. *In personam* jurisdiction will generally not be recognized where someone is duped into entering the state for the purpose of making service. *Townsend v. Smith*, 3 N.W.439 (1879) and *Jacobs/ Kahan & Co. v. Marsh*, 740 F.2d 587 (7th Cir. 1984). Similarly, a person who enters a state to challenge jurisdiction cannot be validly served. *Stewart v. Ramsay*, 242 U.S. 128 (1916).

2. *Burnham v. Superior Court*, 495 U.S. 604 (1990).

3. Senate Select Committee Report on Governmental Operations with Respect to Intelligence Operations, Part IV, Conclusions and Recommendations, p. 290.

4. 28 U.S.C 1391.

V

✳

Civil Procedure

CHAPTER OBJECTIVES

1. *Understand the importance of procedure in our civil legal system.*
2. *Describe the basic steps of the civil litigation process.*
3. *Identify the functions of the complaint, answer, and reply.*
4. *Explain the use of pretrial motions to dismiss and for summary judgment.*
5. *Summarize modern discovery tools and their use.*
6. *Describe the procedural steps in the conduct of a trial.*

Courts are a passive adjudicator of disputes and neither initiate nor encourage litigation. The court system does nothing until one of the parties has called on it through appropriate procedures. Detailed procedural rules create the process that is used to decide the merits of a dispute. At the beginning of the process, these rules explain what a plaintiff must do to start a lawsuit and how the plaintiff can assert a legal claim against a defendant. Defendants are similarly told how to raise defenses and claims once they have been notified of a suit. Procedural rules govern what documents must be prepared, what each must contain, and how they should be presented to the court and the defendant. Once the lawsuit has been initiated, procedures govern how the parties discover relevant information and evidence, especially when it is in the possession of one's opponent. Rules also govern the conduct of trials, any enforcement procedures necessary after trial, the conduct of appeals, and the imposition of sanctions on rule violators. The principal objective of procedural law is to give the parties to a dispute an equal and fair opportunity to present their cases to a nonprejudiced and convenient tribunal. If procedural rules are correctly drafted and implemented, both parties to the dispute should feel that they have been fairly treated.

Although all procedures must satisfy constitutional due process requirements, the state and federal governments, as separate sovereigns, have promulgated separate rules of civil procedure that govern the litigation process in their respective forums. This means, for example, that Oregon lawyers have to learn two sets of procedural rules. If they are litigating in the state courts of Oregon, they comply with the *Oregon Rules of Civil Procedure*, and when litigating in the U.S. District Court for Oregon, they follow the provisions of the *Federal Rules of Civil Procedure* (FRCP).

The purpose of this chapter is to explain the procedures that govern a civil suit from the time a litigant decides to sue until final court judgment. Indispensable to an understanding of these systems is a familiarity with the various stages and terms that are encountered in a civil proceeding.

PROCEEDINGS BEFORE A CIVIL TRIAL

The first step in civil litigation involves a triggering event that injures the plaintiff or damages his or her property (see Figure 5.1). The second step usually involves the plaintiff selecting an attorney. It is important to understand that, in general, each party pays for his or her attorney's fee irrespective of who ultimately prevails in the substantive dispute. This is subject to exceptions where statutory law provides otherwise and where common law judicial doctrines permit the court to order the loser to pay the winner's attorney fees.

Hiring a Lawyer

The period between the event that gives rise to the suit (the triggering event) and the filing of a complaint is known as the **informal discovery** period. The court has neither knowledge of nor interest in the plaintiff's cause of action against the defendant.

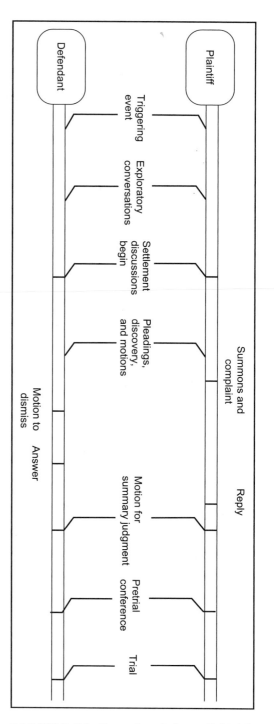

F I G U R E 5.1 Proceedings Before a Civil Trial

During this time, the plaintiff contacts an attorney and describes the circumstances that led to the injury. The attorney discusses in general terms the legal alternatives available and usually asks for an opportunity to conduct an independent investigation to assess the value of the claim. This meeting is known as an exploratory conversation. At this point, the plaintiff and the attorney are not contractually bound to each other.

After the exploratory conversation and further investigation, the plaintiff meets again with the attorney to determine which course of action should be taken. The attorney presents an evaluation of the case in terms of the remedies available, the probability of achieving a favorable verdict, and the nature and probability of the award likely to be granted. At this point, the plaintiff retains the attorney as a representative in the judicial proceedings that are likely to follow.

Attorney's fees may be determined in several ways. Attorneys may charge the client by the hour. They may contract with the client to take a specified percentage of the money collected as compensation pursuant to what is called a **contingent fee** agreement. If no money is recovered for the client, an attorney is not entitled to any fee. However, the client will still be responsible for expenses. An attorney may be on a retainer, in which case the client pays the attorney an agreed-upon sum of money to handle all of or specified portions of a client's legal problems for a specified period of time such as a year. Last, an attorney may charge a flat rate for certain routine services.

After the plaintiff's lawyer has been officially retained, he or she normally contacts the defendant. This information puts the defendant on notice that the plaintiff is preparing to seek an adjudicative settlement of the claim. If the defendant has not already retained an attorney, this is the time to do so. The attorneys meet, with or without their clients, to discuss a reasonable settlement. These discussions are referred to as **settlement conferences**. If they prove unsuccessful, the judicial machinery is set in motion.

Clients always have the right to discharge their lawyers at any time, with or without cause. Readers will see in the next case, however, that discharged attorneys may still be entitled to compensation from their former clients.

Virginia Atkinson and James Howell, the lawyers in the next case, entered into a contingent fee contract with Joy Salmon. After Salmon discharged them, they sued requesting that the court award them a *quantum meruit* **recovery** ("as much as they deserved"). The lawyers, at the client's request, had engaged in legal work prior to their discharge date. Because of their discharge, they argued, the terms of the contingency fee agreement no longer applied. Under these circumstances, they asserted, their former client should have to pay them immediately a reasonable sum for the work they had completed on her behalf. The case was tried to a jury, which found in favor of the attorneys in the amount of $7,200. The client argued that the attorneys were not entitled to recover any fees. The Arkansas Supreme Court was called upon to decide.

Joy Salmon v. Virginia Atkinson
137 S.W.3d 383
Supreme Court of Arkansas
December 11, 2003

Donald L. Corbin, Justice
This case involves an issue of first impression: Whether an attorney who enters into a contingent-fee contract with a client and is later discharged by the client may bring an action for a *quantum-meruit* fee prior to the resolution of the former client's lawsuit. Appellant Joy Salmon contends that the discharged attorney's cause of action does not accrue unless and until the client is successful in recovering an award. She thus contends that the Pulaski County Circuit Court erred in awarding Appellees Virginia Atkinson and James Howell legal fees in the amount of $7,200 for work they performed in representing Appellant prior to date that she discharged them....

The essential facts are not disputed. In June 2000, Appellant hired Appellees to pursue a claim for damages against the estate of George Brown. Appellant had lived with Brown for some time prior to his death and had cared for him as his nurse. Additionally, Appellant believed that she was married to Brown and, as his widow, she wanted to pursue a claim against Brown's estate. Appellees agreed to take Appellant's case on a contingency basis, in which Appellees would receive fifty percent of any recovery awarded to Appellant, plus costs and expenses. The contingent-fee contract was entered into on June 19, 2000, and it provided in pertinent part: "It is understood that in the event of no recovery, no fee shall be charged by Atkinson Law Offices."

Appellees then began to work on Appellant's case. They interviewed multiple witnesses, researched Appellant's claim of marriage to Brown, researched the general law, and negotiated with the estate's attorneys.... Based on their investigation and research, Appellees drew up a petition for Appellant to file in the probate case. Sometime in late July, they presented the petition to Appellant for her signature. Appellant indicated that she wanted to think about filing the claim, and she took the petition with her. The next communication Appellees received from Appellant was a letter, dated August 1, informing them that their services were no longer required.

Thereafter, in a letter dated August 21, 2000, Appellees informed Appellant that she had abrogated the June 19 contract without justification and that, therefore, she was required to pay Appellees for their services from June 19 to July 31. The letter reflects in part: "In investigation of your claims, legal research, and negotiation with the estate we expended 48 hours. At our customary billing rate of $150 per hour, the total fee payable at this time is $7,200." The letter also informed Appellant that the last date for which she could file her claim against Brown's estate was September 1, 2000. The record reflects that on September 1, 2000, Appellant filed a petition against the estate, *pro se*.

On May 10, 2001, Appellees filed suit against Appellant in circuit court, seeking recovery in *quantum meruit* for work they had performed on Appellant's case prior to the date that she discharged them. Following a trial on December 3, 2002, the jury returned a verdict in favor of Appellees. Thereafter, Appellant filed a motion for judgment notwithstanding the verdict (JNOV), arguing that because the contingent-fee contract specifically provided that no fee would be charged unless there was a recovery, and because there had not yet been any recovery, the jury verdict was not supported by substantial evidence. The trial court denied that motion on December 17, 2002. The judgment was also entered of record on that date. On January 2, 2003, Appellant filed a motion for new trial

and a renewed motion for JNOV. The trial court denied those motions on February 4, 2003. Appellant then filed a notice of appeal on February 28, 2003.

On appeal, Appellant argues that allowing Appellees to collect a *quantum meruit* fee directly conflicts with the language of the contract providing that no fee would be charged in the event that Appellant did not recover on her probate claim. Thus, she asserts that because she has not yet recovered on her claim, it was error to award a fee to Appellees. She contends further that the award of fees to Appellees under the circumstances impaired her absolute right, as the client, to discharge Appellees and terminate their services.

As stated above, the issue of when a discharged attorney's cause of action for a *quantum meruit* fee accrues is one of first impression in this court. However, this court has consistently held that a discharged attorney may be paid for the reasonable value of his or her services notwithstanding that the parties originally entered into a contingent-fee contract.... The plain rationale behind this rule is that where the attorney has conferred a benefit upon the client, *i.e.*, legal services and advice, the client is responsible to pay such reasonable fees.

The question in this case is not whether the discharged attorney may recover a *quantum meruit* fee, but whether recovery of such a fee is dependent upon the contingency originally agreed to in the contract, *i.e.*, the successful prosecution of the client's case. There is a split amongst the states on this issue. Some states adhere to the "California rule," which provides that the discharged attorney's cause of action does not accrue unless and until the occurrence of the stated contingency.... Under this rule, a discharged attorney is barred from receiving any fee if the client does not recover on the underlying matter. This is true even if the attorney was discharged without cause.

Other states subscribe to the "New York rule," which provides that the discharged attorney's cause of action accrues immediately upon discharge and is not dependent upon the former client's recovery.... The courts that subscribe to this rule do so primarily for two reasons. First, they reason that when the client terminates the contingent-fee contract by discharging the attorney, the contract ceases to exist and the contingency term, *i.e.*, whether the attorney wins the client's case, is no longer operative. As the New York Court of Appeals explained: "Either [the contract] wholly stands or totally falls."... Because the contract is terminated, the client can no longer use the contract's term to prevent the discharged attorney from recovering a fee in *quantum meruit*. "A client cannot terminate the agreement and then resurrect the contingency term when the discharged attorney files a fee claim."...

The second primary reason that courts subscribe to the "New York rule" is that they believe that forcing the discharged attorney to wait on the occurrence of the contingency is unfair in that it goes beyond what the parties contemplated in the contract. The New York Court of Appeals said it best:

> The value of one attorney's services is not measured by the result attained by another. This one did not contract for his contingent compensation on the hypothesis of success or failure by some other member of the bar.... In making their agreement, the parties may be deemed to have estimated this lawyer's pecuniary merit according to his own character, temperament, energy, zeal, education, knowledge and experience which are the important factors contributing to his professional status and constituting in a large degree, when viewed in relation to the volume of work performed and the result accomplished, a fair standard for gauging the value of services as prudent counsel and skillful advocate....

An additional reason for holding that a discharged attorney does not have to wait on the occurrence of the contingency is that the attorney is not claiming under the contingent-fee contract. The Illinois Supreme Court explained:

> *Quantum meruit* is based on the implied promise of a recipient of services to pay for those services which are of value to him. The recipient would be unjustly enriched if he were able to retain the services without paying for them. The claimant's recovery here should not be linked to a contract contingency when his recovery is not based upon the contract, but upon *quantum meruit*....

We believe that the "New York rule" is the better rule. Applying that rule to the facts of this case, we hold that the trial court did not err in awarding a *quantum meruit* fee to Appellees. The undisputed evidence showed that Appellant hired Appellees to pursue a claim against the estate of George Brown. She entered into a contingency-fee agreement, whereby she agreed to pay Appellees fifty percent of any recovery they obtained for her, plus costs and expenses. For the next six weeks or so, Appellees performed work on Appellant's case, which involved interviewing multiple witnesses, performing document research and general legal research, negotiating with the estate's attorneys, and, finally, preparing a petition for Appellant to file in the probate matter.

Appellees reviewed the prepared petition with Appellant and presented it to her for her signature. She declined to sign the petition at that time, indicating that she wanted to think about it. She then took the petition with her. The next communication Appellees had with Appellant was a letter in which Appellant discharged them without explanation....

Based on the foregoing evidence, we hold that Appellees' cause of action to recover reasonable attorney's fees, under the theory of *quantum meruit*, accrued immediately upon their being discharged by Appellant. While we are mindful of the client's right to discharge his or her attorney at any time, we do not believe that our holding in this case in any way impairs that right. To the contrary, this court has previously determined that the client's right to discharge the attorney is not compromised by allowing the discharged attorney to recover in *quantum meruit*.... We thus affirm the trial court's judgment.

Case Questions

1. How do contracts between attorneys and their clients differ from other contracts?
2. List the pros and cons of contingent fees.
3. Should a court uphold a contingent fee contract between attorney and client that prohibits a settlement by the client?

Assume Attorney Smith orally contracted to represent a client in a real estate transaction and had performed satisfactorily for six months. Assume further that the client, who had been completely satisfied with Smith's work until this point, discharged him from employment without legal cause after learning that Attorney Brown would perform the remaining legal work for 30 percent less than the client was currently obligated to pay Smith.

The Pleadings

The pleading stage begins after the client has chosen a lawyer and decides to bring suit. The role of pleadings in Anglo-American law goes back to the earliest days of the English common law system and writ system.[1] In the twelfth century, persons wishing to litigate in the royal courts had to purchase an original writ (such as the Writ of Right) from the king or chancellor in order to establish the court's jurisdiction. Each writ specified the procedures and substantive law to be followed in deciding the dispute.[2] The writ would often require the plaintiff to make an oral recitation (a **pleading**) in which the claims would be stated, after which the defendant would be entitled to respond orally. In this way the parties would inform the court of the nature of the dispute.[3] In time, the practice of oral pleadings was replaced with written documents, and the common law and equitable pleading process became very complex, overly technical, cumbersome, and long.

In 1848, New York merged the common law and equity courts and replaced its writ system with a newly enacted Code of Civil Procedure. Thus began a reform movement that swept the country and produced modern code pleading at the state level. The popularity of code pleading convinced Congress to enact the Rules Enabling Act in 1934, which led to the development and adoption in 1938 of the Federal Rules of Civil Procedure.

Today's pleadings are written documents and consist of the plaintiff's **complaint**, the defendant's **answer**, and, rarely, the plaintiff's **reply**. The pleadings are somewhat less important under modern rules of civil procedure, because the current procedural rules provide each side of a dispute with the right to engage in extensive discovery. This means that litigants have a variety of available tools for obtaining evidence relevant to the case of which the opponent has knowledge or which is in the possession of an opponent. The pleadings continue to be important, however, because they establish the basis for jurisdiction, briefly state facts giving rise to the complaint, aid in the formulation of the issues, and indicate the relief sought.

The complaint is a document in which the plaintiff alleges jurisdiction, sets forth facts that he or she claims entitle the plaintiff to relief from the defendant, and demands relief. Figure 5.2 provides a sample of a federal complaint. The complaint is filed with the court and served on the defendant.

The answer is a responsive pleading in which the defendant makes admissions or denials, asserts legal defenses, and raises counterclaims. Figure 5.3 provides a sample of a federal answer.

Admissions help to narrow the number of facts that are in dispute. The plaintiff will not have to prove facts at the trial that have been admitted by the defendant in the answer. A denial in the answer, however, creates a factual issue that must be proven at trial. Defendants often will plead one or more **defenses** in the answer. Each defense will consist of facts that the defendant contends may bar the plaintiff from recovery. The defendant may also make a claim for relief against the plaintiff by raising a **counterclaim** in the answer. A counterclaim is appropriate when the defendant has a **cause of action** against a plaintiff arising out of essentially the same set of events that gave rise to the plaintiff's claim. For example, assume that P observes D fishing without permission on P's land and tells D to vacate. If P kicks D in the back as D leaves the property, P is committing a battery against D. P could bring suit against D for trespass, and D could counterclaim against P for the battery. P could file a pleading called the **reply** to the defendant's counterclaim. In this reply, the plaintiff may admit, deny, or raise defenses against the factual allegations raised in the counterclaim.

Methods of Service

The complaint is usually served on the defendant at the same time as the **writ of summons**. (Readers saw an example of a summons in Chapter IV, see Figure 4.2.) A summons warns the defendant that a default judgment can be awarded unless the defendant responds with an answer within a stated period of time (often between twenty and forty-five days).[4]

UNITED STATES DISTRICT COURT
. . . . District of . . . .

. . . . Plaintiff

V.

. . . . Defendant

Civil Action No. . . . .

COMPLAINT

JURY TRIAL DEMANDED

This is a civil action seeking damages under the laws of the State of . . . . . . for injuries to the person of the plaintiff, and to her automobile, caused by the defendant's negligent and/or willful, wanton, or reckless conduct.

1. The court has jurisdiction of this matter by virtue of the fact that the plaintiff is a citizen of the State of . . . . . , and the defendant, ... is a citizen of the State of . . . . . . and the amount in controversy exceeds $75,000 exclusive of interest and costs.

2. This suit is brought pursuant to Section . . . . . . of the Revised Statutes.

3. The plaintiff . . . . is, and at all times material to this action was, a resident of the City of . . . . , State of . . . .

4. The defendant, ... is, and at all times material to this action was, a resident of the City of . . . . , State of . . . .

5. At all times hereinafter mentioned, plaintiff was in the exercise of all due care and caution for her own safety and the safety of others.

6. On January . . . . 200 . . . . at or about . . . . P.M., plaintiff . . . . was operating her automobile in a northerly direction along United States Route . . . . at or about . . . . miles north of . . . .

7. On January . . . . 200 . . . . at or about . . . . P.M., defendant was operating her motor automobile in a southerly direction along United States Route . . . . at or about . . . . miles north of . . . .

8. At that date and time, defendant, ... , negligently operated her vehicle in one or more of the following ways:

    a. Improperly failed to give a signal of her intention to make a turn.

    b. Negligently made an improper left-handed turn, without yielding the right-of-way to traffic coming in the opposite direction.

    c. Negligently failed to yield the right-of-way.

    d. Operated her vehicle on the wrong side of the road.

    e. Negligently failed to keep said vehicle under proper control.

    f. Operated her vehicle in a negligent manner.

    g. Negligently failed to stop her vehicle when danger to the plaintiff was imminent.

9. As a result of one or more of the acts or omissions complained of, the vehicle driven by . . . . . . was caused violently to collide with the vehicle driven by . . . . . .

10. As a direct and proximate result thereof, the plaintiff suffered painful, severe and permanent injuries, loss of income, and has incurred, and will continue to incur expenses for medical care and further was caused to expend the sum of $ . . . . to repair the damages to her automobile caused by the accident.

WHEREFORE, plaintiff prays for judgment against the defendant, ... in the sum of dollars ($ . . . .) plus costs.

Plaintiff requests a jury trial.

. . . .
Attorney for Plaintiff
Office and P.O. Address

. . . .

F I G U R E 5.2 Complaint Document

UNITED STATES DISTRICT COURT
. . . . District of . . . .

. . . . Plaintiff   :
                                             :   Civil Action No. . . . .
                    V.   :   ANSWER
                                             :
. . . . Defendant   :
                                             :   JURY TRIAL DEMANDED

Now comes the defendant in the above-captioned action and gives the following answers to the plaintiff's complaint:

  1. Denies the allegations of paragraphs 1 and 2 of the complaint.
  2. Admits the allegations of paragraphs 3 and 4 of the complaint.
  3. Denies the allegations of paragraphs 5 through 10 of the complaint.

FIRST AFFIRMATIVE DEFENSE

This court lacks subject matter jurisdiction as the amount in controversy does not exceed $75,000, exclusive of interest and cost.

SECOND AFFIRMATIVE DEFENSE

Plaintiff was guilty of negligence which was a contributing cause of the accident in that the plaintiff was negligently operating her automobile at the time that same collided with defendant's automobile. The plaintiff is therefore barred from recovery.

WHEREFORE, the defendant demands that the plaintiff's complaint be dismissed and that the costs of this action be awarded the defendant.

Defendant claims a trial by jury.

                                    . . . .
                                    Attorney for Defendant
                                    Office and P.O. Address
                                    . . . .
                                    . . . .

F I G U R E 5.3 Answer

The summons must be served in time for the defendant to take action in defense. This right is constitutionally guaranteed by the state and federal due process clauses. Several methods to serve the summons can be found in the statute books of each state. These requirements must be precisely followed, and service in *in personam* actions may differ from service in *in rem* actions. Clearly, the most desirable method is to deliver the summons personally to the defendant. Some jurisdictions require that the summons be served within a specified period of time. The Federal Rules of Civil Procedure, for example, require service within 120 days of the filing of the complaint. The summons, sometimes called **process**, is generally served by a process server or sheriff.

The federal rules reward defendants who voluntarily waive their right to be formally served with process. These defendants are allowed sixty days, instead of just twenty days, to respond to the complaint. The benefit to plaintiffs is in not having to pay someone to serve the summons and complaint. Defendants who refuse to honor a requested waiver of service can be required to pay the service costs unless they can show good cause for the refusal.

In addition to having the summons personally served on a defendant, many states permit service by certified or registered mail, return receipt requested. This method is increasingly preferred because it is inexpensive and generally effective.

When **personal service** of a summons and the complaint to a defendant is not possible, the law often permits what is called **substituted service**. This method involves mailing the summons and complaint to the defendant by certified mail and leaving these documents at the defendant's home with a person who resides there and who is of "suitable age and discretion." Traditionally this means someone age fourteen or over. If the plaintiff is suing a corporation, the statutes usually authorize the use of substituted service on a designated agent or even a state official such as the secretary of state or the commissioner of insurance. The agent or official then sends a copy of the documents to the corporation. In some circumstances, the statutes provide for **constructive service**, which means publishing the notice of summons in the legal announcements section of newspapers. Traditionally the law has required that the summons be published for three weeks.

A defendant who has been properly served with a summons and complaint *defaults* by failing to file a written answer in a timely manner. The court can then award judgment to the plaintiff for the sum of money or other legal relief that was demanded in the complaint. In a default judgment, the defendant loses the right to object to anything that is incorrect in the complaint.

In the following case, the plaintiff was awarded a default judgment against the defendant. The defendant in *Dorsey v. Gregg* sought to vacate the default judgment because the trial court lacked jurisdiction over his person due to the inadequacy of the service.

Dorsey v. Gregg
784 P.2nd 154
Court of Appeals of Oregon
January 13, 1988

Richardson, Presiding Judge

Defendant seeks vacation of a default judgment, contending that the trial court lacked jurisdiction over him. We reverse.

Plaintiff's complaint was filed on December 5, 1985. Defendant, a student of the University of Oregon, lived in Eugene. He was a member of a fraternity but did not reside at the fraternity house. Personal service was attempted at the fraternity house from December 29 through February 19, 1986. No attempt was made to serve defendant at his residence even though his address was available from the university. On March 4, the trial court granted plaintiff's motion for alternative service. The motion was supported by the affidavit of Hoyt, which states:

"I am an employee of Barristers' Aid, Inc., a civil process service corporation engaged in delivery of documents among attorneys and in serving civil process in the Lane County area. From on or about December 29, 1985, [to] February 18, 1986, I have made numerous attempts to serve the Defendant, Joseph Gregg, at his fraternity. On various occasions I would call in advance and find that his vehicle was there, or that they expected him to eat dinner at the fraternity that evening. However, upon arriving there in the evening for purposes of serving Mr. Gregg, various individuals there would profess that he no longer resides at the fraternity, nor that he ever eats at the facility nor visits.

"It has become apparent to me and other individuals in our office who have attempted service upon Mr. Gregg, that the members of the fraternity are 'covering' for him, and are not cooperating in allowing us to learn his whereabouts at any given time.

"It is my opinion that, if service was made upon a member of the fraternity, due notice of that would be conveyed to Mr. Gregg from earlier statements of members that he remained in the Eugene-Springfield area, and attended fraternity house functions."

The trial court authorized service "upon a person in charge or other resident member present" at the fraternity and by certified mail, return receipt requested, addressed to defendant's father at a Beaverton address.

Defendant first contends that the trial court erred in ordering the alternative service, because Hoyt's supporting affidavit was insufficient under ORCP 7D(6)(a). That rule provides, in relevant part:

> "On motion upon *a showing by affidavit that service cannot be made by any method otherwise specified in these rules* or other rule or statute, the court, at its discretion, may order service by any method or combination of methods which under the circumstances is most reasonably calculated to apprise the defendant of the existence and pendency of the action, including but not limited to: publication of summons; mailing without publication to a specified post office address of defendant, return receipt requested, deliver to addressee only; or posting at specified locations." (Emphasis supplied.)

In *Dhulst and Dhulst*, 657 P.2d 231 (1983), the trial court ordered alternative service on the husband by publication and registered mail. The supporting affidavit addressed the reasons why the husband could not be personally served, but it was silent about the other types of service authorized by ORCP 7D(3)(a)(I). We held that, because the affidavit was insufficient to support alternative service under ORCP 7D(6)(a), "the trial court [had] erred in ordering [the alternative service]. Because [the alternative service] was improper, the trial court lacked personal jurisdiction over [the] husband." The default decree against the husband was therefore set aside.

Here, Hoyt's affidavit makes no mention of any attempt to locate and serve defendant at his "dwelling house or usual place of abode." ORCP 7D(3)(a)(I). It only details attempts to serve defendant at the fraternity house where he had not resided for at least a year before the filing of this action.... The affidavit fails to comply with the requirement of ORCP 7D(6)(a), and the trial court erred in ordering alternative service. The alternative service was therefore invalid, and the trial court lacked personal jurisdiction over defendant.

Reversed and remanded with instruction to vacate the judgment.

Case Questions

1. Why is the law so concerned with proper service of process?
2. Why did the Oregon Court of Appeals rule that the alternative service of process was invalid?
3. If the circumstances allow a court in the plaintiff's state to assert jurisdiction over an out-of-state defendant, what is the proper method of serving process?

Pretrial Motions

The second stage of the litigation process involves decisions about whether motions are filed prior to trial. Sometimes a defendant's lawyer, after receiving the plaintiff's complaint, will decide to challenge the complaint because of legal insufficiency. For example, the complaint might be poorly drafted and so vague that the defendant can't understand what is being alleged, whether the venue might be wrong, or whether there might be some problem with service. In such situations the attorney may choose to file a **motion to dismiss** (sometimes also called a **demurrer** or a "12(b) motion" in some jurisdictions) prior to preparing the answer. A motion to dismiss is often used by a defendant to challenge perceived defects in the plaintiff's complaint. Common grounds for this motion include the lack of subject matter jurisdiction or *in personam* jurisdiction, improper or inadequate service of the summons, and failure to state a claim upon which relief can be granted. The motion to dismiss is decided by a judge, and jurisdictions differ about permitting the attorneys to argue orally the merits of the motion. If the judge grants the motion, the plaintiff will often try to cure any defect by amending the complaint. If the judge denies the motion, the defendant will normally submit an answer. Alleged defects in the answer and reply can also be raised through a motion to dismiss or an equivalent motion used for that purpose in a particular jurisdiction.

INTERNET TIP

In *DuPont v. Christopher*, the defendants claimed that DuPont had failed to state a claim upon which relief could be granted. The defendants maintained that their conduct was not prohibited by Texas statutory or case law. You can read this "retired case" on the textbook's website.

The **motion for summary judgment** can be made by either or both parties. It is intended to dispose of controversies when no genuine issues of material fact exist, or when the facts necessary to prove the other party's case are not provable or are not true. The motion is supported with proof in the form of affidavits and depositions. This proof is used to illustrate that there is no need to conduct a trial because there is no factual dispute between the parties. The party opposing the motion will present affidavits and depositions to prove the existence of contested issues of fact. Such proof may also be used to show the impossibility of certain facts alleged by an opposing party. For example, a complaint might accuse a defendant of various counts of negligence in operating a car. However, if the defendant was in jail that day, it could be proved that he or she could not possibly have committed the acts in question. The defendant in this instance would move for a summary judgment. Motions for summary judgment are disfavored by courts because, when granted, a party is denied a trial.

Summary judgment should not be granted if there is a genuine issue of material fact because it would deprive the parties of their right to a trial.

Discovery and Pretrial Conference

To prevent surprise at the trial, each party is provided with tools of **discovery** before trial in order to identify the relevant facts concerning the case. Discovery is based on the premise that prior to a civil action each party is entitled to information in the possession of others. This includes the identity and location of persons, the existence and location of documents, known facts, and opinions of experts.

There is a distinction between the right to obtain discovery and the right to use in court the statements or information that are the product of discovery. The restrictions that are made concerning the admissibility in court of the product of discovery are discussed later in the chapter. The requirements for discovery are as follows: The information sought cannot be privileged, it must be relevant, it cannot be the "work product" of an attorney, and if a physical or mental examination is required, good cause must be shown.

The most common tools of discovery are **oral depositions**, written interrogatories to parties, production of documents, physical and mental examinations, and requests for admissions. In an **oral deposition**, a witness is examined under oath outside court before a person legally authorized to conduct depositions (usually a court reporter, or if the deposition is being videotaped, by a video technician who is similarly authorized by law). The party wishing the deposition must give notice to the opposing party to the suit so that person may be present to cross-examine the witness. The questioning of the witness at an oral deposition is thus much the same as it would be in a courtroom. **Written interrogatories** to the parties are lists of questions that must be answered in writing and under oath. Interrogatories are submitted only to the parties to the case, not to witnesses. Because the rules of discovery can differ in federal and state courts, lawyers may take this into consideration in making a choice of forum. A state court, for example, might only permit an attorney to ask a party to answer thirty questions by written interrogatories, whereas fifty questions might be permissible under the federal rules.

One party to the suit may compel the **production of documents** or things in the possession of the other party for inspection. When the mental or physical condition of a party is at issue, a court may order the party to submit to a **mental examination** or **physical examination** by a physician. Finally, one party may send to the other party a **request for admissions or denials** as to certain specified facts or as to the genuineness of certain documents. If no reply is made to such a request, the matters are considered admitted for the purpose of the suit.

All discovery except for physical examinations can be done without a court order. In case of non-compliance, the discovering party may request a court order to compel compliance. Failure to comply with the court order results in imposition of the sanctions provided in the discovery statute.

Discovery may begin after the filing of the complaint, but usually commences after the answer is filed and continues until trial. In addition, a **pretrial conference** may be called by the judge to discuss the issues of the case. A judge and the two opposing lawyers discuss and evaluate the controversy informally. They consider the simplification and sharpening of the issues, the admissions and disclosure of facts, possible amendments to the pleadings, the limitation of the number of witnesses, the possibility of reaching an out-of-court settlement, and any other matters that may aid in the speedy and just disposition of the action.

The importance of discovery cannot be overestimated. Discovery results in the disclosure of unknown facts and reveals the strengths and weaknesses of each side's proof, and is an educational process for the lawyers and their clients. Each side is, in sports terminology, "scouting" their opponent and learning what they plan to prove and how they intend to do it if the case goes to trial. Justice is not supposed to be determined based on surprise witnesses, trickery, and deceit. Discovery allows the parties to identify the core issues, pin witnesses down so they can't easily change their views at trial, determine witness credibility, especially in the case of experts, and clarify where impeachment and cross-examination will be effective.

Lawyers who fail to comply with discovery rules can gain an outcome-determinative tactical advantage over their opponents when a case comes to trial. When this occurs, the injured party has the right to ask for judicial intervention and seek the imposition of sanctions against the offending party.

The defendant in the following case brought a motion to sanction the defendant for not complying with the rules of discovery with respect to written interrogatories. The defendant alleged that because of plaintiff's conduct it had become necessary for the defendant to ask the court to compel defendant to answer the interrogatories. The trial court appointed an attorney to hold a hearing and investigate the facts of this matter and report to the court. The appointed attorney, called the "discovery referee," advised the court that the plaintiff had not acted in good faith and had violated the rules of discovery, and recommended that the court sanction the plaintiff. The trial court followed the discovery referee's recommendation and the plaintiff appealed this decision to the state intermediate appellate court.

Michael H. Clement v. Frank C. Alegre
A123168
Court of Appeals of California, First District, Division Two
September 23, 2009

Kline, P. J.
Twenty-three years ago, the Legislature enacted the Civil Discovery Act of 1986... (the Act), a comprehensive revision of pretrial discovery statutes, the central precept of which is that civil discovery be essentially self-executing. More than 10 years ago, *Townsend v. Superior Court* (1998) ... (*Townsend*) lamented the all too often interjection of "ego and emotions of counsel and clients" into discovery disputes, warning that "[l]ike Hotspur on the field of battle, counsel can become blinded by the combative nature of the proceeding and be rendered incapable of informally resolving a disagreement.... *Townsend* counseled that the

"informal resolution" of discovery disputes "entails something more than bickering with [opposing counsel]."…. Rather, the statute "requires that there be a serious effort at negotiation and informal resolution."…

This case illustrates once again the truth of *Townsend's* observations, as well as highlighting the lengths to which some counsel and clients will go to avoid providing discovery (in this case by responding to straightforward interrogatories with nitpicking and meritless objections), resulting in delaying proceedings, impeding the self-executing operation of discovery, and wasting the time of the court, the discovery referee, the opposing party, and his counsel.

Plaintiffs Michael H. Clement and Michael H. Clement Corp. (plaintiffs) appeal from the Contra Costa County Superior Court's imposition of $6,632.50 as discovery sanctions. The sanctions were awarded against plaintiffs for interposing objections to special interrogatories propounded by defendant and respondent Frank C. Alegre, which objections the discovery referee found to be "unreasonable, evasive, lacking in legal merit and without justification." ....

Background
Plaintiffs sued defendant... in connection with a dispute arising out of the sale of real property by plaintiffs to defendant. (The substantive facts of the underlying action are not relevant to the merits of the issues raised on this appeal.)

On November 12, 2007, defendant Alegre served two identical sets of 23 special interrogatories on plaintiffs: one set to plaintiff Clement, the individual, and one set to plaintiff corporation.... The interrogatories requested information on damages, causation, and the existence of a loan commitment. Plaintiffs answered three of the interrogatories and interposed objections to twenty....

The objection to the term "economic damages" as vague and ambiguous was interposed to interrogatory Nos. 1 and 6. The objection that the interrogatories violated section 2030.060 ... because each was not "full and complete in itself" was interposed to interrogatory Nos. 2 through 5, 7 through 16, 18, 20, 22 and 23....

On January 29, 2008, defendant moved to compel further responses to the special interrogatories, to strike objections, and for sanctions against plaintiff corporation and [plaintiff's] attorney Goldstein....

The matter was heard by discovery referee Laurence D. Kay on August 14, 2008, nine months after the interrogatories had been propounded. On August 20, 2008, the referee found...that plaintiffs had "deliberately misconstrued the question" insofar as they contended the phrase "economic damages" was too vague. He further found with respect to plaintiffs' claim that an interrogatory that referenced a prior interrogatory was not full and complete in itself, that the case cited by plaintiffs was "inapposite and the objection frivolous." The referee determined "the objections and each of them to be unreasonable, evasive, lacking in legal merit and without justification....

Consequently, the referee recommended that plaintiffs be ordered to provide further answers without any of the objections previously interposed and recommended sanctions be imposed by the court as follows: Plaintiffs were to reimburse defendant $4,950

for legal fees, plus $40 for filing the motions to compel and $1,642.50 for defendant's one-half of the referee fee for referee time spent exclusively on the motion (not including one and one-half hours of hearing time on the motion, as other motions were heard at that same hearing). The court adopted the referee's order on September 5, 2008 and the order was entered on September 10, 2008. This timely appeal followed....

Discussion
A. Monetary Sanctions Authorized

"The court may impose a monetary sanction ordering that one engaging in the misuse of the discovery process, or any attorney advising that conduct, or both pay the reasonable expenses, including attorney's fees, incurred by anyone as a result of that conduct.... If a monetary sanction is authorized by any provision of this title, the court shall impose that sanction unless it finds that the one subject to the sanction acted with substantial justification or that other circumstances make the imposition of the sanction unjust." ...

"'Misuse of the discovery process includes failing to respond or submit to authorized discovery, providing evasive discovery responses, disobeying a court order to provide discovery, unsuccessfully making or opposing discovery motions without substantial justification, and failing to meet and confer in good faith to resolve a discovery dispute when required by statute to do so." ...

B. Standard of Review
"We review the trial court's order imposing the sanction for abuse of discretion.... We resolve all evidentiary conflicts most favorably to the trial court's ruling ..., and we will reverse only if the trial court's action was `''`arbitrary, capricious, or whimsical ...'"

C. Vagueness Objection to "Economic Damages" Term
Plaintiffs assert that "economic damages" was not a defined term in defendant's discovery and that the term was, therefore, ambiguous. This contention is preposterous in the circumstances presented...

Ample evidence supports the referee's determination that plaintiffs "deliberately misconstrued the question." Plaintiffs themselves quoted the statute defining the term in their initial response. Yet, they objected, and then deliberately provided an answer using a definition narrower than that provided by statute. Somewhat artfully, plaintiffs urge that Goldstein agreed in his January 23, 2008 letter to respond to any definition of economic damages that plaintiffs chose to provide. However, even after defendant's counsel advised that the term was being used as defined in the statute plaintiffs had cited, plaintiffs did not answer the question, but demanded that defendant supply the definition in writing and allow them an extra 30 days from the date of receipt in which to respond. Clearly this was "game-playing" and supports the referee's findings and the sanctions award....

Sanctions were warranted here, as plaintiffs' objection to the term "economic damages" was without "substantial justification" and their responses to those interrogatories were evasive....

D. Objection That Question Was Not "Full and Complete in and of Itself"
Plaintiffs' objections to most of the interrogatories propounded by defendant were based on the assertion that an interrogatory failed to comply with the statutory requirement that each be "full and complete in and of itself," where it referred to a previous interrogatory....

Plaintiffs do not contend that any of the interrogatories to which they objected on this basis were unclear, or that the interrogatories, considered either singly or collectively, in any way undermined or violated the presumptive numerical limit of 35 interrogatories of section 2030.030. Yet plaintiffs seized on what might have been at most an arguable technical violation of the rule, to object to interrogatories that were clear and concise where the interrogatories did not even arguably violate the presumptive numerical limitation set by statute. In so doing, plaintiffs themselves engaged in the type of gamesmanship and delay decried by the drafters of the Act....

It is a central precept to the Civil Discovery Act of 1986... that civil discovery be essentially self-executing.... A self-executing discovery system is "one that operates without judicial involvement." ... Conduct frustrates the goal of a self-executing discovery system when it requires the trial court to become involved in discovery because a dispute leads a party to move for an order compelling a response.... On many occasions, to be sure, the dispute over discovery between the parties is genuine, though ultimately resolved one way or the other by the court. In such

cases, the losing party is substantially justified in carrying the matter to court. But the rules should deter the abuse implicit in carrying or forcing a discovery dispute to court when no genuine dispute exists. And the potential or actual imposition of expenses is virtually the sole formal sanction in the rules to deter a party from pressing to a court hearing frivolous requests for or objections to discovery....

We have no difficulty in affirming the trial court's determination that in this case plaintiffs forced to court a dispute that was not "genuine." Indeed, the record here strongly indicates that the purpose of plaintiffs' objections was to delay discovery, to require defendants to incur potentially significant costs in redrafting interrogatories that were clear and that did not exceed numerical limits, and to generally obstruct the self-executing process of discovery. That plaintiffs seized upon an arguable deficiency in the interrogatories based on slim authority, does not provide "substantial justification" for their objections. The trial court could look at the whole picture of the discovery dispute and was well within its discretion in rejecting plaintiffs' claim of substantial justification....

...[R]esort to the courts easily could have been avoided here had both parties actually taken to heart Justice Stone's admonitions in Townsend that "the statute requires that there be a serious effort at negotiation and informal resolution." ... Perhaps after 11 years it is necessary to remind trial counsel and the bar once again that "[a]rgument is not the same as informal negotiation"... that attempting informal resolution means more than the mere attempt by the discovery proponent "to persuade the objector of the error of his ways" ...; and that "a reasonable and good faith attempt at informal resolution entails something more than bickering with [opposing] counsel.... Rather, the law requires that counsel attempt to talk the matter over, compare their views, consult, and deliberate." ...

Disposition
Discovery Order No. 1, granting defendant's motions... to compel and awarding sanctions, is affirmed. Defendant shall recover his costs on this appeal...

Case Questions

1. What should a party do when an opponent fails to follow the rules of civil procedure with respect to discovery?
2. The media often depict courtroom lawyers using surprise witnesses and evidence. In reality, thorough discovery usually destroys any possibility of surprise. Is this good or bad?
3. Exhaustive discovery is very expensive. One party will frequently be able to afford more discovery than his or her opponent. Does that change your mind about the value of discovery?

How do the discovery rules seek to encourage ethical conduct in the context of the adversarial process of litigation?

CIVIL TRIALS

A trial is a legal procedure that is available to parties who have been otherwise unwilling or unable to resolve their differences through negotiations, settlement offers, and even mediation attempts. Trials involve the staging of a confrontation between the plaintiff and the defendant as contradicting witnesses, and arguments collide in a courtroom in accordance with procedural and evidentiary rules. The trial process may, as a result of appeals and/or new trials, take many years, but it will ultimately result either in a dismissal of the complaint or in a judgment.

In some cases, parties waive a jury trial, preferring to try their case before a judge. (This is called a **bench trial**.) Bench trials can be scheduled more quickly, and they take less time to conclude because the procedures associated with the jury are eliminated. Bench trials also cost the parties and taxpayers less money than jury trials.

The right to a federal jury trial is provided by the Seventh Amendment to the U.S. Constitution to parties involved in a common law civil action. The right to a jury trial in the state judicial system is determined by state law and may not exist for some types of actions, such as equitable claims and small claims cases. Federal rules permit parties to stipulate to less than twelve jurors, and local court rules often provide for six.

The judge is responsible for making sure that (1) the jury is properly selected in a jury trial, (2) due process requirements for a fair trial are satisfied, (3) proper rulings are made with respect to the admissibility of evidence, (4) the rules of procedure are followed by the parties, and (5) the judgment is awarded in accordance with law.

Selection of the Jury

The procedure discussed here applies only to jury trials (see Figure 5.4). Jurors are selected at random from a fair cross section of the community and summoned to the courthouse for jury duty.[5] After a case has been assigned to a courtroom, the judge calls in a group of prospective jurors, who take their seats in the jury box. A **voir dire** (literally, "to speak the truth") examination is conducted to determine each juror's qualifications for jury duty under the appropriate statute, and any grounds for a challenge for cause, or information on which to base a peremptory challenge. A challenge for cause may be based on prejudice or bias. A juror's relationship, business involvement, or other close connection with one of the parties or attorneys may also be considered cause for replacing a juror. Attorneys for both sides may make as many challenges for cause as they wish, and it is within the judge's sound discretion to replace a juror for cause. In addition to the challenges for cause, each party is given a limited number of peremptory challenges that may be exercised for any reason other than race (*Baton v. Kentucky*, 476 U.S. 79 [1986]) or gender (*J. E. B. v. Alabama* ex rel. T.B., 511 U.S. 127 [1994]).

Opening Statements and Examination of Witnesses

After a jury has been selected and sworn, the trial begins with an opening statement by the plaintiff's attorney. The opening statement explains the case in general, including the attorney's legal theories and what he or she intends to prove. The defendant's lawyer may also present an opening statement introducing legal theories of the case and the facts the defense intends to prove.

In order to win the case, the plaintiff must prove the disputed allegations of the complaint by presenting evidence. Witnesses and exhibits are produced by both parties to the suit. If witnesses do not voluntarily appear to testify, they may be ordered by means of a **subpoena** (see Figure 5.5)

Presentation of Evidence

Proceedings during a civil trial

1 Jury selection
2 Opening statements
3 Plaintiff's case
4 Motion for nonsuit
5 Defendant's case
6 Plaintiff's rebuttal
7 Defendant's rejoinder
8 Motion for directed verdict
9 Closing arguments
10 Instructions to jury
11 Jury verdict
12 Posttrial motions
13 Judgment

1 Prospective jurors are questioned by attorneys and judge. A prospective juror is dismissed if an attorney successfully makes a challenge for cause or exercises a peremptory challenge.

2 Attorneys explain facts of case in general to judge and jury. Plaintiff's attorney's opening argument usually precedes defendant's.

3 Plaintiff's attorney presents witnesses, documents, and other evidence to substantiate allegations in complaint.

4 Defendant's attorney moves for an involuntary dismissal (motion for nonsuit) if it is felt that plaintiff failed to prove allegations. If judge agrees, motion is granted and plaintiff loses. If judge disagrees, motion is denied and trial continues.

5 Defendant's attorney presents witnesses, documents, and other evidence to rebut plaintiff's case.

6 Plaintiff's attorney presents evidence to rebut evidence brought out during presentation of defendant's case.

7 Defendant's attorney presents evidence to rebut any new matters brought out during plaintiff's rebuttal.

8 After both parties rest their case, either or both parties may move for a directed verdict. If judge feels that reasonable persons could not disagree that the moving party should win, judge grants motion. If motion is granted, moving party wins and trial is over. If motion is denied, trial continues.

9 Both attorneys sum up evidence for jury. They suggest how the jury should resolve specific disputed items. Plaintiff's attorney argues first, but may reserve time to rebut defendant's attorney's closing argument.

10 Judge explains substantive law to jury, and tells how it should be applied to facts. Both attorneys may suggest specific instructions to judge, but final instructions are left to judge's discretion.

11 After deliberation, jury returns either a general or special verdict or both. A general verdict is simply a declaration of winner and amount of recovery. A special verdict answers specific factual questions requested by judge.

12 After jury returns its verdict, either or both parties may move to have verdict set aside by filing a motion for a new trial or a motion for a judgment notwithstanding verdict of jury or relief from judgment. If the judge grants the motion, judge renders judgment in accordance with jury verdict.

13 By rendering judgment, judge declares who prevailed at trial and amount of recovery. If losing party does not voluntarily pay prescribed amount, winning party can force payment by obtaining an order of execution.

F I G U R E 5.4 Proceedings During a Civil Trial

UNITED STATES DISTRICT COURT
FOR THE . . . . . DISTRICT OF . . . . .
. . . . DIVISION

. . . .
     Plaintiff,

       v.   Civil Action No. . . . .

. . . .
     Defendant.

To: . . . . *[name and address of witness]*
   You are commanded to appear in the United States District Court for
the . . . . District of . . . . , at . . . . in the City of . . . . ,
State of . . . . . on the . . . . . day of . . . . . , 20 . . . . . at . . . . . o'clock
. . . . . M. to testify on behalf of . . . . . in the above pending action.
Dated . . . . . , 20 . . . . . .
[Name and address of attorney]

                 [Signature and title of clerk]

[Seal]

F I G U R E 5.5 Subpoena—For Attendance of Witness [FRCP 45(a)]

to appear in court. A **subpoena duces tecum** issued by the court commands a witness to produce a document that is in his or her possession. If witnesses refuse to appear, to testify, or to produce required documents, or if they perform any act that disrupts the judicial proceedings, they may be punished for contempt of court.

Judges have much discretion with respect to the order of production of evidence. Normally, a plaintiff's attorney presents the plaintiff's case first. The attorney presents witnesses, documents, and other evidence, and rests the case when he or she decides that enough evidence has been produced to substantiate the allegations. Defendant's lawyer then presents the defendant's case in the same manner. When the defense is finished, the plaintiff's attorney may introduce additional witnesses and exhibits in rebuttal of the defense's case. If new matters are brought out by the rebuttal, the defendant may introduce evidence in rejoinder, limited to answering the new matters.

Both attorneys introduce their own witnesses and question them. This is called **direct examination**. The opposing attorney **cross-examines** the witnesses after the direct examination is completed. Attorneys may conduct **redirect examinations** of their own witnesses following the cross-examinations. Attorneys generally may not ask their own witnesses leading questions (except for preliminary questions to introduce a witness or questions to a hostile witness). A **leading question** is one that suggests the answer to the witness. For instance, if an attorney asks, "You've never seen this gun before, have you?" the witness is almost told to answer no. Leading questions are permissible on cross-examination because they promote the purpose of cross-examination: testing the credibility of witnesses.

Upon cross-examination, for example, an attorney could ask a witness the following question: "Isn't it true, Mr. Smith, that you are a firearms expert?"

RULES OF EVIDENCE

Since 1975, federal trials have been conducted pursuant to the Federal Rules of Evidence (FIRE). Although each state is entitled to promulgate its own rules, most states have chosen to adopt the federal rules as their "state rules." Rules of evidence apply to jury and nonjury trials, although they are applied less strictly in the latter. Many of the so-called "rules" are actually more like policy statements because many provide judges with considerable discretion in their application. Trial judges use the rules to control the admissibility of evidence, and their decisions are generally upheld on appeal unless there has been a clear abuse of discretion. Judges will instruct jurors to disregard evidence that has been improperly presented to them, but it is difficult to evaluate the effect that this excluded evidence has on the jurors' decision-making process. Once jurors have heard testimony, they may not be able to simply forget what they have seen and heard. In some situations, the judge may conclude that significant prejudice has occurred and that instructing the jury is an inadequate remedy. When this occurs, a mistrial will be declared.

Relevance and Materiality

Evidence, whether it be testimony, demonstrative evidence (such as photographs, charts, and graphs), or physical evidence, is admissible only if it is **relevant**. That is, it must logically tend to prove or disprove some issue of consequence that is in dispute at the trial. Irrelevant evidence confuses the jury, wastes court time, and is often prejudicial. Relevancy is sometimes confused with materiality, which has to do with the probative value of evidence. *Probative evidence* tends to prove something of importance to the case. Relevant evidence that has "significant" probative value is "**material**." Evidence that is either immaterial or irrelevant should be excluded.

Competency

Evidence must be **competent** (legally adequate) to be admissible. Competency is a broad concept. To be competent, witnesses have to take an oath or affirm that they will testify truthfully. A nonexpert witness is limited to testimony about what he or she has heard or seen firsthand; the opinions and conclusions of such a witness are "incompetent."

As fact-finder, the jury must draw its own conclusions from the evidence. However, where special expertise is required to evaluate a fact situation, a jury may not be competent to form an opinion. In that case, a person with special training, knowledge, or expertise may be called to testify as an expert witness. Doctors, for example, are frequently called as expert witnesses in personal injury cases. The qualifications and expertise of such witnesses must be established to the court's satisfaction before an expert witness's opinion is admissible.

The Best Evidence Rule

The **best evidence rule** requires that, unless they are unobtainable, original documents rather than copies be introduced into evidence. Even when the original writing is unobtainable, secondary evidence of the contents is admissible only if the unavailability is not the fault of the party seeking to introduce the evidence. In this situation, the best available alternative proof must be presented. For example, a photocopy of a writing is preferred over oral testimony as to its contents.

The Hearsay Rule

The **hearsay evidence rule** excludes witness testimony that does not proceed from the personal knowledge of the witness but instead from the repetition of what was said or written outside court by another person, and is offered for the purpose of establishing the truth of what was written or said. The person who made the out-of-court statement may have been lying, joking, or speaking carelessly. The witness reporting the statement in court may have a poor memory. This exclusionary rule guarantees the opportunity to cross-examine the person who made the out-of-court statement and prevents highly unreliable evidence from being considered.

The hearsay rule contains many exceptions. The **spontaneous declarations exception** (in legalese called *res gestae*) permits courts to admit in court spontaneous declarations uttered simultaneously with the occurrence of an act. The basis for the admission is the belief that a statement made instinctively at the time of an event, without the opportunity for formulation of a statement favorable to one's own cause, is likely to be truthful.

INTERNET TIP

Readers wishing to read an interesting case involving the admissibility of hearsay evidence will want to read *Barbara Harris v. Toys R Us* on the textbook's website. In this case, a children's motorized vehicle weighing ten pounds was alleged to have fallen from the middle shelf of a three-tiered commercial shelving unit in a Toys R Us store. The falling vehicle allegedly struck customer Barbara Harris on her head while she was shopping, knocking her to the floor and causing her injury.

Communicative Privileges

The general rule is that all persons who can provide relevant, competent, and material information that would help the fact finder search for the truth are required to testify at trial. But the law also provides some exceptions where certain communications, for reasons of public policy, are recognized by constitutional provision, statute, judicial decision, or rule of evidence as being privileged. Privileges exist for reasons of public policy. Where a **privilege** exists, a person benefitted by the privilege (called the **holder**) is entitled to refuse to testify or to block some other person from testifying as a witness. Because privileges permit the withholding of important evidence at trial, they are disfavored by courts. This means that privileges are narrowly construed and only recognized when the facts clearly demonstrate that interest being protected by the privilege would be threatened if the testimony were to be given.

Probably the best-known privilege is the privilege against self-incrimination, which is written in the Fifth and Fourteenth Amendments to the U.S. Constitution. This privilege permits individuals to refuse to disclose information (in most circumstances) that might expose them to a criminal prosecution. (This is the privilege against self-incrimination that is protected by the *Miranda* warnings.)

Traditionally the law has recognized two types of privileges that are intended to protect spousal relationships and the institution of marriage: the marital testimonial privilege and the confidential marital communications privilege. The marital testimonial privilege permits one spouse to refuse to testify in a criminal case in which the other spouse is the defendant. The non-accused spouse is the holder of this privilege and decides whether to testify or claim this privilege. The marital communications privilege permits a spouse from being involuntarily forced to testify in any proceeding against the other spouse about the content of a private marital communication between the two. The marital privileges usually can be waived and do not apply to cases in which the spouses clearly have adverse interests (such as in spousal battery, divorce, or child neglect, abuse, or support cases). In cases like these, permitting the spouse's testimony is essential to the action, and there is no intact intimate marital relationship interest to protect. Many states no longer recognize the testimonial privilege, and states differ as to the exact requirements for the confidential marital communications privilege.

The wife of the appellant in the next case claimed the marital testimonial privilege and refused to testify against her criminally accused husband. The prosecution used statements the wife had voluntarily given to the police and a nurse as evidence at the preliminary hearing. The use of these statements in this manner to convict the husband was appealed to the Utah Supreme Court.

State of Utah v. Travis Dee Timmermann
2009 UT 58
Supreme Court of Utah
September 4, 2009

Durham, Chief Justice:

Introduction

Travis Timmerman was charged with attempted rape, forcible sexual abuse, and assault. At the preliminary hearing, the victim, Mrs. Timmerman, invoked her spousal privilege not to testify against her husband. The State then introduced into evidence Mrs. Timmerman's previous statements to the police and to a sexual assault nurse. With those statements, the magistrate bound Mr. Timmerman over for trial. Mr. Timmerman subsequently filed a motion to quash the bindover. The district court denied the motion and held that the admission of Mrs. Timmerman's statements did not violate Mr. Timmerman's constitutional rights or Mrs. Timmerman's spousal testimonial privilege. Mr. Timmerman now appeals the district court's denial of his motion. We are asked to consider whether the Confrontation Clauses of the United States Constitution and Utah Constitution apply to preliminary hearings and whether the spousal testimonial privilege embodied in the Utah Constitution applies to a spouse's voluntary, out-of-court statements. We affirm the trial court.

Background

During the early morning hours of June 30, 2007, the Timmermans' neighbor heard a woman screaming "Stop it!" and "Help me!" The neighbor thought the screams came from the Timmermans' house. Around 7:00 a.m., the neighbor notified the police. Officer McLelland responded and spoke with Mrs. Timmerman. During their conversation, Officer McLelland observed bruises on her arms and face. He asked Mrs. Timmerman to fill out a witness statement. In her three-page statement, Mrs. Timmerman wrote that Mr. Timmerman repeatedly hit her and tried to force her to have ... intercourse.

Another police officer, Detective Harding, interviewed Mrs. Timmerman and asked her to submit to a sexual assault examination at the hospital. When Mrs. Timmerman arrived at the hospital, a sexual assault nurse examined her and filled out a Sexual Assault Nurse Examination (SANE) report. In the report, the nurse cataloged Mrs. Timmerman's bruises and her statements that Mr. Timmerman hit her and tried to have forced sex with her.

Mr. Timmerman was charged with attempted rape, a first-degree felony; forcible sexual abuse, a second-degree felony; and assault, a class B misdemeanor.... At the preliminary hearing, the State called Mrs. Timmerman as a witness, but she invoked her spousal privilege not to testify against her husband. Instead, Officer McLelland and Detective Harding testified for the State, and the State introduced Mrs. Timmerman's witness statement and SANE report. Mr. Timmerman objected to the admission of the statement and the report on the grounds that they violated Mrs. Timmerman's spousal privilege and Mr. Timmerman's confrontation rights under the federal and state constitutions. The magistrate admitted both documents and bound Mr. Timmerman over for trial.

In his motion to quash the bindover before the district court, Mr. Timmerman argued that his confrontation rights under the federal and state constitutions were violated because he could not cross-examine Mrs. Timmerman at the preliminary hearing regarding her out-of-court statements. He also argued that the magistrate had ignored Mrs. Timmerman's spousal privilege when he admitted her out-of-court statements into evidence. Without Mrs. Timmerman's statements, there was insufficient evidence to bind Mr. Timmerman over for trial on the attempted rape charge. The district court held that confrontation rights under the federal and state constitutions do not apply to preliminary hearings and that out-of-court statements made by spouses to third parties are not excluded under the spousal testimonial privilege.

Mr. Timmerman subsequently filed this interlocutory appeal.....

Analysis

Mr. Timmerman argues that the right to confrontation in preliminary hearings is guaranteed by the Sixth Amendment of the United States Constitution and by article 1, section 12 of the Utah Constitution. He also argues that the spousal testimonial privilege found in the Utah Constitution prevents the use of out-of-court, voluntary statements.

[Note: Part I of this opinion which contains the Court's discussion of the right to confrontation has been omitted to focus readers on the spousal privilege discussion]

II. The Trial Court Properly Denied the Motion to Quash Because the Constitutional Spousal Testimonial Privilege Applies only to Compelled, In-Court Testimony

Mr. Timmerman argues that the trial court erred when it allowed Mrs. Timmerman's out-of-court statements into evidence even though Mrs. Timmerman invoked her spousal privilege not to testify against her husband. Utah recognizes two different spousal privileges: the spousal testimonial privilege and the spousal communications privilege. The spousal testimonial privilege is defined in article I, section 12 of the Utah Constitution: "[A] wife shall not be compelled to testify against her husband, nor a husband against his wife." The Utah Rules of Evidence codifies the privilege in rule 502(a). In contrast, the spousal communications privilege, as codified in Utah Code section 78B-1-137 and Rule 502(b) of the Utah Rules of Evidence, protects confidential communications between spouses during their marriage. However, the accused spouse cannot invoke the spousal communications privilege if the accused spouse is charged with a crime.... Mr. Timmerman argues that the privileges were violated, but since Mr. Timmerman is accused of a crime against his spouse, he cannot invoke the spousal communications privilege.... Hence, only the spousal testimonial privilege is at issue here.

Mr. Timmerman argues that Mrs. Timmerman's out-of-court statements were improperly admitted after she invoked her spousal testimonial privilege. ....

Article I, section 12 of the Utah Constitution provides, "[A] wife shall not be compelled to testify against her husband." In examining the language of the privilege, we recognize that a privilege should be "strictly construed in accordance with its object,"... because of its "undesirable effect of excluding relevant evidence." .... Because a privilege withholds "relevant information from the factfinder, it applies only where necessary to achieve its purpose."....

The purpose of the spousal testimonial privilege is to foster "the harmony and sanctity of the marriage relationship.".... If spouses were forced to testify against each other, then "the testifying spouse would be placed in the unenviable position of either committing perjury or testifying to matters that are detrimental to his or her spouse, which could clearly lead to marital strife." ...

Construing the privilege strictly, according to its plain language and in light of its purpose, we interpret the spousal testimonial privilege to apply only to compelled testimony, or in other words, involuntary, in-court testimony. We believe this narrow interpretation

of the privilege will not serve to exclude relevant testimony or extend the privilege beyond its narrow purpose. Further, admitting an out-of-court statement into evidence does not force one spouse to testify against the other or tempt the testifying spouse to commit perjury.

Criticism of the spousal testimonial privilege further bolsters this narrow interpretation. The privilege enables "abusers to silence their victims" and makes the testifying spouse "vulnerable to coercion from the defendant-spouse and his lawyer." Amanda H. Frost, *Updating the Marital Privileges: A Witness-Centered Rationale,* 14 Wis. Women's L.J. 1, 34 (1999). Similarly, the Advisory Committee of the Utah Rules of Evidence is convinced that the justifications for the spousal testimonial privilege are insufficient: "[The privilege] does not promote marital felicity, is based on the outmoded concept that the husband and wife are one, and causes suppression of relevant evidence." ... The Advisory Committee recommends that only the spousal communications privilege be preserved and the spousal testimonial privilege be repealed. However, such a change is dependent on a constitutional amendment to article I, section 12 that would remove the spousal testimonial privilege.

In this case, the introduction of Mrs. Timmerman's statements into evidence at the preliminary hearing did not violate her spousal testimonial privilege, which protects a spouse from giving involuntary, in-court statements. Mrs. Timmerman was not forced to testify at the preliminary hearing. She invoked her privilege and was dismissed from the witness stand. In lieu of her in-court testimony, the State introduced Mrs. Timmerman's witness statement and her statements in the SANE report. Mrs. Timmerman made those statements voluntarily. She was not forced to attend a sexual assault examination or write a witness statement. Because the statements were neither compelled nor in-court, the spousal testimonial privilege does not apply.

We also note that barring the statements would not comport with the justifications for the privilege. Whatever degree of marital harmony that previously existed between the Timmermans was most likely absent when Mrs. Timmerman voluntarily gave her statements to the police and to the sexual assault nurse. Blocking her statements from admission into evidence at the preliminary hearing would promote excluding relevant evidence more than it would promote marital harmony. Furthermore, Mrs. Timmerman was not placed in a position where she had to choose either to perjure herself or harm her husband because she was not forced to testify in court...

Because the spousal testimonial privilege does not apply to the voluntary, out-of-court statements given to the police and to the sexual assault nurse, the trial court properly held that the spousal testimonial privilege was not violated and denied the motion to quash the bindover... We therefore affirm.

Associate Chief Justice Durrant, Justice Wilkins, Justice Parrish, and Justice Nehring concur in Chief Justice Durham's opinion.

Case Questions

1. This case illustrates how recognition of a spousal immunity can result in the exclusion of evidence. In this case, the prosecution was able to introduce the victim/wife's statement in lieu of having her testify at trial. Given that the public policy in Utah is to recognize spousal immunity, should the wife/victim have been "advised of her rights" by the police or hospital personnel prior to giving a statement to the SANE nurse?

2. Chief Justice Durham's opinion points out that one of the spousal immunities has been heavily criticized as bad public policy. Do you believe that there is any continuing need for the recognition of either spousal privilege? Explain and defend your position.

INTERNET TIP

Due to the complexity of the marital privilege, interested readers are invited to read the Florida case of *Dennis and Mary Hill v. State of Florida*. This is a criminal case involving confidential communications between husband and wife as well as the psychotherapist-patient privilege, both of which are also recognized under Florida law. You can read this case on the textbook's website.

Also on the website are the Wisconsin statute containing that state's attorney-client privilege rule, and *Raymond Binkley v. Georgette Allen*, a case in which the appellant claimed that the physician-patient privilege permitted her to refuse to disclose during discovery information relating to her use of prescribed medications....

Other privileges involving confidential communications include the doctor-patient privilege and the attorney-client privilege. The doctor-patient privilege applies to confidential information provided by a patient to a doctor for the purpose of treatment. The attorney-client privilege, the oldest common law privilege, protects confidential communications between lawyers and their clients and thereby encourages clients to speak frankly with their lawyers. The privilege applies to all communications between a client and his/her lawyer relating to professional representation. In addition, the attorney's work product, including all matters considered to be part of the preparation of a case, is privileged. These privileges may be waived by the client for whose protection they are intended.

The communications to clergy privilege protects a parishioner who has divulged confidential information to a member of the clergy while seeking spiritual guidance. If the parishioner reveals confidential information to a member of the clergy who is acting in his or her professional religious capacity, this communication can be excluded from evidence at trial as privileged. The modern version of this privilege has very imprecise boundaries, which will become more clear with the evolution of the case law.

Trial Motions

If, after the plaintiff's attorney presents plaintiff's case, the defendant's attorney believes that the plaintiff was unable to substantiate the essential allegations adequately, the defendant may make a **motion for nonsuit**. The judge grants the motion only if a reasonable person could not find in favor of the plaintiff after considering the evidence most favorable to the plaintiff. If the motion is granted, the case is over and the plaintiff loses.

If the motion for a nonsuit is denied or not made at all, the defendant's lawyer then presents the defendant's case and tries to disprove the plaintiff's evidence or substantiate the defendant's arguments. Witnesses and exhibits are presented, following the same procedure as the plaintiff's direct examination followed by cross-examination. After the defendant rests his or her case, the plaintiff then may produce evidence to rebut the defendant's evidence.

At the end of the presentation of evidence, but before the issues are submitted to the jury, either or both parties may make a motion for a **directed verdict**. The motion is granted for the party making the motion if the judge decides that the case is perfectly clear and that reasonable people could not disagree on the result. If the motion is granted, the moving party wins the dispute without the jury deciding the case. If no motion for a directed verdict is made, or if one is made and denied, the case is submitted to the jury.

Jury Verdict and Posttrial Motions

Both parties' attorneys have an opportunity to make oral arguments to the jury summarizing their cases. The judge then instructs the members of the jury as to how they should proceed. Although jury deliberations are secret, certain restrictions must be observed to avoid possible grounds for setting aside the verdict. These include prohibitions on juror misconduct, such as drunkenness; the use of unauthorized evidence, such as secretly visiting the scene of an accident; or disregarding the judge's instructions, such as discussing the merits of the case over lunch with a friend.

After the verdict has been rendered, a party not satisfied with it may move for judgment notwithstanding the verdict, a new trial, or relief from judgment. A **motion for judgment notwithstanding the verdict (JNOV)** is granted when the judge decides that reasonable people could not have reached the verdict that the jury has reached. A **motion for a new trial** before another jury may be granted by a judge for a variety of reasons, including excessive or grossly inadequate damages, newly discovered evidence, a questionable jury verdict, errors in the production of evidence, or simply the interest of justice. A **motion for relief from judgment** is granted if the judge finds a clerical error in the judgment, newly discovered evidence, or fraud that induced the judgment.

The appellant in the following case made a motion for a directed verdict at the close of all the evidence. She also made postverdict motions for JNOV and a new trial. She appealed from the court's denial of all three motions.

Cody v. Atkins
658 P.2d 59
Supreme Court of Wyoming
February 4, 1983

Raper, Justice
This appeal arose from a negligence action brought by Lois M. Cody (appellant) against Alfred Atkins (appellee) for injuries she allegedly sustained in an automobile collision between her car and appellee's pickup. Appellant appeals from the judgment on a jury verdict entered by the district court in favor of appellee....

At about 7:00 o'clock A.M. on the morning of November 13, 1980, appellant's car was struck from behind by a pickup driven by appellee. At the time of the accident appellant was stopped for a red light in the right-hand, west-bound lane of 16th Street at the intersection of 16th Street and Snyder Avenue in Cheyenne, Wyoming. The right front corner of appellee's vehicle struck the left rear corner of appellant's car. In the words of a police officer who investigated the accident, the lane of traffic in which the accident occurred was ice covered and "very slick." It was overcast and snowing lightly at the time the accident occurred but visibility was not impaired. Neither party complained of injuries when questioned by the investigating officer at the accident scene; however, later that day appellant complained of injuries and was taken to the emergency room at Memorial Hospital where she was examined and released. Appellant was subsequently hospitalized and treated for numerous physical complaints that she alleged resulted from the accident.

Appellant brought suit June 5, 1981, complaining that appellee's negligent operation of his vehicle had caused harm to her. On March 1, 1982, appellant filed an amended complaint against appellee. Appellee answered the complaints by admitting that his pickup collided with appellant's car but denying appellant's remaining allegations of negligence, etc.; there were no counterclaims made nor affirmative defenses asserted by appellee. The matter was tried before a six-person jury May 10 and 11, 1982, in the district court in Cheyenne. At the close of appellee's case, appellant made a motion for directed verdict.... The district court denied the motion. The jury then, after receiving its instructions and deliberating on the matter, returned a verdict in favor of appellee. Following the trial, appellant made timely motions for a new trial... and for a judgment notwithstanding the verdict.... The district court denied both motions; this appeal followed.

I

The first issue appellant raises for our consideration is the propriety of the district court's denial of his motion for a directed verdict.... We ... have held that since a directed verdict deprives the parties of a determination of the facts by a jury, such motion should be cautiously and sparingly granted....

In the majority of our decisions in which directed verdicts are at issue, we have dealt with directed verdicts sought by the defendant; here we are faced with the opposite situation of a plaintiff seeking a directed verdict. In general, the standard in directing a verdict for a plaintiff is similar to the standard used to direct one against him.... It is proper to direct a verdict for the plaintiff in those rare cases where there are no genuine issues of fact to be submitted to a jury.... In a negligence action a verdict may be directed for the plaintiff when there is no evidence that would justify a jury verdict for the defendant.... A directed verdict for the plaintiff is proper when there is no dispute as to a material fact, and when reasonable jurors cannot draw any other inferences from the facts than that propounded by the plaintiff.... In a negligence action, then, we need only determine that there was sufficient evidence to permit a reasonable jury to find that the defendant acted without negligence to hold that appellant's motion was properly denied. We so hold.

In this case appellee presented evidence that the roadway he was traveling on was slippery due to snow and ice; that he had been attempting to slow down and to stop to avoid a collision for some 400 feet prior to impact; that he had slowed from 20 m.p.h. to

5 m.p.h. in the 400 feet prior to impact; that he had attempted to drive to the left and avoid the collision; that his ability to stop was further complicated because he was traveling downhill; and that he was in control of his vehicle at all times prior to the collision. Although we were unable to find where appellee had testified in so many words that he had not been negligent, the jury could have properly inferred as much from the evidence we have outlined. Although appellant contends otherwise, the concept of an automobile accident occurring without a finding of negligence is not novel in our jurisprudence.... The district court could not have, in the face of appellee's evidence showing an absence of negligence, directed a verdict for appellant. Therefore, we hold the district court properly denied appellant's motion for directed verdict.

II

Appellant next argues that the district court erred in denying her motion for a judgment notwithstanding the verdict (J.N.O.V.).... As previously noted, appellant had sought and had been denied a directed verdict at the close of the evidence; therefore, we reach this issue. Before deciding the issue, however, we first set out the standard of review we shall employ....

J.N.O.V. can only be granted where there is an absence of any substantial evidence to support the verdict entered.... The test then for granting a J.N.O.V. is virtually the same as that employed in determining whether a motion for directed verdict should be granted or denied....

The logic behind similar standards of review is that it allows the district court another opportunity to determine the legal question of sufficiency of the evidence raised by the motion after the jury has reached a verdict.... In close cases the J.N.O.V. procedure promotes judicial economy. When a J.N.O.V. is reversed, for example, an appellate court can remand for reinstatement of the original verdict, where a new trial is generally required when a directed verdict is reversed....

In the case before us, we have, in ruling on the directed verdict question, already held that there was sufficient evidence presented to create a question of fact for the jury to determine on the issue of appellee's negligence. For those same reasons we must also hold that the district court correctly denied appellant's motion for a J.N.O.V.

III

We next reach appellant's final argument that the district court erred in denying her motion for a new trial.... Appellant's motion set forth the following grounds for obtaining a new trial:

> "1. That the Verdict is not Sustained by sufficient Evidence and is Contrary to Law.
> 2. That Errors of Law were Committed at the Trial."

Appellant then centers her argument around the first ground. The position appellant takes is that she was entitled to a new trial because the jury's verdict was not consistent with the evidence. We disagree....

A court's exercise of the power to grant a new trial is not a derogation of the right of a jury trial but is one of that right's historic safeguards.... The power to grant a new trial gives the trial court the power to prevent a miscarriage of justice.... Trial courts should grant new trials whenever, in their judgment, the jury's verdict fails to administer substantial justice to the parties....

> "The right of trial by jury includes the right to have the jury pass upon questions of fact by determining the credibility of witnesses and the weight of conflicting evidence. The findings of fact, however, are subject to review by the trial judge who, like the jury, has had the benefit of observing the demeanor and deportment of the witnesses. If he concludes that the evidence is insufficient to support the verdict, he should grant a new trial...."

This court has acknowledged that when a court could have properly granted a J.N.O.V. for insufficient evidence, it was not error to grant a motion for a new trial.... That does not mean, however, that the same standards apply for granting a new trial and a J.N.O.V.; the standard must be more lenient for exercising the power to grant new trials to preserve that power's historic role as a safety valve in our system of justice....

> "When the evidence is wholly insufficient to support a verdict, it is the duty of the trial court to direct a verdict or enter a judgment n.o.v., and the court has no discretion in that respect. But, the granting of a new trial involves an element of discretion which goes further than the mere sufficiency of the evidence. It embraces all the reasons which inhere in the integrity of the jury system itself...."

It is well settled in Wyoming that trial courts are vested with broad discretion when ruling on a motion for new trial, and that on review we will not overturn the trial court's decision except for an abuse of that discretion....

In this case, appellant argues there was not sufficient evidence before the jury to entitle them to find in favor of appellee. As we pointed out in our discussion of appellant's first issue, appellee presented sufficient evidence to permit the jury to reach the issue of negligence. Also, as we said earlier, the mere fact that the collision occurred does not in itself indicate negligence. Therefore, after hearing the testimony of the witnesses and observing their demeanor, the district court exercised its discretion and denied appellant's motion for a new trial. The district court thereby indicated its belief that under the circumstances of the case no substantial injustice would occur in upholding the jury's verdict. Appellant has presented no convincing argument that would persuade us that the district court abused its discretion. Therefore, we hold that the district court did not err when it denied appellant's motion for a new trial.

Affirmed.

Case Questions

1. Does granting a new trial because the jury awarded excessive damages infringe on the plaintiff's constitutional right to a jury trial?
2. Does a reduction of the amount of damages by the court as a condition for denying a new trial invade the province of the jury?
3. When is it proper for a judge to grant a directed verdict motion?
4. What is the purpose of the motion for judgment notwithstanding the verdict (JNOV)?

Additur and Remittitur

On occasion, juries award money damages that are, in the view of the trial or appellate courts, inadequate as a matter of law.

When a jury's award is grossly insufficient, a prevailing party in state court is often entitled to ask the trial court to award the plaintiff an additional sum of money (called **additur**). If the trial court agrees, it will specify an additional amount for the defendant to pay the plaintiff. In that event, the defendant can agree to pay the additur; refuse to pay, in which case the trial court will order a new

trial on damages; or appeal to a higher court. Federal judges cannot award additur because of the Seventh Amendment, which provides that "no fact tried by a jury shall be otherwise reexamined… than according to the rules of the common law." This means that no federal judge can award money damages in an amount above the sum awarded by the jury.

Although the jury in the next case found the defendant negligent, it failed to award the plaintiff any money damages. The plaintiff filed a motion in the trial court asking the court to order additur.

Shirley Junginger v. Rebecca Betts
No. 05C-10-202-JOH.
Superior Court of Delaware, New Castle County.
April 9, 2008.

MEMORANDUM OPINION

Herlihy, Judge.
Plaintiff Shirley Junginger has moved for a new trial complaining that the jury's verdict finding [that] defendant Rebecca Betts negligently caused the accident yet awarding … [plaintiff] no damages is against the great weight of the evidence. Basically … [plaintiff's] contention is that there were objective signs of injury and a zero damage award is inconsistent with that uncontroverted evidence.....

An examination of the record does indicate a few, objective signs of injury. The Court, however, does not find there is a need to retry the case, but will instead award additur in the amount of $13,500.00.

Factual Background
Junginger was backing out of a parking space in the Community Plaza Shopping Center when Betts, driving a van perpendicular to her, struck Junginger's car. The accident was on September 4, 2004. Junginger described the impact as "incredible," and said she was "tossed" to her left side. Her head, she said, hit the passenger window. At the scene, she testified she could not straighten her neck and head. She was taken to Christiana Hospital. There she described the impact as "mild" (according to the hospital records).

Betts was never quite sure she even hit Junginger's car. She testified she did not hear anything. There was, she said further, no jolting or jarring, but since Junginger did not move her car, she assumed something happened. Betts' daughter who was

riding with her sensed her mother braking but nothing else.

Photos of the two vehicles showed no damage to Betts' van but several dents to Junginger's car. One long dent higher up, however, does not correspond to anything on Betts' van.

Junginger had mild pain symptoms at Christiana and was released. She began treatment for her symptoms on September 7, 2004 with Dr. George Buhatiuk. He had treated her in 1998–2000 for a prior accident wherein she had similar problems in some of the same areas: neck and back. Junginger testified these problems resolved, however, prior to the 2004 accident.

Junginger treated with Dr. Buhatiuk from September 7th through May 2005. She had a treatment visit in August that year but did not see him again until a month before the trial. On her first visit, the doctor noted positive foreman's compression and Spurling's tests. These, he testified, are objective findings. But starting with her visit later in September 2004, she had no such positive tests until her visit in 2008. There were times in March, April, and May that she reported she was "guarded" in turning and looking over left shoulder.

Dr. Buhatiuk reported that Junginger told him she had trouble sleeping and that at times when she had slept on her left side, she would wake up with her arm feeling numb or tingly. He also testified she was 90% improved as of February 2005 and many of her symptoms had resolved within two to four weeks of the accident. The only lingering problem, according to the doctor, was mild upper back pain. Since this was present in 2008, he opined it was permanent. Junginger had exhausted her $15,000 PIP [personal injury protection insurance] coverage and owed Dr. Buhatiuk $6,780.

Dr. Buhatiuk has prescribed some therapy for her among other treatment modalities. She was restricted to lifting no more than twenty to twenty-five pounds. Her job at Joy Cleaners, however, meant she had to pick clothes off an overhead rack. At trial, she said she has upper back pain under the left shoulder blade and neck pain. She takes Advil for flare-ups in her pain. She favors her left side. But she was unable to say other activities had been impaired by the accident.

A significant part of this two-day trial involved whether an impact had occurred, who was at fault or whether both parties were at fault. The jury determined that: (1) Betts was negligent, (2) her negligence proximately caused the accident, and (3) her negligence proximately caused injury to Junginger. It did not award damages to Junginger, however, even though it was instructed to award her damages.

Applicable Standard

When considering a motion for new trial which attacks a jury's verdict, there are several key principles the Court must follow. Enormous deference is given to jury verdicts.... A jury's verdict is assumed to be correct.... To be set aside, a jury's verdict must be against the great weight of the evidence.... The Court will not set aside a verdict unless it is clear the jury disregarded the evidence or the rules of law....

Discussion

Junginger appropriately cites *Amalfitano v. Baker* ... in support of her argument that where there are uncontroverted objective findings of injury, a jury must award damages. In this case there is a mixture of a lot of subjective complaints with occasional objective and uncontroverted medical tests. Those tests are foreman's compression and Spurling's. There is mention in March–May 2005, of guarding, which is a report of pain when Junginger turned her head to the left to look over her shoulder. But there is no concurrent physician report of spasm. And when this guarding was noted, the two tests just mentioned either were not done, or they were negative. They were negative, in fact, from September 9, 2004 until next reported positive in February 2008. It is less than clear, therefore,

whether, the "guarding" which Dr. Buhatiuk noted is an "objective" finding in this case.

Many of Junginger's complaints and those reported to her doctor were subjective. This is key for several reasons. The doctor based his opinions about her injuries on subjective complaints, most of which, resolved in late September or early October 2004—just a few weeks after the accident. Respectfully, Junginger was not the most convincing plaintiff. Counsel handling personal injury litigation and judges know how much personal injury cases can rise and fall on the plaintiff's credibility. Further, a jury is entitled to reject a physician's testimony if it is based on a patient's subjective complaints and that patient's credibility is suspect....

There is a strong hint here that the jury's zero damages award reflects its problem with Junginger's credibility; perhaps exaggerating the impact, the pain, its pervasiveness in so many areas of the body and its degree.... This is speculative, of course, but it is a likely explanation considering the brief period many of her injuries lasted and negative results on two objective tests starting September 9, 2004.

The difficulty remains that there were "positive" results on two objective medical tests and uncontroverted medical records from Christiana on September 4th and Dr. Buhatiuk that Junginger suffered injury. This Court has the authority to award additur ... and even do so where there has been zero damages awarded.... In the Court's opinion the amount of that additur must account for three factors: pain and suffering, medical bills above PIP, and the minimal nature of Junginger's injuries (a conclusion supported by the jury's zero damage award). Dr. Buhatiuk testified that all of his treatment was reasonable and necessary and he believed he was appropriately treating what he found and/or was reported to him. Accounting for all of these factors, therefore, the Court will enter an additur award of $13,500.

Accordingly, a new trial on damages will be ordered unless Betts by written filing accepts additur of $13,500 within ten (10) days from the date of this opinion. If no action is taken by Betts, Junginger's motion for a new trial on the issues of damages only will be granted. If Betts accepts the additur, judgment for her will be set aside and a judgment will be entered in favor of Junginger in the amount of $13,500.

IT IS SO ORDERED

Case Questions

1. What is the purpose of additur?
2. If you were Betts' attorney, what would you need to think about as part of the process of determining whether to accept the additur?

Both state and federal judges, with the consent of the plaintiff, can reduce unreasonably high jury verdicts. When a jury finds for the plaintiff and the money damage award is grossly excessive, the defendant is entitled to ask the trial and appellate courts to reduce the size of the award by ordering a **remittitur**. If the trial court awards a remittitur, the plaintiff is given three choices. The plaintiff can accept the reduced sum that was determined by the court, refuse to remit any of the jury's award, in which case the trial court will order a new trial on damages, or appeal to a higher court.

INTERNET TIP

Students wishing to read another additur case, *Ruben Dilone v. Anchor Glass Container Corporation*, or a remittitur case, *Bunch v. King County Department of Youth Services*, can find these cases on the textbook's website.

Judgment and Execution

The trial process concludes with the award of a **judgment**. The judgment determines the rights of the disputing parties and decides what relief is awarded (if any). A judgment is awarded after the trial court has ruled on posttrial motions. Appeals are made from the court's entry of judgment. Either party (or both) may appeal from a trial court's judgment to an appellate court.

A person who wins a judgment is called a **judgment creditor**, and the person who is ordered to pay is called a **judgment debtor**. Many times the judgment debtor will comply with the terms of the judgment and deliver property or pay a specified sum of money to the judgment creditor. If necessary, however, the judgment creditor can enforce the judgment by obtaining a **writ of execution** from the clerk of court where the judgment is filed. The writ will be directed to the sheriff who can then seize the judgment creditor's nonexempt personal property and sell it to satisfy the judgment. An example of a statute exempting specified property from seizure can be seen in Figure 5.6. The statute authorizing judicial sale includes safeguards to prevent abuse of the defendant's rights.

Alternatively, the plaintiff may have a **lien** placed against the judgment debtor's real property.

Vermont Statutes Annotated §§ 2740.
GOODS AND CHATTELS; EXEMPTIONS FROM

The goods or chattels of a debtor may be taken and sold on execution, except the following articles, which shall be exempt from attachment and execution, unless turned out to the officer to be taken on the attachment or execution, by the debtor:

(1) the debtor's interest, not to exceed $2,500.00 in aggregate value, in a motor vehicle or motor vehicles;

(2) the debtor's interest, not to exceed $5,000.00 in aggregate value, in professional or trade books or tools of the profession or trade of the debtor or a dependent of the debtor;

(3) a wedding ring;

(4) the debtor's interest, not to exceed $500.00 in aggregate value, in other jewelry held primarily for the personal, family or household use of the debtor or a dependent of the debtor;

(5) the debtor's interest, not to exceed $2,500.00 in aggregate value, in household furnishings, goods or appliances, books, wearing apparel, animals, crops or musical instruments that are held primarily for the personal, family or household use of the debtor or a dependent of the debtor;

(6) growing crops, not to exceed $5,000.00 in aggregate value;

(7) the debtor's aggregate interest in any property, not to exceed $400.00 in value, plus up to $7,000.00 of any unused amount of the exemptions provided under subdivisions (1), (2), (4), (5) and (6) of this section;

(continued)

F I G U R E 5.6 Vermont Statute Exempting Goods and Chattels from Execution

(8) one cooking stove, appliances needed for heating, one refrigerator, one freezer, one water heater, sewing machines;

(9) ten cords of firewood, five tons of coals or 500 gallons of oil;

(10) 500 gallons of bottled gas;

(11) one cow, two goats, 10 sheep, 10 chickens, and feed sufficient to keep the cow, goats, sheep or chickens through one winter;

(12) three swarms of bees and their hives with their produce in honey;

(13) one yoke of oxen or steers or two horses kept and used for team work;

(14) two harnesses, two halters, two chains, one plow, and one ox yoke;

(15) the debtor's interest, not to exceed $700.00 in value, in bank deposits or deposit accounts of the debtor;

(16) the debtor's interest in self-directed retirement accounts of the debtor, including all pensions, all proceeds of and payments under annuity policies or plans, all individual retirement accounts, all Keogh plans, all simplified employee pension plans, and all other plans qualified under sections 401, 403, 408, 408A or 457 of the Internal Revenue Code. However, an individual retirement account, Keogh plan, simplified employee pension plan, or other qualified plan, except a Roth IRA, is only exempt to the extent that contributions thereto were deductible or excludable from federal income taxation at the time of contribution, plus interest, dividends or other earnings that have accrued on those contributions, plus any growth in value of the assets held in the plan or account and acquired with those contributions. A Roth IRA is exempt to the extent that contributions thereto did not exceed the contribution limits set forth in section 408A of the Internal Revenue Code, plus interest, dividends or other earnings on the Roth IRA from such contributions, plus any growth in value of the assets held in the Roth IRA acquired with those contributions. No contribution to a self-directed plan or account shall be exempt if made less than one calendar year from the date of filing for bankruptcy, whether voluntarily or involuntarily. Exemptions under this subdivision shall not exceed $5,000.00 for the purpose of attachment of assets by the office of child support pursuant to 15 V.S.A. §§ 799;

(17) professionally prescribed health aids for the debtor or a dependent of the debtor;

(18) any unmatured life insurance contract owned by the debtor, other than a credit life insurance contract;

(19) property traceable to or the debtor's right to receive, to the extent reasonably necessary for the support of the debtor and any dependents of the debtor:

(A) Social Security benefits;

(B) veteran's benefits;

(C) disability or illness benefits;

(D) alimony, support or separate maintenance;

(E) compensation awarded under a crime victim's reparation law;

(F) compensation for personal bodily injury, pain and suffering or actual pecuniary loss of the debtor or an individual on whom the debtor is dependent;

(G) compensation for the wrongful death of an individual on whom the debtor was dependent;

(H) payment under a life insurance contract that insured the life of an individual on whom the debtor was dependent on the date of that individual's death;

(I) compensation for loss of future earnings of the debtor or an individual on whom the debtor was or is dependent;

(J) payments under a pension, annuity, profit-sharing, stock bonus, or similar plan or contract on account of death, disability, illness, or retirement from or termination of employment.

It is created when the clerk of courts records the judgment (officially informing interested persons of the existence of the lien). The judgment debtor's property cannot be transferred until the lien is satisfied. This often means that when the judgment debtor's property is sold, part of the sale proceeds is paid to the judgment creditor to satisfy the lien.

Garnishment is another remedy for judgment creditors. It is a process that results in the debtor's employer being ordered to deduct a percentage of the debtor's earnings from each paycheck. These payments are first credited against the debt and then forwarded to the judgment creditor.

CHAPTER SUMMARY

Chapter V introduced readers to the importance of procedure in our civil legal system. Although civil procedure varies somewhat within the fifty-two court systems in this country (federal, state, and District of Columbia), all jurisdictions have adopted rules of civil procedure which serve as the road map for civil litigation. These rules tell attorneys how to move successfully through each stage of the litigation process. Fair procedures are essential to achieving just outcomes.

The basic steps of the litigation process were discussed. The chapter began with a discussion of what lawyers do after being retained by a client contemplating litigation. This was followed by a discussion about the role of the pleadings. Here readers learned about the complaint, answer, and reply. The requirements for serving the summons and consequences of defective service were also discussed.

The use of the pretrial motion to dismiss (for lack of subject matter jurisdiction or *in personam* jurisdiction, improper or inadequate service of the summons and/or complaint, or failure to state a claim upon which relief can be granted) and the motion for summary judgment (which is used to dispose of cases not needing to be tried—such as where no genuine issues of material fact exist) were explained.

Readers will also recall how modern discovery provides attorneys with various tools to identify the relevant facts in the case, especially those in the possession of the opposing party.

The procedural steps in the conduct of a trial, starting with the selection of a jury, the opening statements of the attorneys, the presentation of evidence, the rules of evidence, legal privileges, trial motions (such as the motion for nonsuit and directed verdict), and the closing arguments of the attorneys, were also discussed.

The chapter concluded with explanations of the jury verdict, the award of a judgment, posttrial motions (for JNOV and a new trial), and how a judgment can be enforced.

CHAPTER QUESTIONS

1. Richmond was convicted of sexually assaulting Krell, a woman with whom, according to the court, he had been in an "intimate relationship." In the aftermath of the alleged criminal act, Richmond had contacted a priest, Father Dick Osing, who was also a "part-time unlicensed marriage and family counselor." Richmond and Osing had conversed privately at an Episcopal church at which Osing was a priest. Father Osing testified at trial for the prosecution and disclosed the contents of the private discussion between Richmond and himself. Richmond appealed his conviction for sexual assault in the second degree on the grounds that Father Osing's testimony should have been excluded at the trial because of the

communications with clergy privilege. The facts showed that Richmond had contacted Father Osing for "advice on his relationship with Krell."

John M. Richmond v. State of Iowa, 97-954 Supreme Court of Iowa (1999)

2. The Stars' Desert Inn Hotel filed suit against Richard Hwang, a citizen of Taiwan, to collect on a $1,885,000 gambling debt. The parties were unable to cooperate in scheduling a date for taking defendant Hwang's deposition. The court, aware of the scheduling problem, entered an order requiring that the deposition be taken no later than November 29, 1994. Stars requested that Hwang provide at least two dates prior to the deadline when he would be available to be deposed. When Hwang failed to respond to this request, Stars set the date for November 23. Hwang's lawyers responded on November 21 with a proposal that Hwang be deposed in Taiwan prior to November 29. Stars rejected this proposal and filed a motion asking the court to strike Hwang's answer and enter a default judgment in favor of the plaintiff. Hwang's attorneys explained that their client was not cooperating with them and that he refused to be deposed in Nevada. The court imposed a $2,100 fine against Hwang and ordered him to either be deposed in Nevada or to prepay the plaintiff's expenses (estimated by the plaintiff to be between $20,000 and $40,000), for taking the deposition in Taiwan, no later than February 10, 1995. Hwang failed to pay the fine, asserted that the plaintiff's estimate of the costs of taking the deposition in Taiwan were excessive, and refused to comply with either option contained in the court's order. The plaintiff again requested that the court impose the sanctions. Should the court strike the answer and award a default judgment to the plaintiff in the amount of $1,885,000 (plus interest, costs, attorney's fees, and post-judgment interest)? Are there any less drastic steps that should be taken before imposing such a drastic sanction?

Stars' Desert Inn Hotel & Country Club v. Hwang, 105 F.3d 521 (9th Cir. 1997)

3. Colin Cody, a Connecticut resident, invested $200,000 in the common stock of Phillips Company, a firm that installs video gambling machines in Louisiana casinos. Cody brought suit against the defendant, Kevin Ward, a resident of California, alleging that Ward had used an Internet website called "Money Talk" to perpetrate a fraud on potential investors. The gist of Cody's complaint was that Ward had engaged in false and fraudulent misrepresentations about the Phillips company's impending financial prospects. Cody claimed to have made decisions about whether to buy and hold Phillips stock in partial reliance on Ward's misrepresentations on the Internet and on telephone calls made by Ward that encouraged Cody to buy and hold Phillips stock. Cody further claimed that the Phillips stock was essentially worthless. Ward sought to dismiss the complaint, alleging that he could not be sued in Connecticut because there were insufficient grounds for personal jurisdiction. Cody maintains that a defendant who orally or in writing causes information to enter Connecticut by wire is committing a tortious act within Connecticut and is subject to suit pursuant to the Connecticut long-arm statute. Do you believe that Ward has committed a tortious act within the forum state that would satisfy the requirements of the long-arm statute? Do you believe that there is a constitutional basis for Connecticut to exercise *in personam* jurisdiction over Ward?

Cody v. Ward, 954 F.Supp 43 (D. Conn. 1997)

4. The Stars' Desert Inn Hotel filed suit against Richard Hwang, a citizen of Taiwan, to collect on a $1,885,000 gambling debt. Stars unsuccessfully tried to serve Hwang on six occasions at a guarded and gated housing complex in Beverly Hills. The process server, after verifying with the guard that Hwang was inside, left the summons and complaint with the gate

attendant. Hwang moved to quash the service. Was Hwang properly served?

Stars' Desert Inn Hotel & Country Club v. Hwang, 105 F.3d 521 (9th Cir. 1997)

5. Colm Nolan and others brought suit against two City of Yonkers police officers and the City of Yonkers, New York, for alleged brutality and false arrest. The plaintiff's process server alleged that he had served both defendants at police headquarters (rather than at their place of residence), and also mailed copies of the summons and complaint to each officer at police headquarters. New York law provides that a summons can be delivered to "the actual place of business of the person to be served and by mailing a copy to the person to be served at his actual place of business." One defendant admitted receiving a copy of the summons and complaint at his police mailbox; the second officer denied ever receiving either document at police headquarters. Neither officer suffered any prejudice because both defendants did receive the summons and complaint and both filed answers in a timely manner. Rule 4 of the Federal Rules of Civil Procedure permits service "pursuant to the law of the state in which the district court is located." The two police officers asked the court to dismiss the complaint for lack of personal jurisdiction. Was the service at police headquarters sufficient to confer *in personam* jurisdiction over these defendants?

Nolan v. City of Yonkers, 168 F.R.D. 140 (S.D.N.Y. 1996)

6. A car driven by James Murphy struck a boy and injured him. Immediately after the accident, according to the boy's mother, Murphy told her "that he was sorry, that he hoped her son wasn't hurt. He said he had to call on a customer and was in a bit of a hurry to get home." At trial, Murphy denied telling the boy's mother that he was involved in his employment at the time of the accident. It was shown, however, that part of his normal duties for his employer, Ace Auto Parts Company, included making calls on customers in his car. Can the

mother have the statement admitted in court as a spontaneous exclamation?

7. Carolyn McSwain was driving a vehicle owned by John Denham in New York City on November 5, 1994. In the vehicle with McSwain were John Denham's mother Ollie Denham and John's child, Raesine. All the people in this vehicle were residents of Covington County, Mississippi. This vehicle was in a collision with a commuter van owned by Rockaway Commuter Line and driven by Sylvan Collard. Rockaway was a New York corporation with no significant contacts with Mississippi. As a result of this collision, McSwain and Raesine were injured, and Ollie Denham died. On November 4, 1997, John Denham sued McSwain, Rockaway, and Collard in Smith County, Mississippi for wrongfully causing the death of Ollie and for causing Raesine's injuries. Denham sent process to Rockaway by certified mail in November of 1997. Rockaway waited almost twenty-one months before filing an answer to Rockaway's complaint on August 27, 1999. The answer raised as a defense the lack of personal jurisdiction, improper service of process, and a motion for change of venue from Smith County to New York City. Rockaway's motion to dismiss was denied by the trial court, but Rockaway's petition for interlocutory appeal was granted by the Mississippi Supreme Court. Did Smith County have personal jurisdiction over Rockaway? Did Smith County waive its lack of personal jurisdiction defense by not filing its answer in a timely manner?

Rockaway Commuter Line, Inc. v. Denham, 897 So. 2d 156 (2004)

8. James Duke filed a suit against Pacific Telephone & Telegraph Company (PT&T) and two of its employees for invasion of privacy through unauthorized wiretapping. Duke claimed that defendant's employees installed an interception device on his telephone line without his knowledge or consent for the sole

purpose of eavesdropping. Through the use of the bugging devices, defendants acquired information that they communicated to the police department, resulting in his arrest. Although the charges were dismissed, he was discharged from his job. As part of the plaintiff's discovery, oral depositions were taken of the employees. The defendants refused to answer (1) questions relating to the procedure used in making unauthorized tapes of phone conversations (training of personnel, equipment, authority among employees), (2) questions relating to the deponent's knowledge of the illegality of unauthorized monitoring, (3) questions relating to a possible working relationship between the police and PT&T, and (4) questions relating to the monitoring of telephone conversations of subscribers other than the plaintiff. The defendants claimed that these questions were irrelevant to the litigation and therefore not proper matters for discovery. Do you agree?

Pacific Telephone & Telegraph Co. v. Superior Court, 2 Cal.3d 161, 465 P.2d 854, 84 Cal. Rptr. 718 (1970)

9. W. R. Reeves filed suit under the Federal Employers Liability Act against his employer, Central of Georgia Railway Company, seeking damages he allegedly suffered when the train on which he was working derailed near Griffin, Georgia. The liability of the defendant railroad was established at trial, and the issue of damages remained to be fixed. Several physicians testified regarding the injuries received by Reeves. Reeves also testified. On the witness stand, he said that an examining physician had told him that he would be unable to work because of a weakness in his right arm, a dead place on his arm, stiffness in his neck, and nerve trouble in his back. Why did admission of this testimony into evidence constitute reversible error?

Central of Georgia Ry. Co. v. Reeves, 257 So.2d 839 (Ga. 1972)

10. On December 10, 1962, Rosch obtained a judgment against Kelly from the superior court of Orange County, California. The California Code permits execution of a judgment only within ten years after entry of a judgment. If this is not done, the judgment may be enforced only by leave of court, after notice to the judgment debtors, accompanied by an affidavit setting forth the reasons for the failure to proceed earlier. The plaintiff made no attempt to enforce the judgment in California before Kelly moved to Texas in 1970. On February 15, 1974, the plaintiff attempted to execute on the California judgment in Texas. Does the Texas court have to allow execution under the full faith and credit clause?

Rosch v. Kelly, 527 F.2d 871 (5th Cir. 1976)

NOTES

1. T. F. F. Plucknett, *A Concise History of the Common Law,* 5th ed. (Boston: Little, Brown and Co., 1956), p. 408.
2. Ibid., pp. 408–409.
3. Ibid., p. 400.
4. The Federal Rules of Civil Procedure have significantly altered the service requirement in federal court. Rule 4(d) requires plaintiffs to send a copy of the complaint and a request for waiver of service to the defendant. A defendant who signs the waiver of service is allowed sixty days from the date of the notice to file an answer. A defendant who fails to sign the waiver and cannot prove good cause for this refusal can be required to pay the plaintiffs costs and attorney fees associated with going to court to obtain enforcement.
5. Jurors are generally selected from rosters containing lists of taxpayers, licensed drivers, and/or registered voters.

VI

✳

Limitations in Obtaining Relief

CHAPTER OBJECTIVES

1. *Understand how constitutions, statutes, and judicial doctrines play a role in deciding which cases can be decided in the public courts.*
2. *Explain the case or controversy requirement.*
3. *Summarize what can make a case nonjusticiable.*
4. *Describe how statues of limitations and the equitable doctrine of laches limit plaintiffs.*
5. *Explain the conditions that must be met for a claim to be barred by the res judicata/ claim preclusion doctrine.*
6. *Understand why immunities exist and how they work.*

People with grievances have a variety of options for obtaining relief. Nonjudicial alternatives such as mediation and arbitration, for example, are discussed in Chapter XIV. Access to the public courts, however, is not available to every litigant who would like to have a dispute decided there. We have already seen in Chapter IV, for example, that jurisdictional requirements prevent or limit courts from deciding many cases. In this chapter we learn about other constitutional, statutory, and common law limitations that have been created to determine if suits should be litigated in the public courts.

In some lawsuits courts are asked to provide legal answers to theoretical questions. These suits will generally be dismissed for failure to state a "case or controversy." Cases can also be dismissed for inappropriateness. This occurs, for example, when a plaintiff sues prematurely, takes "too long" to initiate litigation, or tries to relitigate a matter that had been previously decided in a prior suit. Similarly, courts don't want to waste time on cases that are not truly adversarial (such as where **collusion** exists and one party is financing and controlling both sides of the litigation) or where the person bringing the suit has no personal stake in the litigation (such as where the plaintiff is suing on behalf of a friend who is reluctant to sue).

Later in the chapter we will learn that, in some circumstances, the public interest requires that certain defendants receive **immunity** (preferential protection) from lawsuits. Immunities have historically been granted to governments and certain public officials. In some jurisdictions immunities also limit lawsuits between family members.

CASE OR CONTROVERSY REQUIREMENT

To be within the federal judicial power, a matter must be a "case" or "controversy" as required by Article III, Section 2, of the U.S. Constitution. The parties to a lawsuit filed in federal court must truly be adversaries. The U.S. Supreme Court has always construed the **case or controversy** requirement as precluding the federal courts from advising the other branches of the government or anyone else.

Assume that a police chief has devised a new search and seizure strategy for identifying and apprehending terrorists. Assume further that the chief, wishing to know whether this strategy, if implemented, would violate the Fourth Amendment's "reasonableness clause" regarding searches and seizures, sends a letter posing the question to the U.S. Supreme Court. Will the court answer the question? No, it will not. The police chief is asking for a legal opinion. The question posed is based on a set of assumed facts. The facts are limited and entirely "hypothetical," and there are no true adversaries here. The entire matter is premature. The case or controversy requirement would be satisfied, however, if the police chief were to implement the strategy, seize evidence, and make an arrest that resulted in a criminal prosecution.

Many state constitutions follow the federal approach and do not permit state courts to render advisory opinions. Their executive and legislative branches may only seek advice from the state attorney general. However, the constitutions of some states specifically permit the state supreme court to issue advisory opinions to government officials concerning certain matters of law. In this capacity, the court acts only as an adviser; its opinion does not have the effect of a judicial decision.

JUSTICIABILITY—A MATTER OF STANDING, RIPENESS, AND *RES JUDICATA*

Only cases that are **justiciable** can be decided by courts on their merits. To be justiciable, a case must be well suited for judicial determination. Courts use judicial doctrines (policies) such as standing, ripeness, and *res judicata* to weed out cases that lack justiciability. One of the cornerstones of our judicial system is the notion that the parties to a lawsuit must be true adversaries. The underlying assumption is that the best way to determine the truth and do justice in a lawsuit is to require disputing parties to use their full faculties against each other in court. Their interests must collide, and they must be seeking different relief. The ripeness and standing doctrines help courts preserve this essential aspect of the litigation process.

The concepts of ripeness and standing, although distinguishable, are similar and can overlap. A **ripeness** inquiry focuses on whether a case has developed sufficiently to be before a court for adjudication. A challenge to a party's **standing** differs in that it focuses on whether the plaintiff who filed the lawsuit is the right person or entity to be bringing this particular claim before the court.

A lawsuit is not ripe for adjudication, and is therefore nonjusticiable, if it has been filed prematurely. The adversary system works best when the litigants' positions are definite, distinct, and unambiguously adverse. In such a situation, the consequences of ruling for or against each party are more apparent. Where the full facts of a case are unknown or obscured, making a decision becomes much more difficult because the decision maker in such situations has to make too many assumptions in order to reach a well-reasoned conclusion. A just outcome is more likely if more certainty is required.

To have **standing**, a plaintiff must have a legally sufficient personal interest in the dispute and must be adversely affected by the defendant's conduct (i.e., injured in fact). With a few notable exceptions (such as for parents of minor children and guardians of incompetents), one person cannot sue to recover on behalf of another person who has been legally injured. Most people actually refuse to bring lawsuits against individuals they have a legal right to sue. They choose not to take legal action because the persons who have caused them harm are their friends, relatives, neighbors, or acquaintances. The standing requirement ensures that the injured person is in control of the decision to sue, prevents undesired and unnecessary suits, and prevents people who have marginal or derivative interests from filing multiple suits.

The following case, from the state of North Carolina, discusses standing in a case brought by two soldiers who sought to prevent their deployment to Iraq or Afghanistan.

Sullivan v. State
612 S.E.2d 397
Court of Appeals of North Carolina
May 17, 2005

Hunter, Judge.

Lt. Col. Donald Sullivan and Specialist Jeffery S. Sullivan (collectively "plaintiffs") appeal from a dismissal of their claim for injunctive relief entered 1 March 2004....

Plaintiffs are former members of the United States Armed Services. Specialist Sullivan is a current member of the North Carolina National Guard and was deployed in August 2003 to the current United States military operation ongoing in Afghanistan.

On 3 October 2003, plaintiffs sought a temporary restraining order and preliminary injunction against the State of North Carolina, Governor Michael F. Easley, and Major General William E. Ingram, Adjutant General of the North Carolina National Guard (collectively "defendants"), to: (1) rescind orders of deployment for members of the military forces of North Carolina engaged in actions in Iraq and Afghanistan, (2) recall those troops already deployed, and (3) estop defendants from further deployment. Plaintiffs contend such actions violate the state and federal Constitutions.

Defendants moved to dismiss the action, contending that the claim was not justiciable and failed to state a claim on which relief could be granted. The trial court granted defendants' motion to dismiss ... finding plaintiffs lacked standing ... and that the complaint presented political questions not justiciable by the court. Plaintiffs contend the trial court erred in dismissing their claims on these grounds. We disagree.

Standing is among the "justiciability doctrines" developed by federal courts to give meaning to the United States Constitution's "case or controversy" requirement. U.S. Const. Art. 3, § 2. The term refers to whether a party has a sufficient stake in an otherwise justiciable controversy so as to properly seek adjudication of the matter....

"Standing is a necessary prerequisite to a court's proper exercise of subject matter jurisdiction." ...

In order to establish standing to bring a justiciable claim before the court, a plaintiff must show an:

"'(1) "injury in fact"—an invasion of a legally protected interest that is (a) concrete and particularized and (b) actual or imminent, not conjectural or hypothetical; (2) the injury is fairly traceable to the challenged action of the defendant; and (3) it is likely, as opposed to merely speculative, that the injury will be redressed by a favorable decision'."...

Plaintiffs' requested relief in this action is an injunction to rescind orders of deployment for United States military forces, withdrawal of currently deployed troops, and estoppel of future deployments. Such relief is not within the power of the North Carolina state courts to grant.... A member of a state national guard is simultaneously a member of the Army National Guard of the United States.... Further, a guard member ordered to active duty is relieved from duty in the National Guard of his State.... Plaintiffs' remedy of withdrawal of federal troops and estoppel of further deployment is not within the power of the

State of North Carolina to provide, as such deployments of federal troops are entirely within the control of the federal government … art 1, § 8, cl. 16 (stating Congress shall govern the militia when employed in the service of the United States), U.S. Const. art 2, § 2, cl. 1 (stating President is commander in chief of the militia of the several states), U.S. Const. art. 6, § 2 (stating the Constitution is the supreme law of the land

and binding on the judges of every state). Therefore the trial court properly found plaintiffs lacked standing to proceed with their claim.

As both plaintiffs have failed to establish standing, the trial court properly dismissed the action for lack of jurisdiction. We therefore decline to address plaintiffs' additional assignments of error.

Affirmed.

Case Questions

1. What must a plaintiff demonstrate in order to establish standing?
2. Why do Federal courts have a special concern about standing?

INTERNET TIP

Students wishing to read a federal case focusing on both standing and ripeness can read *Thomas v. Anchorage Equal Rights Commission,* 220 F.3d 1134, on the textbook's website.

MOOTNESS

Moot cases are outside the judicial power because there is no case or controversy. Mootness is an aspect of ripeness, in that there is no reason to try a case unless there has been some direct adverse

effect on some party. Deciding when a case is moot is sometimes difficult. An actual controversy must not only exist at the date the action was filed, but it also must exist at the appellate stage. Courts recognize an exception to the mootness rule when an issue is capable of repetition. If a defendant is "free to return to his or her old ways," the public interest in determining the legality of the practices will prevent mootness. In the following case, members of the U.S. Supreme Court debated the "mootness" question within the context of a petition for certiorari brought by Jose Padilla, an American citizen President George W. Bush declared to be an enemy combatant.

Jose Padilla v. C. T. Hanft, U.S. Navy Commander, Consolidated Naval Brig
547 U.S. 1062
Supreme Court of the United States
April 3, 2006

Opinion: The petition for a writ of certiorari is denied. Justice Souter and Justice Breyer would grant the petition for a writ of certiorari.

Concur: Justice Kennedy, with whom the Chief Justice and Justice Stevens join, concurring in the denial of certiorari.

The Court's decision to deny the petition for writ of certiorari is, in my view, a proper exercise of its discretion in light of the circumstances of the case. The history of petitioner Jose Padilla's detention, however, does require this brief explanatory statement.

Padilla is a United States citizen. Acting pursuant to a material witness warrant issued by the United

States District Court for the Southern District of New York, federal agents apprehended Padilla at Chicago's O'Hare International Airport on May 8, 2002. He was transported to New York, and on May 22 he moved to vacate the warrant. On June 9, while that motion was pending, the President issued an order to the Secretary of Defense designating Padilla an enemy combatant and ordering his military detention. The District Court, notified of this action by the Government's ex parte motion, vacated the material witness warrant.

Padilla was taken to the Consolidated Naval Brig in Charleston, South Carolina. On June 11, Padilla's counsel filed a habeas corpus petition in the Southern

District of New York challenging the military detention. The District Court denied the petition, but the
Court of Appeals for the Second Circuit reversed and
ordered the issuance of a writ directing Padilla's
release. This Court granted certiorari and ordered dismissal of the habeas corpus petition without prejudice,
holding that the District Court for the Southern District
of New York was not the appropriate court to consider
it....

The present case arises from Padilla's subsequent
habeas corpus petition, filed in the United States District Court for the District of South Carolina on July 2,
2004. Padilla requested that he be released immediately or else charged with a crime. The District Court
granted the petition on February 28, 2005, but the
Court of Appeals for the Fourth Circuit reversed that
judgment on September 9, 2005. Padilla then filed the
instant petition for writ of certiorari.

After Padilla sought certiorari in this Court, the
Government obtained an indictment charging him
with various federal crimes. The President ordered that
Padilla be released from military custody and transferred to the control of the Attorney General to face
criminal charges. The Government filed a motion for
approval of Padilla's transfer in the Court of Appeals
for the Fourth Circuit. The Court of Appeals denied the
motion, but this Court granted the Government's subsequent application respecting the transfer...The Government also filed a brief in opposition to certiorari,
arguing, among other things, that Padilla's petition
should be denied as moot.

The Government's mootness argument is based
on the premise that Padilla, now having been charged
with crimes and released from military custody, has
received the principal relief he sought. Padilla responds
that his case was not mooted by the Government's
voluntary actions because there remains a possibility
that he will be redesignated and redetained as an
enemy combatant.

Whatever the ultimate merits of the parties'
mootness arguments, there are strong prudential considerations disfavoring the exercise of the Court's certiorari power. Even if the Court were to rule in Padilla's
favor, his present custody status would be unaffected.
Padilla is scheduled to be tried on criminal charges.
Any consideration of what rights he might be able to
assert if he were returned to military custody would be
hypothetical, and to no effect, at this stage of the
proceedings.

In light of the previous changes in his custody
status and the fact that nearly four years have passed
since he first was detained, Padilla, it must be

acknowledged, has a continuing concern that his status
might be altered again. That concern, however, can be
addressed if the necessity arises. Padilla is now being
held pursuant to the control and supervision of the
United States District Court for the Southern District of
Florida, pending trial of the criminal case. In the course
of its supervision over Padilla's custody and trial the
District Court will be obliged to afford him the protection, including the right to a speedy trial, guaranteed to all federal criminal defendants....Were the
Government to seek to change the status or conditions
of Padilla's custody, that court would be in a position
to rule quickly on any responsive filings submitted by
Padilla. In such an event, the District Court, as well as
other courts of competent jurisdiction, should act
promptly to ensure that the office and purposes of the
writ of habeas corpus are not compromised. Padilla,
moreover, retains the option of seeking a writ of
habeas corpus in this Court....

That Padilla's claims raise fundamental issues
respecting the separation of powers, including consideration of the role and function of the courts, also
counsels against addressing those claims when the
course of legal proceedings has made them, at least for
now, hypothetical. This is especially true given that
Padilla's current custody is part of the relief he sought,
and that its lawfulness is uncontested.

These are the reasons for my vote to deny
certiorari.

Justice Ginsburg, dissenting from the denial of certiorari.

This case, here for the second time, raises a question
"of profound importance to the Nation." ...Does the
President have authority to imprison indefinitely a
United States citizen arrested on United States soil dis-
tant from a zone of combat, based on an Executive
declaration that the citizen was, at the time of his
arrest, an "enemy combatant"? It is a question the
Court heard, and should have decided, two years
ago.... Nothing the Government has yet done purports
to retract the assertion of Executive power Padilla
protests.

Although the Government has recently lodged
charges against Padilla in a civilian court, nothing prevents the Executive from returning to the road it earlier constructed and defended. A party's voluntary
cessation does not make a case less capable of repetition or less evasive of review.... Satisfied that this
case is not moot, I would grant the petition for
certiorari.

Case Questions

1. Why did Chief Justice Roberts and Justices Stevens and Kennedy believe that this certiorari petition should not be granted?
2. Why did Justice Ginsburg believe that the petition for certiorari should have been granted?

POLITICAL QUESTIONS

Because of the constitutional separation of powers, the Supreme Court has long recognized a **political question doctrine**. It provides that the judicial branch is not entitled to decide questions that more properly should be decided by the executive and legislative branches of the federal government. U.S. Supreme Court Justice Scalia explained this doctrine in his plurality opinion in *Richard Vieth v. Robert C. Jubelirer*, 541 U.S. 267 (2004):

> As Chief Justice Marshall proclaimed two centuries ago, "It is emphatically the province and duty of the judicial department to say what the law is." *Marbury v. Madison* … (1803). Sometimes, however, the law is that the judicial department has no business entertaining the claim of unlawfulness—because the question is entrusted to one of the political branches or involves no judicially enforceable rights…See, e.g., *Nixon v. United States*, (1993) (challenge to procedures used in Senate impeachment proceedings); *Pacific States Telephone & Telegraph Co. v. Oregon*, … (1912) (claims arising under the Guaranty Clause of Article IV, § 4). Such questions are said to be "nonjusticiable," or "political questions."

The federal constitution allocates separate governmental power to the legislative, executive, and judicial branches. As members of the judicial branch of government, the courts exercise judicial powers. As the political departments, the executive and legislative branches are entrusted with certain functions, such as conducting foreign relations, making treaties, or submitting our country to the jurisdiction of international courts. Such issues fall outside the jurisdiction of the courts. Courts classify an issue as justiciable or as a nonjusticiable political question on a case-by-case basis.

INTERNET TIP

Students wishing to read an interesting case in which the political question doctrine is thoroughly discussed will find *Schneider v. Kissinger* on the textbook's website. The plaintiffs in *Schneider* sought to sue former Secretary of State Henry Kissinger and other prominent governmental officials over the U.S. government's actions in Chile during the Nixon administration. This case was decided in 2005 by the U.S. Court of Appeals for the District of Columbia and certiorari was denied by the U.S. Supreme Court in 2006.

THE ACT OF STATE DOCTRINE

The judicially created **Act of State Doctrine** provides that American courts should not determine the validity of public acts committed by a foreign sovereign within its own territory. This doctrine's roots go back to England in 1674. The doctrine is pragmatic: It prevents our courts from making pronouncements about matters over which they have no power. Judicial rulings about such matters could significantly interfere with the conduct of foreign policy—a matter that the Constitution assigns to the political branches of government. The Constitution does not require the Act of State doctrine; it is based on the relationships among the three branches of the federal government.

Assume, for example, that a foreign dictator confiscates a warehouse containing merchandise belonging to an American corporation. The

American corporation subsequently files suit in an American court to challenge the foreign nation's laws and procedures, alleging that the dictator did not have a valid right to confiscate the merchandise. The American court can apply the Act of State doctrine and refuse to make any pronouncements about the foreign nation's laws or procedures. The law presumes the public acts of a foreign sovereign within its own territory to be valid.

STATUTE OF LIMITATIONS

There is a time period, established by the legislature, within which an action must be brought upon claims or rights to be enforced. This law is known as the **statute of limitations** (see Figure 6.1). The statute of limitations compels the exercise of a right of action within a reasonable time, so that the opposing party has a fair opportunity to defend

| | Contract | | | | Tort | | | | | | | | | | | |
| | | | | | Negligence | | | Intentional Torts | | | | | | | | |
	Breach of Sales Contract	Breach of Warranty	Oral	Written	Personal Injury	Wrongful Death	Medical Malpractice	Assault and Battery	Fraud and Deceit	Libel	Slander	Trespass	Damage to Personal Property	Conversion	False Imprisonment	Malicious Prosecution
Alabama	4	4	6	6	1	2	2	6	2	1	1	6	1	6	6	1
Alaska	4	4	6	6	2	2	2	2	2	2	2	6	6	6	2	2
Arizona	4	4	3	6	2	2	2	2	3	1	1	2	2	2	1	1
Arkansas	4	4	3	5	3	3	2	1	5	3	1	3	3	3	1	5
California	4	4	2	4	1	1	3	1	3	1	1	3	3	3	1	1
Colorado	4	4	3	3	2	2	2	1	1	1	1	2	2	3	1	2
Connecticut	4	4	3	6	2	2	2	3	3	2	2	3	3	3	3	3
Delaware	4	4	3	3	2	2	2	2	3	2	2	3	2	3	2	2
District of Columbia	4	4	3	3	3	1	3	1	3	1	1	3	3	3	1	1
Florida	4	4	4	5	4	2	2	4	4	2	2	4	4	4	4	4
Georgia	4	4	4	6	2	2	2	2	4	1	1	4	4	4	2	2
Hawaii	4	4	6	6	2	2	2	2	6	2	2	2	2	6	6	6
Idaho	4	4	4	5	2	2	2	2	3	2	2	3	3	3	2	4
Illinois	4	4	5	10	2	2	2	2	5	1	1	5	5	5	2	2
Indiana	4	4	6	10	2	2	2	2	6	2	2	6	2	6	2	2
Iowa	5	5	5	10	2	2	2	2	5	2	2	5	5	5	2	2
Kansas	4	4	3	5	2	2	2	1	2	1	1	2	2	2	1	1
Kentucky	4	4	5	15	1	1	1	1	5	1	1	5	2	2	1	1
Louisiana	10	1	10	10	1	1	1	1	1	1	1	1	1	1	1	1

FIGURE 6.1 Statutes of Limitations for Civil Actions (in Years)

| | Contract | | | | Tort | | | | | | | | | | | |
| | | | | | Negligence | | | Intentional Torts | | | | | | | | |
	Breach of Sales Contract	Breach of Warranty	Oral	Written	Personal Injury	Wrongful Death	Medical Malpractice	Assault and Battery	Fraud and Deceit	Libel	Slander	Trespass	Damage to Personal Property	Conversion	False Imprisonment	Malicious Prosecution
Maine	4	4	6	6	6	2	2	2	6	2	2	6	6	6	2	6
Maryland	4	4	3	3	3	3	3	1	3	1	1	3	3	3	3	3
Massachusetts	4	4	6	6	3	3	3	3	3	3	3	3	3	3	3	3
Michigan	4	4	6	6	3	3	2	2	6	1	1	3	3	3	2	2
Minnesota	4	4	6	6	6	3	2	2	6	2	2	6	6	6	2	2
Mississippi	6	6	3	6	6	2	2	1	6	1	1	6	6	6	1	1
Missouri	4	4	5	10	5	3	2	2	5	2	2	5	5	5	2	5
Montana	4	4	5	8	3	3	3	2	2	2	2	2	2	2	2	5
Nebraska	4	4	4	5	4	2	2	1	4	1	1	4	4	4	1	1
Nevada	4	4	4	6	2	2	2	2	3	2	2	3	3	3	2	2
New Hampshire	4	4	3	3	3	3	2	3	3	3	3	3	3	3	3	3
New Jersey	4	4	6	6	2	2	2	2	6	1	1	6	6	6	2	2
New Mexico	4	4	4	6	3	3	3	3	4	3	3	4	4	4	3	3
New York	4	4	6	6	3	2	2½	1	6	1	1	3	3	3	1	1
North Carolina	4	4	3	3	3	2	3	1	3	1	1	3	3	3	1	3
North Dakota	4	4	6	6	6	2	2	2	6	2	2	6	6	6	2	6
Ohio	4	4	6	15	2	2	1	1	4	1	1	4	2	4	1	1
Oklahoma	5	5	3	5	2	2	2	1	2	1	1	2	2	2	1	1
Oregon	4	4	6	6	2	3	2	2	2	1	1	6	6	6	2	2
Pennsylvania	4	4	4	4	2	2	2	2	2	1	1	2	2	2	2	2
Rhode Island	4	4	10	10	3	2	3	10	10	10	1	10	10	10	3	10
South Carolina	6	6	6	6	6	6	3	2	6	2	2	6	6	6	2	6
South Dakota	4	4	6	6	3	3	2	2	6	2	2	6	6	6	2	6
Tennessee	4	4	6	6	1	1	1	1	3	1	½	3	3	3	1	1
Texas	4	4	2	4	2	2	2	2	2	1	1	2	2	2	2	1
Utah	4	4	4	6	4	2	2	1	3	1	1	3	3	3	1	1
Vermont	4	4	6	6	3	2	3	3	6	3	3	6	3	6	3	3
Virginia	4	4	3	5	2	2	2	2	1	1	1	5	5	5	2	1
Washington	4	4	3	6	3	3	3	2	3	2	2	3	3	3	2	3
West Virginia	4	4	5	10	2	2	2	2	2	1	1	2	2	2	1	1
Wisconsin	6	6	6	6	3	3	3	2	6	2	2	6	6	6	2	6
Wyoming	4	4	8	10	4	2	2	1	4	1	1	4	4	4	1	1

FIGURE 6.1 Statutes of Limitations for Civil Actions (in Years) *(Continued)*

and will not be surprised by the assertion of a stale claim after evidence has been lost or destroyed. With the lapse of time, memories fade and witnesses may die or move. The prospects for impartial and comprehensive fact-finding diminish.

The statutory time period begins to run immediately on the accrual of the cause of action, that is, when the plaintiff's right to institute a suit arises. If the plaintiff brings the suit after the statutory period has run, the defendant may plead the statute of limitations as a defense. Although jurisdictions have differing definitions, a cause of action can be generally said to exist when the defendant breaches some legally recognized duty owed to the plaintiff and thereby causes some type of legally recognized injury to the plaintiff.

Generally, once the statute of limitations begins to run, it continues to run until the time period is exhausted. However, many statutes of limitation contain a "saving clause" listing conditions and events that "toll" (suspend) the running of the statute. The occurrence of one of these conditions may also extend the limitations period for a prescribed period of time. In personal injury cases, for example, the statute may start to run from the date of the injury or from the date when the injury is discoverable, depending on the jurisdiction. Conditions that may serve to toll the running of the statute or extend the time period include infancy, insanity, imprisonment, court orders, war, and fraudulent concealment of a cause of action by a trustee or other fiduciary. The statute of limitations often starts to run in medical malpractice cases on the day that the doctor or patient stops the prescribed treatment or on the day that the patient becomes aware (or should have become aware) of the malpractice and subsequent injury. The commencement of an action almost universally tolls the running of the statute of limitations. Thus, once an action is commenced on a claim within the statutory time period, it does not matter if judgment is ultimately rendered after the period of limitations has expired.

In the following case the interests of consumers were pitted against the economic welfare of an important industry (and a major regional employer) within the state. The state legislature used the statute of limitations and a ninety-day notification requirement to further the economic interests of the state's ski industry at the expense of consumers.

Marybeth Atkins v. Jiminy Peak, Inc.
514 N.E.2d 850
Massachusetts Supreme Judicial Court
November 5, 1987

O'Connor, Justice

This case presents the question whether an action by an injured skier against a ski area operator is governed by the one-year limitation of actions provision of G.L.c. 143, § 71P, where the plaintiff's theories of recovery are negligence and breach of warranty, as well as breach of contract, in the renting of defective ski equipment.

In her original complaint, filed on December 5, 1984, the plaintiff alleged that on March 20, 1982, she sustained serious injuries while skiing at the defendant's ski resort, and that those injuries were caused by defective ski equipment she had rented from the rental facility on the premises. She further alleged that the defendant had not inspected or adjusted the equipment, and this failure amounted to negligence

and breach of contract. In an amended complaint filed on February 14, 1986, the plaintiff added counts alleging that the defendant had breached warranties of merchantability and fitness for a particular purpose.

The defendant moved for summary judgment on the ground that the plaintiff's action was barred by the statute of limitations. A judge of the Superior Court granted the motion, and the plaintiff appealed. We transferred the case to this court on our own motion, and now affirm.

The statute we must interpret, G.L.c. 143, § 71P, imposes a one-year limitation on actions "against a ski area operator for injury to a skier." There is no contention that the defendant is not a "ski area operator," or that this action is not "for injury to a skier." The text of the statute, then, seems fully to support the decision of the Superior Court judge. The plaintiff argues, however, that the statute should be construed as governing only actions based on a defendant ski area operator's violation of those duties prescribed by G.L.c.143, § 71N. Section 71N requires that ski areas be maintained and operated in a reasonably safe manner, and prescribes methods by which skiers must be warned about the presence of equipment and vehicles on slopes and trails. The plaintiff thus contends that the statute does not bar her lawsuit because her action does not assert a violation of § 71N but rather was brought against the defendant solely in its capacity as a lessor of ski equipment. We do not interpret the statute in this limited way. Rather, we conclude that the one-year limitation in § 71P applies to all personal injury actions brought by skiers against ski area operators arising out of skiing injuries.

If the Legislature had intended that the one-year limitation apply only to actions alleging breach of a ski area operator's duties under § 71N, it easily could have employed language to that effect instead of the sweeping terms contained in the statute. Nothing in § 71P suggests that its reach is so limited.

The plaintiff contends that there is no sound basis for applying the one-year limitation to her action, because if she "had rented skis from an independently operated ski rental shop which leased space in the Defendant's base lodge, such an independent rental shop could not defend against the Plaintiff's action by relying upon Section 71P." Hence, she argues, it makes no sense to afford special protection to lessors of ski equipment who happen also to be ski operators. We assume for purposes of this case that the plaintiff's assertion that § 71P would not apply to an independent ski rental shop is correct. But we cannot say that, in enacting § 71P, the Legislature could not reasonably have decided that ski area operators require more protection than do other sectors of the ski industry. "Personal injury claims by skiers …may be myriad in number, run a whole range of harm, and constitute a constant drain on the ski industry." …The Legislature appears to have concluded that, in view of this perceived threat to the economic stability of owners and operators of ski areas, not shared by those who simply rent ski equipment, a short period for the commencement of skiers' personal injury actions against ski operators, regardless of the fault alleged, is in the public interest.…

Because § 71P applies to the plaintiff's action, the Superior Court judge correctly concluded that the plaintiff's action was time barred.

Judgment affirmed.

Liacos, J. (dissenting, with whom Wilkins and Abrams, JJ., join)

I respectfully dissent. The court's interpretation of G.L.c. 143, § 71P (1986 ed.), is too broad. The general purpose of G.L.c. 143, § § 71H–71S (1986 ed.), is to set the terms of responsibility for ski area operators and skiers in a sport which has inherent risks of injury or even death. This legislative intent to protect ski area operators was designed, as the court indicates, not only to decrease the economic threat to the ski industry, but also to enhance the safety of skiers.

An examination of the whole statutory scheme reveals, however, that the Legislature did not intend to protect the ski area operators from claims for all harm which occurs in connection with skiing accidents, regardless of where the negligence that caused the harm takes place. Indeed, this court decided not long ago that G.L.c. 143, § 71P, on which it relies to rule adversely on this plaintiff's claim, did not apply to wrongful death actions arising from injuries on the ski slope. *Grass v. Catamount Dev. Corp.*, 390 Mass. 551 (1983) (O'Connor, J.). The court now ignores the wisdom of its own words in *Grass*, supra at 553: "Had the Legislature intended that G.L.c. 143, § 71P, should apply to claims for wrongful death as well as to claims for injuries not resulting in death, we believe it would have done so expressly." …Here, however, the court extends the protective provisions of § 71P to ordinary commercial activity simply because it occurred at the base of a ski area and was conducted by the operator of the ski slope. No such intent can be perceived in this statute. To the contrary, the statute clearly manifests an intent to promote safety on ski slopes by regulating, through the creation of a recreational tramway board and otherwise, the operation of tramways, chair lifts, "J bars," "T bars," and the like (§ § 71H–71M). The statute defines the duties both of ski area operators and skiers (§ § 71K–71O).

In § 71O, liability of ski area operators for ski slope accidents is sharply limited: "A skier skiing down hill shall have the duty to avoid any collision with any other skier, person or object on the hill below him, and, except as otherwise provided in this chapter, the responsibility for collisions by any skier with any other skier or person shall be solely that of the skier or person involved and not that of the operator, and the responsibility for the collision with an obstruction, man-made or otherwise, shall be solely that of the skier and not that of the operator, provided that such obstruction is properly marked pursuant to the regulations promulgated by the board" (emphasis supplied). Clearly, then, the statutory scheme is designed not only to enhance the safety of skiers, but also to limit the liability of a ski area operator for his negligent activities which cause injuries (but not deaths, see *Grass*, supra) on the ski slopes. It is in this context that the court ought to consider the additional protection of a ninety-day notice requirement, as well as the short statute of limitations of one year found in § 71P.

General Laws c. 143, § 71P, imposes a ninety-day notice requirement and a one-year statute of limitations on a party who brings suit against a ski area operator. The imposition in § 71P of the ninety-day notice requirement as a condition precedent to recovery confirms, I think, my view that this statute is designed only to protect the ski area operator as to claims arising from conditions on the ski slope. But there is an even stronger argument against the court's position—that is in the very language of the statute. A "[s]ki area operator" is defined in G.L.c. 143, § 71I(6), as "the owner or operator of a ski area." In the same subsection, a "[s]ki area" is defined as: "[A]ll of the slopes and trails under the control of the ski area operator, including cross-country ski areas, slopes and trails, and any recreational tramway in operation on any such slopes or trails administered or operated as a single enterprise but shall not include base lodges,

motor vehicle parking lots and other portions of ski areas used by skiers when not actually engaged in the sport of skiing" (emphasis supplied).

The alleged negligence and breach of warranty that occurred in this case happened in the rental shop in the base lodge area. It was there that the defendant rented allegedly defective equipment to the plaintiff and failed to check and to adjust that equipment. The injury was not due to ungroomed snow or exposed rocks or any condition on the slopes or trails under the control of the ski area operator. Rather, the injury allegedly was the result of a transaction in the rental shop, not of a defect on the slope. The rental shop is an area excluded from the purview of G.L.c. 143, § 71P, and thus the ninety-day notice requirement and the one-year statute of limitations do not apply.

The Legislature intended to separate the many functions of a ski area operator so as to focus on the business of operating ski slopes and trails. The statute does not apply where the alleged negligent behavior occurs when the ski area operator is acting as a restaurateur, barkeeper, parking lot owner, souvenir vendor, or, as is the case here, rental agent. For this reason, I would reverse the judgment of the Superior Court.

Case Questions

1. Marybeth Atkins severely broke her leg while using skis and ski bindings rented from a shop at a ski resort. The shop was owned and operated by the owners of the resort. What argument did Atkins make to the court in an effort to avoid the one-year statute of limitations?

2. Do you agree with the dissenters, who feel that the negligent action that caused the harm occurred in the rental shop (an area not covered by the statute), or with the majority, who feel that the accident occurred on the slopes (an area covered by the statute)?

The state supreme court stated in its opinion that "The Legislature appears to have concluded that ... a short period for the commencement of skiers' personal injury actions against ski operators ... was in the public interest." It denied recovery to a plaintiff who alleged that she was seriously injured as a result of the defendant's negligence in fitting her with defective ski equipment at its on-premises rental facility. Do you see any utilitarian aspects in the making of public policy in this instance?

EQUITABLE DOCTRINE
OF LACHES

You may recall Chapter I's discussion of the emergence in England, and subsequently in this country, of courts of equity, and that although a few states

continue to maintain separate equitable courts, most states have merged these courts into a single judicial system. In these merged systems, judges are often authorized to exercise the powers of a common law judge as well as the powers of a chancellor in equity. Which "hat" the judge wears is determined by the remedy sought by the plaintiff. Readers will learn about both legal and equitable remedies in Chapter VII, which is entirely devoted to that topic. But for now it is sufficient to know that when a plaintiff requests the court to award an equitable remedy, such as an injunction (a court order mandating or prohibiting specified conduct), the court may resort to equitable doctrines in reaching a decision.

One of the traditional equitable doctrines is called **laches**. This doctrine can be used in some circumstances to deny a plaintiff an equitable remedy. Consider the following hypothetical case: Assume that a plaintiff has brought a tort action against a defendant and is seeking money damages. Assume further that in her complaint this plaintiff, in addition to the money damages, has asked for equitable remedies, such as a declaratory judgment and an injunction. Also assume that the statute of limitations gives the plaintiff ten years within which to file her suit and that she waits eight years before serving the defendant with the summons and complaint. Under these circumstances, the defendant might argue that the plaintiff should be denied equitable relief because of laches. The defendant could support this argument with proof that he suffered legal harm because of the plaintiff's unreasonable delay in bringing suit and for this reason should be limited to her common law remedies.

INTERNET TIP

Students wishing to read a 2005 Indiana Supreme Court decision that illustrates the doctrine of laches can read *SMDFUND, Inc. v. Fort Wayne-Allen County Airport Authority* on the textbook's website.

CLAIM PRECLUSION/*RES JUDICATA*

Many jurisdictions now use the term "claim preclusion" when referring to the judicial doctrine traditionally known as *res judicata*. This doctrine, by either name, provides that a final decision by a competent court on a lawsuit's merits concludes the litigation of the parties and constitutes a bar (puts an end) to a new suit. When a plaintiff wins his or her lawsuit, the claims that he or she made (and could have made, but didn't) merge into the judgment and are extinguished. Thus no subsequent suit can be maintained against the same defendant based on the same claim. This is known as the principle of **bar and merger**. Once a claim has been judicially decided, it is finally decided. The loser may not bring a new suit against the winner for the same claim in any court. The loser's remedy is to appeal the decision of the lower court to a higher court.

The doctrine reduces litigation and prevents harassment of or hardship on an individual who otherwise could be sued twice for the same cause of action. In addition, once the parties realize that they have only one chance to win, they will make their best effort.

For claim preclusion/*res judicata* to apply, two conditions must be met. First, there must be an identity of parties. Identity means that parties to a successive lawsuit are the same as, or in **privity** with, the parties to the original suit. Privity exists, for example, when there is a relationship between two people that allows one not directly involved in the case to take the place of the one who is a party. Thus if a person dies during litigation, the executor of the estate may take the deceased person's place in the lawsuit. Privity exists between the person who dies and the executor, so that as far as this litigation is concerned, they are the same person.

Second, there must be an identity of claims. In other words, for claim preclusion/*res judicata* to bar the suit, the claim—or cause of action—in the first case must be essentially the same the second time the litigation is attempted. For instance, if A sues B for breach of contract and loses, *res judicata* prohibits any further action on that same contract by A and B (except for appeal). A could, however, sue B for the breach of a different contract, because that would be a different cause of action.

In 1982, adjacent neighbors Donald Czyzewski and Paul Harvey went to court over a land dispute. Although both parties were mutually mistaken about the true location of the boundary line that separated their two properties, Donald filed suit against Paul because Paul had dug a ditch along what they believed to be the property line. Donald claimed that the ditch had caused erosion on his land and had damaged his fence. After Paul agreed to plant grass seed to prevent erosion and to pay Donald $1,500, this lawsuit was dismissed. Donald subsequently sold his property to Lawrence Kruckenberg. Lawrence was unaware of the 1982 lawsuit. In 2000 Lawrence had his land surveyed and discovered that the presumed boundary line was incorrect. The survey indicated that Lawrence actually owned a sixteen-foot strip that both he and Paul believed to be part of Paul's parcel. Lawrence filed suit against Paul after Paul cut down some trees in the disputed strip, contrary to Lawrence's wishes. Lawrence thereafter sued for trespass and a judicial determination of his rights to the sixteen-foot strip. The trial and intermediate appellate courts ruled in favor of Paul, and Lawrence appealed to the Wisconsin Supreme Court.

When reading this opinion, you will find that the state supreme court refers to Czyzewski as "plaintiff's predecessor in title." This refers to the fact that Lawrence purchased the parcel of land from Donald and was deeded all of Donald's rights to that parcel. Because their interests in the land were identical, there existed between the two what is called a "privity of estate."

The problem confronting the Wisconsin Supreme Court was that the facts appeared to support the application of the claim preclusion doctrine. Donald, back in 1982, could have and probably should have included in his complaint a request for a judicial determination of the boundary line between the two parcels. He didn't, the trial court dismissed the case, and the boundary line was left where it was, incorrect though it might be, favoring Paul. Donald's omission, because of privity, was thus transferred with the deed to Lawrence. Because a mechanical application of the claim preclusion doctrine would have lead to an unfair result, the Wisconsin Supreme Court refused to apply this doctrine in that manner. The chief justice of that court explains why not in the following opinion.

Lawrence A. Kruckenberg v. Paul S. Harvey
685 N.W.2d 844
Supreme Court of Wisconsin
April 14, 2005

Shirley S. Abrahamson, Chief Justice.
This is a review of a published decision of the court of appeals affirming a judgment and order of the Circuit Court for Green Lake County....

The issue presented is whether the doctrine of claim preclusion bars the plaintiff's action. The prior action brought by the plaintiff's predecessor in title against the defendant was for failing to provide lateral support; the defendant had dug a ditch. The prior action ended in a judgment of dismissal on the merits. The plaintiff's present action against the defendant is for trespass and conversion (the cutting and taking of trees) and for a declaratory judgment regarding the location of the boundary line between the plaintiff's and defendant's land....

For purposes of deciding how to apply the doctrine of claim preclusion to the present case, we set forth the following facts derived from the record on the motion for summary judgment.

The question of claim preclusion in the present case arises from a lawsuit brought by Donald A.

Czyzewski, the plaintiff's predecessor in title, against the defendant in 1982. According to the 1982 complaint, the defendant dug a ditch along the northern boundary of his property, altering the topography and natural watershed, causing Czyzewski's soils and trees to collapse, causing the line fence to collapse ... and causing the water level of Czyzewski's pond to subside.

Czyzewski's 1982 complaint alleged that the defendant breached a duty of lateral support and a duty to maintain a line fence and that his conduct was contrary to Wisconsin Statutes ... §§ 844.01-.21, relating to physical injury to or interference with real property; § 101.111 relating to protection of adjoining property and buildings during excavation; and chapter 90 relating to fences. For the alleged violations, Czyzewski requested: (1) restoration of the line fence, (2) restoration of the eroded portion of his property, (3) restoration of the water level, and (4) $10,000.

The defendant's answer to the 1982 complaint admitted that the defendant and Czyzewski owned adjoining parcels and that the defendant had dug the ditch along the northern boundary of his property. The defendant denied all other allegations of the complaint.

On April 6, 1983, on stipulation of the parties, the circuit court entered an order dismissing the Czyzewski suit on its merits. The defendant agreed to pay Czyzewski $1,500 and plant rye grass along the drainage ditch to prevent erosion.

Czyzewski's sale of his parcel to the plaintiff was completed after the 1982 lawsuit was dismissed, and the plaintiff claims he did not know about the lawsuit.

The plaintiff had his land surveyed in 2000 and learned that the "line fence" was not on the boundary line; the fence was 16 feet north of his property's southern boundary. In other words, the survey showed that the plaintiff's property included a strip of about 16 feet wide that was previously thought to belong to the defendant and on which the defendant had dug a ditch.

Peace between the parties was disturbed in "late winter and early spring of 2001" when the defendant decided to harvest some trees on the south side of the fence; according to the 2000 survey, the trees were on the plaintiff's property. The plaintiff asked the defendant not to cut the trees.

After the defendant removed the trees, the plaintiff, armed with his new survey, sued the defendant for trespass and conversion (cutting and taking the trees), failure to provide lateral support (failing to plant rye grass continually to prevent erosion), and a declaratory judgment regarding the location of the boundary line between their properties. The defendant denied many of the allegations of the complaint....

The circuit court granted summary judgment in the defendant's favor and dismissed the action. The circuit court ruled that the plaintiff could not challenge the location of the line fence as not being the boundary line because of the doctrine of claim preclusion. The circuit court found that the line fence was an issue in the 1982 lawsuit and in effect placed the boundary line at the line fence. The circuit court also ruled that the issue of lateral support was litigated in 1982 and that the doctrine of issue preclusion therefore barred this count....

A divided court of appeals affirmed the circuit court's judgment of dismissal, also on the ground that the lawsuit was barred by the doctrine of claim preclusion....

This court reviews a grant of summary judgment using the same methodology as the circuit court...A motion for summary judgment will be granted "if the pleadings, depositions, answers to interrogatories, and admissions on file, together with the affidavits, if any,

show that there is no genuine issue as to any material fact and that the moving party is entitled to a judgment as a matter of law." ... In the present case no genuine issue of material fact exists.

The only question presented is one of law, namely whether the defendant is entitled to judgment on the ground of claim preclusion. This court determines this question of law independently of the circuit court and court of appeals, benefitting from their analyses...To decide this case we must determine the application of the doctrine of claim preclusion...

The doctrine of claim preclusion provides that a final judgment on the merits in one action bars parties from relitigating any claim that arises out of the same relevant facts, transactions, or occurrences...When the doctrine of claim preclusion is applied, a final judgment on the merits will ordinarily bar all matters "'which were litigated or which might have been litigated in the former proceedings.'"...

Claim preclusion thus provides an effective and useful means to establish and fix the rights of individuals, to relieve parties of the cost and vexation of multiple lawsuits, to conserve judicial resources, to prevent inconsistent decisions, and to encourage reliance on adjudication.... The doctrine of claim preclusion recognizes that "endless litigation leads to chaos; that certainty in legal relations must be maintained; that after a party has had his day in court, justice, expediency, and the preservation of the public tranquillity requires that the matter be at an end."...

In Wisconsin, the doctrine of claim preclusion has three elements:

"(1) identity between the parties or their privies in the prior and present suits;

(2) prior litigation resulted in a final judgment on the merits by a court with jurisdiction; and

(3) identity of the causes of action in the two suits..."

In effect, the doctrine of claim preclusion determines whether matters undecided in a prior lawsuit fall within the bounds of that prior judgment....

The parties do not dispute, and we agree, that the first two elements of claim preclusion have been satisfied in the case at bar. The identities of the parties or their privies are the same in the present and the prior suits. The plaintiff was the successor in interest to the property owned by Czyzewski, and the two are in privity for the purposes of claim preclusion.... The 1982 litigation resulted in a final judgment on the merits by a court with jurisdiction, satisfying the second element of claim preclusion....

The parties' disagreement focuses on the third element of the doctrine of claim preclusion, namely, the requirement that there be an identity of the causes of action or claims in the two suits.

Wisconsin has adopted the "transactional approach" set forth in the Restatement (Second) of Judgments to determine whether there is an identity of the claims between two suits.... Under the doctrine of claim preclusion, a valid and final judgment in an action extinguishes all rights to remedies against a defendant with respect to all or any part of the transaction, or series of connected transactions, out of which the action arose.... The transactional approach is not capable of a "mathematically precise definition," ...and determining what factual grouping constitutes a "transaction" is not always easy. The Restatement (Second) of Judgments § 24 (2) (1982) explains that the transactional approach makes the determination pragmatically, considering such factors as whether the facts are related in time, space, origin, or motivation. Section 24 (2) provides as follows:

> (2) What factual grouping constitutes a "transaction", and what groupings constitute a "series", are to be determined pragmatically, giving weight to such considerations as whether the facts are related in time, space, origin, or motivation, whether they form a convenient trial unit, and whether their treatment as a unit conforms to the parties' expectations or business understanding or usage.

The goal in the transactional approach is to see a claim in factual terms and to make a claim coterminous with the transaction, regardless of the claimant's substantive theories or forms of relief, regardless of the primary rights invaded, and regardless of the evidence needed to support the theories or rights.... Under the transactional approach, the legal theories, remedies sought, and evidence used may be different between the first and second actions.... The concept of a transaction connotes a common nucleus of operative facts....

The transactional approach to claim preclusion reflects "the expectation that parties who are given the capacity to present their 'entire controversies' shall in fact do so." ...One text states that the pragmatic approach that seems most consistent with modern procedural philosophy "looks to see if the claim asserted in the second action should have been presented for decision in the earlier action, taking into account practical considerations relating mainly to trial convenience and fairness."...

At first blush the events giving rise to the two actions (1982 and 2001) do not appear part of the same transaction, as they are separated by time, space, origin, and motivation. The 1982 suit was prompted when the defendant dug a ditch and allegedly caused Czyzewski to claim erosion to his property and damage to the line fence. The 2001 suit was prompted when the defendant cut trees; this time the plaintiff claimed trespass on his property and sought a declaratory judgment concerning the location of the boundary line between the properties.

Because the trees were not cut until 2001, obviously neither Czyzewski nor the plaintiff could have brought a claim for tree cutting and taking (trespass and conversion) in 1982. The plaintiff reasons that the 2001 claim is therefore not part of the same transaction as the 1982 claim, and he should not be barred by the doctrine of claim preclusion.

The plaintiff makes a good point, but he overlooks that the aggregate operative facts in both the 1982 and 2001 claims are the same, namely the defendant's conduct in relation to the location of the boundary line. The facts necessary to establish the location of the boundary line between the plaintiff's and defendant's properties were in existence in 1982.

Czyzewski's 1982 claims and judgment depended on who owned the property south of the line fence upon which the ditch had been dug. Czyzewski's 1982 claim was that the defendant dug a ditch on the defendant's property, injuring Czyzewski's property by removing lateral support.... In 1982, both parties were mistaken about the location of the boundary line and the ownership of the property upon which the defendant had acted when he dug the ditch.

Similarly, the plaintiff's 2001 claims depend on who owned the property south of the line fence upon which the defendant cut trees. The plaintiff's 2001 claim is that the defendant cut trees on the plaintiff's property, an action that constitutes trespass and conversion.

Even though the 1982 litigation did not determine the boundary line, the two lawsuits have such a measure of identity of claims that a judgment in the second in favor of the plaintiff would appear to impair the rights or interests established in the first judgment.

The plaintiff's 2001 action might well be precluded under the well-settled claim preclusion analysis. We need not decide that difficult question, however, because even if claim preclusion were to apply here, we conclude that the plaintiff's 2001 lawsuit should proceed under a narrow exception to the doctrine of claim preclusion.

The parties' current dispute over the common boundary line illustrates that claim preclusion in the present case presents the "classic struggle between the need for clear, simple, and rigid law and the desire for its sensitive application." ...Claim preclusion is a harsh doctrine; it necessarily results in preclusion of some claims that should go forward and it may fail to preclude some claims that should not continue....

Judicial formulation of the doctrine of claim preclusion should seek to minimize the over-inclusion of the doctrine through exceptions that are narrow in scope...This court has previously stated that "[e]xceptions to the doctrine of claim preclusion, confined within proper limits, are 'central to the fair administration of the doctrine.'"

Exceptions to the doctrine of claim preclusion are rare, but in certain types of cases "the policy reasons for allowing an exception override the policy reasons for applying the general rule." ...

Recognizing these truths, the Restatement (Second) of Judgments describes exceptions to the doctrine of claim preclusion. The present case falls within the "special circumstances" exception set forth in § 26(1)(f),...which reads as follows:

> When any of the following circumstances exists, the general rule of § 24 does not apply to extinguish the claim, and part or all of the claim subsists as a possible basis for a second action by the plaintiff against the defendant:...
> (f) It is clearly and convincingly shown that the policies favoring preclusion of a second action are overcome for an extraordinary reason, such as the apparent invalidity of a continuing restraint or condition having a vital relation to personal liberty or the failure of the prior litigation to yield a coherent disposition of the controversy.

We apply Restatement (Second) of Judgments § 26(1)(f) in the present case. We conclude that in the present case the policies favoring preclusion are overcome for an "extraordinary reason," namely, "the failure of the prior litigation to yield a coherent disposition of the controversy."...

The exception we adopt is as follows: When an action between parties or their privies does not explicitly determine the location of a boundary line, the doctrine of claim preclusion will not bar a future declaratory judgment action to determine the proper location of the boundary line.

The narrowly drawn exception we adopt today serves important policy considerations.

First, strict application of the doctrine of claim preclusion in the present case may result in over-litigation in cases involving real property disputes.... Faced with the prospect that they will forever be foreclosed from having boundary lines judicially determined in the future if they fail to litigate the issue in even the most simple lawsuit involving real property, parties will litigate the issue, even when it is apparently not in dispute.

There is no shortage of everyday situations that may implicate the location of a boundary line. The plaintiff's counsel mentioned just a few at oral argument: a pet strays onto a neighbor's property; a child throws his or her ball into the neighbor's flowerbed; trees overhang the neighbor's shed; guests at a party wander onto the neighbor's property. If any of these situations results in a final judgment on the merits without a determination of the boundary line, the parties (and their privies) would, under the defendant's theory of the present case, forever be precluded from determining the location of the boundary line....

Second, strict application of the doctrine of claim preclusion in the present case may discourage individuals from promptly settling lawsuits relating to real property. Parties may fear that without adequate discovery, any stipulated dismissal on the merits could terminate rights or claims they had yet to even discover were potentially implicated.

Lastly, strict application of the doctrine of claim preclusion in the present case places process over truth. The boundary line is important to the parties in the present litigation and future owners of the properties and should be decided on the merits once and for all. Allowing litigation about the boundary line will produce a final judgment that definitively settles the issue and can be recorded to put the public on notice. The legal system should, in the present case, be more concerned with deciding the location of the boundary line than with strictly applying the doctrine of claim preclusion.

The parties in the 1982 action believed the boundary line was at the line fence. A survey in 2000 showed the line fence was not on the boundary line. Neither the parties to the present litigation, nor their predecessors in title, have ever litigated the location of the boundary line. The boundary line can be determined in the present case, without repeating prior litigation.

Claim preclusion is grounded on a desire to maintain reliable and predictable legal relationships. Public policy seeks to ensure that real estate titles are secure and marketable, and therefore the doctrine of claim preclusion ordinarily will apply in property cases. But the strict application of the doctrine of claim preclusion in the present case creates uncertainty. The policies favoring preclusion of the 2001 action are overcome, because the 1982 action, in the words of Restatement (Second) of Judgments, "failed to yield a coherent disposition of the controversy" ... and "has left the parties not in a state of repose but in an unstable and intolerable condition."...

We hold that barring the declaratory judgment action (and the trespass and conversion action) to determine the location of the boundary line, when that line has not been previously litigated, undermines the policies that are at the foundation of the doctrine of claim preclusion. The unique nature of a claim to identify the location of a boundary line warrants this narrow exception.

We therefore conclude that important policy concerns exist that favor creation of a narrowly drawn exception in the present case, namely that when a prior action between the parties or their privies does not explicitly determine the location of a boundary line between the properties, the doctrine of claim preclusion will not bar a later declaratory judgment action to determine the location of the boundary line....

Accordingly, we reverse the decision of the court of appeals and remand the cause to the circuit court for proceedings not inconsistent with this decision.

By the Court. The decision of the court of appeals is reversed and the cause remanded.

Case Questions

1. What must a defendant prove in order to establish a claim preclusion/*res judicata* defense?
2. How did the Wisconsin Supreme Court avoid applying the claim preclusion/*res judicata* doctrine in a mechanical way to the facts of this case?
3. What rationale was given by the Wisconsin Supreme Court for its decision in this case?

IMMUNITY FROM LEGAL ACTION

The law provides immunity from tort liability when to do so is thought to be in the best interest of the public. Immunities are an exception to the general rule that a remedy must be provided for every wrong, and they are not favored by courts. They make the right of the individual to redress a private wrong subservient to what the law recognizes as a greater public good. Immunity does not mean that the conduct is not tortuous in character, but only that for policy reasons the law denies liability resulting from the tort. Today, many courts are willing to abolish or limit an immunity when it becomes apparent that the public is not actually deriving any benefit from its existence.

Sovereign Immunity

It is a basic principle of common law that no sovereign may be sued without its express consent. When a person sues the government, the person is actually suing the taxpayers and him- or herself, because any judgment is paid for out of public revenues. The payment of judgments would require the expenditure of funds raised to provide services to the public.

The doctrine of governmental immunity from liability originated in the English notion that "the monarch can do no wrong." (Ironically, although most U.S. jurisdictions have retained the doctrine, England has repudiated it.) Congress consented to be sued in contract cases in the 1887 Tucker Act. In 1946 the federal government passed the Federal Tort Claims Act, in which the U.S. government waived its immunity from tort liability. It permitted suits against the federal government in federal courts for negligent or wrongful acts committed by its employees within the scope of their employment. Liability is based on the applicable local tort law. Thus the government may be sued in its capacity as a landlord and as a possessor of land, as well as for negligent acts and omissions (concepts explained in Chapter XI). Immunity was not waived for all acts of federal employees, however. Acts within the discretionary function of a federal employee or acts of military and naval forces in time of war are examples of situations in which immunity has not been waived. In addition, members of the armed forces who have suffered a service-related injury due to governmental negligence are denied the right to sue. Permitting such suits has been thought to undermine military discipline. State governments also enjoy **sovereign immunity**.

Courts have made a distinction between governmental and proprietary functions. When a public entity is involved in a governmental function, it is generally immune from tort liability. When the government engages in activity that is usually carried out by private individuals or that is commercial in character, it is involved in a proprietary function, and the cloak of immunity is lost. For example, a state is not immune when it provides a service that a corporation may perform, such as providing electricity.

Courts currently favor limiting or abolishing sovereign immunity. Their rationale is the availability of liability insurance and the perceived inequity of denying relief to a deserving claimant. Many jurisdictions have replaced blanket sovereign immunity with tort claims acts that limit governmental liability. For example, they can reduce exposure to suit by restricting recoveries to the limits of insurance policies or by establishing ceilings on maximum recoveries (often ranging from $25,000 to $100,000). Many states continue to immunize discretionary functions and acts.

Immunity of Governmental Officials

As described in the previous section, executive, legislative, and judicial officers are afforded immunity when the act is within the scope of their authority and in the discharge of their official duties.

Immunity increases the likelihood that government officials will act impartially and fearlessly in carrying out their public duties. Thus, it is in the public interest to shield responsible government officers from harassment or ill-founded damage suits based on acts they committed in the exercise of their official responsibilities. Prosecutors, for example, enjoy immunity when they decide for the public who should be criminally prosecuted. Public defenders, however, are not immunized, because their clients are private citizens and not the general public.

This immunity applies only when public officers are performing discretionary acts in conjunction with official functions. Officials are not immune from liability for tortuous conduct when they transcend their lawful authority and invade the constitutional rights of others. They are legally responsible for their personal torts.

Some argue that granting immunity to officials does not protect individual citizens from harm resulting from oppressive or malicious conduct on the part of public officers. A governmental official may in some jurisdictions lose this protection by acting maliciously or for an improper purpose, rather than honestly or in good faith.

High-level executive, legislative, and judicial officials with discretionary functions enjoy more immunity than do lower-level officials. Judges, for example, are afforded absolute immunity when they exercise judicial powers, regardless of their motives or good faith. But judges are not entitled to absolute immunity from civil suit for their nonjudicial acts.

Police officers, however, are only entitled to qualified immunity from suit because of the discretionary nature of police work and the difficulty of expecting officers to make instant determinations as to how the constitution should be interpreted. As we will see in the next case, the qualified immunity defense is unavailable if the illegality of the officer's constitutionally impermissible conduct has been previously well established and would be clearly understood as such by a properly trained officer.

Solomon v. Auburn Hills Police Department
389 F.3d 167
U. S. Court of Appeals for the Sixth Circuit
August 13, 2004

Damon J. Keith, Circuit Judge.
Defendant Officer David Miller appeals the district court's order denying his motion for summary judgment based on qualified immunity....

1. Background
a. Procedural
This lawsuit arises out of the arrest of Plaintiff Francine Solomon ("Solomon"). After she was arrested, Solomon filed a complaint against the Auburn Hills Police Department ("AHPD") and Officer David Miller ("Officer Miller") alleging violations of 42 U.S.C. § 1983, as well as state law claims for assault and battery and gross negligence. Solomon then filed a motion to amend her complaint, and both defendants moved for summary judgment....

[T]he district court denied Officer Miller's motion for summary judgment after finding that he was not entitled to qualified immunity as to the Fourth Amendment claims because a jury question existed as to whether his conduct was objectively reasonable under the circumstances. The district court also left standing the state claims against Officer Miller for assault and battery and gross negligence.

Officer Miller timely filed an appeal with this court as to the issue of qualified immunity. Our opinion today addresses whether the district court erred when it determined that Officer Miller was not entitled to qualified immunity and consequently denied his motion for summary judgment....

1. Factual
On Saturday, March 24, 2001, Solomon took her six children and several of their friends to see a movie at the Star Theatre at Great Lakes Crossing ("Theatre") in Auburn Hills, Michigan. Because the children ranged in age from three to eighteen, Solomon planned to accompany the younger children to a G-rated movie and Solomon's eighteen-year-old son and his girlfriend planned to accompany the older children to an R-rated movie. Solomon explained this to the ticket seller when she purchased the tickets for the two movies. When her adult son attempted to enter the R-rated movie theater with the other children, the usher informed him that the children would not be allowed into the theater without a parent. Solomon then approached the usher and explained that she was the mother of several of the children and that they had

permission to be in the R-rated movie, but she would be watching the G-rated movie with her younger children. The usher referred Solomon to customer relations.

Solomon then explained her situation to the Theatre manager, who responded that Theatre policy required a parent or guardian to accompany minor children into an R-rated movie. Solomon left customer relations and walked with her younger children toward the movie theater showing the G-rated movie. Before she reached the theater entrance, another Theatre employee informed Solomon that the older children could not see the R-rated movie without her accompanying them. Even though Solomon did not want to take her young children to see an R-rated movie, she went into the R-rated movie theater as instructed by Theatre management.

After Solomon was seated in the R-rated movie theater, the Theatre security guards entered and informed Solomon that she had to leave because she had not purchased tickets for that particular movie. Solomon refused to leave because she was following the manager's instructions. Shortly thereafter, AHPD officers Miller and Raskin—both of whom were between 230 and 250 pounds and at least five-feet-eight-inches tall—arrived. The officers entered the theater, found Solomon sitting with her three young children, and instructed Solomon to leave. Solomon informed the police officers that she had purchased tickets and attempted to explain the situation, but the officers insisted that she leave. After Solomon refused, Officer Miller told her that she was under arrest for trespassing. Officer Miller grabbed her arm to make her leave, and Solomon, pushing her foot against the seat in front of her, backed away from the officer. Officer Miller then informed her that she was under arrest for assaulting a police officer.... At that point, Officer Raskin asked Solomon to speak with the police officers in the lobby and Solomon agreed. Solomon's children and their friends followed Solomon out of the R-rated movie theater.

When Solomon entered the hallway, she handed her toddler to her son's girlfriend, and Solomon explained to her children that she was going to talk with the officers. In the lobby, Officer Raskin motioned for Solomon to walk toward him. As Solomon was walking toward Officer Raskin, Officer Miller came up behind her, grabbed her arm, and attempted to leg sweep her. Solomon tripped but did not fall; when she regained her balance, she folded her arms across her chest. In response to Officer Miller's action, Solomon yelled, "Why are you doing this [?] I did not do anything."

At this point, Officer Miller grabbed her left arm and Officer Raskin grabbed her right arm. The officers threw Solomon up against a wall and knocked her face into a display case. Solomon did not attempt to pull away from them and the Officers gave no directives to Solomon. Officer Raskin then handcuffed Solomon's right arm behind her back. Officer Miller pushed up against Solomon with his entire body weight, shoving his arm against her back and his leg in between hers. Solomon was pinned against the wall and could not move; her right arm was already handcuffed and her left arm was straight along her side. Without uttering any instruction to Solomon, Officer Miller forcibly bent her left arm behind her and "heard a popping sound and her left arm [went] limp."...

Solomon was subsequently taken to Pontiac Osteopathic Hospital, where she was diagnosed with a comminuted fracture of her left elbow; she also had several bruises from being thrown against the wall. Solomon was hospitalized for six days for surgical treatment of the fracture and underwent a second operation at a later date. She also underwent extensive physical therapy and endures continual complications.

Solomon was later charged with resisting arrest, assault on a police officer, and trespass. As part of a plea bargain, Solomon pleaded guilty to trespass and attempted resisting arrest.

II. Discussion
A. Standard of Review...
B. Analysis
Through the use of qualified immunity, the law shields "government officials performing discretionary functions ... from civil damages liability as long as their actions could reasonably have been thought consistent with the rights they are alleged to have violated." ... The United States Supreme Court has constructed a two-part test to determine whether an officer-defendant should be granted qualified immunity... First, a court must consider whether the facts, viewed in the light most favorable to the plaintiff, "show the officer's conduct violated a constitutional right."...If the answer is yes, the court must then decide "whether the right was clearly established." ... "The relevant, dispositive inquiry in determining whether a right is clearly established is whether it would be clear to a reasonable officer that his conduct was unlawful in the situation that he confronted."...

In the case before us, the district court reached the correct decision in denying Officer Miller summary judgment, but its rationale intertwined the standard for determining qualified immunity and the standard for granting summary judgment. The district court failed to completely evaluate ... whether or not Officer Miller acted objectively reasonably under the circumstances, the district court merely found that a jury question exists on that issue....Because we are to review the district court's decision *de novo*, the district court's confusion of the standard does not require reversal. Set forth below is the proper analysis for determining whether qualified immunity should result in summary judgment for a defendant—in this case, Officer Miller.

1. Violation of Constitutional Right
As instructed by the [U.S. Supreme] Court ...this court must "concentrate at the outset on the definition of the constitutional right and [then] determine whether, on the facts alleged, a constitutional violation could be found."...Here, Solomon brought forth a claim that Officer Miller used excessive force when he arrested her, thereby giving rise to a violation of her constitutional protection against unreasonable seizures under the Fourth Amendment. This court has recognized a person's constitutional "right to be free from excessive force during an arrest."...

After the constitutional right has been defined, we still must inquire whether a violation of Solomon's right to be free from excessive force could be found. Solomon walked out of the movie theater into the hallway as instructed by the officers. Once in the hallway, Officer Miller attempted to knock her onto the ground by kicking her legs even though she was not a flight risk and, in fact, was following Officer Raskin's order. Then, Officer Miller, along with Officer Raskin, shoved her into a display case. Even though Officer Raskin had Solomon's right arm handcuffed and even though Solomon was not actively resisting arrest, Officer Miller pushed his entire weight against Solomon's body, shoving his hand into her back and his leg into her legs. Officer Miller then grabbed Solomon's arm and twisted it behind her with such force that he fractured it in several places. Under the circumstances "taken in the light most favorable to the party asserting the injury." ...Officer Miller's overly aggressive actions could have violated Solomon's Fourth Amendment right to be free from excessive force during an arrest.

2. Constitutional Right Clearly Established
Once a potential violation of a plaintiff's constitutional right has been established, we next decide whether

that right was clearly established. In so deciding, we must ask "whether it would be clear to a reasonable officer that his conduct was unlawful in the situation confronted." ... "'The reasonableness' inquiry in an excessive force case is an objective one: the question is whether the officers' actions are objectively reasonable in light of the facts and circumstances confronting them, without regard to their underlying intent or motivation." ... Discerning reasonableness "requires a careful balancing of ...the individual's Fourth Amendment interests' against the countervailing governmental interests at stake." ... We must remember to consider the reasonableness of the officer at the scene, ... and keep in mind that officers must often make split-second judgments because they are involved in "circumstances that are tense, uncertain, and rapidly evolving." ... "It is sometimes difficult for an officer to determine how the relevant legal doctrine, here excessive force, will apply to the factual situation the officer confronts." ... If an officer, therefore, makes a mistake as to how much force is required, he will still be entitled to qualified immunity so long as that mistake was reasonable.... Thus, to find Officer Miller shielded from his actions and therefore entitled to qualified immunity, we must find that Officer Miller's use of force under the circumstances was objectively reasonable.

In determining objective reasonableness of an officer accused of using excessive force, we will consider several factors. We "should pay particular attention to the severity of the crime at issue, whether the suspect poses an immediate threat to the safety of the officers or others, and whether he is actively resisting arrest or attempting to evade arrest by flight." ... In addition, we have also found that "the definition of reasonable force is partially dependent on the demeanor of the suspect." ... In applying these considerations to the facts at hand, it would be clear to a reasonable officer that the amount of force used against Solomon by Officer Miller was unlawful.

First, Solomon was being arrested for trespassing. Therefore, "the reasonableness of the Officer's actions must be weighed against this backdrop." ... The crime at issue here was a minor offense and certainly not a severe crime that would justify the amount of force used by Officer Miller.

Moreover, Solomon posed no immediate threat to the safety of the officers or others. She was surrounded by her children, including toddlers. Solomon bore no weapon, and she made no verbal threats against the officers. We must also consider the size and stature of the parties involved. Here, each of the officers stood at least five-feet-eight-inches tall and weighed between 230 and 250 pounds. By stark contrast, Solomon stood five-feet-five-inches tall and weighed approximately 120 pounds. Under these facts, Solomon posed no immediate threat to the officers' safety.

Finally, it is undisputed that Solomon did not attempt to flee. Solomon cooperated with the officers by leaving the movie theater and accompanying them out into the lobby. She also complied with the request of Officer Raskin, who motioned for her to walk toward him. In taking the facts as Solomon alleges, she did not resist arrest. After she exited the movie theater, she was never told that she was under arrest. The mere fact that she crossed her arms after Officer Miller tried to leg sweep her does not create a presumption of actively resisting arrest that would justify Officer Miller's actions.

Qualified immunity will often operate "to protect officers from the sometimes hazy border between excessive and acceptable force." ... An officer should be entitled to qualified immunity if he made an objectively reasonable mistake as to the amount of force that was necessary under the circumstances with which he was faced.... The facts here, however, do not present one of those hazy cases. The dissent ignores that the officers here were not faced with a tense and uncertain situation where they feared for their safety and the safety of bystanders. In fact, Solomon cooperated with the officers by leaving the movie theater. It was at that point that Officer Miller began to act with unnecessary, unjustifiable, and unreasonable force. He first attempted to leg sweep her when she was walking, as instructed, toward Officer Raskin. Officer Miller then shoved her into the display case, putting his entire weight—nearly twice the amount of her own weight—against her. Finally, without directing Solomon to act, he yanked her arm behind her with such force that it fractured. Officer Miller's actions, in total, were excessive and resulted in Solomon suffering from bruising and a fractured arm. In viewing the facts in favor of Solomon, we conclude that no reasonable officer would find that the circumstances surrounding the arrest of Solomon required the extreme use of force that was used here. Officer Miller is no exception. Because Officer Miller's conduct was unlawful under the circumstances, he is not able to escape liability through qualified immunity.

III. Conclusion

For the foregoing reasons, Officer Miller is not shielded from his actions by qualified immunity and the district court's denial of his motion for summary judgment is AFFIRMED.

Rogers, Circuit Judge, dissenting

At worst, Officer Miller made an objectively reasonable mistake as to the amount of force necessary to handcuff Ms. Solomon. Because Officer Miller is therefore entitled to qualified immunity, I respectfully dissent....

Case Questions

1. Why do police officers receive any form of immunity from civil suit?
2. Why did the U.S. Court of Appeals conclude that Officer Miller should not receive qualified immunity?

INTERNET TIP

The U.S. Supreme Court ruled in *Forrester v. White*, 484 U.S. 219 (1988) that an Illinois Circuit Court judge was not entitled to absolute immunity from a lawsuit filed against him alleging employment discrimination, brought by a discharged court employee. Students can search for this case on the Internet by typing in the case citation.

Immunity among Family Members

American courts have traditionally recognized two types of immunities among family members: interspousal and parental immunities.

Under the common law doctrine of **interspousal immunity**, husbands and wives were immune from liability for negligence and intentional torts perpetrated against their spouses. In part this policy was a byproduct of the old fashioned common law notion that husbands and wives were legally one and the same. But adherents also argued that interspousal immunity was necessary because tort actions between spouses would be harmful to marriages and would disrupt the peace and harmony of the home. They claimed that allowing husbands and wives to sue one another would lead to collusion and fraud. During the twentieth century, reformers successfully argued that married persons and unmarried persons should have equivalent legal rights and remedies. Today, only Georgia and Louisiana continue to adhere in whole or in part to the common law approach. In Georgia, for example, the immunity is limited to personal injury claims, and the immunity will not be recognized if the marital relationship has deteriorated to the point that the spouses are "married" in name only or where it is likely that the spouses are perpetrating a fraud or engaging in collusion.

Author's Commentary

In the late 1920s the author's great-grandfather, August Schubert, while negligently driving one of his company's cars on company business, struck a vehicle in which his wife Jessie, the author's great-grandmother, was a passenger. Jessie was injured as a result of this collision. Prior to 1937, New York recognized interspousal immunity in tort cases. Thus Jessie was not permitted to sue her husband in tort for the damages she sustained resulting from his bad driving. But Jessie (and her lawyers), decided to sue August's company and compel it to pay for her damages. Jessie claimed that the company was financially responsible for the tortious conduct of its employee—her husband, August. Although the company had not directly caused the harm to Jessie, her lawyers argued that the business was still financially responsible for her injury because of a legal doctrine known as *respondeat superior*. Before readers learn about the case it is necessary to explain briefly in general terms the doctrine Jessie relied upon in her suit.

Respondeat Superior

Respondeat superior is an ancient doctrine. The famous American U.S. Supreme Court Justice Oliver Wendell Holmes traced its origin back to the reign of Edward I of England (1272–1307).[1] This doctrine evolved over the centuries. It essentially permits an injured plaintiff, under certain conditions, to hold a company financially responsible for an employee's negligence and intentional torts. Basically, the plaintiff has to prove that the person whose conduct caused the plaintiff's injury was an employee of the company to be sued and not an independent contractor. Secondly, the plaintiff has to prove that the tortious conduct occurred while the employee was acting within the scope of his or her employment. For example if an employee drives a company car for a personal, nonbusiness reason, say to the grocery store, and commits a tort in the parking lot, the employee's personal errand would have amounted to unauthorized travel. An employer is not vicariously liable for an employee's torts that involve unauthorized travel or other nonbusiness–related conduct.

There are three primary arguments by those who favor this doctrine. The first is that the companies are to some extent responsible. They recruit, select, train, and supervise each employee and therefore have the ability to affect how carefully and safely an employee performs his/her job.

The second argument is that the doctrine makes sense as good public policy. Somebody has to pay for the injured person's damages. Of the three alternatives—the injured victim, the employee, or the employer—making employers pay, it is argued, is the best option. Employers are more likely than their employees to have the ability to pay. Companies can purchase liability insurance and pass this expense on to their customers as one of the costs of operating a business.

Thirdly, placing the burden on employers also creates an incentive for them to promote safe conduct by their employees.

Respondeat superior applies at both the state and federal levels of government. As previously mentioned in the discussion of sovereign immunity, the Federal Tort Claims Act provides that the federal government can be sued for tortious conduct committed by federal employees who were acting within the scope of their employment.

Back to the Lawsuit—*Jessie Schubert v. August Schubert Wagon Company,* 164 N.E. 42 (1928)

The company unsuccessfully argued to the trial court that because spousal immunity barred Jessie from suing her husband directly in tort, it made no sense to allow her to do the same thing by suing his company. The company then appealed to New York's highest court, the Court of Appeals. The Court of Appeals agreed with the trial court that Jessie's respondeat superior claim had nothing to do with the spousal immunity relationship. The trial court had properly applied the law to the facts and ruled in her favor. The Court of Appeals opinion was written by Chief Judge Benjamin Cardozo, who ten years later, in 1938, was sworn in by President Hoover as an associate justice of the U.S. Supreme Court. Cardozo's opinion in the *Schubert* case was widely quoted in similar cases throughout the country and played a role in convincing other states to adopt similar policies. It also helped to undermine the continued vitality of spousal immunity in the state of New York. Jessie and August Schubert lived out their lives as husband and wife.

INTERNET TIP

Interested readers can read Judge Cardozo's opinion in *Jessie Schubert v. August Schubert Wagon Company,* 164 N.E. 42 (1928) along with other materials associated with Chapter VI on the textbook's website.

Parental immunity was created to prohibit unemancipated minor children from suing their parents for negligence or intentional torts. This immunity was first recognized in 1891 by the Mississippi Supreme Court in the case of *Hewllette v. George.*[2] The New Hampshire Supreme Court explained in a 1930 case that the "disability of a child to sue the parent for any injury negligently inflicted by the latter upon the former while a minor is not absolute, but is imposed for the protection of family control and harmony, and exists only where the suit, or the prospect of a suit might disturb the family relations."[3].

Courts in many states were reluctant to intrude into the parental right and obligation to determine how their children are raised. They also thought it in society's interest to prohibit unemancipated minor children from maintaining actions for negligence or intentional torts against their parents. At common law, children remained minors until they reached the age of twenty-one. Today, legislation has reduced this age to eighteen. A child is unemancipated until the parents surrender the right of care, custody, and earnings of such child and renounce their parental duties. Many courts believed that subjecting the parent to suit by the child might interfere with domestic harmony, deplete family funds at the expense of the other family members, encourage fraud or collusion, and interfere with the discipline and control of children.

The plaintiff in the next case, Lamoni K. Riordan, was a five-year-old boy who accompanied his father to land owned by the Church of Jesus Christ of Latter-Day Saints. The church had instructed Lamoni's father, Ken, a church employee, to cut the grass at this location. Ken, while carrying out this assignment, accidently backed a riding lawnmower over Lamoni's foot. The damage resulted in the partial amputation of Lamoni's foot.

Lamoni filed suit against the church that employed his father. At the time of the accident, Missouri still recognized parental immunity, thereby making it impossible for the child to sue his father in tort. He claimed that because of the doctrine of respondeat superior the church was legally responsible for the injury to his foot.

Lamoni K. Riordan v. Presiding Bishop, Latter-Day Saints
416 F.3d 825
United States Court of Appeals, Eighth Circuit
August 5, 2005

Riley, Circuit Judge
A jury awarded Lamoni Riordan (Lamoni) over $1.18 million in damages on his claims against the Corporation of the Presiding Bishop of The Church of Jesus Christ of Latter-Day Saints (CPB) for injuries Lamoni sustained when his father, Ken Riordan (Ken), a CPB employee, was operating a riding lawnmower in reverse and backed over Lamoni's foot. CPB appeals, arguing Ken's parental immunity shielded CPB from liability, and the district court... erroneously submitted both a *respondeat superior* and a direct negligence claim to the jury.... We affirm *in toto*.

I. Background
On April 13, 1985, five-year-old Lamoni was injured in an accident involving a riding lawnmower operated by Ken while Ken was mowing at a CPB-owned facility. Because of the accident, Lamoni's foot was partially amputated. Lamoni filed suit against CPB on February 15, 2002, in Missouri state court, claiming ... CPB was liable for Ken's negligence under the doctrine of *respondeat superior*,...and ... CPB negligently failed to train and supervise its employees properly. CPB removed the case to the federal district court.

The district court denied CPB's motion for summary judgment ... [and] concluded Lamoni could bring both the *respondeat superior* and direct negligence claims at trial....
    CPB appeals....

II. Discussion
Exercising diversity jurisdiction, we interpret Missouri law.... We review the district court's interpretation of Missouri law ... attempting to forecast how the Missouri Supreme Court would decide the issues presented....

A. Respondeat Superior Claim
... CPB claims the district court erred in submitting Lamoni's *respondeat superior* claim to the jury. CPB also contends applying parental immunity to bar Lamoni's claims is necessary to prevent collusion between Lamoni and Ken.
    Although the Missouri Supreme Court has... [abolished] parental immunity, the doctrine still applies to causes of action accrued before December 19, 1991.... The parties stipulated "[p]arental immunity applies to this case and, therefore, Plaintiff's parents,

Kenneth and Pearl Riordan, cannot be joined as parties to this action." We find no reason to disagree. Thus, we examine whether Ken's parental immunity shields CPB from liability.

The Missouri Supreme Court has recognized the close and analogous connection between parental immunity and spousal immunity.... Missouri adopted parental immunity on "the belief that allowing children to sue their parents would disturb the unity and harmony of the family." ... Spousal immunity also had underpinnings in notions of family unity and harmony.... In the absence of authority on the applicability of parental immunity in situations like that presented here, it is appropriate for us to consider Missouri courts' rulings on spousal immunity.

In *Mullally v. Langenberg Brothers Grain Co....* (1936), the defendant contended, because a wife could not maintain an action against her husband for damages arising from injuries caused by the husband's negligence, the husband's employer enjoyed ... immunity against the wife's *respondeat superior* claim against the employer. After noting two lines of authority on this question, the Missouri Supreme Court concluded "legal principle and public policy [dictate] the wife has a right of action against the husband's employer." ... The court quoted extensively from the reasoning in [*Jessie*] *Schubert v. August Schubert Wagon Co.*...: "The disability of wife or husband to maintain an action against the other for injuries to the person is not a disability to maintain a like action against the other's principal or master...." (quoting *Schubert*) "The statement sometimes made that it is derivative and secondary ...means this, and nothing more: That at times the fault of the actor will fix the quality of the act. Illegality established, liability ensues." .... (quoting *Schubert*) ...The court reasoned, "A trespass, negligent or willful, upon the person of a wife, does not cease to be an unlawful act, though the law exempts the husband from liability for the damage. Others may not hide behind the skirts of his immunity." *Id.* (quoting *Schubert*).

According to the Restatement (Second) of Agency, in an action against a principal based on an agent's conduct during the course of the agent's employment, "[t]he principal has no defense because of the fact that ...the agent had an immunity from civil liability as to the act." Restatement (Second) of Agency § 217 (1958). These immunities include those "resulting from the relation of parent and child and of husband and wife".... Moreover, "[s]ince the Restatement,...the

trend has been strongly to enforce the liability of the [employer]"....

We believe the Missouri Supreme Court, if confronted with this appeal, would conclude parental immunity does not bar Lamoni's *respondeat superior* claim against CPB. We forecast the Missouri Supreme Court would adopt the majority view, i.e., "the holding that the immunity of a parent is a personal immunity, and it does not, therefore, protect a third party who is liable for the tort." ...Accordingly, the district court did not err in so holding.

CPB also argues application of the parental immunity doctrine is necessary to protect it from collusion between Ken and Lamoni....

...[O]ur review of the record does not convince us collusion occurred. .... Witnesses testified at trial Ken blamed himself for the accident from the moment it occurred, admitted the injury was his fault, and stated he did not realize Lamoni was behind him as he mowed. In his deposition, Ken acknowledged mowing in reverse was more dangerous. During trial, Ken recounted the events surrounding the accident. Although Ken did not state he blamed himself, his testimony clearly demonstrates he accepted the blame for the accident, again acknowledging the danger involved in mowing in reverse.... [W]hatever collusion CPB claims occurred certainly was insufficient to warrant application of the now-abrogated parental immunity doctrine to bar Lamoni's *respondeat superior* claim against CPB.

B. Direct Negligence Claim

CPB argues the court erred in submitting to the jury Lamoni's direct negligence claim based on negligent supervision. CPB contends this claim is inextricably intertwined with the *respondeat superior* claim and is barred by parental immunity, and CPB claims Ken's own negligence was an intervening cause of the injury....

In this case, Ken's negligence resulted from CPB's negligent failure to train or supervise him properly. CPB's failure to train and supervise Ken properly caused Ken to operate the mower negligently.... The jury verdict establishes not only the negligence and causation, but the foreseeability of the failure to train and supervise leading directly to the injury.... The district court did not err in submitting both claims to the jury....

III. Conclusion

We affirm in all respects.

Case Questions

1. What was the traditional rationale for recognizing parental immunity?
2. Why did the U.S. Court of Appeals look to a New York case on spousal immunity to help it decide a Missouri case involving parental immunity?

Author Commentary

The parental immunity doctrine has been significantly eroded in the United States.

According to one source "at least twenty-four states now have either abrogated the doctrine of parental immunity altogether or have held that as a general rule, a parent may be liable to a child for injuries caused by the parent's negligence."[4] It should be emphasized that all states permit the criminal prosecution of parents for child abuse and neglect. Moreover, states that still immunize parents in tort create one or more exceptions for special situations such as where a parent has sexually abused his or her child.

INTERNET TIP

Students wishing to read a case in which the state supreme court creates an exception to the doctrine of parental immunity so that children can sue their parents for sexual abuse can read *Hurst v. Capitell* on the textbook's website.

Immunity through Contract

In addition to the immunities imposed by law, parties can create their own immunities by agreeing not to sue. Because public policy favors freedom of contract, such agreements may be legally enforceable. However, courts are often reluctant to do so. An immunity provision in a contract is construed against the party asserting the contract and is held invalid if the contract is against public policy or is a result of unfair negotiations. Factors that the court considers in determining whether to enforce the agreement are the subject matter involved, the clause itself, the relation of the parties, and the relative bargaining power of the parties.

A basic tenet of freedom of contract is that both parties are free to negotiate the terms of the contract. As a result, the contract should reflect a real and voluntary meeting of the minds. Therefore the equality of bargaining power is an important consideration for courts in determining unfair negotiations. Different courts may accord different degrees of importance to such elements as superior bargaining power, a lack of meaningful choice by one party, take-it-or-leave-it propositions, or exploitation by one party of another's known weaknesses.

In the following case, thieves successfully stole jewels valued at over $1 million from three safe deposit boxes rented by jewelers from a branch of the Firstar Bank. Two of the jewelers had purchased insurance to protect themselves from incidents such as this and collected as provided in their policies from Jewelers Mutual Insurance Company. The insurance company, in turn sought to recover from Firstar Bank. The Bank, although admitting negligence, claimed that it was contractually immune under the circumstances of this case and refused to pay. The question was tried and appealed and ultimately was decided by the Illinois Supreme Court.

Jewelers Mutual Insurance. Co. v. Firstar Bank Ill.
820 N.E.2d 411
Supreme Court of Illinois
November 18, 2004

Justice Thomas delivered the opinion of the court:
At issue is whether the exculpatory clause in defendant Firstar Bank's safety deposit box rental agreement is enforceable under the facts of this case...

Background
More than $1 million worth of loose diamonds and jewelry was stolen from three safety deposit boxes that defendant leased to jewel dealers at one of its Chicago branches. The safety deposit box lease ...agreement contained the following paragraph:

"1. It is understood that said bank has no possession or custody of, nor control over, the contents of said safe and that the lessee assumes all risks in connection with the depositing of such contents, that the sum mentioned is for the rental of said safe alone, and that there shall be no liability on the part of said bank, for loss of, or injury to, the contents of said box from any cause whatever unless lessee and said bank enter into a special agreement in writing to that effect, in which case such additional charges shall be made by said bank as the value of contents of said safe, and the liability assumed on account thereof may justify. The liability of said bank is limited to the exercise of ordinary care to prevent the opening of said safe by any person not authorized and such opening by any person not authorized shall not be inferable from loss of any of its contents."

None of the dealers had entered into the "special agreement" referenced in the first sentence of this paragraph (hereinafter, the exculpatory clause). Two of the dealers, Annaco Corporation and Irving M. Ringel, Inc., had the contents of their boxes insured by plaintiff Jewelers Mutual Insurance Company. The third dealer, Bachu Vaidya, was uninsured. Jewelers Mutual paid losses totaling $887,400.37 to Annaco and Ringel and then brought [suit] ...against defendant. The complaint alleged breach of contract and negligence. Vaidya also separately sued defendant and sought recovery under the same theories. In its answer in both cases, defendant admitted that it had to some extent been negligent and had breached the agreement as alleged by plaintiff.

Relying on the exculpatory clause, defendant moved for and was granted summary judgment in both cases....Plaintiffs appealed, and the two cases were consolidated on appeal.

The appellate court affirmed the dismissal of the negligence count in Vaidya's case.... However, the court reversed the summary judgment in favor of defendant in both cases on the breach of contract counts, holding that the exculpatory clause was unenforceable. The court gave two reasons for finding the clause unenforceable. First, that the contract was ambiguous because the first sentence of paragraph one provided that "there shall be no liability," while the second sentence said that the "liability of said bank is limited to the exercise of ordinary care." ...The court held that the ambiguity had to be resolved against defendant because it drafted the contract... The court stated that defendant had admitted that it allowed unauthorized access to the safety deposit boxes in both cases, and therefore the court granted in part Jewelers Mutual's motion for summary judgment and directed the entry of partial summary judgment for Vaidya. The court remanded for proof of damages...

Presiding Justice McBride dissented from the reversal of summary judgment for defendant. She disagreed with the majority's conclusion that the contract was ambiguous. She believed that the two sentences in paragraph one could be reconciled by reading the second sentence as referring to the "special agreement" mentioned in the first sentence...In other words, the paragraph means that defendant has no liability for any loss whatsoever, unless the parties enter into the special agreement referenced in the first sentence. If they do, then defendant's liability is limited to the exercise of ordinary care to prevent unauthorized access to the box...Finally, she did not believe that the exculpatory clause was void as against public policy because safety deposit companies are not generally insurers of the safety of the box contents...We allowed defendant's petition for leave to appeal...

Analysis
Summary judgment is proper where the pleadings, affidavits, depositions, admissions, and exhibits on file, when viewed in the light most favorable to the nonmoving, reveal that there is no issue as to any material fact and that the movant is entitled to judgment as a matter of law...

We review summary judgment orders *de novo*...

Defendant first argues that the court erred in finding paragraph one ambiguous. According to defendant, although this provision could have been drafted better, its meaning is clear. Defendant contends that the word "liability" is used two different ways in the first and second sentences. In the first sentence, it refers to the amount of damages for which defendant can be held responsible. In the second sentence, the word "liability" addresses the standard of care. Thus, the second sentence means that defendant has a duty to exercise ordinary care to prevent the unauthorized opening of the box, but the first sentence limits the amount of damages that can be collected for a breach of that duty. At oral argument, defendant clarified that its position was that the only damages that a customer could recover if defendant breaches its duty of care would be a return of the rental fee. Defendant argues that this interpretation takes into account the commercial setting in which the parties contracted and also fairly allocates the liability to the party who elected to bear the risk of loss. Here, none of the parties entered into the special agreement referenced in the first sentence to insure the contents of the box. Defendant argues that Annaco Corporation and Irving M. Ringel, Inc., insured the contents of the boxes with Jewelers Mutual and thus elected that Jewelers Mutual would bear the risk of loss. Vaidya did not purchase insurance and thus chose to bear the risk of loss himself.

We disagree with defendant's argument. First, the first sentence of paragraph one is simply not a limitation of damages clause. That sentence provides that the customer assumes all risks of depositing the contents of the box with defendant and that there "shall be no liability on the part of said bank, for loss of, or injury to, the contents of said box from any cause whatever." The clause does not say that, in the event of a breach, the plaintiff's damages are limited to a return of the rental fee. Rather, it is a general exculpatory clause purporting to exculpate defendant from all liability for loss of or damage to the contents of the box. In the very next sentence, however, defendant assumes one particular liability: it must exercise ordinary care to prevent the unauthorized opening of the box. We do not believe that the clauses can be reconciled in the manner suggested by defendant.

Further, defendant's invocation of insurance law "risk of loss" concepts is a red herring. The issue in this case is not a dispute between insurance companies over who bore the risk of loss. The issues are whether defendant breached the contract it entered into with plaintiffs and whether defendant can exculpate itself from all liability for breach of an express obligation assumed in the contract.

The construction placed on paragraph one by the dissenting justice in the appellate court must also be rejected. The dissent argued that the second sentence referred to defendant's liability in the event that the parties entered into the "special agreement" listed in clause one. This obviously cannot be the case because the first sentence provides, in part, that there is "no liability on the part of said bank, for loss of, or injury to, the contents of said box from any cause whatever unless lessee and said bank enter into a special agreement in writing to that effect." ...In other words, there is no liability for loss of or injury to the contents of the box from any cause whatsoever unless the parties enter into an agreement that there will be liability on the part of the bank for loss of, or injury to, the contents of the box from any cause whatsoever. If the parties entered into such an agreement, defendant's liability would not be limited to a failure to exercise ordinary care to keep unauthorized persons out of the box. Rather, defendant would become a general insurer of the contents of the box. Thus, the two sentences cannot be reconciled in the manner suggested by the appellate court dissent.

We believe that paragraph one of the lease agreement is ambiguous and that its two sentences are conflicting. In the first sentence, defendant disclaims liability for any loss whatsoever. In the second sentence, defendant assumes one particular liability. It must exercise ordinary care to prevent unauthorized persons from accessing the box. Defendant argues that, if we find this paragraph ambiguous, then the resolution of its meaning is a question of fact and the case cannot be decided on a motion for summary judgment...Defendant thus contends that, if we find an ambiguity, we must remand the case to the fact finder to resolve the ambiguity.

We disagree.

Whatever the meaning of the exculpatory clause, it clearly cannot be applied to a situation in which defendant is alleged to have breached its duty to exercise ordinary care to prevent unauthorized persons from opening the box. This is a specific duty that defendant assumed in the contract, and it formed the heart of the parties' agreement. A party cannot promise to act in a certain manner in one portion of a contract and then exculpate itself from liability for breach of that very promise in another part of the contract... Here, plaintiffs have received nothing in return for their rental fee if they cannot hold defendant to its contractual obligation to exercise ordinary care to prevent unauthorized persons from accessing their safety deposit boxes.

This same conclusion was reached by the Florida District Court of Appeal in *Sniffen v. Century National Bank of Broward,...* (Fla. App. 1979). In that case, the safety deposit box rental agreement was similar to the one here in that it contained two conflicting provisions. One was a general, broad exculpatory clause denying liability for any loss: "It is expressly understood...that in making this lease the Bank...shall not be liable for loss or damage to, the contents of said box, caused by burglary, fire or any cause whatsoever, but that the entire risk of such of loss or damage is assumed by the lessee." ...In the second provision, the bank assumed a duty to prevent unauthorized access: "No person other than the renter or approved deputy named in the books of Bank ...shall have access to the safe." ...The plaintiff alleged that the bank breached this agreement when it allowed an authorized person, his ex-wife, to access his safety deposit box. She removed over $250,000 worth of bearer bonds and other valuables. The trial judge dismissed the complaint on the ground that the exculpatory clause barred plaintiff's action...

The Florida District Court of Appeal reversed, holding that, "whatever the possible effect of the exculpatory clause in other situations ...it is clear that it cannot be employed, as it was below, to negate the specific contractual undertaking to restrict access to the vault." ...The *Sniffen* court further elaborated on how this principle applies to safety deposit box rental agreements:

> "It should be emphasized that ...an acceptance of the bank's position in this case would render the agreement between the parties entirely nugatory. If a safety deposit customer cannot enforce the bank's undertaking to preclude unauthorized persons from entry to his box which is the very heart of the relationship and the only real reason that such a facility is used at all,...it is obvious that he will have received nothing whatever in return

for his rental fee. The authorities are unanimous in indicating that no such drastic effect may properly be attributed to contractual provisions such as those involved here...."

We agree with the *Sniffen* court's analysis. In this contract, in exchange for plaintiff's rental fee, defendant assumed the obligation to exercise ordinary care to prevent unauthorized access to the safety deposit box. Having assumed this duty, defendant cannot exculpate itself from liability for a breach of that duty. Accepting defendant's argument would mean that, if defendant routinely breached these safety deposit box rental agreements by handing the keys to anyone who came in off the street and asked for them, it would have no liability to its customers except to give them their rental fee back. It is safe to assume that, if defendant explained the agreement this way in the contract, defendant would not have many safety deposit box customers.

Defendant's response to *Sniffen* is two-fold. First, defendant argues that it is distinguishable because it involved an exculpatory clause that conflicted with another provision of the contract, while the contract in the case before us contains no such conflict. This is clearly incorrect. The contract here contains the same conflict as the contract in *Sniffen*: a general exculpatory clause absolving the bank for all liability from any loss whatsoever, and an express obligation to prevent unauthorized opening of the box...Second, defendant argues that *Sniffen* was distinguished in Federal Deposit Insurance Corp...Defendant is correct, but that does not help defendant...

We hold that the exculpatory provision is not applicable to an allegation that defendant breached its duty to exercise ordinary care to prevent unauthorized access to the box...

We affirm the appellate court's judgment reversing the summary judgment for defendant, entering summary judgment for plaintiffs, and remanding for proof of damages.

Affirmed.

Case Questions

1. What was the bank attempting to do in its contract with its safety box customers?
2. Why did the Illinois Supreme Court conclude that this exculpatory clause was unenforceable?

INTERNET TIP

Students may be interested in reading the case of *Gimple v. Host Enterprises, Inc.* in the retired cases section of the textbook's website. The *Gimple* case debuted in this textbook in the fourth edition in 1989. It is a case in which an exculpatory clause contained in a bicycle rental agreement was enforced, despite the fact that the rental bike had bad brakes.

CHAPTER SUMMARY

Chapter VI began with a discussion of the "case or controversy" requirement. This requirement, which is based in the federal constitution, prevents federal courts from advising the legislative and executive branches. The chapter then discussed the umbrella concept known as "justiciability." The court will only decide cases that are well suited to be decided by means of the judicial process. Various judicial doctrines have been developed that are used to exclude disputes that do not lend themselves to judicial determination. Examples included the "standing," "ripeness," "mootness," "political questions," and "act of state" judicial doctrines. Readers also learned about statutes of limitations, which are legislatively created time limits within which plaintiffs must exercise their right to sue. A plaintiff who fails to bring an action within the specified period of time forfeits the right to sue and, in some circumstances, that time period can be extended. The chapter also included a discussion of the equitable doctrine of laches. If a plaintiff is suing for an equitable remedy and the defendant sustains legal injury due to the plaintiff's unreasonable delay in bringing the action, the court may refuse to award the plaintiff any equitable relief because of the doctrine of laches. Next, the chapter addressed the judicial doctrine traditionally known as *res judicata* and, more recently, as claim preclusion. This doctrine prevents the same parties from relitigating the same claims in a second lawsuit. If a judgment has been awarded, generally any claims that were decided or could and should have been litigated in that first action are included in the judgment. Last, the chapter examined some of the more common types of legal immunities from tort liability. Most legal immunities exist to protect some important public interest. This principle is explained in the subsequent discussions of sovereign immunity, the immunities granted to governmental officials, and intrafamily immunities. The chapter concluded with a discussion of immunities that are created by contract and when courts will and will not enforce exculpatory clauses.

CHAPTER QUESTIONS

1. The city of Jacksonville, Florida, sought to increase the percentage of municipal contracts awarded to minority business enterprises (MBEs) and enacted an ordinance containing a 10 percent set aside. Members of the Association of General Contractors brought suit against the city because they thought the set-aside program impermissibly favored one race over another. Such a race-based classification system in the awarding of municipal construction contracts, they contended, violated the Equal Protection Clause of the Fourteenth Amendment. The trial court granted summary judgment in favor of the contractors' association; however, the U.S. Court of Appeals for the Eleventh Circuit vacated the judgment on the grounds that the contractors lacked standing to sue. The appeals court concluded that the contractors' association had "not demonstrated that, but for the

program, any member would have bid successfully for any of the contracts." After the U.S. Supreme Court granted the contractors' association's petition for a writ of certiorari, the city repealed its MBE ordinance and enacted a second ordinance that was very similar in that it provided for contractual set-asides favoring women and black contractors. Is this case moot, inasmuch as the ordinance complained about has been repealed?

Association of General Contractors v. City of Jacksonville, 508 U.S. 656 (1993)

2. Assume the same facts as in question 1. Assume further that the city argued in the Supreme Court that the contractors' association lacked standing in that no member of the association alleged that he or she would have been awarded a city contract but for the set-aside ordinance. Did the contractors' association have standing to sue? Why? Why not?

Association of General Contractors v. City of Jacksonville, 508 U.S. 656 (1993)

3. Paula Piper was a public defender assigned to defend William Aramy. Prior to William's trial, Paula told the judges she thought William was crazy. Bail was set and William was placed in a mental institution. Paula failed to tell William how he could arrange bail. Claiming that his prolonged stay in the mental institution was caused by Paula's negligence, William sued Paula for malpractice. Paula claims that her position as an officer of the court gives her the defense of judicial immunity. Who wins? Why?

4. On February 1, 1999, John Smith bought a car for $10,000. He paid $1,000 down and signed a promissory note for $9,000, due in three years. Assume that the note was never paid and that the applicable statute of limitations is five years. The plaintiff could wait until what date to bring a civil suit for nonpayment of the note?

5. The Endangered Species Act of 1973 authorizes citizens to bring suits against the government to protect threatened wildlife and plant life. When the U.S. Fish and Wildlife Service decided to restrict the amount of water released from an irrigation project along the Oregon–Washington border, Oregon ranchers brought suit against the federal government. The ranchers maintained that their businesses would be severely damaged as a result of this decision. They also alleged that the government had not used the "best scientific and commercial data available," as required by the federal statute. The U.S. Court of Appeals for the Ninth Circuit ruled that the ranchers did not have standing because the statute only provided for citizen suits brought on behalf of endangered species. Should citizens who believe that the government has been overly pro-environment and insufficiently sensitive to the economic consequences of environmental protection have standing to sue the government?

Bennett v. Spear, 520 U.S. 154 (1997)

6. In 1942, Congress amended the Nationality Act of 1940 to make it easier for noncitizens who had fought in World War II and who had been honorably discharged from the U.S. Armed Services to become American citizens. The 1942 act specifically provided that the noncitizen servicemen could complete the naturalization before a designated immigration and naturalization officer and while outside the borders of the United States. This procedure was in lieu of requiring the applicant to come to the United States and appear before a U.S. district court judge. In August 1945, the U.S. vice consul in Manila was designated by the Immigration and Naturalization Service (INS) to perform this responsibility. The government of the Philippines, concerned that too many of its nationals would take advantage of this law, soon prevailed on the United States to restrict this opportunity. The U.S. attorney general responded by revoking the vice consul's authority to process citizenship applications from October 1945 until October 1946. Congress also proceeded to limit the window

of opportunity to those who filed petitions by December 1946. Filipino war veterans brought suit, contending that they were entitled to become citizens under the amended Nationality Act. The INS responded by asserting that the plaintiffs' claims were nonjusticiable because they were political questions. Should the political questions doctrine apply in cases such as this?

Pangilinan v. Immigration and Naturalization Service, 796 F.2d 1091, U.S. Court of Appeals (9th Circuit 1986).

7. Judge Stump, a judge of a circuit court in Indiana (a court of general jurisdiction), approved a mother's petition to have her "somewhat retarded" fifteen-year-old daughter sterilized. The judge approved the mother's petition the same day, without a hearing and without notice to the daughter or appointment of a *guardian ad litem*. The operation was performed on Linda Sparkman, but she was told that she was having her appendix removed. A few years later, after Sparkman married and discovered that she had been sterilized, she and her husband brought suit against Judge Stump. Should Judge Stump be immune under the circumstances?

Stump v. Sparkman, 435 U.S. 349 (1978)

NOTES

1. *Hewllette v. George,* 9 So. 885 (1891).

2. *Lloyd Dunlap v. Dunlap,* 150 A. 905 (1930).

3. R. N. Heath, "The Parental Immunity Doctrine: Is Insurer Bad Faith an Exception or Should the Doctrine Be Abolished," 83 *The Florida Bar Journal* 9, 58 (October 2009).

4. Oliver Wendell Holmes, Harold Joseph Laski, *Collected Legal Papers* (New York: Harcourt, Brace and Howe, 1920), pp. 65–69.

VII

✳

Judicial Remedies

CHAPTER OBJECTIVES

1. *Explain the important differences between equitable and common law relief.*
2. *Describe the function of each remedy.*
3. *Understand what an equitable maxim is and how it is used.*
4. *Identify and explain the three classes of injunctions.*
5. *Explain how compensatory, punitive, nominal, and liquidated damages differ.*

Before addressing the power of the court to award various types of relief, we should establish that courts do not have a monopoly on resolving private disputes. Many disputes within families, for example, are settled without resort to the judiciary by grandparents, parents, or an older sibling. Other peacemakers include religious leaders, coaches, teachers, and other respected persons. Arbitrators, mediators, and private courts also offer disputants alternative procedures for resolving disagreements without involving the public court systems.

Some readers would better understand remedies if they took a few minutes to review the material in Chapter I regarding the development of the English common law and equitable courts. If readers also take another look at Article III, Section 2, of the U.S. Constitution and the Seventh Amendment, they will see that notions of law and equity are specifically mentioned within the text of our Constitution. Lastly, reviewing this historical material will remind readers of the reasons for the traditional rule that a plaintiff who has an adequate legal remedy is not entitled to equitable relief.

We now turn to a discussion of judicial remedies. Once a person has established a substantive right through judicial procedures, the court will award relief.

Judicial relief can assume many different forms, called remedies (see Figure 7.1). The most common remedy is awarding money damages in the form of compensatory damages and, where permissible, punitive damages. Additional remedies include injunctive relief (requiring someone to do or refrain from doing something), restitution (restoring a person to a previous position to prevent unjust enrichment), declaratory judgment (a judicial determination of the parties' rights), and reformation (judicially rewriting a written instrument to reflect the real agreement of the parties).

COMMON LAW REMEDIES

Common law remedies are generally limited to the court's determination of some legal right and the award of money damages. There are some exceptions. For example, when parties want the court's opinion concerning their legal rights but are not seeking damages or injunctive relief, they seek a declaratory judgment. In addition, the common law remedies of ejectment and replevin both seek restitution. An **ejectment** occurs when a trespasser secures full possession of the land and the owner brings an action to regain possession, as well as damages for the unlawful detention of possession. Usually this process involves a title dispute between plaintiff and defendant, and the ejectment action settles this dispute. **Replevin** is an action used to recover possession of personal property wrongfully taken. Once the action is brought, the goods are seized from the defendant after proper notice has been given and held until title has been determined.

Usually, however, a common law court grants relief in the form of damages, a sum of money awarded as compensation for an injury sustained as the consequence of either a tortious act or a breach of a legal obligation. Damages are classified as compensatory, punitive, nominal, and liquidated.

Compensatory Damages

Compensatory damages are awarded to compensate the plaintiff for pecuniary losses that have resulted from the defendant's tortious conduct or breach of contract. Although the permissible damage elements vary by jurisdiction, they typically include awards for loss of time or money, bodily pain and suffering, permanent disabilities or disfigurement, injury to reputation, and mental anguish. Future losses are also recoverable; however, compensation is not allowed for consequences that are remote, indirect, or uncertain (i.e., where speculative).

Damages are usually limited to those reasonably foreseeable by the defendant as a result of the breach. Assume that two plaintiffs have a contract to buy some equipment needed to open their new business, and a defendant breaches by nondelivery. If the plaintiffs sue for lost profits from the delay in opening because they have to procure alternative goods, they would probably not recover, because the defendant could not have foreseen this without knowing that the opening depended on the delivery. Also, future profits are very difficult to measure with any degree of certainty.

In awarding compensatory damages, the court's objective is to put the plaintiff in the same financial position as existed before the commission of the tort or, in a contract case, in the financial position that would have resulted had the promise been fulfilled. In the absence of circumstances giving rise to an allowance of punitive damages, the law will not put the injured party in a better position than the person would have been in had the wrong not been done.

A person who is injured must use whatever means are reasonable to avoid or minimize damages. This rule is called by most the **rule of mitigation** (and by others the avoidable harm doctrine). It prevents recovery for damages that could have been foreseen and avoided by reasonable effort without undue risk, expense, or humiliation. For example, P sues to recover the loss of a crop, because D removed some rails from P's fence, and as a result, cattle escaped and destroyed the crop. Since P, knowing the rails were missing, did not repair the fence, only the cost of repairing the fence is recoverable, because the loss of the crop could have been avoided.

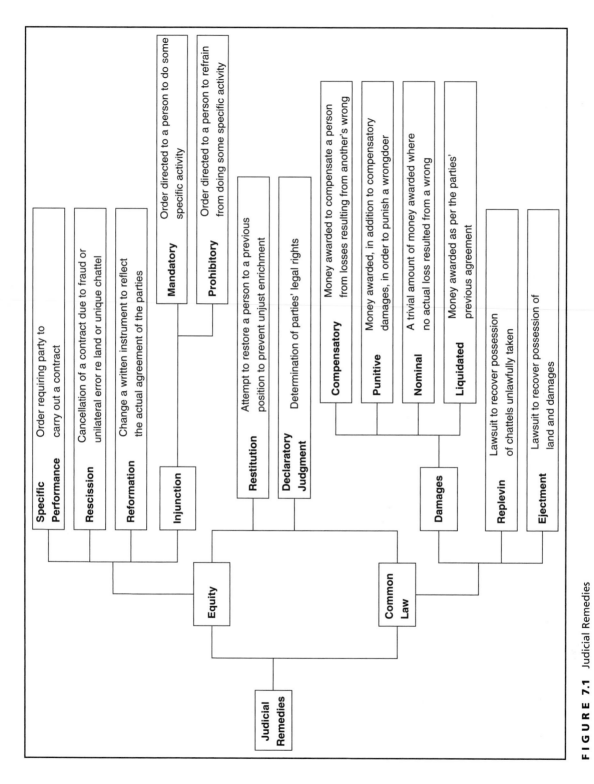

F I G U R E 7.1 Judicial Remedies

When the defendant's misconduct causes damages but also operates directly to confer some benefit on the plaintiff, then the plaintiff's damage claim may be diminished by the amount of the benefit conferred. This policy is called the **benefit rule**. For example, a trespasser digs on plaintiff's land, but the digging works to drain swampy areas and improves the value. The plaintiff may recover for the trespass and any damage it caused, but the defendant gets a credit for the value of the benefit conferred. However, this credit exists only for clear benefits and not for those that are remote and uncertain. Problems arise in deciding what constitutes a benefit and what standard to measure it by.

Compensatory damages may be categorized as either general or special. This distinction is very important to lawyers because general damages do not have to be specifically pleaded, whereas special damages must be listed in the pleadings. **General damages** are those that are the natural and necessary result of the wrongful act or omission, and thus can normally be expected to accompany the injury. Pain and suffering, mental anguish, and the loss of enjoyment of life are damages that occur so frequently in the tort of battery that they do not have to be specifically pleaded. **Special damages** are awarded for injuries that arise from special circumstances of the wrong. A plaintiff in a battery case, for example, would have to plead specifically such special damages as medical and hospital expenses, loss of earnings, and a diminished ability to work.

Putting a dollar value on the plaintiff's loss for the purpose of compensation often becomes a difficult task. Because the amount of damages is a factual question and decisions on factual issues do not create precedent, previous case decisions are not binding. The amount of damages is decided by a jury, unless a jury trial has been waived.

The next case involves a plaintiff who seeks to recover a variety of damages for medical malpractice. The court rules that the state's public policy prohibits her from recovering for all that she claims. The concurrence contains a discussion of the benefits rule and the rule requiring the mitigation of damages.

Macomber v. Dillman
505 A.2d 810
Supreme Judicial Court of Maine
February 27, 1986

Glassman, Justice

In April of 1984, the plaintiffs, Roxanne and Steven Macomber, filed a complaint against the defendants, Carter F. Dillman and the Webber Hospital Association. The complaint alleged, *inter alia*, that as a proximate result of the defendants' negligent and careless failure to comply with the standard of care of medical practice in the performance of a tubal ligation on Roxanne for the purpose of permanent sterilization, Roxanne was not permanently sterilized and had conceived and given birth to a child, Maize. Although the plaintiffs did not allege in their complaint that Maize is a healthy, normal child, they did not allege otherwise, and the parties have agreed to these facts. Plaintiffs sought damages from defendants "including, but not limited to, the cost of raising and educating Maize May Macomber, the medical and other expenses of the pregnancy and childbirth, the medical and other expenses of a subsequent hysterectomy for purposes of sterilization, lost wages, loss of consortium, the medical and other expenses of the unsuccessful tubal ligation, permanent physical impairment to Roxanne Macomber resulting from bearing Maize May, her sixth child, and physical and mental pain and suffering resulting [therefrom]."

Defendants filed motions for dismissal or summary judgment on the grounds that the plaintiffs by their complaint failed to state a claim for which relief could be granted and could not recover damages for the cost of rearing and educating a healthy, normal child. After hearing, the Superior Court entered its order denying the defendants' motions and adopting the analysis that should the plaintiffs prevail they would be entitled to recover "all reasonable, foreseeable, and proximately caused damages, including the expenses of child rearing." The court refused to rule on whether damages so recoverable by plaintiffs "should be offset by benefits" of parenthood.

On a joint motion of the parties, the Superior Court reported the case to this court thereby posing the following questions of law: (1) Did the Superior Court by its order properly deny the defendants' motion to dismiss the plaintiff's complaint for failure to state a claim against the defendants for which relief can be granted? (2) Did the Superior Court by its order properly set forth the damages that the plaintiffs could recover should they prevail in their action against the defendants?

We first address the question of whether the plaintiffs have by their complaint stated a claim against the defendants. Contrary to the defendants' contention, the plaintiffs' action does not represent a new cause of action in the state of Maine. "Since the early days of the common law a cause of action in tort has been recognized to exist when the negligence of one person is the proximate cause of damage to another person." ... When a plaintiff claims he has suffered a personal injury as the result of medical mistreatment, his remedy lies in a complaint for negligence.... The necessary elements of a cause of action for negligence are a duty owed, a breach of that duty proximately causing the plaintiff's injuries and resulting damages.... Applying these principles to the allegations in the plaintiffs' complaint, it is clear that the necessary elements of a cause of action in negligence have been set forth against the defendants.

We next consider whether the Superior Court correctly established the scope of recoverable damages. We are aware that the courts which have considered this type of case have not reached a consensus as to damages, if any, that may be recoverable....

We hold for reasons of public policy that a parent cannot be said to have been damaged or injured by the birth and rearing of a healthy, normal child. Accordingly, we limit the recovery of damages, where applicable, to the hospital and medical expenses incurred for the sterilization procedures and pregnancy, the pain and suffering connected with the pregnancy and the loss of earnings by the mother during that time. Our ruling today is limited to the facts of this case, involving a failed sterilization procedure resulting in the birth of a healthy, normal child.

We also must address whether the plaintiff, Steven Macomber, may recover for loss of consortium of his wife, Roxanne. For centuries courts have recognized a husband's right to recover damages for the loss of consortium when a tortious injury to his wife detrimentally affects the spousal relationship.... Because his wife's cause of action is for negligence, Steven Macomber may recover proven damages for loss of consortium.

The entry is:

The order of the Superior Court is modified to limit the scope of recoverable damages, and as so modified, affirmed. Remanded to the Superior Court for further proceedings consistent with the opinion herein.

McKusik, Nichols, and Roberts, J.J., concurring. Scolnik, Justice, concurring in part and dissenting in part

Although I concur that a cause of action exists for medical malpractice in the performance of a tubal ligation, I am unable to agree with the Court's judicially imposed limitation on the damages that are recoverable. The Court reasons that in no circumstances can a parent be said to have been damaged by the birth and rearing of a healthy, normal child. This rationale, however, is not only plainly inconsistent with the Court's recognition of a cause of action but also totally ignores the fact that many individuals undergo sterilization for the very purpose of avoiding such a birth. Moreover, the Court's opinion is an unwarranted departure from the fundamental principle of tort law that once a breach of duty has been established, the tortfeasor is liable for all foreseeable damages that proximately result from his acts. I dissent because, in my view, the jury should be permitted to consider awarding damages for child rearing costs.

By finding that a parent is not harmed by the birth of a healthy child, the Court's opinion is logically inconsistent. In the first part of its opinion, the Court applies traditional tort principles to recognize a cause of action for negligence resulting in an unwanted conception and subsequent birth of a normal, healthy child. Although the opinion is noticeably silent as to what the required harm is to support the cause of action ... the Court has in effect concluded that the birth of a normal child is recognized as an injury that is directly attributable to the health-care provider's negligence. In the second part of its opinion, however, the Court states that based on unarticulated reasons of public policy, the birth of a normal, healthy child cannot be said to constitute an injury to the parents. As a result, the Court limits the damages that a parent can recover to the hospital and medical expenses incurred for the sterilization procedure and the pregnancy, the pain and suffering connected with the pregnancy and the loss of earnings sustained by the mother during that time. If, however, the birth of a child does not constitute an injury, no basis exists for any award of damages. Damages for "pain and suffering" and medical expenses incidental to childbirth cannot be recoverable if the birth itself is not an injury. Similarly, if the parent is to be compensated for the loss of earnings that result from the pregnancy, should she not equally be compensated for the identical loss following the birth of the child? The Court's opinion fails to reconcile these obvious inconsistencies.

Not only is the Court's opinion internally inconsistent, but its stated rationale to support an artificial limitation on the scope of recoverable damages ignores reality. To hold that a parent cannot be said to have been damaged or injured by the birth and rearing of a normal, healthy child is plainly to overlook the fact that many married couples, such as the plaintiffs, engage in contraceptive practices and undergo sterilization operations for the very purpose of avoiding the birth of [a] child. Many of these couples resort to such conception avoidance measures because, in their particular circumstances, the physical or financial hardships in raising another child are too burdensome. Far from supporting the view that the birth of a child is in all situations a benefit, the social reality is that, for many, an unplanned and unwanted child can be a clear detriment.... "[W]hen a couple has chosen not to have children, or not to have any more children, the suggestion arises that for them, at least, the birth of a child would not be a net benefit." ... This is not to say that there are not many benefits associated with the raising of a child. The point is that it is unrealistic universally to proclaim that the joy and the companionship a parent receives from a healthy child always outweigh the costs and difficulties of rearing that child. As one judge explained:

> "A couple privileged to be bringing home the combined income of a dual professional household may well be able to sustain and cherish an unexpected child. But I am not sure the child's smile would be the most memorable characteristic to an indigent couple, where the husband underwent a vasectomy or the wife underwent a sterilization procedure, not because they did not desire a child, but rather because they faced the stark realization that they could not afford to feed an additional person, much less clothe, educate and support a child when that couple had trouble supporting one another. The choice is not always giving up personal amenities in order to buy a gift for the baby; the choice may only be to stretch necessities beyond the breaking point to provide for a child that the couple had purposely set out to avoid having."...

I know of no instance where we have strayed from the common law principle that a tortfeasor is liable for every foreseeable injury proximately caused by his negligent act and we should avoid doing so here. The Court states that public policy dictates the result it reaches without explaining the source from which it was derived or the foundation on which it rests. This is not a case where change is required in the common law, without legislative help, because of a conflict between an outdated judicially crafted policy and contemporary legal philosophy.... In fact, I am sure that the Court realizes that substantial disagreement exists among the courts as to whether a parent is harmed by the birth of an unexpected child. This fact coupled with the empirical reality that many individuals choose to forego parenthood for economic or other reasons demonstrates that the Court's unexplicated judicial declaration of public policy is unwarranted....

In my view, it is the duty of this Court to follow public policy, not to formulate it, absent a clear expression of public opinion. Moreover, it has always been the public policy of this State to provide relief to those injured by tortfeasors and to allow for compensation for damages caused by their acts. To deprive the plaintiffs in this case of the opportunity to recover compensation for all their damages contravenes this basic policy. Any limitation on the scope of recoverable damages in such cases is best left to the Legislature where the opportunity for wide ranging debate and public participation is far greater than in the Law Court....

Rather than to rely on unstated notions of public policy, the better approach to determine what damages may be recoverable is to apply traditional common-law rules. It is certainly foreseeable that a medical health professional's failure properly to perform a tubal ligation will result in the birth of an unplanned child. As a result of the tortfeasor's act, the parents, who had chosen not to have a child, find themselves unexpectedly burdened both physically and financially. They seek damages not because they do not love and desire to keep the child, but because the direct and foreseeable consequences of the health-care provider's negligence has [sic] forced burdens on them that they sought and had a right to avoid.

In assessing damages for child rearing costs, I would follow those jurisdictions that have adopted the "benefit rule" of the Restatement (Second) of Torts § 920 (1979).... The benefit rule recognizes that various tangible and intangible benefits accrue to the parents of the unplanned child and therefore to prevent unjust enrichment, their benefits should be weighed by the factfinder in determining damages associated with the raising of the unexpected child. The rule provides that "[w]hen the defendant's tortious conduct has caused harm to the plaintiff or to his property and in so doing has conferred a special benefit to the interest of the plaintiff that was harmed, the value of the benefit conferred is considered in mitigation of damages, to the extent that this is equitable." ... The assessment of damages, if any, should focus on the specific interests of the parents that were actually impaired by the physician's negligence. An important factor in making that determination would be the reason that sterilization was sought, whether it was economic, genetic, therapeutic or otherwise.... The advantages of this approach were succinctly stated by the Arizona Supreme Court.

> "By allowing the jury to consider the future costs, both pecuniary and non-pecuniary, of rearing and educating the child, we permit it to consider all the elements of damage on which the parents may present evidence. By permitting the jury to consider the reason for the procedure and to assess and offset the pecuniary and non-pecuniary benefits which will inure to the parents by reason of their relationship to the child, we allow the jury to discount those damages, thus reducing speculation and permitting the verdict to be based upon the facts as they actually exist in each of the unforeseeable variety of situations which may come before the court. We think this by far the better rule. The blindfold on the figure of justice is a shield from partiality, not from reality."...

Although the benefit rule approach requires the jury to mitigate primarily economic damages by weighing them against primarily noneconomic factors, I reject the view that such a process is "an exercise in prophecy, an undertaking not within the specialty of our factfinders." ... The calculation of the benefits a parent could expect to receive from the child is no more difficult than similar computations of damages in wrongful death actions, for extended loss of consortium or for pain and suffering....

As a final note, the parents should not be forced to mitigate their damages by resorting to abortion or to adoption. A doctrine of mitigation of damages known as the avoidable consequences rule requires only that reasonable measures be taken.... Most courts that have considered the matter have held, as a matter of law, neither course of action would be reasonable.... I agree. The tortfeasor takes the injured party as he finds him and has no right to insist that the victims of his negligence have the emotional and mental make-up of a woman who is willing to undergo an abortion or offer her child for adoption. Moreover, the parents should not be precluded from recovering damages because they select the most desirable alternative and raise the child. Accordingly, the avoidable consequences rule is not relevant to the issue of the recovery of child rearing expenses.

Damages recoverable under the cause of action recognized today by this Court should not be limited by unstated notions of public policy so as arbitrarily to limit recovery of proximately caused and foreseeable damages. I recognize that this is an extremely difficult case but I find no public policy declaring that physicians should be partially immunized from the consequences of a negligently performed sterilization operation nor declaring that the birth of a healthy child is in all circumstances a blessing to the parents. Accordingly, I see no justification for supporting a departure from the traditional rules that apply to tort damages.

I would affirm, without modification, the order of the Superior Court and permit the recovery of the potential costs of rearing the child.

Case Questions

1. Why does the court majority hold that the parents could recover damages for hospital and medical expenses, pain, and suffering connected with the unwanted pregnancy, the loss of earnings by the mother during the pregnancy, and loss of consortium, but denies a recovery for the cost of rearing and educating a healthy, normal child?

2. The dissenting justice argues that the majority opinion is inconsistent. Explain the inconsistencies.

3. After carefully reading the majority and dissenting opinions, how would you rule?

 Do you agree with the Court that "a parent cannot be said to have been damaged or injured by the birth and rearing of a healthy, normal child"?

Hedonic Damages

Plaintiffs in recent years have increasingly been seeking compensation for what are called **hedonic damages**, the loss of enjoyment of life. States differ as to whether to recognize the impairment of a person's ability to experience the normal pleasures and enjoyments of life such as being a member of a family, falling in love, becoming a parent or grand-parent, enjoying music, travel, or other common life activities as compensable losses. Supporters would argue that such "losses" are compensable as a stand-alone type of damages. Hedonic damages, they would assert, are different in kind from the physical pain and mental anguish traditionally compensated as pain and suffering. But several states refuse to recognize hedonic damages as compensable. Other states consider hedonic damages to be included within pain and suffering.

INTERNET TIP

Students wishing to learn more about hedonic damages can read *Overstreet v. Shoney's, Inc.*, and *Kansas City Southern Railway Company, Inc. v. Johnson* on the text-book's website.

Punitive Damages

Damages can also be awarded to punish defendants for their conduct and to deter others from similar conduct. These are called **punitive** or **exemplary damages**, and are awarded to the plaintiff beyond the compensatory amount. They are additional damages for a civil wrong and are not imposed as a substitute for criminal punishment. Punitive damages are awarded to plaintiffs to deter them from repeating their conduct, and to deter others from following their example. An award of puni-tive damages also may include an award of attor-neys' fees, although this varies by jurisdiction.

Such an award is appropriate only when a defendant has engaged in aggravated, wanton, reck-less, malicious, or oppressive conduct. This includes all acts done with an evil disposition or a wrong and unlawful motive, or the willful doing of an injuri-ous act without a lawful excuse. Punitive damages

are generally available only for intentional torts and for some statutory wrongs. The reason courts gen-erally refuse to award punitive damages where defendants have acted negligently is that such per-sons did not intend to cause the harmful result that ensued. A person cannot be deterred from causing harms that were never intended in the first place.

Some of the actions that may result in punitive damage awards are copyright and trademark infringe-ment, corporate crimes such as antitrust violations, insurers not paying compensation as required by their policies, employers wrongfully discharging employees, libel and slander, wrongful death, trespass, conversion, battery, and securities fraud. Tradition-ally, punitive damages have not been awarded in contract cases, even in situations in which there has been a malicious breach. Some jurisdictions have modified this rule in some situations: if a breach of contract is accompanied by a malicious tort, exem-plary damages will be awarded for the tort.

The facts in the next case, *Wilen v. Falkenstein,* have been summarized in order to enhance under-standing and to conserve space.

Summary of Facts in *Wilen v. Falkenstein*

William Falkenstein and John Wilen were neigh-bors. Falkenstein planted some thirty trees on his land, two of which were matching trees that he had placed one on each side of his swimming pool. One of these matched trees grew so as to interfere with Wilen's view from the balcony of his house. Wilen tried to work something out with Falkenstein, but his offer to pay for the trim-ming of Falkenstein's tree was rejected. While Falk-enstein was on a trip, the tree in question was reduced in height by some five feet by employees of TLS Landscaping. This fact was discovered by Falkenstein upon returning home after his trip. Falkenstein investigated and concluded that Wilen was responsible for the tree's damage. Falkenstein thereafter filed suit against Wilen, accusing him of trespass and of damaging his tree.

The case was tried to a jury. TLS Landscaping employees testified at the trial. An employee named Story, who actually "trimmed" the tree in question on Falkenstein's property, testified that Wilen had instructed him to cut the top off the tree. Story also testified that because of the manner in which the tree had been cut, it was no longer marketable. Additional testimony indicated that it would cost $4,151.39 to replace the damaged tree with one that matched the surviving poolside tree. Wilen testified that he had assumed that TLS Landscaping had Falkenstein's permission to trim the tree. Wilen admitted to having told the tree cutter "which tree to trim and how much to trim it," but denied ever entering Falkenstein's land or receiving a bill from TLS Landscaping for the tree cut on his neighbor's land. The jury returned a verdict in favor of Falkenstein.

Wilen claimed on appeal that there was insufficient evidence to support the jury's trespass finding. The Texas Court of Appeals disagreed. It ruled that Wilen could be found to be legally responsible in trespass for Story's cutting off the top of the tree on Falkenstein's land. Judge Walker ruled that the jury was entitled to find that Story's actions were directed and controlled by Wilen.

Wilen also claimed that the proof was insufficient to support the jury's compensatory damage

award because there was no evidence that Falkenstein's land had become less valuable in the aftermath of the cutting. Furthermore, argued Wilen, the tree was still alive. The appellate court again disagreed. Judge Walker pointed out that when a tree is damaged in conjunction with a trespass but the land's fair market value is unaffected by the damage, the injured party is still entitled to compensation for "the intrinsic value" of the tree. This would be the amount of money it would take to replace the cut tree with a tree that matched the surviving tree from the original matching pair. The appellate court concluded that the jury's compensatory damage award was reasonable under the circumstances.

The last two issues the appellate court had to resolve had to do with the award of punitive damages and the award of attorneys' fees. Could reasonable jurors, as a matter of law, have found Wilen's actions to have been malicious, spiteful, outrageous, oppressive, or intolerable? Was Falkenstein entitled to an award of attorneys' fees? This case has been substantially edited because of its length.

John C. Wilen v. William Falkenstein
191 S.W.3d. 791
Court of Appeals of Texas, Second District, Fort Worth
April 6, 2006

Sue Walker, J.
Opinion: I. Introduction
This appeal arises from a trespass suit brought by Appellee William Falkenstein against his neighbor, Appellant John C. Wilen, for causing a tree service to trim a tree on Falkenstein's property. The trial court entered judgment in accordance with the jury's verdict, awarding Falkenstein $5,300.00 in actual damages, $18,000.00 in exemplary damages, and attorney's fees of $29,700.00....

3. Sufficiency of the Evidence...
C. Damages ...
2. Exemplary Damages
a. The Malice Finding
... Wilen argues [on appeal] that the evidence is factually insufficient to support the exemplary damages award because his conduct was not malicious. Exemplary damages are recoverable for the tort of trespass

if the trespass was committed maliciously.... The trespass must be initiated by or accompanied with some evil intent or with complete disregard of anyone's rights.... Exemplary damages may not be awarded where it appears that the defendant acted in good faith or without wrongful intention or in the belief that he was exercising his rights....

Here, the trial court asked the jury whether it found by clear and convincing evidence that the harm to Falkenstein resulted from malice. The charge defined malice as including a "specific intent by John C. Wilen to cause substantial injury to William Falkenstein," and the jury answered yes to this question.

We note that the cases prescribing exemplary damages for a "malicious" or "willful" trespass are based on the old, common law "actual malice" definition requiring proof of "ill-will, spite, evil motive, or purposing the injuring of another." ... The common law definition of malice was incorporated into the statutory definition codified in the civil practice and remedies code.... The statutory definition of malice raised the standard of proof required to attain exemplary damages; the statutory definition requires proof of the defendant's specific intent "to cause substantial injury to the claimant."...

Because clear and convincing evidence is required to support the jury's malice finding ... we focus our review on whether there was clear and convincing evidence that Wilen's trespass through TLS Landscaping was performed with malice, that is, performed with a specific intent to cause substantial injury to Falkenstein. The evidence established that Wilen directed TLS Landscaping to enter Falkenstein's yard and to trim five feet off the top of the view-blocking tree. When Wilen told Story how he desired Falkenstein's tree to be trimmed, Story testified that he explained that TLS Landscaping usually did not "top" a tree. Wilen reassured Story that it was "okay" and directed Story to proceed. Wilen's actions in ordering Falkenstein's tree to be trimmed while Falkenstein was on vacation reveal Wilen's disregard for Falkenstein's right to maintain his property in the way he saw fit. The jury was free to discredit Wilen's protestations that no harm was intended.... Additionally, the jury could have discredited Wilen's testimony that he assumed TLS Landscaping had permission to trim the tree as not plausible because when Story arrived, he went to Wilen's house, not to Falkenstein's. And Story did not ask if Wilen knew which of Falkenstein's trees he was supposed to trim, as he would have done if he had obtained Falkenstein's permission to trim his trees. Nor did Story give any indication that Falkenstein had requested TLS Landscaping to trim the view-blocking tree. Instead, Story reported to Wilen's home to perform whatever work Wilen requested, and when Wilen said that he wanted a tree trimmed, Story asked which tree and how much. Wilen pointed out Falkenstein's tree and indicated that five feet should be cut off the top of the tree. This evidence is sufficient to permit the jury to find that the conduct of Wilen, through his use of TLS Landscaping, constituted a specific intent to cause substantial injury to Falkenstein.... We hold that the jury's finding that the harm to Falkenstein resulted from Wilen's malicious trespass is supported by clear and convincing evidence....

b. Amount of Exemplary Damages

...Wilen argues that the exemplary damages award is excessive.... We may only reverse if the exemplary

damages award is so against the great weight and preponderance of the evidence as to be manifestly unjust....

We begin by noting that the jury's award of $18,000.00 in exemplary damages is less than $200,000.00 and is therefore within the statutory exemplary damages cap.... The amount of exemplary damages rests largely in the discretion of the jury and should not be disturbed unless the damages are so large as to indicate that they are the result of passion, prejudice, or corruption.

Here, evidence existed from which the jury could have found that Wilen intentionally disregarded the wishes of his neighbor, Falkenstein. Falkenstein wanted to care for his own trees. Wilen wanted his neighbor's tree to be trimmed back drastically because it blocked Wilen's balcony view of the clubhouse. When Falkenstein rebuffed Wilen's offers to pay to have the tree trimmed, Wilen took matters into his own hands. He directed TLS Landscaping to enter Falkenstein's property and to trim five feet off the top of the tree while his neighbor was vacationing. Despite Story's warning that "topping" the tree was inappropriate and abnormal, Wilen proceeded, disregarding Falkenstein's superior property rights and Story's warning and subjecting his neighbor's property to his own wishes. Evidence further revealed that Wilen had a net worth of over $496,000.00, not including his home and the other assets he owned jointly with his wife. The character of Wilen's conduct, his degree of culpability, the situation and sensibility of the parties involved, and a public sense of justice, as well as Wilen's significant net worth, support the award of $18,000.00 in exemplary damages....

IV. CHARGE ERROR....

A. Attorney's Fees Question

Wilen argues that the trial court erred by overruling his objections to jury charge questions on attorney's fees and by entering judgment on the jury's determination of attorney's fees because attorney's fees are not recoverable in this case....

To recover attorney's fees, a party must prove entitlement by contract or statute....

Falkenstein's action was not founded on the interpretation of a contract, and attorney's fees were not authorized by statute.... Because Falkenstein did not seek recovery of his attorney's fees as a sanction and because attorney's fees are not authorized by statute or contract in this case, we hold that the trial court erred by submitting questions to the jury regarding attorney's fees and by entering judgment on the jury's finding awarding Falkenstein attorney's fees of $29,700.00....

V. Conclusion

... [W]e modify the judgment by deleting the award of attorney's fees to Falkenstein.... As modified, we affirm the trial court's judgment....

Case Questions

1. What must be present to justify an award of punitive damages?
2. What kinds of activities did the court indicate the jury could have considered that would have sustained its conclusion that Wilen acted maliciously in committing the trespass?

ETHICS The Texas Court of Appeals stated in its opinion that "The character of Wilen's conduct, his degree of culpability, the situation and sensibility of the parties involved, and a public sense of justice, as well as Wilen's significant net worth, support the award of $18,000.00 in exemplary damages...." Given the fact that Falkenstein's property value did not decline as a result of the decapitation of his tree, do you think Wilen should have been awarded punitive damages as well as compensatory damages in this case?

Nominal Damages

If a defendant breaches a legal duty owed to the plaintiff and injures that person, compensatory damages may be awarded. The compensatory damages are measured by the amount of the loss. **Nominal damages** are awarded when there has been a breach of an agreement or an invasion of a right but there is no evidence of any specific harm. This occurs, for example, if a person trespasses on your land but causes no actual harm. In such a situation, the plaintiff would only be entitled to a judgment for a trivial amount, such as $1 or $50. The judge awards this token sum to vindicate the plaintiff's claim or to establish a legal right. Nominal damages also are awarded when a plaintiff proves breach of duty and harm but neglects to prove the value of the loss. They are likewise allowable when the defendant's invasion of the plaintiff's rights produces a benefit.

Courts award nominal damages because a judgment for money damages is the only way a common law court can establish the validity of the plaintiff's claim. Students should be careful not to confuse nominal charges with small compensatory damage awards, which are awarded when the actual loss was minor.

Liquidated Damages

Parties may agree, in advance, about the amount to be paid as compensation for loss in the event of a breach of contract. **Liquidated damages** are the stipulated sum contained in such an agreement. An example can be seen in the *Campbell Soup* case (page 237), where Campbell's contract with the Wentz brothers included a provision for damages of $50 per acre if the contract were breached. If the court determines that the amount stipulated in the agreement is a punishment used to prevent a breach rather than an estimate of actual damages, it will deem that sum a penalty and refuse to enforce it. Traditionally, the court upholds a liquidated damage clause only when (1) the damages in case of breach are uncertain or difficult to compute, (2) the parties have agreed in advance to liquidate the damages, and (3) the amount agreed on is reasonable and not disproportionate to the probable loss. Another form of liquidated damages results when money is deposited to guarantee against future damages.

Occasionally, a plaintiff who has suffered no actual damages can recover substantial liquidated damages; however, this occurs only rarely. Some courts require plaintiffs to prove some actual loss before the liquidated damage clause is triggered.

EQUITABLE REMEDIES

An equitable remedy would have been awarded by a court of equity before the merger of equity and the common law courts. Today, most courts in the United States are empowered to grant both equitable and legal relief as required to achieve justice. However, the availability of equitable remedies is a matter for judges and not juries. Traditionally, courts only grant equitable remedies when the common law remedies are inadequate.

Injunctions

An injunction is an equitable remedy in the form of a judicial order directing the defendant to act or refrain from acting in a specified way. An order compelling one to do an act is called a **mandatory injunction**, whereas one prohibiting an act is called a **prohibitory injunction**. An injunction may be enforced by the contempt power of a court, and a defendant may be fined, sent to jail, or deprived of the right to litigate issues if he or she disobeys an injunction. This order must be obeyed until it is reversed, even if it is issued erroneously or the court lacks jurisdiction.

Injunctions may be divided into three classes: (1) permanent, (2) preliminary or interlocutory, and (3) temporary restraining orders. A permanent injunction is a decree issued after a full opportunity to present evidence. It is permanent only in the sense that it is supposed to be a final solution to a dispute. It may still be modified or dissolved later. A preliminary or interlocutory injunction is granted as an emergency measure before a full hearing is held. There must be notice to the defendant and a hearing, usually informal. This remedy is generally limited to situations in which there is a serious need to preserve the status quo until the parties' rights have finally been decided. Thus a preliminary injunction continues only until a further order of the court is issued.

The temporary restraining order, known as a TRO, is an **ex parte** injunction. This means that it is granted without notice to the defendant. The trial judge has heard only the plaintiff's side of the case. Because of the potential for abuse, certain procedures protect a defendant. A TRO may not be granted unless irreparable harm would result and there is no time for notice and a hearing. There must be clear evidence on the merits of the case. The court should look at any damage to the defendant that would be noncompensable in money if the plaintiff's relief is later shown to be improper. This consideration must be balanced with the plaintiff's harm if the TRO is not granted. Factors weigh more heavily against the plaintiff, since there is no notice to defendant.

Certain classes of cases are not considered proper subject matter for injunctions. In general, an injunction is not issued to stop a criminal prosecution or to prevent crimes. However, this policy has been modified in recent years by regulatory statutes and civil rights statutes. Injunctions are usually not proper in defamation cases because they would intrude on the defendant's constitutional right of free speech and would be considered prior restraint.

INTERNET TIP

The case of *Harper v. Poway Unified School District*, which follows, was decided by a panel of three judges assigned to the U.S. Court of Appeals for the Ninth Circuit. Two judges concluded that the federal district court's decision not to enjoin the school district should be affirmed. The third judge, Judge Kozinski, disagreed and wrote a lengthy, thought-provoking dissenting opinion. Judge Kozinski was greatly concerned about the adequacy of the proof and the potential implications of the majority's decision on the legitimate exercise of First Amendment freedoms by high school students.

Students who read both opinions will notice how judges on both sides of the debate engaged in a balancing of the interests and the harm, which is a hallmark of equity courts. An edited version of Judge Kozinski's dissent can be read on the textbook's website.

The facts in the case of *Harper v. Poway Unified School District* have been summarized in order to enhance understanding and to conserve space.

Summary of Facts in *Harper v. Poway Unified School District*

Tyler Chase Harper (hereafter Chase) was a high school sophomore attending a school that had experienced conflict over the issue of sexual orientation. The administration of the school, in conjunction with students who had formed a group called the Gay-Straight Alliance, organized what was called a "Day of Silence," purportedly for the purpose of promoting tolerance between gay and straight students. This first "Day of Silence" was followed shortly thereafter by a "Straight-Pride Day," which was loosely sponsored by an opposing group of students. There were incidents involving name-calling; the wearing of special T-shirts, some of which displayed disparaging statements; and at least one physical confrontation in which the principal had to separate students.

When the Gay-Straight Alliance sought to sponsor a second "Day of Silence" in 2004, the school administration insisted that some planning be undertaken to prevent a repetition of the altercations and confrontations that had occurred in 2003.

On April 21, 2004, the date for the 2004 "Day of Silence," Chase wore a T-shirt to school which contained statements on both the front and back that disparaged homosexuality. The following day he wore the same shirt to school but this time the message on the shirt's front was slightly altered. One of Chase's teachers noticed the shirt, unsuccessfully requested that Chase remove it, and referred Chase to the principal's office for violating the dress code. The vice principal talked to Chase and explained the purported purpose of the "Day of Silence," and said that he could return to class only if he changed his shirt. A similar scenario followed when Chase met with the school principal. When Chase asked to be suspended, the principal declined. Chase spent the remainder of the school day in the office doing homework and then went home. Chase was not sanctioned in any way for not having attended classes on that day.

Forty-two days later, Chase filed suit in federal court claiming that the school had violated his First Amendment rights to freedom of speech and religion, as well as rights protected by the Equal Protection and Due Process Clauses under the federal Constitution and the California Civil Code. The school asked the trial court to dismiss the suit, and Chase asked the court for a preliminary injunction prohibiting the school from violating his constitutionally protected rights.

The district court dismissed Chase's due process and equal protection and civil code claims, and dismissed his damage claim against the school district because of the district's qualified immunity. The court refused to dismiss the First Amendment claims. The judge also denied Chase's preliminary injunction request, which decision he appealed to the U.S. Court of Appeals for the Ninth Circuit.

Tyler Chase Harper v. Poway Unified School District
445 F.3d 1166
U.S. Court of Appeals for the Ninth Circuit
April 20, 2006, as amended May 31, 2006

Reinhardt, Circuit Judge:
May a public high school prohibit students from wearing T-shirts with messages that condemn and denigrate other students on the basis of their sexual orientation? Appellant ... [who] was ordered not to wear [such] a T-shirt to school ... appeals the district court's order denying his motion for a preliminary injunction....

IV. Standard and Scope of Review
For a district court to grant a preliminary injunction, the moving party must demonstrate either "(1) a combination of probable success on the merits and the possibility of irreparable harm; or (2) that serious questions are raised and the balance of hardships tips in its favor."... "Each of these two formulations requires an examination of both the potential merits

of the asserted claims and the harm or hardships faced by the parties." ..."These two alternatives represent extremes of a single continuum, rather than two separate tests,..." Accordingly, "the greater the relative hardship to the moving party, the less probability of success must be shown." ...

We review a district court's grant or denial of a preliminary injunction for abuse of discretion.... Where, as here, the appellant does not dispute the district court's factual findings, we are required to determine "whether the court employed the appropriate legal standards governing the issuance of a preliminary injunction and whether the district court correctly apprehended the law with respect to the underlying issues in the case." ...

V. Analysis
1. Freedom of Speech Claim
The district court concluded that Harper failed to demonstrate a likelihood of success on the merits of his claim that the School violated his First Amendment right to free speech because, under *Tinker v. Des Moines Indep. Cmty. Sch. Dist.*, the evidence in the record was sufficient to permit the school officials to "reasonably ... forecast substantial disruption of or material interference with school activities." ...

a. Student Speech Under Tinker
Public schools are places where impressionable young persons spend much of their time while growing up. They do so in order to receive what society hopes will be a fair and full education—an education without which they will almost certainly fail in later life, likely sooner rather than later.... The public school, with its free education, is the key to our democracy.... Almost all young Americans attend public schools....

The courts have construed the First Amendment as applied to public schools in a manner that attempts to strike a balance between the free speech rights of students and the special need to maintain a safe, secure and effective learning environment.... Although public school students do not "shed their constitutional rights to freedom of speech or expression at the schoolhouse gate," ...the Supreme Court has declared that "the First Amendment rights of students in public schools are not automatically coextensive with the rights of adults in other settings, and must be applied in light of the special characteristics of the school environment." ...Thus, while Harper's shirt embodies the very sort of political speech that would be afforded First Amendment protection outside of the public school setting, his rights in the case before us must be determined "in light of [those] special characteristics." ...

This court has identified "three distinct areas of student speech," each of which is governed by different Supreme Court precedent: (1) vulgar, lewd, obscene, and plainly offensive speech ... (2) school-sponsored speech ... and (3) all other speech....

In *Tinker*, the Supreme Court confirmed a student's right to free speech in public schools.... In balancing that right against the state interest in maintaining an ordered and effective public education system, however, the Court declared that a student's speech rights could be curtailed under two circumstances. First, a school may regulate student speech that would "impinge upon the rights of other students." ...Second, a school may prohibit student speech that would result in "substantial disruption of or material interference with school activities." ...

I. The Rights of Other Students
In *Tinker*, the Supreme Court held that public schools may restrict student speech which "intrudes upon ... the rights of other students" or "collides with the rights of other students to be secure and to be let alone." ...Harper argues that *Tinker*'s reference to the "rights of other students" should be construed narrowly to involve only circumstances in which a student's right to be free from direct physical confrontation is infringed.... Harper contends that ... a student must be physically accosted in order to have his rights infringed.

... The law does not support Harper's argument. This court has explained that vulgar, lewd, obscene, indecent, and plainly offensive speech "by definition, may well 'impinge upon the rights of other students,'" even if the speaker does not directly accost individual students with his remarks.... So too may other speech capable of causing psychological injury....

We conclude that Harper's wearing of his T-shirt "collides with the rights of other students" in the most fundamental way.... Public school students who may be injured by verbal assaults on the basis of a core identifying characteristic such as race, religion, or sexual orientation have a right to be free from such attacks while on school campuses. As *Tinker* clearly states, students have the right to "be secure and to be let alone." ... Being secure involves not only freedom from physical assaults but from psychological attacks that cause young people to question their self-worth and their rightful place in society.... The "right to be let alone" has been recognized by the Supreme Court, of course, as "'the most comprehensive of rights and the right most valued by civilized men.'" ... Although name-calling is ordinarily protected outside the school context, "students cannot hide behind the First

Amendment to protect their 'right' to abuse and intimidate other students at school." ...

Speech that attacks high school students who are members of minority groups that have historically been oppressed, subjected to verbal and physical abuse, and made to feel inferior, serves to injure and intimidate them, as well as to damage their sense of security and interfere with their opportunity to learn.... The demeaning of young gay and lesbian students in a school environment is detrimental not only to their psychological health and well-being, but also to their educational development. Indeed, studies demonstrate that "academic underachievement, truancy, and dropout are prevalent among homosexual youth and are the probable consequences of violence and verbal and physical abuse at school." ... it is well established that attacks on students on the basis of their sexual orientation are harmful not only to the students' health and welfare, but also to their educational performance and their ultimate potential for success in life.

Those who administer our public educational institutions need not tolerate verbal assaults that may destroy the self-esteem of our most vulnerable teenagers and interfere with their educational development.... To the contrary, the School had a valid and lawful basis for restricting Harper's wearing of his T-shirt on the ground that his conduct was injurious to gay and lesbian students and interfered with their right to learn....

We consider here only whether schools may prohibit the wearing of T-shirts on high school campuses and in high school classes that flaunt demeaning slogans, phrases or aphorisms relating to a core characteristic of particularly vulnerable students and that may cause them significant injury. We do not believe that the schools are forbidden to regulate such conduct....

In his declaration in the district court, the school principal justified his actions on the basis that "any shirt which is worn on campus which speaks in a derogatory manner towards an individual or group of individuals is not healthy for young people...." If, by this, the principal meant that all such shirts may be banned under *Tinker*, we do not agree. T-shirts proclaiming "Young Republicans Suck" or "Young Democrats Suck," for example, may not be very civil but they would certainly not be sufficiently damaging to the individual or the educational process to warrant a limitation on the wearer's First Amendment rights. Similarly, T-shirts that denigrate the President, his administration, or his policies, or otherwise invite political disagreement or debate, including debates

over the war in Iraq, would not fall within the "rights of others" *Tinker* prong....

Although we hold that the School's restriction of Harper's right to carry messages on his T-shirt was permissible under *Tinker*, we reaffirm the importance of preserving student speech about controversial issues generally and protecting the bedrock principle that students "may not be confined to the expression of those sentiments that are officially approved." ...Limitations on student speech must be narrow, and applied with sensitivity and for reasons that are consistent with the fundamental First Amendment mandate. Accordingly, we limit our holding to instances of derogatory and injurious remarks directed at students' minority status such as race, religion, and sexual orientation.... Moreover, our decision is based not only on the type and degree of injury the speech involved causes to impressionable young people, but on the locale in which it takes place.... Thus, it is limited to conduct that occurs in public high schools (and in elementary schools). As young students acquire more strength and maturity, and specifically as they reach college age, they become adequately equipped emotionally and intellectually to deal with the type of verbal assaults that may be prohibited during their earlier years. Accordingly, we do not condone the use in public colleges or other public institutions of higher learning of restrictions similar to those permitted here.

Finally, we emphasize that the School's actions here were no more than necessary to prevent the intrusion on the rights of other students. Aside from prohibiting the wearing of the shirt, the School did not take the additional step of punishing the speaker: Harper was not suspended from school nor was the incident made a part of his disciplinary record.

Under the circumstances present here, we conclude that ... the district court did not abuse its discretion in finding that Harper failed to demonstrate a likelihood of success on the merits of his free speech claim....

b. Viewpoint Discrimination

In reaching our decision that Harper may lawfully be prohibited from wearing his T-shirt, we reject his argument that the School's action constituted impermissible viewpoint discrimination. The government is generally prohibited from regulating speech "when the specific motivating ideology or the opinion or perspective of the speaker is the rationale for the restriction." ... However, as the district court correctly pointed out, speech in the public schools is not always governed by the same rules that apply in other circumstances.... Indeed, the Court in *Tinker* held that a school may prohibit student speech, even if the consequence is viewpoint discrimination, if the speech violates the rights of other students or is materially disruptive....

The dissent claims that although the School may have been justified in banning discussion of the subject of sexual orientation altogether, it cannot "gag only those who oppose the Day of Silence." ... As we have explained, however, although *Tinker* does not allow schools to restrict the non-invasive, non-disruptive expression of political viewpoints, it does permit school authorities to restrict "one particular opinion" if the expression would "impinge upon the rights of other students" or substantially disrupt school activities.... Accordingly, a school may permit students to discuss a particular subject without being required to allow them to launch injurious verbal assaults that intrude upon the rights of other students. "A school need not tolerate student speech that is inconsistent with its basic educational mission, even though the government could not censor similar speech outside the school." ... Part of a school's "basic educational mission" is the inculcation of "fundamental values of habits and manners of civility essential to a democratic society." ... For this reason, public schools may permit, and even encourage, discussions of tolerance, equality and democracy without being required to provide equal time for student or other speech espousing intolerance, bigotry or hatred. As we have explained ... because a school sponsors a "Day of Religious Tolerance," it need not permit its students to wear T-shirts reading, "Jews Are Christ-Killers" or "All Muslims Are Evil Doers." ... In sum, a school has the right to teach civic responsibility and tolerance as part of its basic educational mission; it need not as a quid pro quo permit hateful and injurious speech that runs counter to that mission....

2. Free Exercise of Religion Claim

Harper ... asserts that his wearing of the T-shirt was "motivated by sincerely held religious beliefs" regarding homosexuality ... and that the School "punished" him for expressing them, or otherwise burdened the exercise of those views. Additionally, Harper argues that the School "attempted to change" his religious views and that this effort violated both the Free Exercise Clause and the Establishment Clause.

The Free Exercise Clause of the First Amendment provides that Congress shall make no law "prohibiting the free exercise" of religion.... The Clause prohibits the government from "compelling affirmation of religious belief, punishing the expression of religious doctrines it believes to be false, imposing special disabilities on the basis of religious views or religious status, or lending its power to one or the other side in controversies over religious authority or dogma." ...

We seriously doubt that there is "a fair probability or a likelihood" that Harper's claim that a companion right—free speech—has been violated will succeed on the merits.... The record simply does not demonstrate that the School's restriction regarding Harper's T-shirt imposed a substantial burden upon the free exercise of Harper's religious beliefs. There is no evidence that the School "compelled affirmation of a repugnant belief," "penalized or discriminated against [Harper] because [he] holds religious views abhorrent to the authorities," or "conditioned the availability of benefits upon [Harper's] willingness to violate a cardinal principle of [his] religious faith." ... Nor did the School "lend its power to one or the other side in controversies over religious authority or dogma," or "punish the expression of religious doctrines it believes to be false." ...

Schools may prohibit students and others from disrupting the educational process or causing physical or psychological injury to young people entrusted to their care, whatever the motivations or beliefs of those engaged in such conduct. Indeed, the state's interest in doing so is compelling....

Accordingly, we affirm the district court's decision that Harper was not entitled to a preliminary injunction on the basis of his free exercise claim.

3. Establishment Clause Claim

Finally, we consider the district court's conclusion that Harper did not demonstrate a likelihood of success on the merits of his claim that the School violated the Establishment Clause by attempting to "coerce" him into changing his religious beliefs that "homosexuality is harmful to both those who practice it and the community at large." ...

Government conduct does not violate the Establishment Clause when (1) it has a secular purpose, (2) its principal and primary effect neither advances nor inhibits religion, and (3) it does not foster excessive government entanglement in religion.... It is ... clear from the record that the primary effect of the School's banning of the T-shirt was not to advance or inhibit religion but to protect and preserve the educational environment and the rights of other members of the student body....

VI. Conclusion

We hold that the district court did not abuse its discretion in denying the preliminary injunction. Harper failed to demonstrate that he will likely prevail on the merits of his free speech, free exercise of religion, or establishment of religion claims. In fact, such future success on Harper's part is highly unlikely, given the legal principles discussed in this opinion. The Free Speech Clause permits public schools to restrict student speech that intrudes upon the rights of other students. Injurious speech that may be so limited is not immune from regulation simply because it reflects the speaker's religious views. Accordingly, we affirm the district court's denial of Harper's motion for a preliminary injunction. AFFIRMED; REMANDED for further proceedings consistent with this opinion.

Case Questions

1. How did the court of appeals go about determining whether the injunction should have been granted by the district court judge?
2. Why did the Ninth Circuit panel affirm the trial court?
3. If you were writing an opinion in this case, would you agree with the panel majority?

Reformation and Rescission

The equitable remedy of reformation is granted when a written agreement fails to express accurately the parties' agreement because of mistake, fraud, or the drafter's ambiguous language. Its purpose is to rectify or reform a written instrument in order that it may express the real agreement or intention of the parties.

The equitable remedy of rescission is granted when one of the parties consents to a contract because of duress, undue influence, fraud, or innocent misrepresentation, or when either or both of the parties made a mistake concerning the contract. Rescission means the court cancels the agreement. If a court orders rescission, each party normally has to return any property or money received from the other party in performance of the agreement (*restitution*). This topic, with an illustrative case (*Carter v. Matthews*), is addressed in Chapter X.

The following case involves a contractor who was the successful bidder on a public construction contract. The contractor made a unilateral error in computing his bid and subsequently brought suit seeking the equitable remedy of reformation. The appellate court majority ruled that the plaintiff was not entitled to reformation. The dissenting judge disagreed on the basis of the defendant's inequitable conduct. The majority opinion also discusses the equitable remedy of rescission and explains why the plaintiff has waived any claim to that remedy.

Department of Transportation v. Ronlee, Inc.
518 So.2d 1326
District Court of Appeal of Florida, Third District
December 22, 1987

Per Curiam

The threshold question presented is whether the successful bidder for a government road construction contract is entitled to reformation of the contract to increase the price by $317,463 based on a unilateral mistake, after the competing bids are all opened, where the new contract price would still be lower than the second lowest bid.

The Department of Transportation (DOT) solicited bids pursuant to section 337.11, Florida Statutes (1985), for the construction of an interchange at the intersection of State Road 826 and Interstate 75

in Hialeah. On December 7, 1983, DOT declared Ronlee, Inc. the apparent low bidder with a bid of $15,799,197.90. The second lowest bid exceeded Ronlee's bid by $610,148.

On February 13, 1984, DOT entered into a contract with Ronlee to construct the project based on the bid, and on March 7, 1984, gave Ronlee notice to proceed with the project. Five days later, Ronlee advised DOT that the bid contained a "stupid mistake" in the amount of $317,463. The letter alleged an error with respect to the unit price for concrete culverts which occurred when an employee of Ronlee erroneously transcribed a phone quote of $525 for each culvert as $5.25 each. By letter dated March 21, 1984, DOT informed Ronlee that it was aware of the apparently unbalanced unit price for the concrete culverts, but that it was unable, as a matter of state policy, to permit an increase in the contract price.

Nevertheless, on March 22, 1984, having made no effort to withdraw the bid, Ronlee began construction of the project. Twenty-one months later, with the project seventy-five percent completed, Ronlee filed suit against DOT seeking reformation of the contract. Both sides moved for a summary judgment, agreeing that the material facts were not in dispute. Ronlee's motion for summary judgment was granted, the trial court holding that DOT's silence about Ronlee's apparent error in price calculations constituted inequitable conduct and that reformation of the contract would not undermine the competitive bidding process. In addition to the $317,463, the court awarded Ronlee $60,000 in prejudgment interest and costs. We reverse.

Where a contractor makes a unilateral error in formulating his bid for a public contract, the remedy is rescission of the contract…. Florida courts have permitted a contractor to *withdraw* a bid on a public contract, subject to certain equitable conditions. In *State Board of Control v. Clutter Construction Corp.* … a contractor was permitted to withdraw a bid on a showing of the following equitable factors: (1) the bidder acted in good faith in submitting the bid; (2) in preparing the bid there was an error of such magnitude that enforcement of the bid would work severe hardship upon the bidder; (3) the error was not a result of gross negligence or willful inattention; (4) the error was discovered and communicated to the public body, *along with a request for permission to withdraw the bid*, before acceptance.

No reported Florida decision has permitted reformation by belated request of a bid contract for a public project in order to make it profitable to the contractor. *Graham v. Clyde* … is the only case presented by the parties where reformation was even sought as relief for a mistaken bid. There a building contractor was low bidder on a proposal to construct a public school building and was awarded the contract. The following day he notified public officials that he had made a mistake of $5,000 in computing items in his bid and asked to be relieved of his obligation to perform according to the contract terms. He offered to perform the contract for $5,000 more, which was still less than the next low bidder. The circuit court did not grant a reformation but did rescind the contract and enjoined the school board from attempting to enforce it.

The Florida Supreme Court, citing a number of cases from other jurisdictions, reversed, holding that unilateral errors are not generally relieved and that there was no equitable basis for relief. In an opinion by Justice Terrell the court stated the reason for the firm rule:

> "If errors of this nature can be relieved in equity, our system of competitive bidding on such contracts would in effect be placed in jeopardy and there would be no stability whatever to it. It would encourage careless, slipshod bidding in some cases and would afford a pretext for the dishonest bidder to prey on the public…. After the bid is accepted, the bidder is bound by his error and is expected to bear the consequence of it." …

The prevailing view is that reformation is not the appropriate form of relief for unilateral mistakes in public contract bids where the bidder is negligent…. The reason for not permitting reformation of bid contracts for public projects based on unilateral mistake is the same in other jurisdictions—to prevent collusive schemes between bidders, or between bidders and awarding officials, or multiple claims from contractors asserting mistake and claiming inequity at taxpayers' expense….

A written instrument may be reformed where it fails to express the intention of the parties as a result of mutual mistake, or unilateral mistake accompanied by inequitable conduct by the other party…. Because the mistake in this instance was admittedly unilateral, in order to obtain reformation of the contract, Ronlee was obligated to show by clear and convincing evidence that DOT's conduct in not calling Ronlee's attention to a possible error in the bid tabulations was fraudulent or otherwise inequitable…. That burden was not carried. The Department's failure to call Ronlee's attention to the error in calculation was of no consequence since Ronlee discovered its own error shortly after the Department learned of the miscalculation.

Competitive bidding statutes are enacted to protect the public and should be construed to avoid circumvention…. A government unit is not required to act for the protection of a contractor's interest; it is entitled to the bargain obtained in accepting the lowest responsible bid and is under no obligation to examine bids to ascertain errors and to inform bidders accordingly…. Absent an obligation to do so, failure of the government in this case to call the bidder's attention to a relatively minor two percent error in its calculations, after the bids were opened, was not such fraud or imposition as would entitle the bidder to reformation of the contract.

Further, Ronlee forfeited any right it may have had to reformation or rescission. It had knowledge of its own mistake at least ten days before commencement of construction. Ronlee's conduct in performing according to the terms of the agreement for twenty-one months instead of seeking to withdraw the bid, after DOT had advised that it could not administratively correct the error, effected a waiver of rights. *See Farnham v. Blount* ... (any unreasonable or unnecessary delay by a party seeking to cancel an instrument based on fraud or other sufficient cause will be construed as a waiver or ratification)....

Reversed and remanded with instructions to enter judgment for the Department of Transportation.

Hendry and Ferguson, JJ., concur.
Schwartz, Chief Judge, dissenting

With respect, I must dissent. The majority does not say that the record shows and the trial judge found just the inequitable conduct by the DOT which, under principles it acknowledges, renders reformation an entirely appropriate remedy; although the DOT was aware of the mistake when the bids were opened and well before construction commenced, it deliberately failed to inform the contractor of this fact. The final judgment under review contains, among others, the following, essentially undisputed determinations:

"(e) The Defendant acknowledged receipt of notice, *prior* to commencement of construction, of the existence of the error and further acknowledged that the Plaintiff's bid 'error was unintentional' and 'resulted from inexperienced personnel' generating a simple mathematical error by misplacing a decimal point and 'not comprehending the reasonableness of the money figures being used.' (Exhibit 'D' to Plaintiff's Motion).

"(f) Indeed, the Defendant even admitted that *prior* to the Plaintiff's March 12, 1984 notification to the Defendant, the Defendant had already been 'aware of the apparent unbalanced unit price of the item of Class II Concrete Culverts' (Exhibits 'D' and 'C' to Plaintiff's Motion; Plaintiff's Motion at 5–6, 9). Exhibit 'C', a December 19, 1983 computer print-out (entitled 'summary of bids') produced by Defendant during discovery, demonstrates that the 'apparent unbalanced unit price' with respect to the bids 'opened at Tallahassee, Florida on December 7, 1983' was known to Defendant promptly upon examination of the bids.

"3. The Court is therefore of the view that plaintiff has proved inequitable conduct by the Defendant by clear and convincing proof. Clearly, the Defendant was aware, or certainly should have been aware, that the unit item bid price for 400–2–1 Class II Concrete Culverts was one hundred (100) times less than the nearest unit price for the same item. However, the Defendant chose wrongfully to remain silent as to the existence of this error and, further, refused to act equitably after the Plaintiff had discovered the error and promptly acted to notify the Defendant of the error."

On this basis, the trial court held:

"4. While the Court is not unmindful of the fact that competitive bidding statutes should be construed to avoid circumvention, under the unique facts of the case *sub judice*, the integrity of the competitive bidding process will not be undermined with the granting of contract reformation. Where, as here, the differential between the mistaken bid and the second lowest bid exceeds the amount of the error sought to be reformed, no frustration or harm to beneficial purpose can fairly be demonstrated."

I entirely agree.

It is undisputed that, through a simple mistake in decimal point transcription, Ronlee was out and the DOT was in over $300,000 in material expenses. Short of reliance on the well-known playground maxim about keepers and weepers, there is no reason why the state should be entitled to retain this found money. Under ordinary reformation law, the combination of a unilateral mistake and inequitable conduct fully justifies that relief ... and no bases exist or are advanced for the application of a different rule merely because a process of competitive bidding is involved. Since the correction of the mistake would still bring the appellee under the next highest bid, no administratively difficult process of rebidding would be required and none of the purported horribles—"collusive schemes between bidders, or between bidders and awarding officials, or multiple claims from contractors asserting mistake and claiming inequity at taxpayers' expense" ... are even arguably implicated.... I would not refuse to reach a just result here because of the mechanical application of an unsupportable rule or out of a necessarily unjustified fear that someone may in the future misapply our holding in a materially different situation.

The very salutary Florida rule of unilateral mistake—which represents a minority view on the question ...—is that the courts will relieve one of the consequences of such an error and the opposite party should be deprived of any consequent windfall whenever there is neither a detrimental reliance upon the mistake nor an inexcusable lack of due care which led to its commission.... Neither is present in this case. While the law of our state says otherwise, the majority has permitted DOT successfully to play "gotcha" with Ronlee's money. The state, perhaps even more and certainly no less than a private party, should not be permitted to do so.... I would affirm.

Case Questions

1. Why did the trial court grant the plaintiff's summary judgment motion and order reformation in this case?
2. What is the difference between reformation and rescission of a contract?
3. Could Ronlee have rescinded the contract?

 What ethical consideration motivated Chief Judge Schwartz to dissent in this case?

Court of Conscience

In equity's early period, chancellors were almost always members of the clergy attempting to attain justice between parties to a dispute. A court of equity has always been considered to be a court of conscience in which natural justice and moral rights take priority over precedent. For example, a chancellor may decline to grant a plaintiff relief because of the plaintiff's wrongdoing in connection with the dispute. A chancellor may also decline to enforce a contract clause that is too unfair or one-sided. Such a clause would be declared to be **unconscionable**. To enforce it by granting equitable remedies would "shock the conscience of the court."

In the two cases that follow, the plaintiffs/appellants acted inequitably. Why did the courts in these cases decide that equitable relief was inappropriate?

Campbell Soup Company v. Wentz
172 F.2d 80
U.S. Court of Appeals, Third Circuit
December 23, 1948

Goodrich, Circuit Judge

These are appeals from judgments of the District Court denying equitable relief to the buyer under a contract for the sale of carrots....

The transactions which raise the issues may be briefly summarized. On June 21, 1947, Campbell Soup Company (Campbell), a New Jersey corporation, entered into a written contract with George B. Wentz and Harry T. Wentz, who are Pennsylvania farmers, for delivery by the Wentzes to Campbell of *all* the Chantenay red-cored carrots to be grown on fifteen acres of the Wentz farm during the 1947 season.... The contract provides ...for delivery of the carrots at the Campbell plant in Camden, New Jersey. The prices specified in the contract ranged from $23 to $30 per ton according to the time of delivery. The contract price for January 1948 was $30 a ton.

The Wentzes harvested approximately 100 tons of carrots from the fifteen acres covered by the contract. Early in January, 1948, they told a Campbell representative that they would not deliver their carrots at the contract price. The market price at that time was at least $90 per ton, and Chantenay red-cored carrots were virtually unobtainable.

On January 9, 1948, Campbell, suspecting that [defendant] was selling it[s] "contract carrots," refused to purchase any more, and instituted these suits against the Wentz brothers ... to enjoin further sale of the contract carrots to others, and to compel specific performance of the contract. The trial court denied equitable relief. We agree with the result reached, but on a different ground from that relied upon by the District Court.... A party may have specific performance of a contract for the sale of chattels if the legal remedy is inadequate. Inadequacy of the legal remedy is necessarily a matter to be determined by an examination of the facts in each particular instance.

We think that on the question of adequacy of the legal remedy the case is one appropriate for specific performance. It was expressly found that at the time of the trial it was "virtually impossible to obtain Chantenay carrots in the open market." This Chantenay carrot is one which the plaintiff uses in large quantities, furnishing the seed to the growers with whom it makes contracts. It was not claimed that in nutritive value it is any better than other types of carrots. Its blunt shape makes it easier to handle in processing. And its color and texture differ from other varieties. The color is brighter than other carrots.... It did appear that the plaintiff uses carrots in fifteen of its twenty-one soups. It also appeared that it uses these Chantenay carrots diced in some of them and that the appearance is uniform. The preservation of uniformity in appearance in a food article marketed throughout the country and sold under the manufacturer's name is a matter of considerable commercial significance and one which is properly considered in determining whether a substitute ingredient is just as good as the original.

The trial court concluded that the plaintiff had failed to establish that the carrots, "judged by objective standards," are unique goods. This we think is not a pure fact conclusion like a finding that Chantenay carrots are of uniform color. It is either a conclusion of law or of mixed fact and law and we are bound to exercise our independent judgment upon it. That the test for specific performance is not necessarily "objective" is shown by the many cases in which equity has given it to enforce contracts for articles—family heirlooms and the like—the value of which was personal to the plaintiff.

Judged by the general standards applicable to determining the adequacy of the legal remedy we think that on this point the case is a proper one for equitable relief. There is considerable authority, old and new, showing liberality in the granting of an equitable remedy. We see no reason why a court should be reluctant to grant specific relief when it can be given without supervision of the court or other time-consuming processes against one who has deliberately broken his agreement. Here the goods of the special type contracted for were unavailable on the open market, the plaintiff had contracted for them long ahead in anticipation of its needs, and had built up a general reputation for its products as part of which reputation uniform appearance was important. We think if this were all that was involved in the case, specific performance should have been granted.

The reason that we shall affirm instead of reversing with an order for specific performance is found in the contract itself. We think it is too hard a bargain and too one-sided an agreement to entitle the plaintiff to relief in a court of conscience. For each individual grower the agreement is made by filling in names and quantity and price on a printed form furnished by the buyer. This form has quite obviously been drawn by skillful draftsmen with the buyer's interests in mind.

Paragraph 2 provides for the manner of delivery. Carrots are to have their stalks cut off and be in clean sanitary bags or other containers approved by Campbell. This paragraph concludes with a statement that Campbell's determination of conformance with specifications shall be conclusive.

The defendants attack this provision as unconscionable. We do not think that it is, standing by itself. We think that the provision is comparable to the promise to perform to the satisfaction of another and that Campbell would be held liable if it refused carrots which did in fact conform to the specifications.

The next paragraph allows Campbell to refuse carrots in excess of twelve tons to the acre. The next contains a covenant by the grower that he will not sell carrots to anyone else except the carrots rejected by Campbell nor will he permit anyone else to grow carrots on his land. Paragraph 10 provides liquidated damages to the extent of $50 per acre for any breach by the grower. There is no provision for liquidated or any other damages for breach of contract by Campbell.

The provision of the contract which we think is the hardest is paragraph 9.... It will be noted that Campbell is excused from accepting carrots under certain circumstances. But even under such circumstances, the grower, while he cannot say Campbell is liable for failure to take the carrots, is not permitted to sell them elsewhere unless Campbell agrees. This is the kind of provision which the late Francis H. Bohlen would call "carrying a good joke too far." What the grower may do with his product under the circumstances set out is not clear. He has covenanted not to store it anywhere except on his own farm and also not to sell to anybody else.

We are not suggesting that the contract is illegal. Nor are we suggesting any excuse for the grower in this case who has deliberately broken an agreement entered into with Campbell. We do think, however, that a party who has offered and succeeded in getting an agreement as tough as this one is should not come to a chancellor and ask court help in the enforcement of its terms. That equity does not enforce unconscionable bargains is too well established to require elaborate citation.

The plaintiff argues that the provisions of the contract are separable. We agree that they are, but do not think that decisions separating out certain provisions from illegal contracts are in point here. As already said, we do not suggest that this contract is illegal. All we say is that the sum total of its provisions drives too hard a bargain for a court of conscience to assist....

The judgments will be affirmed.

Case Questions

1. If the plaintiff had sued for damages, would the result of the suit have been different?
2. Campbell Soup Company lost this case in its attempt to get equitable relief. May it now sue for money damages?
3. If the contract between Campbell Soup Company and Wentz were not unconscionable, would specific performance of the contract be an appropriate remedy? What is necessary before specific performance will be granted?

ETHICS Why did the court hold the contract to be unconscionable and therefore unenforceable in equity?

Equitable Maxims

Instead of using rules of law in reaching decisions, courts of equity used *equitable maxims*, which are short statements that contain the gist of much equity law. These maxims were developed over the years (with no agreement as to the number or order) and today are used as guides in the decision-making process in disputes in equity. The following are some of the equitable maxims:

Equity does not suffer a wrong to be without a remedy.

Equity regards substance rather than form.

Equality is equity.

Equity regards as done that which should be done.

Equity follows the law.

Equity acts *in personam* rather than *in rem*.

Whoever seeks equity must do equity.

Whoever comes into equity must do so with clean hands.

Delay resulting in a prejudicial change defeats equity (laches).

Isbell v. Brighton Area Schools
500 N.W.2d. 748
Court of Appeals of Michigan
April 5, 1993

Taylor, Judge
Defendants appeal as of right a December 1990 order denying defendants' motion for summary disposition and granting plaintiff's motion for summary disposition, both brought pursuant to MCR 2.116(C)(10). We reverse.

During each semester of the 1988–89 school year, plaintiff's senior year at Brighton High School, plaintiff was absent without excuse on more than six occasions. She was denied course credit under the school's attendance policy, and was ultimately denied a diploma.

Plaintiff sued defendants alleging constitutional, contract, and tort theories, and also raising equitable claims. The trial court ruled that plaintiff lacked an adequate remedy at law and was entitled to equitable relief (issuance of a diploma) because the school attendance policy was unreasonable. Accordingly, the trial court granted plaintiff's (and denied defendants') motion for summary disposition.

Because we conclude that plaintiff is barred from equitable relief by the clean hands doctrine, we need not and do not reach the question whether defendants' attendance policy was reasonable.

One who seeks the aid of equity must come in with clean hands. This maxim is an integral part of any action in equity, and is designed to preserve the integrity of the judiciary. The ... Court [has] described the clean hands doctrine as "a self-imposed ordinance that closes the doors of a court of equity to one tainted with inequitableness or bad faith relative to the matter in which he seeks relief, however improper may have been the behavior of the defendant. That doctrine is rooted in the historical concept of the court of equity as a vehicle for affirmatively enforcing the requirements of conscience and good faith. This pre-supposes a refusal on its part to be "the abettor of iniquity." ...

Plaintiff admittedly forged excuse notes, so she does not have clean hands. In determining whether the plaintiffs come before this Court with clean hands, the primary factor to be considered is whether the plaintiffs sought to mislead or deceive the other party, not whether that party relied upon plaintiff's misre-presentations.... Thus, it is plaintiff's deceit, not defendants' reliance on the forged notes, that deter-mines whether the clean hands doctrine should be applied. As Justice Cooley wrote:

> [I]f there are any indications of overreaching or unfairness on [equity plaintiff's] part, the court will refuse to entertain his case, and turn him over to the usual remedies.

We find that the clean hands doctrine applies to prevent plaintiff from securing the relief she requests. In view of our resolution of this matter, we do not reach the other issues raised.

Reversed.

Case Questions

1.   Why did the trial court believe that the plaintiff was entitled to an equitable remedy?
2.   Why did the appellate court reverse the trial court?

ETHICS   What is the practical significance of the equitable maxim called the *clean hands doctrine*?

Specific Performance

Specific performance is an equitable remedy that is identified with breaches of contract. The plaintiff brings suit to obtain a court order that requires the defendant to fulfill his or her contractual obliga-tions. Specific performance will only be granted where there is a valid contract.[1] It is enforced through the use of the contempt power.

Like all equitable relief, specific performance is limited to situations in which there is no adequate remedy at common law. This means that under the particular circumstances of the case, the plaintiff can establish that a breach of contract action for money damages is inadequate. We saw an example of this in the *Campbell* case. Campbell wanted the court to order the Wentz brothers to live up to their con-tractual obligations to deliver Chantenay carrots to Campbell. Campbell argued that requiring the Wentz brothers to pay Campbell $50 per acre in liquidated damages for breach of contract was an inadequate remedy. Campbell contended that it couldn't go out on the open market and purchase Chantenay carrots from another seller. There was no alternative source of supply.

Specific performance is usually applied in situa-tions involving contracts for the sale of land and unique goods. Common law relief is often inade-quate for unique goods, because one cannot take money damages and go out and purchase the same item. A similar item might be purchased, but that is not what the parties had bargained. The buyer had an agreement to purchase a particu-lar, unique property item. Thus, if a seller and buyer have contracted for the sale of land, a paint-ing, sculpture, an antique car, or a baseball card collection, money damages are just not a substitute for the item. The Chantenay carrot was unique for Campbell soup. It was the only carrot that would work in the machinery. Consumers of Campbell soups were accustomed to that particular carrot's firmness, consistency, color, and taste.

A plaintiff must have substantially performed, or be ready to perform, his or her obligations under the contract in order to be entitled to specific performance. This is referred to as a condition precedent for specific performance.

In addition, equity courts are concerned with practicality. For example, an equitable court generally will not order one person to fulfill a personal service contract and perform work for another. Such a decree would be tantamount to involuntary servitude. It is also impractical for a court to require one person to work for another. Such an order could involve the court in a never-ending series of employer-employee spats.

A defendant can assert various equitable defenses in response to a plaintiff's claim for specific performance. These include (1) unclean hands (see page 239), (2) hardship, and (3) laches. Hardship involves sharp practices where the contractual terms are entirely one-sided and where there is a gross inadequacy of consideration. Hardship exists because one party is attempting to take unfair advantage of the other party. Laches, as we saw in Chapter VI, is an equitable defense that is used to deny equitable relief where a plaintiff's unreasonable delay in bringing the action has caused prejudicial harm to the defendant. This defense is similar to the common law defense of statute of limitations. The equitable defense of *laches* does not involve any specific period of time.

Contracts for the sale of goods are governed by the Uniform Commercial Code (UCC).[2] The UCC provides buyers with a right to specific performance in 2-716, and sellers with an equivalent remedy in 2-709.

In *Bloch v. Hillel Torah North Suburban Day School*, Helen Bloch's parents brought suit to obtain a court order for specific performance of a contract to prevent the expulsion of their grade-school child from a private Jewish school.

Bloch v. Hillel Torah North Suburban Day School
426 N.E.2d 976
Appellate Court of Illinois, First District, Third Division
September 9, 1981

McNamara, Justice

Plaintiffs appeal from an order of the trial court granting summary judgment in favor of defendant Hillel Torah North Suburban Day School. Helen Bloch is a grade school child who was expelled from defendant, a private Jewish school, at mid-year in 1980. Her parents brought this action seeking to enjoin expulsion and for specific performance of defendant's contract to educate Helen.

The complaint alleged that defendant arbitrarily and in bad faith breached its contract, and that Helen's expulsion was motivated by defendant's disapproval of plaintiff's leadership role in combating an epidemic of head lice at the school. The complaint also alleged that the school uniquely corresponded exactly to the religious commitments desired by plaintiffs. Defendant's answer stated that Helen was expelled, pursuant to school regulations, for excessive tardiness and absences. The parties also disputed the duration of the contractual obligation to educate. Defendant contended that the contract was to endure only for a school year since tuition for only that period of time was accepted by it. Plaintiffs maintained that the contract, as implied by custom and usage, was to endure for eight years, the first year's tuition creating irrevocable option contracts for the subsequent school years, provided that Helen conformed to defendant's rules.

After the trial court denied plaintiff's request for a preliminary injunction, both sides moved for summary judgment. The trial court denied plaintiff's motion and granted the motion of the defendant. In the same order, the trial court gave plaintiffs leave to file an amended complaint for money damages.

Whether a court will exercise its jurisdiction to order specific performance of a valid contract is a matter within the sound discretion of the court and dependent upon the facts of each case.... Where the contract is one which establishes a personal relationship calling for the rendition of personal services, the proper remedy for a breach is generally not specific performance but rather an action for money damages.... The reasons for denying specific performance in such a case are as follows: the remedy at law is adequate; enforcement and supervision of the order of specific performance may be problematic and could result in protracted litigation; and the concept of compelling the continuance of a personal relationship to which one of the parties is resistant is repugnant as a form of involuntary servitude....

Applying these principles to the present case, we believe that the trial court properly granted summary judgment in favor of defendant. It is beyond dispute that the relationship between a grade school and a student is one highly personal in nature. Similarly, it is apparent that performance of such a contract requires a rendition of a variety of personal services. Although we are cognizant of the difficulties in duplicating the personal services offered by one school, particularly one like defendant, we are even more aware of the difficulties pervasive in compelling the continuation of a relationship between a young child and a private school which openly resists that relationship. In such a case, we believe the trial court exercises sound judgment in ruling that plaintiffs are best left to their remedy for damages....

Illinois law recognizes the availability of a remedy for monetary damages for a private school's wrongful expulsion of a student in violation of its contract.... And especially, where, as here, the issue involves a personal relationship between a grade school and a young child, we believe plaintiffs are best left to a remedy for damages for breach of contract.

For the reasons stated, the judgment of the circuit court of Cook County is affirmed, and the cause is remanded for further proceedings permitting plaintiffs to file an amended complaint for money damages.

Affirmed and remanded.

Rizzi, P. J., and McGillicuddy, J., concur.

Case Questions

1. What problems might have been encountered had the court ordered specific performance?
2. In what types of cases would specific performance be granted?

Restitution

The remedy of restitution is in some situations an equitable remedy and in other cases a common law remedy. **Restitution** means restoration to the plaintiff of property in the possession of the defendant. The purpose of restitution is to prevent unjust enrichment, which means that a person should not be allowed to profit or be enriched inequitably at another's expense. Thus a person is permitted recovery when another has received a benefit and retention of it would be unjust.

The restoration may be *in specie*, in which a specific item is recovered by the plaintiff from the defendant. In many situations, an *in specie* recovery is impossible or impractical. In such instances, the remedy might have to be "substitutionary," whereby the defendant is ordered to return to the plaintiff as restitution the dollar value of any benefit he or she has received. If so, the amount is determined by the defendant's gain, not by the plaintiff's loss, as in the case of money damages. So if D takes P's car, worth $4,000, and sells it to someone else at $8,000, D may be liable to make restitution to P for the full amount of $8,000. P never had $8,000, only a car worth half as much, but is still entitled to the total amount. If there was cash in the glove compartment, P would be entitled to recover that also.

The following case discusses restitution in both the common law and equitable contexts. The court first determines whether the plaintiff was entitled to a statutory mechanics lien or a common law lien. It is only after ruling the plaintiff ineligible for a lien under the common law that the court turns to equity. The balancing of interests and harm to produce a just result is clearly evidenced here. Observe how damages are computed in an unjust enrichment case. The court said the mechanic's recovery would be limited to the difference in a vehicle's value before and after it was repaired and he would not receive damages reflecting his hourly rate.

Iacomini v. Liberty Mutual Insurance Company
497 A.2d 854
Supreme Court of New Hampshire
August 7, 1985

Douglas, Justice

The issue presented in this case is whether a party may subject an owner's interest in an automobile to a lien for repair and storage charges, without the owner's knowledge, acquiescence, or consent. We hold that no common law or statutory lien may be created under such circumstances but that equitable relief for unjust enrichment may be appropriate.

On August 10, 1983, the plaintiff, Richard Iacomini, d/b/a Motor Craft of Raymond, contracted with one Theodore Zadlo for the towing, storage, and repair of a 1977 Mercedes Benz 450-SL. Mr. Zadlo represented himself to be the owner of the car and presented the plaintiff with a New Hampshire registration certificate for the car bearing Zadlo's name. In fact, the car did not belong to Mr. Zadlo but had been stolen in 1981 from a car lot in New Jersey. The defendant, Liberty Mutual Insurance Company, had earlier fulfilled its policy obligations by reimbursing the owner of the stolen car $22,000. It thereby had gained title to the vehicle.

Extensive damage was done to the car after its theft, and Zadlo brought the car to Mr. Iacomini for the purpose of repairing this damage. The plaintiff kept the car at his garage, where he disassembled it in order to give a repair estimate. He apparently never fully reassembled it. Mr. Zadlo periodically returned to the plaintiff's garage to check the status of the repair work.

In October 1983, the Raymond Police Department notified the plaintiff that the Mercedes was a stolen car and also notified Liberty Mutual of the location of the car. Mr. Iacomini at that point moved the vehicle from the lot to the inside of his garage where it remained for the next several months. Liberty Mutual contacted the plaintiff soon after it learned of the vehicle's location to arrange its pick-up. The plaintiff refused to relinquish the car until he had been reimbursed for repair and storage fees.

...Liberty Mutual instituted a replevin action ... seeking return of the car.... On the basis of facts presented at a hearing ... in the replevin action, the Court ... found that the plaintiff (defendant in that action) did not have a valid statutory lien since the vehicle was brought to the plaintiff by one other than the owner. The court then ordered Mr. Iacomini to make the vehicle available forthwith to Liberty Mutual with the proviso that Liberty Mutual retain the vehicle in its

possession and ownership for a period of at least ninety days in order to allow Mr. Iacomini the opportunity to file an action against Liberty Mutual relating to repairs.

The plaintiff petitioned for an *ex parte* attachment ... claiming approximately $10,000, most of which was for storage fees.... [T]he same court entered judgment in Liberty Mutual's favor finding that "the plaintiff was not authorized or instructed by the legal or equitable owner of the automobile to perform any repair work on the vehicle." On either the day before, or the day of, the hearing ... the plaintiff filed a Motion to Specify Claim to include an action for unjust enrichment. Liberty Mutual objected to the plaintiff's attempt to amend his cause of action at that date, and the court denied the motion. It also denied the plaintiff's requests for findings that the value of the car had been enhanced by the plaintiff and that denial of the plaintiff's claim would result in unjust enrichment. This appeal followed.

The law generally recognizes three types of liens: statutory, common law, and equitable.... The statutes provide as follows:

> For Storage. "Any person who maintains a public garage, public or private airport or hangar, or trailer court for the parking, storage or care of motor vehicles or aircraft or house trailers brought to his premises or placed in his care *by or with the consent of the legal or equitable owner* shall have a lien upon said motor vehicle or aircraft or house trailer, so long as the same shall remain in his possession, for proper charges due him for the parking, storage or care of the same." ...
>
> For Labor. "Any person who shall, by himself or others, perform labor, furnish materials, or expend money, in repairing, refitting or equipping any motor vehicle or aircraft, *under a contract expressed or implied with the legal or equitable owner*, shall have a lien upon such motor vehicle or aircraft, so long as the same shall remain in his possession, until the charges for such repairs, materials, or accessories, or money so used or expended have been paid." ...

"[I]n the case of a statutory lien, the specified requisites must be strictly observed." ...By the language of the statute, no lien may be created on an automobile as to the owner without the owner's knowledge, acquiescence, or consent. Under the present circumstances, where the repairman contracted with the possessor of a stolen vehicle for the repair of the car, it is difficult to imagine how the owner could have consented to, or acquiesced in, the repair of the vehicle. The owner in this case had no idea even where the car was located. Whether the plaintiff was reasonable in believing Mr. Zadlo to be the true owner is irrelevant to whether a contract existed between him and Liberty Mutual.

Prior to the passage of a statute on the subject of mechanics' liens, ... "there existed here and elsewhere a lien at common law in favor of anyone who upon request expended labor and materials upon another's property." ...The statutory lien does not supplant, but supplements, the common law mechanic's lien, so that we must also look to the rights of the plaintiff under the common law....

As with the statutory liens, common law liens on property for repair costs could be created only by the owner or by a person authorized by him. "By common law, every person, who employs labor and skill upon the goods of another, *at the request of the owner*, without a special contract, is entitled to retain the goods until a proper recompense is made." ...New Hampshire common law is consistent with the common law of other jurisdictions which also require the owner's consent or acquiescence before a lien may be established on the property of the owner....

The necessity of the owner's consent is consistent with the contractual relationship between the lienor and the lienee which underlies the establishment of a lien.... As discussed previously, no such contractual

relationship may be inferred where a possessor of a stolen vehicle turns it over to a garageman for repairs; accordingly, no lien is created against the owner. This is the correct result under the common law even though hardships may result to a good faith repairman. "There are many hard cases ... of honest and innocent persons, who have been obliged to surrender goods to the true owners without remedy.... But these are hazards to which persons in business are continually exposed." ...Of course, the repairman would always have a cause of action against the third party who contracted with him for repairs without the owner's consent.

Although the facts of this case do not establish either a statutory or common law lien, the plaintiff may be entitled to restitution under principles of equity. An equitable lien may be imposed to prevent unjust enrichment in an owner whose property was improved, for the increased value of the property.... "In the absence of a contractual agreement, a trial court may require an individual to make restitution for unjust enrichment if he has received a benefit which would be unconscionable to retain." ...The trial court must determine whether the facts and equities of a particular case warrant such a remedy....

We here note that "when a court assesses damages in an unjust enrichment case, the focus is not upon the cost to the plaintiff, but rather it is upon the value of what was actually received by the defendants." ...In this case, the damages would thus be the difference between the value of the vehicle before and after the plaintiff worked on it, regardless of its worth when stolen.

Reversed and remanded.

Case Questions

1. Why should the defendant insurance company be required to pay the plaintiff repairman for services that the plaintiff performed without the defendant's knowledge or consent?
2. What is an equitable lien? How does it work?
3. How does a judge determine the amount of an award in an unjust enrichment case?

Declaratory Judgment

When someone seeks a judicial determination of the rights and obligations of the parties, that person is seeking the remedy of *declaratory judgment*. The court determines what the law is, or the constitutionality or the meaning of the law. For example, if a legislative body passes a statute making your

business activity illegal, you could continue to operate the business and be arrested. You could also try to prevent the enforcement of the law by seeking a declaratory judgment. This action asks a court to determine whether the statute in question is constitutional. Because a judge granting declaratory judgment does not issue any orders telling anyone to act or refrain from acting, people who are seeking declaratory relief often ask for injunctive relief as well.

Declaratory judgment is considered by some courts to be an equitable remedy and by other courts to be a legal remedy.

Jury Trial

Cases are set for a jury trial only if a right to jury trial exists and one or both of the parties properly asserts this right. For the most part, trial by jury is a constitutional right. The Seventh Amendment to the U.S. Constitution guarantees litigants in federal court a jury trial in suits at common law, and most state constitutions make similar provisions. However, there is no constitutional right to a jury trial in equity cases because jury trials were not a part of chancery procedure.

Parties in most U.S. courts may join common law and equitable remedies in the same action without giving up their right to a jury trial. A jury decides the legal issues, and the judge decides the equitable issues.

INTERNET TIP

State v. Yelsen Land Company is a case in which the parties were seeking both equitable and legal relief. The state objected to being denied a jury trial with respect to issues that were inherently legal. Students can read this case on the textbook's website.

CHAPTER SUMMARY

Students were reminded to refresh their memories with respect to the historical characteristics of the law courts and equitable courts in England because their differences continue to have significance today. It is always important when discussing remedies to remember that equitable remedies are not available to a party who has adequate remedies available at law. It was emphasized that the primary common law remedy is the award of money damages. When a plaintiff establishes that the defendant has committed a tort or breached a contract, the remedy most requested is the award of money damages. Although there are some exceptions, it is generally true that a plaintiff so aggrieved is ultimately entitled to have the decision made as to whether money damages should be awarded in tort and contract cases by a jury. Readers learned about the four types of money damages: compensatory, punitive, nominal, and liquidated.

The use of the equitable remedy of injunction was explained, with particular attention paid to each of the three classes: permanent, preliminary (aka interlocutory), and temporary restraining orders. The three equitable remedies that apply to contract cases, reformation, rescission, and specific performance were explained, as were the two remedies that have roots in both equity and law, restitution, and declaratory judgment. The traditional role of equity as a "court of conscience" was also explained. A plaintiff, for example, may have suffered injury at the defendant's hands, but if the plaintiff has also acted inequitably, a judge may decide to deny the plaintiff any remedy in equity. This concept is reflected in two of the equitable maxims contained on page 239, which provide that "whoever seeks equity must do equity," and "whoever comes into equity must do so with clean hands."

CHAPTER QUESTIONS

1. The federal Food and Drug Administration ("FDA"), after warning Lane Labs on multiple occasions that it was marketing three of its products without having obtained necessary FDA approval, filed suit for a permanent injunction. The FDA alleged that the three

Lane Lab products in question were advertised to the public as remedies for cancer, HIV, and AIDS, and none were properly branded nor approved. The FDA's amended complaint requested injunctive relief and an order of restitution for consumers. The district court judge granted the FDA's summary judgment motion, permanently enjoined Lane Labs, and ordered restitution. Lane Labs appealed to the U.S. Court of Appeals for the Third Circuit, maintaining that the Federal Food, Drug and Cosmetic Act ("FDCA") only permitted the FDA to obtain injunctive relief in cases such as this, and did not authorize district courts to order restitution. Assume that there is no statutory provision authorizing federal judges to issue an order of restitution in FDA cases. Assume you are a judge having to decide this question. Based on your knowledge of the history of remedies, how should the court rule?

U.S. v. Lane Labs-USA Inc., 427 F.3d 219 (2005)

2. The plaintiff rented a Halloween costume to Sharp for $20. The rental agreement included a liquidated damages clause which stated, "an amount equal to one-half the rental fee will be charged for each day the costume is returned late." Sharp returned the costume seventy-nine days late and the plaintiff sued in small claims court.

   At a hearing before a referee, the plaintiff testified that he had lost one rental during the seventy-nine days. The referee awarded the plaintiff $500, noting that the plaintiff's complaint sought only that amount. Sharp filed objections to the referee's report, and the matter was brought to the trial court. It entered judgment against Sharp for $400. The case was appealed to the state intermediate appellate court. Should the appellate court affirm the trial court?

Lakewood Creative Costumers v. Sharp, 509 N.E.2d 77 (1986)

3. Richard and Darlene Parker leased an apartment from Sun Ridge Investors for $465 per month. The lease provided that the Parkers

would be charged a $25 late fee if the rent was not paid by the third day of the month, and $5 per day for each additional day until the account was paid in full. The Parkers were late in making their February 1995 rental payment, for which the landlord assessed the monthly and per diem late fees. The Parkers made their subsequent monthly rental payments in a timely manner, but the landlord, after informing the Parkers, applied their payments to the amount that was past due. The Parkers refused to pay the $5 per diem fee. Sun Ridge brought suit in state court seeking the right to forcibly enter and repossess the apartment and $330 in past due rent. The trial court granted judgment to the landlord, and the Parkers unsuccessfully appealed to the intermediate court of appeals. The Parkers appealed to the Supreme Court of Oklahoma. The landlord argued that the per diem fees were additional rent, but the Parkers contended the fees amounted to an unenforceable penalty. Should the Oklahoma Supreme Court affirm or reverse the lower court? Explain your reasoning.

Sun Ridge Investors, Ltd v. Parker, 956 P.2d 876 (1998)

4. El Paso Gas Company transports natural gas through pipelines to points throughout the country. TransAmerican is a natural gas producer. The two companies and their predecessors negotiated various contracts during the 1970s and 1980s. TransAmerica brought suit in 1988 against El Paso when the parties were unable to resolve several disagreements about their respective contractual rights and duties. The trial court entered judgment in favor of TransAmerica. While El Paso's appeal was pending, the parties negotiated a settlement agreement that resulted in the termination of all litigation by both sides, the payment of compensation to TransAmerica by El Paso, and a restructuring of their relationship. The agreement also included a choice of forum clause, which provided that a party, in the event of a breach, would have to bring suit in the Delaware Court of Chancery. In 1993,

TransAmerica filed suit against El Paso, in Texas, alleging, among other claims, breach of the settlement contract. El Paso responded by filing suit against TransAmerica in the Delaware Court of Chancery. The Delaware Chancery Court dismissed the petition on the grounds that it did not have jurisdiction, and the Delaware Supreme Court agreed. What was the fundamental problem that caused the court to rule that it did not have subject matter jurisdiction?

El Paso Natural Gas Company v. TransAmerican Natural Gas Company, 669 A.2d 36 (1995)

5. Plaintiff Whalen discovered upon his return from a trip that someone had left a message on his answering machine from an anonymous caller, to the effect that his dog had been found roaming at large, had been given poison, and would die within twenty-four hours unless the dog were treated immediately. Whalen took the dog to the veterinarian, who examined the animal and concluded that the dog had not ingested poison. Whalen filed suit for damages against Isaacs (the anonymous caller) for intentional infliction of emotional distress, believing that the story about the dog poisoning was a hoax. Under Georgia law, the question as to whether the facts supporting the plaintiff's claim are sufficiently outrageous to constitute the tort of intentional infliction of emotional distress is decided by the trial judge. Both parties moved for summary judgment. The plaintiff's evidence primarily consisted of incidents of conduct in which the defendant demonstrated hostility toward the plaintiff's dog when it was unleashed and allowed to run onto the defendant's property. The defendant, in a deposition, admitted making the telephone call, but explained that he was acting as a good Samaritan and made the call to help save the life of the dog. The defendant further claimed that he was only relaying what he had been told about the dog by an unknown bicyclist. Which party should be awarded judgment? Why?

Whalen v. Isaacs, 504 S.E. 2d. 214 (1998)

6. Chris Titchenal, the plaintiff, and Diane Dexter, the defendant, both women, were in an intimate relationship from 1985 until they broke up in 1994. Their home, cars, and bank accounts were jointly owned, and they had jointly acted as caretakers to Dexter's adopted daughter Sarah (who was named Sarah Ruth Dexter-Titchenal). The plaintiff had not sought to adopt the child jointly. Titchenal alleged that she was a de facto parent and had provided 65 percent of Sarah's care prior to the demise of her personal relationship with Dexter. Titchenal brought suit when Dexter severely cut off Titchenal's visitation opportunities with Sarah. The trial court granted Dexter's motion to dismiss the plaintiff's suit, because it concluded that Titchenal had no common law, statutory, constitutional, or compelling public policy right to visitation with Sarah. Titchenal appealed, contending that the trial court had equitable jurisdiction, in the best interest of the child, to grant "nontraditional" family members visitation rights where a parent-like situation existed, as in this instance. Do you agree with the trial court and the Vermont Supreme Court that equity has no jurisdiction in this case?

Titchenal v. Dexter, 693 A.2d 682 (1997)

NOTES

1. You can learn about the requirements of a valid contract by reading the brief discussion in Chapter I or the more detailed presentation in Chapter X. In general, a valid contract must be clear, the terms must be reasonably certain, and there must have been an agreement between

competent parties supported by consideration, which does not contravene principles of law and which in some circumstances must be in writing.

2. Please see the discussion on the Uniform Commercial Code in Chapter X and in the glossary.

VIII

✳

Criminal Law and Procedure

CHAPTER OBJECTIVES

1. *Understand the sources of American criminal law.*
2. *Describe the different classifications of crimes.*
3. *Explain how the federal constitution limits the imposition of criminal liability and punishment.*
4. *Understand and describe the basic components of a criminal offense.*
5. *Understand each of the justification and excuse defenses and how they differ.*
6. *Explain a defendant's rights to counsel under the Sixth and Fourteenth Amendments.*
7. *Understand why the Supreme Court came to require the Miranda warnings.*
8. *Describe why the Supreme Court created the exclusionary rule.*
9. *Describe the procedural steps in a typical criminal trial.*

This chapter introduces students to some of the fundamental principles of criminal law and criminal procedure. Each of these subjects is a course in itself; in one chapter it is only possible to examine some of the major issues associated with each topic, and even then the discussion has to be limited.

CRIMINAL LAW

William Blackstone, an English judge and author of *Commentaries on the Laws of England* (1765–1769), defined a crime as a wrong committed against the public,[1] a definition that is today still widely recognized as appropriate. Because the general public is injured when a crime is committed, as well as the person who was the perpetrator's targeted victim, the government and not the victim is responsible for deciding whether to initiate a criminal prosecution. It is the government's responsibility, and not the victim's, to investigate, prosecute, and punish those found by the courts to be criminally responsible. This public character of criminal prosecutions means that irrespective of the targeted victim's financial condition the government has an obligation to pay all the costs of investigating and litigating the action. If the accused is convicted and sentenced to incarceration, state-funded correctional institutions will become involved. If the court imposes a sentence of probation, probation officers will be assigned to supervise the probationer at public expense.

Civil remedies, burdens of proof, and court procedures differ significantly from those in criminal cases. Readers might benefit from reviewing Figure 1.2 in Chapter I. Because the actions that are defined as criminal also are recognized as violations of the civil law, it is not uncommon for the victims in criminal cases to maintain separate civil suits against their attackers.

Sources of American Criminal Law

You will recall from the discussion in Chapter I that the colonists along the eastern seaboard of North America were very influenced by the English common law. This diminished because of public opposition to things English.[2] Many of the states that abolished common law crimes converted most of them into statutes.[3] Although these "American" statutes deviated in some respects from the common law, they retained significant aspects of that heritage. Some states continue to recognize common law crimes without statutes, and both federal and state judges are sometimes influenced by the common law when interpreting the meaning of criminal statutes.

In the twentieth century, the legislative branch has replaced the judiciary as the dominant criminal

law policymaker. The inventions of the automobile, fax machine, copying machines, airplanes, computers, the internet, and the growth of sophisticated banking/finance companies and the securities industry, produced as a by-product new and previously unforeseen criminal opportunities. Legislative bodies responded by enacting prodigious numbers of new criminal laws. Some of these laws were well thought out; others were enacted on a piecemeal basis to appease voters without sufficient attention to detail or to appropriate constitutional limitations such as vagueness and overbreadth.

The complexities of modern society and the common law's imprecision led reformers, among them the drafters of the influential Model Penal Code, to call for the abolishment of common law crimes. Today, most states define criminal offenses only through statutes, an approach that is consistent with federal law. In 1812, the U.S. Supreme Court decided that Article I, Section 8, of the U.S. Constitution does not include among the enumerated powers the power to adopt the common law. Thus, all federal crimes have to be statutory.

Classification of Crimes

The common law classified crimes as either **mala in se** or **mala prohibita**. *Mala in se* crimes were offenses that were intrinsically bad, such as murder, rape, arson, and theft. Acts that were criminal only because the law defined them as such were classified as *mala prohibita*. A second way of categorizing crimes is in terms of the harm they cause to society. Today, state statutes are often organized so that crimes of a particular type are clustered, for example, crimes against persons (rape, kidnapping, battery, murder, etc.), crimes against property (larceny, robbery, burglary, arson, etc.), and crimes against government (contempt, perjury, bribery, etc.).

Crimes can also be classified as felonies and misdemeanors, and the distinction between the two is essentially a decision of each state's legislature. In some states, felonies are crimes that are served in state prisons and misdemeanors are offenses served in county jails. Other jurisdictions provide that crimes authorizing a sentence of incarceration of over one year are felonies, whereas those authorizing sentences of one year or less are misdemeanors. The distinction between misdemeanor and felonious theft is usually based on the value of the stolen article. Felony thresholds in theft cases range from $20 in South Carolina to $2,000 in Pennsylvania. In recent years, other classification schemes have gained popularity, for example, white-collar crime (tax evasion, insider trading, kickbacks, defrauding governmental agencies, etc.) and victimless crimes (smoking marijuana, loitering, sodomy, etc.). Other crimes have been reclassified: Driving while intoxicated, a misdemeanor twenty years ago, is today a felony.

Constitutional Limitations on Criminalization

The Constitution limits the imposition of criminal liability and criminal punishments. A criminal statute, for example, must be reasonably precise, since one that is too vague or overly broad (i.e., has an overbreadth problem) violates substantive due process.

Article I, Sections 9 and 10, of the Constitution prohibit federal and state legislative bodies from enacting ex post facto laws—laws that make acts criminal that were not criminal at the time they were committed. Statutes that make a crime greater than when committed, impose greater punishment, or make proof of guilt easier have also been held to be unconstitutional ex post facto laws. Laws also are unconstitutional if they alter the definition of a penal offense or its consequence to the disadvantage of people who have committed that offense. A law is not ex post facto if it "mitigates the rigor" of the law or simply reenacts the law in force when the crime was done. The ex post facto clause restricts only legislative power and does not apply to the judiciary. In addition, the doctrine applies exclusively to penal statutes, whether civil or criminal in form (see *Hiss v. Hampton*, 338 F.Supp. 1141 [1972]).

The Constitution also prohibits **bills of attainder**—acts of a legislature that apply either to named individuals or to easily ascertainable members of a group in such a way as to impose punishments on them without a trial. In *United States v. Brown*, 381 U.S. 437 (1965), for example, an act of Congress that made it a crime for a member of the Communist Party to serve as an officer of a labor union was held unconstitutional as a bill of attainder by the U.S. Supreme Court.

Although no specific provision in the federal Constitution guarantees a general right of personal privacy, the U.S. Supreme Court has recognized that a limited privacy right is implicit in the due process guarantees of life, liberty, and property in the Fourth and Fifth Amendments, and in the First, Ninth, and Fourteenth Amendments. The Court also has recognized that certain fundamental liberties are inherent in the concept of ordered liberty as reflected in our nation's history and tradition and has selected them for special protection. These rights include personal intimacies relating to the family, marriage, motherhood, procreation, and child rearing. The Court has also recognized that a person's home is entitled to special privacy protection. For example, it has been more exacting in assessing the reasonableness of warrantless searches and seizures under the Fourth Amendment that are conducted within a suspect's home.

The limited constitutionally recognized right of privacy is not absolute and is subject to limitations when the government's interest in protecting society becomes dominant. However, a statute affecting a fundamental constitutional right will be subjected to strict and exacting scrutiny, and the statute will fail to pass constitutional muster unless the state proves a compelling need for the law and shows that its goals cannot be accomplished by less restrictive means. If a challenged statute does *not* affect a fundamental constitutional right, the law will be upheld if it is neither arbitrary nor discriminatory, and if it bears a rational relation to a legitimate legislative purpose—protecting the public health, welfare, safety, or morals. A state can satisfy this rational basis test if it can show that there is some conceivable basis for finding such a rational relationship.

The Equal Protection Clause of the Fourteenth Amendment provides that "No state shall … deny to any person within its jurisdiction the equal protection of the laws." This clause was included in the Fourth Amendment in the aftermath of the Civil War for the purpose of securing freedom for black people. On its face, the clause might seem to guarantee individuals as well as groups not only the equal application of the laws, but also equal outcomes. The Supreme Court has rejected such an expansive interpretation and has ruled that the Equal Protection Clause only requires that the laws be applied equally and leaves issues associated with the existence of unequal outcomes to the political branches of government.

The Supreme Court has ruled that classification schemes are inherently suspect if they are based on race, national origin, or alienage, or if they hamper the exercise of fundamental personal rights. When an inherently suspect classification scheme is challenged in court on equal protection grounds, it is subject to "strict scrutiny." This means that the classification scheme will be overturned unless the government can demonstrate that its discriminatory impact is narrowed as much as possible and that the remaining discrimination is necessary to achieve a "compelling" governmental interest.

Discriminatory classifications that are neither suspect, nor based on gender, will be sustained only if they are rationally related to a legitimate governmental interest. When a challenged classification scheme involves gender, the Supreme Court applies a special rule. In these cases, the discriminatory scheme must bear a "substantial relationship to "important governmental objectives."[4]

Although the Equal Protection Clause has rarely been relied upon to strike down criminal statutes, it has played a small, but important role in preventing legislatures from defining crimes in ways that target groups on the basis of race and gender. Examples of criminal statutes that were overturned by the Supreme Court on equal protection grounds include a Massachusetts statute that made it a crime for unmarried adults to use birth control[5] and an Oklahoma statute that allowed females eighteen years or older to consume beer containing 3.2 percent alcohol, while withholding this right from males until they were twenty-one years of age.[6]

The Imposition of Punishment

It is a principle of U.S. law that people convicted of crimes receive only punishments that have been provided by law. Also, legislative bodies are limited in the types of sentences they can provide by the Eighth Amendment's protection against the imposition of cruel and unusual punishments. The Supreme Court has interpreted this provision as preventing the use of "barbaric punishments as well as sentences that are disproportionate to the crime committed." The meaning of "barbaric punishment" has been the subject of much discussion in the debate over capital punishment. The majority of the Supreme Court has consistently rejected arguments that imposition of capital punishment is barbaric, emphasizing that capital punishment was known to the common law and was accepted in this country at the time the Eighth Amendment was adopted. At this time thirty-eight states have enacted statutes providing for the death penalty.

Since 2002, the Supreme Court has reversed course on two capital punishment issues previously decided in 1989. In *Atkins v. Virginia*, 536 U.S. 304 (2002), the Court, by a 6–3 margin, reversed its ruling in *Penry v. Lynaugh*, 492 U.S. 302 (1989), which had permitted the execution of mentally retarded offenders. In *Roper v. Simmons*, 543 U.S. 551 (2005), the Court by a 5–4 margin reversed its ruling in *Stanford v. Kentucky*, 492 U.S. 361, which had permitted states to execute offenders who were as young as sixteen years old. The justices ruled in *Roper* that the Eighth and Fourteenth Amendments prohibited the imposition of capital punishment on criminal offenders who were less than eighteen years of age when their crimes were committed.

The Eighth Amendment's proportionality requirement can be traced to the Virginia Declaration of Rights (1775), the English Bill of Rights (1689), the Statute of Westminster (1275), and even Magna Carta (1215). The Supreme Court in the past has used this principle to strike down sentences imposed pursuant to (1) a statute authorizing a jail sentence for drug addiction (because it is cruel and unusual punishment to incarcerate a person for being ill), (2) a statute authorizing the death penalty for rapists, and (3) a statute authorizing a sentence of life imprisonment without parole for a recidivist who wrote a 100-dollar check on a nonexisting account. In the aftermath of the Supreme Court's decision in *Harmelin v. Michigan*, 501 U.S. 957 (1991), the constitutional importance of proportionality in sentencing decisions, especially in noncapital cases, is very much unclear.

THE BASIC COMPONENTS OF A CRIMINAL OFFENSE

Criminal offenses traditionally consist of the following basic components: (1) the wrongful act, (2) the guilty mind, (3) the concurrence of act and intent, and, in some crimes, (4) causation. To obtain a conviction in a criminal case, the government has to establish each of these components beyond a reasonable doubt.

The Wrongful Act

The wrongful act, or *actus reus*, is most easily defined by example. The wrongful act of larceny includes an unlawful taking and carrying away of another person's property. The wrongful act in a battery is the unjustified, offensive, or harmful touching of another person. The law makes a distinction between acts that are classified as voluntary, and those that result from reflexive acts, epileptic seizures, or hypnotic suggestion (see the Model Penal Code in Figure 8.1). A voluntary act occurs when the accused causes his or her body to move in a manner that produces prohibited conduct. The following case illustrates the requirement that criminal acts be voluntary.

People v. Shaughnessy
319 N.Y.S.2d 626
District Court, Nassau County, Third District
March 16, 1971

Lockman, Judge
On October 9th, 1970, shortly before 10:05 P.M., the Defendant in the company of her boyfriend and two other youngsters proceeded by automobile to the vicinity of the St. Ignatius Retreat Home, Searingtown Road, Incorporated Village of North Hills, Nassau County, New York. The Defendant was a passenger and understood that she was headed for the Christopher Morley Park which is located across the street from the St. Ignatius Retreat Home and has a large illuminated sign, with letters approximately 8 inches high, which identifies the park. As indicated, on the other side of the street the St. Ignatius Retreat Home has two pillars at its entrance with a bronze sign on each pillar with 4- to 5-inch letters. The sign is not illuminated. The vehicle in which the Defendant was riding proceeded into the grounds of the Retreat Home and was stopped by a watchman and the occupants including the Defendant waited approximately

20 minutes for a Policeman to arrive. The Defendant never left the automobile.

The Defendant is charged with violating Section 1 of the Ordinance prohibiting entry upon private property of the Incorporated Village of North Hills, which provides: "No person shall enter upon any privately owned piece, parcel or lot of real property in the Village of North Hills without the permission of the owner, lessee or occupant thereof. The failure of the person, so entering upon, or found to be on, such private property, to produce upon demand, the written permission of the owner, lessee or occupant to enter upon, or to be on, such real property, shall be and shall constitute presumptive evidence of the violation of this Ordinance."

The Defendant at the conclusion of the trial moves to dismiss on the grounds that the statute is unconstitutional. Since the Ordinance is *Malum Prohibitum*, in all likelihood the Ordinance is constitutional.... However, it is unnecessary to pass upon the constitutionality of the Ordinance since there is another basis for dismissal.

The problem presented by the facts in this case brings up for review the primary elements that are required for criminal accountability and responsibility. It is only from an accused's voluntary overt acts that criminal responsibility can attach. An overt act or a specific omission to act must occur in order for the establishment of a criminal offense.

The physical element required has been designated as the *Actus Reus*. The mental element is of course better known as the *Mens Rea*. While the mental element may under certain circumstances not be required as in crimes that are designated *Malum Prohibitum*, the *Actus Reus* is always necessary. It certainly cannot be held to be the intent of the legislature to punish involuntary acts.

The principle which requires a voluntary act or omission to act had been codified ... and reads as follows in part: "The minimal requirement for criminal liability is the performance by a person of conduct which includes a *voluntary act or the omission to perform an act* which he is physically capable of performing."...

The legislature may prescribe that an act is criminal without regard to the doer's intent or knowledge, but an involuntary act is not criminal (with certain exceptions such as involuntary acts resulting from voluntary intoxication).

In the case at bar, the People have failed to establish any act on the part of the Defendant. She merely was a passenger in a vehicle. Any action taken by the vehicle was caused and guided by the driver thereof and not by the Defendant. If the Defendant were to be held guilty under these circumstances, it would dictate that she would be guilty if she had been unconscious or asleep at the time or even if she had been a prisoner in the automobile. There are many situations which can be envisioned and in which the trespass statute in question would be improperly applied to an involuntary act. One might conceive of a driver losing control of a vehicle through mechanical failure and the vehicle proceeding onto private property which is the subject of a trespass.

Although the Court need not pass on the question, it might very well be proper to hold the driver responsible for his act even though he was under the mistaken belief that he was on his way to Christopher Morley Park. The legislature has provided statutes which make mistakes of fact or lack of knowledge no excuse in a criminal action. However, if the driver had been a Defendant, the People could have established an act on the part of the Defendant driver, to wit, turning his vehicle into the private property.

In the case of the Defendant now before the Court, however, the very first and essential element in criminal responsibility is missing, an overt voluntary act or omission to act and, accordingly, the Defendant is found not guilty.

Case Questions

1. Judge Lockman's opinion explains that a voluntary act is normally necessary for criminal liability. What would be an example of an involuntary act?
2. Under what conditions should people be criminally liable for having omitted to act?

Special Rules

When the law recognizes the existence of a legal duty, the failure to act is equivalent to a criminal act. The duty to act can be imposed by statute (filing income tax returns, making child support payments, registering with selective service, registering firearms), by contract (such as that between parents and a day care center), as a result of one's status (parent-child, husband–wife), or because one has assumed a responsibility (voluntarily assuming responsibility for providing food to a person under disability).

Another exception to the requirement of a physical act is recognized in possession offenses in which the law treats the fact of possession as the equivalent of a wrongful act. For example, a person found with a controlled substance in his jacket pocket is not actually engaging in any physical act. Possession can be actual, as when the accused is found with the contraband on his or her person, or constructive, as when the contraband is not on the suspect's person but is under the suspect's dominion and control.

MODEL PENAL CODE*

Official Draft, 1985

Copyright 1985 by The American Law Institute.
Reprinted with the permission of The American Law Institute.

Section 2.01.   Requirement of Voluntary Act; Omission as Basis of Liability; Possession as an Act

(1) A person is not guilty of an offense unless his liability is based on conduct which includes a voluntary act or the omission to perform an act of which he is physically capable.

(2) The following are not voluntary acts within the meaning of this Section:

(a) a reflex or convulsion;

(b) a bodily movement during unconsciousness or sleep;

(c) conduct during hypnosis or resulting from hypnotic suggestion;

(d) a bodily movement that otherwise is not a product of the effort or determination of the actor, either conscious or habitual.

(3) Liability for the commission of an offense may not be based on an omission unaccompanied by action unless:

(a) the omission is expressly made sufficient by the law defining the offense; or

(b) a duty to perform the omitted act is otherwise imposed by law.

(4) Possession is an act, within the meaning of this Section, if the possessor knowingly procured or received the thing possessed or was aware of his control thereof for a sufficient period to have been able to terminate his possession.

*A collection of suggestions for reforming American criminal law, the Model Penal Code was prepared by a private association of professors, lawyers, and judges called the American Law Institute. Over two-thirds of the states have adopted at least some of its provisions and hundreds of courts have been influenced by its suggestions.

FIGURE 8.1 Model Penal Code Section 2.01

Status Crimes

The Supreme Court has emphasized the importance of the wrongful act requirement in its decisions relating to status crimes, ruling that legislatures cannot make the status of "being without visible means of support" or "being ill as a result of narcotic addiction" into crimes. Selling a controlled substance can be made criminal because it involves a voluntary act. The condition of being an addict, however, is a status.

The Criminal State of Mind

The second requirement of a criminal offense (subject to a few exceptions) is that an alleged criminal offender must possess a criminal state of mind (*mens rea*) at the time of the commission of the wrongful act. This is called the concurrence of a wrongful act with a wrongful state of mind. Concurrence is required because some people who commit wrongful acts do not have a wrongful state of mind. For example, if the student sitting next to you mistakenly picks up your copy of a textbook, instead of her copy, and leaves the classroom, there has been a wrongful act but no wrongful intent. While it is theoretically easy to make this distinction between accidental and criminal acts, it is often difficult to prove that a person acted with *mens rea*, and prosecutors often have to prove *mens rea* indirectly and circumstantially. In addition, judges routinely instruct jurors that the law permits them to find that a defendant intended the natural and probable consequences of his or her deliberate acts. This instruction is based on human experience: most people go about their daily affairs intending to do the things they choose to do.

In the United States, *mala in se* offenses require proof of criminal intent. *Mala prohibita* offenses may require criminal intent (in possession of a controlled substance, for instance), or they may involve no proof of intent at all (as in traffic offenses or sales of illegal intoxicating beverages to minors).

There are two major approaches to *mens rea*, one formed by the traditional common law approach, the other by the Model Penal Code. The common law approach recognizes three categories of intent: general intent, specific intent, and criminal negligence. General intent crimes include serious offenses such as rape and arson and less serious offenses such as trespass and simple battery. For conviction of a general intent crime, the prosecution has to prove that the accused intended to commit the *actus reus*. The common law permitted the trier of fact to infer a wrongful state of mind from proof that the actor voluntarily did a wrongful act. Thus a person who punches another person in anger (without any lawful justification or excuse) may be found to have possessed general criminal intent.

A specific intent crime requires proof of the commission of an *actus reus*, plus a specified level of knowledge or an additional intent, such as an intent to commit a felony. A person who possesses a controlled substance (the *actus reus*) and who at the time of the possession has an intent to sell (an additional specified level of intent beyond the commission of the *actus reus*) has committed a specific intent crime.

Criminal negligence results from unconscious risk creation. For example, a driver who unconsciously takes his or her eyes off the road to take care of a crying infant is in fact creating risks for other drivers and pedestrians. Thus the driver's unreasonable conduct created substantial and unjustifiable risks. If the driver is unaware of the risk creation, he or she is acting negligently.

The defendant in the following case was charged and convicted of the specific intent crime of robbery. He appealed his conviction on the ground that he did not have specific intent—the intent to permanently deprive the true owner of his property.

State v. Gordon
321 A.2d 352
Supreme Judicial Court of Maine
June 17, 1974

Wernick, Justice

An indictment returned (on June 27, 1972) by a Cumberland County Grand Jury to the Superior Court charged defendant, Richard John Gordon, with having committed the crime of "armed robbery" in violation of 17 M.R.S.A. § 3401–A. A separate indictment accused defendant of having, with intention to kill, assaulted a police officer, one Harold Stultz. Defendant was arraigned and pleaded not guilty to each charge. Upon motion by the State, and over defendant's objection, the residing Justice ordered a single trial on the two indictments. The trial was before a jury. On the "assault" the jury was unable to reach a verdict and as to that charge a mistrial was declared. The jury found defendant guilty of "armed robbery." From the judgment of conviction entered on the verdict defendant has appealed, assigning ten claims of error.

We deny the appeal.

The jury was justified in finding the following facts.

One Edwin Strode and defendant had escaped in Vermont from the custody of the authorities who had been holding them on a misdemeanor charge. In the escape defendant and Strode had acquired two hand guns and also a blue station wagon in which they had fled from Vermont through New Hampshire into

Maine. Near Standish, Maine, the station wagon showed signs of engine trouble, and defendant and Strode began to look for another vehicle. They came to the yard of one Franklin Prout. In the yard was Prout's 1966 maroon Chevelle and defendant, who was operating the station wagon, drove it parallel to the Prout Chevelle. Observing that the keys were in the Chevelle, Strode left the station wagon and entered the Chevelle. At this time Prout came out of his house into the yard. Strode pointed a gun at him, and the defendant and Strode then told Prout that they needed his automobile, were going to take it but they "would take care of it and see he [Prout] got it back as soon as possible." With defendant operating the station wagon and Strode the Chevelle, defendant and Strode left the yard and proceeded in the direction of Westbrook. Subsequently, the station wagon was abandoned in a sand pit, and defendant and Strode continued their flight in the Chevelle. A spectacular series of events followed—including the alleged assault (with intent to kill) upon Westbrook police officer Stultz, a shoot-out on Main Street in Westbrook, and a high speed police chase, during which the Chevelle was driven off the road in the vicinity of the Maine Medical Center in Portland where it was abandoned, Strode and defendant having commandeered another automobile to resume their flight. Ultimately, both the defendant and Strode were apprehended, defendant having been arrested on the day following the police chase in the vicinity of the State Police Barracks in Scarborough....

[D]efendant maintains that the evidence clearly established that (1) defendant and Strode had told Prout that they "would take care of ... [the automobile] and see [that] he [Prout] got it back as soon as possible" and (2) defendant intended only a temporary use of Prout's Chevelle. Defendant argues that the evidence thus fails to warrant a conclusion beyond a reasonable doubt that defendant had the specific intent requisite for "robbery." (Hereinafter, reference to the "specific intent" necessary for "robbery" signifies the "specific intent" incorporated into "robbery" as embracing "larceny.")

Although defendant is correct that robbery is a crime requiring a particular specific intent ... defendant wrongly apprehends its substantive content.

A summarizing statement appearing in defendant's brief most clearly exposes his misconception of the law. Acknowledging that on all of the evidence the jury could properly

"... have inferred ... that [defendant and Strode] ... intended to get away from the authorities by going to New York or elsewhere *where they would abandon* the car ..." (emphasis supplied)

defendant concludes that, nevertheless, the State had failed to prove the necessary specific intent because it is

"... entirely irrational to conclude ... that the defendant himself intended at the time he and Strode took the car, *to keep the car in their possession for any length of time.*" (emphasis supplied)

Here, defendant reveals that he conceives as an essential element of the specific intent requisite for "robbery" that the wrongdoer must intend: (1) an advantageous relationship between himself and the property wrongfully taken, and (2) that such relationship be permanent rather than temporary.

Defendant's view is erroneous. The law evaluates the "animus furandi" of "robbery" in terms of the detriment projected to the legally protected interests of the owner rather than the benefits intended to accrue to the wrongdoer from his invasion of the rights of the owner....

[M]any of the earlier decisions reveal language disagreements, as well as conflicts as to substance, concerning whether a defendant can be guilty of "robbery" without specifically intending a gain to himself (whether permanent or temporary), so-called "lucri causa." In the more recent cases, there is overwhelming consensus that "lucri causa" is not necessary....

We now decide, in confirmatory clarification of the law of Maine, that "lucri causa" is not an essential element of the "animus furandi" of "robbery." ... [T]he specific intent requisite for "robbery" is defined solely in terms of the injury projected to the interests of the property owner:—specific intent "to deprive permanently the owner of his property." ...

The instant question thus becomes: on the hypothesis, arguendo, that defendant here actually intended to use the Prout automobile "only temporarily" (as he would need it to achieve a successful flight from the authorities), is defendant correct in his fundamental contention that this, *in itself*, negates, *as a matter of law*, specific intent of defendant to deprive permanently the owner of his property? We answer that defendant's claim is erroneous.

Concretely illustrative of the point that a wrongdoer may intend to use wrongfully taken property "only temporarily" and yet, without contradiction, intend that the owner be deprived of his property permanently is the case of a defendant who proposes to use the property only for a short time and then to destroy it. At the opposite pole, and excluding (as a matter of law) specific intent to deprive permanently the owner of his property, is the case of a defendant who intends to make a temporary use of the property and then by his own act to return the property to its owner. Between these two extremes can lie various situations in which the legal characterization of the wrongdoer's intention, as assessed by the criterion of whether it is a specific intent to deprive permanently the owner of his property, will be more or less clear and raise legal problems of varying difficulty.

In these intermediate situations a general guiding principle may be developed through recognition that a "taking" of property is *by definition* "temporary" only if the possession, or control, effected by the taking is relinquished. Hence, measured by the correct criterion of the impact upon the interests of the owner, the wrongdoer's "animus furandi" is fully explored for its true legal significance only if the investigation of the wrongdoer's state of mind extends beyond his anticipated *retention* of possession and includes an inquiry into his contemplated manner of *relinquishing* possession, or control, of the property wrongfully taken.

On this approach, it has been held that when a defendant takes the tools of another person with intent to use them temporarily and then to leave them wherever it may be that he finishes with his work, the fact-finder is justified in the conclusion that defendant had specific intent to deprive the owner permanently of his property....

Similarly, it has been decided that a defendant who wrongfully takes the property of another intending to use it for a short time and then to relinquish possession, or control, in a manner leaving to chance whether the owner recovers his property is correctly held specifically to intend that the owner be deprived permanently of his property.

The rationale underlying these decisions is that to negate, as a matter of law, the existence of specific intent to deprive permanently the owner of his property, a wrongful taker of the property of another must have in mind not only that his retention of possession, or control, will be "temporary" but also that when he will relinquish the possession, or control, he will do it in some manner (whatever, particularly, it will be) he regards as having affirmative tendency toward getting the property returned to its owner. In the absence of such thinking by the defendant, his state of mind is

fairly characterized as *indifference* should the owner *never* recover his property; and such indifference by a wrongdoer who is the moving force separating an owner from his property is appropriately regarded as his "willingness" that the owner *never* regain his property. In this sense, the wrongdoer may appropriately be held to entertain specific intent that the deprivation to the owner be permanent....

On this basis, the evidence in the present case clearly presented a jury question as to defendant's specific intent. Although defendant may have stated to the owner, Prout, that defendant

> "would take care of ... [the automobile] and see [that] ... [Prout] got it back as soon as possible,"

defendant himself testified that

> "[i]n my mind it was just to get out of the area.... Just get out of the area and leave the car and get under cover somewhere."

This idea to "leave the car" and "get under cover somewhere" existed in defendant's mind as part of an uncertainty about where it would happen. Because defendant was "... sort of desperate during the whole day," he had not "really formulated any plans about destination."

Such testimony of defendant, together with other evidence that defendant had already utterly abandoned another vehicle (the station wagon) in desperation, plainly warranted a jury conclusion that defendant's facilely uttered statements to Prout were empty words, and it was defendant's true state of mind to use Prout's Chevelle and abandon it in whatever manner might happen to meet the circumstantial exigencies of defendant's predicament—without defendant's having any thought that the relinquishment of the possession was to be in a manner having some affirmative tendency to help in the owner's recovery of his property. On this finding the jury was warranted in a conclusion that defendant was indifferent should the owner, Prout, *never* have back his automobile and, therefore, had specific intent that the owner be deprived permanently of his property.

Appeal denied.

Case Questions

1. What must a wrongful taker of property do to avoid legal responsibility for having specific intent to deprive the owner permanently of his property?
2. Does a wrongful taker of property have specific intent if the taker does not intend to keep the property for any particular period of time?

The Model Penal Code recognizes four categories of criminal intent. To be criminally culpable, a person must act purposely, knowingly, recklessly, or negligently (see Figure 8 2).

A person acts purposely when he or she has a conscious desire to produce a prohibited result or harm, such as when one person strikes another in order to injure the other person.

A person acts knowingly when he or she is aware that a prohibited result or harm is very likely to occur, but nevertheless does not consciously intend the specific consequences that result from the act. If a person sets a building on fire, the person may be aware that it is very likely that people inside will be injured, and yet hopes that the people escape and that only the building is burned.

A person acts recklessly when he or she consciously disregards the welfare of others and creates a significant and unjustifiable risk. The risk has to be one that no law-abiding person would have consciously undertaken or created. A driver acts recklessly if he or she consciously takes his or her eyes off the road to take care of a crying infant, is aware that this conduct creates risks for other drivers and pedestrians, and is willing to expose others to jeopardy.

As seen in the common law approach, negligence involves unconscious risk creation. A driver acts negligently if he or she unconsciously takes his or her eyes off the road to take care of a crying infant, is unaware that this conduct creates substantial and unjustifiable risks for other drivers and pedestrians, and yet has not acted reasonably while operating a motor vehicle.

Strict Liability

In strict liability offenses there is no requirement that there be a concurrence between the criminal act and criminal intent. In such offenses, the offender poses a generalized threat to society at large. Examples include a speeding driver, a manufacturer who fails to comply with pure food and drug rules, or a liquor store owner who sells alcohol to minors. With respect to such *mala prohibita* offenses, the legislature may provide that the offender is strictly liable. The prosecution need only prove the *actus reus* to convict the accused; there is no intent element.

Causation

There are some criminal offenses that require proof that the defendant's conduct caused a given result. In a homicide case, for example, the prosecution must prove that the defendant's conduct caused death. To be convicted of an assault, the defendant's actions must have caused the victim to fear an impending battery. In a battery, the defendant's conduct must have caused a harmful or offensive touching. In contrast, offenses such as perjury, reckless driving, larceny, and burglary criminalize conduct irrespective of whether any actual harm results.

The prosecution must establish causation beyond a reasonable doubt whenever it is an element of a crime. A key to establishing causation is the legal concept of "proximate cause." Criminal liability only attaches to conduct that is determined to be the proximate or legal cause of the harmful result. This includes both direct and indirect causation. Often the legal cause is the direct cause of harm. If the defendant strikes the victim with his fist and injures him, the defendant is the direct cause of the injury. If the defendant sets in motion a chain of events that eventually results in harm, the defendant may be the indirect cause of the harm.

Proximate cause is a flexible concept. It permits fact finders to sort through various factual causes and determine who should be found to be legally responsible for the result. In addition, an accused is only responsible for the reasonably foreseeable consequences that follow from his or her acts. The law provides, for example, that an accused is not responsible for consequences that follow the intervention of a new, and independent, causal force. The next case, *Commonwealth v. Berggren*, illustrates the legal principle that an accused is only responsible for consequences that are reasonably foreseeable.

MODEL PENAL CODE
Official Draft, 1985

Copyright 1985 by The American Law Institute.
Reprinted with the permission of The American Law Institute.

Section 2.02   General Requirements of Culpability

*   *   *

(2) *Kinds of Culpability Defined.*

(a) *Purposely.*

A person acts purposely with respect to a material element of an offense when:

(i)   if the element involves the nature of his conduct or a result thereof, it is his conscious object to engage in conduct of that nature or to cause such a result; and

(ii) if the element involves the attendant circumstances, he is aware of the existence of such circumstances or he believes or hopes that they exist.

(b) *Knowingly.*

A person acts knowingly with respect to a material element of an offense when:

(i)   if the element involves the nature of his conduct or the attendant circumstances, he is aware that his conduct is of that nature or that such circumstances exist; and

(ii) if the element involves a result of his conduct, he is aware that it is practically certain that his conduct will cause such a result.

(c) *Recklessly.*

A person acts recklessly with respect to a material element of an offense when he consciously disregards a substantial and unjustifiable risk that the material element exists or will result from his conduct. The risk must be of such a nature and degree that, considering the nature and purpose of the actor's conduct and the circumstances known to him, its disregard involves a gross deviation from the standard of conduct that a law-abiding person would observe in the actor's situation.

(d) *Negligently.*

A person acts negligently with respect to a material element of an offense when he should be aware of a substantial and unjustifiable risk that the material element exists or will result from his conduct. The risk must be of such a nature and degree that the actor's failure to perceive it, considering the nature and purpose of his conduct and the circumstances known to him, involves a gross deviation from the standard of care that a reasonable person would observe in the actor's situation.

FIGURE 8.2 Model Penal Code Section 2.2

Commonwealth v. Berggren
496 N.E.2d 660
Supreme Judicial Court of Massachusetts
August 26, 1986

Lynch, Justice

The defendant is awaiting trial before a jury of six in the Barnstable Division of the District Court on a complaint charging him with motor vehicle homicide by negligent operation of a motor vehicle so as to endanger public safety (G.L. c. 90, § 24G(*b*) [1984 ed.]). The District Court judge granted the joint motion to "report an issue" to the Appeals Court pursuant to Mass. R. Crim. P. 34, 378 Mass. 905 (1979). We transferred the report here on our own motion.

We summarize the stipulated facts. On March 29, 1983, about 8:28 P.M., Patrolman Michael Aselton of the Barnstable police department was on radar duty at Old Stage Road in Centerville. He saw the defendant's motorcycle speed by him and commenced pursuit in a marked police cruiser with activated warning devices. The defendant "realized a cruiser was behind him but did not stop because he was 'in fear of his license.'" The pursuit lasted roughly six miles through residential, commercial and rural areas. At one point, the defendant had gained a 100-yard lead and crossed an intersection, continuing north. The patrolman's cruiser approached the intersection at about "76 m.p.h. minimal" and passed over a crown in the roadway which caused the patrolman to brake. The wheels locked and the cruiser slid 170 yards, hitting a tree. Patrolman Aselton died as a result of the impact. The defendant had no idea of the accident which had occurred behind him. "No other vehicles were in any way involved in the causation of the accident." The stipulation further states that the decision to terminate a high-speed chase "is to be made by the officer's commanding officer." No such decision to terminate the pursuit had been made at the time of the accident. The Barnstable police department determined that patrolman Aselton died in the line of duty.

We understand the report to raise the question whether the stipulated facts would be sufficient to support a conviction of motor vehicle homicide by negligent operation under G.L. c. 90, § 24G(*b*). We hold that it is.

A finding of ordinary negligence suffices to establish a violation of § 24G.

The Appeals Court has observed: "It would seem to follow that if the jury's task is to find ordinary negligence, then the appropriate principles of causation to apply are those which have been explicated in a large body of decisions and texts treating the subject in the context of the law of torts." ...

The defendant argues, however, that the "causation theory properly applied in criminal cases is not that of proximate cause." ... If this theory has any application in this Commonwealth ... it does not apply to a charge of negligent vehicular homicide. We adopt instead the suggestion of the Appeals Court and conclude that the appropriate standard of causation to be applied in a negligent vehicular homicide case under § 24G is that employed in tort law.

The defendant essentially contends that since he was one hundred yards ahead of the patrolman's cruiser and was unaware of the accident, his conduct cannot be viewed as directly traceable to the resulting death of the patrolman. The defendant, however, was speeding on a motorcycle at night on roads which his attorney at oral argument before this court characterized as "winding" and "narrow." He knew the patrolman was following him, but intentionally did not stop and continued on at high speed for six miles. From the fact that the defendant was "in fear of his license," it may reasonably be inferred that he was aware that he had committed at least one motor vehicle violation. Under these circumstances, the defendant's acts were hardly a remote link in the chain of events leading to the patrolman's death.... The officer's pursuit was certainly foreseeable, as was, tragically, the likelihood of serious injury or death to the defendant himself, to the patrolman, or to some third party. The patrolman's death resulted from the "natural and continuous sequence" of events caused by the defendant's actions....

We conclude that the proper standard of causation for this offense is the standard of proximate cause enunciated in the law of torts. We further conclude that, should the jury find the facts as stipulated in the instant case, and should the only contested element of the offense of motor vehicle homicide by negligent operation be that of causation, these facts would support a conviction under G.L. c.90, §24G(*b*).

Report answered.

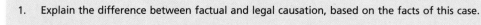
Inchoate Crime

The criminal law recognizes society's need to protect itself from those people who have taken some preliminary steps leading to a criminal act, but who have not yet completed their intended criminal objectives. Thus the law defines as criminal the preparatory activities of solicitation, attempt, and conspiracy and refers to them as inchoate crimes.

Solicitation is a specific intent crime committed by a person who asks, hires, or encourages another to commit a crime. It makes no difference whether the solicited person accepts the offer; the solicitation itself constitutes the *actus reus* for this offense. All jurisdictions treat solicitations to commit a felony as a crime, and some jurisdictions also criminalize solicitations to commit a misdemeanor.

The crime of attempt is committed by a person who has the intent to commit a substantive criminal offense and does an act that tends to corroborate the intent, under circumstances that do not result in the completion of the substantive crime. For example, assume that person Y intends to commit armed robbery of a bank. Y dresses in clothing that disguises his appearance, wears a police scanner on his belt, carries a revolver in his coat pocket, wears gloves, and drives to a bank. Y approaches the front door with one hand in his pocket and the other over his face. When he attempts to open the front door, he discovers that the door is locked and that it is just after the bank's closing time. Y quickly returns to his car, leaves the bank, and is subsequently apprehended by police. Y had specific intent to rob the bank, and took many substantial steps to realize that intent; however, he was unable to complete the crime because of his poor timing. Y has committed the crime of attempted robbery.

The crime of conspiracy is committed when two or more people combine to commit a criminal act. The essential *actus reus* of conspiracy is the agreement to commit a criminal act, coupled with the commission of some overt act by one or more of the coconspirators that tends to implement the agreement. The prosecution can prove the existence of an unlawful agreement either expressly or inferentially. The crime of conspiracy is designed to protect society from group criminality. Organized groups bent on criminal activity pose a greater threat to the public than do the isolated acts of individuals. Conspiracy is a separate crime, and unlike attempt, does not merge into the completed substantive offense. Thus a person can be prosecuted both for murder and conspiracy to murder. If a member of the conspiracy wants to abandon the joint enterprise, he or she must notify every other coconspirator. Conspiracy is a powerful prosecutorial weapon.

The Racketeer Influenced and Corrupt Organization Act

In 1970, the federal government enacted a criminal statute called the Racketeer Influenced and Corrupt Organization Act (RICO). This statute and its state counterparts have been very important weapons in combating organized criminal activity such as drug trafficking, the theft and fencing of property, syndicated gambling, and extortion. A very broad statute, RICO applies to all people and organizations, whether public or private. It focuses on patterns of racketeering activity, the use of money obtained from racketeering to acquire legitimate businesses, and the collection of unlawful debt. The act defines racketeering activity as involving eight state crimes and twenty-four federal offenses called the predicate acts. A person who has committed two or more of the predicate acts within a ten-year period has engaged in a pattern of racketeering activity. People convicted under RICO can be required to forfeit property acquired with money obtained through racketeering, and punished with fines, and up to twenty years' incarceration. Civil penalties, including the award of treble damages, can also be imposed.

INTERNET TIP

An interesting RICO case involving members of the Outlaws Motorcycle Club who allegedly participated in a drug distribution enterprise can be found on the textbook's website. The case of *U.S. v. Lawson* was decided in 2008 by the U.S. Court of Appeals for the Sixth Circuit.

Vicarious Liability

Criminal law recognizes two conditions under which individuals and groups can be held criminally liable for actions committed by other people. Employers can be held responsible for the acts of their employees that occur within the course and scope of employment. For example, if a bartender illegally sells liquor to minors, the bartender's employer (as well as the bartender) can be prosecuted. Vicarious liability helps to impress on employers the importance of insisting that employees comply with legal requirements. However, an employer can be held vicariously liable only for strict liability offenses. In addition, people convicted vicariously can only be subject to a fine or forfeiture.

Corporations can also be held vicariously responsible for criminal acts committed by authorized corporate employees who have acted on behalf of the company to enhance corporate profits. A corporate CEO, for example, who engages in criminal conduct can be prosecuted just like any other person. But additional charges can also be

brought against the corporation itself in order to hold it vicariously liable for the CEO's criminal acts.

INTERNET TIP

Corporations can even be convicted of committing homicides. A trucking company was found guilty by a jury and convicted of the homicide of a police officer in a controversial 2006 Massachusetts case. The truck's driver, whose vehicle lacked a working backup alarm, struck an officer situated in the truck driver's "blind spot." The trucking company was charged with violating the state's vehicular homicide statute. The conviction was appealed to the state's highest court, which affirmed. The majority and dissenting opinions in the case of *Commonwealth vs. Todesca Corporation* can be read on the textbook's website.

Prosecutors usually bring criminal charges against corporations for reasons of deterrence. If a corporation's culture has become corrupted, merely prosecuting the individuals involved is sometimes not enough. Corporations have much to lose if prosecuted and convicted of criminal conduct. They risk public embarrassment, damage to the company's reputation and goodwill, and the risk of devaluation of its stock. The punishment options for corporations are limited, however. The law permits the imposition of fines but these are often inadequate in size, and it is obvious that corporations cannot go to jail.

Defenses

Because of the constitutional presumption of innocence, criminal defendants are not required to prove anything at trial. If the government cannot prove the defendant's guilt beyond a reasonable doubt with its own evidence, the law provides that the accused is not guilty.

One defense strategy is, therefore, to establish reasonable doubt exclusively through the use of the government's own witnesses. It is possible to challenge the credibility of prosecution witnesses on the grounds that their testimony is unbelievable. The defense attorney, for example, may through cross-examination be able to show that a prosecution witness was too far away to have clearly seen what he/she testified to have observed, to be biased against the defendant, or to not really be certain as to the identity of the attacker as was suggested on direct examination. The defense can also challenge the way in which the police obtained evidence by alleging that the police did not comply with the requirements of *Miranda v. Arizona* when they interrogated the defendant, or violated the requirements of the Fourth Amendment when they conducted a search of the defendant's home. Where the prosecution's evidence is insufficient to establish elements of the crime, the defense attorney can move to dismiss, and it is always possible to defend by arguing that the level of *mens rea* required for conviction was not proven or that the prosecution in some other respect has failed its burden of proving the defendant's guilt beyond a reasonable doubt.

Sometimes an accused can call witnesses to testify that the defendant was somewhere other than at the scene of the crime on the date and time that the offense allegedly occurred—thereby raising an alibi defense. Rarely, an accused will present a good character defense. When this occurs, a defendant, for example, who is charged with a crime of violence could introduce reputation or opinion testimony that the defendant is nonviolent and peace loving. From this evidence the defense attorney could argue that the defendant's character is so sterling that he would never have committed the crime with which he was charged.

The law gradually began to recognize that in some situations it would be unfair to impose criminal responsibility on a criminal defendant because of the presence of factors that legitimately mitigated, justified, or excused the defendant's conduct. These special circumstances came to be known as affirmative defenses. The defendant always bears the burden of production with respect to affirmative defenses. Unless the defense affirmatively introduces some evidence tending to establish such a defense, the court will refuse to give the corresponding instruction. Because affirmative defenses do not negate any element of the crime(s) charged by the government, states are constitutionally permitted to decide for themselves whether the defendant should bear the burden of persuasion with respect to affirmative defenses. Some states require the prosecution to disprove affirmative defenses beyond a reasonable doubt. But many other jurisdictions refuse that burden and require that the defendant carry the burden of persuasion regarding such defenses. Jurisdictions differ as to the availability of particular defenses and as to their definitions. Affirmative defenses are often further subdivided into justification defenses and excuse defenses.

Justification Defenses Criminal laws are often written in general terms and without limitations and exceptions. It is understood that exceptions will be made, on a case-by-case basis, where it becomes apparent that a defendant was justified in his/her actions given the then-existing circumstances. Recognized justification defenses often include self-defense, defense of others, defense of property, necessity/choice of evils, and duress/coercion. In each of these defenses, the accused admits to having committed the act which is alleged by the prosecution; however, in each instance the accused claims to have acted correctly.

The law recognizes an individual is justified in defending his or her person and property and others. A person is entitled to use reasonable force in self-defense to protect him- or herself from death or serious bodily harm. Obviously the amount of force that can be used in defense depends on the type of force being used by the attacker. An attack that threatens neither death nor serious bodily harm does not warrant the use of deadly force in defense. When the attack has been repelled, the defender does not have the right to continue using force to obtain revenge. Although the common law required one to "retreat to the wall" before using deadly force in self-defense, the modern rule permits a person to remain on his or her property and to use reasonable force (including the reasonable use of deadly force in defense of others who are entitled to act in self-defense). However, as we saw in *Katko v. Briney*, in Chapter I, it is never justifiable to use force that could cause death or serious bodily injury solely in defense of property. Necessity (also known as the choice of evils defense) traces its lineage to the English common law. Over time it became apparent that in some limited circumstances, committing a criminal act would actually result in a less harmful outcome than would occur were the accused to adhere strictly to the requirements of the law. To be successful with this defense, the accused must be able to establish that there was no reasonable, legal alternative to violating the law. That was the critical question addressed in the following case.

United States v. Juan Donaldo Perdomo-Espana
522 F.3d 983
United States Court of Appeals, Ninth Circuit
April 14, 2008.

Gould, Circuit Judge
Juan Perdomo-Espana ("Perdomo") appeals his jury conviction for one count of illegal entry into the United States as a deported alien in violation of 8 U.S.C. § 1326. In this opinion, we consider whether the defense of necessity that Perdomo advanced must be tested under an objective or subjective standard....

I
In the early morning hours of March 21, 2006, a United States border patrol officer found Perdomo and four others hiding in brush near the United States-Mexican border. Perdomo was wearing dark clothes. Upon discovery, Perdomo admitted that he is a Mexican citizen with no documents to allow him to enter or to remain in the United States. He was found with $598 (USD) and 155 Mexican pesos on his person. Perdomo was arrested and taken to a nearby border patrol station, where he was questioned and fingerprinted.... Immigration records revealed that he had twice previously been deported and had not subsequently applied for reentry.

At trial, Perdomo testified that he had illegally entered the United States for fear of his life. Perdomo stated that in 2000, while in a United States federal prison, he had a stroke precipitated by a high blood sugar level associated with Type 2 diabetes, and thereafter he was treated with insulin injections. Upon his release from prison, Perdomo was given a small insulin supply and was removed to Mexico on March 7, 2006, where his insulin supply soon ran out. While in Tijuana, Perdomo purchased varying kinds of replenishing insulin, but none of the insulin was sufficiently effective, and his blood sugar level began to rise.

According to Perdomo, shortly before the border patrol caught him, he tried to enter the United States via the pedestrian lane at a nearby port of entry, but was turned away despite telling the officers of his need for diabetic-related treatment. Perdomo claims that his blood sugar level soon thereafter rose to 480, the level it had reached when he suffered his diabetes-induced stroke. Perdomo asserted that he then attempted to cross clandestinely into the United States.

Perdomo testified that he entered the United States fearing for his life because of his high blood sugar levels, and did not intend to remain. He believed he was in desperate need of medical treatment which was unavailable in Mexico. Perdomo testified that he did not go to any hospital, church, or the police in Tijuana because he believed that he would not be able to secure the needed treatment in Tijuana, despite the money he carried. According to Perdomo, a person had to be dying on the street to gain medical attention there.

During questioning that took place about four to five hours after his initial capture, Perdomo told a border patrol agent for the first time that he is a Type 2 diabetic and that he had been hospitalized for two weeks in the last six months because of his diabetes....

After questioning, Perdomo was taken to an emergency room, where his blood sugar level was recorded as 340. The emergency room physician who treated Perdomo, Dr. Vincent Knauf, characterized this glucose level as a "severe elevation." However, Dr. Knauf concluded that, in his opinion, Perdomo was not facing serious or imminent risk of bodily harm at that time; although he needed longer-term care, Perdomo was classified as a "non-urgent" patient....

During pre-trial hearings, Perdomo requested to present a necessity defense, which the government moved to preclude. Reserving its final ruling until after the presentation of evidence at trial, the district court allowed Perdomo to testify before the jury about why he had entered the country.

At the conclusion of evidence, Perdomo again requested that the jury be instructed on his proffered defense of necessity. The district court declined to give the requested instruction, reasoning that Perdomo showed no "threat of imminent harm," and that it was "incredulous to suggest that Mexico doesn't have clinics, doctors, [or] hospitals that could manage people who are in need of treatment," especially given that Perdomo "had $600 on him at the time." The district court, instead, instructed the jury that the "theory of the defense" was that Perdomo had come to the United States for medical care. After the jury found Perdomo guilty, Perdomo moved for a new trial, which the district court denied. Perdomo appeals the district court's denial of his request for a necessity defense jury instruction

II

... [W]e review de novo the legal question whether the necessity defense requires an objective inquiry. Once we have resolved that legal question, we review for abuse of discretion whether there is a sufficient factual basis for Perdomo's proffered jury instruction.

III

A defendant is entitled to have the jury instructed on his or her theory of defense, as long as that theory has support in the law and some foundation in the evidence.... A defendant "has the right to have a jury resolve disputed factual issues. However, where the evidence, even if believed, does not establish all of the elements of a defense, ... the trial judge need not submit the defense to the jury." ... ("[It] is well established that a criminal defendant is entitled to have a jury instruction on any defense which provides a legal defense to the charge against him and which has some foundation in the evidence, even though the evidence may be weak, insufficient, inconsistent, or of doubtful credibility. In the necessity context, the proper inquiry is whether the evidence offered by a defendant, if taken as true, is sufficient as a matter of law to support the defense." ...

> "[T]he defense of necessity, or choice of evils, traditionally covered the situation where physical forces beyond [an] actor's control rendered illegal conduct the lesser of two evils." ... In recent years, our case law has expanded the scope of the defense. We have held that a defendant may present a defense of necessity to the jury as long as the defendant "establish[es] that a reasonable jury could conclude: (1) that he was faced with a choice of evils and chose the lesser evil; (2) that he acted to prevent imminent harm; (3) that he reasonably anticipated a causal relation between his conduct and the harm to be avoided; and (4) that there were no other legal alternatives to violating the law."

A defendant must prove each of these elements to present a viable necessity defense....

Perdomo's principal argument is that these elements require a subjective analysis and that the relevant inquiry is thus into his state of mind — i.e., his allegedly genuine fear of the likely, dire medical consequences that he would have faced if he did not illegally reenter the United States. By contrast, the government asserts that the inquiry is an objective one. We agree with the government.

A careful reading of our cases on the subject reveals that we assess a defendant's proffered necessity defense through an objective framework.... In *United States v. Schoon*... (9th Cir.1992), we applied an objective standard in assessing the fourth element of a necessity defense.... We stated that "the law implies a reasonableness requirement in judging whether legal alternatives exist."...

Embedded in our recognition that a person who seeks to benefit from a justification defense must act reasonably is the principle that justification defenses necessarily must be analyzed objectively.

Schoon echoed this principle:

> "Necessity is, essentially, a utilitarian defense. It therefore justifies criminal acts taken to avert a greater harm, maximizing social welfare by allowing a crime to be committed where the social benefits of the crime outweigh the social costs of failing to commit the crime."

... We continued:

> "The law could not function were people allowed to rely on their *subjective* beliefs and value judgments in determining which harms justified the taking of criminal action."

... The latter statement follows logically from the former statement; after all, if the necessity defense were entirely subjective, then allowing a defendant to benefit from it would only advance the common good when the defendant's subjective beliefs were in alignment with an objective perspective.

More recently in *[United States v.] Arellano-Rivera*, we upheld the district court's preclusion of a defendant's proffered necessity defense, reasoning that the defendant had failed to show that he had no legal alternatives other than illegally reentering the United States.... We denied the defendant's appeal, notwithstanding his speculation that the Attorney General would have denied the defendant's application for reentry based on his advanced medical condition; the defendant's subjective belief that this legal alternative was unavailable to him was insufficient to sustain his necessity defense....

We therefore hold that the test for entitlement to a defense of necessity is objective. The defendant must establish that a reasonable jury could conclude that (1) he was faced with a choice of evils and reasonably chose the lesser evil; (2) he reasonably acted to prevent imminent harm; (3) he reasonably anticipated a causal relation between his conduct and the harm to be avoided; and (4) he reasonably believed there were no other legal alternatives to violating the law.... It is not enough, as Perdomo argues, that the defendant had a subjective but unreasonable belief as to each of these elements. Instead, the defendant's belief must be reasonable, as judged from an objective point of view.

IV

Applying an objective standard to Perdomo's case, his argument that he was entitled to a jury instruction on the necessity defense fails on several bases. Dr. Knauf concluded that Perdomo was in no immediately dire medical condition when he was treated in the emergency room soon after crossing the border; thus Perdomo's crossing was not averting any objective, imminent harm, causing his defense to fail on the second element. Additionally, Dr. Knauf testified that there are multiple clinics in Tijuana where Perdomo could have obtained medical treatment, particularly with the money he had, and that, even assuming that his medical condition had been dire, a saline injection would have been the fastest effective means of bringing Perdomo's condition under control; thus there objectively were legal alternatives to violating the law,

causing Perdomo's defense to fail on the fourth prong. Moreover, from an objective perspective, Perdomo's tactic of hiding in bushes, in dark clothing, and in a remote area, trying to escape border patrol's detection, likely thwarted rather than advanced the speedy receipt of medical treatment, meaning that the defense fails on the third prong as well.

Failure on any one of these three bases, let alone all three, was sufficient to support the district court's determination that Perdomo did not present adequate evidence to establish a prima facie case of the necessity defense. Our case law is clear that a trial judge may decline to allow evidence of a necessity defense where the defendant fails to present a prima facie case.... See, e.g., Arellano-Rivera,...("Where the evidence, even if believed, does not establish all of the elements of a defense, ... the trial judge need not submit the defense to the jury." ... All the more so, then, a trial court may preclude a jury instruction after having heard evidence at trial that collectively presents an insufficient factual foundation to establish the defense as a matter of law.

Perdomo was not entitled to a jury instruction regarding necessity in this case because the defense lacked a necessary foundation in evidence. Even if Perdomo's testimony were believed, he did not establish all of the elements of the defense of necessity.... The district court properly analyzed Perdomo's case under an objective framework and did not abuse its discretion when it denied Perdomo's requested jury instruction.

Affirmed.

Case Questions

1. What must a defendant do to be entitled to a jury instruction on the defense of necessity?
2. What is the difference between an objective and a subjective test? Why was that distinction important in this case?

Excuse Defenses In excuse defenses, the defendant admits to having acted unlawfully, but argues that no criminal responsibility should be imposed, given the particular circumstances accompanying the act. Examples of this type of affirmative defense include duress, insanity, and involuntary intoxication.

A person who commits a criminal act only because he or she was presently being threatened with death or serious bodily injury may assert the

defense called duress/coercion. This defense is based on the theory that the person who committed the criminal act was not exercising free will. Most states do not allow the use of this defense in murder cases. In addition, coercion is difficult to establish. It fails, as we see in the next case, if there was a reasonable alternative to committing the crime, such as running away or contacting the police.

United States v. Scott
901 F.2d 871
U.S. Court of Appeals, Tenth Circuit
April 20, 1990

Seay, District Judge

Appellant, Bill Lee Scott, was found guilty by a jury and convicted of one count of conspiracy to manufacture methamphetamine in violation of 21 U.S.C. § 2, and one count of manufacturing methamphetamine in violation of 21 U.S.C. § 841(a)(1), and 18 U.S.C. § 2. Scott appeals his convictions contending that he was denied a fair trial when the district court refused to instruct the jury on the defense of coercion. We disagree, and therefore affirm the judgment of the district court.

I

Between the middle of August 1987, and the early part of January 1988, Scott made approximately six trips to Scientific Chemical, a chemical supply company in Humble, Texas. Scott made these trips at the request of co-defendant Mark Morrow. These trips resulted in Scott purchasing various quantities of precursor chemicals and laboratory paraphernalia from Scientific Chemical. Some trips resulted in Scott taking possession of the items purchased, other trips resulted in the items being shipped to designated points to be picked up and delivered at a future date. These chemicals and laboratory items were purchased to supply methamphetamine laboratories operated by Morrow in New Mexico with the assistance of Silas Rivera and co-defendants George Tannehill, Jerry Stokes, and Robert Stokes.

Scott first became acquainted with Morrow when Morrow helped him move from Portales, New Mexico, to Truth or Consequences, New Mexico, in late July or early August 1987.... Shortly thereafter, Morrow became aware that Scott was going to Houston, Texas, to sell some mercury and Morrow asked Scott if he could pick up some items from Scientific Chemical.... Scott made the trip to Scientific Chemical and purchased the items Morrow requested.... Scott subsequently made approximately five other trips to Scientific Chemical at Morrow's request to purchase various quantities of precursor chemicals and assorted labware.... During the course of one trip on August 31, 1987, Scott was stopped by Drug Enforcement Administration agents after he had purchased chemicals from Scientific Chemical.... The agents seized the chemicals Scott had purchased as well as $10,800 in U.S. currency and a fully loaded .38 Smith and Wesson.... Scott was not arrested at that time.... Scott, however, was subsequently indicted along with the codefendants after the seizure of large quantities of methamphetamine and precursor chemicals from a laboratory site in Portales in January 1988.

At trial Scott claimed that his purchase of the chemicals and labware on behalf of Morrow was the result of a well-established fear that Morrow would kill him or members of his family if he did not act as Morrow had directed. Scott further claimed that he did not have any reasonable opportunity to escape the harm threatened by Morrow. To support this defense of coercion Scott testified on his own behalf as to the nature and circumstances of the threats. Scott testified that approximately one month after the August 31, 1987, trip Morrow called him at his home in Truth or Consequences and talked him into a meeting in Houston to "get that straightened out." It was Scott's contention that Morrow might not have believed that the money and chemicals had been seized and that Morrow might have thought that he had merely kept the money....

After the trip to Houston and Scientific Chemical to confirm Scott's story about the seizure of the chemicals and cash, Morrow contacted Scott at Scott's daughter's house in Portales to have Scott make another trip to Scientific Chemical to make another purchase.... After Scott declined to make another trip, Morrow responded by stating that Scott would not want something to happen to his daughter or her house.... Scott thereafter made the trip for Morrow....

Approximately one week later, Morrow again came by Scott's daughter's house and wanted Scott to make another trip.... At some point during this discussion they decided to go for a ride in separate vehicles.... After traveling some distance, they both stopped their vehicles and pulled off to the side of the road.... Morrow pulled out a machine gun and two banana clips and emptied the clips at bottles and rocks.... Morrow stated "you wouldn't want to be in front of that thing would you?" and "you wouldn't want any of your family in front of that, would you?" ... Scott responded negatively to Morrow's statements and thereafter made another trip to Scientific Chemical for Morrow.... On another occasion, Scott testified that Morrow threatened him by stating that he had better haul the chemicals if he knew what was good for him....

Scott testified that Morrow not only knew his adult daughter living in Portales, but that he knew his wife and another daughter who were living in Truth or Consequences and that Morrow had been to the residence in Truth or Consequences.... Scott testified that he made these trips for Morrow because he feared for the safety of his family in light of the confrontations he had with Morrow.... Scott stated he had no doubt that Morrow would have carried out his threats.... Scott was aware of information linking Morrow to various murders.... Scott further testified that he did not go to the police with any of this information concerning Morrow because he had gone to them before on other matters and they did nothing.... Further, Scott believed that Morrow had been paying a DEA agent in Lubbock, Texas, for information regarding investigations....

On cross-examination Scott testified that all of Morrow's threats were verbal, ... that he saw Morrow only a few times between August 1987 and January 1988, ... that he had an acquaintance by the name of Bill King who was a retired California Highway Patrolman living in Truth or Consequences, ... and that he could have found a law enforcement official to whom he could have reported the actions of Morrow....

II

A coercion or duress defense requires the establishment of three elements: (1) an immediate threat of death or serious bodily injury, (2) a well-grounded fear that the threat will be carried out, and (3) no reasonable opportunity to escape the threatened harm....

Scott proffered a coercion instruction to the district court in conformity with the above elements. Scott ... contended that the testimony before the court concerning coercion was sufficient to raise an issue for the jury and that a coercion instruction should be given. The district court found that Scott had failed to meet his threshold burden as to all three elements of a coercion defense. Accordingly, the district court refused to give an instruction on the defense of coercion.

Scott contends that the district court committed reversible error by substituting its judgment as to the weight of his coercion defense rather than allowing the jury to decide the issue. Scott maintains that he presented sufficient evidence to place in issue the defense of coercion and that it was error for the district court to usurp the role of the jury in weighing the evidence. We disagree and find that the district court acted properly in requiring Scott to satisfy a threshold showing of a coercion defense, and in finding the evidence insufficient to warrant the giving of a coercion instruction. In doing so, we find the evidence clearly lacking as to the third element for a coercion defense—absence of any reasonable opportunity to escape the threatened harm.

Only after a defendant has properly raised a coercion defense is he entitled to an instruction requiring the prosecution to prove beyond a reasonable doubt that he was not acting under coercion when he performed the act or acts charged....

The evidence introduced must be sufficient as to *all* elements of the coercion defense before the court will instruct the jury as to such defense.... If the evidence is lacking as to any element of the coercion defense the trial court may properly disallow the defense as a matter of law and refuse to instruct the jury as to coercion.... Consequently, a defendant who fails to present sufficient evidence to raise a triable issue of fact concerning the absence of any reasonable opportunity to escape the threatened harm is not entitled to an instruction on the defense of coercion....

The evidence in this case as to Scott's ability to escape the threatened harm wholly failed to approach the level necessary for the giving of a coercion instruction. Scott's involvement with Morrow covered a period of time in excess of one hundred twenty-five days. Scott's personal contact with Morrow was extremely limited during this time. Scott had countless opportunities to contact law enforcement authorities or escape the perceived threats by Morrow during this time. Scott made no attempt to contact law enforcement officials regarding Morrow's activities. In fact, Scott even failed to take advantage of his acquaintance, King, a retired law enforcement official, to seek his assistance in connection with Morrow's threats and activities. Scott's failure to avail himself of the readily accessible alternative of contacting law enforcement officials is persuasive evidence of the hollow nature of Scott's claimed coercion defense.... Clearly, the record establishes that Scott had at his disposal a reasonable legal alternative to undertaking the acts on behalf of Morrow....

Morrow did not accompany Scott when he made the purchases nor was there any evidence that Scott was under surveillance by Morrow. In fact, Scott's contact with Morrow was limited and he admitted he saw Morrow only a few times during the course of his involvement on behalf of Morrow between August 1987 and January 1988. Based on all of these circumstances, the district court was correct in finding that Scott had failed to establish that he had no reasonable opportunity to escape the threatened harm by Morrow.

III
In conclusion, we find that Scott failed to present sufficient evidence to establish that he had no reasonable opportunity to escape the harm threatened by

Morrow. Accordingly, the district court properly refused to instruct the jury as to the defense of coercion. We affirm the judgment of the district court.

Case Questions

1. What must a defendant do to be entitled to a jury instruction on the defense of coercion?
2. Given the facts of this case, why did the trial court refuse to give the instruction?

The law also recognizes that occasionally police officers induce innocent people to commit crimes. When this occurs, the person so induced can raise an affirmative defense called entrapment. If an officer provides a person who is previously disposed to commit a criminal act with the opportunity to do so, that is not entrapment. If, however, an officer placed the notion of criminal wrongdoing in the defendant's mind, and that person was previously indisposed to commit the act, entrapment has occurred, and the charges will be dismissed. In entrapment cases, the defendant admits to having committed a criminal act, but the law relieves him or her of criminal responsibility in order to deter police officers from resorting to this tactic in the future.

Intoxication is frequently recognized as a defense in limited circumstances. Most jurisdictions distinguish between voluntary and involuntary intoxication. Most do not recognize voluntary intoxication as a defense to general intent crimes, and some do not recognize it at all—Hawaii is one example. In many states, however, a person who commits a specific intent crime while voluntarily intoxicated may have a defense if the intoxication is quite severe. In those jurisdictions a defendant cannot be convicted of a specific intent crime if the intoxication was so severe that the person was incapable of forming specific intent. Involuntary intoxication, however, completely relieves a defendant of all criminal responsibility. This could occur, for example, when a defendant inadvertently ingests incompatible medicines.

Insanity is one of the least used and most controversial defenses. A defendant who claims insanity admits to having committed the act, but denies criminal responsibility for that act. Because insanity is a legal and not a medical term, jurisdictions use different tests to define insanity. The M'Naghten Rule specifies that a defendant is not guilty if he or she had a diseased mind at the time of the act and was unable to distinguish right from wrong or was unaware of the nature and quality of his or her act due to a diseased mind. The irresistible impulse test specifies that a defendant is not guilty if he or she knows that an act is wrong and is aware of the nature and quality of the act, but cannot refrain from committing the act. The Model Penal Code specifies that a defendant is not criminally responsible for his or her conduct due to either mental disease or defect and if the defendant lacked substantial capacity to understand its criminality or comply with legal requirements. The states of Idaho, Utah, and Montana do not recognize insanity as a defense.

CRIMINAL PROCEDURE

Criminal procedure is that area of the law that deals with the administration of criminal justice, from the initial investigation of a crime and the arrest of a suspect through trial, sentence, and release.

The goal of criminal justice is to protect society from antisocial activity without sacrificing individual rights, justice, and fair play. The procedures used to apprehend and prosecute alleged criminal offenders must comply with the requirements of the law. One objective of using an adversarial system involving prosecutors and defense attorneys is to ensure that procedural justice is accorded the defendant. The judge umpires the confrontation between the litigants and tries to ensure that both parties receive a fair trial—one that accords with the requirements of the substantive and procedural law. The judge or jury determines the guilt or innocence of the accused by properly evaluating the facts presented in open court. Ideally, the truth emerges from adversarial proceedings conducted in a manner consistent with constitutional guarantees. (See Figure 8.3.)

The constitutional limitations on the way governmental officials procedurally go about investigating criminal offenses and prosecuting alleged criminal offenders are primarily contained in the very general statements of the Fourth, Fifth, Sixth, Eighth, and Fourteenth Amendments to the U.S. Constitution. The U.S. Supreme Court, as well as the other federal and state courts, have played a significant role in determining what these amendments actually mean in practice. Does the Constitution mandate that arrested persons who are indigent be provided a court-appointed attorney? Does the Constitution require that twelve-person juries be convened in criminal cases, or are six-person juries sufficient? Do defendants have a constitutional right to be convicted beyond a reasonable doubt by a unanimous jury, or can a guilty verdict be received that is supported by nine out of twelve jurors?

PROCEEDINGS PRIOR TO TRIAL

A criminal trial occurs only after several preliminary stages have been completed. Although there are some jurisdictional variations in the way these stages occur, some generalizations can be made. The "typical" criminal prosecution originates with a police investigation of a crime that has been either reported to officers or that officers have discovered through their own initiative. This investigation establishes if there really was a crime committed, and if so, determines the identity and whereabouts of the offender. In their investigations, officers are limited by federal and state constitutional and statutory law: (1) They are only permitted to make arrests if they have sufficient evidence to constitute probable cause; (2) they are also limited in conducting *searches* making seizures; and (3) they are limited in the way they conduct custodial interrogations and line-ups. The failure to follow correct procedures in the preliminary stages of a criminal case can result in the suppression of evidence and the dismissal of the charges filed against the accused. Violations of a defendant's constitutional rights can also result in a civil and/or criminal lawsuit against the responsible police officers.

Arrest

An arrest occurs when an officer takes someone into custody for the purpose of holding that person to answer a criminal charge. The arrest must be made in a reasonable manner, and the force employed must be reasonable in proportion to the circumstances and conduct of the party being arrested. The traditional rule was that police officers could make arrests in felonies based on probable cause, but officers were required to observe the commission of a misdemeanor offense in order to make a valid arrest. Today, many states have repealed the in-presence requirement and permit officers to make arrests for both misdemeanors and felonies based on probable cause. Probable cause means that the arresting officer has a well-grounded belief that the individual being arrested has committed, or is committing, an offense.

If police officers intend to make a routine felony arrest in a suspect's home, the U.S. Supreme Court has interpreted the U.S, Constitution as requiring that the officers first obtain an arrest warrant. An arrest warrant is an order issued by a judge, magistrate, or other judicial officer commanding the arresting officer to take an individual into custody and to bring the person before the court to answer criminal charges. Before the court will issue a warrant, a complaint containing the name of the accused, or a description of the accused, must be filed. The complaint must be supported by affidavits and contain a description of the offense and the

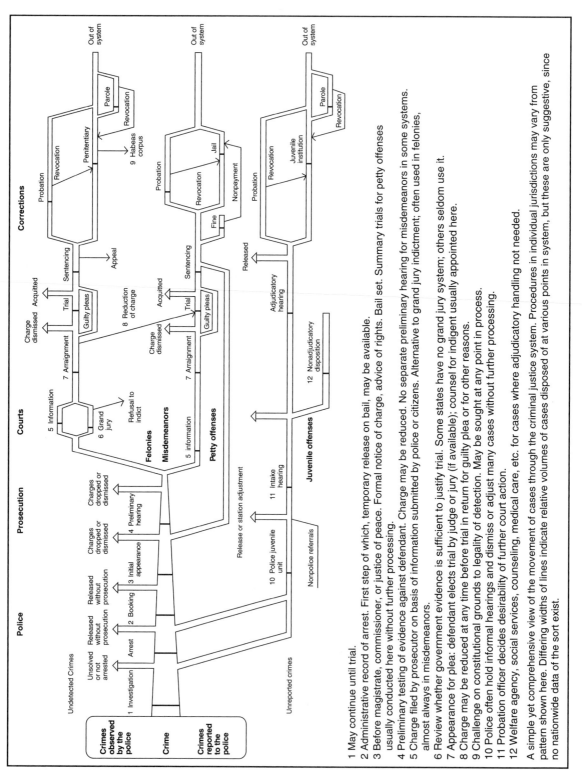

FIGURE 8.3 General View of the Criminal Justice System

1 May continue until trial.
2 Administrative record of arrest. First step of which, temporary release on bail, may be available.
3 Before magistrate, commissioner, or justice of peace. Formal notice of charge, advice of rights. Bail set. Summary trials for petty offenses usually conducted here without further processing.
4 Preliminary testing of evidence against defendant. Charge may be reduced. No separate preliminary hearing for misdemeanors in some systems.
5 Charge filed by prosecutor on basis of information submitted by police or citizens. Alternative to grand jury indictment; often used in felonies, almost always in misdemeanors.
6 Review whether government evidence is sufficient to justify trial. Some states have no grand jury system; others seldom use it.
7 Appearance for plea: defendant elects trial by judge or jury (if available); counsel for indigent usually appointed here.
8 Charge may be reduced at any time before trial in return for guilty plea or for other reasons.
9 Challenge on constitutional grounds to legality of detention. May be sought at any point in process.
10 Police often hold informal hearings and dismiss or adjust many cases without further processing.
11 Probation officer decides desirability of further court action.
12 Welfare agency, social services, counseling, medical care, etc. for cases where adjudicatory handling not needed.

A simple yet comprehensive view of the movement of cases through the criminal justice system. Procedures in individual jurisdictions may vary from pattern shown here. Differing widths of lines indicate relative volumes of cases disposed of at various points in system, but these are only suggestive, since no nationwide data of the sort exist.

surrounding circumstances. A warrant is then issued if the court magistrate decides that (1) the evidence supports the belief that (2) probable cause exists to believe that (3) a crime has been committed and that (4) the suspect is the probable culprit. Many times, the complaining party does not have first-hand information and is relying on hearsay. The warrant may still be issued if the court believes that there is substantial basis for crediting it.

Some policing agencies, such as the FBI, make a large number of arrests based on warrants. Most arrests, however, are made without a warrant, as illustrated in the following *Draper* case. This case also explains what constitutes probable cause to arrest.

Draper v. United States
358 U.S. 307
U.S. Supreme Court
January 26, 1959

Mr. Justice Whittaker delivered the opinion of the Court

The evidence offered at the hearing on the motion to suppress was not substantially disputed. It established that one Marsh, a federal narcotic agent with 29 years' experience, was stationed at Denver; that one Hereford had been engaged as a "special employee" of the Bureau of Narcotics at Denver for about six months, and from time to time gave information to Marsh regarding violations of the narcotic laws, for which Hereford was paid small sums of money, and that Marsh had always found the information given by Hereford to be accurate and reliable. On September 3, 1956, Hereford told Marsh that James Draper (petitioner) recently had taken up abode at a stated address in Denver and "was peddling narcotics to several addicts" in that city. Four days later, on September 7, Hereford told Marsh "that Draper had gone to Chicago the day before [September 6] by train [and] that he was going to bring back three ounces of heroin [and] that he would return to Denver either on the morning of the 8th of September or the morning of the 9th of September also by train." Hereford also gave Marsh a detailed physical description of Draper and of the clothing he was wearing, and said that he would be carrying "a tan zipper bag" and habitually "walked real fast."

On the morning of September 8, Marsh and a Denver police officer went to the Denver Union Station and kept watch over all incoming trains from Chicago, but they did not see anyone fitting the description that Hereford had given. Repeating the process on the morning of September 9, they saw a person, having the exact physical attributes and wearing the precise clothing described by Hereford, alight from an incoming Chicago train and start walking "fast" toward the exit. He was carrying a tan zipper bag in his right hand and the left was thrust in his raincoat pocket. Marsh, accompanied by the police officer, overtook, stopped and arrested him. They then searched him and found the two "envelopes containing heroin" clutched in his left hand in his raincoat pocket, and found the syringe in the tan zipper bag. Marsh then took him (petitioner) into custody. Hereford died four days after the arrest and therefore did not testify at the hearing on the motion.... [T]he Narcotic Control Act of 1956 ... provides in pertinent part:

> "The Commissioner ... and agents, of the Bureau of Narcotics ... may— ...

> "(2) Make arrests without warrant for violations of any law of the United States relating to narcotic drugs ... where the violation is committed in the presence of the person making the arrest or where such person had reasonable grounds to believe that the person to be arrested has committed or is committing such a violation."

The crucial question for us then is whether knowledge of the related facts and circumstances gave Marsh "probable cause" within the meaning of the Fourth Amendment, and "reasonable grounds" ... to believe that petitioner had committed or was committing a violation of the narcotic laws. If it did, the arrest, though without warrant, was lawful....

Petitioner ... contends (1) that the information given by Hereford to Marsh was "hearsay" and, because hearsay is not legally competent evidence in a criminal trial, could not legally have been considered, but should have been put out of mind by Marsh in assessing whether he had "probable cause" and "reasonable grounds" to arrest petitioner without a warrant, and (2) that, even if hearsay could lawfully have been considered, Marsh's information should be held insufficient to show "probable cause" and "reasonable grounds" to believe that petitioner had violated or was violating the narcotic laws and to justify his arrest without a warrant.

Considering the first contention, we find petitioner entirely in error. *Brinegar v. United States*, 338 U.S. 160 ... has settled the question the other way. There, in a similar situation, the convict contended "that the factors relating to inadmissibility of the evidence [for] *purposes of proving guilt at the trial*, deprive[d] the evidence as a whole of sufficiency to show probable cause for the search...." But this Court, rejecting that contention, said: "[T]he so-called distinction places a wholly unwarranted emphasis upon the criterion of admissibility in evidence, to prove the accused's guilt, of facts relied upon to show probable cause. The emphasis, we think, goes much too far in confusing and disregarding the difference between what is required to prove guilt in a criminal case and what is required to show probable cause for arrest or search. It approaches requiring (if it does not in practical effect require) proof sufficient to establish guilt in order to substantiate the existence of probable cause. There is a large difference between the two things to be proved [guilt and probable cause], as well as between the tribunals which determine them, and therefore a like difference in the *quanta* and modes of proof required to establish them." ...

Nor can we agree with petitioner's second contention that Marsh's information was insufficient to show probable cause and reasonable grounds to believe that petitioner had violated or was violating the narcotic laws and to justify his arrest without a warrant. The information given to narcotic agent Marsh by "special employee" Hereford may have been hearsay to Marsh, but coming from one employed for that purpose and whose information had always been found accurate and reliable, it is clear that Marsh would have been derelict in his duties had he not pursued it. And when, in pursuing that information, he

saw a man, having the exact physical attributes and wearing the precise clothing and carrying the tan zipper bag that Hereford had described, alight from one of the very trains from the very place stated by Hereford and start to walk at a "fast" pace toward the station exit, Marsh had personally verified every facet of the information given him by Hereford except whether the petitioner had accomplished his mission and had the three ounces of heroin on his person or in his bag. And surely, with every other bit of Hereford's information being thus personally verified, Marsh had "reasonable grounds" to believe that the remaining unverified bit of Hereford's information—that Draper would have the heroin with him—was likewise true.

"In dealing with probable cause ... as the very name implies, we deal with probabilities. These are not technical; they are the factual and practical considerations of everyday life on which reasonable and prudent men, not legal technicians, act." *Brinegar v. United States*. Probable cause exists where "the facts and circumstances within ... [the arresting officer's] knowledge and of which they had reasonably trustworthy information [are] sufficient in themselves to warrant a man of reasonable caution in the belief that" an offense has been or is being committed....

We believe that, under the facts and circumstances here, Marsh had probable cause and reasonable grounds to believe that petitioner was committing a violation of the laws of the United States relating to narcotic drugs at the time he arrested him. The arrest was therefore lawful, and the subsequent search and seizure, having been made incident to that lawful arrest, were likewise valid. It follows that petitioner's motion to suppress was properly denied and that the seized heroin was competent evidence lawfully received at the trial.

Affirmed.

Case Questions

1. Why did the Supreme Court allow hearsay evidence to be used to establish probable cause, when it would have been inadmissible at trial?
2. Do you believe that an officer who has time to obtain an arrest warrant should have to do so in lieu of making a warrantless arrest in a public place?

Custodial Interrogation

Part of the criminal investigative procedure involves questioning suspects with the aim of obtaining confessions and disclosures of crimes.

The privilege against self-incrimination applies to this questioning done outside the courtroom as well as at the trial. In general, only statements that are voluntarily made by a suspect are admissible.

That is, statements must be the product of free and rational choice. The statements cannot be the result of promises, threats, inducements, or physical abuse. However, the U.S. Supreme Court has ruled that confessions that are neither voluntary nor intelligently made can in some instances be admissible if the coercion amounts to "harmless error."

In the case of *Miranda v. Arizona*, 384 U.S. 436 (1966), the Supreme Court required that people being interrogated while in police custody must first be informed in clear and unequivocal language that they have the right to remain silent, that anything they say can and will be used against them in court, that they have the right to consult with a lawyer and to have a lawyer with them during interrogation, and that they have the right to an appointed lawyer to represent them if they are indigent. If police officers conduct a custodial interrogation without giving these warnings, they violate an accused's Fifth Amendment privilege against self-incrimination. In such a situation, a court may suppress the prosecution's use of the accused's statement at trial to prove his or her guilt. Such statements may, however, be admissible at trial to impeach the credibility of a testifying defendant.

The protections afforded by the *Miranda* warnings may be waived in certain circumstances. The standard is whether a defendant in fact knowingly and voluntarily waived his or her rights.

The *Miranda* decision was very controversial during the late 1960s, and Congress even went so far in 1968 as to enact a statute which was intended to "overrule" the Supreme Court's decision. The lower federal and state courts generally believed that the *Miranda* decision had been grounded in the U.S. Constitution. These courts essentially ignored the statute and went about applying *Miranda*'s principles to the many cases that were brought forward for decision. Things changed, however, in 1999, when the U.S. Court of Appeals for the Fourth Circuit reversed a federal district court's suppression order based on the 1968 statute. The Supreme Court reviewed the Fourth Circuit's action in the following case of *Dickerson v. United States*.

Charles T. Dickerson v. United States
U.S. Supreme Court
No. 99-5525
June 26, 2000

Chief Justice Rehnquist delivered the opinion of the Court

Petitioner Dickerson was indicted for bank robbery, conspiracy to commit bank robbery, and using a firearm in the course of committing a crime of violence, all in violation of the applicable provisions of Title 18 of the United States Code. Before trial, Dickerson moved to suppress a statement he had made at a Federal Bureau of Investigation field office, on the grounds that he had not received "*Miranda* warnings" before being interrogated. The District Court granted his motion to suppress, and the Government took an interlocutory appeal to the United States Court of Appeals for the Fourth Circuit. That court, by a divided vote, reversed the District Court's suppression order. It agreed with the District Court's conclusion that petitioner had not received *Miranda* warnings before making his statement. But it went on to hold that §§3501, which in effect makes the admissibility of statements such as Dickerson's turn solely on whether they were made voluntarily, was satisfied in this case.

It then concluded that our decision in *Miranda* was not a constitutional holding, and that therefore Congress could by statute have the final say on the question of admissibility....

We begin with a brief historical account of the law governing the admission of confessions. Prior to *Miranda*, we evaluated the admissibility of a suspect's confession under a voluntariness test. The roots of this test developed in the common law, as the courts of England and then the United States recognized that coerced confessions are inherently untrustworthy.... Over time, our cases recognized two constitutional bases for the requirement that a confession be voluntary to be admitted into evidence: the Fifth Amendment right against self-incrimination and the Due Process Clause of the Fourteenth Amendment....

> [F]or the middle third of the 20th century our cases based the rule against admitting coerced confessions primarily ... on notions of due process.... The due process test takes into consideration "the totality of all the surrounding

circumstances—both the characteristics of the accused and the details of the interrogation." ...

We have never abandoned this due process jurisprudence, and thus continue to exclude confessions that were obtained involuntarily. But our decisions in *Malloy v. Hogan* ... (1964), and *Miranda* ... (1966) changed the focus of much of the inquiry in determining the admissibility of suspects' incriminating statements. In *Malloy*, we held that the Fifth Amendment's Self-Incrimination Clause is incorporated in the Due Process Clause of the Fourteenth Amendment and thus applies to the States.... We decided *Miranda* on the heels of *Malloy*.

In *Miranda*, we noted that the advent of modern custodial police interrogation brought with it an increased concern about confessions obtained by coercion.... Because custodial police interrogation, by its very nature, isolates and pressures the individual, we stated that "[e]ven without employing brutality, the 'third degree' or [other] specific stratagems, ... custodial interrogation exacts a heavy toll on individual liberty and trades on the weakness of individuals." ... We concluded that the coercion inherent in custodial interrogation blurs the line between voluntary and involuntary statements, and thus heightens the risk that an individual will not be "accorded his privilege under the Fifth Amendment ... not to be compelled to incriminate himself." ... Accordingly, we laid down "concrete constitutional guidelines for law enforcement agencies and courts to follow." ... Those guidelines established that the admissibility in evidence of any statement given during custodial interrogation of a suspect would depend on whether the police provided the suspect with four warnings. These warnings (which have come to be known colloquially as "*Miranda* rights") are: a suspect "has the right to remain silent, that anything he says can be used against him in a court of law, that he has the right to the presence of an attorney, and that if he cannot afford an attorney one will be appointed for him prior to any questioning if he so desires." ...

Two years after *Miranda* was decided, Congress enacted §§3501. That section provides, in relevant part:

"(a) In any criminal prosecution brought by the United States or by the District of Columbia, a confession ... shall be admissible in evidence if it is voluntarily given. Before such confession is received in evidence, the trial judge shall, out of the presence of the jury, determine any issue as to voluntariness. If the trial judge determines that the confession was voluntarily made it shall be admitted in evidence and the trial judge shall

permit the jury to hear relevant evidence on the issue of voluntariness and shall instruct the jury to give such weight to the confession as the jury feels it deserves under all the circumstances.

"(b) The trial judge in determining the issue of voluntariness shall take into consideration all the circumstances surrounding the giving of the confession, including (1) the time elapsing between arrest and arraignment of the defendant making the confession, if it was made after arrest and before arraignment, (2) whether such defendant knew the nature of the offense with which he was charged or of which he was suspected at the time of making the confession, (3) whether or not such defendant was advised or knew that he was not required to make any statement and that any such statement could be used against him, (4) whether or not such defendant had been advised prior to questioning of his right to the assistance of counsel, and (5) whether or not such defendant was without the assistance of counsel when questioned and when giving such confession.

"The presence or absence of any of the above-mentioned factors to be taken into consideration by the judge need not be conclusive on the issue of voluntariness of the confession."

Given §§3501's express designation of voluntariness as the touchstone of admissibility, its omission of any warning requirement, and the instruction for trial courts to consider a non-exclusive list of factors relevant to the circumstances of a confession, we agree with the Court of Appeals that Congress intended by its enactment to overrule *Miranda*.... Because of the obvious conflict between our decision in *Miranda* and §§3501, we must address whether Congress has constitutional authority to thus supersede *Miranda*....

The law in this area is clear. This Court has supervisory authority over the federal courts, and we may use that authority to prescribe rules of evidence and procedure that are binding in those tribunals.... Congress retains the ultimate authority to modify or set aside any judicially created rules of evidence and procedure that are not required by the Constitution....

But Congress may not legislatively supersede our decisions interpreting and applying the Constitution... This case therefore turns on whether the *Miranda* Court announced a constitutional rule or merely exercised its supervisory authority to regulate evidence in the absence of congressional direction.... [T]he Court of Appeals concluded that the protections announced in *Miranda* are not constitutionally required....

We disagree with the Court of Appeals' conclusion....

The *Miranda* opinion itself begins by stating that the Court granted certiorari "to explore some facets of the problems ... of applying the privilege against self-incrimination to in-custody interrogation, and to give concrete constitutional guidelines for law enforcement agencies and courts to follow." ... In fact, the majority opinion is replete with statements indicating that the majority thought it was announcing a constitutional rule.... Indeed, the Court's ultimate conclusion was that the unwarned confessions obtained in the four cases before the Court in *Miranda* "were obtained from the defendant under circumstances that did not meet constitutional standards for protection of the privilege." ...

The dissent argues that it is judicial overreaching for this Court to hold §§3501 unconstitutional unless we hold that the *Miranda* warnings are required by the Constitution, in the sense that nothing else will suffice to satisfy constitutional requirements.... But we need not go farther than *Miranda* to decide this case. In *Miranda*, the Court noted that reliance on the traditional totality-of-the-circumstances test raised a risk of overlooking an involuntary custodial confession ... a risk that the Court found unacceptably great when the confession is offered in the case in chief to prove guilt. The Court therefore concluded that something more than the totality test was necessary.... As discussed above, §§3501 reinstates the totality test as sufficient. Section 3501 therefore cannot be sustained if *Miranda* is to remain the law.

Whether or not we would agree with *Miranda*'s reasoning and its resulting rule, were we addressing the issue in the first instance, the principles of *stare decisis* weigh heavily against overruling it now.... While "*stare decisis* is not an inexorable command," ... particularly when we are interpreting the Constitution ... "even in constitutional cases, the doctrine carries such persuasive force that we have always required a departure from precedent to be supported by some 'special justification.'" ...

We do not think there is such justification for overruling *Miranda*. *Miranda* has become embedded in routine police practice to the point where the warnings have become part of our national culture.... While we have overruled our precedents when subsequent cases have undermined their doctrinal underpinnings, ... we do not believe that this has happened to the *Miranda* decision. If anything, our subsequent cases have reduced the impact of the *Miranda* rule on legitimate law enforcement while reaffirming the decision's core ruling that unwarned statements may not be used as evidence in the prosecution's case in chief.

The disadvantage of the *Miranda* rule is that statements which may be by no means involuntary, made by a defendant who is aware of his "rights," may nonetheless be excluded and a guilty defendant go free as a result. But experience suggests that the totality-of-the-circumstances test which §§3501 seeks to revive is more difficult than *Miranda* for law enforcement officers to conform to, and for courts to apply in a consistent manner....

In sum, we conclude that *Miranda* announced a constitutional rule that Congress may not supersede legislatively. Following the rule of *stare decisis*, we decline to overrule *Miranda* ourselves. The judgment of the Court of Appeals is therefore Reversed.

Case Questions

1. Why did the Fourth Circuit believe the warnings could be dispensed with in Dickerson's case?
2. The Court's opinion defended the *Miranda* warnings requirement on legal grounds, but it went beyond such arguments to advance practical and cultural reasons for not abandoning *Miranda* warnings at this time. What were these arguments?

Searches and Seizures

Examinations of a person or premises are conducted by officers of the law in order to find stolen property or other evidence of guilt to be used by the prosecutor in a criminal action. With some exceptions, a warrant must be obtained by an officer before making a search. (See Figure 8.4.)

As in the case of an arrest warrant, the Fourth Amendment requires probable cause for searches and seizures. Although the Fourth Amendment does not prescribe the forms by which probable cause must be established, evidence of probable cause has traditionally been presented to a magistrate in a written application for warrant supported by oath

---

SEARCH WARRANT

To . . . . *[specify official or officials authorized to execute warrant]:*
    Affidavit having been made before me by . . . . *[affiant]* that he has reason to believe that on the . . . . . [person of *or* premises known as] . . . . *[state name of suspect or specify exact address, including apartment or room number, if any, and give description of premises],* in the City of . . . . , State of . . . . , in the . . . . District of . . . . , there is now being concealed certain property, namely, ... *[specify, such as* certain dies, hubs, molds and plates, fitted and intended to be used for the manufacture of counterfeit coins of the United States, in violation of . . . . *(cite statute)],* and as I am satisfied that there is probable cause to believe that the property so described is being concealed on the . . . . [person *or* premises] above . . . . [named *or* described], and that grounds for issuance of a search warrant exist,
    You are hereby commanded to search within . . . . [ten] days from this date the . . . . [person *or* place] named for the property specified, serving this warrant and making the search . . . . [in the daytime *or* at any time in the day or night], and if the property be found there to seize it, leaving a copy of this warrant and a receipt for the property taken, and prepare a written inventory of the property seized, and promptly return this warrant and bring the property before me, as required by law.
Dated . . . . , 20. . . . .

                                     [Signature and title]

FIGURE 8.4 Sample Search Warrant FRCrP 41(c)

or affirmation, filed by someone who has personal information concerning items to be seized. Today it is increasingly common for statutes to provide for telephonic search warrants as seen in Figure 8.5.

A valid warrant must be specific and sufficiently descriptive. An officer conducting a search is prohibited from going outside the limits set by the warrant.

Courts prefer that searches and seizures are undertaken pursuant to warrants. The warrant process permits a neutral and detached magistrate, in lieu of police officers, to determine if probable cause exists to support a requested search and/or seizure. But the Supreme Court has recognized that warrantless searches and/or seizures are constitutionally reasonable in some circumstances. In an introductory chapter, it is not possible to explain each of the

circumstances in which an exception to the warrant requirement has been recognized. However, the most common of these recognized exceptions can be found in Figure 8.6. Interested students can look up the cases on the Internet or at the library using the case names and corresponding citations.

The Exclusionary Rule

In 1914, the U.S. Supreme Court ruled in the *Weeks* case that the Fourth Amendment prevented the use of evidence obtained from an illegal search and seizure in federal prosecutions. This exclusionary rule remedy was incorporated into the Fourteenth Amendment's Due Process Clause and made binding on the states in the 1961 case of

968.12 Search warrant

(a) *General rule.* A search warrant may be based upon sworn oral testimony communicated to the judge by telephone, radio or other means of electronic communication, under the procedure prescribed in this subsection.

(b) *Application.* The person who is requesting the warrant shall prepare a duplicate original warrant and read the duplicate original warrant, verbatim, to the judge. The judge shall enter, verbatim, what is read on the original warrant. The judge may direct that the warrant be modified.

(c) *Issuance.* If the judge determines that there is probable cause for the warrant, the judge shall order the issuance of a warrant by directing the person requesting the warrant to sign the judge's name on the duplicate original warrant. In addition, the person shall sign his or her own name on the duplicate original warrant. The judge shall immediately sign the original warrant and enter on the face of the original warrant the exact time when the warrant was ordered to be issued. The finding of probable cause for a warrant upon oral testimony shall be based on the same kind of evidence as is sufficient for a warrant upon affidavit.

(d) *Recording and certification of testimony.* When a caller informs the judge that the purpose of the call is to request a warrant, the judge shall place under oath each person whose testimony forms a basis of the application and each person applying for the warrant. The judge or requesting person shall arrange for all sworn testimony to be recorded either by a stenographic reporter or by means of a voice recording device. The judge shall have the record transcribed. The transcript, certified as accurate by the judge or reporter, as appropriate, shall be filed with the court. If the testimony was recorded by means of a voice recording device, the judge shall also file the original recording with the court.

FIGURE 8.5 Excerpt from the Wisconsin Search Warrant Statute [968.12]

Exception	Case	Citation
Abandoned Property	*California v. Greenwood*	486 U.S. 35
Booking Searches	*Illinois v. Lafeyette*	462 U.S. 640
Consent Searches	*Schnecloth v. Bustamonte*	412 U.S. 218
Hot Pursuit	*Warden v. Hayden*	387 U.S. 294
Open Fields	*Oliver v. United States*	466 U.S. 170
	United States v. Dunn	480 U.S. 294
Plain View	*Arizona v. Hicks*	480 U.S. 321
Mobile Vehicles	*Carroll v. United States*	267 U.S. 132
	Chambers v. Maroney	399 U.S. 42
	Ross v. Moffit	417 U.S. 600
	California v. Acevedo	500 U.S. 386
Incident to Arrest	*Chimel v. California*	395 U.S. 752
	United States v. Robinson	414 U.S. 218
	Maryland v. Buie	494 U.S. 325
Vehicle Inventories	*South Dakota v. Opperman*	428 U.S. 364
	Colorado v. Bertine	479 U.S. 367

FIGURE 8.6 Some Common Exceptions to the Search Warrant Requirement

Mapp v. Ohio (367 U.S. 643). Although illegally obtained evidence may not be used by the government to prove the defendant's guilt, such evidence may be used to contradict (impeach) a defendant's trial testimony, thus showing that the defendant's testimony may be untruthful.

The exclusionary rule has been quite controversial because when applied it suppresses evidence which can lead to a failed prosecution. In recent decades, the rule has been severely limited by Supreme Court decisions. Procedural hurdles to its use have been established and judicial doctrines created to narrow the circumstances in which it can be used. Many of these devices are discussed in the next case, *Herring v. United States*. When a recognized exception applies, the evidence can still be admitted as evidence of guilt, despite the violation of the Fourth Amendment. Examples are the independent source exception (when an untainted source of evidence unrelated to the illegal search and seizure is shown to exist) and the good faith exception (which applies if the police acted reasonably in relying on what subsequently turned out to be a defective warrant in obtaining evidence).

The next case highlights a fundamental disagreement that exists among the justices of the U.S. Supreme Court. What is the proper scope of the exclusionary rule? In 2006, the Supreme Court decided *Hudson v. Michigan,* 547 U.S. 586. *Hudson* was a case in which both parties agreed that police officers had violated a Fourteenth Amendment requirement by failing to "knock and announce" their presence prior to forcibly entering Hudson's home and arresting him. Hudson claimed that evidence obtained in this manner should be suppressed. The justices split 5-4 in favor of the government. Justices Scalia (for the majority) and Breyer (joined by Justices Ginsburg, Souter, and Stevens) wrote conflicting opinions as to whether the exclusionary rule applied to these facts. In *Herring* v. *United States*, police officers honestly and reasonably believed that a warrant existed to arrest Herring and did not learn that no valid warrant actually existed until after they had arrested Herring and seized incriminating evidence. Herring sought to suppress the evidence obtained as a result of the arrest. In *Herring* the justices again split 5-4 in favor of the government. Chief Justice Roberts wrote for the majority and Justice Ginsburg authored a dissent which was joined by Justices, Souter, Stevens, and Breyer.

Herring v. United States
555 U.S. 1_(2009)
U.S. Supreme Court
January 14, 2009

Chief Justice Roberts delivered the opinion of the Court

1.
The Fourth Amendment forbids "unreasonable searches and seizures," and this usually requires the police to have probable cause or a warrant before making an arrest. What if an officer reasonably believes there is an outstanding arrest warrant, but that belief turns out to be wrong because of a negligent bookkeeping error by another police employee? The parties here agree that the ensuing arrest is still a violation of the Fourth Amendment, but dispute whether contraband found during a search incident to that arrest must be excluded in a later prosecution.

Our cases establish that such suppression is not an automatic consequence of a Fourth Amendment violation. Instead, the question turns on the culpability of the police and the potential of exclusion to deter wrongful police conduct. Here the error was the result of isolated negligence attenuated from the arrest....

I
On July 7, 2004, Investigator Mark Anderson learned that Bennie Dean Herring had driven to the Coffee County Sheriff's Department to retrieve something from his impounded truck. Herring was no stranger to law enforcement, and Anderson asked the county's warrant clerk, Sandy Pope, to check for any outstanding warrants for Herring's arrest. When she found none, Anderson asked Pope to check with Sharon Morgan, her counterpart in neighboring Dale County. After checking Dale County's computer database,

Morgan replied that there was an active arrest warrant for Herring's failure to appear on a felony charge. Pope relayed the information to Anderson and asked Morgan to fax over a copy of the warrant as confirmation. Anderson and a deputy followed Herring as he left the impound lot, pulled him over, and arrested him. A search incident to the arrest revealed methamphetamine in Herring's pocket, and a pistol (which as a felon he could not possess) in his vehicle....

There had, however, been a mistake about the warrant. The Dale County sheriff's computer records are supposed to correspond to actual arrest warrants, which the office also maintains. But when Morgan went to the files to retrieve the actual warrant to fax to Pope, Morgan was unable to find it. She called a court clerk and learned that the warrant had been recalled five months earlier. Normally when a warrant is recalled the court clerk's office or a judge's chambers calls Morgan, who enters the information in the sheriff's computer database and disposes of the physical copy. For whatever reason, the information about the recall of the warrant for Herring did not appear in the database. Morgan immediately called Pope to alert her to the mixup, and Pope contacted Anderson over a secure radio. This all unfolded in 10 to 15 minutes, but Herring had already been arrested and found with the gun and drugs, just a few hundred yards from the sheriff's office....

Herring was indicted in the District Court for the Middle District of Alabama for illegally possessing the gun and drugs.... He moved to suppress the evidence on the ground that his initial arrest had been illegal because the warrant had been rescinded. The Magistrate Judge recommended denying the motion because the arresting officers had acted in a good-faith belief that the warrant was still outstanding. Thus, even if there were a Fourth Amendment violation, there was "no reason to believe that application of the exclusionary rule here would deter the occurrence of any future mistakes."... The District Court adopted the Magistrate Judge's recommendation,... and the Court of Appeals for the Eleventh Circuit affirmed ....

The Eleventh Circuit found that the arresting officers in Coffee County "were entirely innocent of any wrongdoing or carelessness,..." The court assumed that whoever failed to update the Dale County sheriff's records was also a law enforcement official, but noted that "the conduct in question [wa]s a negligent failure to act, not a deliberate or tactical choice to act." ... Because the error was merely negligent and attenuated from the arrest, the Eleventh Circuit concluded that the benefit of suppressing the evidence "would be marginal or nonexistent," ... and the

evidence was therefore admissible under the good-faith rule of *United States* v. *Leon*, 468 U. S. 897 (1984).

Other courts have required exclusion of evidence obtained through similar police errors, *e.g.*, *Hoay* v. *State*, [Arkansas], 71 S. W. 3d 573, 577 (2002), so we granted Herring's petition for certiorari to resolve the conflict....

II

When a probable-cause determination was based on reasonable but mistaken assumptions, the person subjected to a search or seizure has not necessarily been the victim of a constitutional violation. The very phrase "probable cause" confirms that the Fourth Amendment does not demand all possible precision. And whether the error can be traced to a mistake by a state actor or some other source may bear on the analysis. For purposes of deciding this case, however, we accept the parties' assumption that there was a Fourth Amendment violation. The issue is whether the exclusionary rule should be applied.

A

The Fourth Amendment protects "[t]he right of the people to be secure in their persons, houses, papers, and effects, against unreasonable searches and seizures," but "contains no provision expressly precluding the use of evidence obtained in violation of its commands," ... Nonetheless, our decisions establish an exclusionary rule that, when applicable, forbids the use of improperly obtained evidence at trial.... See, *e.g.*, *Weeks* v. *United States*, 232 U. S. 383, 398 (1914). We have stated that this judicially created rule is "designed to safeguard Fourth Amendment rights generally through its deterrent effect." *United States* v. *Calandra*, 414 U. S. 338, 348 (1974).

In analyzing the applicability of the rule, *Leon* admonished that we must consider the actions of all the police officers involved.... ("It is necessary to consider the objective reasonableness, not only of the officers who eventually executed a warrant, but also of the officers who originally obtained it or who provided information material to the probable-cause determination"). The Coffee County officers did nothing improper. Indeed, the error was noticed so quickly because Coffee County requested a faxed confirmation of the warrant.

The Eleventh Circuit concluded, however, that somebody in Dale County should have updated the computer database to reflect the recall of the arrest warrant. The court also concluded that this error was negligent, but did not find it to be reckless or deliberate....

B

1.

The fact that a Fourth Amendment violation occurred —*i.e.*, that a search or arrest was unreasonable—does not necessarily mean that the exclusionary rule applies.... Indeed, exclusion "has always been our last resort, not our first impulse," ... and our precedents establish important principles that constrain application of the exclusionary rule.

First, the exclusionary rule is not an individual right and applies only where it "'result[s] in appreciable deterrence.' ".... We have repeatedly rejected the argument that exclusion is a necessary consequence of a Fourth Amendment violation. ... Instead we have focused on the efficacy of the rule in deterring Fourth Amendment violations in the future....

In addition, the benefits of deterrence must outweigh the costs.... "We have never suggested that the exclusionary rule must apply in every circumstance in which it might provide marginal deterrence."... "[T]o the extent that application of the exclusionary rule could provide some incremental deterrent, that possible benefit must be weighed against [its] substantial social costs." .... The principal cost of applying the rule is, of course, letting guilty and possibly dangerous defendants go free—something that "offends basic concepts of the criminal justice system." .... "[T]he rule's costly toll upon truth-seeking and law enforcement objectives presents a high obstacle for those urging [its] application."...

These principles are reflected in the holding of *Leon*: When police act under a warrant that is invalid for lack of probable cause, the exclusionary rule does not apply if the police acted "in objectively reasonable reliance" on the subsequently invalidated search warrant.... We (perhaps confusingly) called this objectively reasonable reliance "good faith." ... In a companion case, *Massachusetts* v. *Sheppard*, 468 U. S. 981 (1984), we held that the exclusionary rule did not apply when a warrant was invalid because a judge forgot to make "clerical corrections" to it....

Shortly thereafter we extended these holdings to warrantless administrative searches performed in good-faith reliance on a statute later declared unconstitutional.... Finally ... we applied this good-faith rule to police who reasonably relied on mistaken information in a court's database that an arrest warrant was outstanding. We held that a mistake made by a judicial employee could not give rise to exclusion for three reasons: The exclusionary rule was crafted to curb police rather than judicial misconduct; court employees were unlikely to try to subvert the Fourth Amendment and "most important, there [was] no basis for believing that application of the exclusionary rule in [those]

circumstances" would have any significant effect in deterring the errors.... [L]eft unresolved [was] "whether the evidence should be suppressed if police personnel were responsible for the error,"... an issue not argued by the State in that case, ... but one that we now confront.

2.

The extent to which the exclusionary rule is justified by these deterrence principles varies with the culpability of the law enforcement conduct. As we said in *Leon*, "an assessment of the flagrancy of the police misconduct constitutes an important step in the calculus" of applying the exclusionary rule ... Similarly ... "evidence should be suppressed '... if it can be said that the law enforcement officer had knowledge, or may properly be charged with knowledge, that the search was unconstitutional under the Fourth Amendment."...

Indeed, the abuses that gave rise to the exclusionary rule featured intentional conduct that was patently unconstitutional. In *Weeks*, 232 U. S. 383 ... the officers had broken into the defendant's home (using a key shown to them by a neighbor), confiscated incriminating papers, then returned again with a U. S. Marshal to confiscate even more.... Not only did they have no search warrant, which the Court held was required, but they could not have gotten one had they tried. They were so lacking in sworn and particularized information that "not even an order of court would have justified such procedure...." *Silverthorne Lumber Co.* v. *United States*, 251 U. S. 385 (1920), on which petitioner repeatedly relies, was similar; federal officials "without a shadow of authority" went to the defendants' office and "made a clean sweep" of every paper they could find.... Even the Government seemed to acknowledge that the "seizure was an outrage..."

Equally flagrant conduct was at issue in *Mapp* v. *Ohio*, 367 U. S. 643 (1961), which ... extended the exclusionary rule to the States. Officers forced open a door to Ms. Mapp's house, kept her lawyer from entering, brandished what the court concluded was a false warrant, then forced her into handcuffs and canvassed the house for obscenity... a "flagrant or deliberate violation of rights" ... An error that arises from nonrecurring and attenuated negligence is thus far removed from the core concerns that led us to adopt the rule in the first place. And in fact since *Leon*, we have never applied the rule to exclude evidence... where the police conduct was no more intentional or culpable than this.

3.

To trigger the exclusionary rule, police conduct must be sufficiently deliberate that exclusion can meaningfully deter it, and sufficiently culpable that such deterrence is worth the price paid by the justice system. As laid out in our cases, the exclusionary rule serves to deter deliberate, reckless, or grossly negligent conduct, or in some circumstances recurring or systemic negligence. The error in this case does not rise to that level....

The pertinent analysis of deterrence and culpability is objective, not an "inquiry into the subjective awareness of arresting officers,"... We have already held that "our good-faith inquiry is confined to the objectively ascertainable question whether a reasonably well trained officer would have known that the search was illegal" in light of "all of the circumstances." ...

4.

We do not suggest that all recordkeeping errors by the police are immune from the exclusionary rule. In this case, however, the conduct at issue was not so objectively culpable as to require exclusion. In *Leon* we held that "the marginal or nonexistent benefits produced by suppressing evidence obtained in objectively reasonable reliance on a subsequently invalidated search warrant cannot justify the substantial costs of exclusion." ... The same is true when evidence is obtained in objectively reasonable reliance on a subsequently recalled warrant.

If the police have been shown to be reckless in maintaining a warrant system, or to have knowingly made false entries to lay the groundwork for future false arrests, exclusion would certainly be justified under our cases should such misconduct cause a Fourth Amendment violation. ... Petitioner's fears that our decision will cause police departments to deliberately keep their officers ignorant ... are thus unfounded.

The dissent also adverts to the possible unreliability of a number of databases not relevant to this case.... In a case where systemic errors were demonstrated, it might be reckless for officers to rely on an unreliable warrant system....

Petitioner's claim that police negligence automatically triggers suppression cannot be squared with the principles underlying the exclusionary rule, as they have been explained in our cases. In light of our repeated holdings that the deterrent effect of suppression must be substantial and outweigh any harm to the justice system ... we conclude that when police mistakes are the result of negligence such as that described here, rather than systemic error or reckless disregard of constitutional requirements, any marginal deterrence does not "pay its way." ... In such a case, the criminal should not "go free because the constable has blundered." *People* v. *Defore*,...150 N. E. 585, 587 (1926) (opinion of the Court by Cardozo, J.).

The judgment of the Court of Appeals for the Eleventh Circuit is affirmed.

It is so ordered.

Case Questions

1. What is according to the Chief Justice the primary purpose of the exclusionary rule?
2. How do you believe this opinion will be interpreted by law enforcement officials?
3. Critics claim that court rulings like those in Hudson and Herring establish bad precedents because they allow the prosecution to introduce evidence at trial that officers obtained by violating the Constitution. Do you agree with this argument?

INTERNET TIP

Herring v. United States was a 5-4 decision in the Supreme Court. Chief Justice Roberts on behalf of the court's majority explained its perspective that the exclusionary rule should be strictly confined in scope and rarely applied. The remaining four justices, however had an entirely different view. Justice Ginsburg authored an opinion on behalf of the four dissenters that makes the case in favor of an expansive use of the exclusionary rule. The Ginsburg dissent can be found on the textbook's website.

Investigatory Detentions (Stop and Frisk)

The requirement that police officers have probable cause to arrest makes it difficult for them to investigate individuals whose conduct has aroused their suspicions. The Supreme Court was asked in 1968 to balance police investigative needs against citizen privacy rights in the famous case of *Terry v. Ohio*. In *Terry*, the Supreme Court ruled that it was reasonable under the Fourth Amendment for police officers to make brief seizures of individuals based on reasonable suspicion. The court interpreted the Fourth Amendment as permitting officers to detain suspiciously acting individuals so that their identity could be determined and so that officers could question them about their behavior. However, police officers must be able to articulate the specific facts and circumstances that created a reasonable suspicion in their minds that criminal activity has been, is being, or is about to be committed.

Further, the Supreme Court has ruled that officers who can articulate facts and circumstances that suggest that the stopped individual is armed have a right to make a "frisk." The frisk is less than a full search and consists of the pat-down of the outer clothing of a stopped individual in order to locate weapons that might be used against the officer. If an officer, while conducting the pat-down, feels an object that could be a weapon, the officer is entitled to reach inside the clothing and take the object. If a seized object or weapon is lawfully possessed, it must be returned upon the conclusion of the investigatory detention. If the weapon is unlawfully possessed, it can be seized and used in a criminal prosecution.

Stop and frisk is a very controversial technique in many communities. Police are frequently accused of making stops of individuals based on factors such as race, age, and choice of friends, rather than on actual evidence of impending criminal activity. Officers are also accused of making investigative stops and frisks for the purpose of conducting exploratory searches for evidence.

In the next case, Illinois State Trooper Craig Graham's narcotics detection dog sniffed around Roy Caballes's car while he was being stopped for speeding by Trooper Daniel Gillette. The dog alerted to drugs and the officers discovered marijuana in the trunk. The U.S. Supreme Court granted certiorari to determine "whether the Fourth Amendment requires reasonable, articulable suspicion to justify using a drug-detection dog to sniff a vehicle during a legitimate traffic stop."

Illinois v. Roy I. Caballes
543 U.S. 405
U.S. Supreme Court
January 24, 2005

Justice Stevens delivered the opinion of the Court.
Illinois State Trooper Daniel Gillette stopped respondent for speeding on an interstate highway. When Gillette radioed the police dispatcher to report the stop, a second trooper, Craig Graham, a member of the Illinois State Police Drug Interdiction Team, overheard the transmission and immediately headed for the scene with his narcotics-detection dog. When they arrived, respondent's car was on the shoulder of the road and respondent was in Gillette's vehicle. While Gillette was in the process of writing a warning ticket, Graham walked his dog around respondent's car. The dog alerted at the trunk. Based on that alert, the officers searched the trunk, found marijuana, and arrested respondent. The entire incident lasted less than 10 minutes.

Respondent was convicted of a narcotics offense and sentenced to 12 years' imprisonment and a $256,136 fine. The trial judge denied his motion to suppress the seized evidence and to quash his arrest. He held that the officers had not unnecessarily prolonged the stop and that the dog alert was sufficiently reliable to provide probable cause to conduct the search. Although the Appellate Court affirmed, the Illinois Supreme Court reversed, concluding that because the canine sniff was performed without any "'specific and articulable facts'" to suggest drug activity, the use of the dog "unjustifiably enlarg[ed] the scope of a routine traffic stop into a drug investigation." ...

The question on which we granted certiorari ... is narrow: "Whether the Fourth Amendment requires reasonable, articulable suspicion to justify using a drug-detection dog to sniff a vehicle during a legitimate traffic stop." ... Thus, we proceed on the assumption that the officer conducting the dog sniff had no information about respondent except that he had been stopped for speeding; accordingly, we have omitted any reference to facts about respondent that might have triggered a modicum of suspicion.

Here, the initial seizure of respondent when he was stopped on the highway was based on probable cause, and was concededly lawful. It is nevertheless clear that a seizure that is lawful at its inception can violate the Fourth Amendment if its manner of execution unreasonably infringes interests protected by the Constitution.... A seizure that is justified solely by the interest in issuing a warning ticket to the driver can become unlawful if it is prolonged beyond the time reasonably required to complete that mission. In an earlier case involving a dog sniff that occurred during an unreasonably prolonged traffic stop, the Illinois Supreme Court held that use of the dog and the subsequent discovery of contraband were the product of an unconstitutional seizure.... We may assume that a similar result would be warranted in this case if the dog sniff had been conducted while respondent was being unlawfully detained.

In the state-court proceedings, however, the judges carefully reviewed the details of Officer Gillette's conversations with respondent and the precise timing of his radio transmissions to the dispatcher to determine whether he had improperly extended the duration of the stop to enable the dog sniff to occur. We have not recounted those details because we accept the state court's conclusion that the duration of the stop in this case was entirely justified by the traffic offense and the ordinary inquiries incident to such a stop.

Despite this conclusion, the Illinois Supreme Court held that the initially lawful traffic stop became an unlawful seizure solely as a result of the canine sniff that occurred outside respondent's stopped car. That is, the court characterized the dog sniff as the cause rather than the consequence of a constitutional violation. In its view, the use of the dog converted the citizen-police encounter from a lawful traffic stop into a drug investigation, and because the shift in purpose was not supported by any reasonable suspicion that respondent possessed narcotics, it was unlawful. In our view, conducting a dog sniff would not change the character of a traffic stop that is lawful at its inception and otherwise executed in a reasonable manner, unless the dog sniff itself infringed respondent's constitutionally protected interest in privacy. Our cases hold that it did not.

Official conduct that does not "compromise any legitimate interest in privacy" is not a search subject to the Fourth Amendment.... We have held that any interest in possessing contraband cannot be deemed "legitimate," and thus, governmental conduct that only reveals the possession of contraband

"compromises no legitimate privacy interest." ... This is because the expectation "that certain facts will not come to the attention of the authorities" is not the same as an interest in "privacy that society is prepared to consider reasonable." ... In *United States v. Place* ... (1983), we treated a canine sniff by a well-trained narcotics-detection dog as "sui generis" because it "discloses only the presence or absence of narcotics, a contraband item." ... Respondent likewise concedes that "drug sniffs are designed, and if properly conducted are generally likely, to reveal only the presence of contraband." ... Although respondent argues that the error rates, particularly the existence of false positives, call into question the premise that drug-detection dogs alert only to contraband, the record contains no evidence or findings that support his argument. Moreover, respondent does not suggest that an erroneous alert, in and of itself, reveals any legitimate private information, and, in this case, the trial judge found that the dog sniff was sufficiently reliable to establish probable cause to conduct a full-blown search of the trunk.

Accordingly, the use of a well-trained narcotics-detection dog—one that "does not expose noncontraband items that otherwise would remain hidden from public view,"...—during a lawful traffic stop, generally does not implicate legitimate privacy interests. In this case, the dog sniff was performed on the exterior of respondent's car while he was lawfully seized for a traffic violation. Any intrusion on respondent's privacy expectations does not rise to the level of a constitutionally cognizable infringement.

This conclusion is entirely consistent with our recent decision that the use of a thermal-imaging device to detect the growth of marijuana in a home constituted an unlawful search. *Kyllo v. United States*, ... (2001). Critical to that decision was the fact that the device was capable of detecting lawful activity—in that case, intimate details in a home, such as "at what hour each night the lady of the house takes her daily sauna and bath." ... The legitimate expectation that information about perfectly lawful activity will remain private is categorically distinguishable from respondent's hopes or expectations concerning the nondetection of contraband in the trunk of his car. A dog sniff conducted during a concededly lawful traffic stop that reveals no information other than the location of a substance that no individual has any right to possess does not violate the Fourth Amendment.

The judgment of the Illinois Supreme Court is vacated, and the case is remanded for further proceedings not inconsistent with this opinion.

It is so ordered.

Case Questions

1. Why did the Illinois Supreme Court suppress the marijuana found by Trooper Gillette in the trunk of Roy Caballes's car?
2. Why did the U.S. Supreme Court vacate the Illinois Supreme Court's judgment?
3. Do you think that police officers could use the Supreme Court's ruling in this case to justify the use of dog sniffs of people and luggage on buses, boats, and trains and in public parks? How far do you think they could go before crossing the line and infringing on a reasonable expectation of privacy?

Bail

Although the U.S. Constitution does not guarantee criminal defendants the right to bail, at the present time, bail is authorized for all criminally accused persons except those charged with capital offenses (crimes for which punishment may be death). There is also much constitutional debate about whether legislatures can classify certain other non-capital offenses as nonbailable.

Under the traditional money bail system, the judge sets bail to ensure the defendant's attendance in court and obedience to the court's orders and judgment. The accused is released after he or she deposits with a clerk cash, a bond, or a secured pledge in the amount of bail set by the judge. In 1951 the U.S. Supreme Court declared that the Eighth Amendment prevents federal judges and magistrates from setting bail at a figure higher than an amount reasonably calculated to ensure the defendant's appearance at trial. However, the Eighth Amendment's prohibition against excessive bail has been interpreted to apply only to the federal government and has not been incorporated into the Fourteenth Amendment. Thus it is not binding on the states.

During the early 1960s there was considerable dissatisfaction with the money bail system in this country because it discriminated against low-income people. Reform legislation was enacted in many states. The bail reform statutes made it easier for criminally accused people to obtain their release, since judges were required to use the least restrictive option that would ensure that the accused appeared for trial. In appropriate cases, a defendant could be released on his or her own recognizance (an unsecured promise to appear when required), upon the execution of an unsecured appearance bond, or upon the execution of a secured appearance bond. A judge or magistrate could impose appropriate limitations on the accused's right to travel, as well as his or her contacts with other people. Such laws permitted judges to base their decisions on the defendant's offense, family roots, and employment history. The court was empowered to revoke bail if the accused was found in possession of a firearm, failed to maintain employment, or disregarded the limitations.

Public fear about crimes committed by individuals out on bail resulted in the enactment of legislation authorizing preventive detention in the Bail Reform Act of 1984. Under these laws, people thought to be dangerous who were accused of serious crimes, could be denied bail. The targeted crimes included violent crimes, offenses punishable by life imprisonment, and drug-related crimes punishable by a term of incarceration exceeding ten years. At a hearing a court would determine if the accused was likely to flee and if judicially imposed bail conditions would reasonably protect the public safety. In appropriate cases the court was authorized to deny bail and detain the accused until trial.

The Right to an Attorney

As said earlier, a defendant has an unqualified right to the assistance of retained counsel at all formal stages of a criminal case. An indigent defendant is entitled to a court-appointed attorney under much more limited circumstances. An indigent who is subjected to custodial interrogation by the police is entitled to an appointed attorney in order to protect the Fifth Amendment privilege against self-incrimination. His or her Sixth Amendment right to counsel does not arise until after adversarial judicial proceedings have begun–and the government has formally initiated criminal proceedings against a defendant—usually, after the defendant's initial appearance before a court.

The Supreme Court has ruled that an indigent defendant cannot be sentenced to a term of incarceration for a criminal offense unless appointed counsel was afforded to the defendant at all "critical stages" of a prosecution. Postindictment line-ups for identification purposes, initial appearances, and preliminary hearings, as well as trials and sentencing hearings, are examples of such critical stages. Finally, the Court has recognized that indigents convicted of criminal offenses who want to appeal the trial court's judgment only have a Fourteenth Amendment right to appointed counsel for purposes of a first appeal.

The importance of a nonindigent Missouri defendant's right to be represented by the attorney of his/her choosing (if he or she is paying the bill) was reemphasized in the case of *U.S. v. Gonzalez-Lopez*. The defendant in this case, Cuauhtemoc Gonzalez-Lopez, was accused in federal district court of conspiracy to distribute more than 100 kilograms of marijuana. He rejected the lawyer hired by his parents (Fahle) and hired a California attorney named Low who was not licensed to practice law in Missouri. The district court judge initially permitted Low to represent Gonzalez-Lopez, pro hac vice ("for this case only"), but subsequently revoked this privilege. Gonzalez-Lopez still wanted Low to be his lawyer and so informed Fahle who was allowed to withdraw by the judge. Low made repeated attempts to be permitted to appear pro hac vice, all to no avail. With the trial approaching, Gonzalez-Lopez, while still preferring Low, agreed to be represented by an attorney named Dickhaus. The case was tried to a jury which convicted the defendant. The defendant appealed the district court's refusal to permit him the counsel of his choice to the federal court of appeals which ruled in his favor, reversed his conviction, and ordered a new trial. The U.S. Department of Justice then successfully petitioned the U.S. Supreme Court for certiorari. The government argued in the Supreme Court that while it agreed that Gonzalez-Lopez should have been permitted to be represented by Low, that this was a "harmless error"—it was a trivial mistake that had no bearing on the outcome of the trial. They argued that Gonzalez-Lopez had been effectively represented by Attorney Dickhaus. The government concluded that the appeals court was wrong to have ordered that the conviction be reversed and the case retried. The Supreme Court explains its decision in this case below. This opinion has been extensively edited because of limitations of space.

United States v. Cuauhtemoc Gonzalez-Lopez
548 U.S. 140
U.S. Supreme Court
June 26, 2006

Justice Scalia delivered the opinion of the Court
We must decide whether a trial court's erroneous deprivation of a criminal defendant's choice of counsel entitles him to a reversal of his conviction....

II
The Sixth Amendment provides that "in all criminal prosecutions, the accused shall enjoy the right ... to have the Assistance of Counsel for his defence." We have previously held that an element of this right is the right of a defendant who does not require appointed counsel to choose who will represent him. The Government here agrees ... that "the Sixth Amendment guarantees the defendant the right to be represented by an otherwise qualified attorney whom that defendant can afford to hire, or who is willing to represent the defendant even though he is without funds." ... the Government does not dispute the Eighth Circuit's conclusion in this case that the District

Court erroneously deprived respondent of his counsel of choice.

III

Having concluded, in light of the Government's concession of erroneous deprivation, that the trial court violated respondent's Sixth Amendment right to counsel of choice, we must consider whether this error is subject to review for harmlessness. In *Arizona v. Fulminante*, ... we divided constitutional errors into two classes. The first we called "trial error," because the errors "occurred during presentation of the case to the jury" and their effect may "be quantitatively assessed in the context of other evidence presented in order to determine whether [they were] harmless beyond a reasonable doubt." ... These include "most constitutional errors." ... The second class of constitutional error we called "structural defects." These "defy analysis by 'harmless-error' standards" because they "affect the framework within which the trial proceeds," and are not "simply an error in the trial process itself." ... Such errors include the denial of counsel... , the denial of the right of self-representation, ... the denial of the right to public trial, ... and the denial of the right to trial by jury by the giving of a defective reasonable-doubt instruction.... We have little trouble concluding that erroneous deprivation of the right to counsel of choice, "with consequences that are necessarily unquantifiable and indeterminate, unquestionably qualifies as 'structural error.'" ... Different attorneys will pursue different strategies with regard to investigation and discovery, development of the theory of defense, selection of the jury, presentation of the witnesses, and style of witness examination and jury argument. And the choice of attorney will affect whether and on what terms the defendant cooperates with the prosecution, plea bargains, or decides instead to go to trial. In light of these myriad aspects of representation, the erroneous denial of counsel bears directly on the "framework within which the trial proceeds" ... —or indeed on whether it proceeds at all. It is impossible to know what different choices the rejected counsel would have made, and then to quantify the impact of those different choices on the outcome of the proceedings. Many counseled decisions, including those involving plea bargains and cooperation with the government, do not even concern the conduct of the trial at all. Harmless-error analysis in such a context would be a speculative inquiry into what might have occurred in an alternate universe.

... To determine the effect of wrongful denial of choice of counsel, however, we would not be looking for mistakes committed by the actual counsel, but for differences in the defense that would have been made by the rejected counsel—in matters ranging from questions asked on voir dire and cross-examination to such intangibles as argument style and relationship with the prosecutors. We would have to speculate upon what matters the rejected counsel would have handled differently—or indeed, would have handled the same but with the benefit of a more jury-pleasing courtroom style or a longstanding relationship of trust with the prosecutors. And then we would have to speculate upon what effect those different choices or different intangibles might have had. The difficulties of conducting the two assessments of prejudice are not remotely comparable....

IV

Nothing we have said today casts any doubt or places any qualification upon our previous holdings that limit the right to counsel of choice and recognize the authority of trial courts to establish criteria for admitting lawyers to argue before them. As the dissent too discusses, ... the right to counsel of choice does not extend to defendants who require counsel to be appointed for them.... Nor may a defendant insist on representation by a person who is not a member of the bar.... We have recognized a trial court's wide latitude in balancing the right to counsel of choice against the needs of fairness, ... and against the demands of its calendar.... The court has, moreover, an "independent interest in ensuring that criminal trials are conducted within the ethical standards of the profession and that legal proceedings appear fair to all who observe them." ... None of these limitations on the right to choose one's counsel is relevant here. This is not a case about a court's power to enforce rules or adhere to practices that determine which attorneys may appear before it, or to make scheduling and other decisions that effectively exclude a defendant's first choice of counsel. However broad a court's discretion may be ... the District Court here erred when it denied respondent his choice of counsel. Accepting that premise, we hold that the error violated respondent's Sixth Amendment right to counsel of choice and that this violation is not subject to harmless-error analysis.

The judgment of the Court of Appeals is affirmed, and the case is remanded for further proceedings consistent with this opinion.

It is so ordered.

Case Questions

1. What did the government argue before the Supreme Court?
2. Why did the Supreme Court majority reject this argument?
3. This case was resolved in the Supreme Court on a 5–4 vote because the justices found it to be a very close question. If you were a justice, how would you have voted and why?

Line-ups

The police conduct line-ups before witnesses for the purpose of identifying a suspect. When formal charges are pending, an accused may not be in a line-up before witnesses for identification unless the accused and accused's counsel have been notified in advance. In addition, the line-up may not be conducted unless counsel is present, so that the defendant's counsel is not deprived of the right to effectively challenge the line-up procedures and any identifications that result. It is interesting to note that the U.S. Supreme Court has not required the presence of an attorney where an array of photographs is used in lieu of an actual line-up. Unlike a line-up, a photo array is not a trial-like confrontation that requires the presence of the accused.

Preliminary Hearing and Grand Jury

In order to weed out groundless or unsupported criminal charges before trial, a preliminary hearing is conducted or a grand jury is convened. In a preliminary hearing, the court examines the facts superficially to determine whether there is a strong enough case to hold the arrestee for further proceedings. The prosecution presents evidence before the court, without a jury, in order to determine if there is probable cause. The accused has a right to be present at the preliminary hearing, to cross-examine prosecution witnesses, and to present evidence. If there is no chance of conviction because of lack of evidence, the court dismisses the charges.

A grand jury, composed of people selected at random from the list of registered voters, decides whether there is reason to believe an accused has committed an offense, not whether the person is guilty or innocent. Thus, it determines whether a person should be brought to trial. The decision is based on evidence heard during a secret criminal investigation attended by representatives of the state and witnesses. The grand jury has the right to subpoena witnesses and documents for its investigation. The accused has no right to be present at the proceedings. A grand jury returns an indictment (an accusation in writing) to the court if it believes that the evidence warrants a conviction. (See Figure 8.7.)

For prosecutions involving crimes against the United States, the Fifth Amendment provides that all prosecution for infamous crimes (an offense carrying a term of imprisonment in excess of one year) must be commenced by a grand jury indictment. Virtually all states provide for a preliminary hearing for charges involving a felony. Approximately half of the states require a grand jury indictment, while the remainder use a bill of information (a formal charging document prepared by the prosecutor and filed with the court).

Arraignment

An arraignment follows a grand jury indictment or the judge's finding of probable cause at a preliminary hearing. At arraignments, accused people are advised of the formal charges against them as required by the Sixth Amendment. The description of the charges must be sufficiently clear so that the defendant may be able to enter an intelligent plea. The accused are also asked whether they understand the charges and whether they have an attorney. The court appoints counsel if the accused cannot afford an attorney. Finally, a trial date is set at the arraignment. Defendants and their counsel must be given adequate opportunity to prepare for trial.

```
┌─────────────────────────────────────────────────────────────────────┐
│                    UNITED STATES DISTRICT COURT                       │
│                 FOR THE  . . . . . . DISTRICT OF  . . . . . .          │
│                        . . . . . . . DIVISION                         │
│                                                                       │
│  United States of America,                                            │
│          Plaintiff,                Crim. No.  . . . . . . . . . . . .  │
│              v.                    (. . . . .–USC §  . . . . . . . . . │
│  _____ )                                        │
│          Defendant.                                                   │
│                                                                       │
│                          INDICTMENT                                   │
│       The grand jury charges:                                         │
│       On or about the  . . . . . day of  . . . . . ., 20 . . . . . ., in the . . . . . . │
│  District of . . . . . . . . . . , . . . . . . . [defendant] . . . . . . . [state essential facts │
│  constituting offense charged], in violation of . . . . . . . USC § . . . . . . . . │
│  Dated . . . . . . . , 20. . . . .                                    │
│                                                                       │
│                          A True Bill.                                 │
│                                                                       │
│                                              [Signature],             │
│                                              Foreman                   │
│                                                                       │
│  . . . . . . . ,                                                      │
│  United States Attorney.                                              │
└─────────────────────────────────────────────────────────────────────┘
```

F I G U R E   8.7   Sample Indictment [FRCrP 7(c)]

The defendant is called on to enter a plea at the arraignment. This plea may be guilty, ***nolo contendere***, or not guilty. The plea of guilty is entered in the great majority of situations; it is simply a confession of guilt. The plea of *nolo contendere* is the same as a guilty plea, except that it cannot be used later against the accused as an admission. It is a confession only for the purposes of the criminal prosecution and does not bind the defendant in a civil suit for the same wrong. When the defendant pleads not guilty, the prosecution has the burden of proving him or her guilty beyond a reasonable doubt at the trial.

Plea bargaining is the process by which the accused agrees to enter a plea of guilty, often to a lesser offense, in exchange for a promise by the prosecuting attorney to recommend either a relatively light sentence or a dismissal of part of the charges.

The judge does not have to accept the prosecutor's recommendations and will explain this to the defendant before accepting a negotiated plea.

THE CRIMINAL TRIAL

Every person who is charged with a crime has a constitutional right to a trial. In this way a defendant has the opportunity to confront and cross-examine the witnesses against him or her, testify and present evidence and arguments as a defense against the charges, have the assistance of an attorney in most cases, and take full advantage of the rights and protections afforded all people accused of crimes under the Constitution. Trial procedures are essentially the same in criminal and civil trials.

The prosecution is the plaintiff and must initially present legally sufficient evidence of the defendant's criminal culpability with respect to each element of the crime or the judge will dismiss the charges and terminate the trial. A criminal defendant, unlike a civil defendant, has a constitutional right not to testify at trial. This privilege is often waived by defendants, however, because they wish to explain their version of the facts to the jury or to the judge in a bench trial. Every criminal defendant (and juvenile charged with a criminal offense) is additionally protected by the constitutional due process requirement that the prosecution prove guilt beyond a reasonable doubt in order to be entitled to a judgment of conviction.[7]

The Sixth and Fourteenth Amendments guarantee criminally accused people many important rights, including notice of the charges, trial by jury, a speedy and public trial, and representation by counsel. Also protected by these amendments are the rights to present witnesses and evidence and to cross-examine opposing witnesses.

Trial by Jury

Accused people have a constitutional right to have their guilt or innocence decided by a jury composed of people representing a cross section of their community (this right to a jury trial does not extend to offenses traditionally characterized as petty offenses). The jury trial right is a safeguard against arbitrary and highhanded actions of judges.

Unless a jury trial is waived, the jury is selected at the beginning of the trial. The number of jurors ranges from six to twelve, depending on state law. A unanimous decision is not required for conviction in all states. However, twelve jurors are required in federal criminal courts, and a unanimous decision is necessary for a conviction. If a jury cannot agree on a verdict, it is called a hung jury and the judge dismisses the charges. In this situation, the prosecutor may retry the defendant before a new jury.

If a defendant pleads guilty, there are no questions of fact for a jury to decide, and the judge will proceed to the sentencing phase.

Fair and Public Trial and Cross-Examination

The right to be confronted by their accusers in an adversary proceeding protects accused people from being convicted by testimony given in their absence without the opportunity of cross-examination. The defendant also has a right to a public trial. This constitutional right prevents courts from becoming instruments of persecution through secret action. The right is not unlimited, however. It is subject to the judge's broad power and duty to preserve order and decorum in the courtroom. Judges may limit the number of spectators in order to prevent overcrowding or to prevent disturbances. Judges also have the power to impose sanctions on participants and observers for acts that hinder or obstruct the court in administering justice.

Right to a Speedy Trial

The accused's right to a speedy trial is interpreted as meaning that the trial should take place as soon as possible without depriving the parties of a reasonable period of time for preparation. This right, applicable to both the state and federal courts, protects an accused from prolonged imprisonment prior to trial, prevents long delay that could impair the defense of an accused person through the loss of evidence, and prevents or minimizes public suspicion and anxiety connected with an accused who is yet untried.

The right to speedy trial attaches when the prosecution begins, either by indictment or by the actual restraints imposed by arrest. How much time must elapse to result in an unconstitutional delay varies with the circumstances. The accused has the burden of showing that the delay was the fault of the state and that it resulted in prejudice.

The Prosecutor's Role

The sovereignty has the duty of prosecuting those who commit crimes; its attorney for this purpose is the prosecutor. As trial lawyer for the sovereignty, the prosecutor has extensive resources for investigation and preparation. The prosecutor is not at liberty to distort or misuse this information, and must disclose information that tends to relieve the accused of guilt. Any conduct of a prosecutor or judge that hinders the fairness of a trial to the extent that the outcome is adversely affected violates the defendant's right to due process.

Sentencing

Following conviction or a guilty plea, judges determine the sentence that will be imposed on the convicted defendant in accordance with the laws of that particular jurisdiction. The sentencing options, depending on the sentencing structure of the jurisdiction, usually include confinement, fines, community service, restitution, and probation. A convicted person has the right to challenge the constitutionality of his/her sentence by arguing that it is cruel and unusual and in violation of the Eighth Amendment or that it violates the Equal Protection Clause of the Fourteenth Amendment.

Appeal

The federal and state constitutions guarantee defendants a fair trial, but not an error-free trial. In the federal and state judicial systems appellate courts determine if significant errors that warrant correction were committed by lower courts. The U.S. Constitution does not require states to provide for appellate review, although all defendants who enter a plea of not guilty are granted at least one appeal. The states differ in the number of discretionary appeals that are made available. A defendant who appeals has to exhaust all appellate opportunities at the state level and raise a federal question before petitioning the U.S. Supreme Court for a writ of certiorari. A person convicted of a crime in a federal district court can obtain review in the U.S. Court of Appeals, and then petition the U.S. Supreme Court for certiorari.

The prosecution is prohibited by the Fifth Amendment's double jeopardy clause, and by due process, from appealing a court's entry of a judgment of acquittal based on a jury verdict or on the insufficiency of the evidence. Statutes, however, may permit the prosecution to appeal (1) pretrial court orders suppressing evidence, (2) a trial judge's refusal to enter judgment on the jury's guilty verdict and the entry instead of judgment for the defendant (JNOV), (3) where the sentencing judge abused his or her discretion and imposed an "inadequate" sentence, and (4) from a judgment of acquittal for the sole purpose of clarifying the law.

Habeas Corpus

The writ of *habeas corpus* (Latin for "you have the body") is used to test the legality of a person's detention by government. It is frequently used by prisoners who have been unsuccessful in directly appealing their convictions and who are serving sentences of imprisonment. The writ of *habeas corpus* was recognized in Article 1, Section 9, of the U.S. Constitution. Congress extended the common law writ to federal prisoners in the Judiciary Act of 1789, and to state prisoners in 1867. Congress replaced the common law practices defining prisoners' use of the writ with legislation in 1948, and the U.S. Supreme Court expanded its scope during the 1960s and 1970s.

Federal *habeas corpus* has much strategic importance because it permits convicted people, whether convicted in a federal or state court, to seek collateral review of their sentences in a federal court. The *habeas* process permits local federal district courts to "take a second look" at the functioning of state judicial systems. There have been times when Congress essentially deferred to the judiciary as to the substantive scope of this writ and access to *habeas corpus* expanded when the Supreme Court felt it desirable to exercise more oversight over states. In 1976, however, the Supreme Court decided that the federal judiciary was being flooded with federal *habeas* petitions filed by prisoners in state prisons for drug offenses who wanted to challenge the constitutionality of police searches and seizures that led to their convictions. Because these petitioners' claims had already been fully litigated in state courts (albeit unsuccessfully), the court's majority concluded that there was no reason for continued federal oversight in these cases. The justices announced, in the case of *Stone v. Powell*, 428 U.S. 465 (1976), that district courts could no longer review Fourth Amendment claims by way of *habeas corpus* if "the state has provided an opportunity for full and fair litigation of a Fourth Amendment Claim." This ruling meant that unless the U.S. Supreme Court granted a certiorari petition after a Fourth Amendment claim had been fully litigated in the state courts, the federal judiciary had essentially closed the door to such claims. It is interesting to note that the court has not adopted a similar strategy with respect to *habeas corpus* petitions based on the Fifth and Sixth Amendments. The most recent significant piece of federal legislation relating to *habeas corpus* review was enacted in 1996 when Congress greatly limited the scope of federal *habeas corpus* review in the Antiterrorism and Effective Death Penalty Act of 1996 (AEDPA).[8]

The respondent in the next case, Michael W. Haley, was convicted of stealing a calculator from a Wal-Mart store in 1997, an offense punishable by incarceration for a minimum of six months and up to two years in state prison. Haley was also accused of being a habitual felony offender, because his official conviction records indicated that he had two prior convictions. His first conviction was for delivering amphetamines (October 18, 1991), and his second was for robbery (October 15, 1991). Haley was convicted of theft and found to be a habitual offender. As a convicted habitual offender, he was subject to an enhanced sentence on the theft charge, and he was sentenced to a prison term of sixteen years and 180 days. His appellate lawyer's direct appeal to the intermediate state appellate court was denied, and the Texas Court of Criminal Appeals refused to take the case on discretionary appeal.

Haley began serving his prison sentence. While in prison, he discovered that his sentence exceeded what was statutorily authorized. The sentence enhancement statute, he learned, required that the two convictions prior to the theft offense be chronological. Haley's were not. His conviction for the robbery (his second crime), became final three days prior to when his conviction for the drug offense (his first crime) became final. This mistake went

unnoticed by his trial lawyer and his appellate attorney on direct appeal. Trial lawyers have an obligation to carefully look for error and make the necessary objections and motions in order to clarify the nature of any errors and specify the legal basis for any objections. They do this in order to "protect the record" and thereby "preserve" these issues for appeal. It is important that all alleged errors are identified as such in the official transcript of the proceedings, which is taken down by the official court reporter. The transcript and the documents in the court's file constitute the "record" of the trial. The trial record is the official version of what transpired at the trial and sentencing stages of the case. It is the primary source of factual information about what transpired at the trial level for appellate courts. Errors that are not preserved at trial are likely to be deemed waived and therefore ignored at the appellate level. Constitutional claims not properly preserved at trial become known as "defaulted constitutional claims."

Haley, despite having lost twice on direct appeal, still had one last chance within the Texas judicial process to have his claims heard. This option was to seek *habeas corpus* relief. He petitioned the state court of criminal appeals, claiming that his trial attorney had been ineffective and that because the evidence actually showed that the prior convictions relied upon to enhance his sentence were not chronological, his due process rights had been violated. His petition was denied.

Having no other source of relief under Texas law, Haley petitioned the U.S. District Court for the Eastern District of Texas for a writ of *habeas corpus*. The district court, after being apprised of the sentencing error, found in favor of Haley on due process grounds and according to page 4 of Haley's Supreme Court brief, "the final judgment provided that the State of Texas had ninety days to resentence Mr. Haley without the improper enhancement, and that if it failed to do so, his conviction would be reversed." Having disposed of the case on due process grounds, the district court did not address the ineffective counsel claim. Doug Dretke, who was in charge of Texas's correctional institutions, appealed the district court's decision to the U.S. Court of Appeals for the Fifth Circuit. The Fifth Circuit affirmed the lower court's ruling on the due process claim. Meanwhile, because the ninety-day period established by the district court had expired, that court carried through on its threat and ordered that Haley's conviction be reversed and Haley, after serving six years of incarceration (four years more than the statutory maximum for the theft offense), was released from prison. Dretke decided to seek to overturn the precedent established by the Fifth Circuit, that the "actual innocence exception" to the procedural default doctrine could be applied in noncapital cases, and successfully petitioned the U.S. Supreme Court for a writ of certiorari. According to pages 5 and 6 of Haley's Supreme Court brief, Director Dretke "advised the District Court that he intend[ed] … to reincarcerate Mr. Haley for the remaining ten years of his admittedly erroneous sentence if this Court reverses the Fifth Circuit's decision."[9]

Doug Dretke v. Michael W. Haley
541 U.S. 386
U.S. Supreme Court
May 3, 2004

Justice O'Connor delivered the opinion of the Court.
Out of respect for finality, comity, and the orderly administration of justice, a federal court will not entertain a procedurally defaulted constitutional claim in a petition for *habeas corpus* absent a showing of cause and prejudice to excuse the default. We have recognized a narrow exception to the general rule when the *habeas* applicant can demonstrate that the alleged constitutional error has resulted in the conviction of one who is actually innocent of the underlying offense or, in the capital sentencing context, of the aggravating circumstances rendering the inmate eligible for the death penalty…. The question before us is whether this exception applies where an applicant asserts "actual innocence" of a noncapital sentence. Because the District Court failed first to consider alternative grounds for relief urged by respondent, grounds that might obviate any need to reach the actual innocence question, we vacate the judgment and remand.

I
In 1997, respondent Michael Wayne Haley was arrested after stealing a calculator from a local Wal-Mart and attempting to exchange it for other merchandise. Respondent was charged with, and found guilty at trial of, theft of property valued at less than $1,500, which, because respondent already had two prior theft convictions, was a "state jail felony" punishable by a maximum of two years in prison…. The State also charged respondent as a habitual felony offender. The indictment alleged that respondent had two prior felony convictions and that the first—a 1991 conviction for delivery of amphetamine—"became final prior to

the commission" of the second—a 1992 robbery…. The timing of the first conviction and the second offense is significant: Under Texas' habitual offender statute, only a defendant convicted of a felony who "has previously been finally convicted of two felonies, and the second previous felony conviction is for an offense that occurred subsequent to the first previous conviction having become final, … shall be punished for a second-degree felony." § 12.42(a)(2)…. A second degree felony carries a minimum sentence of 2 and a maximum sentence of 20 years in prison. § 12.33(a).

Texas provides for bifurcated trials in habitual offender cases…. If a defendant is found guilty of the substantive offense, the State, at a separate penalty hearing, must prove the habitual offender allegations beyond a reasonable doubt…. During the penalty phase of respondent's trial, the State introduced records showing that respondent had been convicted of delivery of amphetamine on October 18, 1991, and attempted robbery on September 9, 1992. The record of the second conviction, however, showed that respondent had committed the robbery on October 15, 1991—three days before his first conviction became final. Neither the prosecutor, nor the defense attorney, nor the witness tendered by the State to authenticate the records, nor the trial judge, nor the jury, noticed the 3-day discrepancy. Indeed, the defense attorney chose not to cross-examine the State's witness or to put on any evidence.

The jury returned a verdict of guilty on the habitual offender charge and recommended a sentence of 16½ years; the court followed the recommendation. Respondent appealed. Appellate counsel did not mention the 3-day discrepancy nor challenge the sufficiency of the penalty-phase evidence to support the habitual offender enhancement. The State Court of Appeals affirmed respondent's conviction and sentence; the Texas Court of Criminal Appeals refused respondent's petition for discretionary review.

Respondent thereafter sought state postconviction relief, arguing for the first time that he was ineligible for the habitual offender enhancement based on the timing of his second conviction.... The state *habeas* court refused to consider the merits of that claim because respondent had not raised it, as required by state procedural law, either at trial or on direct appeal.... The state *habeas* court rejected respondent's related ineffective assistance of counsel claim, saying only that "counsel was not ineffective" for failing to object to or to appeal the enhancement.... The Texas Court of Criminal Appeals summarily denied respondent's state *habeas* application....

In August 2000, respondent filed a timely *pro se* application for a federal writ of *habeas corpus* ... renewing his sufficiency of the evidence and ineffective assistance of counsel claims.... The State conceded that respondent was "correct in his assertion that the enhancement paragraphs as alleged in the indictment do not satisfy section 12.42(a)(2) of the Texas Penal Code." ... Rather than agree to resentencing, however, the State argued that respondent had procedurally defaulted the sufficiency of the evidence claim by failing to raise it before the state trial court or on direct appeal.... The Magistrate Judge, to whom the *habeas* application had been referred, recommended excusing the procedural default and granting the sufficiency of the evidence claim because respondent was "'actually innocent' of a sentence for a second-degree felony." ... Because she recommended relief on the erroneous enhancement claim, the Magistrate Judge did not address respondent's related ineffective assistance of counsel challenges.... The District Court adopted the Magistrate Judge's report, granted the application, and ordered the State to resentence respondent "without the improper enhancement." ...

The Court of Appeals for the Fifth Circuit affirmed, holding narrowly that the actual innocence exception "applies to noncapital sentencing procedures involving a career offender or habitual felony offender." ... Finding the exception satisfied, the panel then granted relief on the merits of respondent's otherwise defaulted sufficiency of the evidence claim. In so doing, the panel assumed that challenges to the sufficiency of noncapital sentencing evidence are cognizable on federal *habeas*....

The Fifth Circuit's decision exacerbated a growing divergence of opinion in the Courts of Appeals

regarding the availability and scope of the actual innocence exception in the noncapital sentencing context.... We granted the State's request for a writ of certiorari....

II

The procedural default doctrine, like the abuse of writ doctrine, "refers to a complex and evolving body of equitable principles informed and controlled by historical usage, statutory developments, and judicial decisions." ... [T]he doctrine has its roots in the general principle that federal courts will not disturb state court judgments based on adequate and independent state law procedural grounds.... That being the case, we have recognized an equitable exception to the bar when a *habeas* applicant can demonstrate cause and prejudice for the procedural default.... The cause and prejudice requirement shows due regard for States' finality and comity interests while ensuring that "fundamental fairness [remains] the central concern of the writ of *habeas corpus*." ...

The cause and prejudice standard is not a perfect safeguard against fundamental miscarriages of justice ... [and we have] recognized a narrow exception to the cause requirement where a constitutional violation has "probably resulted" in the conviction of one who is "actually innocent" of the substantive offense.... We subsequently extended this exception to claims of capital sentencing error.... Acknowledging that the concept of "actual innocence" did not translate neatly into the capital sentencing context, we limited the exception to cases in which the applicant could show "by clear and convincing evidence that, but for constitutional error, no reasonable juror would have found the petitioner eligible for the death penalty under the applicable state law." ...

We are asked in the present case to extend the actual innocence exception to procedural default of constitutional claims challenging noncapital sentencing error. We decline to answer the question in the posture of this case and instead hold that a federal court faced with allegations of actual innocence, whether of the sentence or of the crime charged, must first address all nondefaulted claims for comparable relief and other grounds for cause to excuse the procedural default....

Petitioner here conceded at oral argument that respondent has a viable and "significant" ineffective assistance of counsel claim.... Success on the merits would give respondent all of the relief that he seeks—i.e., resentencing. It would also provide cause to excuse the procedural default of his sufficiency of the evidence claim....

[I]t is precisely because the various exceptions to the procedural default doctrine are judge-made rules that courts as their stewards must exercise restraint, adding to or expanding them only when necessary. To hold otherwise would be to license district courts to riddle the cause and prejudice standard with ad hoc exceptions whenever they perceive an error to be "clear" or departure from the rules expedient. Such an approach, not the rule of restraint adopted here, would have the unhappy effect of prolonging the pendency of federal *habeas* applications as each new exception is tested in the courts of appeals. And because petitioner has assured us that it will not seek to reincarcerate respondent during the pendency of his ineffective assistance claim ... the negative consequences for respondent of our judgment to vacate and remand in this case are minimal....

To be sure, not all claims of actual innocence will involve threshold constitutional issues. Even so, as this case and the briefing illustrate, such claims are likely to present equally difficult questions regarding the scope of the actual innocence exception itself. Whether and to what extent the exception extends to noncapital sentencing error is just one example. The judgment of the Court of Appeals is vacated, and the case is remanded for further proceedings consistent with this opinion.

It is so ordered.

Case Questions

1. Why did the Supreme Court refuse to decide whether the actual innocence exception was applicable to this case as held by the Fifth Circuit?
2. Considering the outcome, did the Texas department of corrections really "lose" anything because of this decision?
3. To what extent, if at all, do you believe that federal courts should "oversee" the workings of state judicial systems by means of the writ of *habeas corpus*?

The Remand to the Court of Appeals

In the last sentence of Justice O'Connor's opinion, the Court vacated (set aside) the Court of Appeals' judgment that the "actual innocence exception" to the procedural default doctrine could be applied in noncapital sentencing cases. It left that question for another day. The Court also remanded the case back to the U.S. Court of Appeals for the Fifth Circuit. The Fifth Circuit responded as follows.

Doug Dretke v. Michael W. Haley
376 F.3d 316
U.S. Court of Appeals for the Fifth Circuit
June 25, 2004

Carl E. Stewart, Circuit Judge
On Writ of Certiorari to the United States Court of Appeals for the Fifth Circuit, the United States Supreme Court by an Opinion entered May 3, 2004, ... held that a federal court faced with allegations of actual innocence, whether of the sentence or of the crime charged, must first address all nondefaulted claims of comparable relief and other grounds for cause to excuse the procedural default. Dretke and the State of Texas conceded before the Supreme Court that Haley has a viable and significant ineffective assistance of counsel claim, success on the merits would give respondent all of the relief that he seeks, i.e., resentencing, and also would provide cause to excuse the procedural default of his sufficiency of the evidence claim, and that the State will not reincarcerate Haley during the pendency of his ineffective assistance of counsel claim.

Accordingly, the judgment of this court, 306 F.3d 257, was vacated, and the case remanded for further proceedings consistent with its opinion. It is hereby ordered that this case be remanded to the district court for further proceedings to expeditiously resolve Haley's claim.

Conclusion After Remand to the District Court

Pursuant to the remand order, the U.S. District Court for the Eastern District of Texas subsequently awarded Haley summary judgment on his ineffective assistance of counsel claim and the matter was finally concluded.

CHAPTER SUMMARY

This chapter has provided students with a "taste" of what criminal law and criminal procedure are all about. Readers began with an introduction to the sources of American criminal law and learned about the common law influences, how the legislature came to replace the judiciary as the dominant policymaker, and how the Model Penal Code has greatly influenced the modern development of criminal law. Criminal law classifications such as *mala in se*, *mala prohibita*, felony, and misdemeanor were explained, as were the constitutional limitations on the imposition of criminal liability and criminal punishments.

The focus then shifted to learning about the basic components of a criminal offense: the wrongful act, guilty mind, the concurrence of act and intent, and, in some crimes, causation. This was followed by an overview of the inchoate crimes: solicitation, attempt, and conspiracy, which society relies upon to protect itself from people who have taken some steps toward, but have not yet completed, their intended criminal objectives. The criminal law portion of the chapter concluded with a discussion of some of the common recognized defenses, including affirmative defenses that can mitigate, justify, or excuse a defendant's conduct.

The next discussion focused on criminal procedure, which is the administrative process society has established for determining whether a crime has been committed and whether the person or persons accused are guilty of the crime. Readers learned that constitutional provisions limit this process, in particular the Fourth, Fifth, Sixth, Eighth, and Fourteenth Amendments.

Next was an overview of several procedural stages that occur prior to the commencement of a criminal trial. These included the requirements for a valid arrest, custodial interrogations of suspects (*Miranda* rights), searches and seizures, and investigative detentions (stop and frisk). Other topics discussed included bail and the right to an attorney. The pretrial segment concluded with explanations of the preliminary hearing, the role of the grand jury, and what happens at an arraignment. This was followed by an overview of the criminal trial, the defendant's rights to a trial by jury, a fair and public trial, to cross-examine witnesses, and the right to a speedy trial. The chapter concluded with discussions of the prosecutor's role, sentencing, and a defendant's right to appeal and to petition for a writ of *habeas corpus*.

CHAPTER QUESTIONS

1. Holmes was convicted and received a death sentence for murdering, beating, raping, and robbing an eighty-six-year-old woman. Although his convictions and sentence were affirmed on appeal by the state courts, he was granted a new trial upon postconviction review. Holmes sought at the new trial to introduce evidence that the victim's attacker was another man named White.

   The trial court excluded Holmes's evidence that White had perpetrated the crime. The state supreme court affirmed the trial court ruling "where there is strong evidence of an appellant's guilt, especially where there is strong forensic evidence, the proffered evidence about a third party's alleged guilt does not raise a reasonable inference as to the appellant's own innocence." Holmes successfully petitioned for a writ of certiorari. He argued to the U.S. Supreme Court that he had a constitutionally protected right to introduce proof that White had committed the attack on the victim despite the introduction of forensic which, if believed, would "strongly support a guilty verdict." Was the state supreme court correct?

Holmes v. South Carolina, 126 S. Ct. 1727 (2006)

2. Brandon, a driver, was lawfully stopped by Colorado state police officers for speeding. Besides Brandon, there were two passengers in the vehicle—one male and one female. When the officer asked Brandon to produce evidence that he had the right to operate the vehicle, Brandon only produced an identification card. The officer then contacted his dispatcher to determine if Brandon was a licensed driver. While waiting for the dispatcher's response, the officer asked Brandon and the passengers questions as to their destination and the purpose of their trip. The officer became suspicious when Brandon's and the passengers' answers were inconsistent. The dispatch notified the officer that Brandon was licensed in California.

   The officer then asked for and was given permission to search the car by the vehicle's owner, the female passenger. Brandon, however, refused to consent to a search. The officer then put a police dog into the car and after the dog alerted to the presence of cocaine, it was seized, and Brandon was arrested. Brandon was convicted of possession of a controlled substance. He unsuccessfully moved to suppress the evidence of the cocaine. The trial court ruled that the female passenger had consented to the search that led to the discovery of the cocaine. The defendant then appealed to the state court of appeals. Should the appellate court reverse the trial court and suppress the evidence of cocaine?

   State of Colorado v. Brandon, 03CA1176 (2005)

3. James Brogan was unexpectedly visited one evening at his home by federal investigators. The officers had records indicating that Brogan had received cash payments from a company whose employees were members of a union in which Brogan was an officer. Such an act would have violated federal bribery statutes. The officers asked Brogan if he had received any cash or gifts from the company. Brogan answered "no." Brogan was charged with violating federal bribery laws and with lying to a federal officer who was in the course of performing his or her duty to investigate criminal activity, as prohibited by 18 U.S. Code Section 1001. Do you see any potential for the possible abuse of prosecutorial discretion if persons in Brogan's situation can be convicted of a federal felony for untruthfully answering an incriminating question posed by federal officers in the course of an investigation?

   Brogan v. United States, 96-1579 (1998)

4. Kalb County Police Officer Richardson stopped a motorist named Brown on Candler Road while it was raining for driving without using his headlights because he suspected that Brown might be DUI. Brown explained to the officer that he was not aware the lights were not on. When the officer asked Brown to produce his operator's license and evidence of insurance, Brown began a search for the requested documentation. While looking for the documents, Brown pulled an object out of one of his front pockets that the officer described as a "piece of paper" approximately one to two inches in diameter. When the paper fell in between Brown's legs onto the car seat, Brown immediately closed his legs. The officer asked Brown, "What are you trying to hide?" The trial testimony is silent as to Brown's reply. Officer Richardson then asked Brown to exit the car; however, Brown did not comply. He continued looking in the car for the documents until they were finally found. Brown appeared nervous and shaky while poking around the car. This made Richardson suspicious that Brown was attempting to hide something. After Brown produced the documents, Officer

Richardson asked him to step out of the car. Brown was given a Terry investigative pat-down, which produced neither weapons nor contraband, and he was then placed unarrested inside of Richardson's locked patrol car. The officer then proceeded to enter Brown's car to look for the piece of paper. Richardson found it, in plain view, on the car seat. This search disclosed the existence of several small plastic bags which were subsequently identified from field tests to be rock cocaine. Brown was then arrested for possession of cocaine. The officer did not know that anything was in the piece of paper at the time he conducted his search, and he did not see the cocaine in the paper until the officer subjected it to close examination. Did Officer Richardson have probable cause to make a warrantless search of Brown's car?

Brown v. State of Georgia, 504 S.E.2d 443 (1998)

5. Hillsborough County, New Hampshire, installed a teleconferencing system between the Nashua District Court and the Nashua Police Station. This system made it unnecessary to have police officers physically transport arrested persons to the courthouse for purposes of arraignment and setting bail. This procedure was intended to conserve time as well as money, and was approved by the state supreme court. Jay Larose and two other people were arraigned using this system, and bail was set, but they were unable to make bail. They subsequently petitioned for a writ of *habeas corpus*. The petitioners argued that this high-tech approach to arraignments violated their due process rights under the state and federal constitutions. They also maintained that the teleconferencing procedure violated a state statute which required that arrested persons "… shall be taken before a district or municipal court without unreasonable delay, but not exceeding 24 hours, Sundays and holidays excepted, to answer for the offense." What due process rights could they have claimed were infringed upon, based on these facts? How might the

state respond to the claimed infringement of the statutory right?

Larose v. Hillsborough County, 702 A.2d 326 (1997)

6. Bajakajian tried to take $357,000 in cash out of the United States without completing the necessary paperwork. After his conviction, the federal government asked the court to order that the entire sum be forfeited, as called for by the federal statute. Would this punitive forfeiture violate the requirements of the excessive fines clause of the Eighth Amendment?

United States v. Bajakajian, 96-1487 (1998)

7. The Edmonds Police Department received an anonymous tip contained in a mailed note that Robert Young was growing marijuana in his house. A police detective went to the address. He noted that the windows of the house were always covered, bright lights never could be seen inside, and there was no apparent odor of marijuana detectable from the public sidewalk. The detective obtained records of Young's electric power consumption and believed it to be unusually high—a factor that his prior experience suggested to him was consistent with the cultivation of marijuana. The detective contacted the federal DEA, which supplied an agent trained in the use of infrared thermal detection equipment. This equipment, when used at night, can detect manmade heat sources. Young's house was subjected to thermal surveillance, and the results suggested a pattern consistent with the growth of marijuana; the downstairs, for example, was warmer than the upstairs portion of the house. The detective used this information to establish probable cause for the issuance of a search warrant. Officers executing the search warrant found marijuana within the house, and Young was arrested and charged with possession of marijuana with intent to manufacture or deliver. Young sought to suppress the evidence on the grounds that the infrared surveillance of his home constituted an infringement of his

rights under the Fourth Amendment to the U.S. Constitution and a corresponding right under the Washington State Constitution.

Do you believe the suppression motion should be granted?

State of Washington v. Young, 867 P.2d 593 (1994)

NOTES

1. G. Jones, *The Sovereignty of the Law* (Toronto: University of Toronto Press, 1973), pp. 189–191.

2. Schwartz, *The Law in America* (New York: McGraw-Hill, 1974), p. 9.

3. Schwartz, pp. 12–18, 72, 73.

4. *Craig v. Boren*, 429 U.S. 197 (1976).

5. *Eisenstadt v. Baird*, 405 U.S. 438 (1972).

6. *Craig v. Boren*, 429 U.S. 197 (1976).

7. *In re Winship*, 379 U.S. 358 (1970).

8. The AEDPA was enacted by members of Congress who believed that the writ was being abused by desperate defendants seeking to postpone their execution dates.

9. The sources for this factual statement include Justice O'Connor's opinion and pages 1–5 of the "Statement of the Case" portion of the respondent's brief in the Supreme Court.

IX

✳

Family Law

CHAPTER OBJECTIVES

1. *Understand the antecedents of American family law.*
2. *Describe differing configurations of a family.*
3. *Explain legal obligations that parents have vis-à-vis their children.*
4. *Understand how spousal relationships end.*
5. *Describe the basic stages of the adoption process.*
6. *Explain the two approaches to the division of property in divorce.*

People today conceptualize the family's role in society very differently than they did in seventeenth-century America. Back then, the economy was primarily agrarian. The family unit was responsible for providing care for all its members from the cradle to the grave. There was no social security for the old or unemployment security for those out of work. The family was responsible for performing functions within the home that today are often provided by others outside the home. There were no public schools to educate the young, no day-care centers, no hospitals to care for the sick, and no nursing homes to care for the elderly. Even religious instruction had to be provided by families within the home until churches could be established.[1] In the past, it was common for families to be larger than is typical today. It took many people to take care of the domestic tasks and work the farms. Uneducated children were not as mobile and had fewer opportunities to leave the family home and town. They were also subject to parental discipline for longer periods of time than is the case today.

Today, families headed by a single parent are common. The number of children under eighteen years of age living with a single parent has increased from 19.7 percent in 1980 to 28 percent in 2004, according to the U.S. Census Bureau.[2] Instead of working on a farm, today parents often work outside the home. They sometimes commute long distances to their jobs. It is the norm in two-parent families for both parents to work as they struggle to meet even the most basic needs of the nuclear family. Families today are often unable to provide care for elder family members.[3] Today's children, as they grow into adolescence, become more mobile and independent much sooner than in the past, and parents often find themselves having less ability to exercise influence and control.[4]

These changes in families have been accompanied by changes in society's legal expectations about family life.[5] **Family law**, also called *domestic relations law*, has been recognized as a legal subfield only since the early 1900s.[6] Despite the law's tardiness in formally recognizing family law, legal institutions have long been concerned with the rights and responsibilities of family members.

One of the most enduring features of the western tradition is the deference shown by the law to family self-governance, also called *family autonomy*.[7] This deference was recognized in Roman law[8] and was subsequently incorporated into Anglo-Saxon law;[9] canon law (the law applied in the English ecclesiastical courts, which historically handled domestic relations cases);[10] and the common law.[11]

Also dating from the time of the Roman emperors, however, is the legal recognition that society, through government, has a legitimate right to prevent the maltreatment and abuse of family members.[12] One example of this interest is the existence of laws in every state prohibiting child abuse and neglect. As the U.S. Supreme Court explained, governments today are expected to intervene to prevent "harm to the physical or mental health of [a] child..."[13]

These two legal principles, which accompanied the English immigrants who settled the eastern seaboard of North America, were widely accepted, although they were modified to meet the particular needs of each colony.[14]

In colonial America, the family was the most important unit of society. It was essential to preserving public order and producing economic stability.[15] After the Revolutionary War, the structure of the family was weakened by the ready availability of land, the shortage of labor, and the ease with which individuals could migrate.[16] Independence also brought a greater appreciation for the rights of individuals within the family and a corresponding decline in the outmoded view of a father's traditional rights (see Figure 9.1).[17] This trend has continued to the present time, and today mothers and fathers have equal rights and responsibilities.

Given the complexity of family law, the differences in the laws of the fifty states, and the limitations of available space, this chapter can provide only an introductory overview of the topic. This

---

From *Chapman v. Mitchell*, 44 A2d 392, 393 (1945)

" . . . the plaintiff [husband] is the master of his household. He is the managing head, with control and power to preserve the family relation, to protect its members and to guide their conduct. He has the obligation and responsibility of supporting, maintaining, and protecting the family and the correlative right to exclude intruders and unwanted visitors from the home despite the whims of the wife."

FIGURE 9.1 The Role of the Father—An Old-Fashioned View

discussion focuses on how families are created, the nature of the rights and responsibilities of family members, how family relationships are terminated, and emerging issues such as the evolving dispute about the nature of the family.[18]

WHAT IS A FAMILY?

Although it is apparent that a **family** always includes people in a relationship, major disagreements exist about the precise meaning of the term. There is no single universally accepted legal definition of family. The word is generally defined in operational terms by statute within a particular context (i.e., for purposes of specifying who is entitled to particular benefits).

Traditionally, families have been based on kinship and defined as the "customary legal relationship established by birth, marriage, or adoption."[19] This definition has been challenged recently on the ground that it is too rigid. Critics argue that even if they are unmarried, "two adult lifetime partners whose relationship is long term and characterized by an emotional and financial commitment and interdependence"[20] should receive the same rights and benefits as those who have been married. Anthropologists such as Collier, Rosaldo, and Yanagisako have favored such a functional approach. They think of families as "spheres of human relationships" that "hold property, provide care and welfare, and attend particularly to the young—a sphere conceptualized as a realm of love and intimacy," as contrasted with other more "impersonal" relationships.[21]

The legal definition of family becomes important because special rights, benefits, and privileges favor family membership. Some of these benefits are intangible, such as the societal approval that accompanies birth, marriage, and to some extent adoption. Another example is the sense of identity that family members have as to who they are and how they fit into the larger society.[22] Many other benefits are more tangible. Federal law, for example, favors married taxpayers who file jointly, and it provides social security benefits to family members in some circumstances. State legislatures also provide economic and noneconomic benefits favoring family members. Although states differ greatly as to the nature and scope of the benefits provided, they often include housing rights, homestead acts that protect some family property from creditors, statutory provisions that determine inheritance rights in the event a family member dies without leaving a will, mutual spousal support obligations, evidentiary privileges that prohibit adverse spousal testimony and that protect private spousal communications, and limited tort immunities. Many employers also favor families. Employee fringe-benefit packages frequently provide family members with health and life insurance programs and 401k plans, as well as family leave and educational benefits.

Strong families perform essential tasks and help to create social and economic stability.[23] The family unit is expected to produce, and care for the needs of, the young. This includes raising children who will grow into responsible, well-adjusted, educated, and employable adults. Family members are expected to care for each other from "cradle to grave," especially in times of crisis. When families do not or cannot meet the most basic responsibilities, they have to be met at public expense.

In the following case, the City of East Cleveland sought to enforce a housing ordinance that restricted the occupancy of a dwelling unit to a single family. The ordinance defined "family" so restrictively that it was criminal for a grandmother to live under the same roof with one of her grandsons. As written, the law prohibited a grandmother, her adult son, and his child, Dale Jr., and another grandson, John (who was a first cousin of Dale Jr.), from living as a family. John had moved to his grandmother's house after the death of his mother. The grandmother, Inez Moore, was criminally charged, convicted of the crime, and sentenced to serve a jail term of five days and pay a $25 fine. Mrs. Moore appealed her conviction because she believed the statute violated her rights under the Due Process Clause of the Fourteenth Amendment. Notice the Supreme Court's sympathy for the concept of the extended family, as well as the roles played by race, culture, and economics in defining the nature of a family.

Moore v. City of East Cleveland, Ohio
431 U.S. 494
U.S. Supreme Court
May 31, 1977

Mr. Justice Powell announced the judgment of the Court, and delivered an opinion in which Mr. Justice Brennan, Mr. Justice Marshall, and Mr. Justice Blackmun joined

East Cleveland's housing ordinance, like many throughout the country, limits occupancy of a dwelling unit to members of a single family.... But the ordinance contains an unusual and complicated definitional section that recognizes as a "family" only a few categories of related individuals.... Because her family, living together in her home, fits none of those categories, appellant stands convicted of a criminal offense. The question in this case is whether the ordinance violates the Due Process Clause of the Fourteenth Amendment.

I

Appellant, Mrs. Inez Moore, lives in her East Cleveland home together with her son, Dale Moore, Sr., and her two grandsons, Dale, Jr., and John Moore, Jr. The two boys are first cousins rather than brothers; we are told that John came to live with his grandmother and with the elder and younger Dale Moores after his mother's death.

In early 1973, Mrs. Moore received a notice of violation from the city, stating that John was an "illegal occupant" and directing her to comply with the ordinance. When she failed to remove him from her home, the city filed a criminal charge. Mrs. Moore moved to dismiss, claiming that the ordinance was constitutionally invalid on its face. Her motion was overruled, and upon conviction she was sentenced to five days in jail and a $25 fine. The Ohio Court of Appeals affirmed after giving full consideration to her constitutional claims, and the Ohio Supreme Court denied review....

II

The city argues that our decision in *Village of Belle Terre v. Boraas*, 416 U.S. 1, 94 (1974), requires us to sustain the ordinance attacked here.

But one overriding factor sets this case apart from *Belle Terre*. The ordinance there affected only unrelated individuals. It expressly allowed all who were related by "blood, adoption, or marriage" to live together, and in sustaining the ordinance we were careful to note that it promoted "family needs" and "family values." ...East Cleveland, in contrast, has

chosen to regulate the occupancy of its housing by slicing deeply into the family itself. This is no mere incidental result of the ordinance. On its face it selects certain categories of relatives who may live together and declares that others may not. In particular, it makes a crime of a grandmother's choice to live with her grandson in circumstances like those presented here.

When a city undertakes such intrusive regulation of the family ...the usual judicial deference to the legislature is inappropriate. "This Court has long recognized that freedom of personal choice in matters of marriage and family life is one of the liberties protected by the Due Process Clause of the Fourteenth Amendment." *Cleveland Board of Education v. LaFleur*, 414 U.S. 632 ... (1974) ... But when the government intrudes on choices concerning family living arrangements, this Court must examine carefully the importance of the governmental interests advanced and the extent to which they are served by the challenged regulation....

When thus examined, this ordinance cannot survive. The city seeks to justify it as a means of preventing overcrowding, minimizing traffic and parking congestion, and avoiding an undue financial burden on East Cleveland's school system. Although these are legitimate goals, the ordinance before us serves them marginally, at best. For example, the ordinance permits any family consisting only of husband, wife, and unmarried children to live together, even if the family contains a half dozen licensed drivers, each with his or her own car. At the same time it forbids an adult brother and sister to share a household, even if both faithfully use public transportation. The ordinance would permit a grandmother to live with a single dependent son and children, even if his school-age children number a dozen, yet it forces Mrs. Moore to find another dwelling for her grandson John, simply because of the presence of his uncle and cousin in the same household. We need not labor the point. Section 1341.08 has but a tenuous relation to alleviation of the conditions mentioned by the city.

III

The city would distinguish the cases based on *Meyer* and *Pierce*. It points out that none of them "gives grandmothers any fundamental rights with respect to grandsons," ... and suggests that any constitutional right to live together as a family extends only to the nuclear family—essentially a couple and their dependent children.

To be sure, these cases did not expressly consider the family relationship presented here. They were immediately concerned with freedom of choice with respect to childbearing, e.g., *LaFleur, Roe v. Wade, Griswold, supra*, or with the rights of parents to the custody and companionship of their own children, *Stanley v. Illinois, supra*, or traditional parental authority in matters of child rearing and education. *Yoder, Ginsberg, Pierce, Meyer, supra*. But unless we close our eyes to the basic reasons why certain rights associated with the family have been accorded shelter under the Fourteenth Amendment's Due Process Clause, we cannot avoid applying the force and rationale of these precedents to the family choice involved in this case....

Appropriate limits on substantive due process come not from drawing arbitrary lines but rather from careful "respect for the teachings of history [and], solid recognition of the basic values that underlie our society."

Our decisions establish that the Constitution protects the sanctity of the family precisely because the institution of the family is deeply rooted in this Nation's history and tradition. It is through the family that we inculcate and pass down many of our most cherished values, moral and cultural.

Ours is by no means a tradition limited to respect for the bonds uniting the members of the nuclear family. The tradition of uncles, aunts, cousins, and especially grandparents sharing a household along with parents and children has roots equally venerable and equally deserving of constitutional recognition. Over the years millions of our citizens have grown up in just such an environment, and most, surely, have profited from it. Even if conditions of modern society have brought about a decline in extended family households, they have not erased the accumulated wisdom of civilization, gained over the centuries and honored throughout our history, that supports a larger conception of the family. Out of choice, necessity, or a sense of family responsibility, it has been common for close relatives to draw together and participate in the duties and the satisfactions of a common home. Decisions concerning child rearing, which *Yoder, Meyer, Pierce* and other cases have recognized as entitled to constitutional protection, long have been shared with grandparents or other relatives who occupy the same household—indeed who may take on major responsibility for the rearing of the children. Especially in times of adversity, such as the death of a spouse or economic

need, the broader family has tended to come together for mutual sustenance and to maintain or rebuild a secure home life. This is apparently what happened here.

Whether or not such a household is established because of personal tragedy, the choice of relatives in this degree of kinship to live together may not lightly be denied by the State. *Pierce* struck down an Oregon law requiring all children to attend the State's public schools, holding that the Constitution "excludes any general power of the State to standardize its children by forcing them to accept instruction from public teachers only." ...By the same token the Constitution prevents East Cleveland from standardizing its children—and its adults—by forcing all to live in certain narrowly defined family patterns.

Reversed.

Mr. Justice Brennan, with whom Mr. Justice Marshall joins, concurring

I join the plurality's opinion. I agree that the Constitution is not powerless to prevent East Cleveland from prosecuting as a criminal and jailing a 63-year-old grandmother for refusing to expel from her home her now 10-year-old grandson who has lived with her and been brought up by her since his mother's death when he was less than a year old. I do not question that a municipality may constitutionally zone to alleviate noise and traffic congestion and to prevent overcrowded and unsafe living conditions, in short to enact reasonable land-use restrictions in furtherance of the legitimate objectives East Cleveland claims for its ordinance. But the zoning power is not a license for local communities to enact senseless and arbitrary restrictions which cut deeply into private areas of protected family life. East Cleveland may not constitutionally define "family" as essentially confined to parents and the parents' own children. The plurality's opinion conclusively demonstrates that classifying family patterns in this eccentric way is not a rational means of achieving the ends East Cleveland claims for its ordinance, and further that the ordinance unconstitutionally abridges the "freedom of personal choice in matters of ... family life [that] is one of the liberties protected by the Due Process Clause of the Fourteenth Amendment." ... I write only to underscore the cultural myopia of the arbitrary boundary drawn by the East Cleveland ordinance in the light of the tradition of the American home that has been a feature of our society since our beginning as a Nation—the "tradition" in the plurality's words, "of uncles, aunts, cousins, and especially grandparents sharing a household along with parents and children."...

...The line drawn by this ordinance displays a depressing insensitivity toward the economic and emotional needs of a very large part of our society.

In today's America, the "nuclear family" is the pattern so often found in much of white suburbia.... "The Constitution cannot be interpreted, however, to tolerate the imposition by government upon the rest of us of white suburbia's preference in patterns of family living. The "extended family" that provided generations of early Americans with social services and economic and emotional support in times of hardship, and was the beachhead for successive waves of immigrants who populated our cities, remains not merely still a pervasive living pattern, but under the goad of brutal economic necessity, a prominent pattern—virtually a means of survival—for large numbers of the poor and deprived minorities of our society. For them, compelled pooling of scant resources requires compelled sharing of a household.

The "extended" form is especially familiar among black families. We may suppose that this reflects the truism that black citizens, like generations of white immigrants before them, have been victims of economic and other disadvantages that would worsen if they were compelled to abandon extended, for nuclear, living patterns....

I do not wish to be understood as implying that East Cleveland's enforcement of its ordinance is motivated by a racially discriminatory purpose: The record of this case would not support that implication. But the prominence of other than nuclear families among ethnic and racial minority groups, including our black citizens, surely demonstrates that the "extended family" pattern remains a vital tenet of our society. It suffices that in prohibiting this pattern of family living as a means of achieving its objectives, appellee city has chosen a device that deeply intrudes into family associational rights that historically have been central, and today remain central, to a large proportion of our population.... Indeed, *Village of Belle Terre v. Boraas*, 416 U.S. 1 ... (1974), the case primarily relied upon by the appellee, actually supports the Court's decision. The Belle Terre ordinance barred only unrelated individuals from constituting a family in a single-family

zone. The village took special care in its brief to emphasize that its ordinance did not in any manner inhibit the choice of related individuals to constitute a family, whether in the "nuclear" or "extended" form. This was because the village perceived that choice as one it was constitutionally powerless to inhibit. Its brief stated: "Whether it be the extended family of a more leisurely age or the nuclear family of today the role of the family in raising and training successive generations of the species makes it more important, we dare say, than any other social or legal institution.... If any freedom not specifically mentioned in the Bill of Rights enjoys a 'preferred position' in the law it is most certainly the family." ...The cited decisions recognized, as the plurality recognizes today, that the choice of the "extended family" pattern is within the "freedom of personal choice in matters of ...family life [that] is one of the liberties protected by the Due Process Clause of the Fourteenth Amendment." ...

Mr. Justice Stevens, concurring in the judgment
In my judgment the critical question presented by this case is whether East Cleveland's housing ordinance is a permissible restriction on appellant's right to use her own property as she sees fit...

There appears to be no precedent for an ordinance which excludes any of an owner's relatives from the group of persons who may occupy his residence on a permanent basis. Nor does there appear to be any justification for such a restriction on an owner's use of his property. The city has failed totally to explain the need for a rule which would allow a home-owner to have two children live with her if they are brothers, but not if they are cousins. Since this ordinance has not been shown to have any "substantial relation to the public health, safety, morals, or general welfare" of the city of East Cleveland, and since it cuts so deeply into a fundamental right normally associated with the ownership of residential property—that of an owner to decide who may reside on his or her property ...East Cleveland's unprecedented ordinance constitutes a taking of property without due process and without just compensation. For these reasons, I concur in the Court's judgment.

Case Questions

1. What is the Supreme Court plurality's underlying criticism of the City of East Cleveland ordinance?
2. This case involves due process, a concept discussed in Chapter I. How does due process apply in this instance?
3. Why does Justice Stevens write a concurring opinion?

CREATING FAMILY RELATIONSHIPS

An individual's family relationships are primarily created through marriage, the formation of a civil union/domestic partnership, and parenthood through birth, adoption, or (to a much lesser extent) foster care placements. Each of these relationships is examined in turn.

Marriage

When two people decide to marry, they are voluntarily seeking to enter into a number of relationships involving personal, economic, social, religious, and legal considerations. It is often said that marriage is a contract, and to an extent that is true, but it is unlike other civil contracts because of the extent of governmental regulation. In 1888 the U.S. Supreme Court noted that "[other] contracts may be modified, restricted, or enlarged, or entirely released upon the consent of the parties. Not so with marriage. The relation once formed, the law steps in and holds the parties to various obligations and liabilities. It is an institution, in the maintenance of which in its purity the public is deeply interested, for it is the foundation of the family and of society, without which there would be neither civilization nor progress."[24]

Marriage is regulated by the states, and each state determines who may marry, the duties and obligations of marriage, and how marriages are terminated. Although eligibility requirements for marriage differ from state to state, they generally include minimum age thresholds, prohibitions on marriage between close relatives, monogamy (it is illegal to marry someone who is already married), and competency (neither party can be mentally incompetent). Furthermore, as of this writing, except in Massachusetts, Connecticut, Iowa, New Hampshire, and Vermont, the parties must not be of the same sex. A U.S. District Court's ruling that California's Proposition 8, which prohibits same-sex marriages, is unconstitutional was recently appealed to the U.S. Court of Appeals for the Ninth Circuit. It is widely expected that the losing party in that lawsuit will petition the U.S. Supreme Court for certiorari.

Parties seeking to marry must be acting voluntarily. They indicate their consent to the marriage by jointly applying for a license. Issuance of the license certifies that the applicants have complied with the relevant marriage eligibility requirements. Although states have broad rights to regulate marriage, there are constitutional limitations on this power. This was demonstrated in 1967 in a case argued before the U.S. Supreme Court involving a Virginia criminal statute prohibiting interracial marriages. In the case of *Loving v. Virginia*, the Supreme Court was asked to determine whether such a statute was constitutionally permissible under the Fourteenth Amendment's Due Process and Equal Protection Clauses. The court ruled that the "freedom to marry a person of another race resides with the individual and cannot be infringed by the state."

Loving v. Commonwealth of Virginia
388 U.S. 1
U.S. Supreme Court
June 12, 1967

**Mr. Chief Justice Warren delivered
the opinion of the Court**

This case presents a constitutional question never addressed by this Court: whether a statutory scheme adopted by the State of Virginia to prevent marriages between persons solely on the basis of racial classifications violates the Equal Protection and Due Process Clauses of the Fourteenth Amendment. For reasons which seem to us to reflect the central meaning of those constitutional commands, we conclude that these statutes cannot stand consistently with the Fourteenth Amendment.

In June 1958, two residents of Virginia, Mildred Jeter, a Negro woman, and Richard Loving, a white man, were married in the District of Columbia pursuant to its laws. Shortly after their marriage, the Lovings returned to Virginia and established their marital abode in Caroline County. At the October Term, 1958, of the Circuit Court of Caroline County, a grand jury issued an indictment charging the Lovings with violating Virginia's ban on interracial marriages. On January 6, 1959, the Lovings pleaded guilty to the charge and were sentenced to one year in jail; however, the trial judge suspended the sentence for a period of 25 years on the condition that the Lovings leave the State and not return to Virginia together for 25 years. He stated in an opinion that:

> "Almighty God created the races white, black, yellow, malay and red, and he placed them on separate continents. And but for the interference with his arrangement there would be no cause for such marriages. The fact that he separated the races shows that he did not intend for the races to mix."

After their convictions, the Lovings took up residence in the District of Columbia. On November 6, 1963, they filed a motion in the state trial court to vacate the judgment and set aside the sentence on the ground that the statutes which they had violated were repugnant to the Fourteenth Amendment. The motion not having been decided by October 28, 1964, the Lovings instituted a class action in the United States District Court for the Eastern District of Virginia requesting that a three-judge court be convened to declare the Virginia antimiscegenation statutes unconstitutional and to enjoin state officials from enforcing their convictions. On January 22, 1965, the state trial judge

denied the motion to vacate the sentences, and the Lovings perfected an appeal to the Supreme Court of Appeals of Virginia. On February 11, 1965, the three-judge District Court continued the case to allow the Lovings to present their constitutional claims to the highest state court.

The Supreme Court of Appeals upheld the constitutionality of the antimiscegenation statutes and, after modifying the sentence, affirmed the conviction. The Lovings appealed this decision ... the two statutes under which appellants were convicted and sentenced are part of a comprehensive statutory scheme aimed at prohibiting and punishing interracial marriages. The Lovings were convicted of violating § 20–58 of the Virginia Code:

> "*Leaving State to evade law.*—If any white person and colored person shall go out of this State, for the purpose of being married, and with the intention of returning, and be married out of it, and afterwards return to and reside in it, cohabiting as man and wife, they shall be punished as provided in § 20–59."

Section 20–59, which defines the penalty for miscegenation, provides:

> "*Punishment for marriage.*—If any white person intermarry with a colored person, or any colored person intermarry with a white person, he shall be guilty of a felony and shall be punished by confinement in the penitentiary for not less than one nor more than five years."

...The Lovings have never disputed in the course of this litigation that Mrs. Loving is a "colored person" or that Mr. Loving is a "white person" within the meanings given those terms by the Virginia statutes.

Virginia is now one of 16 States which prohibit and punish marriages on the basis of racial classifications. Penalties for miscegenation arose as an incident to slavery and have been common in Virginia since the colonial period. The present statutory scheme dates from the adoption of the Racial Integrity Act of 1924, passed during the period of extreme nativism which followed the end of the First World War. The central features of this Act, and current Virginia law, are the absolute prohibition of a "white person" marrying other than another "white person," a prohibition against issuing marriage licenses until the issuing official is satisfied that the applicants' statements as to their race are correct, certificates of "racial composition" to be kept by both local and state registrars, and the carrying forward of earlier prohibitions against racial intermarriage.

I

In upholding the constitutionality of these provisions in the decision below, the Supreme Court of Appeals of Virginia referred to its 1955 decision in *Naim v. Naim* … as stating the reasons supporting the validity of these laws. In *Naim*, the state court concluded that the State's legitimate purposes were "to preserve the racial integrity of its citizens," and to prevent "the corruption of blood," "a mongrel breed of citizens," and "the obliteration of racial pride," obviously an endorsement of the doctrine of White Supremacy…. The court also reasoned that marriage has traditionally been subject to state regulation without federal intervention, and, consequently, the regulation of marriage should be left to exclusive state control by the Tenth Amendment.

While the state court is no doubt correct in asserting that marriage is a social relation subject to the State's police power … the State does not contend in its argument before this Court that its powers to regulate marriage are unlimited notwithstanding the commands of the Fourteenth Amendment…. Instead, the State argues that the meaning of the Equal Protection Clause, as illuminated by the statements of the Framers, is only that state penal laws containing an interracial element as part of the definition of the offense must apply equally to whites and Negroes in the sense that members of each race are punished to the same degree. Thus, the State contends that, because its miscegenation statutes punish equally both the white and the Negro participants in an interracial marriage, these statutes, despite their reliance on racial classifications, do not constitute an invidious discrimination based upon race. The second argument advanced by the State assumes the validity of its equal application theory. The argument is that, if the Equal Protection Clause does not outlaw miscegenation statutes because of their reliance on racial classifications, the question of constitutionality would thus become whether there was any rational basis for a State to treat interracial marriages differently from other marriages. On this question, the State argues, the scientific evidence is substantially in doubt and, consequently, this Court should defer to the wisdom of the state legislature in adopting its policy of discouraging interracial marriages.

Because we reject the notion that the mere "equal application" of a statute containing racial classifications is enough to remove t… from the Fourteenth Amendment's proscr… invidious racial discriminations, we do not accep… State's contention that these statutes should be upheld if there is any possible basis for concluding that they serve a rational purpose…. In the case at bar, we deal with statutes containing racial classifications, and the fact of equal application does not immunize the statute from the very heavy burden of justification which the Fourteenth Amendment has traditionally required of state statutes drawn according to race…. There can be no question but that Virginia's miscegenation statutes rest solely upon distinctions drawn according to race. The statutes proscribe generally accepted conduct if engaged in by members of different races. Over the years, this Court has consistently repudiated "[d]istinctions between citizens solely because of their ancestry" as being "odious to a free people whose institutions are founded upon the doctrine of equality." …At the very least, the Equal Protection Clause demands that racial classifications, especially suspect in criminal statutes, be subjected to the "most rigid scrutiny," …and, if they are ever to be upheld, they must be shown to be necessary to the accomplishment of some permissible state objective, independent of the racial discrimination which it was the object of the Fourteenth Amendment to eliminate. Indeed, two members of this Court have already stated that they "cannot conceive of a valid legislative purpose …which makes the color of a person's skin the test of whether his conduct is a criminal offense." …

There is patently no legitimate overriding purpose independent of invidious racial discrimination which justifies this classification. The fact that Virginia prohibits only interracial marriages involving white persons demonstrates that the racial classifications must stand on their own justification, as measures designed to maintain White Supremacy. We have consistently denied the constitutionality of measures which restrict the rights of citizens on account of race. There can be no doubt that restricting the freedom to marry solely because of racial classifications violates the central meaning of the Equal Protection Clause.

These statutes also deprive the Lovings of liberty without due process of law in violation of the Due Process Clause of the Fourteenth Amendment. The freedom to marry has long been recognized as one of the vital personal rights essential to the orderly pursuit of happiness by free men.

Marriage is one of the "basic civil rights of man," fundamental to our very existence and survival…. To deny this fundamental freedom on so unsupportable a basis as the racial classifications embodied in these statutes, classifications so directly subversive of the principle of equality at the heart of the Fourteenth Amendment, is surely to deprive all the State's citizens of liberty without due process of law. The Fourteenth Amendment requires that the freedom of choice to marry not be restricted by invidious racial discriminations. Under our Constitution, the freedom to marry or not marry a person of another race resides with the individual and cannot be infringed by the State.

These convictions must be reversed. It is so ordered. Reversed.

Case Questions

1. Virginia argued to the Supreme Court that its miscegenation statute did not constitute an invidious classification scheme based on race. What was the basis for this position?
2. What response did the Supreme Court make to Virginia's restrictions on an individual's right to decide whether to marry a person of another race?
3. Do you see any merit to the argument often made today that statutes which restrict marriage to heterosexual couples deny same-sex couples wishing to marry the equal protection of the law?

When *Loving v. Virginia* arrived at the U.S. Supreme Court, Virginia and fifteen other states had statutes on the books that made it a crime for blacks and whites to intermarry. These statutes, called *antimiscegenation laws*, were common in former slave states, and had existed in Virginia since Colonial times. The justices of the U.S. Supreme Court declared. "there is patently no legitimate overriding purpose independent of invidious racial discrimination which justifies this classification." Which ethical tradition is most reflected in the Court's opinion in this case?

INTERNET TIP

The Supreme Court in 1978 struck down a Wisconsin statute that required Wisconsin residents who were also parents and who were not current in their child support payments to obtain a court order granting them permission to marry. The court concluded that the statute violated the requirements of the Equal Protection Clause of the Fourteenth Amendment. Persons interested can go to the Internet materials for this chapter and read *Zablocki v. Redhail*.

Marriage Solemnization Ceremonies

States generally require that persons intending to marry solemnize their union with either a civil or a religious ceremony. The solemnization ceremony provides tangible and public evidence that a marriage has occurred. It demonstrates that the parties mutually desire to marry and are legally qualified.[25]

Common Law Marriages

Some jurisdictions recognize privately created, informal marriages by agreement that dispense with licenses and solemnization ceremonies.[26] They are called **common law marriages**.

Although each state that recognizes such marriages has its own particular requirements, most require that the parties be of age, and unmarried. Most important, the parties must have established the relationship of husband and wife, live together as a married couple, and present themselves to the world as being married. Living together, jointly owning property, and having a child are insufficient acts, in themselves, to establish a common law marriage. Montana and Iowa have statutes protecting the validity of such marriages.[27] Other jurisdictions recognize their validity by court decisions. Georgia, Oklahoma, Idaho, Pennsylvania, and Ohio only recognize common law marriages that were formed

---

Title 1 United States Code § 7. Definition of "marriage" and "spouse"

In determining the meaning of any Act of Congress, or of any ruling, regulation, or interpretation of the various administrative bureaus and agencies of the United States, the word "marriage" means only a legal union between one man and one woman as husband and wife, and the word "spouse" refers only to a person of the opposite sex who is a husband or a wife.

F I G U R E 9.2 Definition of "Marriage" and "Spouse" under Federal Law

prior to a specified date, and New Hampshire only recognizes such marriages in conjunction with probating an estate.

Civil Unions, Domestic Partnerships, and Same-Sex Marriage

At the present time, America's ongoing political, social, and cultural disagreement about the definition of marriage continues. This disagreement reflects the reasons for having a federal form of government. It allows for states to differ in significant ways. If one examines how the states line up as to **same-sex marriages**, it is clear that most Americans favor limiting marriage to heterosexual relationships. However, there is considerable support for expanding the traditional concept of marriage in the New England region of the country. Only five states have declared themselves as supporting the concept of same-sex marriages. It was the judiciary that decided the issue in 2003 in Massachusetts (*Goodrich v. Department of Public Health,* 798 N.E.2d 94); in 2005 in Connecticut (*Kerrigan v. Commissioner of Public Health,* 957 A.2d 407); and in 2009 in Iowa (*Varnum v. Brien,* 763 N.W.2d 862). Same-sex marriage laws have been enacted in Vermont and New Hampshire. Such marriages became legal in Vermont on September 1, 2009 (Title 15 V.S.A Sec.8) and in New Hampshire on January 1, 2010 (Title 43 Chapter 457:1)

Several states that continue to prohibit same-sex marriages have enacted laws that permit same-sex couples to enter into state-recognized "**civil unions**" or "**domestic partnerships**." These laws, depending on the state, provide qualifying same-sex couples with some economic benefits and privileges. The scope of the benefits and privileges so conferred vary by jurisdiction. The U.S. Code (the federal statutes) defines marriage in the traditional manner as indicated in Figure 9.2.

It is also important to note that federal law does not recognize same-sex couples as being married. Thus same-sex couples who were lawfully married in New Hampshire and other states recognizing same-sex marriages are not recognized as married by the federal government, and are not entitled to marital benefits under the social security and federal income tax laws (see Figure 9.3).

The Defense of Marriage Acts and Recognition Issues

Although the parameters of the U.S. Constitution's **Full Faith and Credit Clause** (Article IV, Section I) with respect to the enforcement of same-sex marriages remains undefined, all states have traditionally recognized persons as married who were parties to a valid marriage in some other state. But in the aftermath of Vermont's **Civil Union law** and Massachusetts' approval of gay marriage, both Congress and many state legislatures have had second thoughts about this practice.

The federal **Defense of Marriage Act** defines the term "effect," a term used in the U.S. Constitution's Full Faith and Credit Clause, as not requiring any state, against its will, to recognize same-sex marriages as valid. The states overwhelmingly agree with Congress. Thirty-seven states have adopted

---

Defense of Marriage Act—28 USC §1738C

§1738C. Certain acts, records, and proceedings and the effect thereof

No State, territory, or possession of the United States, or Indian tribe, shall be required to give effect to any public act, record, or judicial proceeding of any other State, territory, possession, or tribe respecting a relationship between persons of the same sex that is treated as a marriage under the laws of such other State, territory, possession, or tribe, or a right or claim arising from such relationship.

(Added Sept. 21, 1996, P. L. 104-199, '2(a), 110 Stat. 2419.)

F I G U R E 9.3   Excerpt from the Defense of Marriage Act—28 USC § 1738C

state "Defense of Marriage" statutes and thirty states have constitutional amendments that prohibit same-sex marriages. This opposition creates serious legal problems for same-sex couples because most states that favor "traditional marriage" will not recognize same-sex marriages and civil unions that were created in other states. See *Varnum v. Brien*, 763 N.W. 2d 862.

The next case is illustrative. John Langan and his same-sex partner formally entered into a Vermont civil union. Langan's partner subsequently died after being struck by a car while in New York. Langan then sued St. Vincent's Hospital seeking damages for the wrongful death of his partner. The hospital moved to dismiss the case, claiming that Langan had no standing to bring the suit. The hospital appealed the trial court's ruling in favor of Langan to New York's intermediate appellate court, the Appellate Division of the Supreme Court of New York (which, despite its name, is not New York's court of last resort—that court is called the New York Court of Appeals).

John Langan v. St. Vincent's Hospital
25 A.D.3d 90
Appellate Division of the Supreme Court of New York, Second Department
October 11, 2005

Lifson, J.
The underlying facts of this case are not in dispute. After many years of living together in an exclusive intimate relationship, Neil Conrad Spicehandler (hereinafter Conrad) and John Langan endeavored to formalize their relationship by traveling to Vermont in November 2000 and entering into a civil union. They returned to New York and continued their close, loving, committed, monogamous relationship as a family unit in a manner indistinguishable from any traditional marital relationship.

In February 2002 Conrad was hit by a car and suffered a severe fracture requiring hospitalization at the defendant St. Vincent's Hospital of New York. After two surgeries Conrad died. The plaintiff commenced the instant action which asserted ...a claim ...to recover damages for the decedent's wrongful death. The defendant moved ...to dismiss that cause of action on the ground that the plaintiff and the decedent, being of the same sex, were incapable of being married and, therefore, the plaintiff had no standing as a surviving spouse to institute the present action. The Supreme Court ...denied that motion and the instant appeal ensued.... An action alleging wrongful death, unknown at common law, is a creature of statute requiring strict adherence to the four corners of the legislation.... The relevant portion of EPTL 5-4.1 [Estates, Powers, and Trusts Law] provides as follows:

"The personal representative, duly appointed in this state or any other jurisdiction, of a decedent who is survived by distributees may maintain an action to recover damages for a wrongful act, neglect or default which caused the decedent's death."

...The class of distributees is set forth in EPTL 4-1.1. Included in that class is a surviving spouse. At the time of the drafting of these statutes, the thought that the surviving spouse would be of the same sex as the decedent was simply inconceivable and certainly there was no discriminatory intent to deny the benefits of the statute to a directed class. On the contrary, the clear and unmistakable purpose of the statute was to afford distributees a right to seek compensation for loss sustained by the wrongful death of the decedent....

Like all laws enacted by the people through their elected representatives, EPTL 5-4.1 is entitled to a strong presumption that it is constitutional.... The plaintiff claims that application of the statute in such a manner as to preclude same-sex spouses as potential distributees is a violation of the Equal Protection Clauses of the Constitutions of the United States and the State of New York. However, any equal protection analysis must recognize that virtually all legislation entails classifications for one purpose or another which results in the advantage or disadvantage to the affected groups.... In order to survive constitutional scrutiny a law needs only to have a rational relationship to a legitimate state interest even if the law appears unwise or works to the detriment of one group or the other.... Thus, the plaintiff must demonstrate that the denial of the benefits of EPTL 5-4.l to same-sex couples is not merely unwise or unfair but serves no legitimate governmental purpose. The plaintiff has failed to meet that burden. In the absence of any prior precedent, the court would have to analyze whether the statute imposes a broad and undifferentiated disadvantage to a particular group and if such result is motivated by an animus to that group.... However, in this instance, it has already been established that confining marriage and all laws pertaining either directly or indirectly to the marital relationship to different sex couples is not offensive to the Equal Protection Clause of either the Federal or State constitutions. In *Baker v. Nelson* ...the Supreme Court of Minnesota held that the denial of marital status to same-sex couples did not violate the Fourteenth Amendment of the United States Constitution. The United States Supreme Court refused to review that result.... The plaintiff herein cannot meet his burden of proving the statute unconstitutional and does not refer this court to any binding or even persuasive authority that diminishes the import of the Baker precedent.

On the contrary, issues concerning the rights of same-sex couples have been before the United States Supreme Court on numerous occasions since Baker and, to date, no justice of that court has ever indicated that the holding in Baker is suspect. Although in *Lawrence v. Texas* ...the Supreme Court ruled that laws criminalizing activity engaged in by same-sex couples and potentially adversely affecting their liberty interests could not withstand constitutional scrutiny, every justice of that court expressed an indication that exclusion of marital rights to same-sex couples did promote a legitimate state interest. Justices Scalia, Thomas, and Rehnquist concluded that disapprobation of homosexual conduct is a sufficient basis for virtually any law based on classification of such conduct. The majority opinion of Justices Kennedy, Stevens, Ginsberg, Souter, and Breyer declined to apply an equal protection analysis and nonetheless expressly noted that the holding (based on the penumbra of privacy derived from *Griswold v. Connecticut* ...) did not involve or require the government to give formal recognition to any relationship that homosexuals wish to enter.... Justice O'Connor, in her concurring opinion based on an equal protection analysis, specifically excluded marriage from the import of her conclusions, stating simply "...other reasons exist to promote the institution of marriage beyond mere moral disapproval of an excluded group." ...

Similarly, this court, in ruling on the very same issue ...not only held that the term "surviving spouse" did not include same-sex life partners, but expressly stated as follows:

> Based on these authorities [including Baker ...], we agree with Acting Surrogate Pizzuto's conclusion that 'purported [homosexual] marriages do not give rise to any rights ...pursuant to ... EPTL 5-1.1 [and that] no constitutional rights have been abrogated or violated in so holding'"

.... Although issues involving same-sex spouses have been presented in various contexts since the perfection of this appeal, no court decision has been issued which undermines our obligation to follow our own precedents. Recently, in the somewhat analogous case of *Valentine v. American Airline* ... the Appellate Division, Third Department, in denying spousal status to same-sex couples for purposes of Workers Compensations claims, cited both Baker and Cooper with approval. Thus, no cogent reason to depart from the established judicial precedent of both the courts of the United States and the courts of the State of New York has been demonstrated by the plaintiff or our dissenting colleagues.

The fact that since the perfection of this appeal the State of Massachusetts has judicially created such right for its citizens is of no moment here since the plaintiff and the decedent were not married in that jurisdiction. They opted for the most intimate sanctification of their relationship then permitted, to wit, a civil union pursuant to the laws of the State of Vermont. Although the dissenters equate civil union relationships with traditional heterosexual marriage, we note that neither the State of Vermont nor the parties to the subject relationship have made that jump in logic. In following the ruling of its Supreme Court in the case of *Baker v. State of Vermont* ...the Vermont Legislature went to great pains to expressly decline to place civil unions and marriage on an identical basis. While affording same-sex couples the same rights as those afforded married couples, the Vermont Legislature refused to alter traditional concepts of marriage (i.e., limiting the ability to marry to couples of two distinct sexes).... The import of that action is of no small moment. The decedent herein, upon entering the defendant hospital, failed to indicate that he was married. Moreover, in filing the various probate papers in this action, the plaintiff likewise declined to state that he was married. In essence, this court is being asked to create a relationship never intended by the State of Vermont in creating civil unions or by the decedent or the plaintiff in entering into their civil union. For the same reason, the theories of Full Faith and Credit and comity have no application to the present fact pattern.

The circumstances of the present case highlight the reality that there is a substantial segment of the population of this State that is desirous of achieving state recognition and regulation of their relationships on an equal footing with married couples. There is also a substantial segment of the population of this State that wishes to preserve traditional concepts of marriage as a unique institution confined solely to one man and one woman. Whether these two positions are not so hopelessly at variance (to all but the extremists in each camp) to prevent some type of redress is an issue not for the courts but for the Legislature. Unlike the court, which can only rule on the issues before it, the Legislature is empowered to act on all facets of the issue including, but not limited to, the issues of the solemnization and creation of such relationships, the

dissolution of such relationships and the consequences attendant thereto, and all other rights and liabilities that flow from such a relationship. Any contrary decision, no matter how circumscribed, will be taken as judicial imprimatur of same-sex marriages and would constitute a usurpation of powers expressly reserved by our Constitution to the Legislature. Accordingly, the order must be reversed insofar as appealed from....

ORDERED that the order is reversed insofar as appealed from ...and the cause of action to recover damages for wrongful death is dismissed.

Fisher, J. dissents and votes to affirm the order

The majority's forceful defense of the Legislature's prerogative to define what constitutes a marriage in New York seems to me to miss the point. This case is not about marriage. The plaintiff does not claim to have been married to the decedent, and clearly he was not, either under the laws of New York or in the eyes of Vermont.

What this case is about is the operation of a single statute, New York's wrongful death statute that controls access to the courts for those seeking compensation for the loss of a pecuniary expectancy created and guaranteed by law. The statute provides such access to a decedent's surviving spouse because the wrongful death of one spouse deprives the other of an expectation of continued support which the decedent would have been obligated by law to provide.... But, as applied here, the statute does not permit the surviving member of a Vermont civil union to sue for wrongful death, even though, like spouses, each member of the civil union is obligated by law to support the other.... The principal question presented, therefore, is whether, as it currently operates to permit spouses but not partners in a Vermont civil union to sue for wrongful death, the law draws a distinction between similarly—situated persons on the basis of sexual orientation and, if so, whether the distinction bears some rational relationship to any conceivable governmental objective promoted by the statute. Because I conclude that the statute as applied here does classify similarly-situated persons on the basis of sexual orientation without a rational relationship to any conceivable governmental purpose furthered by the statute, I respectfully dissent.

Case Questions

1. What was the plaintiff's claim in the intermediate appellate court?
2. What was the appellate court's decision?
3. What rationale did the court give for its decision?

Adoption

Informal adoptions existed in this country from its earliest days, and into the 1860s orphans were often apprenticed to masters so that they could pay for their room and board.[28] Since adoption was unknown to the common law, adoption law in the United States is traced to 1851, when Massachusetts enacted the first statute.[29]

Although modern statutes permit the adoption of adults, subject to some exceptions,[30] most adoptions involve children. **Adoption** is both a social and a legal process by which the rights and duties accompanying the parent-child relationship are transferred from birth parents to adoptive parents. State adoption statutes were originally intended primarily to help qualified childless couples "normalize" their marriages,[31] but today the statutes encourage adoption in part to provide families for many abandoned, abused, deserted, neglected, or unwanted children, who might otherwise need to be supported at public expense. Adoptions can be classified as either independent or agency placements. In **agency adoptions**, the birth parents consent to the termination of their parental rights and surrender the child to an adoption agency that selects the adoptive parent(s) and places the child. **An independent adoption** takes place when the birth parent(s) themselves interview prospective adoptive parents and make a selection without agency involvement. Some states prohibit independent adoptions and require that agencies participate in the process.

Becoming an adoptive parent is highly regulated, and the procedures vary by state and by the type of adoption. It often makes a difference whether the adoption involves an agency or is independent, is between relatives, or is of an adult. In adoptions between related persons, for example, where a stepparent wishes to adopt his or her spouse's child, the investigative process is often simplified or eliminated. In an independent adoption, the nature and scope of any investigation is left up to the birth parent(s). They interview prospective adoptive parents and place the child without agency participation. When a public or private agency

licensed by the state places a child for adoption, the law usually requires close scrutiny. Adoptive parents who are unrelated to an adopted child are carefully investigated to determine whether the placement is suitable and in the best interests of the child. This investigation is often very detailed and probes most areas of an applicant's life. The probe results in a report that includes information on the applicant's race, age, marital status, and financial condition, the "adequacy of the home environment," and information about very personal matters such as religious preferences, current romantic interests, and sexuality.[32]

Matching

The investigative process makes it possible for agencies to rank prospective adoptive parents in terms of how closely they match the agency's conception of the ideal family for the child. Those who most closely fit the profile are often matched with the most "desirable" adoptees.[33] Petitioners who are married generally rank higher than those who are unmarried, younger applicants ranked higher than older, able bodied higher than disabled, and heterosexuals higher than homosexuals.[34]

Interracial adoption has long been a topic heavily laden with emotion. Most of the fury arises when whites seek to adopt nonwhite children. Questions are frequently raised about whether white adoptive parents have the ability to develop fully a nonwhite child's racial identity and appreciation for the richness of his or her culture.[35]

Congress, however, declared the nation's public policy as to interracial adoption in 1994 when it enacted the **Multiethnic Placement Act** (MEPA) of 1994, and again in 1996 when it amended MEPA by enacting the **Interethnic Adoption Provisions** (IEP). The two acts are generally known as the MEPA-IEP; these laws essentially

1. Prohibit adoption agencies that receive federal funds from using an aspiring adoptive or foster parent's race, color, or national origin against him or her for purposes of denying such parent the placement of a child.

2. Make it illegal to delay or deny a child an adoptive or foster care placement because of his or her race, color, or national origin.

The MEPA-IEP intends that placement decisions be made on a case-by-case basis, and cultural needs cannot routinely be used to prevent white adoptive parents, for example, from adopting nonwhite children. Congress's intent could not be more clear, because it included a provision in the IEP which repealed language in the original MEPA that expressly permitted agencies to consider a "child's cultural, ethnic, and racial background and the capacity of the prospective foster or adoptive parents to meet the needs of a child from this background" in the making of placement decisions. Many states had to amend their adoption statutes in order to comply with MEPA-IEP. An example of a post MEPA-IEP state adoption statute can be seen in Figure 9.4. Notice how the Arkansas statute prohibits discrimination on the basis of race, color, or national origin, creates legal preferences favoring adult relatives over nonrelatives, and authorizes religious matching.

Despite Congress' clear definition of public policy, it is difficult to determine in practice the extent to which the law is being followed. How can prospective white adoptive parents, who have been told that because of the child's cultural needs they will not be permitted to adopt a nonwhite child, know whether this justification is merely a pretext for invidious racial discrimination? It is likely that categorical discrimination in which placements are based on legally impermissible factors still occur. Similarly, discrimination in placements based on religion, educational levels, and socioeconomic status are other areas in which informal "blanket" policies may continue to exist.

9-9-102. Religious preference—Removal of barriers to interethnic adoption—Preference to relative caregivers for a child in foster care.

(a) In all custodial placements by the Department of Human Services in foster care or investigations conducted by the Department of Human Services pursuant to court order under § 9-9-212, preferential consideration shall be given to an adult relative over a nonrelated caregiver provided that the relative caregiver meets all relevant child protection standards and it is in the child's best interest to be placed with the relative caregiver.

(b) The Department of Human Services and any other agency or entity which receives federal assistance and is involved in adoption or foster care placement shall not discriminate on the basis of the race, color, or national origin of the adoptive or foster parent or the child involved nor delay the placement of a child on the basis of race, color, or national origin of the adoptive or foster parents.

(c) If the child's genetic parent or parents express a preference for placing the child in a foster home or an adoptive home of the same or a similar religious background to that of the genetic parent or parents, the court shall place the child with a family that meets the genetic parent's religious preference, or if a family is not available, to a family of a different religious background which is knowledgeable and appreciative of the child's religious background.

(d) The court shall not deny a petition for adoption on the basis of race, color, or national origin of the adoptive parent or the child involved.

FIGURE 9.4 Arkansas Code Section 9-9-102

The U.S. Supreme Court has strongly indicated that government should remain neutral in religious matters,[36] and has supported parental choice regarding the religious upbringing of children. But the Court has not attempted to answer, as a general proposition, whether religious matching is in the best interest of adoptive children. (see Figure 9.4).

As we have just seen, state statutes sometimes express a preference that adoptive parents be of the same religion as the adoptee or birth parent(s). Should adoptive parents who are of mixed religions, who adhere to obscure faiths, or who are atheists, be legally disadvantaged in placement decisions?[37] Should adoptive parents have the right to choose the religion of their adoptive child, or must they raise the child in the faith chosen by the birth parents? Does it matter whether the adoptive child's religion differs from that of the other members of the adoptive family?[38] Questions like these are easy to ask, but they raise policy issues that are difficult to resolve.

Another area of current controversy involves the placement of adoptees with gay and lesbian adoptive parents. Although many states permit single gays and lesbians to adopt, the laws are unclear as to adoptions by same-sex couples. Florida, explicitly prohibits gay/lesbian adoptions (see Figure 9.5), and Arkansas requires all adoptive parents to be married, which is a back-door way of precluding same-sex couples from adopting.

The Florida statute's constitutionality was affirmed by U.S. Court of Appeals for the Eleventh Circuit in the case of *Steven Lofton v. Secretary of the Department of Children & Family Services*. This court concluded that the determination of public policy regarding gay and lesbian adoptions did not involve the federal constitution and was a matter for the state legislature.

INTERNET TIP

Interested readers can find an edited version of *Steven Lofton v. Secretary of the Department of Children & Family Services* on the textbook's website.

Where no statutes prevent them, gay/lesbian adoptions have been permitted, at least for the most difficult-to-place children.[39] However, the preference of agencies for married couples is sometimes used as a convenient justification for opposing placements that are really rejected because the adoptive parents are gays or lesbians. The stated reasons for rejecting gays and lesbians as adoptive parents are often based on the perceived incompatibility of the "'gay lifestyle' with social mores and on a fear that an adoptive child would be exposed to an increased risk of contracting AIDS."[40] Some courts have been more flexible. One of the earliest was the Massachusetts Supreme Judicial Court, which ruled in the 1993 case *Adoption of Tammy* that two lesbians could jointly become adoptive parents.

INTERNET TIP

Interested readers will find *Adoption of Tammy*, 619N.E.2d 315 (1993), with the Chapter IX Internet materials on the textbook's website.

The next case, *Boseman v. Jarrell,* when viewed narrowly, is simply another legal battle between two parents who, after splitting up, fight about who should have custody and visitation rights with their son. Viewed more broadly, this case is also about the right of lesbians to adopt.

The parties to this action began a same-sex relationship in 1998 and had been domestic partners. Because from the early days of their

---

> **Fla. Stat. § 63.042(3):**
>
> "No person eligible to adopt under this statute may adopt if that person is a homosexual."

F I G U R E 9.5 Florida Statutes Annotated Sec. 63.042

relationship both parties aspired to be parents, Melissa Jarrell was artificially inseminated and gave birth to a son in 2002. Their personal relationship strong at that time, the parties agreed that Julia Boseman would become the child's co-mother through adoption. One significant legal hurdle, however, stood in their path. A state statute provided that in adoptions, the birth mother's parental rights had to be terminated. Jarrell filed suit asking a court to waive this statutory provision. She was successful in 2005 when a court ordered the waiver and declared both women to be the little boy's parents. The parents subsequently ended their

personal relationship and separated. Melissa, after the break-up, no longer wanted Julia to have contact with the child. Julia, still the child's parent, felt it necessary to go to court to establish firmly her right to joint custody of the child and visitation rights. The trial court ultimately ruled that Melissa and Julia would jointly have custody and that the child's primary placement would be with Melissa. Melissa appealed the trial court's decision to the intermediate court of appeals. She claimed, among other things, that the trial court had wrongfully refused to declare the adoption decree void *ab initio* (from the beginning).

Julia Catherine Boseman v. Melissa Ann Jarrell
681 S.E.2d 374
Court of Appeals of North Carolina
August 18, 2009

Bryant, Judge

...Jarrell first contends that the trial court erred in denying her ... motion ... that it [had]... "jurisdiction to declare void an Order or Decree of another District Court Judge sitting in another Judicial District of North Carolina." ... We agree.

Here, the trial court denied Jarrell's motion under the misapprehension that it lacked the necessary jurisdiction to declare the adoption decree void. This constituted an abuse of discretion by a failure to exercise the discretion conferred by law and we vacate the trial court's ...order. In order to expedite resolution of this matter in the best interest of the minor involved, we next address defendant's second argument: whether the adoption decree was in fact void.

Jarrell moved for relief...contending that the adoption decree entered by the District Court in Durham County ("the adoption court") was void ab initio [from the beginning]. After careful review, we conclude that the adoption decree, even if erroneous or contrary to law, was not void....

Jarrell, a party to the adoption, cannot question its validity based on "any defect or irregularity, jurisdictional or otherwise." .... Therefore, the only avenue by which Jarrell can contest the adoption is to show that it was void *ab initio*, a legal nullity....

Our State's case law distinguishing void versus voidable judgments is easy to state, but often thorny

to apply.... "To have validity a judgment must be rendered by a court which has authority to hear and determine the questions in dispute and control over the parties to the controversy or their interest in the property which is the subject matter of the controversy...."

Here, the parties essentially agree on the law as stated above, but differ in their portrayal of the actions of the adoption court. Jarrell argues that the adoption court "had no statutory authority to enter [a] same-sex Adoption Decree," and thus acted in excess of its jurisdiction. Boseman contends that the adoption court had subject matter jurisdiction to handle adoption proceedings involving North Carolina residents pursuant to the explicit terms of Chapter 48, and that any deviations from that Chapter's mandates are, at most, contrary to law. We must look to the language of Chapter 48 as an expression of our General Assembly's intent to determine whether the irregularities in the adoption here exceeded the adoption court's jurisdiction or were merely contrary to law.

Chapter 48 of our General Statutes covers adoptions and establishes subject matter jurisdiction in these special proceedings. The version of section 48-2-100, titled "Jurisdiction," in force at the time of the adoption at issue here..., provided, in pertinent part, that jurisdiction over adoption proceedings commenced under this Chapter exists if, at the commencement of the proceeding:

> (1) The adoptee has lived in this State for at least the six consecutive months immediately preceding the filing of the petition or from birth, and the prospective adoptive parent is domiciled in this State; or
> (2) The prospective adoptive parent has lived in or been domiciled in this State for at least the six consecutive months immediately preceding the filing of the petition.

... Thus, statutory subject matter jurisdiction is determined by the residence of the parties to the adoption. In this case, Jarrell, Boseman and the minor child had all resided in Wilmington, North Carolina for at least several years prior to the adoption proceeding.

Jarrell counters that Chapter 48 does not permit "same-sex adoptions,"... and indeed that phrase appears nowhere in the chapter. Chapter 48 specifically addresses three basic types of adoptions of minors: (1) agency placements, in which the agency has obtained custody of the minor through parental relinquishment or the termination of parental rights; (2) direct placement of a child, in which "a parent or guardian ... personally select[s] a prospective adoptive parent," either with or without the assistance of third-parties; and (3) adoptions by step-parents...

The parties here sought to arrange a direct placement adoption with certain variations from the relevant statutory provisions.... In her motion to the adoption court, Jarrell explained that she wanted her child to have the benefits and protections of "two legal parents" and that obligating Boseman to provide these protections to her child was in the child's best interest and thus consistent with purposes of Chapter 48. The adoption court, after reviewing oral arguments, legal memoranda, a home study and other documents, agreed that the adoption would be in the minor's best interest, granted the waiver, and subsequently entered the decree of adoption. While the factual circumstances of the parties' relationship is discussed in the order granting the waiver, no mention of the parties' sexual orientation is contained in the decree, which merely notes that the petitioner (Boseman) was a "single female." Thus, the adoption here was not explicitly a same-sex adoption; it is better characterized as a direct placement adoption with a waiver of the full terms of parental consent and legal obligations specified in N.C.G.S. §§ 48-1-106(c) and 48-3-606.

While we acknowledge that section 48-3-606 is titled "Content of consent; mandatory provisions," the intent and purpose of subsection (9) quoted above are to ensure that a biological parent or guardian is fully informed about the ramifications of adoption and are intended for the protection of that consenting individual, not the minor.... Similarly, under N.C.G.S. § 48-1-106(c), an adoption decree severs the relationship of parent and child between the individual adopted and that individual's biological or previous adoptive parents. After the entry of a decree of adoption, the former parents are relieved of all legal duties and obligations due from them to the adoptee, except that a former parent's duty to make past-due payments for child support is not terminated, and the former parents are divested of all rights with respect to the adoptee.

As with section 48-3-606(9), any waiver of this provision accrues to the detriment only of the would-be former parent, while actually conferring benefits on the minor who gains an additional adult who is legally obligated to his care and support. Again, Jarrell herself makes this point in her motion for waiver to the adoption court where she notes that the waiver will avail the minor of additional health and governmental benefits, as well as provide stability and "a legal framework for resolving any disputes regarding custody or visitation that may arise after the adoption." This is exactly the end achieved by the adoption in this case. Following unforeseen circumstances, namely the end of the parties' domestic partnership, the minor's interests, both financial and emotional, are protected. Because of the adoption here, the minor will still be entitled to the support and care of the two adults who have acted as his parents and they will both remain fully obligated to his welfare. This result is fully in accord with the stated intent of Chapter 48...

...Here, the evidence before the adoption court tended to show that Boseman and Jarrell planned the conception and birth of the minor and both had acted in a parental capacity providing the minor with "love, care, security, and support." In addition, the General Assembly in Chapter 48 seeks "to promote the integrity and finality of adoptions" and "to encourage prompt, conclusive disposition of adoption proceedings..." Further, our General Assembly has directed that:

> (c) In construing this Chapter, the needs, interests, and rights of minor adoptees are primary. Any conflict between the interests of a minor adoptee and those of an adult shall be resolved in favor of the minor.
> (d) This Chapter shall be liberally construed and applied to promote its underlying purposes and policies.

.... Thus, here we must put the minor's "needs, interests, and rights" above those of either Boseman or Jarrell. Finally, because "the right of adoption is not only beneficial to those immediately concerned but likewise to the public, construction of the statute should not be narrow or technical ... [but rather] fair and reasonable ... where all material provisions of the statute have been complied with...." Having reviewed the intent and purposes of Chapter 48, as well as the specific provisions at issue here, we conclude that the adoption court acted within its authority in granting the direct placement adoption decree, and that the grant of waiver of certain provisions was, at most, erroneous and contrary to law. Thus, the adoption decree is not void. We remand to the trial court for entry of an order containing the required findings of fact and denying defendant's Rule 60(b)(4) on grounds that the adoption decree was not void and that N.C.G.S. § 48-2-607(a) prohibits defendant from contesting its validity.

We note that both parties have made extensive arguments related to the same-sex nature of their former relationship and whether our State and its agencies sanction adoptions by same-sex couples. While acknowledging that such issues are matters of great public interest and of personal significance to Boseman and Jarrell, we emphasize that the specific nature of the parties' relationship or marital status was not relevant to resolution of the instant appeal. The same result would have been reached had the parties been an unmarried heterosexual couple. While Chapter 48 does not specifically address same-sex adoptions, these statutes do make clear that a wide range of adoptions are contemplated and permitted, so long as they protect the minor's "needs, interests, and rights...."

...The order dismissing the declaratory judgment for lack of jurisdiction is vacated and the matter is remanded for entry of an order consistent with this opinion. In addition, based on the validity of the adoption, the trial court did not err in ruling that Boseman was a legal parent of the child. This argument by Jarrell is overruled....

Conclusion
Because the adoption decree was not void and Jarrell may not challenge its validity, Boseman is a legal parent of the child. As discussed above, we affirm in part, and vacate and remand in part for entry of orders consistent with this opinion.

Case Questions

1. Jarrell made essentially two arguments on appeal—what were they?
2. What conclusion did the appeals court reach with respect to each issue?

 Is it morally right for states to disqualify gay men and lesbians categorically from becoming adoptive parents because of moral considerations?

Boseman v. Jarrell Update

The North Carolina Supreme Court has agreed to hear oral arguments in this case during September 2010. That will be too late for inclusion in this textbook. After that court has announced its decision, it will be posted with the Internet materials for Chapter IX on the textbook's website.

Voluntary/Involuntary Adoption

Adoptions may be classified as voluntary or involuntary. Involuntary adoptions occur after a court has formally terminated the parental rights of the birth parent(s) on grounds such as abuse, abandonment, or neglect. In such a situation, an agency is generally responsible for placement. If the adoption is voluntary, the birth parent(s) consent to the termination of their parental rights and surrender the child either to an agency for placement or to adoptive parents of their choosing.

The Adoption Petition

The adoption process starts with the filing of a petition for adoption by the adoptive parents and the serving of a summons on all affected parties (the child, the agency, birth parents, guardian, etc.). In voluntary adoptions, care must be taken to account for all relevant parties, and obtaining the consent of necessary third parties is a major consideration. When both birth parents have an intact marriage, they must jointly consent to a proposed adoption of their child. If the parents are not married to each other, and both the noncustodial and custodial parents have taken an active role in fulfilling parental obligations, each has the right to withhold or grant consent to the adoption of their child.

The birth parents and adoptive parents are not the only individuals who have legal interests in adoptions. An adoptee, if over a specified age (often twelve or fourteen), has a right to refuse to be adopted. Additionally, grandparents may have legally enforceable visitation rights even after the birth father's parental rights have been terminated. We will see more about this topic later on in this chapter when addressing child custody and visitation rights after a divorce.

In addition to providing notice to affected individuals, the petition for adoption will also indicate whether the parental rights have been voluntarily or involuntarily terminated and will allege that the adoption is in the best interests of the child.

INTERNET TIP

Interested readers can find an edited version of *Lehr v. Robertson,* a case in which the U.S. Supreme Court ruled no consent to adopt is required from a noncustodial parent who has only sporadically visited and supported his child and who has otherwise shown little or no interest in functioning as a parent, online at the textbook's website.

Interim Orders

After the adoption petition has been filed, the parties properly served, and all necessary consents obtained, the court will frequently issue interim orders. In voluntary adoptions the court will order the birth parents' rights terminated and grant the adoptive parents temporary legal custody of the child, pending issuance of the final decree. A

hearing can then be scheduled to take testimony about whether the final decree of adoption should be approved by the court. State statutes usually require that the adoptive parents have temporary custody of the adopted child for a statutorily determined minimum period of time so that the court will have evidence that the adoptive parents and child are making a successful adjustment. This waiting period is usually waived in related adoptions. After the waiting time has passed, the court will enter a final decree declaring that the adopted person is now the child of the petitioner(s), and a new birth certificate will be issued to reflect this change.[41]

Confidentiality and Privacy Considerations in Adoptions

One of the most important decisions in adoptions is the extent to which, if at all, the adoptive parent(s) and the birth parent(s) share identification information with one another. This decision as to whether the adoption will be "open." "closed," or something in between has great significance to all involved parties. Whether the adopted child will be able to learn the identity of the birth parents varies from state to state. In recent years, there has been some movement away from permanently sealing such information. Today, although many states maintain the confidentiality of adoption records, the trend is toward more openness.[42] Almost all states have established some type of registry system whereby consenting birth parents and their subsequently adopted children can mutually indicate a desire for contact.[43] Adoptees frequently wish to learn more about their birth parents, not only out of curiosity, but also to gain information about their parents' medical histories.

INTERNET TIP

Readers interested in learning more about state laws regarding open/closed adoptions should visit the following website: http://www.childwelfare.gov/systemwide/laws_policies/statutes/cooperative.cfm

Foster Care

According to U.S. Department of Health and Human Services, preliminary estimates based on fiscal year 2008 **Adoption and Foster Care Analysis and Reporting System (AFCARS)** data indicate that 463,000 children are currently in foster care in the United States.[44] Some parents voluntarily place their children in foster care for a brief time. Most foster placements, however, result from court intervention because of alleged child abuse or neglect.[45] Once a court determines that a child is abused or neglected, it next determines whether foster care is the most appropriate disposition under the circumstances. In many situations, foster care provides temporary care for children while the biological parents work to fulfill the requirements of a case plan. The objective in such situations is reunification of the family, once caseworkers have helped the family to work out its problems. If the birth parents address the problems that gave rise to the judicial intervention in the first place, the child will generally be returned to the parents. If the parents are uncooperative or fail to complete the intervention plan, the court may ultimately decide that it is in the best interests of the child to terminate the parental rights and place the child for adoption.

According to preliminary estimates that were based on fiscal year 2008 AFCARS data, 19 percent of the foster children leaving the foster care system in 2008 were adopted, and over 60 percent were ordered returned to their birth parents or other relatives.[46] State governments license foster homes, and federal and state resources financially support foster children. The foster care system has in the past been criticized as underfunded, overwhelmed with cases, and staffed by persons who are not trained as social workers.[47]

Congress took action to improve this situation when it enacted the Adoption and Safe Families Act of 1997. This legislation created financial incentives and performance expectations for states in an effort to speed up the adoption process and increase the numbers of children placed for adoption.

Critics have complained that federal financial support to the states has been insufficient, especially since the states have moved increasing numbers of children from the foster care system into adoption placements. In September of 2009, however, the U.S. Department of Health and Human Services announced an Adoptive Incentives Program through which it was awarding $35 million dollars to thirty-eight states for the express purpose of increasing the adoption of children currently in foster care. Special incentives rewarded states that were able to move qualifying special needs children and children who are 9 years old or older from foster homes to adoptive families.[48]

FAMILY RELATIONS IN ONGOING FAMILIES

Where families are intact, the law recognizes that spouses and children assume obligations to each other and are entitled to certain rights and benefits. Some of these rights, benefits, and obligations are economic and others are noneconomic.

Spousal Property Rights

Although modern marriages are essentially partnerships, historically husbands and wives were legally considered to be a single unit with the husbands holding the preferred status as head of the household.[49] Before the enactment of married women's property statutes in the 1800s, wives did not generally own property in their own names. Upon marriage, a wife's property was generally controlled by her husband. An exception was created by equitable courts that allowed fathers to establish trusts for their daughters. This device was used to keep family assets out of the control of sons-in-law, but few women from the lower and middle classes were the beneficiaries of such arrangements. A husband, while benefiting from his preferred status as head of the household, was also legally obligated to provide economic support for his wife. The term tradition-ally associated with this responsibility for support is *necessaries,* usually defined to include food, clothing, shelter, and medical care.[50] In earlier times this obligation only applied to husbands; however, it is now shared by both spouses.

Courts were initially resistant to statutory reforms expanding women's property rights, and often construed them very narrowly.[51] Today, in common-law title states, married women have essentially achieved legal equality. Each spouse retains title to property owned prior to marriage, has the separate right to his or her own earnings, and has title to property acquired separately during marriage. The judge in **common-law title** juris-dictions is charged with "equitably" distributing the property between the spouses. This means that fair-ness and not equality is the goal. The court considers each spouse's contributions to the mar-riage and financial circumstances and all other rele-vant factors when determining what constitutes a fair apportionment of the marital assets.

In **community property states** (see Figure 9.6), each spouse is legally entitled to a per-centage of what the state defines as community property, which will vary by jurisdiction. Although states differ, community property is usually defined as including the earnings of both spouses and prop-erty rights acquired with those earnings during the marriage. State statutes, however, usually exclude from community property rights acquired prior to marriage and spousal inheritances and gifts received during the marriage. These are classified as separate property. Community property states differ on whether earnings from separate property should be treated as community property.

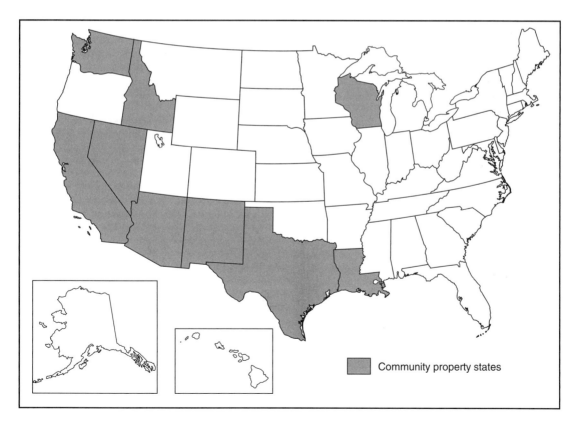

F I G U R E 9.6 Community Property States

Decision Making Within Traditional Families

The U.S. Supreme Court has reinforced family autonomy by ruling that married couples have the right to make decisions regarding the use of birth control[52] and whether they will become parents. If they do, it is they who will decide how many children they will have and how those children will be raised.[53] This right to raise children includes decisions about the nature and extent of their education and their religious upbringing.

Spouses also have great latitude in deciding how their households will operate. Decisions about who is responsible for particular household chores, about how recreational time is used, and about having children and child rearing are often jointly made. Of course, a woman's decision to obtain an abortion early in a pregnancy can be made unilaterally—without regard to the wishes of the putative father. A married woman also has the right to retain her own surname, if she chooses.

Because of **spousal privileges** contained within state and federal rules of evidence, a spouse may refuse to testify against his or her spouse in a criminal trial and may also refuse to testify about confidential communications that occurred between spouses during their marriage.

INTERNET TIP

Parents have traditionally exercised primary responsibility for determining the religious upbringing of their children. In *Yoder v. Wisconsin,* Amish parents were criminally prosecuted by the State of Wisconsin for violating a compulsory school-attendance law. These parents withdrew their children from the public schools after they had completed the eighth grade. The parents appealed their convictions and claimed that the law infringed on their constitutionally protected right to determine the religious development of their children. You can read the U.S. Supreme Court's decision in this case on the textbook's website.

Family Status and the Obligation to Minor Children

Historically, parents have been legally responsible for the financial costs of providing their children with food, clothing, shelter, medical care, and education. This duty exists irrespective of whether the parents are married, divorced, separated, living together, or living apart. The breach of this duty is treated by most states as a criminal offense and can also result in civil actions for nonsupport and child neglect. The government is most eager to identify and locate "deadbeat parents" and to hold them financially accountable for their children so that the public doesn't have to bear these costs.

The exact nature and extent of the parental support obligation varies and depends on the child's needs as well as on each parent's financial condition. Though all states require that parents fulfill support obligations, some have gone so far as to require stepparents[54] and grandparents[55] to provide child support. When marriages break up, a court will usually require the noncustodial parent to pay child support until the child attains the age of majority, marries, becomes emancipated, or dies. Even after a child reaches the age of majority, parents often have a continuing support obligation if their offspring are disabled or haven't completed high school, or if such an obligation exists pursuant to a separation agreement.

One of the areas of recent conflict relates to a parent's duty to pay for a child's college education, an expense that usually isn't payable until after the child has passed the age of majority. Although parents in intact families have no legal duty to fund college educations for their children, as we see in the next case, some courts have ruled that a parent's support obligation can include funding their child's college education.

In re Gilmore
803 A.2d 601
Supreme Court of New Hampshire
July 24, 2002

Dalianis, J.

The respondent, William E. Gilmore, Jr., appeals an order of the Superior Court ... requiring him to pay certain monthly expenses towards his adult child's college education. We reverse and remand.

The record supports the following facts. The parties were divorced in 1991. At the time of their divorce, the parties had two minor children. In the divorce decree the respondent was ordered to pay, among other obligations, "the entire expense of any private schooling or college for the two girls."

By July 2000, the parties' daughter Lindsey was an adult who was commuting to college while living with the petitioner, Nancy J. Gilmore. In September 2000, the petitioner filed a motion requesting that the respondent be ordered to continue paying child support for Lindsey while she attended college.

On November 22, 2000, the trial court dismissed the petitioner's request for child support but ordered the respondent to pay what it characterized as "reasonable college expenses" for Lindsey, including expenses for room and board while she lived at home with the petitioner, as follows:

Tuition, fees and books:	As required
Allowance, as previously established:	$200 per month
Room:	$532 per month
Gas:	$140 per month
Car insurance, repairs, and registration:	$146 per month
Medical and dental expenses:	$ 75 per month
Clothing and shoes:	$200 per month
Food:	$350 per month

The respondent filed a motion for reconsideration and clarification arguing, among other things, that the court did not have jurisdiction to order him to pay for items such as clothing, shoes and an allowance because they are not educational expenses, and that he should not be responsible for Lindsey's educational expenses when she was not in school. The court agreed that the respondent was not responsible for paying Lindsey an allowance, and that he was responsible for her

educational expenses only during the months she was attending college, but otherwise denied the respondent's motion.

On appeal, the respondent argues that the court erred in ordering him to pay for such items as transportation, insurance, medical coverage, clothing and shoes because they are not educational expenses. He also argues that the court erred in requiring payments for Lindsey's room and board to be made to the petitioner.

We afford broad discretion to the trial court in divorce matters, and will not disturb the trial court's rulings regarding child support absent an unsustainable exercise of discretion or an error of law. *Rattee v. Rattee*, 146 N.H. 44, 46, 767 A.2d 415 (2001); *cf. State v. Lambert*, 147 N.H. 295, 296, 787 A.2d 175 (2001) (explaining unsustainable exercise of discretion standard). The party challenging the court's order has the burden of showing that the order was "improper and unfair." *Hunneyman v. Hunneyman*, 118 N.H. 652, 653, 392 A.2d 147 (1978) (quotation omitted).

RSA 458:17, I (1992) (amended 1993) provides that:

> In all cases where there shall be a decree of divorce or nullity, the court shall make such further decree in relation to the support, education, and custody of the children as shall be most conducive to their benefit and may order a reasonable provision for their support and education.

Generally, a parent's obligation to pay child support ceases when the child turns eighteen years old or graduates from high school, whichever is later. ... Both this court and the legislature, however, have recognized the superior court's jurisdiction to order divorced parents, consistent with their means, to contribute toward the educational expenses of their adult children.... The respondent does not dispute the court's authority to order him to provide for Lindsey's educational expenses. He contends, however, that the court erred when it ordered him to pay for, among other things, transportation costs, medical expenses and clothing. He argues that these expenses are tantamount to child support, which he is no longer obligated to pay. The petitioner counters that the trial court's order was proper because RSA 458:20 allows the court to order the respondent to provide for Lindsey's support, maintenance and general welfare while she attends college. We disagree. RSA 458:20, in pertinent part, provides:

> In a proceeding under this chapter, the court may set aside a portion of the property of the parties in a separate fund or trust ... for a child of the parties, who is 18 years of age or older, if the child is in college....

This provision gives the trial court authority, when dividing the property of divorcing parties, to order a portion of that property to be placed into a separate educational trust fund for a child who is both in college and at least eighteen years old.

A divorced parent's support obligation does not automatically terminate when a child reaches eighteen years of age.... However, the nature of that support varies depending upon the circumstances and needs of the child. ... RSA 458:35-c does not place a time limit on a parent's obligation to pay for reasonable college expenses.... This is so because "jurisdiction to award education expenses is not limited as a matter of law to jurisdiction over minors." ...

The issue before us, which is one of first impression, is what constitutes "educational expenses." A number of jurisdictions that have addressed the issue have construed educational expenses to be only those costs directly related to attending college, such as tuition, room and board, and related fees.... . We agree and hold that "educational expenses" are those expenses that are directly related to the child's college education. Such expenses, therefore, include tuition, books, room, board and other directly related fees.

To define "educational expenses" more broadly would essentially require the respondent to pay for Lindsey's general support and maintenance, which would, in this case, conflict with RSA 458:35-c because the petitioner's request for a continuation of child support was dismissed. Consequently, the superior court erred in including amounts for transportation (gas, maintenance and registration), medical and dental coverage, clothing and shoes in its order.....

Moreover, with respect to room and board, we hold that the respondent is not required to pay an amount greater than he would be required to pay if the child resided on campus in college housing. If he is currently paying more than the cost of college housing, then the court must modify its order accordingly. In addition, payments for room and board must ordinarily be made, if Lindsey resides in campus housing, directly to the college, or, if she lives off campus, directly to Lindsey to defray reasonable expenses for "room and board."

We, therefore, reverse the trial court's decision and remand for further proceedings consistent with this opinion.

Case Questions

1. Should a child's aptitude for college level work be considered in cases such as this?
2. Should the obligation to pay for educational expenses include some of the cost of studying abroad?

Noneconomic Obligations

Parents' noneconomic obligations include nurturing and controlling their children, seeing that they attend school, and protecting them from abuse and neglect. Authorities can intervene if parents fail to perform these duties. Although parents generally have the right to make decisions on their child's behalf about religious training and educational and medical needs, this right is limited. When a child's life is threatened, for example, and the parents' religious beliefs prevent them from seeking necessary medical care, the state will often intervene and ensure that the child receives treatment.

Children also have obligations, the single most important of which is to obey their parents. When children perpetually defy their parents, a judicial *CHINS* (child in need of supervision) proceeding may be instituted. Many states also statutorily require adult children to provide their parents with necessaries in the event that the parents become unable to provide for themselves.[56]

Parental Immunity from Suit by Child

As we saw in Chapter VI, parents have traditionally been protected from suit by their children for negligence and intentional torts by an immunity. Over the last thirty years, however, many states have created exceptions to this immunity and have permitted suits in cases of child abuse, neglect, serious batteries, and the negligent operation of automobiles. Today, most states have either abolished the immunity or severely limited its use.

ENDING SPOUSAL RELATIONSHIPS

Spousal relationships can be ended through the legal actions of annulment and divorce, and they can be judicially altered by legal separation.

Annulment

An action to **annul** is appropriate when a marriage partner seeks to prove that no valid marriage ever existed. Thus the plaintiff is not seeking to terminate a valid marriage but, rather, to have a court declare that no valid marriage ever occurred. Annulments were historically important, especially during periods when divorces were difficult to obtain. Obtaining an annulment of a marriage was very useful because it could end the spousal relationship without branding either party as being "divorced," and thus enable each party to remarry. Today, with the advent of no-fault divorce, actions for annulment are much less popular, except among those who for religious reasons prefer to end a marriage legally without going through a divorce.

Although each state has its own grounds for annulments, common reasons include bigamy (where a person who is already married marries yet again); incest (where a person marries someone who is a close blood relative, contrary to law); mental incompetence (such as where the parties were intoxicated at the time of the ceremony);[57]

fraud (such as where one party misrepresents a willingness to engage in sexual relations and have children);[58] coercion; and one or both parties' being underage at the time of the marriage.

Because of the serious potential consequences of an annulment, particularly to property rights, many states have declared the children born to parents whose marriage has been annulled to be legitimate.[59] These states provide by statute that child support and custody matters will be determined in the same way as in divorce cases.[60] Many state courts award temporary alimony, and some award permanent alimony to dependent spouses.[61] Each party to an annulment recovers the property held prior to the marriage and is considered a co-owner of property acquired during the marriage.

Legal Separation

Many states have statutorily recognized an action for **legal separation**, also called a *mensa et thoro* divorce (from table and pillow).[62] The so-called *mensa* divorce can be granted when lawfully married parties have actually separated and when adequate grounds for a legal separation have been shown. Although states differ on what constitute sufficient grounds, common reasons include irreconcilable differences, adultery, desertion, cruelty, and nonsupport. If a court grants a legal separation, the parties remain married to each other but live apart. A criminal action can be brought if one spouse interferes with the other spouse's privacy. Unlike a final divorce, neither party to a legal separation is free to remarry. The court, after considering the financial conditions of each party, can require one spouse to support the other and can determine child custody. States differ about whether a property division should occur. During the legal separation, the possibility of reconciliation still exists, as does the option to proceed with a final divorce. The separation period allows the estranged parties to try to work out their difficulties while living apart.

Divorce/Dissolution

From the perspective of the early twenty-first century, it is difficult to understand the degree to which contemporary expectations of marriage differ from those of our ancestors. Historically, absolute divorce under Anglo-American law was very difficult to obtain. In New York, for example, the legislature had to approve each divorce until 1787, when courts became statutorily authorized to grant divorces in cases of adultery. This was New York's only ground for a lawful divorce until 1966![63] In nineteenth-century America it was assumed that persons were married for life.[64] In 1900 women lived an average of only forty-eight years,[65] so people were married for shorter periods of time. The social, legal, and economic circumstances of that era encouraged husbands and wives to remain formally married despite the existence of dysfunctional relationships and irreparable differences between the parties. Today, people live longer lives and have more choices.[66] There are fewer pressures on people to marry in the first place, and the miserably married are less likely to remain in intolerable relationships.[67] The availability of birth control permits people to be sexually active without conceiving children. Single parenting is common and is no longer considered unusual. Women have more economic opportunities than they did in 1950. The social stigma of being thirty and divorced or unmarried has greatly diminished. People who marry today do so primarily for companionship,[68] a need that can bring people together but can also cause them to follow different paths as their lives evolve with time.

This social transformation has gradually produced legal changes as well. Although many states had liberalized their divorce laws more than New York had by the early 1960s, divorces were generally limited—at least theoretically—to plaintiffs who proved that their spouses had engaged in adultery, cruelty (sometimes interpreted very liberally), and/or desertion.[69] The fact that a married couple had irreconcilable differences and was married in name only was not a sufficient basis under the law for a divorce. The fault-based approach was anti-divorce and existed because of widely held fears about the social consequences to families and society that would result from what was feared might become divorce on demand. When states began to liberalize their laws to meet the increasing demand for divorce, they often required long waiting periods before a divorce became final. During the waiting period it was unlawful for people to remarry, start new families, and get on with their lives.[70] To get around such restrictions, people often went to Nevada to obtain what were called "quickie divorces," because that state required only a six-week waiting period.[71] Reformers pressed for change, urging lawmakers to focus on the marriage relationship itself and to recognize that the adversarial process of proving fault was making a bad situation worse. It was damaging the parties and making the process of ending a marriage more difficult and painful than it ought to be. It encouraged collusion and caused some parties to perjure themselves, "admitting" things they had not done, just in order to qualify for a divorce.[72] In California, proponents of reform carefully drafted and quietly pursued the legislative process[73] and were rewarded with enactment of the nation's first "no-fault" divorce law, which took effect on January 1, 1970.[74] Once that dam was broken, all states adopted some form of no-fault divorce; the last state acted in 1985.[75] Today, in many states, the plaintiff can choose to proceed either on a no-fault basis or on the traditional fault basis. Proving fault can sometimes be advantageous if it makes it possible to avoid the waiting period that some states require before a divorce becomes final. Furthermore, in some jurisdictions proving fault can affect alimony and child custody decisions. Although state no-fault laws differ, a plaintiff usually has to prove marital breakdown and to prove that the parties have been living separately for a statutorily determined minimum period of time. In most states, a divorce can be granted despite the defendant's objection.[76] As a result of the philosophical changes that have occurred in recent years, the term *divorce* is increasingly being replaced with the more neutral term *dissolution*, which denotes the legal ending of the marital relationship.

Jurisdictional and Procedural Considerations

You will recall the discussions of *in personam* and *in rem* jurisdiction in Chapter IV and of civil procedure in Chapter V. Because terminating a marriage often involves some interesting jurisdictional problems and specialized procedures, it is important briefly to revisit these topics as they relate to divorce.

Jurisdiction

If it is determined that a court has granted a divorce, awarded alimony, or determined custody of a child without having jurisdiction, the court's action is void and without effect. Furthermore, this jurisdictional deficiency would make the court's judgment ineligible for full faith and credit in other states. Although constitutional due process often permits the termination of a marriage on the basis of *in rem* jurisdiction, a court must have *in personam* jurisdiction over a person who is to be required to make alimony and child support payments. Thus, a court has jurisdiction to grant a divorce decree where at least one marital party has lived within the forum state long enough to satisfy that state's residency requirement. The residency requirement demonstrates a substantial connection with the forum state and helps to establish the *in rem* notion that the marriage itself (the *res*) is physically located within the forum state.

If the plaintiff seeks to have a court decree alimony or to order child support in addition to terminating the marriage, however, *in rem* jurisdiction is insufficient, and the minimum contacts requirement of *in personam* jurisdiction must be satisfied.

Procedure

Many states statutorily permit a court to issue temporary support orders once a divorce action is initiated. This order may temporarily require one party to pay for an economically dependent spouse's necessaries, determine child custody and support, and determine who is responsible for paying which debts. This order is limited and is intended only to enable both parties to meet their living expenses while the action is pending. These issues are not permanently decided until the divorce and related claims have been acted on and a final judgment and order are entered in the case. Although laypeople generally use the term **divorce** to refer to the entire process of concluding and reordering a couple's marital, parental, and economic relationships, this is actually a misnomer. It is common in many states for each of the divorce-related claims to be decided in segments rather than in one long trial. This approach is called **bifurcation**, and it means that child custody, alimony, property division, and marriage dissolution are taken up separately by the court.

Procedural requirements in a divorce action generally vary with the type and complexity of the claims that must be resolved. Thus a contested divorce will generally be more procedurally cumbersome than an uncontested action, and a no-fault action will often be less procedurally complex than a fault-based action. In some states, cooperating parties can privately negotiate a separation agreement that reflects their mutual decision about how property should be divided, the amounts and types of support to be paid, and even proposals about child custody. If the terms of this contract are not unconscionable, the laws of the state can make this agreement binding on the court except as it relates to child custody provisions. In some states, parties to no-fault divorces who have no children and no substantial assets can end their marriages in a matter of minutes.

Allocation of Financial Obligations

When people divorce, in addition to terminating their marital relationship, there is a need to untangle their financial affairs so that each spouse can function independently. This involves determining whether alimony and child support will be paid and allocating the marital assets and liabilities. In some cases the parties are able to resolve these matters amicably by themselves. They may also benefit from the assistance of a mediator or arbitrator (see

Chapter XIV for more about these options). Where the parties are unable to reach agreement, a judge must ultimately make the decision.

Court-Ordered Alimony

Virtually all states permit a court to require an economically strong spouse to pay financial support to an economically dependent spouse where it is necessary and appropriate. This payment, which is discretionary with the court, is often referred to as **alimony**, although it is also called *spousal support*.[77] Some jurisdictions deny it to any spouse whose marriage ended as a result of that person's marital fault.

One form of spousal support is called *permanent alimony* because it continues until the recipient dies or is remarried. This form of alimony is intended to compensate an economically dependent wife who was married in another era, when homemaking was commonly viewed as a career and when it was reasonable to expect that one's husband would provide support for life. Someone who invested many years taking care of her home and her family, rather than working outside the home, is granted alimony when her marriage is terminated so that she receives economic justice. This form of alimony is on the decline, because public policy today favors sexual equality and because women today generally have the skills and education necessary to get a job and to be self-supporting.

Another type of spousal support, called *rehabilitative alimony,* is awarded for a specified period of years and is intended to provide funds so that the recipient can obtain education or training that will strengthen the person's job prospects. In deciding whether to grant rehabilitative alimony, a court takes into consideration many factors, including the payor's earning capacity; the dependent spouse's health status, work history, and present and future prospects for employment; and the likelihood that the person will take advantage of training and educational opportunities.

A court can order that alimony be paid either in a lump sum or periodically, usually on a monthly basis. If conditions materially change over time, either party can petition for modification. The payor, for example, might seek a reduction because of ill health and unemployment and the fact that the recipient, though not remarried, is cohabiting and has less financial need. The recipient, for example, might argue for an increase to offset inflation's impact on purchasing power and the recipient's need to pay for necessary medical treatment.

Enforcing payment of alimony is very problematic, because courts are reluctant to incarcerate defaulters (how can they earn money while in jail?), and because it is often too expensive for recipients to use the normal remedies available for enforcing civil judgments. (These remedies were discussed in Chapter V.)

Child Custody and Child Support

The general responsibility of parents to support their children was previously addressed in this chapter. The current discussion focuses on child custody and support in the context of a divorce, annulment, or temporary separation.

Although parents can negotiate an agreement and resolve many issues, they can only recommend whether the court should grant custody to both parents (**joint custody**) or grant custody to only one parent. Although the court has the responsibility to protect children, it usually will incorporate into the final judgment the custodial arrangements that have been agreed to by the parents if the arrangements are reasonable and appropriate. The court's decision is of great importance because of the custodial parent's right to make important decisions regarding a child's upbringing. Although judges historically have granted custody of young children to their mothers,[78] most states have discarded the "tender years doctrine," at least as a rigid rule, in response to increasing challenges from fathers during the 1970s.[79] The "best interest of the child" rule, preferred custody statutes (that favor the primary caretaker), and joint custody have become the most widely accepted standards for determining custody.[80] The "best interest of the child" rule requires judges to show no gender preference and to act in the best interest of each child.

When making this decision, the courts consider such matters as each parent's ability to provide, and interest in providing, the child with love, a good home, food, clothing, medical care, and education. Inquiry will be made into the stability of each parent's employment and whether the employment is compatible with the child's needs. Courts also look for instances of parental misconduct (such as substance abuse and sexually and morally questionable behavior), continuity of care,[81] and a sound moral foundation for the child. The following case demonstrates the difficulty of applying the "best interest of the child" rule. Notice how issues of employment, educational and professional accomplishment, and parental bonding bear on the determination of custody.

Shannon Blakely v. Brandon Blakely
218 P.3d 253
Supreme Court of Wyoming
October 20, 2009

Hill, Justice

Shannon Blakely (Mother) appeals from her divorce decree, contending that the district court abused its discretion when it awarded Brandon Blakely (Father) primary residential custody of the parties' two sons, while the half-brother remained in Mother's custody....

Issue

Mother states the single issue as follows:

> Whether the District Court erred when it awarded primary residential custody of the parties' two minor children to [Father]?

Facts

The parties to this action married on January 7, 2003. Mother brought a son, CS, into the marriage, and at the time of the marriage, Mother was pregnant with the couple's first son, CB, who was born in May of 2003. The couple's second son, EB, was born in August of 2005. During the relationship, the family lived in Buffalo, but Father often worked out of town.

The couple separated in October of 2005, with Mother leaving the home and taking all three boys with her. In June of 2007, Mother officially moved to Gillette with the three boys—by this time Mother was engaged to another man and expecting her fourth son, who was born in September of 2007. Father, meanwhile, continued to exercise visitation with his two sons.

Mother filed for divorce in August of 2007, and both parties requested temporary custody, which the district court awarded to Father on January 25, 2008. The case was tried on July 11, 2008, and at the close of evidence, the court made findings on the record. Ultimately, the court awarded primary residential custody to Father, with visitation to Mother. Mother appeals that decision.

Standard of Review

We have stated before that "[c]ustody, visitation, child support, and alimony are all committed to the sound discretion of the district court." ....

This Court has consistently recognized the broad discretion enjoyed by a district court in child custody matters. We will not interfere with the district court's custody determination absent procedural error or a clear abuse of discretion. In determining whether an abuse of discretion has occurred, our primary consideration is the reasonableness of the district court's decision in light of the evidence presented. We view the evidence in the light most favorable to the district court's determination, affording every favorable inference to the prevailing party and omitting from our consideration the conflicting evidence....

Discussion

Mother claims on appeal that in its decision giving primary residential custody to Father, the district court did not "give the welfare and needs of the children paramount consideration." Mother insists that the evidence presented at trial indicated that she was the more appropriate party to have primary residential custody. Essentially, Mother asks us to reweigh the evidence considered by the district court when she points to, and analyzes in detail, each of the statutory factors that guide a custody determination ....

Father contends that the court's decision is supported by the evidence and was a proper exercise of discretion—and, as evidenced by the court's oral ruling, the court thoroughly evaluated the evidence along with the statutory factors.

As we have consistently articulated, "This Court ... does not reweigh evidence. Instead, we view the facts in the light most favorable to the prevailing party." .... In child custody determinations, the district court must base its decision on the factors articulated in § 20-2-201(a), which provides:

(a) In granting a divorce, separation or annulment of a marriage or upon the establishment of paternity pursuant to W.S. 14-2-401 through 14-2-907, the court may make by decree or order any disposition of the children that appears most expedient and in the best interests of the children. In determining the best interests of the child, the court shall consider, but is not limited to, the following factors:

(i) The quality of the relationship each child has with each parent;

(ii) The ability of each parent to provide adequate care for each child throughout each period of responsibility, including arranging for each child's care by others as needed;

(iii) The relative competency and fitness of each parent;

(iv) Each parent's willingness to accept all responsibilities of parenting, including a willingness to accept care for each child at specified times and to relinquish care to the other parent at specified times;

(v) How the parents and each child can best maintain and strengthen a relationship with each other;

(vi) How the parents and each child interact and communicate with each other and how such interaction and communication may be improved;

(vii) The ability and willingness of each parent to allow the other to provide care without intrusion, respect the other parent's rights and responsibilities, including the right to privacy;

(viii) Geographic distance between the parents' residences;

(ix) The current physical and mental ability of each parent to care for each child;

(x) Any other factors the court deems necessary and relevant.

No single factor is determinative.... In fact, depending on the case, different factors will present a greater need for emphasis. The one constant is that the resolution must be in the best interests of the children in that particular family....

With these principles in mind, we turn to the facts of the instant case. The record is clear that each parent had a good relationship with the children. The court stated in its oral findings, "... these are two good parents. They both love their children and want the best for their children." Indeed, each party appears to be more than able to handle the care of the children, and the record contains evidence favorable to each party.

For instance, Mother lives in a four-bedroom, two-bath home on two and a half acres, and is a stay-at-home mom. And even though Father works full-time, he is very responsible regarding daycare and has that "all lined out," according to the district court. The court found both parents to be on equal footing regarding maintaining and strengthening relationships with each other. The court also found to be a positive feature of both parents "the support of their extended families." The phrase "equal footing" was also applied regarding how the parents and each child interact and communicate with each other, as well as the ability and willingness of each parent to allow the other to provide care without intrusion, respecting the other parent's rights and responsibilities, including the right to privacy. By and large, the court found the parents to be on "equal footing" on most of the factors it considered.

Nevertheless, Mother points to a factor in particular that she believes weighs in her favor—that giving custody of EB and CB to Father splits up the four brothers. This Court has addressed the issue of separating siblings:

[G]enerally speaking the separating of siblings through custody awards to different parents is not preferred. Keeping siblings together in the same household is considered the better practice. However, this court clarified that the effect of separating siblings from each other is just one of several factors courts consider in determining the primary issue-the best interests of the children....

The district court addressed this very issue at length on the record:

All right. Another factor I want to take up, under factor 10, which is the general factor that may influence the Court decision is the subject of the half siblings, because it is very important.

... I want the record to reflect I have taken into account the value of half-siblings being raised under the same roof, and I recognize that value....

I am also going to note that right at this moment, that dad has indicated that he has no problem in affording access of these two boys, [CB] and [EB] to their half siblings, and I take that representation at face value.

I want you to know, sir, that if that does not happen, that this Court is going to consider that to be a material and substantial change in circumstances, that could conceivably justify a change in custody later on so that should influence you in the right direction here. These boys need to have a full, deep, and long relationship with their half-siblings. And there is no reason why you and their mother cannot arrange that, particularly when you have the support of your extended families behind you.

The court concluded that it was in the children's overall best interests that Father be awarded custody. Furthermore, the court's oral findings were sufficiently detailed so as to provide an adequate basis for its ultimate determination awarding Father custody of the two boys, effectively separating them from their brothers for much of the time.

Because this was such a close case, we would like to again emphasize:

"The law affords wide discretion to the district court when fashioning custody and visitation provisions for the best interests of the children." ... We recognize such discretion encompasses one of the most difficult and demanding tasks assigned to a trial judge.... Ultimately, the "goal to be achieved is a reasonable balance of the rights and affections of each of the parents, with paramount consideration being given to the welfare and needs of the children...."

Certainly, reasonable minds could reach different conclusions about which parent's custody would be in the best interests of the children....

Seldom if ever does a divorce court have a choice between a parent who is all good on one side and a parent who is all bad on the other side. The matter of awarding custody is a comparative proposition wherein the court exercises its best judgment and discretion and awards custody to one parent or to the other, according to what the court thinks is for the best interest and welfare of the children.

... Here, even the district court admitted this was a close, tough case. This Court will accede to the district court's determination of the admissibility of evidence unless the court clearly abused its discretion.... The burden is on the party asserting an abuse of discretion to establish such an abuse. ... In this instance, Mother has failed to meet the applicable burden and because the record includes sufficient evidence to support the district court's decision, we can find no abuse of discretion in the district court's award of custody to Father.

Conclusion
The district court did not err when it awarded Father primary residential custody of his two sons. This Court can find no abuse of discretion by the district court, and, accordingly, we affirm its decision.

Case Questions

1. Are you satisfied with the Wyoming Supreme Court's reasoning for affirming the trial court's decision?
2. Do you think there is a better way, in cases as close on the merits as this one, to arrive at a just decision as to which parent should have primary physical custody? Which justified rejecting the Iowa preference for not separating siblings in child custody disputes?

 From your perspective, how should a court ethically weigh the economic contributions of a parent who works outside the home against the contributions of the parent who provides a child with primary care and psychological support?

Grandparental Visitation

The question as to what rights, if any, grandparents should have to visit their grandchildren has provoked considerable legislation and litigation throughout the country. In a case decided by the U.S. Supreme Court in 2002, *Troxel v. Granville*, 530 U.S. 57, a trial court in Washington, pursuant to a state statute, granted grandparents named the

Troxels visitation rights with their deceased son's minor children. The children's mother disagreed with the amount of visitation granted by the trial court and appealed to the Washington Supreme Court. That court, believing that the statute was overly broad, concluded that it violated the federal constitution. Although the Troxels successfully petitioned the U.S. Supreme Court for a writ of certiorari, the justices agreed with the Washington Supreme Court and affirmed its decision.

In the aftermath of the *Troxel* decision, many state legislatures redrafted their statutes to accommodate the Supreme Court's concerns. They sought to create a framework for balancing the rights of parents to determine how children should be raised, and with whom they should associate, against denying children and their grandparents, where appropriate and in the best interest of the

children, the right to maintain an existing relationship—even if the parent(s) and grandparents are antagonistic toward one another.

Pennsylvania's post-*Troxel* statute can be seen in Figure 9.7. The constitutionality of this statute was upheld by the Pennsylvania Supreme Court in August of 2006 in the case of *Hiller v. Fausey.*

INTERNET TIP

Readers interested in reading the Pennsylvania Supreme Court's decision in reading *Hiller v. Fausey* can find this case on the textbook's website.

In the next case readers will see how a divorced parent's failure to support his/her minor children financially can also be the determining factor in a contested adoption.

---

§ 5311.   When parent deceased.

If a parent of an unmarried child is deceased, the parents or grandparents of the deceased parent may be granted reasonable partial custody or visitation rights, or both, to the unmarried child by the court upon a finding that partial custody or visitation rights, or both, would be in the best interest of the child and would not interfere with the parent-child relationship. The court shall consider the amount of personal contact between the parents or grandparents of the deceased parent and the child prior to the application.

§ 5312.   When parents' marriage is dissolved or parents are separated.

In all proceedings for dissolution, subsequent to the commencement of the proceeding and continuing thereafter or when parents have been separated for six months or more, the court may, upon application of the parent or grandparent of a party, grant reasonable partial custody or visitation rights, or both, to the unmarried child if it finds that visitation rights or partial custody, or both, would be in the best interest of the child and would not interfere with the parent-child relationship. The court shall consider the amount of personal contact between the parents or grandparents of the party and the child prior to the application.

FIGURE 9.7   Title 23 Pennsylvania Consolidated Statutes

ADA v. SA
132 P.3d 196
Supreme Court of Wyoming
April 20, 2006

Kite, Justice

CJ is the stepfather of ADA and SSA (the children), and SA is their biological father. Stepfather petitioned the district court to adopt the children without father's consent because father had failed to provide adequate child support for the children. The district court denied the petition, finding stepfather failed to prove by clear and convincing evidence that father willfully failed to pay child support....

Facts

The children's mother and father were divorced in 2001, and the divorce decree awarded custody of the children to mother and ordered father to pay $527.46 per month in child support. Mother married stepfather in January 2003, and stepfather assumed responsibility for supporting the children. Father did not comply with his child support obligation; consequently, on February 2, 2004, stepfather filed a petition to adopt the children without father's consent pursuant to Wyo. Stat. Ann. § 1-22-110.

The district court held a hearing on stepfather's petition. Father admitted he had not paid child support in accordance with the order but argued his failure was not willful.... [T]he district court concluded father's failure to pay child support was not willful and, consequently, denied stepfather's petition. Stepfather appealed....

Discussion

Stepfather claims the district court abused its discretion by denying his petition to adopt the children without father's consent. A petition for adoption without parental consent may be granted by the district court if the elements outlined in Wyo. Stat. Ann. § 1-22-110 are satisfied.... Wyo. Stat. Ann. § 1-22-110 states, in pertinent part:

> (a) In addition to the exceptions contained in W.S. 1-22-108, the adoption of a child may be ordered without the written consent of a parent or the putative father if the court finds ... that the putative father or the nonconsenting parent or parents have:...
>
> (iv) Willfully failed to contribute to the support of the child for a period of one (1) year immediately prior to the filing of the petition to

adopt and has failed to bring the support obligation current within sixty (60) days after service of the petition to adopt; or ...

> (ix) Willfully failed to pay a total dollar amount of at least seventy percent (70 percent) of the court-ordered support for a period of two (2) years or more and has failed to bring the support obligation one hundred percent (100 percent) current within sixty (60) days after service of the petition to adopt.

The petition stated the adoption should be allowed without father's permission ...because father had willfully failed to pay a total dollar amount of at least seventy percent of the court-ordered support for a period of two years or more. However, the district court's order denying the petition focused on Wyo. Stat. Ann. § 1-22-110(a)(iv), which allows adoption without the parent's consent if the parent has "willfully failed to contribute to the support of the child for a period of one (1) year immediately prior to the filing of the petition to adopt and has failed to bring the support obligation current within sixty (60) days after service of the petition to adopt." ...Our inquiry, therefore, focuses on the willfulness element and not on the amount of support father did or did not pay.

We have explained the importance of the willfulness requirement as follows:

> Clearly, by inclusion of the modifying term "willfully" the statute draws a distinction, as it must, between the parent who though financially able to pay his court-ordered child support is unwilling to do so, and the parent who though willing to pay his court-ordered child support is financially unable to do so. "A natural parent's failure to support his or her child does not obviate the necessity of the parent's consent to the child's adoption, where the parent's financial condition is such that he or she is unable to support the child." 2 Am.Jur.2d Adoption § 88 (1974).

Moreover, this court has defined willfully in the context of Wyo. Stat. Ann. § 1-22-110 as "intentionally, knowingly, purposely, voluntarily, consciously, deliberately, and without justifiable excuse, as distinguished from carelessly, inadvertently, accidentally, negligently, heedlessly or thoughtlessly." ...

...Father acknowledged he was aware of his child support obligation and did not pay it on a regular basis. He claimed he was unable to consistently pay child support because he had difficulty finding employment ...and he had been incarcerated intermittently on a number of different charges....

Stepfather argues father's actions were willful because his behavior led to his incarceration which prevented him from earning the money to pay child support. We have directly addressed the issue of whether a non-consenting parent's failure to pay child support because he is incarcerated is sufficient to establish willfulness.... We [have] said ... "Incarceration, standing alone, does not provide the direct intent necessary to constitute willful failure to pay under the pertinent statute." ...Instead, "the focus must remain on the parent's intent and ability to pay. The courts should look at whether the parent has demonstrated, through whatever financial means available to him, that the parent has not forgotten his statutory obligation to his child." ...When a parent is incarcerated, "'the proper inquiry to address ...is whether the natural parent intentionally incapacitated himself for the purpose of avoiding the duty imposed by law; if so then imprisonment may constitute justification for dispensing with his consent in the adoption proceeding....'" There is no evidence in this record which indicates father willfully committed any crimes in order to have himself incarcerated so he could avoid his child support obligation. Thus, his incarceration, by itself, does not justify a finding of willfulness.

Of course, even when a parent is incarcerated, he must pay child support if he has the means to do so. "A parent must always pay child support according to his or her financial ability." ...The record indicates father was incarcerated off and on over a period of several years; however, neither the actual dates of his imprisonment nor the total amount of time he spent in jail is shown in the record. Furthermore, stepfather did not present any evidence as to whether father earned wages while incarcerated.... Thus, we do not know if he had the ability to pay any child support while he was incarcerated....

Father testified, when he was not in jail, he attempted to find work in order to earn the funds to pay child support, but was not able to find consistent work in Uinta County. He identified two construction companies for which he had worked as a truck driver and stated, without contradiction, his child support was paid while he was working. Father also testified he had attempted to find work through "the union" and

with "the rigs," but was unsuccessful. After he was unable to secure other employment, he said he started his own business with the hopes of earning a living. At the time of the hearing, the business apparently had not yet yielded any earnings. Father testified he was living with friends because he could not afford his own residence....

The determination of whether father's failure to pay child support was willful involves disputed factual issues; consequently, it was within the district court's province to weigh the evidence and judge the credibility of the witnesses.... Evidence exists in the record supporting father's contention he did not have the means to pay his child support because he had difficulty earning a living and had been incarcerated....

Stepfather also argues the record shows father chose to spend his money on drugs and/or alcohol instead of paying his child support obligation. The record does contain evidence suggesting father's use of intoxicating substances contributed to his difficulties....

Obviously, if a parent has money with which to buy drugs or alcohol and chooses to do so rather than pay child support, an argument could be made that the failure to pay child support was willful.... However, it is important to focus on the proper query when evaluating such an argument. As explained by the Montana Supreme Court when reviewing a lower court's termination of a mother's parental rights:

> [A parent's] admitted drug addiction alone cannot serve as clear and convincing evidence that she had the means to contribute to her children's support. The relevant inquiry is whether she obtained funds which could have been used for the support of the children which, instead, she chose to spend on drugs....

In the case at bar, there was no evidence concerning the extent of father's drug or alcohol use or the actual amount of money he spent on such substances. More importantly, the record does not show father had funds available to him to buy drugs and/or alcohol instead of paying child support.

As we have said before, the right of parents to associate with their children is fundamental, and due process requires we stringently guard this important right. Stepfather was charged with proving, by clear and convincing evidence, father willfully disregarded his child support obligation. The district court concluded he did not meet that onerous burden. Although father's efforts to pay his child support certainly cannot be characterized as model and may have, at times, been willful, stepfather must prove that fact with clear and convincing evidence, and this record does not contain such evidence. When there is a failure of proof, we cannot conclude the district court's denial of the petition for adoption was an abuse of discretion.

Affirmed.

Case Questions

1. What was the stepfather's claim in the intermediate appellate court?
2. What did the appellate court decide?
3. What rationale did the Wyoming Supreme Court give for its decision?

Preferred Custody Statutes

Preferred custody statutes were enacted because it was uncertain whether judges had sufficient reliable information to predict accurately what would be in a child's best interest.[82] Some states require that preference be given to a child's primary caretaker, when the primary caretaker can be established. Such an approach has the advantage of not favoring either gender, and it provides the child with continuity and stability in the parenting role.

When the statutory preference is for joint custody, the public policy provides that even though the marital relationship between the parents has ended, their parenting roles and responsibilities will continue as before. Both parents will share decision making in regard to their child's upbringing. Joint custody produces no winners and losers of a custody battle. The parents continue to share a family, but not a marriage.[83] When joint custody works, the child benefits from the active involvement of both a mother and a father. But it works only where divorcing parents are willing and able to separate their marital and parental relationships and act cooperatively to benefit their child.[84]

Once a court has determined that one parent should have custody, the noncustodial parent will normally be awarded visitation rights. It is important to encourage the noncustodial parent to continue to play an active role in the child's life. Sometimes the custodial parent wants to relocate, which would have the effect of curtailing the visitation opportunities of the noncustodial spouse. Courts are divided on what standard to apply when the parents disagree about making such a move.[85] Although the initial custody determination can be modified at a future date if material changes in the child's circumstances prove harmful, courts are reluctant to unsettle a child unless compelling reasons are shown.

Child Support

Although parents have the right to formally and informally break up with one another, they cannot divorce their minor children. Thus parents will generally be required to support their children until they reach the age of majority. In some special circumstances, however, the support obligation continues even beyond that date. We focus now on the special circumstances that can arise in conjunction with a divorce.

When a marriage that involves children is terminated, the court will examine the earning capacity of each parent and the needs of each child, determine who has custody, and determine each parent's support obligation. Every state has some guidelines to help judges make this determination. Generally, when custody has been awarded to one parent, the noncustodial parent will be ordered to make support payments. This parent is legally required to make the payments irrespective of side issues such as whether the custodial parent has violated the noncustodial parent's visitation rights or whether the custodial parent is spending the support payment money for other purposes than the children. Although child support is awarded to provide for the needs of the child, courts disagree about the exact meaning of that term. It certainly includes a child's necessaries, and there are cases in which noncustodial parents have been required to pay for their children's college educations.[86] Nevertheless, child support has a theoretically different purpose from that of alimony and property awards, which are intended to benefit a spouse.

When parents divorce, remarry, and establish second families, their support obligation to their first family continues, and many states require that the children from the first family receive priority over the children in the second family. Some states are moving away from this traditional approach and are structuring child support so that it benefits both families.[87] As was previously indicated, states differ about whether stepparents have a support liability for stepchildren.

As is the case with alimony, either party can petition for modification of the support order when there is a substantial change of circumstances.

Property Division

As we saw earlier in this chapter, when people divorce, the property that they have accumulated during their marriage is apportioned between them. It is common for married people to own a house, cars, and other tangible personal property concurrently and to have joint accounts at the bank. If they have been married for a long time, they will probably have accumulated much property. States address the distribution problem differently, depending on whether they follow the common law/equitable distribution approach or the community property approach.

Common Law/Equitable Distribution Approach

In most states, what is known as **equitable distribution** has replaced the traditional common law approach to determining property rights. Under the common law, the person who had title to property owned it, and generally this meant the husband. When lawmakers and judges began to look upon marriage as an economic partnership, property acquired during marriage was perceived in different terms. This new perspective produced reforms intended to result in the more equitable distribution of property to each of the divorcing parties. Though not all states that adopt equitable distribution classify property, many do. In those states, property is classified as separate property or as marital property. **Marital property** is nonseparate property acquired during the marriage and is subject to an equitable distribution by a judge. **Separate property**, that which was owned prior to the marriage or was received as a gift or inheritance, is not subject to distribution.

Obviously, the legal definition of property is crucial to any distribution scheme. Many states now treat pensions in which the ownership rights have matured (vested) and medical insurance benefits as also subject to distribution.

Though not all states agree with the holding in the following case, it is looked upon as a landmark decision. In the *O'Brien* case, the court declared that a spouse who has made significant contributions to her husband's medical education and licensing as a doctor was entitled to a property interest in his license at the time of their divorce.

O'Brien v. O'Brien
489 N.E.2d 712
Court of Appeals of New York
December 26, 1985

Simons, Judge

In this divorce action, the parties' only asset of any consequence is the husband's newly acquired license to practice medicine. The principal issue presented is whether that license, acquired during their marriage, is marital property subject to equitable distribution

under Domestic Relations Law § 236(B)(5). Supreme Court held that it was and accordingly made a distributive award in defendant's favor. It also granted defendant maintenance arrears, expert witness fees and attorneys' fees.... On appeal to the Appellate Division, a majority of that court held that plaintiff's medical license is not marital property and that defendant was not entitled to an award for the expert witness fees. It modified the judgment and remitted the case to Supreme Court for further proceedings, specifically for a determination of maintenance and a rehabilitative award.... The matter is before us by leave of the Appellate Division.

We now hold that plaintiff's medical license constitutes "marital property" within the meaning of Domestic Relations Law § 236(B)(1)(c) and that it is therefore subject to equitable distribution pursuant to subdivision 5 of that part....

I

Plaintiff and defendant married on April 3, 1971. At the time both were employed as teachers at the same private school. Defendant had a bachelor's degree and a temporary teaching certificate but required 18 months of postgraduate classes at an approximate cost of $3,000, excluding living expenses, to obtain permanent certification in New York. She claimed, and the trial court found, that she had relinquished the opportunity to obtain permanent certification while plaintiff pursued his education. At the time of the marriage, plaintiff had completed only three and one-half years of college but shortly afterward he returned to school at night to earn his bachelor's degree and to complete sufficient premedical courses and enter medical school. In September 1973 the parties moved to Guadalajara, Mexico, where plaintiff became a full-time medical student. While he pursued his studies defendant held several teaching and tutorial positions and contributed her earnings to their joint expenses. The parties returned to New York in December 1976 so that plaintiff could complete the last two semesters of medical school and internship training here. After they returned, defendant resumed her former teaching position and she remained in it at the time this action was commenced. Plaintiff was licensed to practice medicine in October 1980. He commenced this action for divorce two months later. At the time of trial, he was a resident in general surgery.

During the marriage both parties contributed to paying the living and educational expenses and they received additional help from both of their families. They disagreed on the amounts of their respective contributions but it is undisputed that in addition to performing household work and managing the family finances defendant was gainfully employed throughout the marriage, that she contributed all of her earnings to their living and educational expenses and that her financial contributions exceeded those of plaintiff. The trial court found that she had contributed 76 percent of the parties' income exclusive of a $10,000

student loan obtained by defendant. Finding that plaintiff's medical degree and license are marital property, the court received evidence of its value and ordered a distributive award to defendant. Defendant presented expert testimony that the present value of plaintiff's medical license was $472,000. Her expert testified that he arrived at this figure by comparing the average income of a college graduate and that of a general surgeon between 1985, when plaintiff's residency would end, and 2012, when he would reach age 65. After considering Federal income taxes, an inflation rate of 10 percent and a real interest rate of 3 percent he capitalized the difference in average earnings and reduced the amount to present value. He also gave his opinion that the present value of defendant's contribution to plaintiff's medical education was $103,390. Plaintiff offered no expert testimony on the subject.

The court, after considering the lifestyle that plaintiff would enjoy from the enhanced earning potential his medical license would bring and defendant's contributions and efforts toward attainment of it, made a distributive award to her of $188,800, representing 40 percent of the value of the license, and ordered it paid in 11 annual installments of various amounts beginning November 1, 1982 and ending November 1, 1992. The court also directed plaintiff to maintain a life insurance policy on his life for defendant's benefit for the unpaid balance of the award and it ordered plaintiff to pay defendant's counsel fees of $7,000 and her expert witness fee of $1,000. It did not award defendant maintenance.

A divided Appellate Division ... concluded that a professional license acquired during marriage is not marital property subject to distribution. It therefore modified the judgment by striking the trial court's determination that it is and by striking the provision ordering payment of the expert witness for evaluating the license and remitted the case for further proceedings....

II

The Equitable Distribution Law contemplates only two classes of property: marital property and separate property (Domestic Relations Law § 236[B][1][c], [d]). The former, which is subject to equitable distribution, is defined broadly as "all property acquired by either or both spouses during the marriage and before the execution of a separation agreement or the commencement of a matrimonial action, regardless of the form in which title is held" (Domestic Relations Law § 236[B][1][c] [emphasis added]; see § 236 [B][5][b], [c]). Plaintiff does not contend that his license is excluded from distribution because it is separate property; rather, he claims that it is not property at all but represents a personal attainment in acquiring knowledge. He rests his argument on decisions in similar cases from other jurisdictions and on his view that a license does not satisfy common-law concepts of property. Neither contention is controlling because decisions in other States rely principally on their own statutes, and the legislative history under-lying them, and because the New York Legislature deliberately went beyond traditional property concepts when it formulated the Equitable Distribution Law.... Instead, our statute recognizes that spouses have an equitable claim to things of value arising out of the marital relationship and classifies them as subject to distribution by focusing on the marital status of the parties at the time of acquisition. Those things acquired during marriage and subject to distribution have been classified as "marital property" although, as one commentator has observed, they hardly fall within the traditional property concepts because there is no common-law property interest remotely resembling marital property. "It is a statutory creature, is of no meaning whatsoever during the normal course of a marriage and arises full-grown, like Athena, upon the signing of a separation agreement or the commencement of a matrimonial action. [Thus] [i]t is hardly surprising, and not at all relevant, that traditional common law property concepts do not fit in parsing the meaning of 'marital property.'" ...Having classified the "property" subject to distribution, the Legislature did not attempt to go further and define it but left it to the courts to determine what interests come within the terms of section 236(B)(1)(c). We made such a determination in Majauskas v. Majauskas ...463 N.E.2d 15, holding there that vested but unmatured pension rights are marital property subject to equitable distribution. Because pension benefits are not specifically identified as marital property in the statute, we looked to the express reference to pension rights contained in section 236(B)(5)(d)(4), which deals with equitable distribution of marital property, to other provisions of the equitable distribution statute and to the legislative intent behind its enactment to determine whether pension rights are marital property or separate property. A similar analysis is appropriate here and leads to the conclusion that marital property encompasses a license to practice medicine to the extent that the license is acquired during marriage.

Section 236 provides that in making an equitable distribution of marital property, "the court shall consider: ...(6) any equitable claim to, interest in, or direct or indirect contribution made to the acquisition of such marital property by the party not having title, including joint efforts or expenditures and contributions and services as a spouse, parent, wage earner and homemaker, and to the career or career potential of the other party [and] ...(9) the impossibility or difficulty of evaluating any component asset or any interest in a business, corporation or profession" (Domestic Relations Law § 236 [B][5][d][6], [9] [emphasis added]). Where equitable distribution of marital property is appropriate but "the distribution of an interest in a business, corporation or profession would be contrary to law" the court shall make a distributive award in lieu of an actual distribution of the property (Domestic Relations Law § 236[B][5][e] [emphasis added]). The words mean exactly what they say: that an interest in a profession or professional career potential is marital property which may be represented by direct or indirect contributions of the non-title-holding spouse, including financial contributions and nonfinancial contributions made by caring for the home and family.

The history which preceded enactment of the statute confirms this interpretation. Reform of section 236 was advocated because experience had proven that application of the traditional common-law title theory of property had caused inequities upon dissolution of a marriage. The Legislature replaced the existing system with equitable distribution of marital property, an entirely new theory which considered all the circumstances of the case and of the respective parties to the marriage.... Equitable distribution was based on the premise that a marriage is, among other things, an economic partnership to which both parties contribute as spouse, parent, wage earner or homemaker.... Consistent with this purpose, and implicit in the statutory scheme as a whole, is the view that upon dissolution of the marriage there should be a winding up of the parties' economic affairs and a severance of their economic ties by an equitable distribution of the marital assets. Thus, the concept of alimony, which often served as a means of lifetime support and dependence for one spouse upon the other long after the marriage was over, was replaced with the concept of maintenance which seeks to allow "the recipient spouse an opportunity to achieve [economic] independence." ...

The determination that a professional license is marital property is also consistent with the conceptual base upon which the statute rests. As this case demonstrates, few undertakings during a marriage better qualify as the type of joint effort that the statute's economic partnership theory is intended to address than contributions toward one spouse's acquisition of a professional license. Working spouses are often required to contribute substantial income as wage earners, sacrifice their own educational or career goals and opportunities for child rearing, perform the bulk of household duties and responsibilities and forego the acquisition of marital assets that could have been accumulated if the professional spouse had been employed rather than occupied with the study and training necessary to acquire a professional license. In this case, nearly all of the parties' nine-year marriage was devoted to the acquisition of plaintiff's medical license and defendant played a major role in that project. She worked continuously during the marriage and contributed all of her earnings to their joint effort, she sacrificed her own educational and career opportunities, and she traveled with plaintiff to Mexico for three and one-half years while he attended medical school there. The Legislature has decided, by its explicit reference in the statute to the contributions of one spouse to the other's profession or career ...that these contributions represent investments in the economic partnership of the marriage and that the product of the parties' joint efforts, the professional license, should be considered marital property.

The majority at the Appellate Division held that the cited statutory provisions do not refer to the license held by a professional who has yet to establish a practice but only to a going professional practice.... There is no reason in law or logic to restrict the plain language of the statute to existing practices, however, for it is of little consequence in making an award of marital property, except for the purpose of evaluation, whether the professional spouse has already established a practice or whether he or she has yet to do so. An established practice merely represents the exercise of the privileges conferred upon the professional spouse by the license and the income flowing from that practice represents the receipt of the enhanced earning capacity that licensure allows. That being so, it would be unfair not to consider the license a marital asset.

Plaintiff's principal argument, adopted by the majority below, is that a professional license is not marital property because it does not fit within the traditional view of property as something which has an exchange value on the open market and is capable of sale, assignment or transfer. The position does not withstand analysis for at least two reasons. First, as we have observed, it ignores the fact that whether a professional license constitutes marital property is to be judged by the language of the statute which created this new species of property previously unknown at common law or under prior statutes. Thus, whether the license fits within traditional property concepts is of no consequence. Second, it is an overstatement to assert that a professional license could not be considered property even outside the context of section 236 (B). A professional license is a valuable property right, reflected in the money, effort and lost opportunity for employment expended in its acquisition, and also in the enhanced earning capacity it affords its holder, which may not be revoked without due process of law.... That a professional license has no market value is irrelevant. Obviously, a license may not be alienated as may other property and for that reason the working spouse's interest in it is limited. The Legislature has recognized that limitation, however, and has provided for an award in lieu of its actual distribution....

Plaintiff also contends that alternative remedies should be employed, such as an award of rehabilitative maintenance or reimbursement for direct financial contributions.... The statute does not expressly authorize retrospective maintenance or rehabilitative awards and we have no occasion to decide in this case whether the authority to do so may ever be implied from its provisions.... It is sufficient to observe that normally a working spouse should not be restricted to that relief because to do so frustrates the purposes underlying the Equitable Distribution Law. Limiting a working spouse to a maintenance award, either general or rehabilitative, not only is contrary to the economic partnership concept underlying the statute but also retains the uncertain and inequitable economic ties of dependence that the Legislature sought to extinguish by equitable distribution. Maintenance is subject to termination upon the recipient's remarriage and a working spouse may never receive adequate consideration for his or her contribution and may even be penalized for the decision to remarry if that is the only method of compensating the contribution. As one court said so well, "[t]he function of equitable distribution is to recognize that when a marriage ends, each of the spouses, based on the totality of the contributions made to it, has a stake in and right to a share of the marital assets accumulated while it endured, not because that share is needed, but because those assets represent the capital product of what was essentially a partnership entity" (*Wood v. Wood*, ...465 N.Y. S.3d 475). The Legislature stated its intention to eliminate such inequities by providing that a supporting spouse's "direct or indirect contribution" be recognized, considered and rewarded (Domestic Relations Law § 236 [B][5][d][6]).

Turning to the question of valuation, it has been suggested that even if a professional license is considered marital property, the working spouse is entitled only to reimbursement of his or her direct financial contributions.... If the license is marital property, then the working spouse is entitled to an equitable portion of it, not a return of funds advanced. Its value is the enhanced earning capacity it affords the holder and although fixing the present value of that enhanced earning capacity may present problems, the problems are not insurmountable. Certainly they are no more difficult than computing tort damages for wrongful death or diminished earning capacity resulting from injury and they differ only in degree from the problems presented when valuing a professional practice for purposes of a distributive award, something the courts have not hesitated to do.... The trial court retains the flexibility and discretion to structure the distributive award equitably, taking into consideration factors such as the working spouse's need for immediate payment, the licensed spouse's current ability to pay and the income tax consequences of prolonging the period of payment ...and, once it has received evidence of the present value of the license and the working spouse's contributions toward its acquisition and considered the remaining factors mandated by the statute ..., it may then make an appropriate distribution of the marital property including a distributive award for the professional license if such an award is

warranted. When other marital assets are of sufficient value to provide for the supporting spouse's equitable portion of the marital property, including his or her contributions to the acquisition of the professional license, however, the court retains the discretion to distribute these other marital assets or to make a distributive award in lieu of an actual distribution of the value of the professional spouse's license....

III

...Accordingly, in view of our holding that plaintiff's license to practice medicine is marital property, the order of the Appellate Division should be modified, with costs to defendant, by reinstating the judgment and the case remitted to the Appellate Division for determination of the facts, including the exercise of that court's discretion (CPLR 5613), and, as so modified, affirmed.

Case Questions

1. When Loretta O'Brien sued her husband Michael for divorce, what claim did she make with respect to the marital property of the couple?
2. What was the basis of her claim?
3. How does the court define marital property in this case?

 What moral principles are reflected in the New York equitable distribution statute?

Determining Fairness

For a distribution to be fair, the court must identify, classify, and determine the value of each spouse's assets—or their detriment, in the case of debts. The court must also consider the circumstances and needs of the parties, the length of their marriage, their marital standard of living, their contributions to the marriage, and other similar factors. Although it is possible to take such matters to trial and have them decided by a judge, it is often faster—and the parties have more control over the outcome—if they negotiate a property settlement in lieu of fighting it out in court. Property dispute battles can be very expensive. Appraisals and expensive expert witnesses are

required to establish the value of assets. Litigation costs can also increase dramatically and diminish the assets ultimately available for distribution. Judges frequently incorporate a negotiated agreement that equitably allocates marital assets and debts into the final judgment.

Community Property Approach

The states of Louisiana, Texas, California, New Mexico, Arizona, Nevada, Washington, Idaho, and Wisconsin have statutorily decided to treat all property that is not separate property and that was acquired during the marriage as presumptively community property that belongs equally to both spouses. Under this approach, it doesn't matter who worked and earned the money for a purchase or who purchased the property. Both spouses have the right to make management decisions regarding community property (such as whether it is leased, loaned, invested, etc.). If the parties wish to alter the community property presumption, they may do so by agreement, by gift, and by commingling separate and community assets so that separate property loses its character (such as the merger of a separate stamp collection with a community collection or the deposit of birthday money into the community checking account). In the event of a divorce, the court in a community property state makes an equitable division of all community property to each spouse.

The Decree

Irrespective of whether the issues are negotiated or litigated, at the end of the process the court issues a judgment that dissolves the marriage, distributes the property, and determines claims for alimony, child custody, and child support. The attorneys for the parties then assist the former spouses to implement the orders. Property must be exchanged, ownership rights transferred, money transferred, debts paid, insurance policies obtained, pension rights transferred, and other details wrapped up.

CHAPTER SUMMARY

Chapter IX began with a discussion of the family and its historical roles, as well as its place in contemporary America. Emphasis was given to the many tangible and intangible benefits that accrue to family members but are otherwise unavailable to nonfamily members. The discussion then shifted to the ways in which family relationships are created—through marriage or the formation of civil unions/domestic partnerships, by becoming a parent as a result of the birth of one's child, by adoption, and, to a limited extent, as a consequence of becoming a foster parent. The essential nature of each of these statutes was discussed and each process was explained.

The chapter concluded with an overview of how spousal relationships are legally ended—by way of annulment, legal separation, and divorce/dissolution. The discussion focused on how the divorcing couple's financial affairs are separated so that each spouse is able to function independently—decisions as to alimony, child custody and child support, and the distribution of property.

CHAPTER QUESTIONS

1. Andrea Moorehead was abandoned by her birth mother, a crack cocaine user who had tested positive for venereal disease shortly after birth. Andrea was placed with foster parents when she was nine days old. The foster parents, Melva and Robert Dearth, sought to adopt Andrea when she was ten months old. The county's Children Service Bureau (CSB) opposed this proposed adoption. The Dearths alleged that CSB's decision was predicated on the fact that they were white and Andrea was black. They proved that they lived in an interracial neighborhood, that they attended an interracial church, and that their two children attended an interracial school. They had a stable marriage and financial standing. The Dearths filed a motion for review of this administrative decision in the Common Pleas Court. They requested that CSB's custody be terminated and that permanent custody of Andrea be granted to them. The Court denied the Dearths' motion. The Dearths appealed.

The appeals court found that there was clear evidence that CSB had a documented policy of placing black children with white adoptive parents only when no black parent could be found. Under Ohio law, adoption placements are to be made in the "best interests of the child." To what extent can adoption agencies such as CSB consider factors such as race and culture in determining adoption procedures? Under the law, can the racial factor outweigh all other considerations?

In re Moorhead, 600 N.E.2d 778 (1991)

2. Charles Collins and Bethany Guggenheim began living together in 1977. They were not married to each other. Bethany was recently divorced and had two children from the prior marriage. As part of the property settlement, she had received title to a 68-acre farm, and Charles, Bethany, and the children moved there in 1979. They intended to restore the farmhouse (circa 1740). Charles and Bethany jointly became liable for and made payments on a bank mortgage loan, insurance, and property taxes. They maintained a joint checking account to pay for joint expenses as well as individual checking accounts. They jointly purchased a tractor and other equipment, Charles paying two-thirds of the cost and Bethany one-third. Charles also invested $8,000 of his money in additional equipment and improvements for the farm. For several years they jointly operated a small business that made no profit. Despite Charles's contributions, the title to the farm remained at all times with Bethany. The parties experienced personal difficulties, and when they could not reconcile their differences, they permanently separated in 1986. During their cohabitation period, Charles contributed approximately $55,000 and Bethany $44,500 to the farm. Charles filed suit against Bethany. He claimed that fairness required either that Bethany and he should share title to the farm as tenants in common or that he should receive an equitable distribution of the property acquired during the period of cohabitation.

Charles did not allege that Bethany had breached any contract or engaged in any type of misconduct. The trial court dismissed the complaint. What action should a court take in a situation such as this, where unmarried, cohabiting people go their separate ways?

Collins v. Guggenheim, N.E.2d (1994)

3. James Ellam filed suit for divorce against his wife, Ann, on the ground that they had been living separately and apart. Ann counterclaimed against James for desertion. The facts reveal that James moved out of the marital home on July 5, 1972, because of severe marital discord. He moved back to his mother's home in a nearby city, where he slept, kept his clothes, and ate some of his meals. For the next eighteen months, James had an unusual weekday routine. His mother would drive James early in the morning from her home to the marital home so that James could see his dog, check on the house, take his car out of the garage, and go to work, much as he had done before he and Ann "separated." At the end of the day, James would drive to the marital residence, put the car back in the garage, play with the dog, talk with his wife until she went to bed, and watch television until 12:30 A.M., when his mother would pick him up and take him "home." On weekends, James would do chores at the marital home and even socialize with his wife (although the parties had terminated their sexual relationship). James lived this way because he claimed to love his wife and especially the dog, he wanted to maintain the marital home properly, and he did not want the neighbors to know about his marital problems. New Jersey law provides that persons who have lived separate and apart for a statutory period of time may be granted a divorce. Should the trial court have granted a divorce on the grounds that James and Ann had satisfied the statutory requirements by living "separate and apart in different habitations" as permitted under New Jersey law?

Ellam v. Ellam, 333 A.2d 577 (1975)

4. The Washington Revised Code (Section 26.16.205) provides as follows: "The expenses of the family…are chargeable upon the property of both husband and wife, or either of them, and in relation thereto they may be sued jointly or separately."…

   Should a husband be financially obligated to pay the legal costs resulting from his wife's appeal of criminal convictions?

   State v. Clark, 563 P.2d 1253 (1977)

5. Oregon law provides for "no-fault" divorces. Marie and Max Dunn had been married for twenty years when Marie filed for divorce. After Marie presented evidence of irremediable and irreconcilable differences between herself and her husband, the trial court entered a decree dissolving the marriage. The court also awarded Marie custody of their two minor children and set alimony at $200 per month. Max appealed to the Oregon Court of Appeals on the ground that the trial court's decree was premature and was not supported by adequate proof. Max argued that the court acted without considering the views of both parties to the marriage. The appellate court interpreted the Oregon statute to require only that the trial court determine whether the existing difference "reasonably] appears to the court to be in the mind of the petitioner an irreconcilable one, and based on that difference…whether or not…the breakdown of that particular marriage is irremediable." What public policy arguments can you identify related to the facts in the above case that would favor "no-fault" divorces? What arguments could be brought to bear against them?

   Dunn v. Dunn, 511 P.2d 427 (1973)

6. Two women brought suit against the Jefferson County (Kentucky) Clerk of Courts because the clerk refused to issue them a license to become married to each other. The women alleged that the clerk's refusal denied them various constitutionally protected rights, among these the right to become married, the right to freedom of association, and the right to freedom from cruel and unusual punishment. The trial court ruled that persons seeking to enter into a same-sex marriage were not entitled under the law to a marriage license. The women appealed to the Court of Appeals of Kentucky. The Kentucky statutes do not define the term *marriage*. The appeals court disposed of the case without even reaching the appellants' constitutional claims. Can you surmise on what grounds the appeals court decided the case?

   Jones v. Callahan, 501 S.W.2d 588 (1973)

7. Sixteen-year-old Colleen provided day care for twelve-year-old Shane. The two began a sexual relationship that resulted in Colleen giving birth to a child when the mother and father were seventeen and thirteen years old, respectively. Although Shane was a victim of child abuse himself, a Kansas district court judge ordered him to pay $50 child support per month and found him financially responsible for over $7,000 in other assistance provided to the mother and baby in conjunction with the childbirth. Shane filed an appeal arguing that since he could not legally consent to sexual relations with Colleen, he should not be legally obligated to pay child support.

   What public policies are in conflict in this case? How do you think the Kansas Supreme Court ruled and why?

   State ex rel. Hermesmann v. Seyer, 847 P.2d 1273 (1993)

NOTES

1. J. Demos, "A Little Commonwealth: Family Life in Plymouth," in *Family and State,* ed. L. Houlgate (Totowa, NJ: Rowman & Littlefield, 1988), pp. 30–31.

2. Table 60. Children Under 18 Years by Presence of Parents: 1980–2004. Statistical Abstract of the United States 2006.

3. B. Yorburg, *The Changing Family* (New York: Columbia University Press, 1973), p. 94.

4. D. Castle, "Early Emancipation Statutes: Should They Protect Parents as Well as Children?" 20 *Family Law Quarterly* 3, 363 (Fall 1986).

5. H. Jacob, *Silent Revolution* (Chicago: University of Chicago Press, 1988) p. 1.

6. M. Grossberg, *Governing the Hearth* (Chapel Hill: University of North Carolina Press, 1985) p. 3.

7. L. Houlgate, *Family and State* (Totowa, NJ: Rowman & Littlefield, 1988).

8. E. Pound, "Individual Interests in Domestic Relations," 14 *Michigan Law Review* 177, 179–181 (1916).

9. L. Wardle, C. Blakeseley, and J. Parker, *Contemporary Family Law*, Sec. 1:02 (Deerfield, IL: Clark Boardman Callaghan, 1988).

10. E. Jenks, *A Short History of English Law* (2d rev. ed.) (Boston: Little, Brown & Co., 1922), n. 24 at 20–22.

11. Wardle, Blakeseley, and Parker, Sec. 1:02.

12. Ibid., Sec. 1:03.

13. *Wisconsin v. Yoder,* 406 U.S. 205 (1972), 229–230.

14. P. C. Hoffer, *Law & People in Colonial America* (Baltimore: Johns Hopkins University Press, 1982).

15. Grossberg, pp. 3–4.

16. Ibid., p. 5.

17. Ibid., p. 6.

18. R. Melton, "Evolving Definition of 'Family,'" *Journal of Family Law* 504 (1990–1991).

19. *Braschi v. Stahl Association*, 543 N.E.2d 49 (1989) 58.

20. *Braschi*, 543 N.E.2d at 53–54.

21. J. Collier, M. Rosaldo, and S. Yanagisako, "Is There a Family? New Anthropological Views," in *Rethinking the Family: Some Feminist Questions*, eds. B. Thorne and M. Yalon (New York: Longman, 1982), pp. 25–39.

22. M. Farmer, *The Family* (London: Longmans, Green and Co., 1970), p. 17.

23. H. D. Krause, *Family Law* (2d ed.) (St. Paul: West Publishing, 1986), pp. 31–32.

24. *Maynard v. Hill*, 125 U.S. 190 (1888).

25. Wardle, Blakeseley, and Parker, Sec. 3:02.

26. Alabama, Colorado, the District of Columbia, Iowa, Montana, Oklahoma, Pennsylvania, Rhode Island, South Carolina, Texas, and Utah recognize common law marriages without qualification.

27. Montana Code Annotated 40-1-403 and Iowa Code Ann. 595.11

28. National Commission for Adoption, *Adoption Factbook* 18 (1989).

29. J. Evall, "Sexual Orientation and Adoptive Matching," 24 *Family Law Quarterly* 349 (1991).

30. Some states require that a petitioner be at least ten years or older than the person to be adopted, whereas others require that the adoptee not be related to the petitioner. Some states also refuse to allow an adult petitioner to adopt another adult who happens to be the petitioner's homosexual partner, where the parties may be trying to use the adoption law to circumvent the marriage, contract, and probate laws.

31. Krause, p. 163.

32. E. Bartholet, *Family Bonds* (Boston: Houghton Mifflin, 1993), p. 66.

33. Ibid., p. 71.

34. Ibid., pp. 70–72.

35. L. Schwartz, "Religious Matching for Adoption: Unraveling the Interests Behind the 'Best Interests' Standard," 25 *Family Law Quarterly* 2 (Summer 1991).

36. *Wisconsin v. Yoder,* 406 U.S. 205 (1972), 229–230.

37. Ibid., p. 189.

38. Ibid.

39. J. Evall, "Sexual Orientation and Adoptive Matching," 24 *Family Law Quarterly* 3, 354–355 (1991).

40. Evall, pp. 356–357.

41. Bartholet, p. 48.

42. Ibid., p. 55.

43. Ibid., p. 56.

44. Adoption and Foster Care Analysis & Reporting System (AFCARS), *Interim FY 2008 Estimates as of October 2009*, U.S. Dept. of Health and Human Services.

45. A. Hardin, ed., *Foster Children in the Courts,* Foster Care Project, National Legal Resource Center for Child Advocacy and Protection (Chicago: American Bar Association, 1983), p. 70.

46. *Foster Care Fact Sheet.* Evan B. Donaldson Adoption Institute. (2002).

47. American Public Welfare Association, as quoted in *Newsweek*, April 25, 1994, p. 55.

48. HHS Press Release of September 14, 2009. HHS Awards &35 Million to States for Increasing Adoptions. http://www.hhs.gov/news/press/2009pres/09/20090914a.html.

49. Jacob, p. 1.

50. States differ as to exactly what level of support must be provided. Some states define necessaries to be essentially the most basic needs, whereas other states are more generous in their construction of that term.

51. C. Hused, "Married Woman's Property Law 1800–1850," 71 *Georgetown Law Journal* 1359, n. 4 at 1400 (1983). Also see *Thompson v. Thompson*, 218 U.S. 611 (1910).

52. *Griswold v. Connecticut*, 381 U.S. 479 (1965).

53. *Wisconsin v. Yoder*, 406 U.S. 205 (1972), 229–230.

54. See Kentucky Revised Statutes sec. 205.310, South Dakota Codified Laws Annotated Sec. 25-7-8, and Washington Revised Code Sec. 26.16.205. See also *M. H. B. v. H. T. B.*, 498 A. 2d 775 (1985).

55. See Alaska Statute Sec. 47.25.250, Iowa Code Sec. 252.5, *Estate of Hines*, 573 P.2d 1260 (1978), and Wisconsin Statutes Annotated Sec. 940.27.

56. See Alaska Statute Sec. 25.20.030 and Oregon Revised Statutes Sec. 109.010.

57. See *Mahan v. Mahan,* 88 SO2d 545 (1956).

58. See *Heup v. Heup*, 172 N.W.2d 334 (1969).

59. Maryland Annotated Code Article 16, Sec 27.

60. New Hampshire Revised Statutes annotated Sec. 458:17; Minnesota Sec. 518.57.

61. 4 *American Jurisprudence* 2d, 513.

62. *Posner v. Posner,* 233 So.2d 381 (1970).

63. Jacob, p. 30.

64. Ibid., p. 4.

65. U.S. Bureau of the Census, *Historical Statistics of the United States, Colonial Times to 1957* (Washington, D.C., 1960), p. 25.

66. This is not to suggest that the amount of choice is equally distributed throughout society and is not affected by considerations of race, gender, and socioeconomic status.

67. It is important to emphasize that, in all eras, spouses and parents have deserted their partners and families without bothering with legal formalities. Note also that the primary victims have been women who devoted their lives to their families and homes and who were often left destitute and with children. This has contributed to what is often referred to as the feminization of poverty.

68. Jacob, p. 251.

69. Ibid., p. 47.

70. Ibid., pp. 46–47.

71. Ibid., p. 34.

72. Wadlington, "Divorce Without Fault Without Perjury," 52 *Virginia Law Revue*, 32, 40 (1966).

73. Jacob, pp. 60–61.

74. Ibid., p. 59.

75. Ibid., p. 80.

76. *Hagerty v. Hagerty*, 281 N.W.2d 386 (1979).

77. Freed and Walker, "Family Law in the Fifty States: An Overview." 24 *Family Law Review* 309, 355 (1991).

78. A. Shepard. "Taking Children Seriously: Promoting Cooperative Custody After Divorce," 64 *Texas Law Review* 687 (1985).

79. S. Quinn, "Fathers Cry for Custody," *Juris Doctor* 42 (May 1976).

80. R. Cochran Jr., "Reconciling the Primary Caretaker Preference, and Joint Custody Preference and the Case-by-Case Rule," in *Joint Custody and Shared Parenting*, ed. Jay Folberg (New York: Guilford Press, 1991), pp. 218–219.

81. J. Goldstein, A. Freud, and A. Solnit, *Beyond the Best Interests of the Child* (New York: Free Press, 1970), pp. 107–109.

82. Cochran, p. 222.

83. M. Elkin, in *Joint Custody and Shared Parenting,* ed. Jay Folberg (New York: The Guilford Press, 1991) pp. 12–13.

84. Ibid., p. 13.

85. See *Gruber v. Gruber*, 583 A.2d 434 (1990), and *In re Miroballi*, 589 N.E.2d 565 (1992), for cases supporting parent's right to relocate. See *Plowman v. Plowman*, 597 A.2d 701 (1991), for a contrary opinion.

86. See *Fortenberry v. Fortenberry*, 338 S.E.2d 342 (1985), *Toomey v. Toomey*, 636 S.W.2d 313 (1982), and *Neudecker v. Neudecker*, 577 N.E.2d 960 (1991).

87. H. Krause, *Family Law in a Nutshell* (2d ed.) (St. Paul: West Publishing, 1986), p. 211.

X

✳

Contracts

CHAPTER OBJECTIVES

1. *Understand the origins of the modern contract action.*
2. *Identify and explain the essential requirements of an enforceable contract.*
3. *Explain how contracts are classified in terms of validity and enforceability.*
4. *Identify and explain the legal and equitable remedies available to an injured party when a contract is breached.*
5. *Understand how contractual rights and duties are transferred.*

A BRIEF HISTORY OF AMERICAN CONTRACT LAW

The modern contract action can be traced to the English common law writs of debt, detinue, and covenant, which were created in the twelfth and thirteenth centuries.[1] The **debt** action was used to collect a specific sum of money owed. **Detinue** was used against one who had possessory rights to another's personal property but who refused to return it when requested by the true owner. **Covenant** was initially used to enforce agreements relating to land (especially leases).[2] Later it was employed to enforce written agreements under seal.[3] Gradually, these writs were supplemented by the common law **writ of trespass**, which included trespass to land, assaults, batteries, the taking of goods, and false imprisonment. Each of these acts involved a tortfeasor who directly caused injury to the victim by force and arms and thereby violated the King's peace.

In 1285, Parliament enacted the Statute of Westminster, which authorized the chancery to create a new writ, called **trespass on the case**, to address private wrongs that fell outside the traditional boundaries of trespass.[4] *Case*, as it came to be called, could remedy injuries that resulted from the defendant's failure to perform a professional duty that in turn resulted in harm to the plaintiff. Thus case would be appropriate where A's property was damaged while entrusted to B, as a result of B's failure to exercise proper skill or care.[5] These early writs were based on property rights and were not based on modern contractual notions such as offer, acceptance, and consideration.

In the fifteenth and sixteenth centuries, some breaches of duty (called undertakings) that had been included within the writ of trespass on the case evolved into a new writ called **assumpsit**.[6] For example, in one early case a ferry operator was sued in assumpsit for improperly loading his boat such that the plaintiff's mare drowned while crossing the Humber River.[7] By the early 1500s, a plaintiff could also sue in assumpsit for nonfeasance (failure to perform a promise).[8] During the 1560s, plaintiffs bringing assumpsit actions were generally required to allege that undertakings were supported by consideration.[9] Consideration grew in importance, and in the 1700s chancellors began refusing to order specific performance if they thought the consideration inadequate.[10] This development made the enforceability of contracts uncertain because judges could invalidate agreements reached by the parties and could prevent the parties from making their own bargains.

Assumpsit was the principal "contract" action until the early 1800s, when economic changes and widespread dissatisfaction with the technical requirements and expense of common law pleading resulted in an erosion of the common law approach.[11] The 1800s brought a significant shift in thinking: away from the old writs and toward the emerging new substantive action, called *contract*, which included all types of obligations. Contributing to the demise of assumpsit was the old-fashioned notion that courts had a responsibility to ensure that contracting parties received equivalent value from their bargains.[12] It became apparent that commercial prosperity required that courts protect their expectation damages (the return they had been promised in an agreement).[13] When the courts responded to these changes and demands, contract law rapidly developed. New York's replacement of the writ system in 1848 with its newly enacted Code of Civil Procedure established a trend toward modern code pleading that swept the nation.[14]

By 1850, American courts had accepted the notion that contracts are based on the reciprocal promises of the parties.[15] As courts became increasingly willing to enforce private agreements, they began to recognize the customs of each trade, profession, and business rather than general customs. The courts would often disregard existing legal requirements in favor of the rules created by the contracting parties. This fragmentation of law was bad for business. The absence of a widely accepted code of contract rules resulted in unpredictability and uncertainty in American society, the economy, and the courts. This caused business firms to press for uniform laws dealing with commercial transactions among states.

In the 1890s, the American Bar Association established the National Conference of Commissioners on Uniform State Laws to encourage states to enact uniform legislation. The Uniform Sales Act and the Negotiable Instruments Law were two products of this movement. During this era, Samuel Williston and Arthur Corbin wrote widely accepted treatises on the law of contracts. Then, in 1928, a legal think-tank of lawyers and judges, called the American Law Institute, developed and published the Restatement of Contracts, a proposed code of contract rules that was grounded in the common law.

In 1942, the American Law Institute and the American Bar Association sponsored a project to develop a **Uniform Commercial Code** (UCC), which was completed in 1952. In 1953, Pennsylvania was the first state to adopt the UCC. The code covers sales, commercial paper, bank collection processes, letters of credit, bulk transfers, warehouse receipts, bills of lading, other documents of title, investment securities, and secured transactions. The UCC governs only sales of (and contracts to sell) goods, defined as movables (personal property having tangible form). It does not cover transactions involving realty, services, or the sale of intangibles. If a contract involves a mixed goods/services sale (for example, application of a hair product as part of a beauty treatment), the courts tend to apply the UCC only if the sale-of-goods aspect dominates the transaction. The UCC has been adopted at least partially in all fifty states and is the legislation that has had the largest impact on the law of contracts.

NATURE AND CLASSIFICATION OF CONTRACTS

A **contract** is a legally enforceable agreement containing one or more promises. Not every promise is a contract—only those promises enforceable by law. Although the word *contract* is often used when referring to a written document that contains the terms of the contract, in the legal sense the word *contract* does not mean the tangible document, but rather the legally enforceable agreement itself.

In order to establish an enforceable contract, there must be (1) an agreement, (2) between competent parties, (3) based on genuine assent of the parties, (4) supported by consideration, (5) that does not contravene principles of law, and (6) in writing (in certain circumstances). Each of these requirements is discussed in detail in this chapter.

An **agreement** is an expression of the parties' willingness to be bound to the terms of the contract. Usually, one party offers a proposal, and the other agrees to the terms by accepting it. Both parties to the contract must be **competent**. Some people—because of age or mental disability—are not competent and thus do not have, from the legal standpoint, the capacity to bind themselves contractually. **Genuine assent** of both parties is also necessary. It is presumed to exist unless one of the parties is induced to agree because of

misrepresentation, fraud, duress, undue influence, or mistake.

Consideration on the part of both parties is an essential element of a contract. One party's promise (or consideration) must be bargained for and given in exchange for the other's act or promise (his consideration). The bargain cannot involve something that is prohibited by law or that is against the best interests of society. And, finally, certain contracts, to be enforceable, must be evidenced in writing.

Common law is the primary source of the law of contracts. Many statutes affect contracts, especially specific types of contracts such as employment and insurance. But the overwhelming body of contractual principles is embodied in court decisions.

Valid, Void, Voidable, and Unenforceable Contracts

Contracts can be classified in terms of validity and enforceability. A **valid contract** is a binding and enforceable agreement that meets all the necessary contractual requirements. A contract is said to be valid and enforceable when a person is entitled to judicial relief in case of breach by the other party.

A **void contract** means no contract, because no legal obligation has been created. When an agreement lacks a necessary contractual element—such as consideration—the agreement is without legal effect, and therefore void.

A **voidable contract** exists when one or more persons can elect to avoid an obligation created by a contract because of the manner in which the contract was brought about. For example, someone who has been induced to make a contract by fraud or duress may be able to avoid the obligation created by the contract. Contracts made by those who are not of legal age are also voidable, at the option of the party lacking legal capacity. A voidable contract is not wholly lacking in legal effect, however, because not all the parties can legally avoid their duties under it.

A contract is **unenforceable** (not void or voidable) when a defense to the enforceability of the contract is present. For example, the right of action is lost in a situation in which a sufficient writing is required and cannot be produced. Also, when a party wanting to enforce a contract waits beyond the time period prescribed by law to bring the court action (statute of limitations), the contract is unenforceable.

Bilateral and Unilateral Contracts

All contracts involve at least two parties. **Bilateral contracts** consist simply of mutual promises to do some future act. The promises need not be express on both sides; one of the promises could be implied from the surrounding circumstances.

A **unilateral contract** results when one party makes a promise in exchange for another person performing an act or refraining from doing something. For example, assume that someone wants to buy an item owned by another for $100. If the buyer promises to pay the owner $100 for the item if and when the owner conveys legal title and possession to the buyer, a *uni*lateral contract is created. It is a promise of an act. The contract comes into existence when the act of conveying title and possession is performed. If, however, the buyer promises to pay $100 in exchange for the owner's promise to convey title and possession of the item, a bilateral contract results. A *bi*lateral contract comes into existence when mutual promises are made.

AGREEMENT

In order for a contract to be formed, there must be mutual **agreement** between two or more competent parties who must manifest their intent to be bound to definite terms. The agreement is usually reached by one party making an offer and the other—expressly or impliedly—accepting the terms of the offer.

The intention of the parties is the primary factor determining the nature of the contract. This is ascertained not just from the words used by the parties, but also from the entire situation, including the acts and conduct of the parties. In determining the intent of the parties, the courts generally use an objective rather than a subjective test. In an objective test, the question would be "What would a reasonable person in the position of party A think was meant by the words, conduct, or both of party B?" If a subjective test were used, the question would be "What did party A actually mean by certain expressions?" For example, suppose that one of the parties is not serious about creating a legal obligation, but the other party has no way of knowing this. Under the objective test, a contract would still be created.

In law, invitations to social events lack contractual intention and, when accepted, do not give rise to a binding contract. For example, when two people agree to have dinner together or to go to a baseball game together, each usually feels a moral obligation to fulfill his or her promise. Neither, however, expects to be legally bound by the agreement. An agreement also lacks contractual intent when a party's assent to it is made in obvious anger, excitement, or jest. This is true even when the parties' expressions, if taken literally as stated, would amount to mutual assent. Sometimes it is not obvious that a proposal is made in anger, excitement, or jest. Under the objective test, the surrounding circumstances and context of the expressions would be examined to determine what a reasonably prudent person would believe.

Offer

An **offer** is a proposal to make a contract. It is a promise conditional on a return promise, act, or forbearance being given by the offeree. The return promise, act, or forbearance is acceptance of the offer.

A legally effective offer must be (1) a definite proposal, (2) made with the intent to contract, and (3) communicated to the offeree. The terms of the offer, on acceptance, become the terms of the contract. An offer must be definite and certain, so that when the offeree accepts, both parties understand the obligations they have created.

It is important to distinguish between a definite proposal, which is an offer, and a solicitation of an offer. A willingness to make or receive an offer is not itself an offer, but an invitation to negotiate. For example, the question "Would you be interested in buying my television set for $100?" is considered an invitation to negotiate. A "yes" response would not create a contract, since there was no definite proposal made (form of payment, when due, etc.).

For an offer to be effective, it need not be made to one specific named person. It can be made to the general public, in the form of an advertisement. These may be circulars, quotation sheets, displays, and announcements in publications. However, the publication of the fact that an item is for sale, along with its price, is usually an invitation to negotiate, not an offer.

Termination of an Offer

The **offeree** can bind the **offeror** to his or her proposal for the duration of the offer—the time from the moment an offer is effectively communicated to the offeree until it is terminated. An offer can be terminated by (1) revocation by the offeror, (2) lapse of time, (3) subsequent illegality, (4) destruction of the subject matter, (5) death or lack of capacity, (6) rejection, (7) a counteroffer, and (8) acceptance.

An offeror has the power to terminate the offer by revocation at any time before it is accepted. Even when an offeror promises to hold an offer open for a certain period of time, the offeror can revoke the offer before that time, unless consideration is given to hold the offer open. For example, if a seller promises in an offer to give the offeree one week to accept the offer, the seller still retains the power to withdraw the offer at any time.

A contract whereby an offeror is bound to hold an offer open is called an **option**. In an option contract, consideration is necessary in return for the promise to hold the offer open. For example, if the offeree pays the offeror $10 to hold an offer open for ten days, the offeror does not have the power to withdraw the offer before the ten-day period is up.

If an offer stipulates how long it will remain open, it automatically terminates with the expiration of that period of time. When an offer does not stipulate a time period within which it may be accepted, it is then effective for a "reasonable" length of time.

An offer to enter into an agreement forbidden by law is ineffective and void, even if the offer was legal when made. If the subject matter of an offer is destroyed, the offer is automatically terminated because of impossibility.

An offer is terminated at the death of either the offeror or the offeree. Adjudication of insanity usually has the same effect as death in terminating an offer. The termination is effective automatically without any need for the terminating party to give notice. For example, if a person offers to sell an item at a stated price, but dies before the offer is accepted, there can be no contract, because one of the parties died before a meeting of the minds took place. If the offeree had accepted the offer before the death, however, there would have been a meeting of minds, and the offeror's estate would be responsible under the contract.

An offer is also terminated by a rejection or a counteroffer. When an offeree does not intend to accept an offer and so informs the offeror, the offer is said to have been terminated by rejection. If the offeree responds to an offer by making another proposal, the proposal constitutes a counteroffer and terminates the original offer. For example, if an offer is made to sell merchandise for $300 and the offeree offers to buy this merchandise for $250, the offeree has rejected the original offer by making a counteroffer. However, an *inquiry*, or a request for additional terms by the offeree, is not a counteroffer and does not terminate the offer. Thus, if the offeree had asked whether the offeror would consider reducing the price to $250, this inquiry would not terminate the original offer.

Acceptance

An **acceptance** is the agreement of the offeree to be bound by the terms of the offer. There is no meeting of the minds until the offeree has consented to the proposition contained in the offer. In order for an acceptance to be effective in creating a contract, there must be (1) an unconditional consent, (2) to an open offer, (3) by the offeree only, and (4) communicated to the offeror. In addition, there must be some act of manifestation of the intention to contract. This can be in the form of (1) silence or inaction, (2) a promise, (3) an act or forbearance from an act, or (4) any other manner specifically stipulated in the offer.

In most situations, silence or inaction on the part of the offeree does not constitute acceptance. When a person receives goods or services expecting that they will have to be paid for, the act of receiving the goods or services constitutes acceptance of the offer. An offeror is usually not permitted to word the offer in such a way that silence or inaction of the offeree constitutes acceptance. However, silence or inaction *can* do so in situations in which this method of dealing has been established by agreement between the parties or by prior dealings of the parties.

In an offer to enter into a bilateral contract, the offeree must communicate acceptance in the form of a promise to the offeror. The offeror must be made aware, by the express or implied promise, that a contract has been formed. An offer to enter into a unilateral contract requires an acceptance in the form of an act. A mere promise to perform the act is not an effective acceptance.

The offeror has the power to specify the means and methods of acceptance, and the acceptance must comply with those requirements. For example, an oral acceptance of an offer that called for a written acceptance would be ineffective. If nothing is stated, a reasonable means or method of acceptance is effective. An offer can provide that the acceptance is effective only on the completion of specified formalities. In such a situation, all these formalities must be complied with in order to have an effective acceptance.

At common law, an acceptance must be a "mirror image" of the offer. If it changes the terms of an offer in any way, it acts only as a counteroffer and has no effect as an acceptance. Under the UCC (2-207), an acceptance that adds some new or different terms to contracts involving the sale of goods does create a contract. The new terms are treated as proposals that must be accepted separately.

The next case involves a pest control company that sought to require customers wishing to renew their contracts to thereafter arbitrate rather than litigate contractual disputes between the parties. The company subsequently learned to its chagrin that its customer, the Rebars, had, unknown to company officials, transformed the company's proposed renewal contract into a counteroffer in which the company's arbitration clause was deleted.

Because the Rebars carefully read the company's proposed contract, they detected the presence of the arbitration clause. The Rebars, not wishing to give up their right to litigate any contract-related claims, made some changes to the noneconomic portions of the company's proposal and sent the revised document back to the company along with a check (which the company subsequently cashed). The company, not realizing that their proposal had been rejected, proceeded to provide services to the Rebars, believing that they had accepted the proposal containing the arbitration clause. The Rebars' actions went undiscovered until a contractual dispute arose and the Rebars elected to bring the matter to court.

The moral of this story is that a contracting party cannot assume that another contracting party will shine a spotlight on substantive changes it has decided to include in its contract proposals. Every party to a contract needs to take the time to carefully read an offer, and, if possible, compare it with previous agreements in order to identify changes.

Cook's Pest Control, Inc. v. Robert and Margo Rebar
852 So.2d 730
Supreme Court of Alabama
December 13, 2002

Stuart, Justice

... August 28, 2000, Cook's Pest Control and the Rebars entered into a one-year renewable "Termite Control Agreement." Under the agreement, Cook's Pest Control was obligated to continue treating and inspecting the Rebars' home for termites during the term of the agreement, which, with certain limited exceptions, continued so long as the Rebars continued to pay the annual renewal fee. The agreement contained a mandatory, binding arbitration provision.

When the initial term of the agreement was about to expire, Cook's Pest Control notified the Rebars and requested that they renew the agreement for another year by paying the renewal fee. On August 16, 2001, Mrs. Rebar submitted a payment to Cook's Pest Control; with the payment she included an insert entitled "Addendum to Customer Agreement."... That addendum provided, in part:

> "Addendum to Customer Agreement:
> To: Cook's Pest Control, Inc....
>   Please read this addendum to your Customer Agreement carefully as it explains changes to some of the terms shown in the Agreement. Keep this document with the original Customer Agreement."...

> "Arbitration.
> Cook's [Pest Control] agrees that any prior amendment to the Customer Agreement shall be subject to written consent before arbitration is required. In the event that a dispute arises between Cook's [Pest Control] and Customer, Cook's [Pest Control] agrees to propose arbitration if so desired, estimate the cost thereof, and describe the process (venue, selection of arbitrator, etc.). Notwithstanding prior amendments, nothing herein shall limit Customer's right to seek court enforcement (including injunctive or class relief in appropriate cases) nor shall anything herein abrogate Customer's right to trial by jury. Arbitration shall not be required for any prior or future dealings between Cook's [Pest Control] and Customer.

> "Future Amendments.
> Cook's [Pest Control] agrees that any future amendments to the Customer Agreement shall be in writing and signed by Customer and [an]

authorized representative of Cook's [Pest Control].

> "Effective Date.
> These changes shall be effective upon negotiation of this payment or the next service provided pursuant to the Customer Agreement, whichever occurs first."...

> "Acceptance be [*sic*] Continued Use.
> Continued honoring of this account by you acknowledges agreement to these terms. If you do not agree with all of the terms of this contract, as amended, you must immediately notify me of that fact."

The addendum proposed new terms for the agreement and notified Cook's Pest Control that continued service or negotiation of the renewal-payment check by Cook's Pest Control would constitute acceptance of those new terms. After it received the addendum, Cook's Pest Control negotiated the Rebars' check and continued to perform termite inspections and services at the Rebars' home.

On August 30, 2001, the Rebars filed this action against Cook's Pest Control. The Rebars alleged fraud, negligence, breach of contract, breach of warranty, breach of duty, unjust enrichment, breach of the duty to warn, negligent training, supervision and retention of employees, and bad-faith failure to pay and bad-faith failure to investigate a claim. Those claims were based upon Cook's Pest Control's alleged failure to treat and control a termite infestation in the Rebars' home and to repair the damage to the home caused by the termites.

Cook's Pest Control moved to compel arbitration of the Rebars' claims. In support of its motion, Cook's Pest Control relied upon the arbitration provision contained in the agreement; Cook's Pest Control also submitted the affidavit testimony of the president of the company, who testified regarding the effect of Cook's Pest Control's business on interstate commerce.

The Rebars opposed the motion to compel arbitration, asserting, among other things, that a binding, mandatory arbitration agreement no longer existed. The Rebars asserted that a binding, mandatory arbitration agreement no longer existed because the agreement between the parties had been modified when it was renewed in August 2001. The Rebars presented to the trial court a copy of the addendum and a copy of the canceled check they had written to Cook's Pest Control in payment of their renewal fee, which Cook's Pest Control had accepted and negotiated. The Rebars also submitted the affidavit of Mrs. Rebar, who testified that after Cook's Pest Control had received the addendum and had negotiated the check for the renewal fee, Cook's Pest Control inspected the Rebars' home.

On December 18, 2001, the trial court denied Cook's Pest Control's motion to compel arbitration.... Cook's Pest Control appeals....

Analysis
Cook's Pest Control argues that the trial court incorrectly found that it accepted the terms included in the addendum by continuing to inspect and treat the Rebars' home after it received the addendum and negotiated the Rebars' check for the renewal fee. Cook's Pest Control argues that, under the terms of the agreement, it was already obligated to continue inspecting and treating the Rebars' home. Cook's Pest Control also argues that the addendum was an improper attempt to unilaterally modify an existing contract. We reject those arguments.

First, we reject Cook's Pest Control's argument that the Rebars were attempting unilaterally to modify an existing contract. We note that the parties' original agreement was due to expire on August 28, 2001; Cook's Pest Control had already sent the Rebars a notice of this expiration and had requested that the Rebars renew the agreement by submitting the annual renewal fee.

Upon receiving notice that the agreement was up for renewal, the Rebars responded to Cook's Pest Control's offer to renew that contract with an offer of their own to renew the contract but on substantially different terms. This response gave rise to a counter-offer or a conditional acceptance by the Rebars:

"If the purported acceptance attempts to restate the terms of the offer, such restatement must be accurate in every material respect. It is not a variation if the offeree merely puts into words that which was already reasonably implied in the terms of the offer. But the very form of words used by the offeror is material if the offeror so intended and so indicated in the offer. An acceptance using a different form makes no contract. A variation in the substance of the offered terms is material, even though the variation is slight....

"In the process of negotiation concerning a specific subject matter, there may be offers and counter-offers. One party proposes an agreement on stated terms; the other replies proposing an agreement on terms that are different. Such a counter-proposal is not identical with a rejection of the first offer, although it may have a similar legal operation in part. In order to deserve the name 'counter-offer,' it must be so expressed as to be legally operative as an offer to the party making the prior proposal. It is not a counter-offer unless it is itself an offer, fully complying with all the requirements that have been previously discussed. This does not mean that all of its terms must be fully expressed in a single communication. Often they can be determined only by reference to many previous communications between the two parties. In this, a counter-offer differs in no respect from original offers. But there is no counter-offer, and no power of acceptance in the other party, unless there is a definite expression of willingness to contract on definitely ascertainable terms.

"If the party who made the prior offer properly expresses assent to the terms of the counter-offer, a contract is thereby made on those terms. The fact that the prior offer became inoperative is now immaterial and the terms of that offer are also immaterial except in so far as they are incorporated by reference in the counter-offer itself. Very frequently, they must be adverted to in order to determine what the counter-offer is. Often, the acceptance of a counter-offer is evidenced by the action of the offeree in proceeding with performance rather than by words.

"... If the original offeror proceeds with performance in consequence of the counter-offer, there can be no successful action for breach of the terms originally proposed.

"The terms 'counter-offer' and 'conditional acceptance' are really no more than different forms of describing the same thing. They are the same in legal operation. Whether the word 'offer' is used or not, a communication that expresses an acceptance of a previous offer on certain conditions or with specified variations empowers the original offeror to consummate the contract by an expression of assent to the new conditions and variations. That is exactly what a counter-offer does. Both alike, called by either name, terminate the power of acceptance of the previous offer." Joseph M. Perillo, *Corbin on Contracts* §§ 3.32 at 478-80; §§ 3.35 (rev. ed. 1993) (footnotes omitted).

In this case, the Rebars did not accept the terms proposed by Cook's Pest Control for renewal of the agreement but instead proposed terms for the renewal of that contract that were materially different from the terms of the agreement.... The Rebars did not accept the arbitration provision proposed by Cook's Pest Control; they countered with an arbitration provision of their own.

In addition, the Rebars specified in the addendum the method by which Cook's Pest Control could signify its acceptance of those different terms. Had Cook's Pest Control wished to reject those terms, it could have refused to renew the agreement and forgone receipt of the Rebars' renewal check.

In response, Cook's Pest Control argues that it was obligated under the terms of the original agreement to continue servicing and treating the Rebars' home and that its continued service and treatment should not be regarded as acceptance of modifications to that agreement proposed by the addendum. We disagree.

Because the Rebars did not unconditionally accept the renewal contract as proposed by Cook's Pest Control but rather countered with terms that differed materially from those proposed by Cook's Pest Control, Cook's Pest Control had three options upon receipt of the addendum: (1) reject the Rebars' counteroffer and treat the agreement as terminated on August 28, 2001; (2) respond to the Rebars' counteroffer with a counteroffer of its own; or (3) accept the Rebars' counteroffer. Cook's Pest Control did not reject the counteroffer and treat the agreement as terminated; nor did it respond with its own counteroffer; rather, it deposited the Rebars' check and continued to inspect and treat the Rebars' home—the exact method specified by the Rebars for acceptance of the proposed modifications to the agreement. Those actions constituted acceptance of the Rebars' counteroffer.

Cook's Pest Control also argues that the addendum had no effect upon the renewal of the agreement because none of the employees in the office where the Rebars' payment was processed had the authority to enter into a contract on behalf of Cook's Pest Control. Thus, Cook's Pest Control argues, a properly authorized agent never assented to the modifications proposed by the Rebars. Again, we disagree.

"It is well settled that whether parties have entered a contract is determined by reference to the reasonable meaning of the parties' external and objective actions."... It is also well settled that an agent with actual or apparent authority may enter into a contract and bind his or her principal....

We note that if Cook's Pest Control wished to limit the authority of its employees to enter into contracts on its behalf, Cook's Pest Control, as the drafter of the original agreement, could have included such

limiting language in the agreement. We find nothing in the agreement so limiting the authority of employees of Cook's Pest Control; we find nothing in the agreement requiring that a purported modification to the agreement be directed to any particular office of Cook's Pest Control, and we find nothing in the agreement stating that, to be effective, such a modification must be signed by a corporate officer or by a duly authorized representative of Cook's Pest Control.

Based upon the fact that Cook's Pest Control received the Rebars' proposed modifications to the agreement and that Cook's Pest Control, for some two months thereafter, acted in complete accordance with the Rebars' stated method of accepting those proposed modifications, we conclude that Cook's Pest Control's external and objective actions evidenced assent to the Rebars' proposed modifications. It was reasonable for the Rebars to rely upon those actions as evidence indicating that Cook's Pest Control accepted their proposed changes to the agreement.

We agree with the trial court's conclusion, i.e., that, after receipt of the Rebars' addendum, Cook's Pest Control's continuing inspection and treatment of the Rebars' home and Cook's Pest Control's negotiation of the Rebars' check constituted acceptance of the terms contained in that addendum. Upon acceptance of those new terms, the binding arbitration provision contained in the agreement was no longer in effect. The parties' agreement regarding arbitration had been amended to state:

> "Cook's [Pest Control] agrees that any prior amendment to the Customer Agreement shall be subject to written consent before arbitration is required. In the event that a dispute arises between Cook's [Pest Control] and Customer, Cook's [Pest Control] agrees to propose arbitration if so desired, estimate the cost thereof, and describe the process (venue, selection of arbitrator, etc.). Notwithstanding prior amendments, nothing herein shall limit Customer's right to seek court enforcement (including injunctive or class relief in appropriate cases) nor shall anything herein abrogate Customer's right to trial by jury. Arbitration shall not be required for any prior or future dealings between Cook's [Pest Control] and Customer."

Because the Rebars oppose arbitration of their claims against Cook's Pest Control, the trial court properly denied Cook's Pest Control's motion to compel arbitration....

Affirmed.

Case Questions

1.   Why did the appellate court conclude that the Rebars' addendum constituted a counteroffer?
2.   What steps might Cook's Pest Control take to prevent this from happening in the future?

INTERNET TIP

Students can read a contract formation case entitled *Beaman Pontiac v. Gill* on the textbook's website. This case involves an oral, bilateral contract, and the opinion discusses issues involving the Uniform Commercial Code, the Mailbox Rule, and the existence of consideration.

REALITY OF CONSENT

Genuine assent to be bound by a contract is not present when one of the parties' consent is obtained through duress, undue influence, fraud, or innocent misrepresentation, or when either of the parties, or both, made a mistake concerning the contract. Such contracts are usually voidable, and the injured party has the right to elect to avoid or affirm the agreement. (These defenses against the enforceability of a contract can also be used against other legal documents, such as wills, trust agreements, and executed gifts.)

An injured party who wishes to avoid or rescind a contract should act promptly. Silence beyond a reasonable length of time may be deemed an implied ratification. An injured party who elects to rescind a contract is entitled to *restitution*—the return of any property or money given in performance of the contract. The injured party must also return any property or money received through the contract.

Duress

Freedom of will of both parties to a contract is absolutely necessary. When one of the parties' wills is overcome because of duress, the agreement is voidable. **Duress** is any unlawful constraint exercised on people that forces their consent to an agreement that they would not otherwise have made.

Unlike those situations in which people act as a result of fraud, innocent misrepresentation, or mistake, a person acting under duress does so knowingly. Three elements are necessary for duress to exist: (1) coercion, (2) causing a loss of free will, and (3) resulting in a consent to be bound by a contract.

Any form of constraint improperly exercised in order to get another's consent to contract is sufficient for coercion. Exercise of pressure to contract is not enough; it must be exercised wrongfully. Thus, advice, suggestion, or persuasion are not recognized as coercive. Likewise, causing a person to fear embarrassment or annoyance usually does not constitute duress. In order to amount to coercion, the constraint must entail threatened injury or force. For duress to exist, the person must enter into the agreement while under the influence of this threat.

The threat need not necessarily be to the person or the property of the contracting party. For example, a threat to injure the child of a contracting party could amount to duress. A threat of criminal prosecution gives rise to duress when fear overcomes judgment and deprives the person of the exercise of free will. Making a threat of civil action, however—with the honest belief that it may be successful—is not using duress. For example, assume that an employee embezzles an undetermined amount of money from an employer. The employer estimates that the theft amounts to about $5,000, and threatens to bring a civil suit for damages unless the employee pays $5,000. Even though the employee takes the threat seriously and pays the $5,000, no duress exists. If the employer were to threaten to bring criminal charges under the same circumstances, duress would be present.

Economic distress or business compulsion may be grounds for duress. The surrounding circumstances of the business setting and the relative bargaining positions of the contracting parties are examined in order to determine whether duress is present.

Undue Influence

Undue influence results when the will of a dominant person is substituted for that of the other party, and the substitution is done in an unlawful fashion, resulting in an unfair agreement. Usually, undue influence is found when there is (1) a confidential relationship that is used to create (2) an unfair bargain.

In determining whether a confidential relationship exists, all the surrounding circumstances are examined to find out whether one of the parties dominates the other to the extent that the other is dependent on him or her. Family relationships, such as husband–wife or parent–child, often give rise to confidential relationships. Some relationships involving a special trust—such as trustee–beneficiary or attorney–client—entail a confidential relationship. Sometimes confidential relationships are created between business associates, neighbors, or friends. A person who is mentally weak—because of sickness, old age, or distress—may not be capable of resisting the dominant party's influence.

Whenever there is dominance in a confidential relationship, the court must determine whether the contract was equitable and voluntary. A contract is not invalid simply because there is a confidential relationship. A contract is voidable if one abuses the confidence in a relationship in order to obtain personal gain by substituting one's own will or interest for that of another. Whether the weaker party has had the benefit of independent advice is an important factor in determining fairness in contractual dealings. A legitimate suggestion or persuasion may influence someone, but it is not undue influence; nor, usually, is an appeal to the affections. When methods go beyond mere persuasion and prevent a person from acting freely, undue influence is present.

Fraud

The term **fraud** covers all intentional acts of deception used by one individual to gain an advantage over another. The essential elements of actionable fraud are (1) the misstatement of a material fact, (2) made with knowledge of its falsity, or in reckless disregard of its truth or falsity, (3) with the intention to deceive, (4) that induces reliance by the other party, and (5) that results or will result in injury to the other party.

For fraud, misstatements must be of a fact, a *fact* being something that existed in the past or exists at present. The misstated fact must be material. The often-used definition of a *material fact* is a fact without which the contract would not have been entered into. The speaker, when making the statement of fact, must know that it is false. The stating party must have the intention to deceive, and thereby to induce the other party to enter into the contract.

The deceived party's reliance on the misstatement must be justified and reasonable. A party wishing to rescind a contract need not show actual damages resulting from the fraud. However, a party wishing to sue for damages in addition to rescission must prove that actual damage has been sustained. Assume, for example, that Carlotta purchases a dog from Enrique based on his statements that the dog is a purebred with a pedigree from the American Kennel Club. Carlotta can rescind the contract, return the dog, and recover the purchase price from Enrique if she later discovers that the dog actually is a crossbred. Carlotta may also be able to recover for the dog's medical care, food, and supplies, based on their value to Enrique.

Misrepresentation

When a party to a contract misrepresents a material fact, even if unknowingly, and the other party relies on and is misled by the falsehood, **misrepresentation** is present. If a contract is induced by misrepresentation, the deceived party has the right of rescission. Fraud and misrepresentation are quite similar. However, the intent to deceive is the primary distinction between fraudulent and nonfraudulent misrepresentation. Rescission and restitution are available for both, although damages are not obtainable in cases of misrepresentation.

Mistake

Sometimes one or both of the parties to a contract unintentionally misunderstands material facts. If ignorance is of a fact that is material to the contract, a **mistake** exists, and the contract may be voidable. Although a mistake of material fact related to the contract is sufficient for relief, a mistake of law is not. In addition, the mistake must refer to a past or present material fact, not to a future possibility.

When one enters into a plain and unambiguous contract, one cannot avoid the obligation created by proving that its terms were misunderstood. Carelessness, poor judgment, lack of wisdom, or a mistake as to the true value of an item contracted for are not grounds for relief. Relief based on mistake may not be had simply because one party to a speculative contract expected it to turn out differently.

The court in the following case ordered rescission of an executed agreement and restitution because the parties to the contract made a mutual mistake.

Carter v. Matthews
701 S.W.2d 374
Supreme Court of Arkansas
January 13, 1986

Newbern, Justice

This is a real estate sale case in which the chancellor granted rescission in favor of the appellant on the ground of mutual mistake but did not award the money damages she claimed. The damages she sought were for her expenses in constructing improvements that subsequently had to be removed from the land. The appellant claims it was error for the chancellor to have found she did not rely on misrepresentations made by the appellees through their real estate agent, and thus it was error to refuse her damages for fraud plus costs and an attorney fee. On cross-appeal, the appellees contend the only possible basis for the rescission was fraud, not mistake, and the chancellor erred in granting rescission once he had found there was no reliance by the appellant on any active or constructive misrepresentations of the appellees. We find the chancellor was correct on all counts, and thus we affirm on both appeal and cross-appeal.

1. Rescission

The chancellor found that conversations between the appellant and the appellees' agent showed that both parties were under the mistaken impression that the low, flat portion of land in question was suitable for building permanent structures such as a barn, horse corral and fencing. In fact, however, the area where the appellant attempted to build a barn and corral and which she wanted to use as pasture for horses was subject to severe and frequent flooding. The chancellor held there was thus a mutual mistake of fact making rescission proper. While there was evidence the appellees had known of one instance of severe flooding on the land, the evidence did not show they knew it was prone to the frequent and extensive flooding which turned out to be the case.

Other matters not known to the parties were that the low portion of the land, about two-thirds of the total acreage, is in the 100-year floodplain and that a Pulaski County ordinance...requires a seller of land lying in the floodplain to inform the buyer of that fact no later than ten days before closing the transaction. The county planning ordinance also requires that no structures be built in the floodplain. If the chancellor's decision had been to permit rescission because of the parties' lack of knowledge of these items, we would have had before us the question whether the mistake was one of law rather than fact and thus perhaps irremediable....

While the chancellor mentions these items, his basis for rescission was the mutual lack of knowledge about the extent of the flooding, and misunderstanding of the suitability of the property, as a matter of fact, for the buyer's purposes which were known to both parties. We sustain his finding that there was a mutual mistake of fact. A mutual mistake of fact as to a material element of a contract is an appropriate basis for rescission....

2. Damages for Fraud

The chancellor refused to allow the appellant any damages for the loss she sustained with respect to the improvements she had placed in the floodplain. He found the appellant had made an independent investigation of the propensity of the property to become flooded and had ascertained, erroneously, that the property was not in the floodplain. Thus, in spite of the legal duty on the part of the appellees to tell the appellant that the land was in the floodplain, and what might have been the resultant constructive fraud upon failure to inform her, he held that fraud may not be the basis of a damages award absent reliance on the misrepresentation. For the same reason the chancellor refused to base his decision on any alleged fraud resulting from the appellees' failure to tell the appellant what they may have known about the land's propensity to flood. He was correct. An essential element of an action for deceit is reliance by the plaintiff on the defendant's misrepresentation.... In view of the strong evidence, including her own testimony, that the appellant made her own investigation as to whether the land flooded, the extent to which a creek running through the land was in the floodplain, and the

feasibility of bridging the creek above the floodplain, we can hardly say the chancellor's factual determination that the appellant did not rely on the failure of the appellees to give her information known to them or which they had a duty to disclose to her under the ordinance was clearly erroneous....

When rescission is based on mutual mistake rather than fraud, the recoveries of the parties are limited to their restitutionary interests.... As the appellant could show no benefit conferred on the appellees from her attempted improvements on the land, she was entitled to no recovery in excess of the return of the purchase price, which was awarded to her by the chancellor, as well as cancellation of her note and mortgage....

Affirmed.

Case Questions

1. The plaintiff-appellant in this case went to court seeking rescission as well as damages. What, exactly, is the remedy called rescission?
2. Why did the chancellor agree to grant rescission? What was the rationale behind this ruling?
3. Why did the chancellor refuse to allow the appellant any damages for fraud?
4. What recovery was made by the appellant?

CONSIDERATION

Consideration is simply that which is bargained for and given in exchange for another's promise. Each party to a contract has a motive or price that induces the party to enter into the obligation. This cause or inducement is called consideration. Consideration usually consists of an act or a promise to do an act. **Forbearance** or a promise to forbear may also constitute consideration. Forbearance is refraining from doing an act, or giving up a right.

A person must bargain specifically for the promise, act, or forbearance in order for it to constitute consideration. A promise is usually binding only when consideration is given in exchange. If a person promises to give another $100, this is a promise to make a gift, and it is unenforceable since the promise lacked consideration. If, however, the **promisee** had promised to convey a television set in return for the promise to convey $100, the promise to give $100 would have been supported by consideration and therefore would be enforceable. Although a promise to make a gift is not

enforceable, a person who has received a gift is not required to return it for lack of consideration.

Consideration must be legally sufficient, which means that the consideration for the promise must be either a detriment to the promisee or a legal benefit to the **promisor**. In most situations, both exist. **Benefit** in the legal sense means the receipt by the promisor of some legal right to which the person had not previously been entitled. **Legal detriment** is the taking on of a legal obligation or the doing of something or giving up of a legal right by the promisee.

Assume that an uncle promises to pay a niece $1,000 if she enrolls in and graduates from an accredited college or university. If the niece graduates from an accredited college, she is entitled to the $1,000. The promisee–niece did something she was not legally obligated to do, so the promise was supported by legally sufficient consideration. The legal detriment of the niece certainly did not amount to actual detriment. It can hardly be said that the uncle received any actual benefit either.

Consideration should not be confused with a condition. A condition is an event the happening of which qualifies the duty to perform a promise. A promise to give a person $100 if the person comes to your home to pick it up is a promise to make a gift on the condition that the person picks up the money. A promisee who shows up is not legally entitled to the $100.

When one party to an agreement makes what appears at first glance to be a promise but when on examination no real promise is made, this situation is called an **illusory promise**. A contract is not entered into when one of the parties makes an illusory promise, because there is no consideration. For example, a promise to work for an employer at an agreed rate for as long as the promisor wishes to work is an illusory promise. The promisor is really promising nothing and cannot be bound to do anything.

A court will not concern itself with the terms of a contract as long as the parties have capacity and there has been genuine assent to the terms. Whether the bargain was a fair exchange is for the parties to decide when they enter into the agreement. Consideration need not have a pecuniary or money value. If a mother promises her son $100 if he does not drink or smoke until he reaches the age of twenty-one, there is no pecuniary value to the abstinence; yet it is valid consideration.

It is not necessary to state the consideration on the face of the document when an agreement is put in writing. It may be orally agreed on or implied. Although the recital of consideration is not final proof that consideration exists, it is evidence of consideration that is *prima facie*, or sufficient on its face. Evidence that no consideration existed will, however, overcome the presumption that the recital creates. And a statement of consideration in an instrument does not create consideration where it was never really intended or given.

If a promise is too vague or uncertain concerning time or subject matter, it will not amount to consideration. If a promise is obviously impossible to perform, it is not sufficient consideration for a return promise. When a promise is capable of being performed, even though improbable or absurd, it is consideration.

Consideration must be bargained for and given in exchange for a promise. Past consideration is not consideration. If a person performs a service for another without the other's knowledge, and later the recipient of the service promises to pay for it, the promise is not binding, since the promise to pay was not supported by consideration. A promise to do what one is already legally obligated to do cannot ordinarily constitute consideration. For example, a promise by a father to pay child support payments that are already an existing legal obligation determined by a court will not constitute consideration. Similarly, consideration is also lacking when a promise is made to refrain from doing what one has no legal right to do.

The facts in the following case have been summarized so that you can concentrate on learning about the importance of "consideration" in contract formation.

After Josephine Hopkins died, her estate decided to sell two adjacent parcels of land located in a wealthy neighborhood. One parcel was on Richwood Avenue and had a house on it, and the other was on vacant land on LeBlond Avenue.

Joel and Sandra King, the defendants in the case, decided to buy the Richwood property. Joel King also decided to join with architect Gene Barber to buy the LeBlond Avenue land. Joel King and Barber negotiated an agreement which provided that at the closing on the LeBlond parcel, Joel would promise to relinquish his rights in the LeBlond site to Barber in exchange for Barber's promise to deed a specified 10' by 80' portion of the LeBlond site to Joel for $1. Joel wanted to make sure that his parcel would be large enough to comply with zoning setback requirements.

Barber submitted two offers to the estate. Barber and Joel King made the first offer and Barber and M. Ray Brown made the second offer. King was not an offeror on the second offer. Because no attorneys were involved in the LeBlond Avenue transaction, there were procedural irregularities. The estate, for example, accepted both offers and accepted earnest money from both purchasers. The second offer involving Barber and Brown closed.

The Kings made renovations to the existing house and put on a new addition. Barber and Brown built themselves a new house on the LeBlond parcel and put up a fence along the boundary line between their tract and the Kings' tract. The Kings took offense because the fence was erected on land that the Kings believed to be within "their" 10' by 80' strip. The Kings argued in the ensuing lawsuit that Barber and Brown had breached the contract. The trial court, however, granted summary judgment in favor of Barber and Brown after ruling that the agreement with Joel King was unenforceable due to a lack of sufficient consideration. The Kings appealed.

Brown v. King
869 N.E.2d 35
Court of Appeals of Ohio
December 29, 2006

Mark P. Painter, Judge
This case involves neighbors and the ownership of a 10-foot-by-80-foot strip of land between their properties. The trial court granted summary judgment, holding that there was no consideration to support a contract requiring transfer of the strip...

II. Consideration
In their first assignment of error, the Kings argue that the trial court erred in granting summary judgment for Barber and Brown...

The elements of a contract include an offer, an acceptance, contractual capacity, consideration (the bargained-for legal benefit or detriment), a manifestation of mutual assent, and legality of object and of consideration.... The issue in the present case is whether there was consideration for the contract.

The Ohio Supreme Court has long recognized the rule that a contract is not binding unless it is supported by consideration. Consideration may consist of either a detriment to the promisee or a benefit to the promisor. A benefit may consist of some right, interest, or profit accruing to the promisor, while a detriment may consist of some forbearance, loss, or responsibility given, suffered, or undertaken by the promisee....

In the present case, the contract between Joel King and Barber was supported by consideration. Joel King had a valid contract with Barber to purchase the LeBlond parcel. The estate signed both offers and accepted $1,000 in earnest money. Thus, the contract where Joel King agreed to release all his rights to the LeBlond property in exchange for Barber's transferring a strip of land at the rear of the parcel was valid. The detriment to the promisee (Joel King) was his surrender of his property rights secured by the purchase contract. The surrendering of these rights in exchange for the rear strip of land was a contract supported by consideration.

And when "a contract is clear and unambiguous, then its interpretation is a matter of law and there is no issue of fact to be determined."...

There were no material facts in dispute. The Kings contracted for the rear strip of land and provided consideration by surrendering their remaining property rights in the LeBlond parcel. Thus, the trial court erred by granting summary judgment for Barber and Brown. Summary judgment should have been granted to the Kings because the contract provided them with the property rights to that rear strip. The Kings' first assignment of error is sustained.

Accordingly, we reverse the trial court's grant of summary judgment in favor of Barber and Brown and remand this case so the trial court can enter summary judgment in favor of Joel and Sandra King.

Judgment reversed and cause remanded....

Case Questions

1. Was the contract between Joel King and Barber bilateral or unilateral?
2. What was bargained for and given in exchange by each party?

INTERNET TIP

Interested readers will find another consideration case, *Labriola v. Pollard Group, Inc.*, included with the online materials for Chapter X. In that case, the Washington Supreme Court decided whether a restrictive covenant clause in an employment contract was supported sufficient consideration.

CAPACITY

In order to create a contract that is legally binding and enforceable, the parties must have the legal **capacity to contract**. Not all parties have the same legal capacity to enter into a contract, however. Full contractual capacity is present when a person is of legal age and is not otherwise so impaired as to be substantially incapable of making decisions for him-or herself.

It is presumed that all parties to an agreement have full legal capacity to contract. Therefore, any party seeking to base a claim or a defense on incapacity has the burden of proof with respect to that issue. The principal classes given some degree of special protection on their contracts because of their incapacity are (1) minors, (2) insane people, and (3) intoxicated people.

Minors

At common law, people remained minors until they reached the age of twenty-one. Generally, present legislation has reduced this age to eighteen. The law pertaining to minors entering into contracts formerly held that those contracts were void. Now that law has been almost universally changed, and such contracts are held to be voidable. This law applies not only to contracts, but also to executed transactions such as sales.

The law grants minors this right in order to protect them from their lack of judgment and experience, limited willpower, and presumed immaturity. A contract between an adult and a minor is voidable only by the minor; the adult must fulfill the obligation, unless the minor decides to avoid the contract. Ordinarily, parents are not liable for contracts entered into by their minor children.

Adults contract with minors at their own peril. Thus, an adult party frequently will refuse to contract with or sell to minors because minors are incapable of giving legal assurance that they will not avoid the contract.

Transactions a Minor Cannot Avoid

Through legislation, many states have limited minors' ability to avoid contracts. For instance, many states provide that a contract with a college or university is binding. A purchase of life insurance has also been held to bind a minor. Some statutes take away the right of minors to avoid contracts after they are married. Most states hold that a minor engaging in a business and operating in the same manner as a person having legal capacity will not be permitted to set aside contracts arising from that business or employment. Court decisions or statutes have established this law in order to prevent minors from using the shield of minority to avoid business contracts.

Minors are liable for the reasonable value (not the contract price) of any necessary they purchase, whether goods or services, if they accept and make use of it. The reasonable value of the necessaries, rather than their contract price, is specified to protect them against the possibility that the other party to the agreement has taken advantage of them by overcharging them. If the necessaries have not yet been accepted or received, the minor may disaffirm the contract without liability.

In general, the term **necessaries** includes whatever is needed for a minor's subsistence as measured by age, status, condition in life, and so on. These include food, lodging, education, clothing, and medical services. Objects used for recreation or entertainment and ordinary contracts relating to the property or business of the minor are not classified as necessaries.

Disaffirmance of Contract

Minors may avoid both **executed** (completed) and **executory** (incomplete) contracts at any time during their minority. They may also disaffirm a contract for a reasonable period of time after they attain their majority. In this way, former minors have a reasonable time in which to evaluate transactions made during their infancy. What constitutes a reasonable time depends on the nature of the property involved and the surrounding circumstances. As long as minors do not disaffirm their contracts, they are bound by the terms. They cannot refuse to carry out their part of an agreement, while at the same time requiring the adult party to perform.

Disaffirmance of a contract by a minor may be made by any expression of an intention to repudiate the contract. Disaffirmance need not be verbal or written. If a minor performs an act inconsistent with the continuing validity of a contract, that is considered a disaffirmance. For example, if a minor sells property to Gaskins and later, on reaching majority, sells the same property to Ginger, the second sale to Ginger would be considered a disaffirmance of the contract with Gaskins.

Minors may disaffirm wholly executory contracts, that is, contracts that neither party has performed. In addition, if only the minor has performed, he or she may disaffirm and recover the money or property paid or transferred to an adult. A conflict arises, however, if the contract is wholly executed or if only the adult has performed and the minor has spent what he or she has received and therefore cannot make restitution. As a general rule, minors must return whatever they have in their possession of the consideration under the contract; if the consideration has been destroyed, they may nevertheless disaffirm the contract and recover the consideration they have given. For example, suppose Weldon, a minor, purchases an automobile and has an accident that demolishes the car. She may obtain a full refund by disaffirming the contract; moreover, she will not be liable for the damage to the car.

A few states, however, hold that if the contract is advantageous to the minor and if the adult has been fair in every respect, the contract cannot be disaffirmed unless the minor returns the consideration. In the preceding example, the minor would have to replace the reasonable value of the damaged automobile before she could disaffirm the contract and receive the consideration she gave for the automobile. These states also take into account the depreciation of the property while in the possession of the minor.

Some states have enacted statutes that prevent minors from disaffirming contracts if they have fraudulently misrepresented their age. Generally, however, the fact that minors have misrepresented their age in order to secure a contract that they could not have otherwise obtained will not later prevent them from disaffirming that contract on the basis of their minority. Most courts will hold minors liable for any resulting damage to, or deterioration of, property they received under the contract. Minors are also generally liable for their torts; consequently, in most states, the other party to the contract could recover in a tort action for deceit. In any case, the other party to the contract may avoid it because of the minor's fraud.

Ratification

Although minors may disaffirm or avoid their contracts before reaching their majority, they cannot effectively ratify or approve their contracts until they have attained their majority. **Ratification** may consist of any expression or action that indicates an intention to be bound by the contract, and may come from the actions of a minor who has now reached majority. For example, if a minor acquired property under a contract and, after reaching majority, makes use of or sells the property, he or she will be deemed to have ratified the contract.

Insane People

A person is said to be insane when that individual does not understand the nature and consequences of his or her act at the time of entering into an agreement. In such cases, the person lacks capacity and his or her contracts are either void or voidable.

The contracts of a person who has been judicially declared insane by a court are void. Such a person will have a judicially appointed guardian who is under a duty to transact all business for him or her.

The contracts of insane people who have not been judicially declared insane are generally void-able. Although such people may not ratify or disaffirm a contract during their temporary insanity, they may do so once they regain their sanity. However, if the contract is executed and the sane party to the contract acts in good faith, not knowing that the other party is temporarily insane, most courts refuse to allow the temporarily insane person the right to avoid the contract, unless the consideration that has been received can be returned. On the other hand, if the sane party knows that the other party is mentally incompetent, the contract is voidable at the option of the insane person.

As in the case of minors, the party possessing capacity to contract has no right to disaffirm a contract merely because the insane party has the right to do so. The rule in regard to necessaries purchased by temporarily insane persons is the same as in the case of minors.

Intoxication

If persons enter into a contract when they are so intoxicated that they do not know at the time that they are executing a contract, the contract is voidable at their option. The position of the intoxicated person is therefore much the same as that of the temporarily insane person.

ILLEGALITY

An agreement is **illegal** when either its formation or performance is criminal, tortious, or contrary to public policy. When an agreement is illegal, courts will not allow either party to sue for performance of the contract. The court will literally "leave the parties where it finds them." Generally, if one of the parties has performed, that person can recover neither the value of the performance nor any property or goods transferred to the other party. There are three exceptions to this rule, however.

First, if the law that the agreement violates is intended for the protection of one of the parties, that party may seek relief. For example, both federal and state statutes require that a corporation follow certain procedures before offering stocks and bonds for sale to the public. It is illegal to sell such securities without having complied with the legal requirements. People who have purchased securities from a corporation that has not complied with the law may obtain a refund of the purchase price if they desire to do so.

Second, when the parties are not equally at fault, the one less at fault is granted relief when the public interest is advanced by doing so. This rule is applied to illegal agreements that are induced by undue influence, duress, or fraud. In such cases, the courts do not regard the defrauded or coerced party as being an actual participant in the wrong and will therefore allow restitution.

A third exception occurs within very strict limits. A person who repents before actually having performed any illegal part of an illegal contract may rescind it and obtain restitution. For example, suppose James and Richardo wager on the outcome of a baseball game. Each gives $500 to Smith, the stakeholder, who agrees to give $1,000 to the winner. Prior to the game, either James or Richardo could recover $500 from Smith through legal action, since the execution of the illegal agreement would not yet have occurred.

If the objectives of an agreement are illegal, the agreement is illegal and unenforceable, even though the parties were not aware, when they arrived at their agreement, that it was illegal.

On the other hand, as a general rule, even if one party to an agreement knows that the other party intends to use the subject matter of the contract for illegal purposes, this fact will not make the agreement illegal unless the illegal purpose involves a serious crime. For example, suppose Aiello lends money to Roja, at a legal interest rate, knowing Roja is going to use the money to gamble illegally. After Roja loses her money, she refuses to repay Aiello on the grounds that the agreement was illegal. Aiello can recover her money through court action, even though she knew Roja was going to gamble illegally with the money she lent her.

Contracts against Public Policy

A contract provision is contrary to public policy if it is injurious to the interest of the public, contradicts some established interests of society, violates a statute, or tends to interfere with the public health, safety, or general welfare. The term **public policy** is vague and variable; it changes as our social, economic, and political climates change. One example is the illegal lobbying agreement, an agreement by which one party uses bribery, threats of a loss of votes, or any other improper means to procure or prevent the adoption of particular legislation by a lawmaking body, such as Congress or a state legislature. Such agreements are clearly contrary to the public interest since they interfere with the workings of the democratic process. They are both illegal and void.

The court in the following case ruled that Connecticut's public policy was violated by a "Waiver, Defense, Indemnity and Hold Harmless Agreement, and Release of Liability Agreement" which was intended to shield a ski resort operator from liability for its own negligent conduct.

Gregory D. Hanks v. Powder Ridge Restaurant Corp.
885 A.2d 734
Supreme Court of Connecticut
November 29, 2005

Sullivan, C. J.
This appeal...arises out of a complaint filed by the plaintiff, Gregory D. Hanks, against the defendants, Powder Ridge Restaurant Corporation and White Water Mountain Resorts of Connecticut, Inc., doing business as Powder Ridge Ski Resort, seeking compensatory damages for injuries the plaintiff sustained while snowtubing at the defendants' facility. The trial court rendered summary judgment in favor of the defendants....

The record reveals the following factual and procedural history. The defendants operate a facility in Middlefield, known as Powder Ridge, at which the public, in exchange for a fee, is invited to ski, snowboard and snowtube. On February 16, 2003, the plaintiff brought his three children and another child to Powder Ridge to snowtube. Neither the plaintiff nor the four children had ever snowtubed at Powder Ridge, but the snowtubing run was open to the public generally, regardless of prior snowtubing experience, with the restriction that only persons at least six years old or forty-four inches tall were eligible to participate. Further, in order to snowtube at Powder Ridge, patrons were required to sign a "Waiver, Defense, Indemnity and Hold Harmless Agreement, and Release of Liability" (agreement). The plaintiff read and signed the agreement on behalf of himself and the four children. While snowtubing, the plaintiff's right foot became caught between his snow tube and the man-made bank of the snowtubing run, resulting in serious injuries that required multiple surgeries to repair.

Thereafter, the plaintiff filed the present negligence action against the defendants....

The defendants, in their answer to the complaint, denied the plaintiff's allegations of negligence and asserted two special defenses. Specifically, the defendants alleged that the plaintiff's injuries were caused by his own negligence and that the agreement relieved the defendants of liability, "even if the accident was due to the negligence of the defendants." Thereafter, the defendants moved for summary judgment, claiming that the agreement barred the plaintiff's negligence claim as a matter of law. The trial court agreed and rendered summary judgment in favor of the defendants.... Specifically, the trial court determined...that the plaintiff, by signing the agreement, unambiguously had released the defendants from liability for their allegedly negligent conduct. Thereafter, the plaintiff moved to reargue the motion for summary judgment. The trial court denied the plaintiff's motion and this appeal followed.

The plaintiff raises two claims on appeal. First, the plaintiff claims that the trial court improperly concluded that the agreement clearly and expressly releases the defendants from liability for negligence. Specifically, the plaintiff contends that a person of ordinary intelligence reasonably would not have believed that, by signing the agreement, he or she was releasing the defendants from liability for personal injuries caused by negligence and, therefore...the agreement does not bar the plaintiff's negligence claim. Second, the plaintiff claims that the agreement is unenforceable because it violates public policy. Specifically, the plaintiff contends that a recreational operator cannot, consistent with public policy, release itself from liability for its own negligent conduct where, as in the present case, the operator offers its services to the public generally, for a fee, and requires patrons to sign a standardized exculpatory agreement as a condition of participation....

I

We first address the plaintiff's claim that the agreement does not expressly release the defendants from liability for personal injuries incurred as a result of their own negligence.... Specifically, the plaintiff maintains that an ordinary person of reasonable intelligence would not understand that, by signing the agreement, he or she was releasing the defendants from liability for future negligence. We disagree.... We conclude that the trial court properly determined that the agreement in the present matter expressly purports to release the defendants from liability for their future negligence and, accordingly, satisfies the standard set forth by this court....

II

We next address ... whether the enforcement of a well drafted exculpatory agreement purporting to release a snowtube operator from prospective liability for personal injuries sustained as a result of the operator's negligent conduct violates public policy....

Although it is well established "that parties are free to contract for whatever terms on which they may agree"; ... it is equally well established "that contracts that violate public policy are unenforceable."

As previously noted, "the law does not favor contract provisions which relieve a person from his own negligence...."... This is because exculpatory provisions undermine the policy considerations governing our tort system. "The fundamental policy purposes of the tort compensation system [are] compensation of innocent parties, shifting the loss to responsible parties or distributing it among appropriate entities, and deterrence of wrongful conduct.... It is sometimes said that compensation for losses is the primary function of tort law ... [but it] is perhaps more accurate to describe the primary function as one of determining when compensation [is] required.... An equally compelling function of the tort system is the prophylactic factor of preventing future harm.... The courts are concerned not only with compensation of the victim, but with admonition of the wrongdoer."... Thus, it is consistent with public policy "to posit the risk of negligence upon the actor" and, if this policy is to be abandoned, "it has generally been to allow or require that the risk shift to

another party better or equally able to bear it, not to shift the risk to the weak bargainer."...

Having reviewed the various methods for determining whether exculpatory agreements violate public policy, we conclude ... that "no definition of the concept of public interest can be contained within the four corners of a formula."... Accordingly, we agree with the Supreme Courts of Maryland and Vermont that "the ultimate determination of what constitutes the public interest must be made considering the totality of the circumstances of any given case against the backdrop of current societal expectations."...

We now turn to the merits of the plaintiff's claim. The defendants are in the business of providing snowtubing services to the public generally, regardless of prior snowtubing experience, with the minimal restriction that only persons at least six years old or forty-four inches tall are eligible to participate. Given the virtually unrestricted access of the public to Powder Ridge, a reasonable person would presume that the defendants were offering a recreational activity that the whole family could enjoy safely....

The societal expectation that family oriented recreational activities will be reasonably safe is even more important where, as in the present matter, patrons are under the care and control of the recreational operator as a result of an economic transaction. The plaintiff, in exchange for a fee, was permitted access to the defendants' snowtubing runs and was provided with snowtubing gear. As a result of this transaction, the plaintiff was under the care and control of the defendants and, thus, was subject to the risk of the defendants' carelessness. Specifically, the defendants designed and maintained the snowtubing run and, therefore, controlled the steepness of the incline, the condition of the snow and the method of slowing down or stopping patrons. Further, the defendants provided the plaintiff with the requisite snowtubing supplies and, therefore, controlled the size and quality of the snow tube as well as the provision of any necessary protective gear. Accordingly, the plaintiff voluntarily relinquished control to the defendants with the reasonable expectation of an exciting, but reasonably safe, snowtubing experience.

Moreover, the plaintiff lacked the knowledge, experience and authority to discern whether, much less ensure that, the defendants' snowtubing runs were maintained in a reasonably safe condition.... [The] defendants...have the expertise and opportunity to foresee and control hazards, and to guard against the negligence of their agents and employees. They alone can properly maintain and inspect their premises, and train their employees in risk management. They alone can insure against risks and effectively spread the costs of insurance among their thousands of customers. Skiers, on the other hand, are not in a position to discover and correct risks of harm, and they cannot insure against the ski area's negligence.

"If the defendants were permitted to obtain broad waivers of their liability, an important incentive for ski areas to manage risk would be removed, with the public bearing the cost of the resulting injuries.... It is illogical, in these circumstances, to undermine the public policy underlying business invitee law and allow skiers to bear risks they have no ability or right to control." The concerns expressed by the court in *Dalury* [*v. S-K-I, Ltd.*] are equally applicable to the context of snowtubing, and we agree that it is illogical to permit snowtubers, and the public generally, to bear the costs of risks that they have no ability or right to control. Further, the agreement at issue was a standardized adhesion contract offered to the plaintiff on a "take it or leave it" basis. The "most salient feature [of adhesion contracts] is that they are not subject to the normal bargaining processes of ordinary contracts"... see also Black's Law Dictionary (7th Ed. 1999) (defining adhesion contract as "[a] standard form contract prepared by one party, to be signed by the party in a weaker position, [usually] a consumer, who has little choice about the terms"). Not only was the plaintiff unable to negotiate the terms of the agreement, but the defendants also did not offer him the option of pro-curing protection against negligence at an additional reasonable cost. See Restatement (Third), Torts, Apportionment of Liability 2, comment (e), p. 21 (2000) (factor relevant to enforcement of contractual limit on liability is "whether the party seeking exculpation was willing to provide greater protection against tortious conduct for a reasonable, additional fee"). Moreover, the defendants did not inform prospective snowtubers prior to their arrival at Powder Ridge that they would have to waive important common-law rights as a condition of participation. Thus, the plaintiff, who traveled to Powder Ridge in anticipation of snowtubing that day, was faced with the dilemma of either signing the defendants' proffered waiver of prospective liability or forgoing completely the opportunity to snowtube at Powder Ridge. Under the present factual circumstances, it would ignore reality to conclude that the plaintiff wielded the same bargaining power as the defendants....

In the present case, the defendants held themselves out as a provider of a healthy, fun, family activity. After the plaintiff and his family arrived at Powder Ridge eager to participate in the activity, however, the defendants informed the plaintiff that, not only would they be immune from claims arising from the inherent risks of the activity, but they would not be responsible for injuries resulting from their own carelessness and negligence in the operation of the snowtubing facility. We recognize that the plaintiff had the option of walking away. We cannot say, however, that the defendants had no bargaining advantage under these circumstances.

For the foregoing reasons, we conclude that the agreement in the present matter affects the public interest adversely and, therefore, is unenforceable because it violates public policy.... Accordingly, the trial court improperly rendered summary judgment in favor of the defendants.

The defendants and the dissent point out that our conclusion represents the "distinct minority view."... We acknowledge that most states uphold adhesion contracts releasing recreational operators from prospective liability for personal injuries caused by their own negligent conduct. Put simply, we disagree with these decisions for the reasons already explained in this opinion....

The judgment is reversed and the case is remanded for further proceedings according to law.

Case Questions

1. Why did the Connecticut Supreme Court refuse to enforce the contractual immunity agreement?
2. Do you agree with the Connecticut Supreme Court's argument that the ski resort could purchase liability insurance against negligence and pass the cost on to its patrons, thus making sure that injured patrons are able to obtain compensation for injuries sustained at the ski resort?

Agreements to Commit Serious Crimes

An agreement is illegal and therefore void when it calls for the commission of any act that constitutes a serious crime. Agreements to commit murder, robbery, arson, burglary, and assault are obvious examples, but less obvious violations are also subject to the rule, depending on the jurisdiction.

Agreements to Commit Civil Wrongs

An agreement that calls for the commission of a civil wrong is also illegal and void. Examples are agreements to slander a third person, to defraud another, to damage another's goods, or to infringe upon another's trademark or patent.

A contract that calls for the performance of an act or the rendering of a service may be illegal for one of two reasons. (1) The act or service itself may be illegal (**illegal per se**), and thus any contract involving this act or service is illegal. Prostitution is a good example. (2) Certain other service contracts are not illegal per se, but may be illegal if the party performing or contracting to perform the service is not legally entitled to do so. This latter condition refers to the fact that a license is required before a person is entitled to perform certain functions for others. For example, doctors, dentists, lawyers, architects, surveyors, real estate brokers, and others rendering specialized professional services must be licensed by the appropriate body before entering into contracts with the general public.

All the states have enacted regulatory statutes concerning the practice of various professions and the performance of business and other activities. However, these statutes are not uniform in their working or in their scope. Many of the statutes specifically provide that all agreements that violate them shall be void and unenforceable. When such a provision is lacking, the court will look to the intent of the statute. If the court is of the opinion that a statute was enacted for the protection of the public, it will hold that agreements in violation of the statute are void. If, however, the court concludes that the particular statute was intended solely to raise revenue, then it will hold that contracts entered in violation of the statute are legal and enforceable.

A contract that has for its purpose the restraint of trade and nothing more is illegal and void. A contract to monopolize trade, to suppress competition, or not to compete in business, therefore, cannot be enforced, because the sole purpose of the agreement would be to eliminate competition. A contract that aims at establishing a monopoly is not only unenforceable, but also renders the parties to the agreement subject to indictment for the commission of a crime.

When a business is sold, it is commonly stated in a contract that the seller shall not go into the same or similar business again within a certain geographic area, or for a certain period of time, or both. In early times, such agreements were held void since they deprived the public of the service of the person who agreed not to compete, reduced competition, and exposed the public to monopoly. Gradually, the law began to recognize the validity of such restrictive provisions. To the modern courts, the question is whether, under the circumstances, the restriction imposed upon one party is reasonable, or whether the restriction is more extensive than is required to protect the other party. A similar situation arises when employees agree not to compete with their employers should they leave their jobs.

In the following case, the North Carolina Court of Appeals was asked to determine the validity of a postemployment noncompetition clause, which had been signed by a former employee at the time of his employment by Carolina Pride Carwash, Inc.

Carolina Pride Carwash, Inc. v. Tim Kendrick
COA04-451
Court of Appeals of North Carolina
September 20, 2005

Calabria, Judge

Tim Kendrick ("defendant") appeals from summary judgment entered in favor of Carolina Pride Carwash, Inc. ("Carolina Pride") for breach of an employment contract. We reverse and remand for entry of summary judgment in favor of defendant.

Carolina Pride is a car wash maintenance provider and distributor of car wash equipment and supplies.

Carolina Pride employs approximately forty-five people and operates in North Carolina, South Carolina, and the southern half of Virginia, east of the Blue Ridge Parkway. In late 1999, Carolina Pride was negotiating for the purchase of PDQ Carolina ("PDQ"), a car wash equipment distributor, where defendant was employed as a service technician earning approximately $15.00 per hour. On 20 December 1999, defendant met with the president of Carolina Pride and entered into an employment contract. The contract provided that Carolina Pride would pay defendant $500.00 after signing, employ him beginning in January 2000 as a service technician at $15.00 per hour, and pay him a $1,000.00 bonus after one year of employment. The sixth and seventh provisions of the contract contained a covenant not to compete and a provision for liquidated damages:

> SIXTH: [Defendant] hereby agrees and guarantees to [Carolina Pride], that during the term of this contract and for three years after termination of this contract, [defendant] will not on his own account or as agent, employee or servant of any other person, firm or corporation engage in or become financially interested in the same line of business or any other line of business which could reasonably be considered as being in competition with [Carolina Pride] within North Carolina, South Carolina, or Virginia to-wit: Carwash sales and service of equipment, supplies, parts and any and all related merchandise; and further, that during this period, [defendant] will not directly or indirectly or by aid to others, do anything which would tend to divert from [Carolina Pride] any trade or business with any customer with whom [defendant] has made contracts or associations during the period of time in which he is employed by [Carolina Pride].
>
> SEVENTH: That in the event [defendant] violates the provision of the preceding paragraphs, then [Carolina Pride] shall be entitled to liquidated damages in the amount of $50,000.00 to be paid by [defendant] to [Carolina Pride].

In March 2000, defendant started employment as a technician with Carolina Pride and served customers predominantly in North Carolina and occasionally in South Carolina. The following year, in 2001, defendant left Carolina Pride's employ and took a position with Water Works Management Company, L.L.C. ("Water Works") as manager of repair, maintenance, and supply for several of their car wash facilities in Greensboro, Mt. Airy, Elkin, and Boone.

In January 2002, Carolina Pride filed suit alleging defendant interfered with its customer relationships in violation of the covenant not to compete. In the spring of 2002, Water Works discharged defendant due to Carolina Pride's lawsuit. Defendant answered Carolina Pride's complaint and included counterclaims for the following: (1) fraud; (2) negligent misrepresentation; (3) unfair and deceptive trade practices; and (4) wrongful or tortious interference with business relations.

Both defendant and Carolina Pride subsequently moved for summary judgment, and on 17 October 2003, the trial court granted Carolina Pride's motion based on defendant's alleged breach of the covenant not to compete. In addition, the trial court ordered that defendant pay $50,000.00 in liquidated damages.

Defendant assigns error to the trial court's denial of his motion for summary judgment and grant of Carolina Pride's motion for summary judgment. Defendant argues the covenant not to compete was unenforceable as a matter of law because the time and territorial restrictions of the covenant were unreasonable. We agree, under these facts, that the time and territorial restrictions were greater than reasonably necessary to protect Carolina Pride's legitimate interests....

"[A] covenant not to compete is valid and enforceable if it is '(1) in writing; (2) reasonable as to terms, time, and territory; (3) made a part of the employment contract; (4) based on valuable consideration; and (5) not against public policy.'"... "Although either the time or the territory restriction, standing alone, may be reasonable, the combined effect of the two may be unreasonable. A longer period of time is acceptable where the geographic restriction is relatively small, and vice versa."...

A central purpose of a covenant not to compete is the protection of an employer's customer relationships....Therefore, to prove that a covenant's territorial restriction is reasonable, "an employer must ... show where its customers are located and that the geographic scope of the covenant is necessary to maintain those customer relationships."... "Furthermore, in determining the reasonableness of [a] territorial restriction, when the primary concern is the employee's knowledge of customers, the territory should only be limited to areas in which the employee made contacts during the period of his employment."... "If the territory is too broad, 'the entire covenant fails since equity will neither enforce nor reform an overreaching and unreasonable covenant.'" ...

In the instant case, the covenant not to compete applied to all areas of North Carolina, South Carolina, and Virginia for a term of three years. However, the president of Carolina Pride testified that Carolina Pride's territory included North Carolina, South

Carolina, and "the lower half of Virginia east of the Blue Ridge Parkway." Therefore, by including all of Virginia, the territorial restriction of the covenant encompassed a greater region than necessary to protect Carolina Pride's legitimate interest in maintaining its customer relationships. Moreover, while employed by Carolina Pride, defendant only contacted customers in North and South Carolina but never in Virginia. Therefore, the covenant was unreasonable not only for encompassing a greater region than necessary but also for encompassing any portion of Virginia because defendant never contacted customers in that state while employed by Carolina Pride. Additionally, although the covenant's three-year time period may be valid standing alone, it was unreasonable in this case when coupled with the unnecessarily broad territorial restriction.

Accordingly, we hold the covenant not to compete was unenforceable as a matter of law, and the trial court erred by entering summary judgment for Carolina Pride and failing to enter summary judgment for defendant with respect to Carolina Pride's breach of contract claim. We likewise reverse that portion of the trial court's order requiring defendant to pay liquidated damages and remand the case to the trial court for further proceedings not inconsistent with this opinion.

Reversed and remanded.

Case Questions

1. List some specific employment examples where a postemployment noncompetition agreement would be enforceable.
2. Why did the North Carolina Court of Appeals refuse to enforce the noncompete covenant?

WRITING

Every state has statutes requiring that certain contracts be in writing to be enforceable. Called the **statute of frauds**, these statutes are based on "An Act for the Prevention of Frauds and Perjuries," passed by the English Parliament in 1677. Statutes of frauds traditionally govern six kinds of contracts: (1) an agreement by an executor or administrator to answer for the debt of a decedent, (2) an agreement made in consideration of marriage, (3) an agreement to answer for the debt of another, (4) an agreement that cannot be performed in one year, (5) an agreement for the sale of an interest in real property, and (6) an agreement for the sale of goods above a certain dollar amount.

The writing required by the statute need not be in any special form or use any special language. Usually, the terms that must be shown on the face of the writing include the names of the parties, the terms and conditions of the contract, the consideration, a reasonably certain description of the subject matter of the contract, and the signature of the party, or the party's agent, against whom enforcement is sought. These terms need not be on one piece of paper but may be on several pieces of paper, provided that their relation or connection with each other appears on their face by the physical attachment of the papers to each other or by reference from one writing to the other. At least one, if not all, of the papers must be signed by the party against whom enforcement is sought. (The requirements of memorandums involving the sale of goods differ.)

Agreement by Executor or Administrator

A promise by an executor or administrator to answer for the debt of the decedent is within the statute and must be in writing to be enforced. In order for the statute to operate, the executor's promise must be to pay out of the executor's own personal assets (pocket); a promise to pay a debt out of the assets of a decedent's estate is not required to be in writing.

Agreement in Consideration of Marriage

Agreements made in consideration of marriage are to be in writing. Mutual promises to marry are not within the statute, since the consideration is the exchanged promise, not the marriage itself. However, promises made to a prospective spouse or third party with marriage as the consideration are within the statute. For example, a promise by one prospective spouse to convey property to the other, provided the marriage is entered into, is required to be in writing. Similarly, if a third party, say a rich relative, promises to pay a certain sum of money to a prospective spouse if a marriage is entered into, the promise will be unenforceable unless reduced to writing.

INTERNET TIP

The case of *In re Marriage of DewBerry* involves the statute of frauds. In the case the appellate court has to rule on whether an oral prenuptial agreement that all income acquired by either spouse be strictly considered to be separate property was unenforceable under the statute of frauds as an agreement in consideration of marriage. Interested readers will find this case included with the online Chapter X materials.

Agreement to Answer for the Debt of Another

Agreements to answer for the debt or default of another shall be unenforceable unless in writing. The rationale for this provision is that the guarantor or surety has received none of the benefits for which the debt was incurred and therefore should be bound only by the exact terms of the promise. For example, Bob desires to purchase a new law text on credit. The bookstore is unsure as to Bob's ability to pay, so Bob brings in his friend, Ellen, who says, "If Bob does not pay for the text, I will." In effect, the promise is that the bookstore must first try to collect from Bob, who is primarily liable. After it has exhausted all possibilities of collecting from him, then it may come to Ellen to receive payment. Ellen is therefore secondarily liable. Ellen has promised to answer for Bob's debt even though she will not receive the benefit of the new law text; therefore, her agreement must be in writing to be enforceable.

This situation must be distinguished from those in which the promise to answer for the debt of another is an original promise; that is, the promisor's objective is to be primarily liable. For example, Bob wants to purchase a new law text. When he takes the book to the cashier, his friend Ellen steps in and says, "Give him the book. I will pay for it." Ellen has made an original promise to the bookstore with the objective of becoming primarily liable. Such a promise need not be in writing to be enforceable.

Sometimes it is difficult to ascertain whether the purpose of the promisor is to become primarily liable or secondarily liable. In resolving the issue, courts will sometimes use the leading object rule. This rule looks not only to the promise itself, but also to the individual for whose benefit the promise was made. The logic of the rule is that if the leading object of the promise is the personal benefit of the promisor, then the promisor must have intended to become primarily liable. In such a case, the promise will be deemed to be original and need not be in writing to be enforced.

INTERNET TIP

Readers who wish to read a 2002 Missouri appellate court opinion about whether a promisor's alleged oral agreement to pay another's debt was within or outside the scope of the statute of frauds can find the case of *Douglas D. Owens v. Leonard Goldammer* on the textbook's website.

Agreements Not to Be Performed in One Year

Most statutes require contracts that cannot be performed within one year from the time the contract is formed to be in writing. This determination is made by referring to the intentions of the parties, to the nature of the performance, and to the terms of the contract itself. For example, if Jack agrees to build a house for Betty, the question is whether the contract is capable of being performed within one year. Houses can be built in one year. Therefore, this agreement need not be in writing even if Jack actually takes more than one year to build the house.

It is important to remember that the *possibility* that the contract can be performed within one year is enough to take it out of the operation of the statute regardless of how long performance actually took.

Paul Kocourek, the plaintiff in the next case, filed suit against his employer. Kocourek alleged that although he had intended to hang on to "shadow stock," his employer had forced him to sell it—to his financial detriment—immediately after Kocourek had retired. So-called "shadow stock" is virtual stock and not real shares of stock. It is a device used by some corporations to determine how much additional compensation should be paid to corporate officers. Generally, each share of shadow stock is deemed to be worth whatever a real share of stock trades for on the stock market on the day it is redeemed. Upon redemption, the corporation multiplies the rate at which an actual share of stock was traded by the number of shadow shares "owned."

Paul Kocourek v. Booz Allen Hamilton Inc.
2010 NY Slip Op 02019
Appellate Division of the Supreme Court of New York, First Department.
March 16, 2010

Friedman, J.P., Catterson, McGuire, Acosta, Renwick, JJ.

Plaintiff, an officer employed by the corporate defendants, alleged that the latter promised that the "shadow stock" he received would provide him with benefits equivalent to those provided by the common stock he also received as a corporate officer. According to plaintiff, defendants allegedly "forced" him to redeem the shadow stock shortly after his retirement, and he thereby was injured because he otherwise would have held the shadow stock and profited greatly when, 16 months after his retirement, the company sold a portion of its business to the Carlyle Group for $2.54 billion. It is undisputed, however, that the common stock could not be redeemed for two years after retirement, and thus plaintiff necessarily is contending that defendants breached an agreement not to redeem his shadow stock until he had been retired for two years. That agreement, however, is one which by its very terms has no possibility of being performed within one year.... Accordingly, the absence of a writing violates the statute of frauds, rendering the alleged oral promise as to stock redemption unenforceable....

We have considered plaintiff's remaining arguments on appeal and find them unavailing.

This constitutes the decision and order of the Supreme Court, Appellate Division, First Department.

Case Question

What practical lesson should you remember after reading this case?

Agreement Conveying an Interest in Real Property

The statute of frauds generally renders unenforceable oral agreements conveying interests in real estate. Most problems center on what an interest in real estate is and whether the agreement contemplates the transfer of any title, ownership, or possession of real property. Both must be involved to bring the statute into effect. Real property has commonly been held to include land, leaseholds, easements, standing timber, and under certain conditions, improvements and fixtures attached to the land.

The landlord in the following case brought suit to enforce a written but unsigned two-year lease. The court ruled that there was no leasehold and that only a month-to-month tenancy existed because the requirements of the statute of frauds were not satisfied.

Mulford v. Borg-Warner Acceptance Corp.
495 N.Y.S.2d 493
Supreme Court of New York
Appellate Division
November 21, 1985

Harvey, Justice

Appeal from an order and judgment of the Supreme Court at Special Term (Murphy, J.), entered April 19, 1985 in Madison County, which granted defendant's motion for summary judgment dismissing the complaint.

This is an action involving a written lease for certain office space in the Village of Canastota, Madison County, for a period of two years. The lease was never subscribed by anyone on behalf of defendant. Prior to the lease in issue, there were three written leases between these parties involving space in the same office building owned by plaintiff. Each lease expired on March 31, 1983. Prior to the expiration date, plaintiff proposed a new lease for a three-year period involving the same accommodations. Defendant informed plaintiff that it would not lease one of the office suites previously occupied by it and that, as to the remaining space, it would only be interested in a two-year lease. Thereafter, and on the expiration date of the original lease, plaintiff prepared a written two-year lease, subscribed it and delivered it to defendant. Although defendant retained possession of the property described in the document and paid rent at a rate in accordance with the provisions contained therein, it never signed the new lease. On August 2, 1983, defendant notified plaintiff that it was quitting the premises as of August 31, 1983, and paid the rent for that month.

Plaintiff commenced this action alleging that the unexecuted lease was a valid lease and demanded unpaid rent and other expenses alleged to have resulted from defendant's default. After issue was joined, defendant moved...for summary judgment dismissing the complaint, relying upon General Obligations Law § 5-703(2) as an absolute defense. Special Term granted the motion and this appeal ensued.

General Obligations Law § 5-703(2) provides:

"A contract for the leasing for a longer period than one year, or for the sale, of any real property, or an interest therein, is void unless the contract or some note or memorandum, is in writing, subscribed by the party to be charged, or by his lawful agent thereunto authorized by writing."

Although plaintiff freely admits that the proposed lease was never subscribed by defendant, he contends that signed checks delivered to plaintiff for monthly rentals in the amounts as would have been required by the proposed lease constitute sufficient memoranda to satisfy the Statute of Frauds. We disagree. The law requires that the memoranda embody all the essential and material parts of the lease contemplated with such clarity and certainty as to show that the parties have agreed on all the material parts of the lease contemplated.... The only material factors which could be established by the checks were the fact of possession and the amount of monthly rental. Nothing contained in the checks or any memoranda attached thereto gave any clue as to the term of the lease. The notation on the memo portion of the first check stating "additional rent due for April (new lease)" is consistent with a month-to-month tenancy. This notation is insufficient to establish a tenancy involving all the provisions, including the term, of the proposed written but unsigned lease. We conclude, therefore, that defendant's occupancy of the premises from April 1, 1983 to August 31, 1983 was on the basis of a month-to-month tenancy....

Order and judgment modified, on the law and the facts, without costs, by granting plaintiff judgment for one month's rent for September 1983...and, as so modified, affirmed.

Case Questions

1. What is the rationale behind requiring that contracts for longer than one year satisfy the statute of frauds?
2. The plaintiff argued that the monthly rental checks paid by the defendant to the plaintiff should be held to satisfy the statute of frauds. Why does the appellate court disagree?

Sale of Goods

Generally, a contract for the sale of goods for the price of $500 or more is not enforceable unless there is some writing to serve as evidence that a contract has been entered into. An informal or incomplete writing will be sufficient to satisfy the UCC statute of frauds, providing that it (1) indicates that a contract between the parties was entered into, (2) is signed by the party against whom enforcement is sought, and (3) contains a statement of the quantity of goods sold. The price, time and place of delivery, quality of the goods, and warranties may be omitted without invalidating the writing, as the UCC permits these terms to be shown by outside evidence, custom and usage, and prior dealings between the parties. Thus, the provisions that must be included in a writing that will conform with the UCC statute of frauds are substantially less than those necessary in a writing that evidences one of the other types of contracts governed by the statute of frauds. Under the UCC, the contract will be enforced only as to the quantity of goods shown in the writing (UCC 2-201 [1]).

Parol Evidence Rule

After contracting parties have successfully negotiated a contract, they often sign a written document that contains what they intend to be a definitive and complete statement of the agreed-upon terms (in legalese this means that all terms are "fully integrated"). Courts will usually presume that a fully integrated writing is accurate. Therefore, under the **parol evidence rule**, evidence of alleged prior oral or written agreements or terms not contained in the written document will be inadmissible if offered to change the terms of the document.

There are several exceptions to the parol evidence rule. The parol evidence rule, for example, would not apply where the contracting parties have prepared only a partial memorandum or other incomplete writing. (In legalese the terms of an incomplete agreement are only "partially integrated.") An agreement that is only partially integrated is only intended to be a final and complete statement with respect to the terms actually addressed in the memorandum. Unaddressed terms, in this circumstance, can often be proven extrinsically. Other recognized exceptions exist where parol evidence is used to prove fraud or the absence of consideration in the formation of a contract, and where it helps to explain the meaning of ambiguous words.

Sometimes whether the parol evidence rule applies is a close call. In the next case, the three-judge panel splits 2-1 as to whether the parol evidence rule applies to the particular facts of that case.

Mark Hinkel v. Sataria Distribution & Packaging, Inc.
No. 49A04-0908-CV-473
Court of Appeals of Indiana
February 1, 2010.

Vaidik, Judge
Case Summary
The appellant, Mark Hinkel, was hired to work for the appellee, Sataria Distribution and Packaging, Inc. ("Sataria"). Hinkel was allegedly promised a year's worth of salary and insurance coverage if he were ever terminated involuntarily, but his written employment contract did not provide for severance pay or post-employment benefits. Hinkel was soon terminated, and he did not receive the severance package he says he was promised. Hinkel sued for breach of contract and/or promissory estoppel. The trial court entered summary judgment in favor of Sataria....

Facts and Procedural History
Hinkel was employed by Refractory Engineers, Inc. and Ceramic Technology, Inc. John Jacobs was the owner of Sataria. In late August or September 2005, Hinkel and Jacobs met to discuss working together. Jacobs offered Hinkel a job at Sataria. Hinkel had reservations. Jacobs told him, "Mark, are you worried that I'll f*** you? If so, and things don't work, I'll pay you one (1) year's salary and cover your insurance for the one (1) year as well. But let me make it clear, should you decide this is not for you, and you terminate your own employment, then the agreement is off."... Jacobs later sent Hinkel the following written job offer:

Dear Mark,

This is written as an offer of employment. The terms are as described below:

1. Annual Compensation: $120,000
2. Work Location: Belmont Facility
3. Initial Position: Supervisor Receiving Team
4. Start Date: 08/19/2005
5. Paid Vacation: To be determined
6. Health Insurance: Coverage begins 09/01/2005 pending proper enrollment submission

Please sign and return.

...Hinkel signed the offer and resigned from his other employers. He began working at Sataria in September 2005. According to Hinkel, Jacobs reiterated the severance promise again in November 2005 and December 2005.

Sataria terminated Hinkel's employment involuntarily on January 23, 2006. Sataria paid Hinkel six weeks of severance thereafter. Hinkel brought this action for breach of contract and/or promissory estoppel against Sataria. He claimed that Sataria owed him the severance package that Jacobs promised. Sataria moved for summary judgment. The trial court granted Sataria's motion. Hinkel now appeals....

I. Breach of Contract Claim

According to Hinkel, Jacobs orally promised him a year's salary and insurance coverage if he were ever involuntarily terminated. Sataria argues that any alleged oral promises are barred from consideration by the parol evidence rule.

The parol evidence rule provides that "[w]hen two parties have made a contract and have expressed it in a writing to which they have both assented as the complete and accurate integration of that contract, evidence ... of antecedent understandings and negotiations will not be admitted for the purpose of varying or contradicting the writing." *Dicen v. New Sesco, Inc.*, 839 N.E.2d 684, 688 (Ind. 2005) (quoting 6 Arthur Linton Corbin, *Corbin on Contracts* § 573 (2002 reprint))…. This rule "effectuates a presumption that a subsequent written contract is of a higher nature than earlier statements, negotiations, or oral agreements by deeming those earlier expressions to be merged in to or superseded by the written document."….

The first step when applying the parol evidence rule is determining whether the parties' written contract represents a complete or partial integration of their agreement. See *Restatement* (Second) of Contracts §§ 209, 210 (1981). If the contract is completely integrated, constituting a final and complete expression of all the parties' agreements, then evidence of prior or contemporaneous written or oral statements and negotiations cannot operate to either add to or contradict the written contract…. The preliminary question of integration, either complete or partial, requires the court to hear all relevant evidence, parol or written…. "Whether a writing has been adopted as an integrated agreement is a question of fact to be determined in accordance with all relevant evidence."…

In addition,

The test of [parol evidence] admissibility is much affected by the inherent likelihood that parties who contract under the circumstances in question would simultaneously make both the agreement in writing which is before the court, and also the alleged parol agreement. The point is not merely whether the court is convinced that the parties before it did in fact do this, but whether reasonable parties so situated naturally would or might obviously or normally do so…. The vast majority of courts assessing the admissibility of parol evidence at common law apply this test. This test is commonly known by the adverbs used by the courts which apply it, and might be variously called the "naturally" test, the "naturally and normally" test, the "ordinarily" test, or any of a host of words used by the courts to indicate that parties similarly situated might reasonably have believed it appropriate to keep the two agreements separate. Moreover the test can be stated in the affirmative or the negative; either way the key question is the same. Thus, one way to ask the question is whether the nature of the collateral agreement was such that, if the parties had agreed to it, they would naturally have included it in their writing. Asked in this way, if the answer is that they would have, and they did not, they engaged in "unnatural" behavior, and evidence of the alleged agreement is inadmissible.

11 *Williston on Contracts* § 33:25 (footnotes omitted); …

Here, Jacobs and Hinkel negotiated the terms of Hinkel's employment before completing their written contract. Jacobs allegedly promised Hinkel that he would receive one year of salary and benefits if he were ever terminated involuntarily. The parties then executed their written agreement. The written employment offer specified Hinkel's compensation, work location, title, start date, and the date on which his insurance coverage would begin. It did not provide that Hinkel would receive severance pay or benefits following termination. Hinkel signed the letter and began working at Sataria. In light of all the relevant evidence, we find as a matter of law that Hinkel's contract represented a complete integration of the parties' employment agreement. Jacobs allegedly promised Hinkel a severance package, but the written contract enumerates both compensation and insurance coverage while saying nothing of post-employment salary and/or benefits. The offer leaves one term to be decided—paid vacation—but the contract imports on its face to be a complete expression with respect to salary and insurance. And since a lucrative severance provision would "naturally and normally" be included in an employment contract, its glaring omission here further supports the conclusion that Hinkel's written contract superseded any alleged prior oral promises. We hold that the written contract constituted a final representation of the parties' agreement, and any contemporaneous oral agreements that the parties made as to severance are not subject to interpretation.

To the extent Jacobs may have promised Hinkel a severance package after their written contract was executed, an additional question is whether Jacobs's promise could have constituted a valid contract modification. "The modification of a contract, since it is also a contract, requires all the requisite elements of a contract." *Hamlin v. Steward*, 622 N.E.2d 535, 539 (Ind. Ct. App. 1993). "A written agreement may be changed by a subsequent one orally made, upon a sufficient consideration." ... Consideration consists of either a benefit to the promisor or a detriment to the promisee.... In other words, consideration requires a bargained-for exchange. ... A promise is also valuable consideration, and an exchange of mutual promises is consideration which supports modification of a contract....

Here, if Jacobs promised Hinkel a severance package after the written employment contract was executed, there is no evidence that Hinkel provided additional consideration in exchange for the promise. Hinkel argues that he had to agree "to continue working for Sataria" and "to not voluntarily resign his employment."…. But Hinkel had assumed those duties and employment obligations as consideration for the original agreement…. Any subsequent promise by Jacobs respecting severance was not supported by an independent, bargained-for exchange. Accordingly,

Jacobs's alleged oral promises could not have constituted valid modifications of Hinkel's employment contract.

For the foregoing reasons, Hinkel has failed to raise a genuine issue of material fact on his breach of contract claim, and the trial court properly granted summary judgment in favor of Sataria.

Affirmed.

Crone, Judge, dissenting

I respectfully dissent because I disagree with the majority's conclusion that Jacobs's oral promise to Hinkel regarding a severance package is "barred from consideration by the parol evidence rule." … I do so for two reasons.

First, I believe that a genuine issue of material fact exists regarding whether the parties intended for Jacobs's written job offer to Hinkel to be completely integrated, i.e., a "final and complete expression of all the parties' agreements[.]" … Although not conclusive, the offer—a one-page document with six bullet points for a position paying $120,000 per year—does not contain an integration clause. More persuasive is its statement that Hinkel's vacation terms were yet to be determined, which indicates to me that the parties had not yet reached agreement on that issue. Based on the foregoing, a factfinder reasonably could conclude that the offer is more akin to a memorandum of understanding and represents only a partial integration of the parties' agreements, and that therefore the parol evidence rule would not apply to bar consideration of Jacobs's oral promise regarding the severance package.

Second, the terms of the severance package do not vary from or contradict the terms of the written offer, but merely cover that which was not covered in the offer…. As such, even assuming that the offer is completely integrated, the terms of the severance package would not be barred by the parol evidence rule. … ("[P]arol evidence may be admitted to supply an omission in the terms of the contract…. Using parol evidence to supply an omission will not modify the written agreement, but merely adds to it."). Therefore, I would reverse the trial court's grant of summary judgment in favor of Sataria and remand for further proceedings.

Case Questions

1. Why did two of the judges conclude that contractual terms were completely integrated?
2. Why did the third judge dissent in this case?
3. Which opinion did you find more persuasive?

ASPECTS OF CONTRACT PERFORMANCE

When parties enter into a contract, they generally expect that each side will fully perform in the manner called for in the agreement. Often, however, problems arise and full performance does not occur, as in the following examples.

Accord and Satisfaction

One party may agree to take something less than full performance to satisfy the agreement. For example, suppose that A asks B to pay a debt for services rendered and B states that he is too poor to pay the full amount. A may agree to accept payment for only half of the debt. In this situation, the parties have worked out an accord and satisfaction. An **accord** is the offer of something different from what was due under the original contract. The **satisfaction** is the agreement to take it. Since the law favors a compromise, courts try to uphold any good-faith modification agreement.

Anticipatory Repudiation

Suppose that A, who is one party to a contract, clearly manifests that she will not perform at the scheduled time. The other party, B, has a choice at common law. B may either sue immediately or ignore A's repudiation and wait for the day of performance. If B waits, A may change her mind and still perform according to the original contract. Under UCC section 2-610, the injured party may not wait until the day of performance. B may wait for a change of mind only for a commercially reasonable period of time after repudiation before taking action.

Warranties

A **warranty** is a contractual obligation that sets a standard by which performance of the contract is measured. If the warranties are created by the parties to the contract, they are *express*. Under UCC section 2-313, express warranties exist whenever a seller affirms facts or describes goods, makes a promise about the goods, or displays a sample model.

If warranties are imposed by law, they are implied. There are two types of **implied warranties** under UCC section 2-314 and section 2-315. (1) When a merchant sells goods that are reputed to be fit for the ordinary purpose for which they are intended and are of average quality and properly labeled and packaged, the merchant is bound by an **implied warranty of merchantability**. (2) When the seller has reason to know some particular (nonordinary) purpose for which the buyer has relied on the seller's skill or judgment in making a selection, the seller is bound by an **implied warranty of fitness** for a particular purpose.

Implied warranties may be disclaimed by a conspicuous disclaimer statement that the goods are being sold "as is." Once an express warranty is created, however, it cannot be disclaimed, and any attempt to do so is void. The Magnuson–Moss Federal Warranty Act is an act requiring that written warranties for consumer products be categorized as "full" or "limited" so that consumers know what type of warranty protection they are getting. In addition, under this act, a consumer may sue under both the federal and state warranties to recover actual damages.

Originally, a warranty was enforceable only by purchasers, but the trend has been to extend the warranty to nonbuyers (such as recipients of gifts) who have been injured by the defective product.

Discharge, Rescission, and Novation

A **discharge** from a duty to perform occurs because of objective impossibility, by operation of law, or by agreement. To illustrate, one party may die or become physically incapable of performing, a statute may be passed that prevents a party from performing, or a duty to perform may be discharged in bankruptcy. Parties can also agree to end their contractual relationship through a rescission. In a *rescission* each party gives up its right to performance from the other; this constitutes sufficient consideration for the discharge. A *novation* occurs when a promisee agrees to release the original promisor from a duty and enters into a new agreement with another party.

Transfers of Duties and Rights

Sometimes one of the original parties to a contract decides to transfer its rights or duties to some third person who was not originally a party to the agreement. The transfer of rights is called an **assignment**, and the transfer of duties is called a **delegation**. An assignor assigns his or her rights to an assignee. For example, a creditor (the **assignor**) may decide to transfer her right to collect money owed by a debtor to a finance company (the **assignee**).

In another example, Smith may contract with a builder to construct a garage next to her house using the turnkey method of construction (this means that the developer finances and builds the garage and receives payment when it is completed). The builder would negotiate a bank loan to finance the project, and the bank probably would negotiate a requirement that the contractor transfer his rights to payment to the bank as security for the loan. A right is not assignable if it significantly affects the corresponding duty associated with that right. Thus, Smith probably would not be permitted to assign her right (to have the builder construct a garage) to her sister who lives twenty miles away, since the added distance would be a significant detriment to the building contractor.

A person contractually obligated to perform a duty may often delegate that duty to a third person. If Smith contracts with a painter to paint her new garage, the painter could delegate that duty to other painters. A party cannot delegate a duty if there is a personal component involved such that the duty can only be performed by the party to the original agreement. For example, the personal component exists when a person contracts with a famous photographer to take her portrait. The photographer in this situation would not be permitted to delegate the duty to just any other photographer.

An assignee is legally responsible for any claims that were originally available against the assignor. Thus, the debtor would be entitled to raise the same defenses (such as capacity, duress, illegality, or mistake) against the finance agency that were available against the creditor. The rules are similarly strict vis-à-vis the delegation of a duty. Smith's painter would be responsible if the painter to whom he delegated the painting duty (painter #2) performed inadequately. If Smith agrees to a novation, however, the original contracting painter could be relieved of his duty to perform and painter #2 could be substituted.

Statutory provisions generally require that some assignments be in writing. Statutes also prohibit contractual restrictions on most assignments of rights. The following case illustrates what happens when one original contracting party assigns rights and delegates duties over the objection of the other contracting party.

Macke Company v. Pizza of Gaithersburg, Inc.
270 A.2d 645
Court of Appeals of Maryland
November 10, 1970

Singley, Judge

The appellees and defendants below, Pizza of Gaithersburg, Inc.; Pizzeria, Inc.; The Pizza Pie Corp., Inc. and Pizza Oven, Inc., four corporations under the common ownership of Sidney Ansell, Thomas S. Sherwood and Eugene Early and the same individuals as partners or proprietors (the Pizza Shops) operated at six locations in Montgomery and Prince George's Counties. The appellees had arranged to have installed in each of their locations cold drink vending machines owned by Virginia Coffee Service, Inc., and on 30 December 1966, this arrangement was formalized at five of the locations, by contracts for terms of one year, automatically renewable for a like term in the absence of 30 days' written notice. A similar contract for the sixth location, operated by Pizza of Gaithersburg, Inc., was entered into on 25 July 1967.

On 30 December 1967, Virginia's assets were purchased by The Macke Company (Macke) and the six contracts were assigned to Macke by Virginia. In January, 1968, the Pizza Shops attempted to terminate the five contracts having the December anniversary date, and in February, the contract which had the July anniversary date.

Macke brought suit in the Circuit Court for Montgomery County against each of the Pizza Shops for damages for breach of contract. From judgments for the defendants, Macke has appealed.

The lower court based the result which it reached on two grounds: first, that the Pizza Shops, when they contracted with Virginia, relied on its skill, judgment and reputation, which made impossible a delegation of Virginia's duties to Macke; and second, that the damages claimed could not be shown with reasonable certainty. These conclusions are challenged by Macke.

In the absence of a contrary provision—and there was none here—rights and duties under an executory bilateral contract may be assigned and delegated, subject to the exception that duties under a contract to provide personal services may never be delegated, nor rights be assigned under a contract where *delectus personae** was an ingredient of the bargain....

The six machines were placed on the appellees' premises under a printed "Agreement-Contract" which identified the "customer," gave its place of business, described the vending machine, and then provided:

"TERMS

1. The Company will install on the Customer's premises the above listed equipment in good operating order and stocked with merchandise.
2. The location of this equipment will be such as to permit accessibility to persons desiring use of same. This equipment shall remain the property of the Company and shall not be moved from the location at which installed, except by the Company.
3. For equipment requiring electricity and water, the Customer is responsible for electrical receptacle and water outlet within ten (10) feet of the equipment location. The Customer is also responsible to supply the Electrical Power and Water needed.

4. The Customer will exercise every effort to protect this equipment from abuse or damage.
5. The Company will be responsible for all licenses and taxes on the equipment and sale of products.
6. This Agreement–Contract is for a term of one (1) year from the date indicated herein and will be automatically renewed for a like period, unless thirty (30) day written notice is given by either party to terminate service.
7. Commission on monthly sales will be paid by the Company to the Customer at the following rate: ..."

The rate provided in each of the agreements was "30 percent of Gross Receipts to $300.00 monthly[,] 35 percent over [$]300.00," except for the agreement with Pizza of Gaithersburg, Inc., which called for "40 percent of Gross Receipts."

... We cannot regard the agreements as contracts for personal services. They were either a license or concession granted Virginia by the appellees, or a lease of a portion of the appellees' premises, with Virginia agreeing to pay a percentage of gross sales as a license or concession fee or as rent, ... and were assignable by Virginia unless they imposed on Virginia duties of a personal or unique character which could not be delegated.... [T]he agreements with Virginia were silent as to the details of the working arrangements and contained only a provision requiring Virginia to "install ... the above listed equipment and...maintain the equipment in good operating order and stocked with merchandise."... Moreover, the difference between the service the Pizza Shops happened to be getting from Virginia and what they expected to get from Macke did not mount up to such a material change in the performance of obligations under the agreements as would justify the appellees' refusal to recognize the assignment.... Modern authorities...hold that, absent provision to the contrary, a duty may be delegated, as distinguished from a right which can be assigned, and that the promisee cannot rescind, if the quality of the performance remains materially the same.

Restatement, Contracts § 160(3) (1932) reads, in part:

"Performance or offer of performance by a person delegated has the same legal effect as performance or offer of performance by the person named in the contract, unless, "(a) performance by the person delegated varies or would vary

*Delectus personae means choice of person.—Ed.

materially from performance by the person named in the contract as the one to perform, and there has been no...assent to the delegation."...

In cases involving the sale of goods, the Restatement rule respecting delegation of duties has been amplified by Uniform Commercial Code § 2-210(5), Maryland Code (1957, 1964 Repl. Vol.) Art 95B § 2-210(5), which permits a promisee to demand

assurances from the party to whom duties have been delegated....

As we see it, the delegation of duty by Virginia to Macke was entirely permissible under the terms of the agreements....

Judgment reversed as to liability; judgment entered for appellant for costs, on appeal and below; case remanded for a new trial on the question of damages.

Case Questions

1. When the Virginia Coffee Service sold its assets to the Macke Company, what rights did it assign?
2. What duties were delegated?

Contracts for the Benefit of Third Parties

In some situations, the parties contract with a clear understanding that the agreement is intended to benefit some other, noncontracting person. For example, a son and daughter might contract with a carpenter to repair the back stairs at their elderly mother's house. In another case, a woman might have accidentally damaged a neighbor's fence and agreed to have the fence repaired. The woman might want to discharge this obligation by contracting with a carpenter to repair the damage.

The third person in the first example (the mother) is classified as a **donee beneficiary**, and the third person in the second example (the neighbor) is classified as a **creditor beneficiary**. American law generally permits donee beneficiaries and creditor beneficiaries to sue for breach of contract. The third party's right to sue, however, only exists if that party's rights have "vested," that is, have matured to the point of being legally enforceable. Jurisdictions generally choose one of the following three rules to decide when rights vest: (1) rights vest when the contract is formed, (2) rights vest when the beneficiary acquires knowledge about the contract, or (3) rights vest when the beneficiary relies on the contract and changes his or her position.

INTERNET TIP

Readers can read a New York appellate court opinion in a case in which the deceased plaintiff's estate claimed that she was an intended third-party beneficiary in a contract between her landlord and a contractor. *Castorino v. Unifast Building Products* can be found on the textbook's website.

The Duty to Perform and Breach of Contract

Many agreements include conditions precedent and conditions subsequent that may affect a party's duty to perform. A **condition precedent** exists when some specified event must occur before a duty to perform becomes operative (i.e., obtain a mortgage at a specified rate of interest). A **condition subsequent** exists when a specified event occurs that discharges the parties from their duties.

A breach of contract occurs when a party fails to perform a duty, or inadequately performs what he or she has promised. A breach of contract is a material breach if the nonperforming party totally or substantially fails to perform. Thus, a material breach has occurred if a homeowner contracts with a painter to paint a house with two coats of primer and one finish coat, and the painter quits after painting one coat of primer. The homeowner has not received the substantial benefit of his or her bargain.

In the next case, an exterminating company is found to have breached its contract with a homeowner through inadequate performance of its duty.

Clarkson v. Orkin Exterminating Co., Inc.
761 F.2d 189
U.S. Court of Appeals, Fourth Circuit
May 9, 1985

Haynsworth, Senior Circuit Judge

A jury awarded the plaintiff damages on three separate claims. She claimed breach of a contract to inspect for termites and to treat again if necessary. There was a claim of fraud and of a violation of South Carolina's Unfair Trade Practices Act. § 39–0(a), Code of Laws of South Carolina, 1976.

There was adequate proof that Orkin broke its contract, though an improper measure of damages was applied. There is no evidence in the record, however, to support the finding of fraud or a violation of the Unfair Trade Practices Act. Hence, we reverse in part and affirm in part, but remand the contract claim for an appropriate assessment of damages.

I

In 1976 Mrs. Clarkson purchased a house. Orkin had contracted with her predecessor in title to retreat the house in the event that a termite problem developed. Orkin also promised, for a fee, to inspect the house yearly and, if necessary, retreat it for termites before certifying that the house remained free of termites.

In early 1983, Mrs. Clarkson offered her home for sale. When prospective purchasers noticed evidence of termite infestation, Mrs. Clarkson called Orkin and requested that they inspect the house. Orkin complied with her request and issued a report that the house was free of termites. The report also mentioned the presence of a moisture problem, which had been reported to Mrs. Clarkson on several earlier occasions but which remained uncorrected. For the moisture problem, Orkin had unsuccessfully attempted to sell a protective chemical treatment to Mrs. Clarkson.

The day after Orkin's 1983 inspection, Mrs. Clarkson had the house inspected by the representative of another exterminating company. He found two termite tunnels and damage from water. He attributed the water damage to a drainage problem and expressed the opinion that the water damage would progress unless there were alterations to a porch to prevent drainage of water into the basement.

After a contractor had made the necessary repairs and the recommended alterations, Mrs. Clarkson sought to have Orkin reimburse her for her entire cost of the reconstruction work. She also asked that Orkin reinspect the house and certify that the house was free of termite infestation. Orkin refused both requests.

A jury awarded Mrs. Clarkson $613.47 on the breach of contract claim, $551 on the Unfair Trade Practices Act Claim and $1,148 actual damages and $5,000 punitive damages on the fraud claim. The district judge concluded that the Unfair Trade Practices Act claim was a willful one and tripled the award on that claim and ordered Orkin to pay the plaintiff's attorneys' fees.

II

As proof of a violation of the South Carolina Unfair Trade Practices Act, Mrs. Clarkson points (1) to the fact that Orkin certified in 1983 that the house was free of termites when significant infestation was visible, and (2) the fact that Orkin on several occasions had attempted, though unsuccessfully, to sell to Mrs. Clarkson a "moisture problem treatment package" that would not have been an adequate corrective of an improper drainage problem.

It is abundantly clear that in its 1983 inspection Orkin's representative failed to discover termite infestation which was present and visible. This, however, does not establish a violation of the South Carolina Unfair Trade Practices Act. It shows no more than that Orkin's representative was negligent or incompetent. Mrs. Clarkson had not directed his attention to the area where the infestation was present, though she did direct the attention of the other exterminator to that area....

III

There is enough to support a finding of contract violation. Orkin failed to retreat the house when a termite infestation was present, and it refused Mrs. Clarkson's subsequent request that it reinspect and spray the house after the repairs had been made.

There is no claim that Mrs. Clarkson lost an opportunity to sell the house because of the termite problem. What she claimed was the cost of repairs and alterations. On the breach of contract claim, the jury assessed the damaged at $613.47, which was precisely the cost to Mrs. Clarkson of replacing the wood damaged by the termites. In effect, the jury converted Orkin's retreatment contract into a repair contract.

Orkin offers its customers alternatives. It will promise and guarantee to provide retreatment if there is a later termite infestation. For a higher fee, it will promise and guarantee to effect necessary repairs after a termite infestation has occurred. Mrs. Clarkson's predecessor in title, and she, elected to take the lower option. In Orkin's guarantee to Mrs. Clarkson, there is an express recital of her waiver and release of Orkin from any liability for damage to the structure occasioned by termites. Mrs. Clarkson cannot now claim the benefits of a repair guarantee she chose not to purchase.

Mrs. Clarkson was entitled to a proper performance by Orkin of its contract, which was to inspect and treat again if an infestation was found. That promise was not properly performed, and Mrs. Clarkson is entitled to any damage she suffered by reason of that non-performance. Since she knew of the termite infestation one day after Orkin failed to detect it, her damage would apparently be limited to the cost of inspection by the other exterminator plus the cost of any retreatment she may have procured.

While we agree that the evidence supports a finding of a breach of contract, we remand that claim for further proceedings on damages as may be consistent with this opinion. Judgment in the plaintiff's favor on the unfair trade practice and fraud claims is reversed.

Reversed in part; Affirmed in part, and remanded.

Case Questions

1. In what way did Orkin breach its duty?
2. Why did the court remand the breach of contract claim for further proceedings?

REMEDIES FOR BREACH
OF CONTRACT

An injured party who has established a breach of contract is entitled to turn to a court for legal or equitable relief, as discussed in Chapter VII.

Common Law Remedies

In most cases of breach, the injured party is awarded money damages, which can be compensatory, nominal, or liquidated.

The following case involves breach of contract claims between homeowners and a building contractor. The homeowners discharged the contractor because of defective work. The contractor filed suit against the homeowners to recover the damages. The Maine Supreme Court vacated the trial court's judgment on the counterclaim because of errors in the jury instructions regarding damages.

Anuszewski v. Jurevic
566 A.2d 742
Supreme Judicial Court of Maine
November 28, 1989

Clifford, Justice
Defendants and counterclaim plaintiffs Richard and Judy Jurevic appeal from a judgment entered after a jury trial in Superior Court.... Because we conclude that the court improperly limited the jury's consideration of damages claimed by the Jurevics, we vacate the judgment on the counterclaim.

In early 1987, the Jurevics contracted with the plaintiff, Robert E. Anuszewski, a contractor doing business as Pine Tree Post & Beam, for Anuszewski to construct a home for the Jurevics in Kennebunkport.

The home was to be completed by June 1, 1987, at a cost of $134,000, and the contract called for the Jurevics to make periodic progress payments. The home was only about fifty percent complete on June 1, 1987. In January, 1988, the Jurevics discharged Anuszewski. In March, 1988, Anuszewski brought an action against the Jurevics to recover $39,590.* The Jurevics filed a counterclaim.

At trial, the Jurevics presented evidence that the construction work was defective and testimony in the form of an expert opinion as to the total cost to correct the defects and to complete the house. The testimony indicated that this cost would include a general contractor markup of fifty percent added to the actual cost of the work to be done for overhead and profit, and that this was a usual and customary practice of the industry. The Jurevics also claimed damages for rental and other incidental expenses caused by Anuszewski's delay in completing the house. The court, however, prohibited the Jurevics from presenting evidence of delay damages beyond January 5, 1988, the date the Jurevics terminated the contract with Anuszewski.

At the conclusion of the evidence, the court, in its jury instructions, precluded the jury from considering the general contractor's markup as follows:

> "[I]f you find that the Jurevics are entitled to recover damages from Mr. Anuszewski for completion of the work not done or for repairing work not performed in a workmanlike manner, any amount of damages that you award must be the cost of doing that work by the various workmen without any markup to a general contractor, such as was testified to by [the Jurevics' expert witness]."

The jury returned a verdict awarding Anuszewski damages of $25,000 on his complaint and awarding $22,000 to the Jurevics on their counterclaim. This appeal by the Jurevics followed the denial of their motions for a mistrial, or in the alternative, for a new trial, and for additur.

We find merit in the Jurevics' contention that the court impermissibly restricted the jury's consideration of the full amount of damages that they were entitled to recover. The purpose of contract damages is to place the injured parties in the position they would have been in but for the breach, by awarding the value of the promised performance.... Those damages for breach of a construction contract are measured by either the difference in value between the performance promised and the performance rendered, or the

amount reasonably required to remedy the defect.... The amount reasonably required to remedy the defect may be measured by the actual cost of necessary repairs.... Those costs may be proven by the presentation of expert testimony, as the Jurevics did here....

The court correctly instructed the jury that the Jurevics' measure of recovery for incomplete or defective work was "the amount reasonably required to remedy the defect" as specifically measured by the actual cost of repair.... The court went on, however, to instruct the jury that the cost of repair was to be considered "without any markup to a general contractor." This instruction was given despite testimony from an expert witness that the actual cost to remedy the incomplete and defective construction work of Anuszewski would include a general contractor markup for overhead and profit, and that such a markup was customary and usual in the construction business. Although Anuszewski defends the court's instruction, he did not argue at trial, nor does he now, that the Jurevics were not entitled to have the jury consider their claim that it was reasonable for them to hire a general contractor to supervise the repairs and completion of the house. If the jury concluded that it would be reasonable for the Jurevics to hire a substitute general contractor to supervise the repairs and completion, but was precluded by the court's instruction from considering the award of damages for the reasonable cost of the substitute contractor's overhead, for which the evidence suggests they would be charged as a matter of routine, then the Jurevics could be deprived of full recovery in their breach of contract claim. They would not be placed in the same position they would have been had Anuszewski performed the contract....

In breach of contract cases we have upheld repair or replacement damage awards of the amount required to bring a home into compliance with the contract.... In addition, we have affirmed the computation of indebtedness owed a builder by a homeowner that included a contractor's overhead and profit.... We see no reason to exclude reasonable and customary profit and overhead of a contractor from the cost of repairs to remedy defects in a breach of contract case.

The entry is:

Judgment on the complaint affirmed. Judgment on the counterclaim vacated.

Remanded to the Superior Court for further proceedings consistent with the opinion herein.

---

*The $39,500 represented, alternatively, the unpaid part of the contract price, or the value of the labor and materials provided by Anuszewski for which he had not been paid.

Equitable Remedies

If money damages are deemed to be an inadequate remedy, the court may be persuaded to grant equitable relief. The discussion in Chapter VII addresses the most common forms of equitable relief in breach of contract cases (injunctions, restitution after the court has granted rescission, and specific performance).

UCC Remedies for Breach of Contract for the Sale of Goods

The Uniform Commercial Code provides special rules for breaches of contracts involving the sale of goods. For example, if a seller breaches his or her contract to deliver goods, the buyer is entitled to (1) rescind the contract, (2) sue for damages, and (3) obtain restitution for any payments made. If the goods are unique such as rare artwork, or custom-made, a court may order specific performance. Replevin also is permitted in some situations. If a buyer breaches a sales contract by not accepting delivery of goods, or wrongfully revokes a prior acceptance, the injured seller is entitled to (1) cancel the contract, (2) stop delivery of goods, and (3) recover money damages from the buyer.

CHAPTER SUMMARY

The contracts chapter began with a historical review of the common law antecedents of modern contract law. Included in this overview were the writs of debt, detinue, covenant, trespass, trespass on the case, and assumpsit, as well as the eventual replacement of the writ system with modern code pleading and the development of uniform legislation, such as the Uniform Commercial Code (UCC). Readers then learned that contracts are classified in terms of validity (valid, void, voidable), enforceability, and whether they are bilateral or unilateral. The discussion then turned to an examination of each of the essential requirements of an enforceable contract: (1) an agreement (2) between competent parties (3) based on genuine assent of the parties, (4) supported by consideration, (5) that does not contravene principles of law and (6) that must be in writing in certain circumstances. Attention was also given to several aspects of contract performance, such as accord and satisfaction, anticipatory repudiation, warranties, discharge, recession, and novation, and the transfers of rights and duties to other persons who were not parties to the original agreement. The chapter concluded with a brief return visit to the topic of remedies, which was earlier addressed in Chapter VII.

CHAPTER QUESTIONS

1.   Paul Searle, a former basketball player at St. Joseph's College, brought suit against the college, the basketball coach, and the trainer for breach of contract and negligence. Searle alleged that he had sustained basketball-related injuries to his knees and that St. Joseph's had orally contracted to reimburse him for his basketball-related medical costs. Searle asserted

in his complaint that the college had promised to pay his medical expenses if he continued to play for the team. His proof was a statement that the coach had approached Searle's parents after a game and expressed a willingness to pay for all of the medical bills. Given the above factual record, does Searle have a contract with St. Joseph's College?

Searle v. Trustees of St. Joseph's College, 695 A.2d 1206 (1997)

2. S. Allen Schreiber, having tired of receiving unsolicited phone calls from telemarketers in general, received such a call on November 29, 1989, from Olan Mills, a national family portrait chain. Schreiber promptly sent a "Dear Telemarketer" letter to the defendant.

"Dear Telemarketer:

Today, you called us attempting to sell us a product or a service. We have no interest in the product or service that you are selling. Please don't call us again. Please remove us from your telemarketing list and notify the provider of the list to also remove our name and number since we do not appreciate receiving telemarketing phone calls.

We rely on the availability of our phone lines, which have been installed for our convenience and not for the convenience of telemarketers. We pay for these phone lines and instruments. You do not. Please don't tie up our phone lines.

Should we receive any more calls from you or from anyone connected with your firm of a telemarketing nature, we will consider that you have entered into a contract with us for our listening services and that you have made those calls to us and expect us to listen to your message on a "for hire" basis.

If we receive any additional telemarketing phone calls from you, you will be invoiced in accordance with our rates, which are $100.00 per hour or fraction thereof with a minimum charge. Payment will be due on a net seven (7) day basis.

Late payment charge of 1½ percent per month or fraction thereof on the unpaid balance subject to a minimum late charge of $ 9.00 per invoice per month or fraction thereof will be billed if payment is not made as outlined above. This is an annual percentage rate of 18 percent. In addition, should it become necessary for us to institute collection activities, all costs in connection therewith including, but not limited to, attorney fees will also be due and collectible.

Olan Mill representatives made two additional calls, which resulted in the instant breach of contract suit. Did Olan Mills enter into an enforceable contract with Schreiber?

Schreiber v. Olan Mills, 627 A.2d 806 (1993)

3. George and Mary Jane Graham were driving in a car insured by State Farm when they were forced off the road by an unidentified motorist. The Grahams' vehicle struck a telephone pole and both occupants were injured. When the Grahams were unable to reach an agreement with their insurer, State Farm, regarding the amount they should be paid pursuant to the uninsured motorist provisions of their automobile insurance policy, they filed suit against State Farm. State Farm responded with a motion for summary judgment on the grounds that the policy called for binding arbitration in lieu of litigation in the event of such a dispute. The Grahams did not know about the arbitration clause at the time they paid the first premium. State Farm pointed out that the Grahams, after receiving a copy of the policy, never complained about the arbitration clause at any time during the following two years. The Grahams responded that this was a "take it or leave it" situation, under which they actually had no opportunity to "leave it" because they were denied the information necessary to make a decision at the time they enrolled with State Farm. The court, they contended, should not compel them to arbitrate their claim. They pointed out that this contract was drafted by the insurance company's lawyers and that the terms were written in a one-sided manner, permitting the powerful insurance company to

take advantage of weaker insureds such as the Grahams. Delaware public policy favors the use of arbitration to resolve disputes in situations such as this. Should the court enforce the arbitration clause?

Graham v. State Farm Mutual Co., 565 A.2d 908 (1989)

4. Mr. Lucy and Mr. Zehmer were talking at a restaurant. After a couple of drinks, Lucy asked Zehmer if he had sold the Ferguson farm. Zehmer replied that he had not and did not want to sell it. Lucy said, "I bet you wouldn't take $50,000 cash for that farm," and Zehmer replied, "You haven't got $50,000 cash." Lucy said, "I can get it." Zehmer said he might form a company and get it, "but you haven't got $50,000 to pay me tonight." Lucy asked him if he would put it in writing that he would sell him this farm. Zehmer then wrote on the back of a pad, "I agree to sell the Ferguson Place to W. O. Lucy for $50,000 cash." Lucy said, "All right, get your wife to sign it." Zehmer subsequently went to his wife and said, "You want to put your name to this?" She said no, but he said in an undertone, "It is nothing but a joke," and she signed it. At that time, Zehmer was not too drunk to make a valid contract. The Zehmers refused to convey legal title to the property, and Lucy sued for specific performance. What defense would the Zehmers use in the suit? Who should win the suit?

Lucy v. Zehmer, 196 Va. 493, 84 S.E.2d 516 (1954)

5. National Beverages, Inc., offered to the public prizes to be awarded in a contest known as "Pepsi-Cola Streator-Chevrolet Sweepstakes." The first prize was a Chevrolet Corvair. No order of drawing was announced prior to the close of the contest. After the close of the contest, just prior to the drawing, a sign was displayed stating the order of drawing. The first tickets drawn would receive twelve cases of Pepsi-Cola, and the last ticket drawn would receive the automobile. Walters's ticket was the first ticket to be drawn from the barrel. She claims that her number, being the first qualified number drawn, entitles her to the first prize,

the Chevrolet Corvair. She bases her claim on the wording of the offer, which listed the automobile as the first prize. She accepted the offer by entering the contest. Is Walters entitled to the automobile?

Walters v. National Beverages, Inc., 18 Utah 2d 301, 422 P.2d 524 (1967)

6. Green signed a roofing contract with Clay Tile, agent for Ever-Tite Roofing Company, to have a new roof put on his house. The agreement stated that this contract was subject to Ever-Tite's approval and that the agreement would become binding upon written notice of acceptance or commencement of work. Nine days later, Clay Tile loaded up his truck and drove to Green's house, only to find that someone else was already doing the job. Ever-Tite wishes to sue on the contract for damages. Was Green's offer to Ever-Tite accepted before the offer was revoked?

Ever-Tite Roofing Corporation v. Green, 83 So.2d 449 (La. App. 1955)

7. Workers agreed to work aboard a canning ship during the salmon canning season. The contract, signed individually by each worker, was to last for the length of time it took to sail from San Francisco, California, to Pyramid Harbor, Alaska, and back. Each worker was to receive a stated compensation. They arrived in Alaska at the height of the fishing and canning season. Knowing that every day's delay would be financially disastrous and that it would be impossible to find workers to replace them, the workers refused to work unless they were given substantial wage increases. The owner of the canning ship acceded to their demands. When the ship returned to San Francisco, the owner paid them in accordance with the original agreement. The workers now bring suit to recover the additional amounts due under the second agreement. Will the contract be upheld?

Alaska Packers Association v. Domenico, 117 F.99 (9th Cir. 1902)

8. A little girl found a pretty stone about the size of a canary bird's egg. She had no idea what it was, so she took it to a jeweler, who eventually bought it from her for a dollar, although he too did not know what it was. The stone turned out to be an uncut diamond worth $10,000. The girl tendered back the $1 purchase price and sued to have the sale voided on the basis of mutual mistake. Should mutual mistake be a basis for recovery?

   Wood v. Boynton, 64 Wis. 265, 25 N.W. 42 (1885)

9. William E. Story agreed orally with his nephew that if he would refrain from drinking liquor, using tobacco, swearing, and playing cards or billiards for money until he became twenty-one years old, then he, Story, would pay his nephew $5,000 when the nephew reached age twenty-one. The nephew fully performed his part of the agreement. But when the nephew reached age twenty-one, his uncle stated that he had earned the $5,000 and that he would keep it at interest for his nephew. Twelve years later, Story died, and his nephew brought an action to recover the $5,000 plus interest. Was there sufficient consideration to create a contract?

   Hamer v. Sidway, 124 N.Y. 538, 27 N.E. 256 (1891)

NOTES

1. W. Walsh, *A History of Anglo-American Law* (Indianapolis: Bobbs-Merrill Company, 1932), p. 339; A. W. B. Simpson, *A History of the Common Law of Contract* (Oxford: Clarendon Press, 1975), pp. 12, 53; A. K. R. Kiralfy, *Potter's Historical Introduction to English Law* (London: Sweet and Maxwell Ltd., 1962), pp. 452–457.

2. Kiralfy, p. 456.

3. Ibid., pp. 456–457.

4. Ibid., pp. 305–307; Walsh, p. 344.

5. Walsh, p. 342.

6. Simpson, p. 199; Walsh, p. 344.

7. Simpson, p. 210; Kiralfy, p. 461; Walsh, p. 341.

8. Walsh, p. 340; Simpson, p. 224; T. F. F. Plucknett, *A Concise History of the Common Law* (Boston: Little, Brown, 1956) p. 639.

9. Walsh, pp. 345, 351; Simpson, p. 406; Plucknett, pp. 649–656.

10. Kiralfy, p. 626.

11. B. Schwartz, *The Law in America* (New York: McGraw-Hill, 1974), pp. 59–62; W. E. Nelson, *Americanization of the Common Law* (Cambridge, MA: Harvard University Press, 1975), p. 86.

12. M. Horwitz, *The Transformation of American Law, 1780–1860* (Cambridge, MA: Harvard University Press, 1977), pp. 164–180; Nelson, p. 154.

13. Horwitz, pp. 167, 173.

14. Schwartz, p. 72; Nelson, p. 86.

15. Horwitz, p. 185.

XI

✳

The Law of Torts

CHAPTER OBJECTIVES

1. *Understand the historical origins of the modern tort action.*
2. *Identify the three types of civil wrongs that comprise modern tort law.*
3. *Explain the essential functions of tort law.*
4. *Understand how the named intentional torts differ.*
5. *Understand the elements that a plaintiff must prove to establish negligence.*
6. *Explain how comparative negligence states determine the payment of damages.*
7. *Understand and explain the concept of strict liability in tort.*

A tort is a civil wrong, other than a breach of contract, for which courts provide a remedy in the form of an action for damages. Tort law seeks to provide reimbursement to members of society who suffer losses because of the dangerous or unreasonable conduct of others. Each of the fifty states determines its own tort law, which is divided into the following three categories: intentional torts, negligence, and strict liability.

You may recall from Figure 1.2 and the accompanying discussion in Chapter I that there are important differences between criminal law and tort law. It was there emphasized that criminal prosecutions are brought by the government to convict and then punish offenders who have committed crimes and thereby harmed society as a whole. You should also remember that the Constitution provides defendants in criminal cases with procedural protections that are unavailable in civil litigation. Nevertheless, it is possible for criminal defendants to be sued civilly irrespective of the criminal trial's outcome.

HISTORICAL EVOLUTION OF AMERICAN TORT LAW

The word **tort** (meaning "wrong") is one of many Norman words that became a part of the English and American legal lexicon. American tort law evolved from the writs of trespass[1] and trespass on the case.[2] Trespass covered a variety of acts, which included trespass to land, assaults, batteries, the taking of goods, and false imprisonment. Each of the acts involved a **tortfeasor** directly causing injury to a victim. By the end of Henry III's reign, it was commonplace for plaintiffs to use trespass to recover money damages for personal injuries.[3] In 1285, Parliament enacted the Statute of Westminster,[4] which authorized the chancery to create new writs to address wrongs that fell outside the boundaries of trespass. Because the new writs were designed to remedy the factual circumstances of a particular case, they were called trespass actions on the case (also called "actions on the case"). From trespass on the case came our contemporary concept of negligence.

One of the major drawbacks of the writ system was that it lacked any comprehensive underlying theoretical base. In the 1800s, as the writ system was being replaced with more modern forms of pleading, American law professors and judges began to develop a basic theory for tort law based on fault.

FUNCTIONS OF TORT LAW

Tort law establishes standards of conduct for all members of society. It defines as civil wrongs these antisocial behaviors: the failure to exercise reasonable care (negligence); intentional interference with one's person, reputation, or property (intentional torts); and in some circumstances, liability without fault (strict liability). Tort law deters people from engaging in behavior patterns that the law does not condone and compensates victims for their civil injuries. It is thus a vehicle by which an injured person can attempt to shift the costs of harm to another person. Tort law is not static; courts can create new causes of action to remedy an injustice. Thus, the argument that a claim is novel does not prevent a court from granting relief when it becomes clear that the law should protect the plaintiff's rights.

Because the plaintiffs in tort cases are usually seeking money damages, tort actions that are not settled prior to trial are generally tried to juries. See Table 11.1.

INTENTIONAL TORTS

Intentional torts are based on willful misconduct or intentional wrongs. A tortfeasor who intentionally invades a protected interest of another, under circumstances for which there is no lawful justification or excuse, is legally and morally "at fault." The intent is not necessarily a hostile intent or even a desire to do serious harm. A person acts intentionally if he or she has a conscious desire to produce consequences the law recognizes as tortious. A person who has no conscious desire to cause the consequences, but is aware that the consequences are highly likely to follow, can also be found to have acted intentionally.

Assault

Assault is an intentional tort because as a general proposition, every person should have the right to live his or her life without being placed in reasonable fear of an intentional, imminent, unconsented, harmful, or offensive touching by another person. Assaults occur where the targeted person's anxiety is the product of the actor's threatening conduct, such as stalking. The law also recognizes that an assault has occurred where a targeted person's fear is the product of the actor's unsuccessful attempt to hit the target with a punch or a thrown object. Mere words alone, however, usually will not constitute an assault, no matter how threatening or abusive they may be. Once an actor has committed an

TABLE 11.1   **Tort Cases Disposed of by Bench or Jury Trial in State Courts, by Case Type, 2005**

Case type	Number of tort trials	Percentage disposed of by	
		Jury Trial	Bench Trial
All tort trials	6,397	90.0	10.0
Medical malpractice	2,449	98.7	1.3
Professional malpractice	150	60.0	40.0
Asbestos product liability	87	95.4	4.6
Premises liability	1,863	93.8	6.2
Other product liability	268	92.5	7.5
Automobile accident	9,431	92.2	7.8
Animal attack	138	80.6	19.4
Intentional tort	725	78.2	21.8
Other/unknown tort	664	71.5	28.5
Slander/libel	187	64.2	35.8
False arrest/imprisonment	58	63.8	36.2
Conversion	378	46.3	53.7

Source: U.S. Department of Justice, Bureau of Justice Statistics, Bulletin, November 2009, NCJ 228129. Table 1.

assault, the tort has been committed. An actor cannot, through the abandonment of further assaultive conduct, avoid civil liability for assaultive conduct already committed against a target.

Battery

In the intentional tort called battery, the *tortfeasor* has violated the target's right to be free from harmful or offensive touchings by another. A **battery** is defined as an unpermitted, unprivileged, intentional contact with another's person. This tort includes contact that is actually harmful, as well as conduct that is merely offensive. The standard used to determine offensiveness is not whether a particular plaintiff is offended, but whether an ordinary person who is not unusually sensitive in the matter of dignity would be offended. It is not essential that the plaintiff be conscious of the contact at the time it occurs.

Assault or battery may occur without the other, but usually both result from the same occurrence. As a result of an assault and battery—as well as other intentional torts—the injured party may bring a civil suit for damages and, as has been previously discussed, seek a criminal prosecution for the same act.

The following case illustrates the intentional torts of assault, battery, and invasion of privacy.

Estate of Berthiaume v. Pratt, M.D.
365 A.2d 792
Supreme Judicial Court of Maine
November 10, 1976

Pomeroy, Justice

The appellant, as administratrix, based her claim of right to damages on an alleged invasion of her late husband's "right to privacy" and on an alleged assault and battery of him. At the close of the evidence produced at trial, a justice of the Superior Court granted defendant's motion for a directed verdict. Appellant's seasonable appeal brings the case to this court.

The appellee is a physician and surgeon practicing in Waterville, Maine. It was established at trial without contradiction that the deceased, Henry Berthiaume, was suffering from a cancer of his larynx. Appellee, an otolaryngologist, had treated him twice surgically. A laryngectomy was performed; and later, because of a tumor which had appeared in his neck, a radical neck dissection on one side was done. No complaint is made with respect to the surgical interventions.

During the period appellee was serving Mr. Berthiaume as a surgeon, many photographs of Berthiaume had been taken by appellee or under his direction. The jury was told that the sole use to which these photographs were to be put was to make the medical record for the appellee's use....

Although at no time did the appellee receive any written consent for taking of photographs from Berthiaume or any members of his family, it was appellee's testimony that Berthiaume had always consented to having such photographs made.

At all times material hereto, Mr. Berthiaume was a patient of a physician other than the appellee. Such other physician had referred the patient to appellee for surgery. On September 2, 1970, appellee saw the patient for the last time for the purpose of treatment or diagnosis. The incident which gave rise to this lawsuit occurred on September 23, 1970. It was also on that day Mr. Berthiaume died.

Although appellee disputed the evidence appellant produced at trial in many material respects, the jury could have concluded from the evidence that shortly before Mr. Berthiaume died on the 23rd, the appellee and a nurse appeared in his hospital room. In the presence of Mrs. Berthiaume and a visitor of the patient in the next bed, either Dr. Pratt or the nurse, at his direction, raised the dying Mr. Berthiaume's head and placed some blue operating room toweling under his head and beside him on the bed. The appellee testified that this blue toweling was placed there for the purpose of obtaining a color contrast for the

photographs which he proposed to take. He then proceeded to take several photographs of Mr. Berthiaume.

The jury could have concluded from the testimony that Mr. Berthiaume protested the taking of pictures by raising a clenched fist and moving his head in an attempt to remove his head from the camera's range. The appellee himself testified that before taking the pictures he had been told by Mrs. Berthiaume when he talked with her in the corridor before entering the room that she "didn't think that Henry wanted his picture taken."

It is the raising of the deceased's head in order to put the operating room towels under and around him that appellant claims was an assault and battery. It is the taking of the pictures of the dying Mr. Berthiaume that appellant claims constituted the actionable invasion of Mr. Berthiaume's right to privacy....

The law of privacy addresses the invasion of four distinct interests of the individual. Each of the four different interests, taken as a whole, represent an individual's right "to be let alone." These four kinds of invasion are (1) intrusion upon the plaintiff's physical and mental solitude or seclusion; (2) public disclosure of private facts; (3) publicity which places the plaintiff in a false light in the public eye; [and] (4) appropriation for the defendant's benefit or advantage of the plaintiff's name or likeness....

> "As it has appeared in the cases thus far decided, it is not one tort, but a complex of four. To date the law of privacy comprises four distinct kinds of invasion of four different interests of the plaintiff, which are tied together by the common name, but otherwise have almost nothing in common except that each represents an interference with the right of the plaintiff 'to be let alone.' ...
>
> "Taking them in order—intrusion, disclosure, false light, and appropriation—the first and second require the invasion of something secret, secluded or private pertaining to the plaintiff; the third and fourth do not. The second and third depend upon publicity, while the first does not, nor does the fourth, although it usually involves it. The third requires falsity or fiction; the other three do not. The fourth involves a use for the defendant's advantage, which is not true of the rest." ...

All cases so far decided on the point agree that the plaintiff need not plead or prove special damages. Punitive damages can be awarded on the same basis as in other torts where a wrongful motive or state of mind appears ... but not in cases where the defendant has acted innocently as, for example, in the mistaken but good faith belief that the plaintiff has given his consent....

In this case we are concerned only with a claimed intrusion upon the plaintiff's intestate's physical and mental solitude or seclusion. The jury had a right to conclude from the evidence that plaintiff's intestate was dying. It could have concluded he desired not to be photographed in his hospital bed in such condition and that he manifested such desire by his physical motions. The jury should have been instructed, if it found these facts, that the taking of pictures without decedent's consent or over his objection was an invasion of his legally protected right to privacy, which invasion was an actionable tort for which money damages could be recovered.

Instead, a directed verdict for the defendant was entered, obviously premised on the presiding justice's announced incorrect conclusion that the taking of pictures without consent did not constitute an invasion of privacy and the further erroneous conclusion that no tort was committed in the absence of "proof they [the photographs] were published."

Another claimed basis for appellant's assertion that a right to recover damages was demonstrated by the evidence is the allegations in her complaint sounding in the tort of assault and battery. The presiding justice announced as his conclusion that consent to a battery is implied from the existence of a physician-patient relationship....

There is nothing to suggest that the appellee's visit to plaintiff's intestate's room on the day of the alleged invasion of privacy was for any purpose relating to the *treatment* of the patient. Appellee acknowledges that his sole purpose in going to the Berthiaume hospital room and the taking of pictures was to conclude the making of a photographic record to complete appellee's record of the case. From the evidence, then, it is apparent that the jury had a right to conclude that the physician-patient relationship once existing between Dr. Pratt and Henry Berthiaume, the deceased, had terminated.

As to the claimed assault and battery, on the state of the evidence, the jury should have been permitted to consider the evidence and return a verdict in accordance with its fact-finding. It should have been instructed that consent to a touching of the body of a patient may be implied from the patient's consent to enter into a physician-patient relationship whenever such touching is reasonably necessary for the diagnosis and treatment of the patient's ailments while the physician--patient relationship continues. Quite obviously also, there would be no actionable assault and battery if the touching was expressly consented to. Absent express consent by the patient or one authorized to give consent on the patient's behalf, or absent consent implied from the circumstances, including the physician-patient relationship, the touching of the patient in the manner described by the evidence in this case would constitute assault and battery if it was part of an undertaking which, in legal effect, was an invasion of the plaintiff's intestate's "right to be let alone." ...

We recognize the benefit to the science of medicine which comes from the making of photographs of the treatment and of medical abnormalities found in patients....

> "The court [also] recognizes that an individual has the right to decide whether that which is his shall be given to the public and not only to restrict and limit but also to withhold absolutely his talents, property, or other subjects of the right of privacy from all dissemination."...

Because there were unresolved, disputed questions of fact, which, if decided by the fact finder in favor of the plaintiff, would have justified a verdict for the plaintiff, it was reversible error to have directed a verdict for the defendant.... New trial ordered.

Case Questions

1. Battery is unpermitted, unprivileged, intentional contact with another's person. In a physician-patient relationship, how does a physician receive consent to touch the body of a patient?
2. Could there have been a battery if Dr. Pratt had used rubber gloves in handling Mr. Berthiaume's head in preparation for the pictures? Could there have been a battery if Dr. Pratt had raised Mr. Berthiaume's head by cranking the hospital bed?

3. Could there have been an assault if Mr. Berthiaume was unconscious at the time Dr. Pratt raised his head and placed the blue operating towel under his head?
4. Are plaintiffs able to recover anything in suits for battery if they are unable to prove any actual physical injury?

ETHICS   Does Dr. Pratt have a moral duty to comply with his patient's request? Does acting morally benefit Dr. Pratt?

Conversion

Conversion is an intentional tort which allows owners of tangible personal property (concepts discussed in Chapter XII) to regain possession of their property from other persons who have dispossessed them. Any unauthorized act that deprives an owner of possession of his or her tangible personal property is conversion. There may be liability for the intentional tort of conversion even when the defendant acted innocently. For example, D, an auctioneer, receives a valuable painting from X, reasonably believing that X owns it. D sells the painting for X, but it turns out that P owns the painting. D is liable to P for conversion, even though the mistake is honest and reasonable.

Conversion may be accomplished in a number of ways—for example, if a defendant refuses to return goods to the owner or destroys or alters the goods. Even the use of the chattel may suffice. If you lend your car to a dealer to sell and the dealer drives the car once on business for a few miles, it would probably not be conversion. However, conversion would result if the dealer drives it for 2,000 miles.

Because conversion is considered a forced sale, the defendant must pay the full value, not merely the amount of the actual harm. However, courts consider several factors in determining whether defendant's interference with plaintiff's property is sufficient to require defendant to pay its entire value. These include dominion, good faith, harm, and inconvenience.

The plaintiff in the next case, Consuelo Mickens, claimed that a pawnshop employee committed conversion and breach of contract in transferring possession of her diamond ring to Jesse Colwell, an individual not listed on the pawn ticket.

Consuelo Mickens v. The Pawn Store
723 N.W.2d 450
Court of Appeals of Iowa
July 26, 2006

Vogel, P. J.
Consuelo Mickens appeals from the district court's order following a bench trial denying judgment on her breach of contract and conversion claims against The Pawn Store, Inc. Because we find no error, we affirm the district court.

Mickens and the father of her three children, Jesse Colwell, were regular customers at the Pawn Store (the Store), so much so that the employees were on a first name basis with the couple. Mickens and Colwell held themselves out to be husband and wife to the employees of the Store. Mickens had previously pawned numerous items at the Store, including the diamond ring at question in this case. The Store employees recalled Colwell reclaiming items Mickens had pawned in the past.

On September 25, 2002, Mickens took a pear-shaped, one and a quarter carat diamond ring to pawn at the Store. She received $225 in exchange for the ring. The pawn ticket that was signed by Mickens gave "the grantee" the option to reclaim the ring at a certain price within thirty days. Prior to the expiration of the thirty-day period, Mickens claims Colwell took the pawn ticket without her knowledge or consent and reclaimed the ring from the Store. After Colwell told Mickens he obtained the ring, Mickens attempted to alert the Store employees that Colwell should not be allowed to reclaim the ring. Employee Matt DePhillips informed Mickens that Colwell had already reclaimed the ring, using the pawn ticket. DePhillips thought this was not unusual, as Colwell had regularly picked up items at the Store for Mickens. Mickens quarreled with the Store employees and owner, Jeff Pocock, over the ring in two more visits to the Store. She did not alert the police of Colwell's actions or assert restitution from Colwell for the ring.

Mickens filed suit against the Store in February 2004, with claims for breach of contract [, and] conversion.... After a bench trial, the district court entered judgment in favor of the Store on all claims, finding that Mickens failed to prove breach of contract or conversion due to her implied consent to allow Colwell to reclaim items she had pawned at the Store. Mickens appeals on the breach of contract and conversion claims....

Mickens asserts on appeal that the district court erred by concluding she failed to prove her breach of contract and conversion claims. She argues that the court's finding that Mickens gave implicit permission to the Store for Colwell to redeem her property was not supported by substantial evidence. Mickens's claim for conversion rests on the allegation that the Store's breach of contract amounted to a conversion of the ring when employees turned it over to Colwell. In deciding whether there is an enforceable contract, we consider not only the language used but also the surrounding circumstances and the conduct of the parties.... Contractual obligations may arise from implication as well as from express writing....

Mickens denied that she had allowed Colwell to retrieve pawned items at the Store for her in the past.

The district court found testimony by the Store's employees more credible than Mickens' testimony. Substantial evidence on the record supports the district court's findings that Mickens had previously consented to having Colwell reclaim her various pawned items from the Store. The evidence further supports this arrangement as the couple held themselves out to be husband and wife to the Store's owner and employees. Although the pawn ticket in question was signed by Mickens alone, the parties' repeated past conduct provides substantial evidence that Colwell, having possession of the pawn ticket, was authorized to reclaim the ring pawned by Mickens.... As the district court concluded, "there is nothing in the law or the terms stated on the ticket which would preclude Mickens from giving someone else the right to redeem the ring." We agree and note that Mickens may assign her interest in the pawned item by delivering the pawn ticket to another and transferring the right of redemption.... While Mickens alleges that Colwell took the ticket for the ring without her permission, there is nothing in the record to suggest the Store was aware of this allegation. Rather, the record supports Mickens's and Colwell's past course of dealing with the Store which allowed Colwell to have possession of the ticket and redeem the ring. We conclude the district court did not err by finding no breach of contract or conversion by the Pawn Store and affirm.

Case Questions

1. What facts, according to Mickens, supported her claim that The Pawn Store had committed conversion?
2. Why did Mickens appeal the trial court's judgment to the Court of Appeals?
3. Why did the appellate court reject Mickens's argument and affirm the trial court?

Trespass to Land

Trespass is an intentional tort that protects a lawful owner/occupier's rights to exclusive possession of his or her real property. It occurs when someone makes an unauthorized entry on the land of another. Trespasses to land can occur through either a direct or an indirect entry. A direct entry would occur when one person walks on another person's land without permission. An in-direct entry would occur when one person throws an object on another's land or causes it to flood with water.

The law's protection of the exclusive possession of land is not limited to the surface of real property. It extends below the surface as well as above it. Thus, a public utility that runs a pipe below the surface of a landowner's property without obtaining an easement or consent can commit a trespass. Similarly, overhanging structures, telephone wires, and even shooting across land have been held to be violations of owners' right to the airspace above their land. Although the extent of such rights is still in the process of determination, the legal trend is for landowners to have rights to as much of the airspace that is immediately above their property as they can effectively occupy or use. Trespass may also occur to personal property, but most interference with the possession of personal property would be considered conversion rather than trespass.

The plaintiff in the following case brought suit in trespass after sustaining serious injury when an overhanging limb fell from the defendant's maple tree onto the plaintiff's driveway and struck the plaintiff.

Ivancic v. Olmstead
488 N.E.2d 72
Court of Appeals of New York
November 26, 1985

Jasen, Judge

At issue on this appeal is whether plaintiff, who seeks to recover for injuries sustained when an overhanging limb from a neighbor's maple tree fell and struck him, established a prima facie case of negligence and whether Trial Term erred, as a matter of law, in refusing to submit to the jury the cause of action sounding in common-law trespass.

Plaintiff was working on his truck in the driveway of his parents' home located in the Village of Fultonville, New York. Since 1970, defendant has owned and lived on the property adjoining to the west. A large maple tree stood on defendant's land near the border with plaintiff's parents' property. Branches from the tree had extended over the adjoining property. During a heavy windstorm on September 26, 1980, an overhanging limb from the tree fell and struck plaintiff, causing him serious injuries. As a result, plaintiff commenced this action, interposing causes of action in negligence and common-law trespass.

At trial, the court declined to charge the jury on the common-law trespass cause of action or on the doctrine of *res ipsa loquitur*, submitting the case solely on the theory of negligence. The jury rendered a verdict in favor of the plaintiff in the sum of $3,500. Both parties moved to set aside the verdict, the plaintiff upon the ground of inadequacy, and the defendant upon the ground that the verdict was against the weight of the evidence. The court ultimately... ordered a new trial on the issues of both liability and damages.

Upon cross appeals, the Appellate Division reversed, on the law, and dismissed the complaint. The court reasoned that no competent evidence was presented upon which it could properly be concluded that defendant had constructive notice of the alleged defective condition of the tree. The Appellate Division did not address the correctness of the trial court's ruling in declining to charge the jury on the common-law trespass cause of action....

Considering first the negligence cause of action, it is established that no liability attaches to a landowner whose tree falls outside of his premises and injures another unless there exists actual or constructive knowledge of the defective condition of the tree....

Inasmuch as plaintiff makes no claim that defendant had actual knowledge of the defective nature of the tree, it is necessary to consider whether there was sufficient competent evidence for a jury to conclude that defendant had constructive notice. We conclude, as did the Appellate Division, that plaintiff offered no competent evidence from which it could be properly found that defendant had constructive notice of the alleged defective condition of the tree. Not one of the witnesses who had observed the tree prior to the fall of the limb testified as to observing so much as a withering or dead leaf, barren branch, discoloration, or any of the indicia of disease which would alert an observer to the possibility that the tree or one of its branches was decayed or defective.

At least as to adjoining landowners, the concept of constructive notice with respect to liability for falling trees is that there is no duty to consistently and constantly check all trees for nonvisible decay. Rather, the manifestation of said decay must be readily observable in order to require a landowner to take reasonable steps to prevent harm.... The testimony of plaintiff's expert provides no evidence from which the jury could conclude that defendant should reasonably have realized that a potentially dangerous condition existed. Plaintiff's expert never saw the tree until the morning of the trial when all that remained of the tree was an eight-foot stump. He surmised from this observation and from some photographs of the tree that water had invaded the tree through a "limb hole" in the tree, thus causing decay and a crack occurring below. However, the expert did indicate that the limb hole was about eight feet high and located in the crotch of the tree which would have made it difficult, if not impossible, to see upon reasonable inspection. Although there may have been evidence that would have alerted an expert, upon close observation, that the tree was diseased, there is no evidence that would put a reasonable landowner on notice of any defective condition of the tree. Thus, the fact that defendant landowner testified that she did not inspect the tree for over 10 years is irrelevant. On the evidence presented, even if she were to have inspected the tree, there were no indicia of decay or disease to put her on notice of a defective condition so as to trigger her duty as a landowner to take reasonable steps to prevent the potential harm.

Since the evidence adduced at trial failed to set forth any reasonable basis upon which notice of the tree's defective condition could be imputed to defendant ... we agree with the view of the Appellate Division that plaintiff failed to establish a prima facie case of negligence.

Turning to plaintiff's claim of error by the trial court in declining to submit to the jury the cause of action sounding in common-law trespass, we conclude that there was no error. The scope of the common-law tort has been delineated in *Phillips v. Sun Oil Co.*, ... 121 N.E.2d 249, wherein this court held: "while the trespasser, to be liable, need not intend or expect the damaging consequences of his intrusion, he must intend the act which amounts to or produces the unlawful invasion, and the intrusion must at least be the immediate or inevitable consequence of what he willfully does, or which he does so negligently as to amount to willfulness." In this case, there is evidence that defendant did not plant the tree, and the mere fact that defendant allowed what appeared to be a healthy tree to grow naturally and cross over into plaintiff's parents' property airspace, cannot be viewed as an intentional act so as to constitute trespass. ...

Accordingly, the order of the Appellate Division should be affirmed, with costs.

Case Questions

1. The trial court and the appellate court concluded that the plaintiff was not entitled to an instruction with respect to common law trespass. Why was the instruction refused?
2. Why was the plaintiff's negligence claim rejected?
3. Why should a plaintiff be entitled to recover for a trespass under circumstances where no actual harm has been shown?

Malicious Prosecution

Malicious prosecution is an intentional tort that provides targeted individuals with civil remedies against persons who have filed groundless complaints against the target that result in the target's criminal prosecution. Many states have extended the definition of this tort to permit such suits against individuals who initiate groundless civil actions. The plaintiff in a malicious prosecution case must prove that the defendant maliciously and without probable cause instituted a criminal or civil complaint against the target which resulted in a prosecution or lawsuit, which then resulted in a decision favorable to the target. The target must also establish that he or she suffered legal injury as a result of the groundless charges. Merely threatening to bring a lawsuit against the target is not enough to result in civil liability for malicious prosecution.

In a criminal case, the prosecutor is absolutely immune from malicious prosecution suits. In addition, plea bargaining does not suffice to meet the favorable decision criterion.

False Imprisonment

False imprisonment is an intentional tort that provides targeted individuals with civil remedies against those who unlawfully deprive them of their freedom of movement. Plaintiffs must prove that they were intentionally and unlawfully detained against their will for an unreasonable period of time. The detention need not be in a jail. It may also take place in a mental institution, hospital, restaurant, hotel, store, car, etc. Most courts have held that plaintiffs must be aware of their confinement while suffering it, or if not, then they must suffer some type of actual harm.

The plaintiffs in the following case claimed that they were the victims of false imprisonment by Wal-Mart security personnel.

Kim Gallegly Wesson v. Wal-Mart Stores East, L.P.
No. 2080959.
Court of Civil Appeals of Alabama.
December 4, 2009.

Thomas, Judge

On July 13, 2004, at about 9:30 a.m., Kim Gallegly Wesson and her four children went to the Pell City Wal-Mart discount department store, operated by Wal-Mart Stores East, L.P. ("Wal-Mart"), to have the tires on Wesson's automobile rotated and balanced. Wesson left her automobile at the tire and lube express department ("TLE department") for the service to be performed. Wesson had assumed that the service would take 20–30 minutes, so she and her children walked around the Wal-Mart store awaiting the completion of the service to her automobile. When the automobile was not ready in about 30 minutes, Wesson decided to take her children, who were hungry and requesting breakfast, to the McDonald's fast-food restaurant located inside the store. After finishing breakfast, Wesson checked again to see if her automobile service had been completed; it had not. Wesson and her children proceeded to the pharmacy department of the store, where Wilson dropped off one of her two prescriptions for refilling at the pharmacy counter. Wesson and the children then went to the electronics department of the store, where Wesson purchased additional minutes for her prepaid cellular telephone. When a third check on the status of her automobile yielded further waiting, Wesson dropped off her second prescription at the pharmacy counter for refilling. Wesson then decided to shop for groceries for the family's trip to Florida.

Once Wesson had completed her grocery shopping, she returned to the pharmacy department to retrieve her prescriptions. By this time, the pharmacy associate, Jennifer Vincent, had notified Kyle Jack, the in-store loss prevention associate, that Wesson would be picking up prescriptions from the pharmacy. Because Wal-Mart's policy allows customers to pay for most prescriptions at any check-out counter, the store has a computer system that keeps track of the time and place of the payment to ensure that all prescriptions picked up from the pharmacy department are

ultimately paid for. Wesson's name had appeared on a list of persons who had not paid for prescriptions picked up from the pharmacy department on at least two other occasions, resulting in her placement on a "watch list" of sorts.

Once Wesson arrived at the pharmacy department to retrieve her prescriptions, Wesson said that an announcement came over the loudspeaker to inform her that her automobile service was completed. Wesson informed the pharmacy associate that she would pay for her prescriptions when she checked out her groceries and paid for her car service. Vincent gave Wesson both of her prescriptions; Wesson owed money on both prescriptions. Wesson and her children left the pharmacy department and returned to the TLE department; they were followed by Jack. Once she reached the check-out counter at the TLE department, Wesson proceeded to place her grocery items on the counter and to check out. Wesson did not, however, place her prescriptions on the counter to check out. Once she had paid for her groceries and car service, Wesson and her children left the store.

Tara Swain, the associate who checked out Wesson's groceries at the TLE department, testified that she had asked Wesson whether she wanted to pay for her prescriptions. Swain said that Wesson indicated that she had paid for the prescriptions already. Jack testified that he had seen Swain motion toward the child-seat portion of the cart, in which the prescriptions, Wesson's purse, and some of the children's dolls or toys sat, as she completed checking out Wesson's grocery items. Although he said that he did not hear Swain's exact question or Wesson's first answer to that question, Jack said that he moved closer to Wesson and heard her refer to the items in the child-seat portion of the cart as being her personal items. Jack said that he saw Wesson leave the store without paying for the prescriptions, so he followed her outside to apprehend her.

Once she reached the parking lot, Wesson and her children began to place her purchases into the automobile. Jack and another associate, Nathan Nichols, approached Wesson while she unloaded her groceries. Jack addressed Wesson by name and, according to Wesson, said: "Excuse me, but I don't think you paid for those prescriptions." Wesson said that she admitted that she had not, in fact, paid for the prescriptions.

According to Wesson, Jack told her that she needed to come back inside to fill out some forms and that she would be allowed to pay for the prescriptions. Wesson and her children returned to the store with Jack and the other associate. Once inside the store, Jack led Wesson and her children to the loss-prevention office in the front of the store, where, according to Wesson, Jack locked the door to the office. Wesson said that Jack asked for her driver's license and Social Security number and that he gave her several papers to sign. Wesson admitted that she did not read the papers that Jack gave her to sign other than to notice that the Wal-Mart logo appeared on them. Wesson said that, at that time, she still believed that she was simply going to have to pay for her prescriptions.

However, according to Wesson, once Jack secured her signature on the forms, he raised his voice and told her that she would be trespassing if she ever came back into a Wal-Mart store. She said that Jack accused her of stealing from the store "all the time" and told her, in front of her children, that she would be going to jail. Wesson said that Jack informed her that he had notified the police. Wesson said that she tried to reason with Jack, telling him that she had simply forgotten to pay and that she just wanted to settle the matter by paying for her prescriptions. Wesson further testified that Jack had told her that it did not matter to him whether she was guilty of theft under the law but that his job was loss prevention and that her leaving without paying for the items was a loss to Wal-Mart. Three Pell City police officers responded to Jack's earlier telephone call; they took Wesson into custody when they arrived.

Jack secured a warrant for theft of property in the third degree against Wesson. Wal-Mart then prosecuted Wesson in the municipal court. After a trial, the action was "dismissed by agreement," according to a notation on the case-action-summary sheet of the municipal-court criminal case. That document also indicates that Wesson paid court costs.

Wesson sued Wal-Mart and Jack, asserting claims of malicious prosecution and false imprisonment arising from the events of July 13, 2004, and the resulting criminal prosecution. Wal-Mart and Jack moved for a summary judgment, which Wesson opposed. As exhibits to their motion for a summary judgment, Wal-Mart and Jack submitted Wesson's deposition, Jack's deposition, the trial transcript of the criminal prosecution of Wesson, and the case-action-summary sheet of the municipal-court criminal action. Wal-Mart and Jack argued in their summary-judgment motion that Wesson could not establish the elements of a malicious-prosecution claim or a false-imprisonment claim. The trial court entered a summary judgment in favor of Wal-Mart and Jack. After her postjudgment motion was denied, Wesson appealed to the Alabama Supreme Court, which transferred the appeal to this court, pursuant to Ala. Code 1975, § 12-2-7(6).

On appeal, Wesson challenges the summary judgment in favor of Wal-Mart and Jack because, she says, genuine issues of material fact preclude the entry of a summary judgment. She specifically argues that she can establish the elements of her ... false-imprisonment claim. We disagree....

Turning now to the false-imprisonment claim, we note that.... [p]ursuant to Ala. Code 1975, § 15-10-14(a) and (c), both a merchant and its employee are immune from claims of false imprisonment instituted by a person detained on the suspicion of shoplifting, provided that the merchant or its employee had probable cause for believing that the person detained was attempting to shoplift. Those sections provide:

"(a) A peace officer, a merchant or a merchant's employee who has probable cause for believing that goods held for sale by the merchant have been unlawfully taken by a person and that he can recover them by taking the person into custody may, for the purpose of attempting to effect such recovery, take the person into custody and detain him in a reasonable manner for a reasonable length of time. Such taking into custody and detention by a peace officer, merchant or merchant's employee shall not render such police officer, merchant or merchant's employee criminally or civilly liable for false arrest, false imprisonment or unlawful detention."...

"(c) A merchant or a merchant's employee who causes such arrest as provided for in subsection (a) of this section of a person for larceny of goods held for sale shall not be criminally or civilly liable for false arrest or false imprisonment where the merchant or merchant's employee has probable cause for believing that the person arrested committed larceny of goods held for sale."...

... Jack had probable cause to suspect Wesson had purposefully failed to pay for her prescriptions based on the information he had available to him at the time of Wesson's detention. Wesson admits that she left the Wal-Mart store without paying for her prescriptions. Jack had information compiled by Wal-Mart indicating that Wesson had left the store without paying for her prescriptions on at least two other occasions, and Jack observed Wesson leaving the store on July 13, 2004, after having two opportunities to pay for her prescriptions. Because there existed probable cause to detain Wesson, Wal-Mart and Jack are immune from Wesson's false-imprisonment claim.

Because we have determined that Wesson failed to establish that Wal-Mart and Jack did not have probable cause to institute criminal proceedings against Wesson for theft of the prescriptions, we affirm the summary judgment in Wal-Mart's and Jack's favor on the malicious-prosecution claim. Likewise, because of the existence of probable cause for Wesson's detention, we affirm the summary judgment in favor of Wal-Mart and Jack on the false-imprisonment claim because, under § 15-10-14 (a) and (c), they are immune from that claim.

AFFIRMED.

Case Questions

1. Explain your position as to whether you believe that Wal-Mart employees had probable cause to detain Wesson for shoplifting given that the criminal case against her was dismissed.
2. Although the immunity statute protects merchants from shoplifters, does it make any allowance for the detention of customers? Should forgetful elders, or shoppers who are absent minded or confused, parents preoccupied with keeping track of their children, or people who for other reasons are not adequately focused on the legalities of their conduct be subject to detention by store security to the same extent as professional shoplifters ?

Defamation

Defamation is an intentional tort that is based on the policy that people should be able to enjoy their good names. This tort provides targeted individuals with remedies against persons who intentionally make malicious statements that injure the target's character, fame, or reputation. A publication is defamatory if it tends to lower a person in others' esteem. Language that is merely annoying cannot be defamatory. Generally, the truth of the statement is a complete defense in a suit for defamation because true statements are not considered to be malicious.

Libel and slander are both forms of defamation. **Libel** is defamation expressed by print, writing, signs, pictures, and in the absence of statutory provisions to the contrary, radio and television broadcasts. **Slander** involves spoken words that have been heard by someone other than the target.

The law treats some defamatory expressions as slanderous per se. Examples of **slander per se**

include falsely accusing another of committing a crime of moral turpitude (rape, murder, or selling narcotics); false accusations that another person has contracted a morally offensive communicative disease (such as leprosy, syphilis, gonorrhea, or AIDS), or defamatory expressions that interfere with another person's trade, business, or profession (saying that a banker is dishonest or that a doctor is a "quack"). In defamation cases, the law requires that special damages such as loss of job, loss of customers, or loss of credit be proven before the plaintiff can recover general damages, such as loss of reputation.[5] However, a plaintiff who proves slander per se is not required to prove special damages because such expressions are almost certain to harm the plaintiff's reputation and produce economic loss. Not having to prove special damages is very helpful to the plaintiff because they are difficult to prove. The defendant can usually lessen the amount of damages awarded by publishing a retraction.

Riddle v. Golden Isles Broadcasting, LLC
666 S.E.2d 75
Court of Appeals of Georgia
July 2, 2008

Ellington, Judge

A Glynn County jury found Golden Isles Broadcasting, LLC, liable to Travis S. Riddle for defamatory statements made in a radio broadcast and awarded him $100,000 in damages. Following the grant of a new trial as to damages only, a second jury awarded Riddle $25,000. Riddle appeals....

Riddle contends the trial court abused its discretion in finding that the first jury's award of $100,000 for slander per se was contrary to the preponderance of the evidence adduced in that trial and, therefore, erred in granting a new trial on the issue of damages....

The record reveals that, following a hearing on Golden Isles's motion for new trial, the trial court stated that "I feel like the amount [of the verdict] is excessive, so I am going to—unless [Riddle] agrees to reduce it to sixty thousand dollars, I'm going to grant a new trial." The judge did not explain his basis for concluding that the award was excessive, noting only that he had "never seen or heard about a slander case in any of the jurisdictions where [he] was the trial judge." Riddle did not agree to remit $40,000 of the damages awarded; consequently, the court issued an order finding the award of damages "excessive in that it was inconsistent with the preponderance of the evidence," and granted a new trial "as to the issue of damages."...

As the Supreme Court of Georgia has explained, "an excessive or inadequate verdict is a mistake of fact rather than of law and addresses itself to the discretion of the trial judge who, like the jury, saw the witnesses and heard the testimony."... Consequently, this Court is ordinarily loath to interfere and "[t]he trial court's decision on a motion for a new trial [pursuant to this Code section] will be upheld on appeal unless it was an abuse of discretion."...

In the first trial, the jury found Golden Isles Broadcasting liable to Riddle, a private person, for slander ... and awarded him $100,000 in damages. Riddle produced six witnesses who testified to having heard a Brunswick, Georgia ... WSEG 104.1 radio personality report that Riddle had either killed the mother of his child, that the police were looking for him, or that he had been charged with murder. Jodi Howard, the woman Riddle was alleged to have murdered, was in fact alive and testified at both trials.

Two of Riddle's witnesses testified that while they personally did not believe the broadcast, Riddle's good reputation in the community suffered as a consequence. Riddle, a Brunswick-area rap musician, testified that he had established a positive image in the Brunswick community and with his growing fan base, and that his music did not condone materialism, violence, drug abuse, or the disparaging of women. In fact, in his hit song "Daddy's Little Boy," which WSEG 104.1 played as often as 42 times per week, Riddle presented himself as a positive role model for fathers. Witnesses testified that after the broadcast, radio stations (including Brunswick, Hinesville, and Savannah stations) stopped playing Riddle's music. The evidence showed that Riddle had invested heavily in his nascent music career, and he was beginning to reap the rewards—he had filled local clubs, had successfully promoted his first CD, had appeared on MTV, had launched two commercials on cable television, had moved to Atlanta to join the larger music scene, had begun building a regional fan base, and had been offered a $300,000 distribution deal by a recruiter with Universal Records—but after the Golden Isles broadcast, Riddle's career foundered, the rewards disappeared, and he had to "start over from scratch."

Golden Isles presented the testimony of radio personality Antonio Warrick, who denied making the slanderous statements, and of Golden Isles's business manager, who established the dates and times Warrick was on the air. Golden Isles, through the cross-examination of Riddle's witnesses, attempted to show that he had earned very little as a musician, that he had no written documentation to support his lost income claims, and that he made his living primarily as a part-time banquet server. Golden Isles attempted to demonstrate that Riddle's reputation did not suffer at all, and that Riddle's career suffered not as a consequence of its slander but because Riddle moved away from his Brunswick area fan base and because his one hit song had run its course.

Based on this evidence, the jury found Golden Isles liable for Warrick's slanderous remarks pursuant to OCGA § 51-5-10(a), pertaining to liability for defamatory statements in visual or sound broadcasts. Under this "defamacast" statute, when a slanderous statement is uttered "in or as a part of a visual or sound broadcast, the complaining party shall be allowed only such actual, consequential, or punitive damages as have been alleged and proved."... But as we have explained, "[t]he expression 'actual damages' is not necessarily limited to pecuniary loss, or loss of ability to earn money. Wounding a man's feelings is as much actual damage as breaking his limbs."... "Indeed, the more customary types of actual harm inflicted by defamatory falsehood include impairment of reputation and standing in the community, personal humiliation, and mental anguish and suffering." ... "Those were the damages sought by [Riddle] and they were n[ot] ... forbidden by ... Georgia law."...

And where, as here, the words uttered constituted slander per se by imputing the commission of a crime to another, the law infers an injury to the reputation without proof of special damages.... Such an injury falls within the category of general damages, "those which the law presumes to flow from any tortious act; they may be recovered without proof of any amount."... Therefore, in this case, the "measure or criterion of the general damages which the law infers as flowing from a slanderous statement which is actionable per se is the enlightened consciences of an impartial jury."... The court charged the jury on this law.

We have reviewed the transcript of the first trial, and we cannot say that the jury's award of $100,000 in general damages for slander per se was clearly so excessive as to be inconsistent with the preponderance of the evidence presented, as required by OCGA § 51-12-12(a) and (b). The record does not support an inference that Riddle had a bad reputation such that the imputation that he was a murderer would be less damaging to him than to any other citizen. In fact, that he was building a musical career based on his reputation as a positive role model is some evidence that the slander was especially damaging to his reputation. And although Golden Isles presented some evidence that Riddle's career may have suffered as a result of his own choices or the vagaries of the music industry rather than as a result of the slander broadcast to the heart of his fan base, we cannot say that Golden Isles's damages evidence outweighed that presented by Riddle. Therefore we must conclude that, under these circumstances, the trial court was not authorized to interfere with the jury's verdict and erred in granting a new trial as to damages under OCGA § 51-12-12(a) and (b)....

Judgment reversed.

Case Questions

1. Why were the radio personality's on-air comments about Riddle slanderous per se?
2. According to the appellate court, what types of injury can be considered to be "actual damages" in a slander case?

INTERNET TIP

Readers should consider reading the thought-provoking 2009 slander case of *Williams v. Tharp* on the textbook's website. The case's two plaintiffs were on their way back after an uneventful trip to a neighborhood pizza shop, where they had purchased a carryout pizza. They were utterly unprepared for what was about to transpire. Upon arriving at their intended destination, the home of one plaintiff, the two were apprehended at gunpoint by police officers. With their neighbors and family members looking on, the plaintiffs were ordered to get down on their knees, handcuffed, and detained for a prolonged period of time. They were utterly unaware of what was going on and why. It turned out that one of the pizza store employees, a delivery driver, who had been present when the pizza was purchased, thought that he had seen one of the plaintiffs with a handgun in the shop. This information was relayed to police and ultimately was the reason the police intervened and apprehended the plaintiffs. It turned out that the pizza delivery driver had been mistaken about the handgun. The plaintiffs sued the pizza shop and delivery driver for false imprisonment and defamation (slander per se). The case was ultimately decided by the state supreme court, which ruled 3–2 against the plaintiffs. Both of the judges who voted in favor of the plaintiffs wrote very interesting dissenting opinions in this case. Excerpts from the majority opinion and both dissents are included with the online materials for chapter XI on the textbook's website.

Interference with Contract Relations

The underlying policy reason behind the intentional tort called **interference with contract relations** is the desire to strengthen our economy by promoting the stability of contracts. Strengthening the economy is important to the welfare of Americans both collectively and individually.

The intentional tort of interference with contractual relations takes place when a noncontracting party or third person wrongfully interferes with the contract relations between two or more contracting parties. (See Chapter X for a discussion of contracts.) The tort of interference includes all intentional invasions of contract relations, including any act injuring a person or destroying property that interferes with the performance of a contract. For example, this tort occurs when someone wrongfully prevents an employee from working for an employer or prevents a tenant from paying rent to the landlord.

In order to maintain an action against a third person for interference, the plaintiff must prove that the defendant maliciously and substantially interfered with the performance of a valid and enforceable contract. The motive or purpose of the interfering party is an important factor in determining liability.

Infliction of Mental Distress

The intentional tort called **infliction of mental distress** evolved out of the need to recognize that every person has a right to not be subjected intentionally and recklessly to severe emotional distress caused by some other person's outrageous conduct. A person has a cause of action for infliction of mental distress when the conduct of the defendant is serious in nature and causes anguish in the plaintiff's mind. Because it is difficult to prove mental anguish and to place a dollar amount on that injury, early cases allowed recovery for mental distress only when it was accompanied by some other tort, such as assault, battery, or false imprisonment. Today, the infliction of mental distress is generally considered to be a stand-alone intentional tort.

Recovery for mental distress is allowed only in situations involving extreme misconduct, for example, telling a wife the made-up story that her husband shot himself in the head. Mental worry, distress, grief, and mortification are elements of mental suffering from which an injured person can recover. Recovery is not available for mere annoyance, disappointment, or hurt feelings. For example, the mere disappointment of a grandfather because his grandchildren were prevented from visiting him on account of delay in the transmission of a fax message would not amount to mental distress.

Invasion of Privacy

The law recognizes one's right to be free from unwarranted publicity and, in general, one's right to be left alone. If one person invades the right of another to withhold self and property from public scrutiny, the invading party can be held liable in tort for invasion of the right of privacy. A suit for **invasion of privacy** may involve unwarranted publicity that places the plaintiff in a false light, intrudes into the plaintiff's private life, discloses embarrassing private facts, or uses the plaintiff's name or likeness for the defendant's gain. Generally, the motives of the defendant are unimportant.

The standard used to measure any type of invasion of privacy is that the effect must be highly offensive to a reasonable person. For example, if a frustrated creditor puts up a notice in a store window stating that a named debtor owes money, this is an invasion of the debtor's privacy.

Technological developments in information storage and communications have subjected the intimacies of everyone's private lives to exploitation. The law protects individuals against this type of encroachment. A person who has become a public figure has less protection, however, because society has a right to information of legitimate public interest.

Although invasion of privacy and defamation are similar, they are distinct intentional torts, and both may be included in a plaintiff's complaint. The difference between a right of privacy and a right to freedom from defamation is that the former is concerned with one's peace of mind, whereas the latter is concerned with one's reputation or character. Truth is generally not a defense for invasion of privacy.

INTERNET TIP

Readers can read on the textbook's website the case of *Elli Lake v. Wal-Mart Stores, Inc.* 582 N.W.2d 231. This is a 1998 case in which the Minnesota Supreme Court explains why it decided to recognize only three of the four types of activities that commonly are included in the tort of invasion of privacy.

NEGLIGENCE

The law recognizes a duty or obligation to conform to a certain standard of conduct for the protection of others against unreasonable risk of harm. If the person fails to conform to the required standard, and that failure causes damage or loss, the injured party has a cause of action for **negligence**. Negligence is the unintentional failure to live up to the community's ideal of reasonable care; it is not based on moral fault. The fact that defendants may have suffered losses of their own through their negligent acts does not render them any less liable for plaintiffs' injuries.

An infinite variety of possible situations makes the determination of an exact set of rules for negligent conduct impossible. Conduct that might be considered prudent in one situation may be deemed negligent in another, depending on such factors as the person's physical attributes, age, and knowledge, the person to whom the duty was owed, and the situation at the time. If the defendant could not reasonably foresee any injury as the result of a certain conduct, there is no negligence and no liability.

The elements necessary for a cause of action for the tort of negligence are (1) a duty or standard of care recognized by law, (2) a breach of the duty or failure to exercise the requisite care, and (3) the occurrence of harm proximately caused by the breach of duty. No cause of action in negligence is recognized if any of these elements are absent from the proof.

The plaintiff has the burden of proving, through the presentation of evidence, that the defendant was negligent. Unless the evidence is such that it can reasonably lead to but one conclusion, negligence is primarily a question of fact for the jury. A jury must decide whether the defendant acted as a reasonably prudent person would have under the circumstances—that is, a person having the same information, experience, physique, and professional skill. This standard makes no allowance for a person less intelligent than average.

Children are not held to the same standard as adults. A child must conform merely to the conduct of a reasonable person of like age, intelligence, and experience under like circumstances. This standard is subjective and holds a less intelligent child to what a similar child would do.

Malpractice

The term **malpractice** is a nonlegal term for negligence. Professional negligence takes different forms in different fields. Attorney negligence would include drafting a will but failing to see that it is properly attested; failing to file an answer in a timely manner on behalf of a client, with the result that the plaintiff wins by default; and failing to file suit prior to the running of the statute of limitation, thus barring the client's claim. Accountant negligence would occur if a client paid for an audit but the accountant failed to discover that the client's employees were engaging in embezzlement, exposing the client to postaudit losses that could have been prevented. The case of *Macomber v. Dillman* (Chapter VII) is an example of medical malpractice. In that case, a surgeon improperly performed a tubal ligation and the plaintiff subsequently gave birth to a child.

Plaintiffs in malpractice cases allege that the professional specifically breached a contractual duty (if the suit is in contract) or that the professional breached a duty of care imposed by law (if the suit is in tort). Professionals have a higher degree of knowledge, skills, or experience than a reasonable person and are required to use that capacity. They are generally required to act as would a reasonably skilled, prudent, competent, and experienced member of the profession in good standing within that state. Negligence in this area usually may be shown only by the use of expert testimony.

Duty of Care

There can be no actionable negligence when there is no legal duty. Common law duty is found by courts when the kind of relationship that exists between the parties to a dispute requires the legal recognition of a duty of care. Legislative acts may also prescribe standards of conduct required of a reasonable person. It may be argued that a reasonable person would obey statutes such as traffic laws, ordinances, and regulations of administrative bodies.

In the case of legislative acts, plaintiffs must establish that they are within the limited class of individuals intended to be protected by the statute. In addition, the harm suffered must be of the kind that the statute was intended to prevent. Often the class of people intended to be protected may be very broad. For example, regulations requiring the labeling of certain poisons are for the protection of anyone who may come in contact with the bottle. Many traffic laws are meant to protect other people on the highway. Once it is decided that a statute is applicable, most courts hold that an unexcused violation is conclusive as to the issue of negligence. In other words, it is **negligence per se**, and the issue of negligence does not go to the jury. However, some courts hold that the violation of such a statute is only evidence of negligence, which the jury may accept or reject as it sees fit.

Common law provides that one should guard against that which a reasonably prudent person would anticipate as likely to injure another.

Damages for an injury are not recoverable if it was not foreseen or could not have been foreseen or anticipated. It is not necessary that one anticipate the precise injury sustained, however.

Courts do not ignore the common practices of society in determining the duty or whether due care was exercised in a particular situation. The scope of the duty of care that a person owes depends on the relationship of the parties. For example, those who lack mental capacity, the young, and the inexperienced are entitled to a degree of care proportionate to their incapacity to care for themselves.

As a general rule, the law does not impose the duty to aid or protect another. However, a duty *is* imposed where there is a special relationship between the parties—for example, parents must go to the aid of their children, and employers must render protection to their employees. In addition, if one puts another in peril, that person must render aid. A person can also assume a duty through contract where the duty would not otherwise exist. Although persons seeing another in distress have no obligation to be Good Samaritans, if they choose to do so, they incur the duty of exercising ordinary care. Some states have changed this common law duty by passing Good Samaritan statutes that state that those administering emergency care are liable only if the acts performed constitute willful or wanton misconduct.

In the next case, a patient in a state psychiatric hospital successfully sued the hospital for negligence. The patient claimed that the hospital should have prevented her from injuring herself as a result of falling from a third floor window at the hospital.

Mississippi Department of Mental Health v. Julia R. Hall
2004-CA-01522-SCT
Supreme Court of Mississippi
August 24, 2006

Waller, Presiding Justice, for the Court
Julia Renee Hall filed a complaint against the East Mississippi State Hospital ... alleging that, while she was a patient at East Mississippi, she sustained serious injuries after falling from a third-story window. After

conducting a bench trial pursuant to the Mississippi Tort Claims Act ... the Lauderdale County Circuit Court entered a judgment against East Mississippi in the amount of $250,000....

Facts

Julia Renee Hall, who was 25 years old at the time of the accident, has been institutionalized at different mental health facilities since she was 13 years old. Her latest admitting diagnosis was schizophrenia, disorganized type, borderline; and borderline personality disorder. Her discharge diagnosis from her last stay at East Mississippi ... was Axis One: schizoaffective disorder, bipolar type; alcohol dependency, in remission; amphetamine abuse, in remission; cannabis abuse, in remission; Axis Two: borderline personality disorder. She has been civilly committed to East Mississippi on four different occasions.

On June 4, 2001, Hall became convinced that she would be transferred to the "back building," a facility for chronically ill patients. Hall and other patients believed that the back building was an area where violence and abuse run rampant among the patients and where there was little to no hope for recovery.... Angela Eason, a staff member, filed the following report about what occurred the afternoon of June 4:

> Pam Johnson and I took the patients out for a smoke break at 5:00 o'clock, 1700.... When these patients finished smoking, we returned to the unit on the elevator where the patients started talking about the back building and asking why would a patient get sent to those buildings. I explained it's usually they can't be stabilized on medications or patients that just keep on cycling through the system time and time again.
>
> Julia Hall then laughed and said, You mean like me? I then said, I haven't heard your name come up about going to the back building, but you do keep moving up and down between second (a less restrictive ward) and third and you need to get it together. You are too young to be institutionalized all your life.

When they returned to the third-floor ward, Hall was "hysterical" and "crying" because she thought that the staff was going to transfer her to the back building. Patients Amanda Neal and Regina O'Bryant told Hall that they had a plan in place to escape and coaxed Hall to join them. Neal and O'Bryant's plan was to escape through a third-story window in the all-purpose conference room which adjoined the nurses' station. The door to the room was not locked, and there was no security screen on the window. The window was inoperable, but the women somehow removed a window pane. The group took sheets from a linen closet on the floor which was also unlocked. They entered and exited the conference room several times before Hall actually went out the window and

began climbing down a "rope" created by tying the sheets together. Hall lost her footing and fell to the ground. She suffered multiple fractures of the right leg, necessitating eight surgeries so far. Her right foot and heel have become infected several times due to soft tissue damage. She has undergone bone and skin grafts. At the time of the hearing, her right foot and lower leg were swollen and appeared to be deformed, and she noticeably limped. The circuit judge found that Hall would "never be able to hold gainful employment of any consequence for the rest of her life," and that "she has a future of probable repeated and long-term mental health treatment in institutions."...

The circuit judge found that $1,000,000 for actual and compensatory damages ... was appropriate. He allocated fault as follows: East Mississippi, 50%; Hall, 25%; Neal, 12-1/2%; and O'Bryant, 12-1/2%. Then, applying the cap on compensatory damages as set out in Miss. Code Ann. § 11-46-15 ... the circuit judge entered a judgment against East Mississippi in the amount of $250,000. East Mississippi appealed.

Discussion

"A circuit court judge sitting without a jury is accorded the same deference with regard to his findings as a chancellor, and his findings are safe on appeal where they are supported by substantial, credible, and reasonable evidence." ...

WHETHER EAST MISSISSIPPI HAD A DUTY TO PREVENT HALL FROM HARMING HERSELF BY ATTEMPTING TO ESCAPE THROUGH THE THIRD STORY WINDOW.

To prevail on a negligence claim, a plaintiff must establish by a preponderance of the evidence each of the elements of negligence: duty, breach, causation and injury.... The cause of Hall's injuries was her fall from the third-story window, and the parties stipulate to Hall's injuries. Therefore, at issue is whether East Mississippi had a duty to prevent Hall from harming herself by attempting to escape through the third-story window and whether that duty was breached.

Standard of Care for Patients with Mental Impairments

A state facility providing mental health care is statutorily mandated to provide "proper care and treatment, best adapted, according to contemporary professional standards." ... Neither the Legislature nor Mississippi courts have defined "contemporary professional standards," but, in dicta, this Court, speaking through the learned Presiding Justice Banks, commented, "[p]ersons deemed incapable of making rational judgments, such that they must be committed, are not to be protected by a lesser standard than reasonable care under the circumstances." ... In Texas, "[a] hospital is under a duty to exercise reasonable care to safeguard the patient from any known or reasonably apprehensible danger from herself and to exercise such reasonable care for her safety as her mental and physical condition, if known, may require."...

The Texas standard of care for the duty a hospital owes to a patient is similar to what we enunciated in *Carrington*. It is flexible in that the duty owed to patients may increase depending on the physical or mental condition of the patient. It can therefore be applied to different fact situations. We therefore adopt the Texas standard of care.

Duties Owed to Hall
Wood Hiatt, M.D., a board-certified psychiatrist ... testified that East Mississippi had the duty to protect patients from the consequences of their own dangerous behavior, to lock doors to rooms where a patient could be present without supervision, and to put safety screens on windows in rooms where a patient could be present without supervision. Dr. Hiatt also testified that East Mississippi staff was required to know the location of each patient and the actions in which each patient was engaged. Hall had attempted suicide in March of 2001, and she should have been under "special observation." The May 15, 2001, progress notes concerning Hall state that Hall was a "danger to herself and others." Hall became argumentative with a staff member on May 31 and was placed on the third-floor ward, which was a locked unit.

Dr. Hiatt further testified that East Mississippi breached the above-referenced duties by allowing third-floor ward patients to freely enter and leave an unlocked room without supervision, to have access to the linen closet, and to be without supervision long enough to take sheets out of the linen closet, make a rope out of the sheets, pry the window open in the conference room, take off their pajamas and put on regular clothes, attach the rope to a table in the conference room, and climb out the window. What astounds the Court is that the three women were coming in and out of the supposedly off-limits conference room which was right next to the nurse's station.

Also, each patient was to be checked every thirty minutes. Whoever staffed the nurse's station or monitored the patients during these events should have become suspicious about the women's activities. Someone should have noticed that the three women had pajamas on and then they changed into regular clothes. Hall testified that most of the nurse's aides were "watching television."

We find, as the circuit court did, based on Dr. Hiatt's testimony, East Mississippi breached the duties of care owed to Hall.

Foreseeability
East Mississippi contends that it committed no negligent acts because Hall's injury was unforeseeable....

In response, Hall points out that ... the fact that an injury rarely occurs, or has never happened, is insufficient to protect the actor from a finding of negligence.

The evidence adduced at trial supports the circuit judge's finding that Hall's escape attempt and injuries were foreseeable. Patricia Dudley, M.D., an East Mississippi staff psychiatrist, testified that it is common knowledge that patients will try to climb out windows; a staff nurse testified that any rooms where patients could be present without supervision should have security screens on the windows (all of the patients' rooms had security screens); and another staff psychiatrist testified that the staff was aware that patients would try to leave the third floor ward. Finally, Dr. Hiatt testified that mental hospital staff should know that psychiatric patients will attempt to escape.

The circuit court found that East Mississippi had a duty to keep unsupervised rooms locked, to place safety screens on windows in unsupervised areas, and to monitor patients' activities, that East Mississippi breached these duties on the night in question, and that the injuries suffered by Hall were reasonably foreseeable. We find that the circuit court's findings were supported by substantial and credible evidence....

Conclusion
For these reasons, we affirm the circuit court's judgment in favor of Julia Renee Hall.
AFFIRMED...

Case Questions

1. Why did the Mississippi Supreme Court "adopt" the Texas duty of care for use in Mississippi?
2. Why did Mississippi's highest court determine that Hall's injury was foreseeable?

3. Why did the hospital, which was found by the trial court to be 50 percent responsible for Hall's injuries, end up only having to pay $250,000?

 This case involves an alleged violation of the rule of general application in misfeasance cases that one has a legal duty to exercise ordinary care to prevent others from being injured as a result of one's conduct. How would Immanuel Kant probably react to this legal duty of ordinary care?

Liability Rules for Specialized Activities

The ordinary principles of negligence do not govern occupiers' liability to those entering their premises. For example, the duty the land occupier or possessor owes to a trespasser is less than the duty the possessor owes to the general public under the ordinary principles of negligence. The special rules regarding liability of the possessor of land stem from the English tradition of high regard for land and from the dominance and prestige of the English landowning class. In the eighteenth and nineteenth centuries, owners of land were considered sovereigns within their own boundaries and were privileged to do what they pleased within their domains. The unrestricted use of land was favored over human welfare. Visitors were classified as **invitees, licensees,** or **trespassers**. Although English law has since rejected these distinctions, they remain part of the U.S. common law.

An invitee is either a **public invitee** or a **business visitor**. A public invitee is a member of the public who enters land for the purpose for which the land is held open to the public, for example, a customer who enters a store. A business visitor enters land for a purpose directly or indirectly connected with business dealings with the possessor of the land. Thus, plumbers, electricians, trash collectors, and letter carriers are classified as business invites. Invites are given the greatest protection by the courts. A landowner owes the invitee a duty to exercise ordinary care under the usual principles of negligence liability, and must exercise reasonable care to make the premises safe. This preferred status applies only to the area of invitation.

One who enters or remains on land by virtue of the possessor's implied or express consent is a licensee, for example, door-to-door salespeople or social guests. In addition, police officers and firefighters are usually classified as licensees because they often come on premises unexpectedly and it would not be fair to hold possessors to the standard of care applicable to invites. Licensees must ordinarily accept the premises as they find them and look out for their own welfare. This is based on the principle that land occupiers cannot be expected to exercise a higher degree of care for licensees than they would for themselves. A possessor of land generally owes the licensee only the duty to refrain from willful or wanton misconduct; however, the courts have developed some exceptions to this rule. With respect to active operations, for example, the possessor of land is subject to liability to licensees for injury caused by failure to exercise reasonable care for their safety. What might constitute activities dangerous to licensees depends on the court's interpretation, and knowledge of the nature of the activities normally precludes recovery by the licensee. Generally, the possessor of land is under a duty to give warning of known dangers.

A **trespasser** is one who enters and remains on the land of another without the possessor's expressed or implied consent. Licensees or invades may become trespassers when they venture into an area where they are not invited or expected to venture, or if they remain on the premises for longer than necessary. Generally, possessors of land are not liable to trespassers for physical harm caused by their failure either to exercise reasonable care to make their land safe for their reception or to carry on their activities so as not to endanger them. The only duty that is owed to a trespasser by an occupier of land is to refrain from willful or wanton misconduct. However, a duty of reasonable care is owed to an adult trespasser whose presence has been discovered or who habitually intrudes on a limited area.

Reasonable care is also owed to the child trespasser whose presence is foreseeable.

Many have questioned the legal and moral justification of a rule that determines the legal protection of a person's life and limb according to this classification scheme. Although courts have been reluctant to abandon the land occupier's preferred position set forth by history and precedent, some courts have replaced the common law distinction with ordinary principles of negligence to govern occupiers' liability to those entering their premises.

The following case is from North Dakota, a state that has abandoned the common law distinctions. The defendants in *Schmidt v. Gateway Community Fellowship* were sponsors of an outdoor automotive show that was being held in a shopping mall parking lot. The defendants persuaded the trial court that they were immune from suit under the state's recreational use immunity law and the court granted them summary judgment. The plaintiff, who had injured her ankle while attending the show appealed to the state supreme court. She maintained that the trial court's conclusion was erroneous in that these defendants were not entitled to protection under the recreational immunity statute.

Schmidt v. Gateway Community Fellowship
2010 ND 69
Supreme Court of North Dakota.
April 8, 2010

Kapsner, Justice

Jacqueline and Randall Schmidt appeal from a summary judgment dismissing their personal injury action against Gateway Community Fellowship and North Bismarck Associates II after the district court decided Gateway Community Fellowship and North Bismarck Associates II were entitled to recreational use immunity because Jacqueline Schmidt entered a parking lot at a shopping mall for recreational purposes and she was not charged to enter the premises. The Schmidts argue there are factual issues about whether Jacqueline Schmidt entered the premises for recreational purposes and whether there was a charge for her entry to the premises....

I

The Schmidts alleged Jacqueline Schmidt injured her right ankle on September 14, 2002, when she stepped in a hole in a paved parking lot on the north side of Gateway Mall shopping center in Bismarck while attending an outdoor automotive show and skateboarding exhibition sponsored by Gateway Community Fellowship, a non-profit church affiliated with the Church of God. At the time, Gateway Community Fellowship leased space for church services inside Gateway Mall from North Bismarck Associates II, the mall owner.

On September 14, 2002, Gateway Community Fellowship sponsored an outdoor automotive show and skateboarding exhibition, the "Impact Auto Explosion," on a paved lot on the north side of Gateway Mall from 10 a.m. to 4 p.m., which was during the mall's regular Saturday business hours ... The public was not charged an admission fee for entry to the exhibition, but Gateway Community Fellowship procured exhibition sponsors to defray costs. Additionally, the automotive show included several contests, and Gateway Community Fellowship charged car owners a registration fee to enter the contests.... The ... mall manager for North Bismarck Associates II directed Gateway Community Fellowship to hold the exhibition ... parking lot on the north side of Gateway Mall to increase visibility from Century Avenue in Bismarck. North Bismarck Associates II did not separately charge Gateway Community Fellowship for use of the parking lot.... The parking lot on the north side of Gateway Mall had been part of a lumberyard of a previous mall tenant, and the area had holes and depressions in the concrete from the removal of posts that had formed part of an enclosure around the lumberyard. According to North Bismarck Associates II, the area of the parking lot used for the 2002 exhibition usually was roped off to be less accessible by the public.

On September 14, 2002, Jacqueline Schmidt and her son were driving by ... when they saw activity in the parking lot north of ... Gateway Mall, and they stopped at the exhibition. According to Jacqueline Schmidt, they decided "it would be fun. They had skateboarders, and they had music, and it was a nice day out.... We were enjoying ourselves. We were watching the skateboarders. We were looking around, looking at the vehicles. It was a pleasant day out. It was very nice out, and we were just enjoying spending time together, looking at the activities."

Jacqueline Schmidt and her son were not charged an admission fee for entry to the property or to the exhibition. According to her, she severely injured her right ankle as she walked across the parking lot and stepped in a posthole from the prior tenant's lumberyard.

The Schmidts sued Gateway Community Fellowship and North Bismarck Associates II, alleging they negligently and carelessly failed to eliminate the holes in the parking lot or to warn exhibition attendees about the holes and were liable for the hazardous condition on the premises. Gateway Community Fellowship and North Bismarck Associates II separately answered, denying they were negligent and claiming the Schmidts' action was barred by recreational use immunity under N.D.C.C. ch. 53-08. Gateway Community Fellowship and North Bismarck Associates II separately moved for summary judgment, arguing they were entitled to recreational use immunity ... because the premises were used for recreational purposes and Jacqueline Schmidt was not charged to enter the premises.

The district court granted summary judgment, concluding Gateway Community Fellowship and North Bismarck Associates II were entitled to recreational use immunity, because Jacqueline Schmidt entered the land for the recreational purpose of enjoying the exhibition with her son and she was not charged to enter the premises. The court also decided the statutory provisions for recreational use immunity were not unconstitutional as applied to the Schmidts' action.

II

Summary judgment is a procedural device for promptly resolving a controversy on the merits without a trial if there are no genuine issues of material fact or inferences that reasonably can be drawn from undisputed facts, or if the only issues to be resolved are questions of law....

III

Under North Dakota law for premises liability, general negligence principles govern a landowner's duty of care to persons who are not trespassers on the premises .... See *O'Leary v. Coenen*, ... (N.D. 1977) (abandoning common law categories of licensee and invitee for premises liability and retaining standard that owner owes no duty to trespasser except to refrain from harming trespasser in willful and wanton manner). Thus, a landowner or occupier of premises generally owes a duty to lawful entrants to exercise reasonable care to maintain the property in a reasonably safe condition in view of all the circumstances, including the likelihood of injury to another, the

seriousness of injury, and the burden of avoiding the risk....

Under that formulation, an owner or possessor of commercial property owes a duty to lawful entrants to exercise reasonable care to maintain the property in a reasonably safe condition in view of all the circumstances, including the likelihood of injury to another, the seriousness of injury, and the burden of avoiding the risk... 1 Premises Liability Law and Practice, at § 4.01[2][a] (explaining owner or possessor of commercial property must warn entrants of all known dangers, must inspect premises to discover hidden dangers, and must provide proper warning of known dangers); 62 Am. Jur. 2d Premises Liability, §§ 435, 439 (2005) (discussing commercial property owner's duty to customers and potential customers in shopping centers and malls). Similarly, a church or religious institution generally owes the same duty of care to lawful entrants on its premises....

In 1965, the Legislature enacted recreational use immunity statutes to encourage landowners to open their land for recreational purposes by giving them immunity from suit under certain circumstances.'"

Under N.D.C.C. § 53-08-02, "an owner of land owes no duty of care to keep the premises safe for entry or use by others for recreational purposes, or to give any warning of a dangerous condition, use, structure, or activity on such premises to persons entering for such purposes." Section 53-08-03, N.D.C.C., also provides:

Subject to the provisions of section 53-08-05, an owner of land who either directly or indirectly invites or permits without charge any person to use such property for recreational purposes does not thereby:

1. Extend any assurance that the premises are safe for any purpose;
2. Confer upon such persons the legal status of an invitee or licensee to whom a duty of care is owed; or
3. Assume responsibility for or incur liability for any injury to person or property caused by an act or omission of such persons....

... In 1995 ... the Legislature amended the definition of "recreational purposes" to its present form to cover "all recreational activities."...

IV

The Schmidts argue the district court did not view the evidence in the light most favorable to them and erred in finding, as a matter of law, that Jacqueline Schmidt's use of the land was recreational in character and that there was no charge for her to enter the land. They argue the court erred in failing to weigh the business purposes of Gateway Community Fellowship and North Bismarck Associates II in having the exhibition on the dangerous parking lot. They claim Gateway Community Fellowship's purpose was to increase membership, including tithing, and North Bismarck Associate's purpose was to increase foot traffic for its Gateway Mall tenants.... The Schmidts ... also assert a factual issue exists in this case because, although Gateway Community Fellowship did not directly charge Jacqueline Schmidt to enter the exhibition, it procured sponsors for the exhibition and charged contestants a registration fee to enter the contests in the automotive show....

A common thread under our case law interpreting the recreational use immunity statutes is that the intent of both the owner and the user are relevant to the analysis and that the location and nature of the injured person's conduct when the injury occurs are also relevant.... Other jurisdictions have acknowledged that cases involving claims of recreational use immunity involve fact-driven inquiries in which nonrecreational uses or purposes may be mixed with recreational uses or purposes....

In *Auman v. School Distr. of Stanley-Boyd*, 2001 WI 125, ..., the Wisconsin Supreme Court said the line between recreational and nonrecreational purposes was an intensely fact-driven inquiry and reiterated the test for resolving the issue:

Although the injured person's subjective assessment of the activity is pertinent, it is not controlling. A court must consider the nature of the property, the nature of the owner's activity, and the reason the injured person is on the property. A court should consider the totality of circumstances surrounding the activity, including the intrinsic nature, purpose, and consequences of the activity. A court should apply a reasonable person standard to determine whether the person entered the property to engage in a recreational activity.

Under N.D.C.C. ch. 53-08 and our caselaw interpreting those provisions, we decline to construe our recreational use statutes to necessarily provide a commercial landowner immunity where there is a recreational and commercial component to the landowner's operation. We conclude the rationale and balancing test ... provide persuasive authority for construing our statutes and assessing mixed use cases. We hold that [the Auman] balancing test applies to our recreational use immunity statutes in mixed use cases and that inquiry generally involves resolution of factual issues unless the facts are such that reasonable minds could not differ.

... We conclude the facts in this case are not such that reasonable persons could reach one conclusion and there are disputed factual issues about whether North Bismarck Associates II and Gateway Community Fellowship are entitled to recreational use immunity. We therefore conclude resolution of the issue by summary judgment was inappropriate and a remand is necessary for the trier of fact to apply the balancing test to this mixed use case....

We reverse the summary judgment and remand for proceedings consistent with this opinion.

Case Questions

1. What would it mean to these parties if ultimately the North Dakota courts concluded that the trial court was correct and that the plaintiff was engaging in a recreational activity when attending the auto show in the mall parking lot?
2. The North Dakota Supreme Court felt that the record was insufficient to permit the trial court to decide this case by summary judgment. Assume that the facts revealed upon remand indicate that the auto show contained some elements that were essentially recreational and other elements that were commercial. Which party do you think should ultimately win the lawsuit? Why?

INTERNET TIP

Readers will find *Benejam v. Detroit Tigers, Inc.*, a case in which a state intermediate appellate court concluded that the Tigers had a limited duty to make their stadium reasonably safe for fans, on the textbook's website.

Proximate Cause

For the plaintiff to support a negligence action, there must be a reasonable connection between the negligent act of the defendant and the damage suffered by the plaintiff. For tort liability, however, proof of factual causation is not enough. Tort liability is predicated on the existence of **proximate cause.** Proximate cause means legal cause and consists of two elements: (1) **causation in fact,** and (2) **foreseeability.** A plaintiff must prove that his or her injuries were the actual or factual result of the defendant's actions. Causation in fact may be established directly or indirectly. Courts usually use a "but for" test to establish causation in fact: but for the defendant's negligence, the plaintiff's injuries would not have occurred. This test is an extremely broad one and could have far-reaching results.

Every event has many contributing causes, even though some may be very remote. The defendant is not relieved from liability merely because other causes have contributed to the result. In many situations, application of the "but-for" test will identify several persons who could be placed on a causation continuum. The question before the court in a negligence case is whether the conduct has been so significant and important a cause that the defendant should be legally responsible. For example, in a nighttime automobile accident, the fact that one of the drivers worked late at the office would be a factual cause of the collision. If she hadn't worked late, she wouldn't have been at the location of the accident. But this cause should not be recognized as a legal cause of the collision. Because cause demands that some boundary be set for the consequences of an act, proximate cause, rather than causation in fact, is used to determine liability.

An individual is only responsible for those consequences that are reasonably foreseeable, and will be relieved of liability for injuries that are not reasonably related to the negligent conduct. To illustrate, a driver drives his car carelessly and collides with another car, causing it to explode. Four blocks away, a nurse carrying a baby is startled by the explosion and drops the infant. It is doubtful if any court would hold the driver liable to the infant, even though the driver was negligent and was the factual cause of the infant's injury. The baby's injury is so far removed from the driver that it would be unfair to hold the driver liable. The driver could not reasonably have foreseen the injury sustained by the infant. In other words, the driving would not be the proximate cause of the injury.

If there is more than one cause for a single injury, liability is possible if each alone would have been sufficient to cause the harm without the other. If there are joint tortfeasors of a single injury, each possible tortfeasor's actions must be examined to see if the acts were so closely related to the damage to have proximately caused the plaintiff's injury.

The plaintiffs in the following case, West and Richardson, were injured when their car was involved in a head-on collision with another vehicle operated by an intoxicated driver named Tarver. Tarver had been driving the wrong way at the time of the collision and had just left defendant's nearby gas station, where a store employee assisted him with pumping gas into his vehicle.

Gary L. West v. East Tennessee Pioneer Oil Co.
172 S.W.3d 545
Supreme Court of Tennessee
August 18, 2005

William M. Barker, J.

... The defendant East Tennessee Pioneer Oil Company operates an Exxon convenience store on U.S. Highway 11W, also known as Rutledge Pike, in Knox County, Tennessee. The store consists of three connected portions—a convenience market and gas station, an ice cream counter, and a "Huddle House" restaurant—each owned and operated by the defendant.

On July 22, 2000, Brian Tarver ("Tarver") entered the convenience store. Tarver had been drinking alcohol, and the plaintiffs allege that upon entering the store he was obviously intoxicated. There was [sic] a large number of customers in the store at the time, with a long line of people waiting at the check-out counter. Tarver pushed his way to the front of the line and asked the clerk if she would "go get [him] some beer." The clerk, Dorothy Thomas ("Thomas"), stated in her deposition that Tarver smelled of beer and staggered as he walked. Thomas refused to sell him beer because, in her opinion, Tarver was intoxicated. After being denied beer, Tarver began cursing loudly, talking to Thomas in a threatening manner, and generally causing a disturbance inside the store. Tarver then managed to pull three crumpled one-dollar bills out of his pocket and laid them on the counter. He told Thomas, "we need gas" and then turned to leave. A customer opened the door for Tarver, who staggered out of the store and back toward the gas pump where his car was parked.

A few moments later an alarm began "beeping" inside the store, alerting Thomas that someone was attempting to activate the gasoline pumps outside. After the "beeping" continued, Thomas concluded that a customer was having difficulty with the pump. Although the evidence conflicts on this point, Thomas testified that she could not see the pump ... so she asked the other employees in the store if someone would "go see who doesn't know what they're doing at the gas pump." Two off-duty employees were at the store: Candice Drinnon ("Drinnon"), who worked at both the Huddle House restaurant and the ice cream counter, and Roy Armani ("Armani") ... who worked in the Huddle House portion of the defendant's store. The accounts also differ as to how the events next unfolded. Thomas testified that both Drinnon and Armani were inside the store during this episode, and they went to assist the customer at the pumps at Thomas's request. Drinnon, on the other hand, testified that she and Armani were standing outside on the parking lot when they first saw Tarver and noticed he was having difficulty operating the pump. According to Drinnon, she and Armani walked over to assist Tarver without being asked to do so by Thomas or anyone else.

In any event, Drinnon and Armani came to the aid of the intoxicated Tarver, who could not push the correct button to activate the pump. Drinnon testified that upon approaching Tarver she could tell he had been drinking because she "could smell it on him." Drinnon also states, however, that she and Armani were not fully aware of the degree of Tarver's intoxication until after activating the pump. According to Drinnon, Tarver spoke normally, but, "when we seen him walk away, [we] could tell he was drunk." Drinnon pushed the correct button on the pump and then Thomas, the clerk behind the counter, activated the pump from inside the store which allowed the pump to operate. Tarver then apparently proceeded to operate the nozzle himself, obtaining the gasoline without any further assistance.

Tarver pumped three dollars' worth of gasoline, got back into his vehicle, and prepared to leave. Drinnon and Armani watched as Tarver, without turning on his vehicle's headlights, drove off the parking lot and into the wrong lane of traffic on Rutledge Pike, traveling southbound in the northbound lane. Drinnon then went back into the store and informed Thomas, the clerk, that Tarver had gotten three dollars' worth of gasoline and then driven away on the wrong side of the road. Thomas stated that this was her first indication that Tarver was driving; prior to this point she believed Tarver had been accompanied by another person and was not driving a vehicle himself.

At about the same time as Tarver was traveling south with no headlights on and in the wrong lane of traffic, the plaintiffs' vehicle was traveling north on Rutledge Pike, several miles in front of Tarver. One of the plaintiffs, Gary West, was driving while the other plaintiff, Michell Richardson, was a passenger. Tarver managed to travel 2.8 miles from the convenience store before striking the plaintiffs' vehicle head-on. Both of the plaintiffs sustained serious injuries in the accident....

During their ensuing investigation, the plaintiffs requested Dr. Jeffrey H. Hodgson, a mechanical engineering professor at the University of Tennessee, to examine the fuel tank of Tarver's vehicle. Based upon the results of his examination, Dr. Hodgson determined that at the time Tarver stopped at the defendant's store his vehicle contained only enough fuel to travel another 1.82 miles. Therefore, without the three dollars' worth of gas he obtained at the store, Tarver would have "run out" of gasoline approximately one mile before reaching the accident scene.

On June 1, 2001, the plaintiffs filed suit alleging that the defendant's employees were negligent in selling gasoline to the visibly intoxicated Tarver and assisting him in pumping it into his vehicle. The plaintiffs contended it was reasonably foreseeable that these actions would result in an automobile accident....

The defendant filed a motion for summary judgment.... Specifically, the defendant contended that it owed no duty of care to the plaintiffs while furnishing gasoline to Tarver and that its employees' actions were not a proximate cause of the accident....

Following a hearing on the motion, the trial court entered an order granting summary judgment in favor of the defendant.... Upon appeal, the Court of Appeals ... reversed the trial court on the negligence claim. The intermediate court held, inter alia, that "the affirmative acts of Defendant's employees in both selling gasoline to and in helping a visibly intoxicated Tarver pump the gasoline into his vehicle created a duty to act with due care."

We granted review.

Standard of Review

Summary judgment is appropriate when the moving party establishes that there is no genuine issue as to any material fact and that a judgment may be rendered as a matter of law....

Analysis I. Negligence Principles

A negligence claim requires proof of the following elements: (1) a duty of care owed by the defendant to the plaintiff; (2) conduct by the defendant falling below the standard of care amounting to a breach of that duty; (3) an injury or loss; (4) cause in fact; and (5) proximate or legal cause....

While we will discuss each of these elements in turn, our primary focus is on the first element: duty of care.

I. Duty

Although not a part of the early English common law, the concept of duty has become an essential element in all negligence claims.... The duty owed to the plaintiffs by the defendant is in all cases that of reasonable care under all of the circumstances.... Whether the defendant owed the plaintiffs a duty of care is a question of law to be determined by the court....

If a defendant fails to exercise reasonable care under the circumstances, then he or she has breached his or her duty to the plaintiffs. The term reasonable care must be given meaning in relation to the circumstances.... Reasonable care is to be determined by the risk entailed through probable dangers attending the particular situation and is to be commensurate with the risk of injury.... Thus, legal duty has been defined as the legal obligation owed by a defendant to a plaintiff to conform to a reasonable person standard of care for the protection against unreasonable risks of harm....

The risk involved must be one which is foreseeable; "a risk is foreseeable if a reasonable person could foresee the probability of its occurrence or if the person was on notice that the likelihood of danger to the party to whom is owed a duty is probable." ... "The plaintiff must show that the injury was a reasonably foreseeable probability, not just a remote possibility, and that some action within the [defendant's] power more probably than not would have prevented the injury."...

We employ a balancing approach to assess whether the risk to the plaintiff is unreasonable and thus gives rise to a duty to act with due care.... This Court has held that a risk is unreasonable, "'if the foreseeable probability and gravity of harm posed by defendant's conduct outweigh the burden upon defendant to engage in alternative conduct that would have prevented the harm.'"...

The defendant argues that it owed no duty of care to the plaintiffs because the intoxicated driver was merely a customer at the defendant's convenience store; thus there was no "special relationship" giving rise to a duty on the part of the defendant to control the actions of the customer.... In our view, the defendant misconstrues the plaintiffs' claims as being based upon a "special relationship" arising from the sale of gasoline to Mr. Tarver (the intoxicated driver). The plaintiffs' allegations do not revolve around any duty of the defendant to control the conduct of a customer. Instead, the claims are predicated on the defendant's employees' affirmative acts in contributing to the creation of a foreseeable and unreasonable risk of harm, i.e., providing mobility to a drunk driver which he otherwise would not have had, thus creating a risk to persons on the roadways. Viewed in this light, the balancing test set out above is appropriate to determine whether the defendant owed the plaintiffs a duty.

Simply stated, the defendant convenience store owed a duty to act with reasonable care under all the circumstances. Under the facts of this case, we conclude that the acts of the defendant in selling gasoline to an obviously intoxicated driver and/or assisting an obviously intoxicated driver in pumping gasoline into his vehicle created a foreseeable risk to persons on the roadways, including the plaintiffs. It is common knowledge that drunk driving directly results in accidents, injuries, and deaths....

We next examine the feasibility of alternative, safer conduct and the burdens associated with such alternative conduct. A safer alternative was readily available and easily feasible—simply refusing to sell gasoline to an obviously intoxicated driver. The clerk at the defendant's store had already refused to sell beer to Mr. Tarver. In fact, both state law ... and store policy required her to refuse to sell alcohol to intoxicated persons. It was also the clerk's understanding that she was never required to allow a customer to purchase any item, including gasoline. The relative usefulness and safety of this alternative conduct is obvious. All reasonable persons recognize that refraining from selling gasoline to or assisting intoxicated persons in pumping it into their vehicles will lead to safer roadways.

Based upon the foregoing analysis, we conclude that a convenience store employee owes a duty of reasonable care to persons on the roadways, including the plaintiffs, not to sell gasoline to a person whom the employee knows (or reasonably ought to know) to be intoxicated and to be the driver of the motor vehicle. Similarly, a convenience store employee also owes a duty of reasonable care not to assist in providing gasoline (in this case pumping the gasoline) to a person whom the employee knows (or reasonably ought to know) to be intoxicated and to be the driver of the motor vehicle. We stress that because "Foreseeability is the test of negligence,"... the convenience store employee must know that the individual is intoxicated and that the individual is the driver of the vehicle before a duty arises. It is a question of fact for a jury as to what the employee knew with respect to the individual's intoxication and status as driver. We also hasten to point out, as did the Court of Appeals, that by our decision today we do not hold that convenience store employees have a duty to physically restrain or otherwise prevent intoxicated persons from driving.

II. Breach of Duty, Injury or Loss, Cause in Fact, and Proximate Cause

Our conclusion that the defendant owed a duty to the plaintiffs does not completely resolve this case. The plaintiffs at trial still bear the burden of proving the remaining elements of negligence: breach of duty, injury or loss, cause in fact, and proximate cause. Although we have viewed the facts in the light most favorable to the plaintiffs for purposes of resolving this appeal, the record reflects genuine issues of material fact concerning each of these elements which the jury must resolve.

For instance, the jury must determine whether, in consideration of all the facts and circumstances presented, the employees failed to exercise due care resulting in a breach of their duty of care.... Another question of fact for the jury is whether the employees' actions can be attributed to the defendant, thus making the defendant vicariously liable for the employees' alleged negligence.... Furthermore, the plaintiffs must show that the defendant's employees' acts were the cause in fact of their injuries. While the affidavit from Dr. Hodgson provides probative evidence on this point, the credibility of the witness, the weight given to his testimony and whether this evidence establishes cause in fact are all issues for the jury.

The final element the plaintiffs must prove is proximate cause. While cause in fact establishes that the plaintiff's injury would not have occurred "but for" the defendant's conduct, proximate cause focuses on whether the law will extend responsibility for that conduct.... This Court has previously set out a three-prong test for proximate cause:

(1) the tortfeasor's conduct must have been a "substantial factor" in bringing about the harm being complained of; and (2) there is no rule or policy that should relieve the wrongdoer from liability because of the manner in which the negligence has resulted in the harm; and (3) the harm giving rise to the action could have reasonably been foreseen or anticipated by a person of ordinary intelligence and prudence....

The defendant argues that its employees' actions were not the proximate cause of the plaintiffs' injuries; rather, the injuries were caused solely by the actions of Mr. Tarver. The defendant asserts that its connection to the accident is so tenuous that proximate cause simply does not apply. We note however, "there is no requirement that a cause, to be regarded as the proximate cause of an injury, be the sole cause, the last act, or the one nearest to the injury, provided it is a substantial factor in producing the end result."... Viewing the evidence in the light most favorable to the plaintiffs, we conclude that a reasonable jury could find the acts of the convenience store employees were a substantial factor in bringing about the plaintiffs' accident and that this result was foreseeable. We further conclude there is no rule of law or policy that should relieve the defendant from liability. Accordingly, whether the defendant's employees' acts proximately caused the plaintiffs' injuries is a question for the jury....

Conclusion

In summary, we hold that the convenience store employees owed a duty of reasonable care to persons on the roadways, including the plaintiffs, when selling gasoline to an obviously intoxicated driver and/or assisting an obviously intoxicated driver in pumping the gasoline into his vehicle.... We offer no opinion concerning the ultimate resolution of this case, as the plaintiffs still bear the burden at trial of proving the other elements of negligence. Based upon the foregoing analysis, we conclude that the trial court erred in granting summary judgment in favor of the defendants.... Consequently, the judgment of the Court of Appeals is affirmed ... and the case is remanded for further proceedings consistent with this opinion.

Case Questions

1. What kind of test did the Tennessee Supreme Court say it would use in determining whether the gas station/convenience store operator owed a duty of care to the plaintiff in this case?
2. The defendant gas station/convenience store operator maintained that it owed no duty of care. What was the essence of the defendant's position on this issue?
3. What did the Tennessee Supreme Court conclude with respect to this issue?

INTERNET TIP

Readers visiting the textbook's website will find there the 2002 Texas case of *McClure v. Roch*, a case that discusses the distinction between invitees and licensees, proximate cause, and foreseeability.

Contributory Negligence and Assumption-of-Risk Defenses

Even after a plaintiff has proved that a defendant was negligent and that the negligence was the proximate cause of his or her injury, some states permit the defendant to counter by proving a defense. Contributory negligence and assumption of risk are two such defenses.

Contributory negligence is a defense that exists when the injured persons proximately contributed to their injuries by their own negligence. This defense is based on the theory that the plaintiff is held to the same standard of care as the defendant: that is, that of a reasonable person under like circumstances. When proven, contributory negligence will usually bar any recovery by the plaintiff.

To illustrate, D-1 is driving his car and P is his passenger. Both are injured in a collision with D-2's car. If both cars were driven negligently, D-1 could not recover from D-2 because his own negligence contributed to his own injuries. Yet P could recover from both D-1 and D-2, because they were both joint tortfeasors in causing P's injuries. The burden of proving contributory negligence is on the defendant. The defense of **assumption of risk** exists when the plaintiffs had knowledge of the risk and made the free choice of exposing themselves to it. Assumption of risk may be express or implied. In an express assumption of risk, the

plaintiff expressly agrees in advance that the defendant has no duty to care for him or her and is not liable for what would otherwise be negligent conduct. For example, parents often expressly assume the risk of personal injury to their children in conjunction with youth soccer, basketball, and baseball programs. Where the assumption of risk is implied, consent is manifested by the plaintiff's continued presence after he or she has become aware of the danger involved. The plaintiffs impliedly consent to take their chances concerning the defendant's negligence. For example, baseball fans who sit in unscreened seats at the ballpark know that balls and even bats may strike them; they implicitly agree to take a chance of being injured in this manner.

INTERNET TIP

North Carolina is one of the six states that continue to follow the contributory negligence/assumption of risk approach. Readers can find *Carolyn Alford v. Wanda E. Lowery*, a North Carolina case that illustrates how contributory negligence works, on the textbook's website.

Comparative Negligence

When the defense of contributory negligence is used in a non–comparative-negligence jurisdiction, the entire loss is placed on one party even when both are negligent. For this reason, most states now determine the amount of damage by comparing the negligence of the plaintiff with that of the defendant. Under this doctrine of **comparative negligence,** a negligent plaintiff may be able to recover a portion of the cost of an injury.

In negligence cases, comparative negligence divides the damages between the parties by reducing the plaintiff's damages in proportion to the extent of that person's contributory fault. The trier of fact in a case assigns a percentage of the total fault to the plaintiff, and the plaintiff's total damages are usually reduced by that percentage. For example, a plaintiff who was considered to be 40 percent at fault by the trier of fact would recover $1,200 if the total damages were determined to be $2,000.

The trial court in the following case improperly granted additur to the plaintiff in the next case in spite of the fact that the trial jury found the plaintiff to be 66.75 percent responsible for the collision that caused serious injuries to the plaintiff's eight-year-old son.

Anne Hockema v. J. S.
832 N.E.2d 537
Court of Appeals of Indiana, Second District
August 8, 2005

Vaidik, Judge
Case Summary
Seventeen-year-old Anne Hockema and her father Stanley Hockema appeal the trial court's grant of additur after the jury found Jacob Secrest to be 66.75% at fault and awarded $0 damages....

Facts and Procedural History
In September 2001, Anne was driving along Hanawalt Road in White County, Indiana. As she was driving, eight-year-old Jacob Secrest darted out into the road and collided with Hockema's vehicle. Jacob's nine-year-old sister, Erica Secrest, witnessed the collision, and Jacob's mother, Merri Secrest, came running out of her parents' house to assist Jacob immediately after the collision. Jacob's father, Eric Secrest, was not present at the scene of the accident. Jacob was transported to the hospital by ambulance with his mother accompanying him. As a result of the impact, Jacob broke his right elbow and collarbone, which required him to undergo surgery and attend physical therapy.

The Secrests filed a complaint for damages against Anne and Stanley ... (collectively, "the Hockemas"), which sought recovery for medical expenses; permanent injuries; emotional distress; loss of services; and pain and suffering. A jury trial ensued during which the parties stipulated that Jacob's medical expenses totaled $38,708.44....

The jury returned a defense verdict. In particular, the jury found Jacob to be 66.75% at fault, Anne to be 33.25% at fault, and awarded the Secrests $0 in damages.

The Secrests filed a motion to correct errors seeking additur or a new trial, in which it claimed that the jury erred by not awarding Jacob's parents damages for a percentage of the stipulated medical expenses.

The Hockemas responded by asserting that the Secrests "failed to take into account the expenses and damage claims made by the family members were derivative to Jacob's primary cause of action,"... and consequently, "the 'parent' plaintiffs cannot prevail if a jury decides against the 'child's' claim."... Following a hearing on the motion, the trial court entered judgment in favor of the Secrests for $12,780.56, which is 33.25% of the stipulated amount of medical expenses. In its Order ... the trial court stated:

> The Court instructed the Jury that there was a stipulation as to the medical expenses incurred by the parents in the sum of Thirty-eight Thousand Seven Hundred Eight Dollars Forty-four Cents ($38,708.44), and that the Jury in this matter found that the Defendant, Anne Hockema, was thirty-three point two-five percent (33.25%) negligent in the action.
>
> The Court had previously instructed the Jury that the parent's right of recovery for their medical expenses was not contingent on the child's right of recovery for his injuries.
>
> Therefore, the Court finds that the parents should be entitled to their stipulated expenses of thirty-three point two-five percent (33.25%) of Thirty-eight Thousand Seven Hundred Eight Dollars Forty-four Cents ($38,708.44).
>
> The Court directs that the jury verdict be modified in this matter that the Court now orders a judgment entered against the Defendant, Anne Hockema, in the sum of Twelve Thousand Eight Hundred Seventy Dollars Fifty-six Cents ($12,870.56).
>
> ... The Hockemas now appeal.

Discussion and Decision

The Hockemas argue that the trial court erred by granting the Secrests' request for additur following the jury's award of $0 damages to the Secrests....

The Hockemas claim that the trial court abused its discretion when it granted the Secrests' motion to correct error pursuant to Indiana Trial Rule 59(J)(5) and awarded $12,870.56 to the Secrests notwithstanding the jury's verdict of $0. Trial Rule 59(J)(5) provides:

> The court, if it determines that prejudicial or harmful error has been committed, shall take such action as will cure the error, including without limitation the following with respect to all or some of the parties and all or some of the errors: ... (5) In the case of excessive or inadequate damages, enter final judgment on the evidence for the amount of the proper damages, grant a new trial, or grant a new trial subject to additur or remittitur.

... This remedy is only available when the evidence is insufficient to support the verdict as a matter of law....

Trial courts must afford juries great latitude in making damage award determinations.... A verdict must be upheld if the award determination falls within the bounds of the evidence....

Curiously, the issue with which we are faced today —namely, whether a parent is precluded from recovering necessary medical expenses paid by them on behalf of an injured child whose comparative negligence exceeds the negligence of the tortfeasor—is an issue of first impression in Indiana. The Comparative Fault Act, now codified at Indiana Code 34-51-2, was adopted in Indiana in 1983 and went into effect in 1985... By adopting the Comparative Fault Act, the General Assembly rejected the common law doctrine of contributory negligence as a complete bar to recovery in negligence cases, ... thereby bringing this state in line with the vast majority of states that adhere to some form of a comparative fault law....

There are two basic forms of comparative fault laws, which are designated as "pure" or "modified." Under the "pure" form, a plaintiff may recover a percentage of his damages even though his fault exceeds that of the defendant.... Under "modified" comparative fault statutes, a plaintiff normally may recover a reduced amount of his damages so long as his negligence either does not equal ("modified forty-nine percent") or exceed that of the defendant ("modified fifty percent").... The Indiana statute is a type of modified fifty percent comparative fault law that requires, in some cases, consideration of the degree of fault of non-parties to the action as well as the fault of

the parties.... Thus, if a claimant is deemed to be more than fifty percent at fault, then the claimant is barred from recovery....

The jury found Jacob Secrest to be 66.75% at fault for the accident. Thus, under Indiana's comparative fault scheme, Jacob is barred from recovering any damages from Hockema. Nonetheless, Eric and Merri Secrest argue that they should be able to recover a percentage of the stipulated medical expenses, and therefore the trial court did not err by granting their request for additur. We disagree.

Eric and Merri Secrest, as the parents of Jacob, are responsible for the costs of the medical attention furnished to Jacob by the various providers.... ("The parent also is liable because of his common law and, in some instances, statutory duty to support and maintain his child.... This parental duty includes the provision of necessary medical care."). The obligation to pay medical expenses is not a damage inflicted directly on the parents; rather, the parents' debt arises only because, as parents, they are obligated to contract for necessary medical care for their minor child. If the child was not a minor, the medical expenses would be his own, and the parents would not be obligated to pay them. The right of the parents to recover the child's medical expenses, hence, rests upon the child's right to recover and therefore may be appropriately categorized as a derivative right.... Accordingly, when a child is injured, the parent has a cause of action against the tortfeasor to recover compensation for the necessary medical treatment arising from the tortious conduct.... Because of the derivative nature of this right, however, the right is not absolute. Instead, the right to recover medical expenses may be barred by the child's comparative negligence if it exceeds the negligence of the tortfeasor....

Thus, although Indiana has abandoned contributory negligence in cases such as the one with which we are faced today, the concept of imputation is still viable under our comparative fault scheme. This means that if a child's comparative fault is less than fifty percent, then a parent may recover the appropriate percentage of the medical expenses paid on behalf of the child from the tortfeasors. If, however, the child's comparative fault exceeds fifty percent, the parents are barred from recovering medical expenses.

As mentioned above, the jury determined that Jacob was 66.75% at fault and that Anne was 33.25% at fault. By seeking to recover a percentage of the stipulated medical expenses in spite of Jacob's negligence exceeding that of Anne's, the Secrests essentially are requesting that we abandon the concept of modified comparative fault in favor of a pure comparative fault scheme with regard to medical expenses. The

Indiana General Assembly has chosen to adopt a modified comparative fault system. It is not our province to override the legislature's clear intent of barring recovery when a claimant is more than fifty percent at fault.

Consequently, the trial court erred by granting additur, and we reverse and remand with instructions that the jury verdict be reinstated....

Reversed and remanded.

Case Questions

1. What are the advantages and disadvantages of comparative negligence in comparison to contributory negligence?
2. Under what circumstances will a court disturb a jury's allocation of the percentages of fault?
3. Which of the two basic forms of comparative fault laws do you think to be fairer? Explain your rationale.

Negligence and Product Liability

Plaintiffs can recover in negligence by proving that a manufacturer's conduct violated the reasonable person standard and proximately caused injury. The manufacturer's allegedly tortious conduct could relate to any aspect of product design, manufacturing, quality control, packaging, and/or warnings.

In product liability suits, it is often difficult to prove the defendant's act or omission that caused the plaintiff's injury. Thus, in the interests of justice, courts developed the doctrine of *res ipsa loquitur* ("the thing speaks for itself"). This doctrine permits plaintiffs to circumstantially prove negligence if the following facts are proved: (1) the defendant had exclusive control over the allegedly defective product during manufacture, (2) under normal circumstances, the plaintiff would not have been injured by the product if the defendant had exercised ordinary care, and (3) the plaintiff's conduct did not contribute significantly to the accident. From the proved facts, the law permits the jurors to infer a fact for which there is no direct, explicit proof—the

defendant's negligent act or omission. The trial judge will instruct the jurors that the law permits them to consider the inferred fact as well as the proved facts in deciding whether the defendant was negligent.

The following case illustrates typical problems associated with a case involving negligent failure to warn. A manufacturer's duty to warn consumers depends on the nature of the product. Warnings are unnecessary for products that are obviously dangerous to everyone (knives, saws, and firearms). However, for products that may contain hazards that are not obvious, manufacturers have a duty to warn if the average person would not have known about a safety hazard. If the plaintiff is knowledgeable about the hazard that the warning would have addressed, the manufacturer's negligent failure to warn would not have proximately caused the plaintiff's injuries. Thus in such cases the extent of the plaintiff's actual knowledge and familiarity with the hazard and the product are relevant to the issue of causation.

Laaperi v. Sears Roebuck & Co., Inc.
787 F.2d 726
U.S. Court of Appeals, First Circuit
March 31, 1986

Campbell, Chief Judge

This is an appeal from jury verdicts totaling $1.8 million entered in a product liability suit against defendants Sears, Roebuck & Co. and Pittway Corporation. The actions were brought by Albin Laaperi as administrator

of the estates of his three sons, all of whom were killed in a fire in their home in December 1976, and as father and next friend of his daughter, Janet, who was injured in the fire. Plaintiff's theory of recovery was that defendants had a duty to warn plaintiff that a smoke detector powered by house current, manufactured by Pittway, and sold to Laaperi by Sears might not operate in the event of an electrical fire caused by a short circuit. Defendants contend on appeal that the district court erred in denying their motions for directed verdict and judgment notwithstanding the verdict; that the admission into evidence of purportedly undisclosed expert testimony violated Fed. R. Civ. P. 26(e); and that the award of $750,000 for injuries to Janet Laaperi was excessive and improper. We affirm the judgments in favor of plaintiff in his capacity as administrator of the estates of his three sons, but vacate the judgment in favor of Janet Laaperi, and remand for a new trial limited to the issue of her damages.

In March 1976, plaintiff Albin Laaperi purchased a smoke detector from Sears. The detector, manufactured by the Pittway Corporation, was designed to be powered by AC (electrical) current. Laaperi installed the detector himself in one of the two upstairs bedrooms in his home.

Early in the morning of December 27, 1976, a fire broke out in the Laaperi home. The three boys in one of the upstairs bedrooms were killed in the blaze. Laaperi's 13-year-old daughter, Janet, who was sleeping in the other upstairs bedroom, received burns over 12 percent of her body and was hospitalized for three weeks.

The uncontroverted testimony at trial was that the smoke detector did not sound an alarm on the night of the fire. The cause of the fire was later found to be a short circuit in an electrical cord that was located in a cedar closet in the boys' bedroom. The Laaperi home had two separate electrical circuits in the upstairs bedrooms: one that provided electricity to the outlets and one that powered the lighting fixtures. The smoke detector had been connected to the outlet circuit, which was the circuit that shorted and cut off. Because the circuit was shorted, the AC-operated smoke detector received no power on the night of the fire. Therefore, although the detector itself was in no sense defective (indeed, after the fire the charred detector was tested and found to be operable), no alarm sounded.

Laaperi brought this diversity action against defendants Sears and Pittway, asserting negligent design, negligent manufacture, breach of warranty, and negligent failure to warn of inherent dangers. The parties agreed that the applicable law is that of Massachusetts. Before the claims went to the jury, verdicts were directed in favor of the defendants on all theories of liability other than failure to warn.

Laaperi's claim under the failure to warn theory was that he was unaware of the danger that the very short circuit which might ignite a fire in his home could, at the same time, incapacitate the smoke

detector. He contended that had he been warned of this danger, he would have purchased a battery-powered smoke detector as a backup or taken some other precaution, such as wiring the detector to a circuit of its own, in order better to protect his family in the event of an electrical fire.

The jury returned verdicts in favor of Laaperi in all four actions on the failure to warn claim. The jury assessed damages in the amount of $350,000 in each of the three actions brought on behalf of the deceased sons, and $750,000 in the action brought on behalf of Janet Laaperi. The defendants' motions for directed verdict and judgment notwithstanding the verdict were denied and defendants appealed.

Defendants contend that the district court erred in denying their motions for directed verdict and judgment n.o.v. First, they claim that they had no duty to warn that the smoke detector might not work in the event of some electrical fires. Second, they maintain that even if they had such a duty, there was insufficient evidence on the record to show that the failure to warn proximately caused plaintiff's damages. We address these arguments in turn.

A. Duty to Warn
We must look, of course, to Massachusetts law. While we have found no cases with similar facts in Massachusetts (or elsewhere), we conclude that on this record a jury would be entitled to find that defendants had a duty to warn. In Massachusetts, a manufacturer* can be found liable to a user of the product if the user is injured due to the failure of the manufacturer to exercise reasonable care in warning potential users of hazards associated with use of the product....

The manufacturer can be held liable even if the product does exactly what it is supposed to do, if it does not warn of the potential dangers inherent in the way a product is designed. It is not necessary that the product be negligently designed or manufactured; the failure to warn of hazards associated with foreseeable uses of a product is itself negligence, and if that negligence proximately results in a plaintiff's injuries, the plaintiff may recover....

The sole purpose of a smoke detector is to alert occupants of a building to the presence of fire. The failure to warn of inherent non–obvious limitations of

---

*Defendants make no argument that the duty of Sears is any different from that of Pittway, the actual manufacturer. In the present case, Sears advertised the smoke detector as a "Sears Early One Fire Alarm." Pittway Corp. was not mentioned anywhere in these advertisements or in the 12-page owner's manual packaged with the detector. Where a seller puts out a product manufactured by another as its own, the seller is subject to the same liability as though it were the manufacturer....

a smoke detector, or of non-obvious circumstances in which a detector will not function, can, we believe, "create an unreasonable risk of harm in that the inhabitants of a structure may be lulled into an unjustified sense of safety and fail to be forewarned of the existence of a fire."... In the present case, the defendants failed to warn purchasers that a short circuit which causes an electrical fire may also render the smoke detector useless in the very situation in which it is expected to provide protection: in the early stages of a fire. We believe that whether such a failure to warn was negligent was a question for the jury.

To be sure, it was the fire, not the smoke detector per se, that actually killed and injured plaintiff's children. But as the Second Circuit recently held, the manufacturer of a smoke detector may be liable when, due to its negligence, the device fails to work:

> "Although a defect must be a substantial factor in causing a plaintiff's injuries, it is clear that a 'manufacturer's liability for injuries proximately caused by these defects should not be limited to [situations] in which the defect causes the accident, but should extend to situations in which the defect caused injuries over and above that which would have occurred from the accident, but for the defective design.'"

It is true that, unlike the above, there was no defect of design or manufacture in this case. But there was evidence from which it could be inferred that the absence of a warning enhanced the harm resulting from the fire. Plaintiff testified that if he had realized that a short circuit that caused an electrical fire might at the same time disable the smoke detector, he would have purchased a back-up battery-powered detector or wired the detector in question into an isolated circuit, thus minimizing the danger that a fire-causing short circuit would render the detector inoperative. We find, therefore, a sufficient connection between the children's deaths and injury and the absence of any warning.

Defendants contend that the district court nevertheless erred in denying their motions because, they claim, the danger that an electrical fire will incapacitate an electric-powered smoke detector is obvious. They point out that anyone purchasing a device powered by house electrical current will necessarily realize that if the current goes off for any reason, the device will not work.

In Massachusetts, as elsewhere, a failure to warn amounts to negligence only where the supplier of the good known to be dangerous for its intended use "has no reason to believe that those for whose use the chattel is supplied will realize its dangerous condition."...

Where the risks of the product are discernible by casual inspection, such as the danger that a knife can cut, or a stove burn, the consumer is in just as good a position as the manufacturer to gauge the dangers associated with the product, and nothing is gained by shifting to the manufacturer the duty to warn. Thus, a manufacturer is not required to warn that placing one's hand into the blades of a potato chopper will cause injury ... that permitting a three-year-old child to ride on the running board of a moving tractor risks injury to the child, ... or that firing a BB gun at another at close range can injure or kill.... If a manufacturer had to warn consumers against every such obvious danger inherent in a product, "[t]he list of obvious practices warned against would be so long, it would fill a volume."...

Defendants ask us to declare that the risk that an electrical fire could incapacitate an AC-powered smoke detector is so obvious that the average consumer would not benefit from a warning. This is not a trivial argument; in earlier—some might say sounder—days, we might have accepted it....

Our sense of the current state of the tort law in Massachusetts and most other jurisdictions, however, leads us to conclude that, today, the matter before us poses a jury question; that "obviousness" in a situation such as this would be treated by the Massachusetts courts as presenting a question of fact, not of law. To be sure, it would be obvious to anyone that an electrical outage would cause this smoke detector to fail. But the average purchaser might not comprehend the specific danger that a fire-causing electrical problem can simultaneously knock out the circuit into which a smoke detector is wired, causing the detector to fail at the very moment it is needed. Thus, while the failure of a detector to function as the result of an electrical malfunction due, say, to a broken power line or a neighborhood power outage would, we think, be obvious as a matter of law, the failure that occurred here, being associated with the very risk—fire—for which the device was purchased, was not, or so a jury could find.

... We think that the issue of obviousness to the average consumer of the danger of a fire-related power outage was one for the jury, not the court, to determine. In the present case, the jury was specifically instructed that if it found this danger to be obvious it should hold for the defendants. It failed to do so.

B. Causation

While, as just discussed, the danger the detector would fail in these circumstances was not so obvious as to eliminate, as a matter of law, any need to warn, we must also consider whether Laaperi's specialized electrical knowledge constituted a bar to his own recovery.... [P]laintiff's specialized knowledge is immaterial to whether defendants had a duty to warn, since that duty is defined by the knowledge of the average purchaser. But plaintiff's expertise *is* relevant to whether defendants' failure to warn caused plaintiff's damages. Even though defendants may have been required to provide a warning, plaintiff may not recover if it can be shown that because of his above-average knowledge, he already appreciated the very danger the warning would have described. In such event there would be no connection between the negligent failure to warn and plaintiff's damages.

Defendants here presented considerable evidence suggesting that Laaperi, who was something of an electrical handyman, knew of the danger and still took no precautions. Laaperi, however, offered evidence that he did not know of the danger, and that he would have guarded against it had he been warned....

Self-serving as this testimony was, the jury was free to credit it. In reviewing the denial of a motion for directed verdict or judgment n.o.v., we are obliged to view the evidence in the light most favorable to the verdict winner.... In light of this standard, we cannot say that the district court erred in denying defendants'

motions for directed verdict and judgment n.o.v., for the jury could have believed Laaperi's testimony in the colloquy quoted above, among other evidence, and concluded that had he been properly warned, Laaperi would have instituted different fire detection methods in his home to protect his family against the danger that his smoke detector would be rendered useless in the event of a fire-related power outage.

IV

... Considering Janet's injuries alone, apart from the horrible nature of her brothers' deaths, we find the award of $750,000 was so grossly disproportionate to the injuries of Janet Laaperi as to be unconscionable. It is therefore vacated.

The judgments in favor of Albin Laaperi in his capacity as administrator of the estates of his three sons are affirmed. In the action on behalf of Janet Laaperi, the verdict of the jury is set aside, the judgment of the district court vacated, and the cause remanded to that court for a new trial limited to the issue of damages.

So ordered.

Case Questions

1. What warning should the defendants arguably have given the plaintiffs under the facts of this case?
2. Would the outcome in this case have been different if Albin Laaperi were a licensed electrician?
3. Why didn't the plaintiff base the claim on strict liability?

 What would utilitarians think of the doctrine of res ipsa loquitur?

Imputed Negligence

Although people are always responsible for their own acts, one may be held liable for the negligence of another by reason of some relationship existing between two parties. This is termed **imputed negligence,** or vicarious liability.

Imputed negligence results when one person (the agent) acts for or represents another (the principal) by the latter's authority and to accomplish the latter's ends. A common example is the liability of employers for the torts that employees commit in the scope of their employment.

One should take a liberal view of the scope-of-employment concept, because the basis for

vicarious liability is the desire to include in operational costs the inevitable losses to third persons incident to carrying on an enterprise, and thus distribute the burden among those benefited by the enterprise. Generally, an employee would not be within the scope of employment (1) if the employee is en route to or from home, (2) if the employee is on an undertaking of his own, (3) if the acts are prohibited by the employer, or (4) if the act is an unauthorized delegation by the employer.

One is not accountable for the negligent act of an independent contractor. **Independent contractors** are those who contract to do work according to their own methods and are not subject to the control of employers except with respect to the results. The right of control over the manner in which the work is done is the main consideration in determining whether one employed is an independent contractor or an agent. However, there are certain exceptions to this nonliability; for example, an employer who is negligent in hiring a contractor or who assigns a nondelegable duty may be liable.

Modified No-Fault Liability Statutes

As readers saw in Table 11.1, automobile collision suits account for most of the tort claims filed in the United States. Responding to widespread dissatisfaction with the delay and expense in the litigation of traffic accident cases, some states have enacted **modified no-fault liability statutes** in an attempt to correct the injustices and inadequacies of the fault system in automobile accident cases. Under a modified no-fault liability statute, an injured person normally has no right to file suit to recover money damages for personal injuries and lost wages below a statutorily specified threshold. Instead, the injured party is compensated by his/her own insurance company. The amount of compensation paid is determined by dollar ceilings specified in the injured person's insurance policy. All "no-fault "states, however, permit lawsuits for damages where the injured person has been seriously injured. States differ as to how they determine when this threshold is crossed. The goal of the statutes is to reduce the cost of automobile insurance by saving litigation costs, including attorneys' fees, and by allowing little or no recovery for the pain and suffering and emotional stress that accompany an automobile accident.

STRICT LIABILITY

In addition to intentional torts and negligence, there is a third type of tort called strict liability or absolute liability. This imposes liability on defendants without requiring any proof of lack of due care. Under the early common law, people were held strictly liable for trespass and trespass on the case without regard to their intentions and whether they exercised reasonable care. Although the breadth of strict liability diminished with the emergence of negligence and intentional torts, **strict liability in tort** is applied in cases involving what the common law recognized as abnormally dangerous activities and, more recently, in product liability cases.

Abnormally Dangerous Activities

One who is involved in abnormally dangerous activities is legally responsible for harmful consequences that are proximately caused. The possessor of a dangerous instrumentality is an insurer of the safety of others who are foreseeably within the danger zone. Because of jurisdictional differences, it is impossible to formulate a general definition or complete listing of all dangerous instrumentalities. However, poisons, toxic chemicals, explosives, and vicious animals are examples of items that have been found to fall into this category.

INTERNET TIP

Interested readers can see an example involving strict liability and a dangerous animal in the case of *Westberry v. Blackwell*, which can be found with the Chapter XI materials on the textbook's website.

Strict Liability and Product Liability

A purchaser of tangible, personal property may have a right to recover from the manufacturer for injuries caused by product defects. Product defects include defects in design, manufacturing defects, and warning defects. A person who has been injured by a product defect may be able to recover based on strict liability, as well as on breach of warranty (see discussion in Chapter X) and negligence (see earlier discussion in this chapter).

The use of strict liability in product liability cases occurred because of dissatisfaction with the negligence and warranty remedies. It was very difficult for average consumers to determine whether

> ### § 402A. Special Liability of Seller of Product for Physical Harm to User or Consumer
>
> (1) One who sells any product in a defective condition unreasonably dangerous to the user or consumer or to his property is subject to liability for physical harm thereby caused to the ultimate user or consumer, or to his property, if
>
> (a) the seller is engaged in the business of selling such a product, and
>
> (b) it is expected to and does reach the user or consumer without substantial change in the condition in which it is sold.
>
> (2) The rule stated in Subsection (1) applies although
>
> (a) the seller has exercised all possible care in the preparation and sale of his product, and
>
> (b) the user or consumer has not bought the product from or entered into any contractual relation with the seller.

F I G U R E 11.1 Section 402A of the Restatement (Second) of Torts

manufacturers, wholesalers, or retailers of defective goods were responsible for their injuries. Also, the traditional requirement of privity limited the manufacturer's liability in tort and warranty actions to the person who purchased the defective product, often the wholesaler or retailer. Reformers argued that too often consumers assumed the full cost of the losses. They believed that it would be more just and economically wise to shift the cost of injuries to manufacturers, since manufacturers could purchase insurance and could distribute the costs of the premiums among those who purchased their products.

In contrast to breach of warranty and negligence remedies, which focus on the manufacturer's conduct, modern strict liability focuses on the product itself. A plaintiff who relies on strict liability has to prove that the product was unreasonably dangerous and defective and that the defect proximately caused the injury (although the unreasonably dangerous requirement is disregarded by some courts).

INTERNET TIP

Leichtamer v. American Motors Corporation is a strict liability case involving a Jeep CJ-7 that pitched over while being driven, killing two people and injuring two others. The plaintiffs brought suit, claiming a design defect was responsible for their injuries. The Ohio Supreme Court refers to Section 402A of the Restatement of Torts (see

Figure 11.1) in this case and adopts it as part of Ohio law. You can read this case on the textbook's website.

Tort Reform

The hotly contested battle over tort reform continues to rage on, with "reformers" seeking to limit plaintiff's venue choices; increase the immunities available to physicians, pharmacists, and physician assistants; reduce the liability of pharmaceutical manufacturers in product liability cases; and cap noneconomic and punitive damages. Many advocates of reform insist that trial attorney greed is at the core of the problem. Others maintain that without tort reform it will be impossible to reduce the seemingly unstoppable increases in health costs.

Reform opponents point to reports that thousands of people die annually in the United States because of medical errors.[6] They argue that reforms ultimately seek to arbitrarily deny injured people the just recovery they are entitled to because of the circumstances and the nature and extent of their injuries. They point out that the damage awards are large only in cases in which the injuries are horrific and the tortfeasor's liability is great. They also argue that corporations must be held fully accountable for their tortious acts, or they will not have any economic incentive to act in the public's interest.

The battle has played out at the state level: Thirty-five states have enacted laws intended to lessen recoveries, especially in medical malpractice cases.[7] Reform proposals typically eliminate joint and several liability, limit a plaintiff's choice of venues, cap noneconomic damages, shorten statute of limitations periods, and cap punitive damages.

Joint and Several Liability

Under the common law, if Sarah, Jose, and Soyinni commit a tort at the same time and are at fault, liability for the entire harm is imposed on each of the tortfeasors jointly and individually. This means that the judgment creditors could recover one-third from each judgment debtor, or the entire judgment from one defendant. This common law approach favors plaintiffs. It allows a judgment creditor to collect the entire judgment from the tortfeasor that has the "deepest pockets." This unfortunate person then has to go to court and seek "contribution" from the other tortfeasors (assuming they are neither bankrupt nor judgment proof). Reformers favor modifying the rule so that a judgment debtor who has been found to be only 10 percent liable is not required to pay for 100 percent of the judgment. Virginia is one of the states that still follow the common law rule. The Virginia statute establishing joint and several liability can be seen in Figure 11.2. Most states, however, have made modifications to the common law approach.

INTERNET TIP

Minnesota is one of the states that have modified the common law rule regarding joint and several liability. Interested readers will find Minnesota's apportionment of damages statute included with the Chapter XI materials on the textbook's website. Readers are encouraged to look at both the Virginia statute (Figure 11.2) and the Minnesota statute, and notice how they differ.

A judgment against one of several joint wrongdoers shall not bar the prosecution of an action against any or all the others, but the injured party may bring separate actions against the wrongdoers and proceed to judgment in each, or, if sued jointly, he may proceed to judgment against them successively until judgment has been rendered against, or the cause has been otherwise disposed of as to, all of the defendants, and no bar shall arise as to any of them by reason of a judgment against another, or others, until the judgment has been satisfied. If there be a judgment against one or more joint wrongdoers, the full satisfaction of such judgment accepted as such by the plaintiff shall be a discharge of all joint wrongdoers, except as to the costs; provided, however, this section shall have no effect on the right of contribution between joint wrongdoers as set out in § 8.01-34.

FIGURE 11.2 Va. Code Ann. § 8.01-443. Joint Wrongdoers; Effect of Judgment Against One

Limitations on Venue Choice

Reformers allege that plaintiffs' lawyers are taking advantage of jurisdictions that permit forum shopping. In recent years, certain counties in some states have developed a reputation for consistently awarding large verdicts and have been designated "tort hellholes" by reform advocates.[8] Reformers suggest that plaintiffs be limited to filing suit in the county of the state in which the tort occurred.

Caps on Noneconomic Damages

Many states have tried to lower jury awards by statutorily establishing ceilings on recoveries for noneconomic damages such as pain and suffering, loss of consortium, and loss of enjoyment of life (hedonic damages). Proponents of "tort reform" often urge lawmakers to establish financial "caps" on the amount of damages a successful tort plaintiff can receive. The rationale generally given is that doctors cannot afford to pay the cost of malpractice insurance premiums and establishing ceilings on damage awards will reduce the overall cost of medical care.

The following case from Georgia is illustrative of how this very controversial issue can generate institutional conflict between state legislatures and state supreme courts.

Atlanta Oculoplastic Surgery, P.C. v. Nestlehutt
S09A1432
Supreme Court of Georgia
March 22, 2010.

Hunstein, Chief Justice

This case requires us to assess the constitutionality of OCGA § 51-13-1, which limits awards of noneconomic damages in medical malpractice cases to a predetermined amount. The trial court held that the statute violates the Georgia Constitution by encroaching on the right to a jury trial, ... In January 2006, Harvey P. Cole, M.D., of Atlanta Oculoplastic Surgery, d/b/a Oculus, performed... laser resurfacing and a full facelift on appellee Betty Nestlehutt. In the weeks after the surgery, complications arose, resulting in Nestlehutt's permanent disfigurement. Nestlehutt, along with her husband, sued Oculus for medical malpractice. The case proceeded to trial, ending in a mistrial. On retrial, the jury returned a verdict of $1,265,000, comprised of $115,000 for past and future medical expenses; $900,000 in noneconomic damages for Ms. Nestlehutt's pain and suffering; and $250,000 for Mr. Nestlehutt's loss of consortium. Appellees then moved to have OCGA § 51-13-1, which would have reduced the jury's noneconomic damages award by $800,000 to the statutory limit of $350,000, declared unconstitutional. The trial court granted the motion and thereupon entered judgment for appellees in the full amount awarded by the jury. Oculus moved for a new trial, which was denied, and this appeal ensued.

1. In relevant part, OCGA § 51-13-1 provides,

In any verdict returned or judgment entered in a medical malpractice action, including an action for wrongful death, against one or more health care providers, the total amount recoverable by a claimant for noneconomic damages in such action shall be limited to an amount not to exceed $350,000.00, regardless of the number of defendant health care providers against whom the claim is asserted or the number of separate causes of action on which the claim is based.

... (b). "Noneconomic damages" is defined as damages for physical and emotional pain, discomfort, anxiety, hardship, distress, suffering, inconvenience, physical impairment, mental anguish, disfigurement, loss of enjoyment of life, loss of society and companionship, loss of consortium, injury to reputation, and all other nonpecuniary losses of any kind or nature.

... In addition to capping noneconomic damages against health care providers ... the statute also limits noneconomic damages awards against a single medical facility to $350,000; limits such awards to $700,000 for actions against more than one medical facility; and limits such awards to $1,050,000 for actions against multiple health care providers and medical facilities ....

Enacted as part of a broad legislative package known as the Tort Reform Act of 2005, the damages caps were intended to help address what the General Assembly determined to be a "crisis affecting the provision and quality of health care services in this state." ... Specifically, the Legislature found that health care providers and facilities were being negatively affected by diminishing access to and increasing costs of procuring liability insurance, and that these problems in the liability insurance market bore the potential to reduce Georgia citizens' access to health care services, thus degrading their health and well-being... The provisions of the Tort Reform Act were therefore intended by the Legislature to "promote predictability and improvement in the provision of quality health care services and the resolution of health care liability claims and ... thereby assist in promoting the provision of health care liability insurance by insurance providers."...

2. We examine first the trial court's holding that the noneconomic damages cap violates our state Constitution's guarantee of the right to trial by jury.

Duly enacted statutes enjoy a presumption of constitutionality. A trial court must uphold a statute unless the party seeking to nullify it shows that it "manifestly infringes upon a constitutional provision or violates the rights of the people." The constitutionality of a statute presents a question of law. Accordingly, we review a trial court's holding regarding the constitutionality of a statute de novo....

The Georgia Constitution states plainly that "[t]he right to trial by jury shall remain inviolate."…. It is well established that Article I, Section I, Paragraph XI (a) "guarantees the right to a jury trial only with respect to cases as to which there existed a right to jury trial at common law or by statute at the time of the adoption of the Georgia Constitution in 1798…. Prior to adoption of the 1798 Constitution, the General Assembly had adopted the common law of England and all statutes in force as of 1776 as the law of Georgia… Thus, the initial step in our analysis must necessarily be an examination of the right to jury trial under late eighteenth century English common law…. See Rouse v. State … (1848) (referring to Blackstone, "whose commentaries constituted the law of this State, before and since the Revolution," as authoritative on jury trial right as of 1798)….

(a) The antecedents of the modern medical malpractice action trace back to the 14th century.

The first recorded case in England on the civil [liability] of a physician was an action brought before the Kings Bench in 1374 against a surgeon by the name of J. Mort involving the treatment of a wounded hand. The physician was held not liable because of a legal technicality, but the court clearly enunciated the rule that if negligence is proved in such a case the law will provide a remedy.

… By the mid-18th century, the concept of "mala praxis" [malpractice] was sufficiently established in legal theory as to constitute one of five classes of "private wrongs" described by Sir William Blackstone in his Commentaries…. The concept took root in early American common law, the earliest reported medical negligence case in America dating to 1794…. Given the clear existence of medical negligence claims as of the adoption of the Georgia Constitution of 1798, we have no difficulty concluding that such claims are encompassed within the right to jury trial… under Art. I, Sec. I, Par. XI (a). This conclusion is bolstered by the fact that medical negligence claims appear in Georgia's earliest systematically reported case law…, and the fact that the tort of medical malpractice was included in Georgia's earliest Code. See Code of 1861, § 2915 (effective Jan. 1, 1863)….

As with all torts, the determination of damages rests "peculiarly within the province of the jury."… Because the amount of damages sustained by a plaintiff is ordinarily an issue of fact, this has been the rule from the beginning of trial by jury…. Hence, "[t]he right to a jury trial includes the right to have a jury

determine the amount of … damages, if any, awarded to the [plaintiff]."…

Noneconomic damages have long been recognized as an element of total damages in tort cases, including those involving medical negligence…. Based on the foregoing, we conclude that at the time of the adoption of our Constitution of 1798, there did exist the common law right to a jury trial for claims involving the negligence of a health care provider, with an attendant right to the award of the full measure of damages, including noneconomic damages, as determined by the jury.

(b) We next examine whether the noneconomic damages caps in OCGA § 51-12-1 unconstitutionally infringe on this right. By requiring the court to reduce a noneconomic damages award determined by a jury that exceeds the statutory limit, OCGA § 51-13-1 clearly nullifies the jury's findings of fact regarding damages and thereby undermines the jury's basic function…. Consequently, we are compelled to conclude that the caps infringe on a party's constitutional right, as embodied in Article I, Section I, Paragraph XI (a), to a jury determination as to noneconomic damages…. The fact that OCGA § 51-13-1 permits full recovery of noneconomic damages up to the significant amount of $350,000 cannot save the statute from constitutional attack. "[I]f the legislature may constitutionally cap recovery at [$350,000], there is no discernible reason why it could not cap the recovery at some other figure, perhaps $50,000, or $1,000, or even $1"… The very existence of the caps, in any amount, is violative of the right to trial by jury….

Though we agree with the general principle… that the Legislature has authority to modify or abrogate the common law, we do not agree with the notion that this general authority empowers the Legislature to abrogate constitutional rights that may inhere in common law causes of action… Likewise, while we have held that the Legislature generally has the authority to define, limit, and modify available legal remedies… the exercise of such authority simply cannot stand when the resulting legislation violates the constitutional right to jury trial.

Nor does…the existence of statutes authorizing double or treble damages attest to the validity of the caps on noneconomic damages. While it is questionable whether any cause of action involving an award thereof would constitute an analogue to a 1798 common law cause of action so as to trigger the right to jury trial in the first place,… to the extent the right to jury trial did attach, treble damages do not in any way nullify the jury's damages award but rather merely operate upon and thus affirm the integrity of that award....

In sum, based on the foregoing, we conclude that the noneconomic damages caps in OCGA § 51-13-1 violate the right to a jury trial as guaranteed under the Georgia Constitution....

3. "The general rule is that an unconstitutional statute is wholly void and of no force and effect from the date it was enacted."...

In this case, we do not find that the...factors militate in favor of deviation from the general rule of retroactivity....

4. We find no abuse of the trial court's discretion in granting appellees' motion to exclude certain evidence, because that ruling was necessitated by the trial court's earlier grant of appellant's motion in limine.... As to appellant's claim that the evidence was relevant to establishing the bias of appellee's expert witness, the record establishes that the trial court's ruling in no manner precluded appellant from attempting to show the witness' bias through cross-examination or other means. Accordingly, this enumeration lacks merit.

For the foregoing reasons, we affirm the judgment of the trial court.

Judgment affirmed....

Case Questions

1. Why did the Georgia Supreme Court feel it necessary to examine English legal precedents going back as far as 1374 in order to decide a case before it for decision in 2010?
2. Why did the Georgia Supreme Court conclude that the statute was unconstitutional?

Statutes of Limitations

Legislatures often attempt to limit a potential defendant's exposure to tort liability by shortening the statute of limitations. Although this proposal is intended to benefit defendants, it does so at the expense of injured plaintiffs who will be denied the opportunity for their day in court if they fail to file their suits in a timely manner.

Caps on Punitive Damages

Many states have abolished punitive damages unless such awards are specifically permitted by statute. Increasingly, states are requiring that punitive damages be proven clearly and convincingly rather than by a preponderance of the evidence, and others require bifurcated trials for punitive damages. Reformers urge legislatures to impose dollar ceilings on punitive damage awards in medical malpractice and product liability cases. According to U.S. Bureau of Justice Statistics data, only 3 percent of tort plaintiffs were awarded punitive damages in 2005.[9]

CHAPTER SUMMARY

The chapter began with brief discussions of the historical development of the modern tort action and the functions of tort law in contemporary America. This was followed with an overview of intentional torts in general and discussions and cases focusing on such intentional torts as assault, battery, conversion, trespass to land, malicious prosecution, false imprisonment, defamation, interference with contract relations, infliction of mental distress, and invasion of privacy. The focus then shifted to negligence. The elements of a negligence claim were discussed, with an emphasis on the "duty of care" and "proximate cause" requirements. The workings of the comparative negligence approach, which involves an apportionment of fault between the plaintiff and defendant was explained and illustrated in accompanying cases. The third type of tort, strict liability for abnormally dangerous activities and product defects, was then addressed. The chapter concluded with a brief overview of tort reform.

CHAPTER QUESTIONS

1. Jack McMahon and his wife Angelina decided to take a break from driving and stopped at a Mobil minimart for a take-out coffee. Angelina took the plastic lid off the Styrofoam cup as Jack resumed driving. She spilled coffee on her lap while trying to pour some of the coffee into another cup, and suffered second- and third-degree burns. Angelina experienced considerable pain for several months and sustained scarring on one of her thighs and on her abdomen. The McMahons settled their claims against the manufacturers of the cup and lid, but brought suit against the manufacturer of the coffee-making machine, the Bunn-O-Matic Corporation. The plaintiffs alleged that the machine was defective because it brewed the coffee at too high a tem-perturb, 179 degrees Fahrenheit (the industry average is between 175 and 185), and that the heat caused the cup to deteriorate. They also claimed that Bunn was negligent in failing to warn customers about the magnitude of the injuries (second- and third-degree burns) that could result from spilled coffee at this temperature. Did Bunn, in your opinion, have a legal duty to give plaintiffs the requested warnings?

   McMahon v. Bunn-O-Matic Corp., 150 F.3d 651 (7th Cir. 1998)

2. Patrick Reddell and Derek Johnson, both eighteen years of age, wanted to take part in a BB gun war "game." They agreed not to fire their weapons above the waist and that their BB guns would be pumped no more than three times, thereby limiting the force of the BBs' impact when striking the other person. They also promised each other only to fire a BB gun when the other person was "in the open."

   While participating in this activity, Johnson shot Reddell in the eye, causing seriously impaired vision. Reddell sued Johnson for gross negligence and for recklessly aiming his weapon above the waist. Johnson answered by denying liability and asserting the defenses of *assumption of risk* and *contributory negligence*. Both parties then filed motions for summary judgment. How should the trial judge rule on the motions?

   Reddell v. Johnson, 942 P.2d 200 (1997)

3. Shannon Jackson was injured while driving her car on a farm-to-market road when her vehicle hit and killed a horse named Tiny that was standing in the road. The force of the collision severely damaged her vehicle, which was totaled. Jackson brought a negligence suit against Tiny's owner, Naomi Gibbs, for failing to prevent Tiny from wandering onto the road. Gibbs defended by saying she owed Jackson no duty on a farm-to-market road that was within a "free-range" area. The trial court rejected the defense, and a jury found the defendant negligent and liable for damages of $7,000. The state intermediate appeals court affirmed the trial court, ruling that although there was no statutory duty to keep Tiny off the road, the court recognized a common law duty "to keep domestic livestock from roaming at large on public roads." This was a case of first impression before the state supreme court. Texas courts prior to this case had rejected the English common law rule imposing a duty on the owner of a domestic animal to prevent it from trespassing on a neighbor's property. English common law imposed no corresponding duty to keep an animal from wandering onto a

public road unless the animal had "vicious propensities." In light of the above, Texas law generally permitted healthy, nonvicious animals to roam freely, a condition associated with "free range" jurisdictions. An exception to the free-range law was statutorily recognized where a "local stock law" was enacted to keep animals off of a state highway. What arguments might be made supporting and opposing the new common law rule recognized by the intermediate court of appeals?

Gibbs v. Jackson, 97-0961, Supreme Court of Texas (1998)

4. The plaintiff became ill in the defendant's store. The defendant undertook to render medical aid to the plaintiff, keeping the plaintiff in an infirmary for six hours without medical care. It was determined that when the plaintiff finally received proper medical care, the extended lapse of time had seriously aggravated the plaintiff's illness. Discuss what action, if any, the plaintiff has.

Zelenka v. Gimbel Bros., Inc., 287 N.Y.S. 134 (1935)

5. Plaintiff came into defendant's grocery store and purchased some cigarettes. He then asked if the store had any empty boxes he could use. The defendant instructed the plaintiff that he could find some in the back room and told the plaintiff to help himself. Plaintiff entered the room, which was dark. While searching for a light switch, the plaintiff fell into an open stairwell and was injured. What is the status of the plaintiff (invitee, licensee, trespasser)? How will the status affect the plaintiff's ability to recover from the defendant, if at all? Do you think the fact that the defendant is operating a business should affect his duty?

Whelan v. Van Natta Grocery, 382 S.W.2d 205 (Ky. 1964)

6. Plaintiff's intestate was killed when the roof of the defendant's foundry fell in on him. Plaintiff alleges that the defendant failed to make proper repairs to the roof, and that such neglect of the defendant caused the roof to collapse. The defendant claims, however, that the roof collapsed during a violent storm, and that, even though the roof was in disrepair, the high winds caused the roof to fall. What issue is raised, and how would you resolve it?

Kimble v. Mackintosh Hemphill Co., 59 A.2d 68 (1948)

7. The plaintiff's intestate, who had been drinking, was crossing Broadway when he was negligently struck by one of defendant's cabs. As a result of the accident, the plaintiff's intestate was thrown about twenty feet, his thigh was broken, and his knee injured. He immediately became unconscious and was rushed to a hospital, where he died of delirium tremens (a disease characterized by violent shaking, often induced by excessive alcohol consumption). Defendant argued that the deceased's alcoholism might have caused delirium tremens and death at a later date, even if defendant had not injured him. What is the main issue presented here? Who should prevail and why?

McCahill v. N.Y. Transportation Co., 94 N.E. 616 (1911)

8. Plaintiff, while a spectator at a professional hockey game, is struck in the face by a puck. The defendant shot the puck attempting to score a goal, but shot too high, causing the puck to go into the spectator area. Plaintiff brings suit, and defendant claims assumption of risk. Who prevails? Suppose the defendant had been angry at crowd reaction and intentionally shot the puck into the crowd. Would the outcome change?

9. Clay Fruit, a life insurance salesman, was required to attend a business convention conducted by his employer. The convention included social as well as business events, and Fruit was encouraged to mix freely with out-of-state agents in order to learn as much as possible about sales techniques. One evening, after all scheduled business and social events had concluded, Fruit drove to a nearby bar and restaurant, looking for some out-of-state colleagues. Finding none, he drove back toward his hotel. On the journey back, he negligently

struck the automobile of the plaintiff, causing serious injuries to plaintiff's legs. Was Fruit in the course and scope of his employment at the time of the accident? From whom will the plaintiff be able to recover?

Fruit v. Schreiner, 502 P.2d 133 (Alaska 1972)

NOTES

1. T. F. F. Plucknett, *A Concise History of the Common Law* (Boston: Little, Brown and Co., 1956), p. 372.

2. A. K. R. Kiralfy, *Potter's Historical Introduction to English Law* (4th ed.) (London: Sweet and Maxwell Ltd., 1962), pp. 376–377.

3. R. Walsh, *A History of Anglo-American Law* (Indianapolis: Bobbs-Merrill Co., 1932), p. 323.

4. Kiralfy, pp. 305–307; Walsh, p. 344.

5. More discussion about the different types of damages can be found in Chapter VII.

6. "A tragic error," *Newsweek*, March 3, 2003, p. 22.

7. "Ohio's Tort Reform Law Hasn't Lowered Health-Care Costs," *The Plain Dealer* (March 20, 2010), http//blog.cleveland.com/open/index.ssf/2010/03/ohios_tort_reform_law_hasnt_lo.html

8. "Tort Reform Advances in Mississippi (for starters)," *National Law Journal* (February 3, 2003), pp. A1, A10–A11.

9. U.S. Department of Justice Bureau of Justice Statistics Bulletin, November 2009, NCJ 228129, p. 6.

XII

✳

Property

CHAPTER OBJECTIVES

1. *Understand the historical origins of property law.*
2. *Explain the true meaning of the term "property."*
3. *Identify two ways in which property is classified.*
4. *Understand the importance of intellectual property rights.*
5. *Identify the primary ways that government takes and limits the exercise of private property rights.*
6. *Understand the basic concept of an "estate in land."*
7. *Explain the differences between easements and licenses.*
8. *Identify the different ways personal property can be acquired.*
9. *Understand the essential elements of a bailment.*

Property refers to a person's ownership rights to things and to a person's interests in things owned by someone else. Property includes the rights to possess, use, and dispose of things. These may be tangible objects, such as a car, book, or item of clothing, or they may be intangible—the technology in a camera, a song, or the right of publicity. Although many people refer to the objects themselves as property, "property" actually refers only to ownership rights and interests.

HISTORICAL DEVELOPMENT OF THE REGULATION OF REAL PROPERTY

When we discuss property law, we must remember that the English common law greatly influenced legal thinking in the prerevolutionary colonies and in the new American states.[1] Private property was thought to be essential to individual liberty, a proposition advanced by the English philosopher John Locke (1632–1704). Locke was a "natural law" philosopher who argued that before the creation of governments, people existed in a natural state in which they had total control over their life, liberty, and property. He reasoned that people who established governments retained these inalienable rights and were entitled to resist any government that failed to respect them. Locke's emphasis on the inviolability of private property was reflected in the decisions of colonial legislatures, judges, and political leaders.[2]

Although American law was significantly influenced by the common law, most colonies were willing to take a different path when solutions provided by common law seemed inappropriate. The Puritans in New England, for example, refused to follow a rule of English common law (which was accepted in southern colonies[3]) that prevented a husband from conveying land without his wife's consent. They believed this was a bad social policy because it treated husbands and wives as individuals with separate legal interests rather than as a single, unified entity. They changed the law to allow husbands to make unilateral decisions for the family regarding the sale of real property.[4]

Before the industrial revolution, the economies of America and England were primarily based on agriculture. England's industrial revolution began with the rise of the textile industry in the 1700s. At this time most economic and political power was held by large landowners such as the church, monarchy, military, and landed gentry.[5] There, as in colonial America, the law recognized property owners as having absolute dominion over their land.[6] But no one could use his or her land in a manner that caused injury to any other landowner.

For example, a landowner could not divert the natural flow of a navigable river or stream in order to establish a mill if it created a detriment to another landowner.[7] The fact that economic and social benefits would result from the operation of a new mill was of no consequence.[8]

Legal attitudes toward property began to change as America became industrialized in the 1800s and moved toward a market economy. After the Civil War, courts began to recognize that encouraging competition and economic development benefitted the public.[9] When one landowner's property use conflicted with another's, the courts balanced the nature of the infringement against its socially desirable economic benefits, and the developers usually prevailed.[10] This legal preference for development continued throughout the nineteenth and into the twentieth century. Although it produced new technology, new products, and an expanding economy, it also resulted in environmental pollution, the exploitation of workers, hazardous work environments, and labor–management conflict. These conditions resulted in legislative reform efforts throughout the century designed to protect society. Around 1900, the U.S. Supreme Court began to strike down state laws that interfered with employer–employee contracts with respect to wages, hours, and working conditions.[11] The court concluded that these laws exceeded the state's legislative power because they infringed upon the individual's constitutionally protected due process liberty interest in freedom of contract.

Since the 1930s, the individual's property rights in land have declined as legislatures have acted to protect society from irresponsible and harmful uses of private property. Today, for example, zoning laws regulate land use and building codes regulate building construction. Environmental laws prohibit landowners from filling in wetlands and control the discharge of pollutants into the air, ground, and water.

As environmental regulations have increased in number, they have affected an increasing number of landowners. A heated ongoing national debate has resulted between supporters and opponents of the legal status quo. Opponents have charged that the existing legislation and case law are excessively anti-development and that government agencies are overzealous in enforcing environmental protection regulations. Environmental protection, they conclude, is often achieved without regard for the legitimate rights of landowners. Supporters of current environmental policies maintain that removing the regulations will produce a precipitous decline in habitat for endangered species and, in many instances, will ultimately lead to extinction. They also argue that backsliding from current standards will produce serious environmental hazards to the public's air, water, and land resources. In the 1990s, the Congress, many state legislatures, and federal and state courts, however, began questioning whether our nation's environmental laws properly balanced society's dual interests in protecting the environment and private property rights. We examine this question in more detail later in this chapter when we discuss takings and eminent domain.

CLASSIFICATIONS OF PROPERTY

Property can be classified as real, personal (tangible or intangible), or fixtures. Property interests can also be classified as either contingent or vested. These distinctions matter. Tax rates, for example, often differ for realty, fixtures, and personalty. A second example is the determination of what body of law will be used to determine title. Thus, the common law of each state governs title to real property, whereas the Uniform Commercial Code often governs personalty.[12]

Real property, or realty, includes land and things that are attached permanently to land. It is distinguishable from personal property in that real property is immovable.

Personal property, also called personalty, can classified as either tangible or intangible. **Tangible personal property** consists of physical objects (which are neither realty nor fixtures) such as a book, a boat, or a piece of furniture. **Intangible personal property** is personalty that has no

physical form. Ownership of intangible property is usually evidenced by some type of legal document that sets forth the ownership rights. For example, a bank account is intangible personal property. A person who deposits money into the account receives from the bank intangible rights equal to the amount of the deposit plus interest (if it is an interest-bearing account). The deposit receipt and bank statement are evidence of the holder's title and right to possession of the funds contained in the account. Money, stocks, and bonds are considered to be intangible property because they are paper substitutes for certain ownership rights. Trademarks, patents, and copyrights are also intangible personal property, as are the intangible rights, duties, and obligations arising out of the ownership of physical objects. Thus personal property includes not only a physical or representative object, but also the right to own, use, sell, or dispose of it as provided by law.

Items of personal property are often the subject of both tangible and intangible property rights. For example, suppose that you buy a digital camera, the design and technology of which is protected by valid federal patents. Although you have acquired a piece of tangible personal property that you can use to take pictures, and you can give it as a gift or otherwise dispose of it in any legal manner, the law will recognize that you do not have all the rights vis-à-vis the camera. The patent holders, for example, have intangible property rights in the camera's technology. The purchaser does not have any such rights and therefore cannot sell duplicates of the product or the technology without permission. Thus the patent holders and the purchaser have concurrent property rights in the camera.

A **fixture** is a category of property between realty and personalty. For example, a dishwasher, which is classified as personalty when it is purchased at an appliance store, becomes a fixture when it is permanently built into the buyer's kitchen.

Lastly, property rights are classified in terms of when they become fully effective. A right is said to be **contingent** when some future event must occur for the right to become **vested** (fully effective). For example, employers often require that employees work for a company for a specified period of time before their vacation and pension rights mature. Once pension rights vest, they belong to the employees even if the employees subsequently leave the company.

TRADEMARKS, PATENTS, AND COPYRIGHTS

When one normally thinks of personal property, one generally thinks in terms of tangible property—the rights to things that have a physical existence. However, some of the most valuable property rights have no physical attributes. One who owns intellectual property rights (the rights to trademarks, patents, and copyrights) owns intangible personal property.

Trademarks

The distinctive Nike "Swoosh" is a **trademark** of the Nike Corporation. The company affixes this mark to its many products in order to distinguish them from those of competitors. Customers learn to associate trademarks with quality and style attributes—a matter of great importance to manufacturers and retailers. The name of a type of product, such as "microwave" or "DVD," cannot be a trademark. Sometimes, however, a company's trademark becomes recognized by the public as the name of the product itself and loses its legal status as a trademark. Aspirin, thermos, and escalator are examples of trademarks that lost their trademark status because they became words used for the product category. The Coca-Cola Company works diligently to ensure that the term *Coke* does not lose its status as a trademark by becoming a synonym for "soft drink." Similarly, the Xerox Corporation is most concerned that its trademark *Xerox* does not become a synonym for "photocopy." Trademarks to be used in interstate commerce are required to be registered with the U.S. Department of Commerce's Patent and Trademark Office, pursuant to the Lanham Act of 1946.

An infringement of a trademark occurs, for example, when an infringing mark is so similar to a well-established mark that it is likely to confuse, deceive, or mislead customers into believing that they are doing business with the more established company.

Federal and state statutes create causes of action for trademark infringement. The Lanham Act of 1946 and the Trademark Law Revision Act of 1988 are the principal federal statutes. At the state level, statutes authorize causes of action for trademark infringement and the common law also provides a basis for such suits. Successful plaintiffs can obtain treble damages, injunctive relief, an award of the defendant's profits, damages, costs, and attorney's fees in exceptional cases.

The plaintiff in the following case sought to trademark the words "Best Beer in America," and appealed the Trademark Trial and Appeal Board's decision to reject the proposed trademark application.

In re The Boston Beer Company Ltd. Partnership
198 F.3d 1370
U.S. Court of Appeals, Federal Circuit
December 7, 1999

Mayer, Chief Judge
The Boston Beer Company Limited Partnership ("Boston Beer") appeals from a decision of the U.S. Patent and Trademark Office Trademark Trial and Appeal Board affirming the final rejection of trademark application Serial No. 74/464,118 seeking to register "The Best Beer In America" on the principal register...

Background
On November 30, 1993, the Boston Beer Company filed an application to register "The Best Beer In America" on the principal register for "beverages, namely beer and ale," in Class 32. Boston Beer claimed use since 1985 and asserted that the words sought to be registered have acquired distinctiveness under 15 U.S.C.

§§ 1052(f). Boston Beer claimed secondary meaning based on annual advertising expenditures in excess of ten million dollars and annual sales under the mark of approximately eighty-five million dollars. Specifically, Boston Beer spent about two million dollars on promotions and promotional items which included the phrase "The Best Beer in America."

In support of its claims, Boston Beer submitted an affidavit of its founder and co-president, James Koch, asserting that the words sought to be registered had developed secondary meaning as a source-indicator for its goods by virtue of extensive promotion and sales of beer under the mark since June 1985. It also submitted an advertisement for a competitor's product, Rolling Rock Bock beer, which included an invitation to sample "the beer that bested 'The Best Beer in America,'" as evidence that Rolling Rock regards "The Best Beer in America" as Boston Beer's trademark. The examining attorney rejected the pro-posed mark as merely descriptive and cited articles retrieved from the NEXIS database showing the proposed mark used by Boston Beer and others as a laudatory phrase to refer to superior beers produced by a number of different brewers. All of the beers mentioned had either won comparison competitions or had been touted as the best in America by their makers or others. Boston Beer responded by submitting articles showing its use of the proposed mark to refer to its product and in promoting its beer as a winner of the annual beer competition in Denver. Additionally, it argued that if marks such as "Best Products" and "American Airlines" can be registered even though they are also used descriptively, then the proposed mark should be similarly registered. The examining attorney issued a final refusal to register under 15 U.S.C. §§ 1052(e)(1), holding that Boston Beer had failed to establish that the mark had become distinctive.

Boston Beer filed a notice of appeal and attached further exhibits to its appeal brief. The application was remanded to the examiner on his request for consideration of the new evidence. Another office action was issued denying registration for lack of distinctiveness which noted that the phrase sought to be registered was selected and used after Boston Beer received awards at the Great American Beer Festival. The board then allowed Boston Beer to file a supplemental brief. Action on the appeal was suspended and the board remanded the application.

The examiner concluded that the proposed mark is the name of a genus of goods, namely "beers brewed in America that have won taste competitions or were judged best in taste tests," and included

printouts from the Boston Beer Internet web site to show that it had adopted the proposed mark after it had won such competitions. He therefore issued an office action rejecting the proposed mark as generic and thus incapable of registration. Boston Beer submitted a second supplemental brief to respond to the genericness rejection. After the examiner filed his appeal brief, Boston Beer filed a third supplemental brief arguing against genericness and moved to strike portions of the examiner's brief. Boston Beer argued that the examiner was limited to responding to the issues raised in the second supplemental brief, namely genericness, and could not address descriptiveness and acquired distinctiveness. Boston Beer argued that its proposed mark was not generic because there was no single category at the Great American Beer Festival and thus no "best beer in America" award. The board rejected the motion to strike.

The board found the proposed mark to be merely descriptive because it is only laudatory and "simply a claim of superiority, i.e., trade puffery."... The proposed mark was found not to be generic because the examiner's characterization of the genus or class of goods as "'beers brewed in America which have won taste competitions or were judged best in taste tests' stretches the limits of our language and is inconsistent with common usage."... The board held, however, that the proposed mark inherently cannot function as a trademark because such "claims of superiority should be freely available to all competitors in any given field to refer to their products or services."... Finally, the board said that "even if [it] were to find this expression to be capable of identifying applicant's beer and distinguishing it from beer made or sold by others, [the board] also would find, in view of the very high degree of descriptiveness which inheres in these words, that applicant has failed to establish secondary meaning in them as an identification of source."...This appeal followed.

Discussion

We review the board's legal conclusions, such as its interpretation of the Lanham Act, 15 U.S.C. §§ 1051-1127, de novo. We uphold the board's factual findings unless they are arbitrary, capricious, an abuse of discretion, or unsupported by substantial evidence...

"Marks that are merely laudatory and descriptive of the alleged merit of a product are also regarded as being descriptive.... Self-laudatory or puffing marks are regarded as a condensed form of describing the character or quality of the goods." 2 J. Thomas McCarthy, *McCarthy on Trademarks and Unfair*

Competition §§ 11:17 (4th ed. 1996) (internal quotations omitted). "If the mark is merely descriptive it may nevertheless acquire distinctiveness or secondary meaning and be registrable under Section 1052(f), although ... the greater the degree of descriptiveness the term has, the heavier the burden to prove it has attained secondary meaning."... To acquire secondary meaning, section 1052(f) requires that the mark must have become "distinctive of the applicant's goods." 15 U.S.C. §§ 1052(f) (1994).

Boston Beer provided evidence of advertising expenditures, an affidavit from its co-president, and an advertisement from a competitor. It argues that the use of the mark by others was either referring to Boston Beer's products or merely descriptive of the goods of others and was not used as a trademark. This argument is unavailing. The examples of use of the phrase by others in its descriptive form support the board's conclusion that the mark had not acquired distinctiveness. Therefore, on the facts of this case, and considering the highly descriptive nature of the proposed mark, Boston Beer has not met its burden to show that the proposed mark has acquired secondary meaning.

Boston Beer does not dispute that "The Best Beer in America" is a generally laudatory phrase. We have held that laudation does not per se prevent a mark from being registrable ... As Boston Beer correctly notes, there is an assortment of generally laudatory terms that serve as trademarks. But that is not invariably true; the specific facts of the case control ... As in this case, a phrase or slogan can be so highly laudatory and descriptive as to be incapable of acquiring distinctiveness as a trademark. The proposed mark is a common, laudatory advertising phrase which is merely descriptive of Boston Beer's goods. Indeed, it is so highly laudatory and descriptive of the qualities of its product that the slogan does not and could not function as a trademark to distinguish Boston Beer's goods and serve as an indication of origin. The record shows that "The Best Beer in America" is a common phrase used descriptively by others before and concurrently with Boston Beer's use, and is nothing more than a claim of superiority. Because the board's conclusion of non-registrability is supported by substantial evidence, is not arbitrary and capricious, and is not an abuse of discretion, we agree that "The Best Beer in America" is incapable of registration as a trademark...

Accordingly, the decision of the board is affirmed....

Case Questions

1. Why did the Court of Appeals affirm the examiner and refuse to grant the trademark?
2. The Court of Appeals referred to a provision in the Lanham Act that permits recognition of a mark if the proposed mark has acquired a secondary meaning. What do you think that means?

Patents

A patent is a grant of rights to an inventor from the government. The inventor, or owner of the rights, has the exclusive right to make, use, license others to use, and sell an invention for a period of years (twenty years for most inventions, fourteen years for design patents). After the term of years has expired, the invention goes into the public domain. Patents are only granted for inventions that are beneficial, original, and involve ingenuity. Patents are granted for new machines, methods, uses, and improvements to existing inventions. Patents are also granted for genetically engineered plants.

Copyrights

Authors of literary pieces, musical compositions, dramatic works, photographs, graphic works of various types, video and audio recordings, and computer software can acquire federal legal protection against most unauthorized uses by placing a prescribed copyright notice on publicly disseminated copies of the work. An owner or author of a copyrighted work is required to register with the Copyright Office in Washington, DC, prior to bringing suit for copyright infringement.

Congress enacted its first copyright statute in 1790 and that statute provided authors with exclusive rights to their works for two fourteen-year periods. Although the law has been amended many times, in recent decades substantial revisions occurred in 1978 and 1998. In 1978, Congress abolished common law copyrights and federalized the copyright process, and, in most instances extended the length of the copyright protection from a maximum of fifty-six years after publication to the author's life plus fifty years. In 1998, Congress enacted the Sonny Bono Copyright Extension Act, which extended copyright protections even further, to the life of the author plus seventy years for works that were produced after 1978 and to a maximum of ninety-five years for works produced prior to 1978. Proponents argue that extending the length of U.S. copyright protections brings the United States in line with similar provisions in existing international conventions. Opponents contend that a creator's copyright protections were intended by the founders to be limited. Even the most profitable works should ultimately make their way into the public domain (where anyone can freely use them without having to pay royalties).

The constitutionality of this statute was upheld by the U.S. Supreme Court in the 2003 case of *Eldred v. Ashcroft*. The court ruled that Congress had legal authority to extend the terms of copyright protections as provided in the statute.

The appellant in the following copyright case was sued by BMG Music for downloading music. She appealed the trial court's decision to grant summary judgment in favor of appellees to the U.S. Court of Appeals for the Seventh Circuit, claiming that her conduct should have been recognized by the trial court as fair use under the copyright statute.

BMG Music v. Cecilia Gonzalez
430 F.3d 888
U.S. Court of Appeals for the Seventh Circuit
December 9, 2005

Easterbrook, Circuit Judge.

Last June the Supreme Court held in *MGM Studios, Inc. v. Grokster, Ltd.* ... (2005), that a distributed file-sharing system is engaged in contributory copyright infringement when its principal object is the dissemination of copyrighted material. The foundation of this holding is a belief that people who post or download music files are primary infringers...

In this appeal Cecilia Gonzalez, who downloaded copyrighted music through the Kazaa file-sharing network ... contends that her activities were fair use rather than infringement. The district court disagreed and granted summary judgment for the copyright proprietors (to which we refer collectively as BMG Music).... The court enjoined Gonzalez from further infringement and awarded $22,500 in damages....

A "fair use" of copyrighted material is not infringement. Gonzalez insists that she was engaged in fair use ... or at least that a material dispute entitles her to a trial. It is undisputed, however, that she downloaded more than 1,370 copyrighted songs during a few weeks and kept them on her computer until she was caught. Her position is that she was just sampling music to determine what she liked enough to buy at retail. Because this suit was resolved on summary judgment, we must assume that Gonzalez is telling the truth when she says that she owned compact discs containing some of the songs before she downloaded them and that she purchased others later. She concedes, however, that she has never owned legitimate copies of 30 songs that she downloaded. (How many of the remainder she owned is disputed.)

Instead of erasing songs that she decided not to buy, she retained them. It is these 30 songs about which there is no dispute concerning ownership that formed the basis of the damages award.... The files that Gonzalez obtained ... were posted in violation of copyright law; there was no license covering a single transmission or hearing—and, to repeat, Gonzalez kept the copies....

[Title 17 U.S Code] Section 107 provides that when considering a defense of fair use the court must take into account "(1) the purpose and character of the use, including whether such use is of a commercial nature or is for nonprofit educational purposes; (2) the nature of the copyrighted work; (3) the amount and substantiality of the portion used in relation to the copyrighted work as a whole; and (4) the effect of the use upon the potential market for or value of the copyrighted work."

Gonzalez was not engaged in a nonprofit use; she downloaded (and kept) whole copyrighted songs (for which, as with poetry, copying of more than a couplet or two is deemed excessive); and she did this despite the fact that these works often are sold per song as well as per album. This leads her to concentrate on the fourth consideration: "the effect of the use upon the potential market for or value of the copyrighted work."

As she tells the tale, downloading on a try-before-you-buy basis is good advertising for copyright proprietors, expanding the value of their inventory. The Supreme Court thought otherwise in *Grokster*, with considerable empirical support. As file sharing has increased over the last four years, the sales of recorded music have dropped by approximately 30%. Perhaps other economic factors contributed, but the events likely are related. Music downloaded for free from the Internet is a close substitute for purchased music; many people are bound to keep the downloaded files without buying originals. That is exactly what Gonzalez did for at least 30 songs. It is no surprise, therefore, that the only appellate decision on point has held that downloading copyrighted songs cannot be defended as fair use, whether or not the recipient plans to buy songs she likes well enough to spring for....

Although BMG Music sought damages for only the 30 songs that Gonzalez concedes she has never purchased, all 1,000+ of her downloads violated the statute. All created copies of an entire work. All undermined the means by which authors seek to profit. Gonzalez proceeds as if the authors' only interest were in selling compact discs containing collections of works. Not so; there is also a market in ways to introduce potential consumers to music.

Think of radio. Authors and publishers collect royalties on the broadcast of recorded music, even though these broadcasts may boost sales.... Downloads from peer-to-peer networks such as Kazaa compete with licensed broadcasts and hence undermine the income available to authors. This is true even if a particular person never buys recorded media.... Many radio stations stream their content over the Internet, paying a fee for the right to do so. Gonzalez could have listened to this streaming music to sample songs for purchase; had she done so, the authors would have received royalties from the broadcasters (and reduced the risk that files saved to disk would diminish the urge to pay for the music in the end).

Licensed Internet sellers, such as the iTunes Music Store, offer samples—but again they pay authors a fee for the right to do so, and the teasers are just a portion of the original. Other intermediaries (not only Yahoo! Music Unlimited and Real Rhapsody but also the revived Napster, with a new business model) offer licensed access to large collections of music; customers may rent the whole library by the month or year, sample them all, and purchase any songs they want to keep. New technologies, such as SNOCAP, enable authorized trials over peer-to-peer systems....

Authorized previews share the feature of evanescence: if a listener decides not to buy (or stops paying the rental fee), no copy remains behind. With all of these means available to consumers who want to choose where to spend their money, downloading full copies of copyrighted material without compensation to authors cannot be deemed "fair use." Copyright law lets authors make their own decisions about how best to promote their works; copiers such as Gonzalez cannot ask courts (and juries) to second-guess the market and call wholesale copying "fair use" if they think that authors err in understanding their own economic interests or that Congress erred in granting authors the rights in the copyright statute. Nor can she defend by observing that other persons were greater offenders; Gonzalez's theme that she obtained "only 30" (or "only 1,300") copyrighted songs is no more relevant than a thief's contention that he shoplifted "only 30" compact discs, planning to listen to them at home and pay later for any he liked.

BMG Music elected to seek statutory damages under 17 U.S.C. § 504(c)(1) instead of proving actual injury. This section provides that the author's entitlement, per infringed work, is "a sum of not less than $750 or more than $30,000 as the court considers just." But if an "infringer sustains the burden of proving, and the court finds, that such infringer was not aware and had no reason to believe that his or her acts constituted an infringement of copyright, the court in its discretion may reduce the award of statutory damages to a sum of not less than $200."... Gonzalez asked the district court to reduce the award under this proviso, but the judge concluded that § 402(d) bars any reduction in the minimum award. This subsection provides: "If a notice of copyright in the form and position specified by this section appears on the published phonorecord or phonorecords to which a defendant in a copyright infringement suit had access, then no weight shall be given to such a defendant's interposition of a defense based on innocent infringement in mitigation of actual or statutory damages." It is undisputed that BMG Music gave copyright notice as required—"on the surface of the phonorecord, or on the phonorecord label or container."... It is likewise undisputed that Gonzalez had "access" to records and compact disks bearing the proper notice. She downloaded data rather than discs, and the data lacked copyright notices, but the statutory question is whether "access" to legitimate works was available rather than whether infringers earlier in the chain attached copyright notices to the pirated works. Gonzalez readily could have learned, had she inquired, that the music was under copyright.

As for the injunction: Gonzalez contends that this should be vacated because she has learned her lesson, has dropped her broadband access to the Internet, and

is unlikely to download copyrighted material again. A private party's discontinuation of unlawful conduct does not make the dispute moot, however. An injunction remains appropriate to ensure that the misconduct does not recur as soon as the case ends... The district court did not abuse its discretion in awarding prospective relief.

Affirmed.

Case Questions

1. What was the basis for Gonzalez's appeal?
2. How did the U.S. Court of Appeals for the Seventh Circuit respond to Gonzalez's claim?

An item of personal property that is the subject of both tangible and intangible property rights is called a **fixture.** For example, suppose that you buy a camera, the design of which is protected by a valid federal patent. Although you have acquired a piece of tangible personal property that you can use and dispose of in any legal manner, the law will recognize that you do not have all the right vis-à-vis the camera. The patent holder, for example, has intangible property rights in the camera's technology that prevent a purchaser from selling duplicates of the product or the technology without permission. Thus, both the patent holder and the purchaser have property rights to the same object.

A fixture is a category of property between realty and personality. For example, a dishwasher is classified as personality when it is purchased at an appliance store. When it is permanently built into the buyer's kitchen, however, it becomes a fixture.

Property rights are **contingent** when some future event must occur for the right to become **vested** (fully effective). For example, employers often require that employees work for a company for a specified number of years before their pension rights mature. Once pension rights vest, they belong to the employees even if they subsequently leave the company.

These distinctions are based on practical considerations; for example, tax rates may differ for realty, fixtures, and personality. In addition, the common law of each state governs real property, whereas the Uniform Commercial Code often governs personality.[12]

Property Ownership

Property can be owned in several different forms, including **severalty ownership, concurrent ownership**, and **community property**. Severalty ownership exists when property is owned by one person. Concurrent ownership exists when property is held simultaneously by more than one person. This can occur in one of three ways—**joint tenancy, tenancy in common**, and **tenancy by the entirety**.[13] In joint tenancy, each joint tenant takes an equal, undivided interest in the ownership of property from the same source and at the same time. Each joint tenant also has an undivided right of survivorship. Thus in a joint tenancy involving three tenants, the entire tenancy passes to the two survivors upon the death of the third and bypasses the deceased person's will and heirs. Tenancy in common is similar to a joint tenancy; however, there is no automatic passing of the deceased's rights to the surviving tenants. Instead, the deceased's rights pass according to the will. Tenancies in common can be sold, inherited, and given as a gift. Tenancy by the entirety can exist only between legally married husbands and wives and can be ended only through death, divorce, or mutual consent. Upon the death of one of the tenants, title passes to the surviving spouse. If a divorce occurs, the tenancy is converted into a tenancy in common.

The following case requires that the court determine whether a brother and sister hold title to real property as tenants in common or whether the brother holds title as the severalty owner.

In re Estate of Clayton Gulledge
637 A.2d 1278
District of Columbia Court of Appeals
April 4, 1996.

Schelb, Associate Justice

The issue...is whether the unilateral transfer by one of two joint tenants of his interest to a third party, without the consent of the other joint tenant, converts the joint tenancy into a tenancy in common. We hold that it does.

I.

The dispositive facts are undisputed. Clayton and Margie Gulledge owned a house at 532 Somerset Place, N.W. (the Somerset property) as tenants by the entirety. They had three children—Bernis Gulledge, Johnsie Walker, and Marion Watkins. Margie Gulledge died in 1970. Clayton Gulledge remarried the following year, but his second marriage was apparently unsuccessful.

In order to avert the possible loss, in any divorce proceedings, of the Somerset property, Bernis Gulledge advanced to his father the funds necessary to satisfy the second Mrs. Gulledge's financial demands. In exchange, Clayton Gulledge created a joint tenancy in the Somerset property, naming Bernis and himself as joint tenants. Bernis evidently expected that his father would predecease him, and that the right of survivorship which is the essence of a joint tenancy would enable him to acquire the entire property upon his father's death.

In 1988, however, Clayton Gulledge conveyed his interest in the Somerset property to his daughter, Marion Watkins, "in fee simple tenants in common." In 1991, Clayton Gulledge died, and he was survived by his three children. Bernis Gulledge died in 1993 and Johnsie B. Walker died in 1994. In the now consolidated proceedings relating to the estates of Clayton Gulledge, Bernis Gulledge, and Johnsie Walker, appellant Deborah Walker, Bernis' personal representative claims that when Clayton died, Bernis, as the surviving joint tenant, became the sole owner of the Somerset property. Ms. Watkins, on the other hand, contends that Clayton Gulledge's earlier conveyance of his interest to her severed the joint tenancy, thereby destroying Clayton's right of survivorship, and that Ms. Watkins and Bernis became tenants in common. The trial court agreed with Ms. Watkins....

II

The parties agree that Clayton Gulledge's interest in the joint tenancy was alienable. They disagree only as to the nature of the interest which Clayton transferred to Ms. Watkins. The Estate of Bernis Gulledge (the Estate) argues that an owner cannot convey to a third party a greater interest than his own ... and that because Clayton Gulledge's interest was subject to Bernis' right of survivorship, the interest which Ms. Watkins received from Clayton must be similarly restricted. Ms. Watkins contends, on the other hand, that Clayton's conveyance to her converted the joint tenancy into a tenancy in common by operation of law, and that she received from Clayton an undivided one-half interest in the property.

The question whether a joint tenant severs a joint tenancy by ultimately conveying his interest to a third party without the consent of the other joint tenant has not been squarely decided in the District of Columbia. The issue is one of law, and our review is therefore de novo.... The applicable rule in a large majority of jurisdictions is that either party to a joint tenancy may sever that tenancy by unilaterally disposing of his interest, that the consent of the other tenant is not required, and that the transfer converts the estate into a tenancy in common...

Although no decision by a court in this jurisdiction is directly on point, the discussion of joint tenancy that can be found in District of Columbia cases is consistent with the majority approach. In *Harrington v. Emmerman* ... the court explained that "Joint tenancy cannot exist unless there be present unity of interest, title, time *and possession* that is to say, the interests must be identical, they must accrue by the same conveyance, they must commence at the same time and the estate must be held by the same undivided possession." (Emphasis added.) The interests of Bernis Gulledge and Marion Watkins were not created by the same conveyance, nor did they commence at the same time; the conveyance to Ms. Watkins thus destroyed the unities of title and time...

In *Coleman v. Jackson,* ... the court held that where a marriage was invalid, the deed purporting to convey property to the couple as tenants by the entireties created a joint tenancy instead. Contrasting the two types of estates, the court pointed out that "[o]f course, joint tenancy lacks the feature of inalienability which tenancy by the entireties possesses.... [I]nalienability is an incident only of estates by the entireties..."

In *In re Estate of Wall,* the court restated the principle of *Coleman* and distinguished a tenancy by the entireties from a joint tenancy upon the ground that a tenancy by the entireties creates a "unilateral indestructible right of survivorship," while a joint tenancy does not. The court further stated that "survivorship incidental to joint tenancy differs because it may be frustrated ... by alienation or subjection to debts of a cotenant's undivided share or by compulsory partition."

Although the foregoing authorities do not conclusively settle the question before us, they provide no support for the notion that this court should reject the majority rule. Moreover, "[b]ecause District of Columbia law is derived from Maryland law, decisions of the Court of Appeals of Maryland, and particularly those relating to the law of property, are accorded the most respectful consideration by our courts ... Under Maryland law, the transfer of an interest in a joint tenancy by either joint tenant will sever the joint tenancy and cause the share conveyed to become property held as tenants in common with the other cotenants." ... We adopt the same rule here.

For the foregoing reasons, we conclude that when Clayton Gulledge conveyed his interest to Ms. Watkins, she and Bernis Gulledge both became owners of an undivided one-half interest in the property as tenants in common. Upon Bernis' death, his estate replaced Bernis as a tenant in common with Ms. Watkins. Accordingly, the trial court correctly held that Ms. Watkins and the Estate of Bernis Gulledge are tenants in common, and that each holds an undivided half interest in the Somerset property.

Affirmed.

Case Questions

1. What was the nature of the interest that Clayton transferred to his daughter, Marion Watkins?
2. Why didn't Bernis become the severalty owner of the Somerset property upon Clayton's death?
3. How was it possible for Clayton to create a joint tenancy in the property, with himself and his son Bernis as joint tenants?

Community Property

Community property is recognized by the states of Arizona, California, Idaho, Louisiana, Nevada, New Mexico, Texas, Washington, and Wisconsin. In community property states, each spouse is legally entitled to a percentage of what the state defines as community property, and this varies by jurisdiction. Although states differ, community property is usually defined as including the earnings of both spouses and property rights acquired with those earnings during the marriage. State statutes, however, usually exclude from community property rights acquired prior to marriage, spousal inheritances, and gifts received during the marriage. These are classified as separate property.

Community property states differ on whether earnings from separate property should be treated as community property.

Title

Title refers to ownership rights in property. For example, when a student purchases a textbook from a bookstore, he or she is purchasing the seller's title to the book. This means that the bookstore is selling all its rights in the book to the student. The bookstore will provide the purchaser with a receipt (bill of sale) to evidence the purchase of these rights and the transfer of ownership. If the student purchased the textbook from a thief, however, the student would not obtain title to the book. The larceny victim would still have the title, and the thief would be an unlawful possessor.[14]

A student who has purchased title to a textbook has many rights vis-à-vis that object. The student may decide to loan possessory rights to the book temporarily to another student. The student also has the right to decide whether to dispose of the book after completion of the course. For instance, the student might decide to make a gift of the book, sell his or her rights in the book to another student, or sell it back to the bookstore.

A bookstore does not have to produce a written document to establish its ownership when it sells a textbook to a student. However, the law does require the use of title documents to provide evidence of title for some property items. A seller of a motor vehicle, for example, must have a valid title document from the state to transfer ownership rights to the purchaser, and purchases of land require a title document called a deed.

GOVERNMENT'S RIGHT TO REGULATE AND TAKE PRIVATE PROPERTY

State government bears the primary responsibility for defining and limiting the exercise of private property rights through the police power. The police power refers to the authority of state legislatures to enact laws regulating and restraining private rights and occupations for the promotion of the public health, welfare, safety, and morals. The police power of the states is not a grant derived from a written constitution; the federal Constitution assumes the preexistence of the police power, and the Tenth Amendment reserves to the states any power not delegated to the federal government in Article I. Limitations on the police power have never been drawn with precision or determined by a general formula. But the Fifth and Fourteenth Amendments' Due Process Clauses require that state actions based on the police power be exercised in the public interest, be reasonable, and be consistent with the rights implied or secured in the Constitution. Government uses of the police power with respect to property are promulgated as environmental protection laws, administrative regulations (such as environmental rules), legislation (zoning, eminent domain, taxation), and tort law (for example, nuisance suits). See Figure 12.1 for an overview of the government's role in regulating private property.

Environmental Laws and Natural Resources Regulations: The Northern Spotted Owl Case

Historically, landowners have opposed governmental restrictions that prevent them from developing their land and harvesting its natural resources. In states where logging is big business and a major source of employment, limitations on commercial logging on privately owned timberland are very controversial. Environmentalists counter that it is essential that there be some legal regulation of commercial development on private property. They argue that the cumulative effect of decisions made independently by individual private landowners can produce destruction of critical habitat and cause already endangered species to become extinct.

This problem gained national prominence in 2006 when environmentalists in Washington sought to prevent small private landowners from logging portions of their forest land that threaten the Northern Spotted Owl's habitat. The triggering event was a federal lawsuit brought by the Seattle and Kittitas Audubon Societies against the Weyerhaeuser Company and state officials for allegedly violating the Endangered Species Protection Act. The plaintiffs wanted to prevent further destruction of owl habitat on Weyerhaeuser land and on other privately held forest timberland. They sought declaratory and injunctive relief, and a hearing was held over the granting of a temporary injunction that would prevent any new logging within the targeted forest areas pending the conclusion of the litigation. The plaintiffs explained to the court that they feared that state officials would, if not enjoined, allow private landowners to engage

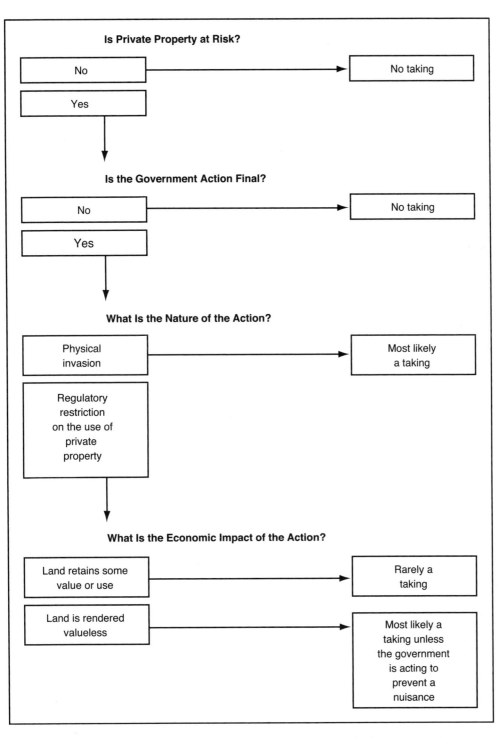

FIGURE 12.1 When Does Government Action Become a Taking of Private Property?

Source: Kathleen C. Zimmerman and David Abelson, "Takings Law: A Guide to Government, Property, and the Constitution," Copyright © 1993 by The Land & Water Fund of the Rockies, Inc.

in logging activities that could harm owls present within owl habitat located on their timberland properties. The plaintiffs identified by location 266 owl habitat administrative zones called "owl circles" that they believed warranted legal protection from logging pending the resolution of the suit. Four of the "owl circles" were located on Weyerhaeuser property, with the remaining 262 situated on other privately owned sites. The district court agreed with the plaintiffs with respect to the Weyerhaeuser owl circles and issued the injunction. But the court refused to enjoin the state, concluding that the plaintiff's proof was legally insufficient to support an injunction. The plaintiffs had only provided evidence that owls were actually present in 44 of the 262 owl circles. Also lacking was proof as to how much owl habitat actually existed in any of the 262 administrative zones. The only habitat-specific evidence presented was limited to the four owl circles on Weyerhaeuser land.[15]

The district judge's rulings on the injunctions may have caused the parties to rethink the wisdom of resolving their differences in a judicial forum. The plaintiffs may have concluded that the cost of obtaining the missing data, paying the costs of a trial, and litigating this and other similar cases in the future just did not make economic sense. What is certain is that in July 2008 the parties jointly announced that they had reached a settlement. Although not all of the settlement terms were revealed, the parties reported that they had agreed to work collaboratively as members of a "policy working group" and to scientifically determine the best strategies for identifying, improving and preserving spotted owl habitat that is located on privately owned land. Weyerhaeuser also agreed to protect the four owl circles on its land.

In 2010, the working group initiated a "pilot project" for eastern Washington that focuses on protecting owl habitat located on privately held land that is frequently subject to forest fires.

The federal government, recognizing the need to encourage small forest landowners to participate voluntarily in protecting endangered species habitat, has attempted to address some of the landowners' concerns. Because many private owners of timberland fear governmental land restrictions, they find it necessary to discourage the presence of an endangered species on their forested land. Having recognized the fear, and wishing to overcome this disincentive, the U.S. Fish and Wildlife Service developed a "Safe Harbor Agreements" program. Under this program, the FWS can negotiate agreements with private landowners to encourage them to manage their private property actively in ways that benefit endangered species. The landowners benefit from these agreements because the government provides them with written "assurances." The government, in essence, promises that landowners who help in building and retaining habitat as specified in the agreement will not be subjected to enhanced levels of land regulation in the future. These agreements can also include provisions allowing a landowner to alter an endangered habitat in specified ways (including some logging), if in the end there is a "net conservation benefit" to the endangered species.

Zoning

State legislatures originally authorized local governments to enact zoning regulations to promote public health and safety by separating housing districts from incompatible commercial and industrial uses. Today, zoning ordinances also preserve a community's historically significant landmarks and neighborhoods and restrict adult entertainment. State and local environmental protection agencies often resort to zoning ordinances in deciding whether to grant licenses to land developers where a proposed land use threatens wetlands or natural habitat, or increases air or water pollution. Zoning ordinances can be very controversial, such as when they prohibit trailer parks or require that structures and lots be large (and therefore often unaffordable to low-income people). In the Family Law chapter (Chapter IX), you can see another example of restrictive zoning. In that 1977 case decided by the U.S. Supreme Court, entitled *Moore v. City of East Cleveland*, governmental authorities unsuccessfully sought to use a zoning ordinance to prohibit a grandmother from living with her two grandchildren.

Eminent Domain

The government can take private property for a public purpose over the objection of a landowner pursuant to what is called the power of **eminent domain.** The Fifth Amendment's Takings Clause provides that whenever the federal government takes property to benefit the public, it must pay just compensation. This constitutional control on government has been incorporated into the Fourteenth Amendment and is also binding on the states. The Takings Clause protects individual private property rights by ensuring that taxpayers, rather than targeted private individuals, pay for public benefits.

Government obtains title to private land through condemnation proceedings in which a court ensures that statutory and constitutional requirements are satisfied. In a related proceeding, a court will determine the fair market value of the land that will be paid to the property owner.

The U.S. Supreme Court has been unsuccessful to date in precisely establishing what constitutes a "taking." It has, however, recognized that takings can assume different forms. One obvious example is where the government takes title to land for the purpose of building a public highway. Other takings, however, are less obvious. The Supreme Court found in 1946 that a taking had occurred where low-flying military aircraft created so much noise while flying over a chicken farm that the farm went out of business.[16] The Court ruled that under these circumstances the government had exploited and in effect taken airspace above it for a flight path (a public purpose), to the commercial detriment of the farmer. The farmer, said the Court, was entitled to compensation.

In a 1978 case, the U.S. Supreme Court had to rule on whether New York City, as part of a historic landmarks preservation program, could impose limitations on the development or redevelopment of historic sites such as Grand Central Station. The city wanted to prevent the construction of a large office building above the station. To the developer, the restrictions imposed by the Landmark Preservation Law amounted to a taking of private property (the airspace above the station) for a public purpose, for which compensation was due. The Court ruled in favor of the city, largely because the law served a public purpose (improving the quality of life for all New Yorkers) and provided the developer with a reasonable economic return on investment.

Historically, landowners have argued that they should be compensated when their property values fall as a result of governmental restrictions that prevent them from commercially developing their land and its natural resources. Defenders maintained that such regulations were necessary because the cumulative effect of the individual actions of private landowners would likely result in endangered species becoming extinct. Legislative initiatives designed to protect the environment, and preserve aesthetic and cultural landmarks, have generally been upheld by the Supreme Court.

The Controversial Decision in the *Kelo* Case

The U.S. Supreme Court's decision in *Susette Kelo v. City of New London*, 545 U.S. 469 (§2005), attracted national attention and considerable outrage throughout the nation. The case arose out of an attempt by the state of Connecticut and the city of New London to revitalize an "economically distressed" area of New London. The proponents of the redevelopment plan sought to use the power of eminent domain to acquire the title to parcels owned by persons who rejected the city's offers to buy them out. Susette Kelo was one of the owners unwilling to sell. Those favoring the plan argued that implementation of the plan would create jobs, improve New London's image, strengthen its tax base and generally enhance its downtown and waterfront areas.

Susette Kelo claimed that the Takings Clause prohibited New London from acquiring her property by way of eminent domain in order to implement an economic development plan. The justices disagreed over whether to commit the federal judiciary to using the Fifth Amendment's Takings Clause to establish national standards for the nation with respect to the potentially endless battles between developers and landowners. The Supreme Court ruled 5–4 that the states should have this responsibility.

Justice Stevens, for the majority, explained that the Takings Clause only required that a condemned parcel be used for a "public purpose" if the taking of the private property occurred pursuant to a "carefully considered development plan." In *Kelo*, Stevens argued that Susette Kelo's house had been taken by eminent domain as part of a comprehensive economic development plan, which had been specifically authorized by Connecticut statute. Justice Stevens acknowledged that many states might believe the federal "public purpose" standard to be too low, and he rejected imposing a "one-size-fits-all" approach on the country. He basically left it up to the states to decide for themselves what standard should apply, explaining it this way:

> We emphasize that nothing in our opinion precludes any State from placing further restrictions on its exercise of the takings power. Indeed, many States already impose "public use" requirements that are stricter than the federal baseline. Some of these requirements have been established as a matter of state constitutional law ... while others are expressed in state eminent domain statutes that carefully limit the grounds upon which takings may be exercised.... As the submissions of the parties and their amici make clear, the necessity and wisdom of using eminent domain to promote economic development are certainly matters of legitimate public debate.... This Court's authority, however, extends only to determining whether the City's proposed condemnations are for a "public use" within the meaning of the Fifth Amendment to the Federal Constitution....

The public reaction to the *Kelo* decision was loud and negative. Within one year, over half of the states took action by statute or constitutional amendment and increased the restrictions on the use of eminent domain. That number has increased to approximately forty states. In this manner, the U.S. Supreme Court kept countless cases out of the federal judicial system, dodged having to define and defend a national standard in these complex cases, and transferred the brunt of the problem to the state legislatures. This will probably mean that a variety of solutions will emerge over time, and the law will continue to evolve to meet the needs of each jurisdiction.

INTERNET TIP

Interested readers can find an edited version of the majority opinion in *Kelo v. New London* and Justice O'Connor's thought-provoking dissent with the Chapter XII materials on the textbook's website.

Introduction to *Goldstein v. Urban Development Corporation*

The petitioners-appellants in *Goldstein v. Urban Development Corporation* are property owners in Brooklyn, New York who had their property taken by eminent domain by the UDC as part of an economic development initiative. They brought suit in state court, saying, in essence, that Justice Sandra Day O'Connor's conclusion in her *Kelo* dissent that "economic development takings" were unconstitutional under the federal constitution was also applicable to the New York constitution. The development project to be completed in Brooklyn was intended to replace the existing lesser-value properties with higher-value uses including an office tower, apartments, and a new arena for the New Jersey Nets NBA basketball team, to be constructed in time for the 2012–2013 season.

The respondent–appellee, Urban Development Corporation (UDC), is a public benefit corporation created by the New York legislature to help finance economic and job development throughout the state of New York. Because it is a hybrid entity (partly governmental and partly private) it can issue bonds for which the state has no responsibility and can circumvent the debt limitation provisions in the state constitution. It can also exercise the power of eminent domain to achieve its public purposes. UDC's claimed justification for using eminent domain to take private homes located on land essential to the completion of this project was similar to New London's rationale in the *Kelo* case . The use of eminent domain was for a public

purpose. It would provide employment, affordable housing (30 percent of the apartments would have to be leased to low- or middle-income people), attract retail businesses to the area, and generate tax revenue for the city and state.

Daniel Goldstein v. Urban Development Corporation
921 N.E.2d 164
Court of Appeals of New York.
November 24, 2009

Chief Judge Lippman

We are asked to determine whether respondent's exercise of its power of eminent domain to acquire petitioners' properties for purposes of the proposed land use improvement project, known as Atlantic Yards, would be in conformity with certain provisions of our State Constitution. We answer in the affirmative.

On December 8, 2006, respondent Empire State Development Corporation (ESDC) issued a determination pursuant to Eminent Domain Procedure Law (EDPL) § 204, finding that it should use its eminent domain power to take certain privately owned properties located in downtown Brooklyn for inclusion in a 22-acre mixed-use development proposed, and to be undertaken, by private developer Bruce Ratner and the real estate entities of which he is a principal, collectively known as the Forest City Ratner Companies (FCRC)....

The project is to involve, in its first phase, construction of a sports arena to house the NBA Nets franchise, as well as various infrastructure improvements—most notably reconfiguration and modernization of the Vanderbilt Yards rail facilities and access upgrades to the subway transportation hub already present at the site. The project will also involve construction of a platform spanning the rail yards and connecting portions of the neighborhood now separated by the rail cut. Atop this platform are to be situated, in a second phase of construction, numerous high rise buildings and some eight acres of open, publicly accessible landscaped space. The 16 towers planned for the project will serve both commercial and residential purposes. They are slated to contain between 5,325 and 6,430 dwelling units, more than a third of which are to be affordable either for low and/or middle income families.

The project has been sponsored by respondent ESDC as a "land use improvement project"... upon findings that the area in which the project is to be situated is "substandard and insanitary"... or, in more

common parlance, blighted. It is not disputed that the project designation and supporting blight findings are appropriate with respect to more than half the project footprint, which lies within what has, since 1968, been designated by the City of New York as the Atlantic Terminal Urban Renewal Area (ATURA). To the south of ATURA, however, and immediately adjacent to the Vanderbilt Yards cut, are two blocks and a fraction of a third which, although within the project footprint, have not previously been designated as blighted. FCRC has purchased many of the properties in this area, but there remain some that it has been unsuccessful in acquiring, whose transfer ESDC now seeks to compel in furtherance of the project, through condemnation. In support of its exercise of the condemnation power with respect to these properties, some of which are owned by petitioners, ESDC, based on studies conducted by a consulting firm retained by FCRC, has made findings that the blocks in which they are situated possess sufficient indicia of actual or impending blight to warrant their condemnation for clearance and redevelopment ... and that the proposed land use improvement project will, by removing blight and creating in its place the above-described mixed-use development, serve a "public use, benefit or purpose."...

The Appellate Division, although rejecting respondent's contention that the proceeding was time-barred, found for respondent on the merits....

I

[The court's decision not to bar this appeal on procedural grounds been omitted to conserve space].

II

Turning now to the merits, petitioners first contend that the determination authorizing the condemnation of their properties for the Atlantic Yards project is unconstitutional because the condemnation is not for the purpose of putting their properties to "public use" within the meaning of article I, § 7 (a) of the State

Constitution—which provides that "[p]rivate property shall not be taken for public use without just compensation"—but rather to enable a private commercial entity to use their properties for private economic gain with, perhaps, some incidental public benefit. The argument reduces to this: that the State Constitution has from its inception, in recognition of the fundamental right to privately own property, strictly limited the availability of condemnation to situations in which the property to be condemned will actually be made available for public use, and that, with only limited exceptions prompted by emergent public necessity, the State Constitution's Takings Clause, unlike its federal counterpart, has been consistently understood literally to permit a taking of private property only for "public use," and not simply to accomplish a public purpose.

Even if this gloss on this State's takings laws and jurisprudence were correct—and it is not … it is indisputable that the removal of urban blight is a proper, and, indeed, constitutionally sanctioned, predicate for the exercise of the power of eminent domain. It has been deemed a "public use" within the meaning of the State Constitution's Takings Clause at least since … 1936 … and is expressly recognized by the Constitution as a ground for condemnation. Article XVIII, § 1 of the State Constitution grants the Legislature the power to "provide in such manner, by such means and upon such terms and conditions as it may prescribe … for the clearance, replanning, reconstruction and rehabilitation of substandard and insanitary areas," and section 2 of the same article provides "[f]or and in aid of such purposes, notwithstanding any provision in any other article of this constitution … the legislature may … grant the power of eminent domain to any … public corporation."… Pursuant to article XVIII, respondent ESDC has been vested with the condemnation power by the Legislature … and has here sought to exercise the power for the constitutionally recognized public purpose or "use" of rehabilitating a blighted area.

Petitioners, of course, maintain that the blocks at issue are not, in fact, blighted and that the allegedly mild dilapidation and inutility of the property cannot support a finding that it is substandard and insanitary within the meaning of article XVIII. They are doubtless correct that the conditions cited in support of the blight finding at issue do not begin to approach in severity the dire circumstances of urban slum dwelling described by the *Muller* court in 1936.… We, however, have never required that a finding of blight by a legislatively designated public benefit corporation be based upon conditions replicating those to which the Court and the Constitutional Convention responded in the midst of the Great Depression. To the contrary, in construing the reach of the terms "substandard and

insanitary" as they are used in article XVIII—and were applied in the early 1950s to the Columbus Circle area upon which the New York Coliseum was proposed to be built—we observed:

"Of course, none of the buildings are as noisome or dilapidated as those described in Dickens' novels or Thomas Burke's 'Limehouse' stories of the London slums of other days, but there is ample in this record to justify the determination of the city planning commission that a substantial part of the area is 'substandard and insanitary' by modern tests."…

And, subsequently, in *Yonkers Community Dev. Agency v Morris* … [1975]), in reviewing the evolution of the crucial terms' signification and permissible range of application, we noted:

"Historically, urban renewal began as an effort to remove 'substandard and insanitary' conditions which threatened the health and welfare of the public, in other words 'slums'…, whose eradication was in itself found to constitute a public purpose for which the condemnation powers of government might constitutionally be employed. Gradually, as the complexities of urban conditions became better understood, it has become clear that the areas eligible for such renewal are not limited to 'slums' as that term was formerly applied, and that, among other things, economic underdevelopment and stagnation are also threats to the public sufficient to make their removal cognizable as a public purpose.…

It is important to stress that lending precise content to these general terms has not been, and may not be, primarily a judicial exercise. Whether a matter should be the subject of a public undertaking—whether its pursuit will serve a public purpose or use—is ordinarily the province of the Legislature, not the Judiciary, and the actual specification of the uses identified by the Legislature as public has been largely left to quasi-legislative administrative agencies. It is only where there is no room for reasonable difference of opinion as to whether an area is blighted, that judges may substitute their views as to the adequacy with which the public purpose of blight removal has been made out for those of the legislatively designated agencies; where, as here, "those bodies have made their finding, not corruptly or irrationally or baselessly, there is nothing for the courts to do about it, unless every act and decision of other departments of government is subject to revision by the courts."…

It is quite possible to differ with ESDC's findings that the blocks in question are affected by numerous conditions indicative of blight, but any such difference would not, on this record, in which the bases for the agency findings have been extensively documented photographically and otherwise on a lot-by-lot basis, amount to more than another reasonable view of the matter; such a difference could not, consonant with what we have recognized to be the structural limitations upon our review of what is essentially a legislative prerogative, furnish a ground to afford petitioners relief....

It may be that the bar has now been set too low—that what will now pass as "blight," as that expression has come to be understood and used by political appointees to public corporations relying upon studies paid for by developers, should not be permitted to constitute a predicate for the invasion of property rights and the razing of homes and businesses. But any such limitation upon the sovereign power of eminent domain as it has come to be defined in the urban renewal context is a matter for the Legislature, not the courts. Properly involved in redrawing the range of the sovereign prerogative would not be a simple return to the days when private property rights were viewed as virtually inviolable, even when they stood in the way of meeting compelling public needs, but a reweighing of public as against private interests and a reassessment of the need for and public utility of what may now be outmoded approaches to the revivification of the urban landscape. These are not tasks courts are suited to perform. They are appropriately situated in the policy-making branches of government....

While there remains a hypothetical case in which we might intervene to prevent an urban redevelopment condemnation on public use grounds—where "the physical conditions of an area might be such that it would be irrational and baseless to call it substandard or insanitary"... this is not that case....

Here too, all that is at issue is a reasonable difference of opinion as to whether the area in question is in fact substandard and insanitary. This is not a sufficient predicate for us to supplant respondent's determination.

III

Petitioners' remaining contention is that the proposed condemnation should not have been authorized because the land use improvement project it is to advance is not in conformity with article XVIII, § 6 of the State Constitution, which states:

"No loan, or subsidy shall be made by the state to aid any project unless such project is in conformity with a plan or undertaking for the clearance, replanning and reconstruction or rehabilitation of a substandard and unsanitary area or areas and for recreational and other facilities incidental or appurtenant thereto. The legislature may provide additional conditions to the making of such loans or subsidies consistent with the purposes of this article. The occupancy of

any such project shall be restricted to persons of low income as defined by law and preference shall be given to persons who live or shall have lived in such area or areas" (emphasis added).

Petitioners understand this provision as requiring that any housing built as part of a land use improvement project receiving a state loan or subsidy be reserved for low income tenants. In alleging that Atlantic Yards, as presently configured, does not comply with article XVIII, § 6, they point out that although it is a land use improvement project expressly governed by article XVIII ... that has already received some $100 million in state financing and is expected to be the recipient of additional state aid earmarked for affordable housing, the majority of the project's housing units are slated to be rented or sold at market rates.

Petitioners' understanding of section 6 does not capture the provision's intendment....

Article XVIII was, as noted, adopted and approved in the late 1930s to empower government, in partnership with private entities, to deal with the emergent problem of slums, which then spread over large portions of the urban landscape like running sores, endangering the health and well-being of their occupants and the civic life of the municipalities in which they were situated. What was envisioned was the use of the condemnation power to clear large swaths of slum dwellings—in some cases entire neighborhoods. The feasibility and ultimate purpose of this scenario, entailing the massive direct displacement of slum dwellers, required the creation of replacement low cost housing, and it is clear from the record of the 1938 Constitutional Convention that it was to address this need that the last sentence of article XVIII, § 6 was crafted... and, after extended separate consideration and revision, agreed upon.... The sentence in essence assures that if housing is created in connection with a slum clearance project, and the project is aided by state loans or subsidies, the new housing will replace the low rent accommodations lost during the clearance....

The situation before us is, as petitioners have elsewhere acknowledged and indeed urged, very different from the scenario addressed by the framers of section 6's occupancy restriction. The land use improvement plan at issue is not directed at the wholesale eradication of slums, but rather at alleviating relatively mild conditions of urban blight principally attributable to a large and, of course, uninhabited subgrade rail cut. The contemplated clearance will not cause direct displacement of large concentrations of low income individuals; only 146 persons lived within the project footprint at the time of the final environmental impact statement, and not all of those were persons of low income. It does not seem plausible that the constitutionality of a project of this sort was meant to turn upon whether its occupancy was restricted to persons of low income. While the creation of low income housing is a generally worthy objective, it is not constitutionally required under article XVIII, § 6 as an element of a land use improvement project that does not entail substantial slum clearance....

Accordingly, the order of the Appellate Division should be affirmed, with costs.

Case Questions

1. What exactly did New York's highest court actually decide in this case?
2. Can you see any consequences that might flow from this decision?
3. Did you agree with the decision? Explain.

INTERNET TIP

Judge Smith dissented in *Goldstein v. Urban Development Corporation*. His opinion can be found with the Chapter XII materials on the textbook's website.

Taxation

A property owner is usually required to pay taxes to the government based on the value and use of the property. Failure to pay these taxes can result in the filing of a lien and eventually in the public taking of the property to satisfy the taxes. Government frequently uses tax concessions to encourage property uses it favors.

Nuisance

A **nuisance** exists when an owner's use of his or her property unreasonably infringes on other persons' use and enjoyment of their property rights. Nuisances are classified as public, private, or both. A **public nuisance** exists when a given use of land poses a generalized threat to the public. It is redressed by criminal prosecution and injunctive relief. Examples of public nuisances include houses of prostitution, actions affecting the public health (such as water and air pollution), crack houses, and dance halls. A **private nuisance** is a tort that requires proof of an injury that is distinct from that suffered by the general public. (It differs from trespass because the offensive activity does not occur on the victim's property.) A party injured by a private nuisance can obtain both damages and injunctive relief.

Hugh and Jackie Evans claimed that the conduct of the defendant, Lochmere Recreation Club, interfered with their right to the enjoyment and use of their property and constituted a private nuisance. They appealed from a trial court's decision to dismiss their complaint for failing to state a claim on which relief could be granted.

Hugh K. Evans v. Lochmere Recreation Club, Inc.
627 S.E.2d 340
Court of Appeals of North Carolina
March 21, 2006

Bryant, Judge.
Hugh K. Evans and Jackie Evans (plaintiffs) appeal from an order entered 27 April 2005 dismissing their claims against Lochmere Recreation Club, Inc. (defendant) ...

Facts & Procedural History
In 1994, plaintiff Hugh Evans (Evans) filed suit against MacGregor Development Co. (MacGregor) and Lochmere Swim & Tennis Club, Inc. (LSTC), claiming the

noise from the speakers and crowds located at the Swim Club interfered with the use and enjoyment of his property. At trial, a jury found in favor of Evans and awarded him $50,000.00 in compensatory damages and $135,000.00 in punitive damages. The trial court further granted a permanent injunction and restraining order against MacGregor and LSTC instructing them to take measures, such as repositioning their speakers, to reduce the noise encroachment on plaintiff's property. This final judgment was affirmed on appeal.... In 1998 defendant Lochmere Recreation Club acquired the property from LSTC.

Plaintiffs initiated the instant civil action against defendant on 22 December 2004, alleging that between May and September of each year from 1998–2004, defendant operated their swim and tennis club in a manner that created a nuisance. Plaintiff's complaint listed several different ways in which plaintiffs assert that defendant caused an unreasonable interference with the enjoyment of their home.... On 13 January 2005, defendant moved to dismiss plaintiffs' complaint...

Defendant's motion was heard on 5 April 2005.... On 27 April 2005, the trial court granted defendant's motion to dismiss.... Plaintiffs appeal.

Plaintiffs argue that the trial court erred in dismissing their claim for private nuisance...

Standard of Review
"The system of notice pleading affords a sufficiently liberal construction of complaints so that few fail to survive a motion to dismiss." In considering a Rule 12 (b)(6) motion to dismiss, the trial court must determine whether the factual allegations in the complaint state a claim for relief.... A plaintiff must state the "substantive elements of a legally recognized claim" in order to survive a Rule 12(b)(6) motion to dismiss.... To support a complaint for private nuisance, a plaintiff must allege "sufficient facts from which it may be determined what liability forming conduct is being complained of and what injury plaintiffs have suffered."... When hearing a motion to dismiss, the trial court must take the complaint's allegations as true and determine whether they are "'sufficient to state a claim upon which relief may be granted under some legal theory.'"...

Sufficiency of Complaint
"[A] private nuisance exists in a legal sense when one makes an improper use of his own property and in that way injures the land or some incorporeal right of one's neighbor." ... In their complaint plaintiffs alleged several specific actions which would support a private nuisance claim against defendant, including that defendant "has used amplified sound from speakers aimed directly at [plaintiffs'] premises" and that when the public address system is used, "it can be clearly heard in plaintiffs' home even with all plaintiffs' doors and windows closed and their television playing."... As the complaint is to be liberally construed, we find it is sufficient on its face to "provide defendant sufficient notice of the conduct on which the claim is based to enable defendant to respond and prepare for trial" and "states enough ... to satisfy the substantive elements" of a private nuisance claim against defendant...

Affirmed in part, reversed in part, and remanded for further proceedings on plaintiffs' claim for private nuisance...

Case Questions

1. What does the court mean when it says that the complaint is to be liberally construed?
2. What is required to change a private nuisance into a public nuisance?

REAL PROPERTY

The laws that govern real property in America have their origins in medieval England. Under feudal law all land was derived from the king; thus it was possible for someone to own an **estate** in land but not the actual land itself. Estates were classified according to their duration, a practice that continues in American law today.

Estates in Land

The word estate is derived from the Latin word for status. An estate in land, therefore, is the amount of interest a person has in land. Some estates in land can be inherited. A person who holds an estate in what is known as **fee simple** can pass his or her interest on to heirs. This represents the maximum ownership right to land that is permissible by law. A person who has an estate in land for the duration of his or her life has a **life estate** in land. Life estates cannot be passed on to heirs.

A person who leases real property has only a possessory interest in land called a leasehold. **Leaseholds** allow tenants to obtain **possessory** interests in real property for a month, a year, or even at will.

A landowner has the right to minerals that exist beneath the surface of the land. Landowners also have the right to control and use the airspace above their land. Governmental regulations regarding the height of buildings, as well as engineering limitations that are associated with a particular property, often limit the exercise of this right.

Easements

Easements and licenses are interests in land that do not amount to an estate but affect the owner's use of land. An **easement** is a nonpossessory property right in land; it is one person's right to use another person's land. For example, B might grant A an easement that permits her to use a private road on B's property. Because B continues to own the land, B can grant similar easements to persons C and D. B can grant these additional easements without having to obtain permission from A because A lacks possessory rights on B's land. Easements are often classified as affirmative or negative. An affirmative easement would exist where landowner A conveys to B the right to lay a pipeline across A's land. A negative easement would exist where A conveys part of her land to B and retains an easement that forbids B to burn trash or plant trees within five yards of A's property line.

An easement also may be created by eminent domain. In such a case, the landowner is constitutionally entitled to receive just compensation. Easements often are created by deed, and usually have to be in writing to be legally enforceable. They can be limited to a specific term or event or they can be of infinite duration. It is commonly said that easements "run with the land," meaning that the burden or benefit of the easement is transferred with the land to the subsequent owners.

Licenses

A **license** is a temporary grant of authority to do specified things on the land of another, for example, hunt or fish. A license can be oral because it is not an actual estate in land and therefore is not subject to the statute of frauds (see Chapter X). Licenses can generally be revoked at will.

Covenants

To protect themselves from sellers who don't have title, purchasers of land often require the seller to make certain promises in the deed that are called **covenants.** The grantor's covenants ensure that he or she has possessory rights to the premises and that the title is good and is free of encumbrances. The grantor will further promise to defend this title against the claims and demands of other people.

Other covenants that affect land use are those that run with the land. Historically, restrictive covenants have discriminated against people because of race, religion, or national origin. Today such covenants are illegal and contrary to public policy and would not be enforced in any court. Courts will, in appropriate cases, enforce nondiscriminatory covenants that run with the land and that create contractual rights in property. Although easements have traditionally been used to affect land use, lawyers began to resort to covenants to augment the kind of restrictions sellers could require of purchasers beyond the scope of easements. A baker, for example, might be willing to sell an adjacent lot that he owns; however, he might protect his business by requiring the purchaser to covenant that the premises conveyed will not be used for the operation or maintenance of a bakery, lunchroom, or restaurant.

Covenants that run with the land are regulated closely by courts because they restrict the use of property. For a covenant to run with the land and bind successive landowners, the original grantor and grantee must have intended that the restrictions on the covenant go with the land. In addition, a close, direct relationship known as **privity of estate** must exist between a grantor and a grantee. The privity requirement is satisfied, for example, when land developer A deeds part of her land to B, and B covenants not to put up a fence on B's land without A's written approval. Finally, covenants must "touch and concern" land; they may not be promises that are personal and unrelated to land. Successors in interest to the original grantor and grantee will be bound by the terms of a properly created covenant that runs with the land.

Adverse Possession

A person who has no lawful right of possession can obtain title to another's land by complying with the rules for **adverse possession** (also known as an **easement by prescription**). The law requires property owners to ensure that no one else uses the land without permission, and a person who fails to use or protect his or her land for many years may one day lose title to an adverse possessor. In order to obtain title by adverse possession, the adverse possessor must take actual possession of the land; the possession must be hostile (without the consent of the owner); the possession must be adverse (against the owner's interest); the possession must be open and notorious (obvious and knowable to anyone who is interested); and the possession must be continuous for a statutorily determined period of time, often twenty years. A successful adverse possessor cannot sell the land until he or she has a marketable title (clear ownership of the land). To obtain a marketable title, the adverse possessor has to file what is called a quiet title action. If the court rules in favor of the adverse possessor, he or she will have a clear title to the land.

Introduction to *Steuk v. Easley*

The defendant/appellant in the next case, Dr. Newell Easley, appealed a trial judge's decision that Easley's neighbors to the east, Peter and Barbara Steuk, had acquired title to seventeen acres of Easley's land by adverse possession. The Steuks had purchased their property from Dale Daggett in 2001, who had in turn purchased this parcel in 1974 from Gordon Daniels. The Daniels/Daggett/Steuk property was adjacent to an essentially undeveloped seventeen-acre parcel which Easley. purchased in 1987. The Steuks (referred to as the plaintiffs in the court's opinion) filed suit claiming that they had acquired title to the seventeen acres through adverse possession. They offered as proof the testimony of their predecessors in title (Daggett and Daniels). Daggett and Daniels testified that while they were owners of the property now owned by the Steuks, they had hunted on the seventeen acres. When their years of hunting were added to the Steuks' possession, it added up to twenty-nine consecutive years on that parcel. Both maintained that throughout that twenty-nine–year period they had been unaware that the land belonged to Easley.

The question before the intermediate court of appeals was: Were the hunters adverse possessors or merely trespassers?

Steuck v. Easley
2009AP757
Court of Appeals of Wisconsin, District IV
May 13, 2010.

Vergeront, J.
This adverse possession claim concerns approximately seventeen acres of undeveloped land in a larger tract of several hundred acres primarily used for hunting by the titleholder, Newell Easley.... Easley appeals the circuit court's determination that the plaintiffs established title to the disputed area by adverse possession....

Background
Easley owns at least 360 acres of undeveloped land in the Township of Shields, Marquette County. He uses his land primarily for hunting and also for activities such as gathering firewood, picking apples, and hiking on the hiking trails. He has set aside some of his land as a sanctuary for the purpose of managing, growing and protecting a deer herd....

The complaint alleges that the use of the disputed area by the plaintiffs' predecessors in title for more than twenty years has established ownership by adverse possession as provided in Wis. Stat. § 893.25....

At the trial to the court, Dale Daggett, the plaintiffs' predecessor in title, testified that when he purchased the property in 2001, he believed he owned the disputed area and he treated it as his. He bow hunted there in the fall of 2003; he went four-wheeling there three or four times in 2003 and a couple times in 2004; he took friends to walk there; and he cleared brush off a trail. He never saw anyone else in that area....

Easley testified that he and one or more of his family and friends are on his land approximately 180 days per year. They do not hunt in the sanctuary, which includes the disputed area. He goes into the disputed area once or twice a year and tries to observe it from a distance because walking through it defeats the purpose of a sanctuary. He never noticed persons trespassing in the disputed area nor saw anything that caused him to believe someone was doing something of a permanent nature. No one in his family or his hunting group gave him any indication there was hunting or other activities going on in the disputed area. He did see two tree stands in the area, but they were very old, and he was sure they had been there for many years prior to his purchase of the property.

The court concluded that the plaintiffs had established title by adverse possession to the disputed area and entered judgment granting full right and title to that property to the plaintiffs....

Discussion

On appeal Easley contends: (1) the circuit court disregarded the presumption in favor of the titleholder and improperly placed the burden on him to prove he had taken measures to keep people off his property; (2) the evidence is insufficient to establish adverse possession when the correct legal standard is applied; and (3) the evidence is insufficient to show he acquiesced to the man-made ditch as the boundary between his property in Lot 6 and the plaintiffs' property....

I. Adverse Possession under WIS. STAT. § 893.25

Pursuant to WIS. STAT. § 893.25(2)(a) and (b), real estate is possessed adversely only if "the person possessing it, in connection with his or her predecessors in interest, is in actual continued occupation under claim of title, exclusive of any other right," and "[o]nly to the extent that it is actually occupied." In addition, the property must be "protected by a substantial enclosure" or "usually cultivated or improved." § 893.25(2)(b). Pursuant to § 893.25(1), the adverse possession must be uninterrupted for twenty years....

In order to constitute adverse possession, "the use of the land must be open, notorious, visible, exclusive, hostile and continuous, such as would apprise a reasonably diligent landowner and the public that the possessor claims the land as his own."... "Hostile" in this context does not mean a deliberate and unfriendly animus; rather, the law presumes the element of hostile intent if the other requirements of open, notorious, continuous, and exclusive use are satisfied.... "Both ... the fact of possession and its real adverse character" must be sufficiently open and obvious to "apprize the true owner ... in the exercise of reasonable diligence of the fact and of an intention to usurp the possession of that which in law is his own.".... The size and nature of the disputed area are relevant in deciding if the use is sufficient to apprise the true owner of an adverse claim....

The party seeking to claim title by adverse possession bears the burden of proving the elements by clear and positive evidence.... The evidence must be strictly construed against the claimant and all reasonable presumptions must be made in favor of the true owner.... One of these presumptions is that "actual possession is subordinate to the right of [the true] owner."...

We consider first Easley's assertion that the circuit court ignored the presumption in favor of the titleholder and improperly placed the burden on him. Easley points to the court's several references to Easley's failure, until 2006, to post no-trespassing signs on the eastern boundary of the disputed area to keep out people entering from the plaintiffs' property. The court contrasted Easley's failure to take "antitrespasser actions" regarding the disputed area with his posting of the rest of his property and his concern with trespassers on the rest of his property. The court also apparently found it significant that there was no trail cut from the lower portion of Lot 6 into the disputed area.

The circuit court acknowledged that a titleholder need not use his or her land at all in order to retain title and that the burden was on the plaintiffs to prove adverse possession. However, we agree with Easley that certain of the court's findings and comments appear to require that Easley prove efforts to keep trespassers out, to post his land, and to patrol it. We clarify here that this is not the law. The elements of adverse possession are directed to the claimant's use of the land, and the claimant has the burden to prove those elements by clear and positive evidence.... If the claimant's use gives the titleholder reasonable notice that the claimant is asserting ownership and the titleholder does nothing, that failure to respond may result in losing title. However, in the absence of such use by the claimant, the titleholder is not obligated to do anything in order to retain title....

We next examine whether the facts as found by the circuit court are sufficient to fulfill the legal standard that the use of the disputed area by Daggett and Daniels was open, notorious, visible, exclusive, hostile, and continuous. The circuit court determined that the regular use of the disputed area for hunting in the various annual hunting seasons by Daggett and Daniels and their friends, the dirt road and trail, and the deer stands should have been noticed by anyone who claimed title to the disputed area. The exclusivity of this use, in the circuit court's opinion, was demonstrated by an incident Daniels described, occurring in approximately 1998, in which he cut down a tree in the disputed area because a tree stand that did not belong to him or his friends was in the tree. The use was continuous, the court determined, because it occurred regularly according to the seasonal nature of hunting.

For the following reasons, we conclude the regular use of the disputed area for hunting, the deer stands, and the dirt road and trail do not constitute open, notorious, visible, exclusive and hostile use. Because of this conclusion, we do not discuss the requirement of continuous use.

There was no finding that Easley ever met Daniels, Daggett or their friends hunting in the disputed area. The circuit court found that Easley could have and should have heard the gunshots during spring and fall gun seasons. We do not agree that the sound of gunshots gives a reasonably diligent titleholder notice of adverse possession. Even assuming that the shots come from the titleholder's property and not from someone else's property beyond, the gunshots would have been consistent with trespassers. As for the deer stands, the testimony was that they were portable deer stands, some kept in place all year. Even if visible, the deer stands, too, are consistent with trespassers. The dirt road and the trail continuing on to the lake are consistent with an easement to the lake rather than adverse possession of the seventeen acres.....

We also do not agree that Daniels' act of cutting down a tree on one occasion because it held someone else's tree stand showed Easley and the public that Daniels was attempting to keep others out of the disputed area. Given the nature and size of the disputed area, this is not reasonable notice of an exclusive claim by another. Notably, neither Daggett nor Daniels posted the disputed area, which would have been notice to Easley that someone else claimed it....

The circuit court and the plaintiffs rely on the statement in Burkhardt [v. Smith, ... (1962)] ... that "actual occupancy" for purposes of adverse possession is "the ordinary use of which the land is capable and such as an owner would make of it." ... The circuit court reasoned, and the plaintiffs argue on appeal, that the "highest and best use" of the disputed area was hunting, and the plaintiffs' predecessors used the area for hunting just as much as a true owner would or could. However, the quoted sentence from Burkhardt is followed by the italicized sentence:

Actual occupancy is not limited to structural encroachment which is common but is not the only physical characteristic of possession. Actual occupancy means the ordinary use of which the land is capable and such as an owner would make of it. *Any actual visible means, which gives notice of exclusion from the property to the true owner or to the public and of the defendant's domination over it, is sufficient....*

In other words, although the use need be only the ordinary use an owner would make of it, the use must also be open, notorious, visible, exclusive, and hostile (as well as continuous)....

The necessary implication of a determination of adverse possession based on the facts here is that a titleholder of large areas of hunting land must either fence or post his or her lands and be diligent about keeping trespassers off in order to avoid the risk of losing title. This result is ... not supported in this case by evidence that satisfies the legal standard for adverse possession with the presumption favoring the titleholder and the burden properly allocated to the plaintiffs.

The next issue we take up is that of the substantial enclosure requirement in WIS. STAT. § 893.25(2)(b)1.... Although we could conclude our discussion of adverse possession without addressing this issue, we choose to address it. Doing so will provide a more complete analysis of the adverse possession arguments of the parties and will be useful in addressing their arguments on acquiescence.

The purpose of the substantial enclosure requirement is to alert a reasonable person to the possibility of a border dispute.... "The boundaries may be artificial in part and natural in part if the circumstances are such as to clearly indicate that the inclosure, partly artificial and partly natural, marks the boundaries of the adverse occupancy." ... In addition, the enclosure "must be of a substantial character in the sense of being appropriate and effective to reasonably fit the premises for some use to which they are adapted." ... However, the enclosure need not actually prevent others from entering....

Given the configuration of the disputed area and the location of the lake, the issue of a substantial enclosure in this case focuses on the southern boundary of the disputed area. As noted above, the court found that there was a substantial enclosure of the disputed property on the south, consisting of the swampy area and a man-made drainage ditch that runs approximately 200 feet from that swampy area to the eastern boundary of Lot 6....

With respect to the swampy area, a natural, swampy area on a titleholder's property does not provide reasonable notice that someone else is or may be claiming title to land on the other side. Therefore, the fact that the swampy area may make it harder to access the disputed area from the southern portion of Lot 6 than from the plaintiffs' property is irrelevant to the issue of a substantial enclosure. This difficulty of natural access does not contribute to providing notice to the Lot 6 titleholder that the owner of the property to the east is or may be claiming ownership of a part of Lot 6.

With respect to the man-made drainage ditch ... this ditch does not alert a reasonable titleholder of Lot 6 that someone else is or might be claiming land on the north side of the ditch in Lot 6. The ditch had already been on Lot 6 for at least three decades when Easley purchased it....

We conclude the evidence does not establish that Daggett's and Daniels' use of the disputed area was open, notorious, visible, exclusive, and hostile, and also does not establish that the disputed area was protected by a substantial enclosure as required by WIS. STAT. § 893.25(2)(b)1.

II. Acquiescence

The parties dispute whether the plaintiffs have established adverse possession by showing that Easley acquiesced for twenty years to the man-made ditch as the northern boundary line of his property in Lot 6. As we explain below, it is not clear whether the doctrine of acquiescence remains a distinct means of proving adverse possession when, as here, there is no issue concerning the twenty-year time period. However, whatever the precise relationship between adverse possession and the doctrine of acquiescence, we conclude the evidence does not establish acquiescence.

As already noted, the "hostile" requirement of adverse possession does not refer to a particular state of mind on the part of the claimant.... However, the law at one time did require a hostile intent—knowledge that the land was owned by another and the intent to dispossess the true owner.... The result was that "one who occupied part of his neighbor's land, due to an honest mistake as to the location of his boundary" could never establish adverse possession.... Thus, courts developed the doctrine of acquiescence under which, even though a hostile intent was absent, a party could acquire land by adverse possession if the

true owner acquiesced in such possession for twenty years.... More specifically, "acquiescence by adjoining owners in the location of a fence as establishing the common boundary line of their respective properties was conclusive as to the location of such line" where the fence had stood in the same location for more than twenty years....

With the focus now on the acts of possession rather than on the subjective intent of the parties, it would appear that the elements of adverse possession —actual occupancy that is open, notorious, visible, exclusive, hostile, and continuous, plus a substantial enclosure—can be established with the evidence that has sufficed under the case law to show occupancy up to a fence line for twenty years, without the need for specific proof of acquiescence by the titleholder....

If we assume the doctrine of acquiescence remains a distinct means of proving adverse possession where there is no dispute regarding the twenty-year requirement, that assumption does not aid the plaintiffs. The cases on which the plaintiffs rely ... all involve visible activities such as gardening, planting, farming or building up to a fence or fence line for twenty years without objection from the titleholder. The visible nature of the activity together with the commonly understood purpose of a fence to define property lines forms the basis for the reasonable inference that the titleholder's lack of objection constitutes acquiescence to that boundary line....

We have already concluded that the activity of the plaintiffs' predecessors in the disputed area was not open and visible. We have also concluded that the swampy area and man-made ditch do not provide reasonable notice to the titleholder of a potential adverse claim. Even if we assume a fence is not essential to the acquiescence doctrine, the boundary must be physically defined in some equivalent way that makes it reasonable to infer the titleholder understood it as the boundary. The swampy area and man-made ditch do not meet this standard....

Accordingly, we conclude the plaintiffs have not established adverse possession under the doctrine of acquiescence, assuming this doctrine remains a distinct means of establishing adverse possession.

Conclusion

We conclude the plaintiffs have not established adverse possession of the disputed area. We therefore reverse and remand for further proceedings consistent with this opinion.

By the Court.—Judgment reversed and cause remanded.

INTERNET TIP

Judge Dykman dissented in the Easley case, saying, "I believe that the majority has re-weighed the evidence, focused on evidence it finds more persuasive than the evidence relied on by the trial court, and therefore is able to reach a conclusion contrary to that of the trial court." Readers can find this dissent included with the Chapter XII materials on the textbook's website.

The Recording System

The **recording system** gives purchasers of land notice of claims against real property. It also helps resolve questions of priority if, for example, a seller deeds land to one person and then deeds the same land to a second person. In every county there is a governmental office called the registry of deeds, usually located in the county courthouse. There the registrar of deeds maintains an index of documents relating to all real property transactions. These include deeds, easements, options, and mortgages. The recording system permits buyers of real property to evaluate the quality of the seller's title. In addition, the purchaser's attorney or a bank's attorney may obtain a document called a title abstract or an insurance company's agreement to insure the title. The abstract is a report that summarizes all the recorded claims that affect the seller's title. If a dispute arises between competing claimants, the recording statutes help the courts resolve who the law will recognize as having title to the property.

PERSONAL PROPERTY

There are many ways by which title to personal property is acquired. These include purchase, creation, capture, accession, finding, confusion, gift, and inheritance. In addition, one person may acquire the personal property of another, though not the title to that property, through bailment.

Purchase

The purchase or sale of goods is the most common means of obtaining or conveying ownership rights to personal property. Most purchases involve an exchange of money for the ownership rights to goods. This is a contractual relationship and is governed by the Uniform Commercial Code.

Creation

A person who manufactures products out of raw materials through physical or mental labor has title to the items created. Thus, a person who builds a boat, writes a song, makes a quilt, or develops a software program will have title to that item. A person who is employed to produce something, however, will not have title; ownership rights will belong to the employer.

Capture

A person who acquires previously unowned property has title to the items captured. For example, a person who catches fish on the high seas has title by way of **capture.** Such captures usually require the purchase of a fishing or hunting license. This license authorizes the holder to take title by way of capture according to established regulations that define the size of the daily catch and determine the season, for example.

Accession

A person can take title to additions that occur to his or her property because of natural increases. This means that the owner of animals has title to the offspring by way of **accession.** Similarly, the owner of a savings account has title to the interest that is earned on that account by way of accession.

Finding

A finder of lost property has title that is good against everyone except the true owner. Some states provide that a finder of a lost item above some designated dollar value has a duty to turn the item over to an agency (often the police) for a period of time. If the true owner fails to claim the item, the finder takes title, and the true owner's ownership rights are severed. A finder has a duty to make reasonable efforts to locate the true owner, although no expenses must be incurred to satisfy this obligation. Lost property differs from mislaid and abandoned property. If you inadvertently leave your jacket in a classroom after a class, you have mislaid it. As we see in the next case, a finder who is a trespasser acquires neither possessory nor ownership rights.

Favorite v. Miller
407 A.2d 974
Supreme Court of Connecticut
December 12, 1978

Bogdanski, Associate Justice
On July 9, 1776, a band of patriots, hearing news of the Declaration of Independence, toppled the equestrian statue of King George III, which was located in Bowling Green Park in lower Manhattan, New York. The statue, of gilded lead, was then hacked apart and the pieces ferried over Long Island Sound and loaded onto wagons at Norwalk, Connecticut, to be hauled some fifty miles northward to Oliver Wolcott's bullet-molding foundry in Litchfield, there to be cast into bullets. On the journey to Litchfield, the wagoners halted at Wilton, Connecticut, and while the patriots were imbibing, the loyalists managed to steal back pieces of the statue. The wagonload of the pieces lifted by the Tories was scattered about in the area of the Davis Swamp in Wilton and fragments of the statue have continued to turn up in that area since that time.

Although the above events have been dramatized in the intervening years, the unquestioned historical facts are: (1) the destruction of the statue; (2) cartage of the pieces to the Wolcott Foundry; (3) the pause at Wilton where part of the load was scattered over the Wilton area by loyalists; and (4) repeated discoveries of fragments over the last century.

In 1972, the defendant, Louis Miller, determined that a part of the statue might be located within property owned by the plaintiffs. On October 16 he entered the area of the Davis Swamp owned by the plaintiffs although he knew it to be private property. With the aid of a metal detector, he discovered a statuary fragment fifteen inches square and weighing twenty pounds which was embedded ten inches below the soil. He dug up this fragment and removed it from the plaintiffs' property. The plaintiffs did not learn that a piece of the statue of King George III had been found on their property until they read about it in the newspaper, long after it had been removed.

In due course, the piece of the statue made its way back to New York City, where the defendant agreed to sell it to the Museum of the City of New York for $5500. The museum continues to hold it pending resolution of this controversy.

In March of 1973, the plaintiffs instituted this action to have the fragment returned to them and the case was submitted to the court on a stipulation of facts. The trial court found the issues for the plaintiffs, from which judgment the defendant appealed to this court. The sole issue presented on appeal is whether the claim of the defendant, as finder, is superior to that of the plaintiffs, as owners of the land upon which the historic fragment was discovered.

Traditionally, when questions have arisen concerning the rights of the finder as against the person upon whose land the property was found, the resolution has turned upon the characterization given the property. Typically, if the property was found to be "lost" or "abandoned," the finder would prevail, whereas if the property was characterized as "mislaid," the owner or occupier of the land would prevail.

Lost property has traditionally been defined as involving an involuntary parting, i.e., where there is no intent on the part of the loser to part with the ownership of the property.

Abandonment, in turn, has been defined as the voluntary relinquishment of ownership of property without reference to any particular person or purpose; i.e., a "throwing away" of the property concerned; ...

while mislaid property is defined as that which is intentionally placed by the owner where he can obtain custody of it, but afterwards forgotten.

It should be noted that the classification of property as "lost," "abandoned," or "mislaid" requires that a court determine the intent or mental state of the unknown party who at some time in the past parted with the ownership or control of the property.

The trial court in this case applied the traditional approach and ruled in favor of the landowners on the ground that the piece of the statue found by Miller was "mislaid." The factual basis for that conclusion is set out in the finding, where the court found that "the loyalists did not wish to have the pieces [in their possession] during the turmoil surrounding the Revolutionary War and hid them in a place where they could resort to them [after the war], but forgot where they put them."

The defendant contends that the finding was made without evidence and that the court's conclusion "is legally impossible now after 200 years with no living claimants to the fragment and the secret of its burial having died with them." While we cannot agree that the court's conclusion was legally impossible, we do agree that any conclusion as to the mental state of persons engaged in events which occurred over two hundred years ago would be of a conjectural nature and as such does not furnish an adequate basis for determining rights of twentieth-century claimants.

The defendant argues further that his rights in the statue are superior to those of anyone except the true owner (i.e., the British government). He presses this claim on the ground that the law has traditionally favored the finder as against all but the true owner, and that because his efforts brought the statue to light, he should be allowed to reap the benefits of his discovery. In his brief, he asserts: "As with archeologists forever probing and unearthing the past, to guide man for the betterment of those to follow, explorers like Miller deserve encouragement, and reward, in their selfless pursuit of the hidden, the unknown."

There are, however, some difficulties with the defendant's position. The first concerns the defendant's characterization of himself as a selfless seeker after knowledge. The facts in the record do not support such a conclusion. The defendant admitted that he was in the business of selling metal detectors and that he has used his success in finding the statue as advertising to boost his sales of such metal detectors, and that the advertising has been financially rewarding. Further, there is the fact that he signed a contract with the City Museum of New York for the sale of the statuary piece and that he stands to profit thereby.

Moreover, even if we assume his motive to be that of historical research alone, that fact will not justify his entering upon the property of another without permission. It is unquestioned that in today's world even archeologists must obtain permission from owners of property and the government of the country involved before they can conduct their explorations. Similarly, mountaineers must apply for permits, sometimes years in advance of their proposed expeditions. On a more familiar level, backpackers and hikers must often obtain permits before being allowed access to certain of our national parks and forests, even though that land is public and not private. Similarly, hunters and fishermen wishing to enter upon private property must first obtain the permission of the owner before they embark upon their respective pursuits.

Although few cases are to be found in this area of the law, one line of cases which have dealt with this issue has held that except where the trespass is trivial or merely technical, the fact that the finder is trespassing is sufficient to deprive him of his normal preference over the owner of the place where the property was found. The presumption in such cases is that possession of the article found is in the owner of the land and that the finder acquires no rights to the article found.

The defendant, by his own admission, knew that he was trespassing when he entered upon the property of the plaintiffs. He admitted that he was told by Gertrude Merwyn, the librarian of the Wilton Historical Society, *before* he went into the Davis Swamp area, that the land was privately owned and that Mrs. Merwyn recommended that he call the owners, whom she named, and obtain permission before he began his explorations. He also admitted that when he later told Mrs. Merwyn about his discovery, she again suggested that he contact the owners of the property, but that he failed to do so.

In the stipulation of facts submitted to the court, the defendant admitted entering the Davis Swamp property "with the belief that part of the 'King George Statue' ... might be located within said property and with the intention of removing [the] same if located." The defendant has also admitted that the piece of the statue which he found was embedded in the ground ten inches below the surface and that it was necessary for him to excavate in order to take possession of his find.

In light of those undisputed facts the defendant's trespass was neither technical nor trivial. We conclude that the fact that the property found was embedded in the earth and the fact that the defendant was a trespasser are sufficient to defeat any claim to the property which the defendant might other-wise have had as a finder.

Where the trial court reaches a correct decision but on mistaken grounds, this court has repeatedly sustained the trial court's action if proper grounds exist to support it. The present case falls within the ambit of that principle of law and we affirm the decision of the court below.

There is no error.

Case Questions

1. On what grounds did the trial court hold for the plaintiff?
2. Why did the Supreme Court of Connecticut disagree with the lower court's reasoning?

 Why, in your opinion, should anyone be expected to act "ethically" unless it is in the person's self-interest to do so?

Confusion

Confusion involves the blending or intermingling of **fungible goods**—goods of a similar character that may be exchanged or substituted for one another; for example, wheat, corn, lima beans, or money. Once similar items are mingled, it is impossible to separate the original owner's money or crops from those of others. In such cases each depositor owns an equivalent tonnage or number of bushels of the crop in an elevator or an equivalent dollar amount on deposit with a bank.

Gift

A person who has title to an item can make a gift by voluntarily transferring all rights in the item to another. A person making a gift is called a donor and the recipient of the gift is called a donee. The donor has donative intent—he or she is parting with all property rights and expects nothing (except love or appreciation) in return. The law requires that a donor make an actual or constructive delivery of the item. This means that if the donor is making a gift of a car, for example, the donor must bring the car to the donee (actual delivery) or present the car keys to the donee (constructive delivery). The donee must accept for a valid gift to occur.

Rick Kenyon believed himself to be the owner of a very valuable painting, which he had purchased for twenty-five dollars at a Salvation Army thrift store. But Claude Abel, the painting's previous owner, claimed that he was still the rightful owner, because the painting had been inadvertently packed and unintentionally shipped with items being donated to the Salvation Army. The Wyoming Supreme Court had to determine who had title to the painting.

Rick Kenyon v. Claude Abel
36 P.3d 1161
Supreme Court of Wyoming
December 27, 2001

Hill, Justice

This dispute concerns the ownership of a painting by the noted Western artist Bill Gollings. Rick Kenyon (Kenyon) purchased the painting, valued between $8,000 and $15,000, for $25 at a Salvation Army thrift store. Claude Abel (Abel) filed suit against Kenyon seeking return of the painting, which had belonged to his late aunt. Abel claimed that the Salvation Army mistakenly took the painting from his aunt's home when the box in which it was packed was mixed with items being donated to the thrift store. Kenyon appeals the district court's decision awarding the painting to Abel....

Abel's aunt, Rillie Taylor (Taylor), was a friend of the artist Bill Gollings, whose works were known for their accurate portrayal of the Old West. Sometime before his death in 1932, Gollings gave a painting to Taylor depicting a Native American on a white horse in the foreground with several other Native Americans on horses in the background traveling through a traditional western prairie landscape. The painting remained in Taylor's possession at her home in Sheridan until her death on August 31, 1999.

After Taylor's death, Abel traveled from his home in Idaho to Sheridan for the funeral and to settle the estate. Abel was the sole heir of Taylor's estate so he inherited all of her personal belongings, including the Gollings painting. Abel and his wife sorted through Taylor's belongings selecting various items they would keep for themselves. Abel and his wife, with the help of a local moving company, packed those items into boxes marked for delivery to their home in Idaho. Items not being retained by Abel were either packed for donation to the Salvation Army or, if they had sufficient value, were taken by an antiques dealer for auction. The scene at the house was apparently one of some confusion as Abel attempted to vacate the residence as quickly as possible while attempting to make sure all of the items went to their designated location. The painting was packed by Abel's wife in a box marked for delivery to Idaho. However, in the confusion and unbeknownst to Abel, the box containing the Gollings painting was inadvertently picked up with the donated items by the Salvation Army. The painting was priced at $25.00 for sale in the Salvation's Army Thrift Store where Kenyon purchased the painting.

After returning to Idaho, Abel discovered that the box containing the painting was not among those delivered by the moving company. Through local sources, Abel learned that the painting had gone to the Salvation Army and was then purchased by Kenyon.... Abel sought possession of the painting through two causes of action: replevin and conversion. Kenyon countered that he was a "good faith purchaser" of the painting under the Uniform Commercial Code (UCC). The district court concluded that Abel was entitled to possession of the painting under either the common law doctrines of gift or conversion or the statutory provisions of the UCC. Kenyon now appeals...

The key to resolving this dispute, under either common law or the UCC, is determining whether or not the painting was voluntarily transferred from Abel to the Salvation Army. The district court concluded that Abel had no intent to give the painting to the Salvation Army. This is a factual conclusion that we will reverse only upon a showing that it is clearly erroneous. Our review convinces us that the district court's conclusion that Abel did not voluntarily transfer the painting to the Salvation Army is supported by the record and is not, therefore, clearly erroneous.

Abel's testimony during the trial disclosed the following facts. Abel's aunt received the painting as a gift from the artist. Abel testified that his aunt often expressed to him the importance of the painting to her and her desire that it remain in the family's possession. He indicated that the painting had a lot of value to him and the family beyond its monetary worth because of his family's personal relationship with the artist. The aunt rejected at least one offer to buy the painting for about $5,000. After inheriting the painting, Abel's wife packed it in a box marked for delivery to their home in Idaho. On the day the painting was packed for moving, there was much confusion around the house as Abel and his wife tried to sort through all of the items and designate them for delivery to the appropriate location. In that confusion, the Salvation Army came to the house to pick up various items. The Salvation Army apparently took the painting, along with the items specifically donated to it. Abel testified that he did not intend to include the painting with the goods that were meant to go to the Salvation Army and, at that time, he had no idea that the painting had been taken by them. According to Abel, he did not learn that the painting was missing until after the moving company had delivered all of the boxes to Idaho. Upon finding that the painting was missing, Abel testified that he immediately contacted an acquaintance in Sheridan who was able to trace the painting from the Salvation Army to Kenyon. Thereupon, Abel attempted to contact Kenyon about the painting's return. Kenyon rebuffed Abel's attempts to discuss the painting thus leading to this action.

The testimony of Abel is sufficient to support the district court's conclusion that the transfer of the painting to the Salvation Army was involuntary. Abel specifically denied any intent to make such a transfer. That denial is supported by reasonable inferences that could be drawn from the painting's acknowledged sentimental value to Abel and his family and from Abel's actions in attempting to recover the painting immediately upon discovery of its loss. Under these circumstances, the district court's conclusion was not clearly erroneous....

The district court awarded Abel possession of the painting on the basis of two common law doctrines: the law of gifts and the law of conversion. A valid gift consists of three elements: (1) a present intention to make an immediate gift; (2) actual or constructive delivery of the gift that divests the donor of dominion and control; and (3) acceptance of the gift by the donee.... The pivotal element in this case is the first one: whether an intention to make a gift existed. As we noted above, we have upheld the district court's conclusion that Abel did not have any intent to donate the painting to the Salvation Army. Therefore, the district court correctly ruled that the transfer of the painting to the Salvation Army did not constitute a valid gift...

The district court held that the sale of the painting constituted conversion by the Salvation Army. The record supports the district court's decision: (1) as the heir to his aunt's estate Abel had legal title to the painting; (2) Abel possessed the painting at the time it was removed from his aunt's residence; (3) the Salvation Army exercised dominion over the property in such a manner that denied Abel the right to enjoy and use the painting, *i.e.*, it sold the painting; (4) Abel demanded the return of the painting from Kenyon, who effectively refused by denying any knowledge of it; and (5) Abel has suffered damages through the loss of a valuable asset without compensation. As a good faith purchaser of converted property, Kenyon is also a converter and must answer in damages to the true owner.... This is true because a converter has no title whatsoever (*i.e.*, his title is void) and, therefore, nothing can be conveyed to a bona fide purchaser for value....

UCC

Kenyon seeks to escape the consequences of the common law doctrines of gifts and conversion by arguing that the UCC is the applicable law in this instance. For purposes of resolving this case, we will assume that the UCC applies to the transaction between Ken-yon and the Salvation Army because, as we shall see, it does not provide the benefit to Kenyon he claims it will.

The district court correctly noted that a distinction exists between a "void" and a "voidable" title. Section 2-403(1)(d) [of the UCC] provides, in effect, that a voidable title is created whenever the transferor voluntarily delivers goods to a purchaser even though that delivery was procured through fraud punishable as larcenous under the criminal law.... [T]his subsection is predicated on the policy that where a transferor has voluntarily delivered the goods to purchaser, he, the transferor, ought to run the risk of the purchaser's fraud as against innocent third parties...

It should be noted that Section 2-403(1)(d) does not create a voidable title where the goods have been wrongfully taken, as by theft or robbery. If the goods have been stolen, the thief acquires no ownership and has no power, except in rare cases of estoppel, to pass a good title to a bona fide purchaser. Nothing in Section 2-403 changes this common-law rule. Section 2-403(1)(d) does not create a situation where the goods are wrongfully taken, as contrasted with delivered voluntarily because of the concepts of "delivery" and "purchaser" which are necessary preconditions. "Delivery" is defined ... to mean "voluntary transfer of possession." By analogy, it should be held that goods are not delivered for purposes of Section 2-403 unless they are voluntarily transferred. Additionally, Section 2-403(1)(d) is limited by the requirement that the goods "have been delivered under a transaction of purchase." "Purchase" is defined ... to include only voluntary transactions. A thief who wrongfully takes goods is not a purchaser within the meaning of this definition.... The Salvation Army, of course, did not steal the painting from Abel. However, the key here is the voluntariness of the transfer from the original owner....

The Salvation Army did not acquire the painting in a voluntary transaction from Abel. A third party purchaser could only acquire rights in the painting to the extent of the interest possessed by the Salvation Army. Since the Salvation Army possessed a void title, the original owner was entitled to recover the painting from the third party purchaser. Accordingly, the district court's order granting possession of the painting to Abel is affirmed.

Case Question

Why wouldn't the appellate court recognize Abel's title to the painting that he purchased from the Salvation Army, which had obtained possession of the painting from Rick Kenyon?

Inheritance

A person can acquire property from the estate of a deceased person. This is called an inheritance.

When a person making a will (a **testator** or **testatrix**) makes a bequest of property, the title to the item will be transferred from a deceased's estate. If the person died without a will (intestate), property is transferred according to a statutory plan enacted by the state legislature (called a statute of descent).

BAILMENT

A **bailment** relationship exists when one person (called the **bailor**) delivers personal property to another person (called the **bailee**) without conveying title. Although the possession of the object is transferred in a bailment, the bailor intends to recover possession of the bailed object, and thus does not part with the title. When a person borrows, loans, or rents a videotape or leaves one's lawn mower or car for repair, for example, a bailment is created.

Some bailments primarily benefit only one person, either the bailee or the bailor. These are called gratuitous bailments. For example, the bailee primarily benefits when he or she borrows a lawn mower from a neighbor. Other bailments primarily benefit the bailor, for example, when he or she asks to leave a motor vehicle in the bailee's garage for a month. Some bailments are mutually beneficial, such as when the bailor leaves shoes for repair at a shoe repair shop or takes clothes to the dry cleaners.

Some bailments are created by contract, such as when a person rents a car from a car rental company. Other bailments are created by a delivery and acceptance of the object, such as when one student loans a textbook to another student. Here there is no contract, because there is no consideration.

All types of bailments involve rights and obligations. In a mutual benefit bailment, the bailee has the duty to exercise reasonable care toward the bailed object. The bailee is not allowed to use the bailed object for his benefit, but may work on the object for the benefit of the bailor. The bailor's duties include paying the bailee and warning the bailee of any hidden dangers associated with the bailed object.

With a gratuitous bailment for the benefit of the bailor, the bailee must exercise at least slight care and store the bailed object in the agreed-upon manner. There is no compensation or quid pro quo involved.

With respect to a bailment for the benefit of the bailee, a bailee must exercise a high degree of care. Since the bailor is acting solely out of friendship and is not receiving any benefit and the bailee is allowed to use the bailed object without charge, the bailee must use the bailed object in the proper manner and return it in good condition when the bailment period ends. The bailee is responsible in negligence for any damages caused to the bailed object. As we see in the next case, the bailor can end the bailment period at any time and ask for the return of the bailed object.

James Croskey and Leach Brothers Automobile Services entered into a contract pursuant to which Leach Brothers was to install an engine and transmission into Croskey's 1985 Buick. When Croskey discovered that the Buick had been stolen and damaged while in Leach Brothers' possession, he brought suit, claiming the breach of a mutual benefit bailment. Leach Brothers lost at trial and appealed to the Ohio Court of Appeals.

James W. Croskey v. Carl Leach
C-010721
Court of Appeals of Ohio
October 18, 2002

Painter, Presiding Judge
Plaintiff-appellee James W. Croskey left his car at a repair shop for installation of an engine and transmission after a first attempted repair failed, only to have his car stolen from the shop's lot twice. The owners of the repair shop, defendants-appellants, Carl Leach and

Joe Leach, d/b/a Leach Brothers Automotive Services and d/b/a Joe Leach Service Center, appeal a Hamilton County Municipal Court judgment in Croskey's favor. The court found the Leaches liable for failure to redeliver Croskey's car due to their failure to exercise ordinary care to protect against loss or damages, further ruling that the Leaches had violated the Ohio Consumer Sales Practices Act. The court awarded treble damages plus reasonable attorney fees to Croskey....

A Failed Repair—And Two Thefts

In June 1999, Croskey and his aunt, Ruth St. Hilaire, took Croskey's 1985 Buick to the Leaches for replacement of the engine and transmission. St. Hilaire agreed to pay for the repairs to Croskey's Buick, with the understanding that Croskey would pay her back over time. The Leaches put in a used engine and transmission, and St. Hilaire paid the $2077.60 bill in cash.

Within two weeks, Croskey brought the Buick back to the Leaches because of noise and leaking fluid from the new transmission. The Leaches added transmission fluid and supplied Croskey with additional quarts of fluid, but otherwise refused to service the car until Croskey could produce the receipt for the previous work. Because St. Hilaire had the receipt and was out of town, Croskey continued to drive the Buick and to replace the leaking transmission fluid. The engine soon died, and the car was towed back to the Leaches' business.

Upon St. Hilaire's return to the city, either the 17th or 18th of August 1999, she delivered the receipt to the Leaches. The Leaches agreed to replace the engine and transmission with used parts. Carl Leach told Croskey and his aunt that he did not have a 1985 Buick engine in his inventory and that he would have to wait until he received one, but they had no knowledge or appreciation of the length of the ensuing delay.

During the delay, which lasted until December 1999, the car was stolen twice from the Leaches' lot. The first time, in September, the North College Hill Police Department contacted Croskey and Carl Leach to inform them that someone had stolen Croskey's Buick, driven it into the wall of the store next door, and then fled from the scene. The police investigation revealed that the Leaches had left the keys in the Buick after closing hours. The car had damage to the bumper and fender, and it was returned to the Leaches' lot.

On October 2, 1999, the Leaches' business was again broken into, and this time keys to customer automobiles were taken. It was not until December 2, however, that either Leach or Croskey realized that Croskey's car had been stolen. On December 2, Croskey, tired of the delay, came to the Leaches' business to retrieve his car. When they could not find the car, Croskey called the police and reported it stolen. The police soon located the stripped Buick and stored it at an impoundment lot.

Croskey sued the Leaches, alleging that they had breached a bailment and violated the Ohio Consumer Sales Practices Act, R.C. Chapter 1345. The trial court ruled that the Leaches were liable for their failure to redeliver Croskey's automobile because they had failed to exercise ordinary care to protect the car from damage or loss, and that the Leaches had breached their repair and ser-vices agreement by failing to install an operable transmission and engine. The court also held that the Leaches had engaged in several unfair and deceptive acts under the Ohio Consumer Sales Practices Act. The court ordered the Leaches to pay treble damages of $6,232.80, plus reasonable attorney fees of $3,450, for a total award of $9,682.80.

A Failed Bailment

In their one assignment of error, the Leaches ... argue that the trial court's judgment was contrary to the manifest weight of the evidence....

The trial court concluded that the transaction between the Leaches and Croskey was, in law, a mutual-benefit bailment. The court then found that the Leaches were liable for their failure to redeliver Croskey's automobile, because they had failed to exercise ordinary care to protect the car from loss or damages.

Where one person delivers personal property to another to be held for a specific purpose, a bailment is created; the bailee must hold the property in accordance with the terms of the bailment. When a bailor delivers property to a bailee and the bailee fails to redeliver the property undamaged, the bailor has a cause of action against the bailee, in either contract or tort. To establish a prima facie case in contract, a bailor must prove (1) the contract of bailment, (2) delivery of the bailed property to the bailee, and (3) failure of the bailee to redeliver the bailed property undamaged at the termination of the bailment.

The record indicates that Croskey left his car with the Leaches after the initial repair failed, with the understanding that the Leaches would install another used engine and transmission. Carl Leach testified that, after the first break-in and robbery of the repair shop, the Leaches took no new or extra precautions to protect the keys from theft, because they believed they were not responsible for cars parked on their outer lots.

After the second theft, the Leaches did not inventory the cars on their lots to determine if Croskey's car had been stolen, and they did not inform Croskey about the theft of his car key. When Croskey finally discovered that his car had been stolen and that it was in the police impoundment lot, the Leaches denied responsibility for recovering it or returning it to their lot.

There is competent and credible evidence in the record to support the trial court's judgment that the Leaches were liable for failing to redeliver Croskey's car. The evidence also supports the court's conclusion that the Leaches had failed to provide minimum security to protect the keys from theft, and that they had breached their agreement to install an operable engine and transmission....

For ... the foregoing reasons, the Leaches' ... assignment of error is not well taken. The trial court's judgment is accordingly affirmed.

Case Questions

1. Why was this bailment a mutual benefit bailment?
2. What duty did the Leach Brothers fail to meet in this case? What should they have done that they didn't do?

CHAPTER SUMMARY

The chapter began with an historical overview of real property law and a discussion of how property is classified. Intellectual property, the law of trademarks, patents, and copyrights, was next. Readers also learned about the common forms of property ownership—severalty, joint tenancies, tenancies in common and tenancies by the entireties. The discussion then turned to the controversial U.S. Supreme Court case of *Kelo v. New London*, and what happened in the aftermath of that decision. Special emphasis was given to the government's use of the power of eminent domain. The section on real property followed, where students learned about estates in land, easements, licenses, covenants, adverse possession, and the recording system.

The discussion of personal property included eight different ways in which personal property is acquired: purchase, creation, capture, accession, finding, confusion, gift, and inheritance. The chapter concluded with an overview of the law of bailments.

CHAPTER QUESTIONS

1. Jackson Chapel Church believed it had ownership rights over a small parcel of land which the church's neighbors, the Mobleys, had begun to develop. The church filed suit seeking ejectment, declaratory judgment, and injunctive relief. The trial court ruled that the church was entitled to a portion of the disputed parcel because it had acquired title by adverse possession. The portion not used by the church still belonged to the Mobleys. The Mobleys appealed to the Georgia Supreme Court. They claimed that their remote predecessor in title, while building on a small portion of the parcel decades ago, had a paper title to the entire parcel. They argued that this gave them the right to possess constructively the entire parcel, despite the trial court's adverse possession ruling in favor of the church. Should the appellate court affirm or reverse the trial court's adverse possession ruling regarding the portion of the Mobleys' parcel that had been used continuously for over 100 years by the church.

Mobley v. Jackson Chapel Church, 636 S.E.2d 535 (2006)

2. C/R TV, Inc. is a cable television company that sought to provide its services to a private housing subdivision (Shannondale). The subdivision had contracted with Mid-Atlantic Cable Services, Inc., one of C/R's competitors, to provide exclusive cable services to Shannondale. C/R, however, believed it had a lawful right to string cable on existing telephone poles in the subdivision pursuant to a 1972 licensing agreement with Potomac Edison. Shannondale had granted easements to Potomac Edison for electrical and telephone services in most of the subdivision in 1955 and in part of the development in 1991. The Shannondale president threatened a trespass action against C/R TV when he learned that the company had installed over six miles of cable wiring in the subdivision. C/R TV responded by bringing a declaratory judgment action against Shannondale. The trial judge ruled in favor of Shannondale, concluding that the 1955 easements were not "sufficiently broad to provide for television cable facilities." The trial court did rule that the part of the subdivision covered by the 1991 easements could be serviced by the plaintiff. C/R TV appealed. Should the 1955 easements, which were granted to Potomac Edison "for the purpose of installation, erection, maintenance, repair and operation of electric transmission and distribution pole lines, and electric service lines, with telephone lines thereon," be interpreted so as to permit Potomac Edison's licensee the right to install cable-television wiring over Shannondale's objections?

C/R TV, Inc. v. Shannondale, Inc., 27 F.3d (1994)

3. Tracy Price took her English bulldog to Dr. Nancy Brown, a veterinarian, for a surgery, which was performed on August 30, 1991. When Tracy visited her dog the next evening at the veterinary hospital, the animal appeared groggy and was panting heavily. Tracy requested that the dog be monitored all day and night and was assured that this would be done. The dog died on the morning of

September 1. Tracy filed suit on May 4, 1993. She claimed that she had entrusted her dog to Dr. Brown based on Brown's assurances that appropriate surgery would be performed and the dog returned to her in a healthy condition. Tracy demanded damages in the amount of $1,200, the fair market value of the animal. She claimed that her dog had been entrusted to the veterinarian for surgical treatment and that it had died while in the doctor's care as a result of the doctor's negligence. Has Tracy stated a cause of action for breach of a bailment agreement?

Price v. Brown, 680 A.2d 1149 (1996)

4. The Kingsmen, a rock band formed in 1958, recorded a rock classic entitled "Louie Louie." The band members contracted with Spector Records in 1968, which provided that the band would receive 9 percent of the future licensing fees and profits generated by the song. Spector subsequently assigned its rights under the agreement to Gusto Records and G.M.L., Inc. In 1993, the Kingsmen sued Gusto, G.M.L., and Highland Music for rescission of the contract and back royalties calculated from the date that the suit was filed. They sought rescission because that would result in the restoration of their title to and possession of the master. The band alleged that the defendants and their predecessors in title had for thirty years failed to pay the band its contracted share of royalties. The defendants argued that the action was barred by the four-year statute of limitations and that the plaintiffs were not entitled to income produced pursuant to licenses that predated the rescission. The trial court ruled in favor of the Kingsmen. The defendants appealed to the U.S. Court of Appeals (9th Circuit). Should the Kingsmen prevail on appeal?

Peterson v. Highland Music, Nos. 95-56393, 97-55597, and 97-55599 (1998)

5. Hiram Hoeltzer, a professional art restorer, sought declaratory relief to quiet title to a large mural that

once was affixed to the walls of the Stamford High School. This mural had been painted as part of the Works Progress Administration (WPA) in 1934. Workers removed the mural when the high school was renovated in the summer of 1970. They cut it into thirty pieces and placed it on top of a heap of construction debris, adjacent to a Dumpster. This was done despite oral and written requests from school officials that the mural be taken down and preserved. A 1970 graduate of Stamford High, recognizing the value of the mural, placed the mural pieces into his car and took them home. The student took the mural to Karel Yasko, a federal official responsible for supervising the restoration of WPA artwork. Yasko suggested that the mural be taken to Hiram Hoeltzer. In 1980, city officials and other interested people began contacting Hoeltzer about the mural. In 1986, the city formally wrote to Hoeltzer and claimed title. Hoeltzer, however, who had retained possession of the mural for ten years, claimed that he was the rightful owner of the mural. Who has legal title to the mural? Why?

Hoeltzer v. City of Stamford, Conn., 722 F.Supp. 1106 (1989)

6. Leonard and Bernard Kapiloff are stamp collectors. In 1976, they purchased two sets of stamps worth $150,400. Robert Ganter found the stamps in a dresser he had purchased for $30 in a used furniture store in 1979 or 1980. Ganter had taken the stamps to an auction house, and they were listed for sale in a nationally distributed catalogue that was read by the Kapiloff brothers. The brothers contacted Ganter and demanded the return of the stamps. Ganter refused. The brothers then contacted the FBI, which took physical possession of the stamps. The brothers then brought a replevin action against Ganter for the stamps and asked the court for a declaratory judgment that they were the true owners of the stamps. The person who originally sold the brothers the stamps supported the brothers' allegations that the stamps Ganter found were

the same stamps that had belonged to the Kapiloffs. Who is the owner of the stamps?

Ganter v. Kapiloff, 516 A.2d 611 (1986)

7. The case of *Clevenger v. Peterson Construction Company* turned on the question of whether forty-four mobile trailers should be classified as personal property or fixtures. The trailers had axles, although they were without hitches or wheels. They were positioned on concrete blocks and not on permanent foundations, and were connected to utilities with flexible hoses. Which classification is more appropriate?

Clevenger v. Peterson Construction Company, Inc., 542 P.2d 470 (1975)

8. The District of Columbia enacted an ordinance that made it unlawful for any hotel to exclude any licensed taxicab driver from picking up passengers at hotel taxicab stands. The Washington Hilton did not have to operate a taxicab stand on its property but elected to do so for the convenience of its guests. The hotel was dissatisfied with the quality of service provided by some of the taxicab drivers and with the cleanliness of some of their vehicles. The hotel wanted to discriminate against some taxis in favor of others. It wanted to require cab drivers to obtain permits and pay an annual fee to use the hotel's taxicab stand. The city's attorney was consulted about these plans and ruled that they violated the Taxicab Act. Does this ordinance constitute a taking of the hotel's property by the district?

Hilton Washington Corporation v. District of Columbia, 777 F.2d 47 (1985)

9. Terry Bohn presented Tommie Louise Lowe with a ring in 1974 when they became engaged to be married. Tommie had a continuing series of strokes over the next ten years, and the marriage never took place. She still possessed the engagement ring at the time of her death in 1984. After her death, Terry brought suit against Tommie's estate to recover the engagement ring. Who has title to the ring?

A Matter of Estate of Lowe, 379 N.W.2d 485 (1985)

10. Robert Lehman and Aki Eveline Lehman were married in 1964. They separated in 1971. They became divorced in 1976. At the time of the separation, Aki retained possession of forty-three art objects that were in the house. Robert and Aki each claimed ownership rights to these objects. Robert claimed that forty-two of the items were either purchased by him or given to him by his father. One item was given to him by Aki. Aki claimed ownership of the items as a result of her purchases made with joint funds, as well as a result of gifts from Robert and Robert's father. Aki took all forty-three items to Paris when she and their children moved there in 1972. Robert demanded that Aki return his property. When she refused, he filed suit against Aki for replevin, conversion, and breach of bailment. At the time the lawsuit was filed, only thirteen items were still in Aki's possession. Aki testified at trial that she didn't know what had happened to the thirty missing items. The court determined that Robert was the exclusive owner of forty of the forty-three items, and Robert and Aki jointly owned the remaining three items. What relief will the court order? Why?

Lehman v. Lehman, 591 F.Supp 1523 (1984)

NOTES

1. P. C. Hoffer, *Law and People in Colonial America* (Baltimore: Johns Hopkins University Press, 1982), pp. 19–24; D. H. Flaherty, *Essays in the History of Early American Law* (Chapel Hill, NC: Institute of Early American History and Culture, 1969), pp. 272–273; B. Schwartz, *The Law in America* (New York: McGraw-Hill Book Co., 1974), pp. 8–18; M. Horwitz, *The Transformation of American Law 1780–1860* (Cambridge, MA: Harvard University Press, 1977), pp. 4–6.

2. Horwitz, pp. 7–9, 84.

3. L. Salmon, *Women and the Law of Property in Early America* (Chapel Hill: University of North Carolina Press, 1986), pp. 18–22.

4. Ibid., pp. 14–15, 22–25.

5. W. Hurst, Law and the Conditions of Freedom in the Nineteenth Century (Madison: University of Wisconsin Press, 1967), p. 8.

6. W. E. Nelson, *Americanization of the Common Law* (Cambridge, MA: Harvard University Press, 1975), p. 47; Horwitz, p. 102.

7. Horwitz, p. 35.

8. Nelson, p. 159; Horwitz, p. 36.

9. Horwitz, p. 102; Hurst, pp. 28–29.

10. Hurst, pp. 24–25.

11. *Lochner v. New York*, 198 U.S. 45 (1905).

12. The Uniform Commercial Code is not uniformly adopted from state to state. Each state legislature decides whether to adopt the Uniform Commercial Code and the extent to which they accept or modify its terms. Other differences can arise from judicial interpretations.

13. Many jurisdictions only recognize the tenancy by the entirety in conjunction with real property.

14. There are two exceptions to this general rule. A good faith purchaser of bearer bonds can take title from a thief, and a buyer in the ordinary course of business who purchases goods from a merchant can take title even if the merchant obtained the items from a thief. Public policy reasons support these exceptions because it is very important to the economy that people who buy goods from merchants can rely on the sellers' claims of title to the goods.

15. *Seattle Audubon Society v. Doug Sutherland* No. C06-1608MJP (W.D. Wash. Aug. 1, 2007).

16. *U.S. v. Causby*, 328 U.S. 256 (1946).

XIII

✴

Administrative Law and Administrative Agencies

CHAPTER OBJECTIVES

1. *Understand the reasons for the creation of administrative agencies.*
2. *Explain the principal ways that federal administrative agencies are organizationally structured.*
3. *Explain the importance of an agency's enabling act.*
4. *Describe the powers typically delegated to administrative agencies.*
5. *Understand the limited role of judicial review of administrative decisions.*

A discussion of the U.S. legal system would not be complete without an examination of the government's use of statutory law and administrative rules to regulate business practices. This chapter addresses administrative law and the role of administrative agencies.

THE RISE OF ADMINISTRATIVE AGENCIES

Administrative agencies have existed at the federal level since the early 1800s, when Congress created the U.S. Patent Office (1802),[1] the Bureau of Indian Affairs (1824),[2] and the Army Corps of Engineers (1824).[3] The greatest growth occurred after 1900, however, when approximately two-thirds of current agencies were created.[4] Before President Franklin Roosevelt's New Deal, this country operated on the premise that the federal government should be kept relatively small. That model of government changed during the 1930s in response to the serious social and economic problems associated with the Great Depression. Newly created agencies included the Federal Deposit Insurance Corporation (1933), the Tennessee Valley Authority (1933), the Federal Communications Commission (1933), the Securities and Exchange Commission (1934), and the National Labor Relations Board (1935). More recently, Congress has created agencies to address important social and public welfare goals, such as the Equal Employment Opportunity Commission (1965), the Occupational Safety and Health Review Commission (1970), and the Environmental Protection Agency (1970). These and a multitude of other commissions, boards, authorities, and departments administer legislation that affects many aspects of daily life (see Figure 13.1).

The enactment of the **Administrative Procedure Act (APA)** in 1946 helped to improve and strengthen the administrative regulatory process in the federal system and served as a model for states as well. The APA requirements vis-à-vis rulemaking, for example, were very influential.

Today, regulatory bodies are well established at both the state and local levels of government. State administrative agencies monitor environmental pollution, license drivers, determine automobile insurance rates, and oversee public utilities. They also regulate a wide range of professions and occupations, including hairdressers, barbers, teachers, doctors, lawyers, and psychologists. At the local level, administrative agencies operate zoning boards, housing authorities, water and sewer commissions, and historical commissions.

This chapter is concerned with the legal framework for administrative law. It does not include political analyses of the role that ideology and resources play in agency decision making. Nor does this chapter focus on process questions, such as how administrative agencies decide which of competing policy alternatives will be adopted. These most interesting issues are often addressed in conjunction with political science courses.

ORGANIZATION AND CLASSIFICATION OF FEDERAL AGENCIES

Administrative agencies are commonly classified in terms of their organizational structure. Agencies that are organized into commissions and boards and directed by commissioners include the Federal Maritime Commission (FMC), the Federal Reserve Board (FRB), the Interstate Commerce Commission (ICC), the National Labor Relations Board (NLRB), the Nuclear Regulatory Commission (NRC), and the Securities and Exchange Commission (SEC). (See, for example, the SEC organizational chart in Figure 13.2.) Agencies that are structured as cabinet-level departments or administrations and are headed by secretaries or administrators include the Department of the Interior, the Department of Agriculture, the Department of Labor, the Department of Homeland Security, and executive agencies such as the Environmental Protection Agency (EPA). (The EPA organizational chart can be seen in Figure 13.3.)

Commissioners, cabinet-level secretaries, and agency head administrators are nominated by the president and are subject to Senate confirmation. In general, commissions and boards are considered to be independent agencies because the commissioners do not serve at the pleasure of the president and can only be removed for cause, such as neglect of duty or inefficiency. In addition, Congress often requires that these agencies be bipartisan. The SEC, for example, has five members. The chairman is chosen by the president and normally is of the president's party. Because the SEC is a bipartisan agency, two Democrats and two Republicans will be chosen for the remaining four seats. Each commissioner serves a five-year staggered term; one term expires each June. Agencies headed by cabinet secretaries and head administrators are not independent, and their leaders serve at the pleasure of the president.

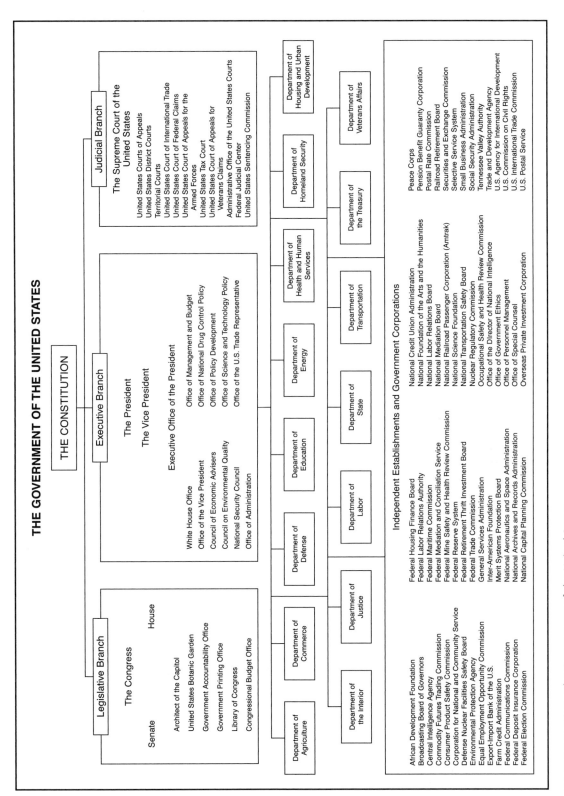

F I G U R E 13.1 The Government of the United States

Source: Office of the Federal Register, National Archives and Records Administration, U.S. Government Manual, 2009–2010, p. 21.

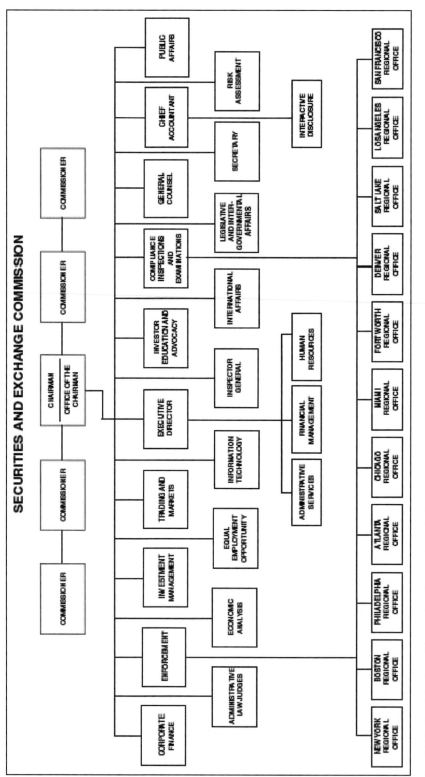

FIGURE 13.2 Securities and Exchange Commission

Source: Office of the Federal Register, National Archives and Records Administration, U.S. Government Manual, 2009–2010, p. 498.

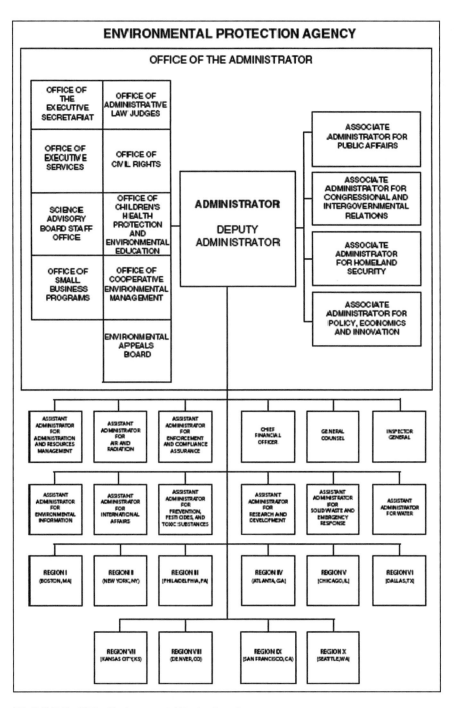

FIGURE 13.3 Environmental Protection Agency

Source: Office of the Federal Register, National Archives and Records Administration, U.S. Government Manual, 2009–2010, p. 369.

Functions of Administrative Agencies

Administrative agencies came into existence because legislative bodies recognized that they could not achieve desired economic and social goals within the existing governmental structure. Although legislatures could provide general policy direction, they possessed limited subject matter expertise and could not devote continuing attention to the multitude of problems that confront our modern society. Agencies, on the other hand, can assemble experts who focus on one area and work toward achieving legislatively determined objectives.

Legislatures establish an administrative agency by enacting a statute called an **enabling act.** In addition to creating the agency, this act determines its organizational structure, defines its functions and powers, and establishes basic operational standards and guidelines. These standards and guidelines help reviewing courts control the abuse of discretion. Courts also use written directives to assess whether an agency is operating according to the legislature's intent. Administrative agencies can also be created by executive orders authorized by statute.

Agencies perform a variety of functions. For example, they monitor businesses and professions in order to prevent the use of unfair methods of competition and the use of deceptive practices; they help ensure that manufacturers produce pure medications and that food products are safe to consume; and they function to protect society from environmental pollution and insider stock-trading practices.

ADMINISTRATIVE AGENCY POWERS

Administrative agencies regulate individual and business decision making by exercising legislatively delegated **rulemaking, investigative,** and **adjudicative powers.** Although the separation of powers doctrine states that the legislative, executive, and judicial functions of government should not exist in the same person or group of persons, the courts have ruled that combining such functions within a single agency does not conflict with the doctrine. Even though a wide range of powers may be delegated to an agency in its enabling act, there are checks on its activities. The creator of the agency, which is generally the legislature, retains the power to eliminate it or to alter the rules governing it. In addition, agency decisions are subject to judicial review.

Rulemaking Power

The rulemaking power of administrative agencies covers a vast range of business and government functions. Rulemaking is often referred to as the quasi-legislative function of administrative agencies. Agencies that have been granted rulemaking powers are authorized to make, alter, or repeal rules and regulations to the extent specified in their enabling statutes. The enabling acts set general standards, authorize the agencies to determine the content of the regulations, and provide general sanctions for noncompliance with the rules. A federal agency possessing the rulemaking power is obliged to comply with duly established procedures when making and promulgating rules, and the rules themselves must be necessary for the agency to fulfill its statutory duties.

There are essentially three types of administrative rules: substantive, interpretive, and procedural.

Substantive rules are used to establish and implement policies that assist an agency in accomplishing its statutorily established objectives. Substantive rules normally apply prospectively but not retroactively. If a federal agency properly exercises its rulemaking power in developing and promulgating substantive rules and the rules are necessary to achieving the objectives established for it by Congress in the enabling act, the rules will have the same legal force and effect as a statute. The "notice and comment" process (which is explained below) is the most common procedure used when agencies develop and promulgate substantive rules.

Courts generally uphold substantive rules if they are satisfied that the agency has examined the issues, appropriately reached its decision, followed established procedures, and acted within the scope of its authority.

An **interpretive rule** is used to explain an agency's interpretation of an ambiguous statute, or its understanding of the meaning of an important term that Congress has neglected to define. Interpretive rules are not to be used to make substantive policy changes. Because of an APA exemption, agencies need not follow the "notice and comment" procedures when developing and promulgating interpretive rules. Although interpretive rules are not enforceable to the same extent as laws, courts will often find interpretive rules persuasive if the agency has relied on its own expertise and experience in the rule's development, and the agency's actions are within its statutory scope of authority.

Procedural rules are developed to establish standard operating procedures within an agency. These process-oriented rules are devoid of substantive content and agencies are exempted by the APA from compliance with the "notice and comment" procedures.

Formal and Informal Rulemaking

Congress sometimes specifies in an agency's enabling statute that formal rulemaking procedures must be followed. The procedural requirements for formal rulemaking are found in Section 554 of the APA and provide for a trial-like hearing process "on the record," complete with witnesses and recorded testimony, as well as findings of fact and conclusions of law.

More commonly, when an agency seeks to make or promulgate substantive rules, it engages in informal rulemaking (also known as "notice and comment" procedures), pursuant to Section 553 of the APA. In informal rulemaking, agencies are required to publish proposed rules in the Federal Register, thereby providing notice of the agency's intended action to anyone interested in the matter. Agencies must also accept written submissions from persons interested in commenting on the proposed rule, and if the agency so desires, permit oral presentations. The APA also provides that the agency publish its final version of each rule and an accompanying explanation of the purpose and rationale for the rule in the Federal Register no less than thirty days prior to when the rule takes effect.

Prelude to *Gonzales v. Oregon*

The next case involves Oregon's judicial challenge to an "interpretive" rule promulgated by former U.S. Attorney General John Ashcroft. The rule purported to "interpret" the federal Controlled Substances Act (CSA) as forbidding licensed physicians in Oregon from prescribing specified drugs when assisting their patients to commit suicide even though the physicians were acting lawfully according to Oregon's Death with Dignity Act.

The State of Oregon and other plaintiffs responded to the promulgation of the interpretive rule by filing suit in federal court. Oregon was successful in the district court in obtaining a permanent injunction and also prevailed in the Court of Appeals.

Many readers of the Oregon case will wonder why a case that focuses on former U.S. Attorney John Ashcroft is captioned *Gonzales v. Oregon*. The explanation is that Ashcroft, in his capacity as the U.S. attorney general, promulgated the interpretive rule at issue. The rule's constitutionality was litigated all the way to the U.S. Supreme Court. Ashcroft resigned his position on February 23, 2005, the very day after the U.S. Supreme Court granted the government's petition for certiorari in this case. His successor, Alberto Gonzales, was nominated by President George W. Bush and confirmed by the Senate, and he replaced Ashcroft as a party in this case.

Alberto Gonzales, Attorney General v. Oregon
546 U.S. 243
U.S. Supreme Court
January 17, 2006

Justice Kennedy delivered the opinion of the Court.
The question before us is whether the Controlled Substances Act allows the United States Attorney General to prohibit doctors from prescribing regulated drugs for use in physician-assisted suicide, notwithstanding a state law permitting the procedure. As the Court has observed, "Americans are engaged in an earnest and profound debate about the morality, legality, and practicality of physician-assisted suicide." *Washington v. Glucksberg*, 521 U.S. 702, 735 (1997). The dispute before us is in part a product of this political and moral debate, but its resolution requires an inquiry familiar to the courts: interpreting a federal statute to determine whether Executive action is authorized by, or otherwise consistent with, the enactment.

In 1994, Oregon became the first State to legalize assisted suicide when voters approved a ballot measure enacting the Oregon Death With Dignity Act (ODWDA).... ODWDA, which survived a 1997 ballot measure seeking its repeal, exempts from civil or criminal liability state-licensed physicians who, in compliance with the specific safeguards in ODWDA, dispense or prescribe a lethal dose of drugs upon the request of a terminally ill patient.

The drugs Oregon physicians prescribe under ODWDA are regulated under a federal statute, the Controlled Substances Act (CSA or Act). 84 Stat. 1242, as amended, 21 U.S.C. § 801 et seq. The CSA allows these particular drugs to be available only by a written prescription from a registered physician. In the ordinary course the same drugs are prescribed in smaller doses for pain alleviation.

A November 9, 2001 Interpretive Rule issued by the Attorney General addresses the implementation and enforcement of the CSA with respect to ODWDA. It determines that using controlled substances to assist suicide is not a legitimate medical practice and that dispensing or prescribing them for this purpose is unlawful under the CSA. The Interpretive Rule's validity under the CSA is the issue before us.

I

A
We turn first to the text and structure of the CSA. Enacted in 1970 with the main objectives of combating drug abuse and controlling the legitimate and

illegitimate traffic in controlled substances, the CSA creates a comprehensive, closed regulatory regime criminalizing the un-authorized manufacture, distribution, dispensing, and possession of substances classified in any of the Act's five schedules.... The Act places substances in one of five schedules based on their potential for abuse or dependence, their accepted medical use, and their accepted safety for use under medical supervision. Schedule I contains the most severe restrictions on access and use, and Schedule V the least.... Congress classified a host of substances when it enacted the CSA, but the statute permits the Attorney General to add, remove, or reschedule substances. He may do so, however, only after making particular findings, and on scientific and medical matters he is required to accept the findings of the Secretary of Health and Human Services (Secretary). These proceedings must be on the record after an opportunity for comment....

The present dispute involves controlled substances listed in Schedule II, substances generally available only pursuant to a written, nonrefillable prescription by a physician. 21 U.S.C. § 829(a). A 1971 regulation promulgated by the Attorney General requires that every prescription for a controlled substance "be issued for a legitimate medical purpose by an individual practitioner acting in the usual course of his professional practice."...

To prevent diversion of controlled substances with medical uses, the CSA regulates the activity of physicians. To issue lawful prescriptions of Schedule II drugs, physicians must "obtain from the Attorney General a registration issued in accordance with the rules and regulations promulgated by him."... The Attorney General may deny, suspend, or revoke this registration if, as relevant here, the physician's registration would be "inconsistent with the public interest."...

Oregon voters enacted ODWDA in 1994. For Oregon residents to be eligible to request a prescription under ODWDA, they must receive a diagnosis from their attending physician that they have an incurable and irreversible disease that, within reasonable medical judgment, will cause death within six months.... Attending physicians must also determine whether a patient has made a voluntary request, ensure a patient's choice is informed, and refer patients to counseling if they might be suffering from a psychological disorder or depression causing impaired judgment.... A second "consulting" physician must examine the patient and the medical record and confirm the attending physician's conclusions.... Oregon physicians may dispense or issue a prescription for the requested drug, but may not administer it....

The reviewing physicians must keep detailed medical records of the process leading to the final prescription.... Physicians who dispense medication pursuant to ODWDA must also be registered with both the State's Board of Medical Examiners and the federal Drug Enforcement Administration (DEA).... In 2004, 37 patients ended their lives by ingesting a lethal dose of medication prescribed under ODWDA....

In 1997, Members of Congress concerned about ODWDA invited the DEA to prosecute or revoke the CSA registration of Oregon physicians who assist suicide. They contended that hastening a patient's death is not legitimate medical practice, so prescribing controlled substances for that purpose violates the CSA. Letter from Sen. Orrin Hatch and Rep. Henry Hyde to Thomas A. Constantine (July 25, 1997).... The letter received an initial, favorable response from the director of the DEA,... but Attorney General Reno considered the matter and concluded that the DEA could not take the proposed action because the CSA did not authorize it to "displace the states as the primary regulators of the medical profession, or to override a state's determination as to what constitutes legitimate medical practice." ... Legislation was then introduced to grant the explicit authority Attorney General Reno found lacking; but it failed to pass....

In 2001, John Ashcroft was appointed Attorney General....

On November 9, 2001, without consulting Oregon or apparently anyone outside his Department, the Attorney General issued an Interpretive Rule announcing his intent to restrict the use of controlled substances for physician-assisted suicide. Incorporating the legal analysis of a memorandum he had solicited from his Office of Legal Counsel, the Attorney General ruled "assisting suicide is not a 'legitimate medical purpose... and that prescribing, dispensing, or administering federally controlled substances to assist suicide violates the Controlled Substances Act. Such conduct by a physician registered to dispense controlled substances may 'render his registration... inconsistent with the public interest' and therefore subject to possible suspension or revocation.... The Attorney General's conclusion applies regardless of whether state law authorizes or permits such conduct by practitioners or others and regardless of the condition of the person whose suicide is assisted."...

There is little dispute that the Interpretive Rule would substantially disrupt the ODWDA regime. Respondents contend, and petitioners do not dispute, that every prescription filled under ODWDA has specified drugs classified under Schedule II. A physician cannot prescribe the substances without DEA registration, and revocation or suspension of the registration would be a severe restriction on medical practice. Dispensing controlled substances without a valid prescription, furthermore, is a federal crime....

In response the State of Oregon, joined by a physician, a pharmacist, and some terminally ill patients, all from Oregon, challenged the Interpretive Rule in federal court. The United States District Court for the District of Oregon entered a permanent injunction against the Interpretive Rule's enforcement.

A divided panel of the Court of Appeals for the Ninth Circuit granted the petitions for review and held the Interpretive Rule invalid....

We granted the Government's petition for certiorari....

II.

Executive actors often must interpret the enactments Congress has charged them with enforcing and implementing. The parties before us are in sharp disagreement both as to the degree of deference we must accord the Interpretive Rule's substantive conclusions and whether the Rule is authorized by the statutory text at all. Although balancing the necessary respect for an agency's knowledge, expertise, and constitutional office with the courts' role as interpreter of laws can be a delicate matter, familiar principles guide us. An administrative rule may receive substantial deference if it interprets the issuing agency's own ambiguous regulation. *Auer v. Robbins, 519 U.S. 452... (1997).* An interpretation of an ambiguous statute may also receive substantial deference. *Chevron U.S.A. Inc. v. Natural Resources Defense Council, Inc., 467 U.S. 837 (1984).* Deference in accordance with *Chevron*, however, is warranted only "when it appears that Congress delegated authority to the agency generally to make rules carrying the force of law, and that the agency interpretation claiming deference was promulgated in the exercise of that authority."... Otherwise, the interpretation is "entitled to respect" only to the extent it has the "power to persuade."...

The Government first argues that the Interpretive Rule is an elaboration of one of the Attorney General's own regulations, 21 CFR § 1306.04 (2005), which requires all prescriptions be issued "for a legitimate medical purpose by an individual practitioner acting in the usual course of his professional practice." As such, the Government says, the Interpretive Rule is entitled to considerable deference in accordance with *Auer*.

In our view *Auer* and the standard of deference it accords to an agency are inapplicable here.... Here... the underlying regulation does little more than restate the terms of the statute itself. The language the Interpretive Rule addresses comes from Congress, not the Attorney General, and the near-equivalence of the statute and regulation belies the Government's argument for *Auer* deference....

The regulation uses the terms "legitimate medical purpose" and "the course of professional practice"... but this just repeats two statutory phrases and attempts to summarize the others. It gives little or no instruction on a central issue in this case: Who decides whether a particular activity is in "the course of professional practice" or done for a "legitimate medical purpose"? Since the regulation gives no indication how to decide this issue, the Attorney General's effort to decide it now cannot be considered an interpretation of the regulation. Simply put, the existence of a parroting regulation does not change the fact that the question here is not the meaning of the regulation but the meaning of the statute. An agency does not acquire special authority to interpret its own words when, instead of using its expertise and experience to formulate a regulation, it has elected merely to paraphrase the statutory language....

Just as the Interpretive Rule receives no deference under *Auer*, neither does it receive deference under *Chevron*. If a statute is ambiguous, judicial review of administrative rule making often demands *Chevron* deference; and the rule is judged accordingly. All would agree, we should think, that the statutory phrase "legitimate medical purpose" is a generality, susceptible to more precise definition and open to varying constructions, and thus ambiguous in the relevant sense. *Chevron* deference, however, is not accorded merely because the statute is ambiguous and an administrative official is involved. To begin with, the rule must be promulgated pursuant to authority Congress has delegated to the official....

The Attorney General has rule-making power to fulfill his duties under the CSA. The specific respects in which he is authorized to make rules, however, instruct us that he is not authorized to make a rule declaring illegitimate a medical standard for care and treatment of patients that is specifically authorized under state law....

The CSA gives the Attorney General limited powers, to be exercised in specific ways. His rule-making authority under the CSA is described in two

provisions: (1) "The Attorney General is authorized to promulgate rules and regulations and to charge reasonable fees relating to the registration and control of the manufacture, distribution, and dispensing of controlled substances and to listed chemicals,"... and (2) "The Attorney General may promulgate and enforce any rules, regulations, and procedures which he may deem necessary and appropriate for the efficient execution of his functions under this subchapter,"... As is evident from these sections, Congress did not delegate to the Attorney General authority to carry out or effect all provisions of the CSA. Rather, he can promulgate rules relating only to "registration" and "control," and "for the efficient execution of his functions" under the statute.

Turning first to the Attorney General's authority to make regulations for the "control" of drugs, this delegation cannot sustain the Interpretive Rule's attempt to define standards of medical practice. Control is a term of art in the CSA. "As used in this subchapter," § 802—*the subchapter that includes § 821*—

> "The term 'control' means to add a drug or other substance, or immediate precursor, to a schedule under part B of this subchapter, whether by transfer from another schedule or otherwise." § 802(5)

To exercise his scheduling power, the Attorney General must follow a detailed set of procedures, including requesting a scientific and medical evaluation.... The statute is also specific as to the manner in which the Attorney General must exercise this authority: "Rules of the Attorney General under this subsection [regarding scheduling] shall be made on the record after opportunity for a hearing pursuant to the rule making procedures prescribed by [the Administrative Procedure Act.] ... The Interpretive Rule now under consideration does not concern the scheduling of substances and was not issued after the required procedures for rules regarding scheduling, so it cannot fall under the Attorney General's "control" authority.

... [T]he CSA's express limitations on the Attorney General's authority, and other indications from the statutory scheme, belie any notion that the Attorney General has been granted this implicit authority. Indeed, if "control" were given the expansive meaning required to sustain the Interpretive Rule, it would transform the carefully described limits on the Attorney General's authority over registration and scheduling into mere suggestions....

The Interpretive Rule ... is ... an interpretation of the substantive federal law requirements (under 21 CFR § 1306.04 (2005)) for a valid prescription. It begins by announcing that assisting suicide is not a "legitimate medical purpose"... and that dispensing controlled substances to assist a suicide violates the CSA.... Violation is a criminal offense, and often a felony.... The Interpretive Rule thus purports to declare ... that using controlled substances for physician-assisted suicide is a crime, an authority that goes well beyond the Attorney General's statutory power to register or deregister....

The problem with the design of the Interpretive Rule is that it cannot, and does not, explain why the Attorney General has the authority to decide what constitutes an underlying violation of the CSA in the first place. The explanation the Government seems to advance is that the Attorney General's authority to decide whether a physician's actions are inconsistent with the "public interest" provides the basis for the Interpretive Rule.

By this logic, however, the Attorney General claims extraordinary authority. If the Attorney General's argument were correct, his power ... would include the greater power to criminalize even the actions of registered physicians, whenever they engage in conduct he deems illegitimate. This power to criminalize... would be unrestrained. It would be anomalous for Congress to have so painstakingly described the Attorney General's limited authority to deregister a single physician or schedule a single drug, but to have given him, just by implication, authority to declare an entire class of activity outside "the course of professional practice," and therefore a criminal violation of the CSA....

... It is not enough that the terms "public interest," "public health and safety," and "Federal law" are used in the part of the statute over which the Attorney General has authority. The statutory terms "public interest" and "public health" do not call on the Attorney General, or any other Executive official, to make an independent assessment of the meaning of federal law. The Attorney General did not base the Interpretive Rule on an application of the five-factor test generally, or the "public health and safety" factor specifically. Even if he had, it is doubtful the Attorney General could cite the "public interest" or "public health" to deregister a physician simply because he deemed a controversial practice permitted by state law to have an illegitimate medical purpose....

The limits on the Attorney General's authority to define medical standards for the care and treatment of patients bear also on the proper interpretation of § 871(b). This section allows the Attorney General to best determine how to execute "his functions." It is quite a different matter, however, to say that the Attorney General can define the substantive standards of medical practice as part of his authority. To find a delegation of this extent in *§ 871* would put that part of the statute in considerable tension with the narrowly defined delegation concerning control and registration. It would go, moreover, against the plain language of the text to treat a delegation for the "execution" of his functions as a further delegation to define other functions well beyond the statute's specific grants of authority. When Congress chooses to delegate a power of this extent, it does so not by referring back to the administrator's functions but by giving authority over the provisions of the statute he is to interpret....

The structure of the CSA... conveys unwillingness to cede medical judgments to an Executive official who lacks medical expertise. In interpreting statutes that divide authority, the Court has recognized: "Because historical familiarity and policymaking expertise account in the first instance for the presumption that Congress delegates interpretive lawmaking power to the agency rather than to the reviewing court, we presume here that Congress intended to invest interpretive power in the administrative actor in the best position to develop these attributes." This presumption works against a conclusion that the Attorney General has authority to make quintessentially medical judgments.

The Government contends the Attorney General's decision here is a legal, not a medical, one. This generality, however, does not suffice. The Attorney General's Interpretive Rule, and the Office of Legal Counsel memo it incorporates, place extensive reliance on medical judgments and the views of the medical community in concluding that assisted suicide is not a "legitimate medical purpose." This confirms that the authority claimed by the Attorney General is both beyond his expertise and incongruous with the statutory purposes and design.

The idea that Congress gave the Attorney General such broad and unusual authority through an implicit delegation in the CSA's registration provision is not sustainable. "Congress, we have held, does not alter the fundamental details of a regulatory scheme in vague terms or ancillary provisions—it does not, one might say, hide elephants in mouseholes."...

The importance of the issue of physician-assisted suicide, which has been the subject of an "earnest and profound debate" across the country ... makes the oblique form of the claimed delegation all the more suspect. Under the Government's theory, moreover, the medical judgments the Attorney General could make are not limited to physician-assisted suicide. Were this argument accepted, he could decide whether any particular drug may be used for any particular purpose, or indeed whether a physician who administers any controversial treatment could be deregistered. This would occur, under the Government's view, despite the statute's express limitation of the Attorney General's authority to registration and control, with attendant restrictions on each of those functions, and despite the statutory purposes to combat drug abuse and prevent illicit drug trafficking.

We need not decide whether *Chevron* deference would be warranted for an interpretation issued by the Attorney General concerning matters closer to his role under the CSA, namely preventing doctors from engaging in illicit drug trafficking. In light of the foregoing, however, the CSA does not give the Attorney General authority to issue the Interpretive Rule as a statement with the force of law....

The Government, in the end, maintains that the prescription requirement delegates to a single Executive officer the power to effect a radical shift of authority from the States to the Federal Government to define general standards of medical practice in every locality. The text and structure of the CSA show that Congress did not have this far-reaching intent to alter the federal-state balance and the congressional role in maintaining it.

The judgment of the Court of Appeals is Affirmed.

Case Questions

1. What was the Justice Department's argument on behalf of the Attorney General's Interpretive Regulation?
2. According to the Supreme Court majority, what rulemaking powers does the U.S. Attorney General possess?
3. Why did the Supreme Court reject the Justice Department's arguments and affirm the lower courts?

INTERNET TIP

Justices Scalia, Roberts, and Thomas dissented in this case. Interested readers can find Justice Scalia's dissent on the textbook's website.

Investigative Power

Agencies cannot operate without access to facts for intelligent regulation and adjudication. Thus, the **investigative power** is conferred on practically all administrative agencies. As regulation has expanded and intensified, the agencies' quest for facts has gained momentum.

Statutes commonly grant an agency the power to use several methods to carry out its fact-finding functions, such as requiring reports from regulated businesses, conducting inspections, and using judicially enforced subpoenas.

The power to investigate is one of the functions that distinguishes agencies from courts. This power is usually exercised in order to perform another primary function properly. However, some agencies are created primarily to perform the fact-finding or investigative function. Like any other power or function of the government, it must be exercised so as not to violate constitutionally protected rights.

The inspector general of the U.S. Department of Agriculture is statutorily charged with auditing federal programs and exposing fraud and abuse in federal disaster relief programs. In the following case, the inspector general served Ann Glenn and others with subpoenas to turn over specified records, documents, and reports. Glenn and the others, believing that the inspector general did not have the right to subpoena such information, sought relief in the Eleventh Circuit U.S. Court of Appeals.

Inspector General of U.S. Department of Agriculture v. Glenn
122 F.3d 1007
U.S. Court of Appeals, Eleventh Circuit
September 18, 1997

Floyd R. Gibson, Senior Circuit Judge

1. Background
In 1993, in response to a hotline complaint alleging questionable disaster program payments to program participants in Mitchell County, Georgia, the United States Department of Agriculture's ("USDA") Inspector General audited the Consolidated Farm Service Agency's ("CFSA") Mitchell County disaster program. The Inspector General sought to determine whether CFSA program participants were complying with regulatory payment limitations. As a result of the audit, the Inspector General determined that $1.3 million in questionable disaster payments were awarded to Mitchell County program participants. As part of the audit, the Inspector General requested various information from appellants to determine their compliance with the payment limitations. When appellants repeatedly refused to provide the requested information, the Inspector General issued subpoenas to require production of the information. The Inspector General sought summary enforcement of the subpoenas in the United States District Court for the Middle District of Georgia. The district court ordered enforcement, and appellants challenge that order on appeal.

II. Discussion
Due to a concern that fraud and abuse in federal programs was "reaching epidemic proportions,"... Congress created Offices of Inspectors General in several governmental departments "to more effectively combat fraud, abuse, waste and mismanagement in the programs and operations of those departments and agencies,"... 5 U.S.C. app. §§ 1–12 (1994). The Inspector General Act of 1978,... enables Inspectors General to combat such fraud and abuse by allowing "audits of Federal establishments, organizations, programs, activities, and functions," and by authorizing broad subpoena powers.... We will enforce a subpoena issued by the Inspector General so long as (1) the Inspector General's investigation is within its authority; (2) the subpoena's demand is not too indefinite or overly burdensome; (3) and the information sought is reasonably relevant.... Although appellants recognize that the scope of the Inspector General's subpoena power is broad, they contend that the USDA's

Inspector General exceeded the scope of this power when he subpoenaed information as part of a payment limitation review. Appellants argue that a payment limitation review is a "program operating responsibilit[y]" which section 9(a)(2) of the IGA prohibits agencies from transferring to the Inspector General....

The IGA specifically directs Inspector General to coordinate "activities designed ... to prevent and detect abuse" in departmental programs.... To enable the Inspector General to carry out this function, the IGA authorizes the Inspector General to conduct "audits,"... for the purpose of promoting "efficiency" and detecting "fraud and abuse."... The IGA's legislative history suggests that audits are to have three basic areas of inquiry:

> (1) examinations of financial transactions, accounts, and reports and reviews, compliance with applicable laws and regulations,
> (2) reviews of efficiency and to determine whether the audited is giving due consideration to economical and efficiency management, utilization, and conservation of its resources and to minimum expenditure of effort, and
> (3) reviews of program results to determine whether programs or activities meet the objectives established by Congress or the establishment....

To enable the Inspector General to conduct such audits in an effective manner, the IGA provides the Inspector General with broad subpoena power which is "absolutely essential to the discharge of the Inspector ... General's functions," for "[w]ithout the power necessary to conduct a comprehensive audit the Inspector ... General could have no serious impact on the way federal funds are expended."...

This case illustrates the necessity of the Inspector General's auditing and subpoena powers. The Inspector General received a hotline complaint regarding questionable payments in the CFSA's Mitchell County disaster program. The Inspector General appropriately began an investigation of the program to detect possible abuse. As part of the audit, the Inspector General requested information from program participants to determine whether the payments they received were warranted. When appellants, who were program participants, refused to produce the requested information, the Inspector General utilized its subpoena powers to acquire the necessary information. Without this ability to issue subpoenas, the Inspector General would be largely unable to determine whether the program and its benefit recipients were operating in an appropriate manner. Thus, an abuse of the system, which the Inspector General was specifically created to combat, could possibly go undetected, and government waste and abuse could continue unchecked. The subpoena power, which the Inspector General appropriately invoked in this case, is vital to the Inspector General's function of investigating fraud and abuse in federal programs.

Appellants contend that the Inspector General is only authorized to detect fraud and abuse within government programs, and that program administrators are responsible for detecting abuse among program participants. While we agree that IGA's main function is to detect abuse within agencies themselves, the IGA's legislative history indicates that Inspectors General are permitted and expected to investigate public involvement with the programs in certain situations. Congressman Levitas, a co-sponsor of the IGA, stated that the Inspector General's "public contact would only be for the beneficial and needed purpose of receiving complaints about problems with agency administration and in the investigation of fraud and abuse by those persons who are misusing or stealing taxpayer dollars." ... From this statement, we conclude that the Inspector General's public contact in this case was appropriate because it occurred during the course of an investigation into alleged misuse of taxpayer dollars. In sum, we conclude that the subpoenas issued by the Inspector General did not exceed the statutory authority granted under the IGA.

Appellants also claim that the subpoenas were too indefinite and were unduly burdensome. CFSA regulations require participants to retain records for a period of two years following the close of the program year.... Appellants argue that the Inspector General cannot subpoena records which predate the required retention period. We do not agree with appellants' argument. While appellants are not required to retain records beyond the two-year period, no indication exists that records created prior to the retention period should be free from the Inspector General's subpoena powers.

Appellants further contend that the subpoenas are unduly burdensome because the 1990 and 1991 records sought by the Inspector General "were maintained and controlled by [appellant] J. C. Griffin, Sr., who had no mental capacity to explain the record-keeping system utilized in 1990 and 1991 in his dealings with the USDA during [that] time period."... We do not believe that Mr. Griffin's mental incapacity has any bearing on the enforceability of the Inspector General's subpoenas. At this stage, the Inspector General is merely requesting information from appellants as part of a large investigation involving many program participants in Mitchell County. The Inspector General has not requested that Griffin explain the contents of his records or his system for maintaining them. Consequently, we are unable to conclude that subpoenas create an undue burden upon Griffin or any of the other appellants....

III. Conclusion
For the reasons set forth in this opinion we AFFIRM the district court's decision to enforce the Inspector General's subpoenas.

Case Questions

1. What argument did Glenn make to the appellate court regarding the Inspector General's statutory authority?
2. How did the appeals court rule, and why?
3. Why do you think that the appellants were unsuccessful with their claims that the subpoenas were both indefinite and unduly burdensome?

Adjudicative Power

When an agency's action involves the rulemaking function, it need not make use of judicial procedures. The **adjudicative power** delegated to administrative agencies, however, requires it to make determinations of a targeted person's legal rights, duties, and obligations and for this reason adjudicatory hearings resemble a court's decision-making process. Thus, when an agency is intent on obtaining a binding determination or adjudication that affects the legal rights of an individual or individuals, it must use some of the procedures that have traditionally been associated with the judicial process.

Before sanctions can be imposed, an alleged violator is entitled to an administrative hearing that is conducted according to APA procedures (or other procedures specified in the enabling act) and that complies with the due process requirements of the Fifth and Fourteenth Amendments. This means that the accused has to receive notice and a fair and open hearing before an impartial and competent tribunal. Parties affected by the agency action must be given the opportunity to confront any adverse witnesses and present oral and written evidence on their own behalf. An agency may confine cross-examination to the essentials, thus avoiding the discursive and repetitive questioning common to courtroom cross-examinations.

Administrative agencies employ **administrative law judges (ALJs)** to conduct adjudicatory hearings. Like judges, ALJs decide both questions of fact and issues of law, and they are limited to the evidence that is established on the record. ALJs are authorized to issue subpoenas, administer oaths, make evidentiary rulings, and conduct hearings. ALJs are not, however, members of the federal judiciary. They perceive their function as that of implementing and administering a legislative purpose rather than as judges impartially deciding between two litigants. In some agencies, ALJs are quite active in questioning witnesses, so a thorough record of the proceedings is developed for the benefit of the agency's administrator or board.

However, administrative law judges *are* empowered to make findings of fact and to recommend a decision. The recommendation is sent to the board of final review in the administrative agency, which ultimately decides whether the agency will retain the power to adopt, alter, or reverse it.

In theory, the decision of an administrative law judge is thoroughly reviewed before the agency's board of final review adopts it as its opinion. In reality, however, because of a board's heavy workload, the review may be delegated to members of its staff, and board members may never even read the administrative law judge's opinion. Although this has been challenged as a lack of due process for the defendant, the courts often permit delegation of review to agency staff members. The courts require only that the board members make decisions and understand the positions taken by the agency.

JUDICIAL REVIEW

Judicial review is a relatively minor aspect of administrative law. In part, this is because judges lack expertise in the very technical and specialized subject area that is subject to agency regulation. The sheer volume of agency adjudications also makes it unrealistic to expect the judiciary to review more than a small percentage of such decisions. Third, the expense of obtaining judicial review is a barrier to many potential appellants.

Courts and administrative agencies are collaborators in the task of safeguarding the public interest. Thus, unless exceptional circumstances exist, courts are reluctant to interfere with the operation of a program administered by an agency. As the courts' respect of the administrative process increases, judicial self-restraint also increases.

The petitioner in the next case, the National Mining Association, asked the U.S. Court of Appeals to review a final rule promulgated by the Federal Mine Safety and Health Administration. The rule came into being after two fatal incidents occurred in West Virginia coal mines in 2006. The Association objected to procedural and substantive provisions of the rule, which had been adopted to help miners survive mining disasters.

National Mining Ass'n v. Mine Safety and Health Admn.
512 F.3d 696
United States Court of Appeals, District of Columbia Circuit
January 11, 2008.

Randolph, Circuit Judge:

Two fatal accidents at West Virginia coal mines in January 2006 prompted the Mine Safety and Health Administration—MSHA—to adopt emergency safety measures.... MSHA, an agency within the Department of Labor, concluded that the West Virginia miners might have survived if there had been portable oxygen devices ... in the escapeways to protect them from toxic fumes for at least an hour. Acting quickly, MSHA issued an emergency temporary standard requiring mine operators to place such rescue devices, one for each miner, in the primary and emergency escapeways of the mine.... This petition for judicial review, brought by the National Mining Association, seeks to set aside the final rule that replaced the temporary standard.

The Mine Act authorizes MSHA to issue the temporary rules without notice and comment in response to emergencies.... In this case, in order to make its temporary standard permanent, MSHA engaged in notice-and-comment rulemaking, with the published temporary standard serving as the proposed rule.... The resulting product—the final emergency mine evacuation rule ... altered the temporary standard with respect to rescue devices.... The final rule required either that one additional device be provided for each miner in each emergency escapeway or that one additional device be provided in a "hardened room" cache located between two adjacent emergency escapeways and accessible from both.... A "hardened room" is a reinforced room built to the "same explosion force criteria as seals" and serviced by an independent, positive pressure source of ventilation from the surface.... The National Mining Association urges us to set the final rule aside. One of its objections is that MSHA failed to give adequate notice of the hardened room option.

The objection rests on § 101(a)(2) of the Mine Act. 30 U.S.C. § 811(a)(2). This section requires MSHA, in putting out proposed rules for notice and comment, to publish "the text of such rules proposed in their entirety" in the Federal Register.... Because MSHA never published the hardened room option in the Federal Register before issuing the final rule, National

Mining concludes that this aspect of the final rule is invalid.

That the final rule differed from the one MSHA proposed is hardly unusual. An agency's final rules are frequently different from the ones it published as proposals. The reason is obvious. Agencies often "adjust or abandon their proposals in light of public comments or internal agency reconsideration.".... Whether in such instances the agency should have issued additional notice and received additional comment on the revised proposal "depends, according to our precedent, on whether the final rule is a `logical outgrowth' of the proposed rule."... While we often apply the doctrine simply by comparing the final rule to the one proposed, we have also taken into account the comments, statements and proposals made during the notice-and-comment period.... In *South Terminal Corp. v. EPA,* the case that gave birth to the "logical outgrowth" formulation, the court did the same ... (1st Cir. 1974). The court held that the final rule was "a logical outgrowth"—not simply of the proposed rule—but "of the hearing and related procedures" during the notice and comment period....

Here MSHA's proposed rule—the emergency temporary standard—required that a rescue device be provided for each miner in both the primary and the alternative escapeways. That proposal left open several questions. Where in the escapeways should the devices be stored? How should they be made available to the miners? When the two escapeways are close together, will it suffice to have one common cache of devices rather than two separate caches? Given these considerations, interested persons must have been alerted to the possibility of a hardened room option. And the record shows that they were so alerted. Mine operators inquired about the potential of using a common cache of rescue devices located between adjacent emergency escapeways. They submitted questions, to MSHA about whether such a common cache would suffice. Four public meetings were held as part of the rulemaking. At each, the MSHA official's opening statement addressed the possibility of a hardened room alternative directly and sought comments from interested parties. A representative of the National Mining Association attended the Washington, D.C., meeting and indicated that his organization would respond to the opening statement by the end of the comment period. The Mining Association never submitted comments, but several interested parties did—including several of the Mining Association's members. MSHA later extended the comment period by thirty days so that "interested parties could adequately address issues contained in MSHA's opening statements."...

The hardened room option was thus a logical outgrowth of the proposed rule, or put differently, the Mining Association had adequate notice. Even if we were less than certain about this conclusion, the actual notice the Mining Association received would have cured any inadequacy....

The Mining Association alleges that the hardened room option—as opposed to an option allowing a common cache with less stringent safeguards—is arbitrary and capricious because MSHA did not sufficiently explain its decision.

The Mine Act incorporates the rulemaking requirements of the APA. 30 U.S.C. § 811(a)... Under the APA, an agency must "incorporate in the rules adopted a concise general statement of their basis and purpose."... This requirement is not meant to be particularly onerous.... It is enough if the agency's statement identifies the major policy issues raised in the rulemaking and coherently explains why the agency resolved the issues as it did... MSHA's statement did just that. As to the hardened room option, the main controversy was about whether less stringent common storage measures could be used instead.... The claim was that these less stringent requirements would provide incremental safety benefits over placing the rescue devices in the escapeways and that the options would be cheaper than the hardened room alternative, making common caches feasible for more mines.

MSHA referred to those comments in the preamble to its final rule, ... It explained that its primary concern with approving a common cache of devices was that the cache needed to be "secured against damage from explosions in either escapeway."... Underlying MSHA's analysis is the apparent belief that the redundancy provided by having separate sets of devices results in an increased likelihood that at least one set would survive an explosion. Thus, in order to justify collapsing the two sets into one, additional steps are required to ensure that an explosion would not destroy the devices in a common cache. Hardened rooms achieve this end because they are built to more rigorous specifications.... While other options might be cheaper, the hardened room meets the primary concern MSHA identified.

Though MSHA's explanation of its decision is short, it adequately addresses the major policy concerns raised and demonstrates a course of reasoned decision making. The final rule, including the hardened room option, is not arbitrary and capricious.

IV.

The Mining Association argues that MSHA failed to comply with the Regulatory Flexibility Act ... because it did not analyze the economic impact of the hardened room option. When promulgating a rule, an agency must perform an analysis of the impact of the rule on small businesses, or certify, with support, that the regulation will not have a significant economic impact on them.... When it published the temporary standard, MSHA certified that the primary method of compliance—placing a separate set of rescue devices in each emergency escapeway—would not have a significant economic impact on small businesses.... The Mining Association does not challenge the sufficiency of that certification. Since the primary method of compliance did not create a significant economic burden on small businesses, there was no reason for MSHA to undertake an economic analysis of the alternative. If the hardened room option is considerably more expensive, small businesses can simply refuse to choose it. *Compare Envtl. Def. Ctr., Inc. v. EPA, 344 F.3d 832, 879 (9th Cir. 2003)* (noting that the creation of cheaper alternative methods of compliance is one way to minimize the impact on small businesses).

For the foregoing reasons, the petition for review is denied.

So ordered.

Case Questions

1. What were the Association's objections to the final rule?
2. Why did the court deny the petition and sustain the final rule?

INTERNET TIP

The case of *Chao v. Occupational Safety Health Review Commission* has been included in the Chapter XIII materials found on the textbook's website. In that case, the Secretary of the Department of Labor challenged a final ruling made by the Occupational Safety and Health Review Commission. The Commission had overturned three OSHA citations issued to a bridge painting contractor who was removing lead paint from the bridge. OSHA inspectors had issued the citations after inspecting the worksite and discovering problems with the protective scaffolding installed at that location. The Secretary asked the Court of Appeals to reverse the Review Commission's decision with respect to these citations. In this case, the court had to determine whether to defer to a statutory interpretation made by the administrative agency.

Timing of Review

Parties must address their complaints to administrative tribunals and explore every possibility for obtaining relief through administrative channels **(exhaust administrative remedies)** before appealing to the courts. The courts will generally not interrupt an agency's procedure until the agency has issued a final decision, because if the administrative power has not been finally exercised, no irreparable harm has occurred; therefore, the controversy is not ripe.

The courts will hear a case before a final agency decision if the aggrieved party can prove that failure to interrupt the administrative process would be unfair. To determine the extent of fairness, the court will consider (1) the possibility of injury if the case is not heard, (2) the degree of doubt of the agency's jurisdiction, and (3) the requirement of the agency's specialized knowledge.

The requirements of exhaustion of administrative remedies and ripeness are concerned with the timing of judicial review of administrative action, but the two requirements are not the same. Finality and exhaustion focus on whether the administrative position being challenged has crystallized and is, in fact, an institutional decision. Ripeness asks whether the issues presented are appropriate for judicial resolution. Although each doctrine has a separate and distinct aim, they frequently overlap.

INTERNET TIP

Interested readers can find the case of *Sturm, Ruger & Company v. Chao* in the Internet materials for Chapter XIII on the textbook's website. Sturm, Ruger attempted to litigate claims against the Occupational Safety and Health Administration without having first exhausted all of their administrative remedies. The company was unsuccessful in the U.S. District Court, which dismissed their complaint. The company then appealed to the U.S. Court of Appeals for the District of Columbia Circuit. You can read that court's opinion online.

Judicial Deference and the Scope of Judicial Review

In general, courts are willing to show **deference** to an agency's competence. Courts will uphold administrative findings if they are satisfied that the agency has examined the issues, reached its decision within the appropriate standards, and followed the required procedures.

It is impossible for a reviewing court to consider more than the highlights of the questions actually argued before an administrative agency since the fact situations are often complex and technical, and the time available for argument short. Instead, courts rely on an agency's expertise. Even when a court holds an original determination invalid, it usually remands the case for further consideration by the agency, rather than making its own final decision.

The courts have established standards as to the scope of judicial review. In general, questions of law are ultimately determined by courts and questions of fact are considered only to a very limited extent. Questions of law must be reserved for the courts because the power of final decision on judicial matters involving private rights cannot constitutionally be taken from the judiciary. However, this does not mean that courts will review every issue of law involved in an administrative determination.

Agency findings with respect to questions of fact, if supported by substantial evidence on the record considered as a whole, are conclusive. Substantial evidence exists when the agency's conclusion is reasonably supported by the facts of record. Legal conclusions are judicially reversed only because of arbitrariness, capriciousness, an abuse of discretion, or a denial of due process.

INTERNET TIP

Students may wish to read a case involving the judicial review of a final decision by the Occupational Safety and Health Review Commission to issue citations to one of the contractors involved in the "Big Dig" project in downtown Boston. This case includes discussions of many of the topics addressed in this chapter in the context of an actual dispute. The case is *Modern Continental Construction Co. Inc v. Occupational Safety and Health Review Comm.*, and it can be found on the textbook's website.

Introduction to *Ahmed v. Sebelius*

Dr. Ahmed, a Massachusetts dermatologist, was prosecuted in federal court in conjunction with a Medicare fraud investigation. The prosecution alleged that the doctor had fraudulently falsified and backdated patient documents. Prosecutors claimed that Ahmed intentionally misled CMS, the governmental agency administering Medicare, into paying him for treating patients afflicted with a disease called pemphigoid, a malady not covered by Medicare. Ahmed was accused of falsely reporting that some of the pemphigoid patients were also

afflicted with a Medicare-authorized disease called "pemphigus." Ahmed entered a plea of guilty to one count of a fifteen-count indictment and was convicted of feloniously obstructing a health care investigation. Shortly after his conviction and sentencing, Dr. Ahmed's billing privileges were revoked by Medicare.

Dr. Ahmed decided to challenge the billing revocation decision via administrative proceedings. The first step in the review process involved asking NHIC, the Medicare contractor that had issued the revocation, to reconsider. A hearing officer reviewed the matter and affirmed the revocation decision. The next step was to request that the Department of Health and Human Services conduct an administrative hearing before an administrative law judge (ALJ). The ALJ also sustained the revocation order. The third step was an appeal from the ALJ's decision to the Health and Human Services Department Appeals Board (DAB), which would be the last administrative step. The DAB made the final decision on behalf of the Department and reaffirmed the revocation decision. Having exhausted all administrative remedies, Dr. Ahmed was entitled to seek judicial review, in this case to the U.S. District Court for Massachusetts.

Dr. Ahmed alleged in his complaint that Secretary Sebelius's Department of Health and Human Services had violated the Administrative Procedures Act, the Medicare Act, and the Fifth Amendment's Due Process Clause.

Abdul Razzaque Ahmed v. Kathleen Sebelius
9-CV-11441-DPW
United States District Court, District of Massachusetts.
May 10, 2010

MEMORANDUM AND ORDER
Douglas Woodlock, District Judge

I. BACKGROUND
...Ahmed is a Massachusetts dermatologist who specializes in the diagnosis and treatment of autoimmune skin blistering diseases. Prior to the commencement of the administrative action in this case, Ahmed was an approved Medicare supplier ... treated Medicare patients, and received reimbursements from Medicare

for those treatments. A. The Medicare Program The Medicare program provides health insurance benefits to individuals over age sixty-five and to certain disabled persons.... Medicare is administered by the Centers for Medicare and Medicaid Services ("CMS"), an agency of HHS. Congress has granted the Secretary broad authority to issue regulations relating to the administration of Medicare pursuant to Sections 1102 and 1871 of the Social Security Act.... (authorizing the

Secretary to "make and publish such rules and regulations ... as may be necessary to the efficient administration of the functions" of Medicare); ... [and] § 1395 ... ("The Secretary shall prescribe such regulations as may be necessary to carry out the administration of the [Medicare] insurance programs."...). A physician wishing to participate in Medicare must first enroll in the program to receive Medicare billing privileges and a billing number....

To maintain billing privileges, physicians must complete the applicable enrollment application and revalidate their Medicare enrollment information every five years.... The application requires the physician to list any "final adverse actions" including any felony convictions.... CMS also may perform "off cycle revalidations."... In addition, CMS has regulatory authority to revoke a physician's Medicare enrollment and billing privileges in certain instances.... Relevant to this case is the regulation permitting revocation if, "within the 10 years preceding enrollment or revalidation of enrollment," the physician "was convicted of a Federal or State felony offense that CMS has determined to be detrimental to the best interests of the [Medicare] program and its beneficiaries."...

II. STANDARD OF REVIEW

Any Medicare provider or supplier whose billing privileges are revoked may have a hearing and judicial review under... 42 U.S.C. § 1395cc(j). ...

Under the review provision, the district court has the "power to enter, upon the pleadings and transcript of the record, a judgment affirming, modifying, or reversing the decision of the [Secretary], with or without remanding the cause for a rehearing." The Secretary's findings "as to any fact, if supported by substantial evidence, shall be conclusive,"... and must be upheld "if a reasonable mind, reviewing the evidence in the record as a whole, could accept it as adequate to support his conclusion."... Questions of law, however, are reviewed de novo....

III. DISCUSSION

In order for the Secretary to revoke Ahmed's billing privileges properly ... two conditions must be satisfied: first, the supplier must have been convicted of a designated federal or state felony offense that CMS has determined to be detrimental to the best interests of the Medicare program and its beneficiaries, and second, the conviction must have occurred within the ten years preceding enrollment or revalidation of enrollment. Ahmed challenges the Secretary's decision to revoke his Medicare billing privileges on the grounds that neither condition was met, and that the decision

violated his due process rights. I review the Secretary's decision against this challenge and assess whether it is supported by substantial evidence and is legally correct.

A. Relevant Criminal Conduct

1. The Designated Crimes

Ahmed argues that CMS improperly revoked his Medicare enrollment and billing privileges based on the "erroneous conclusion" that his conviction for obstruction constituted a "financial crime" under 42 C.F.R. § 424.535.... That regulation designates "[f]inancial crimes, such as extortion, embezzlement, income tax evasion, insurance fraud and other similar crimes" as offenses that "CMS has determined to be detrimental to the best interests of the [Medicare] program and its beneficiaries."... Obstruction of a criminal investigation of a health care offense, he suggests, is not such an offense. Ahmed attempts to distinguish his felony conviction for obstruction of the criminal investigation of a health care offense from the four financial crimes listed in the regulation, each of which purportedly requires a showing of actual or intended financial harm to another. I agree with the Secretary, however, that the regulation should not be interpreted so narrowly.... The regulation uses nonexclusive, illustrative language to enumerate the various felony convictions that permit revocation of Medicare privileges: "[o]ffenses *include* ... [f]inancial crimes, *such as* extortion, embezzlement, income tax evasion, insurance fraud *and other similar crimes*."... The DAB [Department Appeals Board] concluded—in my view, correctly—that Ahmed's conviction under § 1518 was "similar" to the listed financial crimes, specifically insurance fraud. The obstruction charge for which Ahmed was convicted is a criminal offense that bears the DNA of insurance fraud in the health care setting. Ahmed created and submitted false documents that could support claims for Medicare coverage of his patients' IVIg treatments. The DAB properly concluded that this conduct, as does insurance fraud, "involves a false statement or misrepresentation in connection with a claim or application for insurance or insurance benefits." Moreover, as recited in the DAB decision, Ahmed stated in briefing to the ALJ [administrative law judge] that he had "placed false letters and immunopathology reports into his patients' files to bolster the reimbursements he received from Medicare." The offense involves the cover up (sic) dimension of criminal conduct striking at the essential financial integrity of the Medicare insurance program.... Ahmed sought to throw investigators off the scent in their pursuit of a core financial fraud. It is not merely similar to insurance fraud; it is of a piece with it.

2. Regulatory Revocation Versus Statutory Exclusion
Ahmed also relies on the separate Medicare participation exclusion statute to distinguish obstruction from financial crimes.... The "mandatory exclusion" provision requires the Secretary to exclude individuals who were convicted of certain crimes, including "*a felony relating to fraud,* theft, embezzlement, breach of fiduciary responsibility, *or other financial misconduct,*" from participation in Medicare.... Under the "permissive exclusion" provision, by contrast, the Secretary *may* exclude individuals who have been "convicted, under Federal or State law, in connection with the interference with or *obstruction of any investigation* into" certain criminal offenses, including health care fraud.... Ahmed contends that "Congress's deliberate, separate treatment of obstruction of justice demonstrates that NHIC may not view Dr. Ahmed's actions as falling into the category of 'financial crimes' set forth in 42 CFR § 424.535 ... and should not automatically revoke his privileges on that basis."

I reject Ahmed's argument because, as the DAB correctly explained, the regulatory revocation ... and the statutory exclusion ... are "distinct remedial tools, each with its own set of prerequisites and consequences."... Under the revocation provision, the physician is barred from participating in Medicare from the effective date of the revocation until the end of the re-enrollment bar, which ranges between one and three years depending on the severity of the basis for revocation.... To re-enroll after revocation, the physician must complete and submit a new enrollment application and applicable documentation as a new supplier for validation by CMS....

The exclusion of a physician from participation in Medicare also has a finite time period, but the duration of exclusion differs depending on the crime committed. For mandatory exclusion ... based on a felony conviction relating to health care fraud, the minimum period of exclusion is not less than five years.... For permissive exclusion ... for a conviction relating to obstruction of an investigation, the exclusion period is three years, "unless the Secretary determines in accordance with published regulations that a shorter period is appropriate because of mitigating circumstances or that a longer period is appropriate because of aggravating circumstances."... At the end of the exclusion period, the physician may apply to the Secretary for termination of the exclusion, or the Secretary may terminate the exclusion in certain instances....

Although there are a variety of differences in details, a primary difference between revocation and exclusion appears to be in the collateral consequences. Revocation bars a supplier from participation in the Medicare program.... Exclusion extends beyond Medicare to Medicaid and all other federal health care programs.... "Federal health care program" is defined as "any plan or program providing health care benefits, whether directly through insurance or otherwise, that is funded directly, in whole or part, by the United States Government ... or any State health care program."...

3. Detrimental to the Best Interests of Medicare
In the final analysis, even if Ahmed's felony conviction is somehow conceived as not expressly financial in nature, I am persuaded that his admitted obstruction of a criminal investigation of a health care offense here is the type of similar felony that CMS would properly consider "to be detrimental to the best interests" of Medicare and its beneficiaries because of its financial implications....

I therefore conclude ... that substantial evidence supports the Secretary's determination that Ahmed's conviction ... fell within the scope of relevant financial crimes detrimental to the best interests of Medicare and that the Secretary applied the correct construction of her regulations in reaching this conclusion.

B. Revalidation
Ahmed next argues that even if the Secretary properly determined that he committed a relevant crime, she should not have revoked his Medicare privileges without first engaging in some sort of revalidation process. To revoke Ahmed's Medicare billing privileges, his felony conviction must have occurred "within the 10 years preceding enrollment or revalidation of enrollment."... Neither party disputes that Ahmed's initial enrollment in Medicare occurred over ten years before his felony conviction. Therefore, the issue is whether revalidation occurred.

Section 424.515 outlines two types of revalidations. First, a provider or supplier "must resubmit and recertify the accuracy of its enrollment information every 5 years," and they "are required to complete the applicable enrollment application." ... Second, "CMS reserves the right to perform off cycle revalidations in addition to the regular 5-year revalidations and may request that a provider or supplier recertify the accuracy of the enrollment information when warranted to assess and confirm the validity of the enrollment information maintained by CMS." ...

... Specifically, Ahmed objects to the conclusion that "even the passive act of receiving information that a physician was convicted of a felony can constitute revalidation" because that "nonsensical" reading would render the revalidation requirement meaningless. I find, to the contrary, that § 424.515 expressly provides for event-triggered revalidation: "[o]ff cycle revalidations may be triggered as a result of random checks, information indicating local health care fraud problems, national initiatives, complaints, or other reasons that cause CMS to question the compliance of the provider or supplier with Medicare enrollment requirements."... That is precisely what happened here and it made a great deal of sense. Ahmed's conviction triggered an off-cycle revalidation in November 2007, when CMS and/or NHIC acquired or reviewed information that Ahmed had pled guilty to a felony related to health care reimbursement. The deliberative process did not end there because the felony conviction did not automatically require revocation; rather the regulation *permits*, but does not require, revocation if a physician is convicted of specified felonies.... The revocation based on Ahmed's felony conviction was assessed by three successive layers of administrative decision makers before reaching finality with the DAB decision. Ahmed was afforded the opportunity to submit materials he believed to bear upon the decision. Given the circumstances, those decision makers understandably did not consider Ahmed's several arguments against revocation compelling. I therefore conclude that the revocation of Ahmed's privileges was well within the Secretary's authority as a procedural matter.

C. Due Process
More broadly, Ahmed contends that his due process rights were violated because a revalidation process did not occur *before* CMS and/or NHIC made the revocation decision. He insists that revalidation is "an important procedural safeguard that provides Medicare participants and their patients with notice and an opportunity to be heard before a provider's billing privileges are revoked." Ahmed claims that if given that opportunity, he would have clarified "the true circumstances of his crime" and demonstrated "that his

Medicare patients had access to few, if any, comparable treatment sources." The constitutional right to due process requires notice and a meaningful opportunity to respond.... Both of these requirements were met in this case. With respect to notice, Ahmed received a letter from NHIC on November 8, 2007 before his billing privileges were revoked on December 9, 2007. That letter also detailed an opportunity for Ahmed to obtain "an independent review" by requesting "an on-the-record reconsideration." With respect to a meaningful opportunity to respond, the Supreme Court "has recognized, on many occasions, that... where it would be impractical to provide predeprivation process, postdeprivation process satisfies the requirements of the Due Process Clause."... *Gilbert v. Homar*,... (1997) ..."An important government interest, accompanied by a substantial assurance that the deprivation is not baseless or unwarranted, may in limited cases demanding prompt action justify postponing the opportunity to be heard until after the initial deprivation." *FDIC v. Mallen* ... (1988).... Once Ahmed was convicted of a crime manifesting an intent to manipulate the Medicare reimbursement system and to obstruct the criminal justice system which polices it, there was more than adequate need for prompt action to revoke his privileges to participate in the system. An elaborate pre-revocation process before the initiation of a felony-based revocation is not required for those convicted, as Ahmed was, of any felony within the terms of § 424.535(a)(3).... [T]he regulation expressly rejects pre-revocation process for physicians, like Ahmed, whose billing privileges are revoked due to a felony conviction.... The sole remedies are post-revocation administrative and judicial review, which have been pursued vigorously by Ahmed through all their layers and fully satisfy his constitutional right to due process.

IV. Conclusion
For the reasons set forth more fully above, I GRANT the Defendant's motion ... for judgment on the pleadings, or in the alternative, for summary judgment. I DENY the Plaintiff's cross-motion for judgment on the pleadings.

Case Questions

1. Why did Ahmed believe his billing privileges should not have been revoked?
2. Why did the U.S. District Court reject Ahmed's arguments?

ADMINISTRATIVE AGENCIES AND THE REGULATION OF BUSINESS

Congress has neither the time nor the expertise to regulate business. Congress has also decided that the judicial process is not well suited to the task. Instead it has entrusted the day-to-day responsibility for regulating business to administrative agencies. The following material focuses on two administrative agencies and how they perform this function.

Occupational Safety and Health Administration

Historically, the common law provided an employee injured on the job with little recourse against an employer who could use the assumption-of-risk and contributory-negligence defenses or who invoked the fellow servant doctrine. With little incentive for employers to reduce employment-related injuries, the number of industrial injuries increased as manufacturing processes became more complex. Legislation was passed to improve job safety for coal miners during the late 1800s, and most states had enacted job safety legislation by 1920. Maryland and New York were the first states to establish workers' compensation laws, which have now been adopted in all fifty states. Although these laws modified the common law to enable injured employees to recover, they didn't change the practices that caused the dangerous conditions. Furthermore, state legislatures were reluctant to establish strict safety regulations, fearing that such actions would cause industry to move to other, less restrictive states.

In response to the problem, in 1970 Congress passed the Occupational Safety and Health Act to improve employees' safety and working conditions. The act established the National Institute of Occupational Safety and Health to conduct research in the area of employee health and safety. The act also created an administrative agency, called the **Occupational Health and Safety Administration (OSHA),** to set and enforce environmental standards within the workplace.

An employee who suspects that there is a safety violation at his or her place of work can contact the local OSHA office. An OSHA inspector makes an unannounced visit to the premises and conducts an inspection. If the inspection reveals violations, appropriate citations—either civil or criminal—are issued.

For civil citations, OSHA may impose fines up to $70,000 for each willful and repeated violation and $7,000 for less serious violations. As we saw earlier in this chapter in the case of *Sturm, Ruger & Co., Inc. v. Elaine Chao, Sec., U.S. Dept. of Labor,* an employer may contest an OSHA citation at a hearing before an administrative law judge. The ALJ's decision is appealable to the Occupational Health Review Commission, whose decision is appealable to the U.S. Court of Appeals.

Criminal prosecutions for OSHA violations are rare; however, when brought they are tried in federal district court. Convicted offenders can be fined up to $500,000 for each count and sentenced to a maximum of six months in prison.

OSHA inspectors also have the right to post a job site as imminently dangerous and obtain injunctions where necessary to shut down a work site because of the existence of dangerous working conditions.

Federal Trade Commission and Consumer Credit Protection

The first multiuse credit cards, Visa and Master-Card, came into existence only in 1959. Initially, businesses that extended credit to consumers were subject to few regulations. They often imposed unduly high interest charges, failed to disclose their interest rates and associated credit charges, and mailed unsolicited credit cards to potential users. Because debt collection practices were unregulated, consumers were often harassed and threatened at home and at work. As a result, in 1968 Congress passed the **Consumer Credit Protection Act (CCPA).**

Designed to promote the disclosure of credit terms and to establish the rights and responsibilities of both creditors and consumers, the CCPA is much more protective of the consumer than was the common law. Although several agencies share authority for enforcing and controlling the CCPA, the Federal

Trade Commission bears primary responsibility for the CCPA enforcement.

Under the CCPA, many early credit card and loan practices became illegal. Issuers of credit cards, for example, were no longer permitted to mail unsolicited cards. Many of the questions about the apportionment of duties between the merchants who accepted credit cards and the card-issuing banks were clarified. For example, under the CCPA, a bank may not withdraw funds from a cardholder's savings or checking accounts to cover a credit card charge without the cardholder's authorization. Also, under the CCPA a cardholder's liability for unauthorized charges is limited to $50 in most cases.

The CCPA is extremely lengthy and complex and is better known under its various subsections. Title 1 of the CCPA is known as the Truth in Lending Act. The Fair Credit Reporting Act was added in 1970, the Equal Credit Opportunity Act in 1974, the Fair Credit Billing Act in 1975, and the Fair Debt Collection Practices Act in 1977.

The Truth in Lending Simplification and Reform Act was signed into law in 1980. It primarily regulates the disclosure of credit terms and conditions in conjunction with household purchases and common real estate transactions. Congress intended to make it easier for consumers to shop for credit. Before the passage of this act, many lenders did not disclose interest rates, finance charges, or other charges in ways that could be easily compared with those of their business competitors. Under the Truth in Lending Act, creditors must disclose information about interest rates and other finance charges in a highly regulated and uniform manner. A knowing and willful violator of the Truth in Lending Act may be criminally prosecuted and penalized with fines and incarceration. However, the most effective and most commonly used method of enforcing this act is through private suit. A successful plaintiff can recover a fine, an award of compensatory damages, and an order that the creditor pay the consumer's attorney fees.

The Fair Credit Reporting Act of 1970 (FCRA) is designed to ensure that consumers are treated fairly by credit reporting agencies and medical information businesses. Prior to its enactment, agencies that investigated individuals in order to provide companies with credit, insurance, employment, or other consumer reports were subject to few restraints. Individuals not only had no right to know the contents of the report, but businesses had no duty to disclose the fact that a report even existed. Hence, many individuals were denied credit, employment, or other benefits without knowing that an investigation had been made. Consumers now have the right to know the contents of any adverse report used by a business, the name of the agency that compiled the report, and when such information has resulted in an adverse decision that has been made based on such a report. Consumers may also require compiling agencies to investigate disputed facts, correct the report, or include a consumer's own explanation of disputed facts as part of its report. Investigating agencies must follow "reasonable procedures" in compiling the report, and comply with provisions intended to protect the consumer's privacy.

The Fair Credit Billing Act (FCBA) provides that a credit cardholder is financially responsible only for the first $50 of unauthorized charges. Many credit card issuers, as a matter of company policy, will even waive a bona fide customer's obligation to make this payment. The FCBA also addresses a cardholder's rights vis-à-vis a creditor where the cardholder has discovered that items purchased with a credit card were received in damaged condition or were of poor quality. In general (and there are exceptions), the FCBA provides a cardholder with the same remedies against the creditor as exist under state law in the cardholder's state (which will frequently include the right to withhold payment) if certain requirements are met. First, the credit card purchase must have cost more than $50; second, the purchase must have been made either in the cardholder's own state or within 100 miles of his or her home; third, the cardholder must have attempted to resolve the dispute with the merchant; and fourth, the cardholder must have given the credit card issuer a detailed written explanation of the facts within sixty days of receiving the credit card bill containing the disputed charge.

The **Equal Credit Opportunity Act (ECOA)** of 1974 is designed to eradicate discrimination in the granting of credit when the decision to grant it or refuse it is based on an individual's sex, marital status, race, color, age, religion, national origin, or receipt of public assistance. The major effect of this act had been to eliminate sex discrimination. Under the ECOA, a married woman can now obtain credit in her own name. A prospective creditor may not ask about an individual's marital status, childbearing plans, spouse or former spouse, or other similar criteria. Questions regarding alimony and child support are proper only if the applicant will rely on those sums to repay the obligation.

Because the ECOA is modeled after the Equal Employment Opportunity Act, facially neutral practices that have the effect of discriminating against a protected class are also prohibited.

The ECOA requires creditors to notify consumers of any decision about the extension or denial of credit, along with the creditor's reasons or a statement indicating that the individual is entitled to know the reasons. An individual may bring suit against a creditor for noncompliance with the ECOA to recover actual and punitive damages.

As previously stated, the Federal Trade Commission bears primary responsibility for the CCPA enforcement. We see an example of the FTC attempting to enforce one of the various consumer protection acts for which it is responsible in the following case. Trans Union, the appellant, is one of the nation's largest credit reporting companies. What follows is its appeal of an FTC determination that the Fair Credit Reporting Act prohibits credit reporting agencies from compiling and selling certain types of information that have been collected for purposes of credit-worthiness determinations to marketing firms who deal directly with consumers.

Trans Union Corporation v. Federal Trade Commission
245 F.3d 809
U.S. Court of Appeals, District of Columbia Circuit
April 13, 2001

Tatel, Circuit Judge

Petitioner, a consumer reporting agency, sells lists of names and addresses to target marketers—companies and organizations that contact consumers with offers of products and services. The Federal Trade Commission determined that these lists were "consumer reports" under the Fair Credit Reporting Act and thus could no longer be sold for target marketing purposes. Challenging this determination, petitioner argues that the Commission's decision is unsupported by substantial evidence and that the Act itself is unconstitutional....

I

Petitioner Trans Union sells two types of products. First, as a credit reporting agency, it compiles credit reports about individual consumers from credit information it collects from banks, credit card companies, and other lenders. It then sells these credit reports to lenders, employers, and insurance companies. Trans Union receives credit information from lenders in the form of "tradelines." A tradeline typically includes a customer's name, address, date of birth, telephone number, Social Security number, account type, opening date of account, credit limit, account status, and payment history. Trans Union receives 1.4 to 1.6 billion records per month. The company's credit database contains information on 190 million adults.

Trans Union's second set of products—those at issue in this case—are known as target marketing products. These consist of lists of names and addresses of individuals who meet specific criteria such as possession of an auto loan, a department store credit card, or two or more mortgages. Marketers purchase these lists, then contact the individuals by mail or telephone to offer them goods and services. To create its target marketing lists, Trans Union maintains a database known as MasterFile, a subset of its consumer credit database. MasterFile consists of information about every consumer in the company's credit database who has (A) at least two tradelines with activity during the previous six months, or (B) one tradeline with activity during the previous six months plus an address confirmed by an outside source. The company compiles target marketing lists by extracting from MasterFile the names and addresses of individuals with characteristics chosen by list purchasers. For example, a department store might buy a list of all individuals in a particular area code who have both a mortgage and a credit card with a $10,000 limit. Although target marketing lists contain only names and addresses, purchasers know that every person on a list has the characteristics they requested because Trans Union uses those characteristics as criteria for culling individual files from its database. Purchasers also know that every individual on a target marketing list satisfies the criteria for inclusion in MasterFile.

The Fair Credit Reporting Act of 1970 ("FCRA"),... regulates consumer reporting agencies like Trans Union, imposing various obligations to protect the privacy and accuracy of credit information. The Federal Trade Commission, acting pursuant to its authority to enforce the FCRA ... determined that Trans Union's target marketing lists were "consumer reports" subject to the Act's limitations....

... Finding that the information Trans Union sold was "collected in whole or in part by [Trans Union] with the expectation that it would be used by credit grantors for the purpose of serving as a factor in establishing the consumer's eligibility for one of the transactions set forth in the FCRA," and concluding that target marketing is not an authorized use of consumer reports ... the Commission ordered Trans Union to stop selling target marketing lists....

Trans Union petitioned for review. In *Trans Union Corp. v. FTC,*... (D.C. Cir. 1996) ("*Trans Union I*"), we agreed with the Commission that selling consumer reports for target marketing violates the Act.... We nevertheless set aside the Commission's determination that Trans Union's target marketing lists amounted to consumer reports.... The Commission, we held, failed to justify its finding that Trans Union's lists, by conveying the mere fact that consumers had a tradeline, were communicating information collected for the purpose of determining credit eligibility. We found that the Commission had failed to provide evidence to support the proposition that "the mere existence of a tradeline, as distinguished from payment history organized there-under," was used for credit-granting decisions or was intended or expected to be used for such decisions....

On remand, following extensive discovery, more than a month of trial proceedings, and an initial decision by an Administrative Law Judge, the Commission found that Trans Union's target marketing lists contain information that credit grantors use as factors in granting credit. Accordingly, the Commission concluded, the lists are "consumer reports" that Trans Union may not sell for target marketing purposes.... The Commission also rejected Trans Union's argument

that such a restriction would violate its First Amendment rights. Applying intermediate scrutiny, the Commission found that the government has a substantial interest in protecting private credit information, that the FCRA directly advances that interest, and that the Act's restrictions on speech are narrowly tailored.... The Commission thus ordered Trans Union to "cease and desist from distributing or selling consumer reports, including those in the form of target marketing lists, to any person unless [the company] has reason to believe that such person intends to use the consumer report for purposes authorized under Section [1681b] of the Fair Credit Reporting Act." *In re Trans Union Corp.*, Final Order, No. 9255 (Feb. 10, 2000). Trans Union again petitions for review.

II

As we pointed out in *Trans Union I*, the first element of the FCRA's definition of consumer report—"bearing on a consumer's credit worthiness, credit standing, credit capacity, character, general reputation, personal characteristics, or mode of living," 15 U.S.C. §§ 1681a(d)(1)—"does not seem very demanding," for almost any information about consumers arguably bears on their personal characteristics or mode of living.... Instead, Trans Union does not challenge the Commission's conclusion that the information contained in its lists meets this prong of the definition of consumer report.

Whether the company's target marketing lists qualify as consumer reports thus turns on whether information they contain "is used or expected to be used or collected in whole or in part for the purpose of serving as a factor in establishing the consumer's eligibility for [credit]." ... According to the Commission, "a factor in establishing the consumer's eligibility for [credit]," *id.*, includes any type of information credit grantors use in their criteria for "prescreening" or in "credit scoring models." ... "Prescreening" involves selecting individuals for guaranteed offers of credit or insurance.... "Credit scoring models" are statistical models for predicting credit performance that are developed by observing the historical credit performance of a number of consumers and identifying the consumer characteristics that correlate with good and bad credit performance.... Applying its prescreening/credit scoring model standard, the Commission found that Trans Union's lists contain the type of information "'used' and/or 'expected to be used'... as a factor in establishing a consumer's eligibility for credit." ...

Trans Union urges us to reject the Commission's interpretation of the Act in order to avoid what the company calls "serious constitutional questions."... But as we demonstrate in Section III, *infra*, Trans Union's constitutional arguments are without merit, so we have no basis for rejecting the Commission's statutory interpretation on that ground.

Nor has Trans Union offered a basis for questioning the Commission's statutory interpretation on other grounds....

We have the same reaction to the brief's occasional suggestions that the Commission's decision was arbitrary and capricious.... [T]he list of issues presented for review neither mentions the arbitrary and capricious standard nor otherwise questions the reasonableness of the Commission's decision.

We thus turn to the one non-constitutional argument that Trans Union clearly mounts: that the Commission's decision is unsupported by substantial evidence....

Instead of challenging the Commission's findings regarding specific target marketing products, Trans Union points to evidence relating to the general question of whether the information in its target marketing lists is used to determine credit worthiness. This is not the question before us. As we indicate above, the Commission interprets "factors in establishing the consumer's eligibility for credit,"... to include any information considered by lenders in prescreening, which, as two witnesses testified, can involve consideration of criteria other than credit worthiness, e.g., whether a given consumer is likely to respond to an offer of credit. Because Trans Union has not challenged the Commission's interpretation of the statute, its argument that the information the company sells is not actually used to determine credit worthiness is beside the point. Moreover, Trans Union cites no testimony refuting the Commission's finding that the information in its target marketing lists is used in prescreening.

...Trans Union [has] thus failed to mount a proper substantial evidence challenge to the Commission's finding that lenders take list information into account in credit models and prescreening, but we have no doubt that the decision does find support in the record. Consider, for example, Trans Union's "Master-File/Selects" product line, which allows marketers to request lists based on any of five categories of information: (1) credit limits (e.g., consumers with credit cards with credit limits over $10,000), (2) open dates of loans (e.g., consumers who took out loans in the last six months), (3) number of tradelines, (4) type of tradeline (e.g., auto loan or mortgage), and (5) existence of a tradeline. The Commission cites testimony and other record evidence that support its finding that lenders consider each of these five categories of information in prescreening or credit scoring models.... To support its finding that information about the number of tradelines in a consumer's credit file is a consumer report, the Commission cites the testimony of a vice

president in charge of direct mail processing for a bank's credit card department who explained that, in its credit making decisions, her bank considers the number of tradelines consumers possess.... The Commission also points to record evidence demonstrating that Trans Union itself uses the number of tradelines as a predictive characteristic in its credit scoring models.... As to the type of tradeline, the Commission cites the testimony of representatives of companies that design credit models who explained that some credit scoring models, including two used by Trans Union, take into account possession of a bank card.... One witness testified that Trans Union scoring models also consider possession of a finance company loan to be a predictive characteristic. Another witness, this one representing a credit card company, testified that his company's scoring models assign points for possession of a mortgage, retail tradeline, or bank card....

The record also contains sufficient evidence to support the Commission's resolution of the issue remanded by *Trans Union I*: whether mere existence of a tradeline is "a factor in credit-granting decisions." ... An employee of a bank that issues credit cards testified that to be eligible for credit, an individual must have at least one tradeline.... The vice president of credit scoring at another credit card issuer testified that the very first question her company asks in prescreening is whether the consumer has a tradeline that has been open for at least a year. Challenging the implications of this testimony, Trans Union argues that banks ask whether consumers have tradelines not because the existence of a tradeline is itself a factor in determining credit eligibility, but because banks want to determine whether there is enough information in consumer files to make credit eligibility determinations. This may be true. But as we explain above, our task is limited to determining whether substantial record evidence supports the Commission's finding that banks consider the existence of a tradeline as a factor in prescreening or credit models. Because the record contains such evidence, we have no basis for questioning the Commission's decision....

III

Trans Union's constitutional challenge consists of two arguments. It claims first that the FCRA is vague, thus running afoul of the due process guarantee of the Fifth Amendment. Trans Union also argues that the statute violates the free speech guarantee of the First Amendment because it restricts its ability to disseminate information.

Beginning with the Fifth Amendment challenge, we are guided by *Village of Hoffman Estates v. Flipside, Hoffman Estates, Inc.*... (1982). "Laws," the

Court said, must not only "give the person of ordinary intelligence a reasonable opportunity to know what is prohibited," but in order to prevent "arbitrary and discriminatory enforcement," they must also "provide explicit standards for those who apply them.".... Emphasizing that these principles should not "be mechanically applied," the Court held that "economic regulation is subject to a less strict vagueness test because its subject matter is often more narrow, and because businesses, which face economic demands to plan behavior carefully, can be expected to consult relevant legislation in advance of action.".... The "regulated enterprise," the Court added, "may have the ability to clarify the meaning of the regulation by its own inquiry, or by resort to an administrative process." ... Finally, "the consequences of imprecision are qualitatively less severe" when laws have "scienter requirements" and "civil rather than criminal penalties."...

Applying this standard, we see no merit in Trans Union's vagueness argument. To begin with, because the FCRA's regulation of consumer reporting agencies is economic, it is subject to "a less strict vagueness test.".... Moreover, Trans Union has "the ability to clarify the meaning of the [FCRA]"... through the Commission's advisory opinion procedures. *See* 16 C.F.R. §§ 1.1–1.4 (establishing general procedures for obtaining advisory opinions); *id.* §§ 2.41(d) (establishing procedures for obtaining guidance regarding compliance with FTC orders)....

Trans Union's First Amendment challenge fares no better. Banning the sale of target marketing lists, the company says, amounts to a restriction on its speech subject to strict scrutiny. Again, Trans Union misunderstands our standard of review. In *Dun & Bradstreet, Inc. v. Greenmoss Builders, Inc*.... (1985), the Supreme Court held that a consumer reporting agency's credit report warranted reduced constitutional protection because it concerned "no public issue." ... "The protection to be accorded a particular credit report," the Court explained, "depends on whether the report's 'content, form, and context' indicate that it concerns a public matter."... Like the credit report in *Dun & Bradstreet*, which the Supreme Court found "was speech solely in the interest of the speaker and its

specific business audience,"... the information about individual consumers and their credit performance communicated by Trans Union target marketing lists is solely of interest to the company and its business customers and relates to no matter of public concern. Trans Union target marketing lists thus warrant "reduced constitutional protection."...

We turn then to the specifics of Trans Union's First Amendment argument. The company first claims that neither the FCRA nor the Commission's Order advances a substantial government interest. The "Congressional findings and statement of purpose" at the beginning of the FCRA state: "There is a need to insure that consumer reporting agencies exercise their grave responsibilities with ... respect for the consumer's right to privacy."... Contrary to the company's assertions, we have no doubt that this interest—protecting the privacy of consumer credit information—is substantial.

Trans Union next argues that Congress should have chosen a "less burdensome alternative," i.e., allowing consumer reporting agencies to sell credit information as long as they notify consumers and give them the ability to "opt out."... Because the FCRA is not subject to strict First Amendment scrutiny, however, Congress had no obligation to choose the least restrictive means of accomplishing its goal.

Finally, Trans Union argues that the FCRA is underinclusive because it applies only to consumer reporting agencies and not to other companies that sell consumer information. But given consumer reporting agencies' unique "access to a broad range of continually-updated, detailed information about millions of consumers' personal credit histories,"... we think it not at all inappropriate for Congress to have singled out consumer reporting agencies for regulation.... To survive a First Amendment underinclusiveness challenge ... "neither a perfect nor even the best available fit between means and ends is required." ... The FCRA easily satisfies this standard....

IV
Having considered and rejected Trans Union's other arguments, we deny the petition for review.
So Ordered.

Case Questions

1. What consumer interest was the FTC seeking to protect in ruling as it did vis-à-vis Trans Union?
2. Why did the appeals court uphold the agency's determination that Trans Union's actions were contrary to the requirements of the Fair Credit Reporting Act?

CHAPTER SUMMARY

The chapter began with a historical overview of the evolution of federal administrative agencies and why they came into being. This was followed with a discussion of the ways federal agencies are organized and how agencies are legally delegated rulemaking, investigative, and adjudicative powers in an enabling act. Explanations as to how each of these delegated powers is exercised were then followed by an overview of the judiciary's limited role in reviewing agency decisions. The chapter concluded with a look at how two federal agencies regulate business activity.

CHAPTER QUESTIONS

1. The Secretary of Commerce, pursuant to rulemaking authority contained in the Atlantic Tunas Convention Act of 1975 (the "ATCA"), adopted regulations regarding the use of "spotter aircraft" by fishing permit holders. The purposes of the ATCA included preventing the overfishing of the Atlantic Bluefin Tuna (ABT), setting quotas on the ABT catch per country, and increasing ABT scientific research. The regulations prohibited persons holding "general" category fishing permits from using "spotter" aircraft to locate Atlantic Bluefin Tuna (ABT), but permitted the use of such planes by persons licensed to catch ABT with harpoons or seine nets. The ABT is a very valuable fish, each one being worth up to $50,000. The Atlantic Fish Spotters Association brought suit, maintaining that this regulation should be overturned. What standard will the plaintiffs have to meet to persuade the U.S. District Court to overturn the regulation? What type of evidence will the plaintiffs need to produce to be successful?

   Atlantic Fish Spotters Association v. Dailey, 8 F. Supp.2d 113 (1998)

2. Faustino Ramos, Michael Beal, and Francisco Marila were employees of Mavo Leasing, Inc. Mavo and the Production Workers Union (PWU) of Chicago were parties to a collective bargaining agreement that required that all employees pay union dues to the PWU. Mavo discharged the above-named employees for not paying their union dues in accordance with a clause in the collective bargaining agreement. The three employees claimed that the union had not given them notice of their right to challenge certain union expenditures that were not made in furtherance of collective bargaining. They argued that they did not have to pay dues for nonrepresentation expenses. The employees complained about this lack of notice to the National Labor Relations Board (NLRB). An ALJ heard the complaint and ruled that the union did not have an affirmative obligation to provide the employees with the requested notice. An NLRB three-member appeals panel ruled in favor of the employees and interpreted the National Labor Relations Act as requiring the union to affirmatively provide the employees with notice of the right to object to paying dues to fund nonrepresentation expenditures, prior to discharge from employment for nonpayment of union dues. The issue was appealed to the U.S. Court of Appeals for the Seventh Circuit. How should the Court decide this appeal, and why?

   Production Workers Union of Chicago v. N.L.R.B., 161 F.3d 1047 (1998)

3. The Fertilizer Institute (TFI) is a trade organization that represents members of the fertilizer industry. TFI filed suit in U.S. District Court against the EPA, contesting the agency's decision to list nitrate compounds on the toxic release inventory that is compiled by the EPA pursuant to the "Emergency Planning and Community Right to Know Act of 1986."

The EPA listed these compounds because there was evidence that they posed a chronic health threat to human infants. TFI argued that the record did not support the EPA's decision. What evidence would the trial court need to conclude that the EPA had acted arbitrarily in reaching its decision? Why?

Fertilizer Industry v. Browner, 163 F.3d 774 (1998)

4. New York's Aid to Families with Dependent Children (AFDC) program, stressing "close contact" with beneficiaries, requires home visits by caseworkers as a condition for assistance "in order that any treatment or service tending to restore [beneficiaries] to a condition of self-support and to relieve their distress may be rendered and … that assistance or care may be given only in such amount and as long as necessary." Visitation with a beneficiary, who is the primary source of information to welfare authorities about eligibility for assistance, is not permitted outside working hours, and forcible entry and snooping are prohibited. The appellee was a beneficiary under the AFDC program. Although she had received several days' advance notice, she refused to permit a caseworker to visit her home. Following a hearing and advice that assistance would consequently be terminated, she brought suit for injunctive and declaratory relief, contending that home visitation is a search and, when not consented to or supported by a warrant based on probable cause, would violate her Fourth and Fourteenth Amendment rights. The district upheld the appellee's constitutional claim. Was the district court correct? Why or why not?

Wyman v. James, 400 U.S. 309 (1971)

5. Columbia East, Inc., the owner of 34.3 acres of farmland, wanted its zoning changed so it could develop a mobile home park. The board of zoning appeals granted a preliminary approval of the application for a special exception to develop a mobile home park in an area zoned as agricultural. Final approval by the board of zoning appeals could only be granted after the plans and specifications for the

development of the proposed trailer court had been completed and approved by the appropriate agencies. Neighboring landowners filed a suit in court challenging the board's preliminary approval, claiming the decision was made without adequate provision for sewage treatment. What should the court decide?

Downing v. Board of Zoning Appeals, 274 N.E.2d 542 (Ind. 1971)

6. The Occupational Safety and Health Act empowers agents of the Secretary of Labor to search the work area of any employment facility within the act's jurisdiction. No search warrant or other process is expressly required under the act. An OSHA inspector entered the customer service area of Barlow's, Inc., an electrical and plumbing installation business, and stated that he wished to conduct a search of the working areas of the business. Barlow, the president and general manager, asked the inspector whether he had received any complaints about the working conditions and whether he had a search warrant. The inspector answered both questions in the negative. The inspector was denied entry into the working areas. Marshall, Secretary of Labor, argued that warrantless inspections to enforce OSHA regulations are reasonable within the meaning of the Fourth Amendment, and relied on the act, which authorizes inspection of business premises without a warrant. Should the court accept Marshall's argument?

Marshall v. Barlow's, Inc., 436 U.S. 307 (1978)

7. Under the U.S. Community Health Centers Act, the secretary of the Department of Health, Education, and Welfare was empowered to award monetary grants to health centers that complied with federal regulations. Temple University received funds under the act and was therefore required to meet the federal regulations. In addition, the Pennsylvania Department of Public Welfare and the County Mental Health and Retardation Board were charged with the responsibility of administering county health programs. In 1970, the Temple

University Mental Health Center was required to cut back services and impose strict security measures because of campus riots. Members of the surrounding community brought suit against Temple University, charging that the center was not providing required services and that members of the community were deprived of access to the facility. What should the court's decision be?

North Philadelphia Community Board v. Temple University, 330 F.Supp. 1107 (1971)

NOTES

1. *Federal Regulatory Directory* (Washington, D.C.: Congressional Quarterly, Inc., 1990), p. 621.

2. Ibid., p. 687.

3. Ibid., p. 2.

4. Ibid., p. 3.

XIV

❋

Alternative Dispute Resolution

CHAPTER OBJECTIVES

1. *Understand the rationale supporting the use of ADR methods as a substitute for litigation.*
2. *Explain the differences between voluntary and court-annexed arbitration.*
3. *Describe the key features of arbitration, mediation, minitrials, summary jury trials, and private trials.*

Litigation is not the only mechanism available for the resolution of a dispute. Disputants who are unable to negotiate a solution to a pending conflict but who wish to avoid a public court trial can choose what is currently called **alternative dispute resolution (ADR).** ADR has gained in popularity largely because many people are dissatisfied with the workings of the traditional legal system. This dissatisfaction has many origins. Plaintiffs, in particular, dislike litigation's snail-like pace and complain about the volume of cases clogging up the court system and producing gridlock.[1] In federal district courts, for example, 276,397 civil cases were filed in the twelve-month period ending September 30, 2009, up from 244,343 filings in 2006.[2] Dissatisfaction also results when lawyers adopt a strategy of winning by exhausting an opponent's financial resources. Although case preparation generally will not compensate for a weak case, sometimes a weak case can be won if the client has vastly superior resources. An attorney may take such a case to trial in order to drag out the proceedings, dramatically increase the opponent's litigation expenses, and force the opponent to settle the case on unfavorable terms.

As a factual matter, a very small percentage of cases filed actually go to trial. The data from federal courts are illustrative. Of the 263,049 civil cases terminated in U.S. district courts during the twelve-month period ending September 30, 2009, only 1.2 percent actually went to trial. The percentage of federal cases reaching trial was 1.3 percent in 2006 and 2.2 percent in 2000.[3]

Many attorneys, while acknowledging that few cases are actually resolved at trial, continue to prepare each case as if it will be. They overprepare for a variety of professional and strategic reasons. Because litigation is an adversarial process, lawyers assume that opponents will resort to every legal device to win. Attorneys anticipate a continuing series of battles with the opponent at the pretrial, trial, and appellate stages of a process that can take years to determine an ultimate winner. They know that there are many ways to lose a case, and they worry about malpractice claims. Trial victories require more than good facts and sound legal arguments; they result from careful preparation and thorough discovery. Discovery also consumes large amounts of an attorney's time, which often translates into billable hours paid by the client.

The fact that lawyers become heavily involved in preparing attacks upon their client's opponent often means that they avoid looking at possible weaknesses in their own cases until just before trial. Lawyers often view themselves as their client's champion, and they frequently engage in posturing and puffery. Some refuse to initiate settlement discussions with the opponents because they fear that this might be interpreted by their clients, as well as their client's opponents, as a sign of weakness. If settlement discussions do occur, neither side is likely to be candid and reveal the amount that would be accepted in settlement of the case. Further, a tactical advantage can be gained by responding to an opponent's proposal rather than being the first to suggest a settlement figure. This game-like approach to litigation only compounds costs in money and time as the parties prepare for a trial that statistically is unlikely to occur.

Many litigants often find the judicial system's traditional "winner-take-all" approach unsatisfactory because it produces a costly victory. Both parties can lose when the disputants have an ongoing relationship, as in business, labor–management, or child custody cases, and one party clobbers the other in court. Because ADR methods can often resolve disputes more satisfactorily than trials—at less expense and in less time—some lawyers are required to explain the existence of options to litigation to their clients.[4]

Businesses have been looking for ways to resolve disputes that avoid class action lawsuits and jury trials, which expose them to the possibility of high damage awards. Congress's enactment of the Alternative Dispute Resolution Act (ADRA) in 1998) has increased judicial interest in ADR. In the ADRA, Congress explicitly required the federal district courts and courts of appeals to implement ADR procedures. Its reasoning is clearly explained in the excerpt found in Figure 14.1.

State courts also have been looking for cost-efficient ways to reduce the length of their burgeoning dockets, given the low percentage of their civil cases that are actually tried. California, Florida, and Texas, for example, have established statewide ADR systems. Other states permit local jurisdictions to experiment with ADR if they wish to do so. Some jurisdictions offer a menu of ADR options; others focus on a preferred procedure, such as mediation or arbitration.[5]

Thus, many disputants participate in ADR either because they have been required to do so by legislation or court rule **(court-annexed ADR)**.

VOLUNTARY ADR

When parties to a dispute decide to avoid the negative aspects of a court trial, they may voluntarily choose to resort to ADR, because it can often produce a fair result faster and at less cost than a public court trial involves. In fact, several major corporations will contract only with vendors who agree to participate in ADR. Disputants often prefer ADR

Sec. 651. Authorization of alternative dispute resolution

(a) Definition.—For purposes of this chapter, an alternative dispute resolution process includes any process or procedure, other than an adjudication by a presiding judge, in which a neutral third party participates to assist in the resolution of issues in controversy, through processes such as early neutral evaluation, mediation, minitrial, and arbitration as provided in sections 654 through 658.

(b) Authority.—Each United States district court shall authorize, by local rule adopted under section 2071(a), the use of alternative dispute resolution processes in all civil actions, including adversary proceedings in bankruptcy, in accordance with this chapter, except that the use of arbitration may be authorized only as provided in section 654. Each United States district court shall devise and implement its own alternative dispute resolution program, by local rule adopted under section 2071(a), to encourage and promote the use of alternative dispute resolution in its district.

(c) Existing Alternative Dispute Resolution Programs.—In those courts where an alternative dispute resolution program is in place on the date of the enactment of the Alternative Dispute Resolution Act of 1998, the court shall examine the effectiveness of that program and adopt such improvements to the program as are consistent with the provisions and purposes of this chapter.

(d) Administration of Alternative Dispute Resolution Programs.—Each United States district court shall designate an employee, or a judicial officer, who is knowledgeable in alternative dispute resolution practices and processes to implement, administer, oversee, and evaluate the court's alternative dispute resolution program. Such person may also be responsible for recruiting, screening, and training attorneys to serve as neutrals and arbitrators in the court's alternative dispute resolution program. . . .

F I G U R E   14.1   Excerpt from the Alternative Dispute Resolution Act of 1998
Source: Public Law 105-315, 105th Congress.

because they can choose the procedure that seems most appropriate to their needs. They may also like having their dispute resolved by a person or persons who have particular expertise in that subject area.

When parties voluntarily participate in ADR, they negotiate a contract that sets forth the rules that will govern the proceedings. There are several agencies to which they can turn for model ADR rules and procedures. This is helpful because attorneys who are inexperienced with ADR are sometimes reluctant to negotiate an ADR agreement with a more seasoned opponent. Model rules are evenhanded, and their terms provide either side with an advantage. They establish reasonable and simplified discovery rules and simplified rules of evidence that allow the parties to introduce

documents that might otherwise be inadmissible hearsay. The rules also can provide for confidentiality: Businesses and individuals often would prefer to deny competitors, the general public, and the news media access to private and potentially embarrassing information that would be revealed in conjunction with public court litigation.[6]

Traditional ADR practitioners and firms often advertise in trade publications and list themselves in many metropolitan-area telephone directories under "arbitration." To attract customers, increasing numbers of automobile manufacturers, local home contractors, businesses, and professionals advertise that they participate in ADR. The American Arbitration Association and the Federal Conciliation and Mediation Service are prominent examples of institutions that maintain panels of arbitrators and impartial third parties (called neutrals) who can be engaged to provide ADR services. National dispute resolution firms have offices in major cities, have employed hundreds of retired judges (even state supreme court justices), and have annual revenues exceeding $40 million.[7]

ONLINE DISPUTE RESOLUTION

In recent years, the Internet explosion and advances in computer hardware and software have contributed to the expansion of online dispute resolution (ODR). Well-known organizations such as the American Arbitration Association and the Better Business Bureau now provide ODR services, as do private companies such as Square Trade and Cybersettle. The speed, flexibility, and relatively low costs of ODR are especially appealing to online retailers seeking another option for handling customer disputes that cannot be easily resolved by customer service representatives.

INTERNET TIP

The American Arbitration Association has a wonderful website explaining both traditional ADR and the expanding ODR options.

COURT-ANNEXED ADR

Participation in ADR is legislatively or judicially authorized in many jurisdictions. As mentioned above, the federal Alternative Dispute Resolution Act, for example, provides for ADR programs in the U.S. District Courts as well as the U.S. Courts of Appeals.

Where federal and state judges claim authority to compel ADR participation, they usually promulgate court rules. Such rules are justified as being necessary and an appropriate exercise of a court's inherent power to manage its docket. Local rules often require that parties participate in nonbinding, court-annexed ADR programs before they are permitted access to a jury trial. Such programs encourage settlements, reduce court dockets, and lessen the financial burdens on taxpayers, who pay for the operation of the public judicial systems. The Alternative Dispute Resolution Act requires every federal district court to adopt at least one ADR method by local rule.

Most ADR methods are undertaken in the expectation that such programs will result in reducing the number of cases that are tried to juries. Any proposals to deny plaintiffs pursuing common law relief access to a trial by jury will clearly collide with the traditional right to a jury trial enshrined in the Seventh Amendment to the U.S. Constitution. The scope of the Seventh Amendment's jury trial right is deeply rooted in our history. Under our law, the right to a jury trial is recognized for all actions that were tried by English juries at the time of the Constitution's ratification and for other actions that are closely related to common law claims. There is no jury trial right for litigants who seek equitable relief or for actions that were unknown to the common law. Compulsory ADR has been structured so that there is no infringement of the right to a jury trial. Litigants are required to participate in pretrial ADR, but they can reject ADR solutions and then proceed to a trial by jury.

In the following case, the petitioner, Atlantic Pipe Corporation (APC), petitioned for a writ of prohibition from the district court's ruling that APC was required to participate in, and share in the cost of, court-annexed mediation conducted by a neutral appointed by the court.

In re Atlantic Pipe Corporation
304 F.3d 135
U.S. Court of Appeals, First Circuit
September 18, 2002

Selya, Circuit Judge

...January 1996, Thames-Dick Superaqueduct Partners (Thames-Dick) entered into a master agreement with the Puerto Rico Aqueduct and Sewer Authority (PRASA) to construct, operate, and maintain the North Coast Superaqueduct Project (the Project). Thames-Dick granted subcontracts for various portions of the work, including a subcontract for construction management to Dick Corp. of Puerto Rico (Dick-PR), a subcontract for the operation and maintenance of the Project to Thames Water International, Ltd. (Thames Water), and a subcontract for the fabrication of pipe to Atlantic Pipe Corp. (APC). After the Project had been built, a segment of the pipeline burst. Thames-Dick incurred significant costs in repairing the damage. Not surprisingly, it sought to recover those costs from other parties. In response, one of PRASA's insurers filed a declaratory judgment action in a local court to determine whether Thames-Dick's claims were covered under its policy. The litigation ballooned, soon involving a number of parties and a myriad of issues above and beyond insurance coverage....

...Thames-Dick asked that the case be referred to mediation and suggested Professor Eric Green as a suitable mediator. The district court granted the motion over APC's objection and ordered non-binding mediation to proceed before Professor Green.... The court also stated that if mediation failed to produce a global settlement, the case would proceed to trial.

After moving unsuccessfully for reconsideration of the mediation order, APC ... alleged that the district court did not have the authority to require mediation ... and, in all events, could not force APC to pay a share of the expenses of the mediation. We invited the other parties and the district judge to respond.... Several entities ... opposed the petition. Two others ... filed a brief in support of APC. We assigned the case to the oral argument calendar and stayed the contemplated mediation pending our review....

The Merits

There are four potential sources of judicial authority for ordering mandatory non-binding mediation of pending cases, namely, (a) the court's local rules, (b) an applicable statute, (c) the Federal Rules of Civil Procedure, and (d) the court's inherent powers. Because the district court did not identify the basis of its assumed authority, we consider each of these sources.

A. The Local Rules

A district court's local rules may provide an appropriate source of authority for ordering parties to participate in mediation.... In Puerto Rico, however, the local rules contain only a single reference to any form of alternative dispute resolution (ADR). That reference is embodied in the district court's Amended Civil Justice Expense and Delay Reduction Plan (CJR Plan)....

The district court adopted the CJR Plan on June 14, 1993, in response to the directive contained in the Civil Justice Reform Act of 1990 (CJRA),... Rule V of the CJR Plan states:

> Pursuant to 28 U.S.C. §§ 473(b)(4), this Court shall adopt a method of Alternative Dispute Resolution ("ADR") through mediation by a judicial officer. Such a program would allow litigants to obtain from an impartial third party—the judicial officer as mediator—a flexible non-binding, dispute resolution process to facilitate negotiations among the parties to help them reach settlement.

... In addition to specifying who may act as a mediator, Rule V also limns the proper procedure for mediation sessions and assures confidentiality....

The respondents concede that the mediation order in this case falls outside the boundaries of the mediation program envisioned by Rule V... because it involves mediation before a private mediator, not a judicial officer.... APC argues that the ... court exceeded its authority... by issuing a non-conforming mediation order (i.e., one that contemplates the intervention of a private mediator). The respondents counter by arguing that the rule does not bind the district court because, notwithstanding the unambiguous promise of the CJR Plan (which declares that the district court "shall adopt a method of Alternative Dispute Resolution"), no such program has been adopted to date.

This is a powerful argument. APC does not contradict the respondents' assurance that the relevant portion of the CJR Plan has remained unimplemented.... Because that is so, we conclude that the District of Puerto Rico has no local rule in force that dictates the permissible characteristics of mediation orders. Consequently, APC's argument founders....

B. The ADR Act

There is only one potential source of statutory authority for ordering mandatory non-binding mediation here: the Alternative Dispute Resolution Act of 1998 (ADR Act), 28 U.S.C. §§ 651–658. Congress passed the ADR Act to promote the utilization of alternative dispute resolution methods in the federal courts and to set appropriate guidelines for their use. The Act lists mediation as an appropriate ADR process.... Moreover, it sanctions the participation of "professional neutrals from the private sector" as mediators .... Finally, the Act requires district courts to obtain litigants' consent only when they order arbitration ... not when they order the use of other ADR mechanisms (such as non-binding mediation).

Despite the broad sweep of these provisions, the Act is quite clear that some form of the ADR procedures it endorses must be adopted in each judicial district by local rule.... (directing each district court to "devise and implement its own alternative dispute resolution program, by local rule adopted under [28 U.S.C.] section 2071(a), to encourage and promote the use of alternative dispute resolution in its district"). In the absence of such local rules, the ADR Act itself does not authorize any specific court to use a particular ADR mechanism. Because the District of Puerto Rico has not yet complied with the Act's mandate, the mediation order here at issue cannot be justified under the ADR Act....

Although the ADR Act was designed to promote the use of ADR techniques, Congress chose a very well-defined path: it granted each judicial district, rather than each individual judge, the authority to craft an appropriate ADR program. In other words, Congress permitted experimentation, but only within the disciplining format of district-wide local rules adopted with notice and a full opportunity for public comment.... To say that the Act authorized each district judge to disregard a district-wide ADR plan (or the absence of one) and fashion innovative procedures for use in specific cases is simply too much of a stretch....

We add, however, that ... we know of nothing in either the ADR Act or the policies that undergird it that can be said to restrict the district courts' authority to engage in the case-by-case deployment of ADR procedures. Hence, we conclude that where, as here, there are no implementing local rules, the ADR Act neither authorizes nor prohibits the entry of a mandatory mediation order.

C. The Civil Rules

The respondents next argue that the district court possessed the authority to require mediation by virtue of the Federal Rules of Civil Procedure. They concentrate their attention on Fed. R. Civ. P. 16, which states in pertinent part that "the court may take appropriate action with respect to ... (9) settlement and the use of special procedures to assist in resolving the dispute when authorized by statute or local rule...."... Because there is no statute or local rule authorizing mandatory private mediation in the District of Puerto Rico ... Rule 16(c)(9) does not assist the respondents' cause....

D. Inherent Powers

...[D]istrict courts have substantial inherent power to manage and control their calendars.... This inherent power takes many forms.... By way of illustration, a district court may use its inherent power to compel represented clients to attend pretrial settlement conferences, even though such a practice is not specifically authorized in the Civil Rules....

Although many federal district courts have forestalled ... debate by adopting local rules that authorize specific ADR procedures and outlaw others ... [because] the District of Puerto Rico is not among them ... we have no choice but to address the question head-on.

We begin our inquiry by examining the case law. In *Strandell v. Jackson County* ... (7th Cir. 1987), the Seventh Circuit held that a district court does not possess inherent power to compel participation in a summary jury trial.... In the court's view, Fed. R. Civ. P. 16... prevented a district court from forcing "an unwilling litigant [to] be sidetracked from the normal course of litigation...." But the group that spearheaded the subsequent revision of Rule 16 explicitly rejected that interpretation.... Thus, we do not find *Strandell* persuasive on this point....

... [T]he Sixth Circuit also has found that district courts do not possess inherent power to compel participation in summary jury-trials.... The court thought the value of a summary jury trial questionable when parties do not engage in the process voluntarily, and it worried that "too broad an interpretation of the federal courts' inherent power to regulate their procedure ... encourages judicial high-handedness...."

The concerns articulated by these two respected courts plainly apply to mandatory mediation orders. When mediation is forced upon unwilling litigants, it stands to reason that the likelihood of settlement is diminished. Requiring parties to invest substantial amounts of time and money in mediation under such circumstances may well be inefficient....

The fact remains, however, that none of these considerations establishes that mandatory mediation is always inappropriate. There may well be specific cases in which such a protocol is likely to conserve judicial resources without significantly burdening the objectors" rights to a full, fair, and speedy trial. Much depends on the idiosyncrasies of the particular case and the details of the mediation order.

In some cases, a court may be warranted in believing that compulsory mediation could yield significant benefits even if one or more parties object. After all ... negotiations could well produce a beneficial outcome, at reduced cost and greater speed, than would a trial. While the possibility that parties will fail to reach agreement remains ever present, the boon of settlement can be worth the risk.

This is particularly true in complex cases involving multiple claims and parties. The fair and expeditious resolution of such cases often is helped along by creative solutions—solutions that simply are not available in the binary framework of traditional adversarial litigation. Mediation with the assistance of a skilled facilitator gives parties an opportunity to explore a much wider range of options, including those that go beyond conventional zero-sum resolutions. Mindful of these potential advantages, we hold that it is within a district court's inherent power to order non-consensual mediation in those cases in which that step seems reasonably likely to serve the interests of justice....

E. The Mediation Order

Our determination that the district courts have inherent power to refer cases to non-binding mediation is made with a recognition that any such order must be crafted in a manner that preserves procedural fairness and shields objecting parties from undue burdens. We thus turn to the specifics of the mediation order entered in this case....

As an initial matter, we agree with the lower court that the complexity of this case militates in favor of ordering mediation. At last count, the suit involves twelve parties, asserting a welter of claims, counterclaims, cross-claims, and third-party claims predicated on a wide variety of theories. The pendency of nearly parallel litigation in the Puerto Rican courts, which features a slightly different cast of characters and claims that are related to but not completely congruent with those asserted here, further complicates the matter. Untangling the intricate web of relationships among the parties, along with the difficult and fact-intensive arguments made by each, will be time-consuming and will impose significant costs on the

parties and the court. Against this backdrop, mediation holds out the dual prospect of advantaging the litigants and conserving scarce judicial resources.

In an effort to parry this thrust, APC raises a series of objections.... APC posits that the appointment of a private mediator proposed by one of the parties is per se improper (and, thus, invalidates the order). We do not agree. The district court has inherent power to "appoint persons unconnected with the court to aid judges in the performance of specific judicial duties...." In the context of non-binding mediation, the mediator does not decide the merits of the case and has no authority to coerce settlement. Thus, in the absence of a contrary statute or rule, it is perfectly acceptable for the district court to appoint a qualified and neutral private party as a mediator. The mere fact that the mediator was proposed by one of the parties is insufficient to establish bias in favor of that party....

We hasten to add that the litigants are free to challenge the qualifications or neutrality of any suggested mediator (whether or not nominated by a party to the case). APC, for example, had a full opportunity to present its views about the suggested mediator both in its opposition to the motion for mediation and in its motion for reconsideration of the mediation order. Despite these opportunities, APC offered no convincing reason to spark a belief that Professor Green, a nationally recognized mediator with significant experience in sprawling cases, is an unacceptable choice. When a court enters a mediation order, it necessarily makes an independent determination that the mediator it appoints is both qualified and neutral. Because the court made that implicit determination here in a manner that was procedurally fair (if not ideal), we find no abuse of discretion in its selection of Professor Green....

APC also grouses that it should not be forced to share the costs of an unwanted mediation. We have held, however, that courts have the power under Fed. R. Civ. P. 26(f) to issue pretrial cost-sharing orders in complex litigation....

The short of the matter is that, without default cost-sharing rules, the use of valuable ADR techniques (like mediation) becomes hostage to the parties" ability to agree on the concomitant financial arrangements. This means that the district court's inherent power to order private mediation in appropriate cases would be rendered nugatory absent the corollary power to order the sharing of reasonable mediation costs. To avoid this pitfall, we hold that the district court, in an appropriate case, is empowered to order the sharing of reasonable costs and expenses associated with mandatory non-binding mediation.

....[A] mediation order [,] [however,] must contain procedural and substantive safeguards to ensure fairness to all parties involved. The mediation order in this case does not quite meet that test. In particular, the order does not set limits on the duration of the mediation or the expense associated therewith....

... As entered, the order ... does not set forth either a timetable for the mediation or a cap on the fees that the mediator may charge. The figures that have been bandied about in the briefs—$900 per hour or $9,000 per mediation day—are quite large and should not be left to the mediator's whim. Relatedly, because the mediator is to be paid an hourly rate, the court should have set an outside limit on the number of hours to be devoted to mediation. Equally as important, it is trite but often true that justice delayed is justice denied. An unsuccessful mediation will postpone the ultimate resolution of the case—indeed, the district court has stayed all discovery pending the completion of the mediation—and, thus, prolong the litigation. For these reasons, the district court should have set a definite time frame for the mediation....

To recapitulate, we rule that a mandatory mediation order issued under the district court's inherent power is valid in an appropriate case. We also rule that this is an appropriate case. We hold, however, that the district court's failure to set reasonable limits on the duration of the mediation and on the mediator's fees dooms the decree.

IV. Conclusion
We admire the district court's pragmatic and innovative approach to this massive litigation. Our core holding—that ordering mandatory mediation is a proper exercise of a district court's inherent power, subject, however, to a variety of terms and conditions—validates that approach. We are mindful that this holding is in tension with the opinions of the Sixth and Seventh Circuits in NLO and Strandell, respectively, but we believe it is justified by the important goal of promoting flexibility and creative problem-solving in the handling of complex litigation.

That said, the need of the district judge in this case to construct his own mediation regime ad hoc underscores the greater need of the district court as an institution to adopt an ADR program and memorialize it in its local rules. In the ADR Act, Congress directed that "each United States district court shall authorize, by local rule under section 2071(a), the use of alternative dispute resolution processes in all civil actions...." 28 U.S.C. §§ 651(b). While Congress did not set a firm deadline for compliance with this directive, the statute was enacted four years ago. This omission having been noted, we are confident that the district court will move expediently to bring the District of Puerto Rico into compliance.

We need go no further. For the reasons set forth above, we vacate the district court's mediation order and remand for further proceedings consistent with this opinion. The district court is free to order mediation if it continues to believe that such a course is advisable or, in the alternative, to proceed with discovery and trial.

Vacated and remanded....

Case Questions

1. Should a court have the power to compel litigants to participate in (and pay for) mediation before permitting a jury trial? Isn't this a waste of time and money?
2. Did reading this case expose any problems with the Alternative Dispute Resolution Act?
3. What exactly did the Sixth Circuit Court of Appeals decide in this case? How did the court justify its decision?

ADR TECHNIQUES

The demand for trial-avoidance methods to resolve disputes has resulted in increasing reliance on settlement conferences, arbitration, and mediation—three of the oldest and the most popular ADR options—as well as the development of newer techniques such as private trials, minitrials, and summary jury trials.

Settlement Conferences

Rule 1 of the Federal Rules of Civil Procedure states that judges are expected to promote "the just, speedy, and inexpensive determination of every action." This very general charge gives judges considerable flexibility in determining how they will achieve this goal. Many judges use **settlement conferences,** which are a traditional step in the litigation process, as an informal method for resolving a dispute without a trial.[8]

A judge who is willing to be assertive can help parties explore a lawsuit's settlement potential. The judge can initiate the process or respond to a request for assistance from one or more of the parties. This intervention can be helpful when neither of the opposing attorneys is willing to make the first move toward a settlement. The parties, however, often leap at an opportunity to discuss settlement if the judge broaches the subject. An assertive judge may personally convene a settlement conference, carefully review the case, and emphasize each side's weaknesses and strengths. This is important because the evidence is frequently inconclusive. A judge who is knowledgeable about the relevant law can be very influential. He or she can point out the costs of going to trial and emphasize the risks each side incurs by trying the matter to an unpredictable jury.[9] The judge may know about recent verdicts in similar cases that went to trial and may suggest ADR options that could help each side avoid the necessity of a trial. Some judges, if requested by the parties, will propose a settlement figure. Judges who have the time, skill, and interest to function as mediators may meet privately with each side. They may even request that the clients meet without their attorneys being present. The judge's participation is the key ingredient. It is one thing for an attorney to engage in puffery with a client or an opponent. It is another matter to refuse to acknowledge the weaknesses of one's case to an experienced trial judge. Many judges, however, don't define their role in this way, believing that settlement is a matter to be decided solely by the parties without judicial involvement.

Serious issues arise regarding the judge's proper role in the settlement conference. Many lawyers are concerned that a party who refuses to settle may encounter bias if the matter is subsequently set for trial before the settlement judge. They fear that the judge might rule against the "uncooperative" party on motions and evidence admissibility at trial. One solution to this problem is to make sure that the judge conducting the settlement conference does not sit as the trial judge. Another is to use a lawyer–mediator instead of the judge at the settlement conference.

INTERNET TIP

In *Estate of John Skalka v. Mark Skalka*, the Indiana Court of Appeals has to decide whether a state trial judge acted improperly when conducting a settlement conference. Interested readers will find this case included with the Chapter XIV materials on the textbook's website.

Arbitration

Arbitration is the most used form of ADR[10] and was in existence long before the emergence of the English common law.[11] It was well known in the eighteenth century, and George Washington's will even contained an arbitration clause in the event that disputes arose between his heirs.[12]

American courts traditionally opposed arbitration because the parties were in effect thumbing their noses at the judicial system. Many judges believed that people who chose arbitration over the judicial system should not be entitled to come to the judiciary for enforcement of nonjudicial decisions. In the 1925 **Federal Arbitration Act** (FAA), however, Congress established a national policy favoring the arbitration of commercial transactions. In the act, Congress provided that arbitration contracts "shall be valid, irrevocable, and enforceable save upon such grounds as exist at law or equity for the revocation of any contract" and required that courts enforce most arbitration awards.[13] Congress subsequently amended the FAA in 1947, 1954, 1970, and 1990 to recognize and enforce arbitration awards involving commercial arbitration agreements between Americans and citizens of other countries. Congress also enacted the **Labor–Management Relations Act** in 1947, which extended the use of arbitration to disputes arising out of collective bargaining. The U.S. Supreme Court has generally gone along with Congress and the executive branch in supporting the expansion of this and other forms of ADR.[14]

Some disputants end up in arbitration because it is required by a court-annexed program or Is a condition of being employed. In other instances, parties contract to submit their disputes to an arbitrator for resolution.

INTERNET TIP

The plaintiff in *Linda James v. McDonald's Corporation* challenged McDonald's claim that by participating in that company's "Who Wants to Be a Millionaire" promotion she had contracted to resolve any dispute with the company via arbitration and could not litigate her claim. The U.S. Court of Appeals for the Seventh Circuit's opinion in this 2005 case can be found on the textbook's website.

Voluntary Arbitration

Voluntary arbitration is increasingly used to resolve business disputes because it provides prompt decisions at a reasonable cost. The voluntary arbitration process is very different from the judicial process. In voluntary arbitrations, for example, the arbitrator makes a binding decision on the merits of the dispute and can base his or her decision on a lay or business sense of justice rather than on the rules of law that would be applied in court. A private arbitration proceeds pursuant to a contract in which the parties promise to bind themselves to arbitrate their controversy and abide by the arbitrator's decision (which is called an **award**). Because a person who chooses to arbitrate waives the right to a jury trial, arbitration agreements must be in writing to be enforceable in court. Some parties agree to arbitrate their agreements prior to the existence of any dispute.[15] Contracts between unions and management, investors and stockbrokers,[16] and banks and their customers[17] often include arbitration clauses. Many major corporations routinely include arbitration clauses in contracts they make with their suppliers. Arbitration agreements can also be negotiated after a controversy has arisen.

Arbitrators are selected by agreement of the parties. The nonprofit American Arbitration Association has been a supplier of arbitrators since 1926.[18] Arbitrators in business disputes are often chosen because of their expertise in a specific field. This better enables them to render a reasonable and proper decision. This should be contrasted with the trial decisions that are made by a randomly selected judge and jury. The parties can choose a person who they believe will conduct the proceedings fairly and with integrity. However, the legal continuity of the judicial system is not necessarily present in a voluntary arbitration. Arbitrators, for example, do not have to follow precedent in their decision-making process, nor do they have to prepare written explanations for their award (although they often do both).

Each arbitration hearing is convened for the sole purpose of deciding a particular dispute. Arbitration hearings are often conducted in hotels, motels, and offices and, unlike court trials, are generally not open to the public. Although the formalities of a court proceeding need not be followed, arbitration hearings usually follow the sequence of opening statements by the opposing parties, direct and cross-examination of the witnesses, introduction of exhibits, and closing arguments. Arbitrators base their decisions on the evidence and the arguments made before them. However, they are generally not bound by the rules of evidence used in litigation.

Although the parties to an arbitration usually comply with the terms of the arbitrator's award, judicial enforcement action can be taken against a party who reneges.

In the next case, Shelly Sullivan, the plaintiff at trial, sought to litigate rather than arbitrate her claims against a pest control company. The company contended that Sullivan had contractually agreed to arbitrate any claims she might have and thus the lawsuit should be abated.

Sears Authorized Termite and Pest Control, Inc. v. Shelly J. Sullivan
816 So. 2d 603
Supreme Court of Florida
May 2, 2002

Wells, C. J

We have for review the ... issue of whether a provision requiring arbitration in an agreement to provide exterminating services for pests, including spiders, includes claims for personal injury allegedly caused by being bitten by spiders which were to be eradicated in the performance of the agreement....

In this case, petitioner Sears Authorized Termite & Pest Control, Inc. (Sears) and respondent Shelly Sullivan (Sullivan) executed a pest control agreement in which Sears agreed to provide services for the control of various pests, including spiders. Sullivan filed suit, essentially alleging in her complaint that Sears treated and retreated for spiders but failed to control the population of spiders at her residence. The failure to control the population of spiders resulted in Sullivan being bitten by spiders, causing her personal injuries and damages. Sears responded by moving to abate and compel arbitration based upon the following arbitration provision in the pest control agreement:

Arbitration

The purchaser and ... Sears Authorized Termite & Pest Control agree that any controversy or claim between them arising out of or related to the interpretation, performance or breach of any provision of this agreement shall be settled exclusively by arbitration. This contract/agreement is subject to arbitration pursuant to the Uniform Arbitration Act of the American Arbitration Association. The arbitration award may be entered in any court having jurisdiction. In no event shall either party be liable to the other for indirect, special or consequential damages or loss of anticipated profits.

The trial judge held a hearing and entered an order granting Sears' motion. In his order the trial judge stated:

The key case seems to be *Seifert v. U.S. Home Corporation*.... The two closest cases to the present case are *Terminix International Company v. Michaels* ... (Fla. 4th DCA 1996), and *Terminix International Company v. Ponzio* ... (Fla. 5th DCA 1997).

The present case hinges on an arbitration provision in a pest control customer agreement. The Court's view of the pertinent portion of the agreement is that: regarding any provision of this contract for which a controversy exists concerning its interpretation, performance or breach, arbitration is required. The Court analyzes the pertinent provisions of the contract to require the pest control company to provide necessary service for the control of spiders. The allegations in this complaint are essentially that the pest control company treated and retreated for spiders but failed to control the spiders. The counts are counts for breach of warranty which are clearly contractual counts and counts for negligence, fraud in the inducement, fraud, and negligent misrepresentation.

This case differs from *Michaels* in that *Michaels* had to do with the use of ultra hazardous chemicals. A general duty is imposed on the producer and distributor of hazardous chemicals which is independent of and unrelated to any contractual obligations. Personal injuries claimed in that case were the result of poisoning from these ultra hazardous chemicals. In the present case the cause of action is based on the inability of the pest control services to effectively poison the spiders. In *Michaels* the duty to avoid poisoning persons with ultra hazardous chemicals existed whether or not there was a contract between the parties.

Ponzio is factually like the present case in that it was a lawsuit on a pest control contract for failure to eradicate brown recluse spiders, the same spiders in the present case. Like *Ponzio*... the allegations of the present complaint are that the pest control service had a duty to control certain pests and that it failed to do so resulting in bodily injury. There is no assertion of strict liability or of a failure to warn and the claims and controversy herein derive from the contract.

Seifert is the most important case. It involves an inherently dangerous design of an air conditioning system so that carbon monoxide gas from a vehicle in the garage circulated through the house and killed Mr. Seifert. The court held that the tort claim related to duties wholly independent of the agreement by the builder to construct the house. *Seifert* recognized that carbon monoxide poisoning was not related to any of the contemplated terms of the contract. In the present case the contemplated terms of the contract call for the control of spiders. The issue is whether the spiders were properly controlled or not. This at least, raises some issue, the resolution of which requires a reference to or construction of a portion of the contract, namely the portion that obligates the pest control service to control the pests. It involves a disagreement or a controversy relating to the performance or breach of this requirement of the contract as well as the interpretation of how much treatment was necessary in order to effectuate control of the pests.

Unlike an ultra hazardous chemical, or a latent fatally dangerous condition in a home, the present condition is not one imposed by general law or public policy but arises from the contract in question. The obligation is based on a new duty that did not exist without the contract. The tort claims are therefore directly related to the contract. The contract explicitly refers to the control of spiders. It is not necessary to stretch the scope of the arbitration clause in order to encompass these claims. Consequently the arbitration clause is not interfering with a right to jury trial since arbitration clauses are enforceable and favored when the disagreement falls within the scope of the arbitration agreement....

... [T]he... Court of Appeal... reversed.... [It]... found that *Seifert* and *Michaels* should be read to mean that Sullivan's claim for personal injuries and damages resulting from the spider bites were not covered by the arbitration provision....

In this case, it is clear that the intent of the agreement was to "control" spiders, among other "pests." Thus, Sullivan's cause of action rests upon the failure to perform the agreement. The plain language of this arbitration clause covers the "performance" of the agreement. This clearly is distinct from *Seifert*, in which we specifically held: "The tort claim filed in this case neither relies on the agreement nor refers to any provision within the agreement. Rather, the petitioner's tort claim relates to duties wholly independent from the agreement..." We likewise find this case to be distinguishable from the Fourth District Court of Appeal's decision in *Michaels*, in which the factual allegation was based on the use of ultra-hazardous chemicals.... Rather, we find this case to be similar to the Fifth District Court of Appeal's decision in *Ponzio*.

Accordingly, we quash the Fourth District Court of Appeal's decision in *Sullivan*, approve *Ponzio* to the extent it is consistent with this opinion, and remand this case with instructions that the trial court's order compelling arbitration be affirmed.

It is so ordered.

Case Questions

1. Why does the Florida Supreme Court reverse the Court of Appeals?
2. How were the *Seifert* and *Michaels* cases distinguished on their facts from the facts of the Sullivan case?

Judicial Review of Arbitration Awards

Either party to an arbitration may institute a court action seeking confirmation (judicial enforcement) or modification of the award. Federal and state laws provide for jurisdiction in specified courts to (1) recognize and enforce arbitration, (2) provide standards of conduct for arbitration hearings, (3) make arbitration agreements irrevocable, and (4) provide that court action cannot be initiated until the arbitration has concluded.

States differ about the powers judges reviewing arbitration awards should possess. Most state courts and the federal courts will usually confirm an arbitration award unless the arbitrator violated the terms of the arbitration contract, the arbitration procedures offended fundamental due process, or the award violated public policy. Even the traditional rule prohibiting appellate courts from reviewing an arbitrator's findings of fact is subject to reconsideration, as we will see in the following precedent-setting case.

Cable Connection, Inc. v. DIRECTV, Inc.
190 P.3d 586
California Supreme Court
August 25, 2008

Corrigan, J.

This case presents two questions regarding arbitration agreements. (1) May the parties structure their agreement to allow for judicial review of legal error in the arbitration award? (2) Is classwide arbitration available under an agreement that is silent on the matter? ...

Defendant DIRECTV, Inc. broadcasts television programming nationwide, via satellite. It contracts with retail dealers to provide customers with equipment needed to receive its satellite signal. In 1996, DIRECTV employed a "residential dealer agreement" for this purpose. A new "sales agency agreement" was used in 1998. Both agreements included arbitration clauses; neither mentioned classwide arbitration.

In 2001, dealers from four states filed suit in Oklahoma, asserting on behalf of a nationwide class that DIRECTV had wrongfully withheld commissions and assessed improper charges. DIRECTV moved to compel arbitration. As the Oklahoma court was considering whether the arbitration could be conducted on a classwide basis, the United States Supreme Court decided *Green Tree Financial Corp. v. Bazzle* (2003).... A plurality in *Bazzle* held that the arbitrator must decide whether class arbitration is authorized by the parties' contract.... Accordingly, the Oklahoma court directed the parties to submit the matter to arbitration in Los Angeles as provided in the sales agency agreement....

After the dealers presented a statement of claim and demand for class arbitration in March 2004, a panel of three AAA [American Arbitration Association] arbitrators was selected. Following the procedure adopted by the AAA in response to *Bazzle,* the panel first addressed whether the parties' agreement permitted the arbitration to proceed on a classwide basis.

After briefing and argument, a majority of the panel decided that even though "the contract is silent and manifests no intent on this issue," arbitration on a classwide basis was authorized.... The award emphasized that class arbitration was not necessarily required in this case; it was merely permitted by the contract. Whether the arbitration would actually be maintained on a classwide basis would be the subject of a future hearing....

DIRECTV petitioned to vacate the award, contending (1) the majority had exceeded its authority by substituting its discretion for the parties' intent regarding class arbitration; (2) the majority had

improperly ignored extrinsic evidence of contractual intent; and (3) even if the majority had not exceeded the authority generally granted to arbitrators, the award reflected errors of law that the arbitration clause placed beyond their powers and made subject to judicial review.... The trial court vacated the award, essentially accepting all of DIRECTV's arguments.

The Court of Appeal reversed, holding that the trial court exceeded its jurisdiction by reviewing the merits of the arbitrators' decision....

We granted DIRECTV's petition for review.

II. DISCUSSION
A. Contract Provisions for Judicial Review of Arbitration Awards
1. The CAA, the FAA, and Prior Case Law

"In most important respects, the California statutory scheme on enforcement of private arbitration agreements is similar to the FAA [Federal Arbitration Act]; the similarity is not surprising, as the two share origins in the earlier statutes of New York and New Jersey....

Consistent with that purpose, the CAA [California Arbitration Act] and the FAA provide only limited grounds for judicial review of an arbitration award. Under both statutes, courts are authorized to vacate an award if it was (1) procured by corruption, fraud, or undue means; (2) issued by corrupt arbitrators; (3) affected by prejudicial misconduct on the part of the arbitrators; or (4) in excess of the arbitrators' powers.... An award may be corrected for (1) evident miscalculation or mistake; (2) excess of the arbitrators' powers; or (3) imperfection in form.....

...[I]n *Moncharsh* [*v. Heily & Bliss* (1992] we declared that "in the absence of some limiting clause in the arbitration agreement, the merits of the award, either on questions of fact or of law, may not be reviewed except as provided in the statute."... In the years following the *Moncharsh* decision, our Courts of Appeal have rejected claims that review of the merits was authorized inferentially, by contract clauses stating that "the award will be in the form of a statement of decision"... In each of these cases, however, the courts noted that an expanded scope of review *would* be available under a clause specifically tailored for that purpose...

Nevertheless, when the issue has been squarely presented, no Court of Appeal has enforced a contract clause calling for judicial review of an arbitration award on its merits…. In *Crowell* [*v. Downey Community Hospital Foundation* (2002)] … the parties' contract included an arbitration clause requiring the arbitrator to make written findings and conclusions "supported by law and substantial evidence."… The award was to be "final, binding and enforceable …, except that upon the petition of any party to the arbitration, a court shall have the authority to review the transcript of the arbitration proceedings and the arbitrator's award and shall have the authority to vacate the arbitrator's award, in whole or in part, on the basis that the award is not supported by substantial evidence or is based upon an error of law."…

The *Crowell* court, in a split decision, decided the statutory bases for vacating and correcting arbitration awards are exclusive, and permitting the parties to expand those grounds by agreement would undermine the purpose of reducing expense and delay….

2. Hall Street and the Question of Preemption

The *Hall Street* case arose from an arbitration agreement negotiated during litigation, to resolve an indemnification claim. The agreement was approved and entered as an order by the trial court. It provided:

> "The Court shall vacate, modify or correct any award: (i) where the arbitrator's findings of facts are not supported by substantial evidence, or (ii) where the arbitrator's conclusions of law are erroneous…."

The trial court vacated the arbitrator's award and remanded for further consideration; at the time, the Ninth Circuit approved of contract provisions for expanded judicial review…. After the arbitrator ruled a second time, both parties sought modification, and both appealed from the trial court's judgment modifying the award. By that time, the Ninth Circuit had changed its view on the enforceability of judicial review provisions…. It reversed the judgment….

… [T]he Supreme Court granted certiorari. A majority of the court agreed with the Ninth Circuit that the grounds for vacatur and modification provided by sections 10 and 11 of the FAA are exclusive. … First, the majority rejected the argument that the nonstatutory "manifest disregard of the law" standard of review recognized by some federal courts supports the enforceability of contract provisions for additional grounds to vacate or modify an arbitration award. ….

Next, the *Hall Street* majority disposed of the contention that allowing parties to contract for an expanded scope of review is consistent with the FAA's primary goal of ensuring the enforcement of arbitration agreements. … The majority … characterized the statutory grounds for review as remedies for "egregious departures from the parties' agreed-upon arbitration," such as corruption and fraud…. It viewed the directive in section 9 of the FAA, that the court "must grant" confirmation "unless the award is vacated, modified, or corrected as prescribed in sections 10 and 11," as a mandatory provision leaving no room for the parties to agree otherwise….

Despite this strict reading of the FAA, the *Hall Street* majority left the door ajar for alternate routes to an expanded scope of review…."… [H]ere we speak only to the scope of the expeditious judicial review under §§ 9, 10, and 11, deciding nothing about other possible avenues for judicial enforcement of arbitration awards…."

Furthermore, the *Hall Street* majority recognized that the trial court's case management authority under rule 16 of the Federal Rules of Civil Procedure might support its order adopting the parties' agreement to review of the merits. However, it remanded for further proceedings on this point, concluding that it was "in no position to address the question now, beyond noting the claim of relevant case management authority independent of the FAA…."

The dealers in this case urge us to follow the rationale of the *Hall Street* majority. They contend that any other construction of the CAA would result in its preemption by the FAA. Alternatively, they argue that *Hall Street* provides a persuasive analysis of the FAA that should be applied to the similar CAA provisions governing judicial review….

We conclude that the *Hall Street* holding is restricted to proceedings to review arbitration awards under the FAA, and does not require state law to conform with its limitations. Furthermore, a reading of the CAA that permits the enforcement of agreements for merits review is fully consistent with the FAA "policy guaranteeing the enforcement of private contractual arrangements"…

3. Moncharsh and the California Rule

In *Moncharsh* … [w]e reaffirmed "the general rule that an arbitrator's decision is not ordinarily reviewable for error by either the trial or appellate courts"… and held that the statutory grounds for review were intended to implement that rule…. To that extent, our conclusions were consistent with those of the *Hall Street* majority. However, in several respects *Moncharsh* reflects a very different view of arbitration agreements and the arbitration statutes, as applied to the scope of judicial review. Therefore, we disagree with the dealers' argument that *Hall Street* is persuasive authority for a restrictive interpretation of the review provisions in the CAA.

Moncharsh began from the premise that "[t]he scope of arbitration is ... a matter of agreement between the parties' [citation], and "[t]he powers of an arbitrator are limited and circumscribed by the agreement or stipulation of submission."...

"The policy of the law in recognizing arbitration agreements and in providing by statute for their enforcement is to encourage persons who wish to avoid delays incident to a civil action to obtain an adjustment of their differences by a tribunal of their own choosing... "Because the decision to arbitrate grievances evinces the parties' intent to bypass the judicial system and thus avoid potential delays at the trial and appellate levels, arbitral finality is a core component of the parties' agreement to submit to arbitration. Thus, an arbitration decision is final and conclusive *because the parties have agreed that it be so.* By ensuring that an arbitrator's decision is final and binding, courts simply assure that the parties receive the benefit of their bargain...."

"Thus, both because it vindicates the intentions of the parties that the award be final, and because an arbitrator is not ordinarily constrained to decide according to the rule of law, it is the general rule that, "The merits of the controversy between the parties are not subject to judicial review...."

Our reasoning in *Moncharsh* centered not on statutory restriction of the parties' contractual options, but on the parties' intent and the powers of the arbitrators as defined in the agreement. These factors support the enforcement of agreements for an expanded scope of review. If the parties constrain the arbitrators' authority by requiring a dispute to be decided according to the rule of law, *and* make plain their intention that the award is reviewable for legal error, the general rule of limited review has been displaced by the parties' agreement. Their expectation is not that the result of the arbitration will be final and conclusive, but rather that it will be reviewed on the merits at the request of either party. ...

We have consistently recognized that "[a]n exception to the general rule assigning broad powers to the arbitrators arises when the parties have, in either the contract or an agreed submission to arbitration, explicitly and unambiguously limited those powers.... Our review in *Moncharsh* of the CAA's legislative history confirms that while the statutory grounds for correction and vacation of arbitration awards do not ordinarily include errors of law,

contractual limitations on the arbitrators' powers can alter the usual scope of review.

The current version of the CAA was enacted following a study by the California Law Revision Commission, undertaken at the Legislature's direction....

"The Arbitration Study emphasized that arbitration should be the end of the dispute and that 'the ordinary concepts of judicial appeal and review are not applicable to arbitration awards. Settled case law is based on this assumption....'" After surveying the state of the law, the report concluded that although the California statutes do not 'attempt to express the exact limits of court review of arbitration awards, ... no good reason exists to codify into the California statute the case law as it presently exists.' ... Further, the report recommended that the 'present grounds for vacating an award should be left substantially unchanged.' ... Considering the nature of the revisions incorporated in the CAA, this court concluded that the Legislature intended to "adopt the position taken in case law and endorsed in the Arbitration Study, that is, 'that in the absence of some limiting clause in the arbitration agreement, the merits of the award, either on questions of fact or of law, may not be reviewed except as provided in the statute."' ... (*Moncharsh* ... quoting *Crofoot* ...)

The *Crofoot* rule does not suggest that review of the merits must rest on a nonstatutory basis. As discussed below, *Crofoot's* reference to a limiting clause in the agreement pertains to limits on the arbitrators' powers. Thus, the merits of an award may come within the ambit of the statutory grounds of review for excess of the arbitrators' powers. (§§ 1286.2, subd. (a)(4); 1286.6, subd. (b).) However, absent such a limitation, the scope of review provided by statute is quite limited. In *Moncharsh*, we noted that section 1286.2 includes no provision for review of the merits like that found in section 1296, governing public construction contract arbitrations.... The *Crowell* court, and the Court of Appeal below, considered section 1296 an indication that the Legislature did not intend to permit review of the merits by agreement.... This view is mistaken. In *Moncharsh* we inferred from section 1296 that "the Legislature did not intend to confer traditional judicial review in private arbitration cases...." However, the failure to provide for that scope of review *by statute* does not mean the parties themselves may not do so *by contract*.... Our holding in *Moncharsh* that the CAA incorporates the *Crofoot* rule is irreconcilable with the notion that the parties are barred from agreeing to limit the arbitrators' authority by subjecting their award to review on the merits. The history of the FAA, as reviewed by the *Hall Street* majority, includes no similar indication that Congress intended the statutory grounds for review to operate as default provisions, providing only limited review unless the parties agree otherwise.... Therefore, *Hall Street's* FAA analysis is inapposite.

In California, the policy favoring arbitration without the complications of traditional judicial review is based on the parties' expectations as embodied in their agreement, and the CAA rests on the same foundation. "Accordingly, policies favoring the efficiency of private arbitration as a means of dispute resolution must sometimes yield to its fundamentally contractual nature, and to the attendant requirement that arbitration shall proceed *as the parties themselves have agreed.*" ... The scope of judicial review is not invariably limited by statute; rather, "the parties, simply by agreeing to arbitrate, are deemed to accept limited judicial review *by implication...*" It follows that they may expressly agree to accept a broader scope of review...

The Arbitration Study discussed in *Moncharsh* includes a similar observation. Regarding the statutory ground of review for excess of the arbitrators' powers, the study stated: "Arbitrators may base their decision upon broad principles of justice and equity, but if the submission agreement specifically requires an arbitrator to act in conformity with rules of law, the arbitrator exceeds his authority if his decision is not based on rules of law."...

A provision requiring arbitrators to apply the law leaves open the possibility that they are empowered to apply it "wrongly as well as rightly." ... As we recently observed: "When parties contract to resolve their disputes by private arbitration, their agreement ordinarily contemplates that the arbitrator will have the power to decide any question of contract interpretation, historical fact or general law necessary, in the arbitrator's understanding of the case, to reach a decision.... Inherent in that power is the possibility the arbitrator may err in deciding some aspect of the case. Arbitrators do not ordinarily exceed their contractually created powers simply by reaching an erroneous conclusion on a contested issue of law or fact, and arbitral awards may not ordinarily be vacated because of such error, for "[t]he arbitrator's resolution of these issues is what the parties bargained for in the arbitration agreement."...

Therefore, to take themselves out of the general rule that the merits of the award are not subject to judicial review, the parties must clearly agree that legal errors are an excess of arbitral authority that is reviewable by the courts. Here, the parties expressly so

agreed, depriving the arbitrators of the power to commit legal error. They also specifically provided for judicial review of such error.... We do not decide here whether one or the other of these clauses alone, or some different formulation, would be sufficient to confer an expanded scope of review. However, we emphasize that parties seeking to allow judicial review of the merits, and to avoid an additional dispute over the scope of review, would be well advised to provide for that review explicitly and unambiguously....

Review on the merits has been deemed incompatible with the goals of finality and informality that are served by arbitration and protected by the arbitration statutes.... However ... those policies draw their strength from the agreement of the parties. It is the parties who are best situated to weigh the advantages of traditional arbitration against the benefits of court review for the correction of legal error....

To the extent the concern with reviewability arises from apprehension that permitting review on the merits would open the door to contracts imposing unfamiliar standards of review, it appears to be unfounded. We have discovered no case where the parties attempted to make the courts apply an unusual standard of review. Instead, as in this case, they have required the arbitrators to apply legal standards, resulting in awards that can be reviewed in traditional fashion....We need not speculate about provisions calling for bizarre modes of decision, but we note that arbitration agreements are "as enforceable as other contracts, but not more so."... Thus, just as the parties to any contract are limited in the constraints they may place on judicial review, an arbitration agreement providing that a "judge would review the award by flipping a coin or studying the entrails of a dead fowl" would be unenforceable....

The benefits of enforcing agreements like the one before us are considerable, for both the parties and the courts. The development of alternative dispute resolution is advanced by enabling private parties to choose procedures with which they are comfortable. Commentators have observed that provisions for expanded judicial review are a product of market forces operating in an increasingly "judicialized" arbitration setting, with many of the attributes of court proceedings. The desire for the protection afforded by review for legal error has evidently developed from the experience of sophisticated parties in high stakes cases, where the arbitrators' awards deviated from the parties' expectations in startling ways....

The judicial system reaps little benefit from forcing parties to choose between the risk of an erroneous arbitration award and the burden of litigating their dispute entirely in court. Enforcing contract provisions for review of awards on the merits relieves pressure on congested trial court dockets.... Courts are spared not only the burden of conducting a trial, but also the complications of discovery disputes and other pretrial proceedings. Incorporating traditional judicial review by express agreement preserves the utility of arbitration as a way to obtain expert factual determinations without delay, while allowing the parties to protect themselves from perhaps the weakest aspect of the arbitral process, its handling of disputed rules of law....

There are also significant benefits to the development of the common law when arbitration awards are made subject to merits review by the parties' agreement. "[I]f courts are reduced to the function of merely enforcing or denying arbitral awards, without an opportunity to discuss the reasoning for the arbitral decision, the advancement of the law is stalled, as arbitral decisions carry no precedential value.... Thus, expansion of judicial review gives the courts of first instance the opportunity to establish a record, and to include the reasoning of expert arbitrators into the body of the law in the form of written decisions. This procedure better advances the state of the law and facilitates the necessary beneficial input from experts in the field...."

These advantages, obtained with the consent of the parties, are substantial. As explained in *Moncharsh*, the drafters of the CAA established the statutory grounds for judicial review with the expectation that arbitration awards are ordinarily final and subject to a restricted scope of review, but that parties may limit the arbitrators' authority by providing for review of the merits in the arbitration agreement.... The Court of Appeal erred by refusing to enforce the parties' clearly expressed agreement in this case.

B. The Award Permitting Classwide Arbitration
Two of the three arbitrators below decided the dealers could pursue arbitration on a classwide basis, although the parties' contract did not mention classwide arbitration. The Court of Appeal agreed with this

determination. The contract calls for the arbitrators to apply California substantive law, while following the procedural requirements of AAA rules and the FAA....

The Court of Appeal, and the arbitrators in the majority, viewed the right to pursue classwide arbitration as a substantive one... The court concluded that these cases "give[ ] arbitrators discretion to order classwide arbitration even where the arbitration agreement is silent on that issue, in divergence from the general rules of contract interpretation that terms are not to be inserted into contracts."...

DIRECTV claims that ...the arbitrators in the majority violated a provision of the AAA rules stating: "In construing the applicable arbitration clause, the arbitrator shall not consider the existence of ... AAA rules, to be a factor either in favor of or against permitting the arbitration to proceed on a class basis." ...

DIRECTV appears to be correct.... AAA's class arbitration policy is based on the *Bazzle* decision.... The *Bazzle* plurality declared: "[T]he relevant question here is what *kind of arbitration proceeding* the parties agreed to. That question does not concern a state statute or judicial procedures.... It concerns contract interpretation and arbitration procedures. Arbitrators are well situated to answer that question...." We express no view on whether the terms of this arbitration clause are consistent with conducting arbitration on a classwide basis. Instead of deciding that question, the majority arbitrators misapplied AAA rules and policy as well as the *Keating* rule. Under the circumstances, we deem it appropriate to permit the arbitration panel to reconsider the availability of classwide arbitration as a matter of contract interpretation and AAA arbitration procedure.

III. DISPOSITION
We reverse the judgment of the Court of Appeal, with directions to instruct the trial court to vacate the award so that the arbitrators may redetermine whether the arbitration may proceed on a classwide basis.

Case Question
Why did the California Supreme Court refuse to adopt the U.S. Supreme Court's reasoning in the Hall Street case?

Court-Annexed Arbitration

Court–annexed arbitration includes both voluntary and mandatory procedures. Mandatory arbitrations,

however, for reasons founded in the right to jury trial contained in both federal and state constitutions, can only produce nonbinding decisions.

The type of cases that can be arbitrated is increasingly determined by statute, but in many jurisdictions this is determined pursuant to local court rules. Traditionally, arbitrations are most common in commercial, personal injury, and property damage cases in which the amount does not exceed a designated sum. That sum, called the jurisdictional amount, varies by jurisdiction.

The rules of arbitration often provide for limited discovery and modified rules of evidence. In brief, trial-like hearings lasting only a few hours, attorneys offer documentary evidence, present witness testimony, and cross-examine opposing witnesses. Arbitrators, who are often retired judges and local attorneys, are selected in various ways. In some courts, the clerk of court randomly assigns arbitrators. In other jurisdictions the parties participate in the selection process.

Arbitrators listen to the presentations, ask questions of the presenters, and determine the liability and damages issues. They generally do not make findings of fact or conclusions of law (as would judges in bench trials). Depending on local practice, the arbitrator may—or may not—attempt to mediate the dispute, critique the parties, or propose settlement terms.

An arbitrator's award becomes a final judgment unless the parties reject it within a prescribed period of time and demand a traditional jury trial (called a **trial de novo**). Unless the trial judgment exceeds the arbitration award, a party demanding a trial de novo often will be penalized and required to pay the arbitration costs.

The following case contains a discussion of the rights of the parties to a court-annexed arbitration proceeding to reject the arbitrator's decision and insist on a trial de novo.

Allstate Insurance Company v. A. William Mottolese
803 A.2d 311
Supreme Court of Connecticut
August 20, 2002

Sullivan, C. J.

This case is before us on a writ of error brought by the named plaintiff in error, Allstate Insurance Company (plaintiff) ... the insurer of the defendant in the underlying action, seeking reversal of an order of the trial court, *Mottolese. J.*, the defendant in error (trial court), imposing sanctions against the plaintiff pursuant to Practice Book §§ 14-13. The dispositive issue in this case is whether a party's proper exercise of its right to a trial de novo ... following a nonbinding arbitration proceeding may serve as the grounds for the imposition of sanctions under Practice Book §§ 14-13....

The plaintiff claims that the trial court's order of sanctions against it is void because it is not a party to the underlying action and never consented to the court's personal jurisdiction over it. Further, the plaintiff contends that: (1) the trial court violated its due process rights by failing to give notice that court would be considering whether to impose sanctions upon the plaintiff for its refusal to increase its settlement offer; and (2) the order of sanctions was an improper attempt by the trial court to coerce and intimidate the

plaintiff to settle the underlying defendant's case and, as such, violated the underlying defendant's constitutional right of access to the courts. We agree that, under the circumstances of this case, the plaintiff's conduct, which was grounded in its insured's exercise of his right to a trial de novo, cannot serve as the basis for an order of sanctions, and we reverse the order sanctioning the plaintiff.

The record discloses the following relevant facts and procedural history. In December, 1997, Robert Morgan filed the underlying action against David Distasio, the plaintiff's insured, to recover damages for injuries sustained in a December 5, 1995 automobile accident.... After a pretrial conference at which no settlement was reached, the trial court referred the case to nonbinding arbitration... the court annexed arbitration program. In December, 1999, the arbitrator issued a memorandum of decision in which he found... that Distasio negligently had rear-ended Morgan's vehicle, that Morgan had sustained minor physical injuries and property damage, and that judgment should be rendered in favor of Morgan in the amount of $2450. Distasio thereafter timely filed a claim for a trial de novo ... requesting that the trial court vacate the arbitration award and restore the case to the jury trial list.

On April 4, 2001, a pretrial conference was held before the trial court, Mottolese, J. The trial court continued the conference to April 11, 2001, with the instruction that Distasio produce his insurance claims representative on that date. On April 11, 2001, Distasio, Morgan and their respective counsel, along with the claims representative for the plaintiff, Stephen Coppa, appeared before the court in accordance with a written notice of pretrial conference. Coppa acknowledged that the plaintiff had made its initial settlement offer of $2050 to Morgan after evaluating the case, and that, at the time the offer was made, he had told Morgan that the offer was final. After discussion, the trial court found that the plaintiff's refusal "to pay anything more than $2050... is conduct which may fairly be characterized as unfair and in bad faith." The trial court further stated that "this court deems [the plaintiff's] refusal to participate in a resolution of this case in a reasonable manner as the functional equivalent of a failure to attend a pretrial," and that "it's unreasonable for any insurance carrier, any tortfeasor, to require judicial resources to be put in place and for thousands and thousands of taxpayers' money to be expended in order to save you, [the plaintiff], $400.00." The trial court held that the plaintiff's conduct was an "unwarranted imposition upon scarce judicial resources... a gross abuse of the civil justice system; and [that it made] a mockery of Connecticut's court annexed arbitration program." Accordingly, pursuant to Practice Book §§ 14-13 ... the trial court awarded Morgan attorney's fees of $250 for the April 4 pretrial conference and $250 for the April 11 hearing.

Distasio moved for articulation, requesting that the trial court clarify whether the ruling on attorney's fees was directed at the plaintiff, Distasio or Distasio's counsel. In response, the trial court appointed H. James Pickerstein, an attorney, "as a special master to conduct discovery on behalf of the court and to assist the court in preparing its articulation." The court ordered that the scope of discovery was to include, but not be limited to, the plaintiff's settlement policies and practices as they related to the underlying case, the extent to which Distasio's counsel had participated in the settlement process, and the policies and practices of the court annexed arbitration program and de novo trials....

...Distasio filed an appeal in the Appellate Court challenging the appointment of the special master.

In the meantime, the plaintiff moved for permission to amend the writ to address the sanction order....

The plaintiff claims that the order of sanctions was an improper attempt to coerce and intimidate it into settling the matter, thereby violating its constitutional right to a trial by jury. Specifically, the plaintiff argues that Distasio's assertion of his statutory right to a trial de novo following the court-ordered nonbinding arbitration proceeding preserved his right to a trial by jury guaranteed by the Connecticut constitution, and that a party's decision not to be bound by an arbitrator's decision regarding settlement cannot be the basis for the imposition of sanctions under Practice Book §§ 14-13.

Conversely, the trial court argues that, because the arbitrator's award of $2450 in damages was a mere $400 more than the plaintiff was originally willing to pay, the plaintiff took a defiant approach to the settlement process that was interpreted by the trial court as being disrespectful to it, harmful to the opposing party and implicitly contemptuous. The trial court further argues that it is within that court's inherent authority to sanction all who appear before it whose actions may be characterized as unfair and in bad faith.

We agree with the plaintiff and conclude that Distasio's exercise of his right to file for a trial de novo after the completion of arbitration proceedings cannot provide the basis for sanctions pursuant to Practice Book §§ 14-13. Accordingly, we conclude that the trial court abused its discretion when it sanctioned the plaintiff....

We begin with a review of the nonbinding arbitration program. Section 52-549u permits the judges of the Superior Court to refer certain civil actions to an arbitrator for nonbinding arbitration. The arbitrator's decision, however, is not binding on the parties and does not limit either party's access to a trial.... Pursuant to §§ 52-549z (d) and Practice Book §§ 23-66(c), a party that participated in nonbinding arbitration may appeal from the arbitrator's decision by requesting a trial de novo, in which case the arbitrator's decision becomes null and void.

The statutory right to a trial de novo has its underpinnings in the Connecticut constitution. "Article IV of the amendments to the constitution of Connecticut provides, inter alia, that the right of trial by jury shall remain inviolate. It is clear that the right to a jury trial may not be abolished as to causes triable to the jury prior to the constitution of 1818, and extant at the time of its adoption.... Nevertheless, such a right may be subjected to reasonable conditions and regulations.... The provision by the legislature for an alternative means of dispute resolution through the use of arbitrators to hear cases claimed for jury trial was but part of an effort to alleviate court congestion.... The right to a trial by jury in these cases is preserved inviolate by General Statutes §§ 52-549z and Practice Book §§ [23-66]. Each of these sections provides for a claim for a trial de novo within twenty days of the filing of the arbitrator's decision. Once a claim for trial de novo is filed in accordance with the rules, a decision of an arbitrator becomes null and void...."

Although both parties to the arbitration have an inviolable right to a trial de novo, that right is subject to reasonable conditions and regulations.... Attendance at a pretrial hearing is one such condition. Thus, Practice Book §§ 14-13 provides in relevant part that "when a party against whom a claim is made is insured, an insurance adjuster for such insurance company shall be available by telephone at the time of such pretrial session unless the judge... in his or her discretion, requires the attendance of the adjuster at the pretrial. If any person fails to attend or to be available by telephone pursuant to this rule, the judicial authority may make such order as the ends of justice require, which may include the entry of a nonsuit or default against the party failing to comply and an award to the complying party of reasonable attorney's fees...."

We further recognize, as the trial court claimed, that "our courts have long been recognized to have an inherent power, independent of any statute, to hold a defendant in contempt of court.... The purpose of the contempt power is to enable a court to preserve its dignity and to protect its proceedings...." The sanction created by Practice Book §§ 14-13 and relied upon by the trial court in this case, however, was intended to serve a different function, namely to ensure the insurer's presence to assist in the settlement of the case.

Public policy favors and encourages the voluntary settlement of civil suits.... *Krattenstein v. G. Fox & Co.* ... (1967) ("It is a proper exercise of the judicial office to suggest the expediency and practical value of adjusting differences and compromising and settling suits at law. The efficient administration of the courts is subserved by the ending of disputes without the delay and expense of a trial, and the philosophy or ideal of justice is served in the amicable solution of controversies. Our rules specifically provide for the procedure to be followed in pretrial sessions designed to encourage the settlement of cases.") We view with disfavor, however, all pressure tactics, whether employed directly or indirectly, to coerce settlement by litigants, their counsel

and their insurers. The failure to concur with what a trial court may consider an appropriate settlement should not result in the imposition of any retributive sanctions upon a litigant, his or her counsel or his or her insurer. As our sister state, New York, has recognized, "the function of courts is to provide litigants with an opportunity to air their differences at an impartial trial according to law.... [The court should not be able] to exert undue pressure on litigants to oblige them to settle their controversies without their day in court."...

We recognize that Practice Book §§ 14-13 grants the trial court the authority to sanction an insurance company for its failure to attend or be available by telephone at a pretrial session. In this case, however, the plaintiff was not unavailable or otherwise absent from the proceedings. Moreover, its actual presence, through its agent,... cannot be transformed into the functional equivalent of an absence, as the trial court ruled,... simply because the insurer decided not to abide by the arbitrator's assessment of damages and to insist, as its insured's agent, on the insured's right to a trial.

Although we sympathize with the trial court's concern that merely attending a pretrial conference while refusing, at the same time, to participate meaningfully in the negotiation or settlement process is not within the spirit of the settlement process, the plaintiff's refusal, on the basis of a validly exercised right to a trial de novo, to abide by the arbitrator's nonbinding decision that the plaintiff should pay $400 more than its original offer does not fall within the parameters of sanctionable behavior under §§ 14-13. To conclude otherwise would undermine the insured's constitutional right to a trial of the claims. Practice Book §§ 14-13 authorizes the court to use its discretion to require an insurer to be present or available because the insurer's presence might assist in the settlement of the case. Under these circumstances, however, the failure to negotiate is not equivalent to the failure to appear in court. Distasio indicated, by requesting a trial de novo, that he wanted his dispute to be resolved by trial. The plaintiff's rejection of the arbitration award evidences the same preference, in accordance with §§ 52-549z (d) and Practice Book §§ 23-66 (c). Accordingly, because Distasio properly exercised his statutory right to a trial de novo and the plaintiff properly complied with the trial court's request to be present at the pretrial hearing, we conclude that the trial court abused its discretion when it imposed sanctions....

The writ of error is granted and the matter is remanded with direction to vacate the order of sanctions....

Case Questions

1.   What was the arbitrator's decision in this case?
2.   Why did Judge Mottolese want to sanction the insurance company in this case for contempt of court?
3.   Why did the state supreme court order that the order imposing sanctions be vacated?

JOINTLY USED ADR METHODS

Mediation, minitrials, and arbitration are used with both court-annexed and voluntary ADR. The following discussion briefly examines each of these methods.

Mediation

Mediation is a technique in which one or more neutral parties, called mediators, help disputants to find ways to settle their dispute.[19] Parties often attempt to resolve their disagreements by mediation before participating in binding arbitration or litigation. Informal, unstructured, and inexpensive, mediation focuses on settlement, not on victory at trial. Mediators have no formal power to make a decision: Their role is that of facilitator, and different mediators use different styles and techniques to help parties come to an agreement. There is no formal hearing in a mediation. Instead, using joint meetings and private caucuses, mediators (1) help the parties identify their real goals, (2) narrow the issues, (3) look for alternatives and options as well as areas of common interest, and (4) prevent the parties from focusing on only one solution.

Court-annexed mediation often involves using trial attorneys as mediators. Mediators in some jurisdictions are paid and in others are volunteers. The theory is that neutral, experienced trial attorneys will be able to persuade litigants to look at their cases realistically and moderate their monetary demands. These are important hurdles that often stand in the way of a settlement.

Court-annexed mediation procedures vary. Lawyer-mediators are used in some jurisdictions and three-person panels in others. In complex cases, the court may appoint a person called a special master to serve as a mediator. Mediators vary in their approaches, but they tend to evaluate each case and predict what would happen if the case went to trial. They also indicate what they believe to be the settlement value of the case. These two determinations serve as a catalyst in starting settlement discussions between the parties.

In some jurisdictions the court refers most cases to mediation. In other jurisdictions, mediation occurs pursuant to stipulation or a suggestion from the court. Mediation is nonbinding, and parties retain their rights to attempt other ADR methods and to go to trial.

There is a big difference between the focus of a trial and that of a mediation. Trials exist to produce a winner and a loser. Mediation exists to help the parties settle their dispute in an amicable and expeditious manner. The objective is to find a solution to the dispute that is more acceptable to each party than going to trial. Mediation is more flexible than a trial and can produce a result that is more attuned to the underlying facts. Another advantage to mediation is that there are fewer enforcement problems. Because mediation produces an agreement between the parties, many problems that result when a judgment creditor attempts to enforce a judgment are avoided.

As states have begun to implement court-annexed mediation, questions have arisen regarding the procedures to be employed when using the ADR method. The following case from Tennessee is illustrative.

Team Design v. Anthony Gottlieb
104 S.W.3d 512
Court of Appeals of Tennessee
July 18, 2002

William C. Koch

This appeal raises important issues regarding the permissible range of court-annexed alternative dispute resolution procedures available under Tenn. S. Ct. R. 31....

Michael J. Bonagura and Kathie Baillie Bonagura perform country music in a group known as "Baillie and the Boys." When the transactions giving rise to this lawsuit arose, they were managed by Anthony Gottlieb, who did business as Morningstar Management. On January 22, 1996, the Bonaguras signed an "Exclusive Artist Agreement" with Intersound Entertainment, Inc. ("Intersound"), a Minnesota corporation whose principal place of business was in Roswell, Georgia. This agreement obligated Intersound to be responsible for the artwork and graphic design for the Baillie and the Boys albums.

With Intersound's knowledge and consent, the Bonaguras hired Harris Graphics, Inc. and Team Design to develop the artwork and graphics for an upcoming album called "Lovin' Every Minute." They believed that Intersound would be responsible for paying for this work. However, unbeknownst to the Bonaguras, Mr. Gottlieb had delivered a letter to Intersound agreeing that the Bonaguras would be responsible for paying for the artwork and graphic design for this album.

When Harris Graphics and Team Design were not paid for their work, they filed suit in the Davidson County General Sessions Court against Intersound and Mr. Gottlieb seeking payment and an injunction against the use of their work until they were paid. The general sessions court later permitted Harris Graphics and Team Design to add the Bonaguras as defendants. Following a hearing, the general sessions court granted Team Design a $4,086.75 judgment against Intersound and the Bonaguras. It also granted Harris Graphics a $2,200 judgment against Inter-sound and a $2,760 judgment against the Bonaguras.

All the parties perfected de novo appeals to the Circuit Court for Davidson County....

The trial was originally set for September 1998 but, at the trial court's initiative, was continued twice to February 16, 1999. Approximately one month before trial, the lawyer representing the Bonaguras requested his fellow lawyers to agree to preserve the Bonaguras' trial testimony by taking their depositions because Cactus Pete's in Jackpot, Nevada had declined to release them from a previous contractual commitment that conflicted with the rescheduled court date. The lawyers agreed, and the Bonaguras' depositions were scheduled for January 19, 1999. However, before the depositions could be taken, Mr. Gottlieb changed his mind and insisted that the Bonaguras be present at the trial. On January 21, 1999, the Bonaguras filed a motion seeking a continuance and an order enforcing the agreement permitting them to present their testimony by deposition. Team Design and Harris Graphics agreed to the use of the depositions at trial but objected to another continuance.

The trial court conducted a hearing on the Bonaguras' motion on February 5, 1999.... After the trial court agreed to the Bonaguras' request for a continuance, the lawyers and the trial court began discussing another trial date. During this discussion, the trial court offered the alternative of "binding mediation" and stated that it would be available to conduct the mediation on March 11, 1999. The record contains no indication that the trial court informed the parties of the specific procedures that would be used for this mediation or the legal consequences of their agreement to participate in the mediation.... The lawyers for all the parties accepted the court's offer, and on February 16, 1999, the trial court entered an order referring the case to "binding mediation before this Court" on March 11, 1999.

Thereafter, the trial court directed the parties to submit confidential statements outlining their respective positions. When the parties returned to court on March 14, 1999,... a clerk explained the procedure the trial court intended to follow which consisted of separate meetings with each of the parties and their lawyers in chambers. Over the next four hours, the trial court met separately with each of the parties and their lawyer. According to one of the lawyers, the trial court "made no attempt to seek a mutual agreement as to a resolution of the issues among the parties, but, after the final interview, announced that she would make a decision and enter an order reflecting her decision." On March 19, 1999, the trial court entered an order awarding Team Design a $4,086.75 judgment against Intersound and awarding Harris Graphics a $5,044.45 judgment against Intersound. The trial court also awarded Intersound a judgment against Mr. Gottlieb for one-third of the total amount of Team Design's and Harris Graphics' judgments to be paid from moneys he received from the "Lovin' Every Minute" album. Likewise, the trial court awarded Intersound a judgment against the Bonaguras for one-third of the of Team Design's and Harris Graphics' judgments to be paid from the royalties generated from their "Lovin' Every Minute" album.

On March 31, 1999, Intersound filed a … motion based on its lawyer's assertion that he had understood that the "binding mediation" offered by the trial court would be the sort of mediation authorized by Tenn. S. Ct. R. 31 in which he had previously participated in other cases. He also asserted that he never would have agreed to mediation had he understood the procedure that the court planned to follow. Team Design, Harris Graphics, and Mr. Gottlieb opposed the motion. They argued (1) that all the parties had agreed to "binding mediation," (2) that Intersound had not objected to the procedure prior to the entry of the March 19, 1999 order, and (3) that it would be unfair to permit Intersound to object to the proceeding at this point. The trial court entered an order on April 29, 1999, denying Intersound's post-trial motion. Intersound has perfected this appeal.

II. The Trial Court's Authority to Conduct Binding Mediation

We turn first to the question of a Tennessee trial court's authority to conduct "binding mediation." Intersound asserts that any sort of mediation conducted by a trial court in Tennessee must be consistent with Tenn. S. Ct. R. 31. In response, Team Design, Harris Graphics, and Mr. Gottlieb assert that the parties and the trial court may, by agreement, agree upon an alternative dispute procedure that does not meet all the requirements of Tenn. S. Ct. R. 31 and that the trial court and the parties did precisely that. We have determined that all court-annexed alternative dispute resolution procedures must be consistent with Tenn. S. Ct. R. 31 and that the "binding mediation" procedure used in this case was not consistent with Tenn. S. Ct. R. 31.

A.

Public policy strongly favors resolving disputes between private parties by agreement. Private parties may, of course, decide to submit their disputes to the courts for resolution; however, a broad range of other formal and informal alternatives are available before they resort to litigation. These procedures are, as a practical matter, limited only by the parties' imaginations because the parties themselves may agree on virtually any mutually satisfactory procedure that is not illegal or contrary to public policy. Thus, alternative dispute resolution procedures may range from formal procedures such as arbitration under Tennessee's

version of the Uniform Arbitration Act… to far less formal procedures such as "splitting the difference," flipping a coin, or, for that matter, arm wrestling. At least with regard to formal agreements to resolve disputes, the courts will require the parties to follow their agreed-upon dispute resolution procedure as long as they are competent and are dealing at arm's length. When the parties have agreed to be bound by the outcome of their agreed-upon procedure, the courts will require them to accept the result by declining to try their dispute de novo and by limiting the scope of judicial review of the outcome….

The parties' ability to manipulate the contours of the procedure to resolve their disputes narrows considerably once they submit their dispute to the courts for resolution. Judicial proceedings must be conducted in accordance with the ancient common-law rules, applicable constitutional principles, statutes, and court rules.

In Tennessee prior to 1995, traditional litigation was the only procedure available to parties who turned to the courts for resolution of their disputes. The trial courts lacked express authority to provide judicial oversight over pending cases other than the sort of oversight traditionally provided by American judges. They certainly did not have express authority to offer or require the use of alternative dispute resolution procedures. This changed on July 1, 1995, when amendments to Tenn. R. Civ. P. 16 greatly expanded the trial courts' case management authority. For the first time, Tenn. R. Civ. P. 16.03(7) specifically empowered trial courts to discuss "the possibility of settlement or the use of extrajudicial procedures, including alternative dispute resolution, to resolve the dispute." These amendments did not, however, empower trial courts to require the parties to engage in any sort of alternative dispute resolution procedure or to participate in any such procedure themselves. These changes were to come five months later.

On December 18, 1995, the Tennessee Supreme Court filed Tenn. S. Ct. R. 31 establishing procedures for court-annexed alternative dispute resolution in Tennessee's trial courts…. The original version of the rule represented an incremental approach to court-annexed alternative dispute resolution. The procedures… were intended to be alternatives, not replacements, to traditional litigation….

Under the original version of the rule … [ADR] procedures became available only after "all parties are before the court."… At that time, any or all of the parties could request authorization to engage in an alternative dispute resolution procedure…. The rule also permitted the trial court, even without the parties' request or consent but after consultation with the lawyers and the parties ... to require the parties to participate in a judicial settlement conference, a mediation, or a case evaluation.... In addition, with the consent of all parties, the trial court could refer the case for "non-binding arbitration, mini-trial, summary jury trial, or other appropriate alternative dispute resolution proceedings." ...

The original version of Tenn. S. Ct. R. 31, like the current version, specifically defined each of the alternative dispute resolution methods contemplated by the rule. Consistent with the Commission's recommendation that court-annexed alternative dispute proceedings should be non-binding ... each of these methods were intended to promote negotiated settlements between the parties themselves. They were not intended to require the parties to relinquish their decision-making right to any third party who would make the decision for them.

The fact that all proposed alternative dispute resolution methods are non-binding is an essential attribute of the court-annexed procedures.... The rule specifically defines mediation as "an informal process in which a neutral person... conducts discussions among the disputing parties designed to enable them to reach a mutually acceptable agreement among themselves on all or any part of the issues in dispute." ...The arbitration permitted by the rule must be "non-binding."... Likewise, a "case evaluation" is advisory only; a "mini-trial" envisions that "the parties or their representatives [will] seek a negotiated settlement of the dispute"... and a "summary jury trial" envisions only an "advisory verdict" followed by a "negotiated settlement."... In 1996, the Tennessee Supreme Court reaffirmed that all court-annexed alternative dispute resolution proceedings permitted by Tenn. S. Ct. R. 31 were premised on the principle of "self-determination."...

Another essential attribute of alternative dispute resolution is the neutrality and impartially of the mediators, arbitrators, or other neutral persons conducting the process.... The importance of neutrality is reflected in the fact that Tenn. S. Ct. R. 31 refers to persons conducting court-annexed alternative dispute resolution proceedings as "dispute resolution neutrals."... It is also reflected in the Standards of Professional Conduct for Rule 31 Mediators adopted by the Tennessee Supreme Court... which state that "integrity, impartiality, and professional competence are essential qualifications of any mediator."...

A third essential attribute of the court-annexed procedures... is confidentiality. All parties in a mediation proceeding trust that the proceeding will be confidential because these proceedings permit them to "bare their soul" to the mediator and provide them

the opportunity to vent which, in some instances, is all that stands in the way of a negotiated settlement.... Accordingly, a vast majority of the proponents of alternative dispute resolution view confidentiality of the proceedings as a central issue....

The Tennessee Supreme Court recognized the importance of confidentiality when it first authorized court-annexed alternative dispute resolution. Tenn. S. Ct. R. 31,... required that a "mediator, settlement judge, or other dispute resolution neutral shall preserve and maintain the confidentiality of all alternative dispute resolution proceedings except where required by law to disclose the information."...

The principles of self-determination, neutrality, and confidentiality influenced the Tennessee Supreme Court's view of the role trial judges should properly play in court–annexed alternative dispute resolution proceedings. While the court gave trial courts the authority to require litigants, with or without their consent, to participate in a case evaluation, mediation, or judicial settlement conference ... the court carefully limited the trial court's role in these proceedings. First, the court permitted trial judges to participate only in judicial settlement conferences. All other proceedings being presided over by a "neutral person" or a "neutral panel."... Secondly, with regard to judicial settlement conferences, the court stated clearly that judges presiding over a pending case could not also conduct the judicial settlement conference. The definition of "judicial settlement conference" makes it clear that these proceedings must be "conducted by a judicial officer other than the judge before whom the case will be tried."...

The policy reasons for not permitting the trial judge who could eventually try the case to preside over the mediation or other alternative dispute resolution procedure ... are evident and compelling. A judge who presides over a judicial settlement conference is not acting as a judge but as a neutral.... The success of the settlement "depends largely on the willingness of the parties to freely disclose their intentions, desires, and the strengths and weaknesses of their case" with the neutral.... Thus, a judge conducting a settlement conference becomes a confidant of the parties ... with whom the parties share information that would normally be shared only with their lawyers.

Generally, knowledge gained in a prior judicial proceeding is not a sufficient ground to require the recusal or disqualification of a trial judge in a later judicial proceeding.... However, much of the information imparted during a mediation is not the sort of information that would normally be disclosed to the other parties or the court. Accordingly, should the judge who conducts the judicial settlement conference later be called upon to decide the issues of liability or damages, it is impossible to avoid questions as to whether he or she can disregard the matters disclosed during the conference or put aside any opinions or judgments already formed based on this information....

The Tennessee Supreme Court recognized these confidentiality and predisposition concerns in its September 1996 revisions to Tenn. S. Ct. R. 31. The court added a provision to the rule stating:

> A person serving as a Rule 31 dispute resolution neutral in an alternative dispute resolution proceeding shall not participate as attorney, advisor, judge, guardian ad litem, master or in any other judicial or quasi-judicial capacity in the matter in which the alternative dispute resolution proceeding was conducted....

B.

The "binding mediation" proceeding at issue in this case did not comply with... Tenn. S. Ct. R. 31 as it stood in early 1999 in four fundamental particulars. First, [it]... did not authorize "binding mediation"... as a method for court-annexed alternative dispute resolution.... Second, the procedure actually used by the trial court bore no resemblance to a judicial settlement conference or mediation because the parties' decision-making rights were supplanted by the trial court, and there was no apparent effort to assist the parties in reaching their own voluntary settlement of their differences.... Third, the proceeding was conducted by the trial judge to whom the case had been assigned notwithstanding the clear requirement... that it be "conducted by a judicial officer other than the judge before whom the case will be tried." Fourth, the judge who conducted the alternative dispute resolution proceeding entered a final order disposing of the parties' claims even though it did not have the authority to do so....

These departures are not just minor deviations from Tenn. S. Ct. R. 31. Each of them is inconsistent with one or more of the fundamental principles that impelled the Tennessee Supreme Court to authorize court-annexed alternative dispute resolution in the first place. They undermined the principles carefully designed to preserve the parties' right of self-determination. They also raised the specter of possible repercussions for the parties who objected to referring the case to alternative dispute resolution or who objected to its outcome. Accordingly, we have concluded that these deviations are substantive and material and that they affected the outcome of this proceeding.

A judgment is considered void if the record demonstrates that the court entering it lacked jurisdiction over either the subject matter or the person, or did not have the authority to make the challenged judgment.... A void judgment lacks validity anywhere and is subject to attack from any angle....

A trial court cannot exercise authority it has not been granted expressly or by necessary implication.... At the time of this proceeding, Tenn. S. Ct. R. 31 did not permit the judge who conducted the judicial settlement conference to enter an order disposing of the case. Accordingly, the order disposing of the parties' claims entered on March 19, 1999, by the judge who conducted the mediation was void,... and the trial court erred when it declined to grant Intersound's... motion....

We vacate the March 19, 1999 and April 29, 1999 orders and remand the case to the trial court for further proceedings consistent with this opinion. We tax the costs to Team Design; Harris Graphics, Inc.; Anthony Gottlieb; and Intersound Entertainment, Inc. and its surety for which execution, if necessary, may issue.

Case Questions

1. What was the mediator's decision in this case?
2. Why did the state court of appeals vacate the trial court's orders?

MINITRIALS

The **minitrial,** used primarily to resolve business disputes, actually isn't a trial at all. It is a process in which each party makes an abbreviated presentation to a panel, generally consisting of a senior manager or decision maker from each side and a judge (in the case of a court–ordered minitrial) or jointly selected neutral (in the case of a voluntary minitrial). The theory behind this process is that the presenters for each side will educate the managers about the dispute.[20] The strength of this process is that the business managers, rather than lawyers, judges, and juries, make the decisions. The managers can often design creative solutions that make it possible to resolve the dispute. They are not restricted to the types of relief that courts can award after a trial. If the managers fail to agree, minitrial rules often require a judge or neutral to forecast what he or she believes would happen if the case were to go to trial and indicate what he or she believes to be a reasonable settlement proposal. The parties in a court-annexed minitrial can reject the judge's proposal but may incur a penalty. A party who insists on a trial but fails to recover a judgment more favorable than the judge's proposal may be assessed a substantial fine for each day that it takes to try the case.[21] The parties in a voluntary minitrial can reject the neutral's proposal without a penalty.

Some courts schedule minitrials only after the parties agree to participate. Other courts require parties to take part. Minitrials are primarily used in complex, time-consuming cases where the substantial savings of money and time realized by limiting discovery and presentations are strong incentives. Minitrials are most likely to succeed when both parties are serious about resolving the underlying issues with a minimum of acrimony.

The parties in a minitrial have control over the procedures and can disregard the formal rules of civil procedure and evidence that apply in litigation. For example, they can set their own rules regarding the nature and scope of discovery and determine whether position papers will be exchanged prior to the hearing. They can also determine the procedures to be used at the hearing. For example, they can decide whether written summaries will be submitted in lieu of witness testimony, how many hours each side will have to present its case, how long opening statements will be, and whether cross-examination will be allowed.

The typical procedures for a minitrial include an abbreviated presentation of each side's case to a panel of decision makers selected by the parties and the neutral. The decision makers then meet privately after the presentations have concluded and work to negotiate a solution to the dispute.

SUMMARY JURY TRIALS

An Ohio federal district court judge developed the **summary jury trial** (SJT) process in 1980 as a court-annexed, mandatory procedure. It operates pursuant to local court rules and is used in cases that have proved difficult to settle—primarily damage cases. The key elements in the typical SJT are an advisory jury, an abbreviated, two-hour hearing, and a nonbinding verdict. The SJT procedure can be helpful when parties agree on the defendant's liability but disagree about the damages. In such cases, the plaintiff's attorney doesn't want to settle for less than what he or she estimates a jury will award. Similarly, the defendant's lawyer will not want to settle for more than what a jury would probably require.

SJT procedures are similar to those at trial.[22] A judge presides, and each side has one or two hours to present its case. Case presentations include oral summaries of the evidence and the reading of witness depositions. Each side also has an opportunity to argue the case to the jury, which consists of five or six jurors. The judge gives the jury abbreviated oral instructions. The SJT juries are composed of persons summoned to court but not chosen to sit on a regular trial jury that day.

After the judge's instructions, the SJT jurors retire and deliberate on both liability and damages. The jurors often are asked to discuss the case with the attorneys and clients after they return with a nonbinding verdict. The process works best when the client or some person with settlement authority attends the SJT and participates in this settlement conference.

The SJT process allows the attorneys to have a practice trial and the opportunity to see how a group of regular jurors reacts to each side's presentation. It also gives the parties "a day in court," which helps to satisfy some litigants' emotional needs. The fact that neutral jurors establish a damage figure is an additional plus. The SJT has had an impact on insurance companies, as well as the attorneys and parties. Insurance companies are often more willing to settle after they have seen an SJT jury's verdict because they then have a dollar figure that can serve as a basis for settlement negotiations.

If the parties are unable to settle the dispute, the case remains on the calendar for a regular trial.

One criticism of summary jury trials is that SJT presentations compress cases to such an extent that the jurors can't absorb the evidence and argument. In response, a few judges now allow one-week summary "trials." Others permit the use of live witness testimony.

Introduction to *Griffin v. Yonkers*

The plaintiff and defendant in the following case were involved in a motor vehicle collision. The lawyers for both parties stipulated to having the matter decided by a summary jury trial. The plaintiff won the summary jury trial and the defendant filed a motion asking to delay the entry of judgment. The defendant explained that he wanted the court to schedule a hearing and determine whether any third party (such as an insurance company) had a legal obligation to contribute along with the defendant to paying for the plaintiff's damages. The plaintiff urged the court to enter judgment immediately and opposed the plaintiff's motion, claiming that the motion was forbidden by the judicial district's summary jury trial rules.

Derik Griffin v. Richard A. Yonkers
891 N.Y.S.2d 896
Supreme Court, Bronx County.
December 21, 2009.

Lucindo Suarez, J.
Review of defendant Richard A. Yonkers's motion pursuant to CPLR 4545 (c) for a collateral source setoff with respect to the jury verdict concerning loss of earnings and medical expenses; and same defendant's [motion] ... to stay entry of the judgment pursuant to CPLR 2201 until defendant's motion pursuant to CPLR 4545 (c) for a collateral source hearing is determined.

The issue in these motions to stay enforcement of the judgment until a collateral source hearing is held is whether the court is precluded from conducting such a hearing where the parties have agreed to waive any motions for directed verdicts or to set aside the verdict pursuant to the summary jury trial rules and procedures of the Twelfth Judicial District. This court holds it is not so prevented, as such a motion is not addressed to the validity or sufficiency of the substantive evidence and proof adduced at trial, but to the quantum of compensation pursuant to the verdict; and upon consideration denies the application as defendant has not demonstrated that the relevant portion of the jury's verdict will, with reasonable certainty, be replaced or indemnified from any collateral source.

The underlying action arises from an automobile accident where plaintiff claims various injuries. The attorneys stipulated to a summary jury trial.

A summary jury trial is a voluntary, innovative and streamlined form of alternative dispute resolution that combines the flexibility and cost-effectiveness of arbitration with the structure of a conventional trial. The primary mission of New York's Summary Jury Trial Program is to give cost-conscious litigants a reliable, trial-tested option guaranteed to resolve civil cases fairly, quickly and economically by one-day jury trials. Jury selection is abbreviated, each litigant may offer documentary, demonstrative, and limited testimonial evidence without calling expert witnesses, and the attorneys are permitted to deliver condensed opening and closing statements. The parties may stipulate to a summary jury trial providing for: the extent, dates and period for discovery; the mode and method of the trial; a waiver of the right of appeal and motions directed to the verdict; and high/low verdict parameters. In the absence of agreement of counsel and approval by the trial court, the process provided in the rules of the jurisdiction apply....

The summary jury trial achieves its economy of time by limiting the presentation by each side to one hour, absent a court rule or an agreement to the contrary. During the one hour, each side may call one or two witnesses, who are subject to cross-examination. Other testimony may be presented through deposition transcripts or sworn affidavits. The rules of evidence are relaxed but not abrogated. The key to the saving of time and especially expense is the submission of medical evidence through the affidavits or reports of providers, rather than through live testimony. Police, hospital, and accident reports, as well as other documentary or demonstrative evidence are allowed to be introduced without certification or authentication, subject to all items having been exchanged, and objections to the introduction of evidence and rulings thereto having been made before trial at an evidentiary hearing.

The overarching theme to be borne in mind is that the parties themselves, with the permission of the trial judge, may fashion their own parameters for their summary jury trial, by using, augmenting and/or disregarding the rules existing in the jurisdiction, as well as by creating rules of their choosing. The parties are allowed to shape a format that will allow them to fully explore all the issues or to focus on a particular issue without spending the time and money to bring in myriad witnesses, doctors and other experts.

The parties here did not stipulate to abide by any parameters other than the rules of the Twelfth Judicial District... with respect to motion practice, which explicitly preclude motions for a directed verdict and motions to set aside the verdict, both of which are addressed to the sufficiency of the substantive evidence and proof at trial.... For example, a trial court may set aside a verdict "only if there was "no valid line of reasoning and permissible inferences which could possibly lead rational men to the conclusion reached by the jury on the basis of the evidence presented."....

A motion pursuant to CPLR 4545 (c), however, addresses the sufficiency and propriety of plaintiff's recovery of damages.... It does not question the validity or weight of the substantive evidence adduced at trial. "Under CPLR 4545 (c), if the court finds that any portion of a personal injury award for economic loss "was or will, with reasonabl[e] certainty, be replaced or indemnified from any collateral source, it shall reduce the amount of the award by such finding."" (Brewster v Prince Apts.... [2000].)

The only New York cases answering this question are found in the Fourth Department, emanating from the Eighth Judicial District, the jurisdiction that pioneered the use of the summary jury trial in New York State. Although that jurisdiction's summary jury trial rules are essentially similar to those followed in the Bronx, the cases establish that posttrial motion practice is not per se disallowed in the summary jury trial setting. For example, in *Conroe v Barmore-Sellstrom, Inc.* ... [4th Dept 2004]), the court allowed motion practice to challenge the admission into evidence of documents that had not been exchanged pursuant to the summary jury trial rules. In addition, where neither the parties' stipulation to submit the action to summary jury trial nor the administrative judicial materials in the jurisdiction addressed the particular type of motion made in the summary jury trial setting, and while dismissing the appeal, the court stated that it would not have been error to rule on the motion....

Accordingly, as collateral source motions are not specifically excluded by the rules under which the parties stipulated to submit the action to a summary jury trial, defendant's motion may be entertained. Furthermore, "[t]o assure that plaintiffs are fully compensated—but not overcompensated—a "direct correspondence between the item of loss and the type of collateral reimbursement must exist before the required statutory offset may be made.'" (*Fisher v Qualico Contr. Corp.*, ... [2002]..., Ordinarily, a hearing would be required to determine the amount of the collateral source offset, if any, from the jury's verdict.

Here, however, movant, pursuant to the court's directive, provided the insurance carrier's denial of benefits of proposed collateral source. As benefits were already denied, and the time to appeal the denial has long since passed, movant has not demonstrated that the relevant portion of the jury's verdict "will, with reasonable certainty, be replaced or indemnified ... from any collateral source."... Therefore, defendant's motion for a stay of enforcement of the judgment is denied as moot.

Accordingly, it is ordered that the motion...of defendant Richard A. Yonkers for a collateral source hearing and reduction of the verdict by collateral source payment is denied; and it is further ordered, that the motion ... of defendant Richard A. Yonkers for a stay of enforcement of the judgment is denied as moot.

Case Question

These parties had three choices. They could have chosen a bench trial, a regular jury trial, or a summary jury trial. Why do you think that the lawyers for both parties stipulated that their dispute be resolved via a summary jury trial as opposed to a regular jury trial?

Private Trials

Parties that have failed to resolve their dispute with mediation and/or arbitration may choose to litigate in a private court system. Provided by commercial firms that employ retired federal, state, and local judges, such trials are held in hotels, law schools, and even office buildings in which courtrooms that replicate public courtrooms have been constructed. These firms exist to provide timely, confidential, and affordable trials. In thirteen states, the parties can employ jurors selected from the public jury rolls to hear the case. The **private trial system** allows the parties to select a judge who has experience appropriate to the case. It also allows the parties to conduct their trial in private, an important advantage in many contract, employment rights, professional liability, and divorce actions. The parties to a private trial often contract to use simplified evidentiary and procedural rules and to cooperate in discovery, saving time and money for both parties. The parties also decide whether the decision of the private judge or jury will be final or appealable. Some private court systems even provide for private appeals.

Critics of the private court system maintain that it allows the wealthy to avoid the delays and conditions that others must endure in the public court system. They also express concern that the higher compensation that is paid to private judges could result in a two-tier system of justice. The best judges would handle the litigation of the wealthy in the private sector, while others would litigate before less able judges in underfunded, overworked public-sector courts.

Does ADR Really Work?

The question as to the extent to which ADR programs have produced the benefits that were advertised remains unresolved. In 1996, the Rand Corporation evaluated ten ADR pilot programs created pursuant to the Civil Justice Reform Act. Rand found no statistical evidence that the districts with pilot programs had been more successful than ten comparison districts in reducing cost or delay.[23]

A 1997 study conducted by the Federal Judicial Center, however, was more favorable and encouraged continued federal participation.[24] Students interested in reading an excellent article summarizing the effectiveness of ADR in federal district courts and critiquing its use by federal administrative agencies should read a 1997 article in the *Duke Law Journal* written by Judge Patricia M. Wald of the U.S. Court of Appeals for the District of Columbia. This brief and very informative article can be found on the Internet.[25]

In 2005, the National Arbitration Forum and the American Bar Association surveyed members of two of the ABA's thirty practice-oriented sections, the Tort Trial and Insurance Practice Section (TIPS) and the General Practice Solo and Small Firm Section (GPSolo), to ask their views about and experience with ADR techniques.

When asked about the extent to which they had used ADR techniques to resolve cases in 2004, slightly over 53 percent of the TIPs respondents indicated that they had done so in one to five cases, but only 4.5 percent reported using ADR methods in at least twenty-six cases (see Figure 14.2).

When TIPS respondents were asked if "clients' interests are sometimes served by offering ADR solutions," only 10.6 percent answered in the negative. And when asked about ADR's long-term prospects, almost 60 percent of TIPS respondents believed it would be utilized more frequently in the future (see Figure 14.3).

When GPSolo respondents were asked the same questions as the TIPS respondents, 65.4 percent indicated that they had used ADR techniques to resolve between one and five cases in 2004, but only 1.7 percent reported using ADR methods in at least twenty-six cases. Only 13.8 percent of GPSolo respondents answered that offering ADR solutions would not benefit their client's interest. And when asked about ADR's long-term prospects, over 66 percent of GPSolo respondents reported they expected it would be utilized more frequently in future years.

It is important to note that the lawyers participating in these two surveys were chosen because of their membership in the targeted ABA sections.

In your role as client counsel, how many cases did you resolve through ADR last year (mediation, arbitration, and other forms of ADR)?

Response	Percent
5 or fewer	53.2
6–25	39.0
26–50	4.5
Over 50	3.4
Total	100.0

F I G U R E 14.2 Use of ADR in 2004 by Tort Trial and Insurance Practice Section Members of ABA

Source: National Arbitration Forum in collaboration with Tort Trial and Insurance Practice Section of the American Bar Association, "ADR Use and Preference Survey," Copyright 2006 by the American Arbitration Forum.

Overall View of ADR among TIPS Respondents

Response	Percent
Clients' interests are sometimes best served by offering ADR solutions	89.4
My practice will necessarily include offering ADR solutions to clients in the future	60.5
Offering clients ADR is an ethical obligation as a practitioner	59.8
ADR use will increase in the future	59.8
Offering clients ADR solutions has improved my law practice financially	21.4
Clients frequently inquire about ADR solutions	20.7

F I G U R E 14.3 Overall View of ADR by Tort Trial and Insurance Practice Section Member of ABA

Source: National Arbitration Forum in collaboration with Tort Trial and Insurance Practice Section of the American Bar Association, "ADR Use and Preference Survey," Copyright 2006 by the American Arbitration Forum.

Their responses may or may not reflect the views of ABA member lawyers not surveyed. It is also important to note that mediation and arbitration were the only ADR methods explicitly included in either survey's questions. It can be said that most respondents, while including ADR methods in their practices and professing confidence that ADR methods would play a more prominent role in the practice of law in the future, reported having used them infrequently to resolve cases in 2004.

INTERNET TIP

The contents of both surveys can be found on the Internet as follows:

- ADR Preference and Usage Survey (in collaboration with Tort Trial and Insurance Practice Section [TIPS] of the American Bar Association) (National Arbitration Forum, 2006; data collected by Surveys and Ballots, Inc.): http://www.adrforum.com/users/naf/resources/2006TIPSSurvey.pdf

- ADR Preference and Usage Report (in collaboration with General Practice Solo and Small Firm Section [GPSolo] of the American Bar Association) (National Arbitration Forum, 2006; data collected by Surveys and Ballots, Inc.): http://www.adrforum.com/users/naf/resources/GPSoloADRPreferenceAndUsageReport.pdf

CHAPTER SUMMARY

The chapter began with an explanation of some of the disadvantages of resolving disputes by public court trial. These include the public nature of the process, the length of time it often takes for a case to get to trial, the cost of preparing for a trial that will most likely never occur, and the potential dissatisfaction with the consequences of litigation's "winner-take-all" approach. Next, the chapter covered the differences between voluntary participation in ADR and participation that is mandated by law (court-annexed ADR). The majority of the chapter focused on explaining various ADR methods such as settlement conferences, arbitration, mediation, minitrials, and summary jury trials. The chapter concluded with a brief discussion of how well ADR works.

CHAPTER QUESTIONS

1. Frances J. Vukasin was employed by D. A. Davidson & Co. in August 1979. The company implemented an annual performance review in 1985, which rated her performance in each of six areas, gave her an overall rating, and indicated a recommended salary increase. Included in Vukasin's 1986 and 1987 performance reviews, directly above the employee's signature line, was a provision that read, "Employment with D. A. Davidson & Co. is subject to arbitration." The review also provided that she or her employer could terminate employment at any time for any reason. There was also a statement that "I [the employee] … acknowledge and agree that any controversy between myself and the Company arising out of my employment or the termination of my employment with the Company for any reasons whatsoever shall be determined by arbitration." On December 12, 1988, Vukasin filed a complaint in a state court against the company. She alleged in the complaint that another employee had assaulted and battered her at the company's offices on April 30, 1988. She claimed damages for mental and emotional distress, pain and suffering, loss of wages, and various medical and therapy expenses. Is the allegation of assault and battery outside the scope of the arbitration clause and appropriate for litigation?

   Vukasin v. D. A. Davidson & Co., 785 P.2d 713 (Mont. 1990)

2. James Clawson contracted with Habitat, Inc., to build a retaining wall and driveway at his home. The contract contained an arbitration clause. A dispute arose regarding the construction, and the matter was submitted to binding arbitration. The parties continued negotiation throughout the arbitration process. When it appeared that they were close to a settlement, they entered into a new agreement. The new

agreement provided that the parties would retract the arbitration if they could negotiate a settlement by 3:00 P.M. on October 21, 1988. Clawson and Habitat disagreed about whether an agreement had been reached by that date. The arbitrator's decision was released on November 1, 1988. Both parties filed motions in the circuit court, Habitat to confirm the award, and Clawson to vacate the award. Should the circuit court confirm the award?

Clawson v. Habitat, Inc., 783 P.2d 1230 (Hawai'i 1989)

3. The Medford (Oregon) Firefighters Association and the City of Medford reached a stalemate while negotiating a collective bargaining agreement. They unsuccessfully tried to mediate their dispute. Pursuant to state law, the Oregon Employment Relations Board appointed an arbitrator, who held a hearing, prepared an agreement, and submitted it to the parties. The firefighters petitioned the circuit court for a writ of *mandamus* when the city refused to sign the agreement. The city claimed that the state law providing for binding arbitration was unconstitutional. Can the state legislature constitutionally delegate legislative power to a private person as an arbitrator?

Medford Firefighters Association v. City of Medford, 595 P.2d 1268 (1979)

4. Roger Lockhart, a teenager, lost the sight in one of his eyes. He alleged that this was due to the negligence of Dr. Ramon Patel. A summary jury trial was conducted, and the advisory jury awarded the plaintiff $200,000. The court held several formal and informal settlement conferences following the SJT. The court directed that the defense attorney attend a settlement conference on November 3, 1986 and that he bring with him a representative of Dr. Patel's liability insurance carrier, who possessed authority to settle the case. The defense attorney appeared on November 3, but the insurance representative with settlement authority did not. The insurance carrier sent an adjuster instead. The court responded by (1) striking the defendant's pleadings, (2) declaring the

defendant in default, (3) setting the trial for the following day, limited to the question of damages, and (4) set a hearing to show cause why the insurance carrier should not be punished for criminal contempt of the court. Does the court have the right to strike the defendant's pleadings because of the insurance carrier's failure to send a representative to attend the settlement conference?

Lockhart v. Patel, 115 F.R.D. 44 (E.D. Ky. 1987)

5. Elizabeth Garfield brought suit against her former employer, Thomas McKinnon Securities, Inc., claiming that McKinnon had discharged her on account of her age in violation of the Age Discrimination in Employment Act. McKinnon moved to dismiss the complaint and compel arbitration because Garfield had agreed to arbitrate any controversy arising out of her employment. Garfield responded that she and all registered brokers are required to execute arbitration agreements as a condition of employment. She maintained that Congress did not intend to permit persons to waive their statutory right to sue for ADEA violations in federal court via the execution of an arbitration agreement. Should the court dismiss the complaint and compel arbitration?

Garfield v. Thomas McKinnon Securities, Inc., 731 F.Supp. 841 (N.D. Ill. 1988)

6. Irmis Achong was hired as a nursing attendant by the Cabrini Medical Center. He became a member of Local 1199 of the Drug, Hospital and Health Care Employees Union, which was party to a collective bargaining agreement. On November 4, 1986, a disoriented and distraught patient kicked Achong as he walked by her stretcher. Cabrini claimed that Achong, who had a perfect performance record at the time, responded by cursing the patient and striking her on the leg. Cabrini discharged Achong for abusing the patient. The collective bargaining agreement provided for binding arbitration whenever the union and Cabrini disagreed upon whether an employee was discharged for just cause. Achong's dismissal was

submitted to arbitration. The arbitrator made careful and detailed findings and conclusions. He ruled that just cause did not exist for Achong's discharge, because Cabrini failed to establish how hard Achong touched the patient. He believed that summary discharge was too harsh a penalty under the circumstances and based on the limited evidence. He ruled that Achong should be reinstated without back pay (thereby imposing a forfeiture of nine months' pay) and given a warning against future conduct. Cabrini brought an action in federal court to set aside the award, and the union brought an action in state court to confirm. Cabrini removed the state action to federal court, where the two actions were consolidated. Cabrini argued that the award violated public policy based on a statutory provision that patients "shall be free from mental and physical abuse." Should the award be confirmed?

Cabrini Medical Center v. Local 1199 Drug, Hospital and Health Care Employees Union, 731 F.Supp. 612 (S.D.N.Y. 1990)

NOTES

1. R. Samborn, "In Courts: Caseloads Still Rise," *National Law Journal* (July 5, 1993).

2. Judicial Business 2009. Administrative Office of U.S. Courts. Statistical Table for the Federal Judiciary, Table S-7, September 30, 2009.

3. Judicial Business 2009. Administrative Office of the U.S. Courts. Statistical Table for the Federal Judiciary, Tables C-4 and C-4A, September 30, 2009.

4. As early as 1991, for example, Colorado amended its Code of Professional Responsibility and required lawyers to advise their clients of this option.

5. Massachusetts Supreme Judicial Court Rule 1:18, May 1, 1998.

6. W. H. Schroeder Jr., "Private ADR May Offer Increased Confidentiality," *National Law Journal* C14–16 (July 25, 1995).

7. J. H. Kennedy, "Merger Aimed at Settling Out of Court," *Boston Globe*, May 16, 1994, pp. 18–19.

8. D. M. Provine, *Settlement Strategies for Federal District Judges* (Federal Judicial Center, 1986).

9. H. N. Mazadoorian, "Widespread Disgust With Civil Justice Is Boon to ADR," *Corporate Legal Times* 17 (April 1994).

10. Ibid.

11. J. W. Keltner, *The Management of Struggle* (Cresskill, NJ: Hampton Press, 1994), p. 152.

12. J. W. Cooley, "Arbitration vs. Mediation— Explaining the Differences," *Judicature* 69, 264 (1986).

13. Federal Arbitration Act, 9 U.S.C. Sec. 1.

14. See *Eastern Associated Coal Corp v. United Mine Workers*, 531 U.S. 57 (2000) and *Circuit City Stores, Inc. v. Adams*, 99–1379 (2001).

15. Some states have, in the past, refused to enforce arbitration agreements entered into before the existence of any dispute.

16. *Shearson Lehman Hutton v. McMahon*, 482 U.S. 220 (1987).

17. R. C. Reuben, "Decision Gives Banking ADR a Boost," *American Bar Association Journal* 32 (December 1994), pp. 32–33.

18. Mazadoorian, p. 17.

19. Cooley, p. 266.

20. J. Davis and L. Omlie, "Mini-trials: The Courtroom in the Boardroom," *Willamette Law Review* 21, 531 (1985).

21. The extent to which judges can order parties to participate in a minitrial remains a hotly contested issue.

22. "Mandatory and Summary Jury Trial Guidelines for Ensuring Fair and Effective Process," *Harvard Law Review* 103, 1086 (1993).

23. J. S. Kakalik, *Implementation of the Civil Justice Reform Act in Pilot and Comparison Districts,* Rand Institute for Civil Justice (1996).

24. Federal Judicial Center, *Report to the Judicial Conference Committee on Court Administration and Case Management: A Study of the Five Demonstration Programs Established Under the Civil Justice Reform Act of 1990* (1997).

25. P. M. Wald, "ADR and the Courts: An Update," 46 *Duke Law Journal* 1445 (1997), www.law.duke .edu/journals/dlj/articles/ dlj46p1445.

Appendix

✳

The Constitution of the United States

We the people of the United States, in order to form a more perfect union, establish justice, insure domestic tranquility, provide for the common defense, promote the general welfare, and secure the blessings of liberty to ourselves and our posterity, do ordain and establish this Constitution for the United States of America.

ARTICLE I

Section 1

All legislative powers herein granted shall be vested in a Congress of the United States, which shall consist of a Senate and House of Representatives.

Section 2

1. The House of Representatives shall be composed of members chosen every second year by the people of the several States, and the electors in each State shall have the qualifications requisite for electors of the most numerous branch of the State Legislature.

2. No person shall be a representative who shall not have attained to the age of twenty-five years, and been seven years a citizen of the United States, and who shall not, when elected, be an inhabitant of that State in which he shall be chosen.

3. Representatives and direct taxes[1] shall be apportioned among the several States which may be included within this Union, according to their respective numbers, which shall be determined by adding to the whole number of free persons, including those bound to service for a term of years, and excluding Indians not taxed, three fifths of all other persons.[2] The actual enumeration shall be made within three years after the first meeting of the Congress of the United States, and within every subsequent term of ten years, in such manner as they shall by law direct. The number of representatives shall not exceed one for every thirty thousand, but each State shall have at least one representative; and until such enumeration shall be made, the State of New Hampshire shall be entitled to choose three, Massachusetts eight, Rhode Island and Providence Plantations one, Connecticut five, New York six, New Jersey four, Pennsylvania eight, Delaware one, Maryland six, Virginia ten, North Carolina five, South Carolina five, and Georgia three.

4. When vacancies happen in the representation from any State, the executive authority thereof shall issue writs of election to fill such vacancies.

5. The House of Representatives shall choose their speaker and other officers; and shall have the sole power of impeachment.

Section 3

1. The Senate of the United States shall be composed of two senators from each State, chosen by the legislature thereof,[3] for six years; and each senator shall have one vote.

2. Immediately after they shall be assembled in consequence of the first election, they shall be divided as equally as may be into three classes. The seats of the senators of the first class shall be vacated at the expiration of the second year, of the second class at the expiration of the fourth year and of the third class at the expiration of the sixth year, so that one third may be chosen every second year; and if vacancies happen by resignation, or otherwise, during the recess of the legislature of any State, the executive thereof may make temporary appointments until the next meeting of the legislature, which shall then fill such vacancies.[4]

3. No person shall be a senator who shall not have attained to the age of thirty years, and been nine years a citizen of the United States, and who shall not, when elected, be an inhabitant of that State for which he shall be chosen.

4. The Vice President of the United States shall be President of the Senate, but shall have no vote, unless they be equally divided.

5. The Senate shall choose their other officers, and also a president pro tempore, in the absence of the Vice President, or when he shall exercise the office of the President of the United States.

6. The Senate shall have the sole power to try all impeachments. When sitting for that purpose, they shall be on oath or affirmation. When the President of the United States is tried, the chief justice shall preside: And no person shall be convicted without the concurrence of two thirds of the members present.

7. Judgment in cases of impeachment shall not extend further than to removal from office, and disqualifications to hold and enjoy any office of honor, trust or profit under the United States:

---

1. Altered by the 16th Amendment.

2. Altered by the 14th Amendment.

3. Superseded by the 17th Amendment.

4. Altered by the 17th Amendment.

But the party convicted shall nevertheless be liable and subject to indictment, trial, judgment and punishment, according to law.

Section 4

1. The times, places, and manner of holding elections for senators and representatives, shall be prescribed in each State by the legislature thereof: But the Congress may at any time by law make or alter such regulations, except as to the places of choosing senators.

2. The Congress shall assemble at least once in every year, and such meeting shall be on the first Monday in December, unless they shall by law appoint a different day.

Section 5

1. Each House shall be the judge of the elections, returns and qualifications of its own members, and a majority of each shall constitute a quorum to do business; but a smaller number may adjourn from day to day, and may be authorized to compel the attendance of absent members, in such manner, and under such penalties as each House may provide.

2. Each House may determine the rules of its proceedings, punish its members for disorderly behavior, and, with the concurrence of two thirds, expel a member.

3. Each House shall keep a journal of its proceedings, and from time to time publish the same, excepting such parts as may in their judgment require secrecy; and the yeas and nays of the members of either House on any question shall, at the desire of one fifth of those present, be entered on the journal.

4. Neither House, during the session of Congress, shall, without the consent of the other, adjourn for more than three days, nor to any other place than that in which the two Houses shall be sitting.

Section 6

1. The senators and representatives shall receive a compensation for their services, to be ascertained by law, and paid out of the Treasury of the United States. They shall in all cases, except treason, felony, and breach of the peace, be privileged from arrest during their attendance at the session of their respective Houses, and in going to and returning from the same; and for any speech or debate in either House, they shall not be questioned in any other place.

2. No senator or representative shall, during the time for which he was elected, be appointed to any civil office under the authority of the United States, which shall have been created, or the emoluments whereof shall have been increased, during such time; and no person holding any office under the United States shall be a member of either House during his continuance in office.

Section 7

1. All bills for raising revenue shall originate in the House of Representatives; but the Senate may propose or concur with amendments as on other bills.

2. Every bill which shall have passed the House of Representatives and the Senate, shall, before it become a law, be presented to the President of the United States; If he approves he shall sign it, but if not he shall return it, with his objections, to that House in which it shall have originated, who shall enter the objections at large on their journal, and proceed to reconsider it. If after such reconsideration two thirds of that House shall agree to pass the bill, it shall be sent, together with the objections, to the other House, by which it shall likewise be reconsidered, and if approved by two thirds of that House, it shall become a law. But in all such cases the votes of both Houses shall be determined by yeas and nays, and the names of the persons voting for and against the bill shall

be entered on the journal of each House respectively. If any bill shall not be returned by the President within ten days (Sundays excepted) after it shall have been presented to him, the same shall be a law, in like manner as if he had signed it, unless the Congress by their adjournment prevent its return, in which case it shall not be a law.

3. Every order, resolution, or vote to which the concurrence of the Senate and the House of Representatives may be necessary (except on a question of adjournment) shall be presented to the President of the United States; and before the same shall take effect, shall be approved by him, or being disapproved by him, shall be repassed by two thirds of the Senate and House of Representatives, according to the rules and limitations prescribed in the case of a bill.

Section 8

The Congress shall have the power

1. To lay and collect taxes, duties, imposts, and excises, to pay the debts and provide for the common defense and general welfare of the United States; but all duties, imposts, and excises shall be uniform throughout the United States;

2. To borrow money on the credit of the United States;

3. To regulate commerce with foreign nations, and among the several States, and with the Indian tribes;

4. To establish an uniform rule of naturalization, and uniform laws on the subject of bankrupt-cies throughout the United States;

5. To coin money, regulate the value thereof, and of foreign coin, and fix the standard of weights and measures;

6. To provide for the punishment of counter-feiting the securities and current coin of the United States;

7. To establish post offices and post roads;

8. To promote the progress of science and useful arts, by securing for limited times to authors and inventors the exclusive right to their respective writings and discoveries;

9. To constitute tribunals inferior to the Supreme Court;

10. To define and punish piracies and felonies committed on the high seas, and offenses against the law of nations;

11. To declare war, grant letters of marque and reprisal, and make rules concerning captures on land and water;

12. To raise and support armies, but no appro-priations of money to that use shall be for a longer term than two years;

13. To provide and maintain a navy;

14. To make rules for the government and regu-lation of the land and naval forces;

15. To provide for calling forth the militia to execute the laws of the Union, suppress insur-rections and repel invasions;

16. To provide for organizing, arming, and disciplining the militia, and for governing such part of them as may be employed in the service of the United States, reserving to the States respectively, the appointment of the officers, and the authority of training the militia according to the discipline prescribed by Congress.

17. To exercise exclusive legislation in all cases whatsoever, over such district (not exceeding ten miles square) as may, by cession of partic-ular States and the acceptance of Congress, become the seat of the government of the United States, and to exercise like authority over all places purchased by the consent of the legislature of the State in which the same shall be, for the erection of forts, magazines, arsenals, dockyards, and other needful buildings; and

18. To make all laws which shall be necessary and proper for carrying into execution the forego-ing powers, and all other powers vested by the Constitution in the government of the United States, or any department or officer thereof.

Section 9

1. The migration or importation of such persons as any of the States now existing shall think proper to admit, shall not be prohibited by the Congress prior to the year one thousand eight hundred and eight, but a tax or duty may be imposed on such importation, not exceeding ten dollars for each person.

2. The privilege of the writ of habeas corpus shall not be suspended unless when in cases of rebellion or invasion the public safety may require it.

3. No bill of attainder or ex post facto law shall be passed.

4. No capitation, or other direct, tax shall be laid, unless in proportion to the census or enumeration hereinbefore directed to be taken.[5]

5. No tax or duty shall be laid on articles exported from any State.

6. No preference shall be given by any regulation of commerce or revenue to the ports of one State over those of another: Nor shall vessels bound to, or from, one State be obliged to enter, clear, or pay duties in another.

7. No money shall be drawn from the treasury, but in consequence of appropriations made by law; and a regular statement and account of the receipts and expenditures of all public money shall be published from time to time.

8. No title of nobility shall be granted by the United States: And no person holding any office of profit or trust under them, shall, without the consent of the Congress, accept of any present, emolument, office, or title, of any kind whatever, from any king, prince, or foreign State.

Section 10

1. No State shall enter into any treaty, alliance, or confederation; grant letters of marque and reprisal; coin money; emit bills of credit; make any thing but gold and silver coin a tender in payment of debts; pass any bill of attainder, ex post facto law, or law impairing the obligation of contracts, or grant any title of nobility.

2. No State shall, without the consent of the Congress, lay any imposts or duties on imports or exports, except what may be absolutely necessary for executing its inspection laws: And the net produce of all duties and imposts laid by any State on imports or exports, shall be for the use of the treasury of the United States; and all such laws shall be subject to the revision and control of the Congress.

3. No State shall, without the consent of the Congress, lay any duty of tonnage, keep troops, or ships of war in time of peace, enter into any agreement or compact with another State, or with a foreign power, or engage in war, unless actually invaded, or in such imminent danger as will not admit of delay.

ARTICLE II

Section 1

1. The executive power shall be vested in a President of the United States of America. He shall hold his office during the term of four years, and, together with the Vice President, chosen for the same term, be elected as follows:

2. Each State shall appoint, in such manner as the legislature thereof may direct, a number of electors, equal to the whole number of senators and representatives to which the State may be entitled in the Congress: But no senator or representative, or person holding an office of trust or profit under the United States, shall be appointed an elector.

   The electors shall meet in their respective States, and vote by ballot for two persons, of

5. Superseded by the 16th Amendment.

whom one at least shall not be an inhabitant of the same State with themselves. And they shall make a list of all the persons voted for, and of the number of votes for each; which list they shall sign and certify, and transmit sealed to the seat of the government of the United States, directed to the president of the Senate. The president of the Senate shall, in the presence of the Senate and House of Representatives, open all the certificates, and the votes shall then be counted. The person having the greatest number of votes shall be President, if such number be a majority of the whole number of electors appointed; and if there be more than one who have such majority, and have an equal number of votes, then the House of Representatives shall immediately choose by ballot one of them for President; and if no person have a majority, then from the five highest on the list the said House shall in like manner choose the President. But in choosing the President, the votes shall be taken by States, the representation from each State having one vote; a quorum for this purpose shall consist of a member or members from two thirds of the States, and a majority of all the States shall be necessary to a choice. In every case, after the choice of the President, the person having the greatest number of votes of the electors shall be the Vice President. But if there should remain two or more who have equal votes, the Senate shall choose from them by ballot the Vice President.[6]

3. The Congress may determine the time of choosing the electors, and the day on which they shall give their votes; which day shall be the same throughout the United States.

4. No person except a natural born citizen, or a citizen of the United States, at the time of the adoption of this Constitution, shall be eligible to the office of President; neither shall any person be eligible to that office who shall not have attained to the age of thirty-five years, and been fourteen years a resident within the United States.

5. In case of the removal of the President from office, or of his death, resignation, or inability to discharge the powers and duties of the said office, the same shall devolve on the Vice President, and the Congress may by law provide for the case of removal, death, resignation or inability, both of the President and Vice President, declaring what officer shall then act as President, and such officer shall act accordingly, until the disability be removed, or a President shall be elected.

6. The President shall, at stated times, receive for his services a compensation, which shall neither be increased nor diminished during the period for which he shall have been elected, and he shall not receive within that period any other emolument from the United States, or any of them.

7. Before he enter on the execution of his office, he shall take the following oath or affirmation: "I do solemnly swear (or affirm) that I will faithfully execute the office of President of the United States, and will to the best of my ability, preserve, protect, and defend the Constitution of the United States."

Section 2

1. The President shall be commander in chief of the army and navy of the United States, and of the militia of the several States, when called into the actual service of the United States; he may require the opinion, in writing, of the principal officer in each of the executive departments, upon any subject relating to the duties of their respective offices, and he shall have power to grant reprieves and pardons for offenses against the United States, except in cases of impeachment.

---

6. Superseded by the 12th Amendment.

2. He shall have power, by and with the advice and consent of the Senate, to make treaties, provided two thirds of the senators present concur; and he shall nominate, and by and with the advice and consent of the Senate, shall appoint ambassadors, other public ministers and consuls, judges of the Supreme Court, and all other officers of the United States, whose appointment are not herein otherwise provided for, and which shall be established by law: But the Congress may by law vest the appointment of such inferior officers, as they think proper, in the President alone, in the courts of law, or in the heads of departments.

3. The President shall have power to fill up all vacancies that may happen during the recess of the Senate, by granting commissions which shall expire at the end of their next session.

Section 3

He shall from time to time give to the Congress information of the state of the Union, and recommend to their considerations such measures as he shall judge necessary and expedient; he may, on extraordinary occasions, convene both Houses, or either of them, and in case of disagreement between them with respect to the time of adjournment, he may adjourn them to such time as he shall think proper; he shall receive ambassadors and other public ministers; he shall take care that the laws be faithfully executed, and shall commission all the officers of the United States.

Section 4

The President, Vice President, and all civil officers of the United States, shall be removed from office on impeachment for, and conviction of, treason, bribery, or other high crimes and misdemeanors.

ARTICLE III

Section 1

The judicial power of the United States shall be vested in one Supreme Court, and in such inferior courts as the Congress may from time to time ordain and establish. The judges, both of the Supreme and inferior courts, shall hold their offices during good behavior, and shall, at stated times, receive for their services, a compensation, which shall not be diminished during their continuance in office.

Section 2

1. The judicial power shall extend to all cases, in law and equity, arising under this Constitution, the laws of the United States, and treaties made, or which shall be made, under their authority;—to all cases affecting ambassadors, other public ministers and consuls;—to all cases of admiralty and maritime jurisdiction;—to controversies to which the United States shall be a party;[7]—to controversies between two or more States;—between a State and citizens of another State;—between citizens of different State;—between citizens of the same State claiming lands under grants of different States, and between a State, or the citizens thereof, and foreign States, citizens or subjects.

2. In all cases affecting ambassadors, other public ministers and consuls, and those in which a State shall be party, the Supreme Court shall have original jurisdiction. In all the other cases before mentioned, the Supreme Court shall have appellate jurisdiction, both as to law and fact, with such exceptions, and under such regulations as the Congress shall make.

3. The trial of all crimes, except in cases of impeachment, shall be by jury; and such trial shall be held in the State where the said crimes shall have been committed; but when not

---

7. Cf. the 11th Amendment.

committed within any State, the trial shall be at such place or places as the Congress may by law have directed.

Section 3

1. Treason against the United States shall consist only in levying war against them, or in adhering to their enemies, giving them aid and comfort. No person shall be convicted of treason unless on the testimony of two witnesses to the same overt act, or on confession in open court.

2. The Congress shall have power to declare the punishment of treason, but no attainder of treason shall work corruption of blood, or forfeiture except during the life of the person attained.

ARTICLE IV

Section 1

Full faith and credit shall be given in each State to the public acts, records, and judicial proceedings of every other State. And the Congress may by general laws prescribe the manner in which such acts, records and proceedings shall be proved, and the effect thereof.

Section 2

1. The citizens of each State shall be entitled to all privileges and immunities of citizens in the several States.[8]

2. A person charged in any State with treason, felony, or other crime, who shall flee from justice, and be found in another State, shall on demand of the executive authority of the State from which he fled, be delivered up to be removed to the State having jurisdiction of the crime.

3. No person held to service or labor in one State under the laws thereof, escaping into another, shall in consequence of any law or regulation therein, be discharged from such service or labor, but shall be delivered up on claim of the party to whom such service or labor may be due.[9]

Section 3

1. New States may be admitted by the Congress into this Union; but no new State shall be formed or erected within the jurisdiction of any other State; nor any State be formed by the junction of two or more States, or parts of States, without the consent of the legislatures of the States concerned as well as the Congress.

2. The Congress shall have power to dispose of and make all needful rules and regulations respecting the territory or other property belonging to the United States; and nothing in this Constitution shall be so construed as to prejudice any claims of the United States, or of any particular State.

Section 4

The United States shall guarantee to every State in this Union a republican form of government, and shall protect each of them against invasion; and on application of the legislature, or of the executive (when the legislature cannot be convened) against domestic violence.

ARTICLE V

The Congress, whenever two thirds of both Houses shall deem it necessary, shall propose amendments to this Constitution, or, on the application of the legislatures of two thirds of the several States, shall call a convention for proposing amendments,

---

8. Superseded by the 14th Amendment, Sec. 1.

9. Voided by the 13th Amendment.

which in either case shall be valid to all intents and purposes, as part of this Constitution, when ratified by the legislatures of three fourths of the several States, or by conventions in three fourths thereof, as the one or the other mode of ratification may be proposed by the Congress; Provided that no amendment which may be made prior to the year one thousand eight hundred and eight shall in any manner affect the first and fourth clauses in the ninth section of the first article; and that no State, without its consent, shall be deprived of its equal suffrage in the Senate.

ARTICLE VI

1. All debts contracted and engagements entered into, before the adoption of this Constitution, shall be as valid against the United States under this Constitution, as under the Confederation.

2. This Constitution, and the laws of the United States which shall be made in pursuance thereof; and all treaties made, or which shall be made, under the authority of the United States, shall be supreme law of the land; and the Judges in every State shall be bound thereby, any thing in the Constitution or laws of any State to the contrary notwithstanding.

3. The senators and representatives before mentioned, and the members of the several State legislatures, and all executives and judicial officers, both of the United States and of the several States, shall be bound by oath or affirmation to support this Constitution; but no religious test shall ever be required as a qualification to any office or public trust under the United States.

ARTICLE VII

The ratification of the conventions of nine States shall be sufficient for the establishment of this Constitution between the States so ratifying the same.

Done in Convention by the unanimous consent of the States present the seventeenth day of September in the year of our Lord one thousand seven hundred and eighty-seven, and of the independence of the United States of America the twelfth. In witness thereof we have hereunto subscribed our names. [Names omitted.]

. . .

Articles in addition to, and amendment of, the Constitution of the United States of America, proposed by Congress, and ratified by the legislatures of the several States, pursuant to the fifth article of the original Constitution.

AMENDMENT I [FIRST TEN AMENDMENTS RATIFIED DECEMBER 15, 1791]

Congress shall make no law respecting an establishment of religion, or prohibiting the free exercise thereof; or abridging the freedom of speech, or of the press; or the right of the people peaceably to assemble, and to petition the government for a redress of grievances.

AMENDMENT II

A well regulated militia, being necessary to the security of a free State, the right of the people to keep and bear arms, shall not be infringed.

AMENDMENT III

No soldier shall, in the time of peace be quartered in any house, without the consent of the owner, nor in time of war, but in a manner to be prescribed by law.

AMENDMENT IV

The right of the people to secure in their persons, houses, papers, and effects, against unreasonable searches and seizures, shall not be violated, and no warrants shall issue, but upon probable cause, supported by oath or affirmation, and particularly describing the place to be searched, and the persons or things to be seized.

AMENDMENT V

No person shall be held to answer for a capital, or otherwise infamous crime, unless on a presentment or indictment of a grand jury, except in cases arising in the land or naval forces, or in the militia, when in actual service in time of war or public danger; nor shall any person be subject for the same offense to be twice put in jeopardy of life or limb; nor shall be compelled in any criminal case to be a witness against himself; nor be deprived of life, liberty, or property, without due process of law; nor shall private property be taken for public use, without just compensation.

AMENDMENT VI

In all criminal prosecutions, the accused shall enjoy the right to a speedy and public trial, by an impartial jury of the State and district wherein the crime shall have been committed, which district shall have been previously ascertained by law, and to be informed of the nature and cause of the accusation; to be confronted with the witnesses against him; to have compulsory process for obtaining witnesses in his favor, and to have the assistance of the counsel for his defense.

AMENDMENT VII

In suits at common law, where the value in controversy shall exceed twenty dollars, the right of trial by jury shall be preserved, and no fact tried by a jury shall be otherwise reexamined in any court of the United States, than according to the rules of the common law.

AMENDMENT VIII

Excessive bail shall not be required, nor excessive fines imposed, nor cruel and unusual punishments inflicted.

AMENDMENT IX

The enumeration in the Constitution of certain rights shall not be construed to deny or disparage others retained by the people.

AMENDMENT X

The powers not delegated to the United States by the Constitution, nor prohibited by it to the States, are reserved to the States respectively, or to the people.

AMENDMENT XI [RATIFIED JANUARY 8, 1798]

The judicial power of the United States shall not be construed to extend to any suit in law or equity, commenced or prosecuted against one of the United States by citizens of another State, or by citizens or subjects of any foreign State.

AMENDMENT XII [RATIFIED SEPTEMBER 25, 1804]

The electors shall meet in their respective States, and vote by ballot for President and Vice President, one of whom, at least, shall not be an inhabitant of the same State with themselves; they shall name in their ballots the person voted for as President, and in distinct ballots the person voted for as Vice President, and they shall make distinct lists of all persons voted for as President and of all persons voted for as Vice President, and of the number of votes for each, which lists they shall sign and certify, and transmit sealed to the seat of the government of the United States, directed to the President of the Senate;—The President of the Senate shall, in the presence of the Senate and House of Representatives, open all the certificates and the votes shall then be counted;—The person having the greatest number of votes for President, shall be the President, if such number be a majority of the whole number of electors appointed; and if no person have such majority, then from the persons having the highest numbers not exceeding three on the list of those voted for as President, the House of Representatives shall choose immediately, by ballot, the President. But in choosing the President, the votes shall be taken by States, the representation from each State having one vote; a quorum for this purpose shall consist of a member or members from two thirds of the States, and a majority of all the States shall be necessary to a choice. And if the House of Representatives shall not choose a President whenever the right of choice shall devolve upon them, before the fourth day of March next following, then the Vice President shall act as President, as in the case of the death or other constitutional disability of the President. The person having the greatest number of votes as Vice President shall be the Vice President, if such number be a majority of the whole number of electors appointed, and if no person have a majority, then from the two highest numbers on the list, the Senate shall choose the Vice President; a quorum for the purpose shall consist of two thirds of the whole number of Senators, and a majority of the whole number shall be necessary to a choice. But no person constitutionally ineligible to the office of President shall be eligible to that of Vice President of the United States.

AMENDMENT XIII [RATIFIED DECEMBER 18, 1865]

Section 1

Neither slavery nor involuntary servitude, except as punishment for crime whereof the party shall have been duly convicted, shall exist within the United States, or any place subject to their jurisdiction.

Section 2

Congress shall have power to enforce this article by appropriate legislation.

AMENDMENT XIV [RATIFIED JULY 28, 1868]

Section 1

All persons born or naturalized in the United States, and subject to the jurisdiction thereof, are citizens of the United States and of the State wherein they reside. No State shall make or enforce any law which shall abridge the privileges or immunities of citizens of the United States; not shall any State deprive any person of life, liberty, or property, without due process of law; nor deny to any person within its jurisdiction the equal protection of the laws.

Section 2

Representatives shall be apportioned among the several States according to their respective numbers, counting the whole number of persons in each States, excluding Indians not taxed. But when the right to vote at any election for the choice of electors for President and Vice President of the United States, representatives in Congress, the executive and judicial officers of a State, or the members of the legislature thereof, is denied to any of the male inhabitants of such State, being twenty-one years of age, and citizens of the United States, or in any way abridged, except for participating in rebellion, or other crime, the basis of representation therein shall be reduced in the proportion which the number of such male citizens shall bear to the whole number of male citizens twenty-one years of age in such State.

Section 3

No person shall be a senator or representative in Congress, or elector of President and Vice President, or hold any office, civil or military, under the United States, or under any State, who having previously taken an oath as a member of Congress, or as an officer of the United States, or as a member of any State legislature, or as an executive or judicial officer of any State, to support the Constitution of the United States, shall have engaged in insurrection or rebellion against the same, or given aid or comfort to the enemies thereof. But Congress may by a vote of two thirds of each House, remove such disability.

Section 4

The validity of the public debt of the United States, authorized by law, including the debts incurred for payment of pensions and bounties for services in suppressing insurrection or rebellion, shall not be questioned. But neither the United States nor any State shall assume or pay any debt or obligation incurred in aid of insurrection or rebellion against the United States, or any claim for the loss or emancipation of any slave; but all such debts, obligations, and claims shall be held illegal and void.

Section 5

Congress shall have power to enforce, by appropriate legislation, the provisions of this article.

AMENDMENT XV [RATIFIED MARCH 30, 1870]

Section 1

The right of citizens of the United States to vote shall not be denied or abridged by the United States or by any State on account of race, color, or previous condition of servitude.

Section 2

The Congress shall have power to enforce this article by appropriate legislation.

AMENDMENT XVI [RATIFIED FEBRUARY 25, 1913]

The Congress shall have power to lay and collect taxes on incomes, from whatever source derived, without apportionment among the several States, and without regard to any census or enumeration.

AMENDMENT XVII [RATIFIED MAY 31, 1913]

The Senate of the United States shall be composed of two senators from each State, elected by the people thereof, for six years; and each senator shall have one vote. The electors in each State shall have the qualifications requisite for electors of the most numerous branch of the State legislature.

When vacancies happen in the representation of any State in the Senate, the executive authority of such State shall issue writs of election to fill such vacancies: *Provided*, That the legislature of any State may empower the executive thereof to make temporary appointments until the people fill the vacancies by election as the legislature may direct.

This amendment shall not be so construed as to affect the election or term of any senator chosen before it becomes valid as part of the Constitution.

AMENDMENT XVIII[10] [RATIFIED JANUARY 29, 1919]

After one year from the ratification of this article, the manufacture, sale, or transportation of intoxicating liquors within, the importation thereof into, or the exportation thereof from the United States and all territory subject to the jurisdiction thereof for beverage purposes is thereby prohibited.

The Congress and the several States shall have concurrent power to enforce this article by appropriate legislation.

This article shall be inoperative unless it shall have been ratified as an amendment to the Constitution by the legislature of the several States, as provided in the Constitution, within seven years from the date of the submission hereof to the States by Congress.

---

10. Repealed by the 21st Amendment.

AMENDMENT XIX [RATIFIED AUGUST 26, 1920]

The right of citizens of the United States to vote shall not be denied or abridged by the United States or by any State on account of sex.

Congress shall have the power to enforce this article by appropriate legislation.

AMENDMENT XX [RATIFIED JANUARY 23, 1933]

Section 1

The terms of the President and Vice President shall end at noon on the 20th day of January, and the terms of Senators and Representatives at noon on the 3d day of January, of the year in which such terms would have ended if this article had not been ratified; and the terms of their successors shall then begin.

Section 2

The Congress shall assemble at least once in every year, and such meeting shall begin at noon on the 3d day of January, unless they shall by law appoint a different day.

Section 3

If, at the time fixed for the beginning of the term of President, the President-elect shall have died, the Vice President-elect shall become President. If a President shall not have been chosen before the time fixed for the beginning of his term, or if the President-elect shall have failed to qualify, then the Vice President-elect shall act as President until a President shall have qualified; and the Congress may by law provide for the case wherein neither a President-elect nor a Vice President-elect shall have qualified, declaring who shall then act as President, or the manner in which one who is to act shall be selected, and such person shall act accordingly until a President or Vice President shall have qualified.

Section 4

The Congress may by law provide for the case of the death of any of the persons from whom the House of Representatives may choose a President whenever the right of choice shall have devolved upon them, and for the case of the death of any of the persons from whom the Senate may choose a Vice President whenever the right of choice shall have devolved upon them.

Section 5

Sections 1 and 2 shall take effect on the 15th day of October following the ratification of this article.

Section 6

This article shall be inoperative unless it shall have been ratified as an amendment to the Constitution by the legislatures of three-fourths of the several States within seven years from the date of its submission.

AMENDMENT XXI [RATIFIED DECEMBER 5, 1933]

Section 1

The Eighteenth Article of amendment to the Constitution of the United States is hereby repealed.

Section 2

The transportation or importation into any State, Territory, or possession of the United States for delivery or use therein of intoxicating liquors in violation of the laws thereof, is hereby prohibited.

Section 3

This article shall be inoperative unless it shall have been ratified as an amendment to the Constitution by conventions in the several States as provided in the Constitution, within seven years from the date of the submission thereof to the States by the Congress.

AMENDMENT XXII [RATIFIED MARCH 1, 1951]

No person shall be elected to the office of the President more than twice, and no person who has held the office of President, or acted as President, for more than two years of a term to which some other person was elected President shall be elected to the office of President more than once.

But this article shall not apply to any person holding the office of President when this article was proposed by the Congress, and shall not prevent any person who may be holding the office of President, or acting as President, during the term within which this article becomes operative from holding the office of President or acting as President during the remainder of such term.

This article shall be inoperative unless it shall have been ratified as an amendment to the Constitution by the legislature of three-fourths of the several States within seven years from the date of its submission to the States by the Congress.

AMENDMENT XXIII [RATIFIED MARCH 29, 1961]

Section 1

The District constituting the seat of Government of the United States shall appoint in such manner as the Congress may direct:

A number of electors of President and Vice President equal to the whole number of Senators and Representatives in Congress to which the District would be entitled if it were a State, but in no event more than the least populous State; they shall be in addition to those appointed by the States, but they shall be considered, for the purposes of the election of President and Vice President, to be electors appointed by a State; and they shall meet in the District and perform such duties as provided by the twelfth article of amendment.

Section 2

The Congress shall have power to enforce this article by appropriate legislation.

AMENDMENT XXIV [RATIFIED JANUARY 24, 1964]

Section 1

The right of citizens of the United States to vote in any primary or other election for President or Vice President, for electors for President or Vice President, or for Senator or Representative in Congress, shall not be denied or abridged by the United States or any State by reason of failure to pay any poll tax or other tax.

Section 2

The Congress shall have power to enforce this article by appropriate legislation.

AMENDMENT XXV [RATIFIED FEBRUARY 10, 1967]

Section 1

In case of the removal of the President from office or of his death or resignation, the Vice President shall become President.

Section 2

Whenever there is a vacancy in the office of the Vice President, the President shall nominate a Vice President who shall take office upon confirmation by a majority vote of both Houses of Congress.

Section 3

Whenever the President transmits to the President pro tempore of the Senate and the Speaker of the House of Representatives his written declaration that he is unable to discharge the powers and duties of his office, and until he transmits to them a written declaration to the contrary, such powers and duties shall be discharged by the Vice President as Acting President.

Section 4

Whenever the Vice President and a majority of either the principal officers of the executive departments or of such other body as Congress may by law provide, transmit to the President pro tempore of the Senate and the Speaker of the House of Representatives their written declaration that the President is unable to discharge the powers and duties of his office, the Vice President shall immediately assume the powers and duties of the office as Acting President.

Thereafter, when the President transmits to the President pro tempore of the Senate and the Speaker of the House of Representatives his written declaration that no inability exists, he shall resume the powers and duties of his office unless the Vice President and a majority of either the principal officers of the executive departments or of such body as Congress may by law provide, transmit within four days to the President pro tempore of the Senate and the Speaker of the House of Representatives their written declaration that the President is unable to discharge the powers and duties of his office. Thereupon Congress shall decide the issue, assembling within forty-eight hours for that purpose if not in session. If the Congress, within twenty-one days after receipt of the latter written declaration, or, if Congress is not in session, within twenty-one days after Congress is required to assemble, determines by two-thirds vote of both Houses that the President is unable to discharge the powers and duties of his office, the Vice President shall continue to discharge the same as Acting President; otherwise, the President shall resume the powers and duties of his office.

AMENDMENT XXVI [RATIFIED JULY 1, 1971]

Section 1

The right of citizens of the United States, who are eighteen years of age or older, to vote shall not be denied or abridged by the United States or by any State on account of age.

Section 2

The Congress shall have powers to enforce this article by appropriate legislation.

AMENDMENT XXVII [RATIFIED MAY 7, 1992]

No law varying the compensation for the services of the senators and representatives shall take effect until an election of representatives shall have intervened.

Glossary of Selected Terms from *The Law Dictionary* with Augmentation by the Textbook Author*

Acceptance Agreement of the offeree to be bound by the terms of the offer.

Accession A natural increase in one's property. Examples include the interest earned on money deposited in a bank account, or crops grown on one's land, or newborn puppies delivered by one's dog.

Accord An agreement between two (or more) persons, one of whom has a right of action against the others that the latter should do or give, and the former accept, something in satisfaction of the right of action. When the agreement is executed, and satisfaction has been made, it is called accord and satisfaction, and operates as a bar to the right of action. Accord, Restatement (Second) of Contracts § 281(1).

Act of State Doctrine Provides that American courts should not determine the validity of public acts committed by a foreign sovereign within its own territory.

Actus Reus An overt wrongful act.

Additur A motion made by a prevailing party in state court asking that the trial court award the plaintiff an additional sum of money because the jury's verdict is grossly inadequate.

Adjudicative Power A delegated power contained in an enabling act authorizing an administrative agency to determine legal rights, duties, and obligations, and to impose sanctions on those subject to its jurisdiction.

Administrative Law Judges Administrative law judges (ALJs) are employed by administrative agencies to conduct adjudicatory hearings. Like judges, ALJs decide questions of fact and issues of law, and issue subpoenas, administer oaths, make evidentiary rulings, and conduct hearings. ALJs are not, however, members of the federal judiciary. They perceive their function as that of implementing and administering a legislative purpose rather than as judges impartially deciding between two litigants.

Administrative Procedure Act A 1946 federal statute enacted to improve and strengthen the administrative process. Section 553 of the APA establishes notice and comment procedures for informal rule making and Section 554 establishes trial-like procedures for formal rule making.

Adoption A social and a legal process by which the rights and duties accompanying the parent-child

The Law Dictionary (*Cochran's Law Lexicon*, Sixth Edition), revised by Wesley Gilmer, Jr., Anderson Publishing Co., Cincinnati. Reprinted by permission. Additional terms have been incorporated into this glossary by the author of this text, Frank A. Schubert.

relationship are transferred from birth parents to adoptive parents.

Adverse Possession Also known as "easement by prescription." One whose possession of another's realty is open and notorious, hostile, adverse, and continuous for a legally specified period of time can bring a "quiet title action" in court at the end of the time period and, if successful, obtain a marketable title.

Advisory Opinion (1) In some jurisdictions, the formal opinion of a higher court concerning a point at issue in a lower court. (2) The formal opinion of a legal officer, e.g., Attorney General, concerning a question of law submitted by a public official. (3) In some jurisdictions, the opinion of a court concerning a question submitted by a legislative body.

Aesthetics The study of beauty.

Affirm An appellate court affirms a lower court when it concludes that the lower court's judgment is valid.

Affirmative Defenses Defenses in which a criminal defendant admits to the act but claims that special circumstances mitigate, justify, or excuse the defendant's conduct.

Agency Adoptions Birth parents consent to the termination of their parental rights and surrender child to an adoption agency that selects the adoptive parent(s) and places the child.

Agent A person authorized by another (the principal) to do an act or transact business for him or her, and to bind the principal within the limits of that authority. An agent may be authorized to do all business of a particular kind, or limited to one particular act. The agent's power to bind the principal is confined to the scope of his/her authority.

Agreement An expression of the parties' willingness to be bound to the terms of a contract.

Alibi A defense in which a criminal defendant proves that he/she was somewhere other than at the scene of the crime on the date and time that the offense allegedly occurred.

Alimony Court order requiring that an economically strong spouse pay financial support to an economically dependent spouse where it is necessary and appropriate. Some jurisdictions deny alimony to a spouse whose marriage ended as a result of that person's marital fault.

Alternative Dispute Resolution A term that refers to a variety of techniques adherents claim can in some cases resolve disputes more quickly, at less cost, and with less acrimony than would be true if the case were litigated in a court.

Analytical Positivism Adherents of this philosophical approach view law as a self-sufficient system of legal rules that the sovereign issues in the form of commands to the governed. Judgments about the intrinsic morality of the sovereign's commands are viewed as extra-legal.

Annulment An action in which a marriage partner seeks to prove that no valid marriage ever existed.

Answer (1) A pleading in which a civil defendant responds to the allegations of the complaint and states the defenses on which he/she intends to rely. (2) A statement under oath in response to written interrogatories, i.e., questions, or oral questions.

Appeal A process for obtaining review by a higher court of a lower court's decision.

Appellant A person who initiates an appeal from one court to another.

Appellee The party in a lawsuit against whom an appeal has been taken.

Arbitration The voluntary submission of a matter in dispute to the nonjudicial judgment of one, two, or more disinterested persons, called arbitrators, whose decision is binding on the parties.

Arbitrator's Award An arbitrator's decision is called an award.

Arraign To bring a criminally accused person formally before a court for the purpose of having him/her answer charges brought by the prosecution.

Arrest (1) The seizing and detaining of a person in custody by lawful authority. (2) Taking of another into the custody for the actual or purported purpose of bringing the other before a court, or of otherwise securing the administration of the law. (3) The seizure and detention of personal chattels, especially ships and vessels libeled in a court of admiralty.

Assault (1) Strictly speaking, threatening to strike or harm. (2) A threatening gesture, with or without verbal communication. If a blow is struck, it is battery. (3) Attempting to cause or purposely, knowingly, or recklessly causing bodily injury to another, or negligently causing bodily injury to another with a deadly weapon, or attempting by physical menace to put another in fear of imminent serious bodily injury; also called simple assault.

Assignee The person to whom an assignment is made.

Assignment The transfer of contractual rights to another person.

Assignor The person making an assignment.

Assumpsit A common law writ used to remedy some breaches of duty (called undertakings) that had previously been actionable under the old writ of trespass on the case.

Assumption of Risk A defense to a claim for negligent injury to a person or property, i.e., a person who voluntarily exposes himself or his property to a known danger may not recover for injuries thereby sustained.

Attempt A crime committed by a person who has the intent to commit a substantive criminal offense and does an act that tends to corroborate the intent, under circumstances that do not result in the completion of the substantive crime.

At-Will Doctrine A legal doctrine in employment law that permits an employee who has no contractual rights to employment to quit without notice or be fired by the employer at any time, for any reason or for no reason at all.

Avoidable Harm Doctrine Also known as the rule of mitigation, this rule prevents the recovery of damages that could have been foreseen and avoided by reasonable effort without undue risk, expense, or humiliation.

Bail To set at liberty a person arrested or imprisoned, on written security taken for his appearance on a day and at a place named. The term is applied, as a noun, to the persons who become security for the defendant's appearance; to the act of delivering such defendant to his bondsmen; and also to the bond given by the sureties to secure his release. A person who becomes someone's bail is regarded as his jailer, to whose custody he is committed. The word "bail" is never used with a plural termination.

Bailment A broad expression which describes the agreement, undertaking, or relationship which is created by the delivery of personal property by the owner, i.e., the bailor, to someone who is not an owner of it, i.e., the bailee, for a specific purpose, which includes the return of the personal property to the person who delivered it, after the purpose is otherwise accomplished. In a bailment, dominion and control over the personal property usually pass to the bailee. The term is often used to describe, e.g.: (1) The gratis loaning of an automobile for the borrower's use. (2) The commercial leasing of an automobile for a fee. (3) The delivery of an automobile to a repairman for the purpose of having it repaired.

(4) The delivery of an automobile to a parking attendant for storage, when the keys are left with the attendant.

Bailor A person who commits goods to another person (the bailee) in trust for a specific purpose.

Bar and Merger A judicial doctrine which provides that claims made by the plaintiff and claims that could have made, but were not, merge into the judgment and are extinguished. A subsequent suit against the same defendant based on the same claim is barred.

Battery An unlawful touching, beating, wounding, or laying hold, however trifling, of another's person or clothes without his consent.

Bench Trial A case is litigated before a judge instead of a jury.

Benefit The receipt by the promisor of some legal right to which the person had not previously been entitled.

Benefit Rule When a plaintiff is both damaged and benefitted by the defendant's conduct, the plaintiff's damage award should be reduced by the amount of the benefit conferred.

Best Evidence A rule of evidence that requires the production of original documents in court unless they are unobtainable.

Best Interest of the Child Doctrine A rule requiring judges to show no gender preference and to act on ability to provide, and interest in providing, the child with love, a good home, food, clothing, medical care, and education.

Bifurcation A trial is broken up into segments.

Bilateral Contract Contracts in which the parties exchange mutual promises to do some future act.

Bill of Attainder A legislative act that declares a person guilty of a crime and imposes punishment (generally capital punishment). Used in lieu of the judicial process.

Breach of Contract A flexible term for the wrongful failure to perform one or more of the promises that a person previously undertook when he or she made a contract, e.g., failure to deliver goods.

Burden of Proof The duty of proving facts disputed in the trial of a case. It commonly lies on the person who asserts the affirmative of an issue, and is sometimes said to shift when sufficient evidence is furnished to raise a presumption that what is alleged is true. The shifting of the burden of proof is better characterized as the creation of a burden of going forward with the evidence; however, because the total burden of proof is not thereby changed, the burden of going forward with the evidence is apt to revert to the other party and change from time to time.

Canon Law Church law.

Capacity Where a person is of legal age and is not otherwise so impaired as to be substantially incapable of making decisions for himself/herself.

Capias A writ that orders law enforcement to take a person into custody and bring him/her before the court.

Capture A method of obtaining title to previously unowned property such as catching fish on the high seas or netting a butterfly. Capture often requires that the captor purchase a license, such as when one goes hunting or fishing.

Case of First Impression A case presenting a legal question that has not previously been answered in a reported appellate opinion.

Cases And Controversies Article III, Section 2, of the U.S. Constitution requires that a matter must be a "case" or "controversy" to be within the federal judicial power. This means that the parties must truly be adverse, the plaintiff's claims of having suffered legal injuries are real and not hypothetical, and the issues raised are neither abstract nor hypothetical.

Causation An element that must be proved in some, but not all, criminal cases and in negligence and some strict liability cases in tort.

Causation in Fact A causal connection does exist between the defendant and the plaintiff's injuries—i.e., but for the defendant's negligence, the plaintiff's injuries would not have occurred.

Caveat Emptor Let the buyer beware.

Chancellor As used in this textbook, an equitable court judge, or a judge exercising the powers of an equitable court judge.

Child Support This term refers to a parent's duty to provide necessaries to one's child and to the sum of money one parent must pay to the other pursuant to a court order in the aftermath of a divorce.

Civil Suit All legal actions other than criminal prosecutions.

Civil Union A legally recognized relationship that permits qualifying same-sex partners to obtain economic benefits that in some states are equal to those afforded married people. Only a few states recognize civil unions.

Clause A provision in a document such as a contract or constitution containing a subject and a finite verb, for

example, the Due Process Clause of the Fourteenth Amendment.

Code Napoleon A civil code developed at the direction of Napoleon Bonaparte in 1804. This code, as amended, is the basis of French law and is still a source of law in Louisiana.

Collusion A term used to describe parties to a lawsuit who are not truly adverse, for example, one party is financing and controlling both sides of a lawsuit.

Common Law This term is used in three different contexts in this textbook. (1) It refers to the right of judges, particularly in contract and tort cases, to declare the law based on principles and precedents established over several centuries in Anglo-American case law. (2) It refers to the system of law established in England and subsequently adopted in most American states that features judge-made law and considers case precedents as an important source of law. This text distinguishes the common law approach to lawmaking from the civil law approach, which is derived from detailed legislative codes rather than judicial precedents. (3) Lastly, this term refers to differences in rights, remedies, and procedures that distinguish the common law courts (law courts) from courts of equity.

Common Law Lien A legally enforceable claim against property recognized under the common law.

Common Law Marriage Informal marriage by agreement that dispenses with licenses and solemnization ceremonies. The parties must have established the relationship of husband and wife, live together as a married couple, and present themselves to the world as being married.

Community Property A system used in some states when apportioning property between the parties in a divorce. The earnings of both spouses and property rights acquired with those earnings during the marriage are lumped together and each party receives a percentage of the whole. State statutes usually exclude from community property any rights acquired prior to marriage and spousal inheritances and gifts received during the marriage.

Comparative Negligence The approach to determining damages in negligence cases followed by most states. These states apportion damages between the plaintiff and defendant in proportion to each party's contributory fault. Thus the trier of fact in a case determines the total damages and then assigns a percentage of the total fault to the plaintiff, as well as well as the defendant; the plaintiff's total damage award is usually reduced by that percentage.

Compensatory Damages Damages awarded to compensate the plaintiff for actual monetary losses resulting from the defendant's conduct.

Competent Legally adequate.

Competent Party A person who has the legal capacity to bind himself or herself contractually.

Complaint Under modern rules of civil and criminal procedure, a pleading that is filed to commence an action.

Concurrent Ownership Property held simultaneously by more than one person.

Concurring Opinion An opinion written by a judge who, while voting with the majority, has additional comments to make that go beyond what is included in the majority opinion.

Condition Precedent A contractual requirement that some specified event must occur before a duty to perform becomes operative.

Condition Subsequent A contractual requirement that discharges the parties from their duties if a specified event occurs.

Conflict of Laws The variance between the laws of two states or countries relating to the subject matter of a suit brought in one of them, when the parties to the suit, or some of them, or the subject matter, belong to the other.

Consideration An essential element of contracts. That which is bargained for and given in exchange for another's promise, usually consisting of the performance of an act or promise to do an act, or to refrain from doing an act or to give up a right.

Conspiracy A crime committed when two or more people agree to commit a criminal act and one or more of the conspirators takes a significant step in furtherance of the intended criminal objective.

Constructive Service Service is accomplished by publishing the notice of summons in the legal announcements section of newspapers.

Construe To interpret the meaning of words.

Consumer Credit Protection Act (CCPA) A statute enacted by Congress in 1968 to promote the disclosure of credit terms and to establish the rights and responsibilities of both creditors and consumers.

Contingent Fee Agreement A method of compensation for lawyers. The lawyer takes a contractually agreed upon percentage of the damages collected in lieu of other forms of compensation. The attorney receives nothing for his or her time if the client recovers nothing.

Contingent Property Rights Property rights that accrue only after the occurrence of some specified future event.

Contract A legally enforceable agreement containing one or more promises.

Contributory Negligence (1) The failure to exercise care by a plaintiff, which contributed to the plaintiff's injury. Even though a defendant may have been negligent, in some jurisdictions, contributory negligence will bar a recovery by the plaintiff. (2) Conduct on the part of a plaintiff that falls below the standard to which the plaintiff should conform for his or her own protection, and which is a legally contributing cause cooperating with the negligence of the defendant in bringing about the plaintiff's harm.

Conversion A flexible term. (1) The wrongful appropriation of the goods of another. (2) An intentional exercise of dominion or control over a chattel that so seriously interferes with the right of another to control it that the actor may justly be required to pay the other the full value of the chattel.

Copyright A grant of rights to an author from the federal government. Authors of literary pieces, musical compositions, dramatic works, photographs, graphic works of various types, video and audio recordings, and computer software are protected against most unauthorized uses by placing a prescribed copyright notice on publicly disseminated copies of the work.

Corpus Juris Civilis Sixth-century Roman Code that was promulgated by the Emperor Justinian.

Counterclaim A defendant's claim against the plaintiff, which is usually included in the answer; it is essentially a defendant's "complaint."

Court of Equity Originally a court of equity headed by the Chancellor that came into being in the 14th century in England and lasted until 1875. Today, most states confer on their judges both the powers traditionally exercised by law judges as well as the powers traditionally exercised by the chancellor in the equity courts.

Court-Annexed Adr ADR participation is required either by legislation or court rule.

Covenant A common law writ initially used to enforce agreements pertaining to land and later used to enforce written agreements under seal; in other contexts, a promise contained in a deed or contract.

Creation A method for acquiring title to personalty. A person who manufactures products out of raw materials through physical or mental labor has title to the items created. However, someone who is employed to produce something does not take title to the thing produced.

Creditor Beneficiary A noncontracting person who is the intended beneficiary of a contract entered into between two other people.

Criminal Law Jurisprudence concerning crimes and their punishment.

Criminal Negligence A level of negligence greater than ordinary negligence in which the actor unconsciously creates risk of harm.

Cruel and Unusual Punishment A clause in the Eighth Amendment to the U.S. Constitution.

Curia Regis A 12th-century royal court established by Henry I which eventually became known as the Court of Kings/Queen's Bench.

Custodial Interrogation Police initiated questioning of a person who has been deprived of his liberty in a "significant" way. This term originated in the famous case of *Miranda v. Arizona.*

Custodial Parent A parent awarded primary physical placement of a child.

Damages A flexible term for the reparation in money that is allowed by law on account of damage. They may be general, such as necessarily and by implication of law arise from the act complained of; or special, such as under the peculiar circumstances of the case arise from the act complained of, but are not implied by law; compensatory, sufficient in amount to cover the loss actually sustained; exemplary, punitive, or vindictive, when in excess of the loss sustained and allowed as a punishment for torts committed with fraud, actual malice, or violence; nominal, when the act was wrong, but the loss sustained was trifling; substantial, when the loss was serious; liquidated, fixed by agreement of the parties, as when it is agreed beforehand what amount one shall receive in case of a breach of contract by the other.

Debt A common law writ used to collect a specific sum of money owed by another.

Declaratory Judgment A determination or decision by a court, which states the rights of the parties to a dispute, but does not order or coerce any performance relative to those rights. The procedural and substantive conditions of the usual action must be present. The relief that the court grants is the distinguishing characteristic.

Defamation (1) A flexible term for the uttering of spoken or written words concerning someone that tend to injure that person's reputation and for which an action for damages may be brought. (2) To create liability for defamation there must be (a) a false and defamatory statement concerning another, (b) an unprivileged publication to a third party, (c) fault amounting at least to negligence on the part of the publisher, and (d) either actionability of the statement irrespective of special harm or the existence of special harm caused by the publication.

Default Judgment The failure to plead or otherwise defend an action, by a party against whom a judgment for affirmative relief is sought.

Defendant A person against whom an action is brought, a warrant is issued, or an indictment is found.

Delegate (1) A person authorized to act for another. (2) A person elected to represent others in a deliberative assembly, such as a political convention.

Delegation The transfer of contractual duties to another person.

Demurrer A synonym for motion to dismiss.

Deposition A written record of oral testimony, in the form of questions and answers, made before a public officer for use in a lawsuit. They are used for the purpose of discovery of information, or for the purpose of being read as evidence at a trial, or for both purposes.

Detainer A writ requiring that a person be retained in custody.

Detinue A writ used to recover possession of personal property from someone who had possessory rights but refused to return it when requested.

Dicta Plural of dictum.

Dictum A statement by a judge concerning a point of law that is not necessary for the decision of the case in which it is stated. Usually, dictum is not as persuasive as its opposite, i.e., holding.

Direct Examination The initial questioning of a witness by the party who calls that witness.

Directed Verdict A determination by a jury made at the direction of the court, in cases where there has been a failure of evidence, an overwhelming weight of the evidence, or where the law, as applied to the facts, is for one of the parties.

Disaffirm (A Contract) A party to a contract elects to back out of the agreement.

Discharge (1) A flexible term that connotes finality, e.g., cancellation, rescission, or nullification. (2) The court order by which a person held to answer a criminal charge is set free. (3) The court order by which a jury is relieved from further consideration of a case.

Discovery A pliant method by which the opposing parties to a lawsuit may obtain full and exact factual information concerning the entire area of their controversy, via pretrial depositions, interrogations, requests for admissions, inspection of books and documents, physical and mental examinations, and inspection of land or other property. The purpose of these pretrial procedures is to disclose the genuine points of factual dispute and facilitate adequate preparation for trial. Either party may compel the other party to disclose the relevant facts that are in his possession, prior to the trial.

Discretion The use of private independent judgment; the authority of a trial court that is not controlled by inflexible rules, but can be exercised one way or the other as the trial judge believes to be best in the circumstances. It is subject to review, however, if it is abused.

Dissenting Opinion An opinion written by a judge who disagrees with the court's majority. In the opinion the dissenting judge explains why he/she believes the majority has wrongfully decided the case.

Diversity of Citizenship Jurisdiction One of two categories of federal subject matter jurisdiction. For this type of jurisdiction to exist the lawsuit must be between citizens of different states or between a citizen of a state and an alien, and the amount in controversy must exceed $75,000.

Divorce A term used to describe the entire process of concluding and reordering a couple's marital, parental, and economic relationships.

Doctrine of Forum Non Conveniens A judicial policy that permits a court to decline to exercise jurisdiction where it believes that the case can proceed more conveniently in another court.

Doctrine of Substituted Judgment An equitable doctrine that provides that a chancellor in equity has the right to act for an incompetent in the same manner as the incompetent would if he/she were competent.

Domicile The state in which the defendant has established his or her permanent home and to which the defendant returns after temporary absences.

Donee Beneficiary A noncontracting person who is intended to receive the benefit of an agreement between the contracting parties, i.e., if A and B contract to replace a window in C's house, C is the donee beneficiary.

Due Process A concept traced back to Magna Carta that has traditionally stood for the notion that government has to treat people fairly when attempting to deprive them of "life, liberty, or property." The determination of what fairness requires in any given context is determined by courts on a case-by-case basis. This principle of due process is included in both federal and state constitutions. This fairness requirement applies both in procedural and substantive contexts.

Due Process Clause Clauses found in both the Fifth and Fourteenth Amendments to the U.S. Constitution expressly providing that people are entitled to due process of law when government is seeking to deprive them of "life, liberty or property." The Fifth Amendment due process clause applies to the federal government and the Fourteenth Amendment applies to the state governments.

Duress (1) Imprisonment; compulsion; coercion. (2) Threats of injury or imprisonment.

Easement A nonpossessory property right in land; it is one person's right to use another person's land.

Egoist One who believes it is ethically proper to act on ones own self interest, irrespective of the consequences to others.

Ejectment Formerly a mixed action at common law, which depended on fictions in order to escape the inconveniences in the ancient forms of action. It was a mixed action, because it sought to recover both possession of land (a real property claim), and also damages (a personal property claim). Various statutory proceedings for the recovery of land, some of which bear the same name, have taken place in most of the United States.

Embezzlement A crime in which a criminal actor who has been entrusted with another person's money or property uses the money or property to his/her own advantage, without permission, and in a manner adverse to the true owner's interests.

Eminent Domain The right of the government to take private property for a public purpose over the objection of a landowner. This governmental right is limited by the Fifth and Fourteenth Amendments to the federal constitution, which provide that government must pay just compensation to the objecting landowner whenever property is taken to benefit the public by way of the power of eminent domain.

En Banc All judges assigned to a court hear the case as a group

Enabling Act A statute defining and guiding an administrative agency's structure, functions, powers, and objectives.

Entrapment A defense raised in a criminal prosecution where an officer induces a person who was not otherwise so disposed to commit a criminal act. The purpose of this defense is to deter this form of police misconduct.

Epistemology The study of knowledge.

Equal Credit Opportunity Act (ECOA) A statute enacted by Congress in 1974 to eradicate discrimination in the granting of credit when the decision to grant it or refuse it is based on an individual's sex, marital status, race, color, age, religion, national origin, or receipt of public assistance.

Equal Protection Clause The Fourteenth Amendment's equal protection clause prohibits discrimination on the basis of race, national origin, gender, or religion.

Equitable Court A court with jurisdiction to decide equitable claims and award equitable remedies. Also known as a court of chancery.

Equitable Distribution An alternative method for apportioning property in a divorce. The court ignores which party has title to marital property and based on the totality of the circumstances treats each divorcing party "fairly" after considering each party's contributions, needs, and the duration of the marriage.

Equitable Lien An equitable remedy used to avoid an unjust enrichment that would otherwise result because no other lien is provided by statute or under the common law.

Equitable Maxims Short statements of principle used to determine if an equitable remedy should be awarded.

Equitable Remedy A remedy traditionally available in equity but not under the common law.

Equity (1) Fairness. A type of justice that developed separately from the common law, and which tends to complement it. The current meaning is to classify disputes and remedies according to their historical relationship and development. Under modern rules of civil procedure, law and equity have been unified. Historically, the courts of equity had a power of framing and

adapting new remedies to particular cases, which the common law courts did not possess. In doing so, they allowed themselves latitude of construction and assumed, in certain matters such as trusts, a power of enforcing moral obligations that the courts of law did not admit or recognize. (2) A right or obligation attaching to property or a contract. In this sense, one person is said to have a better equity than another.

Erie Doctrine A judicial policy that is applied in federal court when adjudicating state matters. This policy provides that where federal jurisdiction is based on diversity of citizenship, a federal court should normally apply the substantive law that would be applied in the state courts of the district in which the federal court is situated.

Estate The amount of interest a person has in land.

Ethics The study of morality.

Ex Parte Injunction An injunction granted without notice to the party being enjoined.

Ex Post Facto Laws that make acts criminal that were not criminal at the time they were committed.

Exclusionary Rule A judicial remedy that under some circumstances excludes from trial evidence obtained by the prosecution. The evidence is suppressed because it was obtained by the police as a byproduct of infringing a criminal defendant's constitutionally protected rights.

Excuse Defenses The defendant acted unlawfully, but argues that no criminal responsibility should be imposed, given the particular circumstances accompanying the act; examples include duress, insanity, and involuntary intoxication.

Executed Contract A contract in which both parties have performed as agreed; a completed contract.

Execution (1) The writ, order, or process issued to a sheriff directing him to carry out the judgment of a court. (2) To complete a contract.

Executory Contract A contract that is incomplete.

Exemplary Damages A synonym for punitive damages.

Exhaustion of Administrative Remedies A requirement that all aggrieved persons pursue to conclusion all opportunities for administrative relief prior to seeking relief from the judiciary.

Express Contract A contract in which none of the terms is implied.

False Arrest; False Imprisonment (1) A tort consisting of restraint imposed on a person's liberty, without proper legal authority. (2) False imprisonment is a misdemeanor consisting of knowingly restraining another unlawfully so as to interfere substantially with his or her liberty.

Family There is no single universally accepted legal definition of family. The word is generally defined by statute in operational terms, within a particular context (i.e., to specify which people are entitled to specified economic benefits). In Vermont, two same-sex partners in a civil union can qualify for family leave benefits. Under Social Security, a step child can sometimes qualify for family benefits. The traditional notion that a family consists of people sharing kinship and cohabitation is outdated. It is common for people to recognize more than one type of family (notably the nuclear family and the extended family, the nuclear family plus the grandparents, cousins, aunts and uncles). Many employers today refer to their employees as members of a business "family."

Federal Arbitration Act A 1925 federal statute that establishes a policy of favoring the arbitration of disputes over commercial transactions.

Federal Register This daily publication of the federal government is where administrative agencies give notice of proposed rule making, publish proposed rules, and publish promulgated substantive rules not less than thirty days before the rule's effective date.

Fee Simple The maximum ownership right to land that is permissible by law. A person who holds an estate in what is known as fee simple can pass his or her interest on to heirs.

Felony Although jurisdictional variations exist, a felony is generally regarded as any criminal offense for which a defendant is subject to execution or may be imprisoned for more than one year.

Feudalism A military, political, and social structure that ordered relationships between people. Under feudalism, a series of duties and obligations existed between a lord and his vassals.

Final Decision A decision that is not or cannot be appealed.

Fixture Formerly, an article which was a personal chattel, but which, by being physically annexed to a building or land, became accessory to it and part and parcel of it. It was treated as belonging to the owner of the freehold, and passed with it to a vendee, and, though annexed by a tenant for his own convenience in the occupation of the premises, could not be removed by

him. The rule has been modified by statute in many of the states, and is significantly relaxed in practice, especially as between landlord and tenant. Trade fixtures and ornamental fixtures may usually be removed by the tenant at the end of his term, provided he does no material injury to the freehold. Written leases often make specific provisions concerning the matter.

Forbearance Refraining from doing an act, or giving up a right.

Foreign Laws Those enacted and in force in a foreign state, or country.

Foreseeability An individual is only responsible in negligence for those consequences that are reasonably foreseeable, and will be relieved of liability for injuries that are not reasonably related to the negligent conduct.

Formal Rule Making The procedural requirements that provide for a trial-like hearing process "on the record," complete with witnesses and recorded testimony, as well as findings of fact and conclusions of law.

Forum (1) A court of justice; the place where justice must be sought. (2) Formerly, an open space in Roman cities, where the people assembled, markets were held, and the magistrates sat to transact their business.

Forum State The state in which a lawsuit has been filed.

Foster Care A child care placement with a family (the foster family) or group home, that is willing to provide an unadopted child with short-term "parenting" in the foster family's home. Some parents voluntarily place their children in foster care for a brief time. Most foster placements, however, result from court intervention because of alleged child abuse or neglect.

Fraud Intentional acts of deception used by one individual to gain an advantage over another.

Full Faith and Credit The requirement that the public acts, records, and judicial proceedings of every state shall be given the same effect by the courts of another state that they have by law and usage in the state of origin. U.S. Const., Art. IV, Sec. I. Congress has prescribed the manner in which they may be proven.

Fundamental Liberties Fundamental rights are rights that have been given "heightened protection" by the U.S. Supreme Court. These include most of the protections expressly included in the Bill of Rights. The Court has also added other rights to the list that it has found by implication to be deserving of fundamental constitutional protection. Some examples include the rights to marry, to determine how one's children are raised and educated, to marital privacy, and to abortion.

Garnishment A judgment enforcement process that results in the debtor's employer being ordered to deduct a percentage of the debtor's earnings from each paycheck.

General Appearance A person makes a general appearance by not objecting to in personam jurisdiction and by arguing the substantive facts of the case. Such a person is implicitly consenting to personal jurisdiction.

General Damages Damages that are the natural and necessary result of the wrongful act or omission, and thus can normally be expected to accompany the injury.

General or Residual Jurisdiction The authority of a court to hear and decide an action or lawsuit, except for those cases that are within the exclusive jurisdiction of another court.

Genuine Assent Agreement to contract that is not induced because of misrepresentation, fraud, duress, undue influence, or mistake.

Good Character Defense Defense proves character traits and argues that the defendant's character is so sterling that he/she would never have committed the crime as charged.

Grand Jury A body of persons, not less than twelve, nor more than twenty-four, freeholders of a county, whose duty it is, on hearing the evidence for the prosecution in each proposed bill of indictment, to decide whether a sufficient case is made out, on which to hold the accused for trial. It is a body that is convened by authority of a court and serves as an instrumentality of the court. It has authority to investigate and to accuse, but it is not authorized to try cases. It is a creature of the common law that was instituted to protect the people from governmental oppression. In a few states, it has been partially abolished, but in others it exists by constitutional mandate. No person shall be held to answer for a capital or otherwise infamous federal crime, unless on a presentment or indictment of a grand jury, except in cases arising in the land or naval forces, or in the militia, when in actual service in time of war or public danger; U.S. Const., Fifth Amendment.

Grantee The recipient of a grant.

Grantor The person making a grant.

Guardian A person appointed by a court, to have the control or management of the person or property, or

both, of another who is incapable of acting on his own behalf, e.g., an infant or a person of unsound mind.

Habeas Corpus A writ used to require that a detained person be brought before the court. The purpose of habeas review is to test the legality of the detention.

Harmless-Error Doctrine A judicial doctrine that provides that a criminal conviction need not be automatically reversed just because it has been proved that constitutional error occurred during the trial. There should be no reversal, according to the U.S. Supreme Court, where the quantity and quality of the factual evidence introduced at trial is consistent with the jury's verdict and is so strong that appellate courts can forecast beyond a reasonable doubt that the error was not included in the jury's calculus in reaching its verdict. Errors of this sort are classified as "harmless."

Hearing A flexible term for a court proceeding or trial.

Hearsay Evidence A statement other than one made by the declarant while testifying at the trial or hearing, offered in evidence to prove the truth of the matter asserted. Usually, such evidence is inadmissible, but exceptions are made, e.g., in questions of pedigree, custom, reputation, dying declarations, and statements made against the interest of the declarant.

Hedonic Damages Damages awarded to compensate for the loss of enjoyment of life.

Historical Jurisprudence Adherents of this philosophical approach believe that law is only valid to the extent that the will of the sovereign is compatible with long-standing social practices, customs, and values.

Holding The rule of law that the court says applies to the facts of the case.

Hundred The lowest unit of governmental organization in Anglo-Saxon England. Its primary function was judicial. It operated a court that met monthly and handled civil and criminal matters according to local custom. Hundreds were grouped into shires.

Illegal Contract An agreement's formation or performance is criminal, tortious, or contrary to public policy.

Immunity Preferential protection from lawsuits.

Impeach (1) To charge a public official with crime or misdemeanor, or with misconduct in office. (2) To undermine a witness's testimony by proving lack of veracity, prior inconsistent statement, bias, or that the witness is otherwise unworthy of belief.

Implied Contract Contract presumed by law to have been made from the circumstances and the conduct of the parties.

Imputed Negligence A person can be held vicariously liable for the negligence of another when one person (the agent) acts for or represents another (the principal) by the latter's authority and to accomplish the latter's ends.

In Camera A hearing held in a judge's office or in a closed courtroom.

In Personam Jurisdiction Jurisdiction over the persons of the plaintiff and defendant.

In Rem Jurisdiction Jurisdiction over property.

Inchoate Crimes Solicitation, attempt, and conspiracy.

Independent Adoption Birth parent(s) interview and select prospective adoptive parents without agency involvement. Some states prohibit independent adoptions.

Independent Contractor A person who agrees with another to do something for the other, in the course of his or her occupation, but who is not controlled by the other, nor subject to the other's right to control with respect to the performance of the undertaking, and is thereby distinguished from an employee.

Indictment A written accusation that one or more persons have committed a crime, presented upon oath, by a grand jury. The person against whom the indictment is returned is said to be indicted.

Infamous Crimes An offense carrying a term of imprisonment in excess of one year.

Infliction of Mental Distress An intentional tort in which the tortfeasor's outrageous conduct intentionally and recklessly subjects someone to severe emotional distress. The tortfeasor's conduct must be serious in nature and cause anguish in the plaintiff's mind.

Informal Rule Making Procedural requirements in the Administrative Procedures Act that provide for "notice and comment" rule making. In informal rule making, agencies are required to publish proposed rules in the Federal Register, so that interested persons can receive notice of the agency's intentions and have an opportunity to submit written submissions in which they comment on the proposed rule, and if the agency so desires, make oral presentations.

Injunction A flexible, discretionary process of preventive and remedial justice, which is exercised by courts that have equity powers. Courts issue injunctions when it appears that the ordinary remedy usually provided by law is not a full, adequate, and complete one. Injunctions are preventive if they restrain a person from doing something, or mandatory if they command something to be done. They are preliminary, provisional, or interlocutory if they are granted on the filing of a bill, or while the suit is pending, to restrain the party enjoined from doing or continuing to do the acts complained of, until final hearing or the further order of the court. They are final, perpetual or permanent if they are awarded after full hearing on the merits, and as a final determination of the rights of the parties.

Insanity Defendant claims to lack the capacity to commit the crime with which he/she is charged; the meaning of capacity varies by jurisdiction.

Insurance People contract with insurance companies and pay premiums in exchange for economic protection against specified risks. Common examples include automobile, property, life, health, and professional liability insurance.

Intangibles A kind of property that is nonphysical and not subject to being sensed (e.g., touched or felt), but which exists as a concept of people's minds (e.g., promissory notes, bank accounts, and corporate stock).

Integrity Quality of a person whose behavior is consistent with moral principles.

Intentional Torts Civil wrongs in which he defendant is alleged to have intentionally interfered with the plaintiff's person, reputation, or property.

Interference With Contract Relations An intentional tort in which a noncontracting party or third person wrongfully interferes with the contract relations between two or more contracting parties.

Intermediate Appellate Court An appellate court above trial courts and below the highest appellate court in a judicial system.

Interpretive Rule Administrative rule used to explain an agency's interpretation of an ambiguous statute or its understanding of the meaning of an important term which the legislature body has neglected to define.

Invasion of Privacy An intentional tort in which the tortfeasor invades someone's right to be free from unwarranted publicity that places the plaintiff in a false light, intrudes into the plaintiff's private life, discloses embarrassing private facts, or uses the plaintiff's name or likeness for the defendant's gain.

Investigative Power A delegated power contained in an enabling act authorizing an administrative agency to engage in fact-finding.

Investigatory Detentions (Stop and Frisk) An investigative stop is a warrantless, nonprobable cause based seizure of a person by police for investigative purposes. The U.S. Supreme Court approved brief seizures by police for investigative purposes where officers have reasonable suspicion to believe that a person has committed, is about to commit, or is committing a crime. The Court ruled that officers have the right to make such brief stops so that they can engage in brief questioning. The Court has further approved a limited frisk of the detained person if officers can articulate reasonable suspicion to believe that the detained person possesses a weapon. The officers are then permitted to conduct a pat-down of the detained person's outer clothing for self protection while questioning the suspect. If the frisk discloses anything that feels like a weapon, the frisking officer can reach into the detained person's garments to remove the object/s identified in the frisk. An officer who has finished questioning the detained person is required to return any seized object that was legally possessed, and can retain any object that was illegally possessed.

Invitee (1) A person who goes upon land or premises of another by invitation, express or implied. (2) Either a public invitee or a business visitor: (a) Public invitee is a person who is invited to enter or remain on land as a member of the public for a purpose for which the land is held open to the public. (b) Business visitor is a person who is invited to enter or remain on land for a purpose directly or indirectly connected with business dealings with the possessor of the land.

Involuntary Adoption Adoption occurs after a court has formally terminated the parental rights of the birth parent(s) on grounds such as abuse, abandonment, or neglect.

Involuntary Intoxication A criminal defense available to a person who is not responsible for having become intoxicated due to the actions of others or circumstances beyond his/her knowledge and/or control.

Irresistible Impulse Test This test provides that a criminal defendant is not guilty by reason of insanity if the defendant, although knowing that an act is wrong and aware of the nature and quality of the act, cannot refrain from committing the act due to mental disease or defect. Used to determine insanity in some jurisdictions.

Joint and Severable Liability Persons who commit a tort at the same time are both individually and collectively liable for the entire harm.

Joint Custody Court grants custody to both parents instead of just one. Both parents share decision-making responsibilities in regard to their child's upbringing. The parents, although no longer married to each other, continue to share a family.

Joint Tenancy Each tenant takes an equal, undivided interest in the ownership of property from the same source and at the same time. Includes a right of survivorship, which means that a deceased joint tenant's rights automatically pass to the surviving joint tenants and not through the deceased's will.

Judgment A judgment determines the rights of the disputing parties and decides what relief is awarded (if any).

Judgment Creditor Person awarded a money judgment.

Judgment Debtor Person who has been ordered in a judgment to pay money to a judgment creditor.

Judicial Deference A court's willingness to show deference to an agency's competence. Courts generally sustain administrative findings if satisfied that the agency has examined the issues, reached its decision appropriately, and followed required procedures.

Jurisdiction The power or authority of a court to determine the merits of a dispute and to grant relief.

Jurisprudence The study of legal philosophy.

Justiciable A case is justiciable if it is well-suited for judicial determination.

Justification Defenses Criminal defenses in which the defendant claims to have acted correctly. Examples include self-defense, defense of others, defense of property, necessity/choice of evils, and duress/coercion.

Knowingly A criminally accused person is aware that a prohibited result or harm is very likely to occur as a result of his/her act, but does not consciously intend the specific consequences that result from the act.

Labor Management Relations Act A 1947 federal statute providing for the arbitration of disputes arising from collective bargaining.

Laches An equitable doctrine that can be used to bar equitable relief to a plaintiff who has unreasonably delayed filing suit under circumstances that unfairly prejudiced the defendant.

Larceny The unlawful taking and carrying away of another's personal property without color of right, and with intent to deprive the rightful owner of the same. Larceny is commonly classified as grand or petty, according to the value of the object taken. Usually defined and classified by various state statutes.

Leading Question An improper question on direct examination that suggests the answer to the witness.

Leasehold In general, a possessory interest in real property for a specified period of time (often a month or year) held by a person who leases property.

Legal Detriment The taking on of a legal obligation, the performance of an act, or the giving up of a legal right.

Legal Duty A legal obligation created by statute, contract, case law, or which has been voluntarily assumed.

Legal Realists Adherents of this philosophical approach focus on the extent to which actual practices vary from the formal legal rules. They believe that judges are more influenced by their personal convictions than by established and immutable rules.

Legal Separation Granted when lawfully married parties have actually separated and when adequate grounds for a legal separation have been shown. The parties remain married to each other but live apart. During the legal separation, the possibility of reconciliation still exists, as does the option to proceed with a final divorce. The separation period allows the estranged parties to try to work out their difficulties while living apart. Also known as a mensa et thoro divorce.

Legal Sociologists Adherents of this philosophical approach use quantitative methodological tools to explain legal outcomes. They use measurements of such factors as the financial standing, race, social class, respectability, and cultural differences of those involved in disputes to explain why some people win lawsuits and others do not.

Lex Fori The law of the place where the action was instituted.

Lex Loci Contractus The law of the state where the last act necessary to complete the contract was done and which created a legal obligation.

Lex Loci Delicti Commissi The substantive law of place where the last event necessary to make the actor liable takes place or where the person or thing harmed is situated at the time the wrong is committed.

Lex Loci Solutionis The law of the place where the contract was to be performed.

Libel (1) Defamatory writing; any published matter that tends to degrade persons in the eyes of their neighbors, or to render them ridiculous, or to injure their properties or businesses. It may be published by writing, effigy, picture, or the like. (2) Broadcasting of defamatory matter by means of radio or television, whether or not it is read from a manuscript.

License In property law, a temporary grant of authority to do specified things on the land of another.

Licensee A person who enters or remains on the land of another with express or implied consent.

Lien A security device, by which there is created a right (1) to retain that which is in a person's possession, belonging to another, until certain demands of the person in possession are satisfied; or (2) to charge property in another's possession with payment of a debt, e.g., a vendor's lien.

Life Estate An estate in land held for the duration of the holder's life but which cannot be passed on to heirs.

Line-Ups A police investigative procedure in which an array of people or an array of photographs of people, including the suspect, are displayed as a group before a victim or witness who may or may not be able to make an identification.

Liquidated Damages The exact amount of money, which the parties to a contract expressly agree must be paid, or may be collected, in the event of a future default or breach of contract.

Logic The study of correct reasoning.

Long-Arm Statute A state statute that permits the exercise of personal jurisdiction over nonresident defendants who have had sufficient minimum contacts with the forum state.

Magna Carta The first Magna Carta was issued in 1215 by the English monarch King John. It is the original source of the protections imbedded in the Due Process Clauses found in the U.S. Constitution.

Majority Opinion An opinion that explains the Court's decision in the case and the majority's reasoning for reaching that outcome.

Mala in Se Traditional label for criminal offenses that are intrinsically wrong.

Mala Prohibita Traditional label for illegal acts which are not intrinsically bad. They are criminal only because the law defines them as such.

Malicious Prosecution An intentional tort in which the plaintiff alleges that the defendant maliciously and without probable cause instigated a civil or criminal action against the plaintiff. The plaintiff must prevail in the original dispute and must have suffered legal injury due to the groundless nature of the defendant's original allegations.

Malpractice A nonlegal term for a professional person's negligence.

Mandamus A writ that commands a public official to perform a non-discretionary duty.

Mandatory Injunction A judicial order compelling a person to act in a specified way.

Marital Property Nonseparate property acquired during a marriage that is subject to distribution by a judge in conjunction with a divorce.

Marriage In 49 states, a state sanctioned relationship in which a man and woman after complying with relevant marriage eligibility requirements become husband and wife. In Massachusetts, a state sanctioned relationship between two people (irrespective of gender) who have complied with relevant marriage eligibility requirements.

Matching Investigative process in which agency ranks prospective adoptive parents in terms of how closely they match the agency's conception of the ideal family for the child.

Material Evidence that has significant probative value.

Maxim An axiom; a general or leading principle.

Mediation The settlement of disputes by the amicable intervention of an outside party who is a stranger to the controversy.

Medical Malpractice An allegation that a physician has either breached a contract or has been professionally negligent in diagnosing and/or treating a patient.

Mens Rea Criminal state of mind.

Mensa Et Thoro Divorce *See* legal separation.

Metaethics The study of ethical terms and arguments.

Metaphysics The study of the nature of reality or being.

Minitrial A misnomer because it is a process used in business disputes and is an alternative to a trial. In this process each party makes a short presentation to a panel comprised of senior managers or decision makers (i.e., employees of the respective parties who have been selected to participate by their employers) and a neutral.

After the presentations are concluded, the panel negotiates a resolution of the dispute.

Misdemeanor Generally, any crime or offense greater than an ordinance violation but not amounting to a felony.

Misprision A common law crime in which the accused failed to tell authorities about the commission of a felony of which the person had knowledge.

Misrepresentation One party to a contract either knowingly or unknowingly misrepresents a material fact that misleads the other contracting party into relying on false facts.

Mistake Where one or both contracting parties unintentionally misunderstand or are ignorant of a fact that is material to their agreement.

Money Damages A sum of money claimed by a plaintiff as recompense for injuries sustained as a result of an alleged breach of contract or the commission of a tort.

Moot Case A case that is no longer justiciable because no present case or controversy continues to exist. Mootness is an aspect of ripeness.

Moral Duty A universally accepted moral obligation.

Motion for Directed Verdict A motion made by the defendant at the end of all the evidence. The motion is granted if the court concludes that evidence favors one side to such an extent that no reasonable juror could find in favor of the other party. This motion is not available to the prosecution in a criminal case but is available to criminal defendants.

Motion for Judgment Notwithstanding the Verdict A motion made after a jury verdict is returned. It is granted when the judge decides that reasonable people could not have reached the verdict that the jury has reached.

Motion for New Trial This motion may be granted by a judge for a variety of reasons, including excessive or grossly inadequate damages, newly discovered evidence, questionable jury verdict, errors in the production of evidence, or simply in the interest of justice.

Motion for Relief from Judgment A motion for relief from judgment is granted only if the judge finds a clerical error in the judgment, newly discovered evidence, or that fraud induced the judgment.

Motion for Summary Judgment A motion made to dispose of controversies that can be decided without a full trial because either no genuine issues of material fact exist or because facts necessary to prove the opponent's case are not provable or are not true.

Motion to Dismiss Sometimes also called a demurrer or a "12(b) motion." A motion used to challenge perceived defects in the plaintiff's complaint.

Natural Law Adherents of this philosophical approach believe that every person possesses a moral barometer that gives him or her the capacity to discover independently moral truth.

Natural Parent Birth parents.

Necessaries (1) Generally defined as the food, clothing, shelter, and medical care that one spouse is legally responsible for providing the other spouse. (2) What a parent is legally responsible to provide for his/her minor child's subsistence as measured by age, status, and condition in life, such as food, lodging, education, clothing, and medical services.

Negligence (1) A flexible term for the failure to use ordinary care, under the particular factual circumstances revealed by the evidence in a lawsuit. (2) Conduct that falls below the standard established by law for the protection of others against unreasonable risk of harm. It does not include conduct recklessly in disregard of an interest of others.

Nominal Damages A token sum awarded where a breach of duty or an infraction of plaintiffs' rights is shown, but no substantial injury is proven to have been sustained.

Noncustodial Parent The parent in a custody dispute not awarded primary physical placement with a child.

Nonsuit A trial motion made by the defendant in a civil case at the end of the plaintiff's case-in-chief. It is granted where the court rules that the plaintiff's case is too weak to continue with the trial. The court must conclude that no reasonable person could find in favor of the plaintiff even if all disputed facts are found to be in the plaintiff's favor. If the motion is granted, the court awards a judgment to the defendant.

Normative Ethics The study of whether particular conduct should be classified as moral or immoral.

Notary Public A state official authorized to administer oaths and to authenticate documents.

Notice (1) Information given to a person of some act done, or about to be done; knowledge. Notice may be actual, when knowledge is brought home to the party to be affected by it; or constructive, when certain acts are done in accordance with law, from which, on grounds of

public policy, the party interested is presumed to have knowledge. It may be written or oral, but written notice is preferable to avoid disputes as to its terms. (2) A person has notice of a fact when he or she has actual knowledge of it, or has received a notice or notification of it, or, from all the facts and circumstances known to him or her at the time in question, has reason to know that it exists.

Novation The substitution of a new obligor or obligation for an old one, which is thereby extinguished, e.g., the acceptance of a note of a third party in payment of the original promisor's obligation, or the note of an individual in lieu of that of a corporation.

Nuisance A nuisance exists when one person's use of real property injures or infringes on another person's use and/or enjoyment of land or infringes on the general public's rights.

Occupational Health and Safety Administration (OSHA) An administrative agency created by Congress in 1970 to set and enforce environmental standards within the work place that would improve employees' safety and working conditions.

Offer A definite proposal to make a contract that is communicated to another person.

Offeree The recipient of an offer to contract.

Offeror A person who makes an offer to contract.

Open Adoption An adoption in which the adoptive parents permit the birth mother to remain in contact with the adopted child.

Option A contract in which an offeror is bound to hold an offer open for a specified period of time in exchange for consideration, usually a sum of money.

Oral Deposition A discovery tool in which a witness is examined under oath, by the lawyers for each party and the testimony is transcribed by a certified court reporter.

Pardon The remission by the chief executive of a state or nation of the punishment to which the person to be pardoned has been sentenced.

Parole Supervised suspension of the execution of a convict's sentence, and release from prison, conditional upon his continued compliance with the terms of parole. Statutes generally specify when and if a prisoner will be eligible to be considered for parole and detail the standards and procedures applicable.

Parole Evidence Rule Evidence of alleged prior agreements or terms not contained in the written document will be inadmissible if offered to change the terms of the document.

Patent A grant of rights to an inventor from the federal government. The inventor, or owner of the rights, has the exclusive right to make, use, license others to use, and sell an invention for a period of years (twenty years for most inventions). Patents are only granted for inventions that are beneficial, original, and involve ingenuity.

Penal Statutes Statutes that command or prohibit certain acts and establish penalties for their violation.

Per Curiam Opinion Usually a brief appellate court opinion for the entire court that does not identify any jurist as author. For example, if nine justices of the Supreme Court agree on the outcome of the case but completely disagree as to why that outcome is correct, the Court might announce its decision in a per curium opinion and then each justice could write a concurring opinion explaining that justice's views as to the rationale supporting the decision.

Personal Property Tangible objects that are not realty or fixtures and all intangible rights, duties, and obligations arising out of the ownership of tangible objects. Personal property also includes intangible property, such as money, stocks, and bonds, that are paper substitutes for certain ownership rights.

Personal Service Delivering summons personally to a defendant.

Personalty Personal property.

Petitioner (1) A party wishing to have its case reviewed by the U.S. Supreme Court who has petitioned the Court for a writ of certiorari. (2) Someone who petitions a court.

Physical Custody Rightful possession.

Plaintiff A person who initiates a lawsuit.

Plea Bargaining A process by which the accused agrees to enter a plea of guilty, often to a lesser offense, in exchange for a promise by the prosecuting attorney to recommend a lesser sentence or a dismissal of part of the charges.

Plea of Nolo Contendere A plea that is equivalent to a guilty plea, except that it cannot be used as an admission in any subsequent civil action admission.

Pleadings The alternate and opposing written statements of the parties to a lawsuit. The typical pleadings include the complaint, answer, and occasionally a reply.

Police Power A flexible term for the authority of state legislatures to enact laws regulating and restraining private rights and occupations for the promotions of public health, safety, welfare, and morals.

Political Question Doctrine Political issues should be resolved by the political branches of government and not by the judiciary.

Positive Law Legislated rules or law.

Possessory Interest The right of possession.

Preferred Custody Statutes Some states require that preference be given to a child's primary caretaker, when the primary caretaker can be established. Such an approach favors neither gender, and provides the child with continuity and stability in parenting.

Preliminary Hearing A hearing at which the prosecution must establish the existence of probable cause to believe that a felony was committed and that the accused was the person who committed the crime.

Pretrial Conference A meeting between the judge and counsel for the parties, preliminary to the trial of a lawsuit. Under modern rules of civil procedure, in any lawsuit, the court may in its discretion direct the attorneys for the parties to appear before it for a conference, to consider any matters that may aid in the disposition of the lawsuit.

Preventive Detention Preventive detention occurs when criminally accused persons are denied bail because they are alleged to have committed very serious crimes and because they allegedly pose a serious threat of danger to particular individuals or to the public safety in general.

Prima Facie Evidence Proof of a fact or collection of facts from which other facts can be presumed. In most situations the presumed fact(s) can be rebutted by other relevant proof.

Principal The leading, or most important; the original; a person, firm or corporation from whom an agent derives his authority; a person who is first responsible, and for whose fulfillment of an obligation a surety becomes bound; the chief, or actual, perpetrator of a crime, as distinguished from the accessory, who may assist him; the important part of an estate, as distinguished from incidents, or accessories; a sum of money loaned, as distinguished from the interest paid for its use.

Private Nuisance A tort that requires proof of an injury that is distinct from that suffered by the general public. (It differs from trespass because the offensive activity does not occur on the victim's property.) A party injured by a private nuisance can obtain both damages and injunctive relief.

Private Trial The parties to the dispute contract with a private business to conduct a private trial before a private judge (often well reputed and recently retired) who has experience appropriate to the case or a private jury. The news media and general public have no right to attend these trials. The parties often use simplified evidentiary and procedural rules, cooperate with discovery, and decide whether the decision of the private judge or jury will be appealable.

Privilege (1) An exceptional right, or exemption. It is either (a) personal, attached to a person or office; or (b) attached to a thing, sometimes called real. The exemption of ambassadors and members of Congress from arrest, while going to, returning from, or attending to the discharge of their public duties, is an example of the first. (2) The fact that conduct which, under ordinary circumstances, would subject an actor to liability, under particular circumstances does not subject him to liability. A privilege may be based upon (a) the consent of the other affected by the actor's conduct, or (b) the fact that its exercise is necessary for the protection of some interest of the actor or of the public that is of such importance as to justify the harm caused or threatened by its exercise, or (c) the fact that the actor is performing a function for the proper performance of which freedom of action is essential.

Privileged Communication A confidential communication that cannot be introduced at trial because the law recognizes the existence of a privilege. Privileges exist to protect legally favored rights (such as the privilege against self incrimination) and relationships (i.e., attorney-client, doctor-patient, clergy-parishioner). Because privileges permit the withholding of important evidence at trial, they are disfavored by courts.

Privity Participation in knowledge or interest. Persons who so participate are called privies.

Privity of Contract A legal term referring to the existence of a special relationship between the parties to a contract.

Privity of Estate The direct relationship between grantor and grantee.

Pro Se A person who appears without a lawyer and chooses to represent himself or herself appears pro se.

Probable Cause (1) A reasonable ground for suspicion, supported by circumstances sufficiently strong to warrant a cautious man to believe that an accused person is guilty of the offense with which he is charged. (2) Concerning a search, probable cause is a flexible, common-sense standard. It merely requires that the facts available to the officer would warrant a person of reasonable caution in the belief that certain items may be contraband or stolen property or useful as evidence of a crime; it does not demand any showing that the belief is correct or more likely true than false. A practical, nontechnical probability that incriminating evidence is involved is all that is required.

Procedural Due Process The premise underlying procedural due process is that justice is more likely to occur if correct procedures are employed when government seeks to deprive someone of life, liberty, or property. The U.S. Supreme Court has ruled that what procedures are due varies with the context. In criminal cases, for example, the procedures are quite extensive and the process is very formal. But when a school board decides to suspend a student for violating school rules, the procedures are much less extensive and the process is much less formal. But irrespective of context it is clear that procedural due process requires at a minimum an "impartial" decision maker, some kind of notice, some kind of hearing (although the Court has permitted the government in some contexts to take away financial benefits before conducting the requisite hearing).

Procedural Rule Administrative rule used to establish "standard operating procedures" within an agency.

Process The means whereby a court enforces obedience to its orders. Process is termed (a) original, when it is intended to compel the appearance of the defendant; (b) mesne, when issued pending suit to secure the attendance of jurors and witnesses; and (c) final, when issued to enforce execution of a judgment.

Production of Documents Showing of the documents in a court.

Prohibitionary Injunction *See* prohibitory injunction.

Prohibitory Injunction A judicial order requiring a person to refrain from acting in a specified way.

Promisee The person to whom a promise is made.

Promisor The person making a promise.

Property Property includes the rights to possess, use, and dispose of things. These may be tangible objects, such as a car, book, or item of clothing, or they may be intangible, e.g., the technology in a camera, a song, or the right of publicity. Although many people refer to the objects themselves as property, "property" actually refers only to ownership rights and interests.

Property Right A person's ownership rights to things and to a person's interests in things owned by someone else.

Prosecutor A person who brings an action against another in the name of the government. A public prosecutor is an officer appointed or elected to conduct all prosecutions in behalf of the government.

Prospective Effect A new rule applies to all questions subsequently coming before that court and the lower courts of the jurisdiction.

Proximate Cause (1) Something that produces a result, without which the result could not have occurred. (2) Any original event that in natural unbroken sequence produces a particular foreseeable result, without which the result would not have occurred.

Public Nuisance This exists when a land use poses a generalized threat to the public as a whole or to a substantial segment of the community. An action to redress a public nuisance is brought by government, oftentimes by criminal prosecution and injunctive relief.

Public Policy (1) A highly flexible term of imprecise definition, for the consideration of what is expedient for the community concerned. (2) The principle of law that holds that no person can do that which has a tendency to be injurious to the public, or against the public good.

Punitive Damages Damages awarded in excess of the general damages or economic loss, intended solely to punish the offender.

Purposely A conscious desire to produce a prohibited result or harm.

Quantum Meruit As much as he or she deserves. An equitable means for determining what sum is due where there is no actual agreement between parties but where fairness requires that a contract be implied in order to avoid an unjust enrichment.

Quasi-Contract An obligation that arises without express agreement between the parties; an implied contract.

Ratification of Contract An expression or action that indicates an intention to be contractually bound.

Realty Land and things that are attached permanently to land.

Recklessly Acts by a person with utter indifference to the welfare of others and that pose a significant and unjustifiable risk of harm to other people.

Recognizance An unsecured promise to appear in court when so required.

Record A written memorial of the actions of a legislature or of a court.

Recording System The process by which purchasers of realty can evaluate the quality of the seller's title to a parcel.

Redirect Examination A second direct examination of a witness conducted by the attorney or party who first called this witness to testify. This examination occurs after the cross-examination of the witness.

Reeve The official heading the hundred in Anglo Saxon England.

Reformation An action brought requesting that a judge correct a provision contained in a written instrument, so that the instrument expresses the true agreement or intention of the parties. Also known as rectification.

Rehabilitative Alimony A sum of money that, when appropriate, a judge will award a dependent spouse in a divorce action so that the recipient can obtain education or training to strengthen job skills.

Relevant Evidence that logically tends to prove or disprove some issue of consequence that is in dispute at the trial or hearing.

Remand Return of a case by an appellate court to a lower court with instructions to the lower court to take further specified action.

Remedy (1) The legal means to declare or enforce a right or to redress a wrong. (2) Any remedial right, to which an aggrieved party is entitled.

Remittitur For purposes of this textbook (because it has more than one meaning), remittitur refers to a non-prevailing party's post verdict motion to reduce a jury's award of money damages. The motion is granted by a trial or appellate court that has been convinced that the jury's verdict is grossly excessive.

Replevin A writ used to recover possession of personal property wrongfully in the possession of another.

Reply A pleading in which the plaintiff admits, denies, or raises defenses against the factual allegations raised in the defendant's counterclaim.

Request for Admissions A method of discovery in which one party sends to the other party a request that the other party admit that certain facts are true and/or that specified documents are genuine.

Request for Waiver Of Service Defendants who voluntarily waive their right to be formally served with process are allowed 60 days, instead of just 20 days, to respond to the complaint.

Res Ipsa Loquitur A judicial doctrine which permits plaintiffs to circumstantially prove negligence if the following facts are proved: (1) the defendant had exclusive control over the allegedly defective product during manufacture, (2) under normal circumstances, the plaintiff would not have been injured by the product if the defendant had exercised ordinary care, and (3) the plaintiff's conduct did not contribute significantly to the accident. From the proved facts, the law permits the jurors to infer a fact for which there is no direct, explicit proof: the defendant's negligent act or omission.

Res Judicata In general, a judicial policy that once a valid judgment has been rendered on the merits in one jurisdiction, the claims adjudicated in that lawsuit cannot be relitigated by the same parties in some other jurisdiction.

Rescission The cancellation of or putting an end to a contract by the parties, or by one of them, e.g., for any reason mutually acceptable to the parties, or on the ground of fraud.

Residual Jurisdiction A court with residual jurisdiction exercises original jurisdiction over subject matter that has not been assigned by the legislature to a court of original, limited, subject matter jurisdiction.

Respondent (1) The name given one of the parties in a case before the U.S. Supreme Court. The petitioner is the party asking the Court to grant a writ of certiorari. The respondent is the party opposing the granting of the petition. (2) The name given a party in any court who is before the court in response to another party's petition.

Restitution The restoring of property, or a right, to a person who has been unjustly deprived of it. A writ of restitution is the process by which an appellant may recover something of which he has been deprived under a prior judgment.

Restoration in Specie The meaning of this term varies with the context in which it is used. In this textbook it refers to requiring a person wrongfully in possession of property to return the property or its monetary equivalent to the person who rightfully is entitled to possession.

Retroactive Effect A new rule applies to causes of action arising before the announcement of the decision.

Reversal An appellate court enters a judgment of reversal when it rules that a lower court's judgment should be overturned.

Ripeness A case is ripe if it has developed sufficiently to be before a court for adjudication. If a lawsuit has been filed prematurely it is not ripe for adjudication.

Rule of Mitigation An injured person must make a reasonable effort to avoid or minimize damages. Also called "avoidable harm" doctrine.

Rule-Making Power A delegated power contained in an enabling act authorizing an administrative agency to make, alter, or repeal rules and regulations on those subject to its terms.

Satisfaction The payment of owed money.

Separate Property Property not classified as "community property" because it was owned prior to the marriage or was received as a gift or inheritance.

Separation Agreement An agreement between divorcing parties as to the allocation of financial obligations and how property should be divided. It often contains recommendations on how the court should decide child custody and support, spousal support, and visitation rights. Although the court is ultimately responsible for determining each of the aforementioned issues, it is often greatly influenced by the proposals in a separation agreement.

Separation of Powers The federal constitution delegates the legislative power to the Congress in Article I, the executive power to the President in Article II, and the judicial power to the federal judiciary in Article III. The founders believed that dispersing power in this way would result in a system of checks and balances and prevent abuse.

Settlement Conference A pretrial meeting attended by the lawyers for the contesting parties and sometimes the judge to explore the possiblity of settlement.

Severalty Ownership Property owned by one person.

Shire English counties are called shires.

Significant Relationship The law of the place that has the most significant contacts with the incident or event in dispute.

Slander The malicious defamation of a person in his reputation, profession, or business by spoken words. Usually, the truth of the words spoken is a defense. Statutorily defined in many states' statutes.

Sociological Jurisprudence Adherents of this approach believe that law is not just the formal rules, but also the informal rules that actually influence social behavior. The sociological school maintains that law can only be understood when the formal system of rules is considered in conjunction with social realities (or facts).

Solicitation A specific intent crime committed by a person who asks, hires, or encourages another to commit a crime.

Sovereign Immunity A rule of law holding that a nation or state, or its political subdivisions, is exempt from being sued, without its consent, in its own courts or elsewhere. Often criticized as being erroneously conceived, anachronistic, and unjust. Occasionally modified by court decisions, and various state and federal statutes, e.g., Tort Claims Act.

Sovereignty The supreme authority of an independent nation or state. It is characterized by equality of the nation or state among other nations or states, exclusive and absolute jurisdiction and self-government within its own territorial limits, and jurisdiction over its citizens beyond its territorial limits.

Special Appearance If a person appears in court to challenge a court's in personam jurisdiction, he/she is making a special appearance for that limited purpose and is not consenting to personal jurisdiction by arguing that issue.

Special Damages Damages awarded for injuries that arise from the particular circumstances of the wrong.

Special Verdict A verdict that requires the jury to answer specific questions related to certain factual issues in the case.

Specific Intent An additional specified level of intent beyond the commission of the actus reus.

Specific Performance The actual carrying out of a contract in the particular manner agreed upon. Courts of equity will compel and coerce specific performance of a contract in many cases, where damages payable in money, the usual remedy at law, would not adequately compensate for its nonperformance, e.g., in the case of contracts concerning land, or for the sale of a unique chattel.

Spontaneous Declarations An exception to the hearsay rule that permits courts to admit in court spontaneous declarations uttered simultaneously with the occurrence of an act.

Spousal Privileges The right to refuse to testify against a spouse in a criminal trial and to refuse to testify about confidential communications that occurred between spouses during their marriage.

Standing To have standing a plaintiff must have a legally sufficient personal stake in the outcome of the litigation and must be adversely affected by the defendant's conduct.

Stare Decisis In general a judicial policy that guides courts in making decisions. The doctrine normally requires lower-level courts to follow the legal precedents that have been established by higher-level courts.

Status Crimes Status crimes punish people for being in a condition rather than for what they are doing or have done. Examples include being without visible means of support and being found addicted to narcotics.

Statute of Frauds Various state legislative acts, patterned after a 1677 English act, known by the same name. Because of the variations in each state, reference must be made to the specific state statutes. The main object was to take away the facilities for fraud, and the temptation to perjury, that arose in verbal obligations, the proof of which depended upon oral evidence. Its most common provisions are these: (a) all leases, excepting those for less than three years, shall have the force of leases at will only, unless they are in writing and signed by the parties or their agents; (b) assignments and surrenders of leases and interests in land must be in writing; (c) all declarations and assignments of trusts must be in writing, signed by the party (trusts arising by implication of law are, however, excepted); (d) no action shall be brought upon a guarantee, or upon any contract for sale of lands, or any interest in or concerning them, or upon any agreement that is not to be performed within a year, unless the agreement is in writing and signed by the party to be charged or his agent; (e) no contract for the sale of goods for a certain price or more, shall be good, unless the buyer accept part, or give something in part payment, or some memorandum thereof be signed by the parties to be charged or their agents.

Statute of Limitations Various periods of time, fixed by different state and federal statutes, called statutes of limitations, within which a lawsuit must be commenced, and after the expiration of which, the claimant will be forever barred from the right to bring the action. Generally, a statute of limitations is a procedural bar to a plaintiff's action that does not begin to run until after the cause of action has accrued and the plaintiff has a right to maintain a lawsuit.

Statute of Repose A statute of repose is similar to a statute of limitation in that it sets a maximum time within which a lawsuit can be brought. A statute of repose, however, is often broader than a statute of limitations in that its cut-off date is rigidly enforced and cannot be "tolled" as can a statute of limitations. For example, a statute of limitations begins to run in a products liability case when the plaintiff is injured as a result of the defendant's breach of a legal duty. A statute of repose would begin to run when the plaintiff took possession of the product. If the plaintiff rarely uses a product and then several year later while using the product becomes injured, the statute of limitations may not have elapsed because it would start to run on the date of the injury. If the state has enacted a statute of repose it might well have elapsed and would then bar any suit against the product's manufacturer. Statutes of repose are often included in proposals for tort reform in that they absolutely cut off liability on a date certain irrespective of any other considerations.

Statutory Lien A lien created by statute.

Strict Construction A rule of statutory construction, particularly used in criminal cases where the language of a criminal statute is vague. A court should not enlarge the meaning of a criminal statute by implication beyond the fair meaning of the language used nor construe its meaning so as to defeat the obvious intention of the legislature.

Strict Liability Crime A mala prohibita offense that requires no proof of mens rea.

Strict Liability in Tort Liability for negligence imposed on defendant irrespective of defendant's lack of fault, where injury occurred as a result of defendant's abnormally dangerous activities or because a purchaser of manufacturer's product was injured as a result of a product defect (i.e., a product liability case).

Subpoena A writ that requires a person to appear in court to give testimony.

Subpoena Duces Tecum A writ requiring that a witness appear in court with a document that is in his or her possession.

Substantive Due Process A label that is used to refer to the ongoing constitutional debate over what should be included within the scope of the Due Process Clause of the Fourteenth Amendment. At this time, most but not all of the rights enumerated in the Bill of Rights have been incorporated into the Fourteenth Amendment Due Process Clause and made binding on the states. Far more contentious, however, is the debate about which unenumerated rights should also be incorporated into the Fourteenth Amendment Due Process Clause. Students can get a taste of this debate by reading the excerpts from the opinions written by Chief Justice Rehnquist and

Justice Souter in the assisted suicide case in Chapter One—*Washington v. Glucksberg*.

Substantive Rule Administrative rule used to establish and implement policies that assist an agency to accomplish its statutorily established objectives.

Substituted Service The summons and complaint are mailed to the defendant by certified mail; these documents are left at the defendant's home with a person who resides there and who is of "suitable age and discretion."

Summary Jury Trial An abbreviated "practice trial" allows disputing parties to see how a group of regular jurors reacts to each side's presentation and produces an non binding "verdict." Useful when parties agree about liability but disagree as to damages.

Supremacy Clause As a general rule, Article VI, Section 2 of the federal constitution makes the U.S. Constitution, federal laws, and treaties "the supreme law of the land" taking precedence over state constitutions and laws where a direct conflict exists.

Suspect Classification Legislatively established classifications based on race, religion, national origin, alienage, and classifications that trammel on fundamental rights are likely to violate the provisions of the Equal Protection Clause of the Fourteenth Amendment. Suspect classifications are subject to strict scrutiny and can be justified only by a compelling state interest.

Tangible Descriptive of something that may be felt or touched; corporeal.

Tenancy by the Entirety A tenancy by the entirety is limited to married husbands and wives and is ended only upon death, divorce, or mutual consent. When a tenant spouse dies, title passes to the surviving spouse. If a divorce occurs, the tenancy is converted into a tenancy in common.

Tenancy in Common Similar to a joint tenancy; however, there is no automatic passing of the deceased's rights to the surviving tenants (right of survivorship). Instead, the deceased's rights pass according to his/her will.

Tender Years Doctrine An outdated view that courts should generally award custody of young children to their mother.

Title Ownership rights in property.

Tort A wrongful act, not involving a breach of an agreement, for which a civil action may be maintained.

Tortfeasor A person who commits a tort.

Trade Secret A plan, process, tool, mechanism, or compound, known only to its owner and those of his employees to whom it is necessary to confide it, in order to apply it to the uses intended. It is distinguishable from a patent in that it may be used by anyone who is able to discover its nature.

Trademark A unique symbol, term, phrase, or design that a company uses to help customers identify and distinguish its products from competitors.

Trespass (1) At common law, any offense less than treason, felony, or misprision of either. (2) Especially, trespass quare clausum fregit, i.e., entry on another's close or land without lawful authority. (3) Trespass on the case. (4) Criminal trespass is entering or surreptitiously remaining in a building or occupied structure, or separately secured or occupied portion thereof, knowing that he or she is not licensed or privileged to do so.

Trespass on the Case A statutory writ created by the English Parliament to redress private wrongs not addressed by the writ of trespass where the failure to perform a duty resulted in harm to a victim.

Trial Court's Jury Instructions The judge's instructions explain to the jury the elements of the claims and defenses that were raised by the parties, which party has the burden of proof with respect to each issue, and the forms of verdict being submitted to the jury, etc. After the close of the evidence in a jury trial, the parties will submit suggested jury instructions to the judge. The judge then holds a hearing out of the presence of the jury and after argument, rules as to which instructions are accepted. The accepted jury instructions are subsequently read to the jury.

Trial De Novo In some jurisdictions, a party who has had a trial in a local court can elect to have a county court with general jurisdiction decide the case afresh. This second trial is called a trial de novo because this second trial proceeds "from the beginning" just as if the first trial had not occurred.

Unconscionable Contract A contract clause that is too unfair or one-sided.

Undue Influence The will of a dominant person is substituted for that of the other party, and the substitution is done in an unlawful fashion, resulting in an unfair agreement.

Unenforceable A contract that courts will not enforce. Examples include oral agreements that have not been reduced to writing under circumstances where a writing is required and breach of contract lawsuits that are barred by a statute of limitations.

Uniform Commercial Code A model code which has been substantially adopted by all states except Louisiana (which has not adopted those portions of the UCC which are based on common law notions because they are incompatible with that state's civil law approach to commercial law).

Unilateral Contract A contract in which one party makes a promise in exchange for another person performing or refraining from performing an act.

Unjust Enrichment The doctrine that places a legal duty of restitution upon a defendant who has acquired something of value at the expense of the plaintiff.

U.S. Courts of Appeals Normally the court to which appeals are directed from the federal district courts. There are thirteen federal judicial circuits.

U.S. District Courts Federal courts of original jurisdiction that function as the trial courts for the federal judiciary. Federal district courts are given limited subject matter jurisdiction by the Constitution and by Congress.

Utilitarianism A philosophical approach that focuses on the social usefulness of legislation rather than on natural law ideas of goodness and justice.

Valid Contract A binding and enforceable agreement that meets all the necessary contractual requirements.

Venue The place where judicial authority should be exercised.

Vested Fully effective.

Vicarious Liability Substituted or indirect responsibility, e.g., the responsibility of an employer for the torts committed by his employee within the scope of his employment.

Void Contract No contract, because no enforceable legal obligation has been created.

Void For Vagueness Doctrine Legislation that fails to establish minimal guidelines that structure and confine police discretion and/or that fail to provide citizens with fair notice of what is prohibited. Such legislation is too vague and violates substantive due process.

Voidable Contract An agreement in which one or more of the parties can elect to avoid an obligation created by contract because of the manner in which the contract was brought about (such as fraud, duress, or lack of capacity).

Voir Dire A pretrial oral examination of prospective jurors conducted to determine their qualifications.

Voluntary Adoption Birth parent(s) consent to the termination of their parental rights and surrender the child either to an agency for placement or to adoptive parents of their choosing.

Waiver The voluntary relinquishment of a legal right.

Wanton Misconduct Behavior that manifests a disposition to perversity. It must be under such circumstances and conditions that the party doing the act, or failing to act, is conscious that his or her conduct will, in all common probability, result in injury.

Warrant A written order from a court to an officer, directing the officer to arrest a person, or search specified premises for items subject to lawful seizure.

Writ of Account An old common law writ used to obtain a reconciliation statement of receipts and payments and to recover any money due.

Writ of Certiorari (1) "To be more fully informed," an original writ or action whereby a cause is removed from an inferior to a superior court for review. The record of the proceedings is then transmitted to the superior court. (2) A discretionary appellate jurisdiction that is invoked by a petition for certiorari, which the appellate court may grant or deny in its discretion. The petition for a writ of certiorari is the legal vehicle used to obtain review from the United States Supreme Court.

Writ of Covenant An old common law writ used to enforce agreements relating to land, especially leases.

Writ of Debt An old common law writ used to collect a specific sum of money owed.

Writ of Entry An old common law writ used to regain possession of land.

Writ of Execution A court order commanding the sheriff to take possession of a judgment debtor's non-exempt property so that it can be sold to satisfy a judgment.

Writ of Right A twelfth-century common law writ that required communal/manorial courts to conduct a trial according to specified royal procedures to determine if the demandant (the previous possessor who sought the writ) had been wrongfully dispossessed.

Writ of Summons The summons warns the defendant that a default judgment can be awarded to the plaintiff unless the defendant responds with a pleading (usually an answer) within a specified period of time.

Written Deposition A deposition in which the questions and answers are written down. Written depositions are significantly less expensive than oral depositions but can be useful for third party discovery.

Written Interrogatories Written questions propounded on behalf of one party in an action to another party, or to someone who is not a party, before the trial thereof. The person interrogated must give his answers in writing, and upon oath.

Year Books Annual series of important cases collected by English lawyers and students during the fourteenth and fifteenth centuries.

Zoning Laws and regulations that restrict the use of real property. They serve many purposes including protecting housing districts from industrial pollution, and the preservation of historically significant landmarks and agriculture. Zoning has also been used to exclude low income housing and adult entertainment establishments, and to reduce population density (and therefore the need for additional schools).

✳

Introduction to Law & the Legal System 1975–2010: A Short Chronicle

Authors

    Harrold J. Grilliot   editions 1–3

    Frank August Schubert   editions 4–10

Publisher

    Houghton Mifflin Company   editions 1–9

    Cengage Learning   edition 10

AUTHOR'S COMMENTARY

I assumed responsibility for the textbook in 1988 and since then have produced editions 4–10. I was a professor at Northeastern University when Harold Grilliot died, and was using the third edition of the textbook in my own classes. I greatly liked the book and how well it worked in the classroom. I liked the succinct textual discussions and the way Professor Grilliot's case selections captured my students and helped them to overcome their fear of law, legal jargon, and complex procedures. I particularly appreciated *DuPont v. Christopher*, Grilliot's first case in Chapter One of his first edition (it really was on page 3). I always enjoyed that second day of class when we would plunge into the case. My students were initially convinced they could never survive that case, let alone the course. Yet with help they discovered they could and did overcome the challenge and when they emerged from the fog, having survived this ordeal, they believed they could handle anything that was to come. Later on in the course, usually after discussing the Erie Doctrine, I would have students reread the DuPont case so that they could appreciate how much they had learned in the interim. They could not believe how easy it then seemed.

I was honored to have been asked to become the textbook's second author. Because I believed in Grilliot's philosophy, I have retained most of Grilliot's structure and approach. Over the years I have made changes which I believed were necessary for undergraduates and reflective of what was happening in the country.

The biggest changes occurred in the fifth edition. English legal history, philosophy of law, and the sample brief were added to Chapter One. Criminal law was added to the criminal procedure chapter. Three new chapters were written including property law, alternative dispute resolution, and employment discrimination. The sixth edition included a procedural primer and, because the economy and employment situation had improved by the mid-1990s, Family Law replaced Employment and Discrimination. The most recent "new" chapter was the Ethics chapter, which debuted in the seventh edition.

I have included two figures in the Appendix (Figures A.1 and A.2) that illustrate the comings and goings of the chapters and the cases that have made at least seven appearances in the textbook during the last thirty-five years.

F.A.S.

CHAPTER HISTORY BY EDITION

EDITION	Grilliot Era					Schubert Era				
	one	two	three	four	five	six	seven	eight	nine	ten
YEAR PUBLISHED	1975	1979	1983	1988	1992	1996	2000	2004	2006	2010
Introduction	x	x	x	x	x	x	x	x	x	x
The Judicial System	x	x	x	x	x	x	x	x	x	x
Limitations on Judicial Relief	x	x	x	x	x	x	x	x	x	x
Judicial Remedies	x	x	x	x	x	x	x	x	x	x
Civil Procedure	x	x	x	x	x	x	x	x	x	x
The Administrative Process/Law	x	x	x	x	x	x	x	x	x	x
Torts	x	x	x	x	x	x	x	x	x	x
Judicial Decisionmaking	x	x	x	x	x					
Criminal Procedure	x	x	x	x						
Legislation	x	x	x	x						
Government Reg of Business		x	x	x						
Contracts			x	x	x	x	x	x	x	x
Property				x	x	x	x	x	x	x
ADR				x	x	x	x	x	x	x
Criminal Law & Procedure					x	x	x	x	x	x
Family Law						x	x	x	x	x
Institutional Sources of US Law						x	x	x	x	x
Ethics							x	x	x	x
Employment Law & Discrimination					x	x				
Antitrust Law					x					

F I G U R E A.1 Chapters Appearing in the Textbook 1975–2010

	Grilliot Era						Schubert Era				
EDITION	one	two	three	four	five	six	seven	eight	nine	ten
YEAR PUBLISHED	1975	1979	1983	1988	1992	1996	2000	2004	2006	2010
CASE										
Katko v. Briney	x	x	x	x	x	x	x	x	x	x
Strunk v. Strunk	x	x	x	x	x	x	x	x	x	x
Campbell Soup v. Wentz	x	x	x	x	x	x	x	x	x	x
DuPont v. Christopher	x	x	x	x	x	x	x	x		
Carson v. National Bank		x	x	x	x	x	x	x		
Cody v. Atkins				x	x	x	x	x	x	x
Dorsey v. Greg				x	x	x	x	x	x	x
Macomber v. Dillman				x	x	x	x	x	x	x
Iacomini v. Liberty Mutual				x	x	x	x	x	x	x
Berthiaume v. Pratt				x	x	x	x	x	x	x
Carter v. Mathews				x	x	x	x	x	x	x

F I G U R E A.2   Cases Appearing in Seven or More Editions 1975–2010

✳

Case Index

Subject Index